Wrongful Conviction

Wrongful Conviction

Law, Science, and Policy

James R. Acker
Distinguished Teaching Professor,
School of Criminal Justice, University at Albany

Allison D. Redlich
Associate Professor,
School of Criminal Justice, University at Albany

Carolina Academic Press
Durham, North Carolina

Library of Congress Cataloging-in-Publication Data

Acker, James R., 1951-
Wrongful conviction : law, science, and policy / James R. Acker, Allison D. Redlich.
p. cm.
Includes bibliographical references and index.
ISBN 978-1-59460-753-0 (alk. paper)
1. Judicial error--United States. 2. Compensation for judicial error--United States. 3. Clemency--United States. 4. Criminal justice, Administration of--United States. I. Redlich, Allison D. II. Title.

KF9756.A25 2011
345.73'05--dc23

2011016117

Carolina Academic Press, LLC
700 Kent Street
Durham, North Carolina 27701
Telephone (919) 489-7486
Fax (919) 493-5668
www.cap-press.com

Printed in the United States of America
2016 Printing

Dedication

To Jenny, Elizabeth, and Anna. "Innocent: 1. free from moral wrong; without sin; pure. 2. freedom from legal or specific wrong; guiltless.... 11. a simpleton or idiot." *Webster's Collegiate Dictionary* 695 (New York: Random House 1991). You embrace the first meaning. May this book make some small contribution so that those allied with the second category are not wrongly convicted. To the third definition I plead guilty and can only hope that justice is tempered by mercy.

—JRA

To John, Isaac, and Lucie. Thanks for understanding how important my work is to me and for knowing that when I cannot be with you, I still wish that I was. To all those who have been exonerated, those waiting to be, and those who work tirelessly to right the wrongs of our criminal justice system, words cannot express my admiration for your courage, perseverance, and heroism. To those who stymie the factually innocent becoming free, I hope that you find this book enlightening.

—ADR

Contents

Part II
The Leading Correlates and Causes of Wrongful Convictions

Part III
Adjudication; Capital Cases; Post-adjudication Detection and Redress

Table of Cases

E

F

G

H

I

J

K

L

M

Acknowledgments

It has been a true delight for us to be able to work on this book from start to finish with the many good people at Carolina Academic Press.

In particular, Beth Hall's enthusiasm and support from the outset, and throughout the writing and production stages, were indispensable in allowing *Wrongful Conviction* to get out of the starting gate. When we justifiably might have heard grumbling about a deadline or two that came and went, Beth's good humor and understanding in acquiescing to our requested extensions were a welcome and much-appreciated reprieve.

Kelly Miller somehow transformed the patchwork of files that we provided into the book's now highly professional (bordering on artistic) countenance. She went extraordinarily beyond what was necessary and into the realm of making innumerable creative enhancements, always coupled with good cheer.

We were lucky to be able to work with such fine colleagues.

We also thank Laura Dewey, who produced a comprehensive and tightly organized Index, in very timely fashion.

To the others who have been so supportive and important to us, we have so noted in our Dedications and take the opportunity once again to say how much you mean to us.

—JRA
—ADR

Part I

Introduction and Overview of the Criminal Justice Decision-Making Process

Chapter 1

The Problem of Wrongful Conviction

A. What Is a "Wrongful Conviction"?

We must be clear about our subject matter. What, precisely, is a "wrongful conviction"? Agreeing about the meaning of a "conviction" should not be difficult; we take that term to mean a judicial determination that an individual is guilty of a crime. Defining a "wrongful" conviction, on the other hand, is not so straightforward. For example, well into the 20th century blacks in several states who sought equal access to public accommodations were convicted of crimes and punished under "Jim Crow" laws that have since been condemned as both morally offensive and unconstitutional. It might be argued that such convictions, although lawful when rendered, were inherently unjust and hence wrongful. Alternatively, we might not quarrel in principle with legislation that makes designated conduct a crime, such as laws prohibiting the use of controlled substances, but nevertheless recoil at their enforcement in exceptional cases, such as when an acutely ill individual ingests marijuana to alleviate the disease's pernicious symptoms. Whether a conviction obtained under such circumstances should be considered wrongful is certainly debatable, but our focus will be elsewhere. We will be examining cases in which factually innocent people are convicted of crimes.

Yet even this more restricted category requires further definition. We now must concur about what it means to be innocent of a crime. In this context, which of the following cases should be classified as wrongful convictions?

Jesse and Stephen Boorn. Russell Colvin, the brother-in-law of Jesse and Stephen Boorn as a result of having married their sister Sally, disappeared without explanation from Manchester, Vermont in 1812. It was widely known that Jesse and Stephen disliked Colvin, and his disappearance followed a heated argument involving the men. Years later, in 1819, a relative of the Boorns reported that Colvin had visited him in a series of dreams and revealed that he had been murdered. The apparition disclosed where his remains had been buried on the Boorns' farm. Follow-up investigations led to the discovery at the dreamed burial site of personal items that apparently belonged to Colvin and, at another site, of bones. With community interest rekindled, Jesse Boorn was jailed and an arrest warrant issued for Stephen, who had relocated in New York. After Jesse's jail cellmate claimed that Jesse had implicated Stephen as well as the brothers' father in Colvin's murder, Jesse confessed to participating in the killing and identified his brother as the principal. Although Jesse later recanted his confession, Stephen returned to Vermont where he, too, confessed to killing Colvin although he maintained that he struck the lethal blow amidst mutual combat. Both of the brothers were found guilty of murder and sentenced to death, but Jesse's sentence later was commuted to life imprisonment. The publicity inspired by the case, and particularly by the dream visitation that had triggered the renewed investigation, included a *New York Evening Post* article that fortuitously came to the attention of a man in New York City who was acquainted with a Russell Colvin who had frequently spoken about his Vermont heritage. Colvin thereafter was located in New Jersey, very much alive. He was duped into returning to Vermont in December 1819, just three weeks prior to Stephen Boorn's scheduled date with the gallows. With this turn of events, both Jesse's and Stephen's murder convictions were vacated.[1]

Kirk Bloodsworth. A nine-year-old girl was found dead in Fontana Village, a small town in Baltimore County, Maryland, on July 25, 1984. Her skull had been crushed, and she had been strangled and sexually assaulted. Five witnesses later testified that they had seen Kirk Bloodsworth with the girl shortly before her murder. Police officers who questioned Bloodsworth reported that he had told them that he had done something terrible that would threaten his marriage and had mentioned a bloody rock, a previously unpublicized item of evidence that had been found at the murder scene. Although he denied having anything to do with the child's death, Bloodsworth was found guilty of rape and capital murder in 1985. He was sentenced to death. His conviction was overturned on appeal because the prosecution had failed to disclose potentially exculpatory evidence. He was convicted once again at his 1987 retrial and was sentenced to two consecutive terms of life imprisonment. Following nearly nine years of incarceration, Bloodsworth was released from prison and pardoned in 1993 after DNA testing revealed that he was not the source of the semen found in the girl's body. A decade later, the DNA found in the victim was matched to another man, Kimberly Shay Ruffner, who was serving a prison sentence for other crimes. Ruffner pled guilty to the child's murder in 2004.[2]

Andrea Yates. A horrified nation learned in June 2001 that five children, ranging between six months and seven years of age, had been drowned in a bathtub in their home in Clear Lake, Texas, just outside of Houston. Their mother, Andrea Yates, had a lengthy history of mental illness and suffered from severe depression. She admitted to having filled the bathtub and then holding each of her struggling children under water until they died. She summoned the police by making a 911 call and then telephoned her husband Rusty, who was at work, and told him to come home. When he asked whether anyone was hurt, she responded, "The kids.... All of them." Yates was charged with three counts of capital murder (the district attorney elected not to join all five children's cases at the trial). She entered a plea of not guilty by reason of insanity which, under Texas law, required her to prove that when she drowned her children she suffered from severe mental illness and, as a result, did not know that her actions were wrong. The trial jury heard from numerous mental health experts who agreed that Yates was psychotic when she immersed her children in the bath water. She reportedly believed that by killing her children she was saving them from Satan's influence and perishing in the fires of hell. Four psychiatrists and a psychologist testified that, in their opinion, her mental illness prevented her from knowing that her actions were wrong. Dr. Park Dietz, the prosecution's sole mental health expert, concurred that Yates was psychotic. He disagreed that she failed to understand that drowning her children was wrong. On cross-examination, Dr. Dietz testified that shortly before Yates had acted, the television show "Law & Order," which Yates regularly watched, featured a woman suffering from post-partum depression who had been found insane after drowning her children in a bathtub. At the conclusion of more than three weeks of testimony, the jury took less than four hours to find Yates guilty as charged. The same jury deliberated just 35 minutes before rejecting the prosecution's call for the death penalty. Yates was sentenced to life imprisonment. Three years later, the Texas Court of Appeals reversed Yates's convictions. The reversals were based on the revelation that Dr. Dietz's testimony about the "Law & Order" episode was erroneous—in fact, no show had aired portraying a depressed woman drowning her children and being acquitted by reason of insanity. The court concluded that this misinformation was likely to have influenced the jury's verdict. At her 2006 retrial, a jury found Yates not guilty by reason of insanity.[3]

Francesco Caruso. In February 1927, Francesco Caruso was convicted following trial in a Brooklyn court of the intentional, deliberate, and premeditated murder of a physician, Dr. Pendola, who had attended to his ill son. Under New York law then in effect, Caruso was sentenced to death. The facts supporting Caruso's first-degree murder conviction are described in *People v. Caruso*, 159 N.E. 390 (N.Y. 1927).

Francesco Caruso, an illiterate Italian, 35 years old, came to this country about 1911. He worked as a laborer, and in the early part of 1927 was living with his wife and six small children in an apartment in Brooklyn. On Friday, February 11th, one of these children, a boy of six, was ill with a sore throat. That day and the next he treated the boy with remedies bought at a drug store. The child grew worse, and at 10 o'clock of the night of the 12th he sent for a Dr. Pendola, who had been recommended to him, but with whom he was not acquainted....

Some time between 10:30 and 11 in the evening Dr. Pendola arrived. The child had diptheria (sic). Caruso was sent out to buy some antitoxin, and, when he returned, the doctor administered it. He then gave Caruso another prescription with instructions as to its use, and left promising to return in the morning.

Caruso watched the child all night, giving remedies every half hour. 'About 4 o'clock in the morning,' he testified, 'my child was standing up to the bed, and asked me to, he he says, 'Papa' he said, 'I am dying.' I say that time, I said, 'You don't die.' I said, 'I will help you every time.' The same time that child he will be crazy—look like crazy, that time—don't want to stay any more inside. All I can do, I keep my child in my arms, and I held him in my arms from 4 o'clock until 8 o'clock in the morning. After 8 o'clock in the morning the poor child getting worse—the poor child in the morning he was'—(slight interruption in the testimony while the defendant apparently stops to overcome his emotion). 'The poor child that time, and he was asking me, 'Papa,' he said, 'I want to go and sleep.' So I said, 'All right, Giovie, I will put you in the sleep.' I take my Giovie, and I put him in the bed, and he started to sleep, to wait until the doctor came, and the doctor he never came. I waited from 10 o'clock, the doctor he never came.'

Then, after trying in vain to get in touch with the doctor, he sent for an ambulance from a drug store.

'When I go home I seen my child is got up to the bed that time, and he says to me, 'Papa, I want to come with you.' I take my child again up in my arms, and I make him look to the backyard to the window. He looked around the yard about a couple of minutes, and after, when he looked around, he says to me, 'Papa, I want to go to sleep again.' I said, 'All right, Giovie, I will put you in the sleep.' I put my child on the bed. About a few seconds my child is on the bed, my child says to me, he says, 'Papa, I want to go to the toilet.' I said, 'All right, Giovie, I will take you to the toilet.' So I was trying to pick up the child, and make him go to the toilet, when I held that child I felt that leg—that child started to shake up in my arms. My wife know about better than me—I cannot see good myself in the face, so she tell what kind of shakes he do, and she has told me, she says, 'Listen, Frank, why, the child has died already.' I said, 'All right, you don't cry. No harm, because you make the child scared.' That time I go right away and put the child on the bed. When I put the child, before I put my hand to the pillow, my child said to me, 'Good-bye, Papa, I am going already.' So that time I put my hands to my head—I said, 'That child is dead. I don't know what I am going to do myself now.' That time I never said nothing, because I said, 'Jesus, my child is dead now. Nobody will get their hands on my child."

About 12 o'clock Dr. Pendola arrived. The child had been dead for some time. He was told, and then Caruso says the doctor laughed, and he 'lost his head.' This seems incredible. Yet Caruso apparently believed it, for his testimony on the stand is a repetition of the same charge made in his statement that same night, before it is likely that a man of Caruso's mentality would be preparing a false defense. The probability is there was, from one cause or another, some twitching of the facial muscles that might be mistaken for a smile.

Besides the delay of the doctor and the smile was another circumstance, which, if true, would exasperate Caruso. He says, and again this appears in the statement as well as in his testimony on the trial, that, when he was buying the antitoxin, the druggist told him that the dose was too large for a child of the age of his son. This he told the doctor. The latter was indignant, and paid no heed to the warning. The druggist denied any such conversation, and apparently the dose was proper. But it seems probable that something occurred that left on Caruso's mind the impression that the death of his child was caused by malpractice. At least, immediately after the death, he told an ambulance surgeon that Dr. Pendola had killed his child by an injection, and also complained of his delay in not coming that morning. And within a short time he made the same charge to others.

Then followed some talk. Caruso accused the doctor of killing his child. The doctor denied it. Caruso attacked him in anger, choked him until he fell to the floor, then went to a closet ten or twelve feet away, took a knife, and stabbed him twice in the throat, so killing him. Caruso then took his family to the janitor's apartment downstairs, and himself went to his brother's house on Staten Island, where he was arrested that night. He made no attempt whatever to conceal the facts of the homicide....

The court unanimously reversed Caruso's conviction.

Conviction here of murder in the first degree is not justified by the weight of the evidence. The jury might find that the intent to kill existed....

But was there premeditation and deliberation? This seems to have been the question which troubled the jury. They considered their verdict for six hours—twice returning for definitions of homicide and of deliberation and premeditation. Time to deliberate and premeditate there clearly was. Caruso might have done so. In fact, however, did he?

Until the Saturday evening Caruso had never met Dr. Pendola. Nothing occurred at that interview that furnished any motive for murder. Then came nervous strain and anxiety culminating in grief, deep and genuine, for the death of his child. Brooding over his loss, blaming the doctor for his delay in making the promised visit, believing he had killed the boy by his treatment, the doctor finally enters. And, when told of the child's death he appears to laugh. This, added to his supposed injuries, would fully account for the gust of anger that Caruso says he felt. Then came the struggle and the homicide.

As has been said, Caruso had the time to deliberate, to make a choice whether to kill or not to kill—to overcome hesitation and doubt—to form a definite purpose. And, where sufficient time exists, very often the circumstances surrounding the homicide justify—indeed require—the necessary inference. Not here, however. No plan to kill is shown, no intention of violence when the doctor arrived—only grief and resentment. Not until the supposed laugh did the assault begin. 'If the defendant inflicted the wound in a sudden transport of passion, excited by what the deceased then said and by the preceding events which, for the time, disturbed her reasoning faculties and deprived her of the capacity to reflect, or while under the influence of some sudden and uncontrollable emotion excited by the final culmination of her misfortunes, as indicated by the train of events which have been related, the act did not constitute murder in the first degree. Deliberation and premeditation imply the capacity at the time to think and reflect, sufficient volition to make a choice, and by the use of these powers to refrain from doing a wrongful act.' People v. Barberi, 149 N. Y. 256, 43 N. E. 635. When the supposed laugh came, there was apparent cause for excitement and anger. There was enough to indicate hot blood and unreflecting action. There was immediate provocation. The attack seems to have been the instant effect of impulse. Nor does the fact that the stabbing followed the beginning of the attack by some time affect this conclusion. It was all one transaction under the peculiar facts of this case. If the assault was not deliberated or premeditated, then neither was the infliction of the fatal wound.

With due consideration of all the facts presented there is insufficient evidence to justify a conviction of murder in the first degree. Doubtless, on this record the defendant might be convicted of some crime, either murder in the second degree, or, if his testimony on the stand is accepted, manslaughter in the first degree. Either verdict might be sustained on the facts. Not the one actually rendered.

The judgment of conviction should be reversed, and a new trial ordered.

On remand, Caruso pled guilty to first-degree manslaughter. He was sentenced to five- to ten-years in prison, and received an additional five- to ten-year sentence for committing a felony while armed.[4]

Robert Williams. A ten-year-old girl accompanied her family to watch a wrestling tournament at a YMCA in Des Moines, Iowa on Christmas Eve in 1968. When she failed to return from a trip to the restroom her parents became alarmed and began searching for her. A boy subsequently reported seeing Robert Williams, who recently had escaped from a mental hospital and had taken up residence at the YMCA, carrying a blanket from which two legs were protruding. Williams loaded the blanket into his car and drove away. The car was found abandoned in Davenport, Iowa, approximately 160 miles away, on Christmas Day. Williams telephoned a Des Moines attorney on December 26, and at the lawyer's urging Williams turned himself in to the Davenport police. He was arrested, given his *Miranda* rights, and arraigned. Pursuant to discussions with two separate attorneys who represented Williams, the police agreed that they would not interrogate Williams while they transported him from Davenport to Des Moines. During that trip, one of the detectives in the squad car engaged Williams in conversation, including what would become known as "the Christian burial speech."

> I want to give you something to think about while we're traveling down the road.... Number one, I want you to observe the weather conditions, it's raining, it's sleeting, it's freezing, driving is very treacherous, visibility is poor, it's going to be dark early this evening. They are predicting several inches of snow for tonight, and I feel that you yourself are the only person that knows where this little girl's body is, that you yourself have only been there once, and if you get a snow on top of it you yourself may be unable to find it. And, since we will be going right past the area on the way into Des Moines, I feel that we could stop and locate the body, that the parents of this little girl should be entitled to a Christian burial for the little girl who was snatched away from them on Christmas [E]ve and murdered. And I feel we should stop and locate it on the way in rather than waiting until morning and trying to come back out after a snow storm and possibly not being able to find it at all.

In short order, Williams directed the police to the child's body, which lay in a ditch approximately two miles from the Interstate highway connecting Davenport and Des Moines. Williams subsequently was convicted of the child's murder, with testimony concerning the discovery of her body and its condition admitted as evidence at his trial. By vote of 5–4, the United States Supreme Court ruled that Williams's incriminating statements in response to the Christian burial speech had been secured in violation of his Sixth Amendment right to counsel and thus were inadmissible at his trial, requiring reversal of his murder conviction. In his dissenting opinion, Chief Justice Burger argued that "Williams is guilty of the savage murder of a small child...." He maintained that "[t]he result in this case ought to be intolerable in ... an organized society."[5]

* * *

Applying even our narrow definition, which focuses on the conviction of individuals who are factually innocent of the charged crime, there should be little difficulty in concluding that the cases of Jesse and Stephen Boorn represent wrongful convictions. When Russell Colvin, their alleged victim, materialized in good health, it was crystal clear that the Boorns were innocent and that their convictions for murdering him could not be sustained. Their convictions are classic examples of "no crime" cases, which perhaps are most dramatic in the homicide context.[6] However, cases in which people have been convicted although no crime was committed also occur under other circumstances, such as when the fire supporting an arson conviction actually was of natural origin rather than the result of unlawful human agency, or when money allegedly stolen by a person convicted of larceny had, in fact, simply been misplaced by its owner.[7]

Nor should classifying Kirk Bloodsworth's case as a wrongful conviction be controversial. In addition to "no crime" cases, the other straightforward instance of a factually innocent person suffering a wrongful conviction is a so-called "wrong man" case—*i.e.*, where a crime has been committed but the wrong person is held responsible for it. Bloodsworth's wrongful conviction for the rape and murder of a child occurred before DNA analysis was applied to crime scene evidence. Nine years after his conviction, DNA test results were critical to his exoneration, and several years later to identifying the truly guilty party. As Bloodsworth's case illustrates, justice is doubly confounded when "the wrong man" is found guilty of a crime. Not only does an innocent person suffer, but the actual perpetrator may remain at large and escape conviction and punishment for years, if not entirely.

The original conviction of Andrea Yates, for murder, presents a more difficult classification decision. Suppose that Yates's first trial had not been tainted by Dr. Dietz's faulty testimony and the jury had simply (but "erroneously") rejected her insanity defense and found her guilty of the murder charges. Conceptually, it would seem eminently justifiable to consider a conviction "wrongful" that is based on the fact-finder's erroneous failure to credit an affirmative defense—such as insanity in Yates's case, or in another case, self defense, or duress. In the eyes of the law, having a valid defense negates guilt. Nevertheless, traditional definitions of wrongful convictions are not so expansive. Most commentators consider wrongful convictions to encompass only cases in which the accused did not physically engage in the charged conduct; under this restrictive definition, the erroneous rejection of a strictly "legal" defense does not qualify.[8]

If we accept that limitation, we would not consider Yates to have been wrongfully convicted of murder at her first trial even if she met the legal definition of insanity. By similar reasoning, Francesco Caruso's conviction for murdering Dr. Pendola would not be classified as wrongful. Indeed, Caruso's claim would seemingly be even more tenuous than Yates's, who would have been "not guilty" of a crime had her insanity defense been accepted. In contrast, Caruso could properly have been convicted of second-degree murder or manslaughter based on the evidence presented at his trial; the New York Court of Appeals acknowledged as much, while ruling only that the facts did not support a conviction for first-degree murder. Most crimes include a mental element, which cannot directly be observed. When the *mens rea* required to support a conviction involves such elusive constructs as "deliberation," "premeditation," or "malice," errors inevitably will be made.[9] Such errors can be highly consequential; in Caruso's case, for example, the difference was between death as punishment for first-degree murder, and a five- to ten-year prison sentence for manslaughter. Notwithstanding the significant factual and legal distinctions, if we follow convention we will not classify as a "wrongful conviction" the erroneous determination that an individual committed a more serious crime if he or she could properly be found guilty of a lesser offense.

Finally, there is general agreement that "wrongful convictions," in the present context, do not include those tainted by procedural error alone—even errors that contribute directly to a guilty verdict or involve the violation of a fundamental constitutional right. Robert Williams's murder conviction, although contaminated by what a majority of the Supreme Court concluded was a deliberate breach of his Sixth Amendment right to counsel, thus would not qualify. We might agree with the majority opinion in *Brewer v. Williams* that important constitutional values must be upheld even at the cost of establishing guilt in the case of a "savage murder." Yet we still would not offer Williams's case as an example of a wrongful conviction. We will be concerned exclusively with the conviction of factually innocent persons.

B. Operational Definitions and Measurement

Assuming that we can reach conceptual agreement about the meaning of a "wrongful conviction," we must still confront important practical questions, such as how to identify and measure wrongful convictions when they occur. This is no easy task. One approach would simply be to ask people who have been convicted of crimes whether they in fact are innocent. The obvious drawback to this strategy is our inability in most cases to corroborate the self-reported information and thus to confirm its validity. Researchers nevertheless have employed this essential methodology. An analysis of surveys completed by nearly 1300 prisoners in California, Michigan, and Texas in 2000 revealed that 15.4% (197 of 1282) of the inmates reported that they had been convicted and incarcerated despite not having committed a crime. While acknowledging that "some prisoners ... have a variety of self-serving motives for underreporting their crimes,"[10] the analysis also highlighted the revealing corollary finding that roughly 85% of the prisoners did not claim to be innocent. The authors of the study suggested that the 15.4% rate of self-reported wrongful convictions represents a useful benchmark as the uppermost estimate of wrongfully incarcerated individuals.[11]

Other researchers have asked criminal justice practitioners for their opinions regarding the prevalence of wrongful convictions. A survey administered in 2002–03 to several hundred police officers, prosecutors, defense attorneys, and judges in Ohio produced estimates that wrongful convictions occur nationally in approximately 1% to 3% of felony cases, and in 0.5% to 1% of felony cases within the respondents' own, local jurisdictions.[12] Twenty years earlier, a similarly comprised sample of Ohio criminal justice practitioners, supplemented by three-quarters of the country's state attorneys general, estimated that, on average, wrongful felony convictions occurred in approximately 0.5% of cases nationally.[13] The researchers who completed the latter study noted that even if "these apparently conservative estimates" of a 99.5% accuracy rate are reasonable, the resulting absolute number of erroneous convictions would be eye-opening. Using 1990 conviction data, and limiting their analysis to "index crimes" (murder and non-negligent manslaughter, robbery, forcible rape, aggravated assault, burglary, larceny/theft, motor vehicle theft, and arson), they calculated that a 0.5% error rate would "still generate about 10,000 erroneous convictions for index crimes in a single year. And this figure does not includ[e] the many erroneous convictions that occur in cases involving crimes not in the index...."[14]

Other estimates of how frequently wrongful convictions occur rely on different methodologies. These studies focus our attention on the difficult, intertwined issues of measurement and definition. While avoiding the drawbacks associated with asking people convicted of crimes if they in fact are guilty, or crediting the informed guesses of criminal justice practitioners, we confront other problems if we require some form of extrinsic, objective evidence—such as a judicial reversal or an executive pardon—that a wrongful conviction has occurred. For starters, an unknown number of wrongful convictions inevitably will escape official detection and correction, leaving a "dark figure" of uncertain size. But the threat of underinclusiveness, or failing to identify wrongful convictions that should have been counted, is not the only problem we encounter. When we rely on official measures, we simultaneously incur a risk of overinclusiveness, or erroneously labeling convictions as wrongful even though the defendants actually committed the crimes.

We might readily appreciate the concern that we will undercount, perhaps dramatically, the number of innocent people convicted of crimes if we demand that the same system of justice that produced an erroneous conviction officially recognize its mistake. Most wrongful convictions almost certainly are the product of a mistaken belief that the defendant was in fact guilty rather than a deliberate design to punish individuals who were known to be innocent. Consequently, the witnesses and criminal justice officials who helped cause a wrongful conviction, even if unwittingly, may resist efforts to overturn the conviction even in the face of new evidence that suggests the defendant is innocent. Various legal doctrines that reinforce the importance of achieving finality in the criminal justice process also serve as barriers to re-examining guilty verdicts. And, of course, in many cases there will be no new evidence; only the defendant's protestation of innocence, which already has been rejected. Some commentators thus argue that the wrongful convictions officially recognized by the judiciary or executive authorities almost certainly represent "only the tip of a very large iceberg."[15]

While official measures of wrongful convictions may be too restrictive, failing to account for untold numbers of innocent people convicted of crimes, they suffer from another serious shortcoming: they do not necessarily exclude the factually guilty. Proxies for actual innocence based on such official measures as a defendant's acquittal on retrial following a successful appeal, the judicial reversal of a conviction based on insufficient evidence of guilt or newly discovered evidence of innocence, a prosecutor's decision to forgo retrial following a reversal, or a gubernatorial pardon, are imperfect. Timothy Hennis's case is illustrative. Hennis, then a soldier stationed at Fort Bragg, was convicted of capital murder in 1985 following trial in a Cumberland County, North Carolina court. The crimes were horrific; a woman and her two children, ages 3 and 5, were stabbed to death. The woman also had been sexually assaulted. The evidence against Hennis included tenuous eyewitness identification testimony but was largely circumstantial. The trial court admitted 35 crime scene and autopsy photographs into evidence, many of which were gruesome. Hennis was sentenced to death and spent more than two years on death row before the North Carolina Supreme Court reversed his conviction in 1988. The court ruled that the combination of weak evidence and the cumulative, prejudicial photographs created "'a reasonable possibility that, had the error in question not been committed, a different result would have been reached at the trial....'"[16]

The prosecution elected to retry Hennis. In 1989, a second jury found him not guilty and Hennis was released from custody. The Death Penalty Information Center (DPIC) thus included Hennis on its list of individuals who had been convicted of capital murder, sentenced to death, and later determined to be innocent. DPIC began compiling its "innocence list" following a request for information from a congressional Subcommittee on Civil and Constitutional Rights about erroneous convictions for capital murder. The organization purposefully adopted an objective measure of innocence, relying on the actions of criminal justice officials.

> Since DPIC assumed a primary role in keeping this list, the only cases that have been added are those involving former death row inmates who have:
>
> a. Been **acquitted** of all charges related to the crime that placed them on death row, or
>
> b. Had all charges related to the crime that placed them on death row **dismissed** by the prosecution, or

> c. Been granted a complete **pardon** based on evidence of innocence.
>
> Cases are included in DPIC's list based on objective criteria. These criteria differ markedly from subjective judgments about who is "actually innocent." For example, some commentators have suggested that if the original prosecutor still thinks the defendant is "guilty," even though the defendant has been unanimously acquitted, then such a person should be excluded from the list. But DPIC's list avoids such personal suspicions and relies instead on the traditional source given the authority to separate guilt from innocence—our justice system. Our principal role has been to assemble these cases. We avoid subjective judgments or a hierarchy of innocence.[17]

Hennis remained on DPIC's "innocence list" for more than 20 years. But a DNA analysis performed in 2006, which employed more sophisticated technology than was available in the 1980s, linked Hennis to the original sexual assault and murders. Double jeopardy principles prevented North Carolina from bringing Hennis to trial again in its state courts. However, because Hennis had been in the Army at the time of the murders, the U.S. Military asserted jurisdiction and prosecuted him for the crimes. He was convicted by a military jury and sentenced to death in April 2010.[18] Hennis's unusual case illustrates "the stark difference between a jury's not finding guilt beyond a reasonable doubt and actual proof of innocence."[19] Indeed, in Scotland and some other countries, fact-finders in criminal trials are given three verdict options—guilty, not guilty, and "not proven"—to enable them to reflect this important distinction more clearly.[20] Hennis's name was removed from DPIC's innocence list in 2010.[21]

Measures of wrongful convictions based on definitions of innocence such as the one employed by the Death Penalty Information Center thus risk being both under- and over-inclusive. A compensating virtue is their objective nature. Other researchers have chosen more subjective measures in preference over official criteria. For example, in their widely cited study, "Miscarriages of Justice in Potentially Capital Cases," Professors Hugo Adam Bedau and Michael Radelet "found no instance in which the government has officially acknowledged that an execution carried out under lawful authority was in error."[22] Yet they reasoned, with considerable logical force, that the "failure by the authorities to acknowledge error is not very convincing evidence that errors have not occurred."[23] They consequently opted for a different measure of innocence.

> Apart from those few cases where it was later established that no capital crime was committed, or that the defendant had an ironclad alibi, or that someone else was incontrovertibly guilty, there is no quantity or quality of evidence that could be produced that would definitively prove innocence. The most one can hope to obtain is a consensus of investigators after the case reaches its final disposition. Consensus can be measured in degrees, and the cases that we have included in our catalogue are those in which we believe a majority of neutral observers, given the evidence at our disposal, would judge the defendant in question to be innocent.[24]

Is such a standard—the authors' belief that "a majority of neutral observers, given the evidence at our disposal, would judge the defendant in question to be innocent"—to be preferred over more objective criteria premised on official recognition of a wrongful conviction? Not surprisingly, the measure has been criticized: "The overwhelming problem with the Bedau-Radelet study is the largely subjective nature of its methodology and therefore of its conclusions.... [N]either the standard they use to determine innocence nor the proof they offer to meet that standard permits ... assurance," argue skeptics, that the cases they identified involve factually innocent individuals who were wrongfully convicted of crimes.[25]

We are left with no ideal solution to these definitional issues. Drawbacks are evident in using either the objective or more subjective definitions of wrongful convictions and innocence.[26] Most sources tend to rely on official, objective measures of these important constructs, while acknowledging their limitations.[27] The criteria invoked by DPIC to identify innocent persons who have been convicted of murder and sentenced death in this country during the modern era of capital punishment are representative. Professor Samuel Gross and colleagues used similar measures in their broad-based study of exonerations in the United States between 1989 and 2003.

> As we use the term, "exoneration" is an official act declaring a defendant not guilty of a crime for which he or she had previously been convicted. The exonerations we have studied occurred in four ways: (1) ... [G]overnors (or other appropriate officers) issued pardons based on evidence of the defendants' innocence. (2) ... [C]riminal charges were dismissed by courts after new evidence of innocence emerged, such as DNA. (3) ... [T]he defendants were acquitted at a retrial on the basis of evidence that they had no role in the crimes for which they were originally convicted. (4) ... [S]tates posthumously acknowledged the innocence of defendants who had already died in prison.... [28]

Definitional and measurement issues are of vital concern to our subject matter. The revealed portrait is essential to allowing us to understand the scope of the problem of wrongful convictions, and also to helping establish the framework for our investigation of the case and systemic variables that contribute to miscarriages of justice. We consider these issues next.

C. Wrongful Convictions: Incidence and Contributing Factors

The Innocence Project, founded in 1992 by Barry Scheck and Peter Neufeld at Cardozo Law School, "is a national litigation and public policy organization dedicated to exonerating wrongfully convicted people through DNA testing and reforming the criminal justice system to prevent future injustice."[29] In addition to investigating and assisting with legal challenges in potential wrongful conviction cases where DNA analysis can be probative of guilt or innocence, the Innocence Project maintains and updates a national roster of DNA-based exonerations. Through early March 2011, that list included 266 post-conviction DNA exonerations.[30] The first such exoneration occurred in Illinois in 1989, when Gary Dotson's 1979 convictions for aggravated kidnapping and rape were vacated following the analysis of DNA based on semen found in the underwear of the alleged victim (who four years earlier had recanted her trial testimony accusing Dotson of the crimes, explaining that she had instead engaged in consensual sexual relations with her boyfriend).[31]

Of course, even a DNA-based exoneration may not conclusively establish innocence. Even if the scientific validity of the analysis is conceded, it can be argued that a DNA exclusion does not demonstrate that a convicted defendant did not participate in a crime, but rather only that he or she was not the source of the biological evidence.[32] Still, exonerations such as Dotson's, in which DNA analysis either was not available or was not performed at the time of conviction but later was employed to exclude the defendant as the source of biological material associated with the alleged crime, normally are considered among the most trustworthy because the testing is both scientifically authoritative and highly discriminate. Consequently, the Innocence Project's list of DNA-based exonerations is frequently consulted to help shed light on the factors that, in retrospect, appear to have helped produce wrongful convictions. The Innocence Project identifies the following "contributing causes" of the wrongful convictions exposed through DNA analysis:

- "Eyewitness misidentification is the single greatest cause of wrongful convictions nationwide, playing a role in more than 75% of convictions overturned through DNA testing."[33]
- "[U]nvalidated or improper forensic science ... is the second-greatest contributor to wrongful convictions. In more than 50% of DNA exonerations, unvalidated or improper forensic science contributed to the wrongful conviction."[34]
- False confessions: "In about 25% of DNA exoneration cases, innocent defendants made incriminating statements, delivered outright confessions or pled guilty."[35]
- "In more than 15% of cases of wrongful conviction overturned by DNA testing, an informant or jailhouse snitch testified against the defendant."[36]
- Government misconduct: "The cases of wrongful convictions uncovered by DNA testing are replete with evidence of fraud or misconduct by prosecutors or police departments.... This misconduct has included: deliberate suggestiveness in identification procedures[;] the withholding of evidence from defense[;] the deliberate mishandling, mistreatment or destruction of evidence[;] the coercion of false confessions[; and] the use of unreliable government informants or snitches[.]" Police misconduct was identified as a factor contributing to a wrongful conviction in 37 of the first 74 (50%) DNA exonerations, and prosecutorial misconduct was identified as a contributing factor in 33 (45%) of those cases.[37]
- Bad lawyering: One of the contributing factors to wrongful convictions exposed through DNA analysis is representation "by an ineffective, incompetent or overburdened defense lawyer. The failure of overworked lawyers to investigate, call witnesses or prepare for trial has led to the conviction of innocent people.... Shrinking funding and access to resources for public defenders and court-appointed attorneys is only making the problem worse."[38]

The breakdown of contributing factors in the Innocence Project's list of DNA-based exonerations is interesting and potentially quite useful as we begin to anticipate mechanisms designed to help prevent, detect, and correct wrongful convictions. We must nevertheless attach important caveats to this information; cautionary notes that relate back to the definitional and measurement issues that we have introduced. The nub of the problem is that unless our sample is truly representative, we cannot safely assume that the findings are more widely generalizable to all cases of wrongful convictions. There are many reasons to be hesitant about inferring that the wrongful convictions exposed through DNA analysis—the only cases compiled and considered by the Innocence Project—are typical of the much larger universe of cases in which innocent people are convicted of crimes.

In the first place, the forensic use of DNA of course presumes that biological evidence, such as blood, saliva, semen, skin, or hair, has been retrieved from the crime scene or the victim and preserved for analysis. Yet such evidence is available in only a minority of crimes, perhaps between 10% and 20%,[39] and is typically associated with a skewed array of offenses. Sexual assaults, in particular, and other personal injury crimes are far more likely to yield evidence that is susceptible to DNA analysis than many other offenses such as robbery, property crimes, and public order violations—crimes which are much more prevalent. Moreover, for a variety of reasons, including resource constraints, the failure to collect or preserve evidence, the relatively minor nature of a crime or a defendant's lacking incarcerated status, a conviction being based on a guilty plea, and many others, post-conviction DNA analysis will not be conducted in many criminal cases even when biological evidence existed and might have been tested. We must be cautious about concluding that the factors contributing to the more than 260 wrongful convictions documented by later DNA testing and reported by the Innocence Project occur with comparable frequency in the considerably different and larger universe of cases of innocent people convicted of crimes.

Relying on the criteria noted previously (executive pardon, the vacating of a conviction and the dismissal of charges in light of newly discovered evidence of innocence, acquittal following retrial based on evidence that the defendant was not involved in the alleged crime, and a state's acknowledgment of innocence posthumously), Professor Gross and his colleagues identified 340 wrongful convictions that came to light in the United States between 1989 and 2003. Relying on media reports and various other sources, they generated "the most comprehensive compilation of exonerations available," while readily acknowledging the inevitability that their listing "is not exhaustive."[40] Indeed, they speculated that "many defendants who are not on this list, no doubt thousands, have been falsely convicted of serious crimes but have not been exonerated."[41] Their study focused only on exonerations involving case-specific evidence of innocence, thus excluding "mass exonerations of innocent defendants who were falsely convicted as a result of large scale patterns of police perjury and corruption"[42] as well as daycare cases. The wrongful convictions Gross *et al.* uncovered were not confined to DNA exonerations and thus went beyond those included on the Innocence Project list. Even so, their sample is unlikely to be representative of wrongful convictions generally.

For example, fully 96% of the exonerations they discovered were in murder cases (including murder accompanied by a sexual assault) (60%) or involved rape or sexual assault (36%)[43]—crimes "which together account for about 2% of all felony convictions, and a smaller proportion of all criminal convictions."[44] As Gross *et al.* explain, it would be fanciful to argue from these findings that almost all wrongful convictions are confined to murder and rape cases.

> At the end of 2001, about 118,000 prisoners in state prisons were serving sentences for rape and sexual assault, less than 10% of the total prison population. There were also over 155,000 prisoners who had been convicted of robbery, nearly 119,000 who were in prison for assault, more than 27,000 for other violent felonies, and over 600,000 for property, drug and public order offenses. Why are 90% of the exonerations for non-homicidal crimes concentrated among the rape cases?
>
> The comparison between rape and robbery is particularly telling. Robbery and rape are both crimes of violence in which the perpetrator is often a stranger to the victim. As a result, robberies and rapes alike are susceptible to the well-known danger of eyewitness misidentification. In fact there is every reason to believe that misidentifications in robberies outnumber those in rapes, by a lot....
>
> ...We have 121 exonerations in rape cases; in 88% of them (107/121) the defendant was the victim of eyewitness misidentification. But we have only six robbery exonerations, all of which include eyewitness misidentifications. What changed? The answer is obvious: DNA.... Since 1989, ... 87% of exonerated rape defendants were cleared by DNA evidence....

The implication is clear. If we had a technique for detecting false convictions in robberies that was comparable to DNA identification for rapes, robbery exonerations would greatly outnumber rape exonerations, and the total number of falsely convicted defendants who were exonerated would be several times what we report. And even among rape cases, DNA is only useful if testable samples of biological evidence were preserved and can be found, which is not always true.[45]

Our misgivings must extend beyond having an incomplete understanding about the true incidence of wrongful convictions or how miscarriages of justice are distributed among different offense types. Owing to the almost certainly skewed nature of the samples, we cannot safely assume that the factors contributing to the wrongful convictions exposed by DNA analysis, or even the larger number of cases compiled by Gross *et al.*, have comparable significance with respect to wrongful convictions generally. For instance, Gross *et al.* identified three principal "causes" of the false convictions in the murder and rape cases within their sample, as follows:[46]

	Murder (n = 205)*	Rape (n = 121)*
Eyewitness Misidentification	50%	88%
Reported Perjury	56%	25%
False Confession	20%	7%

(*Columns total to > 100% because some wrongful convictions had multiple causes)

Eyewitness misidentification played a part in roughly 75% of the wrongful convictions included on the Innocence Project's list of DNA-based exonerations, and in 50% of the murder and 88% of the rape wrongful convictions identified by Gross *et al.* The differential influence of eyewitness errors reported for these samples is one indication that we must exercise caution before drawing conclusions about the factors that most commonly give rise to wrongful convictions. An obvious reason for the reflected differences is that, unlike most rape prosecutions, homicide cases do not involve a surviving victim capable of offering identification testimony. Thus, if murder cases and rape cases are over- or underrepresented in the samples of known wrongful convictions, we risk having a correspondingly distorted picture of how large a role eyewitness misidentifications play in contributing to miscarriages of justice in criminal cases generally. Professors Gross and O'Brien elaborate:

> Nearly 90 percent of the rape exonerations in these data ... included eyewitness misidentifications—but how could it be otherwise? If the victim had been killed, the case would have been classified as murder rather than rape. Since these rape cases all included victims who survived, in all but a handful the victim testified and identified her attacker.... [R]ape cases are rarely prosecuted unless the victim is prepared to identify the defendant. That is also true, however, in the great majority of *all* rape prosecutions, most of which lead to conviction of guilty defendants. These aggregate data do not suggest that at the time of trial anything about the content of the victim's identification testimony should have alerted the court to the danger of misidentification. We now know that these were *mis*identifications because we now know from other evidence, usually DNA, that these 107 rape defendants were all innocent. In retrospect, looking only at cases in which a convicted rape defendant was ultimately exonerated, misidentification and innocence are almost synonymous.[47]

Other studies of known or presumed wrongful convictions, relying on different samples of cases, present still different pictures about the underlying contributing factors. An analysis completed in 2004 of the first 111 death row exonerations occurring in the modern (post-*Furman v. Georgia* (1972)[48]) era of capital punishment, reported that: "The snitch cases [involving the testimony of witnesses with incentives to lie, including jailhouse informants motivated by the prospect of leniency in their cases and killers seeking to divert suspicion from themselves] account for 45.9% of those [exonerations]. That makes snitches the leading cause of wrongful convictions in U.S. capital cases—followed by erroneous eyewitness identification testimony in 25.2% of the cases, false confessions in 14.4%, and false presentation of misleading scientific evidence in 9.9%."[49]

An earlier study that focused on wrongful convictions in both capital and potentially capital cases produced generally similar findings. Employing the standard described earlier, their belief that "a majority of neutral observers, given the evidence at our disposal, would judge the defendant in question to be innocent," Professors Bedau and Radelet identified 350 wrongful convictions in capital and potentially capital cases in the United States between 1900 and 1985, including 326 criminal homicide cases and 24 rape cases.[50] Consistent with other studies, they concluded that multiple factors contributed to many of the wrongful convictions. They summarized the sources of error and their respective frequency as follows:[51]

Type of Error	Number of Cases	
Police Error		*82*
Coerced or other false confession	49	
Negligence	11	
Other overzealous police work	22	
Prosecutor Error		*50*
Suppression of exculpatory evidence	35	
Other overzealous prosecution	15	
Witness Error		*193*
Mistaken eyewitness identification	56	
Perjury by prosecution witness	117	
Unreliable or erroneous prosecution testimony	20	
Other Error		*209*
Misleading circumstantial evidence	30	
Incompetence of defense counsel	10	
Judicial denial of admissibility of exculpatory evidence	7	
Inadequate consideration of alibi evidence	45	
Erroneous judgment on cause of death	16	
Fraudulent alibi or false guilty plea made by defendant	17	
Conviction demanded by community outrage	70	
Unknown	14	

Perjury committed by prosecution witnesses emerged as the factor contributing most frequently to wrongful convictions, occurring in 117 of the 350 cases (33%) in this sample.

Other leading factors included "community outrage" (70 cases, or 20%), eyewitness misidentification (56 cases, or 16%), and coerced or other false confessions (49 cases, or 14%).

It is easy to understand why a significant amount of attention has been given to wrongful convictions in death penalty cases, as reflected in DPIC's innocence list, and to potential death penalty cases, as included in the Bedau and Radelet study. Capital punishment is a uniquely severe and irrevocable sanction. Nevertheless, just as we suspect that the Innocence Project's compilation of DNA-based exonerations is not likely to be representative of wrongful convictions generally, we must be cautious about drawing general inferences about the prevalence and causes of wrongful convictions based on what is known about capital cases. For instance, it is possible that errors occur more frequently in capital cases than others because greater pressure is placed on the police to make arrests and on prosecutors to secure convictions, because jurors are influenced by the attendant publicity or the heinous nature of the crimes, because accomplices and other informants have heightened incentives to lie to deflect attention from themselves, because there is no surviving victim to offer testimony, and for a host of other reasons.[52] On the other hand, it could be true that enhanced procedural safeguards in capital prosecutions help prevent erroneous convictions,[53] which would suggest that the error rate is likely to be higher in more routine matters. Another possibility is that heightened judicial review is afforded capital cases on appeal and post-conviction challenges, simply making it more likely that miscarriages of justice will be detected when they happen to occur.[54]

Relying on the documented death row exonerations during capital punishment's modern era, some researchers have estimated that innocent people may account for as many as 2.3%[55] or an even higher percentage (between 3.3% and 5%)[56] of individuals under sentence of death in this country. Yet, for the reasons we have just considered, we would be ill-advised to extrapolate from what is known about either the incidence of wrongful convictions in death-penalty cases or the factors contributing to them, to the much broader context of non-capital crimes. Our limited understanding of the prevalence and causes of wrongful convictions is significant, not only for untold numbers of innocent people adjudged guilty of crimes they did not commit, but because it compromises our ability to construct and implement effective policies to prevent, detect, and correct miscarriages of justice.

D. Wrongful Convictions: Past, Present, and Future

The emergence of DNA testing as a tool in the investigation and prosecution of crimes, and for exonerating the innocent, represented a watershed, commanding public recognition that wrongful convictions occur and have profound human consequences. This seemingly incontrovertible science demonstrated unequivocally that miscarriages of justice embody tragic consequences for factually innocent people, rather than entailing just procedural irregularities and so-called legal technicalities. By linking previously unknown perpetrators to crimes, DNA analyses also highlighted the compound injustices associated with wrongful convictions: not only were innocent people falsely imprisoned, but truly guilty parties escaped conviction and punishment. The number of additional crimes committed by offenders who remain at large while others are convicted in their stead is unknown, but the threat is a significant public safety concern. The true perpetrators were identified in

91 of the nation's first 233 DNA-based exonerations; it has been estimated that they were responsible for committing an additional 49 rapes and 19 murders.[57] Although wrongful convictions were certainly acknowledged prior to DNA's criminal justice application in the late 20th century, claims that innocent people suffered prosecution and conviction historically were greeted with skepticism and commanded much less urgency as a legal and social policy issue.

Yale Law School Professor Edwin Borchard published his seminal book, *Convicting the Innocent*, in 1932. In it, he described 65 cases of wrongful conviction for crimes that had occurred throughout the country in recent years. The book was motivated in part by Borchard's desire to substantiate the problem of wrongful convictions. He explained: "A district attorney in Worcester County, Massachusetts, a few years ago is reported to have said: 'Innocent men are never convicted. Don't worry about it, it never happens in the world. It is a physical impossibility.' The present collection of sixty-five cases, which have been selected from a much larger number, is a refutation of this supposition."[58] In 1923, United States District Court Judge Learned Hand had expressed similar certitude that justice systems did not produce wrongful convictions: "Our dangers do not lie in too little tenderness to the accused. Our procedure has been always haunted by the ghost of the innocent man convicted. It is an unreal dream. What we need to fear is the archaic formalism and the watery sentiment that obstructs, delays, and defeats the prosecution of crime."[59]

Borchard's method involved collecting and providing capsule summaries of recognized wrongful convictions. In so doing, he both demonstrated the existence of miscarriages of justice and attached a human face to them. Borchard's essential approach was replicated in ensuing decades, as more and more cases accumulated of innocent people being convicted of crimes. Erle Stanley Gardner, an attorney and writer who created the famous fictional defense attorney Perry Mason, was prominent among those who perpetuated Borchard's tradition. Gardner wrote frequently of cases of suspected or known wrongful convictions in articles appearing in *Argosy* magazine. In 1952, he published *The Court of Last Resort*, a book that discussed many such cases and his investigation of them.[60]

Gardner purposefully wrote in a journalistic, non-technical fashion so as to appeal to a general audience of readers. In their 1957 book, *Not Guilty*, Judge Jerome Frank and his daughter Barbara Frank used different case histories but the same format in describing instances of wrongful conviction and analyzing their causes. Their objective, likewise, was "to get each of you [addressing their readers] keenly interested, to stir you to a lively sense of injustice about the plight of the wrong man convicted of a crime."[61]

Every few years another such work would materialize, invoking different case studies yet representing a similar variation on what had become a familiar theme regarding the existence, causes, and consequences of wrongful convictions. More systematic, scholarly study concerning the prevalence and correlates of wrongful convictions began taking root in the 1980s and received increasing attention thereafter.[62] This social scientific research focus coincided with the dawning of DNA as an evidentiary tool, which in turn spurred renewed legal interest in miscarriages of justice and their correction. Social scientists have since begun developing explanatory theories and probing for the underlying fundamental or root causes of wrongful convictions—including perceptual, organizational, and institutional factors that may help spawn their more immediate causes such as eyewitness misidentification, false confessions, forensic errors, and the like.[63] Through the proliferation of Innocence Projects, the convening of Task Forces, the creation of Innocence Commissions, and many related developments, the legal community also has increasingly embraced case-specific and systemic issues endemic to the causes and prevention of wrongful convictions.[64] The many complex and intertwined issues of law, science, and policy that inhere in the study of wrongful convictions comprise our studies in the ensuing pages of this volume.

The book is formatted into an edited casebook approach. In each chapter, we have selected some watershed and some little-known, but important, cases that define and illustrate the focal issues. The full case opinions are not presented, but rather relevant excerpts. In connection with these cases, we discuss the results of relevant social science research and their policy implications. We also pose discussion questions and topics for further study.

Chapter 2

Wrongful Convictions and the Criminal Justice Process: Decision Points and Decision-Makers

A. Introduction

Wrongful convictions are the product of numerous interrelated decisions made by diverse actors in the criminal justice system. The police ordinarily are at the front end of the process as they investigate reported crimes and exercise their powers of arrest. Then, prosecutors, working closely with the police, typically oversee formal charging decisions and determine which cases will proceed to disposition, to be resolved either through guilty pleas or contested trials. The accused, of course, is an active participant in deciding how to plead to a charged offense. If a guilty plea is tendered the case will come before a judge for final resolution. A not guilty plea sets the stage for a trial before a judge or jury. The defendant is entitled to be acquitted unless the prosecution sustains its burden of proving guilt beyond a reasonable doubt. If it meets its burden of persuasion and judgment is entered on the guilty verdict, the defendant—even if innocent in fact—will stand convicted under law.

Once guilt is formally adjudicated, the defendant, no longer cloaked in a legal presumption of innocence, must affirmatively demonstrate that error tainted the conviction if the judgment is later to be disturbed. In this respect, innocent defendants face a peculiar disadvantage on appeal because, for the most part, appellate review focuses on detecting procedural error rather than re-examining the facts supporting a guilty verdict. An appellate court nevertheless may be asked to review the sufficiency of the evidence that underlies a conviction, and federal courts on habeas corpus review are empowered to decide whether a constitutionally adequate quantum of evidence supports a judgment of guilt. New evidence bearing on a defendant's professed innocence sometimes surfaces after a trial has been completed. Since that evidence is not part of the record reviewed on appeal, it may serve as the basis for a petition for a hearing and request for a new trial on post-conviction review. The federal courts also may be asked to issue a writ of habeas corpus (a legal remedy for prisoners protesting unfair or illegal detainment) to prisoners who maintain their innocence, coupled with a claim that their constitutional rights have been violated. Finally, executive clemency (such as a pardon issued by a state governor or, in federal cases, the President) may be available to individuals who have been denied judicial relief notwithstanding their claims of innocence.

In this chapter we introduce several of the decision points and decision-makers in the criminal justice process that are instrumental in producing and perpetuating wrongful convictions. More positively, these same decision-makers can help guard against and correct wrongful convictions when the process works effectively. We begin by considering the police decision to arrest.

B. The Police and the Decision to Arrest

The decision to arrest is momentous. An arrest sets in motion a chain of events that, in the normal sequence, immerses the suspect increasingly deeper in a process that can entail pre-trial incarceration, the filing of formal criminal charges, adjudication, and punishment. The police exercise vast discretion and are entrusted with broad authority in making arrests. Although statutes frequently constrain some of their arrest powers, the federal Constitution permits the police to make custodial arrests even for minor offenses that are not punishable by jail time.[1] The police normally are entrusted to make arrests without prior judicial authorization in the form of a warrant as long as they have probable cause to believe that the suspect has committed a crime.[2] And, significantly, the "probable cause" standard is a forgiving one. It does not require the police to be correct that the person arrested is in fact guilty of committing a crime, but only that ample, objective reasons support their decisions. The Supreme Court elaborated on the meaning of probable cause to arrest in *Maryland v. Pringle*, 540 U.S. 366, 124 S.Ct. 795, 157 L.Ed.2d 769 (2003), a case in which the defendant—a front-seat passenger in a car stopped for speeding around 3:00 a.m., who was arrested after the police found cocaine hidden in the vehicle's back seat—disputed the lawfulness of his arrest.

The long-prevailing standard of probable cause protects "citizens from rash and unreasonable interferences with privacy and from unfounded charges of crime," while giving "fair leeway for enforcing the law in the community's protection." *Brinegar v. United States,* 338 U.S. 160, 176 (1949). On many occasions, we have reiterated that the probable-cause standard is a "'practical, nontechnical conception'" that deals with "'the factual and practical considerations of everyday life on which reasonable and prudent men, not legal technicians, act.'" *Illinois v. Gates,* 462 U.S. 213, 231 (1983) (quoting *Brinegar, supra,* at 175–176). "[P]robable cause is a fluid concept—turning on the assessment of probabilities in particular factual contexts—not readily, or even usefully, reduced to a neat set of legal rules." *Gates,* 462 U.S., at 232.

The probable-cause standard is incapable of precise definition or quantification into percentages because it deals with probabilities and depends on the totality of the circumstances. We have stated, however, that "[t]he substance of all the definitions of probable cause is a reasonable ground for belief of guilt," [*Brinegar, supra,* at 175] and that the belief of guilt must be particularized with respect to the person to be searched or seized, *Ybarra v. Illinois,* 444 U.S. 85, 91 (1979). In *Illinois v. Gates,* we noted:

> "As early as *Locke v. United States,* 7 Cranch 339, 348 (1813), Chief Justice Marshall observed, in a closely related context: '[T]he term "probable cause," according to its usual acceptation, means less than evidence which would justify condemnation.... It imports a seizure made under circumstances which warrant suspicion.' More recently, we said that 'the *quanta* ... of proof' appropriate in ordinary judicial proceedings are inapplicable to the decision to issue a warrant. *Brinegar,* 338 U.S., at 173. Finely tuned standards such as proof beyond a reasonable doubt or by a preponderance of the evidence, useful in formal trials, have no place in the [probable-cause] decision." 462 U.S., at 235.

To determine whether an officer had probable cause to arrest an individual, we examine the events leading up to the arrest, and then decide "whether these historical facts, viewed from the standpoint of an objectively reasonable police officer, amount to" probable cause, *Ornelas* [*v. United States*, 517 U.S. 690, 696 (1996)].

In this case, Pringle was one of three men riding in a Nissan Maxima at 3:16 a.m. There was $763 of rolled-up cash in the glove compartment directly in front of Pringle. Five plastic glassine baggies of cocaine were behind the back-seat armrest and accessible to all three men. Upon questioning, the three men failed to offer any information with respect to the ownership of the cocaine or the money.

We think it an entirely reasonable inference from these facts that any or all three of the occupants had knowledge of, and exercised dominion and control over, the cocaine. Thus, a reasonable officer could conclude that there was probable cause to believe Pringle committed the crime of possession of cocaine, either solely or jointly.

With these observations in mind, we consider a Louisiana case in which a man who was convicted of murder and served several years in prison before his conviction was vacated and he gained release sued the police for damages on the ground that he had been wrongfully arrested.

Gibson v. State

758 So.2d 782 (La. 2000)

TRAYLOR, Justice.

In 1968, Plaintiff, Roland Gibson was convicted of first degree murder and received a life sentence. He subsequently filed an application for post conviction relief and, in 1993, was granted a new trial based upon the failure of the District Attorney to furnish *Brady* material. Lloyd West, the sole witness testifying against Gibson, recanted his previous testimony and confession wherein he implicated Gibson as the triggerman in the murder. Gibson, his wife, and two sons filed the instant suit for false arrest and imprisonment, malicious prosecution, and personal injury for Gibson's twenty-five-year incarceration. Without West's testimony, the District Attorney entered a *nolle prosequi* as to Gibson's indictment on March 31, 1993.

After the civil trial in the instant matter, the trial court found the Police lacked probable cause for Gibson's 1967 arrest and awarded Plaintiffs in excess of eleven million dollars in damages.... The court of appeal affirmed the trial court, but ... apportioned forty-five percent of the fault to the State, forty-five percent to the City, and ten percent to West....

We granted writs to determine whether, after being duly convicted of a crime and later released, a party may succeed in a suit for civil damages against the municipality for his arrest, prosecution, and incarceration on the basis of an alleged wrongful arrest.... [W]e answer this question in the negative. We hold that the City cannot be found at fault for Plaintiff's alleged wrongful arrest and prosecution and, therefore, vacate the contrary findings of the lower courts.

FACTS AND PROCEDURAL HISTORY

Murder Investigation and Trial

On December 30, 1967, at approximately 8:30 p.m. Charles Reinecke, Jr., a New Orleans Yellow Cab driver, was shot and killed in his taxi during an armed robbery. On January 1, 1968, the New Orleans Police (Police) completed an Offense Against Person Case Report detailing that an unknown five-foot, eleven-inch tall white male, twenty-five to thirty years of age, and weighing approximately 160 pounds was wanted in connection with the investigation "for questioning only." The Police lifted a fingerprint from a rear cab window and later determined it belonged to Lloyd West.

West, who was already in Police custody for an unrelated crime, initially denied any knowledge of the incident and gave the names of two persons with whom he claimed to have been at the time of the murder. These individuals denied being with West. West named a third individual, Thomas Crayton, who denied being with West at the time of the murder but informed the Police that on December 29, 1967 West and an AWOL Army soldier named "Roland" spent the night at his home. Crayton stated that he left West and "Roland" at his home when he left at noon on December 30, 1967. The Police contacted the Army and confirmed that as of

7:00 a.m. on December 30, 1967, a soldier named Roland Gibson was reported AWOL from his company in Fort Campbell, Kentucky, and could have been missing for up to forty-eight hours.

West was again interviewed and confronted with the discrepancies in his statements. At this point, he changed his story and claimed he was with his mother at the time of the murder. His mother was summoned to the police station, refused to be his alibi, and told Police that her son was lying. The Police apprized West of his mother's statement and asked him to submit to a polygraph test. Only after the polygraph test indicated deception did West confess his involvement in the murder and implicate Gibson as the triggerman. West repeated this confession on video, in the presence of his mother and uncle. West told Police that the murder weapon, a gun, was under a mattress at Gibson's residence.[3]

On March 30, 1968, the Police obtained a search warrant for Gibson's residence and served it on Gibson's mother. During the search, the Police found no weapon but remained at the residence and arrested Gibson when he arrived home at 6:20 a.m., intoxicated from a night of drinking. The Police arrested Gibson and took him to the police station.... On April 1, 1968, Gibson was advised of his rights and questioned by the Police. He repeatedly denied any knowledge of the murder and claimed to have left Fort Campbell by bus at 10:00 p.m. on the day of the murder. According to this story, Gibson could not have reached New Orleans by the time of the murder. Gibson told Police he arrived in New Orleans at approximately 3:00 a.m. the day after the murder. In an attempt to corroborate his story, Gibson told Police he was paid on the morning of December 30, 1967 but later produced an Army pay stub showing he was in fact paid on December 29, 1967. Gibson also produced a bus ticket which bore a date that did not substantiate his story. When confronted with conflicting information provided by the Army, Gibson admitted he was paid on December 29, went AWOL, and arrived in New Orleans before the murder took place.

On May 10, 1968, the Police concluded their investigation and turned all evidence and reports over to the District Attorney. The District Attorney did not provide the defense with the supplemental police report which detailed the numerous conflicting stories and alibis West provided the Police before he confessed and implicated Gibson in the murder.

Gibson and West were indicted for first degree murder. At Gibson's criminal trial, West testified that although he participated in the murder, Gibson was the triggerman. For the first time, Gibson, his wife, and his mother related that Gibson was alternately with his mother and wife the entire night of the murder. When asked the reason for their failure to inform the Police of this alibi during the pendency of the investigation and Gibson's incarceration, the wife and mother responded that they were never asked to do so. Several police officers testified that Gibson had given a different alibi when he was questioned in 1968. Following trial, the jury found Gibson guilty as charged and sentenced him to life imprisonment at hard labor. Two days later, West pled guilty to first degree murder, was sentenced to life imprisonment, and remains incarcerated.

Throughout the years, West and Gibson have filed appeals and numerous requests for post conviction relief. On June 3, 1985, Gibson drew up and gave West an affidavit to sign that recanted his prior testimony. In the affidavit, West swore that he lied at Gibson's trial and falsely accused Gibson to avoid receiving the death penalty. West signed the affidavit and, since that time, maintains Gibson was neither present during nor his accomplice in the murder.

Hearings on Application for Post Conviction Relief

In 1992, approximately seven years after Gibson effected West's affidavit and twenty-four years after his conviction, Gibson filed the instant application for post conviction relief and, for the first time, revealed West's June 3, 1985 affidavit. In it, Gibson claimed the District Attorney withheld a supplemental police report containing exculpatory *Brady* material.

The criminal court held three hearings on Gibson's motion for post conviction relief.... At the third and final hearing held on February 16, 1993, ... West represented for the first time that a man named George Carter, not Roland Gibson, was the triggerman. West stated he had not previously implicated George Carter because the Police beat him into submission of a statement implicating Gibson.

The presiding judge granted Gibson's application for post-conviction relief, finding that the District Attorney withheld the supplemental

3. Later, West confessed that the gun was at his home. The gun was never retrieved.

police report which contained exculpatory *Brady* material in the form of West's numerous conflicting statements to Police and could have denied Gibson a fair trial. The judge ordered a new trial. The District Attorney, bereft of the testimony of its sole witness, West, entered a *nolle prosequi* as to Gibson's indictment on March 31, 1993. Thereafter, Gibson was released from prison.

Civil Trial

On February 12, 1993, the Plaintiffs, Roland Gibson, his wife and two sons, filed the instant civil suit against the State of Louisiana, Lloyd West, the New Orleans District Attorney's Office, and the City seeking damages for false arrest and imprisonment, malicious prosecution, and personal injury in connection with Roland Gibson's twenty-five-year incarceration. The trial court found the State and District Attorney to be immune under La.Rev.Stat. 42:1441 A and dismissed all claims against them. On February 18, 1998, after a bifurcated trial, the trial court found the Police "did not have reasonable and trustworthy information sufficient to believe Mr. Gibson had committed a crime." The court rendered judgment awarding Plaintiffs a total of $11,674,624, with fault allocated ten percent to West and ninety percent to the City.

The City appealed.... The court of appeal, amended fault to include comparative fault of the District Attorney regardless of immunity as required by the La. Civ.Code art. 2323. The court of appeal found "the trial court erred in holding the Police, rather then [sic] the District Attorney, primarily liable for Gibson's wrongful conviction and incarceration" and re-apportioned forty-five percent of the fault to the State, forty-five percent to the City, and ten percent to West. The court of appeal affirmed the remainder of the trial court judgment. The City sought writs with this court.

STANDARD OF REVIEW

... The facts of this case are not disputed, therefore, this court must determine whether the lower court was manifestly erroneous in finding the Police lacked probable cause to arrest Gibson....

LAW AND DISCUSSION

The main issue presented for review is whether a municipality, through its police department, may be held liable in tort for wrongful arrest after the arrestee has been indicted, prosecuted, found guilty, and convicted of the crime with which he was charged....

Probable Cause to Arrest

At the outset, we note without hesitation that no police officer should fear that doing his duty in good faith will subject him to liability. An officer satisfies his duty of good faith in making an arrest if the arrest is based on probable cause. Probable cause exists when the facts and circumstances within the arresting officer's knowledge, and of which he has reasonable and trustworthy information, are sufficient to justify a man of average caution in the belief that the person to be arrested has committed or is committing an offense. *Beck v. Ohio,* 379 U.S. 89 (1964).

The determination of probable cause, unlike the determination of guilt at trial, does not require the fine resolution of conflicting evidence required at trial, and credibility determinations are seldom crucial in deciding whether available evidence supports a reasonable belief that the person to be arrested has committed a crime. Probable cause, as the very name implies, deals with probabilities. *Brinegar v. United States,* 338 U.S. 160 (1949). The probable cause standard recognizes that a degree of uncertainty may exist and that an officer need not have sufficient proof to convict but must have more than a mere suspicion. The facts need not eliminate all possible innocent explanations in order to support a finding of probable cause.

While verification may be required to establish probable cause where the source of the information seems untrustworthy, it is well established that the reputation of the accused, his opportunity to offer explanation, and the need for prompt action are all factors in determining whether unverified information furnishes probable cause. However, admissions of criminal activity carry their own indicia of reliability sufficient to support a finding of probable cause. Where a person confesses to a crime, the confession and implication of another is to be deemed highly credible and *more* reliable and trustworthy than previous statements disavowing any knowledge of the murder, because confessions are statements against penal interest....

In its reasons for judgment, the trial court asserted five reasons why it found the Police lacked probable cause to arrest Gibson: 1) the Police report detailed that a white male was "wanted for questioning only," a description which did not fit Gibson; 2) the Police reports did not mention two individuals were suspected of committing the crime; 3) there was no physical evidence against Gibson; 4) the Police believed West, a "convicted felon"; and 5) the Police failed to contact Greyhound to secure an alibi on Gibson's behalf.

After a thorough analysis of these points, we find no merit to any of the reasons for judgment and address each one in turn. First, the fact that the Police report contained the physical description of a white male wanted "for questioning only" does not refute the existence of probable cause for Gibson's arrest in light of other evidence against Gibson. The police report did not specify whether the white male was a suspect in the murder or merely a witness of some kind.... [T]he Police do not need to eliminate all possible innocent explanations in order to support a finding of probable cause. For this reason, we find the trial court erred in this finding.

Second, we do not find compelling the trial court's desire for an "explanation in police reports as to why or when police [concluded] that the crime was committed by two individuals rather than one." The Police are not precluded from arresting those whom they reasonably believe to have committed a crime and need not restrict themselves to investigating, questioning or arresting only those individuals they have previously designated as suspects in their reports. As evidence avails itself, the Police are required to act on that evidence and arrest any individual they reasonably suspect of having committed a crime. This is a basic tenet of the probable cause standard.

Third, regarding the trial court's requirement of physical evidence to arrest, clearly, just as an individual can be convicted solely on circumstantial evidence, so too can probable cause exist without physical evidence linking an individual to a crime. Under *Beck v. Ohio* and its progeny, the probable cause standard does not require the police to have direct, physical evidence; it only requires that the reasonable and trustworthy facts and circumstances within the arresting officer's knowledge are sufficient to justify a man of average caution in the belief that the arrestee has committed a crime. The trial court erred in requiring physical evidence to prove probable cause for the arrest.

Fourth, the trial court's repeated criticism of the Police for believing West's statements are disingenuous at best because the trial court later found West to be "a highly credible witness." The court cannot in one breath chastise the Police for their reliance on the statements of a "convicted felon" and in the next breath hold in high esteem the same individual's candor.... In light of all the reasonably reliable facts known to the Police at the time of the arrest,[8] the trial court erred in finding otherwise.

Lastly, the trial court censured the Police for not contacting Greyhound to substantiate Gibson's alibi.... [T]he Police need not exhaust all innocent explanations in order for probable cause to exist. Furthermore, Gibson later admitted he was in town at the time of the murder, so the Police's alleged failure is irrelevant. The trial court erred in unjustifiedly placing this burden upon the Police.

Under our analysis, each of the trial courts' reasons for judgment fail and we find the civil trial court committed manifest error in re-determining the probable cause issue. Plaintiffs failed to prove that no reasonable police officer would have concluded probable cause was present.

All information known to the Police at the time of Gibson's arrest was sufficient to justify a man of ordinary caution in believing Gibson had committed a crime. *See* n. 8. Furthermore, probable cause was conclusively proven by Gib-

8. The following facts were known to the Police at the time of the arrest and upon which they based that arrest: West implicated Gibson in his confession which was, as earlier discussed, properly regarded by the Police as highly credible ... regardless of West's prior false statements. This alone provided Police sufficient probable cause to effect a valid arrest. Further fortifying the existence of probable cause for the arrest, the Police received information from Mr. Crayton and the Army that corroborated the Police's belief that Gibson was in New Orleans and with West on the day of the murder. Gibson had no valid alibi and those he attempted to provide Police never materialized. The witnesses' statements against Gibson were uncontradicted and further bolstered the Police's reasonable belief that Gibson was involved in the murder, providing probable cause. As previously discussed, the trial court erred in finding West's inconsistent statements and confession negated the existence of probable cause for Gibson's arrest. It is not uncommon for an accused to deny guilt when first questioned by the Police. However, we consider the information provided by West in his confession to be more reliable and trustworthy than his previous conflicting statements because his confession was a statement against penal interest which carried its own indicia of reliability sufficient to support a finding of probable cause.

son's indictment and conviction in the criminal case. It is well settled that an indictment is conclusive proof of probable cause which connotes that probable cause existed for the underlying arrest. *Gerstein v. Pugh*, 420 U.S. 103 (1975). After indictment or conviction, the defendant can no longer allege lack of probable cause for his arrest. The jurisprudence of this state allows civil damages for false arrest only where there has been insufficient probable cause to sustain the arrest and the party has not been convicted of the crime with which they were charged....

Because the standard of proof for the determination of probable cause for a criminal case is more onerous than that for a civil case, it is, therefore, not the province of the civil court to later second-guess or redetermine this finding after the convict has been released, acquitted, or *nolle prosequied.* Absolute certainty of conviction is not the benchmark by which probable cause is determined, and we decline to go so far even where, as in this case, the conviction is later overturned and Plaintiff was not again convicted of the crime. Consequently, we conclude that probable cause existed at the time of Plaintiff's arrest and thereafter, notwithstanding the fact that plaintiff was granted post conviction relief and his indictment *nolle prosequied*....

CONCLUSION

Based on the totality of the circumstances, the Police had probable cause to believe Gibson had committed first degree murder and were therefore justified in arresting him. The trial court and court of appeal erred in assessing any fault to the City. Therefore, we reverse the portions of the rulings of the civil court and court of appeal finding the Police liable for false arrest based upon a lack of probable cause....

LEMMON, J., Concurring.

Although the majority frames the issue in this case as whether a party who has been convicted of a crime may recover civil damages based on his allegedly wrongful arrest, this decision should not be taken as holding that the conviction precludes recovery even if a wrongful arrest is proved. The critical issue is whether the police had probable cause to arrest plaintiff at the time he was arrested, and not whether the State had sufficient evidence to convict him eight months after his arrest.

The majority correctly determines that there was probable cause to arrest plaintiff at the time of the arrest. However, if probable cause had not existed at the critical time and an investigation subsequent to the arrest had developed evidence to support the eventual conviction, plaintiff would be entitled to some amount of damages for wrongful arrest, irrespective of the fact that he was subsequently convicted.

CALOGERO, C.J., concurring.

Mistakes happen in our less-than-perfect criminal justice system. Occasionally, innocent people serve time. Some people serve their entire sentence, and others, after serving a portion of their sentence, find relief through conclusive proof of innocence, or through a post-conviction proceeding that is simply designed to maintain a fair system, not necessarily to establish innocence. In either event, proven innocence or faulty process in securing the conviction, the State, some other public institution, or public officers are sometimes sued for recompense for harm caused by wrongful conduct or negligence on the part of their agents.

Counterbalanced against the law's affording relief in the form of monetary damages arising out of failures in the criminal justice system is a fear that the State will be subject to a flood of litigation and huge judgments threatening to drain its resources for the negligence and misdeeds of criminal justice agents while performing their jobs, as well as the fact that exposure to damage awards may have a chilling effect on vigorous prosecutions. It is for this reason that the legislature has seen fit to grant immunity to the State for the damages caused by district attorneys within the course and scope of their official duties. La.Rev.Stat. 42:1441....

On the other hand, State agencies or political subdivisions, *e.g.*, municipalities, are not afforded the same immunity. Thus, in the instant case, although the State does not have to pay for bad or substandard district attorney conduct, the City has to pay for its police officers' actions, provided Plaintiff bears his burden of showing that his damages were a consequence of the police officers' negligence or other fault-based conduct....

I concur in the judgment in favor of the City because the law and the evidence do not support the district court's ruling in this civil case. If Plaintiff's arrest by the New Orleans Police Department was without probable cause, then that misdeed or police officer failure may have caused or contributed to Plaintiff's short, legally unsupportable period of confinement following his arrest. Following that brief period—Plaintiff's arrest to the issuance of the indictment—the district attorney alone, with the evidence assembled and during the conduct of the trial, was responsible for Plaintiff's prosecution and conviction. Assuming Plaintiff was wrongfully arrested, and assuming the prosecutor procured Plaintiff's conviction and incarceration by misconduct or negligence on his part, the City would not likely be liable for more than a minimal sum for the short period of confinement prompted but the police officers' arrest without probable cause.

More significantly, however, the evidence in this case does not support the trial judge's determination that the police officers did not have probable cause to arrest Mr. Gibson for the armed robbery and murder of Charles Reinecke, Jr....

Although there may have been some evidence, gathered during the early part of the investigation, which did not implicate Plaintiff, other evidence did strongly point to Roland Gibson. On the negative side, the initial police report indicated that the police were looking for an unknown white male, twenty-five to thirty years old, five feet eleven inches tall, with blond hair for questioning. Nevertheless, on the positive side, the police had the evidence of Lloyd West's fingerprint found on the inside of the victim's cab and West's statement implicating Plaintiff as the gunman. Additionally, the police were able to corroborate these pieces of evidence with the statement of Thomas Crayton, who explained that he saw West and a friend named "Roland," an alleged AWOL Army soldier, which description fits Plaintiff, together in an apartment shortly before noon on December 30, 1967, just hours before the murder. Thus, the information available to the police at the time they chose to arrest Plaintiff established probable cause....

Notes and Questions

1. If the police had arrested Gibson without probable cause, would his subsequent indictment and conviction have exempted them from civil liability? How do the majority and concurring opinions appear to answer this question?

2. How persuasive is the reasoning in the majority opinion concerning West's credibility in implicating Gibson in the murder? In this regard, what should we make of the assertion that: "admissions of criminal activity carry their own indicia of reliability sufficient to support a finding of probable cause. Where a person confesses to a crime, the confession and implication of another is to be deemed highly credible ... because confessions are statements against penal interest"?

3. Are you persuaded by the facts presented in this case that Gibson was factually innocent? Does the answer to this question have any bearing on whether the police had probable cause to arrest him? On whether he should be entitled to recover money damages from the State of Louisiana or one of its subdivisions for his 25 years of incarceration? Does Gibson's case represent a "wrongful conviction" as we defined that term in Chapter One?

The arrest decision, if erroneous, can escalate rapidly and culminate in a wrongful conviction through a series of self-fulfilling prophecies as later actors—prosecutors, jurors, and even defense attorneys—succumb (perhaps subconsciously) to the belief that the police are unlikely to have taken an innocent person into custody. Yet, as we have seen, probable cause to arrest is far less demanding than the proof required to establish guilt. Innocent people sometimes are arrested. The police often must make decisions based on incomplete, conflicting, and ambiguous information, and while under intense pressure to restore order and quell community unrest following a crime. Like other actors in the criminal justice system, the police can be prone to "tunnel vision," a tendency that can help explain their erroneous focus on an innocent suspect and prematurely closing an investigation by making an arrest.

Tunnel vision is a well-researched and ubiquitous phenomenon; so ubiquitous that it goes by many additional names, including self-fulfilling prophecy, expectancy theory, and confirmation bias.[3] As defined by Findley and Scott, tunnel vision is a "compendium of common heuristics and logical fallacies to which we are all susceptible, that lead actors in the criminal justice system to focus on a suspect, select and filter the evidence that will build a case for conviction, while ignoring or suppressing evidence that points away from guilt."[4] In other words, once police and other criminal justice actors internalize that they have found "their man," a natural and unconscious tendency to focus exclusively on that suspect takes over. Information and evidence that supports their position is *actively* sought out, whereas information and evidence (*e.g.*, other possible suspects) that is contrary to or inconsistent with the guilt of the main suspect is ignored, discounted, mis-remembered, and re-interpreted. Tunnel vision, or confirmation bias, among police investigators is particularly pernicious because it sets the course for future investigation further down the criminal justice pipeline. Indeed, confirmation bias early in the investigation can enhance the effects of the phenomenon in later stages. As stated by Findley and Scott:

> Tunnel vision that might have led police investigators to focus on a suspect and to develop evidence against that suspect and disregard inconsistent or disconfirming evidence, shapes the information upon which prosecutors base their judgments. Prosecutors see the evidence generated by the police investigation, but often do not see the evidence about alternative suspects who were rejected too quickly, about eyewitnesses who failed to identify the defendant, or about other disconfirming evidence that police dismissed as insignificant.[5]

C. The Prosecutor: Charging and Trial Decisions

Robert H. Jackson had a distinguished legal career, serving as United States Solicitor General, United States Attorney General, and as an Associate Justice on the United States Supreme Court from 1941 through 1954. He took leave from the Supreme Court in 1945 to act as the chief United States prosecutor of Nazi war criminals in Nuremburg, Germany. In remarks delivered in 1940, while he was the nation's Attorney General, he made the following observations about the extensive power residing in the prosecutor's office.

> The prosecutor has more control over life, liberty, and reputation than any other person in America. His discretion is tremendous. He can have citizens investigated and, if he is that kind of person, he can have this done to the tune of public statements and veiled or unveiled intimations. Or the prosecutor may choose a more subtle course and simply have a citizen's friends interviewed. The prosecutor can order arrests, present cases to the grand jury in secret session, and on the basis of his one-sided presentation of the facts, can cause the citizen to be indicted and held for trial. He may dismiss the case before trial, in which case the defense never has a chance to be heard. Or he may go on with a public trial. If he obtains a conviction, the prosecutor can still make recommendations as to sentence, as to whether the prisoner should get probation or a suspended sentence, and after he is put away, as to whether he is a fit subject for parole. While the prosecutor at his best is one of the most beneficent forces in our society, when he acts from malice or other base motives, he is one of the worst.[6]

As the key figure in deciding whether to pursue formal charges against criminal suspects, in plea negotiations, and in representing the government's interests at trial, the prosecutor has enormous potential impact in helping to produce, or to avert wrongful convictions. In *Imbler v. Pachtman*, presented below, the Supreme Court rendered an important decision regarding the scope of a prosecutor's liability for damages under the federal civil rights statute, 42 U.S.C. § 1983, for allegedly violating the defendant's constitutional rights by contributing to his wrongful conviction and incarceration.

Imbler v. Pachtman

424 U.S. 409, 96 S.Ct. 984, 47 L.Ed.2d 128 (1976)

Mr. Justice POWELL delivered the opinion of the Court.

The question presented in this case is whether a state prosecuting attorney who acted within the scope of his duties in initiating and pursuing a criminal prosecution is amenable to suit under 42 U.S.C. § 1983 for alleged deprivations of the defendant's constitutional rights. The Court of Appeals for the Ninth Circuit held that he is not. We affirm.

I

The events which culminated in this suit span many years and several judicial proceedings. They began in January 1961, when two men attempted to rob a Los Angeles market run by Morris Hasson. One shot and fatally wounded Hasson, and the two fled in different directions. Ten days later Leonard Lingo was killed while attempting a robbery in Pomona, Cal., but his two accomplices escaped. Paul Imbler, petitioner in this case, turned himself in the next day as one of those accomplices. Subsequent investigation led the Los Angeles District Attorney to believe that Imbler and Lingo had perpetrated the first crime as well, and that Imbler had killed Hasson. Imbler was charged with first-degree felony murder for Hasson's death.

The State's case consisted of eyewitness testimony from Hasson's wife and identification testimony from three men who had seen Hasson's assailants fleeing after the shooting. Mrs. Hasson was unable to identify the gunman because a hat had obscured his face, but from police photographs she identified the killer's companion as Leonard Lingo. The primary identification witness was Alfred Costello, a passerby on the night of the crime, who testified that he had a clear view both as the gunman emerged from the market and again a few moments later when the fleeing gunman after losing his hat turned to fire a shot at Costello and to shed his coat before continuing on. Costello positively identified Imbler as the gunman. The second identification witness, an attendant at a parking lot through which the gunman ultimately escaped, testified that he had a side and front view as the man passed. Finally, a customer who was leaving Hasson's market as the robbers entered testified that he had a good look then and as they exited moments later. All of these witnesses identified Imbler as the gunman, and the customer also identified the second man as Leonard Lingo. Rigorous cross-examination failed to shake any of these witnesses.

Imbler's defense was an alibi. He claimed to have spent the night of the Hasson killing bar-hopping with several persons, and to have met Lingo for the first time the morning before the attempted robbery in Pomona. This testimony was corroborated by Mayes, the other accomplice in the Pomona robbery, who also claimed to have accompanied Imbler on the earlier rounds of the bars. The jury found Imbler guilty and fixed punishment at death.

Shortly thereafter Deputy District Attorney Richard Pachtman, who had been the prosecutor at Imbler's trial and who is the respondent before this Court, wrote to the Governor of California describing evidence turned up after trial by himself and an investigator for the state correctional authority. In substance, the evidence consisted of newly discovered corroborating witnesses for Imbler's alibi, as well as new revelations about prime witness Costello's background which indicated that he was less trustworthy than he had represented originally to Pachtman and in his testimony. Pachtman noted that leads to some of this information had been available to Imbler's counsel prior to trial but apparently had not been developed, that Costello had testified convincingly and withstood intense cross-examination, and that none of the new evidence was conclusive of Imbler's innocence. He explained that he wrote from a belief that "a prosecuting attorney had a duty to be fair and see that all true facts whether helpful to the case or not, should be presented."[5]

Imbler filed a state habeas corpus petition shortly after Pachtman's letter. The Supreme Court of California appointed one of its retired justices as referee to hold a hearing, at which Costello was the main attraction. He recanted his trial identification of Imbler, and it also was established that on cross-examination and redirect he had painted a picture of his own background that was more flattering than true. Imbler's corroborating witnesses, uncovered by prosecutor Pachtman's investigations, also testified.

In his brief to the Supreme Court of California on this habeas petition, Imbler's counsel described Pachtman's post-trial detective work as "(i)n the highest tradition of law enforcement and justice," and as a premier example of "devotion to duty." But he also charged that the prosecution had knowingly used false testimony and suppressed material evidence at Imbler's trial. In a thorough opinion by then Justice Traynor, the Supreme Court of California unanimously rejected these contentions and denied the writ. The California court noted that the hearing record fully supported the referee's finding that Costello's recantation of his identification lacked credibility compared to the original identification itself, and that the new corroborating witnesses who appeared on Imbler's behalf were unsure of their stories or were otherwise impeached.

In 1964, the year after denial of his state habeas petition, Imbler succeeded in having his death sentence overturned on grounds unrelated to this case. Rather than resentence him, the State stipulated to life imprisonment. There the matter lay for several years, until in late 1967 or early 1968 Imbler filed a habeas corpus petition in Federal District Court based on the same contentions previously urged upon and rejected by the Supreme Court of California.

The District Court ... found eight instances of state misconduct at Imbler's trial, the cumulative effect of which required issuance of the writ. Six occurred during Costello's testimony and amounted in the court's view to the culpable use by the prosecution of misleading or false testimony. The other two instances were suppressions of evidence favorable to Imbler by a police fingerprint expert who testified at trial and by the police who investigated Hasson's murder. The District Court ordered that the writ of habeas corpus issue unless California retried Imbler within 60 days, and denied a petition for rehearing.

... The Court of Appeals affirmed, ... and certiorari was denied. California chose not to retry Imbler, and he was released.

... In April 1972, Imbler filed a civil rights action, under 42 U.S.C. § 1983 and related statutes, against respondent Pachtman, the police fingerprint expert, and various other officers of the Los Angeles police force. He alleged that a conspiracy among them unlawfully to charge and convict him had caused him loss of liberty and other grievous injury. He demanded $2.7 million in actual and exemplary damages from each defendant, plus $15,000 attorney's fees.

... The gravamen of his complaint against Pachtman was that he had "with intent, and on other occasions with negligence" allowed Costello to give false testimony as found by the District Court, and that the fingerprint expert's suppression of evidence was "chargeable under federal law" to Pachtman. In addition Imbler claimed that Pachtman had prosecuted him with knowledge of a lie detector test that had "cleared" Imbler, and that Pachtman had used at trial a police artist's sketch of Hasson's killer made shortly after the crime and allegedly altered to resemble Imbler more closely after the investigation had focused upon him.

Pachtman moved under Fed. Rule Civ. Proc. 12(b)(6) to have the complaint dismissed as to him. The District Court, noting that public prosecutors repeatedly had been held immune from civil liability for "acts done as part of their traditional official functions," found that Pachtman's alleged acts fell into that category and granted his motion.... [T]he Court of Appeals for the Ninth Circuit ... affirmed.... We granted

5. The record does not indicate what specific action was taken in response to Pachtman's letter. We do note that the letter was dated August 17, 1962, and that Imbler's execution, scheduled for September 12, 1962, subsequently was stayed. The letter became a part of the permanent record in the case available to the courts in all subsequent litigation.

certiorari to consider the important and recurring issue of prosecutorial liability under the Civil Rights Act of 1871.

II

Title 42 U.S.C. § 1983 provides that "(e)very person" who acts under color of state law to deprive another of a constitutional right shall be answerable to that person in a suit for damages.[10] The statute thus creates a species of tort liability that on its face admits of no immunities, and some have argued that it should be applied as stringently as it reads. But that view has not prevailed.

This Court first considered the implications of the statute's literal sweep in Tenney v. Brandhove, 341 U.S. 367 (1951).... The Court concluded that immunities "well grounded in history and reason" had not been abrogated "by covert inclusion in the general language" of § 1983....

The decision in Tenney established that § 1983 is to be read in harmony with general principles of tort immunities and defenses rather than in derogation of them. Before today the Court has had occasion to consider the liability of several types of government officials.... The common-law absolute immunity of judges for "acts committed within their judicial jurisdiction," was found to be preserved under § 1983 in Pierson v. Ray, 386 U.S. 547 (1967). In the same case, local police officers sued for a deprivation of liberty resulting from unlawful arrest were held to enjoy under § 1983 a "good faith and probable cause" defense coextensive with their defense to false arrest actions at common law. We found qualified immunities appropriate in two recent cases.[13] ...

III

This case marks our first opportunity to address the § 1983 liability of a state prosecuting officer....

[O]ur earlier decisions on § 1983 immunities were ... predicated upon a considered inquiry into the immunity historically accorded the relevant official at common law and the interests behind it. The liability of a state prosecutor under § 1983 must be determined in the same manner.

A

The function of a prosecutor that most often invites a common-law tort action is his decision to initiate a prosecution, as this may lead to a suit for malicious prosecution if the State's case misfires. The first American case to address the question of a prosecutor's amenability to such an action was Griffith v. Slinkard, 146 Ind. 117, 44 N.E. 1001 (1896). The complaint charged that a local prosecutor without probable cause added the plaintiff's name to a grand jury true bill after the grand jurors had refused to indict him, with the result that the plaintiff was arrested and forced to appear in court repeatedly before the charge finally was nolle prossed. Despite allegations of malice, the Supreme Court of Indiana dismissed the action on the ground that the prosecutor was absolutely immune.

The Griffith view on prosecutorial immunity became the clear majority rule on the issue....

The common-law immunity of a prosecutor is based upon the same considerations that underlie the common-law immunities of judges and grand jurors acting within the scope of their duties. These include concern that harassment by unfounded litigation would cause a deflection of the prosecutor's energies from his public duties, and the possibility that he would shade his decisions instead of exercising the independence of judgment required by his public trust....

B

The common-law rule of immunity is thus well settled. We now must determine whether the same considerations of public policy that underlie the common-law rule likewise countenance absolute immunity under § 1983. We think they do.

If a prosecutor had only a qualified immunity, the threat of § 1983 suits would undermine performance of his duties no less than would the threat of common-law suits for malicious pros-

10. 42 U.S.C. § 1983, originally passed as § 1 of the Civil Rights Act of 1871, reads in full:

"Every person who, under color of any statute, ordinance, regulation, custom, or usage, of any State or Territory, subjects, or causes to be subjected, any citizen of the United States or other person within the jurisdiction thereof to the deprivation of any rights, privileges, or immunities secured by the Constitution and laws, shall be liable to the party injured in an action at law, suit in equity, or other proper proceeding for redress."

13. The procedural difference between the absolute and the qualified immunities is important. An absolute immunity defeats a suit at the outset, so long as the official's actions were within the scope of the immunity. The fate of an official with qualified immunity depends upon the circumstances and motivations of his actions, as established by the evidence at trial.

ecution. A prosecutor is duty bound to exercise his best judgment both in deciding which suits to bring and in conducting them in court. The public trust of the prosecutor's office would suffer if he were constrained in making every decision by the consequences in terms of his own potential liability in a suit for damages. Such suits could be expected with some frequency, for a defendant often will transform his resentment at being prosecuted into the ascription of improper and malicious actions to the State's advocate. Further, if the prosecutor could be made to answer in court each time such a person charged him with wrongdoing, his energy and attention would be diverted from the pressing duty of enforcing the criminal law.

Moreover, suits that survived the pleadings would pose substantial danger of liability even to the honest prosecutor. The prosecutor's possible knowledge of a witness' falsehoods, the materiality of evidence not revealed to the defense, the propriety of a closing argument, and ultimately in every case the likelihood that prosecutorial misconduct so infected a trial as to deny due process, are typical of issues with which judges struggle in actions for post-trial relief, sometimes to differing conclusions. The presentation of such issues in a § 1983 action often would require a virtual retrial of the criminal offense in a new forum, and the resolution of some technical issues by the lay jury. It is fair to say, we think, that the honest prosecutor would face greater difficulty in meeting the standards of qualified immunity than other executive or administrative officials. Frequently acting under serious constraints of time and even information, a prosecutor inevitably makes many decisions that could engender colorable claims of constitutional deprivation. Defending these decisions, often years after they were made, could impose unique and intolerable burdens upon a prosecutor responsible annually for hundreds of indictments and trials.

The affording of only a qualified immunity to the prosecutor also could have an adverse effect upon the functioning of the criminal justice system. Attaining the system's goal of accurately determining guilt or innocence requires that both the prosecution and the defense have wide discretion in the conduct of the trial and the presentation of evidence. The veracity of witnesses in criminal cases frequently is subject to doubt before and after they testify, as is illustrated by the history of this case. If prosecutors were hampered in exercising their judgment as to the use of such witnesses by concern about resulting personal liability, the triers of fact in criminal cases often would be denied relevant evidence.[24]

The ultimate fairness of the operation of the system itself could be weakened by subjecting prosecutors to § 1983 liability. Various post-trial procedures are available to determine whether an accused has received a fair trial. These procedures include the remedial powers of the trial judge, appellate review, and state and federal post-conviction collateral remedies. In all of these the attention of the reviewing judge or tribunal is focused primarily on whether there was a fair trial under law. This focus should not be blurred by even the subconscious knowledge that a post-trial decision in favor of the accused might result in the prosecutor's being called upon to respond in damages for his error or mistaken judgment.[25]

We conclude that the considerations outlined above dictate the same absolute immunity under § 1983 that the prosecutor enjoys at common law. To be sure, this immunity does leave the genuinely wronged defendant without civil redress against a prosecutor whose malicious or dishonest action deprives him of liberty. But the alternative of qualifying a prosecutor's immunity would disserve the broader public interest. It would prevent the vigorous and fearless performance of the prosecutor's duty that is essential to the proper functioning of the criminal justice

24. A prosecutor often must decide, especially in cases of wide public interest, whether to proceed to trial where there is a sharp conflict in the evidence. The appropriate course of action in such a case may well be to permit a jury to resolve the conflict. Yet, a prosecutor understandably would be reluctant to go forward with a close case where an acquittal likely would trigger a suit against him for damages.

25. The possibility of personal liability also could dampen the prosecutor's exercise of his duty to bring to the attention of the court or of proper officials all significant evidence suggestive of innocence or mitigation. At trial this duty is enforced by the requirements of due process, but after a conviction the prosecutor also is bound by the ethics of his office to inform the appropriate authority of after-acquired or other information that casts doubt upon the correctness of the conviction. Indeed, the record in this case suggests that respondent's recognition of this duty led to the post-conviction hearing which in turn resulted ultimately in the District Court's granting of the writ of habeas corpus.

system. Moreover, it often would prejudice defendants in criminal cases by skewing post-conviction judicial decisions that should be made with the sole purpose of insuring justice. With the issue thus framed, we find ourselves in agreement with Judge Learned Hand, who wrote of the prosecutor's immunity from actions for malicious prosecution:

"As is so often the case, the answer must be found in a balance between the evils inevitable in either alternative. In this instance it has been thought in the end better to leave unredressed the wrongs done by dishonest officers than to subject those who try to do their duty to the constant dread of retaliation." Gregoire v. Biddle, 177 F.2d 579, 581 (C.A.2 1949), cert. denied, 339 U.S. 949 (1950).

We emphasize that the immunity of prosecutors from liability in suits under § 1983 does not leave the public powerless to deter misconduct or to punish that which occurs. This Court has never suggested that the policy considerations which compel civil immunity for certain governmental officials also place them beyond the reach of the criminal law. Even judges, cloaked with absolute civil immunity for centuries, could be punished criminally for willful deprivations of constitutional rights on the strength of 18 U.S.C. § 242, the criminal analog of § 1983. The prosecutor would fare no better for his willful acts. Moreover, a prosecutor stands perhaps unique, among officials whose acts could deprive persons of constitutional rights, in his amenability to professional discipline by an association of his peers. These checks undermine the argument that the imposition of civil liability is the only way to insure that prosecutors are mindful of the constitutional rights of persons accused of crime.

IV

It remains to delineate the boundaries of our holding.... [T]he Court of Appeals emphasized that each of respondent's challenged activities was an "integral part of the judicial process." The purpose of the Court of Appeals' focus upon the functional nature of the activities rather than respondent's status was to distinguish and leave standing those cases, in its Circuit and in some others, which hold that a prosecutor engaged in certain investigative activities enjoys, not the absolute immunity associated with the judicial process, but only a good-faith defense comparable to the policeman's. We agree with the Court of Appeals that respondent's activities were intimately associated with the judicial phase of the criminal process, and thus were functions to which the reasons for absolute immunity apply with full force. We have no occasion to consider whether like or similar reasons require immunity for those aspects of the prosecutor's responsibility that cast him in the role of an administrator or investigative officer rather than that of advocate.[33] We hold only that in initiating a prosecution and in presenting the State's case, the prosecutor is immune from a civil suit for damages under § 1983. The judgment of the Court of Appeals for the Ninth Circuit accordingly is affirmed.

Mr. Justice STEVENS took no part in the consideration or decision of this case.

Mr. Justice WHITE, with whom Mr. Justice BRENNAN and Mr. Justice MARSHALL join, concurring in the judgment.

I concur in the judgment of the Court and in much of its reasoning. I agree with the Court that the gravamen of the complaint in this case is that the prosecutor knowingly used perjured testimony; and that a prosecutor is absolutely immune from suit for money damages under 42 U.S.C. § 1983 for presentation of testimony later determined to have been false, where the presentation of such testimony is alleged to have been unconstitutional solely because the prosecutor did not believe it or should not have believed it to be true.... [H]owever, ... I disagree with any implication that *absolute* immunity for prosecutors extends to suits based on claims of unconstitutional suppression of evidence because I believe such a rule would threaten to *injure* the

33. We recognize that the duties of the prosecutor in his role as advocate for the State involve actions preliminary to the initiation of a prosecution and actions apart from the courtroom. A prosecuting attorney is required constantly, in the course of his duty as such, to make decisions on a wide variety of sensitive issues. These include questions of whether to present a case to a grand jury, whether to file an information, whether and when to prosecute, whether to dismiss an indictment against particular defendants, which witnesses to call, and what other evidence to present. Preparation, both for the initiation of the criminal process and for a trial, may require the obtaining, reviewing, and evaluating of evidence. At some point, and with respect to some decisions, the prosecutor no doubt functions as an administrator rather than as an officer of the court. Drawing a proper line between these functions may present difficult questions, but this case does not require us to anticipate them.

judicial process and to interfere with Congress' purpose in enacting 42 U.S.C. § 1983, without any support in statutory language or history.

I

... [T]he central purpose of § 1983 is to "give a remedy to parties deprived of constitutional rights, privileges and immunities by an Official's abuse of his position." Monroe v. Pape, 365 U.S. 167, 172 (1961). The United States Constitution among other things, places substantial limitations upon state action, and the cause of action provided in 42 U.S.C. § 1983 is fundamentally one for "[m]isuse of power, possessed by virtue of state law and made possible only because the wrongdoer is clothed with the authority of state law." It is manifest then that all state officials as a class cannot be immune absolutely from damage suits under 42 U.S.C. § 1983 and that to extend absolute immunity to any group of state officials is to negate *pro tanto* the very remedy which it appears Congress sought to create. Thus, as there is no language in § 1983 extending *any* immunity to any state officials, the Court has not extended *absolute* immunity to such officials in the absence of the most convincing showing that the immunity is necessary. Accordingly, we have declined to construe § 1983 to extend absolute immunity from damage suits to a variety of state officials. Instead, we have construed the statute to extend only a qualified immunity to these officials, and they may be held liable for unconstitutional conduct absent "good faith." Any other result would "deny much of the promise of § 1983." Nonetheless, there are certain absolute immunities so firmly rooted in the common law and supported by such strong policy reasons that the Court has been unwilling to infer that Congress meant to abolish them in enacting 42 U.S.C. § 1983....

In justifying absolute immunity for certain officials, both at common law and under 42 U.S.C. § 1983, courts have invariably rested their decisions on the proposition that such immunity is necessary to protect the decision-making process in which the official is engaged.... [A]bsolute immunity for judges was justified on the ground that no matter how high the standard of proof is set, the burden of defending damage suits brought by disappointed litigants would "contribute not to principled and fearless decision-making but to intimidation." ...

The majority articulates other adverse consequences which may result from permitting suits to be maintained against public officials. Such suits may expose the official to an unjust damage award; such suits will be expensive to defend even if the official prevails and will take the official's time away from his job; and the liability of a prosecutor for unconstitutional behavior might induce a federal court in a habeas corpus proceeding to deny a valid constitutional claim in order to protect the prosecutor. However, these adverse consequences are present with respect to suits against policemen, school teachers, and other executives, and have never before been thought sufficient to immunize an official absolutely no matter how outrageous his conduct.... Thus, unless the threat of suit is also thought to injure the governmental decision-making process, the other unfortunate consequences flowing from damage suits against state officials are sufficient only to extend a qualified immunity to the official in question. Accordingly, the question whether a prosecutor enjoys an absolute immunity from damage suits under § 1983, or only a qualified immunity, depends upon whether the common law and reason support the proposition that extending absolute immunity is necessary to protect the judicial process.

II

... [T]he risk of injury to the judicial process from a rule permitting malicious prosecution suits against prosecutors is real. There is no one to sue the prosecutor for an erroneous decision *not* to prosecute. If suits for malicious prosecution were permitted, the prosecutor's incentive would always be not to bring charges. Moreover, the "fear of being harassed by a vexatious suit, for acting according to their consciences" would always be the greater "where powerful" men are involved. Accordingly, I agree with the majority that, with respect to suits based on claims that the prosecutor's decision to prosecute was malicious and without probable cause at least where there is no independent allegation that the prosecutor withheld exculpatory information from a grand jury or the court, the judicial process is better served by absolute immunity than by any other rule.

Public prosecutors were also absolutely immune at common law from suits for defamatory remarks made during and relevant to a judicial proceeding, and this immunity was also based on the policy of protecting the judicial process.... It is precisely the function of a judicial proceeding to determine where the truth lies. The ability of courts, under carefully developed procedures, to separate truth from falsity, and the importance of accurately resolving factual disputes in criminal (and civil) cases are such that those involved in judicial proceedings should be "given every encouragement to make a full disclosure of all pertinent information within their knowledge." For a witness, this means he must be permitted to testify without fear of being sued if his testimony is disbelieved. For a lawyer, it means that he must be permitted to call witnesses without fear of being sued if the witness is disbelieved and it is alleged that the lawyer knew or should have known that the witness' testimony was false.... [I]f the risk of having to defend a civil damage suit is added to the deterrent against such conduct already provided by criminal laws against perjury and subornation of perjury, the risk of self-censorship becomes too great. This is particularly so because it is very difficult if not impossible for attorneys to be absolutely certain of the objective truth or falsity of the testimony which they present. A prosecutor faced with a decision whether or not to call a witness whom he believes, but whose credibility he knows will be in doubt and whose testimony may be disbelieved by the jury, should be given every incentive to submit that witness' testimony to the crucible of the judicial process so that the factfinder may consider it, after cross-examination, together with the other evidence in the case to determine where the truth lies....

For the above-stated reasons, I agree with the majority that history and policy support an absolute immunity for prosecutors from suits based solely on claims that they knew or should have known that the testimony of a witness called by the prosecution was false; and I would not attribute to Congress an intention to remove such immunity in enacting 42 U.S.C. § 1983.

... However, insofar as the majority's opinion implies an absolute immunity from suits for constitutional violations other than those based on the prosecutor's decision to initiate proceedings or his actions in bringing information or argument to the court, I disagree. Most particularly I disagree with any implication that the absolute immunity extends to suits charging unconstitutional suppression of evidence. Brady v. Maryland, 373 U.S. 83 (1963).

III

There was no absolute immunity at common law for prosecutors other than absolute immunity from suits for malicious prosecution and defamation. There were simply no other causes of action at common law brought against prosecutors for conduct committed in their official capacity.... Secondly, it is by no means true that such blanket absolute immunity is necessary or even helpful in protecting the judicial process. It should hardly need stating that, ordinarily, liability in damages for unconstitutional or otherwise illegal conduct has the very desirable effect of deterring such conduct.... Absent special circumstances, such as those discussed in Part II, *supra*, with respect to actions attacking the decision to prosecute or the bringing of evidence or argument to the court, one would expect that the judicial process would be protected and indeed its integrity enhanced by denial of immunity to prosecutors who engage in unconstitutional conduct.

The absolute immunity extended to prosecutors in defamation cases is designed to encourage them to bring information to the court which will resolve the criminal case. That is its single justification. Lest they withhold valuable but questionable evidence or refrain from making valuable but questionable arguments, prosecutors are protected from liability for submitting before the court information later determined to have been false to their knowledge. It would stand this immunity rule on its head, however, to apply it to a suit based on a claim that the prosecutor unconstitutionally *withheld* information from the court. Immunity from a suit based upon a claim that the prosecutor suppressed or withheld evidence would *discourage* precisely the disclosure of evidence sought to be encouraged by the rule granting prosecutors immunity from defamation suits. *Denial* of immunity for unconstitutional withholding of evidence would encourage such disclosure. A prosecutor seeking to protect himself from liability for failure to disclose evidence may be induced to disclose more than is required. But, this will hardly injure the judicial process. Indeed, it will help it....

Equally important, unlike constitutional violations committed in the courtroom—improper summations, introduction of hearsay evidence in violation of the Confrontation Clause, knowing presentation of false testimony—which truly are an "integral part of the judicial process," the judicial process has no way to prevent or correct the constitutional violation of suppressing evidence. The judicial process will by definition be ignorant of the violation when it occurs; and it is reasonable to suspect that most such violations never surface. It is all the more important, then, to deter such violations by permitting damage actions under 42 U.S.C. § 1983 to be maintained in instances where violations do surface....

IV

The complaint in this case, while fundamentally based on the claim that the prosecutor knew or should have known that his witness had testified falsely in certain respects, does contain some allegations that exculpatory evidence and evidence relating to the witness' credibility had been suppressed. Insofar as the complaint is based on allegations of suppression or failure to disclose, the prosecutor should not, for the reasons set forth above, be absolutely immune. However, as the majority notes, the suppression of fingerprint evidence and the alleged suppression of information relating to certain pretrial lineups is not alleged to have been known in fact to the prosecutor it is simply claimed that the suppression is legally chargeable to him. While this may be so as a matter of federal habeas corpus law, it is untrue in a civil damage action. The result of a lie-detector test claimed to have been suppressed was allegedly known to respondent, but it would have been inadmissible at Imbler's trial and is thus not constitutionally required to be disclosed. The alteration of the police artist's composite sketch after Imbler was designated as the defendant is not alleged to have been suppressed and in fact appears not to have been suppressed.... The other items allegedly suppressed all relate to background information about only one of the three eyewitnesses to testify for the State, and were in large part concededly known to the defense and thus may not be accurately described as suppressed. The single alleged fact not concededly known to the defense which might have been helpful to the defense was that the State's witness had written some bad checks for small amounts and that a criminal charge based on one check was outstanding against him. However, the witness had an extensive criminal record which was known to but not fully used by the defense. Thus, even taken as true, the failure to disclose the check charges is patently insufficient to support a claim of unconstitutional suppression of evidence.... Thus, the only constitutional violation adequately alleged against the prosecutor is that he knew in his mind that testimony presented by him was false; and from a suit based on such a violation, without more, the prosecutor is absolutely immune. For this reason, I concur in the judgment reached by the majority in this case.

Notes and Questions

1. Given the procedural posture of this case, we must assume that Imbler's allegations are true; that is, that Deputy District Attorney Pachtman knew that the State's trial witnesses presented perjured testimony and that he had a hand in suppressing exculpatory evidence, misconduct which directly contributed to Imbler's conviction for capital murder in 1961, his sentence of death (subsequently vacated), and his nine years of incarceration until his conviction was vacated. California opted not to retry him, and he was released from prison by a federal court order. Yet, when Imbler sought money damages in compensation for his wrongful conviction and incarceration he was greeted with the response that prosecutors enjoy absolutely immunity under 42 U.S.C. § 1983 for such misconduct and that his complaint accordingly would be dismissed. Is this result unfair? Is it necessary? Can the answer to both of those questions be, "Yes"?

2. Justice Powell suggests that alternative deterrents exist for prosecutors who might be tempted to procure convictions by knowingly presenting perjured testimony or covering up exculpatory evidence, even if they need not fear civil liability under 42 U.S.C. § 1983. What might help deter such misconduct? How likely are those alternatives to be pursued? Even if employed, would they help repair the harm caused to someone like Imbler?

3. Within the context of recognizing absolute immunity from civil damages, should a distinction be made between a prosecutor's deliberately presenting false testimony and deliberately suppressing exculpatory evidence? Is Justice White's position on this issue persuasive?

4. What is the meaning of the caveat at the end of the majority opinion: "[R]espondent's activities were intimately associated with the judicial phase of the criminal process, and thus were functions to which the reasons for absolute immunity apply with full force. We have no occasion to consider whether like or similar reasons require immunity for those aspects of the prosecutor's responsibility that cast him in the role of an administrator or investigative officer rather than that of advocate"? What are the implications of this statement?

Ten-year old Jeanine Nicarico was abducted from her home in Naperville, Illinois, a suburb of Chicago, on February 25, 1983. She had stayed out of school that day due to illness. While she was home alone, an unidentified person or persons kicked in the front door of her house sometime during the afternoon. Her body was discovered two days later close to a hiking trail in the nearby town of Eola. She had been viciously beaten and sexually assaulted. Authorities eventually focused suspicion on three men: Alejandro Hernandez, Stephen Buckley, and Rolando Cruz. Months passed before each was indicted for the child's murder, in March 1984. The three men were jailed pending their joint trial, which began in January 1985. Hernandez and Cruz were found guilty and were sentenced to death. The jury was unable to reach a verdict in Buckley's case and charges against him were dropped, although not for another two years, during which time he remained incarcerated.

The Illinois Supreme Court overturned Hernandez's and Cruz's convictions on appeal in 1988. Cruz was retried in 1990 and was again convicted and sentenced to death. Hernandez's retrial ended in a hung jury. He was found guilty following a third trial in May 1991 and sentenced to 80 years in prison. Both men's convictions were again reversed on appeal. Cruz was tried a third time, in 1995, and was found not guilty. All charges against Hernandez subsequently were dismissed. Amidst the lengthy proceedings, DNA testing linked another man, Brian Dugan, to Jeanine Nicarico's rape and murder. Dugan, who committed numerous additional crimes before being arrested on other charges in 1985, including murder and rape, pled guilty to murdering Jeanine Nicarico in 2009. A jury sentenced him to death. Dugan's death sentence, along with all others on Illinois' death row, was commuted to life imprisonment without parole in March 2011 when Governor Pat Quinn signed legislation abolishing capital punishment in that state.

The circumstances surrounding the wrongful convictions and death sentences of Alejandro Hernandez and Rolando Cruz, and Stephen Buckley's arrest and incarceration, included numerous allegations of police and prosecutorial misconduct. The allegations resulted in the criminal prosecution of several of the involved DuPage County, Illinois law enforcement officers and prosecutors, who became known as the DuPage Seven. All were brought to trial and all were acquitted.[7] The following United States Supreme Court case involves Stephen Buckley's suit for civil damages filed under 42 U.S.C. § 1983 in connection with this case, and the justices' consideration of whether absolute immunity should be recognized for the claimed prosecutorial misconduct based on the alleged facts.

Buckley v. Fitzsimmons

509 U.S. 259, 113 S.Ct. 2606, 125 L.Ed.2d 209 (1993)

Justice STEVENS delivered the opinion of the Court.

In an action brought under 42 U.S.C. § 1983, petitioner seeks damages from respondent prosecutors for allegedly fabricating evidence during the preliminary investigation of a crime and making false statements at a press conference announcing the return of an indictment. The questions presented are whether respondents are absolutely immune from liability on either or both of these claims.

As the case comes to us, we have no occasion to consider whether some or all of respondents' conduct may be protected by qualified immunity. Moreover, we make two important assumptions about the case: first, that petitioner's allegations are entirely true; and, second, that they allege constitutional violations for which § 1983 provides a remedy....

I

Petitioner commenced this action on March 4, 1988, following his release from jail in Du Page County, Illinois. He had been incarcerated there for three years on charges growing out of the highly publicized murder of Jeanine Nicarico, an 11-year-old child, on February 25, 1983. The complaint named 17 defendants, including Du Page County, its sheriff and seven of his assistants, two expert witnesses and the estate of a third, and the five respondents.

Respondent Fitzsimmons was the duly elected Du Page County State's Attorney from the time of the Nicarico murder through December 1984, when he was succeeded by respondent Ryan, who had defeated him in a Republican primary election on March 21, 1984. Respondent Knight was an assistant state's attorney under Fitzsimmons and served as a special prosecutor in the Nicarico case under Ryan. Respondents Kilander (who came into office with Ryan) and King were assistant prosecutors, also assigned to the case.

The theory of petitioner's case is that in order to obtain an indictment in a case that had engendered "extensive publicity" and "intense emotions in the community," the prosecutors fabricated false evidence, and that in order to gain votes, Fitzsimmons made false statements about petitioner in a press conference announcing his arrest and indictment 12 days before the primary election. Petitioner claims that respondents' misconduct created a "highly prejudicial and inflamed atmosphere" that seriously impaired the fairness of the judicial proceedings against an innocent man and caused him to suffer a serious loss of freedom, mental anguish, and humiliation.

The fabricated evidence related to a bootprint on the door of the Nicarico home apparently left by the killer when he kicked in the door. After three separate studies by experts from the Du Page County Crime Lab, the Illinois Department of Law Enforcement, and the Kansas Bureau of Identification, all of whom were unable to make a reliable connection between the print and a pair of boots that petitioner had voluntarily supplied, respondents obtained a "positive identification" from one Louise Robbins, an anthropologist in North Carolina who was allegedly well known for her willingness to fabricate unreliable expert testimony. Her opinion was obtained during the early stages of the investigation, which was being conducted under the joint supervision and direction of the sheriff and respondent Fitzsimmons, whose police officers and assistant prosecutors were performing essentially the same investigatory functions.

Thereafter, having failed to obtain sufficient evidence to support petitioner's (or anyone else's) arrest, respondents convened a special grand jury for the sole purpose of investigating the Nicarico case. After an 8-month investigation, during which the grand jury heard the testimony of over 100 witnesses, including the bootprint experts, it was still unable to return an indictment. On January 27, 1984, respondent Fitzsimmons admitted in a public statement that there was insufficient evidence to indict anyone for the rape and murder of Jeanine Nicarico. Although no additional evidence was obtained in the interim, the indictment was returned in March, when Fitzsimmons held the defamatory press conference so shortly before the primary election. Petitioner was then arrested, and because he was unable to meet the bond (set at $3 million), he was held in jail.

Petitioner's trial began 10 months later, in January 1985. The principal evidence against him was provided by Robbins, the North Carolina anthropologist. Because the jury was unable to reach a verdict on the charges against petitioner, the trial judge declared a mistrial. Petitioner remained in prison for two more years, during which a third party confessed to the crime and the prosecutors prepared for petitioner's retrial. After Robbins died, however, all charges against him were dropped. He was released, and filed this action.

II

We are not concerned with petitioner's actions against the police officers (who have asserted the defense of qualified immunity), against the expert witnesses (whose trial testimony was granted absolute immunity by the District Court), and against Du Page County (whose motion to dismiss on other grounds was granted in part). At issue here is only the action against the prosecutors, who moved to dismiss based on their claim to absolute immunity. The District Court held that respondents were entitled to absolute immunity for all claims except the claim against Fitzsimmons based on his press conference. With respect to the claim based on the alleged fabrication of evidence, the District Court framed the question as whether the effort "to obtain definitive boot evidence linking [petitioner to the crime] was in the nature of acquisition of evidence or in the nature of evaluation of evidence for the purpose of initiating the criminal process." The Court concluded that it "appears" that it was more evaluative than acquisitive.

Both petitioner and Fitzsimmons appealed, and a divided panel of the Court of Appeals for the Seventh Circuit ruled that the prosecutors had absolute immunity on both claims....

We granted Buckley's petition for certiorari, vacated the judgment, and remanded the case for further proceedings in light of our intervening decision in *Burns v. Reed,* 500 U.S. 478 (1991). On remand, the same panel, again divided, reaffirmed its initial decision....

We granted certiorari for a second time, limited to issues relating to prosecutorial immunity. We now reverse.

III

The principles applied to determine the scope of immunity for state officials sued under 42 U.S.C. § 1983 are by now familiar. Section 1983, on its face admits of no defense of official immunity. It subjects to liability "[e]very person" who, acting under color of state law, commits the prohibited acts. In *Tenney v. Brandhove,* 341 U.S. 367, 376 (1951), however, we held that Congress did not intend § 1983 to abrogate immunities "well grounded in history and reason." ...

Since *Tenney,* we have recognized two kinds of immunities under § 1983. Most public officials are entitled only to qualified immunity. *Harlow v. Fitzgerald,* 457 U.S. 800 (1982). Under this form of immunity, government officials are not subject to damages liability for the performance of their discretionary functions when "their conduct does not violate clearly established statutory or constitutional rights of which a reasonable person would have known." *Harlow v. Fitzgerald,* 457 U.S., at 818. In most cases, qualified immunity is sufficient to "protect officials who are required to exercise their discretion and the related public interest in encouraging the vigorous exercise of official authority."

We have recognized, however, that some officials perform "special functions" which, because of their similarity to functions that would have been immune when Congress enacted § 1983, deserve absolute protection from damages liability....

In determining whether particular actions of government officials fit within a common-law tradition of absolute immunity, or only the more general standard of qualified immunity, we have applied a "functional approach," which looks to "the nature of the function performed, not the identity of the actor who performed it." We have twice applied this approach in determining whether the functions of contemporary prosecutors are entitled to absolute immunity.

In *Imbler v. Pachtman,* 424 U.S. 409 (1976), we held that a state prosecutor had absolute immunity for the initiation and pursuit of a criminal prosecution, including presentation of the state's case at trial. Noting that our earlier cases had been "predicated upon a considered inquiry into the immunity historically accorded the relevant official at common law and the interests behind it," we focused on the functions of the prosecutor that had most often invited common-law tort actions. We concluded that the common-law rule of immunity for prosecutors was "well settled" and that "the same considerations of public policy that underlie the common-law rule likewise countenance absolute immunity under § 1983." Those considerations supported a rule of absolute immunity for conduct of prosecutors that was "intimately associated with the judicial phase of the criminal process." In concluding that "in initiating a prosecution and in presenting the State's case, the prosecutor is immune from a civil suit for damages under § 1983," we did not attempt to describe the line between a prosecutor's acts in preparing for those functions, some of which would be absolutely immune, and his acts of investigation or "administration," which would not.

We applied the *Imbler* analysis two Terms ago in *Burns v. Reed,* 500 U.S. 478 (1991). There the § 1983 suit challenged two acts by a prosecutor: (1) giving legal advice to the police on the propriety of hypnotizing a suspect and on whether probable cause existed to arrest that suspect, and

(2) participating in a probable-cause hearing. We held that only the latter was entitled to absolute immunity. Immunity for that action under § 1983 accorded with the common-law absolute immunity of prosecutors and other attorneys for eliciting false or defamatory testimony from witnesses or for making false or defamatory statements during, and related to, judicial proceedings. Under that analysis, appearing before a judge and presenting evidence in support of a motion for a search warrant involved the prosecutor's "'role as advocate for the State.'" Because issuance of a search warrant is a judicial act, appearance at the probable-cause hearing was "'intimately associated with the judicial phase of the criminal process.'"

We further decided, however, that prosecutors are not entitled to absolute immunity for their actions in giving legal advice to the police. We were unable to identify any historical or common-law support for absolute immunity in the performance of this function. We also noted that any threat to the judicial process from "the harassment and intimidation associated with litigation" based on advice to the police was insufficient to overcome the "[a]bsen[ce] [of] a tradition of immunity comparable to the common-law immunity from malicious prosecution, which formed the basis for the decision in *Imbler.*" And though we noted that several checks other than civil litigation prevent prosecutorial abuses in advising the police, "one of the most important checks, the judicial process," will not be effective in all cases, especially when in the end the suspect is not prosecuted. In sum, we held that providing legal advice to the police was not a function "closely associated with the judicial process."

IV

In this case the Court of Appeals held that respondents are entitled to absolute immunity because the injuries suffered by petitioner occurred during criminal proceedings. That holding is contrary to the approach we have consistently followed since *Imbler*....

A

We first address petitioner's argument that the prosecutors are not entitled to absolute immunity for the claim that they conspired to manufacture false evidence that would link his boot with the bootprint the murderer left on the front door. To obtain this false evidence, petitioner submits, the prosecutors shopped for experts until they found one who would provide the opinion they sought. At the time of this witness shopping the assistant prosecutors were working hand in hand with the sheriff's detectives under the joint supervision of the sheriff and state's attorney Fitzsimmons.

Petitioner argues that *Imbler's* protection for a prosecutor's conduct "in initiating a prosecution and in presenting the State's case," extends only to the act of initiation itself and to conduct occurring in the courtroom. This extreme position is plainly foreclosed by our opinion in *Imbler* itself. We expressly stated that "the duties of the prosecutor in his role as advocate for the State involve actions preliminary to the initiation of a prosecution and actions apart from the courtroom," and are nonetheless entitled to absolute immunity. We noted in particular that an out-of-court "effort to control the presentation of [a] witness' testimony" was entitled to absolute immunity because it was "fairly within [the prosecutor's] function as an advocate." To be sure, *Burns* made explicit the point we had reserved in *Imbler*: A prosecutor's administrative duties and those investigatory functions that do not relate to an advocate's preparation for the initiation of a prosecution or for judicial proceedings are not entitled to absolute immunity. We have not retreated, however, from the principle that acts undertaken by a prosecutor in preparing for the initiation of judicial proceedings or for trial, and which occur in the course of his role as an advocate for the State, are entitled to the protections of absolute immunity. Those acts must include the professional evaluation of the evidence assembled by the police and appropriate preparation for its presentation at trial or before a grand jury after a decision to seek an indictment has been made.

On the other hand, as the function test of *Imbler* recognizes, the actions of a prosecutor are not absolutely immune merely because they are performed by a prosecutor. Qualified immunity "'represents the norm'" for executive officers, so when a prosecutor "functions as an administrator rather than as an officer of the court" he is entitled only to qualified immunity. *Imbler,* 424 U.S., at 431, n. 33. There is a difference between the advocate's role in evaluating evidence and interviewing witnesses as he prepares for trial, on the one hand, and the detective's role in searching for the clues and corroboration that might give him probable cause to recommend that a suspect be arrested, on the other hand. When a prosecutor performs the investigative functions normally performed by a detective or police officer, it is "neither appropriate nor justifiable that, for the same act, immunity should protect the one and not the other." Thus, if a prosecutor plans and executes a raid on a suspected weapons cache, he "has no greater claim to complete immunity than activities of police officers allegedly acting under his direction."

The question, then, is whether the prosecutors have carried their burden of establishing that they were functioning as "advocates" when they were endeavoring to determine whether the bootprint at the scene of the crime had been made by petitioner's foot. A careful examination of the allegations concerning the conduct of the prosecutors during the period before they convened a special grand jury to investigate the crime provides the answer. The prosecutors do not contend that they had probable cause to arrest petitioner or to initiate judicial proceedings during that period. Their mission at that time was entirely investigative in character. A prosecutor neither is, nor should consider himself to be, an advocate before he has probable cause to have anyone arrested.[5]

It was well after the alleged fabrication of false evidence concerning the bootprint that a special grand jury was empaneled. And when it finally was convened, its immediate purpose was to conduct a more thorough investigation of the crime — not to return an indictment against a suspect whom there was already probable cause to arrest. Buckley was not arrested, in fact, until 10 months after the grand jury had been convened and had finally indicted him. Under these circumstances, the prosecutors' conduct occurred well before they could properly claim to be acting as advocates. Respondents have not cited any authority that supports an argument that a prosecutor's fabrication of false evidence during the preliminary investigation of an unsolved crime was immune from liability at common law.... It therefore remains protected only by qualified immunity.

After *Burns,* it would be anomalous, to say the least, to grant prosecutors only qualified immunity when offering legal advice to police about an unarrested suspect, but then to endow them with absolute immunity when conducting investigative work themselves in order to decide whether a suspect may be arrested. That the prosecutors later called a grand jury to consider the evidence this work produced does not retroactively transform that work from the administrative into the prosecutorial. A prosecutor may not shield his investigative work with the aegis of absolute immunity merely because, after a suspect is eventually arrested, indicted, and tried, that work may be retrospectively described as "preparation" for a possible trial; every prosecutor might then shield himself from liability for any constitutional wrong against innocent citizens by ensuring that they go to trial. When the functions of prosecutors and detectives are the same, as they were here, the immunity that protects them is also the same.

B

We next consider petitioner's claims regarding Fitzsimmons' statements to the press. Petitioner alleged that, during the prosecutor's public announcement of the indictment, Fitzsimmons made false assertions that numerous pieces of evidence, including the bootprint evidence, tied Buckley to a burglary ring that committed the Nicarico murder. Petitioner also alleged that Fitzsimmons released mug shots of him to the media, "which were prominently and repeatedly displayed on television and in the newspapers."

---

5. Of course, a determination of probable cause does not guarantee a prosecutor absolute immunity from liability for all actions taken afterwards. Even after that determination, as the opinion dissenting in part, points out, a prosecutor may engage in "police investigative work" that is entitled to only qualified immunity.

Furthermore, there is no "true anomaly," in denying absolute immunity for a state actor's investigative acts made before there is probable cause to have a suspect arrested just because a prosecutor would be entitled to absolute immunity for the malicious prosecution of someone whom he lacked probable cause to indict. That criticism ignores the essence of the function test. The reason that lack of probable cause allows us to deny absolute immunity to a state actor for the former function (fabrication of evidence) is that there is no common-law tradition of immunity for it, whether performed by a police officer or prosecutor. The reason that we grant it for the latter function (malicious prosecution) is that we have found a common-law tradition of immunity for a prosecutor's decision to bring an indictment, whether he has probable cause or not. By insisting on an equation of the two functions merely because a prosecutor might be subject to liability for one but not the other, the dissent allows its particular policy concerns to erase the function test it purports to respect....

Petitioner's legal theory is that "[t]hese false and prejudicial statements inflamed the populace of DuPage County against" him, thereby defaming him, resulting in deprivation of his right to a fair trial, and causing the jury to deadlock rather than acquit.

Fitzsimmons' statements to the media are not entitled to absolute immunity. Fitzsimmons does not suggest that in 1871 there existed a common-law immunity for a prosecutor's, or attorney's, out-of-court statement to the press.... Indeed, while prosecutors, like all attorneys, were entitled to absolute immunity from defamation liability for statements made during the course of judicial proceedings and relevant to them, most statements made out of court received only good-faith immunity. The common-law rule was that "[t]he speech of a counsel is privileged by the occasion on which it is spoken...." *Flint v. Pike,* 4 Barn. & Cress. 473, 478, 107 Eng.Rep. 1136, 1138 (K.B. 1825).

The functional approach of *Imbler,* which conforms to the common-law theory, leads us to the same conclusion. Comments to the media have no functional tie to the judicial process just because they are made by a prosecutor. At the press conference, Fitzsimmons did not act in "'his role as advocate for the State.'" The conduct of a press conference does not involve the initiation of a prosecution, the presentation of the state's case in court, or actions preparatory for these functions. Statements to the press may be an integral part of a prosecutor's job, and they may serve a vital public function. But in these respects a prosecutor is in no different position than other executive officials who deal with the press, and, as noted above, qualified immunity is the norm for them....

V

... As to the two challenged rulings on absolute immunity, ... the judgment of the United States Court of Appeals for the Seventh Circuit is reversed, and the case is remanded for further proceedings consistent with this opinion....

Justice KENNEDY, with whom the Chief Justice, Justice WHITE, and Justice SOUTER join, concurring in part and dissenting in part.

I agree there is no absolute immunity for statements made during a press conference. But I am unable to agree with the Court's conclusion that respondents are not entitled to absolute immunity on petitioner's claim that they conspired to manufacture false evidence linking petitioner to the bootprint found on the front door of Jeanine Nicarico's home....

I

... There is a reason even more fundamental than that stated by the Court for rejecting Buckley's argument that *Imbler* applies only to the commencement of a prosecution and to in-court conduct. This formulation of absolute prosecutorial immunity would convert what is now a substantial degree of protection for prosecutors into little more than a pleading rule. Almost all decisions to initiate prosecution are preceded by substantial and necessary out-of-court conduct by the prosecutor in evaluating the evidence and preparing for its introduction, just as almost every action taken in the courtroom requires some measure of out-of-court preparation. Were preparatory actions unprotected by absolute immunity, a criminal defendant turned civil plaintiff could simply reframe a claim to attack the preparation instead of the absolutely immune actions themselves....

Applying these principles to the case before us, I believe that the conduct relating to the expert witnesses falls on the absolute immunity side of the divide. As we recognized in *Imbler* and *Burns,* and do recognize again today, the functional approach does not dictate that all actions of a prosecutor are accorded absolute immunity. "When a prosecutor performs the investigative functions normally performed by a detective or police officer, it is 'neither appropriate nor justifiable that, for the same act, immunity should protect the one and not the other.'" *Ante.* Nonetheless, while Buckley labels the prosecutors' actions relating to the bootprint experts as "investigative," I believe it is more accurate to describe the prosecutors' conduct as preparation for trial. A prosecutor must consult with a potential trial witness before he places the witness on the stand, and if the witness is a critical one, consultation may be necessary even before the decision whether to indict. It was obvious from the outset that the bootprint was critical to the prosecution's case, and the prosecutors' consultation with experts is best viewed as a step to ensure the bootprint's admission in evidence and to bolster its probative value in the eyes of the jury.

Just as *Imbler* requires that the decision to use a witness must be insulated from liability, it requires as well that the steps leading to that decision must be free of the distortive effects of potential liability, at least to the extent that the prosecutor is engaged in trial preparation. Actions in "obtaining, reviewing, and evaluating" witness testimony, are a classic function of the prosecutor as advocate. Pretrial and even preindictment consultation can be "intimately associated with the judicial phase of the criminal process." Potential liability premised on the prosecutor's early consultation would have "an adverse effect upon the functioning of the criminal justice system." Concern about potential liability arising from pretrial consultation with a witness might "hampe[r]" a prosecutor's exercise of his judgment as to whether a certain witness should be used. The prospect of liability may "induc[e] [a prosecutor] to act with an excess of caution or otherwise to skew [his] decisions in ways that result in less than full fidelity to the objective and independent criteria that ought to guide [his] conduct." Moreover, "[e]xposing the prosecutor to liability for the initial phase of his prosecutorial work could interfere with his exercise of independent judgment at every phase of his work, since the prosecutor might come to see later decisions in terms of their effect on his potential liability." That distortion would frustrate the objective of accuracy in the determination of guilt or innocence.

Furthermore, the very matter the prosecutors were considering, the decision to use particular expert testimony, was "subjected to the 'crucible of the judicial process.'" ...

Our holding in *Burns v. Reed* is not to the contrary.... The premise of *Burns* was that, in providing advice to the police, the prosecutor acted to guide the police, not to prepare his own case. In those circumstances, we found an insufficient link to the judicial process to warrant absolute immunity. But the situation here is quite different. For the reasons already explained, subjecting a prosecutor's pretrial or preindictment witness consultation and preparation to damages actions would frustrate and impede the judicial process, the result *Imbler* is designed to avoid....

III

In recognizing a distinction between advocacy and investigation, the functional approach requires the drawing of difficult and subtle distinctions, and I understand the necessity for a workable standard in this area. But the rule the Court adopts has created more problems than it has solved. For example, even after there is probable cause to arrest a suspect or after a suspect is indicted, a prosecutor might act to further police investigative work, say by finding new leads, in which case only qualified immunity should apply. The converse is also true: Even before investigators are satisfied that probable cause exists or before an indictment is secured, a prosecutor might begin preparations to present testimony before a grand jury or at trial, to which absolute immunity must apply. In this case, respondents functioned as advocates, preparing for prosecution before investigators are alleged to have amassed probable cause and before an indictment was deemed appropriate. In my judgment respondents are entitled to absolute immunity for their involvement with the expert witnesses in this case. With respect, I dissent from that part of the Court's decision reversing the Court of Appeals judgment of absolute immunity for respondents' conduct in relation to the bootprint evidence.

Notes and Questions

1. In *Kalina v. Fletcher*, 522 U.S. 118, 118 S.Ct. 502, 139 L.Ed.2d 471 (1997), the Supreme Court revisited the scope of a prosecutor's absolute immunity from civil liability under 42 U.S.C. § 1983. Rodney Fletcher was arrested for burglary in connection with the theft of computer equipment from a school in King County, Washington. A judge had issued a warrant for his arrest based on the sworn allegations of a deputy prosecuting attorney, Lynne Kalina, which were included in a certificate attached to the warrant application. Kalina's allegations included material factual errors. The charges against Fletcher subsequently were dismissed, although they resulted in his spending a day in jail after he was arrested. Fletcher sought damages against Kalina under § 1983 for violating his constitutional right to be free from unreasonable seizures. The lower federal courts rejected Kalina's claim of absolute immunity. A unanimous Supreme Court affirmed. Justice Stevens' opinion distinguished between a prosecutor's preparing and filing court documents such as a charging instrument or an application for an arrest warrant—actions which

are integral to the prosecutor's function as an advocate in a judicial proceeding and hence entitled to absolute immunity—and the conduct in this case.

Although the law required that [certificate supporting the arrest warrant application] to be sworn or certified under penalty of perjury, neither federal nor state law made it necessary for the prosecutor to make that certification. In doing so, petitioner performed an act that any competent witness might have performed....

[P]etitioner argues that the execution of the certificate was just one incident in a presentation that, viewed as a whole, was the work of an advocate and was integral to the initiation of the prosecution. That characterization is appropriate for her drafting of the certification, her determination that the evidence was sufficiently strong to justify a probable-cause finding, her decision to file charges, and her presentation of the information and the motion to the court. Each of those matters involved the exercise of professional judgment; indeed, even the selection of the particular facts to include in the certification to provide the evidentiary support for the finding of probable cause required the exercise of the judgment of the advocate. But that judgment could not affect the truth or falsity of the factual statements themselves. Testifying about facts is the function of the witness, not of the lawyer.... [T]he evidentiary component of an application for an arrest warrant is a distinct and essential predicate for a finding of probable cause. Even when the person who makes the constitutionally required "Oath or affirmation" is a lawyer, the only function that she performs in giving sworn testimony is that of a witness.

2. In 1978, Curtis W. McGhee, Jr. and Terry Harrington were convicted of murder in Iowa and sentenced to life imprisonment. Twenty-four years later their convictions were vacated and they were freed from prison following the revelation that the trial prosecutor had suppressed material, exculpatory evidence in violation of *Brady v. Maryland,* 373 U.S. 83, 83 S.Ct. 1194, 10 L.Ed.2d 215 (1963). The prosecutor in office when the convictions were vacated elected not to retry Harrington. McGhee pled guilty to second-degree murder pursuant to an agreement that he would be sentenced to the time he already had served in prison.[8] Thereafter, in reliance on 42 U.S.C. § 1983, McGhee and Harrington sued the two county attorneys involved in their original trial, alleging that the prosecutors had violated their "due process rights by obtaining, manufacturing, coercing and fabricating evidence before filing formal charges" against them. A federal district court rejected the prosecutors' contention that they were entitled to absolute immunity from damages under *Imbler v. Pachtman.* The Eighth Circuit Court of Appeals affirmed, concluding that the alleged misconduct "is not 'a distinctly prosecutorial function.' The district court was correct in denying [the prosecutors immunity] for their acts before the filing of formal charges." *McGhee v. Pottawattamie County,* 547 F.3d 922, 933 (8th Cir. 2008). The Supreme Court granted *certiorari,* in *Pottawattamie County v. McGhee,* 129 S.Ct. 2002, 173 L.Ed.2d 1083 (2009), to address "[w]hether a prosecutor may be subjected to a civil trial and potential damages for a wrongful conviction and incarceration where the prosecutor allegedly violated a criminal defendant's 'substantive due process' rights by procuring false testimony during the criminal investigation and then introduced that same testimony against the defendant at trial."[9] The case was argued in November 2009. The parties subsequently agreed to a $12 million settlement,[10] causing the Supreme Court to dismiss the case without reaching a decision.[11]

3. John Thompson was convicted of a 1985 murder committed in New Orleans and sentenced to death. A few weeks before his murder trial, he had been convicted of committing an unrelated attempted armed robbery. Not wanting this conviction to be brought to the jury's attention as impeachment evidence, Thompson declined to testify at his murder trial. Just one month before Thompson's scheduled execution, an investigator for the defense discovered a New Orleans Police Department Crime Laboratory report

that revealed that the blood left by the robber on the victim's pants was type B, thereby excluding Thompson, who had type A blood. The Louisiana Court of Appeals ruled that the prosecution's failure to disclose the lab report in connection with the robbery trial represented a *Brady* violation, and the court vacated both the robbery and the murder convictions. At his retrial on the murder charge in 2003, Thompson testified in his own defense and the jury found him not guilty, thereby exonerating him. He had spent 18 years in prison, including 14 years on death row. Thompson subsequently filed a § 1983 suit seeking damages against Harry Connick, the Orleans Parish District Attorney, alleging that "Connick had failed to train his prosecutors adequately about their duty to produce exculpatory evidence and that the lack of training had caused the nondisclosure in Thompson's robbery case. The jury awarded Thompson $14 million and the Court of Appeals for the Fifth Circuit affirmed...." In *Connick v. Thompson*, ___ U.S. ___, 131 S.Ct. 1350, ___ L.Ed.2d ___ (2011), the Supreme Court granted *certiorari* "to decide whether a district attorney's office may be held liable under § 1983 for failure to train based on a single *Brady* violation." Writing for the majority in a 5–4 decision, Justice Thomas announced, "We hold that it cannot."

Plaintiffs who seek to impose liability on local governments under § 1983 must prove that "action pursuant to official municipal policy" caused their injury. [*Monell v. New York City Dept. of Social Servs.*, 436 U.S. 658, 691, 98 S.Ct. 2018, 56 L.Ed.2d 611 (1978)]. Official municipal policy includes the decisions of a government's lawmakers, the acts of its policymaking officials, and practices so persistent and widespread as to practically have the force of law....

In limited circumstances, a local government's decision not to train certain employees about their legal duty to avoid violating citizens' rights may rise to the level of an official government policy for purposes of § 1983. A municipality's culpability for a deprivation of rights is at its most tenuous where a claim turns on a failure to train. To satisfy the statute, a municipality's failure to train its employees in a relevant respect must amount to "deliberate indifference to the rights of persons with whom the [untrained employees] come into contact." [*Canton v. Harris*, 489 U.S. 378, 388, 109 S.Ct. 1197, 103 L.Ed.2d 412 (1989)] Only then "can such a shortcoming be properly thought of as a city 'policy or custom' that is actionable under § 1983." *Id.*, at 389.

"'[D]eliberate indifference' is a stringent standard of fault, requiring proof that a municipal actor disregarded a known or obvious consequence of his action." [*Board of Comm'rs of Bryan Cty. v. Brown*, 520 U.S. 397, 410, 117 S.Ct. 1382, 137 L.Ed.2d 626 (1997)]. Thus, when city policymakers are on actual or constructive notice that a particular omission in their training program causes city employees to violate citizens' constitutional rights, the city may be deemed deliberately indifferent if the policymakers choose to retain that program. The city's "policy of inaction" in light of notice that its program will cause constitutional violations "is the functional equivalent of a decision by the city itself to violate the Constitution." *Canton*, 489 U.S., at 395 (O'Connor, J., concurring in part and dissenting in part). A less stringent standard of fault for a failure-to-train claim "would result in *de facto respondeat superior* liability on municipalities...." *Id.*, at 392.

B

A pattern of similar constitutional violations by untrained employees is "ordinarily necessary" to demonstrate deliberate indifference for purposes of failure to train.... Without notice that a course of training is deficient in a particular respect, decisionmakers can hardly be said to have deliberately chosen a training program that will cause violations of constitutional rights.

Although Thompson does not contend that he proved a pattern of similar *Brady* violations, he points out that, during the ten years preceding his armed robbery trial, Louisiana courts had overturned four convictions because of *Brady* violations by prosecutors in Connick's office. Those four reversals could not have put Connick on notice that the office's *Brady* training was inadequate with respect to the sort of *Brady* violation at issue here. None of those cases involved failure to disclose blood evidence, a crime lab report, or physical or scientific evidence of any kind. Because those incidents are not similar to the violation at issue here, they could not have put Connick on notice that specific training was necessary to avoid this constitutional violation.

C

1

Instead of relying on a pattern of similar *Brady* violations, Thompson relies on the "single-incident" liability that this Court hypothesized in *Canton*. He contends that the *Brady* violation in his case was the "obvious" consequence of failing to provide specific *Brady* training, and that this showing of "obviousness" can substitute for the pattern of violations ordinarily necessary to establish municipal culpability....

The District Court and the Court of Appeals panel erroneously believed that Thompson had proved deliberate indifference by showing the "obviousness" of a need for additional training. They based this conclusion on Connick's awareness that (1) prosecutors would confront *Brady* issues while at the district attorney's office; (2) inexperienced prosecutors were expected to understand *Brady*'s requirements; (3) *Brady* has gray areas that make for difficult choices; and (4) erroneous decisions regarding *Brady* evidence would result in constitutional violations. This is insufficient.

It does not follow that, because *Brady* has gray areas and some *Brady* decisions are difficult, prosecutors will so obviously make wrong decisions that failing to train them amounts to "a decision by the city itself to violate the Constitution." *Canton,* 489 U.S., at 395 (O'Connor, J., concurring in part and dissenting in part). To prove deliberate indifference, Thompson needed to show that Connick was on notice that, absent additional specified training, it was "highly predictable" that the prosecutors in his office would be confounded by those gray areas and make incorrect *Brady* decisions as a result. In fact, Thompson had to show that it was *so* predictable that failing to train the prosecutors amounted to *conscious disregard* for defendants' *Brady* rights. See *Bryan Cty.,* 520 U.S., at 409; *Canton, supra,* at 389. He did not do so.

III

The role of a prosecutor is to see that justice is done. *Berger v. United States,* 295 U.S. 78, 88, 55 S.Ct. 629, 79 L.Ed. 1314 (1935). "It is as much [a prosecutor's] duty to refrain from improper methods calculated to produce a wrongful conviction as it is to use every legitimate means to bring about a just one." *Ibid.* By their own admission, the prosecutors who tried Thompson's armed robbery case failed to carry out that responsibility. But the only issue before us is whether Connick, as the policymaker for the district attorney's office, was deliberately indifferent to the need to train the attorneys under his authority.

We conclude that this case does not fall within the narrow range of "single-incident" liability hypothesized in *Canton* as a possible exception to the pattern of violations necessary to prove deliberate indifference in § 1983 actions alleging failure to train. The District Court should have granted Connick judgment as a matter of law on the failure-to-train claim because Thompson did not prove a pattern of similar violations that would "establish that the 'policy of inaction' [was] the functional equivalent of a decision by the city itself to violate the Constitution." *Canton, supra,* at 395, 109 S.Ct. 1197 (opinion of O'Connor, J.).

The judgment of the United States Court of Appeals for the Fifth Circuit is reversed.

Justice Ginsburg, joined by Justices Breyer, Sotomayor, and Kagan, issued a lengthy dissent. She summarized her reasoning as follows:

In *Brady v. Maryland,* 373 U.S. 83 (1963), this Court held that due process requires the prosecution to turn over evidence favorable to the accused and material to his guilt or punishment. That obligation, the parties have stipulated, was dishonored in this case; consequently, John Thompson spent 18 years in prison, 14 of them isolated on death row, before the truth came to light: He was innocent of the charge of attempted armed robbery, and his subsequent trial on a murder charge, by prosecutorial design, was fundamentally unfair.

The Court holds that the Orleans Parish District Attorney's Office (District Attorney's Office or Office) cannot be held liable, in a civil rights action under 42 U.S.C. § 1983, for the grave injustice Thompson suffered. That is so, the Court tells us, because Thompson has shown only an aberrant *Brady* violation, not a routine practice of giving short shrift to *Brady*'s requirements. The evidence presented to the jury that awarded compensation to Thompson, however, points distinctly away from the Court's assessment. As the trial record in the § 1983 action reveals, the conceded, long-concealed prosecutorial transgressions were neither isolated nor atypical.

From the top down, the evidence showed, members of the District Attorney's Office, including the District Attorney himself, misperceived *Brady's* compass and therefore inadequately attended to their disclosure obligations. Throughout the pretrial and trial proceedings against Thompson, the team of four engaged in prosecuting him for armed robbery and murder hid from the defense and the court exculpatory information Thompson requested and had a constitutional right to receive. The prosecutors did so despite multiple opportunities, spanning nearly two decades, to set the record straight. Based on the prosecutors' conduct relating to Thompson's trials, a fact trier could reasonably conclude that inattention to *Brady* was standard operating procedure at the District Attorney's Office.

What happened here, the Court's opinion obscures, was no momentary oversight, no single incident of a lone officer's misconduct. Instead, the evidence demonstrated that misperception and disregard of *Brady's* disclosure requirements were pervasive in Orleans Parish. That evidence, I would hold, established persistent, deliberately indifferent conduct for which the District Attorney's Office bears responsibility under § 1983.

I dissent from the Court's judgment mindful that *Brady* violations, as this case illustrates, are not easily detected. But for a chance discovery made by a defense team investigator weeks before Thompson's scheduled execution, the evidence that led to his exoneration might have remained under wraps. The prosecutorial concealment Thompson encountered, however, is bound to be repeated unless municipal agencies bear responsibility—made tangible by § 1983 liability—for adequately conveying what *Brady* requires and for monitoring staff compliance. Failure to train, this Court has said, can give rise to municipal liability under § 1983 "where the failure ... amounts to deliberate indifference to the rights of persons with whom the [untrained employees] come into contact." *Canton v. Harris*, 489 U.S. 378, 388 (1989). That standard is well met in this case....

4. In Chapter 8, we will consider another Supreme Court case involving a district attorney's claim of absolute immunity under 42 U.S.C. § 1983 for allegedly failing to train and share information among assistant district attorneys regarding the use of jailhouse informants, and thereby contributing to a man's wrongful conviction and incarceration. *Van de Kamp v. Goldstein*, 129 S.Ct. 855, 172 L.Ed.2d 706 (2009).

D. The Criminal Trial: Proof Beyond a Reasonable Doubt

A person charged with a crime is presumed to be innocent unless and until he or she stands convicted. The presumption of innocence does not guarantee unfettered freedom. Indeed, many "legally innocent" people accused of crimes are incarcerated before trial when they cannot post bail, and some are not even entitled to be released on bail.[12] Although the Supreme Court has ruled that persons charged with but not convicted of crimes cannot be punished, it has simultaneously reasoned that many onerous restraints do not amount to "punishment" and can be inflicted notwithstanding the legal presumption of innocence. In *Bell v. Wolfish*, 441 U.S. 520, 99 S.Ct. 1861, 60 L.Ed.2d 447 (1979), the Court overturned a lower court ruling and rejected a pretrial detainee's contentions that the conditions of jail confinement that he was forced to endure violated his constitutional rights. Justice Rehnquist's majority opinion included the following observations about the presumption of innocence.

[T]he Court of Appeals and the District Court seem to have relied on the "presumption of innocence" as the source of the detainee's substantive right to be free from conditions of confinement that are not justified by compelling necessity. But the presumption of innocence provides no support for such a rule.

The presumption of innocence is a doctrine that allocates the burden of proof in criminal trials; it also may serve as an admonishment to the jury to judge an accused's guilt or innocence solely on the evidence adduced at trial and not on the basis of suspicions that may arise from the fact of his arrest, indictment, or custody, or from other matters not introduced as proof at trial. It is "an inaccurate, shorthand description of the right of the accused to 'remain inactive and secure, until the prosecution has taken up its burden and produced evidence and effected persuasion; ...' an 'assumption' that is indulged in the absence of contrary evidence." *Taylor v. Kentucky,* [436 U.S., 478, 484, n. 12 (1978)]. Without question, the presumption of innocence plays an important role in our criminal justice system. "The principle that there is a presumption of innocence in favor of the accused is the undoubted law, axiomatic and elementary, and its enforcement lies at the foundation of the administration of our criminal law." *Coffin v. United States,* 156 U.S. 432, 453 (1895). But it has no application to a determination of the rights of a pretrial detainee during confinement before his trial has even begun.

Much as its legal significance is limited, the presumption of innocence is apt to be perceived with some skepticism among the general public, including prospective jurors. Many people have difficulty accepting that a person whom the authorities have charged with a crime is innocent. They may, in fact, presume precisely the opposite. For example, in one of the earliest psycho-legal studies, Weld and Roff[13] demonstrated that the subjects in their study experienced difficulty in affording persons charged with committing a crime a presumption of innocence. Across four separate samples, subjects presented with no other information than an indictment from an actual legal case held slight to strong feelings that the defendant was guilty. In addition, a large empirical literature exists about the influence of pre-trial publicity, which in general indicates the damaging effects of media reports on the presumption of innocence.[14] When indulged, such a working "presumption of guilt" has obvious and regrettable implications for helping induce wrongful convictions.

Nevertheless, as the Court observed in *Bell v. Wolfish,* the presumption of innocence at a minimum entitles one accused of a crime "to 'remain inactive and secure, until the prosecution has taken up its burden and produced evidence and effected persuasion'...." We next learn more about the prosecution's burden of persuasion in criminal trials. Ironically, the case cementing "proof beyond a reasonable doubt" as the constitutional standard for establishing guilt did not involve a criminal trial, but rather a juvenile delinquency proceeding.

In re Winship

397 U.S. 358, 99 S.Ct. 1068, 51 L.Ed.2d 323 (1970)

Mr. Justice BRENNAN delivered the opinion of the Court.

... This case presents the single, narrow question whether proof beyond a reasonable doubt is among the 'essentials of due process and fair treatment' required during the adjudicatory stage when a juvenile is charged with an act which would constitute a crime if committed by an adult.

Section 712 of the New York Family Court Act defines a juvenile delinquent as 'a person over seven and less than sixteen years of age who does any act which, if done by an adult, would constitute a crime.' During a 1967 adjudicatory hearing, conducted pursuant to § 742 of the Act, a judge in New York Family Court found that appellant, then a 12-year-old boy, had entered a locker and stolen $112 from a woman's pocketbook.... The judge acknowledged that the proof might not establish guilt beyond a reasonable doubt, but rejected appellant's contention that such proof was required by the Fourteenth

Amendment. The judge relied instead on § 744(b) of the New York Family Court Act which provides that '[a]ny determination at the conclusion of [an adjudicatory] hearing that a [juvenile] did an act or acts must be based on a preponderance of the evidence.'[2] During a subsequent dispositional hearing, appellant was ordered placed in a training school for an initial period of 18 months, subject to annual extensions of his commitment until his 18th birthday-six years in appellant's case. The Appellate Division of the New York Supreme Court, First Judicial Department, affirmed without opinion. The New York Court of Appeals then affirmed by a four-to-three vote.... We reverse.

I

The requirement that guilt of a criminal charge be established by proof beyond a reasonable doubt dates at least from our early years as a Nation. The 'demand for a higher degree of persuasion in criminal cases was recurrently expressed from ancient times, [though] its crystallization into the formula 'beyond a reasonable doubt' seems to have occurred as late as 1798. It is now accepted in common law jurisdictions as the measure of persuasion by which the prosecution must convince the trier of all the essential elements of guilt.' C. McCormick, Evidence § 321, pp. 681–682 (1954); see also 9 J. Wigmore, Evidence, § 2497 (3d ed. 1940). Although virtually unanimous adherence to the reasonable-doubt standard in common-law jurisdictions may not conclusively establish it as a requirement of due process, such adherence does 'reflect a profound judgment about the way in which law should be enforced and justice administered.' Duncan v. Louisiana, 391 U.S. 145, 155 (1968).

Expressions in many opinions of this Court indicate that it has long been assumed that proof of a criminal charge beyond a reasonable doubt is constitutionally required....

The reasonable-doubt standard plays a vital role in the American scheme of criminal procedure. It is a prime instrument for reducing the risk of convictions resting on factual error. The standard provides concrete substance for the presumption of innocence—that bedrock 'axiomatic and elementary' principle whose 'enforcement lies at the foundation of the administration of our criminal law.' Coffin v. United States, 156 U.S. [432], 453 [(1895)]. As the dissenters in the New York Court of Appeals observed, and we agree, 'a person accused of a crime * * * would be at a severe disadvantage, a disadvantage amounting to a lack of fundamental fairness, if he could be adjudged guilty and imprisoned for years on the strength of the same evidence as would suffice in a civil case.'

The requirement of proof beyond a reasonable doubt has this vital role in our criminal procedure for cogent reasons. The accused during a criminal prosecution has at stake interest of immense importance, both because of the possibility that he may lose his liberty upon conviction and because of the certainty that he would be stigmatized by the conviction. Accordingly, a society that values the good name and freedom of every individual should not condemn a man for commission of a crime when there is reasonable doubt about his guilt. As we said in Speiser v. Randall, 357 U.S. [513], 525–526: 'There is always in litigation a margin of error, representing error in factfinding, which both parties must take into account. Where one party has at stake an interest of transcending value—as a criminal defendant his liberty—this margin of error is reduced as to him by the process of placing on the other party the burden of * * * persuading the factfinder at the conclusion of the trial of his guilt beyond a reasonable doubt. Due process commands that no man shall lose his liberty unless the Government has borne the burden of * * * convincing the factfinder of his guilt.' To this end, the reasonable-doubt standard is indispensable, for it 'impresses on the trier of fact the necessity of reaching a subjective state of certitude of the facts in issue.' Dorsen & Rezneck, In Re Gault and the Future of Juvenile Law, 1 Family Law Quarterly, No. 4, pp. 1, 26 (1967).

Moreover, use of the reasonable-doubt standard is indispensable to command the respect and confidence of the community in applications of the criminal law. It is critical that the moral force of the criminal law not be diluted by a stan-

2. The ruling appears in the following portion of the hearing transcript:

Counsel: 'Your Honor is making a finding by the preponderance of the evidence.'

Court: 'Well, it convinces me.'

Counsel: 'It's not beyond a reasonable doubt, Your Honor.'

Court: 'That is true * * * Our statute says a preponderance and a preponderance it is.'

dard of proof that leaves people in doubt whether innocent men are being condemned. It is also important in our free society that every individual going about his ordinary affairs have confidence that his government cannot adjudge him guilty of a criminal offense without convincing a proper factfinder of his guilt with utmost certainty.

Lest there remain any doubt about the constitutional stature of the reasonable-doubt standard, we explicitly hold that the Due Process Clause protects the accused against conviction except upon proof beyond a reasonable doubt of every fact necessary to constitute the crime with which he is charged.

II

We turn to the question whether juveniles, like adults, are constitutionally entitled to proof beyond a reasonable doubt when they are charged with violation of a criminal law. The same considerations that demand extreme caution in factfinding to protect the innocent adult apply as well to the innocent child....

Reversed.

Mr. Justice HARLAN, concurring....

I

Professor Wigmore, in discussing the various attempts by courts to define how convinced one must be to be convinced beyond a reasonable doubt, wryly observed: 'The truth is that no one has yet invented or discovered a mode of measurement for the intensity of human belief. Hence there can be yet no successful method of communicating intelligibly * * * a sound method of self-analysis for one's belief,' 9 J. Wigmore, Evidence 325 (3d ed. 1940).

Notwithstanding Professor Wigmore's skepticism, we have before us a case where the choice of the standard of proof has made a difference: the juvenile court judge below forthrightly acknowledged that he believed by a preponderance of the evidence, but was not convinced beyond a reasonable doubt, that appellant stole $112 from the complainant's pocketbook. Moreover, even though the labels used for alternative standards of proof are vague and not a very sure guide to decisionmaking, the choice of the standard for a particular variety of adjudication does, I think, reflect a very fundamental assessment of the comparative social costs of erroneous factual determinations.

To explain why I think this so, I begin by stating two propositions, neither of which I believe can be fairly disputed. First, in a judicial proceeding in which there is a dispute about the facts of some earlier event, the factfinder cannot acquire unassailably accurate knowledge of what happened. Instead, all the fact-finder can acquire is a belief of what probably happened. The intensity of this belief—the degree to which a factfinder is convinced that a given act actually occurred—can, of course, vary. In this regard, a standard of proof represents an attempt to instruct the fact-finder concerning the degree of confidence our society thinks he should have in the correctness of factual conclusions for a particular type of adjudication. Although the phrases 'preponderance of the evidence' and 'proof beyond a reasonable doubt' are quantitatively imprecise, they do communicate to the finder of fact different notions concerning the degree of confidence he is expected to have in the correctness of his factual conclusions.

A second proposition, which is really nothing more than a corollary of the first, is that the trier of fact will sometimes, despite his best efforts, be wrong in his factual conclusions. In a lawsuit between two parties, a factual error can make a difference in one of two ways. First, it can result in a judgment in favor of the plaintiff when the true facts warrant a judgment for the defendant. The analogue in a criminal case would be the conviction of an innocent man. On the other hand, an erroneous factual determination can result in a judgment for the defendant when the true facts justify a judgment in plaintiff's favor. The criminal analogue would be the acquittal of a guilty man.

The standard of proof influences the relative frequency of these two types of erroneous outcomes. If, for example, the standard of proof for a criminal trial were a preponderance of the evidence rather than proof beyond a reasonable doubt, there would be a smaller risk of factual errors that result in freeing guilty persons, but a far greater risk of factual errors that result in convicting the innocent. Because the standard of proof affects the comparative frequency of these two types of erroneous outcomes, the choice of the standard to be applied in a particular kind of litigation should, in a rational world, reflect an assessment of the comparative social disutility of each.

When one makes such an assessment, the reason for different standards of proof in civil as opposed to criminal litigation becomes apparent. In a civil suit between two private parties for money damages, for example, we view it as no more serious in general for there to be an erroneous verdict in the defendant's favor than for there to be an erroneous verdict in the plaintiff's favor. A preponderance of the evidence standard therefore seems peculiarly appropriate for, as explained most sensibly, it simply requires the trier of fact 'to believe that the existence of a fact is more probable than its nonexistence before [he] may find in favor of the party who has the burden to persuade the [judge] of the fact's existence.'

In a criminal case, on the other hand, we do not view the social disutility of convicting an innocent man as equivalent to the disutility of acquitting someone who is guilty....

In this context, I view the requirement of proof beyond a reasonable doubt in a criminal case as bottomed on a fundamental value determination of our society that it is far worse to convict an innocent man than to let a guilty man go free. It is only because of the nearly complete and long-standing acceptance of the reasonable-doubt standard by the States in criminal trials that the Court has not before today had to hold explicitly that due process, as an expression of fundamental procedural fairness, requires a more stringent standard for criminal trials than for ordinary civil litigation.

II

When one assesses the consequences of an erroneous factual determination in a juvenile delinquency proceeding in which a youth is accused of a crime, I think it must be concluded that, while the consequences are not identical to those in a criminal case, the differences will not support a distinction in the standard of proof....

Mr. Chief Justice BURGER, with whom Mr. Justice STEWART joins, dissenting....

Mr. Justice BLACK, dissenting....

Notes and Questions

1. What is the precise meaning of "proof beyond a reasonable doubt"? Whatever the proper understanding might be, it seems clear that beyond a "*reasonable*" doubt does not mean beyond "*all*" doubt, and hence that the law does not demand absolute certainty before a person can be convicted of a crime. The "proof beyond a reasonable doubt" standard is one acknowledgment that wrongful convictions are an inevitable consequence of maintaining systems of criminal justice. Indeed, errors of justice are likely inevitable no matter where the proof threshold is established. As Justice Scalia noted in *Kansas v. Marsh*, 548 U.S. 163, 199, 126 S.Ct. 2516, 165 L.Ed.2d 429 (2006) (concurring opinion): "Like other human institutions, courts and juries are not perfect. One cannot have a system of criminal punishment without accepting the possibility that someone will be punished mistakenly. That is a truism, not a revelation." Still, setting the bar for conviction at "proof beyond a reasonable doubt" is considered an important safeguard in protecting innocent people against conviction. As *Winship* illustrates, even though the precise meaning of "proof beyond a reasonable doubt" is elusive, it is more demanding than the "preponderance of the evidence" standard the juvenile court judge applied in adjudicating Sam Winship delinquent.

In *Victor v. Nebraska,* 511 U.S. 1, 114 S.Ct. 1239, 127 L.Ed.2d 583 (1994), the Supreme Court considered the constitutional sufficiency of jury instructions defining "proof beyond a reasonable doubt" given in two cases that resulted in capital murder convictions and death sentences—one from California (*Sandoval*), and the other from Nebraska (*Victor*).

The jury in Sandoval's case was given the following instruction on the government's burden of proof:

> "A defendant in a criminal action is presumed to be innocent until the contrary is proved, and in case of a reasonable doubt whether his guilt is satisfactorily shown, he is entitled to a verdict of not guilty. This presumption places upon the State the burden of proving him guilty beyond a reasonable doubt.
>
> "Reasonable doubt is defined as follows: It is *not a mere possible doubt;* because everything relating to human affairs, and *depending on moral*

evidence, is open to some possible or imaginary doubt. It is that state of the case which, after the entire comparison and consideration of all the evidence, leaves the minds of the jurors in that condition that they cannot say they feel an abiding conviction, *to a moral certainty,* of the truth of the charge." (emphasis added) ...

At Victor's trial, the judge instructed the jury that "[t]he burden is always on the State to prove beyond a reasonable doubt all of the material elements of the crime charged, and this burden never shifts." The charge continued:

"'Reasonable doubt' is such a doubt as would cause a reasonable and prudent person, in one of the graver and more important transactions of life, to pause and hesitate before taking the represented facts as true and relying and acting thereon. It is such a doubt as will not permit you, after full, fair, and impartial consideration of all the evidence, to have an abiding conviction, *to a moral certainty,* of the guilt of the accused. At the same time, absolute or mathematical certainty is not required. You may be convinced of the truth of a fact beyond a reasonable doubt and yet be fully aware that possibly you may be mistaken. You may find an accused guilty upon the *strong probabilities of the case,* provided such probabilities are strong enough to exclude any doubt of his guilt that is reasonable. A reasonable doubt is an *actual and substantial doubt* reasonably arising from the evidence, from the facts or circumstances shown by the evidence, or from the lack of evidence on the part of the State, as distinguished from a doubt arising from mere possibility, from bare imagination, or from fanciful conjecture." (emphasis added).

The justices unanimously endorsed the California instructions and approved the Nebraska instructions by vote of 7–2. Are the offered definitions helpful? Are they likely to provide sufficient guidance to lay jurors concerning the magnitude of the prosecution's burden in proving guilt? A comprehensive discussion of jury instructions defining "proof beyond a reasonable doubt," including studies assessing their interpretation, is offered in *Vargas v. Keane,* 86 F.3d 1273 (2d Cir. 1996).

2. Legal scholars and social scientists alike have often tried to quantify "proof beyond a reasonable doubt" as well as "preponderance of the evidence," and other legal standards. As reviewed by Dane,[15] several methods to quantify reasonable doubt have been investigated. These methods include: (1) rank ordering (in which probabilities of guilt are compared to dichotomous (guilty-not guilty) ratings; 70–74%); (2) self-report (asking individuals to assign a minimum value of reasonable doubt, 82–90%); (3) decision theory (based on subjective, expected utility decision-making and weighing false positive against false negatives, 50–90%); and (4) interpretations of U.S. Supreme Court decisions (*e.g., Johnson v. Louisiana,* 406 U.S. 356, 92 S.Ct. 1620, 32 L.Ed.2d 152 (1972), translated into 75%). In essence, there is no standard definition of "reasonable doubt," but rather the concept is quantified and qualified differently by different individuals. When asked directly, individuals tend to respond that reasonable doubt can range from 50% to 100% certainty of guilt.[16]

In addition, there is some empirical support that jurors have difficulty discriminating between reasonable doubt, clear and convincing evidence, and a preponderance of the evidence. Specifically, Kagehiro and Stanton[17] found that when mock jurors were presented with legal definitions of these three evidentiary standards, verdicts were unaffected. However, when jurors were presented with quantified thresholds (*i.e.,* 91% vs. 71% vs. 51% probability), their verdicts were different and in line with expectations.

3. Justice Brennan's majority opinion in *Winship* instructs that "[t]he reasonable-doubt standard ... is a prime instrument for reducing the risk of convictions resting on factual error." Justice Harlan's concurring opinion makes explicit that our choices concerning which party in a legal proceeding is assigned the burden of persuasion, and how demanding that burden is, tell us a great deal about society's tolerance for the different kinds of error that can be made. "In a criminal case ... we do not view the social disutility of convicting an innocent man as equivalent to the disutility of acquitting someone who is guilty." His

opinion asserts further that the respective errors are interdependent: "If, for example, the standard of proof for a criminal trial were a preponderance of the evidence rather than proof beyond a reasonable doubt, there would be a smaller risk of factual errors that result in freeing guilty persons, but a far greater risk of factual errors that result in convicting the innocent." More than a century ago, in *Coffin v. United States,* 156 U.S. 432, 455–456, 15 S.Ct. 394, 39 L.Ed. 481 (1895), the Supreme Court relied on several common law authorities in endorsing and elaborating on the important values underpinning these assessments.

Fortescue says: 'Who, then, in England, can be put to death unjustly for any crime? since he is allowed so many pleas and privileges in favor of life. None but his neighbors, men of honest and good repute, against whom he can have no probable cause of exception, can find the person accused guilty. Indeed, one would much rather that twenty guilty persons should escape punishment of death than that one innocent person should be condemned and suffer capitally.' De Laudibus Legum Angliae (Amos' translation, Cambridge, 1825).

Lord Hale (1678) says: 'In some cases presumptive evidence goes far to prove a person guilty, though there be no express proof of the fact to be committed by him; but then it must be very warily pressed, for it is better five guilty persons should escape unpunished than one innocent person should die.' 2 Hale, P. C. 290. He further observes: 'And thus the reasons stand on both sides; and, though these seem to be stronger than the former, yet in a case of this moment it is safest to hold that in practice, which hath least doubt and danger,—Quod dubitas, ne feceris." 1 Hale, P. C. 24.

Blackstone (1753–1765) maintains that 'the law holds that it is better that ten guilty persons escape than that one innocent suffer.' 2 Bl. Comm. c. 27, marg. p. 358, ad finem.

Note the different ratios employed by these distinguished writers. Fortescue asserts that it is better "that twenty guilty persons should escape punishment of death than that one innocent person should ... suffer capitally." For Hale, "it is better five guilty persons should escape unpunished than one innocent person should die." And Blackstone's conclusion is "that it is better that ten guilty persons escape than that one innocent suffer." Alexander Volokh canvasses these and many other related assessments in his clever and comprehensive article, "N Guilty Men," 143 *University of Pennsylvania Law Review* 173 (1997). Another contemporary writer, Professor D. Michael Risinger, whose study of DNA-based exonerations for individuals sentenced to death for capital murder-rape in the 1980s led him to conclude that as many as 3.3% to 5% of all persons convicted and given capital sentences under such circumstances might be innocent, raises a number of challenging questions concerning societal tolerance for wrongful conviction in his article, "Innocents Convicted: An Empirically Justified Factual Wrongful Conviction Rate," 97 *Journal of Criminal Law & Criminology* 761 (2007). With respect to a numerical ratio expressing society's relative distaste for convicting the innocent and acquitting the guilty—*e.g.,* "It is better that (a) 20, (b) 10, (c) 5, or (d) some other value of 'N' guilty persons escape than one innocent suffer"—should it matter what type of offense or alleged offender is at issue? For instance, should it make a difference whether Sam Winship is (a) a 12-year-old boy accused of stealing money from a woman's purse, as opposed to (b) an alleged terrorist accused of plotting to bomb a government building, or (c) a man with a lengthy history of committing sex crimes against children who has been charged with the rape of a child, or (d) an alleged killer who is apprehended in a community that is being terrorized by a serial murderer?

4. Note that although *Winship* requires the prosecution to prove all elements of a crime beyond a reasonable doubt, it says nothing directly about the burden of persuasion regarding affirmative defenses. The Supreme Court has ruled, for example, that Due

Process is not offended by requiring a defendant charged with a crime to bear the burden of proof in establishing the insanity defense, *Leland v. Oregon*, 343 U.S. 790, 72 S.Ct. 1002, 96 L.Ed. 1302 (1952) (defendant required to prove insanity beyond a reasonable doubt); self defense, *Martin v. Ohio*, 480 U.S. 228, 107 S.Ct. 1098, 94 L.Ed.2d 267 (1987) (by a preponderance of the evidence); or the existence of extreme emotional disturbance to demonstrate that manslaughter, and not murder, has been committed following the state's proof of an unlawful, intentional killing, *Patterson v. New York*, 432 U.S. 197, 97 S.Ct. 2319, 53 L.Ed.2d 281 (1977) (by a preponderance of the evidence).

E. Appellate Review and the Sufficiency of the Evidence

The adversaries' positions change dramatically following the defendant's conviction for a crime. With the prosecution having proven the essential facts of the alleged offense beyond a reasonable doubt, the guilty verdict strips the defendant of the legal presumption of innocence. The onus of removing the judgment of guilt now falls squarely on the convict. Appellate review only encompasses issues of law. In this respect, factually innocent defendants whose trials were untainted by procedural error are in a perilous legal position.

> [T]he adversarial system places much greater emphasis on *process* than on simple truth-finding. This is apparent in a number of cases involving wrongful convictions, wherein the convicted defendants sought reversals of their verdicts on the grounds that they were factually innocent ... only to learn that since they claimed no procedural violations, their chances for success were remote at best.[18]

The facts contested at the trial cannot be relitigated on appeal; they are strongly presumed to have been resolved in favor of the prosecution. Defendants nevertheless can argue on appeal that the evidence offered at trial is legally insufficient to support a guilty verdict, even when construed most favorably to the prosecution. In light of *In re Winship's* holding that Due Process requires the prosecution to prove all elements of a crime beyond a reasonable doubt to support a conviction, this argument can assume constitutional dimensions.

In *Thompson v. Louisville*, 362 U.S. 199, 80 S.Ct. 624, 4 L.Ed.2d 654 (1960), which was decided a decade prior to *Winship*, the Court considered the claim raised by a man found guilty of loitering and disorderly conduct that the charges against him "were so totally devoid of evidentiary support as to render his conviction unconstitutional under the Due Process Clause of the Fourteenth Amendment." Justice Black's opinion emphasized that, "Decision of this question turns not on the sufficiency of the evidence, but on whether this conviction rests upon any evidence at all." On reviewing the evidence offered in support of the convictions, the justices unanimously voted to overturn them. "[W]e find no evidence whatever in the record to support these convictions. Just as 'Conviction upon a charge not made would be sheer denial of due process,' so is it a violation of due process to convict and punish a man without evidence of his guilt." *Id.*, 362 U.S., at 206 (footnotes and citations omitted).

The justices revisited the *Thompson* "no evidence" test in *Jackson v. Virginia*, 443 U.S. 307, 99 S.Ct. 2781, 61 L.Ed.2d 560 (1979), where they considered the argument "that under *In re Winship*, a federal habeas corpus court must consider not whether there was *any* evidence to support a state-court conviction, but whether there was sufficient evidence to justify a rational trier of the facts to find guilt beyond a reasonable doubt."

The *Winship* doctrine requires more than simply a trial ritual. A doctrine establishing so fundamental a substantive constitutional standard must also require that the factfinder will rationally apply that standard to the facts in evidence. A "reasonable doubt," at a minimum, is one based upon "reason." Yet a properly instructed jury may occasionally convict even when it can be said that no rational trier of fact could find guilt beyond a reasonable doubt, and the same may be said of a trial judge sitting as a jury....

After *Winship* the critical inquiry on review of the sufficiency of the evidence to support a criminal conviction must be not simply to determine whether the jury was properly instructed, but to determine whether the record evidence could reasonably support a finding of guilt beyond a reasonable doubt. But this inquiry does not require a court to "ask itself whether *it* believes that the evidence at the trial established guilt beyond a reasonable doubt." Instead, the relevant question is whether, after viewing the evidence in the light most favorable to the prosecution, *any* rational trier of fact could have found the essential elements of the crime beyond a reasonable doubt. This familiar standard gives full play to the responsibility of the trier of fact fairly to resolve conflicts in the testimony, to weigh the evidence, and to draw reasonable inferences from basic facts to ultimate facts. Once a defendant has been found guilty of the crime charged, the factfinder's role as weigher of the evidence is preserved through a legal conclusion that upon judicial review *all of the evidence* is to be considered in the light most favorable to the prosecution. The criterion thus impinges upon "jury" discretion only to the extent necessary to guarantee the fundamental protection of due process of law.

That the *Thompson* "no evidence" rule is simply inadequate to protect against misapplications of the constitutional standard of reasonable doubt is readily apparent.... The *Thompson* doctrine simply fails to supply a workable or even a predictable standard for determining whether the due process command of *Winship* has been honored....

We hold that in a challenge to a state criminal conviction brought under 28 U.S.C. § 2254—if the settled procedural prerequisites for such a claim have otherwise been satisfied—the applicant is entitled to habeas corpus relief if it is found that upon the record evidence adduced at the trial no rational trier of fact could have found proof of guilt beyond a reasonable doubt....

Turning finally to the specific facts of this case, we reject the petitioner's claim that under the constitutional standard dictated by *Winship* his conviction of first-degree murder cannot stand. A review of the record in the light most favorable to the prosecution convinces us that a rational factfinder could readily have found the petitioner guilty beyond a reasonable doubt of first-degree murder under Virginia law....

We next consider two cases in which defendants found guilty at state criminal trials claimed on appeal (in *Corbin v. State*) or on federal habeas corpus (in *Tucker v. Palmer*) that their respective convictions were based on legally insufficient evidence.

Corbin v. State

585 So.2d 713 (Miss. 1991)

PITTMAN, Justice, for the Court: ...

I.

During the evening hours of September 9, 1988, M & M Grocery in Greenville, Mississippi, was burglarized. The crime was discovered at approximately 5:40 a.m. on September 10, 1988, by Sgt. Lon Pepper of the Greenville Police Department. Entry into the local business had been forced.

Before discovering the M & M Grocery burglary, Officer T.C. Meyers of the Greenville Police Department was on patrol when he noticed a black male walking along Hughes Street. As Officer Meyers approached this person, the man dropped the various items that he was carrying and ran away from the approaching officer. This person was never identified. The items thrown down by this person, however, were identified as the goods that had been stolen from M & M Grocery that same night. These items included several cartons of cigarettes, a coin box, a bag of quarters and a glove. Upon recovery of the above goods, they were immediately processed for fingerprints by detectives from the Greenville Police Department. The stolen merchandise was found within two blocks of M & M Grocery.

Although the suspect was observed by two police officers, no witness was able to identify the person that dropped the stolen goods and ran.

The proprietor of M & M Grocery, Mr. Major Norman of Greenville, testified that he had indeed been burglarized on September 10, 1988. He stated that entry had been gained through the back door of his building by prying open both an iron door and an inner wooden door. Mr. Norman testified that he was able to determine that several items of merchandise had been stolen from his store, including several cartons of cigarettes, change from the video machine and a small change box. The stolen items, according to Norman, totalled around $150.00 in merchandise and cash.

Officer Ken Winter of the Greenville Police Department, a certified fingerprint examiner, testified that on October 7, 1988, he matched four latent fingerprints taken from the cartons of cigarettes stolen from M & M Grocery with the known fingerprints of Walter L. Corbin. At trial, Captain Winter testified that Walter Corbin, "at some point in time," touched the three cigarette cartons from which the fingerprints were lifted.

Based upon the evidence above, Walter Corbin was convicted in the Circuit Court of Washington County for the burglary of M & M Grocery [and was sentenced to a term of seven years imprisonment]. Aggrieved by that conviction, he appeals to this Court.

II.

Walter Corbin argues on appeal that the lower court was in error when it did not sustain his motions for Directed Verdict and Judgment of Acquittal Notwithstanding the Verdict. These motions, according to appellant, challenged the sufficiency of the State's proof concerning the elements of the crime of burglary. Those elements, under Miss. Code Ann. § 97-17-33 (Supp.1989), are the unlawful breaking and entering of any structure with the intent to steal or commit a felony therein. Appellant argues that the State wholly failed to prove these elements in the case *sub judice*. We agree.

When one argues on appeal concerning the legal sufficiency of the evidence supporting a conviction, the standard is as follows:

This Court has often stated the standard of review to be used on motions for a directed verdict:

> In passing upon a motion for a directed verdict, all evidence introduced by the State is accepted as true, together with any reasonable inferences that may be drawn from that evidence, and, if there is sufficient evidence to support a verdict of guilty, the motion for directed verdict must be overruled.

Guilbeau v. State, 502 So.2d 639, 641 (Miss. 1987).

A motion for judgment notwithstanding the verdict, after the jury verdict is returned, essentially tests the legal sufficiency of the evidence that supports a guilty verdict. The standard of review for such a claim is familiar:

> Where a defendant has moved for jnov, the trial court must consider all of the evidence which supports the State's case—in a light most favorable to the State. The State must be given the benefit of all favorable inferences that may reasonably be drawn from the evidence. If the facts and inferences 'so considered' point in favor of the defendant with sufficient force that reasonable men could not have found 'beyond a reasonable doubt' that the defendant was guilty, granting the motion is required. On the other hand, if there is substantial evidence opposed to the motion—that is, evidence of such quality and weight that having in mind the beyond a reasonable doubt burden of proof standard, reasonable fairminded men in the exercise of impartial judgment might reach different conclusions—the motion should be denied.

Parker v. State, 484 So.2d 1033, 1036 (Miss. 1986)....

The facts of the case at bar reveal the following: (1) that M & M Grocery was burglarized sometime between closing hours September 9, 1988, and 4:50 a.m. September 10, 1988; (2) that an unidentified black male was seen dropping the items stolen from M & M Grocery and running from a police officer at 4:50 a.m. on September 10, 1988; (3) that the fingerprints of Walter Corbin were found on three of the six cartons of cigarettes recovered by the Greenville Police Department; and (4) that these cartons were generally inaccessible to the public during business hours at M & M Grocery.

These facts, standing alone, do not prove beyond a reasonable doubt that Walter Corbin was the person who unlawfully entered M & M Grocery with the intent to steal merchandise in that business. No fingerprints were recovered at M & M Grocery to place him at the scene of the crime. In fact, the State did not present any evidence placing Walter Corbin at the business at any time. The State will not be required to disprove every hypothesis in a criminal trial. The State here, however, did nothing to focus the possibilities of the fingerprints being concurrent with the robbery....

... [A] fingerprint as the sole and only proof of guilt is insufficient. Fingerprint evidence must be coupled with some other evidence, especially so when the fingerprint was not found at the crime scene but on some object away from the scene. The State must corroborate this physical evidence with other proof of guilt. Here the State failed in this regard. Therefore, the judgment of the trial court will be reversed, and appellant discharged.

REVERSED AND RENDERED

J.BANKS, Justice, concurring:

I concur in the result reached by the majority. I write separately only to disassociate myself from any implication that the state need disprove less than all reasonable hypotheses consistent with innocence in any case.

The state is required to prove guilt beyond a reasonable doubt as a matter of federal constitutional law, *Jackson v. Virginia,* 443 U.S. 307 (1979) and the law of this state. That task requires that the evidence produced be such that we can conclude that a rational, fair-minded jury could find the essential elements of the crime charged beyond a reasonable doubt. *Id.* Put another way the evidence must be such that a rational jury could exclude all inferences consistent with innocence.

I agree with the majority that evidence that Walter Corbin, at some point, handled the cartons of cigarettes included in the contraband is insufficient, standing alone, to conclude that he committed the burglary in question....

Here Corbin could have picked up the goods after they were dropped by the burglar and before they were dropped by the individual seen by the officer; the burglar or some other person may have offered them to Corbin for sale or had him handle them for some other reason; or Corbin's prints may have gotten on the cartons of cigarettes even before they were delivered to the store. The state asks that we draw an inference from the fingerprints, first that Corbin had possession after the burglary and then, from that inference, that he broke into the store. That inference upon an inference is too tenuous to rise to the level of certainty necessary to convict one of a crime.

DAN M. LEE, P.J., and PRATHER and SULLIVAN, JJ., join this opinion.

HAWKINS, Presiding Justice, dissenting:

Because there was sufficient evidence to support Corbin's conviction, I would affirm, and respectfully dissent.

APPELLATE REVIEW OF CIRCUMSTANTIAL EVIDENCE

Under settled case law in a circumstantial evidence case, the accused is always entitled to an instruction that the jury must acquit unless they are convinced of his guilt beyond a reasonable doubt and to the exclusion of every other reasonable hypothesis than that of guilt.

Where there is circumstantial evidence of guilt, however, it is the function of *the jury,* not the trial judge or the appellate court, to determine whether or not there is a reasonable hypothesis of innocence. This is peculiarly within the province of the jury. When there is strong circumstantial evidence of guilt, the Court does not look over the jury's shoulder to try and ascertain whether there is some hypothesis of innocence when the jury has found none....

When there have been sufficient facts introduced into evidence from which a jury can reasonably conclude the accused guilty, he is nevertheless entitled to have that jury also told that they must acquit unless in their own minds they can exclude every reasonable hypotheses except that of guilt.

But he is not entitled to have the trial judge or this Court make the *same* inquiry. Whether, under those circumstances, there exists some reasonable hypothesis of innocence is within the province of the jury.

THE EVIDENCE

.... There can be no real argument as to the following facts:

(1) Norman's store was burglarized some time during the night or early morning hours.
(2) Around his counter there was disarray.
(3) An unidentified black man was seen carrying the stolen property from his store, approximately two blocks distance, and walking away from the store.
(4) When the man saw the officer, he ran.

Surely, there can be no argument but that *a jury was entitled* to conclude *from this evidence* that the man seen carrying the stolen loot was in fact the burglar.

If a jury does not have the right to conclude that a man in possession of freshly stolen loot who, when he sees a law enforcement officer, drops it and runs, was in fact the thief, that this does not make a jury issue on guilt, then we have departed the world of common sense.

The only question is the identity of this man.

Therefore, the *core question* in this case is whether or not a jury issue was made on the *fleeing man's identity.*

This brings us to the next evidence in the record.

There is no dispute in the record but that:

(1) Corbin's left ring finger and left little finger prints were on one of the cartons of cigarettes,
(2) his left thumb print on another carton of cigarettes, and
(3) his right ring finger print on another carton of cigarettes.

Three separate cartons of these cigarettes had his fingerprints, *all different.* These were the *only* fingerprints lifted off the recovered property.

And whose fingerprints were these?

Corbin's.

Why, then, was not a Washington County jury entitled to conclude that the man carrying the loot was Corbin?

If this did not make a circumstantial case calling for some kind of defense, what would?

Suppose Officer Myers had testified, "Yes, I recognized the man who dropped the merchandise and ran. It was Corbin."? Could it then be maintained that at least a jury issue was not made on whether or not Corbin was indeed the man? Of course not.

Well, what about those fingerprints on three separate, loose cartons being carried by Mr. X by hand? No other person's fingerprints were found on the cartons or other merchandise.

To me this is stronger evidence than eyewitness identification. An eyewitness may be mistaken. There is no mistake about those being Corbin's fingerprints on the three cartons....

If somebody else burglarized the store and stole the merchandise, why weren't the other fingerprints on the cartons? If some other person than Corbin was carrying the loot, why weren't his fingerprints on the loot?

If there were in fact some innocent explanation, if Corbin's fingerprints got on those cartons in some manner other than his breaking in the store and stealing them, he is the one person who can give it. Put slightly differently, if there *is* an *innocent* explanation for Corbin's fingerprints on the cigarette cartons, the *only* person in the entire world we *absolutely* know could give it is Corbin.

The State should not be required to rule out some other explanation of innocence when Corbin is the only person we know who can furnish it. And that's not the law....

FAILURE TO EXPLAIN

An accused has a constitutional right not to take the stand in his own behalf. He is presumed innocent until proof is offered to the contrary.

But, there is not a thing in the world wrong with a rule of law which says that when certain facts are proved, which *only* the defendant can explain, it is up to him to offer some explanation. Otherwise, the jury has the right to find him guilty.

We do that in murder prosecutions. A and B go into a room together. A shot is fired, and A is seen walking out with a smoking pistol. B is dead, a bullet through his head.

The law presumes A *murdered* B unless he offers some rational explanation....

In *Moore v. U.S.,* 271 F.2d 564, 568 (4th Cir. 1959), the Court held:

> In a criminal case the accused is protected, at every stage of the trial, with a presumption of innocence and until he is proven guilty beyond a reasonable doubt by proper and competent evidence. No inference of guilt can be drawn from the mere fact that the accused did not testify in his own behalf. These are fundamental principles which require no citation of authority. But other principles have not been overlooked or disregarded in

> reaching our decision. Circumstantial evidence may support a verdict of guilty, though it does not exclude every reasonable hypothesis consistent with innocence. *Holland v. United States,* 1954, 348 U.S. 121. If it be sufficient to support an inference of guilt and the defendant fails to offer a reasonable explanation consistent with innocence, such failure may be considered by the trier of fact. *Wilson v. United States,* 1896, 162 U.S. 613. It is not necessary, in appraising the sufficiency of the evidence, that this court be convinced beyond a reasonable doubt of the guilt of the defendant. The question is whether the evidence, construed most favorably for the prosecution, is such that a jury (or trial judge) might find the defendant guilty beyond a reasonable doubt....

The significance the majority attaches to Corbin's fingerprints is reminiscent of an episode in Mark Twain's book, *A Connecticut Yankee in King Arthur's Court,* where the hero, Hank, must fight two heavily armored knights in a tournament.

Rather than encumber himself or his nimble horse in heavy metal, Hank dons his "long handles" and readies himself for the fray. He initially plans to lasso his opponents as they lope past and do them no serious harm, but Merlin steals his rope. Hank has prepared himself for this eventuality, however. He has two .45 caliber revolvers in good working order.

As each knight approaches, he whips out a revolver and fires. Wham! A knight is on the ground. Stone dead.

The curious onlookers cannot understand his being dead. They see nothing of any significance about the dead knight. Well, there *is* a little hole in the chain metal on his chest, but that is meaningless.

The majority attaches the same importance to these three little sets of Corbin's fingerprints.

I apprehend my esteemed colleagues have done the State an injustice.

I would affirm.

ROY NOBLE LEE, C.J., and McRAE, J., join this opinion.

Tucker v. Palmer

541 F.3d 652 (6th Cir. 2008)

ACKERMAN, District Judge.

This case involves the conviction of a man for second-degree home invasion based exclusively upon the testimony of the homeowner, who saw the defendant climbing over the back yard fence and running away from the house. Here, we face the sobering issue of whether a man was unconstitutionally deprived of his liberty. We recognize that such an issue should never be addressed lightly, and so we have endeavored to carefully and thoroughly review, with the appropriate level of deference, the evidence adduced at trial. Having engaged in such review, we conclude that the state court conviction of Raymond Tucker for second-degree home invasion is supported by sufficient evidence, albeit circumstantial. For the following reasons, we will reverse the District Court's grant of Tucker's habeas petition.

I.

At trial, the prosecution's only witness, Nicholas Sutliff, testified to the following facts. On August 18, 2003, Sutliff was mowing his yard in Dearborn Heights, Michigan when he saw a man jump over a low fence out of Sutliff's back yard and into Sutliff's side yard where Sutliff was located. Sutliff recognized the man as Defendant Raymond Tucker, someone with whom he was familiar because Tucker's family lived next door to Sutliff.[1] After clearing the fence, Tucker ran in Sutliff's general direction and passed within six feet of Sutliff, at which point the two men made eye contact before Tucker continued running without exchanging a word with Sutliff.

After this incident, Sutliff went into his back yard, and as he approached his back door, noticed that it was ajar. This fact is significant because Sutliff remembered having locked the front door, and closed, but not locked, the back door. He remembers having closed the door completely

1. Apparently, Tucker used to live in the same neighborhood as Sutliff, but had moved out many years before the 2003 incident.

because his air conditioning was on in the house. Sutliff entered his house, did not notice anything unusual, then left his house to ask his neighbors if they had seen Tucker that day. After returning to his house, Sutliff noticed that his dresser drawer was open where previously it had been closed. In addition, Sutliff noticed that where he had left two rings and a watch on top of the dresser, only the watch remained.

Police arrested Tucker on September 24, 2003 in connection with the incident at Sutliff's home.... On February 3, 2004, after signing and filing a waiver of trial by jury, Tucker was tried in a bench trial, and convicted of second-degree home invasion, in violation of Michigan Comp. Laws § 750.110a(3). On February 26, 2004, the trial judge sentenced Tucker to 7 to 15 years imprisonment.

After his conviction in this case, Tucker filed an appeal with the Michigan Court of Appeals, which issued a summary order on May 13, 2005 denying his appeal.... On November 29, 2005, the Michigan Supreme Court similarly denied Tucker's appeal....

On January 19, 2006, Tucker filed his federal habeas petition in the Eastern District of Michigan. On December 15, 2006, Magistrate Judge Paul J. Komives issued a Report and Recommendation ("R & R"), in which he recommended that the District Court grant Tucker's petition for habeas relief on the grounds that there was insufficient evidence for the trial court to conclude that Tucker entered Sutliff's home. On March 22, 2007, District Judge Lawrence P. Zatkoff adopted the Magistrate Judge's R & R, entered it as "the findings and conclusions of this Court," and concomitantly granted Tucker's petition for a writ of habeas corpus....

II.

We review *de novo* a district court's decision to grant or deny habeas corpus relief. "Under the Antiterrorism and Effective Death Penalty Act of 1996 ('AEDPA'), a federal court may grant a writ of habeas corpus only if the state courts ruled in a way contrary to, or involving an unreasonable application of, clearly established federal law as determined by the United States Supreme Court." *Parker v. Renico,* 506 F.3d 444, 447 (6th Cir. 2007). "A state-court decision is an unreasonable application of clearly established federal law if it 'correctly identifies the governing legal rule but applies it unreasonably to the facts of a particular prisoner's case.'" [*Id.,* at 447–48.] "When assessing unreasonableness, 'a federal habeas court may not issue the writ simply because that court concludes in its independent judgment that the relevant state-court decision applied clearly established federal law erroneously or incorrectly. Rather, that application must also be unreasonable.'" [*Id.,* at 448.] Furthermore, "[f]indings of fact made by the state court are presumed correct, and this presumption may be rebutted only by 'clear and convincing evidence.'" [*Tinsley v. Million,* 399 F.3d 796, 801–02 (6th Cir. 2005).]

As framed by AEDPA, the issue before this Court is whether the District Court erred in concluding that the state court unreasonably applied *Jackson v. Virginia,* 443 U.S. 307 (1979).... [A] reviewing court's task is to determine whether the record evidence could reasonably support a finding of guilt beyond a reasonable doubt.... [T]he relevant question is whether, after viewing the evidence in the light most favorable to the prosecution, *any* rational trier of fact could have found the essential elements of the crime beyond a reasonable doubt. This familiar standard gives full play to the responsibility of the trier of fact fairly to resolve conflicts in testimony, to weigh the evidence, and to draw reasonable inferences from basic facts to ultimate facts.

443 U.S. at 318–19 (emphasis in original). In other words, "[u]nder *Jackson,* habeas corpus relief is appropriate based on insufficient evidence only where the court finds, after viewing the evidence in the light most favorable to the prosecution, that no rational trier of fact could have found the essential elements of the crime beyond a reasonable doubt." *Parker,* 506 F.3d, at 448....

III.

Tucker was charged with, and convicted of, second-degree home invasion, which is defined by the statute in the following terms:

> A person who breaks and enters a dwelling with intent to commit a felony, larceny, or assault in the dwelling, a person who enters a dwelling without permission with intent to commit a felony, larceny, or assault in the dwelling, or a person who breaks and enters a dwelling or enters a dwelling without permission and, at any time while he or she is entering, present in, or exiting the dwelling, commits a felony, larceny, or assault is guilty of home invasion in the second degree.

Mich. Comp. Laws § 750.110a(3). Parsing the statutory language to fit this case, Tucker could be found guilty only if it was proved beyond a reasonable doubt that he: (1) entered a dwelling without permission; and (2) had the intent to commit a larceny therein. There is no dispute that Sutliff's home qualifies as a dwelling under the statute. Furthermore, there is no dispute that Tucker's presence in Sutliff's home would have been without permission. Thus, as to the first element, the only question for the trier-of-fact was whether there was proof beyond a reasonable doubt that Tucker in fact had entered Sutliff's home.

In assessing the adduced proof, the Court may sustain a conviction based upon nothing more than circumstantial evidence. Indeed, the Supreme Court has explained that circumstantial evidence is "intrinsically no different from testimonial evidence," and that both "may in some cases point to a wholly incorrect result." *Holland v. United States*, 348 U.S. 121, 140 (1954). "Yet ... [i]n both instances, a jury is asked to weigh the chances that the evidence correctly points to guilt against the possibility of inaccuracy or ambiguous inference." *Id.* at 137–38. To accomplish this, "the jury must use its experience with people and events in weighing the probabilities. If the jury is convinced beyond a reasonable doubt, we can require no more." *Id.* at 138.

On the first element, the District Court declared that "[s]imply put, there was no evidence whatsoever that [Tucker] entered [Sutliff's] home, nor was there any evidence from which such an inference could be made." The District Court then characterized the evidence as consisting "merely" of testimony that "[Tucker], whose family lived next door to [Sutliff] and who thus had reason to be in the area, was 25–30 feet from [Sutliff's] door, and sometime thereafter Sutliff noticed that two rings were missing." Indeed, such a characterization lends strong credence to the District Court's conclusion that Tucker's habeas petition be granted. Based upon such reading of the evidence, the District Court thereafter explained that the "prosecution's case rested simply on the supposition that [Tucker] must have entered the home ... based on his temporal and geographic proximity." But this characterization omits crucial facts found by the trier-of-fact, upon which a reasonable inference can be made that Tucker entered the home....

Specifically, the District Court's recitation suggests that Tucker was perambulating down a public sidewalk that placed him about 25–30 feet from Sutliff's door. Importantly, however, Tucker was not so innocently observed, but instead Sutliff saw Tucker jump out of Sutliff's back yard, which alone would arouse strong suspicion in any factfinder. Then, Tucker began running away from the fence he just scaled, and when he came within six feet of the homeowner standing in his own yard, Tucker made eye contact with Sutliff, but then kept running without so much as even trying to explain why he had just come out of the homeowner's fenced property. This interaction, or lack thereof, between the perpetrator and the homeowner would heighten a rational factfinder's suspicion because it is demonstrative of guilty conduct of some kind, even if that conduct is merely trespassing. Indeed, even the dissent appears to acknowledge that proximity plus flight would be sufficient evidence of entry.

Contrary to the District Court's characterization, there is more. Indeed, after seeing Tucker flee the scene, Sutliff then went into his back yard to enter his house through the back door because he had locked the front door. Sutliff testified at trial that, it being a hot August day, he had the air conditioning on in his house, and thus remembered having closed the back door before he went outside to mow the yard. Approaching his back door after having seen Tucker exiting Sutliff's back yard, Sutliff observed the back door standing ajar. This fact alone might make Sutliff, or a rational factfinder, believe that Sutliff was simply mistaken in his belief that he had closed the door before going out to mow. But, of course, this is not a lone fact. Instead, it is added to the previous observations of Tucker jumping over the fence from Sutliff's back yard, and Tucker declining to explain such behavior when he immediately thereafter saw Sutliff observing him. If Sutliff is believable in his testimony that he observed Tucker, and not someone else; and if Sutliff is also believable in his testimony that he had closed the door, but then found it open after observing Tucker, then these facts combined provide a strong inference that Tucker entered Sutliff's home.

The dissent expresses concern that the only evidence is that of the testimony of Sutliff.... Sutliff's testimony was all that the prosecutor had available, and the Constitution does not require anything more than a credible eyewitness. But wait, there is more.

The District Court noted that Sutliff observed Tucker "and sometime thereafter Sutliff noticed that two rings were missing." Of course, that is a characterization in the light most favorable to *Tucker*, rather than the prosecution; but the law requires the latter, not the former. Viewed less charitably towards Tucker, Sutliff's testimony at trial showed that Sutliff entered his house and did not immediately notice anything unusual, so he went to his next-door neighbors to ask if they had seen Tucker in the area that day. After returning to his house, Sutliff this time did notice something unusual. First, he observed that two rings that he had left on top of his dresser were no longer there. Second, Sutliff noticed that the top two drawers of the dresser were open a couple of inches, which is not the way Sutliff remembered leaving them. The missing items and the disturbed dresser drawers provide further circumstantial evidence from which a rational factfinder could conclude that Tucker had entered Sutliff's home.[4]

Indeed, the combination of all these facts—Tucker jumping over the fence *from* Sutliff's back yard; Tucker failing to explain his behavior to the person he knew to be the homeowner; Sutliff thereafter finding the back door ajar, when it had been closed; Sutliff observing that two rings were missing from his dresser; and Sutliff noticing that his top two dresser drawers were open, when they had been closed—provides a strong basis upon which to conclude that the prosecution proved its case beyond a reasonable doubt as to the first element of second-degree home invasion, namely that Tucker entered Sutliff's home without permission. Stated differently, the above evidence is strongly indicative that *someone* entered Sutliff's home without permission that day, and that the *only* person observed leaving the property was Tucker, and that he left at a rapid pace. Thus, it was not unreasonable for the trier-of-fact to link all these facts together to conclude that Tucker had entered Sutliff's home that day without permission.

As previously noted, to be found guilty of second-degree home invasion in Michigan, the prosecution had to prove beyond a reasonable doubt that Tucker: (1) entered a dwelling without permission; and (2) had the intent to commit a larceny therein. Mich. Comp. Laws §750.110a(3).... But the record provides sufficient evidence to support a finding that Tucker, having entered Sutliff's home, had the intent to commit a larceny....

Here, Sutliff testified that the top two drawers to his dresser were open, as though Tucker had gone through them. Furthermore, the two rings that were on top of the dresser were missing. These two facts provide sufficient evidence that Tucker had not innocently entered Sutliff's house thinking it was his own and then casually walked out when he realized it was not, but instead entered Sutliff's house with the intent to commit a larceny. Furthermore, while it is not unreasonable to conclude that Tucker in fact did commit a larceny by taking the rings, it is enough that Tucker simply had the intent, as demonstrated by the rifling through drawers. It is irrelevant that the rings were never found in Tucker's possession....

The District Court erred in finding that there was insufficient evidence to support Tucker's state conviction.... [W]e review *de novo* a district court's decision to grant or deny habeas corpus relief, and deference, AEDPA tells us, goes to the three state courts that considered this matter. Accordingly, under the strict standards applied to habeas petitions, we cannot ignore the principles of federalism that undergird deference to the *state court's* findings, especially in terms of credibility of a witness, which is so difficult to ascertain from a cold record. In sum, we conclude

4. The dissent accepts the District Court's characterization that "the evidence [offered] showed nothing more than that petitioner was *near the home* at about the time the rings went missing." In addition, the dissent declares that "[t]o infer that Tucker took the rings Sutliff allegedly owned solely based on the averred proximity of Tucker to Sutliff's house is to infer a fact from an inference." But as the trial transcript demonstrates, and the trial judge articulated, the evidence shows much more than Tucker casually strolling down the sidewalk. Instead, it shows that he was not merely "near the home," but *fleeing the back yard.* Moreover, we need not agree on whether the evidence sufficiently proves that Tucker *actually stole* the rings—or that the rings ever existed—to conclude that there is evidence sufficient to support a finding that Tucker *entered* the home. Indeed, the testimony that the drawers were disturbed, combined with Tucker fleeing the back yard, is sufficient to conclude that he entered Sutliff's home because the statute merely requires proof of entry into the dwelling without permission, with *intent* to commit a larceny, not that a larceny *actually* occurred. And the trial judge found that "the address was entered without permission and that it was done with the *intent* to commit a larceny."

that, based upon the evidence adduced at trial, a rational trier of fact could have found the essential elements of the crime beyond a reasonable doubt. *See Jackson,* 443 U.S. at 318....

DAMON J. KEITH, Circuit Judge, dissenting.

The majority's opinion flagrantly violates the Fourteenth Amendment. I therefore vehemently DISSENT. It is "[b]etter that ten guilty persons escape than that one innocent suffer." 4 William Blackstone, Commentaries at 358. This powerful and wise axiom reveals that a court commits the ultimate injustice by convicting and imprisoning a person based on insufficient evidence. Such a judicial transgression contravenes the most important right our Constitution affords the accused: "the Due Process Clause [of the Fourteenth Amendment] protects the accused against conviction except upon proof beyond a reasonable doubt of every fact necessary to constitute the crime with which he is charged." *In re Winship,* 397 U.S. 358, 364 (1970). Apparently neither the state trial judge nor the majority ever read or understood the Constitution, for in the instant matter, they recklessly disregarded this fundamental requirement of proof beyond a reasonable doubt by convicting Defendant Raymond Tucker of home invasion without any evidence sufficient to prove his guilt.

In a bench trial with no jury, absolutely no physical evidence, and no witnesses aside from the accuser himself, the trial judge astonishingly convicted Tucker of home invasion without any evidence that Tucker *ever entered the accuser's home....*

It is frightening that, in a case this devoid of facts, the prosecutor could have ever prosecuted Tucker in the first place. No reasonable jury (or judge), by any stretch of the imagination, could come to the conclusion that Tucker committed home invasion beyond a reasonable doubt....

Tucker's conviction and the majority's affirmation of that conviction constitute an egregious miscarriage of justice....

I.

Given the majority's terse and incomplete recitation of the facts, I feel it necessary to give a more comprehensive account of the trial court proceedings. At Tucker's trial, Sutliff testified that on August 18, 2003, he was mowing his lawn when he saw a man "scale[ ] the small fence that encloses [his] backyard and [come] over into the front [yard]." Sutliff said that the fence the man scaled is about 20 to 25 feet from the back door of his home. Sutliff claimed that in coming to his front yard, the man passed within six feet of him. He claimed that the man was running, but had slowed down momentarily after having passed him. However, Sutliff, upon seeing the man, did not speak to him. Sutliff claims that he recognized the man as Raymond Tucker, the son of the family living next door to him. Sutliff also testified, however, that he could not remember the last time he had seen Tucker but that it had probably been "several years," that Tucker had moved out of his neighborhood over twenty years ago, and that his eyes "fluctuate" because he is diabetic, sometimes requiring glasses to see clearly. He was not wearing glasses at the time he claimed he saw Tucker. Moreover, Sutliff testified that he had actually been "looking for [Tucker]," in response to a recent rash of break-ins in his neighborhood. In fact, he had just recently told police that Tucker "was paroled in March (2003) and had *absconded* a week later," suggesting that perhaps they too should be on the look out for Tucker. Sutliff said that he believed this information to be correct because he had been "tracking" Tucker using the Department of Corrections's Offender Tracking Information System.

After allegedly seeing Tucker, Sutliff went into his house through the back door. Sutliff testified that he remembered having previously shut the back door and claimed that, after having seen Tucker, the door was "ajar." He also claimed that the "top two drawers [of his dresser] were open about just a couple of inches which is unusual." In his initial search of his home, however, Sutliff did not notice anything missing. He then went to his neighbor's house, where Tucker's parents lived, and asked them if they had seen Tucker. The neighbors informed him that they had not. Afterward, Sutliff returned to his house and searched his home again, this time noticing that two rings he allegedly had placed on top of his dresser were missing.... Shortly thereafter, Tucker was arrested for breaking into Sutliff's house and stealing his rings.

Following a bench trial with only Sutliff's testimony submitted as evidence, the state trial court found that the prosecution had proven its case beyond a reasonable doubt, and convicted Tucker of home invasion in the second degree....

III.

... The Due Process Clause of the Fourteenth Amendment "protects the accused against conviction except upon proof beyond a reasonable doubt of every fact necessary to constitute the crime with which he is charged." *In re Winship*, 397 U.S. at 364. Thus, in an insufficiency of evidence habeas claim, "[t]he relevant question is whether, after viewing the evidence in the light most favorable to the prosecution, *any* rational trier of fact could have found the essential elements of the crime beyond a reasonable doubt." *Jackson v. Virginia*, 443 U.S. 307, 319 (1979) (emphasis in original). In reviewing a state court's application of the *Jackson* standard, a federal habeas court must determine whether the state court's application of the law was reasonable. 28 U.S.C. § 2254(d)(1). Thus, the question here is whether the Michigan Court of Appeals's application of the *Jackson* standard was reasonable....

The facts presented at trial consisted solely of the testimony of the alleged victim, Sutliff. Sutliff testified that he saw Tucker running from his backyard, he noticed that his back door was "ajar," two rings he thought he placed on his dresser were missing, and the drawers of his dresser were slightly open. However, the federal district court found that none of these alleged facts could be used by any reasonable trier of fact to find beyond a reasonable doubt that Tucker entered Sutliff's home, the first element of the home invasion statute. As noted above, the federal district court stated:

> There was *no evidence*—either eyewitness testimony or physical evidence—presented that petitioner was actually in Sutliff's home, nor was there evidence which connected petitioner to the rings that were taken. The prosecution's case rested simply on the supposition that petitioner must have entered the home and stolen the rings based on his temporal and geographic proximity to the crime. This *supposition alone cannot constitute sufficient evidence to prove beyond a reasonable doubt* that petitioner entered the home, nor can the Michigan courts' conclusion that the evidence was sufficient be deemed reasonable.

Tucker, 2007 WL 869164, at *5 (emphasis added)....

Given the absence of any evidence that Tucker entered the home, I am compelled to agree with the federal district court's ruling that no reasonable fact-finder could find *beyond a reasonable doubt* that Tucker was guilty of home invasion. There was no evidence showing that Tucker damaged Sutliff's property to gain entrance into his house, there were no fingerprints placing Tucker in the Sutliff's home, there was no one who claims they saw Tucker in the Sutliff's home, there was no one who claims they saw Tucker exiting the Sutliff's home, the rings Sutliff claims Tucker stole were never found, and there was no evidence found on Tucker's person or in his possession that could link him to Sutliff's home....

... [T]he majority suggests that the federal district court did not properly consider the fact that Tucker was seen "fleeing" Sutliff's back yard. The federal district court, however, did not consider this "fact" because Tucker was never seen "fleeing" the backyard. The state trial court did not find, nor did Sutliff testify, that Tucker was seen "fleeing" anything. As previously stated, Tucker was allegedly seen jumping a fence and running. To conclude that Tucker was "fleeing" is the very act of inferring a fact from an inference, and perhaps the act of an active imagination. Finally, the majority seems to give great weight to the fact that Tucker did not speak to Sutliff as he passed him in his yard. It is beyond my understanding why this is relevant. With Sutliff being so suspicious of Tucker, it defies reason that Sutliff himself, upon seeing Tucker in his backyard, would not speak to Tucker. A defendant does not have to explain his alleged actions, before, during, or after they take place. Again, as emphasized throughout this dissent, it is the *government's* burden to prove a defendant's guilt, not the defendant's burden to prove his innocence....

This Court's habeas jurisprudence in cases involving insufficiency of evidence has repeatedly distinguished between evidence that can lead to *reasonable speculation* of guilt and *evidence sufficient to prove guilt beyond a reasonable doubt.* Here, the government's sparse evidence, at best, provided *speculation* that Tucker committed the crime. This Court is to grant habeas relief when convictions are based solely upon mere reasonable speculation instead of evidence sufficient to prove guilt beyond a reasonable doubt....

The government, however, claims that if we find that insufficient evidence supported Tucker's conviction, we will essentially be eliminating the possibility of convicting a defendant on circumstantial evidence. Nothing could be further from the truth.... In vacating Tucker's sentence, we would simply be holding that the circumstantial evidence presented in the instant matter, standing alone, was insufficient to support a conviction, not that a conviction can never be based on circumstantial evidence....

IV.

I am saddened, outraged, and in fact embarrassed for our judicial system that this case has reached this point. That this Court could affirm a state trial judge's conviction and sentence of seven to fifteen years in prison without a semblance of evidence of wrongdoing is a pathetic and dismal reflection of our judicial system. The trial judge, the state courts that affirmed his conviction, and indeed this Court have ruined Tucker's life (and likely that of his family as well). This case is so devoid of evidence that Tucker should never have been prosecuted, much less convicted....

To conclude, I would like again to quote the sage words that "[b]etter that ten guilty persons escape than that one innocent suffer." 4 William Blackstone, Commentaries at 358.... Where a state trial court ignores and abuses the fundamental constitutional requirement and meaning of proof beyond a reasonable doubt, it is the responsibility of this Court to restore that constitutional guarantee. The majority turns a blind eye to this basic constitutional responsibility and undermines the concept of equal justice under law. I vigorously DISSENT.

Notes and Questions

1. One reason that appellate courts exhibit deference to the implicit or explicit findings of fact that help support a trial verdict is that the fact-finder—the jury or the trial judge—is able to observe the testifying witnesses' demeanor and thus presumably can assess their credibility better than the reviewing court, which is confined to examining a cold, written record. Does this rationale appear to be relevant in either *Corbin* or *Tucker*? Are these decisions more directly concerned with the facts found at the respective trials, or with the inferences that reasonably can be drawn from the facts? If the latter, should the measure of deference exhibited to the jury's or the trial judge's conclusions be the same as when only the resolution of facts is at issue? To what extent does a judgment about whether inferences are "reasonable" involve questions of fact or a question of law?

2. If you were a member of the jury in *Corbin*, or if you were the trial judge in *Tucker*, how would you have voted in each case: guilty or not guilty? How does this question differ from the one that an appellate court asks when evaluating the sufficiency of the evidence to support a conviction, or a federal habeas court asks when reviewing a state criminal conviction under *Jackson v. Virginia*?

F. Post-Conviction Review

In the preceding section we examined cases that considered whether the evidence presented at trials was legally sufficient to support the resulting convictions. Courts addressing that issue are confined to reviewing the evidence admitted at the trial, consisting primarily of the witnesses' transcribed testimony. However, evidence supporting a claim of innocence sometimes does not surface until after the defendant has been convicted. We then must consider a host of important questions pertaining to post-conviction review. These issues include whether the newly discovered evidence can be presented at all—for example, whether there is an adequate excuse for the defendant's failure to offer the evidence at the trial, or whether a defendant who pled guilty should be allowed to offer post-conviction evidence of innocence—and, if it can, how important it must be before a court will be justified in vacating the conviction and ordering a new trial.

People v. Tankleff

49 A.D.3d 160, 848 N.Y.S.2d 286 (2d Dept. 2007)

RIVERA, J.P.

On the instant appeal, the primary issue presented is whether the County Court erroneously denied, after a hearing, the defendant's motion pursuant to CPL 440.10(1)(g) and (h) to vacate two judgments of the same court, both rendered October 23, 1990, convicting him of murder in the second degree (two counts; one count as to each indictment), upon jury verdicts. For the reasons that follow, we grant that branch of the defendant's motion pursuant to CPL 440.10(1)(g) which was to vacate the judgments based upon newly-discovered evidence, vacate the judgments and the sentences imposed thereon, and remit the matter to the County Court, Suffolk County, for a new trial.

I. *FACTUAL AND PROCEDURAL BACKGROUND*

A. *TRIAL AND INITIAL APPELLATE PROCEEDINGS*

On September 7, 1988, Seymour Tankleff and Arlene Tankleff (hereinafter the victims or the Tankleffs) were fatally attacked in their home in Belle Terre, New York. Upon the arrival of the police at the crime scene, the defendant, the victims' son—who was then 17 years of age—repeatedly and consistently asserted that Seymour Tankleff's business partner, Jerard Steuerman (hereinafter Jerry Steuerman), committed the murders. The defendant was taken to the headquarters of the Suffolk County Police Department in Yaphank, where he was questioned extensively. James McCready, one of the lead detectives in the investigation and interrogation, utilized a ruse wherein he falsely advised the defendant that his father was alive and had accused the defendant of the crimes. During the questioning, the defendant asked, "[c]ould I have blacked out ... and done this?" and "[c]ould I be possessed?" At that point, a second detective, Norman Rein, responded, "Marty, I think that's what happened to you." The defendant then confessed to both killings and almost immediately thereafter recanted.

At the ensuing, highly-contested jury trial, the prosecution's evidence consisted primarily of this repudiated confession. The defense's theory at trial was that Jerry Steuerman, not the defendant, killed the Tankleffs. Jerry Steuerman had been present at a card game at the Tankleffs' residence which lasted until approximately 3:00 A.M. on the morning of September 7, 1988. Furthermore, evidence was elicited at the trial that Jerry Steuerman owed Seymour Tankleff a substantial amount of money and that, one week after the Tankleff murders, he staged his own death, changed his appearance, and suddenly fled to California. Moreover, at trial, Detective McCready denied that he knew Jerry Steuerman prior to this case, testimony that would become a point of contention over the ensuing years.

After seven days of deliberations by the jury between June 21, 1990, and June 28, 1990, the defendant was convicted of murder in the second degree (intentional murder) with regard to Seymour Tankleff and murder in the second degree (depraved indifference murder) with regard to Arlene Tankleff. On October 23, 1990, he was sentenced to two consecutive terms of incarceration of 25 years to life. The defendant remains incarcerated to date, having served more than 17 years in prison....

[On appeal, the state courts affirmed the defendant's convictions. The United States District Court for the Eastern District of New York thereafter denied his petition for a writ of habeas corpus and the Second Circuit Court of Appeals affirmed, *Tankleff v. Senkowski,* 135 F.3d 235 (2d Cir. 1998).]

B. *THE OCTOBER 2003 CPL 440.10 MOTION IN THE COUNTY COURT*

On October 3, 2003, the defendant moved in the County Court, Suffolk County, to vacate the judgments of conviction pursuant to CPL 440.10(1)(g) and (h), on the grounds of newly-discovered evidence and actual innocence....

In support of his motion, the defendant proffered, inter alia, the affidavits of Karlene Kovacs, sworn to August 10, 1994, and Glenn Harris, sworn to August 29, 2003....

In her affidavit, Kovacs averred that, after the Tankleff murders, she and her friend John Guarascio went to the house of John Guarascio's sister, where they "smoked a joint" of marijuana. Kovacs asserted that, while there, "Joe [referring to one Joseph Creedon]," admitted that he was "involved in the Tankleff murders in some way." Kovacs recalled Creedon saying "something about hiding behind trees and bushes at the Tankleff house during the time of the murders" and that he was with someone named "Steuerman." As Kovacs explained it in her affidavit, Creedon described to Kovacs how, after the murders, "they [sic] had to make a quick dash to avoid being caught."

In February 2002 Glenn Harris was contacted by representatives of the defense. Thereafter, he corresponded with, among others, both the defendant and the defendant's retained investigator, Jay Salpeter.... Essentially, in the correspondence, Harris contended that he drove Creedon and another individual, Peter Kent, to the Tankleffs' residence on the night of the murder.

In a letter dated July 8, 2002, and delivered to Salpeter, Harris wrote: "I lied, fabricated, concocted the whole ... story."

Subsequently, however, Harris provided Salpeter with an affidavit, sworn to August 29, 2003, wherein he related in great detail how he drove Creedon and Kent to the Tankleff residence on the night of the murders. In that affidavit, Harris specifically averred that, in early September 1988, he ran into Kent and Creedon. He stated that, after smoking crack, he drove Creedon and Kent to a house in Belle Terre because Creedon knew that there was a "safe" at that house. Harris asserted that he parked his car on the street near that house. He averred that Creedon and Kent exited the car and walked towards the Tankleff house. According to Harris, approximately 10 to 30 minutes later, Creedon and Kent came running back to the car. Harris asserted that Creedon had gloves in the left-hand pocket of his windbreaker, and told him "lets [sic] go." According to Harris, Creedon and Kent were "both" nervous and Kent was "winded."

In his affidavit, Harris stated that he thereafter drove Kent to Kent's mother's house. Harris asserted that, once there, he observed Kent burning his clothing. At this point, Harris "realized that something more than a burglary occurred." He averred that he later heard on the radio that "something happened to an elderly couple" in Belle Terre. Harris explained that he was "on parole" at that time and was "afraid to go to the police." ...

D. *THE CPL 440.10 HEARING*

On May 12, 2004, the People consented to a CPL 440.10 hearing, on the condition that Harris not be granted transactional immunity. The hearing commenced on July 19, 2004. At the hearing, the defendant's case consisted of a total of 23 witnesses. The People presented 16 witnesses. Several of the witnesses who testified admitted that they had criminal histories and/or had abused drugs....

3. *THE ORDER APPEALED FROM*

In an order dated March 17, 2006, the County Court denied the defendant's motion in its entirety on the following grounds:

a. *Due Diligence*

The County Court found that the defendant did not exercise due diligence in moving for a new trial.

b. *Hearsay*

The County Court determined that statements purportedly made by Creedon to "nefarious scoundrels," many with "extensive criminal histories that included illegal drug use and sales, burglary, robbery, assault and other similar crimes," were hearsay and not admissible as declarations against penal interest.

The court also found that the witnesses who testified about Creedon's confession were shown to be "unreliable, incredible, contradictory, and possibly motivated to harm Creedon by having him convicted of these murders." ...

The court analyzed the admissibility of the affidavit sworn to by Harris. It held that "the affidavit provided by Harris would not be admissible at trial since it lacks trustworthiness and reliability, and even were he to testify at a new trial, it would appear that his testimony would lack any credibility."

c. *The Pipe and McCready's Credibility*

The County Court held that the pipe introduced by the defendant as the actual murder weapon had no probative value because there was no physical evidence connecting it to the murders, and because the People's investigator found other pipes in the same location....

The court concluded "the bulk of the evidence which the defendant seeks to have presented at a new trial would be inadmissible, and that what is left would be insufficient for a jury to render a different verdict." ...

IV. *LEGAL ANALYSIS*

It is abhorrent to our sense of justice and fair play to countenance the possibility that someone innocent of a crime may be incarcerated or otherwise punished for a crime which he or she did not commit. A motion pursuant to CPL 440.10 is a vehicle which "enables convicted defendants to fully vindicate their rights" (34 N.Y. Jur. 2d, Criminal Law § 3047, at 838)....

A. *CPL 440.10(1)(g)*

CPL 440.10(1)(g) provides as follows:

"1. At any time after the entry of a judgment, the court in which it was entered may, upon motion of the defendant, vacate such judgment upon the ground that:

> (g) New evidence has been discovered since the entry of a judgment based upon a verdict of guilty after trial, which could not have been produced by the defendant at the trial even with due diligence on his part and which is of such character as to create a probability that had such evidence been received at the trial the verdict would have been more favorable to the defendant; provided that a motion based upon such ground must be made with due diligence after the discovery of such alleged new evidence."

... As explained by the Court of Appeals in *People v. Crimmins,* 38 N.Y.2d 407, 413, 381 N.Y.S.2d 1, 343 N.E.2d 719, "[u]nlike a post-conviction application for a new trial under [prior law], which had to be made within one year after judgment, no time limitation is prescribed for a motion to vacate judgment under CPL 440.10."

The power to vacate a judgment of conviction upon the ground of newly-discovered evidence and concomitantly grant a new trial rests within the discretion of the hearing court.... [T]his Court is not bound by the hearing court's factual determinations and may make its own credibility determinations....

Thus, this Court's jurisdiction is not limited to reviewing errors of law, but extends to the power to reverse or modify a judgment on the facts and as a matter of discretion in the interest of justice....

1. *Newly Discovered Evidence—The Six Criteria*

"'Newly-discovered evidence in order to be sufficient must fulfill all the following requirements: 1. It must be such as will probably change the result if a new trial is granted; 2. It must have been discovered since the trial; 3. It must be such as could have not been discovered before the trial by the exercise of due diligence; 4. It must be material to the issue; 5. It must not be cumulative to the former issue; and, 6. It must not be merely impeaching or contradicting the former evidence.'" *People v. Salemi,* 309 N.Y. 208, 215–16, 128 N.E. 377, *cert. denied,* 348 U.S. 845. At a hearing on a motion pursuant to CPL 440.10(1)(g), the defendant has the burden of proving by a preponderance of the evidence every fact essential to support the motion.

2. *DUE DILIGENCE REQUIREMENT*

With regard to his motion to vacate the judgment of conviction on the basis of "newly-discovered evidence," the defendant was required to show that the motion was made "with due diligence after the discovery of the alleged new evidence." [CPL 440.10(1)(g)] The County Court found that the defendant failed to make this motion with due diligence. We disagree.

"[T]he due diligence requirement is measured against the defendant's available resources and the practicalities of the particular situation" (34 N.Y. Jur. 2d § 3064, at 866). Under the unique facts of this case, the defendant should not be charged with a lack of due diligence in finding the multiple witnesses who implicated Creedon and/or Jerry Steuerman. The defendant's investigation resulted in a body of new evidence which required time to accumulate. He should not be penalized for waiting to amass all of the new evidence and then presenting it cumulatively to the County Court. Such conduct avoided separate motions upon the discovery of each witness, obviated the squandering of resources, and preserved judicial economy.

3. *THE EVALUATION OF THE EVIDENCE*

A review of the record on appeal reveals that the County Court's determination amounted to a misapplication of its gatekeeper function relative to the evaluation and admissibility of the proffered "new evidence."

The resolution of the inquiry into whether the evidence adduced at the hearing "is of such character as to create a probability that had such evidence been received at the trial the verdict would have been more favorable to the defendant" (CPL 440.10[1][g]) is dispositive of a court's determination of a motion pursuant to CPL 440.10(1)(g). In carrying out this task, the hearing court is obligated to conduct a critical analysis of the evidence. It cannot merely engage in the mechanical exclusion of such evidence.

The County Court completely disregarded a crucial fact which is pivotal to our determination. Namely, many of the witnesses who testified at the CPL 440 hearing were *unrelated* to each other, and their genesis as witnesses was separated by both space and time.... Notably, although clearly not connected to one another, each of those witnesses implicated Creedon and/or Jerry Steuerman in the Tankleff murders.

Moreover, a court must view and evaluate all of the evidence in its entirety. In its determination as to the "impact of evidence unavailable at trial, a court must make its final decision based on the likely cumulative effect of the new evidence had it been presented at trial" (*Amrine v. Bowersox,* 128 F.3d 1222, 1230, *cert denied,* 523 U.S. 1123).

In this case, the County Court failed in this regard. Instead, it erroneously applied both a narrow approach and methodology in evaluating the evidence. It appears that the County Court never considered that the cumulative effect of the new evidence created a probability that, had such evidence been received at the trial, the verdict would have been more favorable to the defendant.

The County Court, in effect, applied a blanket disqualification of all of the defendant's proffered evidence. It viewed almost all of the defendant's witnesses as questionable, untrustworthy, or unreliable. It dismissed, outright, the possibility that witnesses with criminal records, drug addictions, and/or psychiatric issues may nevertheless be capable of testifying truthfully. A witness's "unsavory background" does not render his or her "testimony incredible as a matter of law." As noted by my learned colleague, the Honorable Gabriel Krausman, at the oral argument before this Court, the People "use [such witnesses] all the time."

Similarly, the County Court dismissed as incredible the testimony of certain witnesses on the ground that they were biased against Creedon. We cannot conclude that multiple witnesses who admittedly expressed fear of or contempt for Creedon perjured themselves in order to implicate Creedon in the murders.

On a related topic, we reject the People's assertion, made at the oral argument of the instant appeal, that certain witnesses came forth because this was a highly-publicized case. The claim that intense media coverage somehow played a role in this case and the implication that this prompted individuals to testify falsely is sheer conjecture and speculation.

Additionally, the County Court disparaged the testimony of several witnesses on the ground that it would constitute inadmissible hearsay. "Implicit in th[e] ground for vacating a judgment of conviction is that the newly discovered evidence be admissible" (34 N.Y. Jur. 2d, Criminal Law § 3963, at 863; *see People v. Boyette,* 201 A.D.2d 490, 491, 607 N.Y.S.2d 402).

At this juncture, there is no basis to conclude that all of the subject evidence is inadmissible. In fact, significant competent evidence in admissible form was elicited at the CPL 440 hearing from disparate and wholly unrelated sources. This evidence warrants a new trial.

At the original trial, the defendant's repudiated confession was the most compelling evidence elicited by the prosecution. Arguably, it was the linchpin of the prosecution's case. The *Miranda* aspects of this case have been extensively litigated and will not be revisited. However, when the evidence presented at the CPL 440 hearing is evaluated against the backdrop of the trial evidence, including the defendant's confession, how the confession was obtained, and the fact that the defendant almost immediately recanted the confession, the newly-discovered evidence is "of such character as to create a probability that had such evidence been received at the trial the verdict would have been more favorable to the defendant" (CPL 440.10[1][g]).

B. *CPL 440.10(1)(h)*

Nonetheless, the County Court properly denied that branch of the defendant's motion pursuant to CPL 440.10(1)(h) which was to vacate the judgments of conviction on the ground of actual innocence. The defendant did not establish entitlement to this relief. In making our determination, we do not decide the contention, advanced by the defendant, that New York recognizes a free-standing claim of actual innocence that is cognizable by, or which may be addressed within the parameters of, CPL 440.10(1)(h).

V. *CONCLUSION*

Accordingly, ... the two judgments rendered October 23, 1990, and the sentences imposed thereon are vacated, and we remit the matter to the County Court, Suffolk County, for a new trial, to be conducted with all convenient speed....

Notes and Questions

1. The New York statute authorizing "the court in which [judgment] was entered" to vacate a criminal conviction based on newly discovered evidence, N.Y. Criminal Procedure Law § 440.10 (1)(g), includes the fairly standard prerequisite that the new evidence could

not have been produced with "due diligence" at the original trial. The section's materiality requirement (the evidence would "create a probability that had [it] been received at the trial the verdict would have been more favorable to the defendant") also is typical of standards used in other jurisdictions. State statutes and court decisions commonly demand that the new evidence would "probably" result in a different outcome to justify a new trial, and frequently specify that the evidence cannot merely be cumulative or of value only to impeach a trial witness's credibility. Unlike many states, New York imposes no time limits within which a motion for a new trial based on newly discovered evidence must be filed; the statute allows such motions to be made "[a]t any time after the entry of a judgment...."[19] Finally, the statutory limitation that the "[n]ew evidence has been discovered since the entry of a judgment based upon a verdict of guilty after trial" has been interpreted by New York courts to deny defendants who pled guilty the chance to petition for a new trial based on newly discovered evidence.[20]

2. The court in *Tankleff* found it unnecessary to reach the defendant's argument "that New York recognizes a free-standing claim of actual innocence that is cognizable by, or which may be addressed within the parameters of, CPL 440.10(1)(h)." That section of the statute provides:

> (1) At any time after the entry of a judgment, the court in which it was entered may, upon motion of the defendant, vacate such judgment upon the ground that:
>
> (h) The judgment was obtained in violation of a right of the defendant under the constitution of this state or of the United States.

We will consider "free-standing" claims of actual innocence in the next section, in connection with our discussion of *Herrera v. Collins*, 506 U.S. 390, 113 S.Ct. 853, 122 L.Ed.2d 203 (1993).

3. Prosecutors elected not to retry Martin Tankleff following the court order granting him a new trial. The indictments in his case were dismissed "in the interest of justice" in July 2008.[21] Tankleff, 17 years old at the time his parents were slain, spent 17 years in prison after being convicted of the murders. For a book chronicling the case, co-authored by the investigator responsible for uncovering much of the new evidence that resulted in Tankleff's exoneration, *see* Richard Firstman & Jay Salpeter, *A Criminal Injustice: A True Crime, a False Confession, and the Fight to Free Marty Tankleff* (New York: Ballantine Books 2008).

G. Federal Habeas Corpus and Free-Standing Claims of Actual Innocence

On the heels of the United States Constitution's ratification, the First Congress enacted the Judiciary Act of 1789, authorizing the federal courts to issue writs of habeas corpus to examine claims raised by prisoners held "under or by colour of the authority of the United States" that their detention was unlawful.[22] The federal courts' habeas corpus authority was expanded dramatically at the conclusion of the Civil War, through the Judiciary Act of 1867. This landmark legislation granted state prisoners access to the federal courts to challenge the constitutionality of their confinement. The Act provided:

> ... [T]he several courts of the United States, ... in addition to the authority already conferred by law, shall have power to grant writs of habeas corpus in all

> cases where any person may be restrained of his or her liberty in violation of the constitution, or of any treaty or law of the United States....[23]

Subsequent statutory revisions and Supreme Court decisions have imposed a number of substantive and procedural restrictions on the federal courts' authority to review state prisoners' claims for relief on habeas corpus. Significant changes accompanied passage of the Anti-Terrorism and Effective Death Penalty Act of 1996, 28 U.S.C. §§ 2254 (d) and (e), which specified that:

> (d) An application for a writ of habeas corpus on behalf of a person in custody pursuant to the judgment of a State court shall not be granted with respect to any claim that was adjudicated on the merits in State court proceedings unless the adjudication of the claim—
>
> (1) resulted in a decision that was contrary to, or involved an unreasonable application of, clearly established Federal law, as determined by the Supreme Court of the United States; or
>
> (2) resulted in a decision that was based on an unreasonable determination of the facts in light of the evidence presented in the State court proceeding.
>
> (e)(1) In a proceeding instituted by an application for a writ of habeas corpus by a person in custody pursuant to the judgment of a State court, a determination of a factual issue made by a State court shall be presumed to be correct. The applicant shall have the burden of rebutting the presumption of correctness by clear and convincing evidence.
>
> (2) If the applicant has failed to develop the factual basis of a claim in State court proceedings, the court shall not hold an evidentiary hearing on the claim unless the applicant shows that—
>
> (A) the claim relies on—
>
> (i) a new rule of constitutional law, made retroactive to cases on collateral review by the Supreme Court, that was previously unavailable; or
>
> (ii) a factual predicate that could not have been previously discovered through the exercise of due diligence; and
>
> (B) the facts underlying the claim would be sufficient to establish by clear and convincing evidence that but for constitutional error, no reasonable factfinder would have found the applicant guilty of the underlying offense.

The failure to adhere to procedural rules that limit successive filings, impose time deadlines, and require the exhaustion of potential state remedies, among others, ordinarily bars federal habeas corpus review of state prisoners' claims.[24] The Supreme Court nevertheless has excused petitioners' procedural defaults when habeas corpus review may be necessary to correct a fundamental miscarriage of justice. The miscarriage of justice exception comes into play when a habeas petitioner may be "actually innocent" of the offense for which he or she was convicted. Most of the constitutional claims raised on federal habeas corpus involve procedural violations—for instance, ineffective assistance of counsel, the admission of a coerced confession, or being denied the right to confront accusing witnesses. A prisoner who seeks to present a procedurally defaulted constitutional claim to a federal court on habeas corpus to prevent a fundamental miscarriage of justice, in reliance on the "actual innocence" exception, is said to be invoking innocence as a "gateway" to be allowed to raise the alleged error. "A petitioner's burden at the gateway stage is to demonstrate that more likely than not, in light of the new evidence, no reasonable juror would find him guilty beyond a reasonable doubt—or, to remove the double negative, that more likely than not any reasonable juror would have a reasonable doubt."[25]

"Gateway" claims of actual innocence are fundamentally different from "free-standing" claims of actual innocence. Under the former, a habeas petitioner who ordinarily would be denied access to federal court is allowed to present a claimed rights violation that otherwise would have been defaulted. In contrast, a "free-standing" claim of innocence asks the court to do much more. It essentially is an assertion that, "I am innocent, and since the State cannot constitutionally punish an innocent person, I am entitled to habeas corpus relief."

Leonel Herrera was convicted of capital murder and sentenced to death in Texas. When the state courts refused to grant him a hearing to enable him to offer newly discovered evidence of his innocence, he filed a petition for a writ of habeas corpus in federal court, alleging that the United States Constitution prohibits the execution of an innocent person. The Supreme Court considered the federal courts' authority to reach free-standing claims of actual innocence on habeas corpus, in *Herrera v. Collins.*

Herrera v. Collins

506 U.S. 390, 113 S.Ct. 853, 122 L.Ed.2d 203 (1993)

Chief Justice REHNQUIST delivered the opinion of the Court.

Petitioner Leonel Torres Herrera was convicted of capital murder and sentenced to death in January 1982. He unsuccessfully challenged the conviction on direct appeal and state collateral proceedings in the Texas state courts, and in a federal habeas petition. In February 1992—10 years after his conviction—he urged in a second federal habeas petition that he was "actually innocent" of the murder for which he was sentenced to death, and that the Eighth Amendment's prohibition against cruel and unusual punishment and the Fourteenth Amendment's guarantee of due process of law therefore forbid his execution. He supported this claim with affidavits tending to show that his now-dead brother, rather than he, had been the perpetrator of the crime. Petitioner urges us to hold that this showing of innocence entitles him to relief in this federal habeas proceeding. We hold that it does not.

Shortly before 11 p.m. on an evening in late September 1981, the body of Texas Department of Public Safety Officer David Rucker was found by a passer-by on a stretch of highway about six miles east of Los Fresnos, Texas, a few miles north of Brownsville in the Rio Grande Valley. Rucker's body was lying beside his patrol car. He had been shot in the head.

At about the same time, Los Fresnos Police Officer Enrique Carrisalez observed a speeding vehicle traveling west towards Los Fresnos, away from the place where Rucker's body had been found, along the same road. Carrisalez, who was accompanied in his patrol car by Enrique Hernandez, turned on his flashing red lights and pursued the speeding vehicle. After the car had stopped briefly at a red light, it signaled that it would pull over and did so. The patrol car pulled up behind it. Carrisalez took a flashlight and walked toward the car of the speeder. The driver opened his door and exchanged a few words with Carrisalez before firing at least one shot at Carrisalez' chest. The officer died nine days later.

Petitioner Herrera was arrested a few days after the shootings and charged with the capital murder of both Carrisalez and Rucker. He was tried and found guilty of the capital murder of Carrisalez in January 1982, and sentenced to death. In July 1982, petitioner pleaded guilty to the murder of Rucker.

At petitioner's trial for the murder of Carrisalez, Hernandez, who had witnessed Carrisalez' slaying from the officer's patrol car, identified petitioner as the person who had wielded the gun. A declaration by Officer Carrisalez to the same effect, made while he was in the hospital, was also admitted. Through a license plate check, it was shown that the speeding car involved in Carrisalez' murder was registered to petitioner's "live-in" girlfriend. Petitioner was known to drive this car, and he had a set of keys to the car in his pants pocket when he was arrested. Hernandez identified the car as the vehicle from which the murderer had emerged to fire the fatal shot. He also testified that there had been only one person in the car that night.

The evidence showed that Herrera's Social Security card had been found alongside Rucker's patrol car on the night he was killed. Splatters of blood on the car identified as the vehicle involved in the shootings, and on petitioner's blue jeans and wallet were identified as type A blood —the same type which Rucker had. (Herrera has type O blood.) Similar evidence with respect to strands of hair found in the car indicated that the hair was Rucker's and not Herrera's. A handwritten letter was also found on the person of petitioner when he was arrested, which strongly implied that he had killed Rucker.[1]

Petitioner appealed his conviction and sentence, arguing, among other things, that Hernandez' and Carrisalez' identifications were unreliable and improperly admitted. The Texas Court of Criminal Appeals affirmed, *Herrera v. State,* 682 S.W.2d 313 (1984), and we denied certiorari, 471 U.S. 1131 (1985). Petitioner's application for state habeas relief was denied. *Ex parte Herrera,* No. 12,848-02 (Tex.Crim.App., Aug. 2, 1985). Petitioner then filed a federal habeas petition, again challenging the identifications offered against him at trial. This petition was denied, see 904 F.2d 944 (CA5), and we again denied certiorari, 498 U.S. 925 (1990).

Petitioner next returned to state court and filed a second habeas petition, raising, among other things, a claim of "actual innocence" based on newly discovered evidence. In support of this claim petitioner presented the affidavits of Hector Villarreal, an attorney who had represented petitioner's brother, Raul Herrera, Sr., and of Juan Franco Palacious, one of Raul, Senior's former cellmates. Both individuals claimed that Raul, Senior, who died in 1984, had told them that he—and not petitioner—had killed Officers Rucker and Carrisalez. The State District Court denied this application, finding that "no evidence at trial remotely suggest[ed] that anyone other than [petitioner] committed the offense." *Ex parte Herrera,* No. 81-CR-672-C (Tex. 197th Jud.Dist., Jan. 14, 1991). The Texas Court of Criminal Appeals affirmed, *Ex parte Herrera,* 819 S.W.2d 528 (1991), and we denied certiorari, *Herrera v. Texas,* 502 U.S. 1085 (1992).

In February 1992, petitioner lodged the instant habeas petition—his second—in federal court, alleging, among other things, that he is innocent of the murders of Rucker and Carrisalez, and that his execution would thus violate the Eighth and Fourteenth Amendments. In addition to proffering the above affidavits, petitioner presented the affidavits of Raul Herrera, Jr., Raul Senior's son, and Jose Ybarra, Jr., a schoolmate of the Herrera brothers. Raul, Junior, averred that he had witnessed his father shoot Officers Rucker and Carrisalez and petitioner was not present. Raul, Junior, was nine years old at the time of the killings. Ybarra

1. The letter read: "To whom it may concern: I am terribly sorry for those I have brought grief to their lives. Who knows why? We cannot change the future's problems with problems from the past. What I did was for a cause and purpose. One law runs others, and in the world we live in, that's the way it is.

"I'm not a tormented person.... I believe in the law. What would it be without this [*sic*] men that risk their lives for others, and that's what they should be doing—protecting life, property, and the pursuit of happiness. Sometimes, the law gets too involved with other things that profit them. The most laws that they make for people to break them, in other words, to encourage crime.

"What happened to Rucker was for a certain reason. I knew him as Mike Tatum. He was in my business, and he violated some of its laws and suffered the penalty, like the one you have for me when the time comes.

"My personal life, which has been a conspiracy since my high school days, has nothing to do with what has happened. The other officer that became part of our lives, me and Rucker's (Tatum), that night had not to do in this [*sic*]. He was out to do what he had to do, protect, but that's life. There's a lot of us that wear different faces in lives every day, and that is what causes problems for all. [Unintelligible word].

"You have wrote all you want of my life, but think about yours, also. [Signed Leonel Herrera].

"I have tapes and pictures to prove what I have said. I will prove my side if you accept to listen. You [unintelligible word] freedom of speech, even a criminal has that right. I will present myself if this is read word for word over the media, I will turn myself in; if not, don't have millions of men out there working just on me while others—robbers, rapists, or burglars—are taking advantage of the law's time. Excuse my spelling and writing. It's hard at times like this."

alleged that Raul, Senior, told him one summer night in 1983 that he had shot the two police officers....

The District Court dismissed most of petitioner's claims as an abuse of the writ. However, "in order to ensure that Petitioner can assert his constitutional claims and out of a sense of fairness and due process," the District Court granted petitioner's request for a stay of execution so that he could present his claim of actual innocence, along with the Raul, Junior, and Ybarra affidavits, in state court....

The Court of Appeals vacated the stay of execution. 954 F.2d 1029 (CA5 1992).... Absent an accompanying constitutional violation, the Court of Appeals held that petitioner's claim of actual innocence was not cognizable because, under *Townsend v. Sain,* 372 U.S. 293 (1963), "the existence merely of newly discovered evidence relevant to the guilt of a state prisoner is not a ground for relief on federal habeas corpus." We granted certiorari, 502 U.S. 1085 (1992), and the Texas Court of Criminal Appeals stayed petitioner's execution. We now affirm.

Petitioner asserts that the Eighth and Fourteenth Amendments to the United States Constitution prohibit the execution of a person who is innocent of the crime for which he was convicted. This proposition has an elemental appeal, as would the similar proposition that the Constitution prohibits the imprisonment of one who is innocent of the crime for which he was convicted. After all, the central purpose of any system of criminal justice is to convict the guilty and free the innocent. But the evidence upon which petitioner's claim of innocence rests was not produced at his trial, but rather eight years later. In any system of criminal justice, "innocence" or "guilt" must be determined in some sort of a judicial proceeding. Petitioner's showing of innocence, and indeed his constitutional claim for relief based upon that showing, must be evaluated in the light of the previous proceedings in this case, which have stretched over a span of 10 years.

A person when first charged with a crime is entitled to a presumption of innocence, and may insist that his guilt be established beyond a reasonable doubt. Other constitutional provisions also have the effect of ensuring against the risk of convicting an innocent person. In capital cases, we have required additional protections because of the nature of the penalty at stake. All of these constitutional safeguards, of course, make it more difficult for the State to rebut and finally overturn the presumption of innocence which attaches to every criminal defendant. But we have also observed that "[d]ue process does not require that every conceivable step be taken, at whatever cost, to eliminate the possibility of convicting an innocent person." *Patterson v. New York,* 432 U.S. 197, 208 (1977). To conclude otherwise would all but paralyze our system for enforcement of the criminal law.

Once a defendant has been afforded a fair trial and convicted of the offense for which he was charged, the presumption of innocence disappears. Here, it is not disputed that the State met its burden of proving at trial that petitioner was guilty of the capital murder of Officer Carrisalez beyond a reasonable doubt. Thus, in the eyes of the law, petitioner does not come before the Court as one who is "innocent," but, on the contrary, as one who has been convicted by due process of law of two brutal murders.

Based on affidavits here filed, petitioner claims that evidence never presented to the trial court proves him innocent notwithstanding the verdict reached at his trial. Such a claim is not cognizable in the state courts of Texas. For to obtain a new trial based on newly discovered evidence, a defendant must file a motion within 30 days after imposition or suspension of sentence. Tex.Rule App.Proc. 31(a)(1) (1992). The Texas courts have construed this 30-day time limit as jurisdictional.

Claims of actual innocence based on newly discovered evidence have never been held to state a ground for federal habeas relief absent an independent constitutional violation occurring in the underlying state criminal proceeding. Chief Justice Warren made this clear in *Townsend v. Sain, supra,* 372 U.S., at 317 (emphasis added):

"Where newly discovered evidence is alleged in a habeas application, evidence which could not reasonably have been presented to the state trier of facts, the federal court must grant an evidentiary hearing. Of course, such evidence must bear upon the constitutionality of the applicant's detention; *the existence merely of newly discovered evidence relevant to the guilt of a state prisoner is not a ground for relief on federal habeas corpus.*"

This rule is grounded in the principle that federal habeas courts sit to ensure that individuals are not imprisoned in violation of the Constitution—not to correct errors of fact.... The guilt or innocence determination in state criminal trials is "a decisive and portentous event." *Wain-*

wright v. Sykes, 433 U.S. 72, 90 (1977). "Society's resources have been concentrated at that time and place in order to decide, within the limits of human fallibility, the question of guilt or innocence of one of its citizens." *Ibid.* Few rulings would be more disruptive of our federal system than to provide for federal habeas review of freestanding claims of actual innocence....

Petitioner is understandably imprecise in describing the sort of federal relief to which a suitable showing of actual innocence would entitle him. In his brief he states that the federal habeas court should have "an important initial opportunity to hear the evidence and resolve the merits of Petitioner's claim." Acceptance of this view would presumably require the habeas court to hear testimony from the witnesses who testified at trial as well as those who made the statements in the affidavits which petitioner has presented, and to determine anew whether or not petitioner is guilty of the murder of Officer Carrisalez. Indeed, the dissent's approach differs little from that hypothesized here....

The dissent fails to articulate the relief that would be available if petitioner were to meets its "probable innocence" standard. Would it be commutation of petitioner's death sentence, new trial, or unconditional release from imprisonment? The typical relief granted in federal habeas corpus is a conditional order of release unless the State elects to retry the successful habeas petitioner, or in a capital case a similar conditional order vacating the death sentence. Were petitioner to satisfy the dissent's "probable innocence" standard, therefore, the District Court would presumably be required to grant a conditional order of relief, which would in effect require the State to retry petitioner 10 years after his first trial, not because of any constitutional violation which had occurred at the first trial, but simply because of a belief that in light of petitioner's new-found evidence a jury might find him not guilty at a second trial.

Yet there is no guarantee that the guilt or innocence determination would be any more exact. To the contrary, the passage of time only diminishes the reliability of criminal adjudications....

This is not to say that our habeas jurisprudence casts a blind eye toward innocence. In a series of cases culminating with *Sawyer v. Whitley*, 505 U.S. 333 (1992), ... we have held that a petitioner otherwise subject to defenses of abusive or successive use of the writ may have his federal constitutional claim considered on the merits if he makes a proper showing of actual innocence. This rule, or fundamental miscarriage of justice exception, is grounded in the "equitable discretion" of habeas courts to see that federal constitutional errors do not result in the incarceration of innocent persons. But this body of our habeas jurisprudence makes clear that a claim of "actual innocence" is not itself a constitutional claim, but instead a gateway through which a habeas petitioner must pass to have his otherwise barred constitutional claim considered on the merits.

Petitioner in this case is simply not entitled to habeas relief based on the reasoning of this line of cases. For he does not seek excusal of a procedural error so that he may bring an independent constitutional claim challenging his conviction or sentence, but rather argues that he is entitled to habeas relief because newly discovered evidence shows that his conviction is factually incorrect. The fundamental miscarriage of justice exception is available "only where the prisoner *supplements* his constitutional claim with a colorable showing of factual innocence." We have never held that it extends to freestanding claims of actual innocence. Therefore, the exception is inapplicable here.

Petitioner asserts that this case is different because he has been sentenced to death. But we have "refused to hold that the fact that a death sentence has been imposed requires a different standard of review on federal habeas corpus." *Murray v. Giarratano*, 492 U.S. 1, 9 (1989) (plurality opinion). We have, of course, held that the Eighth Amendment requires increased reliability of the process by which capital punishment may be imposed. But petitioner's claim does not fit well into the doctrine of these cases, since, as we have pointed out, it is far from clear that a second trial 10 years after the first trial would produce a more reliable result.

Perhaps mindful of this, petitioner urges not that he necessarily receive a new trial, but that his death sentence simply be vacated if a federal habeas court deems that a satisfactory showing of "actual innocence" has been made. But such a result is scarcely logical; petitioner's claim is not that some error was made in imposing a capital sentence upon him, but that a fundamental error was made in finding him guilty of the underlying murder in the first place. It would be a rather strange jurisprudence, in these circumstances, which held that under our Constitution he could not be executed, but that he could spend the rest of his life in prison....

Alternatively, petitioner invokes the Fourteenth Amendment's guarantee of due process of law in support of his claim that his showing of actual innocence entitles him to a new trial, or at least to a vacation of his death sentence.... [W]e have found criminal process lacking only where it "'offends some principle of justice so rooted in the traditions and conscience of our people as to be ranked as fundamental.'" "Historical practice is probative of whether a procedural rule can be characterized as fundamental."

The Constitution itself, of course, makes no mention of new trials.... The First Congress provided for new trials for "reasons for which new trials have usually been granted in courts of law." ... One of the grounds upon which new trials were granted was newly discovered evidence.

The early federal cases adhere to the common-law rule that a new trial may be granted only during the term of court in which the final judgment was entered.... In 1934, this Court departed from the common-law rule and adopted a time limit—60 days after final judgment—for filing new trial motions based on newly discovered evidence. Four years later, we amended Rule II(3) to allow such motions in capital cases "at any time" before the execution took place.

There ensued a debate as to whether this Court should abolish the time limit for filing new trial motions based on newly discovered evidence to prevent a miscarriage of justice, or retain a time limit even in capital cases to promote finality. In 1946, we set a 2-year time limit for filing new trial motions based on newly discovered evidence and abolished the exception for capital cases. Rule 33, Federal Rules of Criminal Procedure ("A motion for a new trial based on the ground of newly discovered evidence may be made only before or within two years after final judgment"). We have strictly construed the Rule 33 time limits. And the Rule's treatment of new trials based on newly discovered evidence has not changed since its adoption.

The American Colonies adopted the English common law on new trials. Thus, where new trials were available, motions for such relief typically had to be filed before the expiration of the term during which the trial was held. Over time, many States enacted statutes providing for new trials in all types of cases. Some States also extended the time period for filing new trial motions beyond the term of court, but most States required that such motions be made within a few days after the verdict was rendered or before the judgment was entered.

The practice in the States today, while of limited relevance to our historical inquiry, is divergent. Texas is one of 17 States that requires a new trial motion based on newly discovered evidence to be made within 60 days of judgment. One State adheres to the common-law rule and requires that such a motion be filed during the term in which judgment was rendered. Eighteen jurisdictions have time limits ranging between one and three years, with 10 States and the District of Columbia following the 2-year federal time limit. Only 15 States allow a new trial motion based on newly discovered evidence to be filed more than three years after conviction. Of these States, four have waivable time limits of less than 120 days, two have waivable time limits of more than 120 days, and nine States have no time limits.

In light of the historical availability of new trials, our own amendments to Rule 33, and the contemporary practice in the States, we cannot say that Texas' refusal to entertain petitioner's newly discovered evidence eight years after his conviction transgresses a principle of fundamental fairness "rooted in the traditions and conscience of our people." *Patterson v. New York,* 432 U.S., at 202. This is not to say, however, that petitioner is left without a forum to raise his actual innocence claim. For under Texas law, petitioner may file a request for executive clemency. Clemency is deeply rooted in our Anglo-American tradition of law, and is the historic remedy for preventing miscarriages of justice where judicial process has been exhausted.

In England, the clemency power was vested in the Crown and can be traced back to the 700s.... Clemency provided the principal avenue of relief for individuals convicted of criminal offenses—most of which were capital—because there was no right of appeal until 1907. It was the only means by which one could challenge his conviction on the ground of innocence.

Our Constitution adopts the British model and gives to the President the "Power to grant Reprieves and Pardons for Offences against the United States." Art. II, § 2, cl. 1. In *United States v. Wilson,* 32 U.S. (7 Pet.) 150, 160–161 (1833), Chief Justice Marshall expounded on the President's pardon power:

..."A pardon is an act of grace, proceeding from the power entrusted with the execution of the laws, which exempts the individual, on whom it is bestowed, from the punishment the law inflicts for a crime he has committed. It is the private, though official act of the executive magistrate, delivered to the individual for whose benefit it is intended, and not communicated officially to the court...."

Of course, although the Constitution vests in the President a pardon power, it does not require the States to enact a clemency mechanism. Yet since the British Colonies were founded, clemency has been available in America.... Today, all 36 States that authorize capital punishment have constitutional or statutory provisions for clemency.

Executive clemency has provided the "fail safe" in our criminal justice system. It is an unalterable fact that our judicial system, like the human beings who administer it, is fallible. But history is replete with examples of wrongfully convicted persons who have been pardoned in the wake of after-discovered evidence establishing their innocence. In his classic work, Professor Edwin Borchard compiled 65 cases in which it was later determined that individuals had been wrongfully convicted of crimes. Clemency provided the relief mechanism in 47 of these cases; the remaining cases ended in judgments of acquittals after new trials. E. Borchard, Convicting the Innocent (1932). Recent authority confirms that over the past century clemency has been exercised frequently in capital cases in which demonstrations of "actual innocence" have been made. See M. Radelet, H. Bedau, & C. Putnam, In Spite of Innocence 282–356 (1992).[15]

... As the foregoing discussion illustrates, in state criminal proceedings the trial is the paramount event for determining the guilt or innocence of the defendant. Federal habeas review of state convictions has traditionally been limited to claims of constitutional violations occurring in the course of the underlying state criminal proceedings. Our federal habeas cases have treated claims of "actual innocence," not as an independent constitutional claim, but as a basis upon which a habeas petitioner may have an independent constitutional claim considered on the merits, even though his habeas petition would otherwise be regarded as successive or abusive. History shows that the traditional remedy for claims of innocence based on new evidence, discovered too late in the day to file a new trial motion, has been executive clemency.

We may assume, for the sake of argument in deciding this case, that in a capital case a truly persuasive demonstration of "actual innocence" made after trial would render the execution of a defendant unconstitutional, and warrant federal habeas relief if there were no state avenue open to process such a claim. But because of the very disruptive effect that entertaining claims of actual innocence would have on the need for finality in capital cases, and the enormous burden that having to retry cases based on often stale evidence would place on the States, the threshold showing for such an assumed right would necessarily be extraordinarily high. The showing made by petitioner in this case falls far short of any such threshold.

Petitioner's newly discovered evidence consists of affidavits. In the new trial context, motions based solely upon affidavits are disfavored because the affiants' statements are obtained without the benefit of cross-examination and an opportunity to make credibility determinations. Petitioner's affidavits are particularly suspect in this regard because, with the exception of Raul Herrera, Jr.'s affidavit, they consist of hearsay. Likewise, in reviewing petitioner's new evidence, we are mindful that defendants often abuse new trial motions "as a method of delaying enforcement of just sentences." ...

The affidavits filed in this habeas proceeding were given over eight years after petitioner's trial. No satisfactory explanation has been given as to why the affiants waited until the 11th hour—and, indeed, until after the alleged perpetrator of the murders himself was dead—to make their statements. Equally troubling, no explanation has been offered as to why petitioner, by hypothesis an innocent man, pleaded guilty to the murder of Rucker.

Moreover, the affidavits themselves contain inconsistencies, and therefore fail to provide a

15. The dissent points to one study concluding that 23 innocent persons have been executed in the United States this century as support for the proposition that clemency requests by persons believed to be innocent are not always granted. See *post,* at 876, n. 1 (citing Bedau & Radelet, Miscarriages of Justice in Potentially Capital Cases, 40 Stan.L.Rev. 21 (1987)). Although we do not doubt that clemency—like the criminal justice system itself—is fallible, we note that scholars have taken issue with this study. See Markman & Cassell, Protecting the Innocent: A Response to the Bedau-Radelet Study, 41 Stan.L.Rev. 121 (1988).

convincing account of what took place on the night Officers Rucker and Carrisalez were killed. For instance, the affidavit of Raul, Junior, who was nine years old at the time, indicates that there were three people in the speeding car from which the murderer emerged, whereas Hector Villarreal attested that Raul, Senior, told him that there were two people in the car that night. Of course, Hernandez testified at petitioner's trial that the murderer was the only occupant of the car. The affidavits also conflict as to the direction in which the vehicle was heading when the murders took place and petitioner's whereabouts on the night of the killings.

Finally, the affidavits must be considered in light of the proof of petitioner's guilt at trial—proof which included two eyewitness identifications, numerous pieces of circumstantial evidence, and a handwritten letter in which petitioner apologized for killing the officers and offered to turn himself in under certain conditions. That proof, even when considered alongside petitioner's belated affidavits, points strongly to petitioner's guilt.

This is not to say that petitioner's affidavits are without probative value. Had this sort of testimony been offered at trial, it could have been weighed by the jury, along with the evidence offered by the State and petitioner, in deliberating upon its verdict. Since the statements in the affidavits contradict the evidence received at trial, the jury would have had to decide important issues of credibility. But coming 10 years after petitioner's trial, this showing of innocence falls far short of that which would have to be made in order to trigger the sort of constitutional claim which we have assumed, *arguendo,* to exist.

The judgment of the Court of Appeals is *Affirmed.*

Justice O'CONNOR, with whom Justice KENNEDY joins, concurring.

I cannot disagree with the fundamental legal principle that executing the innocent is inconsistent with the Constitution. Regardless of the verbal formula employed—"contrary to contemporary standards of decency," "shocking to the conscience," or offensive to a """principle of justice so rooted in the traditions and conscience of our people as to be ranked as fundamental,"""—the execution of a legally and factually innocent person would be a constitutionally intolerable event. Dispositive to this case, however, is an equally fundamental fact: Petitioner is not innocent, in any sense of the word.

As the Court explains, petitioner is not innocent in the eyes of the law because, in our system of justice, "the trial is the paramount event for determining the guilt or innocence of the defendant." In petitioner's case, that paramount event occurred 10 years ago. He was tried before a jury of his peers, with the full panoply of protections that our Constitution affords criminal defendants. At the conclusion of that trial, the jury found petitioner guilty beyond a reasonable doubt. Petitioner therefore does not appear before us as an innocent man on the verge of execution. He is instead a legally guilty one who, refusing to accept the jury's verdict, demands a hearing in which to have his culpability determined once again.

Consequently, the issue before us is not whether a State can execute the innocent. It is, as the Court notes, whether a fairly convicted and therefore legally guilty person is constitutionally entitled to yet another judicial proceeding in which to adjudicate his guilt anew, 10 years after conviction, notwithstanding his failure to demonstrate that constitutional error infected his trial. In most circumstances, that question would answer itself in the negative. Our society has a high degree of confidence in its criminal trials, in no small part because the Constitution offers unparalleled protections against convicting the innocent. The question similarly would be answered in the negative today, except for the disturbing nature of the claim before us. Petitioner contends not only that the Constitution's protections "sometimes fail," but that their failure in his case will result in his execution—even though he is factually innocent and has evidence to prove it.

Exercising restraint, the Court and Justice WHITE assume for the sake of argument that, if a prisoner were to make an exceptionally strong showing of actual innocence, the execution could not go forward. Justice BLACKMUN, in contrast, would expressly so hold; he would also announce the precise burden of proof.... Resolving the issue is neither necessary nor advisable in this case. The question is a sensitive and, to say the least, troubling one. It implicates not just the life of a single individual, but also the State's powerful and legitimate interest in punishing the guilty, and the nature of state-federal relations....

Nonetheless, the proper disposition of this case is neither difficult nor troubling. No matter what the Court might say about claims of actual innocence today, petitioner could not obtain relief. The record overwhelmingly demonstrates that petitioner deliberately shot and killed Officers Rucker and Carrisalez the night of September 29, 1981; petitioner's new evidence is bereft of credibility.... The record makes it abundantly clear that petitioner is ... the established perpetrator of two brutal and tragic [murders]....

... At some point in time, the State's interest in finality must outweigh the prisoner's interest in yet another round of litigation. In this case, that point was well short of eight years.

Unless federal proceedings and relief—if they are to be had at all—are reserved for "extraordinarily high" and "truly persuasive demonstration[s] of 'actual innocence'" that cannot be presented to state authorities, the federal courts will be deluged with frivolous claims of actual innocence....

Ultimately, two things about this case are clear. First is what the Court does *not* hold. Nowhere does the Court state that the Constitution permits the execution of an actually innocent person. Instead, the Court assumes for the sake of argument that a truly persuasive demonstration of actual innocence would render any such execution unconstitutional and that federal habeas relief would be warranted if no state avenue were open to process the claim. Second is what petitioner has not demonstrated. Petitioner has failed to make a persuasive showing of actual innocence. Not one judge—no state court judge, not the District Court Judge, none of the three judges of the Court of Appeals, and none of the Justices of this Court—has expressed doubt about petitioner's guilt. Accordingly, the Court has no reason to pass on, and appropriately reserves, the question whether federal courts may entertain convincing claims of actual innocence. That difficult question remains open. If the Constitution's guarantees of fair procedure and the safeguards of clemency and pardon fulfill their historical mission, it may never require resolution at all.

Justice SCALIA, with whom Justice THOMAS joins, concurring.

We granted certiorari on the question whether it violates due process or constitutes cruel and unusual punishment for a State to execute a person who, having been convicted of murder after a full and fair trial, later alleges that newly discovered evidence shows him to be "actually innocent." I would have preferred to decide that question, particularly since, as the Court's discussion shows, it is perfectly clear what the answer is: There is no basis in text, tradition, or even in contemporary practice (if that were enough) for finding in the Constitution a right to demand judicial consideration of newly discovered evidence of innocence brought forward after conviction. In saying that such a right exists, the dissenters apply nothing but their personal opinions to invalidate the rules of more than two-thirds of the States, and a Federal Rule of Criminal Procedure for which this Court itself is responsible. If the system that has been in place for 200 years (and remains widely approved) "shock[s]" the dissenters' consciences, perhaps they should doubt the calibration of their consciences, or, better still, the usefulness of "conscience shocking" as a legal test.

I nonetheless join the entirety of the Court's opinion, including the final portion—because there is no legal error in deciding a case by assuming, *arguendo,* that an asserted constitutional right exists, and because I can understand, or at least am accustomed to, the reluctance of the present Court to admit publicly that Our Perfect Constitution lets stand any injustice, much less the execution of an innocent man who has received, though to no avail, all the process that our society has traditionally deemed adequate. With any luck, we shall avoid ever having to face this embarrassing question again, since it is improbable that evidence of innocence as convincing as today's opinion requires would fail to produce an executive pardon.

My concern is that in making life easier for ourselves we not appear to make it harder for the lower federal courts, imposing upon them the burden of regularly analyzing newly-discovered evidence-of-innocence claims in capital cases (in which event such federal claims, it can confidently be predicted, will become routine and even repetitive)....

Justice WHITE, concurring in the judgment.

In voting to affirm, I assume that a persuasive showing of "actual innocence" made after trial, even though made after the expiration of the time provided by law for the presentation of newly discovered evidence, would render unconstitutional the execution of petitioner in this case. To be entitled to relief, however, petitioner would at the very least be required to show that based on proffered newly discovered evidence and the entire record before the jury that convicted him, "no rational trier of fact could [find] proof of guilt beyond a reasonable doubt." *Jackson v. Virginia,* 443 U.S. 307, 324 (1979). For the reasons stated in the Court's opinion, petitioner's showing falls far short of satisfying even that standard, and I therefore concur in the judgment.

Justice BLACKMUN, with whom Justice STEVENS and Justice SOUTER join with respect to Parts I–IV, dissenting.

Nothing could be more contrary to contemporary standards of decency, or more shocking to the conscience, than to execute a person who is actually innocent.

I therefore must disagree with the long and general discussion that precedes the Court's disposition of this case. That discussion, of course, is dictum because the Court assumes, "for the sake of argument in deciding this case, that in a capital case a truly persuasive demonstration of 'actual innocence' made after trial would render the execution of a defendant unconstitutional." Without articulating the standard it is applying, however, the Court then decides that this petitioner has not made a sufficiently persuasive case. Because I believe that in the first instance the District Court should decide whether petitioner is entitled to a hearing and whether he is entitled to relief on the merits of his claim, I would reverse the order of the Court of Appeals and remand this case for further proceedings in the District Court.

I

The Court's enumeration of the constitutional rights of criminal defendants surely is entirely beside the point. These protections sometimes fail.[1] We really are being asked to decide whether the Constitution forbids the execution of a person who has been validly convicted and sentenced but who, nonetheless, can prove his innocence with newly discovered evidence. Despite the State of Texas' astonishing protestation to the contrary, I do not see how the answer can be anything but "yes."

A

The Eighth Amendment prohibits "cruel and unusual punishments." This proscription is not static but rather reflects evolving standards of decency. I think it is crystal clear that the execution of an innocent person is "at odds with contemporary standards of fairness and decency." Indeed, it is at odds with any standard of decency that I can imagine....

The protection of the Eighth Amendment does not end once a defendant has been validly convicted and sentenced....

Respondent and the United States as *amicus curiae* argue that the Eighth Amendment does not apply to petitioner because he is challenging his guilt, not his punishment.... What respondent and the United States fail to recognize is that the legitimacy of punishment is inextricably intertwined with guilt....

The Court also suggests that allowing petitioner to raise his claim of innocence would not serve society's interest in the reliable imposition of the death penalty because it might require a new trial that would be less accurate than the first. This suggestion misses the point entirely. The question is not whether a second trial would be more reliable than the first but whether, in light of new evidence, the result of the first trial is sufficiently reliable for the State to carry out a death sentence....

B

Execution of the innocent is equally offensive to the Due Process Clause of the Fourteenth Amendment. The majority's discussion misinterprets petitioner's Fourteenth Amendment claim as raising a procedural, rather than a substantive, due process challenge.

... "The Due Process Clause of the Fifth Amendment provides that 'No person shall ... be deprived of life, liberty, or property, without due process of law....' This Court has held that the Due Process Clause protects individuals against two types of government action. So-called 'substantive due process' prevents the government from engaging in conduct that 'shocks the conscience,' *Rochin v. California,* 342 U.S. 165, 172 (1952), or interferes with rights 'implicit in the

1. One impressive study has concluded that 23 innocent people have been executed in the United States in this century, including one as recently as 1984. Bedau & Radelet, Miscarriages of Justice in Potentially Capital Cases, 40 Stan.L.Rev. 21, 36, 173–179 (1987); Radelet, Bedau, & Putnam, In Spite of Innocence 282–356 (1992). The majority cites this study to show that clemency has been exercised frequently in capital cases when showings of actual innocence have been made. But the study also shows that requests for clemency by persons the authors believe were innocent have been refused. See, *e.g.,* Bedau & Radelet, 40 Stan.L.Rev., at 91 (discussing James Adams who was executed in Florida on May 10, 1984); Radelet, Bedau, & Putnam, In Spite of Innocence, at 5–10 (same).

concept of ordered liberty,' *Palko v. Connecticut,* 302 U.S. 319, 325–326 (1937). When government action depriving a person of life, liberty, or property survives substantive due process scrutiny, it must still be implemented in a fair manner. *Mathews v. Eldridge,* 424 U.S. 319, 335 (1976). This requirement has traditionally been referred to as 'procedural' due process." *United States v. Salerno,* 481 U.S. 739, 746 (1987)....

... Execution of an innocent person is the ultimate "'arbitrary impositio[n].'" It is an imposition from which one never recovers and for which one can never be compensated. Thus, I also believe that petitioner may raise a substantive due process challenge to his punishment on the ground that he is actually innocent....

II

The majority's discussion of petitioner's constitutional claims is even more perverse when viewed in the light of this Court's recent habeas jurisprudence....

Having adopted an "actual-innocence" requirement for review of abusive, successive, or defaulted claims, ... the majority would now take the position that "a claim of 'actual innocence' is not itself a constitutional claim, but instead a gateway through which a habeas petitioner must pass to have his otherwise barred constitutional claim considered on the merits." In other words, having held that a prisoner who is incarcerated in violation of the Constitution must show he is actually innocent to obtain relief, the majority would now hold that a prisoner who is actually innocent must show a constitutional violation to obtain relief. The only principle that would appear to reconcile these two positions is the principle that habeas relief should be denied whenever possible.

III

The Eighth and Fourteenth Amendments, of course, are binding on the States, and one would normally expect the States to adopt procedures to consider claims of actual innocence based on newly discovered evidence....

A

Whatever procedures a State might adopt to hear actual-innocence claims, one thing is certain: The possibility of executive clemency is *not* sufficient to satisfy the requirements of the Eighth and Fourteenth Amendments. The majority correctly points out: "'A pardon is an act of grace.'" The vindication of rights guaranteed by the Constitution has never been made to turn on the unreviewable discretion of an executive official or administrative tribunal.... The possibility of executive clemency "exists in every case in which a defendant challenges his sentence under the Eighth Amendment. Recognition of such a bare possibility would make judicial review under the Eighth Amendment meaningless." ... It is understandable, therefore, that the majority does not say that the vindication of petitioner's constitutional rights may be left to executive clemency.

B

... Texas provides no judicial procedure for hearing petitioner's claim of actual innocence and his habeas petition was properly filed in district court under § 2254.... If, as is the case here, the petition raises factual questions and the State has failed to provide a full and fair hearing, the district court is required to hold an evidentiary hearing....

C

The question that remains is what showing should be required to obtain relief on the merits of an Eighth or Fourteenth Amendment claim of actual innocence. I agree with the majority that "in state criminal proceedings the trial is the paramount event for determining the guilt or innocence of the defendant." I also think that "a truly persuasive demonstration of 'actual innocence' made after trial would render the execution of a defendant unconstitutional." The question is what "a truly persuasive demonstration" entails, a question the majority's disposition of this case leaves open....

I think the standard for relief on the merits of an actual-innocence claim must be higher than the threshold standard for merely reaching that claim or any other claim that has been procedurally defaulted or is successive or abusive. I would hold that, to obtain relief on a claim of actual innocence, the petitioner must show that he probably is innocent....

[T]he court charged with deciding such a claim should make a case-by-case determination about the reliability of the newly discovered evidence under the circumstances. The court then should weigh the evidence in favor of the prisoner against the evidence of his guilt. Obviously, the stronger the evidence of the prisoner's guilt, the more persuasive the newly discovered evidence of innocence must be....

It should be clear that the standard I would adopt would not convert the federal courts into "'forums in which to relitigate state trials.'" ... I believe that if a prisoner can show that he is probably actually innocent, in light of all the evidence, then he has made "a truly persuasive demonstration," and his execution would violate the Constitution. I would so hold.

IV

I would reverse the order of the Court of Appeals and remand the case to the District Court to consider whether petitioner has shown, in light of all the evidence, that he is probably actually innocent....

V

I have voiced disappointment over this Court's obvious eagerness to do away with any restriction on the States' power to execute whomever and however they please. I have also expressed doubts about whether, in the absence of such restrictions, capital punishment remains constitutional at all. Of one thing, however, I am certain. Just as an execution without adequate safeguards is unacceptable, so too is an execution when the condemned prisoner can prove that he is innocent. The execution of a person who can show that he is innocent comes perilously close to simple murder.

Notes and Questions

1. Leonel Herrera was executed on May 12, 1993, less than five months after the Supreme Court's ruling and more than 11 years after his trial, conviction, and death sentence for Officer Carrisalez's murder. No court, state or federal, heard evidence in support of his post-conviction claim of innocence.

2. What, precisely, is the state of the law governing the federal courts' consideration of free-standing claims of innocence on habeas corpus?

3. In 1991, Troy Davis was tried in Georgia for the capital murder of Mark MacPhail, an off-duty police officer who was shot at close range after coming to the aid of a homeless man who was being assaulted and robbed. Davis maintained that he was innocent and that an acquaintance, Sylvester "Red" Coles, had shot and killed the officer. Several prosecution witnesses testified otherwise, and Davis was convicted and sentenced to death. Years later, many of the trial witnesses recanted their testimony and additional evidence surfaced suggesting that Coles was the shooter. In 2007, based on this new evidence, Davis filed an extraordinary motion for a new trial in the state court in which he had been convicted. As summarized by the federal appeals court that subsequently reviewed his claims:[26]

> This evidence consisted of: (1) seven affidavits containing recantations of eyewitnesses who testified at trial; (2) three affidavits averring post-trial confessions to the murder by another man, Sylvester "Red" Coles (hereinafter "Red Coles"); (3) several affidavits of persons who had not previously testified who were either present at the scene of the murder or in the general area immediately following the crime; (4) two expert affidavits addressing ballistic evidence and eyewitness identifications; (5) affidavits of jurors; and (6) a general cache of additional affidavits.

The trial court denied Davis's motion for a new trial without conducting a hearing on the new evidence, and the Georgia Supreme Court affirmed that ruling in a 4–3 decision.[27] Davis thereafter sought authorization from the Eleventh Circuit Court of Appeals "to file a second or successive 28 U.S.C. § 2254 federal habeas petition, raising for the first time a freestanding actual innocence claim."[28] By a 2–1 vote, the Eleventh Circuit denied Davis's application. In dissent, Judge Barkett protested:[29]

> While we must deal with the thorny constitutional and statutory questions before us, we also cannot lose sight of the underlying issue in this case. Simply put, the issue is whether Troy Anthony Davis may be lawfully executed when *no* court has ever conducted a hearing to assess the reliability of the score of affidavits that, if reliable, would satisfy the "threshold showing" for

"a truly persuasive demonstration of actual innocence," thus entitling Davis to habeas relief. *Herrera v. Collins,* 506 U.S. 390, 417 (1993).

In the affidavits, seven of nine key trial witnesses recanted their testimony which pointed to Davis as Officer MacPhail's murderer. The two remaining non-recanting witnesses were Sylvester "Red" Coles, who was himself alleged to have been the shooter in affidavits, and Steve Sanders, who identified Davis at trial two years after the incident despite admitting to police immediately following the shooting that he would not be able to recognize the shooter.

The majority of the affidavits support the defense's theory that, after Coles raced to the police station to implicate Davis, the police directed all of their energy towards building a case against Davis, failing to investigate the possibility that Coles himself was the actual murderer.... Additionally, three affiants now state that Coles confessed to the killing. To execute Davis, in the face of a significant amount of proffered evidence that may establish his actual innocence, is unconscionable and unconstitutional....

Davis, who at one point during the protracted litigation in his case had come within two hours of execution, then pursued an avenue of relief that had not been successfully utilized for nearly a half century by filing a petition for a writ of habeas corpus directly with the United States Supreme Court. The High Court issued its summary order in August 2009.

In re Davis

130 S.Ct. 1, 174 L.Ed.2d 614 (2009).

ON PETITION FOR WRIT OF HABEAS CORPUS

... The petition for a writ of habeas corpus is transferred to the United States District Court for the Southern District of Georgia for hearing and determination. The District Court should receive testimony and make findings of fact as to whether evidence that could not have been obtained at the time of trial clearly establishes petitioner's innocence.

Justice STEVENS, with whom Justice GINSBURG and Justice BREYER join, concurring.

Justice SCALIA's dissent is wrong in two respects. First, he assumes as a matter of fact that petitioner Davis is guilty of the murder of Officer MacPhail. He does this even though seven of the State's key witnesses have recanted their trial testimony; several individuals have implicated the State's principal witness as the shooter; and "*no* court," state or federal, "has ever conducted a hearing to assess the reliability of the score of [postconviction] affidavits that, if reliable, would satisfy the threshold showing for a truly persuasive demonstration of actual innocence," 565 F.3d 810, 827 (C.A.11 2009) (Barkett, J., dissenting) (internal quotation marks omitted). The substantial risk of putting an innocent man to death clearly provides an adequate justification for holding an evidentiary hearing. Simply put, the case is sufficiently "exceptional" to warrant utilization of this Court's Rule 20.4(a), 28 U.S.C. § 2241(b), and our original habeas jurisdiction.

Second, Justice SCALIA assumes as a matter of law that, "[e]ven if the District Court were to be persuaded by Davis's affidavits, it would have no power to grant relief" in light of 28 U.S.C. § 2254(d)(1). For several reasons, however, this transfer is by no means "a fool's errand." The District Court may conclude that § 2254(d)(1) does not apply, or does not apply with the same rigidity, to an original habeas petition such as this. The court may also find it relevant to the AEDPA analysis that Davis is bringing an "actual innocence" claim. Even if the court finds that § 2254(d)(1) applies in full, it is arguably unconstitutional to the extent it bars relief for a death row inmate who has established his innocence. Alternatively, the court may find in such a case that the statute's text is satisfied, because decisions of this Court clearly support the proposition that it "would be an atrocious violation of our Constitution and the principles upon which it is based" to execute an innocent person. 565 F.3d, at 830 (Barkett, J., dissenting); cf. *Teague v. Lane,* 489 U.S. 288, 311–313 (1989) (plurality opinion).

Justice SCALIA would pretermit all of these unresolved legal questions on the theory that we must treat even the most robust showing of actual innocence identically on habeas review to an accusation of minor procedural error. Without briefing or argument, he concludes that Congress chose to foreclose relief and that the Constitution permits this. But imagine a petitioner in Davis's situation who possesses new evidence conclusively and definitively proving, beyond any scintilla of doubt, that he is an innocent man. The dissent's reasoning would allow such a petitioner to be put to death nonetheless. The Court correctly refuses to endorse such reasoning.

Justice SCALIA, with whom Justice THOMAS joins, dissenting.

Today this Court takes the extraordinary step—one not taken in nearly 50 years—of instructing a district court to adjudicate a state prisoner's petition for an original writ of habeas corpus. The Court proceeds down this path even though every judicial and executive body that has examined petitioner's stale claim of innocence has been unpersuaded, and (to make matters worst) even though it would be impossible for the District Court to grant any relief. Far from demonstrating, as this Court's Rule 20.4(a) requires, "exceptional circumstances" that "warrant the exercise of the Court's discretionary powers," petitioner's claim is a sure loser. Transferring his petition to the District Court is a confusing exercise that can serve no purpose except to delay the State's execution of its lawful criminal judgment. I respectfully dissent.

Eighteen years ago, after a trial untainted by constitutional defect, a unanimous jury found petitioner Troy Anthony Davis guilty of the murder of Mark Allen MacPhail. The evidence showed that MacPhail, an off-duty police officer, was shot multiple times after responding to the beating of a homeless man in a restaurant parking lot. Davis admits that he was present during the beating of the homeless man, but he maintains that it was one of his companions who shot Officer MacPhail. It is this claim of "actual innocence"—the same defense Davis raised at trial but now allegedly supported by new corroborating affidavits—that Davis raises as grounds for relief. And (presumably) it is this claim that the Court wants the District Court to adjudicate once the petition is transferred.

Even if the District Court were to be persuaded by Davis's affidavits, it would have no power to grant relief. Federal courts may order the release of convicted state prisoners only in accordance with the restrictions imposed by the Antiterrorism and Effective Death Penalty Act of 1996. Insofar as it applies to the present case, that statute bars the issuance of a writ of habeas corpus "with respect to any claim that was adjudicated on the merits in State court proceedings unless the adjudication of the claim ... resulted in a decision that was contrary to, or involved an unreasonable application of, clearly established Federal law, as determined by the Supreme Court of the United States." 28 U.S.C. § 2254(d)(1).

The Georgia Supreme Court rejected petitioner's "actual-innocence" claim on the merits, denying his extraordinary motion for a new trial. Davis can obtain relief only if that determination was contrary to, or an unreasonable application of, "clearly established Federal law, as determined by the Supreme Court of the United States." It most assuredly was not. This Court has *never* held that the Constitution forbids the execution of a convicted defendant who has had a full and fair trial but is later able to convince a habeas court that he is "actually" innocent. Quite to the contrary, we have repeatedly left that question unresolved, while expressing considerable doubt that any claim based on alleged "actual innocence" is constitutionally cognizable. See *Herrera v. Collins,* 506 U.S. 390, 400–401, 416–417 (1993); see also *House v. Bell,* 547 U.S. 518, 555 (2006); *District Attorney's Office for Third Judicial Dist. v. Osborne,* 129 S.Ct. 2308, 2321–2322 (2009). A state court cannot possibly have contravened, or even unreasonably applied, "clearly established Federal law, as determined by the Supreme Court of the United States," by rejecting a type of claim that the Supreme Court has not once accepted as valid.

Justice STEVENS says that we need not be deterred by the limitations that Congress has placed on federal courts' authority to issue the writ, because we cannot rule out the possibility that the District Court might find those limitations unconstitutional as applied to actual-innocence claims.... But acknowledging that possibility would make a nullity of § 2254(d)(1). There is no sound basis for distinguishing an actual-innocence claim from any other claim that is alleged to have produced a wrongful conviction. If the District Court here can ignore § 2254(d)(1) on the theory that otherwise Davis's actual-innocence claim would (unconstitutionally) go unaddressed, the same possibility would exist for *any* claim going beyond "clearly established Federal law." ...

... [T]he argument that the Constitution requires federal-court screening of all state convictions for constitutional violations is frivolous. For much of our history, federal habeas review was not available even for those state convictions claimed to be in violation of clearly established federal law. It seems to me improper to grant the extraordinary relief of habeas corpus on the possibility that we have approved-indeed, directed—the disregard of constitutional imperatives in the past. If we have new—found doubts regarding the constitutionality of § 2254(d)(1), we should hear Davis's application and resolve that question (if necessary) ourselves.

Transferring this case to a court that has no power to grant relief is strange enough. It becomes stranger still when one realizes that the allegedly new evidence we shunt off to be examined by the District Court has already been considered (and rejected) multiple times. Davis's postconviction "actual-innocence" claim is not new. Most of the evidence on which it is based is almost a decade old. A State Supreme Court, a State Board of Pardons and Paroles, and a Federal Court of Appeals have all considered the evidence Davis now presents and found it lacking....

Today, without explanation and without any meaningful guidance, this Court sends the District Court for the Southern District of Georgia on a fool's errand. That court is directed to consider evidence of actual innocence which has been reviewed and rejected at least three times, and which, even if adequate to persuade the District Court, cannot (as far as anyone knows) form the basis for any relief. I truly do not see how the District Court can discern what is expected of it. If this Court thinks it possible that capital convictions obtained in full compliance with law can never be final, but are always subject to being set aside by federal courts for the reason of "actual innocence," it should set this case on our own docket so that we can (if necessary) resolve that question. Sending it to a district court that "might" be authorized to provide relief, but then again "might" be reversed if it did so, is not a sensible way to proceed.

In June 2010, a federal district court in Savannah received evidence on Davis's habeas corpus petition in compliance with the Supreme Court's directive.[30] Two months later, the district court denied relief, ruling that Davis's factual showing failed to establish his innocence. *In re Davis*, 2010 WL 3385081 (S.D.Ga. 2010). The 11th Circuit Court of Appeals subsequently ruled that it lacked jurisdiction to hear an appeal. *Davis v. Terry*, 625 F.3d 716 (11th Cir. 2010). In March 2011, the Supreme Court denied *certiorari* without comment, *Davis v. Humphrey*, ___ U.S. ___, 2011 WL 220685 (2011), presumably marking the end of judicial review and leaving a decision about executive clemency as the final one to be made in the case.

4. Some state courts have interpreted their state constitutions or other sources of state law to authorize proceedings to allow persons convicted of crimes to present free-standing claims of innocence based on newly discovered evidence. *See, e.g., Montoya v. Ulibarri*, 163 P.3d 476 (N.M. 2007); *People v. Washington*, 665 N.E.2d 1330 (Ill. 1996).

5. We will consider executive clemency, identified by Chief Justice Rehnquist in his majority opinion in *Herrera v. Collins* as providing "the 'fail safe' in our criminal justice system" with respect to wrongful convictions, in Chapter 11.

H. Conclusion

The criminal justice system is not perfect. Errors can and will be made, even by individuals with the best of intentions, that result in wrongful convictions. In this chapter we have reviewed several important decisions, from arrest, prosecution, and trial through appellate, post-conviction, and habeas corpus review, that can contribute to—or potentially prevent and/or correct—the conviction and punishment of innocent persons. In the ensuing chapters, we turn to more detailed consideration of the principal causes and correlates of wrongful convictions.

Part II

The Leading Correlates and Causes of Wrongful Convictions

Chapter 3

Eyewitness Identification

A. Introduction

In Chapter One we noted the difficulties associated with being able to identify wrongful conviction cases and measure their true incidence. Those limitations greatly compromise our ability to pinpoint and understand their principal causes. Consider, for example, the following statement: "Eyewitness misidentification is the single greatest cause of wrongful convictions nationwide, playing a role in more than 75% of convictions overturned through DNA testing."[1] The Innocence Project has reported that 175 of the first 239 wrongful conviction cases revealed by later DNA testing involved misidentification of the defendant by one or more eyewitnesses.[2] We could quibble with the computation included in the statement: 175 out of 239 (73.2%) is close to, but not "more than 75% of convictions overturned through DNA testing." However, our real concern lies with the logic of conjoining that computation with the assertion that "[e]yewitness misidentification is the single greatest cause of wrongful convictions nationwide...." We have no reliable means of assessing that conclusion. For the several reasons that we previously considered, it is hazardous to generalize from what is known about wrongful convictions exposed by DNA analysis—which necessarily are confined to crimes that yield biological evidence, and consist largely of sexual assaults—to the unknown but vastly more expansive universe of all cases of wrongful conviction.

Our admittedly imperfect knowledge nevertheless leaves us with little hesitation in concluding that eyewitness errors are a very important source of wrongful convictions. Many courts and policymakers have recognized as much, leading them to design procedures to try to prevent suggestiveness and enhance reliability when witnesses are first asked to identify suspects, and to help judges and jurors evaluate witnesses' subsequent identification testimony. We begin this chapter by examining Supreme Court decisions governing the admissibility of eyewitness identification testimony. We then consult social science research findings bearing on perception, memory, and recall, and consider related policy initiatives regarding eyewitness identification procedures. Next, we consider evolving legal doctrine in the state courts. We conclude by exploring the admissibility in criminal trials of expert testimony bearing on the reliability of eyewitness identification.

B. Supreme Court Doctrine Governing the Admissibility of Eyewitness Identification Testimony

1. Line-Ups and Show-Ups

"Corporeal" identifications, in contrast to photo arrays, computer-generated imagery, or the work of a sketch artist, involve the physical presentation of a suspect before one or more witnesses to a crime. They are conducted by using line-ups (which include multiple individuals) or show-ups (usually involving the display of a single suspect). In 1967, toward the end of Earl Warren's tenure as Chief Justice, the Supreme Court announced three decisions on the same day bearing on corporeal eyewitness identification. Known as "the *Wade* trilogy," *United States v. Wade,* 388 U.S. 218, 87 S.Ct. 1926, 18 L.Ed.2d 1149 (1967), *Gilbert v. California,* 388 U.S. 263, 87 S.Ct. 1951, 18 L.Ed.2d 1178 (1967), and *Stovall v. Denno,* 388 U.S. 293, 87 S.Ct. 1967, 18 L.Ed.2d 1199 (1967) signaled the justices' concerns about suggestive identification procedures, yet also their recognition that eyewitness testimony is indispensable to effective law enforcement and the prosecution of crimes. The three cases presented significantly different legal issues.

In *Wade*, a man wearing "a small strip of tape on each side of his face" robbed a bank in September 1964. He pointed a pistol at the two employees present, a cashier and a vice president, ordered them to "put the money in the bag," and then fled in a stolen car driven by an accomplice. Six months later, on March 23, 1965, Billy Joe Wade was indicted for the crime. He was arrested ten days later and an attorney was appointed to represent him on April 26.

> Fifteen days later an FBI agent, without notice to Wade's lawyer, arranged to have the two bank employees observe a lineup made up of Wade and five or six other prisoners and conducted in a courtroom of the local county courthouse. Each person in the line wore strips of tape such as allegedly worn by the robber and upon direction each said something like 'put the money in the bag,' the words allegedly uttered by the robber. Both bank employees identified Wade in the lineup as the bank robber.
>
> At trial the two employees, when asked on direct examination if the robber was in the courtroom, pointed to Wade. The prior lineup identification was then elicited from both employees on cross-examination....
>
> [T]he testimony of the identifying witnesses elicited on cross-examination revealed that those witnesses were taken to the courthouse and seated in the courtroom to await assembly of the lineup. The courtroom faced on a hallway observable to the witnesses through an open door. The cashier testified that she saw Wade 'standing in the hall' within sight of an FBI agent. Five or six other prisoners later appeared in the hall. The vice president testified that he saw a person in the hall in the custody of the agent who 'resembled the person that we identified as the one that had entered the bank.

After rejecting Wade's argument that his compelled appearance in the line-up and utterance of the words violated his 5th Amendment right against compelled self-incrimination, the justices considered whether, under the 6th Amendment, the "courtroom identifications of an accused at trial are to be excluded from evidence because the accused was exhibited to the witnesses ... at a post-indictment line-up ... without notice to and in the absence of [his] court-appointed counsel." Justice Brennan's opinion for the Court included a lengthy discussion of recognized threats to reliable identification testimony.

> [T]he confrontation compelled by the State between the accused and the victim or witnesses to a crime to elicit identification evidence is peculiarly riddled with innumerable dangers and variable factors which might seriously, even crucially, derogate from a fair trial. The vagaries of eyewitness identification are well-known; the annals of criminal law are rife with instances of mistaken identification. Mr. Justice Frankfurter once said: 'What is the worth of identification testimony even when uncontradicted? The identification of strangers is proverbially untrustworthy. The hazards of such testimony are established by a formidable number of instances in the records of English and American trials. These instances are recent—not due to the brutalities of ancient criminal procedure.' The Case of Sacco and Vanzetti 30 (1927). A major factor contributing to the high incidence of miscarriage of justice from mistaken identification has been the degree of suggestion inherent in the manner in which the prosecution presents the suspect to witnesses for pretrial identification. A commentator has observed that '(t)he influence of improper suggestion upon identifying witnesses probably accounts for more miscarriages of justice than any other single factor—perhaps it is responsible for more such errors than all other factors combined.' Wall, Eye-Witness Identification in Criminal Cases 26. Suggestion can be created intentionally or unintentionally in many subtle ways. And the dangers for the suspect are particularly grave when the witness' opportunity for observation was insubstantial, and thus his susceptibility to suggestion the greatest.
>
> Moreover, '[i]t is a matter of common experience that, once a witness has picked out the accused at the line-up, he is not likely to go back on his word later on, so that in practice the issue of identity may (in the absence of other relevant evidence) for all practical purposes be determined there and then, before the trial.'[8]
>
> ... Since it appears that there is grave potential for prejudice, intentional or not, in the pretrial lineup, which may not be capable of reconstruction at trial, and since presence of counsel itself can often avert prejudice and assure a meaningful confrontation at trial, there can be little doubt that for Wade the postindictment lineup was a critical stage of the prosecution at which he was 'as much entitled to such aid (of counsel) * * * as at the trial itself.' Powell v. State of Alabama, 287 U.S. 45, at 57. Thus both Wade and his counsel should have been notified of the impending lineup, and counsel's presence should have been a requisite to conduct of the lineup, absent an 'intelligent waiver.' ...

In the companion case of *Gilbert v. California,* which similarly involved a post-indictment line-up conducted in the absence of the accused's counsel, the Court announced a rule of automatic, or *per se* exclusion of the testimony of the witnesses' line-up, or "out-of-court" identification of the defendant.

> Only a per se exclusionary rule as to such testimony can be an effective sanction to assure that law enforcement authorities will respect the accused's constitutional right to the presence of his counsel at the critical lineup. In the absence of legislative regulations adequate to avoid the hazards to a fair trial which inhere in lineups as presently conducted, the desirability of deterring the constitutionally objectionable practice must prevail over the undesirability of excluding relevant evidence.

In *Wade,* however, the Court adopted a more nuanced approach regarding whether witnesses who had participated in a pre-trial identification conducted in violation of the accused's right to counsel would be permitted to testify at the trial that they recognized the defendant as the perpetrator of the crime. *Wade* held as follows concerning the admissibility of the "in-court" identification of the defendant:

8. Williams & Hammelmann, Identification Parades, Part I, (1963) Crim.L.Rev. 479, 482.

We come now to the question whether the denial of Wade's motion to strike the courtroom identification by the bank witnesses at trial because of the absence of his counsel at the lineup required, as the Court of Appeals held, the grant of a new trial at which such evidence is to be excluded. We do not think this disposition can be justified without first giving the Government the opportunity to establish by clear and convincing evidence that the in-court identifications were based upon observations of the suspect other than the lineup identification. Where, as here, the admissibility of evidence of the lineup identification itself is not involved, a per se rule of exclusion of courtroom identification would be unjustified. A rule limited solely to the exclusion of testimony concerning identification at the lineup itself, without regard to admissibility of the courtroom identification, would render the right to counsel an empty one. The lineup is most often used, as in the present case, to crystallize the witnesses' identification of the defendant for future reference.... The State may then rest upon the witnesses' unequivocal courtroom identifications, and not mention the pretrial identification as part of the State's case at trial. Counsel is then in the predicament in which Wade's counsel found himself realizing that possible unfairness at the lineup may be the sole means of attack upon the unequivocal courtroom identification, and having to probe in the dark in an attempt to discover and reveal unfairness, while bolstering the government witness' courtroom identification by bringing out and dwelling upon his prior identification. Since counsel's presence at the lineup would equip him to attack not only the lineup identification but the courtroom identification as well, limiting the impact of violation of the right to counsel to exclusion of evidence only of identification at the lineup itself disregards a critical element of that right.

We think it follows that the proper test to be applied in these situations is that quoted in Wong Sun v. United States, 371 U.S. 471, 488, "[W]hether, granting establishment of the primary illegality, the evidence to which instant objection is made has been come at by exploitation of that illegality or instead by means sufficiently distinguishable to be purged of the primary taint." Application of this test in the present context requires consideration of various factors; for example, the prior opportunity to observe the alleged criminal act, the existence of any discrepancy between any pre-lineup description and the defendant's actual description, any identification prior to lineup of another person, the identification by picture of the defendant prior to the lineup, failure to identify the defendant on a prior occasion, and the lapse of time between the alleged act and the lineup identification. It is also relevant to consider those facts which, despite the absence of counsel, are disclosed concerning the conduct of the lineup.[33]

The Court remanded the case so the district court could conduct "a hearing to determine whether the in-court identifications had an independent source, or whether, in any event, the introduction of the evidence was harmless error."

In the third case of the *Wade* trilogy, *Stovall v. Denno*, the Court declined to give retroactive application to the rules governing the exclusion of identification evidence that were announced in *Wade* and *Gilbert*. However, the justices did address the "further question ... whether ... on the facts of the particular confrontation involved in this case, petitioner was denied due process of law in violation of the Fourteenth Amendment." Dr. Paul Behrendt was stabbed to death by an intruder in his Long Island home on the night of August 23, 1961. His wife was stabbed 11 times by the same intruder and underwent major surgery at a hospital where doctors worked to save her life. Theodore Stovall was arrested for the crimes on the afternoon of August 24.

33. Thus it is not the case that '(i)t matters not how well the witness knows the suspect, whether the witness is the suspect's mother, brother, or long-time associate, and no matter how long or well the witness observed the perpetrator at the scene of the crime.' Such factors will have an important bearing upon the true basis of the witness' in-court identification....

The police, without affording petitioner time to retain counsel, arranged with [Mrs. Behrendt's] surgeon to permit them to bring petitioner to her hospital room about noon of August 25, the day after the surgery. Petitioner was handcuffed to one of five police officers who, with two members of the staff of the District Attorney, brought him to the hospital room. Petitioner was the only Negro in the room. Mrs. Behrendt identified him from her hospital bed after being asked by an officer whether he 'was the man' and after petitioner repeated at the direction of an officer a 'few words for voice identification.'... Mrs. Behrendt and the officers testified at the trial to her identification of the petitioner in the hospital room, and she also made an in-court identification of petitioner in the courtroom.

Petitioner was convicted and sentenced to death.

...

The Court concluded that Stovall's due process rights were not violated by the admission of the identification testimony on these facts, notwithstanding the highly suggestive nature of the show-up.

We turn now to the question whether petitioner, although not entitled to the application of Wade and Gilbert to his case, is entitled to relief on his claim that in any event the confrontation conducted in this case was so unnecessarily suggestive and conducive to irreparable mistaken identification that he was denied due process of law. This is a recognized ground of attack upon a conviction independent of any right to counsel claim. The practice of showing suspects singly to persons for the purpose of identification, and not as part of a lineup, has been widely condemned. However, a claimed violation of due process of law in the conduct of a confrontation depends on the totality of the circumstances surrounding it, and the record in the present case reveals that the showing of Stovall to Mrs. Behrendt in an immediate hospital confrontation was imperative. The Court of Appeals ... stated:

"Here was the only person in the world who could possibly exonerate Stovall. Her words, and only her words, 'He is not the man' could have resulted in freedom for Stovall. The hospital was not far distant from the courthouse and jail. No one knew how long Mrs. Behrendt might live. Faced with the responsibility of identifying the attacker, with the need for immediate action and with the knowledge that Mrs. Behrendt could not visit the jail, the police followed the only feasible procedure and took Stovall to the hospital room. Under these circumstances, the usual police station line-up, which Stovall now argues he should have had, was out of the question." [355 F.2d, at 735] ...

In 1972, then under the stewardship of Chief Justice Warren Burger, the Supreme Court revisited the right to counsel at pre-trial identifications and imposed important qualifications on the *Wade-Gilbert* rules that had been announced five years earlier. In *Kirby v. Illinois,* 406 U.S. 682, 92 S.Ct. 1877, 32 L.Ed.2d 411 (1972), Chicago police arrested Thomas Kirby and a companion, Ralph Bean, after finding them in possession of traveler's checks and a Social Security card bearing the name of Willie Shard. The two men were taken to a police station, where the arresting officers learned that Shard previously had reported being robbed.

A police car was then dispatched to Shard's place of employment, where it picked up Shard and brought him to the police station. Immediately upon entering the room in the police station where the petitioner and Bean were seated at a table, Shard positively identified them as the men who had robbed him two days earlier. No lawyer was present in the room, and neither the petitioner nor Bean had asked for legal assistance, or been advised of any right to the presence of counsel.

More than six weeks later, the petitioner and Bean were indicted for the robbery of Willie Shard. Upon arraignment, counsel was appointed to represent them, and they pleaded not guilty. A pretrial motion to suppress Shard's identification testimony was denied, and at the trial Shard testified as a witness for the prosecution. In his testimony he described his identification of the two men at the police station ... and identified them again in the courtroom as the men who had robbed him.... He was cross-examined at length regarding the circumstances of his identification of the two defendants. The jury found both defendants guilty, and the petitioner's conviction was affirmed on appeal. The Illinois appellate court held that the admission of Shard's testimony was not error, ... holding that the Wade-Gilbert per se exclusionary rule is not applicable to preindictment confrontations. We granted certiorari, limited to this question....

Justice Stewart's plurality opinion concluded that Kirby was not entitled to the assistance of counsel at the show-up conducted shortly after his arrest, since that 6th Amendment right applies only to "critical stages" of a criminal prosecution. At a minimum, a "critical stage" connotes a "time at or after the initiation of adversary judicial criminal proceedings—whether by way of formal charge, preliminary hearing, indictment, information, or arraignment."

The initiation of judicial criminal proceedings is far from a mere formalism. It is the starting point of our whole system of adversary criminal justice. For it is only then that the government has committed itself to prosecute, and only then that the adverse positions of government and defendant have solidified. It is then that a defendant finds himself faced with the prosecutorial forces of organized society, and immersed in the intricacies of substantive and procedural criminal law. It is this point, therefore, that marks the commencement of the 'criminal prosecutions' to which alone the explicit guarantees of the Sixth Amendment are applicable.[7]

In this case we are asked to import into a routine police investigation an absolute constitutional guarantee historically and rationally applicable only after the onset of formal prosecutorial proceedings. We decline to ... [impose] a per se exclusionary rule upon testimony concerning an identification that took place long before the commencement of any prosecution whatever.

While thus limiting the 6th Amendment right to counsel to "critical stage" corporeal identifications, Justice Stewart's opinion noted that Kirby and others similarly situated had recourse to other constitutional protections.

The Due Process Clause of the Fifth and Fourteenth Amendments forbids a lineup that is unnecessarily suggestive and conducive to irreparable mistaken identification. When a person has not been formally charged with a criminal offense, Stovall [v. Denno, 388 U.S. 293 (1967)] strikes the appropriate constitutional balance between the right of a suspect to be protected from prejudicial procedures and the interest of society in the prompt and purposeful investigation of an unsolved crime.

Justice Brennan, the author of the majority opinions in each of the cases comprising the *Wade* trilogy, complained in his dissent that the *Kirby* plurality had essentially abandoned the previously articulated rationale for ensuring the presence of counsel at pre-trial identifications.

7. 'In all criminal prosecutions, the accused shall enjoy the right to a speedy and public trial, by an impartial jury of the State and district wherein the crime shall have been committed, which district shall have been previously ascertained by law, and to be informed of the nature and cause of the accusation; to be confronted with the witnesses against him; to have compulsory process for obtaining witnesses in his favor, and to have the Assistance of Counsel for his defence.' U.S.Const., Amdt. VI.

While it should go without saying, it appears necessary, in view of the plurality opinion today, to re-emphasize that Wade did not require the presence of counsel at pretrial confrontations for identification purposes simply on the basis of an abstract consideration of the words 'criminal prosecutions' in the Sixth Amendment. Counsel is required at those confrontations because 'the dangers inherent in eyewitness identification and the suggestibility inherent in the context of the pretrial identification,' [388 U.S.,] at 235, mean that protection must be afforded to the 'most basic right (of) a criminal defendant—his right to a fair trial at which the witnesses against him might be meaningfully cross-examined,' id., at 224.... Hence, 'the initiation of adversary judicial criminal proceedings,' is completely irrelevant to whether counsel is necessary at a pretrial confrontation for identification in order to safeguard the accused's constitutional rights to confrontation and the effective assistance of counsel at his trial.

Because line-ups and show-ups have principal value as investigative tools, by allowing the police to confirm or rule out a suspect as the likely perpetrator of a crime, they assume greatest significance and are used far more often before formal charges are lodged than after. Consequently, the ruling in *Kirby*, which confines the right to counsel to post-critical stage corporeal identifications, means that most challenges to the admissibility of eyewitness identification testimony must be premised on Due Process rather than 6th Amendment grounds. The Due Process test enunciated in *Stovall* and reaffirmed in *Kirby* requires examination of the "totality of the circumstances" to assess whether the line-up or show-up was "unnecessarily suggestive and conducive to irreparable mistaken identification." The burden is on the defendant to make that showing.

As we have seen, the tests governing the admissibility of eyewitness identification testimony are different under *Wade-Gilbert* when the accused's 6th Amendment right to the assistance of counsel at a line-up or show-up has been violated. *Gilbert* imposed a *per se* rule of exclusion for testimony involving the witness's "out-of-court" (*i.e.*, the line-up or show-up) identification to encourage police compliance with the suspect's right to counsel. But in deference to the potential value of eyewitness testimony, the *Wade* Court devised a different test for the admissibility of in-court identifications following a line- up or show-up conducted in violation of the accused's right to counsel: "[T]he Government [must] ... establish by clear and convincing evidence that the in-court identifications were based upon observations of the suspect other than the lineup identification."

Neither the Due Process test governing the admissibility of eyewitness identification testimony nor the corresponding *Wade* test is self-executing. That is, it is not immediately apparent how a trial judge is to determine whether an identification procedure was "unnecessarily suggestive" or "conducive to irreparable mistaken identification," or whether a witness's identification of the defendant in court is "based upon observations ... other than the lineup identification." The following case—involving a contest over the admissibility of a witness's photographic identification of the defendant as the perpetrator of a crime, rather than a corporeal (line-up or show-up) identification—presents several factors the Supreme Court has deemed relevant to assessing the reliability, and hence the admissibility of eyewitness testimony. It also is significant for its resolution of an important legal issue: whether law enforcement's reliance on "unnecessarily suggestive" procedures should result in the automatic exclusion of a witness's out-of-court identification of the defendant, or whether the admissibility of such testimony should instead hinge on indicia of its reliability.

Manson v. Brathwaite

432 U.S. 98, 97 S.Ct. 2243, 53 L.Ed.2d 140 (1977)

Mr. Justice BLACKMUN delivered the opinion of the Court.

This case presents the issue as to whether the Due Process Clause of the Fourteenth Amendment compels the exclusion, in a state criminal trial, apart from any consideration of reliability, of pretrial identification evidence obtained by a police procedure that was both suggestive and unnecessary. This Court's decisions in Stovall v. Denno, 388 U.S. 293 (1967), and Neil v. Biggers, 409 U.S. 188 (1972), are particularly implicated.

I

Jimmy D. Glover, a full-time trooper of the Connecticut State Police, in 1970 was assigned to the Narcotics Division in an undercover capacity. On May 5 of that year, about 7:45 p.m., e.d.t., and while there was still daylight, Glover and Henry Alton Brown, an informant, went to an apartment building at 201 Westland, in Hartford, for the purpose of purchasing narcotics from "Dickie Boy" Cicero, a known narcotics dealer. Cicero, it was thought, lived on the third floor of that apartment building. Glover and Brown entered the building, observed by back-up Officers D'Onofrio and Gaffey, and proceeded by stairs to the third floor. Glover knocked at the door of one of the two apartments served by the stairway.[2] The area was illuminated by natural light from a window in the third floor hallway. The door was opened 12 to 18 inches in response to the knock. Glover observed a man standing at the door and, behind him, a woman. Brown identified himself. Glover then asked for "two things" of narcotics. The man at the door held out his hand, and Glover gave him two $10 bills. The door closed. Soon the man returned and handed Glover two glassine bags. While the door was open, Glover stood within two feet of the person from whom he made the purchase and observed his face. Five to seven minutes elapsed from the time the door first opened until it closed the second time.

Glover and Brown then left the building. This was about eight minutes after their arrival. Glover drove to headquarters where he described the seller to D'Onofrio and Gaffey. Glover at that time did not know the identity of the seller. He described him as being "a colored man, approximately five feet eleven inches tall, dark complexion, black hair, short Afro style, and having high cheekbones, and of heavy build. He was wearing at the time blue pants and a plaid shirt." D'Onofrio, suspecting from this description that respondent might be the seller, obtained a photograph of respondent from the Records Division of the Hartford Police Department. He left it at Glover's office.... Glover, when alone, viewed the photograph for the first time upon his return to headquarters on May 7; he identified the person shown as the one from whom he had purchased the narcotics....

Respondent was arrested on July 27 while visiting at the apartment of a Mrs. Ramsey on the third floor of 201 Westland. This was the apartment at which the narcotics sale had taken place on May 5.

Respondent was charged, in a two-count information, with possession and sale of heroin ... At his trial in January 1971, the photograph from which Glover had identified respondent was received in evidence.... Glover also testified that, although he had not seen respondent in the eight months that had elapsed since the sale, "there [was] no doubt whatsoever" in his mind that the person shown on the photograph was respondent. Glover also made a positive in-court identification without objection.

No explanation was offered by the prosecution for the failure to utilize a photographic array or to conduct a lineup.

Respondent, who took the stand in his own defense, testified that on May 5, the day in question, he had been ill at his Albany Avenue apartment ... and that at no time on that particular day had he been at 201 Westland. His wife testified that she recalled, after her husband had refreshed her memory, that he was home all day on May 5....

The jury found respondent guilty on both counts of the information. He received a sentence of not less than six nor more than nine years.

2. It appears that the door on which Glover knocked may not have been that of the Cicero apartment. Petitioner concedes, in any event, that the transaction effected "was with some other person than had been intended."

His conviction was affirmed per curiam by the Supreme Court of Connecticut....

Fourteen months later, respondent filed a petition for habeas corpus in the United States District Court for the District of Connecticut. He alleged that the admission of the identification testimony at his state trial deprived him of due process of law to which he was entitled under the Fourteenth Amendment. The District Court ... dismissed respondent's petition. On appeal, the United States Court of Appeals for the Second Circuit reversed ...

In brief summary, the court felt that evidence as to the photograph should have been excluded, regardless of reliability, because the examination of the single photograph was unnecessary and suggestive. And, in the court's view, the evidence was unreliable in any event. We granted certiorari.

II

Stovall v. Denno ... concerned a petitioner who had been convicted in a New York court of murder. He was arrested the day following the crime and was taken by the police to a hospital where the victim's wife, also wounded in the assault, was a patient. After observing Stovall and hearing him speak, she identified him as the murderer. She later made an in-court identification.... Stovall claimed the identification testimony violated his Fifth, Sixth, and Fourteenth Amendment rights.... This Court ... reviewed the practice of showing a suspect singly for purposes of identification, and the claim that this was so unnecessarily suggestive and conducive to irreparable mistaken identification that it constituted a denial of due process of law. The Court noted that the practice "has been widely condemned," but it concluded that "a claimed violation of due process of law in the conduct of a confrontation depends on the totality of the circumstances surrounding it." In that case, showing Stovall to the victim's spouse "was imperative." ...

Neil v. Biggers ... concerned a respondent who had been convicted in a Tennessee court of rape, on evidence consisting in part of the victim's visual and voice identification of Biggers at a station house showup seven months after the crime. The victim had been in her assailant's presence for some time and had directly observed him indoors and under a full moon outdoors. She testified that she had "no doubt" that Biggers was her assailant. She previously had given the police a description of the assailant. She had made no identification of others presented at previous showups, lineups, or through photographs. On federal habeas, the District Court held that the confrontation was so suggestive as to violate due process.... This Court reversed ... and held that the evidence properly had been allowed to go to the jury.... The Court concluded that general guidelines emerged from these cases "as to the relationship between suggestiveness and misidentification." The "admission of evidence of a showup without more does not violate due process." ... The "central question" ... was "whether under the 'totality of the circumstances' the identification was reliable even though the confrontation procedure was suggestive." Applying that test, the Court found "no substantial likelihood of misidentification. The evidence was properly allowed to go to the jury."

Biggers well might be seen to provide an unambiguous answer to the question before us: The admission of testimony concerning a suggestive and unnecessary identification procedure does not violate due process so long as the identification possesses sufficient aspects of reliability.... The question before us ... is simply whether the Biggers analysis applies to post-Stovall confrontations as well to those pre-Stovall.

III

In the present case the District Court observed that the "sole evidence tying Brathwaite to the possession and sale of the heroin consisted in his identifications by the police undercover agent, Jimmy Glover." On the constitutional issue, the court stated that the first inquiry was whether the police used an impermissibly suggestive procedure in obtaining the out-of-court identification. If so, the second inquiry is whether, under all the circumstances, that suggestive procedure gave rise to a substantial likelihood of irreparable misidentification.... The court concluded that there was no substantial likelihood of irreparable misidentification. It referred to the facts: Glover was within two feet of the seller. The duration of the confrontation was at least a "couple of minutes." There was natural light from a window or skylight and there was adequate light to see clearly in the hall. Glover "certainly was paying attention to identify the seller." He was a trained police officer who realized that later he would have to find and arrest the person with whom he was dealing. He gave a detailed description to D'Onofrio. The reliability of this description was supported by the fact that it enabled D'Onofrio to pick out a single photograph that was thereafter positively identified by Glover. Only two days elapsed between the crime and the photographic identification. Despite the fact that another eight months passed before the in-court identification, Glover had "no doubt" that Brathwaite was the person who had sold him heroin.

The Court of Appeals confirmed that the exhibition of the single photograph to Glover was "impermissibly suggestive," and felt that, in addition, "it was unnecessarily so." There was no emergency and little urgency...."Evidence of an identification unnecessarily obtained by impermissibly suggestive means must be excluded under Stovall.... No rules less stringent than these can force police administrators and prosecutors to adopt procedures that will give fair assurance against the awful risks of misidentification." ...

IV

Petitioner at the outset acknowledges that "the procedure in the instant case was suggestive (because only one photograph was used) and unnecessary" (because there was no emergency or exigent circumstance). The respondent ... proposes a per se rule of exclusion that he claims is dictated by the demands of the Fourteenth Amendment's guarantee of due process....

Since the decision in Biggers, the Courts of Appeals appear to have developed at least two approaches to such evidence. The first, or per se approach, employed by the Second Circuit in the present case, focuses on the procedures employed and requires exclusion of the out-of-court identification evidence, without regard to reliability, whenever it has been obtained through unnecessarily suggested confrontation procedures. The justifications advanced are the elimination of evidence of uncertain reliability, deterrence of the police and prosecutors, and the stated "fair assurance against the awful risks of misidentification."

The second, or more lenient, approach is one that continues to rely on the totality of the circumstances. It permits the admission of the confrontation evidence if, despite the suggestive aspect, the out-of-court identification possesses certain features of reliability.... This second approach, in contrast to the other, is ad hoc and serves to limit the societal costs imposed by a sanction that excludes relevant evidence from consideration and evaluation by the trier of fact....

There are, of course, several interests to be considered and taken into account. The driving force behind United States v. Wade, 388 U.S. 218 (1967), Gilbert v. California, 388 U.S. 263 (1967) (right to counsel at a post-indictment line-up), and Stovall, all decided on the same day, was the Court's concern with the problems of eyewitness identification. Usually the witness must testify about an encounter with a total stranger under circumstances of emergency or emotional stress. The witness' recollection of the stranger can be distorted easily by the circumstances or by later actions of the police. Thus, Wade and its companion cases reflect the concern that the jury not hear eyewitness testimony unless that evidence has aspects of reliability. It must be observed that both approaches before us are responsive to this concern. The per se rule, however, goes too far since its application automatically and peremptorily, and without consideration of alleviating factors, keeps evidence from the jury that is reliable and relevant.

The second factor is deterrence. Although the per se approach has the more significant deterrent effect, the totality approach also has an influence on police behavior. The police will guard against unnecessarily suggestive procedures under the totality rule, as well as the per se one, for fear that their actions will lead to the exclusion of identifications as unreliable.

The third factor is the effect on the administration of justice. Here the per se approach suffers serious drawbacks. Since it denies the trier reliable evidence, it may result, on occasion, in the guilty going free....

The standard, after all, is that of fairness as required by the Due Process Clause of the Fourteenth Amendment....

We therefore conclude that reliability is the linchpin in determining the admissibility of identification testimony for both pre- and post-Stovall confrontations. The factors to be considered are set out in Biggers. These include the opportunity of the witness to view the criminal at the time of the crime, the witness' degree of attention, the accuracy of his prior description of the criminal, the level of certainty demonstrated at the confrontation, and the time between the crime and the confrontation. Against these factors is to be weighed the corrupting effect of the suggestive identification itself.

V

We turn, then, to the facts of this case and apply the analysis:

1. The opportunity to view. Glover testified that for two to three minutes he stood at the apartment door, within two feet of the respondent. The door opened twice, and each time the man stood

at the door. The moments passed, the conversation took place, and payment was made. Glover looked directly at his vendor. It was near sunset, to be sure, but the sun had not yet set, so it was not dark or even dusk or twilight. Natural light from outside entered the hallway through a window. There was natural light, as well, from inside the apartment.

2. The degree of attention. Glover was not a casual or passing observer, as is so often the case with eyewitness identification. Trooper Glover was a trained police officer on duty and specialized and dangerous duty when he called at the third floor of 201 Westland in Hartford on May 5, 1970. Glover himself was a Negro and unlikely to perceive only general features of "hundreds of Hartford black males," as the Court of Appeals stated. It is true that Glover's duty was that of ferreting out narcotics offenders and that he would be expected in his work to produce results. But it is also true that, as a specially trained, assigned, and experienced officer, he could be expected to pay scrupulous attention to detail, for he knew that subsequently he would have to find and arrest his vendor. In addition, he knew that his claimed observations would be subject later to close scrutiny and examination at any trial.

3. The accuracy of the description. Glover's description was given to D'Onofrio within minutes after the transaction. It included the vendor's race, his height, his build, the color and style of his hair, and the high cheekbone facial feature. It also included clothing the vendor wore. No claim has been made that respondent did not possess the physical characteristics so described. D'Onofrio reacted positively at once. Two days later, when Glover was alone, he viewed the photograph D'Onofrio produced and identified its subject as the narcotics seller.

4. The witness' level of certainty. There is no dispute that the photograph in question was that of respondent. Glover, in response to a question whether the photograph was that of the person from whom he made the purchase, testified: "There is no question whatsoever." This positive assurance was repeated.

5. The time between the crime and the confrontation. Glover's description of his vendor was given to D'Onofrio within minutes of the crime. The photographic identification took place only two days later. We do not have here the passage of weeks or months between the crime and the viewing of the photograph.

These indicators of Glover's ability to make an accurate identification are hardly outweighed by the corrupting effect of the challenged identification itself. Although identifications arising from single-photograph displays may be viewed in general with suspicion, we find in the instant case little pressure on the witness to acquiesce in the suggestion that such a display entails. D'Onofrio had left the photograph at Glover's office and was not present when Glover first viewed it two days after the event. There thus was little urgency and Glover could view the photograph at his leisure. And since Glover examined the photograph alone, there was no coercive pressure to make an identification arising from the presence of another. The identification was made in circumstances allowing care and reflection....

Surely, we cannot say that under all the circumstances of this case there is "a very substantial likelihood of irreparable misidentification." Short of that point, such evidence is for the jury to weigh. We are content to rely upon the good sense and judgment of American juries, for evidence with some element of untrustworthiness is customary grist for the jury mill. Juries are not so susceptible that they cannot measure intelligently the weight of identification testimony that has some questionable feature....

We conclude that the criteria laid down in Biggers are to be applied in determining the admissibility of evidence offered by the prosecution concerning a post-Stovall identification, and that those criteria are satisfactorily met and complied with here.

The judgment of the Court of Appeals is reversed....

Mr. Justice MARSHALL, with whom Mr. Justice BRENNAN joins, dissenting.

Today's decision can come as no surprise to those who have been watching the Court dismantle the protections against mistaken eyewitness testimony erected a decade ago in United States v. Wade, Gilbert v. California, and Stovall v. Denno. But it is still distressing to see the Court virtually ignore the teaching of experience embodied in those decisions and blindly uphold the conviction of a defendant who may well be innocent.

I

... The foundation of the Wade trilogy was the Court's recognition of the "high incidence of miscarriage of justice" resulting from the admission of mistaken eyewitness identification evidence at criminal trials. Relying on numerous studies made over many years by such scholars as Professor Wigmore and Mr. Justice Frankfurter, the Court concluded that "[t]he vagaries of eyewitness identification are well-known; the annals of criminal law are rife with instances of mistaken identification." It is, of course, impossible to control one source of such errors—the faulty perceptions and unreliable memories of witnesses—except through vigorously contested trials conducted by diligent counsel and judges. The Court in the Wade cases acted, however, to minimize the more preventable threat posed to accurate identification by "the degree of suggestion inherent in the manner in which the prosecution presents the suspect to witnesses for pretrial identification."

The Court did so in Wade and Gilbert v. California by prohibiting the admission at trial of evidence of pretrial confrontations at which an accused was not represented by counsel. Further protection was afforded by holding that an in-court identification following an uncounseled lineup was allowable only if the prosecution could clearly and convincingly demonstrate that it was not tainted by the constitutional violation. Only in this way, the Court held, could confrontations fraught with the danger of misidentification be made fairer, and could Sixth Amendment rights to assistance of counsel and confrontation of witnesses at trial be effectively preserved. The crux of the Wade decisions, however, was the unusual threat to the truth-seeking process posed by the frequent untrustworthiness of eyewitness identification testimony. This, combined with the fact that juries unfortunately are often unduly receptive to such evidence, is the fundamental fact of judicial experience ignored by the Court today.

Stovall v. Denno ... recognized that, regardless of Sixth Amendment principles, "the conduct of a confrontation" may be "so unnecessarily suggestive and conducive to irreparable mistaken identification" as to deny due process of law. The pretrial confrontation in Stovall was plainly suggestive, and evidence of it was introduced at trial along with the witness' in-court identification. The Court ruled that there had been no violation of due process, however, because the unusual necessity for the procedure outweighed the danger of suggestion....

... Stovall and Simmons [v. United States, 390 U.S. 377 (1968)] established two different due process tests for two very different situations. Where the prosecution sought to use evidence of a questionable pretrial identification, Stovall required its exclusion, because due process had been violated by the confrontation, unless the necessity for the unduly suggestive procedure outweighed its potential for generating an irreparably mistaken identification. The Simmons test, on the other hand, was directed to ascertaining due process violations in the introduction of in-court identification testimony that the defendant claimed was tainted by pretrial procedures. In the latter situation, a court could consider the reliability of the identification under all the circumstances....

III

Despite my strong disagreement with the Court over the proper standards to be applied in this case, I am pleased that its application of the totality test does recognize the continuing vitality of Stovall. In assessing the reliability of the identification, the Court mandates weighing "the corrupting effect of the suggestive identification itself" against the "indicators of [a witness'] ability to make an accurate identification." The Court holds ... that a due process identification inquiry must take account of the suggestiveness of a confrontation and the likelihood that it led to misidentification, as recognized in Stovall and Wade. Thus, even if a witness did have an otherwise adequate opportunity to view a criminal, the later use of a highly suggestive identification procedure can render his testimony inadmissible....

I consider first the opportunity that Officer Glover had to view the suspect. Careful review of the record shows that he could see the heroin seller only for the time it took to speak three sentences of four or five short words, to hand over some money, and later after the door reopened, to receive the drugs in return. The entire face-to-face transaction could have taken as little as 15 or 20 seconds. But during this time, Glover's attention was not focused exclusively on the seller's face. He observed that the door was opened 12 to 18 inches, that there was a window in the room behind the door, and, most importantly, that there was a woman standing behind the man. Glover was, of course, also concentrating on the details of the transaction he must have looked away from the seller's face to hand him the money and receive the drugs. The observation during the conversation thus may have been as brief as 5 or 10 seconds.

As the Court notes, Glover was a police officer trained in and attentive to the need for making accurate identifications. Nevertheless, both common sense and scholarly study indicate that while a trained observer such as a police officer "is somewhat less likely to make an erroneous identification than the average untrained observer, the mere fact that he has been so trained is no guarantee that he is correct in a specific case. His identification testimony should be scrutinized just as carefully as that of the normal witness." [P. Wall, Eye-Witness Identification in Criminal Cases 14 (1965)]. Moreover, "identifications made by policemen in highly competitive activities, such as undercover narcotic agents ..., should be scrutinized with special care." [*Id.*] Yet it is just such a searching inquiry that the Court fails to make here.

Another factor on which the Court relies the witness' degree of certainty in making the identification is worthless as an indicator that he is correct. Even if Glover had been unsure initially about his identification of respondent's picture, by the time he was called at trial to present a key piece of evidence for the State that paid his salary, it is impossible to imagine his responding negatively to such questions as "is there any doubt in your mind whatsoever" that the identification was correct. As the Court noted in Wade: "'It is a matter of common experience that, once a witness has picked out the accused at the [pretrial confrontation], he is not likely to go back on his word later on.'" 388 U.S., at 229.

Next, the Court finds that because the identification procedure took place two days after the crime, its reliability is enhanced. While such temporal proximity makes the identification more reliable than one occurring months later, the fact is that the greatest memory loss occurs within hours after an event. After that, the dropoff continues much more slowly. Thus, the reliability of an identification is increased only if it was made within several hours of the crime. If the time gap is any greater, reliability necessarily decreases.

Finally, the Court makes much of the fact that Glover gave a description of the seller to D'Onofrio shortly after the incident. Despite the Court's assertion that because "Glover himself was a Negro and unlikely to perceive only general features of 'hundreds of Hartford black males,' as the Court of Appeals stated," the description given by Glover was actually no more than a general summary of the seller's appearance. We may discount entirely the seller's clothing, for that was of no significance later in the proceeding. Indeed, to the extent that Glover noticed clothes, his attention was diverted from the seller's face. Otherwise, Glover merely described vaguely the seller's height, skin color, hairstyle, and build. He did say that the seller had "high cheekbones," but there is no other mention of facial features, nor even an estimate of age. Conspicuously absent is any indication that the seller was a native of the West Indies, certainly something which a member of the black community could immediately recognize from both appearance and accent.[12]

From all of this, I must conclude that the evidence of Glover's ability to make an accurate identification is far weaker than the Court finds it. In contrast, the procedure used to identify respondent was both extraordinarily suggestive and strongly conducive to error. In dismissing "the corrupting effect of the suggestive identification" procedure here, the Court virtually grants the police license to convict the innocent. By displaying a single photograph of respondent to the witness Glover under the circumstances in this record almost everything that could have been done wrong was done wrong....

Worse still than the failure to use an easily available corporeal identification was the display to Glover of only a single picture, rather than a photo array....

I must conclude that this record presents compelling evidence that there was "a very substantial likelihood of misidentification" of respondent Brathwaite. The suggestive display of respondent's photograph to the witness Glover likely erased any independent memory that Glover had retained of the seller from his barely adequate opportunity to observe the criminal.

IV

Since I agree with the distinguished panel of the Court of Appeals that the legal standard of Stovall should govern this case, but that even if it does not, the facts here reveal a substantial likelihood of misidentification in violation of respondent's right to due process of law, I would affirm the grant of habeas corpus relief. Accordingly, I dissent from the Court's reinstatement of respondent's conviction.

12. Brathwaite had come to the United States from his native Barbados as an adult....

Notes and Questions

1. The "*Brathwaite* factors" for assessing the reliability of an eyewitness's identification of the suspected perpetrator of a crime have been thoroughly scrutinized by researchers and we later will summarize their principal findings. Do the factors appear to be logical? Comprehensive? Does the Court offer any assistance about how the factors are "to be weighed against the corrupting effect of the suggestive identification"?

2. Note that the Due Process test and application of the *Brathwaite* criteria concern only the *admissibility* of the identification testimony. The relative *weight* afforded identification testimony in the event of its admission presents an importantly different question. The jury might embrace the identification as highly credible, dismiss it as fatally suspect, or consider it to be equivocal. Justice Blackmun's opinion declared: "We are content to rely upon the good sense and judgment of American juries.... Juries are not so susceptible that they cannot measure intelligently the weight of identification testimony that has some questionable feature." In *Brathwaite,* Officer Glover testified, "There is no question whatsoever" that the photo he examined was of the person who had sold him the heroin. How sanguine should we be about a jury's ability to discriminate between reliable and unreliable identification testimony, particularly when the witness exhibits such confidence?

3. In *Neil v. Biggers*, 409 U.S. 188, 93 S.Ct. 375, 34 L.Ed.2d 401 (1972), which is cited in *Brathwaite*, an intruder accosted a woman in the kitchen of her home. It was night and the kitchen was dark but the woman reported that she could see the man because a light was on in another room. The assailant commandeered her by knifepoint into a nearby woods and raped her. A full moon helped illuminate the wooded area. She estimated that they were together for 15 to 30 minutes. On being released she returned home and called the police, providing a description of her assailant and the sound of his voice. Over the next several months she viewed numerous line-ups, show-ups, and photographs but did not identify any of the suspects. Approximately seven months after the crime, she observed Biggers during a show-up, while he was accompanied by two detectives. She listened as he repeated the words used by her rapist, "Shut up or I'll kill you." She then indicated that she had "no doubt" that Biggers was the man who had raped her. Her identification testimony was admitted at Biggers' state trial, which took place in 1965 and thus preceded *Stovall v. Denno*, 388 U.S. 293 (1967). Biggers was convicted and sentenced to 20 years imprisonment. A federal district court subsequently ruled that the trial testimony concerning the out-of-court identification should have been excluded because the show-up was unnecessarily suggestive. The Supreme Court reversed in a 5–3 decision. Applying the same factors deemed relevant in *Brathwaite,* the majority opinion reasoned:

> The victim spent a considerable period of time with her assailant, up to half an hour. She was with him under adequate artificial light in her house and under a full moon outdoors, and at least twice, once in the house and later in the woods, faced him directly and intimately. She was no casual observer, but rather the victim of one of the most personally humiliating of all crimes. Her description to the police, which included the assailant's approximate age, height, weight, complexion, skin texture, build, and voice, might not have satisfied Proust but was more than ordinarily thorough. She had 'no doubt' that respondent was the person who raped her. In the nature of the crime, there are rarely witnesses to a rape other than the victim, who often has a limited opportunity of observation. The victim here, a practical nurse by profession, had an unusual opportunity to observe and identify her assailant. She testified at the habeas corpus hearing that there was something about his face 'I don't think I could ever forget.'

There was, to be sure, a lapse of seven months between the rape and the confrontation. This would be a seriously negative factor in most cases. Here, however, the testimony is undisputed that the victim made no previous identification at any of the showups, lineups, or photographic showings. Her record for reliability was thus a good one, as she had previously resisted whatever suggestiveness inheres in a showup. Weighing all the factors, we find no substantial likelihood of misidentification. The evidence was properly allowed to go to the jury.

2. Photo Identifications

Manson v. Brathwaite involved Officer Glover's photographic identification of the man who sold him heroin. The police often must rely on photos, computer-generated composites, or an artist's sketch work because no suspect has been taken into custody, making an attempted corporeal identification impossible. However, presenting a single photograph to the officer for identification, instead of using an array consisting of photos of several different individuals, distinguished the procedure used in *Brathwaite* as "unnecessarily suggestive." In *Simmons v. United States,* 390 U.S. 377, 88 S.Ct. 967, 19 L.Ed.2d 1247 (1968), while approving of the investigation at issue, the Court acknowledged that, just as with corporeal identifications, the reliability of photographic identifications can be undermined by suggestive procedures.

It must be recognized that improper employment of photographs by police may sometimes cause witnesses to err in identifying criminals. A witness may have obtained only a brief glimpse of a criminal, or may have seen him under poor conditions. Even if the police subsequently follow the most correct photographic identification procedures and show him the pictures of a number of individuals without indicating whom they suspect, there is some danger that the witness may make an incorrect identification. This danger will be increased if the police display to the witness only the picture of a single individual who generally resembles the person he saw, or if they show him the pictures of several persons among which the photograph of a single such individual recurs or is in some way emphasized. The chance of misidentification is also heightened if the police indicate to the witness that they have other evidence that one of the persons pictured committed the crime. Regardless of how the initial misidentification comes about, the witness thereafter is apt to retain in his memory the image of the photograph rather than of the person actually seen, reducing the trustworthiness of subsequent lineup or courtroom identification.

In cases such as *Simmons* and *Brathwaite,* where the police have no one in custody and ask witnesses to view photos of suspects to assist their investigation, it would be impractical to try to involve defense counsel to monitor the identification process. Moreover, even if a suspect is under arrest when the police ask a witness to attempt a photo identification—which they might do because of logistical difficulties in locating enough suitable "fillers" for a fair line-up and because they want to avoid a suggestive show-up—the ruling in *Kirby v. Illinois* would foreclose the argument that defense counsel's presence is required prior to arraignment or the filing of formal charges. However, should a defendant be entitled to counsel's involvement during a post-indictment photographic identification procedure, when counsel's presence would be required under *Wade-Gilbert* for a corporeal identification procedure?

United States v. Ash

413 U.S. 300, 93 S.Ct. 2568, 37 L.Ed.2d 619 (1973)

Mr. Justice BLACKMUN delivered the opinion of the Court.

In this case the Court is called upon to decide whether the Sixth Amendment[1] grants an accused the right to have counsel present whenever the Government conducts a post-indictment photographic display, containing a picture of the accused, for the purpose of allowing a witness to attempt an identification of the offender. The United States Court of Appeals for the District of Columbia Circuit, sitting en banc, held, by a 5-to-4 vote, that the accused possesses this right to counsel.... We reverse and remand.

I

On the morning of August 26, 1965, a man with a stocking mask entered a bank in Washington, D.C., and began waving a pistol. He ordered an employee to hang up the telephone and instructed all others present not to move. Seconds later a second man, also wearing a stocking mask, entered the bank, scooped up money from tellers' drawers into a bag, and left. The gunman followed, and both men escaped through an alley. The robbery lasted three or four minutes.

A Government informer, Clarence McFarland, told authorities that he had discussed the robbery with Charles J. Ash, Jr., the respondent here. Acting on this information, an FBI agent, in February 1966, showed five black-and-white mug shots of Negro males of generally the same age, height, and weight, one of which was of Ash, to four witnesses. All four made uncertain identifications of Ash's picture. At this time Ash was not in custody and had not been charged. On April 1, 1966, an indictment was returned charging Ash and a codefendant, John L. Bailey, in five counts related to this bank robbery....

Trial was finally set for May 1968, almost three years after the crime. In preparing for trial, the prosecutor decided to use a photographic display to determine whether the witnesses he planned to call would be able to make in-court identifications. Shortly before the trial, an FBI agent and the prosecutor showed five color photographs to the four witnesses who previously had tentatively identified the black-and-white photograph of Ash. Three of the witnesses selected the picture of Ash, but one was unable to make any selection. None of the witnesses selected the picture of Bailey which was in the group. This post-indictment[3] identification provides the basis for respondent Ash's claim that he was denied the right to counsel at a 'critical stage' of the prosecution.

... Ash and Bailey were tried jointly. The trial judge held a hearing on the suggestive nature of the pretrial photographic displays. The judge did not make a clear ruling on suggestive nature, but held that the Government had demonstrated by 'clear and convincing' evidence that in-court identifications would be 'based on observation of the suspect other than the intervening observation.'

At trial, the three witnesses who had been inside the bank identified Ash as the gunman, but they were unwilling to state that they were certain of their identifications. None of these made an in-court identification of Bailey. The fourth witness, who had been in a car outside the bank and who had seen the fleeing robbers after they had removed their masks, made positive in-court identifications of both Ash and Bailey. Bailey's counsel then sought to impeach this in-court identification by calling the FBI agent who had shown the color photographs to the witnesses immediately before trial. Bailey's counsel demonstrated that the witness who had identified Bailey in court had failed to identify a color photograph of Bailey. During the course of the examination, Bailey's counsel also, before the jury, brought out the fact that this witness had selected another man as one of the robbers. At this point the prosecutor became concerned that the jury might believe that the witness had selected a third person when, in fact, the witness had selected a photograph of Ash. After a conference at the bench, the trial judge ruled that all five color photographs would be admitted into evidence.

1. 'In all criminal prosecutions, the accused shall enjoy the right ... to have the Assistance of Counsel for his defence.'

3. Respondent Ash does not assert a right to counsel at the black-and-white photographic display in February 1966 because he recognizes that Kirby v. Illinois, 406 U.S. 682, (1972), forecloses application of the Sixth Amendment to events before the initiation of adversary criminal proceedings.

The Court of Appeals held that this constituted the introduction of a post-indictment identification at the prosecutor's request and over the objection of defense counsel.

McFarland testified as a Government witness. He said he had discussed plans for the robbery with Ash before the event and, later, had discussed the results of the robbery with Ash in the presence of Bailey. McFarland was shown to possess an extensive criminal record and a history as an informer.

The jury convicted Ash on all counts. It was unable to reach a verdict on the charges against Bailey, and his motion for acquittal was granted. Ash received concurrent sentences on the several counts, the two longest being 80 months to 12 years....

II

... The right to counsel in Anglo-American law has a rich historical heritage, and this Court has regularly drawn on that history in construing the counsel guarantee of the Sixth Amendment....

This historical background suggests that the core purpose of the counsel guarantee was to assure 'Assistance' at trial, when the accused was confronted with both the intricacies of the law and the advocacy of the public prosecutor. Later developments have led this Court to recognize that 'Assistance' would be less than meaningful if it were limited to the formal trial itself.

This extension of the right to counsel to events before trial has resulted from changing patterns of criminal procedure and investigation that have tended to generate pretrial events that might appropriately be considered to be parts of the trial itself. At these newly emerging and significant events, the accused was confronted, just as at trial, by the procedural system, or by his expert adversary, or by both....

The Court consistently has applied a historical interpretation of the guarantee, and has expanded the constitutional right to counsel only when new contexts appear presenting the same dangers that gave birth initially to the right itself....

Throughout this expansion of the counsel guarantee to trial-like confrontations, the function of the lawyer has remained essentially the same as his function at trial. In all cases considered by the Court, counsel has continued to act as a spokesman for, or advisor to, the accused. The accused's right to the 'Assistance of Counsel' has meant just that, namely, the right of the accused to have counsel acting as his assistant....

The function of counsel in rendering 'Assistance' continued at the lineup under consideration in Wade and its companion cases. Although the accused was not confronted there with legal questions, the lineup offered opportunities for prosecuting authorities to take advantage of the accused. Counsel was seen by the Court as being more sensitive to, and aware of, suggestive influences than the accused himself, and as better able to reconstruct the events at trial. Counsel present at lineup would be able to remove disabilities of the accused in precisely the same fashion that counsel compensated for the disabilities of the layman at trial. Thus, the Court mentioned that the accused's memory might be dimmed by 'emotional tension,' that the accused's credibility at trial would be diminished by his status as defendant, and that the accused might be unable to present his version effectively without giving up his privilege against compulsory self-incrimination. It was in order to compensate for these deficiencies that the Court found the need for the assistance of counsel.

This review of the history and expansion of the Sixth Amendment counsel guarantee demonstrates that the test utilized by the Court has called for examination of the event in order to determine whether the accused required aid in coping with legal problems or assistance in meeting his adversary....

III

... Although Wade did discuss possibilities for suggestion and the difficulty for reconstructing suggestivity, this discussion occurred only after the Court had concluded that the lineup constituted a trial-like confrontation, requiring the 'Assistance of Counsel' to preserve the adversary process by compensating for advantages of the prosecuting authorities....

... The Government had argued in Wade that if counsel was required at a lineup, the same forceful considerations would mandate counsel at other preparatory steps in the 'gathering of the prosecution's evidence,' such as, for particular example, the taking of fingerprints or blood samples.

The Court concluded that there were differences. Rather than distinguishing these situations from the lineup in terms of the need for counsel to assure an equal confrontation at the time, the Court recognized that there were times when the subsequent trial would cure a one-sided confrontation between prosecuting authorities and the uncounseled defendant. In other words, such stages were not 'critical.' Referring to fingerprints, hair, clothing, and other blood samples, the Court explained:

'Knowledge of the techniques of science and technology is sufficiently available, and the variables in techniques few enough, that the accused has the opportunity for a meaningful confrontation of the Government's case at trial through the ordinary processes of cross-examination of the Government's expert witnesses and the presentation of the evidence of his own experts.' 388 U.S., at 227–228.

The structure of Wade, viewed in light of the careful limitation of the Court's language to 'confrontations,' makes it clear that lack of scientific precision and inability to reconstruct an event are not the tests for requiring counsel in the first instance. These are, instead, the tests to determine whether confrontation with counsel at trial can serve as a substitute for counsel at the pretrial confrontation. If accurate reconstruction is possible, the risks inherent in any confrontation still remain, but the opportunity to cure defects at trial causes the confrontation to cease to be 'critical.' The opinion of the Court even indicated that changes in procedure might cause a lineup to cease to be a 'critical' confrontation....

IV

A substantial departure from the historical test would be necessary if the Sixth Amendment were interpreted to give Ash a right to counsel at the photographic identification in this case. Since the accused himself is not present at the time of the photographic display, and asserts no right to be present, no possibility arises that the accused might be misled by his lack of familiarity with the law or overpowered by his professional adversary. Similarly, the counsel guarantee would not be used to produce equality in a trial-like adversary confrontation....

Even if we were willing to view the counsel guarantee in broad terms as a generalized protection of the adversary process, we would be unwilling to go so far as to extend the right to a portion of the prosecutor's trial-preparation interviews with witnesses.... The traditional counterbalance in the American adversary system for these interviews arises from the equal ability of defense counsel to seek and interview witnesses himself.

That adversary mechanism remains as effective for a photographic display as for other parts of pretrial interviews. No greater limitations are placed on defense counsel in constructing displays, seeking witnesses, and conducting photographic identifications than those applicable to the prosecution. Selection of the picture of a person other than the accused, or the inability of a witness to make any selection, will be useful to the defense in precisely the same manner that the selection of a picture of the defendant would be useful to the prosecution. In this very case, for example, the initial tender of the photographic display was by Bailey's counsel, who sought to demonstrate that the witness had failed to make a photographic identification. Although we do not suggest that equality of access to photographs removes all potential for abuse, it does remove any inequality in the adversary process itself and thereby fully satisfies the historical spirit of the Sixth Amendment's counsel guarantee.

The argument has been advanced that requiring counsel might compel the police to observe more scientific procedures or might encourage them to utilize corporeal rather than photographic displays. This Court has recognized that improved procedures can minimize the dangers of suggestion. Commentators have also proposed more accurate techniques.

Pretrial photographic identifications, however, are hardly unique in offering possibilities for the actions of the prosecutor unfairly to prejudice the accused. Evidence favorable to the accused may be withheld; testimony of witnesses may be manipulated; the results of laboratory tests may be contrived. In many ways the prosecutor, by accident or by design, may improperly subvert the trial. The primary safeguard against abuses of this kind is the ethical responsibility of the prosecutor,[16] who, as so often has been said, may 'strike hard blows' but not 'foul ones.' Berger v. United States, 295 U.S. 78, 88 (1935). If that safeguard fails, review remains available under due process standards. See Giglio v. United States, 405 U.S. 150 (1972); Mooney v. Holohan, 294 U.S. 103 (1935); Miller v. Pate, 386 U.S. 1 (1967).

16. Throughout a criminal prosecution the prosecutor's ethical responsibility extends, of course, to supervision of any continuing investigation of the case. By prescribing procedures to be used by his agents and by screening the evidence before trial with a view to eliminating unreliable identifications, the prosecutor is able to minimize abuse in photographic displays even if they are conducted in his absence.

These same safeguards apply to misuse of photographs.

We are not persuaded that the risks inherent in the use of photographic displays are so pernicious that an extraordinary system of safeguards is required.

We hold, then, that the Sixth Amendment does not grant the right to counsel at photographic displays conducted by the Government for the purpose of allowing a witness to attempt an identification of the offender....

Reversed and remanded.

Mr. Justice STEWART, concurring in the judgment....

The Court held in Wade that a post-indictment, pretrial lineup at which the accused was exhibited to identifying witnesses was ... a critical stage, because of the substantial possibility that the accused's right to a fair trial would otherwise be irretrievably lost....

The Court held..that counsel was required at a lineup, primarily as an observer, to ensure that defense counsel could effectively confront the prosecution's evidence at trial. Attuned to the possibilities of suggestive influences, a lawyer could see any unfairness at a lineup, question the witnesses about it at trial, and effectively reconstruct what had gone on for the benefit of the jury or trial judge.

A photographic identification is quite different from a lineup, for there are substantially fewer possibilities of impermissible suggestion when photographs are used, and those unfair influences can be readily reconstructed at trial. It is true that the defendant's photograph may be markedly different from the others displayed, but this unfairness can be demonstrated at trial from an actual comparison of the photographs used or from the witness' description of the display. Similarly, it is possible that the photographs could be arranged in a suggestive manner, or that by comment or gesture the prosecuting authorities might single out the defendant's picture. But these are the kinds of overt influence that a witness can easily recount and that would serve to impeach the identification testimony. In short, there are few possibilities for unfair suggestiveness—and those rather blatant and easily reconstructed. Accordingly, an accused would not be foreclosed from an effective cross-examination of an identification witness simply because his counsel was not present at the photographic display. For this reason, a photographic display cannot fairly be considered a 'critical stage' of the prosecution....

Preparing witnesses for trial by checking their identification testimony against a photographic display is little different, in my view, from the prosecutor's other interviews with the victim or other witnesses before trial. While these procedures can be improperly conducted, the possibility of irretrievable prejudice is remote, since any unfairness that does occur can usually be flushed out at trial through cross-examination of the prosecution witnesses. The presence of defense counsel at such pretrial preparatory sessions is neither appropriate nor necessary under our adversary system of justice 'to preserve the defendant's basic right to a fair trial as affected by his right meaningfully to cross-examine the witnesses against him and to have effective assistance of counsel at the trial itself.' United States v. Wade, supra, 388 U.S. at 227.

Mr. Justice BRENNAN, with whom Mr. Justice DOUGLAS and Mr. Justice MARSHALL join, dissenting.

... I must reluctantly conclude that today's decision marks simply another[1] step towards the complete evisceration of the fundamental constitutional principles established by this Court, only six years ago, in United States v. Wade, 388 U.S. 218 (1967); Gilbert v. California, 388 U.S. 263 (1967); and Stovall v. Denno, 388 U.S. 293 (1967). I dissent....

III

As the Court of Appeals recognized, 'the dangers of mistaken identification ... set forth in Wade are applicable in large measure to photographic as well as corporeal identifications.' To the extent that misidentification may be attributable to a witness' faulty memory or perception, or inadequate opportunity for detailed observation during the crime, the risks are obviously as great at a photographic display as at a lineup. But '[b]ecause of the inherent limitations of photography, which presents its subject in two dimensions rather than the three dimensions of reality, ... a photographic identification, even when properly obtained, is clearly inferior to a properly obtained corporeal identification.' P. Wall, Eye-witness Identification in Criminal Cases 70 (1965). Indeed, noting 'the hazards of initial identification by photograph,' we have expressly recognized that 'a corporeal

1. See Kirby v. Illinois, 406 U.S. 682 (1972).

identification ... is normally more accurate' than a photographic identification. Simmons v. United States, 390 U.S. 377, 384, 386 n. 6 (1968). Thus, in this sense at least, the dangers of misidentification are even greater at a photographic display than at a lineup.

Moreover, as in the lineup situation, the possibilities for impermissible suggestion in the context of a photographic display are manifold. Such suggestion, intentional or unintentional, may derive from three possible sources. First, the photographs themselves might tend to suggest which of the pictures is that of the suspect. For example, differences in age, pose, or other physical characteristics of the persons represented, and variations in the mounting, background, lighting, or markings of the photographs all might have the effect of singling out the accused.

Second, impermissible suggestion may inhere in the manner in which the photographs are displayed to the witness....

Third, gestures or comments of the prosecutor at the time of the display may lead an otherwise uncertain witness to select the 'correct' photograph.... More subtly, the prosecutor's inflection, facial expressions, physical motions, and myriad other almost imperceptible means of communication might tend, intentionally or unintentionally, to compromise the witness' objectivity. Thus, as is the case with lineups, '[i]mproper photographic identification procedures, ... by exerting a suggestive influence upon the witnesses, can often lead to an erroneous identification....' P. Wall, supra, at 89.[12] And '[r]egardless of how the initial misidentification comes about, the witness thereafter is apt to retain in his memory the image of the photograph rather than of the person actually seen....' As a result, "the issue of identity may [in the absence of other relevant evidence] for all practical purposes by determined there and then, before the trial" United States v. Wade, supra, 388 U.S., at 229.

Moreover, as with lineups, the defense can 'seldom reconstruct' at trial the mode and manner of photographic identification.... [P]reservation of the photographs affords little protection to the unrepresented accused. For, although retention of the photographs may mitigate the dangers of misidentification due to the suggestiveness of the photographs themselves, it cannot in any sense reveal to defense counsel the more subtle, and therefore more dangerous, suggestiveness that might derive from the manner in which he photographs were displayed or any accompanying comments or gestures....

Finally, and unlike the lineup situation, the accused himself is not even present at the photographic identification, thereby reducing the likelihood that irregularities in the procedures will ever come to light....

Thus, the difficulties of reconstructing at trial an uncounseled photographic display are at least equal to, and possibly greater than, those involved in reconstructing an uncounseled lineup.[15] And, as the Government argued in Wade, in terms of the need for counsel, '[t]here is no meaningful difference between a witness' pretrial identification from photographs and a similar identification

12. The Court maintains that 'the ethical responsibility of the prosecutor' is in itself a sufficient 'safeguard' against impermissible suggestion at a photographic display. The same argument might, of course, be made with respect to lineups. Moreover, it is clear that the 'prosecutor' is not always present at such pretrial displays. Indeed, in this very case, one of the four eye-witnesses was shown the color photographs on the morning of trial by an agent of the FBI, not in the presence of the 'prosecutor.' And even though 'the ethical responsibility of the prosecutor' might be an adequate 'safeguard' against intentional suggestion, it can hardly be doubted that a 'prosecutor' is, after all, only human. His behavior may be fraught with wholly unintentional and indeed unconscious nuances that might effectively suggest the 'proper' response. And, of course, as Wade itself makes clear, unlike other forms of unintentional prosecutorial 'manipulation,' even unintentional suggestiveness at an identification procedure involves serious risks of 'freezing' the witness' mistaken identification and creates almost insurmountable obstacles to reconstruction at trial.

15. The Court's assertion, that these difficulties of reconstruction are somehow minimized because the defense can 'duplicate' a photographic identification reflects a complete misunderstanding of the issues in this case.... [There is] a critical difference between 'systematized or scientific analyzing of the accused's fingerprints, blood sample, clothing, hair, and the like,' on the one hand, and eyewitness identification, on the other.... [I]n the former situations, the accused can preserve his right to a fair trial simply by 'duplicating' the tests of the Government, thereby enabling him to expose any errors in the Government's analysis. Such 'duplication' is possible, however, only because the accused's tests can be made independently of those of the Government—that is, any errors in the Government's analyses cannot affect the reliability of the accused's

made at a lineup.' For in both situations, 'the accused's inability effectively to reconstruct at trial any unfairness that occurred at the [pretrial identification] may deprive him of his only opportunity meaningfully to attack the credibility of the witness' courtroom identification.' United States v. Wade, supra, 388 U.S. at 231–232. As a result, both photographic and corporeal identifications create grave dangers that an innocent defendant might be convicted simply because of his inability to expose a tainted identification. This being so, considerations of logic, consistency, and, indeed, fairness compel the conclusion that a pretrial photographic identification, like a pretrial corporeal identification, is a 'critical stage of the prosecution at which (the accused is) 'as much entitled to such aid (of counsel) ... as at the trial itself.'" Id., at 237.

IV

... [T]he Court holds today that, in order to be deemed 'critical,' the particular 'stage of the prosecution' under consideration must, at the very least, involve the physical 'presence of the accused,' at a 'trial-like confrontation' with the Government, at which the accused requires the 'guiding hand of counsel.' According to the Court a pretrial photographic identification does not, of course, meet these criteria....

The fundamental premise underlying all of this Court's decisions holding the right to counsel applicable at 'critical' pretrial proceedings, is that a 'stage' of the prosecution must be deemed 'critical' for the purposes of the Sixth Amendment if it is one at which the presence of counsel is necessary 'to protect the fairness of the trial itself.' ...

This established conception of the Sixth Amendment guarantee is, of course, in no sense dependent upon the physical 'presence of the accused,' at a 'trial-like confrontation' with the Government, at which the accused requires the 'guiding hand of counsel.' ...

There is something ironic about the Court's conclusion today that a pretrial lineup identification is a 'critical stage' of the prosecution because counsel's presence can help to compensate for the accused's deficiencies as an observer, but that a pretrial photographic identification is not a 'critical stage' of the prosecution because the accused is not able to observe at all. In my view, there simply is no meaningful difference, in terms of the need for attendance of counsel, between corporeal and photographic identifications. And applying established and well-reasoned Sixth Amendment principles, I can only conclude that a pretrial photographic display, like a pretrial lineup, is a 'critical stage' of the prosecution at which the accused is constitutionally entitled to the presence of counsel.

Notes and Questions

1. Are the potential suggestiveness and threats to reliability associated with photographic and corporeal identification procedures meaningfully different? Do other considerations relevant to the 6th Amendment justify the different outcomes in *Ash* and *Wade*?

2. Is allowing the jurors to examine the array of photos used in an identification procedure, so they can assess the similarities and differences of the included subjects, coupled with cross-examination of the participants in the procedure, a sufficient reliability check? Would allowing defense counsel to be present during post-indictment photo identifications impede or burden law enforcement? In what ways, if any, could allowing defense counsel's presence influence police behavior?

3. Is there a reason to prefer corporeal identifications over photo identifications, or the converse, from a perspective of maximizing either reliability or administrative efficiency?

---

tests. That simply is not the case, however, with respect to eyewitness identifications, whether corporeal or photographic. Due to the 'freezing effect' recognized in Wade, once suggestion has tainted the identification, its mark is virtually indelible. For once a witness has made a mistaken identification, "he is not likely to go back on his word later on." United States v. Wade, supra, 388 U.S., at 229. As a result, any effort of the accused to 'duplicate' the initial photographic display will almost necessarily lead to a reaffirmation of the initial misidentification....

C. Eyewitness Identification Procedures: Research Evidence, Policy Directives, and Developments in the State Courts

1. Eyewitness Identification: Social Science Research and Related Policy Directives

As alluded to throughout this chapter, the reliability and validity of eyewitness identification have received a great deal of research attention. The research dates back at least to the beginning of the 20th century with studies completed by Louis William Stern.[3] The modern era of eyewitness research, however, can be dated back to the mid-1970s with the seminal work of Professor Elizabeth Loftus.[4] In one of her early studies, she demonstrated how misleading questions and other post-event information can alter what eyewitnesses remember and subsequently report.

In its simplest form, memory can be considered to include three phases: encoding, storage, and retrieval. At any and all three of these phases, the potential for error can be introduced. In 1978 Professor Gary Wells established the terms "system variables" and "estimator variables."[5] System variables are factors within the control of law enforcement officers or other criminal justice officials that can affect the reliability of eyewitness identifications, including the use of suggestive identification procedures. System variables are known and can be manipulated, and thus, in principle, can also be prevented. Estimator variables are factors that can influence the reliability of eyewitness identification, but are neither alterable nor preventable. Estimator variables tend to be situational—such as, for example, whether the crime was committed in the dark of night or in broad daylight, or whether the witness had a split second or several minutes to observe the perpetrator—or personal—involving, for example, the witness's eyesight, age, degree of fright, and whether the witness and perpetrator were different races. In a general, but not exclusive sense, system variables are relevant to memory retrieval, whereas estimator variables are relevant to memory encoding and storage. Because system variables have the potential to be controlled, more research has been devoted to identifying and understanding them than estimator variables.

In 1998, the American Psychology-Law Society, a division of the American Psychological Association, approved and published a scientific white paper on eyewitness identifications.[6] This paper, which represented the current corpus of scientific knowledge about eyewitness identifications, offered four independent rules for reform:

Rule 1) Who conducts the lineup: "The person who conducts the lineup or photospread should not be aware of which member of the lineup or photospread is the suspect." In other words, "double-blind" procedures should be implemented as intentional and unintentional bias can alter the reliability of the procedure.

Rule 2) Instructions on viewing: "Eyewitnesses should be told explicitly that the person in question might not be in the lineup or photospread and therefore should not feel that they must make an identification. They should also be told that the person administering the lineup does not know which person is the suspect in the case." Several empirical studies have demonstrated that such a warning decreases rates of witnesses identifying innocent foils.

Rule 3) Structure of lineup or photospread: "The suspect should not stand out in the lineup or photospread as being different from the distractors based on the eyewitness's previous description of the culprit or based on other factors that would draw extra attention to the suspect." Within this recommended rule, the authors stress that innocent distractors in the lineup should be chosen on the basis of the original eyewitness description (*e.g.*, White, mid-20s male with scar on face) rather than on the basis of matching the suspect, which can make the suspect stand out.

Rule 4) Obtaining confidence statements: "A clear statement should be taken from the eyewitness at the time of the identification and prior to any feedback as to his or her confidence that the identified person is the actual culprit." Extensive research has demonstrated that whereas eyewitness confidence has a powerful effect on the trier of fact's credibility assessments, it often has little to do with the accuracy of an identification. Thus, documenting witness certainty at the time of the initial identification decision is critical.

With this white paper in hand, science was translated into policy. Then-Attorney General Janet Reno assembled an expert, technical working group comprised of social scientists, law enforcement officials, and legal practitioners. This group produced the National Institute of Justice's *Eyewitness Evidence: A Guide for Law Enforcement* (1999).[7] The Guide, which explicitly claimed to be "supported by social science research" and a combination of "research and practical perspectives," contained numerous recommendations, including those for the preliminary investigator (*e.g.*, 911 call-takers), for preparing mugshot books and composite sketches, for interviewing and instructing witnesses, and for conducting line-ups. At each phase of the investigation, emphasis was placed on asking open-ended questions, avoiding exposure to possible sources of contamination, and documenting all procedures.

Both the white paper and the NIJ Guide fell short of recommending or requiring the use of sequential over simultaneous lineups.[8] Sequential lineups require eyewitnesses to view suspects (either corporeal or photo) one at a time, rather than in a row or in a "six-pack" (*i.e.*, simultaneously). The theorized benefits of sequential procedures are that the eyewitness must make an absolute judgment about the suspect rather than a relative judgment. An absolute judgment is an independent, dichotomous judgment ("this is the perpetrator or this is not the perpetrator"). In contrast, relative judgments foster eyewitnesses choosing the suspect that looks *most* like the perpetrator from among the several people presented. At the time, several laboratory studies had demonstrated that the sequential lineup procedure is more diagnostic than the simultaneous procedure in that the number of inaccurate identifications decreased but the number of accurate identifications was unaffected.

When the white paper and the NIJ Guide were published, the benefits of the sequential procedure over the simultaneous were shown in the laboratory but not the field (*i.e.*, actual eyewitness identifications). In the early part of the 21st century, Illinois undertook a pilot program (in the cities of Evanston, Chicago, and Joliet) to test whether the scientifically recommended procedures (*i.e.*, double-blind and sequential) were superior to the in-practice procedures (*i.e.*, non-blind and simultaneous). In 2006, the "Mecklenburg Report" was published (named after the author, who was general counsel for the Chicago police).[9] The Report indicated that in two of the three cities, the standard practice procedures resulted in higher suspect identification rates and lower innocent foil rates; in other words, that the standard practices were superior to the scientific ones.

The Mecklenburg Report has generated considerable controversy. Scientists who have and have not been involved in eyewitness identification research have criticized the validity of the study design and its conclusions.[10] Most notably, the intrusion of other factors may have confounded a comparison of the different practices. Professor Nancy Steblay[11] recently secured 100 of the eyewitness identification reports from the Evanston study site. She was able to determine that in comparison to the double-blind, sequential lineups, the simultaneous non-blind lineups contained more confirmatory and non-stranger identifications, shorter delays between the event and lineup, and that verbatim eyewitness comments were less frequently recorded. Many view this Illinois pilot study as a failed experiment and a squandered opportunity to evaluate the comparative value of sequential and simultaneous identification procedures in the field.[12]

Based on research findings and related policy recommendations, several states have enacted legislation to regulate eyewitness identification procedures. For example, an Ohio statute requires, *inter alia*, that lineups and photo arrays be conducted by a blinded administrator "[u]nless impracticable," and that a written record be preserved of "eyewitnesses' confidence statements made immediately at the time of identification." Trial courts are to consider noncompliance with mandated procedures in ruling on suppression motions and can instruct jurors to consider such noncompliance in their determination of the reliability of a witness's identification. Ohio Rev. Code Ann. §§ 2933.83 (B)(1), (4)(a), (C)(1), (3) (2010). In Wisconsin, law enforcement agencies are required to adopt written policies designed to enhance the reliability of eyewitness identifications and to consider "[t]o the extent feasible, having a person who does not know the identity of the suspect administer the eyewitness' viewing of individuals[;] ... and showing individuals ... sequentially rather than simultaneously to an eyewitness." Wis. Stat. Ann. § 175.50 (2), (5)(a), (b) (2008). West Virginia legislation addresses various aspects of identification procedures and creates "a task force to study and identify best practices for eyewitness identification." W. Va. Code § 62-1E-2 (c) (2008). Reforms legislated in North Carolina are among the most comprehensive. N.C.G.S. § 15A-284.52 (2008) provides:

(a) Definitions.—The following definitions apply in this Article:
(1) Eyewitness.—A person whose identification by sight of another person may be relevant in a criminal proceeding.
(2) Filler.—A person or a photograph of a person who is not suspected of an offense and is included in a lineup.
(3) Independent administrator.—A lineup administrator who is not participating in the investigation of the criminal offense and is unaware of which person in the lineup is the suspect.
(4) Lineup.—A photo lineup or live lineup.
(5) Lineup administrator.—The person who conducts a lineup.
(6) Live lineup.—A procedure in which a group of people is displayed to an eyewitness for the purpose of determining if the eyewitness is able to identify the perpetrator of a crime.
(7) Photo lineup.—A procedure in which an array of photographs is displayed to an eyewitness for the purpose of determining if the eyewitness is able to identify the perpetrator of a crime.
(b) Eyewitness Identification Procedures.—Lineups conducted by State, county, and other local law enforcement officers shall meet all of the following requirements:
(1) A lineup shall be conducted by an independent administrator or by an alternative method as provided by subsection (c) of this section.
(2) Individuals or photos shall be presented to witnesses sequentially, with each individual or photo presented to the witness separately, in a previously determined order, and removed after it is viewed before the next individual or photo is presented.
(3) Before a lineup, the eyewitness shall be instructed that:
a. The perpetrator might or might not be presented in the lineup,

b. The lineup administrator does not know the suspect's identity,
c. The eyewitness should not feel compelled to make an identification,
d. It is as important to exclude innocent persons as it is to identify the perpetrator, and
e. The investigation will continue whether or not an identification is made.

The eyewitness shall acknowledge the receipt of the instructions in writing. If the eyewitness refuses to sign, the lineup administrator shall note the refusal of the eyewitness to sign the acknowledgement and shall also sign the acknowledgement.

(4) In a photo lineup, the photograph of the suspect shall be contemporary and, to the extent practicable, shall resemble the suspect's appearance at the time of the offense.

(5) The lineup shall be composed so that the fillers generally resemble the eyewitness's description of the perpetrator, while ensuring that the suspect does not unduly stand out from the fillers. In addition:

a. All fillers selected shall resemble, as much as practicable, the eyewitness's description of the perpetrator in significant features, including any unique or unusual features.
b. At least five fillers shall be included in a photo lineup, in addition to the suspect.
c. At least five fillers shall be included in a live lineup, in addition to the suspect.
d. If the eyewitness has previously viewed a photo lineup or live lineup in connection with the identification of another person suspected of involvement in the offense, the fillers in the lineup in which the current suspect participates shall be different from the fillers used in any prior lineups.

(6) If there are multiple eyewitnesses, the suspect shall be placed in a different position in the lineup or photo array for each eyewitness.

(7) In a lineup, no writings or information concerning any previous arrest, indictment, or conviction of the suspect shall be visible or made known to the eyewitness.

(8) In a live lineup, any identifying actions, such as speech, gestures, or other movements, shall be performed by all lineup participants.

(9) In a live lineup, all lineup participants must be out of view of the eyewitness prior to the lineup.

(10) Only one suspect shall be included in a lineup.

(11) Nothing shall be said to the eyewitness regarding the suspect's position in the lineup or regarding anything that might influence the eyewitness's identification.

(12) The lineup administrator shall seek and document a clear statement from the eyewitness, at the time of the identification and in the eyewitness's own words, as to the eyewitness's confidence level that the person identified in a given lineup is the perpetrator. The lineup administrator shall separate all witnesses in order to discourage witnesses from conferring with one another before or during the procedure. Each witness shall be given instructions regarding the identification procedures without other witnesses present.

(13) If the eyewitness identifies a person as the perpetrator, the eyewitness shall not be provided any information concerning the person before the lineup administrator obtains the eyewitness's confidence statement about the selection. There shall not be anyone present during the live lineup or photographic identification procedures who knows the suspect's identity, except the eyewitness and counsel as required by law.

(14) Unless it is not practical, a video record of live identification procedures shall be made. If a video record is not practical, the reasons shall be documented, and an audio record shall be made. If neither a video nor audio record are practical, the reasons shall be documented, and the lineup administrator shall make a written record of the lineup.

(15) Whether video, audio, or in writing, the record shall include all of the following information:

a. All identification and nonidentification results obtained during the identification procedure, signed by the eyewitness, including the eyewitness's confidence statement. If the eyewitness refuses to sign, the lineup administrator shall note the refusal of the eyewitness to sign the results and shall also sign the notation.
b. The names of all persons present at the lineup.
c. The date, time, and location of the lineup.
d. The words used by the eyewitness in any identification, including words that describe the eyewitness's certainty of identification.

e. Whether it was a photo lineup or live lineup and how many photos or individuals were presented in the lineup.

f. The sources of all photographs or persons used.

g. In a photo lineup, the photographs themselves.

h. In a live lineup, a photo or other visual recording of the lineup that includes all persons who participated in the lineup.

(c) Alternative Methods for Identification if Independent Administrator Is Not Used.—In lieu of using an independent administrator, a photo lineup eyewitness identification procedure may be conducted using an alternative method specified and approved by the North Carolina Criminal Justice Education and Training Standards Commission. Any alternative method shall be carefully structured to achieve neutral administration and to prevent the administrator from knowing which photograph is being presented to the eyewitness during the identification procedure. Alternative methods may include any of the following:

(1) Automated computer programs that can automatically administer the photo lineup directly to an eyewitness and prevent the administrator from seeing which photo the witness is viewing until after the procedure is completed.

(2) A procedure in which photographs are placed in folders, randomly numbered, and shuffled and then presented to an eyewitness such that the administrator cannot see or track which photograph is being presented to the witness until after the procedure is completed.

(3) Any other procedures that achieve neutral administration.

(d) Remedies.—All of the following shall be available as consequences of compliance or noncompliance with the requirements of this section:

(1) Failure to comply with any of the requirements of this section shall be considered by the court in adjudicating motions to suppress eyewitness identification.

(2) Failure to comply with any of the requirements of this section shall be admissible in support of claims of eyewitness misidentification, as long as such evidence is otherwise admissible.

(3) When evidence of compliance or noncompliance with the requirements of this section has been presented at trial, the jury shall be instructed that it may consider credible evidence of compliance or noncompliance to determine the reliability of eyewitness identification.

2. State Court Developments

In *Manson v. Brathwaite,* the Supreme Court declined to require the automatic suppression of unnecessarily suggestive out-of-court identifications, opting instead to allow identification testimony unless found to be unreliable under a totality of the circumstances test. Does this approach strike the appropriate balance between deterring the police from using unnecessarily suggestive procedures and admitting identification testimony that satisfies a minimum reliability threshold? In the following case, the New Jersey Supreme Court was asked to depart from the *Brathwaite* framework in favor of a *per se* rule of exclusion of identification testimony rooted in unnecessarily suggestive show-ups.

State v. Herrera

902 A.2d 177 (N.J. 2006)

Justice WALLACE, JR. delivered the opinion of the Court.

... On February 26, 2002, Benjamin Valentin, a sixty-three-year-old private security guard, was assigned to work the 4:00 p.m. to 12:00 a.m. shift in a Hoboken housing complex. He had been working in that area for approximately one month. At the conclusion of his shift, Valentin entered his car and drove to the exit to wait for traffic to pass. While stopped, Valentin observed a man, later identified as defendant Carmelo Herrera, approach on his bicycle before stopping near the front of Valentin's car and yelling something. Valentin did not hear what defendant said to him and lowered his window. Defendant walked to the window and asked Valentin for five dollars. When Valentin replied that he had no money, defendant punched him twice, once in the face and once on the back of the neck, knocking Valentin unconscious. When Valentin regained consciousness, his car was missing and he was bleeding. He walked to a nearby security booth and called the police.

Officer James Miller of the Hoboken Police Department arrived at the scene a short while later. Valentin related the incident and described his assailant as a Hispanic male, about 5'7", with a husky build, and a scar on his face, who was wearing something white and red.[1] Valentin was taken to St. Mary's hospital in Hoboken for treatment.

Meanwhile, Officer Joseph Carr of the Harrison Police Department was called to an accident scene shortly after 1:00 a.m. He observed a damaged vehicle in the roadway with the front passenger side tire missing. A man, later identified as defendant, was standing in front of the vehicle. Because defendant appeared intoxicated, Officer Carr arrested and transported him to the police station to administer a breathalyzer test. A search of his person revealed four black belt keepers, which are used by police or security personnel to secure their belts to gun holsters. While preparing his report, Officer Carr received information that the damaged vehicle was stolen from Hoboken.

After the Hoboken police were informed that Valentin's car had been recovered, Lieutenant Edward Mecka contacted the Hudson County Prosecutor's Office to request a "showup" between the victim and the person found with the victim's car. Following that conversation, Lieutenant Mecka and Detective Padilla traveled to St. Mary's Hospital where they informed Valentin of the situation and asked him to go to the police station to identify the man who attacked him. Lieutenant Mecka transported Valentin to the station, where, on arrival, Lieutenant Mecka learned that defendant had been taken to West Hudson Hospital, so the Lieutenant drove Valentin there. As soon as Valentin entered the emergency room of the hospital, he looked around and identified defendant, who was sitting on a hospital bed about six feet away, as the man who had attacked him. The only other persons in the emergency room were two police officers and nurses.

Defendant was indicted for first-degree carjacking, and third-degree receiving stolen property. Prior to trial, he moved to suppress Valentin's out-of-court identification.... The trial court found that Valentin had seen defendant in the neighborhood prior to the incident and the police did not cause Valentin to misidentify or identify defendant. The court concluded that the out-of-court identification was admissible....

At trial, the jury found defendant guilty of both counts....

II.

... [D]efendant ... urges that because showup identifications are by their nature suggestive and more likely to yield false identifications compared to properly conducted lineups and photo arrays, they should be admissible only when the showup is necessary. That is, showup identification evidence should be admitted only if exigent circumstances that require immediate identification are present. Under that approach, defendant argues that a showup conducted without exigent circumstances would be inadmissible regardless of any indication of reliability. Applying that standard here, defendant concludes that the showup identification testimony should be excluded because of the absence of exigent circumstances to justify the showup....

... In support of that approach, defendant urges that the fallibility of eyewitness identifications cannot be ignored and that current studies of post-conviction DNA exonerations show that a large majority of those wrongful convictions involved eyewitness error....

Preliminarily, we note that at least three states have deviated from the United States Supreme Court's precedent on the admission of eyewitness showup identification.... *People v. Adams,* 423 N.E.2d 379 (N.Y. 1981) ... ; *Commonwealth v. Johnson,* 650 N.E.2d 1257 (Mass. 1995) ... ; *State v. Dubose,* 699 N.W.2d 582 (Wis. 2005)....

We have no reason to doubt that if defendant had raised these arguments before the trial court

1. At trial Officer Miller testified that Valentin described defendant as a "Hispanic male about five-seven in height, wearing blue jeans, white sneakers, black jacket with red lettering, and he had a short style cut black hair." On cross-examination, Officer Miller stated the "red lettering" was not referenced in his report, but he recalled Valentin saying red lettering.

and submitted the current research in support of his request for a new standard for determining the admissibility of showup identification, a different record would have been made.... In the absence of such a record, and in light of our consistent application of federal constitutional precedent in deciding the admissibility of identification evidence, we decline to adopt a new standard under our state constitution.

IV.

We turn now to defendant's alternative argument that the victim's out-of-court identification was both impermissibly suggestive and lacked reliability....

V.

... We start with the commonsense notion that one-on-one showups are inherently suggestive. Those showups by definition are suggestive because the victim can only choose from one person, and, generally, that person is in police custody....

In the present case, during the pretrial hearing, Valentin testified that while he was being treated at the hospital, a police officer told him they had located his car and that they would take him "to Harrison to identify the person." On cross-examination, Valentin agreed that he told the grand jury the police had said "we found your car, we located your car with somebody in it, we want you to come with us to identify the person." Valentin also testified that while he was at the police station, an officer told him that the individual was now in the hospital and that they would take him to "the hospital to identify [the man]." In addition, Lieutenant Mecka testified that he informed Valentin "that his vehicle was recovered, ... there was an occupant, and that we were going to go out there to look, let him look at the occupant."

We conclude that in combination with the suggestiveness inherent in a showup, the added comments by the police rendered the showup procedures in the out-of-court identification of defendant impermissibly suggestive. Those comments made by the police to the victim were inappropriate because they may have influenced the victim to develop a firmer resolve to identify someone he might otherwise have been uncertain was the culprit.

We turn now to determine whether the impermissibly suggestive showup procedure was nevertheless sufficiently reliable to warrant the admissibility of the identification by the victim. We must consider the totality of the circumstances surrounding the identification procedure. Moreover, we have emphasized that "the factors listed in *Manson* [*v. Brathwaite,* 432 U.S. 98 (1977)] must be weighed against the corrupting effect of the suggestive procedure." The *Manson* factors are "the opportunity of the witness to view the criminal at the time of the crime, the witness's degree of attention, the accuracy of his prior description of the criminal, the level of certainty demonstrated at the confrontation, and the time between the crime and the confrontation." ...

Weighing the above factors in favor of reliability against the corrupting effects of the impermissibly suggestive procedure, we are satisfied that the identification procedure was reliable and did not result in a substantial likelihood of misidentification. In particular, the evidence that Valentin had seen defendant on a daily basis in the month prior to the incident is strong evidence in support of reliability of Valentin's identification of defendant. Based on the totality of the circumstances, we conclude that the trial court properly admitted Valentin's out-of-court identification of defendant.

VI.

Lastly, we note that other jurisdictions have expanded upon and refined the *Manson* factors in evaluating reliability. For example, the Utah Supreme Court replaced the *Manson* factor of "the level of certainty demonstrated by the witness at the confrontation" with "whether the witness's identification was made spontaneously and remained consistent thereafter, or whether it was the product of suggestion." *State v. Ramirez,* 817 P.2d 774, 781 (1991). That court also considered "the nature of the event being observed and the likelihood that the witness would perceive, remember and relate it correctly." *Ibid.* Under the latter factor, the Utah court included "whether the event was an ordinary one in the mind of the observer during the time it was observed, and whether the race of the actor was the same as the observer's." *Ibid.*

In *State v. Cromedy,* 727 A.2d 457 (N.J. 1999), we required a cross-racial identification jury charge and relied in part on the Utah Supreme Court's view expressed in *State v. Long,* 721 P.2d 483 (1986). Subsequently, our model jury charge was amended to include a cross-racial identification provision when appropriate.

To be sure, our model jury charge on out-of-court identification instructs the jury to consider "[a]ny other factor based on the evidence or lack of evidence in the case which you consider relevant to your determination whether the out-of-court identification was reliable." *Model Jury Charges (Criminal),* "Out-of-Court Identification" (1999). Nevertheless, we note that the charge on identification has not been amended since 1999. Some members of the Court agree with the Utah approach that the jury charge on identification should expressly address whether the identification was the product of suggestion. Accordingly, we request that the Criminal Practice Committee and the Model Jury Charge Committee consider whether our charge on identification should expressly include a reference to suggestibility, as well as any other factor the Committees deem appropriate.

VII.

The judgment of the Appellate Division is affirmed.

Justice ALBIN, dissenting.

Misidentification is the single greatest source of error leading to wrongful convictions in this country. In recent years, capital convictions have been overturned in a number of jurisdictions because DNA evidence has irrefutably established that the defendants condemned to death were wrongly convicted based on mistaken identification testimony. Fair identification procedures cannot fully ensure that mistaken identifications will not occur, for any ultimate judgment that relies on human perception and memory is fraught with the potential for error. Highly suggestive identification procedures, however, exponentially increase the possibility of misidentifications and unjust convictions....

Under the present constitutional standard followed by the majority, a suggestive identification procedure, however unnecessary, will not lead to the exclusion of an identification if a court finds the identification otherwise reliable. To minimize the number of wrongful convictions in our system of justice, the time has come for this Court to set new standards that prohibit highly suggestive identification procedures, such as the showing of a single suspect to a witness, when they are unnecessary —that is, when they are not warranted by any exigency. Nevertheless, even under current law, the identification of defendant should have been excluded because the showup procedure was so impermissibly suggestive as to give rise to a very substantial likelihood of irreparable misidentification. I therefore respectfully dissent....

II.

I agree with the majority that the identification procedures were impermissibly suggestive. I disagree with the majority's conclusion that the suggestive identification procedures did not give rise to a very substantial likelihood of irreparable misidentification. First, Herrera was under arrest at the hospital. Because he was not about to be released and the police had photographs of him which could have been placed in an array and shown to Valentin, there was no need for a showup. Second, it was inexcusable for the police to tell Valentin that the suspect he would be shown was found in his car.... The subliminal message conveyed by the police was, "We found the man who attacked you." ... It is difficult to imagine a more unnecessarily suggestive identification procedure, a procedure more likely to fatally distort the memory of a witness.

Under those circumstances, whatever certainty Valentin expressed in identifying Herrera is suspect. It bears mentioning that whether a witness makes a correct identification or a mistaken identification, the witness invariably is certain about his or her selection.[4] In light of the impermissibly suggestive techniques, it is impossible to credit the reliability of the identification in this case. Valentin caught only a brief glimpse of his attacker, he was knocked unconscious, and he gave a description of his attacker that did not conform in significant ways to the appearance or dress of Herrera. Moreover, only after Valentin was told that the person he would be shown was found in his car did he say that he knew his assailant.

III.

...

A.

Commonsense and a multitude of social science studies tell us that "the one-person 'showup,' in which the eyewitness confronts a single

4. *See, e.g.,* Elizabeth F. Loftus & James M. Doyle, *Eyewitness Testimony: Civil and Criminal* 141 (3d ed. 1997) ("Research suggests that witness certainty sometimes has little or no correlation with accuracy."); 2 Wayne R. LaFave et al., *Criminal Procedure* § 7.4(c), at 675 (2d ed. 1999) ("The level of certainty demonstrated at the confrontation by the witness ... is not a valid indicator of the accuracy of the recollection." (internal quotation marks omitted)).

suspect, is particularly conducive to misidentifications." Charles A. Pulaski, *Neil v. Biggers: The Supreme Court Dismantles the Wade Trilogy's Due Process Protection,* 26 *Stan. L.Rev.* 1097, 1104 (1974)....

Despite the widespread condemnation of the unnecessary use of showups, the police continue to employ the technique in unwarranted circumstances....

In light of the increased likelihood of misidentifications by the use of showups, this Court should not be timid about barring that highly suggestive procedure in circumstances when its use is not warranted....

If a suspect has been in custody for days and a photographic or in-person lineup is feasible, it is inexcusable for the police to use a procedure pregnant with the possibility of error. On the other hand, the showup still has a place in appropriate cases, as evidenced by the facts in *Stovall v. Denno....*

B.

To a person whose fate depends on the accuracy of an identification, it is fundamentally unfair for the police to unnecessarily employ a technique that maximizes the potential for error....

It is time for this Court to announce that the use of unnecessarily suggestive identification procedures violates the due process guarantees of Article I, Paragraph 1 of the New Jersey Constitution. By doing so, we will be in step with a number of other states that have rejected the United States Supreme Court's approach and relied on their own state constitutions to ensure that unnecessarily suggestive identification procedures are not used by the police. *See Commonwealth v. Botelho,* 343 *N.E.*2d 876, 880 (Mass. 1976) (barring prosecution from introducing "confrontation that was unnecessarily suggestive"); *State v. Leclair,* 385 *A.*2d 831, 833 (N.H. 1978) (finding that "[t]here is no legitimate reason for the police to use unnecessarily suggestive identification procedures" and condemning use of one-man showups "absent exigent circumstances"); *People v. Riley,* 517 *N.E.*2d 520, 523 (N.Y. 1987) (declaring showups "permissible if exigent circumstances require immediate identification, or if the suspects are captured at or near the crime scene and can be viewed by the witness immediately" (citation omitted)); *State v. Dubose,* 699 *N.W.*2d 582, 584 (Wis. 2005) (holding that "evidence obtained from [an out-of-court] showup will not be admissible unless, based on the totality of the circumstances, the showup was necessary"). In one form or another, those jurisdictions all have found that by overly focusing on the reliability of the identification itself, the federal approach has inadequately protected against "unnecessarily suggestive identification procedures, ... mistaken identifications and, ultimately, wrongful convictions."

Those jurisdictions recognize what Justices Marshall and Brennan understood in *Manson v. Brathwaite*:

> [I]mpermissibly suggestive identifications are not merely worthless law enforcement tools. They pose a grave threat to society at large in a more direct way than most governmental disobedience of the law. For if the police and the public erroneously conclude, on the basis of an unnecessarily suggestive confrontation, that the right man has been caught and convicted, the real outlaw must still remain at large. Law enforcement has failed in its primary function and has left society unprotected from the depredations of an active criminal.
>
> [432 *U.S.* at 127 (Marshall, J., dissenting).]

Like those jurisdictions, I would preclude the introduction into evidence of an identification that is the product of an unnecessarily suggestive identification procedure. *See id.* at 127 ("[E]xclusion both protects the integrity of the truth-seeking function of the trial and discourages police use of needlessly inaccurate and ineffective investigatory methods.")....

V.

I ... would hold that Article I, Paragraph 1 of our State Constitution does not allow for the admission into evidence of identifications made through unnecessarily suggestive procedures. For those reasons, I respectfully dissent.

Justice LONG joins in this opinion.

Notes and Questions

1. In 2001, the New Jersey Attorney General distributed a set of "General Guidelines for Preparing and Conducting Photo and Live Lineup Identification Procedures" to all state law enforcement officers. Those Guidelines are reproduced as an Appendix in *State*

v. Herrera, 902 A.2d 177, 187–194 (N.J. 2006).[13] Although non-binding, they prescribe numerous procedures derived from social science studies that are designed to enhance the reliability of identifications, including double-blind administration, an instruction to the witness that the perpetrator may or may not be present, that identifications be conducted sequentially rather than simultaneously, that the witness's degree of certainty should be recorded when an identification is made, and many others. In June 2010, a Special Master appointed by the New Jersey Supreme Court issued a lengthy report addressing eyewitness identification issues. Among other recommendations, the report urged rejection of the *Brathwaite* test and included factors, and proposed that the prosecution be required to bear the burden of establishing the reliability of identification testimony at a pretrial hearing.[14] The report was prepared by order of the New Jersey Supreme Court in *State v. Henderson*, 2009 WL 510409 (N.J. 2009), *on appeal from* 937 A.2d 988 (N.J. Super. 2008), a pending case involving a challenge to the admissibility of eyewitness identification testimony. The eventual state high court decision in *Henderson* has the potential to result in significant reforms in the eyewitness identification procedures used in New Jersey.

2. In *Commonwealth v. Johnson*, 650 N.E.2d 1257 (Mass. 1995), the Massachusetts Supreme Judicial Court, relying on state constitutional grounds, rejected the *Brathwaite* approach in favor of a *per se* rule excluding testimony of an eyewitness's out-of-court identification of the defendant following unnecessarily suggestive procedures.

[S]tudies conducted by psychologists and legal researchers since *Brathwaite* have confirmed that eyewitness testimony is often hopelessly unreliable. Permitting the admission of an identification obtained through unnecessarily suggestive procedures can only serve to exacerbate this problem. Furthermore, contrary to the *Brathwaite* Court's unsubstantiated claim, the per se approach does not keep relevant and reliable identification evidence from the jury. Subsequent identifications shown to come from a source independent of the suggestive identification remain admissible under the per se approach. The per se approach excludes only the unnecessarily suggestive identification and subsequent tainted identifications.... If, for example, the prosecution is able to demonstrate that the witness got a good look at his assailant and his initial description matches a description of the defendant, the court may conclude that there was an independent source and may admit evidence of any identification subsequent to the unnecessarily suggestive one ...

[I]t appears clear to us that the reliability test does little or nothing to discourage police from using suggestive identification procedures....

[In *People v. Adams*, 53 N.Y.2d 241, 251, 440 N.Y.S.2d 902, 423 N.E.2d 379 (1981), the New York Court of Appeals explained]: "A reliable determination of guilt or innocence is the essence of a criminal trial. A defendant's right to due process would be only theoretical if it did not encompass the need to establish rules to accomplish that end. Permitting the prosecutor to introduce evidence of a suggestive pretrial identification can only increase the risks of convicting the innocent in cases where it has the desired effect of contributing to a conviction. In most instances, where the witness is able to make an untainted identification in court, proof of the suggestive showup only serves to bolster the People's case. However, if the jury finds the in-court identification not entirely convincing it should not be permitted to resolve its doubts by relying on the fact that the witness had identified the defendant on a prior occasion if that identification was made under inherently suggestive circumstances. Similarly, if the witness is unable to identify the defendant at trial the defendant's conviction should not rest solely upon evidence of a pretrial identification made under circumstances which were likely to produce an unreliable result."

... [T]he Court of Appeals concluded: "Excluding evidence of a suggestive showup does not deprive the prosecutor of reliable evidence of guilt. The witness would still be permitted to identify the defendant in court if that identification is based on an independent source." *Id.*...

.... Only a rule of per se exclusion can ensure the continued protection against the danger of mistaken identification and wrongful convictions. Accordingly, we reject *Brathwaite*....

3. In *People v. Adams,* 423 N.E.2d 379 (N.Y. 1981), cited in *Commonwealth v. Johnson, supra,* the New York Court of Appeals departed from *Brathwaite* in favor of a rule of automatic exclusion of eyewitness testimony about out-of-court identifications following unnecessarily suggestive procedures. The Wisconsin Supreme Court has done the same, in *State v. Dubose,* 699 N.W.2d 582 (Wis. 2005).

We conclude that evidence obtained from an out-of-court showup is inherently suggestive and will not be admissible unless, based on the totality of the circumstances, the procedure was necessary. A showup will not be necessary ... unless the police lacked probable cause to make an arrest or, as a result of other exigent circumstances, could not have conducted a lineup or photo array.

In the following case, the Alaska Court of Appeals gives extensive consideration to social science research findings in considering a challenge to eyewitness identification testimony, and discusses the highly publicized case of Ronald Cotton, who was twice convicted of rape in North Carolina based on the victim's erroneous identification of him. Following his exoneration, Cotton and Jennifer Thompson-Cannino, the woman who had misidentified him, became friends and advocates for reforms of eyewitness identification procedures. Their joint experiences are described in Jennifer Thompson-Cannino, Ronald Cotton & Erin Torneo, *Picking Cotton: Our Memoir of Injustice and Redemption* (New York: St. Martin's Griffin 2009).

Tegoseak v. State

221 P.3d 345 (Alaska App. 2009)

MANNHEIMER, Judge.

[On June 19, 2005, while driving their car in Anchorage, Robert and Michelle Maestas observed a Ford Bronco being driven erratically. Suspecting that the driver was intoxicated, they used their cell phone to call the police and they followed the Bronco until it parked in a lot at Bell's Nursery. While they watched, the Bronco's driver and the front-seat passenger emerged from the vehicle, switched places, and the Bronco then resumed travel on the roads under the control of the new driver. Shortly thereafter, Officer Gerald Asselin of the Anchorage Police stopped the Bronco. He determined that the man driving it, who was wearing a white T-shirt, was Edgar Henry. The front-seat passenger, wearing a black T-shirt, was the defendant Frank Tegoseak. In response to the officer's questioning, Henry volunteered that "he had taken over driving the Bronco after the stop at Bell's nursery because Tegoseak had been driving so poorly that he thought Tegoseak was going to kill them." A subsequent breath test revealed that Tegoseak's blood alcohol content (BAC) was .227 percent, or nearly three times Alaska's BAC limit for intoxication of .10 percent.

[One week later, on June 26, Officer Asselin asked Mr. and Mrs. Maestas to observe photo arrays to see if they could identify the men they had observed in the Bronco. He prepared two separate arrays, each of which included six photos. The first array included a photo of Edgar Henry, in position number 5. The second array included Frank Tegoseak's photo, in position number 5.]

Asselin showed the photo arrays to Mr. and Mrs. Maestas separately. He told them that he would show them two photo arrays, and he asked them to let him know if they "recognize[d] any of those individuals as being involved." When Asselin showed the first array to Mr. and Mrs. Maestas, he reminded them that, if they did not recognize anyone from the first array of six photographs, he had a second set of photographs to show them.

After Michelle Maestas examined the two arrays of photographs, she picked one person from among the twelve photographs as having been in the Bronco—but that person was neither Henry nor Tegoseak.

After Michelle Maestas failed to identify either Henry or Tegoseak, Officer Asselin showed the photographs to Robert Maestas.

When Robert Maestas was shown the first array of six photographs, he selected *three* people from this array as the possible occupants of the Bronco. Maestas told Asselin, "[I]t could have been [number] 1 or 3 that was driving [the Bronco originally], and [number] 5 that was in the passenger seat.... I think [that], between 1 and 3, those two [photographs] kind of look like the driver that we originally pulled up next to."

The three photographs that Maestas selected were of Edgar Henry and two "fillers"—that is, two people whose photographs were included, not because the police suspected that they were connected to this incident, but rather to fill out the six-photograph array.

At this point, that is, after Maestas had apparently identified both the original driver and the original passenger from among the photographs in the first array, Asselin said to Maestas, "Let me try to at least show you [the second array of photographs]; then you can see the entire compilation of photos. So far, you've said [that] 1 and 3 [in the first array] could be the driver." Asselin then showed Maestas the second array of six photographs.

When Maestas looked at the second array of photos, he told Asselin that photograph number 5 in this second array could also potentially be the initial driver of the Bronco (that is, the man who was driving before the driver and passenger switched places in the nursery parking lot). Maestas told Asselin that the man "originally driving the car" was "either [number] 5 in [the second array] or [number] 1 in [the first array]." (... Tegoseak's picture was number 5 in the second photo array.)

Asselin asked Maestas to memorialize his identifications on two different "Photographic Lineup" forms. These forms (one for each of the two arrays) apparently had boxes on them that corresponded to the photographs in the arrays. Asselin asked Maestas to place a check mark on the boxes that corresponded to the photographs he had selected.

On the first of these forms (*i.e.*, the form that corresponded to the first photo array), Maestas stated that he identified photograph number 5 in the first array as the man who began driving the Bronco *after* the car stopped at the nursery. (... [T]his photograph was of Edgar Henry.)

Asselin then handed Maestas the second form (*i.e.*, the form corresponding to the second photo array). Although Maestas had told Asselin that he was uncertain whether the original driver of the Bronco was photograph number 1 from the first array or photograph number 5 from the second array, Asselin directed Maestas to put a check mark in only one box—the box corresponding to photograph number 5 from the second array.

Asselin invited Maestas to add a handwritten notation explaining his uncertainty about the identification. Maestas wrote on the form, "When looking at the photos, both [photograph] # 5 on [the second array] and [photograph] # 1 on [the first array] look similar to the original driver that we ... first [saw]."

However, Officer Asselin added his own separate notation to this form. In the officer's notation, he indicated that Maestas had made an identification from the photographs, and that the person Maestas had identified was Frank Tegoseak ... Maestas signed this form.

This same ambiguity concerning the nature or precision of Maestas's identification is reflected in the testimony given by Asselin and Maestas at the evidentiary hearing.

At the hearing, Asselin testified that he did not remember the exact exchange between himself and Maestas, "but it was clear to [him], based upon the [conversation], that [Maestas] identified [photograph] number 5 [in the second array] as being ... the person who was originally driving the vehicle." Asselin conceded that, while he was showing the photographs to Maestas, "there was some conversation ... where [Maestas] would say, 'Well, [photograph] number 1 [in the first array] looks very similar', but [Maestas] came back to it being [photograph] number 5 [in the second array]."

When Maestas testified at the evidentiary hearing, he acknowledged that he was hesitant to positively identify either photograph 1 from the first array or photograph 5 from the second array "because the two photos look similar, ... and [because it was] a week [after the incident]." When Maestas was asked whether he had made a "positive identification", he responded, "I wouldn't say it was 100 percent positive; no."

After hearing this testimony, and after listening to Officer Asselin's tape recording of the photo lineup procedure, Superior Court Judge Michael L. Wolverton concluded that the photo lineup procedure was not unduly suggestive.

In particular, Judge Wolverton found that the "filler" photographs were well-selected (in the sense that the people depicted in these filler photographs were visually similar to the two suspects).

The judge suggested that this fact (the good selection of fillers) was potentially the explanation for Robert and Michelle Maestas's difficulty in selecting Henry and Tegoseak from among the photographs.

Judge Wolverton also concluded that there was nothing wrong in Officer Asselin's act of drawing Robert Maestas's attention to the second array after Maestas had already declared that the first array contained photographs of both suspects. The judge found that Asselin was not trying to suggest that Maestas had chosen prematurely, or to suggest that the second array contained a photograph of at least one of the suspects. Rather, Judge Wolverton found that Asselin was simply "trying to explain" the procedure (*i.e.,* the need to examine both arrays) and to request that Maestas withhold his final judgement until he had seen all twelve of the photographs.

Judge Wolverton also concluded that, given the circumstances of the case, there was essentially no possibility of a misidentification. The judge remarked that "this might [have been] a different situation if [the occupants of the Bronco] had not been followed and [immediately arrested]—almost like a hand-off to the police- [but] we know who was in the vehicle [when] it was stopped, [and the photo lineup] was [merely] a determination as to ... who was driving when" —a determination that was made "easier ... because one [man] was wearing a white shirt and [the other] was wearing a black shirt." ...

[Following a jury trial, at which Robert Maestas's identification testimony was admitted over objection, Tegoseak was convicted of felony driving under the influence and driving with a suspended license.]

The photographic lineup in this case does not appear to be overtly suggestive. As Judge Wolverton noted when he denied Tegoseak's suppression motion, the ten filler photographs are quite similar to the two suspects' photographs in facial characteristics and hair style....

But even though a photographic lineup may not be overtly suggestive, the procedure by which the photographs are selected, the procedure by which a photo lineup is displayed to a witness, and the procedure by which the witness's identification is elicited, can engender suggestiveness —even when this is not the intention of the officer conducting the lineup.

Medical researchers have long recognized the phenomenon that testers influence the persons they are testing. Even though one might think that a test subject's physical reaction to an experimental drug or therapy would remain the same regardless of the mental attitude or desires of the researchers, the truth is that the researchers' expectations regarding the experiment *do* make a difference to the result.

One well-known problem is the "placebo effect": the recognized phenomenon that when a person *believes* that they are receiving an effective drug or therapy, their body will physically react in accordance with their belief—even though the substance or treatment they are receiving would ordinarily do nothing to alleviate their condition.

But the placebo effect is compounded by another difficulty known as the "Clever Hans effect." This is the problem that researchers, because of their knowledge of the experiment and their expectations concerning the outcome, can unintentionally influence the responses of the test subjects by unconscious signaling, or by small differences in how they interact with test subjects who are receiving the real drug or therapy as opposed to a placebo.[7]

7. In 1891, William von Osten began displaying his horse, "Clever Hans," to the public. Hans would answer questions by tapping his hoof—either by tapping out a number, or by tapping out the letters of the alphabet that corresponded to the answer (with one tap equaling "A," two taps equaling "B," and so on). Hans could apparently perform mathematical calculations, tell time, identify musical intervals, and name people.

Von Osten did not intend to trick people. He believed that animals possessed an intelligence equal to that of humans—and, in his quest to prove this, he attempted to teach many animals how to do simple calculations. However, Clever Hans was the only animal who showed any ability.

The first scientific test of Hans's ability was conducted in 1904 by Professor Carl Stumpf. Stumpf looked for evidence of cheating or trickery to explain Hans's ability, but he found none, and he subsequently endorsed Hans's abilities as genuine. Following Professor Stumpf's endorsement, Clever Hans became a sensation, and people flocked to see him.

In 1907, a group of thirteen scientists (the "Hans Commission") re-tested Clever Hans. Their test is now recognized as a classic experiment in psychology.

In the late 1980s (that is, approximately ten years after the Supreme Court issued its decision in [*Manson v. Brathwaite*, 432 U.S. 98 (1977)], Professor Gary L. Wells of Iowa State University noted that photographic lineups could be affected by these same difficulties that the police officers who conducted photographic lineups could unwittingly be influencing the witnesses they were interviewing. Professor Wells accordingly proposed that photo lineups (like medical trials) should be conducted using a double-blind procedure. In other words, (1) the lineup should be conducted by an officer who does not know which photograph in the lineup represents the suspect and which photographs are fillers, and (2) because witnesses will naturally assume that any photo lineup will contain a photograph of the person whom the police suspect, the witness must affirmatively be told that the lineup may not contain a photograph of the perpetrator.

In his article, "The Double-Blind Lineup: General Comments and Observations" (2008),[9] Professor Wells notes that police officers can inadvertently (and often unconsciously) influence witnesses by such seemingly innocuous comments as, "I noticed you paused on photograph number 3." Or, when a witness hesitates between two or three photographs, the officer might say to the witness, "Tell me about photograph 2"—directing the witness's attention to the photograph that the officer knows is the suspect, rather than to one of the fillers. Or, when the witness has picked a filler, the officer might ask, "Is there any other photograph that stands out to you?"—a question that obviously would not be asked if the witness had selected the suspect.

According to Professor Wells, there are currently close to 200 cases in which (1) the police identified a person as the suspected perpetrator of a crime, (2) the suspect was included in a photographic or live lineup, (3) the witness who viewed the lineup identified the suspect as the perpetrator, (4) the suspect was convicted, but (5) post-trial DNA testing proved that the suspect was innocent.

Because there was no evidence of connivance or cheating, the scientists began with the assumption that Hans did have an ability of some kind, and they designed their experiment to find out what this ability was.

Hans was tested inside a large tent to avoid outside distractions, such as spectators. The experiment was designed in the following way:

- A large number of questions were used, to eliminate the effects of chance;
- Different people posed these questions, in case Hans was picking up signals from his owner, von Osten;
- The questioners sometimes knew the answers to the questions they were asking, but other times they did not;
- The questioners would stand at different distances from Hans during different trials; and
- Some trials were run with Hans blinkered.

The first important finding was that Clever Hans needed to have visual contact with the questioner in order to answer correctly. The farther away the questioner stood, the less accurate Hans became. And when Hans's peripheral vision was obstructed by blinkers, his ability to answer was diminished even further.

The other major finding was that Hans could only answer a question correctly if the questioner also knew the answer to the question. When the questioner did not know the answer to the question, Hans could not give the answer.

These facts—that Hans could only answer a question correctly if it was posed by a questioner who knew the answer, and only if Hans could see the questioner-led the psychologists to perceive that Hans was not using intelligence to work out the answers; rather, he was responding to visual cues given unwittingly by the questioner. These unwitting visual cues took the form of increases or decreases in the tension of the questioner's body, changes in the questioner's facial expression, and other involuntary movements that the questioner would make when Hans reached the right answer.

The results of the experiment with Clever Hans led the scientists to the key insight that an animal's—or a person's—behavior can be influenced by subtle and unintentional cues given by a questioner or researcher.

This effect—now known as the "Clever Hans effect"—is one of the primary reasons why scientific tests (and, in particular, clinical trials) must be done using a "double-blind" method: a procedure in which neither the questioner/researcher nor the subject being tested knows the nature of the information required or the treatment being administered.

Source: John Jackson, "Clever Hans" (2005), available at: www.skeptics.&1forg.uk/article.php?dir=articles &article=clever-hans.php.

9. Available at: www.psychology.iastate.edu/%25glwells/homepage.htm, through the link "Meet the double-blind lineup."

One of these cases recently received national publicity through the publication of the book, *Picking Cotton*,[10] and the related story that aired in March 2009 on the CBS television news show "60 Minutes."[11]

As described in the 60 Minutes story, in the summer of 1984, a man broke into Jennifer Thompson's apartment and raped her at knifepoint. During the attack, Thompson forced herself to stay alert and study this man carefully—his physical characteristics, his voice, his accent—so that, if she survived, she could make sure that he was convicted and sentenced to prison. After about half an hour, Thompson tricked the rapist into letting her get up to fix him a drink; she then took the opportunity to escape from her apartment through the back door.

Police Detective Mike Gauldin interviewed Thompson at the hospital, and he worked with Thompson to assemble a composite sketch of the rapist. After the sketch was broadcast, the police started to receive tips about the crime. One of these tips was about a young man named Ronald Cotton. Cotton worked at a restaurant near Thompson's apartment, and he had a previous conviction for breaking and entering, as well as a juvenile record for sexual assault.

Three days after the rape, Detective Gauldin assembled a six-photograph lineup that contained Cotton's picture, and then he called Thompson to come view the lineup. Thompson studied the photographs for about five minutes, and then she identified Cotton as the man who had raped her.

Thompson subsequently picked Cotton from a live lineup. After Thompson made the live lineup identification, the police informed her that she had picked the same man that she previously selected from the photo lineup. When she heard this, Thompson remembers thinking, "Bingo! I did it right; I did it right."

Later, Thompson identified Cotton again when she testified at his trial. Cotton was convicted and sentenced to life imprisonment plus 50 years.

While in prison, Cotton met a man named Bobby Poole. Poole looked very similar to Cotton; in fact, some of the prison stewards mistook them for each other. Then Cotton heard, from a fellow inmate, that Poole had admitted raping Thompson. Based on this information, Cotton received a new trial.

At the new trial, Cotton's lawyers summoned Bobby Poole to court so that Jennifer Thompson could see him. But when Thompson looked at Poole, she did not recognize him. Indeed, she felt nothing but anger toward Cotton and his attorneys. She remembers thinking, "How dare you question me? How dare you [suggest that I] could possibly have forgotten what my rapist looked like? ... The one person [I] would never forget?"

Cotton was again convicted. This time, he received two life sentences.

Seven years later (ten years after the rape), Cotton watched the O.J. Simpson trial on television and learned about DNA. He convinced his lawyer to investigate the possibility of DNA testing. By luck, the Birmingham, North Carolina police still had the rape kit, and the kit contained enough viable sperm to conduct a DNA test. The result: Bobby Poole was indeed the rapist—and Ronald Cotton was innocent.

For people who care about our justice system, this is a bittersweet tale. A man spent a decade in prison for a crime he did not commit—and yet he was finally exonerated, and he has even become reconciled with the woman whose testimony sent him to prison. Cotton and Thompson are now friends; they co-authored the book *Picking Cotton,* which describes the case, and they are prominent advocates of reform in police identification practices.

But for the judges and lawyers who administer and actively participate in the criminal justice system, this story has a more fundamental and disquieting aspect. What happened in Ronald Cotton's case lends anecdotal support to the scientific research that casts doubt on the validity of the *Brathwaite* method for assessing the reliability of eyewitness identifications....

In *Brathwaite,* the Supreme Court rejected a rule of *per se* suppression and instead held that the witness's identification would be admissible if the State could demonstrate the reliability of the identification under the "totality of the cir-

10. Jennifer Thompson-Cannino & Ronald Cotton, with Erin Torneo, *Picking Cotton: Our Memoir of Injustice and Redemption* (St. Martin's Press, 2009).

11. Both the video and the text of the 60 Minutes story, "Picking Cotton" (originally aired in March 2009) are available at: www.cbsnews.com/stories/2009/03/06/60minutes/main4848039.shtml.

cumstances." The Supreme Court defined this phrase, "totality of the circumstances," as encompassing the five factors....

- the witness's opportunity to view the perpetrator during the crime,
- the witness's degree of attention,
- the accuracy of any prior description given by the witness,
- the witness's level of certainty when making the identification, and
- the length of time between the crime and the witness's identification.

With the *Brathwaite* reliability test in mind, we now return to the facts of the Ronald Cotton case.

One of the crucial events in that case occurred after Bobby Poole was finally identified as a suspect in the case and Ronald Cotton was granted a second trial. At that second trial, Poole was summoned to court so that Jennifer Thompson would have the opportunity to view Cotton and Poole together.

... Thompson spent half an hour in Poole's presence during the rape. During that half hour, Thompson consciously paid attention to, and made a point of remembering, Poole's physical features and the nuances of his voice and speech, so that she could be sure to identify him later. Nevertheless, when Thompson saw the two men together in court, she did not recognize Poole as her attacker. Indeed, even though the two men apparently had similar physical features, Thompson did not even experience any uncertainty. She reaffirmed that Cotton was the rapist—and Cotton was convicted again.

Years later, when the DNA test results finally proved Cotton's innocence, Detective Gauldin (the detective who conducted the photo lineup) was the one who went to tell Thompson that Poole was the rapist and that Cotton was innocent. Thompson's reaction was, "No, that can't be true; it's not possible.... I know Ronald Cotton raped me. There's no question in my mind."

Moreover, even after Thompson knew the truth, her memory of the event remained the same: whenever she thought about the rape, or dreamed about it, it was still Cotton's face that she saw.

This last aspect of the case is particularly troubling: the fact that Thompson's false memory of Cotton as her attacker persisted even after Thompson knew (intellectually) that Cotton was innocent and that Poole had committed the rape. This false memory was clearly the result of the identification procedures employed during the investigation ... But if the five *Brathwaite* factors are applied to this case, it is obvious that a court would have allowed Thompson to testify and identify Cotton as her assailant—even if the court had found that the photo lineup was unnecessarily suggestive.

Thompson had plenty of opportunity (a half an hour) to view the rapist. And during the attack, she consciously devoted her attention to the rapist, so that she would remember his physical characteristics and voice. Shortly after the rape, when Thompson was interviewed at the hospital, she worked with the police to develop a composite drawing of her attacker—a drawing that resembled Ronald Cotton. And when Thompson was shown the photo lineup three days after the rape, she declared she was certain that Cotton was her attacker.

One might conclude that this is simply a rare and unfortunate instance where application of the *Brathwaite* factors would lead a court to admit evidence of a mistaken identification. But there is another, more troubling conclusion that could be drawn: that the *Brathwaite* factors are inadequate to the task of sorting reliable identifications from unreliable identifications.

A photographic lineup is generally conducted in private between a police investigator and a witness. As Professor Wells notes in the recent article he co-authored with Deah S. Quinlivan concerning the validity of the *Brathwaite* factors, when a police investigator conducts a photographic lineup, the investigator interacts directly with the witness: in effect, they have a conversation about the photos.[14] If the police investigator knows which photograph represents the person who is under suspicion, there is a danger that the witness's identification will be influenced by the officer's knowledge and expectations, even though, seemingly, there is nothing suggestive about the procedure:

14. Gary L. Wells & Deah S. Quinlivan, "Suggestive Eyewitness Identification Procedures and the Supreme Court's Reliability Test in Light of Eyewitness Science: Thirty Years Later" [*i.e.*, 30 years after *Brathwaite*], 33 Law and Human Behavior 1–24 (2009).

[When the police investigator knows which photograph is the suspect's photograph, this] creates a situation very similar to one that has been extensively studied by psychological scientists in other contexts in which a tester's knowledge or expectations influence the person being tested in a direction that is consistent with the tester's knowledge or expectations.... There is no presumption that these tester effects are the result of intentional efforts by the tester or that the tester is aware of influencing the person being tested.... [T]he concern here is with the kinds of influences that are unintentional, natural by-products of the [personal] interaction. Wells & Quinlivan at 7–8.

Moreover, the *Brathwaite* decision appears to be premised on the assumption that, despite the suggestiveness of an identification procedure, a witness retains a "true" memory of the event which may be independently sufficient to reliably identify the perpetrator—if the witness had an adequate opportunity to observe the perpetrator, if the witness was paying attention, etc. In effect, the five *Brathwaite* factors are the test that a court uses to determine if the witness is relying on this presumed independent memory rather than on the result suggested by the identification procedure....

But as Professors Wells and Quinlivan point out in their article on *Brathwaite,* "the dominant view among psychological scientists [is] that, once an eyewitness has mistakenly identified someone, that [mis-identified] person 'becomes' the witness' memory[,] and the error will simply repeat itself [in subsequent identifications]."

This observation is vividly corroborated by the facts of the Ronald Cotton case. Even when Jennifer Thompson was confronted with Bobby Poole (the real rapist) in court, she had no recollection of him, and she re-affirmed her identification of Ronald Cotton as her attacker. Indeed, this false memory persisted even after Thompson *knew* that the memory was false: she continued to see Ronald Cotton's face when she thought back to the rape even after she learned that the DNA testing had demonstrated Cotton's innocence.

Moreover, even assuming that a "true" memory exists independently of a witness's exposure to a suggestive identification procedure, there is reason to doubt whether the five *Brathwaite* factors are a valid method for judging whether a witness's testimony reflects that independent memory.

For instance, according to the Wells and Quinlivan article, when a witness is asked to estimate how long they were able to observe the perpetrator of a crime, the witness will often grossly over-estimate the amount of time the perpetrator was in their view—especially if the witness was under stress or anxiety at the time they observed the events. Similarly, a witness will often inaccurately minimize the amount of time that their view of the perpetrator was blocked by another person or a physical obstruction.

Perhaps more troubling are the results of experiments showing that the comments of a police investigator can alter a witness's perception or memory of how long they were able to view the perpetrator, and how good their view was. In a series of experiments, witnesses were given a poor view of a simulated crime, and then they were shown a photo lineup that did *not* include the culprit. The experiment centered on those witnesses who (mistakenly) identified one of the people in the lineup as having committed the crime. The lineup administrator would tell some of these witnesses, "Good; you identified the suspect in this case," while the administrator would make no suggestive remark to the others.

Later, when all of these witnesses were asked, "How good was the view that you had of the culprit?" and "How well could you make out the details of the culprit's face?", the overwhelming majority of witnesses who heard no confirmatory remark conceded that, even though they had made an identification from the lineup, their view was not very good and they could not easily make out the details of the culprit's face. On the other hand, the witnesses who received a confirmatory remark from the lineup administrator had very different perceptions of their own experience. Even though these witnesses had the same poor view of the crime, about 25 percent of them reported that they had a "good" or "excellent" view of the crime, and 20 percent of them declared that they could easily make out the details of the culprit's face.

The results of these experiments suggest that if the evidence in support of the first *Brathwaite* factor—opportunity to view—is based solely on the self-reporting of the witness, then a court would need to know (and try to take account of) what was said to the witness during the identification procedure. In other words, there is reason to believe that this first *Brathwaite* factor is *not* independent of the suggestive identification procedure.

Similarly, many experiments have shown that when a witness receives a confirmatory suggestive remark following their identification of a person in a lineup, this tends to inflate the witness's own perception of how much attention they were paying to the perpetrator of the crime—the second *Brathwaite* factor.

The third *Brathwaite* factor—the witness's degree of certainty in their identification—is obviously crucial to all stages of a criminal investigation. A witness's certainty (or lack of certainty) may influence whether a person is charged at all, or whether the prosecutor takes the case to trial, and if the case goes to trial, how much weight the jury will give to the witness's testimony.

Of course, life provides many instances of people who are certain about something but who are nevertheless mistaken. The question is: is there a valid correlation between a witness's certainty and the correctness of their identification?

Studies have shown that, among witnesses who make an identification (either correct or mistaken) from a lineup, the statistical correlation between the witness's certainty and the correctness of their identification can be as high as 0.41. (Some studies suggest that the correlation is lower.) To put this figure in perspective, the statistical correlation between height and sex in human beings is considerably higher than 0.4. In other words, these studies suggest that you would have much better success in predicting a person's sex if you knew their height than you would have in predicting the accuracy of a witness's identification if you knew the witness's degree of certainty.

Nevertheless, the fact that there is a positive correlation between a witness's certainty and the accuracy of their identification means that a witness's degree of certainty is *some* indication of the accuracy of their identification.

However, as is the case with *Brathwaite* factors one and two, a lineup administrator's confirmatory remark can have a substantial influence on a witness's degree of certainty. In one study, for example, witnesses who mistakenly identified someone from a lineup were later asked whether they had been "positive" or "nearly positive" when they made their identification. Of the witnesses who did not receive a confirmatory remark from the lineup administrator, only 15 percent reported that they had been "positive" or "nearly positive" when they made their selection from the lineup. However, among the witnesses who received a confirmatory remark following their mistaken identification, 50 percent reported that they had been "positive" or "nearly positive" when they made their selection.

As Professors Wells and Quinlivan observe, one crucial aspect of this experiment is that these witnesses were asked *after the fact* to report on their degree of certainty *at the time they made their identification*. In other words, the lineup administrator's suggestive confirmatory remark was not altering the witness's degree of certainty at the time they made their selection from the lineup. Rather, the confirmatory remark was altering the witness's memory—their *recollection* of their degree of certainty at that earlier time.

This finding has potential importance to a judge's evaluation of a witness's testimony—in particular, the witness's self-report of their degree of certainty—at any pre-trial hearing on the *Brathwaite* factors. It suggests that a witness's self-reported degree of certainty is not necessarily trustworthy.

The fourth *Brathwaite* factor—the "accuracy" of the witness's pre-lineup description of the perpetrator—suggests a logical error. One can not know whether a witness's description of the perpetrator is "accurate" unless one knows who the perpetrator is.

As illustrated by the Ronald Cotton case, the fact that a witness may have accurately described the defendant in advance of the lineup, and then selected the defendant's photograph from the lineup, does not prove guilt unless the witness's recollection of the perpetrator is accurate. To conclude that a witness's pre-lineup description was "accurate" (in the sense of describing the true perpetrator of the crime) simply because the witness's description fits the physical characteristics of the defendant is to assume the very fact that needs to be proved.

Instead of the "accuracy" of a witness's pre-lineup description, the fourth *Brathwaite* factor is more properly concerned with the *consistency* between the witness's pre-lineup description of the perpetrator and the physical characteristics of the person whom the witness later selects in the lineup, as well as the *degree* of this consistency (*i.e.*, the amount of detail in the witness's pre-lineup description, and how much of that detail is consistent with physical characteristics of the person whom the witness selected in the lineup).

This fourth *Brathwaite* factor suffers from an underlying analytical weakness. The probative value of this fourth factor—*i.e.*, the consistency between a witness's pre-lineup description of the culprit and the physical characteristics of the person who is later selected in the lineup—hinges in large measure on the assumption that the composition of the lineup has not been influenced by the witness's pre-lineup description of the culprit. This assumption is often false. It is common for the police to rely on the witness's pre-lineup description when they select which photographs to include in a lineup—because the witness's description is often one of the primary clues that the police rely on when they begin to narrow the field of potential suspects.

Moreover, some studies have shown that when witnesses are confronted with a photo lineup, they tend to select the person who looks most like their memory of the culprit, even when none of the photos matches their memory exactly. This is apparently what happened in the Ronald Cotton case.

Even though Detective Gauldin did not expressly tell Thompson that the photo lineup contained a photograph of the person whom the police suspected, Thompson made the assumption that her attacker's photograph was among the six photos displayed to her, and she believed that her job was to identify the correct photograph. She later told "60 Minutes" reporter Leslie Stahl, "I ... remember almost feeling like I was [taking] an SAT [multiple choice] test. You know, where you start narrowing down your choices. You can [immediately] discount A and B, [and then you work on the others]."

What does this mean in terms of *Brathwaite's* fourth factor? Professors Wells and Quinlivan suggest the following hypothetical: The police assemble a photo lineup, and they include a photo of the defendant because the defendant seems to match the witness's description of the perpetrator. The witness views the lineup and identifies the defendant. A judge later rules that the lineup was unnecessarily suggestive because the filler photographs were too dissimilar to the photograph of the defendant. But then, based on the consistency between the witness's pre-lineup description of the culprit and the defendant's physical characteristics, the judge concludes that the witness's identification of the defendant is reliable. One might well question whether courts should indulge in this form of circular reasoning....

Despite the tension between the *Brathwaite* analysis of reliability and the results of the past three decades' psychological research into the dynamics of eyewitness identification, few courts have conducted a critical re-examination of the *Brathwaite* approach....

Beginning in the early 1990s, courts began to demonstrate awareness of the growing scientific criticism of the *Brathwaite* approach....

The year 2005 appears to have been a turning point of sorts in the judicial recognition of the growing body of research into the psychological dynamics of eyewitness identification. In that year, two state supreme courts issued opinions that contained lengthy citations and discussions of the research literature: *State v. Ledbetter,* 881 A.2d 290, 311–13 (Conn. 2005), and *State v. Dubose,* 699 N.W.2d 582, 591–92 (Wis. 2005). The Connecticut court in *Ledbetter* concluded that the research data was not convincing enough to abandon the *Brathwaite* analysis, but the Wisconsin court in *Dubose* held that an eyewitness identification arising from an unnecessarily suggestive showup must be suppressed, without regard to any *Brathwaite* reliability analysis....

In addition to these few courts that have responded to the psychological research on eyewitness identification, several legislatures and police agencies have enacted new laws or policies based on this research.

In September 2005, the Wisconsin Attorney General issued a "Model Policy and Procedure for Eyewitness Identification." This policy recommended that all police agencies utilize a double-blind, sequential photo lineup procedure. The salient details of this procedure are: (1) the officer conducting the photo lineup does not know who the suspect is, (2) the witness being interviewed is told that the culprit may not be included among the photographs, (3) the photographs are shown to the witness one at a time, rather than in a group, (4) the witness is not told in advance how many photographs they will see, and (5) the witness is asked to rate each photograph separately (*e.g.,* "yes," "no," or "unsure")—thus minimizing the danger that the witness will view the procedure as a "multiple choice" test where their task is to pick the one photo that best matches their memory of the culprit.[32]

In April 2006, the California Commission on the Fair Administration of Justice issued its "Report

32. [*See*: www.doj.state.wi.us/dles/tns/eyewitness public.pdf.] ...

and Recommendations Regarding Eye Witness Identification Procedures." In this report, the California Commission likewise recommended that all police agencies in the state adopt a double-blind, sequential photo lineup procedure.[33]

... In September 2009, USA Today reported that five other states (Connecticut, Georgia, Maryland, North Carolina, and West Virginia) and several major metropolitan police departments are changing their identification procedures in response to the psychological research and the wealth of information confirming that innocent people are indeed being convicted based on mistaken eyewitness identifications.[35]

In particular, North Carolina has enacted a statute that mandates double-blind, sequential photo lineup procedures. *See* North Carolina Statute 15A-284.52....

There can be little doubt that these recent changes in the legal system have been prompted by the confluence of two forces: the increasing amount of psychological research in this area, and the concurrent development of forensic DNA testing....

A re-examination of the photo lineup in Tegoseak's case

... Officer Asselin—the lead investigator in this case—knew that Edgar Henry was photograph number 5 in the first array of six photos and that Frank Tegoseak was photograph number 5 in the second array. Asselin first showed the two photographic arrays to Michelle Maestas, but she failed to identify either Edgar Henry or Frank Tegoseak. Thus, when Asselin next showed the photographs to Robert Maestas, Asselin knew that this was his final opportunity to get an identification of either Henry or Tegoseak from an eyewitness.

... [W]hen Robert Maestas was shown the first array, he "correctly" identified the photograph of Henry (photograph number 5) as being the original passenger in the Bronco, but Maestas also "incorrectly" identified photographs 1 and 3 of this first array as being the original driver.

Asselin knew that this was "wrong," so he said to Maestas, "Let me try to at least show you [the second array of photographs]; then you can see the entire compilation of photos. So far, you've said [that] 1 and 3 [in the first array] could be the driver." Asselin then showed Maestas the second array of six photographs....

If—as appears likely—Maestas knew or suspected that the photo arrays contained photographs of the two men whom Asselin knew to be the culprits (the two men who had been found in the Bronco), then when Asselin told Maestas to keep looking at more photos even though Maestas had apparently identified both men, Asselin's remark could well have suggested to Maestas that his initial selection was "wrong," and that he had not yet identified the true culprit....

The potential suggestiveness of Asselin's remark could only have been amplified later, when Maestas viewed the second array and told Asselin that the original driver of the Bronco was either photograph 1 in the first array (a filler) or photograph 5 in the second array (Tegoseak). Rather than have Maestas place an "X" in the two boxes representing these two photos, Asselin directed Maestas to place an "X" in only one box, the box representing Tegoseak's photo—although Asselin invited Maestas to add a written notation explaining that Maestas thought that the other photo might also be the driver.

Asselin's reaction to Maestas's ambiguous identification was not necessarily an attempt to manipulate Maestas. Rather, it might be attributed to the phenomenon of "observer bias". Both scientific researchers and police investigators can fall prey to the normal human tendency to pay attention to, or to overemphasize, the results that they expect or hope to see—and the converse tendency to fail to observe, or to ignore the significance of, results they do not expect or hope to see.

But while Asselin may not have intended to manipulate Maestas, his directions to Maestas may have affected Maestas's perception of the identification procedure. Asselin's directions to Maestas potentially constituted an inadvertent suggestion that photograph number 5 in the second array (*i.e.*, Tegoseak) was Maestas's "real" selection, and that photograph number 1 in the first array was only a subsidiary alternative selection....

... [O]ne of the important findings of the psychological research in this area is that, if a witness makes an identification during a suggestive lineup procedure and then the witness

---

33. ... Available at: www.psychology.iastate.edu/%25glwells/$1fCalifornia-commission.pdf.

35. Kevin Johnson, "States Change Police Lineups After Wrongful Convictions," USA Today, September 17, 2009. Available at: www.usatoday.com/news/nation/009-09-16-police-line ups-N.htm.

receives some kind of confirmation from the officer administering the lineup, the witness's after-the-fact perception of their identification can be altered: the witness can become artificially more confident in their identification. There is reason to believe that this is what happened to Robert Maestas....

Why we conclude that the potential suggestiveness of the photo lineup is harmless beyond a reasonable doubt

We have covered a lot of ground in this opinion: a lengthy discussion of the Ronald Cotton case, a look at some of the scientific research on the subject of eyewitness identification, and a description of the recent efforts in various states and cities to improve eyewitness identification procedures. All of this naturally leads to the question: What, if anything, should this Court do in response to what society has learned in the thirty years since *Brathwaite?*

We first wish to clarify that the Ronald Cotton case is simply one case, albeit a prominent one. What happened in that case may provide reason to question the *Brathwaite* analysis, but it does not constitute scientific proof that the *Brathwaite* analysis is flawed.

Second, we acknowledge that our examination of the past three decades' research has not been an exhaustive one. There are many studies in this area that we have not mentioned. And, of course, there are questions in the scientific community about the methodology of particular studies, as well as questions regarding the significance that should be attributed to the results of various studies.

We do not intend to endorse a particular viewpoint or reach a definitive conclusion at this time. Rather, our goals are more modest: to acknowledge that psychological research into eyewitness identification has furnished new insights into the potential suggestiveness of identification procedures, and to point out that this research has illuminated the related problem that a suggestive identification procedure can work an after-the-fact alteration of a witness's memory of a criminal episode.

We need go no further at the present time—because, even assuming that the photo lineup procedure in Tegoseak's case was unnecessarily suggestive, any error was harmless beyond a reasonable doubt.

When Judge Wolverton ruled on Tegoseak's suppression motion, he noted that "this might [have been] a different situation if [Tegoseak and Henry] had not been followed and almost [handed]-off to the police." As Judge Wolverton correctly pointed out, the case against Tegoseak was not a "whodunit"—not a case where the police knew that a crime had been committed but did not know the identity of the perpetrator. Rather, the State's evidence clearly established (1) that the Bronco was being driven in an erratic manner, (2) that two men—one wearing a white shirt and one wearing a black shirt—got out of the Bronco in the nursery parking lot and switched places before getting back in the vehicle and driving off, (3) that only two men were in the Bronco when the police stopped the vehicle minutes later—one wearing a white shirt and one wearing a black shirt, and (4) that, following the stop, both men initially admitted to having just driven the car. In addition, Officer Asselin testified that Edgar Henry told the police that he had taken over driving the Bronco after the stop at Bell's Nursery because Tegoseak had been driving so poorly that he thought Tegoseak was going to kill them.

Given all of this, we have no doubt that the jury would have convicted Tegoseak even if Maestas had been unable to identify Tegoseak at trial, and even if the jurors had been told that Maestas was unable to identify the driver in the photo lineup, or that Maestas had identified one of the filler photos as being the driver. In other words, even if the superior court should have granted Tegoseak's motion to suppress Robert Maestas's identification of him as the initial driver of the Bronco, any error was harmless beyond a reasonable doubt.

The judgement of the superior court is AFFIRMED....

Notes and Questions

1. In *State v. Marquez,* 967 A.2d 57 (Conn. 2009), following an extensive review of research studies, the Connecticut Supreme Court declined to exercise its supervisory authority to mandate "three specific procedural changes" requested by the defendant pertaining to eyewitness identification procedures: "(1) the double-blind procedure; (2)

the sequential display of live suspects or photographs; and (3) a prohibition on police informing witnesses, after they identify a suspect, that the individual that they chose is the person whom police believe is the culprit." *Id.*, 967 A.2d, at 165. In reliance on *State v. Ledbetter*, 881 A.2d 290 (Conn. 2005), the *Marquez* majority opinion concluded: "We believe that the development and implementation of identification procedures 'should continue to be the province of the law enforcement agencies of this state.'" Justice Katz's concurring opinion elaborated:

It is ... clear that witness identification research, although evolving, is converging toward a consensus. It is equally clear that, in light of the evolving research, this court should avoid closing off debate on witness identification procedures by signaling its approval of procedures on which research currently casts doubt, especially when there is no need to do so. Ultimately, as science progresses and is able to offer more concrete recommendations, witness identification procedures may need to be revised to ensure that they produce accurate results in accordance with due process guarantees.

In light of these concerns, I would reaffirm the case-by-case approach that we endorsed in *State v. Ledbetter*, allowing trial courts to examine the studies presented to them and to consider those studies under the particular facts as they arise in any given case.

D. Expert Testimony

Defendants sometimes seek to enlist expert witnesses, typically social scientists familiar with research evidence bearing on perception, memory, and recall, to testify before juries and explain the system and estimator variables that can affect the reliability of eyewitness identification. The following decision by the Utah Supreme Court announces a new rule to govern the admissibility of expert testimony about the reliability of eyewitness identification in that state's criminal trials.

State v. Clopten

223 P.3d 1103 (Utah 2009)

DURHAM, Chief Justice:

Defendant, Deon Lomax Clopten, appeals his conviction for murder on grounds that the trial court abused its discretion when it excluded expert testimony regarding the reliability of eyewitness identification.... We reverse..., vacate the conviction, and remand for a new trial.

In February 2006, Clopten was convicted of first-degree murder for the shooting of Tony Fuailemaa outside a Salt Lake City nightclub. At trial, Clopten maintained that someone else—a man named Freddie White—was responsible for the shooting. The testimony of several individuals who witnessed the murder and who identified Clopten as the perpetrator countered this assertion. In the absence of strong physical or forensic evidence against Clopten, the State leaned heavily on the eyewitness testimony to secure a conviction.

As part of his defense, Clopten sought to introduce the testimony of Dr. David Dodd, an expert on eyewitness identification. Clopten intended to elicit testimony from Dr. Dodd regarding various factors that can affect the accuracy of eyewitness identifications, including cross-racial identification, the impact of violence and stress during an event, the tendency to focus on a weapon rather than an individual's facial features, and the suggestive nature of certain identification procedures used by police....

[T]he court excluded the expert testimony. The trial court reasoned that the testimony was unnecessary since potential problems with eyewitness identification could be explained using a jury instruction, as has been the common practice in Utah since this court's decision in *State v. Long*, 721 P.2d 483 (Utah 1986). The trial court concluded that the jury instruction (hereinafter a "*Long* instruction") "does an adequate job" and that Dr. Dodd's testimony would be "superfluous" and "would only confuse the issue." ...

We granted certiorari review on whether expert testimony regarding the reliability of eyewitness identification should be presumed admissible when timely requested....

When we decided *State v. Long* in 1986, it was already apparent that "[a]lthough research has convincingly demonstrated the weaknesses inherent in eyewitness identification, jurors are, for the most part, unaware of these problems." 721 P.2d 483, 490. Thus we confronted a troubling quandary: while eyewitness identifications are frequently crucial to the State's case against a criminal defendant, the human ability to perceive and remember accurately is subject to numerous limitations. In addition, it appears that jury members are frequently unaware of these limitations and thus give eyewitness identifications a disproportionate weight....

Prior to *Long*, the decision to issue a cautionary instruction regarding the infirmities of eyewitness testimony was left entirely to the trial court's discretion.... We ... reversed Long's conviction, and ... directed trial courts to provide instructions "whenever eyewitness identification is a central issue in a case and such an instruction is requested by the defense."

It was never the intent of this court to establish cautionary instructions as the sole means for educating juries about eyewitness fallibility.... With the benefit of hindsight, however, it is clear that *Long* actually discouraged the inclusion of eyewitness expert testimony by failing to dispel earlier notions that such testimony would constitute a "lecture to the jury about how they should perform their duties." [*State v. Malmrose*, 649 P.2d 56, 61 (Utah 1982).] ...

Subsequent decisions reinforced this bias. In *State v. Hubbard*, we held that the substance of expert testimony "can be just as adequately conveyed to the jury through the judge in a jury instruction." 48 P.3d 953 (Utah 2002). Further, we affirmed trial court rulings that "such evidence could cause confusion of the issues and could cause undue delay." *State v. Butterfield*, 27 P.3d 1133 (Utah 2001). Proponents of eyewitness expert testimony also found themselves in a dilemma regarding the specificity of the proffered testimony. On one hand, eyewitness expert testimony that was too specific was excluded as having "a significant tendency to cause the jury to abdicate its role as fact finder." *Hubbard*, 48 P.3d 953. If, on the other hand, the eyewitness expert only gave general testimony about memory phenomena, then it could be excluded because it "did not deal with the specific facts from this case but rather would constitute a lecture to the jury about how it should judge the evidence." *Butterfield*, 27 P.3d 1133. In addition, we held that a *Long* instruction is enough to render an erroneous exclusion harmless, even if the instruction failed to mention significant portions of the proffered expert testimony. Finally, in a continuation of our history prior to *Long*, neither this court nor the court of appeals has ever reversed a conviction for failure to admit eyewitness expert testimony. Given this history, it is not surprising that there is a de facto presumption against eyewitness expert testimony in Utah's trial courts.

This trend ... is troubling in light of strong empirical research suggesting that cautionary instructions are a poor substitute for expert testimony....

... Decades of study, both before and particularly after *Long*, have established that eyewitnesses are prone to identifying the wrong person as the perpetrator of a crime, particularly when certain factors are present. For example, people identify members of their own race with greater accuracy than they do members of a different race. In addition, accuracy is significantly affected by factors such as the amount of time the culprit was in view, lighting conditions, use of a disguise, distinctiveness of the culprit's appearance, and the presence of a weapon or other distractions. Moreover, there is little doubt that juries are generally unaware of these deficiencies in human perception and memory and thus give great weight to eyewitness identifications. Indeed, juries seemed to be swayed the most by the confidence of an eyewitness, even though such confidence correlates only weakly with accuracy. That the empirical data is conclusive on these matters is not disputed by either party in this case and has not been questioned by this court in the decisions that followed *Long*.

The remaining issue is whether expert testimony is generally necessary to adequately educate a jury regarding these inherent deficiencies.... [W]e are now convinced that it is. In the absence of expert testimony, a defendant is left with two tools—cross-examination and cautionary instructions—with which to convey the possibility of mistaken identification to the jury. Both of these tools suffer from serious shortcomings when it comes to addressing the merits of eyewitness identifications.[7] Additionally, the admission of eyewitness expert testimony is gaining support in courts throughout the country.

The most troubling dilemma regarding eyewitnesses stems from the possibility that an inaccurate identification may be just as convincing to a jury as an accurate one. In one study, subjects watched a mock trial of a defendant accused of armed robbery. One group of subjects heard only circumstantial evidence against the defendant —they convicted at a rate of only 18 percent. The conviction rate jumped to 72 percent for a second group, which heard an eyewitness identify the defendant. A third group heard the same evidence and the same eyewitness, but was also told that the eyewitness was legally blind and had not been wearing glasses at the time of the crime. Despite the obvious unreliability of the eyewitness, 68 percent of this group still voted to convict.[8] As one leading researcher said: "[T]here is almost nothing more convincing than a live human being who takes the stand, points a finger at the defendant, and says 'That's the one!'" Elizabeth F. Loftus, *Eyewitness Testimony* 19 (1979). Because of this overreliance on questionable eyewitnesses, juries will often benefit from assistance as they sort reliable testimony from unreliable testimony.

The challenge arises in determining how best to provide that assistance in cases where mistaken identification is a possibility. It is apparent from the research that the inclusion of expert testimony carries significant advantages over the alternatives, namely cross-examination and jury instructions.[9]

Typically, an expert is called by a criminal defendant to explain how certain factors relevant to the identification in question could have produced a mistake. The expert may or may not be familiar with the facts of the case prior to the testimony, and in any case will not offer an opinion on whether the specific eyewitness identification is accurate or not. Instead, the relevant research is discussed in more general terms, thus allowing the jury to apply the information to whatever degree it sees fit.

Such testimony performs two beneficial functions. First, it teaches jurors about certain factors —such as "weapon focus" and the weak correlation between confidence and accuracy—that have a strong but counterintuitive impact on the reliability of an eyewitness. In other words, the testimony enables jurors to avoid certain common pitfalls, such as believing that a witness's statement of certainty is a reliable indicator of accuracy. Second, it assists jurors by quantifying what most people already know. An expert may discuss, for example, the degree to which accuracy is affected by a disguise or a long lapse between the crime and the identification. Importantly, expert testimony does not unfairly favor the defendant by making the jury skeptical of all eyewitnesses. In fact, when a witness sees the perpetrator under favorable conditions, expert testimony actually makes jurors more likely to convict. When expert testimony is used correctly, the end result is a jury that is better able to reach a just decision.

In the absence of expert testimony, the method most commonly used to challenge the veracity of eyewitnesses is cross-examination. But because eyewitnesses may express almost absolute certainty about identifications that are inaccurate, research shows the effectiveness of cross-examination is badly hampered. Cross-examination will often expose a lie or half-truth, but may be far less effective when witnesses, although mistaken, believe that what they say is true. In addition, as we recognized in *Long*, eyewitnesses are likely to use their "expectations,

7. There is significant dispute over how often mistaken eyewitness identification results in a wrongful conviction. Some researchers estimate that thousands of wrongful convictions occur across the country each year, while others argue that they are far more rare. Daniel S. Medwed, *Innocentrism*, 2008 U. Ill. L.Rev. 1549, 1552–53 nn. 13–18. We need not come down on one side or the other to justify our decision today. Jury misperceptions about eyewitness identifications create the possibility of wrongful convictions. Regardless of how often it actually occurs, the seriousness of that possibility is enough to justify the remedy [we] prescribe[]....

8. Steven Penrod, Elizabeth Loftus & John Winkler, *The Reliability of Eyewitness Testimony: A Psychological Perspective*, in *The Psychology of the Courtroom* 119, 154–55 (Norbert L. Kerr & Robert M. Bray eds., 1982).

9. For general discussion of eyewitness experts, *see* Brian L. Cutler & Steven D. Penrod, *Mistaken Identification: The Eyewitness, Psychology and the Law*, 250 (1995); Henry F. Fradella, *Why Judges Should Admit Expert Testimony on the Unreliability of Eyewitness Testimony*, 2006 Fed. Cts. L.Rev. 3, 24–25, 28 (June 2006); Richard A. Wise & Martin A. Safer, *What U.S. Judges Know and Believe About Eyewitness Testimony*, 18 Applied Cognitive Psychol. 427, 435 (2004).

personal experience, biases, and prejudices" to fill in the gaps created by imperfect memory. 721 P.2d at 489. Because it is unlikely that witnesses will be aware that this process has occurred, they may express far more confidence in the identification than is warranted.

Even if cross-examination reveals flaws in the identification, expert testimony may still be needed to assist the jury. Cross-examination might show, for example, that the perpetrator was a different race than the eyewitness and was also wearing a disguise. Without the assistance of expert testimony, a jury may have difficulty assessing the import of those factors in gauging the reliability of the identification. For these reasons, we cannot rely on cross-examination as a surefire way to uncover the possibility of mistaken identification.

Trial courts in Utah and around the nation have often tried to remedy the possibility of mistaken identification by giving cautionary instructions to the jury.... The standard *Long* instruction consists of general cautions about many factors known to contribute to mistaken identifications, such as brief exposure time, lack of light, presence of disguises and distractions, and effects of stress and cross-racial identification. *Id.* At the time, it seemed logical that this measure would substantially enhance a jury's ability to evaluate eyewitness accuracy.

Subsequent research, however, has shown that a cautionary instruction does little to help a jury spot a mistaken identification. While this result seems counterintuitive, commentators and social scientists advance a number of convincing explanations. First, instructions "given at the end of what might be a long and fatiguing trial, and buried in an overall charge by the court" are unlikely to have much effect on the minds of a jury. Second, instructions may come too late to alter the jury's opinion of a witness whose testimony might have been heard days before. Third, even the best cautionary instructions tend to touch only generally on the empirical evidence. The judge may explain that certain factors are known to influence perception and memory, but will not explain how this occurs or to what extent. As a result, instructions have been shown to be less effective than expert testimony....

The admissibility of eyewitness expert testimony was first considered by the nation's courts starting in the 1970s. In general, these early decisions excluded the testimony on grounds that have since been undercut by the research cited above. The majority of courts that have considered the issue since then have held that admission or exclusion of the evidence is within the broad discretion of the trial court. Starting in the 1980s, however, numerous state and federal courts recognized that the statistical evidence on eyewitness inaccuracy was too substantial to ignore. Many of these appellate courts instructed trial judges that, under certain circumstances, it would be an abuse of discretion not to allow expert testimony on the subject....

In short, a growing number of courts have recognized that eyewitness expert testimony is both reliable and helpful to the jury. Numerous courts have also rejected the idea that such testimony is impermissible because it is misleading or because it "invades the province" of the jury....

Our previous holdings have created a de facto presumption against the admission of eyewitness expert testimony, despite persuasive research that such testimony is the most effective way to educate juries about the possibility of mistaken identification.... We [now] hold that the testimony of a qualified expert regarding factors that have been shown to contribute to inaccurate eyewitness identifications should be admitted whenever it meets the requirements of rule 702 of the Utah Rules of Evidence. We expect this application of rule 702 will result in the liberal and routine admission of eyewitness expert testimony, particularly in cases where, as here, eyewitnesses are identifying a defendant not well known to them.

We conclude that this approach best conforms to the intent of rule 702....[21] ... [R]ule 702 consists of two basic parts. First, the trial judge

21. The current version of rule 702 reads:
(a) Subject to the limitations in subsection (b), if scientific, technical, or other specialized knowledge will assist the trier of fact to understand the evidence or to determine a fact in issue, a witness qualified as an expert by knowledge, skill, experience, training, or education may testify thereto in the form of an opinion or otherwise.
(b) Scientific, technical, or other specialized knowledge may serve as the basis for expert testimony if the scientific, technical, or other principles or methods underlying the testimony meet a threshold showing that

must find that the expert testimony will "assist the trier of fact." Utah R. Evid. 702(a). Second, the testimony must "meet a threshold showing" of reliability. *Id.* 702(b)....

... We now hold that, in cases where eyewitnesses are identifying a stranger and where one or more established factors affecting accuracy are present,[22] the testimony of an eyewitness expert will meet rule 702's requirement to "assist the trier of fact." As the research makes clear, the topics covered by eyewitness experts are often beyond the common knowledge of ordinary jurors and usually cannot be effectively elicited through cross-examination alone. It is therefore inappropriate for a trial judge to exclude an eyewitness expert merely on grounds that the jurors' life experiences already provide enough information, that cross-examination will suffice to reveal weaknesses with the identification, or that the testimony presented will be misleading or confusing.

We are not mandating the admission of eyewitness expert testimony in every case. Trial judges must still analyze whether the testimony will assist the jury, and in some cases it will not. The research on eyewitness identifications, for example, almost exclusively focuses on individuals who are attempting to identify a stranger. If the eyewitness is identifying someone with whom he or she has been acquainted over a substantial period of time (for example, a family member, long-time business associate, neighbor, or friend), then expert testimony is not likely to assist the jury in evaluating the accuracy of a witness's testimony. Similarly, there may be cases in which a witness viewed the perpetrator under such ideal conditions that an expert would not be able to identify factors that could have contributed to a misidentification. In such cases, the trial judge retains the discretion to exclude the testimony. We expect, however, that in cases involving eyewitness identification of strangers or near-strangers, trial courts will routinely admit expert testimony.

In addition, the testimony of an eyewitness expert should not be considered cumulative or duplicative of cautionary instructions to the jury. To reconcile this holding with our previous decision in *Long*, we modify our guidance regarding cautionary instructions. In cases where the defense does not call an eyewitness expert, the holding in *Long* still applies. In other words, the trial judge must provide a cautionary instruction if one is requested by the defense and eyewitness identification is a "central issue." *State v. Long*, 721 P.2d 483, 492 (Utah 1986). Where eyewitness expert testimony is heard, however, *Long* no longer applies and the inclusion of a cautionary instruction, if requested, is a matter for the trial judge's discretion....

[T]he State concedes that the testimony of eyewitness experts is based on sufficiently reliable principles to merit admission....

Finally, we hold that eyewitness expert testimony should not be excluded as intruding on the province of the jury or as an impermissible "lecture." ... It is therefore acceptable for an eyewitness expert to "give a dissertation or exposition"

---

they (i) are reliable, (ii) are based upon sufficient facts or data, and (iii) have been reliably applied to the facts of the case.

(c) The threshold showing required by subparagraph (b) is satisfied if the principles or methods on which such knowledge is based, including the sufficiency of facts or data and the manner of their application to the facts of the case, are generally accepted by the relevant expert community....

22. An illustrative but not exhaustive list of such factors can be broken down into several categories. The first category pertains to the eyewitness and includes factors such as uncorrected visual defects, fatigue, injury, intoxication, presence of a bias, an exceptional mental condition such as an intellectual disability or extremely low intelligence, age (if the eyewitness is either a young child or elderly), and the race of the eyewitness relative to the race of the suspect (cross-racial identification). The second category relates to the event witnessed and includes the effects of stress or fright, limited visibility, distance, distractions, the presence of a weapon (weapon focus), disguises, the distinctiveness of the suspect's appearance, the amount of attention given to the event by the eyewitness, and whether the eyewitness was aware at the time that a crime was occurring. The third category pertains to the identification itself. This category includes such factors as the length of time between observation and identification, any instances in which the eyewitness failed to identify the suspect or gave an inconsistent description, the value of lineups compared to showups, the value of photo identifications compared to in-person identifications, and any exposure of the eyewitness to influences such as news reports or interaction with other witnesses. It also includes potentially suggestive police conduct, such as the instructions given to the eyewitness by police, the composition of the lineup, the way in which the lineup was carried out, and the behaviors of the person conducting the lineup....

of factors found in the case that are understood to contribute to eyewitness inaccuracy. *Id.* As long as the expert does not attempt to tell the jury that a specific eyewitness identification either is or is not accurate, then the expert has not impinged on the jury's duty as the sole evaluator of witness credibility....

Tony Fuailemaa, the victim in this case, was shot and killed outside a nightclub following a rap concert. An undercover police officer responded and was told by the victim's girlfriend, Shannon Pantoja, that the shooter was "the guy in the red." The officer gave chase and saw several men jump into a Ford Explorer and drive away at high speed. A police pursuit ensued and resulted in the capture of Clopten and three other men. Clopten was in the driver's seat of the Explorer at the time of the arrest. Freddie White, the individual identified by Clopten as the shooter, was in the rear passenger seat. Both Clopten and White are African-American. Clopten was wearing both a red hooded sweatshirt and red pants at the time of arrest, while White was wearing a red T-shirt. Another red hooded sweatshirt was later found in the Explorer near where White had been sitting; the evidence suggested that White had been wearing it earlier in the evening. The handgun was found on the side of a road, having been thrown from the Explorer during the pursuit.

The State was unable to link Clopten to the handgun using fingerprints or other forensic evidence. Instead, the State relied heavily on eyewitness testimony....

In short, the circumstances found in the Clopten trial are exactly those under which the testimony of an eyewitness expert is most helpful to a jury. Dr. Dodd, the proffered expert in this case, could have testified about research into how eyewitness identification of a stranger is affected by stress, disguises, darkness and length of exposure. He could have quantified the impact of factors such as weapon focus and cross-racial identification. Dr. Dodd could also have testified as to the impact that comments made by police officers may have on an eyewitness making an identification. Additionally, he could have discussed a common phenomenon in which witnesses fill gaps in their memory with information obtained later and thus, over time, become more and more certain of identifications that may be inaccurate. All of these factors were present here, and thorough testimony by a qualified expert as to their nature would have significantly assisted the jury in evaluating the accuracy of the State's most important witnesses.... [W]e hold that the court of appeals erred in concluding that the exclusion of Dr. Dodd's testimony was not an abuse of discretion....

We are always reluctant to reverse a jury's decision to convict, particularly when the crime in question is as serious as this one. The seriousness of the crime, however, makes it only more imperative that the jury's decisionmaking abilities are supported by the best information available. If unreliable identifications are not addressed properly at trial, then there exists an unacceptable risk of the innocent being punished and dangerous criminals remaining at large. We therefore hold that, in cases where eyewitnesses are identifying a stranger and one or more established factors affecting accuracy are present, the testimony of a qualified expert is both reliable and helpful, as required by rule 702. Such eyewitness expert testimony should therefore be routinely admitted, regardless of whether the trial judge decides to issue a cautionary instruction. Given the circumstances present in this case, we hold that the court of appeals erred; the trial court's decision to exclude eyewitness expert testimony was an abuse of discretion that cannot be considered harmless. Accordingly, we reverse the decision of the court of appeals, vacate Clopten's conviction and remand for a new trial in accordance with our decision today....

Notes and Questions

1. In most jurisdictions, trial courts retain considerable discretion in determining whether to admit expert testimony, including testimony addressing the reliability of eyewitness identification. *See, e.g., United States v. Bartlett,* 567 F.3d 901 (7th Cir. 2009), *cert. denied,* 130 S.Ct. 1137 (2010). That discretion, however, can be abused, requiring reversal if a defendant is prejudiced by the testimony's exclusion. *See, e.g., Benn v. United States,* 978 A.2d 1257 (D.C. App. 2009); *People v. Abney,* 918 N.E.2d 486 (N.Y. 2009); *United States v. Brownlee,* 454 F.3d 131 (3d Cir. 2006).

2. Witnesses' tendency to make a "relative" judgment by selecting whichever person or photo before them bears the closest resemblance to the individual they recall observing previously is a danger commonly associated with the simultaneous presentation of suspects in a corporeal or photographic display. The sequential presentation of suspects or their photos, in contrast, is designed to minimize this risk and help ensure that witnesses make an "absolute" judgment that the person or photo selected matches their recollection of the perpetrator. The defendant in *State v. Shomberg*, 709 N.W.2d 370 (Wis. 2006) argued that the testimony of a trial witness (S.B., the victim of an outdoor, nighttime sexual assault) who identified him as her assailant exhibited the confounding influence of the simultaneous presentation of suspects in a line-up that she viewed. His appeal challenged the trial court's decision to exclude expert testimony that, he argued, was important to help the judge understand this alleged threat to the reliability of the witness's identification of him. A portion of the cross-examination suggested that S.B. may have identified the defendant by making a "relative" judgment at the line-up:

Q And when they brought the six people in, you knew right away it couldn't be number one, three, and six because they were too big, right?
A Right.
. . . .
Q And that left two, four, and five, right?
A Right.
Q And you knew it couldn't be two and four because they were too old, right?
A Right.
Q What did that leave?
A Five.
Q Number five, and that's why you picked him out, right?
A Right.
Q He was the best, and in fact, he was the only one left after you eliminated the other five people?
A That's right.
Q And you didn't pick him out because for sure that was the guy, just he was the best of the six?
A Right.

The majority opinion concluded that the court's exclusion of the proffered expert testimony did not constitute an abuse of discretion, and even if it had, the error would have been harmless. In dissent, Chief Judge Abrahamson argued:

> The defense expert witness sought to emphasize the weakness of an identification made in a lineup in which all persons are shown to an eyewitness at the same time (a simultaneous lineup), as compared to an identification made when the persons are shown to an eyewitness one at a time (sequential lineup) and the eyewitness is asked to state after seeing each person whether that person is or is not the suspect.
>
> . . . Instead of focusing on the weaknesses inherent in a simultaneous lineup in determining whether to admit expert testimony, the circuit court kept returning to the expert's testifying to other weaknesses of eyewitness identification, many familiar to triers of fact, such as the effect of stress, darkness, and limited opportunity to observe on the reliability of eyewitness identification. The circuit court then excluded the expert's testimony as not helpful. . . .
>
> When Shomberg's trial was held in 2002, many judges and counsel in Wisconsin evidently had not yet explored the problems associated with simultaneous lineups. Indeed, simultaneous lineups were the norm and any attack on a well-conducted lineup was counter to then-held views. . . .
>
> The circuit court did not fully appreciate, as the expert witness would have testified, that when a witness is given a simultaneous presentation of subjects, the witness tends to make relative judgments, comparing one person in the lineup with the others and identifying the person who looks most like the actual perpetrator. This tendency to make relative judgments does not usually pose a problem if the actual perpetrator is present; the witness will ordinarily identify the perpetrator. But if the perpetrator is not in the lineup, the witness will tend to identify the person in the

lineup who looks most like the witness's recollection of the suspect. A simultaneous lineup thus encourages a witness to select the "best" match, making a comparative judgment about the persons in the lineup, rather than making an absolute judgment about each person presented....

The majority opinion asserts that the defense was able to convey through cross-examination of Detective Marion Morgan, a state witness, "the concept that some experts believe sequential lineups are relatively more reliable than simultaneous lineups." The detective's testimony on cross-examination was based on attending training on eyewitness identification given by Shomberg's proffered expert. It is extraordinarily weak. The cross-examination fails to explain the research or to make the points that the defense's expert witness could have made about a witness's relative judgment in a simultaneous lineup....

For the reasons set forth, I dissent....

E. Conclusion

Eyewitness errors are unquestionably important in contributing to wrongful convictions. United States Supreme Court opinions have recognized the risks of eyewitness misidentification and their potential corrupting influence in criminal trials. Nevertheless, critics on and off the Court have expressed skepticism about whether the constitutional rules crafted by the justices—particularly those developed after 1967 and the *Wade* trilogy—are sufficient in guarding against suggestive identification procedures and the admission of potentially unreliable identification testimony. Some state courts have relied on state constitutional interpretation to reject the rule of *Manson v. Brathwaite* and require the automatic exclusion of out-of-court identifications that follow unnecessarily suggestive procedures, without further inquiry into their reliability. An impressive body of empirical research evidence has documented how witnesses' perceptions of events can be flawed and how identification procedures can affect the reliability of eyewitnesses' memory and recall of what they observed.

The courts, legislatures, and law enforcement agencies in several states have implemented reforms designed to improve identification procedures and enhance the reliability of eyewitness testimony. The procedural revisions include such relatively innocuous and straightforward measures as double-blind administration of identifications and cautioning witnesses that the perpetrator may or may not be in the line-up or photo array, and more controversial initiatives such as presenting suspects (or photos) to witnesses sequentially instead of simultaneously. We concluded this chapter by considering how expert witnesses can help educate jurors about research findings pertaining to the accuracy of eyewitness identifications and the reliability of eyewitness testimony, and how trial judges typically have broad discretion regarding the admissibility of expert testimony.

Chapter 4

False Confessions

A. Introduction

> "The idea that a rational being should confess that he had committed a most wanton murder, and thereby expose himself to the awful doom which must consequently follow, and the whole be a fictitious story, is, to many, a mystery they are unable to unravel." —*Rutland [Vermont] Herald*, commenting in 1820 on the exoneration of Jesse and Stephen Boorn following their confessions and convictions for murdering Russell Colvin, who subsequently appeared alive, shortly before Stephen was to be hanged.[1]
>
> "People just do not confess, particularly to something of this magnitude, this heinous, this vicious, without having participated in it. It's just not natural, it's just not reasonable." —Assistant Commonwealth Attorney D.J. Hansen, closing argument in the 2003 trial of Derek Tice, one of "the Norfolk Four," who had confessed to and was convicted of murder and rape; DNA evidence and another man's confession that he had committed the crimes alone resulted in Virginia Governor Timothy Kaine granting "partial clemency" to Tice and two other men convicted of the crimes, who also had confessed.[2]

To many, it is unthinkable that anyone would confess to a crime—especially a capital crime—that he or she did not commit. To do so would, at a minimum, represent "a mystery," if not also be "just not natural [or] ... reasonable." Yet, false confessions happen. The Innocence Project reports that defendants' false confessions or other damning admissions, including guilty pleas, were a factor in 51 of the first 225 wrongful convictions (23%) confirmed through DNA testing.[3] In this chapter, we explore legal rules and psychological principles that relate to this fascinating, and troubling, topic.

False confessions are made under diverse circumstances and have different causes. Researchers have distinguished "voluntary," "compliant," and "internalized" false confessions.

> Voluntary false confessions are those in which people claim responsibility for crimes they did not commit without prompting from police.... There are several reasons why innocent people volunteer confessions, such as a pathological need for attention or self-punishment, feelings of guilt or delusions, the perception of tangible gain, or the desire to protect someone else.
>
> In contrast, people are sometimes induced to confess through the processes of police interrogation. In compliant false confessions, the suspect acquiesces in order to escape from a stressful situation, avoid punishment, or gain a promised or implied reward.... [T]his confession is an act of public compliance by a suspect who perceives that the short-term benefits of confession outweigh the long-term costs....

> [I]nternalized false confessions are those in which innocent but vulnerable suspects, exposed to highly suggestive interrogation tactics, not only confess but come to believe they committed the crime.... [4]

False confessions have the potential to cascade rapidly into wrongful convictions. Once the police secure a confession, they are likely to curtail further investigation of a crime, believing that they have the perpetrator in custody. Prosecutors sometimes decline to go forward with a case supported by a confession because corroborating evidence is lacking, but they similarly are apt to accept the suspect's incriminating statements as strong evidence of guilt and follow up by filing charges. Defense attorneys, persuaded that a confession points singularly to guilt, can refrain from investigating further, abandon thoughts of preparing for trial, and concentrate on negotiating a guilty plea.[5] Even in the face of evidence strongly suggesting innocence, jurors often give determinative weight to a defendant's confession and vote to convict.[6] Appellate courts may rely on the defendant's confession to conclude that errors committed during a trial are harmless and thus affirm convictions.[7] In short, false confessions can easily become self-fulfilling prophecies.

We will focus on legal doctrine most directly associated with the risk of "compliant" false confessions, in which innocent suspects incriminate themselves after succumbing to the pressure of being questioned by the police or to specific interrogation tactics. We first examine several issues associated with the voluntariness of confessions, relying on Due Process principles. We next turn to the rules developed by the Supreme Court in *Miranda v. Arizona*, 384 U.S. 436, 86 S.Ct. 1602, 16 L.Ed.2d 694 (1966) and follow-up decisions, safeguards that are designed to protect the Fifth Amendment right against compelled self-incrimination. Then we consider an increasingly popular reform designed to help ensure compliance with the legal rules governing police interrogation, and that, concomitantly, can be expected to help judges and juries evaluate the reliability of confessions: requirements that the police make an electronic recording of interrogation sessions. We conclude by examining the courts' receptivity to allowing expert testimony in criminal trials to help educate jurors about false confessions and their causes. Throughout, we combine our consideration of the legal and policy issues with relevant insights from social science research.

B. Voluntariness

1. The Due Process Test

In *Brown v. Mississippi*, 297 U.S. 278, 279, 56 S.Ct. 461, 80 L.Ed. 682 (1936), the Supreme Court ruled that the 14th Amendment Due Process Clause prohibits state criminal courts from admitting into evidence "confessions shown to have been extorted by officers of the state by brutality and violence...." The justices thus invalidated the murder convictions and death sentences of three men notwithstanding their confessions. Chief Justice Hughes, quoting from the dissenting opinion written by a member of the Mississippi Supreme Court, described how the incriminating admissions were obtained.

'The crime with which these defendants, all ignorant negroes, are charged, was discovered about 1 o'clock p.m. on Friday, March 30, 1934. On that night one Dial, a deputy sheriff, accompanied by others, came to the home of Ellington, one of the defendants, and requested him to accompany them to the house of the deceased, and there a number of white men were gathered, who began to accuse the defendant of the crime. Upon his denial they seized him, and with the participation of the deputy they hanged him by a rope to the limb of a tree, and, having let him down, they hung him again, and when he was let down the second time, and he still protested his innocence, he was tied to a tree and whipped, and, still declining to accede to the demands that he confess, he was finally released, and he returned with some difficulty to his home, suffering intense pain and agony. The record of the testimony shows that the signs of the rope on his neck were plainly visible during the ... trial. A day or two thereafter the said deputy, accompanied by another, returned to the home of the said defendant and arrested him, and departed with the prisoner towards the jail in an adjoining county, but went by a route which led into the state of Alabama; and while on the way, in that state, the deputy stopped and again severely whipped the defendant, declaring that he would continue the whipping until he confessed, and the defendant then agreed to confess to such a statement as the deputy would dictate, and he did so, after which he was delivered to jail.

'The other two defendants, Ed Brown and Henry Shields, were also arrested and taken to the same jail. On Sunday night, April 1, 1934, the same deputy, accompanied by a number of white men, one of whom was also an officer, and by the jailer, came to the jail, and the two last named defendants were made to strip and they were laid over chairs and their backs were cut to pieces with a leather strap with buckles on it, and they were likewise made by the said deputy definitely to understand that the whipping would be continued unless and until they confessed, and not only confessed, but confessed in every matter of detail as demanded by those present; and in this manner the defendants confessed the crime, and, as the whippings progressed and were repeated, they changed or adjusted their confession in all particulars of detail so as to conform to the demands of their torturers. When the confessions had been obtained in the exact form and contents as desired by the mob, they left with the parting admonition and warning that, if the defendants changed their story at any time in any respect from that last stated, the perpetrators of the outrage would administer the same or equally effective treatment....

'All this having been accomplished, on the next day, that is, on Monday, April 2, when the defendants had been given time to recuperate somewhat from the tortures to which they had been subjected, the two sheriffs, one of the county where the crime was committed, and the other of the county of the jail in which the prisoners were confined, came to the jail, accompanied by eight other persons, some of them deputies, there to hear the free and voluntary confession of these miserable and abject defendants.... [T]he solemn farce of hearing the free and voluntary confessions was gone through with, and these two sheriffs and one other person then present were the three witnesses used in court to establish the so-called confessions, which were received by the court and admitted in evidence over the objections of the defendants....

'The defendants were brought to the courthouse of the county on the ... morning [of] April 5th, and the ... trial was opened, and was concluded on the next day, April 6, 1934, and resulted in a ... conviction with death sentences. The evidence upon which the conviction was obtained was the so-called confessions.... [T]he same deputy, Dial, under whose guiding hand and active participation the tortures to coerce the confessions were administered, was ... put on the stand by the state ... and admitted the whippings. It is interesting to note that in his testimony with reference to the whipping of the defendant Ellington, and in response to the inquiry as to how severely he was whipped, the deputy stated, 'Not too much for a negro; not as much as I would have done if it were left to me.'...

No great imagination is required to understand that confessions extracted in the manner described in *Brown v. Mississippi* might be false. Although the danger that coerced confessions are unreliable is one reason they are excluded from evidence, the Due Process principles on which *Brown* rests implicate other important interests as well. Justice Frankfurter addressed these concerns in *Rogers v. Richmond,* 365 U.S. 534, 540–541, 81 S.Ct. 735, 5 L.Ed.2d 760 (1961).

> Our decisions under [the Fourteenth] Amendment have made clear that convictions following the admission into evidence of confessions which are involuntary, i.e., the product of coercion, either physical or psychological, cannot stand. This is so not because such confessions are unlikely to be true but because the methods used to extract them offend an underlying principle in the enforcement of our criminal law: that ours is an accusatorial and not an inquisitorial system—a system in which the State must establish guilt by evidence independently and freely secured and may not by coercion prove its charge against an accused out of his own mouth. To be sure, confessions cruelly extorted may be and have been, to an unascertained extent, found to be untrustworthy. But the constitutional principle of excluding confessions that are not voluntary does not rest on this consideration. Indeed, in many of the cases in which the command of the Due Process Clause has compelled us to reverse state convictions involving the use of confessions obtained by impermissible methods, independent corroborating evidence left little doubt of the truth of what the defendant had confessed. Despite such verification, confessions were found to be the product of constitutionally impermissible methods in their inducement. Since a defendant had been subjected to pressures to which, under our accusatorial system, an accused should not be subjected, we were constrained to find that the procedures leading to his conviction had failed to afford him that due process of law which the Fourteenth Amendment guarantees.

During the three decades that ensued between *Brown v. Mississippi* and *Miranda v. Arizona*, the courts regularly scrutinized confessions under the Due Process "involuntariness" standard discussed in *Rogers v. Richmond.* This test requires careful attention to the "totality of the circumstances" surrounding the confession, including both the suspect's characteristics and the police interrogation tactics. As we shall see, this analysis frequently remains relevant even in contemporary, post-*Miranda* cases. The test presents special challenges because of the difficulty in defining the elusive concept of "voluntariness" and because its application depends on having an unambiguous understanding of the facts—reasons that were instrumental to the justices' decision to develop a different approach in *Miranda.* Justice Powell elaborated on the meaning of a "voluntary" confession in his opinion for the Court in *Schneckloth v. Bustamonte,* 412 U.S. 218, 223–225, 93 S.Ct. 2041, 36 L.Ed.2d 854 (1973).

> In some 30 different cases decided during the era that intervened between Brown [v. Mississippi] and Escobedo v. Illinois, 378 U.S. 478 [(1964)] the Court was faced with the necessity of determining whether in fact the confessions in issue had been 'voluntarily' given....
>
> Those cases yield no talismanic definition of 'voluntariness,' mechanically applicable to the host of situations where the question has arisen. 'The notion of "voluntariness," Mr. Justice Frankfurter once wrote, 'is itself an amphibian.' Culombe v. Connecticut, 367 U.S. 568, 604–605 [(1961)]. It cannot be taken literally to mean a 'knowing' choice. 'Except where a person is unconscious or drugged or otherwise lacks capacity for conscious choice, all incriminating statements—even those made under brutal treatment—are 'voluntary' in the sense of representing a choice of alternatives. On the other hand, if 'voluntariness' incorporates notions of 'but for' cause, the question should be whether the statement would have been made even absent inquiry or other official action. Under such a test, virtually no statement would be voluntary because very few people give incriminating statements in the absence of official action of some kind.'[7] It is thus evident that neither linguistics nor epistemology will provide a ready definition of the meaning of 'voluntariness.'
>
> Rather, 'voluntariness' has reflected an accommodation of the complex of values implicated in police questioning of a suspect. At one end of the spectrum is the acknowledged need for police questioning as a tool for the ef-

7. Bator & Vorenberg, Arrest, Detention, Interrogation and the Right to Counsel: Basic Problems and Possible Legislative Solutions, 66 Col.L.Rev. 62, 72–73. See also 3 J. Wigmore, Evidence § 826 (J. Chadbourn rev. 1970): 'When, for example, threats are used, the situation is one of choice between alternatives, either one disagreeable, to be sure, but still subject to a choice. As between the rack and a confession, the latter would usually be considered the less disagreeable; but it is nonetheless a voluntary choice.'

fective enforcement of criminal laws. Without such investigation, those who were innocent might be falsely accused, those who were guilty might wholly escape prosecution, and many crimes would go unsolved. In short, the security of all would be diminished. At the other end of the spectrum is the set of values reflecting society's deeply felt belief that the criminal law cannot be used as an instrument of unfairness, and that the possibility of unfair and even brutal police tactics poses a real and serious threat to civilized notions of justice. '(I)n cases involving involuntary confessions, this Court enforces the strongly felt attitude of our society that important human values are sacrificed where an agency of the government, in the course of securing a conviction, wrings a confession out of an accused against his will.' Blackburn v. Alabama, 361 U.S. 199, 206–207 [(1960)].

This Court's decisions reflect a frank recognition that the Constitution requires the sacrifice of neither security nor liberty. The Due Process Clause does not mandate that the police forgo all questioning, or that they be given carte blanche to extract what they can from a suspect. 'The ultimate test remains that which has been the only clearly established test in Anglo-American courts for two hundred years: the test of voluntariness. Is the confession the product of an essentially free and unconstrained choice by its maker? If it is, if he has willed to confess, it may be used against him. If it is not, if his will has been overborne and his capacity for self-determination critically impaired, the use of his confession offends due process.' Culombe v. Connecticut, supra, 367 U.S., at 602.

In determining whether a defendant's will was overborne in a particular case, the Court has assessed the totality of all the surrounding circumstances—both the characteristics of the accused and the details of the interrogation. Some of the factors taken into account have included the youth of the accused, his lack of education or his low intelligence, the lack of any advice to the accused of his constitutional rights, the length of detention, the repeated and prolonged nature of the questioning, and the use of physical punishment such as the deprivation of food or sleep. In all of these cases, the Court determined the factual circumstances surrounding the confession, assessed the psychological impact on the accused, and evaluated the legal significance of how the accused reacted.

The significant fact about all of these decisions is that none of them turned on the presence or absence of a single controlling criterion; each reflected a careful scrutiny of all the surrounding circumstances.... While the state of the accused's mind, and the failure of the police to advise the accused of his rights, were certainly factors to be evaluated in assessing the 'voluntariness' of an accused's responses, they were not in and of themselves determinative.

2. State Action

For constitutional purposes, should only the conduct of government agents in creating pressures or inducements for an individual to confess be relevant to assessing the statement's voluntariness, or should other factors—such as the person's mental illness or other idiosyncratic circumstances—also be considered? In answering this question, should the possible unreliability of a confession, with the attendant risk that it will produce a wrongful conviction, be a consideration independent of the police conduct that may have helped induce the statement? Consider the following case.

Colorado v. Connelly

479 U.S. 157, 107 S.Ct. 515, 93 L.Ed.2d 473 (1986)

Chief Justice REHNQUIST delivered the opinion of the Court.

In this case, the Supreme Court of Colorado held that the United States Constitution requires a court to suppress a confession when the mental state of the defendant, at the time he made the confession, interfered with his "rational intellect" and his "free will." ... We conclude that the admissibility of this kind of statement is governed by state rules of evidence, rather than by our previous decisions regarding coerced confessions and *Miranda* waivers. We therefore reverse.

I

On August 18, 1983, Officer Patrick Anderson of the Denver Police Department was in uniform, working in an off-duty capacity in downtown Denver. Respondent Francis Connelly approached Officer Anderson and, without any prompting, stated that he had murdered someone and wanted to talk about it. Anderson immediately advised respondent that he had the right to remain silent, that anything he said could be used against him in court, and that he had the right to an attorney prior to any police questioning. See *Miranda v. Arizona,* 384 U.S. 436 (1966). Respondent stated that he understood these rights but he still wanted to talk about the murder. Understandably bewildered by this confession, Officer Anderson asked respondent several questions. Connelly denied that he had been drinking, denied that he had been taking any drugs, and stated that, in the past, he had been a patient in several mental hospitals. Officer Anderson again told Connelly that he was under no obligation to say anything. Connelly replied that it was "all right," and that he would talk to Officer Anderson because his conscience had been bothering him. To Officer Anderson, respondent appeared to understand fully the nature of his acts.

Shortly thereafter, Homicide Detective Stephen Antuna arrived. Respondent was again advised of his rights, and Detective Antuna asked him "what he had on his mind." Respondent answered that he had come all the way from Boston to confess to the murder of Mary Ann Junta, a young girl whom he had killed in Denver sometime during November 1982. Respondent was taken to police headquarters, and a search of police records revealed that the body of an unidentified female had been found in April 1983. Respondent openly detailed his story to Detective Antuna and Sergeant Thomas Haney, and readily agreed to take the officers to the scene of the killing. Under Connelly's sole direction, the two officers and respondent proceeded in a police vehicle to the location of the crime. Respondent pointed out the exact location of the murder. Throughout this episode, Detective Antuna perceived no indication whatsoever that respondent was suffering from any kind of mental illness.

Respondent was held overnight. During an interview with the public defender's office the following morning, he became visibly disoriented. He began giving confused answers to questions, and for the first time, stated that "voices" had told him to come to Denver and that he had followed the directions of these voices in confessing. Respondent was sent to a state hospital for evaluation. He was initially found incompetent to assist in his own defense. By March 1984, however, the doctors evaluating respondent determined that he was competent to proceed to trial.

At a preliminary hearing, respondent moved to suppress all of his statements. Dr. Jeffrey Metzner, a psychiatrist employed by the state hospital, testified that respondent was suffering from chronic schizophrenia and was in a psychotic state at least as of August 17, 1983, the day before he confessed. Metzner's interviews with respondent revealed that respondent was following the "voice of God." This voice instructed respondent to withdraw money from the bank, to buy an airplane ticket, and to fly from Boston to Denver. When respondent arrived from Boston, God's voice became stronger and told respondent either to confess to the killing or to commit suicide. Reluctantly following the command of the voices, respondent approached Officer Anderson and confessed.

Dr. Metzner testified that, in his expert opinion, respondent was experiencing "command hallucinations." This condition interfered with respondent's "volitional abilities; that is, his ability to make free and rational choices." Dr. Metzner further testified that Connelly's illness did not significantly impair his cognitive abilities. Thus, respondent understood the rights he had when Officer Anderson and Detective Antuna advised him that he need not speak. Dr. Metzner admitted that the "voices" could in reality be Connelly's interpretation of his own guilt, but explained that in his opinion, Connelly's psychosis motivated his confession.

On the basis of this evidence the Colorado trial court decided that respondent's statements must be suppressed because they were "involuntary." Relying on our decisions in *Townsend v. Sain,* 372 U.S. 293 (1963), and *Culombe v. Connecticut,* 367 U.S. 568 (1961), the court ruled that a confession is admissible only if it is a product of the defendant's rational intellect and "free will." Although the court found that the police had done nothing wrong or coercive in securing respondent's confession, Connelly's illness destroyed his volition and compelled him to confess. The trial court also found that Connelly's mental state vitiated his attempted waiver of the right to counsel and the privilege against compulsory self-incrimination. Accordingly, respondent's initial statements and his custodial confession were suppressed.

The Colorado Supreme Court affirmed. 702 P.2d 722 (1985)....

II

The Due Process Clause of the Fourteenth Amendment provides that no State shall "deprive any person of life, liberty, or property, without due process of law." Just last Term, in *Miller v. Fenton,* 474 U.S. 104, 109 (1985), we held that by virtue of the Due Process Clause "certain interrogation techniques, either in isolation or as applied to the unique characteristics of a particular suspect, are so offensive to a civilized system of justice that they must be condemned."

Indeed, coercive government misconduct was the catalyst for this Court's seminal confession case, *Brown v. Mississippi,* 297 U.S. 278 (1936). In that case, police officers extracted confessions from the accused through brutal torture. The Court had little difficulty concluding that even though the Fifth Amendment did not at that time apply to the States, the actions of the police were "revolting to the sense of justice." *Id.,* at 286. The Court has retained this due process focus, even after holding, in *Malloy v. Hogan,* 378 U.S. 1 (1964), that the Fifth Amendment privilege against compulsory self-incrimination applies to the States.

Thus the cases considered by this Court over the 50 years since *Brown v. Mississippi* have focused upon the crucial element of police overreaching.[1] While each confession case has turned on its own set of factors justifying the conclusion that police conduct was oppressive, all have contained a substantial element of coercive police conduct. Absent police conduct causally related to the confession, there is simply no basis for concluding that any state actor has deprived a criminal defendant of due process of law. Respondent correctly notes that as interrogators have turned to more subtle forms of psychological persuasion, courts have found the mental condition of the defendant a more significant factor in the "voluntariness" calculus. See *Spano v. New York,* 360 U.S. 315 (1959). But this fact does not justify a conclusion that a defendant's mental condition, by itself and apart from its relation to official coercion, should ever dispose of the inquiry into constitutional "voluntariness." ...

Our "involuntary confession" jurisprudence is entirely consistent with the settled law requiring some sort of "state action" to support a claim of violation of the Due Process Clause of the Fourteenth Amendment.... [T]he Supreme Court of Colorado, however, concluded that sufficient state action was present by virtue of the admission of the confession into evidence in a court of the State.

The difficulty with the approach of the Supreme Court of Colorado is that it fails to recognize the essential link between coercive activity of the State, on the one hand, and a resulting confession by a defendant, on the other. The flaw in respondent's constitutional argument is that it would expand our previous line of "voluntariness" cases into a far-ranging requirement that courts must divine a defendant's motivation for speaking or acting as he did even though there be no claim that governmental conduct coerced his decision.

The most outrageous behavior by a private party seeking to secure evidence against a defendant does not make that evidence inadmissible under the Due Process Clause.... Moreover, suppressing respondent's statements would serve absolutely no purpose in enforcing constitutional guarantees. The purpose of excluding evidence

1. *E.g., Mincey v. Arizona,* 437 U.S. 385 (1978) (defendant subjected to 4-hour interrogation while incapacitated and sedated in intensive-care unit); *Greenwald v. Wisconsin,* 390 U.S. 519 (1968) (defendant, on medication, interrogated for over 18 hours without food or sleep); *Beecher v. Alabama,* 389 U.S. 35 (1967) (police officers held gun to the head of wounded confessant to extract confession); *Davis v. North Carolina,* 384 U.S. 737 (1966) (16 days of incommunicado interrogation in closed cell without windows, limited food, and coercive tactics); *Reck v. Pate,* 367 U.S. 433 (1961) (defendant held for four days with inadequate food and medical attention until confession obtained); *Culombe v. Connecticut,* 367 U.S. 568 (1961) (defendant held for five days of repeated questioning during which police employed coercive tactics); *Payne v. Arkansas,* 356 U.S. 560 (1958) (defendant held incommunicado for three days with little food; confession obtained when officers informed defendant that Chief of Police was preparing to admit lynch mob into jail); *Ashcraft v. Tennessee,* 322 U.S. 143 (1944) (defendant questioned by relays of officers for 36 hours without an opportunity for sleep).

seized in violation of the Constitution is to substantially deter future violations of the Constitution. Only if we were to establish a brand new constitutional right—the right of a criminal defendant to confess to his crime only when totally rational and properly motivated—could respondent's present claim be sustained.

We have previously cautioned against expanding "currently applicable exclusionary rules by erecting additional barriers to placing truthful and probative evidence before state juries...." *Lego v. Twomey,* 404 U.S. 477, 488–489 (1972). We abide by that counsel now. "[T]he central purpose of a criminal trial is to decide the factual question of the defendant's guilt or innocence," *Delaware v. Van Arsdall,* 475 U.S. 673, 681 (1986), and while we have previously held that exclusion of evidence may be necessary to protect constitutional guarantees, both the necessity for the collateral inquiry and the exclusion of evidence deflect a criminal trial from its basic purpose. Respondent would now have us require sweeping inquiries into the state of mind of a criminal defendant who has confessed, inquiries quite divorced from any coercion brought to bear on the defendant by the State. We think the Constitution rightly leaves this sort of inquiry to be resolved by state laws governing the admission of evidence and erects no standard of its own in this area. A statement rendered by one in the condition of respondent might be proved to be quite unreliable, but this is a matter to be governed by the evidentiary laws of the forum, and not by the Due Process Clause of the Fourteenth Amendment....

We hold that coercive police activity is a necessary predicate to the finding that a confession is not "voluntary" within the meaning of the Due Process Clause of the Fourteenth Amendment. We also conclude that the taking of respondent's statements, and their admission into evidence, constitute no violation of that Clause....

The judgment of the Supreme Court of Colorado is accordingly reversed, and the cause is remanded for further proceedings not inconsistent with this opinion....

Justice STEVENS, concurring in the judgment in part and dissenting in part....

Justice BRENNAN, with whom Justice MARSHALL joins, dissenting....

... Because I believe that the use of a mentally ill person's involuntary confession is antithetical to the notion of fundamental fairness embodied in the Due Process Clause, I dissent.

I

The respondent's seriously impaired mental condition is clear on the record of this case. At the time of his confession, Mr. Connelly suffered from a "longstanding severe mental disorder," diagnosed as chronic paranoid schizophrenia. He had been hospitalized for psychiatric reasons five times prior to his confession; his longest hospitalization lasted for seven months. Mr. Connelly heard imaginary voices and saw nonexistent objects. He believed that his father was God, and that he was a reincarnation of Jesus.

... Dr. Metzner testified that Mr. Connelly was unable "to make free and rational choices" due to auditory hallucinations: "[W]hen he was read his *Miranda* rights, he probably had the capacity to know that he was being read his *Miranda* rights [but] he wasn't able to use that information because of the command hallucinations that he had experienced." ...

II

...

A

Today's decision restricts the application of the term "involuntary" to those confessions obtained by police coercion. Confessions by mentally ill individuals or by persons coerced by parties other than police officers are now considered "voluntary." The Court's failure to recognize all forms of involuntariness or coercion as antithetical to due process reflects a refusal to acknowledge free will as a value of constitutional consequence. But due process derives much of its meaning from a conception of fundamental fairness that emphasizes the right to make vital choices voluntarily: "The Fourteenth Amendment secures against state invasion ... the right of a person to remain silent unless he chooses to speak in the unfettered exercise of his own will...." *Malloy v. Hogan,* 378 U.S. 1, 8 (1964). This right requires vigilant protection if we are to safeguard the values of private conscience and human dignity....

But even if state action is required, police overreaching is not its only relevant form. The Colorado Supreme Court held that the trial court's admission of the involuntary confession into evidence is also state action.... Police conduct constitutes but one form of state action. "The objective of deterring improper police conduct is only part of the larger objective of safeguarding the integrity of our adversary system." *Harris v. New York,* 401 U.S. 222, 231 (1971) (BRENNAN, J., dissenting).

The only logical "flaw" which the Court detects in this argument is that it would require courts to "divine a defendant's motivation for speaking or acting as he did even though there be no claim that governmental conduct coerced his decision." Such a criticism, however, ignores the fact that we have traditionally examined the totality of the circumstances, including the motivation and competence of the defendant, in determining whether a confession is voluntary.... The Court's holding that involuntary confessions are only those procured through police misconduct is thus inconsistent with the Court's historical insistence that only confessions reflecting an exercise of free will be admitted into evidence.

B

Since the Court redefines voluntary confessions to include confessions by mentally ill individuals, the reliability of these confessions becomes a central concern. A concern for reliability is inherent in our criminal justice system, which relies upon accusatorial rather than inquisitorial practices. While an inquisitorial system prefers obtaining confessions from criminal defendants, an accusatorial system must place its faith in determinations of "guilt by evidence independently and freely secured." *Rogers v. Richmond,* 365 U.S. 534, 541 (1961)....

Our distrust for reliance on confessions is due, in part, to their decisive impact upon the adversarial process. Triers of fact accord confessions such heavy weight in their determinations that "the introduction of a confession makes the other aspects of a trial in court superfluous, and the real trial, for all practical purposes, occurs when the confession is obtained." E. Cleary, McCormick on Evidence 316 (2d ed. 1972). No other class of evidence is so profoundly prejudicial....

Because the admission of a confession so strongly tips the balance against the defendant in the adversarial process, we must be especially careful about a confession's reliability. We have to date not required a finding of reliability for involuntary confessions only because *all* such confessions have been excluded upon a finding of involuntariness, regardless of reliability. The Court's adoption today of a restrictive definition of an "involuntary" confession will require heightened scrutiny of a confession's reliability.

The instant case starkly highlights the danger of admitting a confession by a person with a severe mental illness.... Mr. Connelly was found incompetent to stand trial because he was unable to relate accurate information, and the court-appointed psychiatrist indicated that Mr. Connelly was actively hallucinating and exhibited delusional thinking at the time of his confession....

Moreover, the record is barren of any corroboration of the mentally ill defendant's confession. No physical evidence links the defendant to the alleged crime. Police did not identify the alleged victim's body as the woman named by the defendant. Mr. Connelly identified the alleged scene of the crime, but it has not been verified that the unidentified body was found there or that a crime actually occurred there. There is not a shred of competent evidence in this record linking the defendant to the charged homicide. There is only Mr. Connelly's confession.

Minimum standards of due process should require that the trial court find substantial indicia of reliability, on the basis of evidence extrinsic to the confession itself, before admitting the confession of a mentally ill person into evidence. I would require the trial court to make such a finding on remand. To hold otherwise allows the State to imprison and possibly to execute a mentally ill defendant based solely upon an inherently unreliable confession....

Notes and Questions

1. As with the voluntariness of Connelly's confession, the majority opinion concluded that only government action is relevant to assessing the voluntariness of a waiver of *Miranda* rights. There was no evidence to suggest that Connelly failed to comprehend his rights; his mental illness apparently interfered with his volition but not his cognitive abilities. "There is no reason to require more in the way of a 'voluntariness' inquiry in the *Miranda* waiver context than in the Fourteenth Amendment confession context. The sole concern of the Fifth Amendment, on which *Miranda* was based, is governmental coercion.... The voluntariness of a waiver of this privilege has always depended on the absence of police overreaching, not on 'free choice' in any broader sense." *Colorado v. Connelly,* 479

U.S., at 169–170. Justice Stevens dissented from this portion of the Court's ruling, as did Justices Brennan and Marshall.

2. Justice Brennan's dissenting opinion expresses concern about allowing "the State to imprison and possibly to execute a mentally ill defendant based solely upon an inherently unreliable confession." 479 U.S., at 183. Following the Supreme Court's reversal of the state court rulings, Connelly's case was remanded for trial. In 1987, he pled guilty to second-degree murder and was sentenced to prison. Is there a risk that Connelly was wrongfully convicted of murder based on a false confession? A commentator familiar with the evidence in the case has concluded that there was "overwhelming corroborating evidence" of the confession and that "Justice Brennan's insistence that there was not 'a shred of competent evidence in this record linking the defendant to the charged homicide'... is a serious mischaracterization of the facts...."[8]

3. Some state courts, in reliance on state constitutional or common law grounds, have declined to follow *Connelly's* holding that only governmental conduct should be considered in determining the voluntariness of a confession. *See, e.g., State v. Rees,* 748 A.2d 976 (Me. 2000); *State v. Bowe,* 881 P.2d 538 (Ha. 1994); *State v. Marczak,* 782 A.2d 440 (N.J. Super. 2001).

3. The Totality of the Circumstances: Characteristics of the Suspect

As we have seen, where there is sufficient governmental or "state action" to trigger federal constitutional protections, the voluntariness of a confession hinges on the totality of the circumstances, including the suspect's characteristics as well as the interrogation techniques employed by the police. Those factors figure prominently in the following case, involving a civil rights action in the aftermath of a wrongful conviction and an allegedly involuntary (and false) confession.

Wilson v. Lawrence County

260 F.3d 946 (8th Cir. 2001)

BEAM, Circuit Judge.

Johnny Lee Wilson brought this 42 U.S.C. § 1983 civil rights action against Lawrence County and several law enforcement officials for allegedly violating his constitutional rights in conducting a murder investigation, which resulted in Wilson spending over nine years in jail for a crime he did not commit. The district court denied appellants' motion for summary judgment asserting qualified immunity. We affirm.

I. BACKGROUND

On April 13, 1986, Cuba Pauline Martz was found murdered in her home in Aurora, Missouri. An intruder (or intruders) had apparently broken into her home, tied her up, beat her, and then started the house on fire with her inside. The next day, a major case squad composed of officers from several local law enforcement agencies was assembled to investigate the murder. Appellants are law enforcement officers who participated in the squad. The fruit of their investigation was a confession from Wilson, who is mentally retarded. In order to avoid the death penalty, Wilson entered an *Alford* plea, was convicted of the murder and spent over nine years in prison. In 1995, after conducting an independent investigation, the late Mel Carnahan, then Missouri Governor, granted Wilson a full pardon, stating: "As a result of an intense investigation conducted by my office, I have decided to issue a pardon to Johnny Lee Wilson because it is clear he did not commit the crime for which he has been incarcerated."

In the days following the murder, officers interviewed Wilson twice. During these initial interviews Wilson consistently stated that he knew nothing about the crime and had been shopping with his mother prior to the fatal fire. Through their investigation, the appellants discovered that Wilson was twenty years old, still lived at home, worked occasional odd-jobs, was mentally impaired,[4] had attended mostly, if not exclusively, special education classes in high school and that some people believed he could be "talked into anything."

During this time, the officers began to focus on another local youth, Gary Wall, because he seemed to know early in the evening of April 13 that the victim had been tied and beaten. This was before such information was made public. Officers knew that Wall was a junior in high school, involved in special education classes, and was slightly mentally impaired. They also knew that he had disciplinary problems at his school and had been described as a "very skilled liar" by school officials. As a result of several custodial interrogations in the days following the murder, Wall told the officers on April 18 that Wilson had confessed to Wall that he committed the crime. That same day, Wall passed a polygraph examination regarding this issue. Wilson challenges the efficacy of the polygraph test, based not only on the fact that Wall's statement proved to be false, but also on the insufficient amount of time allowed for the numerous polygraph tests Wall was given on April 18, and the difficulty the examiner had in interpreting the tests.

Wall has since signed an affidavit asserting: he did not talk to Wilson at the scene of the fire or in the days following the crime and Wilson never confessed to him; the appellants first suggested Wilson's name to him as the criminal (not the other way around as the appellants contend); through leading questions, the appellants "tricked" him into giving details about the crime he did not know; the appellants threatened to put him in jail if he did not implicate Wilson in the crime and promised a reward if he did; and he did not come forward earlier to correct his statement because he was afraid of the police. The appellants contest Wall's account of the interrogations. The tapes of the interrogations, which were supposed to be in the appellants' possession, have inexplicably disappeared.

After extracting the statement from Wall, Deputy Seneker devised a plan to have Officer Owens pick up Wilson under the pretense of having him identify a lost wallet, and then question him about the murder. Owens found Wilson at a local movie theater and transported him to the police headquarters. Wilson was then taken to a windowless interrogation room. Appellants told him that he was not under arrest, but that department policy required them to read him his Miranda rights. Officers Kahre and Merritt interrogated Wilson for an hour. They played him portions of Wall's statement to convince him he had been implicated in the murder. During this time, Wilson denied any involvement and consistently repeated that he had been at the store with his mother prior to the fire.

Then, Deputy Seneker and Officer Wegrzyn took over the interrogation for approximately three more hours. Seneker falsely told Wilson that he knew what Wilson was thinking because he had a psychiatrist analyze him and that they had an eyewitness who could put him at the scene of the crime before the fire. They began to ask Wilson leading questions about the murder, strongly rebuking and threatening him when he gave answers inconsistent with the facts of the crime or was unable to give an answer, and affirming him whenever his answers matched the details of the murder. Ultimately, a collection of discombobulated facts about the murder evolved into a confession. Wilson has stated that he only confessed because he was extremely scared, nervous, anxious, and was pressured to make a confession.

The record does not mention any independent physical or circumstantial evidence linking Wilson to the crime, or corroborating his confession. After Wilson's motion to suppress his confession was denied, he entered an *Alford* plea to avoid the death penalty and was convicted.

II. ANALYSIS

Wilson asserts ... that appellants violated his Fifth and Fourteenth Amendment rights by coercing a false confession from him....

B. Qualified Immunity

... In determining if appellants are entitled to qualified immunity we must ask whether Wil-

4. Subsequent testing of Wilson indicates his overall mental abilities are in the bottom two percent of the population and that his adaptive behavior (communication, daily living skills, etc.) is in the lowest one percent of the general population.

son states a violation of a constitutional right, and whether that right was clearly established at the time, such that a reasonable officer would have known that his conduct violated the law....

At the summary judgment stage, we must view the facts in the light most favorable to Wilson, the nonmoving party below, and "take as true those facts asserted by [Wilson] that are properly supported in the record." Therefore, although many of the facts recounted herein are contested by the appellants, we view them most favorably to Wilson.

1. Wilson's Confession

Wilson alleges the appellants violated his Fifth Amendment right against self-incrimination and his Fourteenth Amendment right to due process by coercing an involuntary false confession from him. Fundamental to our system of justice is the principle that a person's rights are violated if police coerce an involuntary confession from him, truthful or otherwise, through physical or psychological methods designed to overbear his will. *See Blackburn v. Alabama,* 361 U.S. 199, 206 (1960) ("coercion can be mental as well as physical ... the blood of the accused is not the only hallmark of an unconstitutional inquisition"). The Supreme Court has long held "that certain interrogation techniques, either in isolation or *as applied to the unique characteristics of a particular suspect,* are so offensive to a civilized system of justice that they must be condemned under the Due Process Clause of the Fourteenth Amendment." *Miller v. Fenton,* 474 U.S. 104, 109 (1985) (emphasis added).

Whether a confession is the involuntary product of coercion is judged by the totality of the circumstances—including an examination of both the conduct of the officers and the characteristics of the accused. The Supreme Court has long indicated that one of the key concerns in judging whether confessions were involuntary, or the product of coercion, was the intelligence, mental state, or any other factors possessed by the defendant that might make him particularly suggestible, and susceptible to having his will overborne. *See Colorado v. Connelly,* 479 U.S. 157 (1986) (stating that mental condition is surely relevant to an individual's susceptibility to police coercion); *Spano v. New York,* 360 U.S. 315 (1959) (reversing conviction because confession was involuntary because of effect of psychological coercion on suspect who was foreign-born, completed one-half year of high school, and had a history of mental instability); *Fikes v. Alabama,* 352 U.S. 191, 196–98 (1957) (reversing a conviction because the coercion applied against a person who was "weak of will or mind" deprived him of due process of law)....

The appellants' own investigative reports reveal they were aware that although Wilson graduated from high school, he had attended largely, if not exclusively, special education classes; school officials considered him mentally handicapped; school officials believed he had difficulty distinguishing between fantasy and reality and believed he could be talked into anything. Armed with this knowledge, appellants proceeded to interrogate Wilson for over four hours. The district court described it thus:

> Four different officers interrogated Wilson; he was never left alone and no friend, family member, guardian or advisor was ever present. The officers lied to Wilson. They told him that there were eyewitnesses placing him at the scene prior to the time of the fire. They told him about Gary Wall's statement that Wilson had told Wall, before anyone else knew, that Ms. Martz had been tied and burned in the fire. They offered to help Wilson obtain leniency if he confessed to the murder. They falsely informed him that their psychiatrist had analyzed him. They insisted that he would undoubtedly be found guilty if he did not confess. Then, when Wilson failed to provide correct details about the crime, they rebuked him for not cooperating and offered those details to him in a leading question format. Through the entire interrogation, Defendants used threatening tones and language. They restricted Wilson's freedom of movement and refused to accept his repeated protestations of innocence. They even threatened to use these protestations against him by claiming that his "lies" could subject him to even harsher penalties.

Of particular concern, in addition to the general threats and intimidation that may have been employed to overbear Wilson's will, is the fact that the officers relied largely on leading questions to secure this confession from Wilson. *Spano,* 360 U.S. at 322 (noting that involuntary confession was not delivered in narrative fashion, but rather in response to "leading questions of a skillful prosecutor in a question and answer confession"); *Fikes,* 352 U.S. at 195 (describing involuntary confession that was delivered in response to yes-or-no questions, "some of which were quite leading or suggestive"). There are sufficient facts in the record to support the conclusion that the officers set out to secure a confession from Wilson, and succeeded only by overreaching. Against this background case law, in light of Wilson's limited intelligence and mental capacities, no officer could have reasonably thought this conduct consistent with Wilson's constitutional rights.

Appellants refer us to several cases that have held a confession is not involuntary simply because officials created a fear of imminent arrest, or expressed disbelief in the statements of a suspect in order to elicit further statements, or lied to the accused about the evidence against him. However, none of the cases involve a confessor who was mentally handicapped. Also, a totality of the circumstances analysis does not permit state officials to cherry-pick cases that address individual potentially coercive tactics, isolated one from the other, in order to insulate themselves when they have combined all of those tactics in an effort to overbear an accused's will.

Lastly, appellants assert that one must take into account the fact that they repeatedly advised Wilson of his rights during the interrogation. They are correct that this is part of the totality of the circumstances and must be considered. However, one must also consider that they downplayed the importance of those rights to Wilson, whom they knew was unlikely to understand them because of his low intelligence. Advising a suspect of his rights does not automatically mean that any subsequent confession is voluntary or that officers may use any methods to secure a confession, particularly when they know the suspect is unlikely to fully understand those rights. *See Sims v. Georgia,* 389 U.S. 404 (1967) (holding that where suspect had only third grade education, was deprived of contact with anyone outside, and was subjected to earlier physical violence by officers, advising him of his right not to speak was of little significance); *Fikes,* 352 U.S. at 193 (stating that the fact an officer advised a suspect of his rights must be considered in light of suspect's experience and mental ability); *see also Miller,* 474 U.S. at 110 (stating that even after the Court ruled *Miranda* warnings must be given in custodial interrogations, the Court continued to judge whether confessions were voluntary under due process). Thus, the *Miranda* warnings are but one factor to consider in evaluating the totality of the circumstances.

We affirm the denial of qualified immunity on this claim....

Notes and Questions

1. An "*Alford* plea," the basis of Wilson's conviction, is a guilty plea in which the defendant does not acknowledge committing the crime, and may even protest innocence. It is named after the Supreme Court case upholding the acceptance of such pleas, *North Carolina v. Alford,* 400 U.S. 25, 91 S.Ct. 160, 27 L.Ed.2d 162 (1970), which we discuss in Chapter 9.

2. In *Singletary v. Fischer,* 365 F.Supp.2d 328 (E.D.N.Y. 2005), a federal district court concluded that the petitioner, a mentally retarded individual who had confessed to and was convicted of murder at a state trial, had been provided ineffective assistance of counsel because his attorney had failed to investigate and challenge his potentially false and unreliable admissions to the police following lengthy interrogation.

[T]rickery by the police, particularly when applied to those of immature minds, may cause, with a substantial degree of probability, false confessions.

Criminal interrogators are warned not to do what the police apparently did in the instant case. *See* FRED E. INBAU ET AL., CRIMINAL INTERROGATION AND CONFESSIONS 405 (Jones and Bartlett Publishers, Inc. 4th ed.2004) (2001). The authors of this standard work on the subject caution:

> [P]ersons who are unintelligent, uneducated, and come from a low cultural background engage in criminal behavior. The investigator must particularly avoid any theme or interrogation technique designed to persuade such a suspect ... that he is guilty of the offense

> despite his alleged lack of recall committing it, or statements that threaten inevitable consequences or offer promises of leniency.

In *Mental Retardation, Competency to Waive* Miranda *Rights, and False Confessions,* Professors Solomon M. Fulero and Caroline Everington warn that "confessions are frequently entered by persons with mental retardation in police interrogations without full understanding of their rights," and their statements must be "evaluated closely for reliability." Solomon M. Fulero & Caroline Everington, *Mental Retardation, Competency to Waive* Miranda *Rights, and False Confessions, in* INTERROGATIONS, CONFESSIONS AND ENTRAPMENT 163, 163 (G. Daniel Lassiter, ed., 2004) (citation omitted). The authors remind us,

> While there is no work directly finding that persons with mental retardation are more likely to render false confessions than those without mental retardation, all of the evidence ... suggests that this is likely. Persons with mental retardation are susceptible to non-physical forms of coercion, pressure and intimidation by the police that people with normal intelligence can more readily withstand. They are less able to handle the stress and fear of a police interrogation, particularly if the questioning is prolonged. They are also less likely to resist the efforts of an apparently "friendly" police questioner. Their characteristic desire to please figures of authority can lead them to do whatever they think necessary to gain approval. *Id.* at 171.

They point out,

In the British system, when a person with a disability is being interrogated, a neutral person is required in the interrogation to ensure that the individual understands the questions and the implications of any statements that he/she makes. *Id.* at 176 (citations omitted).

The petitioner, as the literature and the expert testimony indicated, might well have believed that his confession was accurate, his memory having been sufficiently influenced by the situation and his own mental deficiencies. Without expert testimony on the subject there is no way the jury could have appreciated and evaluated the probative force of the confession.

Should special rules be devised to help protect juveniles—whose lack of maturity, experience, and cognitive development might leave them especially susceptible to pressure to confess, and perhaps confess falsely—during police interrogation? Is it sufficient simply to take account of a suspect's youth among the "totality of the circumstances" in determining the voluntariness of a juvenile's confession? Consider the following decision of the Wisconsin Supreme Court, which involves a confession to participating in an armed robbery that was given by a 14-year-old boy.

In the Interest of Jerrell C.J.

699 N.W.2d 110 (Wis. 2005)

ANN WALSH BRADLEY, J.

[Three young men, armed and wearing masks, robbed a McDonald's restaurant in Milwaukee on Saturday, May 26, 2001. Fourteen-year-old Jerrell C.J. was arrested at his home two days later at 6:20 a.m. and taken to the police station, where he was booked and then placed in an interrogation room.]

In the interrogation room, Jerrell was handcuffed to a wall and left alone for approximately two hours. At 9:00 a.m., Police Detectives Ralph Spano and Kurt Sutter entered the interrogation room. The detectives introduced themselves, removed Jerrell's handcuffs, and asked him some background questions. Jerrell stated that he was 14 years old and in eighth grade. He also provided the names, addresses, and phone numbers of his parents and siblings.

At 9:10 a.m., Detective Spano advised Jerrell of his *Miranda* rights. The detectives then began to question Jerrell about the armed robbery at McDonald's. Jerrell denied his involvement. The detectives challenged this denial and encouraged Jerrell to be "truthful and honest" and "start standing up for what he did." Jerrell again denied his involvement. The detectives again challenged this denial.

At times in this exchange, Detective Spano raised his voice. He later explained, "I'm raising my voice short of yelling at him ... there were points I needed to make, and I needed to make them with a strong voice. But not yelling." Jerrell described the "raised voice," stating, "I'm not quite sure but it's like he was angry with me. That sort of tone in his voice." Jerrell indicated that it made him feel "kind of frightened."

During the questioning, Jerrell was afforded food and bathroom breaks. He was kept in the interrogation room until lunchtime. At lunch, he was placed in a bullpen cell for about 20 minutes where he ate. The questioning resumed about 12:30 p.m. In the interrogation room, Detective Spano said Jerrell "started opening up about his involvement and everybody else's" somewhere between 1:00 and 1:30 p.m.

It is undisputed that "several times" during the interrogation, Jerrell asked "if he could make a phone call to his mother or father." Each time Detective Spano said "no." Detective Spano later testified that he "never" in 12 years allowed a juvenile to contact parents during interrogation because it could stop the flow or jeopardize it altogether. He explained:

> If I don't have any control about what he can say over the phone or what he can do when he has got the phone in his hand, I don't think it is prudent or proper to let him do that.

At 2:40 p.m., over five-and-a-half hours after interrogation began, and eight hours after he was taken into custody, Jerrell signed a statement prepared by Detective Spano. In it, he admitted his involvement in the McDonald's robbery.

Jerrell subsequently moved to suppress his written confession, claiming that it was involuntary, unreliable, and a product of coercion. The circuit court denied the motion. Jerrell was then tried with a co-defendant and adjudged delinquent for committing armed robbery, party to a crime.

After his adjudication, Jerrell filed a postdisposition motion seeking a new trial on the basis that his confession was unreliable, untrustworthy, and involuntary. The motion focused on inconsistencies between Jerrell's statement and that of eyewitnesses and other participants. Again, the circuit court denied the motion....

The court of appeals affirmed the circuit court ... [but] wrote separately to express its grave concern with the issue of false confessions made by juveniles during custodial interrogation. Its opinion concludes with a call for action:

> It is this court's opinion that it is time for Wisconsin to tackle the false confession issue. We need to take appropriate action so that the youth of our state are protected from confessing to crimes they did not commit. We need to find safeguards that will balance necessary police interrogation techniques to ferret out the guilty against the need to offer adequate constitutional protections to the innocent.

... The first issue presented for our review is whether Jerrell's written confession to police was constitutionally voluntary....

The voluntariness of a confession is evaluated on the basis of the totality of the circumstances surrounding that confession....

When applying this test to a juvenile interrogation, we note that "[t]he Supreme Court in the past has spoken of the need to exercise 'special caution' when assessing the voluntariness of a juvenile confession, particularly when there is prolonged or repeated questioning or when the interrogation occurs in the absence of a parent, lawyer, or other friendly adult." *Hardaway v. Young,* 302 F.3d 757, 762 (7th Cir.2002) (citing *In re Gault,* 387 U.S. 1, 45 (1967); *Gallegos v. Colorado,* 370 U.S. 49, 53–55 (1962); *Haley v. Ohio,* 332 U.S. 596, 599–601 (1948))....

In assessing the totality of the circumstances, we first examine Jerrell's relevant personal characteristics. Here, these include his age, education and intelligence, and prior experience with law enforcement. We then consider the pressures and tactics used by the police such as the refusal of Jerrell's requests to talk to his parents, the length of the custody, and the psychological techniques applied to Jerrell.

Courts have long recognized the importance of age in determining whether a juvenile confession is voluntary. For example, in *Haley,* 332 U.S. at 599, the juvenile's "tender and difficult age" of 15 was a significant factor favoring the Supreme Court's suppression of his confession....

We agree with the case law's recognition that "youth is more than a chronological fact." *Eddings v. Oklahoma,* 455 U.S. 104, 115 (1982). While not necessarily dispositive, "youth remains a critical factor for our consideration, and the younger the child the more carefully we will scrutinize police questioning tactics to determine if excessive coercion or intimidation or simple immaturity that would not affect an adult has tainted the juvenile's confession." *Hardaway,* 302 F.3d at 765. Simply put, children are different than adults, and the condition of being a child renders one "uncommonly susceptible to police pressures." *[State v.] Hoppe,* 661 N.W.2d 407 [(Wis. 2003)].[6] We therefore view Jerrell's young age of 14 to be a strong factor weighing against the voluntariness of his confession.

Another factor weighing against the voluntariness of Jerrell's confession is his education and intelligence. At the time of the interrogation, Jerrell was in eighth grade and earning a 3.6 grade point average. Although such academic achievement is usually consistent with a high degree of aptitude, postdisposition standard IQ testing revealed that Jerrell had an IQ of 84, indicating a low average range of intelligence. The reliability of the IQ test is supported by Jerrell's previous school records, showing average to failing grades, as well as testing completed by the Ethan Allen School. Accordingly, we consider Jerrell's limited education and low average intelligence as additional reasons for why he was susceptible to police pressure.

Finally, we examine Jerrell's prior experience with law enforcement. In cases where courts have found that prior experience weighs in favor of a finding of voluntariness, the juvenile's contacts with police have been extensive....

In this case, Jerrell's experience with law enforcement was more limited and may have contributed to his willingness to confess in the case at hand. Jerrell had been arrested twice for misdemeanor offenses prior to his interrogation for the armed robbery. In both instances, he answered police questions, admitted to involvement, and was allowed to go home. Significantly, he was never adjudged delinquent. We note the argument of Jerrell's counsel that such an experience may have taught him a dangerous lesson that admitting involvement in an offense will result in a return home without any significant consequences.

Having examined Jerrell's relevant personal characteristics, we now consider the pressures and tactics used by the police during the interrogation, beginning with the refusal of Jerrell's requests to talk to his parents. Thirty years ago this court rejected a per se rule requiring parental presence in juvenile interrogations. *Theriault,* 223 N.W.2d 850. In doing so, however, the court stressed the importance of parental presence in the totality of the circumstances analysis:

> The failure to promptly notify [parents] and the reasons therefore may be a factor, however, in determining whether the confession was coerced or voluntary. If the police fail to call the parents for the purpose of depriving the juvenile of the opportunity to receive advice and counsel, that would be strong evidence that coercive tactics were used to elicit the incriminating statements.

Here, the police specifically denied Jerrell's requests to call his parents. Detective Spano later testified that he "never" in 12 years allowed a juvenile to contact parents during interrogation because it could stop the flow of, or jeopardize the interrogation. We are troubled by this tactic,

6. Scholarly research supports this. For example, one commentator has observed that juveniles may be more susceptible than adults to making false confessions for a number of reasons. See Jennifer J. Walters, Comment, *Illinois' Weakened Attempt to Prevent False Confessions by Juveniles: The Requirement of Counsel for the Interrogations of Some Juveniles,* 33 Loy. U. Chi. L.J. 487, 504–05 (2002). Because their intellectual capacity is not fully developed, children are less likely to understand their *Miranda* rights. *Id.* Additionally, minors are more likely to want to please and believe police officers because they are authority figures. *Id.* at 505. Finally, because juveniles are incapable of fully realizing the consequences of their decisions, they may confess because they believe it is the only way to end a psychologically coercive interrogation. *Id.*

See also Steven A. Drizin & Richard A. Leo, *The Problem of False Confessions in the Post DNA World,* 82 N.C. L.Rev. 891, 944 (2004) (documenting 40 proven false juvenile confessions, including five from the infamous Central Park Jogger case); Welsh S. White, *False Confessions and the Constitution: Safeguards Against Untrustworthy Confessions,* 32 Harv. C.R.-C.L.Rev. 105, 131 (1997) ("Empirical data suggest that suspects who are especially vulnerable for other reasons such as youth, brain damage, or compliant personalities may be similarly prone to give false confessions.").

as parents are often the very people children turn to for advice.... [W]e view the denial of Jerrell's requests to talk to his parents as strong evidence of coercive police conduct.

The length of the custody is also an important factor in evaluating police behavior....

In this case, Jerrell was handcuffed to a wall and left alone for approximately two hours. He was then interrogated for five-and-a-half more hours before finally signing a written confession prepared by Detective Spano. The duration of Jerrell's custody and interrogation was longer than the five hours at issue in *Haley,* 332 U.S. 596. Indeed, it was significantly longer than most interrogations.[7] Under these circumstances, it is easy to see how Jerrell would be left wondering "if and when the inquisition would ever cease." *Woods v. Clusen,* 794 F.2d 293, 298 (7th Cir.1986). Thus, Jerrell's lengthy custody and interrogation is additional evidence of coercive conduct.

The final factor we address is the psychological techniques applied....

Not only did the detectives refuse to believe Jerrell's repeated denials of guilt, but they also joined in urging him to tell a different "truth," sometimes using a "strong voice" that "frightened" him. Admittedly, it does not appear from the record that Jerrell was suffering from any significant emotional or psychological condition during the interrogation. Nevertheless, we remain concerned that such a technique applied to a juvenile like Jerrell over a prolonged period of time could result in an involuntary confession.

Weighing the above personal characteristics against the pressures and tactics used by the police, we determine that the State has not met its burden of proving that Jerrell's written confession was "the product of a free and unconstrained will, reflecting deliberateness of choice." *Hoppe,* 661 N.W.2d 407. Rather, we conclude that it was "the result of a conspicuously unequal confrontation in which the pressures brought to bear on the defendant by representatives of the State exceeded the defendant's ability to resist." *Id.* Accordingly, we determine that the written confession was involuntary under the totality of the circumstances.

We turn next to the second issue in this case concerning whether this court should adopt a per se rule, excluding in-custody admissions from any child under the age of 16 who has not been given the opportunity to consult with a parent or interested adult. Jerrell asserts that such a requirement is critical to leveling the playing field between juveniles and the police in an interrogation....

[W]e decline to abandon the "totality of the circumstances" approach at this time in favor of Jerrell's per se rule regarding consultation with a parent or interested adult. Instead, we choose to reaffirm our warning in *Theriault,* 223 N.W.2d 850, that the failure "to call the parents for the purpose of depriving the juvenile of the opportunity to receive advice and counsel" will be considered "strong evidence that coercive tactics were used to elicit the incriminating statements." ...

[W]e exercise our supervisory power to require that all custodial interrogation of juveniles in future cases be electronically recorded where feasible, and without exception when questioning occurs at a place of detention....

The decision of the court of appeals is reversed.

SHIRLEY S. ABRAHAMSON, C.J. (concurring).

... [U]nlike the majority, I would adopt a per se rule excluding in-custody admissions from any child under the age of 16 who has not been given the opportunity to consult with a parent or interested adult.

The court of appeals, the defendant, the Children and Family Justice Center at Northwestern University School of Law's Bluhm Legal Clinic,[4] the Juvenile Law Center,[5] and University of Wisconsin Law School Professor Marygold S. Melli[6] all agree that it is time to take appropriate action to protect the youth of our state from confessing to crimes they did not commit.

The State does not question the merits of a per se rule, but argues that the formulation of

---

7. In *Inside the Interrogation Room,* 86 J.Crim. L. & Criminology 266, 279 (1996), Richard A. Leo reported that more than 70% of the interrogations he observed lasted less than an hour, and only 8% lasted more than two hours. These figures were taken from a sample of 153 interrogations. *Id.*

4. *See* Brief of Amicus Curiae Children & Family Justice Center, Professor Emerita Marygold S. Melli, & The Juvenile Law Center.

5. *See id.*

6. *See id.*

such a rule should be left to the legislature, as a matter of policy ... I reject the State's leave-it-to-the-legislature approach on this parental issue.

... [T]he majority opinion's holding that an adult's presence is a significant factor under the totality of circumstances test does not go far enough. I would adopt a per se rule excluding in-custody admissions from any child under the age of 16 who has not been given the opportunity to consult with a parent or interested adult. Here are my top 8 (interrelated and overlapping) reasons for adopting a per se rule:

Reason No. 1. A per se rule should be adopted because Wisconsin law enforcement officers have not heeded the warning this court issued 30 years ago in *Theriault v. State,* 223 N.W.2d 850 (1974), that law enforcement's failure to call a juvenile's parents would be viewed as "strong evidence that coercive tactics were used to elicit the incriminating statements." ... As the present case demonstrates, the long-time practice of Milwaukee police officers to exclude parents from the interrogation of juveniles has continued ... [and] the practice of excluding parents during juvenile interrogation is apparently widespread throughout the state.

... [T]here is no reason to think a second clarion call by this court re-announcing *Theriault's* totality of the circumstances rule will change police practices, especially when a leading police interrogation manual recommends that police interrogate suspects in privacy whenever possible.[42]

Reason No. 2. A per se rule should be adopted because Wisconsin courts have not heeded this court's warning from *Theriault* that law enforcement's failure to call a juvenile's parents would be viewed as "strong evidence that coercive tactics were used to elicit incriminating statements." Courts have inconsistently applied the totality of circumstances test and have tended to haphazardly exclude only the most egregiously obtained confessions....

Reason No. 3. A per se rule should be adopted because juveniles do not have the decision-making capacity and understanding of adults. Emerging studies demonstrate that the area of the brain governing decision making and the weighing of risks and rewards continues to develop into the late teens and the early twenties.[46] Further studies show that children under the age of 16 are less capable than adults of understanding their *Miranda* rights,[47] have a propensity to confess to police,[48] and are less capable than adults of making long range decisions.[49] As the United States Supreme Court observed over 40 years ago, adult advice would put a juvenile "on a less unequal footing with his [or her] interrogators."[50]

---

42. *See* Fred E. Inbau et al., *Criminal Interrogation and Confessions* 51–56, 521 (4th ed.2001).

46. *See, e.g.,* Elizabeth R. Sowell et al., *Mapping Continued Brain Growth and Gray Matter Density Reduction in Dorsal Frontal Cortex: Inverse Relationships during Postadolescent Brain Maturation,* 21 J. Neurosci. 8819, 8828 (2001).

Information about juvenile brain development is available on the ABA's Juvenile Justice Center's website at http://www.aban et.org/crimjust/juvjus/resources#brain.

47. *See, e.g.,* Barbara Kaban & Ann E. Tobey, *When Police Question Children: Are Protections Adequate?,* 1 J. Ctr. for Child. & Cts. 151 (1999); Barry C. Field, *Competence, Culpability, and Punishment: Implications of Atkins for Executing and Sentencing Juveniles,* 32 Hofstra L.Rev. 463, 530–535 (Winter 2003); David T. Huang, *Less Unequal Footing: State Courts' Per Se Rules for Juvenile Waivers During Interrogations and the Case For Their Implementation,* 86 Corn. L.Rev. 437, 449 (2001); Robert E. McGuire, *A Proposal to Strengthen Juvenile Miranda Rights: Requiring Parental Presence in Custodial Interrogation,* 53 Vand. L.Rev. 1355, 1381–82 (2000); Thomas Grisso, *Juveniles' Capacities to Waive Miranda Rights: An Empirical Analysis,* 68 Cal. L.Rev. 1134, 1160–61 (1980).

48. *See, e.g.,* Allison D. Redlich & Gail S. Goodman, *Taking Responsibility for an Act Not Committed: The Influence of Age and Suggestibility,* Law & Human Behavior 141, 152–53 (April 2003); Kaban & Tobey, *supra* note 47; Jennifer J. Walters, Comment, *Illinois' Weakened Attempt to Prevent False Confessions by Juveniles: The Requirement of Counsel for the Interrogations of Some Juveniles,* 33 Loy. U. Chi. L.J. 487, 504–05 (2002); McGuire, *supra* note 47, at 1381–82; Maggie Bruck & Stephen J. Ceci, *The Suggestibility of Children's Memory,* 50 Ann. Rev. Psychol. 419 (1999); Amy Bach, *True Crime, False Confession,* The Nation (Feb. 8, 1999, at 21).

49. *See, e.g.,* Elizabeth S. Scott & Lawrence Steinberg, *Blaming Youth,* 81 Tex. L.Rev. 799, 814–15 (Feb. 2003). *See* Wis. Stat. § 48.375 (requiring parental consent for abortion, finding that "[i]mmature minors often lack the ability to make fully informed choices that take account of both immediate and long-range consequences").

50. *Gallegos v. Colorado,* 370 U.S. 49, 54 (1962).

Courts using the totality of circumstances test have not considered this evidence and have not weighed factors that make children uniquely vulnerable during interrogation.

Reason No. 4. A per se rule should be adopted to prevent false confessions. Although it is difficult for many of us to understand what leads an innocent person to confess to a crime, especially a serious felony, researchers have documented that false confessions are "a leading cause of the wrongful convictions of the innocent in America."[52]

When used against vulnerable suspects, standard police interrogation techniques are especially apt to lead to false confessions.[53] Juveniles and the mentally retarded are the most vulnerable to modern psychological interrogation techniques.[54] It follows that juveniles "appear with some regularity in false confession cases."[55]

Although it is difficult to quantify the exact number of false juvenile confessions, the court of appeals referred to one study in which over a two-year period almost a dozen juveniles in the United States who confessed to committing murder were subsequently proven innocent.[56] The majority opinion acknowledges false confessions and notes the Central Park jogger rape case in which five youths ages 14 to 16 (interrogated in the absence of their parents) falsely confessed to rape.

The U.S. Supreme Court has accepted that parental counsel and advice are crucial protections for juveniles against coercion and intimidation during police interrogation and are crucial to the voluntariness analysis. The Supreme Court has urged that the "greatest care must be taken to assure that the admission was voluntary,"[58] and that a juvenile needs someone to lean on "lest the overpowering presence of the law, as he knows it, may not crush him."[59]

At least two state courts have concluded that when a parent is deliberately excluded from interrogation of a juvenile, a confession almost invariably will be suppressed.[60]

Given the limited mental abilities of juveniles and their heightened susceptibility to suggestion, a per se rule is needed to increase the likelihood that a guilty verdict will not be based on a false confession and be overturned on appeal. A per se rule thus fosters the fair administration of justice.

Reason No. 5. A per se rule should be adopted to protect parental and family values. One of the oldest fundamental liberty interests recognized by the U.S. Supreme Court is that of parents to direct the care, control, and upbringing of their children. This constitutional protection extends to parents' right to be consulted in decisions that have potentially traumatic and permanent consequences....

Reason No. 6. A per se rule should be adopted because it comports with Wisconsin legislative policy evidenced in numerous statutes requiring parents or guardians to have a say in a variety of significant decisions affecting their children....

Reason No. 7. A per se rule should be adopted because it has proven to function well in other states and in England. According to one commentator, thirteen states have adopted, by case law or legislative action, some form of a per se parental consultation rule.[64] In 1998 the Kansas supreme court[65] reviewed court-imposed rules

52. Steven A. Drizin & Richard A. Leo, *The Problem of False Confessions in the Post-DNA World,* 82 N.C. L.Rev. 891, 906 (2004).

53. *See, e.g.,* Welsh S. White, *False Confessions and the Constitutional Safeguards Against Untrustworthy Confessions,* 32 Harv. C.R.-C.L. L.Rev. 105, 120 (1997).

54. Drizin & Leo, *supra* note 52, at 919.

55. John E. Reid and Associates, *False Confession Cases—The Issues,* available at http://www.reid.com/educational_info/r_tips.html?serial=1080 839438473936&print.

56. *Jerrell C.J.,* 674 N.W.2d 607, citing Walters, *supra* note 48, at 489.

58. *In re Gault,* 387 U.S. 1, 55 (1967).

59. *Haley v. Ohio,* 332 U.S. 596, 600 (1948).

60. *State v. Farrell,* 766 A.2d 1057, 1062 (N.H. 2001); *State v. Presha,* 748 A.2d 1108, 1118 (N.J. 2000).

64. Thomas J. Von Wald, Note, *No Questions Asked! State v. Horse: A Proposition for a Per Se Rule When Interrogating Juveniles,* 48 S.D. L.Rev. 143, 164 n. 237 (2002–03).

65. *In re B.M.B.,* 264 Kan. 417, 955 P.2d 1302 (1998). Counsel for B.M.B. argued that the following states have statutory restrictions on the admissibility of unadvised juvenile statements: Colorado, Connecticut, Iowa, Montana, North Carolina, Oklahoma, and West Virginia. *See id.* at 1310.

from Massachusetts, Missouri, New York, Indiana, Vermont, and Florida and adopted a per se rule.

Great Britain's Police and Criminal Evidence Act of 1984 details a Code of Practice for the Detention, Treatment, and Questioning of Persons by Police Officers, including those persons under 17 years of age. Juveniles must have an "appropriate adult" present during interrogation....

Reason No. 8. A per se rule should be adopted because such a rule is the right, just, and fair way to operate the Wisconsin judicial system.

Police and law television dramas may lead us to believe that interrogations using psychological tactics (including trickery) lead to sound and reliable confessions. Television is not reality. What may be compelling entertainment (as we cheer for the good guys and applaud the capture and successful prosecution of the bad guys) is far removed from the complications of the real world that sadly includes unreliable and false confessions.

Wisconsin must do more than apply the "totality of the circumstances" rule to protect children and families and tackle the problem of false confessions. Mandating electronic recording of juvenile interrogations is a very important step, but it is only one step. I would have the court fashion a rule requiring the participation of an interested adult in the interrogation process of juveniles. Other jurisdictions provide good working models. Such a rule will provide desperately needed procedural safeguards to protect children and families and to ensure the validity of confessions and the sound administration of justice....

Notes and Questions

1. Do you find persuasive the reasons that Chief Justice Abrahamson advances in support of a *per se* rule that an interested adult must be involved when the police interrogate a juvenile? What sort of advice is apt to be offered by parents or a guardian to a child whom the police want to question about criminal activity? Would the presence of an interested adult likely be helpful in guarding against false confessions? Would the presumed benefits of involving an interested adult outweigh the potential costs to law enforcement?

2. In a portion of the majority opinion in *In the Interest of Jerrell C.J.* that we have omitted, lengthy discussion is devoted to whether the police should be required to electronically record their interrogation of juvenile suspects. Relying on its supervisory powers, rather than constitutional or common law grounds, the Wisconsin Supreme Court announced that such recording would prospectively be required of interrogation sessions that involve juveniles and occur in a place of detention. We consider additional issues concerning the electronic recording of custodial interrogation sessions later in this chapter.

The two most oft-cited populations at risk for false confessions are juveniles and persons with mental impairment (*i.e.*, intellectual disabilities and mental illness). There are numerous confirmatory case examples, including the five juveniles involved in the Central Park Jogger case, Michael Crowe, Martin Tankleff, Earl Washington, Jr., Eddie Joe Lloyd, Ron Williamson, and many others.[9] It is important to note that, although certain populations, like juveniles, are overrepresented among proven false confession cases (in comparison to prevalence rates for their arrests or convictions), the majority of proven and probable cases are of adults without any obvious vulnerabilities present. For example, of 125 proven false confession cases,[10] 33% involved juveniles, meaning the remaining 67% were adults, although a portion had known mental impairments.

Social scientists have begun to investigate the reasons why certain groups are especially vulnerable to the risk of falsely confessing. In general, the characteristics that typify juveniles and persons with mental impairment, such as suggestibility, the tendency to obey authority, impulsivity, and deficiencies in abstract thinking, are the same characteristics that serve to increase risk. Although relatively few direct studies exist, large literatures in basic developmental science, psychopathology, and intellectual disability are available for insights. In one laboratory study, researchers demonstrated that minors between the ages of 12 and 16 years were more likely than young adults (aged 18 to 24) to take responsibility for an act they did not commit.[11] In addition, in this study, the presentation of false evidence—an allowable police interrogation tactic—had especial influence on the minors, serving to increase the rate of false admissions.

Regardless of an individual's inherent vulnerabilities, it is quite often the combination of intrinsic qualities (*i.e.*, dispositional characteristics) and modern-day police interrogation techniques (*i.e.*, situational characteristics) that produce false confessions. With the exception of truly voluntary false confessions (such as could have occurred in the *Connelly* case discussed above), most false confessors do not walk into the police station, offer incriminating statements, and become wrongfully convicted. Rather, false confessions emerge when inappropriate and/or impermissible interrogation techniques are employed on those erroneously assumed to be guilty. Although all misjudged suspects are susceptible to false confessions under the right confluence of circumstances, those deemed vulnerable because of age, cognitive abilities, physical need, lack of sleep, etc. are even more susceptible. In the next section, we will see how many of the standard police interrogation techniques used today are psychologically manipulative in nature.

4. The Totality of the Circumstances: Police Interrogation Tactics

Individuals who have committed a crime understandably may be reluctant to volunteer that information to the police. Interrogators who meet with suspects' denials accordingly may press ahead with their questioning and employ techniques designed to overcome resistance and secure a confession. In *Brown v. Mississippi*, which reached the Supreme Court in 1936, the police resorted to whippings, beatings, and other acts of violence to produce confessions. As we saw, the justices in *Brown* had no difficulty in concluding that such overbearing conduct rendered the confessions involuntary. As the 20th century progressed, fewer claims reached the courts that the police used physical coercion to extract confessions from crime suspects.

In 1966, Chief Justice Warren observed in his opinion for the Court in *Miranda v. Arizona*, 384 U.S. 436, 448, 86 S.Ct. 1602, 16 L.Ed.2d 694 (1966) "that the modern practice of in-custody interrogation is psychologically rather than physically oriented." He offered numerous examples, gleaned from leading instructional manuals, of the contemporary interrogation practices commonly used by the police. As a part of this discussion, the Chief Justice recognized that the same psychological techniques employed by the police to elicit confessions from the guilty simultaneously risked inducing false confessions from the innocent.

The officers are told by the manuals that the 'principal psychological factor contributing to a successful interrogation is privacy—being alone with the person under interrogation.'[10] The efficacy of this tactic has been explained as follows:

'If at all practicable, the interrogation should take place in the investigator's

10. Inbau & Reid, Criminal Interrogation and Confessions (1962), at 1.

office or at least in a room of his own choice. The subject should be deprived of every psychological advantage. In his own home he may be confident, indignant, or recalcitrant. He is more keenly aware of his rights and more reluctant to tell of his indiscretions of criminal behavior within the walls of his home. Moreover his family and other friends are nearby, their presence lending moral support. In his office, the investigator possesses all the advantages. The atmosphere suggests the invincibility of the forces of the law.'[11]

To highlight the isolation and unfamiliar surroundings, the manuals instruct the police to display an air of confidence in the suspect's guilt and from outward appearance to maintain only an interest in confirming certain details. The guilt of the subject is to be posited as a fact. The interrogator should direct his comments toward the reasons why the subject committed the act, rather than court failure by asking the subject whether he did it. Like other men, perhaps the subject has had a bad family life, had an unhappy childhood, had too much to drink, had an unrequited desire for women. The officers are instructed to minimize the moral seriousness of the offense,[12] to cast blame on the victim or on society.[13] These tactics are designed to put the subject in a psychological state where his story is but an elaboration of what the police purport to know already—that he is guilty. Explanations to the contrary are dismissed and discouraged.

The texts thus stress that the major qualities an interrogator should possess are patience and perseverance. One writer describes the efficacy of these characteristics in this manner:

> 'In the preceding paragraphs emphasis has been placed on kindness and stratagems. The investigator will, however, encounter many situations where the sheer weight of his personality will be the deciding factor. Where emotional appeals and tricks are employed to no avail, he must rely on an oppressive atmosphere of dogged persistence. He must interrogate steadily and without relent, leaving the subject no prospect of surcease. He must dominate his subject and overwhelm him with his inexorable will to obtain the truth. He should interrogate for a spell of several hours pausing only for the subject's necessities in acknowledgment of the need to avoid a charge of duress that can be technically substantiated. In a serious case, the interrogation may continue for days, with the required intervals for food and sleep, but with no respite from the atmosphere of domination. It is possible in this way to induce the subject to talk without resorting to duress or coercion. The method should be used only when the guilt of the subject appears highly probable.'[14]

The manuals suggest that the suspect be offered legal excuses for his actions in order to obtain an initial admission of guilt. Where there is a suspected revenge-killing, for example, the interrogator may say:

> 'Joe, you probably didn't go out looking for this fellow with the purpose of shooting him. My guess is, however, that you expected something from him and that's why you carried a gun—for your own protection. You knew him for what he was, no good. Then when you met him he probably started using foul, abusive language and he gave some indication that he was about to pull a gun on you, and that's when you had to act to save your own life. That's about it, isn't it, Joe?'[15]

Having then obtained the admission of shooting, the interrogator is advised to refer to circumstantial evidence which negates the self-defense explanation. This should enable him to secure the entire story. One text notes that

11. O'Hara, [Fundamentals of Criminal Investigation (1956)], at 99.

12. Inbau & Reid, at 34–43, 87. For example, in Leyra v. Denno, 347 U.S. 556 (1954), the interrogator-psychiatrist told the accused, 'We do sometimes things that are not right, but in a fit of temper or anger we sometimes do things we aren't really responsible for,' id., at 562, and again, 'We know that morally you were just in anger. Morally, you are not to be condemned,' id., at 582.

13. Inbau & Reid, at 43–55.

14. O'Hara, at 112.

15. Inbau & Reid, at 40.

'Even if he fails to do so, the inconsistency between the subject's original denial of the shooting and his present admission of at least doing the shooting will serve to deprive him of a self-defense 'out' at the time of trial.'[16]

When the techniques described above prove unavailing, the texts recommend they be alternated with a show of some hostility. One ploy often used has been termed the 'friendly-unfriendly' or the 'Mutt and Jeff' act:

> '* * * In this technique, two agents are employed. Mutt, the relentless investigator, who knows the subject is guilty and is not going to waste any time. He's sent a dozen men away for this crime and he's going to send the subject away for the full term. Jeff, on the other hand, is obviously a kindhearted man. He has a family himself. He has a brother who was involved in a little scrape like this. He disapproves of Mutt and his tactics and will arrange to get him off the case if the subject will cooperate. He can't hold Mutt off for very long. The subject would be wise to make a quick decision. The technique is applied by having both investigators present while Mutt acts out his role. Jeff may stand by quietly and demur at some of Mutt's tactics. When Jeff makes his plea for cooperation, Mutt is not present in the room.'[17]

The interrogators sometimes are instructed to induce a confession out of trickery. The technique here is quite effective in crimes which require identification or which run in series. In the identification situation, the interrogator may take a break in his questioning to place the subject among a group of men in a line-up. 'The witness or complainant (previously coached, if necessary) studies the line-up and confidently points out the subject as the guilty party.'[18] Then the questioning resumes 'as though there were now no doubt about the guilt of the subject.' A variation on this technique is called the 'reverse line-up':

> 'The accused is placed in a line-up, but this time he is identified by several fictitious witnesses or victims who associated him with different offenses. It is expected that the subject will become desperate and confess to the offense under investigation in order to escape from the false accusations.'[19]

The manuals also contain instructions for police on how to handle the individual who refuses to discuss the matter entirely, or who asks for an attorney or relatives. The examiner is to concede him the right to remain silent. 'This usually has a very undermining effect. First of all, he is disappointed in his expectation of an unfavorable reaction on the part of the interrogator. Secondly, a concession of this right to remain silent impresses the subject with the apparent fairness of his interrogator.'[20] After this psychological conditioning, however, the officer is told to point out the incriminating significance of the suspect's refusal to talk:

> 'Joe, you have a right to remain silent. That's your privilege and I'm the last person in the world who'll try to take it away from you. If that's the way you want to leave this, O.K. But let me ask you this. Suppose you were in my shoes and I were in yours and you called me in to ask me about this and I told you, 'I don't want to answer any of your questions.' You'd think I had something to hide, and you'd probably be right in thinking that. That's exactly what I'll have to think about you, and so will everybody else. So let's sit here and talk this whole thing over.'[21]

Few will persist in their initial refusal to talk, it is said, if this monologue is employed correctly.

---

16. Ibid.

17. O'Hara, at 104, Inbau & Reid, at 58–59. See Spano v. People of State of New York, 360 U.S. 315 (1959). A variant on the technique of creating hostility is one of engendering fear. This is perhaps best described by the prosecuting attorney in Malinski v. People of State of New York, 324 U.S. 401, 407 (1945): 'Why this talk about being undressed? Of course, they had a right to undress him to look for bullet scars, and keep the clothes off him. That was quite proper police procedure. That is some more psychology—let him sit around with a blanket on him, humiliate him there for a while; let him sit in the corner, let him think he is going to get a shellacking.'

18. O'Hara, at 105–106.

19. Id., at 106.

20. Inbau & Reid, at 111.

21. Ibid.

In the event that the subject wishes to speak to a relative or an attorney, the following advice is tendered:

> '[T]he interrogator should respond by suggesting that the subject first tell the truth to the interrogator himself rather than get anyone else involved in the matter. If the request is for an attorney, the interrogator may suggest that the subject save himself or his family the expense of any such professional service, particularly if he is innocent of the offense under investigation. The interrogator may also add, 'Joe, I'm only looking for the truth, and if you're telling the truth, that's it. You can handle this by yourself.'[22]

From these representative samples of interrogation techniques, the setting prescribed by the manuals and observed in practice becomes clear. In essence, it is this: To be alone with the subject is essential to prevent distraction and to deprive him of any outside support. The aura of confidence in his guilt undermines his will to resist. He merely confirms the preconceived story the police seek to have him describe. Patience and persistence, at times relentless questioning, are employed. To obtain a confession, the interrogator must 'patiently maneuver himself or his quarry into a position from which the desired objective may be attained.'[23] When normal procedures fail to produce the needed result, the police may resort to deceptive stratagems such as giving false legal advice. It is important to keep the subject off balance, for example, by trading on his insecurity about himself or his surroundings. The police then persuade, trick, or cajole him out of exercising his constitutional rights.

Even without employing brutality, the 'third degree' or the specific stratagems described above, the very fact of custodial interrogation exacts a heavy toll on individual liberty and trades on the weakness of individuals.[24] This fact may be illustrated simply by referring to three confession cases decided by this Court in the Term immediately preceding our Escobedo decision. In Townsend v. Sain, 372 U.S. 293 (1963), the defendant was a 19-year-old heroin addict, described as a 'near mental defective,' id., at 307–310. The defendant in Lynumn v. State of Illinois, 372 U.S. 528 (1963), was a woman who confessed to the arresting officer after being importuned to 'cooperate' in order to prevent her children from being taken by relief authorities. This Court as in those cases reversed the conviction of a defendant in Haynes v. State of Washington, 373 U.S. 503 (1963), whose persistent request during his interrogation was to phone his wife or attorney. In other settings, these individuals might have exercised their constitutional rights. In the incommunicado police-dominated atmosphere, they succumbed.

In light of the Court's apparent concerns that the techniques of interrogation described above can produce uncommon pressures on suspects to confess, including to confess falsely, we might inquire whether tactics that involve deceit and psychological manipulation undermine the voluntariness of an incriminating admission. In *Frazier v. Cupp*, 394 U.S. 731, 89 S.Ct. 1420, 22 L.Ed.2d 684 (1969), which came to the Supreme Court three years after *Miranda* was decided, the police arrested Frazier on suspicion of murder. Frazier denied involvement during the initial stages of questioning, insisting that he had been alone with his cousin, Jerry Rawls. "At this point, the officer questioning [Frazier] told him, falsely, that Rawls had been brought in and that he had confessed. [Frazier] still was reluctant to talk, but after the officer sympathetically suggested that the victim had started

22. Inbau & Reid, at 112.

23. Inbau & Reid, Lie Detection and Criminal Interrogation 185 (3d ed. 1953).

24. Interrogation procedures may even give rise to a false confession. The most recent conspicuous example occurred in New York, in 1964, when a Negro of limited intelligence confessed to two brutal murders and a rape which he had not committed. When this was discovered, the prosecutor was reported as saying: 'Call it what you want—brain-washing, hypnosis, fright. They made him give an untrue confession. The only thing I don't believe is that Whitmore was beaten.' N.Y. Times, Jan. 28, 1965, p. 1, col. 5. In two other instances, similar events had occurred. N.Y. Times, Oct. 20, 1964, p. 22, col. 1; N.Y. Times, Aug. 25, 1965, p. 1, col. 1. In general, see Borchard, Convicting the Innocent (1932); Frank & Frank, Not Guilty (1957).

a fight by making homosexual advances, [Frazier] began to spill out his story.... A full confession [eventually] was obtained...." 394 U.S., at 737–738. The confession was admitted into evidence at Frazier's trial and he was convicted of second-degree murder.

Among other grounds urged for reversal, Frazier maintained that his confession, secured by the police's deliberate misrepresentation that his cousin already had admitted to the murder, was involuntary and should not have been admitted into evidence. The justices disagreed.

Before petitioner made any incriminating statements, he received partial warnings of his constitutional rights; this is, of course, a circumstance quite relevant to a finding of voluntariness. The questioning was of short duration, and petitioner was a mature individual of normal intelligence. The fact that the police misrepresented the statements that Rawls had made is, while relevant, insufficient in our view to make this otherwise voluntary confession inadmissible. These cases must be decided by viewing the 'totality of the circumstances,' see, e.g., Clewis v. Texas, 386 U.S. 707, 708 (1967), and on the facts of this case we can find no error in the admission of petitioner's confession.

What limits, if any, should be placed on police trickery and deception during interrogation; tactics that are designed to create pressures or incentives for suspects to confess? Would condoning such tactics create an undue risk that some suspects will confess falsely? Consider the following case.

Lincoln v. State

882 A.2d 944 (Md. App.), *cert. denied,* 888 A.2d 342 (Md. 2005)

EYLER, J.

A jury in the Circuit Court for Baltimore City found Leroy Lincoln, Jr., the appellant, guilty of conspiracy to commit murder. The court sentenced the appellant to life imprisonment with all but 25 years suspended.

On appeal, the appellant presents one question: Did the circuit court err in denying his motion to suppress his statement to the police? Perceiving no error, we shall affirm the judgment.

FACTS AND PROCEEDINGS

On February 27, 1995, Leroy Lincoln, Sr., was murdered in his home on East Northern Parkway, in Baltimore City. The cause of death was blunt force trauma to the head.

Lincoln, Sr., was the appellant's father. The appellant was 18 years old when the murder took place. Also at the time of the murder, Lincoln, Sr., was married to Geralene Lincoln, the appellant's mother, although it is not clear from the record whether Lincoln, Sr., and Geralene were living together.

The murder case remained unsolved for several years, until Baltimore City Police Detective Tyrone Francis, of the "Cold Case Unit," reopened the investigation. He tracked down Monique Peterson, who was the appellant's girlfriend at the time of the murder. On August 23, 2003, Francis interviewed Peterson and obtained a tape-recorded statement from her.

Peterson told Francis that, sometime before the murder, she heard Geralene say she wanted to kill Lincoln, Sr. Also, Peterson had had a conversation with the appellant in which he said that he, his mother, and his friend "John," were planning to kill Lincoln, Sr. Peterson identified a picture of one John Ulrich as the friend in question. Peterson further stated that, after the murder, the appellant said his father was dead and that Ulrich had killed him. The appellant told her that he and Ulrich had gone to Lincoln, Sr.'s house and that Ulrich had hit Lincoln, Sr. with the back of an ax handle. The appellant also told Peterson the murder had been carried out so his mother could obtain his father's insurance money.

Francis attempted to interview Ulrich. Ulrich would not give a statement....

By the time the investigation was reopened, the appellant was 26 years old and was living in North Carolina. His mother was living in North Carolina also. They had moved there in late 1995.

As a result of Francis's investigation, the appellant and Geralene Lincoln were arrested in North Carolina, on October 3 and October 6, 2002, respectively. Francis and Detective J.T. Brown, also of the "Cold Case Unit," traveled to that state and, on October 8, 2002, obtained a tape-recorded statement from Geralene. That afternoon, they interviewed the appellant at the Wilkes County Sheriff's Department in Wilkesboro.

The appellant gave oral and tape-recorded statements during that interview. After he was charged, in the Circuit Court for Baltimore City, with murder and conspiracy to commit murder in the death of his father, he moved to suppress the statements, on the ground that they were not voluntarily made.

At the suppression hearing, Francis testified as follows about the interview of the appellant and the statements he made.

The interview took place in a 6x9 room. The appellant was sitting in a chair at the table in the room. He was not handcuffed. Francis ascertained that the appellant was not under the influence of alcohol or drugs and that he was a high school graduate.

Francis advised the appellant of his *Miranda* rights.... He waived his rights and agreed to answer questions without having an attorney present.

According to Francis, neither he nor Brown threatened or coerced the appellant into waiving his rights or giving a statement. During the interview, they did not make any promises to the appellant, or say or do anything to make him think they would advocate for him with the Maryland or North Carolina authorities. They did not otherwise suggest that they might recommend the appellant's release if he waived his rights and gave them a statement. They did not threaten to use or use physical force. During the interview, the appellant never asked to use the bathroom, for medicine, or for food or beverages. The entire interview lasted one hour and 30 minutes, from when the appellant waived his *Miranda* rights through the conclusion of his tape-recorded statement.

At the outset of the interview, Francis told the appellant the detectives were there to discuss Lincoln, Sr.'s murder. He placed two large files for the case on the table in front of the appellant. He told the appellant he was "willing to discuss the contents of the case files" with him. The appellant denied having any knowledge about the murder.

Francis removed three photographs from the files and showed them to the appellant. The first was a photograph of the appellant. On the back was written, in messy script that looks to have been written using an opposite writing hand: "That's Junior whose father he and I killed for Ms. Geralene." The statement was signed, "John Ulrich, 9-6-02." Although worded as if written by Ulrich, the statement, signature, and date all were written by Francis.

The second photograph was of John Ulrich. On the back was written, in print, "This is John[.] Junior Said He Hit Junior's Father in the Head, While They Smoked Weed With Him And Killed Him[,]" followed by the signature and date, "Monique Peterson, 8-22-02." Although seeming to have been written by Peterson, the statement, signature, and date all were written by Francis.

The third photograph was of the appellant's mother. On the back was written, in the same messy script on the reverse of photograph one: "That's Ms. Geralene. She set up the murder of Junior's dad." The statement was unsigned, but was dated 9-6-02. This statement and date also were written by Francis. The appellant did not ask Francis who wrote the statement and Francis did not identify the writer.

Francis made plain on direct examination that the writings on the reverse sides of the photographs were "fake," in that, at least for photographs one and two, the statements, signatures, and dates were made to look like they were written by Ulrich and Peterson, respectively, when in fact they were written by him. He testified that the writings were "true," in that the information they conveyed was "[b]ased on what was done in determining the investigation." He acknowledged, however, that Ulrich had not admitted to killing Lincoln, Sr.

According to Francis, after the appellant was shown the photographs and writings on their reverse sides, he continued to deny knowing anything about the murder. He did not make any admissions and his demeanor did not change.

Francis then played for the appellant excerpts of the tape-recorded statement the appellant's mother had given earlier that day. The excerpts did not implicate the appellant in the murder. Francis told the appellant that Geralene in fact had given a statement confessing to the murder and implicating him and Ulrich, however. According to Francis, at that point, the appellant's "shoulders slumped," he "appeared defeated," and he said he wanted to talk about the murder.

The appellant proceeded to tell Francis that, on the night of the murder, he and Ulrich went to Lincoln Sr.'s house, where all three smoked marijuana. Ulrich then produced a wooden ax handle and hit Lincoln, Sr. on the head with it. The appellant left the house, walked outside, and waited for Ulrich to come out.

After making the oral statement, untaped, the appellant made a statement that was tape-recorded, to the same effect. In the taped statement, the appellant said he was speaking freely and voluntarily and that he had not been made any promises or coerced or threatened. The tape-recorded statement was moved into evidence at the hearing.

The appellant testified about the interview. Much of his version of what happened was rejected by the hearing judge....

On cross-examination, the appellant acknowledged that he had a prior conviction of possession with intent to distribute crack cocaine.

The hearing court made its ruling the day after the hearing ended, and after the judge had had an opportunity to listen to the tape-recorded statement. The court found that Francis had engaged in "a form of a ruse" that involved "a series of clever misrepresentations" designed to mislead the appellant by "suggesting things to him that ... were sort of consistent with the State's theory of what had occurred[,]" but were not true, and at the same time creating a "sense of security." The court viewed the ruse as probably being "within the range of potential ruses that are acceptable ruses" and not "reach[ing] the level of being impermissible." The court was persuaded, by the total circumstances, that the appellant's "will was not overborne" and his statement "was voluntary."

... We accept the suppression court's findings of first-level fact unless clearly erroneous, giving due regard to the court's opportunity to assess the credibility of witnesses. "[B]ecause the issue of voluntariness is a mixed one of law and fact, we undertake a *de novo* review of the trial judge's ultimate determination."

DISCUSSION

The appellant contends his statement was involuntary because, after creating an environment that made it appear safe for him to speak, the police deceived him by using fabricated documents about the evidence against him....

Upon a proper challenge, the State bears the burden of showing, affirmatively, that the defendant's inculpatory statement was made freely and voluntarily; and must so prove by a preponderance of the evidence, if the challenge is made pretrial.

Ordinarily, we look to the "totality of the circumstances" in determining whether a statement was given voluntarily. Among the non-exhaustive list of factors to be considered in determining voluntariness are the defendant's age, physical condition, mental capacity, background, intelligence, education, and experience; the length of the interrogation and the number of officers present; and the manner in which the interrogation was conducted.

Not all of the multitude of factors that may bear on voluntariness are necessarily of equal weight. *Williams v. State*, 375 Md. 404, 429, 825 A.2d 1078 (2003). The Court of Appeals has held that, when a confession is "preceded or accompanied by threats or a promise of advantage," those factors are "transcendent and decisive," and the confession will be deemed involuntary "unless the State can establish that such threats or promises in no way induced [it]." *Id.*

Other factors, such as creating an atmosphere that is conducive to making a statement, in that it appears safe and friendly, do not automatically render a confession involuntary.

In *Rowe v. State*, 41 Md.App. 641, 644, 398 A.2d 485 (1979), we rejected the defendant's assertion that his statement was involuntary because "the atmosphere surrounding the interrogation was too compatible." There,

> the interrogating officer explained to the [defendant] that the officer had known what a "no good son-of-a-bitch" the victim had been, and "that the only thing that we wanted to do really was to shake the hand of the man that murdered him...." With a classic non-verbal act which in itself might have constituted a confession, the [defendant] offered his hand to the officer.

Id. The defendant argued that the officer's statement was proscribed "psychological coercion." Disagreeing, we stated, "An enticement is only improper when 'the behavior of the State's law enforcement officials was such as to overbear [the appellant's] will to resist and bring about confessions not freely self-determined....'" *Id.* at 645 (quoting *Rogers v. Richmond*, 365 U.S. 534, 544 (1961))....

The use of deception by the police also is a factor to be considered in determining whether, given the totality of the circumstances, the defendant's will was overborne. Trickery or deceit "short of an overbearing inducement is a 'valid weapon of the police arsenal.'" *Ball v. State,* 347 Md. 156, 178, 699 A.2d 1170 (1997).

In *Ball,* the defendant argued on appeal that a police detective had used "psychological coercion" to obtain his confession to a murder. The detective wrote out two scenarios of how the murder had taken place, one of which implicated the defendant as the killer, but portrayed him positively, and the other of which implicated him as the killer, but portrayed him negatively; the defendant reacted by confessing to the positive portrayal. Concluding that there was "no indication that [Ball's] will was overborne" by the police tactic, the Court observed:

> A confession clearly is not voluntary if it is the product of physical or psychological coercion. A person who has committed an illegal act, however, is not always eager to admit his or her wrongdoing. *Police officers, charged with investigating crimes and bringing perpetrators to justice, are permitted to use a certain amount of subterfuge, when questioning an individual about his or her suspected involvement in a crime.*

Id. at 178–79 (emphasis added).

The Court of Appeals has warned, however, that, although "[a] degree of police deception to obtain a confession is tolerated," there are "limits to the type of police deception which will be tolerated without rendering a confession involuntary, particularly with regard to deception concerning constitutional rights." *Lewis v. State,* 285 Md. 705, 721–722, 404 A.2d 1073 (1979). In that case, the defendant was interviewed by the police on and off for two days about the murder of his wife and daughter, during which the police allegedly told him that, "if he requested a lawyer he would be labeled a murderer"; and that "asking for a lawyer amounted to an admission of guilt," accusations the police denied. The trial court never resolved the factual dispute over whose story it believed about the interrogation, and the Court of Appeals reversed Lewis's conviction on another basis. In doing so, it found "[p]articularly troublesome" "the allegations of the police mis-statements concerning requests for an attorney." *Id.* at 720.

In a number of cases, this Court has held that confessions were voluntarily obtained notwithstanding the use of deceptive police tactics....

In *Finke v. State,* 56 Md.App. 450, 489–90, 468 A.2d 353 (1983), we held that the defendant's confession to murder was voluntary even though the interrogating officer told him numerous lies about the state of the evidence against him: that he had failed a polygraph test; that his three-year-old cousin could identify him as the killer; that his fingerprints were recovered from the crime scene; that two eyewitnesses had seen him enter the house where the murder was committed and two eyewitnesses had seen him leave; and that "according to an expert he would be unable to remember the incident[.]"

More recently, in *Whittington v. State,* 147 Md.App. 496, 525–27, 809 A.2d 721 (2002), we held that a defendant's confession was voluntary even though an interrogating officer staged a fake "blow back" test, in which a police evidence technician purported to show the defendant, scientifically, that she had gunshot residue on her hands, and even though the defendant was told, falsely, that she had "failed miserably" a "polygraph test." The defendant confessed 15 hours after the "blow back" test was administered.

This Court rejected the defendant's contention that "police deception with regard to the use of bogus scientific procedures is inherently more coercive than other forms of deception" and therefore should render consequent confessions involuntary *per se. Id.* at 518, 809 A.2d 721. We disagreed, adhering to "the totality of the circumstances" test for voluntariness and concluding that the "total circumstances" in that case, including the fake gunshot residue test and the passage of time between the test and the confession, showed that the defendant's confessions had been made freely and willingly.

In the case at bar, the appellant concedes that "[s]ome deception is permitted in police interrogations." He argues, however, that the deception used by the officers against him, which he characterizes as "the creation of false documents," "is about as bad an instance of deception as can be found," and should be a transcendent factor that renders his statement involuntary *per se.* He relies upon *State v. Cayward,* 552 So.2d 971 (Fla.Dist.Ct.App.1989).

Cayward was an appeal by the State from a ruling suppressing the defendant's confession to sexually assaulting and murdering his five-year-old niece. The police had interrogated the 19-year-old defendant using phony scientific reports they had fabricated, one on stationery of the Florida Department of Criminal Law Enforcement, and the other on stationery of Life Codes, Inc., a scientific testing organization. The reports stated, falsely, that the defendant's semen had been found on the victim's underwear. The defendant repeatedly denied involvement in the crime until he was confronted with the fake reports, at which point he admitted his involvement.

The Florida Court of Appeals affirmed the suppression ruling. It agreed with the State that, generally, police use of deception does not render a confession involuntary *per se,* and voluntariness is assessed based on the total circumstances surrounding the confession. It held, however, that the "intrinsic distinction" between police use of verbal misrepresentations and police use of manufactured documents requires a "bright-line" rule that says "that the type of deception engaged in here has no place in our criminal justice system."

The court offered three reasons to support adopting a bright-line rule. First, it opined that a "tangible, official looking report[ ]" "purport[ing] to be authoritative" is more likely to "impress" a suspect, when presented to him in the "atmosphere of confrontation" that exists during police interrogation, and hence is inherently coercive psychologically, much as the threat or application of force is inherently coercive physically. Second, while the suspect and the public expect that the police will use some deception in interrogations, they do not expect that police will manufacture documents to induce confessions: "This is precisely one of the parade of horrors civics teachers have long taught their pupils that our modern judicial system was designed to correct."

Finally, the court expressed practical concerns about the police use of false documents "beyond the inducement of a confession"; namely that, "[u]nlike oral misrepresentations, manufactured documents have the potential of indefinite life and the facial appearance of authenticity. A report falsified for interrogation purposes might well be retained and filed in police paperwork. Such reports have the potential of finding their way into the courtroom[,]" and otherwise being mistakenly accepted as authentic.

In *State v. Patton,* 362 N.J.Super. 16, 49, 826 A.2d 783 (2003), the New Jersey intermediate appellate court, relying on *Cayward,* held that the defendant's confession, which was elicited by use of "police-fabricated tangible evidence," was involuntary. The defendant was brought in for questioning about a shooting, and was held for 19 hours before he was interrogated. Between the time of the arrest and the interrogation, the police manufactured an audiotape of an "eyewitness" identifying the defendant as the shooter. In fact, the "eyewitness" was a police officer posing as a witness to the crime. The "eyewitness" recounted the version of events the police had come to believe, from their investigation, had happened. To lend authenticity to the statement, the "eyewitness" spiced the account with other information about the defendant that was true, including information about prior bad acts he had committed, some against the same victim. When the defendant heard the tape, he confessed on the spot.

The appellate court reversed the conviction, holding that the confession had been induced by improper psychological coercion, in violation of the defendant's due process rights. *Id.* The court concluded that the use of police-fabricated documents rendered the confession involuntary *per se. See also State v. Farley,* 192 W.Va. 247, 257 n. 13, 452 S.E.2d 50 (1994) (commenting in *dicta* that court would "draw a demarcating line between police deception generally, which does not render a confession involuntary *per se,* and the manufacturing of false documents by the police, which 'has no place in our criminal justice system'" (quoting *Cayward, supra,* 552 So.2d at 974)).

Other courts have declined to adopt the bright-line rule drawn in *Cayward,* however. In *State v. Von Dohlen,* 322 S.C. 234, 471 S.E.2d 689 (1996), the police showed the defendant a "composite sketch" of himself to make him think they had an eyewitness to the murder he was being questioned about. In fact, the "composite sketch" was drawn by a police artist looking at the defendant through a one-way window in the interrogation room. The defendant also was shown spent shell casings that the police falsely told him had been found at the crime scene. The defendant maintained his innocence after being confronted with those items, but confessed about an hour and a half later.

The court agreed with the defendant that the police tactics were "reprehensible." Without drawing any distinction between written and verbal misrepresentations of the evidence, the court applied the totality of the circumstances test, and concluded that "the present record simply does not sustain [the defendant's] claim that his will was overborne, so as to render his confession involuntary."

In *Sheriff, Washoe County v. Bessey,* 112 Nev. 322, 914 P.2d 618 (1996), during interrogation about the sexual assault of a minor, a police officer presented the defendant with a false crime lab report, prepared by the police, showing that the defendant's semen was found on the couch at the apartment where the assault took place. In fact, the police did not have any scientific evidence linking the defendant to the crime. When shown the fabricated report, the defendant made a number of inculpatory statements. The trial court suppressed the statements from evidence.

In an appeal by the State, the Supreme Court of Nevada reversed, holding that the statements were not involuntary. *Id.* at 327, 914 P.2d 618. The court drew a distinction between the use of a deliberate falsehood *intrinsic* to the facts of the alleged offense (*i.e.,* a lie about the existence of incriminating evidence) and the use of a deliberate falsehood *extrinsic* to the facts of the alleged offense, of a type reasonably likely to procure an untrue statement or to influence an accused to make a confession regardless of guilt (*i.e.,* a promise or threat about preferential or detrimental treatment by the authorities, that welfare benefits or mental health treatment will be given or withdrawn, or of benefit or harm to someone) and held that the former is one item to be regarded in the totality of circumstances relevant to voluntariness, while the latter will be regarded as coercive *per se. Id.* at 326–27, 914 P.2d 618 (citing and applying *State v. Kelekolio,* 74 Haw. 479, 849 P.2d 58 (1993), and *Holland v. McGinnis,* 963 F.2d 1044 (7th Cir.1992)).

The *Bessey* court declined to place emphasis, as the *Cayward* court had, on the use of written rather than verbal misrepresentations by the police, calling the distinction one without a real difference. It criticized the *Cayward* court for ignoring what the *Bessey* court viewed as the basic test for voluntariness of confessions: whether the deception, whatever its nature, would have induced a false confession under the circumstances. The court further disagreed with the *Cayward* court's concerns about the "indefinite life" of fabricated documents and their potential for being misused or mistaken for real. It reasoned that the rules of evidence work to differentiate between authentic and fabricated documents, and so although "[f]alse documents may 'go astray,'... our evidentiary rules are designed to prevent their use in our legal forums."

Holding that the police detective's use of the falsified lab report "went to the strength of the evidence against [the defendant], a consideration intrinsic to the facts of the alleged offense[,]" the court in *Bessey* concluded that the voluntariness of the confession was to be assessed under the totality of the circumstances standard. It found that, applying that standard, the defendant's statements were not involuntary. "The false report would not have implicated any concerns on [the defendant's] part other than consideration of his own guilt or innocence and the evidence against him. There is nothing about the fabricated document presented to [the defendant] in this case which would have produced a false confession."

In *Arthur v. Commonwealth,* 24 Va.App. 102, 105, 480 S.E.2d 749 (1997), the police prepared "'dummy' reports" showing that a fingerprint and hair found at the scene of a murder matched the defendant's. A police detective confronted the defendant with the fake reports, but he continued to deny that he had been at the scene of the murder. He did confess, however, after the detective told him that the police and the victim's family believed that he loved the victim and that the killing was unintentional, and that the victim's family wanted to know what had happened.

On appeal, the defendant urged the court to "draw a 'bright line' where false *documents* are used." (emphasis in original). The court rejected that approach in favor of the totality of the circumstances test, and concluded that the use of the fabricated fingerprint and DNA reports "did not overcome [the defendant's] will or critically impair his capacity for self-determination." ...

The appellant urges us to establish a bright-line rule, as the *Cayward* court did, that police deception by use of fabricated documents is a transcendent factor that is so inherently psychologically coercive that it makes a resulting confession involuntary *per se.* We decline to do so. We shall hold that the use of a police-fabricated document as a ploy to deceive a defendant into thinking the State has evidence of guilt, or greater knowledge than it actually has, is a relevant factor to be considered in deciding whether, in the totality of the circumstances, the defendant's confession was freely and voluntarily made; but it is not, in and of itself, dispositive of the issue.

We do not find merit in the central assumption underlying the *Cayward* court's bright-line rule: that a false statement about the state of the evidence, presented in writing, necessarily exerts such influence over a suspect's mind so as to overcome his free will when the same false statement, presented verbally, does not. It is well settled that when the police deceive a suspect by telling him, falsely, that other suspects have given written statements targeting him in the crime, that deception is not trickery that, in and of itself, will render the suspect's later inculpatory statements involuntary. If the same false information were to be communicated in writing, the *Cayward* court's bright-line rule would automatically ascribe a coercive effect to it.

Not all fabricated documents carry the same weight of authority and have the same influential power to affect thinking, however, and therefore not all deceptions involving fabricated documents should be treated identically. Fabricated documents may run the gamut in appearance from seemingly official and authentic, on the one hand, to amateurish in their fakery, on the other. In addition, the circumstances of the interrogation and the facts peculiar to the suspect's background, including his level of education and past experiences with law enforcement, may affect how he perceives the document and whether it has any effect on his will.

It is a simplistic generality that a written false assertion by the police, regardless of its substance, always will have a greater impact on a suspect's thinking than an oral assertion, and that every written false assertion by the police will have precisely the same coercive effect as all other false written assertions by the police. If our objective in applying the law of confessions merely were to discourage the practice of police deception by use of fabricated documents in interrogation, the generality would be helpful, because it furnishes the rationale for an exclusionary rule. Our objective is more focused, however: it is to ensure that inculpatory statements only are admissible in evidence if they are given voluntarily, as the product of free will. The generality is not useful for this purpose, because its application will render inadmissible both voluntary and involuntary statements alike.

We also are not persuaded by the *Cayward* Court's rationale that, because fabricated documents have a potential for indefinite life, their admissibility into evidence in a hearing or trial raises the specter that they will be mistakenly used, in some other context, as real. This consideration overlooks that the fabricated documents used as part of a police ruse will be identified as such in the litigation of the case to which they apply; that they will not become part of the evidence as disembodied items but as exhibits to testimony explaining their creation and use; and that the rules of evidence are designed to prevent the use of fabricated or unauthenticated documents as genuine documents.

We find the reasoning of the court in *Bessey* more sound, and more compatible with the Maryland non-constitutional law of confessions, than the bright-line rule approach of the court in *Cayward*. The *Bessey* court rejected a rule that treats a police lie "embodied in a piece of paper" as necessarily coercive, 112 Nev. at 327, 914 P.2d 618, instead tailoring the test to be used for voluntariness around the substance of the falsehood: whether the falsehood was about the facts of the crime or the evidence or strength of the evidence against the suspect, in which the totality of the circumstances test applies; or whether the falsehood was about a topic apart from the crime that would be likely to influence the suspect to make a confession regardless of guilt....

Likewise, under Maryland non-constitutional law, the factors that the Court of Appeals has identified as "transcendent and decisive," so as to render a confession involuntary (so long as the State cannot prove an absence of a causal nexus between the factor and the confession), have been extrinsic to the facts of the case, the evidence against the suspect, and the strength or supposed strength of the evidence against the defendant: the use or threat of force or lack of protection against force and improper promises of advantage and leniency. The holdings recognize implicitly ... that extrinsic considerations introduced into a police interrogation are more likely to direct a suspect's thought process about whether to confess away from a rational self-evaluation to an irrational exercise that is no longer the product of free thought. The *Cayward* bright-line rule about the use of fabricated writings as ruses elevates the form of a deception over its substance and overlooks the common thread about extrinsic inducements that runs through the Maryland common law of confessions.

We hold that the use by police of fabricated documents as a means to trick a suspect about the evidence against him, or the weight of the evidence against him, during interrogation, is not a practice that is necessarily so highly psychologically coercive as to deem involuntary any resulting inculpatory statement. The totality of the circumstances standard applies to whether a confession resulting from the deception was voluntarily made. The use of police-fabricated writings is one factor to be considered in the totality of the circumstances in deciding whether the suspect's will was overborne, or whether his statement was the product of a free decision to speak. In assessing the coercive effect *vel non* of a ruse carried out by use of a police-fabricated document, as one factor in the total circumstances, the following may be relevant: the type of document, including whether it has been made to appear authentic or official; the identity of the supposed author of the document; the substance and nature of the information imparted in the document; the manner in which the document was presented to the suspect; and the truth or falsity of the information imparted in the document.

We now return to the facts in the case at bar, as credited by the hearing court, to assess whether, given the total circumstances surrounding the appellant's interrogation and statements, including that the police showed him fabricated witness statements to misrepresent the evidence against him to trick him into confessing, the appellant's statements were made voluntarily.

The photographs presented to the appellant were genuine, but the handwritten statements on their reverse sides were fabricated. The statements ostensibly were written by the witnesses (Peterson and Ulrich) and were meant to look as such. The fabrications thus were of handwritten statements, not of official, scientific, or government documents. They did not create an appearance of authority and reliability as would, for example, DNA tests presented on the stationery of a police crime laboratory. As mentioned above, the statement designed to look like it had been written by Ulrich was an amateurish fakery (which prompted the hearing judge to ask Francis whether the writing really was his, after Francis had said it was). The "unsigned" statement on the reverse of the photograph of Geralene was in the same handwriting. The appellant claimed not to have been shown that photograph or statement at all.

The information imparted in the fabricated "statements" was for the most part true, in that it represented information learned by the police in the course of their "Cold Case Unit" investigation. The information on the back of the photograph of Ulrich, for example, was information the police had learned by interviewing Peterson. Although Ulrich had not confessed to killing Lincoln, Sr., Peterson had told the police that the appellant had told her that Ulrich had done so. The ruse was to inflate the strength of the evidence by making the appellant think not only that Peterson had implicated him and Ulrich, but also that she had committed her accusation to writing; and that Ulrich had turned on him and Geralene and also had committed his account to writing. While underhanded, we cannot say that this trick would have dominated the appellant's will so he could no longer freely decide what to say.

Significantly, ... the appellant did not immediately confess after being presented with the officer's ruse. The appellant continued to deny knowledge of the murder after Francis showed him the photographs and statements. Indeed, he did not display any change of demeanor when the false statements were presented to him. It was not until the appellant heard excerpts from his mother's tape-recorded statement and was told by Francis that she had implicated him in his father's murder that he revealed that he had been present when Ulrich killed Lincoln, Sr.

Other than the use of police-fabricated statements, there was nothing out of the ordinary and certainly nothing coercive about the circumstances surrounding the interrogation. The appellant was 26 years old and a high school graduate. He had been advised of his *Miranda* rights, initialed each of the rights on the "Explanation of Rights" form, and signed his name stating that he understood all his rights. Further, during his taped statement, the appellant said he was speaking freely and voluntarily and had not been made any promises or coerced. The appellant was not under the influence of any substance. No threats or promises were made. The appellant was not denied use of the bathroom or food or drink or medicine. The appellant was not a newcomer to the criminal justice system. The entire interview lasted only an hour and a half. It was conducted in the middle of the afternoon. Only two officers were present.

Upon our independent review, under the totality of the circumstances test of the voluntariness of the appellant's inculpatory statements, we conclude that the use of the police-fabricated "statements" against him did not overcome his will. Accordingly, the hearing court did not err in denying the appellant's motion to suppress the statements from evidence....

Notes and Questions

1. The court in *Lincoln* discusses two cases, *State v. Cayward,* 552 So.2d 971 (Fla. App. 1989) and *State v. Patton,* 826 A.2d 763 (N.J. Super. 2003), in which courts drew a sharp distinction between the police orally misrepresenting facts and their fabricating scientific reports or other physical evidence as a ploy to induce suspects to confess. *Lincoln,* of course, declines to attribute significance to the difference between those techniques of interrogation and cites other authority in support of its decision. Which approach works the better balance between law enforcement's investigation of crimes, observing suspects' rights, and producing reliable (as opposed to false) confessions?

2. In *People v. Mays,* 95 Cal. Rptr.3d 219 (Cal. App. 2009), the defendant, age 17, denied being involved in a murder under a police detective's questioning and offered to take a polygraph test to demonstrate that he was telling the truth. "Because no polygraph examiner was available, the detective's supervisor authorized a mock polygraph test, *i.e.,* the police placed on his body patches connected to wires, pretended to administer a lie detector test, fabricated written test results, showed defendant the fake results, and told him the results showed he failed the test." The defendant then admitted to being present when the murder occurred and this admission was allowed into evidence at his trial. He was convicted of first-degree murder and sentenced to life imprisonment without parole. He argued on appeal, in reliance on *State v. Cayward* and *State v. Patton, supra,* that the police's falsification and use of physical evidence, in the form of the mock polygraph results, to induce his admission rendered the statement involuntary. The California Court of Appeal rejected the claim, adopting the essential reasoning of *Lincoln* and similar case holdings. It also relied on California precedent, quoting *People v. Chutan,* 85 Cal. Rptr.2d 744 (Cal. App. 1999) for the proposition: "'So long as a police officer's misrepresentations or omissions are not of a kind likely to produce a *false* confession, confessions prompted by deception are admissible in evidence.'" 95 Cal. Rptr.3d, at 227 (emphasis in original). How, precisely, might a court, or a police officer, determine whether deceptive interrogation tactics are "of a kind likely to produce a *false* confession"?

3. Do ruses such as the one employed in *Lincoln,* and those used in other cases discussed in that opinion, risk producing "internalized" false confessions, *i.e.,* of persuading innocent parties—particularly those operating under a disability such as mental retardation or mental illness, a vulnerability such as youth, or persons whose recollection may be impaired because of alcohol or drug use—to accept responsibility for crimes they did not, in fact, commit? In 1988, seventeen-year-old Martin (Marty) Tankleff's parents were bludgeoned and stabbed in their Long Island, New York home. The police and medical assistance arrived in response to Tankleff's urgent 911 call that his parents had been gravely injured. During homicide detectives' subsequent questioning of Tankleff in an interrogation room at the police station, one of the officers briefly left to answer a telephone call. On his return, the detective told Tankleff, falsely, that his father had emerged from his coma at the hospital and had identified Marty as his assailant. Then:

> [T]he defendant [*i.e.,* Tankleff] asked, "[c]ould I have blacked out ... and done this?" and "[c]ould I be possessed?" At that point a second detective ... responded,

> "Marty, I think that's what happened to you." The defendant then confessed to both killings and almost immediately thereafter recanted.

People v. Tankleff, 848 N.Y.S.2d 286, 289 (App. Div. 2007). As we discussed in Chapter Two, Tankleff's confession was admitted into evidence and he was convicted for murdering his parents. The convictions were vacated when newly discovered evidence of his innocence was presented, and the charges against him were dismissed. He spent 6,338 days in prison—more than 17 years—before he was exonerated.[12]

4. Modern-day interrogation techniques are more art than science. The techniques used today have typically been handed down from one interrogator to the next, and thus have largely been developed independently of scientific inquiry or verification.[13] This absence of the scientific method is particularly problematic when decision-making about suspects' guilt, deception, and involvement may be based on perceptions of how the guilty and the innocent *should* act, and what has "worked" or been accepted in the past. These stereotypes about how the innocent and guilty behave include assumptions such as innocent people waive their rights because they have nothing to hide, that guilty people who killed their relatives show predictable "inappropriate" reactions, and others. Like all stereotypes, there may be some truth underlying these perceptions but problems arise when the stereotyped behaviors are applied to all persons. As discussed in Chapter 2, initial perceptions of guilt can lead to stunted investigations, confirmation bias, and tunnel vision that continue through the remainder of the case.

In the past two decades or so, research on police interrogations and false confessions has exploded. Social scientists and legal scholars have identified several problems with modern-day interrogation techniques. One of the primary concerns is that formal interrogations are conducted with suspects already presumed to be guilty. Specifically, police first conduct an *interview* with persons of interest, and then if and only if the person is considered to be deceptive during the interview, will a formal *interrogation* commence. This pathway is problematic for at least two reasons. First, deception detection techniques, particularly the ones employed by law enforcement, are generally unreliable.[14] Police often interpret verbal, non-verbal and paralinguistic cues, such as certain postures and the use of contractions, to indicate the presence or absence of veracity. But, the overwhelming majority of scientific studies has demonstrated that individuals, including law enforcement officers, are poor at distinguishing between truth-tellers and deceivers.

The second problem arises when police, relying on potentially invalid indicators of veracity, employ psychologically manipulative interrogation techniques on suspects whom they already have decided are guilty. Two leading researchers, Kassin and Gudjonsson,[15] break down the interrogation process into three parts: (1) custody and isolation, in which the suspect is detained in a small, windowless room alone; (2) confrontation, in which a suspect who has been determined to be deceptive or "guilty" is confronted with the interrogator's unshakable belief in his guilt and the inevitability of detection: and (3) minimization, in which the interrogator devises ways to minimize the suspect's culpability or involvement, thereby making it easier for the suspect to confess. In essence, the objective of an interrogation is to obtain a confession, not to obtain the truth—and this goal facilitates and helps reinforce tunnel vision and confirmation bias. It also is important to keep in mind that interrogation techniques may be effective with the guilty (in that they confess) but these same techniques can also be "effective" with the innocent and lead to false confessions.

5. Voluntariness: The Burden of Proof

In *Lego v. Twomey*, 404 U.S. 477, 92 S.Ct. 619, 30 L.Ed.2d 618 (1972), the defendant argued that Due Process requires the government to prove beyond a reasonable doubt that a confession was given voluntarily for the statement to be admissible into evidence. But in a 4–3 decision (Justices Powell and Rehnquist did not participate), the Court disagreed. The justices ruled that this heightened standard of proof is not necessary to safeguard the constitutional values advanced by suppressing coerced confessions, and that criminal defendants are already protected against conviction unless their guilt is established beyond a reasonable doubt. While concluding that "the prosecution must prove at least by a preponderance of the evidence that the confession was voluntary," Justice White's majority opinion also noted that, "[o]f course, the States are free, pursuant to their own law, to adopt a higher standard." 404 U.S., at 489.

Is the preponderance of the evidence standard adequate to ensure that involuntary—and potentially false or unreliable—confessions are shielded from the fact-finder's consideration? Consider the following case.

State v. Lawrence

920 A.2d 236 (Conn. 2007)

[David Lawrence and his wife Beverly lived in Waterbury, Connecticut with their two minor children and four minor grandchildren. The couple had become the legal guardians of the grandchildren after their daughter, the grandchildren's mother, had become involved in illegal drug activity and lost custody of them. The Lawrences only gained their status as legal guardians after a "lengthy and arduous process" that involved what David Lawrence described as "a nightmare" experience with the state Department of Children and Families. In June 2001, Waterbury police executed a search warrant at the Lawrences' residence that authorized them to look for controlled substances. They found cocaine and related paraphernalia in a bureau drawer in the master bedroom and in Beverly's purse. David subsequently made oral and written statements admitting that the cocaine and other items belonged to him.

[After criminal charges were filed against him, Lawrence testified at a pretrial suppression hearing that he had admitted ownership of the drugs because he was threatened by one of the police officers that his children and grandchildren would be removed from his home unless he did so. He thus claimed that his confessions, made in response to this alleged threat, were involuntary. Police officers who testified at the suppression hearing denied issuing any threats. Relying on the standard approved by the Connecticut Supreme Court in *State v. James*, 678 A.2d 1338 (Conn. 1996), the trial court ruled that the prosecution had satisfied its burden of proving by a preponderance of the evidence that Lawrence had confessed voluntarily. The confessions were admitted into evidence and Lawrence was convicted.

[On appeal, Lawrence urged the Connecticut Supreme Court to overrule *State v. James* and, in reliance on the state constitution, to require the prosecution to establish the voluntariness of a confession beyond a reasonable doubt to enable its admission into evidence. The court declined to overrule *State v. James* and affirmed Lawrence's conviction. Justice Borden's majority opinion cited several reasons supporting this decision before addressing Lawrence's argument that a heightened standard of proof was required to help guard against wrongful convictions based on false confessions.]

... [T]he defendant and the amicus curiae Connecticut Criminal Defense Lawyers Association claim that the reasonable doubt standard is necessary both to protect adequately a criminal defendant's right to be free from self-incrimination, and to ensure the accuracy and reliability of a jury verdict based on confession evidence. In support of this claim, the amicus curia relies on various sociological studies indicating that juries are unable to recognize and disregard false confessions. See, e.g., S. Drizin & R. Leo, "The

Problem of False Confessions In the Post-DNA World," 82 N.C. L.Rev. 891, 962–63, 996 (2004); R. Leo & R. Ofshe, "The Consequences of False Confessions: Deprivations of Liberty and Miscarriages of Justice in the Age of Psychological Interrogation," 88 J.Crim. L. & Criminology 429 (1998). Even assuming arguendo the validity of these studies,[18] we are not compelled to conclude that the public policy of this state requires the voluntariness of a confession to be proven beyond a reasonable doubt.

As a preliminary matter, we note that neither the defendant, the amicus curiae nor the dissenting opinion have pointed to a single case in which a defendant was convicted wrongfully in the state of Connecticut on the basis of false confession evidence. Accordingly, we can perceive no reason to conclude that the existing procedural safeguards in this state against the admission of false confession evidence are inadequate, or that the juries of this state are unable to recognize and disregard false confessions.

Assuming arguendo, however, that the studies on which the amicus curiae and the dissenting opinion rely do not reflect isolated incidences in which justice was miscarried, but, rather, reflect a national trend concerning the undue weight afforded to false confession evidence by juries generally, we note that it is unclear what percentage, if any, of the false confessions identified in these studies were elicited by governmental coercion and, thus, were involuntary. Indeed, the studies establish that the "false confession problem is ... not pandemic in the American criminal justice system, but rather concentrated among a narrow and vulnerable population: persons with mental disabilities." P. Cassell, "The Guilty and the 'Innocent': An Examination of Alleged Cases of Wrongful Conviction from False Confessions," 22 Harv. J.L. & Pub. Policy 523, 526 (1999); see also S. Drizin & R. Leo, supra, 82 N.C. L.Rev. at 963–74 (observing that false confessions are concentrated among following vulnerable populations: children, juveniles, mentally ill and mentally retarded). In light of the fact that a deficient mental condition alone is insufficient to render a confession involuntary, and that establishing involuntariness requires evidence of "police conduct, or official coercion, causally related to the confession," these studies appear to belie, rather than support, the proposition that false confessions necessarily are obtained by coercive means.

The dissenting opinion states that, "the significant role of false confessions in wrongful convictions necessarily implicates the voluntariness concern" because "[w]hile the strong-arm tactics that often led to false confessions before the Supreme Court's decision effectively abolishing that practice in *Miranda v. Arizona* may no longer be prevalent, anecdotal evidence shows that the deceptive interrogation techniques currently employed by police interrogators are equally capable of coercing innocent suspects into false confessions." It is well established, however, that although "some types of police trickery can entail coercion ... trickery is not automatically coercion." *United States v. Byram,* 145 F.3d 405, 408 (1st Cir. 1998) (confession voluntary despite police assurances to defendant that "he was not implicated in [the victim's] death")....

For the reasons articulated in *James* and herein, we remain convinced that requiring the state to prove the voluntariness of a confession by a preponderance of the evidence, rather than by proof beyond a reasonable doubt, "strikes the appropriate balance, in light of our historical background and contemporary policy concerns, between the various interests at stake." *State v. James,* 678 A.2d 1338. Accordingly, we reject the defendant's invitation to overrule *James* and "to enshrine, as a constitutional mandate, the highest standard of proof for the preliminary determination of voluntariness." Id., 678 A.2d 1338....

The judgment is affirmed....

KATZ, J., dissenting.

As expressed in my concurring opinion in *State v. James,* 678 A.2d 1338 (Conn. 1996) (concurring in result upon concluding that trial court determined that confession was voluntary beyond reasonable doubt), I remain convinced that article first, § 8, of the constitution of Connecticut requires the state to prove beyond a reasonable doubt that a defendant's confession was voluntary

18. We note that the methodology employed in these studies and, therefore, the reliability of the conclusions drawn, has met with profound criticism in the academic community. See P. Cassell, "The Guilty and the 'Innocent': An Examination of Alleged Cases of Wrongful Conviction from False Confessions," 22 Harv. J.L. & Pub. Policy 523, 578, 583 (1999) (criticizing Leo and Ofshe's reliance on secondary sources to establish defendant's proven "'innocence'" and noting that, of remaining proven false confession cases, all but one case involved individuals with serious mental illness).

before that confession may be admitted as evidence against the defendant at trial. Given the growing body of evidence that has come to light since *James* demonstrating the problem of erroneous convictions generally and false confessions specifically, I would use this opportunity to overrule this court's holding in *James* ... I believe that Connecticut should join the significant minority of states that have concluded that their state constitutions require that, in order to use a confession against a defendant, the state must prove beyond a reasonable doubt that the confession was "the product of an essentially free and unconstrained choice by its maker...." *Culombe v. Connecticut,* 367 U.S. 568, 602 (1961)....

Recent studies demonstrating the significant role of admissions of involuntary and false confessions in wrongful convictions in this country provide compelling evidence that our conclusion in *James* as to the admissibility of confessions fails to promote just verdicts. Therefore, stare decisis should not control our decision in this case.

There is, for example, a considerable and growing body of anecdotal evidence regarding wrongful convictions that has been exposed through recent DNA exonerations. According to one authoritative source, as of April 12, 2007, 198 wrongfully convicted persons have been exonerated though the use of postordination DNA testing in the United States. See http://innocence project.org/know (last visited April 12, 2007).[2] False confessions played a role in at least forty-one of those wrongful convictions. See R. Leo, S. Drizin & P. Neufeld et al., "Bringing Reliability Back In: False Confessions and Legal Safeguards in the Twenty-First Century," 2006 Wis. L.Rev. 479, 516. DNA exonerations, however, represent only a fraction of the actual number of wrongful convictions in this country.[3]

Indeed, in a survey attempting to analyze all exonerations in the United States between 1989 and 2003, researchers uncovered a total of 340 exonerations, in which 144 of those wrongly convicted persons were exonerated by DNA evidence and 196 were exonerated by other means. See S. Gross, K. Jacoby & D. Matheson et al., "Exonerations in the United States 1989 through 2003," 95 J.Crim. L. & Criminology 523, 524 (Winter 2005).[4] In 51 of those 340 exonerations, the defendants had confessed falsely to crimes they did not commit. In 28 of the 51 false confessions, police coercion was apparent from the record. Although in 18 of the cases the record is unclear as to the motivation for the false confession, in only 5 instances did the confessions appear to have been given freely and voluntarily. False confessions are most common among the most vulnerable groups of defendants—juveniles and people with mental disabilities. see also R. Leo, S. Drizin & P. Neufeld et al., supra, 2006 Wis. L.Rev. at 512 (concluding that DNA evidence has revealed that false confessions are leading cause of wrongful convictions, citing B. Scheck, P. Neufeld & J. Dwyer, Actual Innocence [2000] p. 92); R. Leo & R. Ofshe, "The Consequences of False Confessions: Deprivations of Liberty and Miscarriages of Justice in the Age of Psychological Interrogations," 88 J.Crim. L. & Criminology 429 (1998); P. Cassell, "The Guilty and the 'Innocent': An Examination of Alleged Cases of Wrongful Conviction from False Confessions,"

2. The Innocence Project is a national litigation and public policy organization that handles cases involving claims of actual innocence in which post-conviction DNA testing can yield conclusive proof of innocence or guilt and, through exposure of the causes of wrongful conviction, seeks to initiate criminal justice reform. See http://innocenceproject.org (last visited April 12, 2007).

3. See, e.g., S. Drizin & R. Leo, "The Problem of False Confessions in the Post-DNA World," 82 N.C. L.Rev. 891, 955–56 (2004). According to the data collected to date by the Innocence Project; see footnote 2 of this opinion; Connecticut has had two wrongfully convicted persons exonerated through DNA testing, neither of whom falsely confessed. See http://innocenceproject.org/Content/240.php (Mark Reid case profile) and http://innocence project.org/Content/272.php (James Tillman case profile). According to another survey, two additional criminal defendants in Connecticut also were exonerated of the crimes for which they had been convicted: Rickey Hammond was exonerated through DNA evidence in 1992; and Lawrence J. Miller, Jr., was exonerated through other means in 1997. See S. Gross, K. Jacoby & D. Matheson et al., "Exonerations in the United States 1989 through 2003," 95 J.Crim. L. & Criminology 523, 555 (Winter 2005). Disparities in such statistics are not uncommon, however, due to the difficulty in collecting comprehensive data from the various criminal justice institutions in the United States.

4. Although the survey is the most comprehensive available for that time period, the authors caution that it should not be considered exhaustive due to the fragmentation of the United States criminal justice system. S. Gross, K. Jacoby & D. Matheson et al., supra, at 95 J.Crim. L. & Criminology 525.

22 Harv. J.L. & Pub. Policy 523, 526 (1999) (criticizing Leo and Ofshe study, but admitting that "false confession problem is ... concentrated among a narrow and vulnerable population: persons with mental disabilities").

In a 2003 study of wrongful homicide convictions in Illinois, which, like Connecticut, uses a preponderance voluntariness standard for admission of confessions, it was found that twenty-five out of forty-two wrongful murder convictions since 1970 were based on false confessions, fourteen of those cases involved confessions by the defendants themselves and eleven cases involved confessions principally by codefendants. R. Warden, "The Role of False Confessions in Illinois Wrongful Murder Convictions Since 1970," Center on Wrongful Convictions, at http://www.law.northwestern.edu/depts/clinic/wrongful/FalseConfessions2.htm (last modified March 8, 2004). A 2004 study analyzed 125 "interrogation-induced false confessions that can be classified as 'proven'—that is, confessions that are indisputably false because at least one piece of dispositive evidence objectively establishes, beyond any doubt, that the confessor could not possibly have been the perpetrator of the crime." S. Drizin & R. Leo, "The Problem of False Confessions in the Post-DNA World," 82 N.C. L.Rev. 891, 925 (2004).[5] Ten of these 125 people were arrested but never charged, seventy-one were unsuccessfully prosecuted, and forty-four were convicted of crimes they did not commit.[6]

Given this overwhelming evidence regarding the acute problem of false confessions, I believe that we must reexamine whether the Connecticut constitution requires the state to prove the voluntariness of a defendant's confession beyond a reasonable doubt....

... [A]lthough the petitioner in *Lego* may not have been able to produce evidence that "admissibility rulings [had] been unreliable or otherwise wanting in quality"; [404 U.S.], at 488; the flood of evidence collected by scholars and researchers regarding false confessions impacting wrongful convictions since *Lego* was decided demonstrably undermines the propriety of the preponderance standard....

The Supreme Court decided *Lego* in 1972, long before the use of DNA testing exposed the significant problem of wrongful conviction in the criminal justice system. In light of the substantial evidence uncovered regarding the considerable role of false confessions in this alarming and widespread phenomenon, it is reasonable to imagine that the *Lego* court would come to a different conclusion today. At the very least, the court would have to acknowledge and reconcile the evidence that we currently confront. Certainly, there is a distinction to be made between involuntary confessions and false confessions. The *Lego* court explicated that distinction thoroughly in its decision. As the court also recognized, however, the two issues are closely related. If the primary purpose of the voluntariness determination is to evaluate whether a defendant confessed of his or her own volition and to exclude all confessions that are involuntary, both true and false involuntary confessions would be identified as

5. The authors explain that their study included confessions that were proven false in four dispositive situations: when a person confessed to a crime that did not occur; when it was proven that it was physically impossible for the suspect to commit the crime; when the true perpetrator was found and his or her guilt objectively established; and when scientific evidence, most commonly DNA evidence, established the false confessor's innocence. S. Drizin & R. Leo, supra, 82 N.C. L.Rev. at 925–26.

6. As compelling as the wrongful conviction statistic is, the authors of the 2004 survey note: "[V]irtually all false confessions result in some deprivation of the false confessor's liberty. Some scholars have focused only on false confession cases leading to wrongful conviction, but this neglects the amount of harm the system imposes on those who are not convicted. Individuals who are coerced into falsely confessing but ultimately not convicted may still lose their freedom for extended periods of time and suffer a number of other significant corollary harms as well: the stigma of criminal accusation (particularly if the person has falsely confessed to serious crimes such as murder or rape), the ongoing damage to their personal and professional reputation (even if charges are dropped or the innocent defendant is eventually acquitted), loss of income, savings, a job or career (sometimes resulting in bankruptcy), and the emotional strain of being apart from one's friends and family (which sometimes results in marital separation or divorce). To those innocents who suffer these unjust fates, the assertion by some scholars that only false confessions leading to wrongful convictions should count for scholarly inquiry or public policy reform or that only false confessions leading to wrongful convictions impose any meaningful harm is obviously misguided and myopic, if not downright cruel." S. Drizin & R. Leo, supra, 82 N.C. L.Rev. at 949–50.

inadmissible. All involuntary confessions are equally abhorrent to our criminal law. The anecdotal evidence of the significant role of false confessions in wrongful convictions necessarily implicates the voluntariness concern. While the strong-arm tactics that often led to false confessions before the Supreme Court's decision effectively abolishing that practice in *Miranda v. Arizona* may no longer be prevalent, anecdotal evidence shows that the deceptive interrogation techniques currently employed by police interrogators are equally capable of coercing innocent suspects into false confessions.[10]

... In light of the copious evidence of wrongful convictions and admission of false confessions in this country, the claim that admission of confessions should be divorced from any consideration of reliability is, at a minimum, socially irresponsible. Undeniably, many unreliable confessions have been admitted for consideration by triers of fact. The majority's reiteration of the *James* court's affirmation of its "confidence in the ability of juries to discern the proper weight to be afforded to conflicting evidence" regarding whether to credit a confession "and if so, whether it is sufficient with other evidence to demonstrate guilt beyond a reasonable doubt," plainly has been discredited by several scholarly studies conducted subsequent to that case. Statistics have shown not only that juries are unable to identify false confessions, but that they regularly base their verdicts on such confessions despite other evidence pointing to innocence.

One recent study demonstrated that in a sample of thirty proven false confession cases, 73 percent of the defendants were convicted even in the absence of any physical or other significant credible evidence to corroborate the confession. See R. Leo & R. Ofshe, supra, 88 J.Crim. L. & Criminology 481–82;[11] see also S. Drizin & R. Leo, supra, 82 N.C. L.Rev. at 960 (in study of 125 proven false confession cases, 81 percent of those

10. See M. Gohara, "A Lie for a Lie: False Confessions and the Case for Reconsidering the Legality of Deceptive Interrogation Techniques," 33 Ford-ham Urb. L.J. 791, 816 (March 2006) ("A number of critiques of the leading interrogation techniques... described the reasons that the use of deception and trickery during interrogations leads to false confessions. Most of these critiques describe the kinds of cost/benefit analyses suspects undertake before deciding to incriminate themselves, regardless of guilt or innocence. The critiques and related theories help illustrate the impact trickery and deception, particularly an exaggeration or misrepresentation of the existence or quantum of independent incriminating evidence, have on even innocent suspects."); R. Ofshe & R. Leo, "The Decision to Confess Falsely: Rational Choice and Irrational Action," 74 Denv. U. L. Rev. 979, 985 (1997) ("Psychological interrogation is effective at eliciting confessions because of a fundamental fact of human decision-making-people make optimizing choices given the alternatives they consider. Psychologically-based interrogation works effectively by controlling the alternatives a person considers and by influencing how these alternatives are understood. The techniques interrogators use have been selected to limit a person's attention to certain issues, to manipulate his perceptions of his present situation, and to bias his evaluation of the choices before him. The techniques used to accomplish these manipulations are so effective that if misused they can result in decisions to confess from the guilty and innocent alike.").

11. The majority cites an article in which one scholar criticizes the methodology of the study by Leo and Ofshe that formed the basis for this article. See P. Cassell, supra, at 22 Harv. J.L. & Pub. Policy 526. Cassell's main criticism of Leo and Ofshe is their reliance on secondary sources for factual information underpinning the claims of innocence in some of their case studies. See id., at 525, 580. In support of his claim that "[e]ven among the fifteen 'proven' cases of wrongful conviction from false confession [cited in the Leo and Ofshe article], many are disputed"; id., at 581; however, Cassell cites the opinions of the prosecutors, district attorneys, and state police who worked on these cases that those people whom they helped to prosecute were in fact guilty, despite the fact that two of those people were officially exonerated by DNA evidence. Id., at 581–82. Though there may be dispute about the accuracy of the media in reporting *details* of crimes, it hardly can be argued that those people with a personal stake in winning convictions are less biased than the members of the media. For example, Steven Linscott had his conviction overturned twice before prosecutors submitted biological evidence to DNA testing that proved conclusively that he could not have been the source of the seminal fluid in the murder for which he was convicted, leading the prosecutors to decline to try him a third time. See http://www.innocenceproject.org/Content/200.php. Earl Washington, who has an I.Q. of approximately sixty-nine and was questioned by police for two days before producing "confessions" to five different crimes, four of which were dismissed by the commonwealth of Virginia as being unreliable, eventually conclusively was excluded as the source of the seminal fluid in the capital murder for which he was convicted (based on the fifth "confession"), and received an absolute pardon from the governor of Virginia. See http://innocenceproject.org/Content/282.php. It is, therefore, difficult to imagine how the belief of the prosecutors in those cases that these men are in fact guilty has *any* bearing on their actual innocence.

defendants who went to trial were convicted by juries even though their confessions were later proven false). Mock jury studies have shown that confession evidence has greater impact than eyewitness testimony, character testimony and other forms of evidence. See S. Kassin & K. Neumann, "On the Power of Confession Evidence: An Experimental Test of the 'Fundamental Difference' Hypothesis," 21 Law & Hum. Behav. 469 (1997). These studies demonstrate that jurors are unable to detect false confessions because of the commonsense expectation of self-serving behavior in others and the accompanying disinclination to believe that a person would falsely confess. S. Kassin & G. Gudjonsson, "The Psychology of Confessions: A Review of the Literature and Issues," 5 Psychol. Sci. in Pub. Int. 33, 56 (November 2004); see also S. Kassin & H. Sukel, "Coerced Confessions and the Jury: An Experimental Test of the 'Harmless Error' Rule," 21 Law & Hum. Behav. 27, 44 (1997) (mock jury study demonstrated that false confession increased conviction rate even when jury recognized it as coerced, court ruled it inadmissible and jurors claimed it did not affect verdict).

... [T]he facts of the present case would appear to exemplify a scenario in which the trial court very well might have been convinced that the confession by the defendant, David Lawrence, was more likely than not voluntary, and yet still have harbored a reasonable doubt as to its voluntariness. The defendant testified that, while he was being interrogated alone in his bedroom by Detective Michael Goggin of the Waterbury police department, Goggin threatened to have the department of children and families remove the defendant's children if he did not admit to possession of the drugs found in his home. Although other police officers testified that Goggin did not threaten the defendant, they were not in the room at the time of the interrogation, and it is not surprising that Goggin did not admit that he threatened the defendant when he testified at the probable cause hearing. While I make no assumptions about the internal deliberations of the trial court on this issue, it is far from inconceivable that the facts presented to the court regarding the voluntariness deliberation could have raised a reasonable doubt in the court's mind.

Justice Brennan was all too accurate when he stated that "[t]riers of fact accord confessions such heavy weight in their determinations that the introduction of a confession makes the other aspects of a trial in court superfluous...." *Colorado v. Connelly,* 479 U.S. 157, 182 (1986) (Brennan, J., dissenting). As the Supreme Court recognized in *Arizona v. Fulminante,* 499 U.S. 279, 296 (1991), "[a] confession is like no other evidence." Thus, the *James* court's contention, reiterated with approval by the majority in its opinion, that the defendant is free "to familiarize a jury with circumstances that attend the taking of his confession, including facts bearing upon its weight and voluntariness" is unavailing. Although the jury must decide whether to credit a confession and must weigh whether the other evidence adduced at trial is in accordance with the confession or demands acquittal, as discussed previously, experience shows that a jury's ability to evaluate that evidence is biased dramatically by the introduction of a confession, no matter how incredible it appears in light of other evidence. Requiring the state to prove the voluntariness of a confession beyond a reasonable doubt before it is submitted to the jury increases the chances that, when a jury does consider a confession, that confession will be reliable and voluntary. There is simply no reason not to utilize every opportunity our legal system affords to ensure the accuracy of jury verdicts and avoid wrongful convictions....

In the context of this case, the cost of the higher burden of proof does not outweigh the benefit to society. Although some voluntary and reliable confessions may be barred from introduction when there is doubt about their voluntariness, the overall effect will be to hold police officers and prosecutors to the highest standard when prosecuting their cases for the state. It is difficult to fathom the argument against assuring the protection of our citizens from unduly coercive police tactics in interrogation,[13] especially if we are concerned with protecting the innocent from unwarranted prosecution....

... Although I am unaware of studies examining the connection between the admission of false confessions and the requisite burden of proof for admissibility, I believe it is safe to assume that raising the burden of proof decreases

13. Indeed, legal scholars have argued against the efficacy and constitutionality of current police interrogation tactics, urging reform in this area. See generally M. Gohara, supra, at 33 Fordham Urb. L.J. 791 (2006); R. Leo, S. Drizin & P. Neufeld et al., supra, 2006 Wis. L.Rev. at 479.

the chance of admitting both a coerced false confession and a coerced true confession, either of which, according to the United States Supreme Court and this court, is equally offensive to constitutional due process rights. As noted previously, studies have been conducted, however, examining the persuasive power of confessions, even when much if not all of the additional evidence points to the defendant's innocence. These studies show the vast disproportionate credence allotted to confessions by juries weighing evidence. Thus, it is inconceivable, given the demonstrated problem of wrongful convictions and the concomitant role of false confessions in that epidemic, that this court would refuse the opportunity it is offered to combat this constitutionally abhorrent scourge.

Accordingly, I respectfully dissent.

Notes and Questions

1. Is the dissenting opinion's contention persuasive that, "the cost of the higher burden of proof [for determining the voluntariness of a confession] does not outweigh the benefit to society"? Does the answer to this question depend, at least in part, on how capable juries are in distinguishing between reliable and unreliable confessions?

2. As noted in the dissenting opinion, jury members as well as other triers of fact are not very adept at discriminating between reliable and unreliable confessions. For example, Professors Steven Drizin and Richard Leo found that 81% of proven false confessors whose cases went before a jury or judge were convicted despite their actual innocence.[16] And in one creative study, Professor Saul Kassin and his colleagues had prisoners confess to the crimes for which they were currently serving time (*i.e.*, true confessions) and confess to crimes they did not commit. The confessions, which were videotaped, were shown to college students and police officers. Although neither group was especially accurate in determining which confessions were true and which were false, the students actually performed better than the police officers.[17]

In large part, the inability to discern true from false confessions, especially those that find their way into the courtroom, owes to the fact that false confessions often have indicators of reliability and veracity. That is, they sound like the real thing, frequently containing credible statements of remorse, motivation, and apologies. However, upon closer examination, these statements are pre-scripted by police or derive from other sources. Professor Brandon Garrett completed an in-depth examination of 34 false confessions (as confirmed by subsequent DNA exonerations) and documented how all had been contaminated through media reports, the interrogation itself, crime scene visits, or other such input.[18] These contaminated confessions, often purported to include non-public facts that only the true perpetrators would know, hold considerable weight with jurors and judges and serve to obfuscate the difference between true and false confessions. One example is the case of Earl Washington, Jr., a man with intellectual disabilities who falsely confessed to committing a murder. In addition to feeding him many case facts during the interrogation, the police took Mr. Washington to the crime scene. As described by Garrett:

> Earl Washington, Jr. led police to locations all around Culpepper, Virginia, having had no idea where the victim was murdered. Even after being driven right in front of the victim's building several times, he did not identify it. When the police then asked him to point to her building once in the apartment complex he pointed to "the exact opposite end" of the complex, and it was only when the officer pointed to her apartment and asked if that was it, he finally "said that it was."[19]

Despite not even knowing the location of the crime or other basic information (such as the victim's race), Washington was convicted, sentenced to death, and spent 18 years in prison before being exonerated.

Social scientists have also conducted surveys to gain insights about what jurors and judges know about false confessions, including their knowledge about who is vulnerable and under what circumstances. One interesting finding that emerged is that whereas individuals recognize that others are susceptible to confessing falsely, they do not believe themselves to be. For example, Costanzo and his colleagues surveyed a representative sample of individuals eligible for jury service about their interrogation-related beliefs and found that more than 90% felt that they were immune from making a false confession regardless of the severity of the crime.[20] However, the same sample thought that between 19 and 24% of confessions are false, a rate which almost certainly is higher than the actual prevalence. Costanzo *et al.* identified other misconceptions as well, including that law enforcement officers are more adept at lie detection than those not in law enforcement and that the police should not be allowed to lie during interrogations. These misconceptions can contribute to jurors' decreased abilities to discern true from false confessions. Interestingly, the Costanzo *et al.* survey and other similar ones[21] have found that most respondents believe that it would be useful to hear from experts, suggesting that the prospective jurors who were surveyed acknowledged their limited understanding of false confessions.

C. *Miranda* and False Confessions

By the mid-1960s, the justices had become increasingly dissatisfied with the nebulous Due Process "voluntariness" test. As the general standard governing the admissibility of confessions, the test offered little guidance to the police and the lower courts. Its application depended on accurately reconstructing often-disputed facts, which further compromised the judiciary's ability to monitor police interrogation practices. Those concerns, in combination with the ruling in *Malloy v. Hogan*, 378 U.S. 1, 84 S.Ct. 1489, 12 L.Ed.2d 653 (1964) that the Fifth Amendment's guarantee against compelled self-incrimination was binding on the States, paved the way for the Court's landmark decision in *Miranda v. Arizona*, 384 U.S. 436, 86 S.Ct. 1602, 16 L.Ed.2d 694 (1966).

Chief Justice Warren summarized the *Miranda* ruling in his majority opinion for the divided (5–4) Court:

[B]riefly stated [our holding] is this: the prosecution may not use statements, whether exculpatory or inculpatory, stemming from custodial interrogation of the defendant unless it demonstrates the use of procedural safeguards effective to secure the privilege against self-incrimination. By custodial interrogation, we mean questioning initiated by law enforcement officers after a person has been taken into custody or otherwise deprived of his freedom of action in any significant way. As for the procedural safeguards to be employed, unless other fully effective means are devised to inform accused persons of their right of silence and to assure a continuous opportunity to exercise it, the following measures are required. Prior to any questioning, the person must be warned that he has a right to remain silent, that any statement he does make may be used as evidence against him, and that he has a right to the presence of an attorney, either retained or appointed. The defendant may waive effectuation of these rights, provided the waiver is made voluntarily, knowingly and intelligently. If, however, he indicates in any manner and at any stage of the process that he wishes to consult with an attorney before speaking there can be no questioning. Likewise, if the individual is alone and indicates in any manner that he does not wish to be interrogated, the police may not question him. The mere fact that he may have answered some questions or volunteered some statements on his own does not deprive him of the right to refrain from answering any further inquiries until he has consulted with an attorney and thereafter consents to be questioned.

The Court sought to clarify the law governing police interrogations through its decision in *Miranda*. Although the new requirements promised to be more straightforward than the practice of assessing the voluntariness of confessions by using a case-by-case, totality of the circumstances approach, it soon became apparent that *Miranda* was bedeviled by complexities of its own. Later decisions had to grapple with such fundamental issues as the meaning of "custody"[22] and "interrogation,"[23] the sufficiency of different statements of the promised rights,[24] how suspects can effectively invoke or relinquish their rights,[25] and numerous other questions. In operation, the essential *Miranda* prerequisites for the admissibility of confessions—having the police administer the rights and then securing the suspect's knowing, intelligent, and voluntary waiver—might also have fallen short in affording individuals the protections envisioned by the majority opinion.

We cannot cover the full complement of *Miranda*-related issues. We instead focus on suspects' comprehension and waiver of their *Miranda* rights, and how such issues might affect individuals' propensity to confess falsely in response to police interrogation. *Miranda* violations normally result in confessions being inadmissible in evidence even if they were made voluntarily under Due Process standards. The issues we now confront thus take on added significance.

In 1983, Fauquier County, Virginia sheriff's deputies and state and local police officers secured the signed confession of Earl Washington, Jr. to the rape and murder of 19-year-old Rebecca Lynn Williams, crimes which had been committed almost a year earlier. We have discussed aspects of Washington's case earlier. Washington had recently been arrested for breaking and entering the home of an elderly woman, threatening to assault her, and stealing her money. Believing that he might have committed other crimes, police questioned him about the 1982 slaying of Ms. Williams. Washington, who had dropped out of school at age 15 and whose IQ measured somewhere between 58 and 68, waived his *Miranda* rights prior to answering questions. His responses to initial police questioning concerning the 1982 rape-murder included several significant misstatements, including that the victim was black (she was white) and that he had stabbed her once or twice (38 stab wounds were inflicted). Based largely on his confession, which gradually was molded to reflect facts corresponding to the crime scene evidence as Washington responded to more and more questions, he was convicted of capital murder and sentenced to death. His conviction and death sentence were affirmed on appeal. Among other issues it considered, the Virginia Supreme Court found no error in the trial court's determination that Washington had made an effective waiver of his *Miranda* rights.[26]

On appeal, the defendant argues that he received insufficient *Miranda* warnings when his statements were given to the police, that he made no waiver of his right to counsel on May 22, 1983, and that he was, in any event, incapable of making a voluntary and intelligent waiver of his constitutional rights....

These contentions lack merit. The record clearly shows that *Miranda* warnings were given to Washington on at least three occasions and that he gave his questioners clear indications that he understood and waived his rights, both orally and in writing. At no time before or during his questioning did he request the assistance of counsel.

Dr. Centor testified that the defendant, when asked, correctly defined the roles of judge, jury, commonwealth's attorney, defense counsel, and witnesses. He was basically familiar with pleas, plea bargaining, and the consequences of each. He demonstrated more familiarity with the criminal justice system than many intelligent laymen. Dr. Centor's expert testimony, together with the testimony of the interviewing officers and the defendant's own responses on the witness stand, was unrefuted and furnishes ample factual support for the trial court's finding of voluntariness, which we will not disturb on appeal unless plainly wrong. The defendant conceded that he was not subjected to physical or psychological coercion of any kind. His only complaint was that he was tired when first interviewed. If so, he gave no outward sign of it. He went to sleep by 3:00 p.m. on May 21, and told the officers, when questioning resumed at 10:00 a.m. on May 22, that he had slept well. His relatively low intelligence and limited education were factors to be weighed, along with all surrounding circumstances, in determining whether he voluntarily and intelligently waived his constitutional rights, and whether his confession was voluntary. The entire record, however, furnishes strong factual support for the trial court's findings that the defendant made knowing and intelligent waivers and that his confession and admissions were voluntary.

Washington's "confession" was false. Following his conviction, he spent nearly 18 years in prison, including close to ten years on Virginia's death row, once coming within nine days of a scheduled execution. He was released after DNA testing linked another man to the rape-murder. Governor Jim Gilmore pardoned him in 2001. He received $1.9 million in damages after a jury ruled that the confession that Washington had signed had included details that had been supplied or fabricated by law enforcement officers.[27]

Mentally retarded individuals, such as Earl Washington, Jr., juveniles, the mentally ill, and others with cognitive disabilities are especially susceptible to giving false confessions. Although by no means alone in this respect, they may also be unlikely to comprehend their *Miranda* rights when administered by the police. Earlier in this chapter, we considered *Wilson v. Lawrence County*, involving a claim made by a mentally retarded individual that the police had taken advantage of his disability to secure his involuntary, and false, confession to a murder.

In *Murray v. Earle*, 405 F.3d 278 (5th Cir. 2005), 11-year-old LaCresha Murray, who was reported to have an IQ of 77, was convicted following a jury trial in a Texas "juvenile criminal adjudication" and sentenced to 25 years in the custody of the Texas Youth Commission. Her conviction stemmed from the death of a two-year-old child, Jayla Belton, who suffered severe abdominal injuries while under day care supervision by LaCresha's grandparents, who also were LaCresha's adoptive parents. Detectives administered *Miranda* warnings to LaCresha, who had been removed from her grandparents' home following Jayla's injuries and placed in Texas Baptist Children's home, "a private shelter for children which contracts with the State to provide foster care." The detectives questioned LaCresha for approximately three hours and elicited her confession that she had accidentally dropped Jayla and then kicked her. The confession was admitted into evidence at LaCresha's trial. Three years later, the Texas Court of Criminal Appeals reversed her conviction, ruling that LaCresha had been in custody when questioned by the detectives, and that Texas law prohibited her interrogation because she had not yet appeared before a magistrate. The court thus concluded that her confession was inadmissible at her trial. LaCresha thereafter filed a civil action against several state officials, alleging, *inter alia*, that they had violated her Fifth Amendment right against compelled self-incrimination.

A federal district court denied the officials' motion for summary judgment. The Fifth Circuit Court of Appeals reversed, reasoning that the state trial judge's ruling that LaCresha's confession was admissible into evidence, although erroneous, was the proximate cause of the violation of her constitutional rights and gave the police officers immunity from liability. In the process, however, the court concurred that LaCresha's purported waiver of her *Miranda* rights was invalid and her confession was involuntary.

Once we have concluded that a juvenile's interrogation was custodial, we determine whether such a suspect's confession is coerced or involuntary by examining the totality of the circumstances surrounding the child's interrogation.[29] In addition to the fact that the interrogation was conducted in violation of state law, our examination includes consideration of the juvenile's "age, experience, education, background, and intelligence, and into whether he has the capacity to understand the warnings given him, the nature of his Fifth Amendment rights, and the consequences of waiving those rights."[30] The Supreme Court has admonished that the police are required to take special care to ensure the voluntariness of a minor suspect's confession:

> If counsel was not present for some permissible reason when an admission was obtained, the greatest care must be taken to assure that the admission was voluntary, in the sense not only that it was not coerced or suggested, but also that it was not the product of ignorance of rights or of adolescent fantasy, fright or despair.[31]

Every factor weighed in our analysis militates against the conclusion that LaCresha's statement was voluntary. At eleven years of age, she was far younger than the fifteen-year-old juvenile suspect whom we held to have voluntarily confessed in *Gachot v. Stadler.*[32] She had no experience with the criminal justice system, had been held in the custody of the State for three days, was unaccompanied by any parent, guardian, attorney, or other friendly adult, and was found to have below-normal intelligence by the court-appointed psychiatrist prior to her criminal trial, also in contrast to the *Gachot* defendant.[33]

LaCresha cannot be held to have knowingly and voluntarily waived her rights to be represented by counsel and to remain silent. Other than having LaCresha sign a *Miranda* card, and briefly explaining her rights to her at the outset of the interrogation, the police took no precautions to ensure the voluntariness of her statement, let alone "special care." The police made no effort to contact LaCresha's adoptive parents, and the shelter, which had assumed responsibility for her care, sent no representative with her to the interrogation. LaCresha was never told that she was free to leave or that she could call her adoptive parents or any other friendly adult. In addition, the police officers represented to LaCresha that they had already talked to everyone in her family, that everyone "knew" what happened, and that she could help her family only by telling the truth. We hold that LaCresha's statement was involuntary, and that its admission at trial violated her Fifth Amendment right against self-incrimination.

29. *Fare v. Michael C.,* 442 U.S. 707 (1979); *Gachot v. Stadler,* 298 F.3d 414, 418 (5th Cir.2002).

30. *Fare,* 442 U.S. at 725.

31. *In re Gault,* 387 U.S. 1, 55 (1967).

32. 298 F.3d at 416, 421.

33. *Id.* (noting that the defendant was accompanied by his brother during the interrogation, voluntarily went to the police station for questioning, and was there for approximately four hours). *Compare Fare,* 442 U.S. at 726–27 (holding 16½-year-old juvenile voluntarily and knowingly waived his Fifth Amendment rights during an interrogation as he had considerable experience with the police, having a record of several arrests, sufficient intelligence to understand the rights he was waiving, and was not worn down by improper interrogation tactics or lengthy questioning by trickery or deceit) *with Haley v. Ohio,* 332 U.S. 596 (1948) (holding that a 15-year-old who had been arrested at midnight, taken to a police station and subjected to continuous interrogation by a rotation of several police officers, without counsel or friend, until he confessed to participating in a robbery and shooting, had not voluntarily confessed).

The potential link between false confessions and *Miranda* violations is not confined to incriminating statements made by youths or individuals with mental disabilities. Consider the following case.

Ross v. State

45 So.3d 403 (Fla. 2010)

Per Curiam.

[Based in part on a confession secured by the police, Blaine Ross was convicted of the capital murder of his parents and sentenced to death. On January 7, 2004, the 21-year-old Ross made a 911 call to the police to report finding his parents' bodies in their Bradenton, Florida home. They had suffered extensive head injuries, apparently inflicted by a baseball bat, while asleep in their bed. Ross, not then under arrest, was questioned by the police on January 7 and 8. After telephoning the police on January 9 and indicating that he had questions about the case, Ross arrived at the sheriff's office and met with Detective William Waldron.]

Detective Waldron believed that the January 9 interrogation was his last chance to talk to Ross without an attorney present, so he decided to change the location to a room where the interrogation could be videotaped. The room was much smaller than the room where Ross was initially interviewed. Inside the room, there was a small desk and three chairs. Detective Waldron sat relatively close to Ross. Ross's chair was in the corner of the room and he was, in essence, blocked in with a desk at one side and Detective Waldron in front of him. Ross was ... barefoot. At least one other law enforcement officer was in the room, and at various times throughout the interview, other officers entered and exited the room, passing notes to Detective Waldron.

Detective Waldron was the primary interrogator throughout the questioning. Initially, he answered many of Ross's questions concerning the process of an investigation. After they talked about Ross's concerns, Detective Waldron questioned Ross about his prior statements given on January 7 and 8. The questioning became more accusatory, and at times, Detective Waldron raised his voice. Detective Waldron confronted Ross with evidence that Ross had lied regarding significant aspects of Ross's prior statements. He then informed Ross that police had found the pants that Ross wore on the night his parents were killed and the pants had blood on them that matched the crime scene. The interrogation continued for about four hours in the same small room with Detective Waldron and other officers before *Miranda* warnings were finally administered. During the unwarned portion of the interrogation, Detective Waldron constantly referred to the bloody pants and emphasized that this evidence could not be disputed. Ross finally acknowledged that this evidence "[p]uts me at the crime scene." Shortly after that, Ross admitted that it was a possibility that he killed his parents:

> You made me dig inside and think about it, and you've also given me hard evidence that puts me at the crime. And I can't—I can't—I can't—I can't remember if I did this or not. I don't know. I mean, you—you have solid evidence, blood on my pants and everything, but I don't remember doing this, if I did it.

From this point on, Ross repeatedly asserted that he may have committed the crime but "blacked out" and had no memory of it. He further provided additional statements that implied he had reason to commit the murders:

> I can tell you that I didn't plan to kill my parents. I can tell you that I do bottle things up, and things that you've said does [sic] make sense. They do make sense to me, that I can [sic] have done this. I could have been so angry, done this. But I don't—I can't put myself there. I don't remember if I was there, so I can't tell you if I did it or not.

At approximately 7 p.m., Detective Waldron left the interrogation room. About fifteen minutes later, he returned and Ross asked, as he had done previously, if he could see his sister "one more time." Detective Waldron left the room again and returned shortly telling Ross, "I can't find her." Although Detective Waldron left the room for the ostensible purpose of checking if Ross's sister was still in the building, at trial he testified that he did not believe that she was in the building and he personally was not making any efforts to find her. When Detective Waldron returned, he eventually administered *Miranda* warnings and ... Ross signed a written waiver. After more questioning by Detective Waldron based on the prior interrogation and further equivocation by Ross, Ross finally confessed that he killed his parents but did not remember committing the act.

> Ross: You were right about a couple of things. I was angry at my dad. I wasn't angry with my mom, she was trying to help me, she was giving me money. But when—you were right that I didn't do this on purpose. I remember dropping Mikey off—[unintelligible]—his neighborhood, I remember being in my house. I didn't do this on purpose.
>
> Waldron: I know you didn't.
>
> Ross: It was like I had just woken up, and I was standing there, not next—not next to my parents, but in front of their bed. I had a [unintelligible]—I don't know why, I don't know what triggered me to do it. I know I was angry at my dad, but I don't know why I did this....

He stated that he "woke up" after the murders, realized what he had done, and tried to make it look like a robbery. When he discussed what happened after the murders, he also confessed to certain actions that later evidence showed that he did not do. Specifically, when Detective Waldron asked about Kathleen Ross's missing jewelry, Ross stated that he "[j]ust grabbed it" in order to "cover [his] tracks." In fact, Ross did not take the jewelry.

Ross was subsequently arrested for the murder of his parents. On January 12, Detective Waldron arrived at the jail to talk to Ross based on a request made by Ross. After an initial discussion, the detective provided new *Miranda* warnings to Ross. During their discussion, Ross further answered additional questions as to where he disposed of the evidence. However, none of this evidence was ever discovered....

On appeal, Ross raises [several] issues ... Because we conclude that multiple statements made by Ross during the January 9 interrogation should have been suppressed and that the admission of those statements was not harmless beyond a reasonable doubt, we address only that issue in depth.

... Following an evidentiary hearing, which included the admission of the recorded interrogation of Ross by the police, the trial court denied the motion to suppress [the confession]....

[T]he trial court concluded that Ross was not in custody on January 9 prior to the reading of the *Miranda* warnings, that Ross voluntarily waived his rights, and that the statements were made voluntarily....

A. Pre-Miranda Statements—Custodial Interrogation

The first issue centers on whether the interrogation became custodial on January 9 prior to the time the *Miranda* warnings were administered, particularly after the detective confronted Ross with evidence that the victims' blood was found on his pants. Determining whether the defendant was "in custody" so as to require the administration of *Miranda* warnings involves a mixed question of law and fact subject to independent review....

For *Miranda* purposes, custodial interrogation means "questioning initiated by law enforcement officers after a person has been taken into custody or otherwise deprived of his freedom of action in any significant way." *Miranda,* 384 U.S. at 444. The determination of whether a person was in custody for purposes of *Miranda* depends on "how a reasonable person in the suspect's situation would perceive his circumstances." *Yarborough v. Alvarado,* 541 U.S. 652, 662 (2004). The United States Supreme Court explained this analysis as follows:

> Two discrete inquiries are essential to the determination: first, what were the circumstances surrounding the interrogation; and second, given those circumstances, would a reasonable person have felt he or she was not at liberty to terminate the interrogation and leave. Once the scene is set and the players' lines and actions are reconstructed, the court must apply an objective test to resolve the ultimate inquiry: was there a formal arrest or restraint on freedom of movement of the degree associated with a formal arrest. *Id.* at 663.

This Court has adopted the same objective, reasonable-person framework in determining whether a suspect was in custody. *See Connor* [*v. State,* 803 So.2d 598, 605 (Fla. 2001)]. "[I]t must be evident that, under the totality of the circumstances, a reasonable person in the suspect's position would feel a restraint of his or her freedom of movement, fairly characterized, so that the suspect would not feel free to leave or to terminate the encounter with police." *Id.* To analyze the case-specific facts that are relevant to determining this issue, the Court considers the following four factors:

> (1) the manner in which police summon the suspect for questioning; (2) the purpose, place, and manner of the interrogation; (3) the extent to which the suspect is confronted with evidence of his or her guilt; [and] (4) whether the suspect is informed that he or she is free to leave the place of questioning.

Ramirez [*v. State,* 739 So.2d 568, 574 (Fla. 1999)]....

The first of the four factors, the manner in which police summon the suspect for questioning, weighs in favor of the State. Ross voluntarily came to the sheriff's office for a meeting with a victim's advocate. While he was at the office, Detective Waldron requested that Ross see him before he left, and Ross agreed.

We next turn to the second factor—the purpose, place, and manner of questioning. Initially, Detective Waldron asked Ross to again provide a statement of Ross's activities regarding the last day he was with his mother and questioned him as to inconsistencies in his story. However, at the point when Detective Waldron informed Ross about the bloody pants, the detective's focus shifted from merely questioning a witness to attempting to obtain a confession and pressuring Ross to admit his involvement in the crime. The detective repeatedly told Ross that he knew Ross committed the crime and the only question remaining was why. This type of questioning, which was highly confrontational and accusatorial, lasted for hours and took place in a very small room at the station with at least two officers in the room. Moreover, at this point, when Ross asked for a smoke break, the detective told him to smoke in the room, while the questioning continued. This factor clearly supports a conclusion that the defendant was in custody.

The third factor to consider is the extent to which Ross was confronted with evidence of his guilt. This factor also weighs in favor of a finding that Ross was in custody. Ross was confronted with very strong evidence of his guilt during the January 9 interview—most importantly, that pants Ross wore on the night in question had blood on them that matched the crime scene. Detective Waldron referred to the bloody pants throughout the interview and how this evidence could not be disputed. Ross finally acknowledged that this evidence "[p]uts me at the crime scene."

At various points after this time, when Ross denied having any involvement in his parents' murders, Detective Waldron stressed, "The evidence says you did." Detective Waldron constantly referred to the blood on the pants as proof that Ross was at the crime scene that night and, throughout the interview, accused Ross of killing his parents. Questioning by Detective Waldron included:

> Waldron: *I know how that blood got there, Blaine. When you brutally, cold-blooded beat your parents to death, when you smashed in their heads and beat them to death....*
>
> Waldron: And then you put that rope that was in the garage and you put it around your mother's neck, and you put it around your father's neck, and you slowly methodically, cold-bloodedly pulled it tighter and tighter and tighter, Blaine. After smashing in their heads. That's how you got that blood on your pants, those black Dickies that you were wearing Tuesday....
>
> Waldron: You want to see [your girlfriend] Erin go to prison now? ... Is that what you want? You want to bring all these people down with you? For what you did? The time is now to be a man. *And the evidence doesn't lie.*

Detective Waldron repeated variations of this type of accusatorial questioning over a period of hours before the *Miranda* warnings were given and after Ross was confronted with the blood on his pants.

The fourth and final factor to consider is that Ross was never informed he was free to leave. At the point when Ross was informed that the police had evidence that blood on his pants matched the crime scene, a reasonable person would not believe he or she was free to leave. Moreover, all of the circumstances after this point conveyed the clear impression that he was not free to leave. After the interview turned accusatory and Ross asked for a cigarette break, Detective Waldron told Ross that he could simply smoke in the room. Ross responded, "I was also going to say you could handcuff me or something to make sure I don't run." This situation stands in contrast to how Ross was handled in his prior interviews, where he was permitted to go outside, take a break from the interrogation, and smoke a cigarette.

Later during the January 9 interrogation, Ross asked to speak with his sister who had accompanied him to the station. He was not permitted to talk to her outside the interrogation room—she was brought to Ross. He asked for her again, and he was left in the room while Detective Waldron said that he would try to find her. When Ross asked if he was being charged with the crime, Detective Waldron avoided a direct answer by asking Ross what he thought should happen. Only once did Detective Waldron assure Ross that he was not currently being arrested, but this was moments before Detective Waldron provided Ross with *Miranda* warnings and after Ross made the admissions that he could have killed his parents. Therefore, the final factor weighs in favor of concluding that the interrogation was custodial.

Ultimately, as we have stated, the factors enunciated provide the basis for the twofold inquiry: (1) the "circumstances surrounding the interrogation"; and (2) "given those circumstances, would a reasonable person have felt he or she was not at liberty to terminate the interrogation and leave." *Yarborough,* 541 U.S. at 663. In considering these factors in conjunction with each other, we conclude that the January 9 interview became a custodial interrogation....

Once the police informed Ross that they had his bloody pants that matched the crime scene, a reasonable person would not have felt at liberty to terminate the interrogation and leave. At this point the officer should have advised Ross as to his *Miranda* rights....

In accordance with the case law governing when *Miranda* warnings must be given, we conclude that the officers should have provided *Miranda* warnings during the January 9 interrogation before the interrogation turned accusatorial and the officers confronted Ross with the bloody pants. Accordingly, any prewarning statements made by Ross after this point should have been suppressed.

B. Validity of Statements After Miranda Waiver

We next address the issue of whether, under the totality of the circumstances, the waiver of the *Miranda* rights was voluntary, knowing, and intelligent and whether the statements made after the waiver were voluntary....

In the ordinary case, the teachings of *Miranda* dictate that the warnings will be administered once custodial interrogation begins and thus the prophylactic effect of *Miranda* will be served. This, however, is a case where the administration of the *Miranda* warnings was delayed for several hours into the custodial interrogation. *See Missouri v. Seibert,* 542 U.S. 600, 609 (2004) (plurality opinion) ("The technique of interrogating in successive, unwarned and warned phases raises a new challenge to *Miranda.*").

Miranda was intended to address and minimize the coercive effects of interrogation and guard against police techniques "likely ... to disable [an individual] from making a free and rational choice" about speaking. *Miranda,* 384 U.S. at 464–65. Whether a defendant validly waived his rights is a twofold inquiry:

> First, the relinquishment of the right must have been voluntary in the sense that it was the product of free and deliberate choice rather than intimidation, coercion, or deception. Second, the waiver must have been made with a full awareness of both the nature of the right being abandoned and the consequences of the decision to abandon it. Only if the totality of the circumstances surrounding the interrogation reveal both an uncoerced choice and the requisite level of comprehension may a court properly conclude that the *Miranda* rights have been waived.

Ramirez, 739 So.2d at 575 (quoting *Moran v. Burbine,* 475 U.S. 412, 421 (1986)).

In reviewing such challenges, courts must remain vigilant regarding whether a defendant was given an actual choice in order to guard against the potential danger of violating a defendant's constitutional right against self-incrimination. Ensuring that police do not use intimidation, coercion, or deception in obtaining a waiver also helps to protect the integrity of the truth-seeking process, including guarding against the danger of false confessions....

In *Oregon v. Elstad,* 470 U.S. 298 (1985), the United States Supreme Court held that the failure to administer the *Miranda* warnings before eliciting a confession does not necessarily render any subsequently warned statement inadmissible and that the admissibility of such statements must turn on whether the subsequent waiver is voluntarily, knowingly, and intelligently made. *Id.* at 310–11, 314–15....

The circumstances of the police conduct in *Elstad* ... stand in stark contrast to the circumstances in *Missouri v. Seibert,* 542 U.S. 600 (2004), which involves the intentionally delayed administration of *Miranda* warnings....

[W]e conclude that the issue before us is not *only* whether the police deliberately withheld the *Miranda* warnings in an impermissible "question first and warn later" technique under *Seibert* but whether under the totality of the circumstances the waiver was voluntary, knowing, and intelligent and whether the statements made after the waiver were voluntary under *Elstad* and our own precedent in *Ramirez*....

Focusing on whether the statements were voluntarily given is consistent with the holdings in both *Elstad* and *Seibert*.... *Seibert* applies once the determination is made that the police deliberately delayed administration of the *Miranda* warnings. However, the totality of the circumstances analysis under *Elstad* also includes a multiplicity of factors that impacts the ultimate determination of voluntariness. We thus disagree ... that administration of the *Miranda* warnings alone will suffice to render the statements admissible, absent a deliberate delay....

... [T]he analysis of the admissibility of statements made following a custodial interrogation and after the delayed administration of *Miranda* warnings is based on the totality of the circumstances, with the following being factors important in making this determination: (1) whether the police used improper and deliberate tactics in delaying the administration of the *Miranda* warnings in order to obtain the initial statement; (2) whether the police minimized and downplayed the significance of the *Miranda* rights once they were given; and (3) the circumstances surrounding both the warned and unwarned statements including "the completeness and detail of the questions and answers in the first round of interrogation, the overlapping content of the two statements, the timing and setting of the first and second [interrogations], the continuity of police personnel, and the degree to which the interrogator's questions treated the second round as continuous with the first." In addition, there are other circumstances to consider on a case-by-case basis, such as the suspect's age, experience, intelligence, and language proficiency....

First, we review whether the police used improper and deliberate tactics in delaying the administration of the *Miranda* warnings in order to obtain the initial statement. This record in fact affirmatively establishes that, in marked contrast to ... *Elstad*..., the police conducted the January 9 interrogation in a manner that arose from a deliberate decision among numerous officers, including the sheriff himself, to delay the administration of the *Miranda* warnings in order to attempt to elicit a confession. As mentioned above, Detective Waldron believed that this would be his last opportunity to question Ross before Ross obtained an attorney. Before the interview, the sheriff spoke to Detective Waldron, informing Detective Waldron that he was counting on him to "get closure on this." Detective Waldron and the sheriff discussed how the interview should be conducted, and the sheriff, along with numerous other officers, watched the entire proceeding from another room.

Further, Detective Waldron testified at trial that he knew his department's general orders required him to read *Miranda* rights to a suspect before the questioning turned to an accusatory stage. However, he deliberately chose not to follow this policy, asserting that it was merely a guideline. In defending this decision, Detective Waldron asserted that while the sheriff did not explicitly tell him to violate the general policies, the sheriff gave him guidance on how this interview should proceed and since the sheriff was watching the entire interview, he would have stepped in if he disagreed with the detective's decisions.

Finally, the manner of questioning before *Miranda* rights were given and the length of time that the highly accusatorial questioning lasted demonstrate that this delay was deliberate. Prior to the time when the *Miranda* warnings were administered, Detective Waldron constantly accused Ross of committing the crimes based on blood found on Ross's pants. After hours of intense and highly accusatorial questioning, the police eventually wore down Ross's will until Ross responded to repeated questioning: "This is the scary part, now I think that I did do it." The detective repeatedly attempted to elicit a full confession from Ross, telling him that confessing to a crime that happened in the heat of the moment was different from confessing to a premeditated murder.

The length of time this interrogation continued without *Miranda* warnings distinguishes this case from *Elstad*.... While the length of time is not determinative, it bears noting that cases in which no intentional conduct was found involved what appeared to be relatively brief initial interrogations and certainly nothing approximating the several hours of custodial interrogation without *Miranda* warnings involved in this case....

In addition, this improper questioning lasted for several hours after this point and continued in an extremely accusatorial manner where Ross was repeatedly told that his denials were not accepted. Other officers at times entered the room during the interrogation and also watched the interrogation from a separate video room. In addition, prior to receiving the ski mask, the police had the following incriminatory evidence: Ross's recent admissions that it was possible that he killed his parents, Ross's bloody pants, evidence that Ross was attempting to take his mother's money, and prior incriminating statements from Ross.

Based on the above analysis, we conclude that rather than merely making a good-faith mistake, the police used improper and deliberate tactics in delaying the administration of the *Miranda* warnings in order to obtain the initial statement....

We next review whether the police minimized and downplayed the significance of the *Miranda* rights once they were given. This factor is important to ensure that a suspect who is provided with a tardy administration of the *Miranda* warnings truly understands the importance and the effect of the *Miranda* warnings in light of the problems faced when warnings are delivered midstream.... [W]here police minimize and downplay the significance of the warnings, the very purpose of *Miranda* is undermined.

... [W]e conclude that the significance of the *Miranda* rights was minimized and downplayed based on the following facts: (1) prior to providing Ross with his *Miranda* rights, Detective Waldron minimized the significance of the rights by asserting they were only a matter of procedure; (2) prior to the warnings, the detective lulled Ross into a false sense of security by asserting that he was not arresting him at that time; (3) when Ross indicated a hesitancy in talking, the detective did not stop the interrogation immediately; and (4) rather than informing Ross that his prior incriminating statements could not be used against him, Ross was reminded about his earlier admissions, implying that exercising the right to remain silent would be futile.

Immediately prior to providing Ross with his *Miranda* rights, Detective Waldron stated to Ross:

> Waldron: There's a couple of things that I need to go over with you *real quick*. There's a couple of things I discovered, and before we go any further I want to cover this with you, *it's just a matter of procedure, um, based on everything we're talking about.*
>
> Ross: So am I being arrested?
>
> Waldron: Nope. *At this time you and I are talking, okay?* And I would like to talk to you some more. But before I can do that I need to go over this. You're not in handcuffs or anything like that, okay?

This strategy, employed after the hours of unwarned interrogation, de-emphasized the significance of the *Miranda* warnings. By referring to it as a matter of procedure, the detective conveyed the clear impression that the warnings were merely a bureaucratic formality. After making the remarks to Ross, Detective Waldron then showed Ross a written *Miranda* form and told Ross, "I got to read this to you, Blaine." The following colloquy ensued:

> Waldron: Having these rights in mind you wish to talk to us now?
>
> Ross: I don't—I can't tell you anything different.
>
> Waldron: And that's up to you.
>
> Ross. So, I'm—
>
> Waldron: I can't make your decision for you.
>
> Ross: I want—I'd really like to talk to my sister, and since she's not here—
>
> Waldron: We tried to get in touch with her, get her back here.
>
> Ross: I don't know what I'm going to do. I don't know what's going to happen, and—
>
> Waldron: Well, I'm willing to talk to you if you want. We're trying to get in touch with your sister now so—you're indicating that you do want to talk to me; correct?
>
> Ross: Yes.
>
> Waldron: Okay, if you would, please sign right there.

After having Ross sign the waiver of *Miranda* warnings, Detective Waldron then asked Ross about a ski mask that they found in his car with blood on it, and Ross provided an innocent explanation for the ski mask. At that point, the interview turned back to their prior discussion. Detective Waldron reminded Ross of his prior statements as follows:

Like I was saying before, earlier, *there's a lot of things that happened today,* and there's a lot of things that have come at you, *and a lot of things that you've admitted to now,* that you've kept bottled up inside before, hidden, that you're now having to deal with. I know this is very difficult. I do know that you loved your parents. (Emphasis supplied.)

Detective Waldron continued his prior line of questioning that was established before the warnings without any break in the interrogation. He asked many of the same or similar questions. He played on the same themes and employed many of the same techniques, such as stressing that he would not think less of Ross and that he had compassion and understanding because he knew people have tempers and can hurt those they love.

Ross initially asserted that he did not believe that he committed the murders and asserted that he did not think he had anything else to say:

> Ross: Well, I told you—you—you're right, about a lot of things. I, I, I don't think I did this. I don't know—(unintelligible).
>
> Waldron: I know you say you don't think you did this, but there's the blood on your pants. This wasn't a burglary, somebody who broke into that house.
>
> Ross: I don't think I can help you anymore. I don't think I have anything else to say.

In response, Detective Waldron stressed that Ross had to make this "right," that the evidence already told a story as to what happened, and that Ross had to make it right by accepting responsibility for his actions. After he brought up the bloody pants again and discussed additional inferences that he could make based on the crime scene, Ross confessed that he killed his parents.

As the record establishes, Detective Waldron minimized the significance of the warning when it was given by telling Ross that reading the rights was "just a matter of procedure." Further, when Ross asked whether he was going to be arrested, Detective Waldron told him not at that time. However, based on statements made during the evidentiary hearing, Detective Waldron clearly knew he had probable cause to arrest Ross at that time and thus his statements to the contrary were an attempt to lull Ross into a false sense of security.... According to Detective Waldron, it was the discovery of the ski mask that allegedly provided this probable cause and prompted Detective Waldron to advise Ross as to his rights. Yet at this very point during the interrogation, when Ross asked if he was being arrested, Detective Waldron explicitly denied it, telling Ross that he was not being arrested at that time but that they were merely "talking."

We have previously found troubling such attempts to lull a defendant into a false sense of security. In addition, when Ross first hesitated about his desire to talk to the detective and said he did not wish to talk, Detective Waldron did not immediately stop the interrogation. Instead, the detective continued in his request for Ross to talk with him, letting him know that he understood that the decision belonged to Ross, that he would not make Ross's decision for him, that he was attempting to locate Ross's sister, and that he was still "willing" to talk to him.

Finally, prior to resuming the interrogation relating to the bloody pants, rather than informing Ross that his prior admissions could not be used against him, Detective Waldron did the opposite, reminding Ross about everything that happened that day and that there were "a lot of things that [Ross] admitted to now." Detective Waldron continued his prior questioning without any break from the prewarning interrogation, playing on the same themes and using the same tactics as earlier. Based on the tactics used and the fact that Detective Waldron reminded Ross about his admissions immediately after providing him with his *Miranda* warnings, Ross would likely have had the misimpression that his prior incriminating statements could be used against him. Such a tactic downplayed the significance of the *Miranda* warnings.

We conclude that ... the police minimized and downplayed the significance of the *Miranda* rights once they were finally administered. In *Seibert,* the plurality stressed the danger of providing *Miranda* warnings in the middle of an interrogation, particularly after incriminating statements have already been made:

> Upon hearing warnings only in the aftermath of interrogation and just after making a confession, a suspect would hardly think he had a genuine right to remain silent, let alone persist in so believing once the police began to lead him over the same ground again. A more likely reaction on a suspect's part would be perplexity about the reason for discussing rights at that point, bewilderment being an unpromising frame of mind for knowledgeable decision. What is worse, telling a suspect that "anything you say can and will be used against you," without expressly excepting the statement just given, could lead to an entirely reasonable in-

> ference that what he has just said will be used, with subsequent silence being of no avail. *Seibert,* 542 U.S. at 613.

Similarly in this case, when Ross was finally given his *Miranda* warnings, he was told, "Anything you say may be used against you in a court of law." Ross could have reasonably believed that all of his prior statements would be admissible regardless as to what he said in the future. Thus, providing *Miranda* warnings at this point to Ross could have misled Ross about the consequences of the decision to abandon his rights. If Ross believed that what he stated in the previous few hours could have been used against him, any attempt to invoke his "right" to remain silent would have been futile....

As we have made clear, any waiver must be "the product of free and deliberate choice rather than intimidation, coercion, or deception ... and must have been made with a full awareness of both the nature of the right being abandoned and the consequences of the decision to abandon it." *Ramirez,* 739 So.2d at 575 (quoting *Moran,* 475 U.S. at 421). Based on all of the circumstances regarding the delay in administering *Miranda* and the manner of administering *Miranda,* we conclude that the officers minimized and downplayed the significance of the warnings so as to undermine the effectiveness of *Miranda*....

Finally, as addressed in both *Elstad* and *Seibert,* courts review the circumstances surrounding both the warned and unwarned statements including "the completeness and detail of the questions and answers in the first round of interrogation, the overlapping content of the two statements, the timing and setting of the first and second [interrogations], the continuity of police personnel, and the degree to which the interrogator's questions treated the second round as continuous with the first." *Seibert,* 542 U.S. at 615; *see also Elstad,* 470 U.S. at 310....

In contrast to *Elstad,* in this case, the accusatory questioning on January 9 took place in the same small room where Ross had previously been for hours, during which he had already made incriminatory statements. He was questioned not only in the same place, but by the same law enforcement officer, and the substance of the questioning was the same. The questioning was nothing more than one continuous round of interrogation with no meaningful break. Moreover, as emphasized above, after providing *Miranda* warnings, Detective Waldron again reminded Ross of his prior admissions, which also shows that the second round of questioning was treated as continuous with the first round. Thus, the first and second interrogations (if they can be divided) were conducted in the same manner, in the same room, with the same officers, with only a very short break in between. This is the very problem noted by the *Seibert* plurality:

> Thus, when *Miranda* warnings are inserted in the midst of coordinated and continuing interrogation, they are likely to mislead and "depriv[e] a defendant of knowledge essential to his ability to understand the nature of his rights and the consequences of abandoning them." *Moran v. Burbine,* 475 U.S. 412, 424 (1986). By the same token, it would ordinarily be unrealistic to treat two spates of integrated and proximately conducted questioning as independent interrogations subject to independent evaluation simply because *Miranda* warnings formally punctuate them in the middle.

Seibert, 542 U.S. at 613–14. This danger was present under the facts of this case, particularly in light of the fact that the interrogation consisted of "integrated and proximately conducted questioning" with no meaningful break and with constant reminders of the preceding multihour interrogation....

While police eventually provided Ross with his complete *Miranda* warnings, the timing and circumstances of the warnings undermined the intent and effectiveness of *Miranda,* particularly in light of the following: (1) the initial *Miranda* warnings were deliberately delayed and no warnings were given until after Ross made incriminating statements; (2) police downplayed the significance of the *Miranda* rights and misled Ross by assuring him that he was not being arrested "at the time" despite the incriminating evidence and Ross's prior statements; (3) before continuing the postwarning interrogation, the police reminded Ross about his earlier admissions; (4) police did nothing to counter the probable misimpression that Ross's prior incriminating statements could be used against him; and (5) police treated the pre- and postwarning interrogation as one continuing round of questioning with only a minimal break but no change in circumstances. In addition, we also take into account that Ross was only twenty-one at the time with no indication of any prior experience with the criminal justice system.

As we explained, the danger of police engaging

in the type of tactics exhibited in this case is not only that the prophylactic purpose of *Miranda* is undermined but that the confession itself is unreliable. Dr. DeClue, Ross's false confession expert, explained the factors that increase likelihood of false confessions, many of which were present in Ross's case, such as increasing the pressure, exaggerating evidence, challenging a person's memory, continuing an interrogation for a lengthy amount of time, showing photographs of the crime scene, and using isolation. The very fact that Ross confessed that he might have taken his mother's jewelry when in fact the evidence reveals that Kathleen Ross herself had actually taken the jewelry from her house and placed it in her mother's house highlights this danger.

Miranda was designed to combat pressures in custodial interrogations and holds that "to permit a full opportunity to exercise the privilege against self-incrimination, the accused must be adequately and effectively apprised of his rights." *Miranda,* 384 U.S. at 467. The inquiry when *Miranda* warnings are delayed, after a lengthy custodial interrogation, is whether the warnings functioned effectively to apprise the defendant that he or she has the "right to choose between silence and speech." *Id.* at 469. When the *Miranda* warnings are purposely delayed after hours of custodial interrogation, when *Miranda* warnings are given in such a way as to minimize and downplay their significance, and when the postwarning interrogation is treated as a continuation of the prewarning interrogation, the risk is that the suspect will not understand the rights and the consequences of waiving the rights. The risk is that the very purpose of *Miranda* is undermined and that the warnings will not function effectively as *Miranda* requires.

In conclusion, the State must prove that the defendant voluntarily, knowingly, and intelligently waived his *Miranda* rights and that the postwarning statements were voluntary. Here, the State did not meet that burden based on an analysis of the totality of the circumstances. We reach this conclusion both under an analysis of *Elstad* and *Seibert* and under our precedent in *Ramirez.* Thus, the statements provided after the *Miranda* warnings were likewise required to be suppressed....

[Three judges dissented.]

Notes and Questions

1. Although an expert witness apparently testified at Ross's trial about factors associated with false confessions, Ross was convicted and sentenced to death, suggesting that the jury and trial judge credited his confession. Does the court's ruling appear to treat the *Miranda* issues and the reliability of the confession as independent? Should those issues be kept separate?

2. As discussed in *Ross, Miranda* warnings are not necessary unless the person being questioned by the police is "in custody." Unlike the inquiry into a confession's "voluntariness," which depends in part on the suspect's unique characteristics, the "custody" determination is based primarily (or exclusively) on objective considerations. In *Yarborough v. Alvarado,* 541 U.S. 652, 124 S.Ct. 2140, 158 L.Ed.2d 938 (2004), five members of the Court declined to attribute significance to the fact that Michael Alvarado was "five months short of his 18th birthday" when questioned by the police about a murder, in assessing whether he was "in custody" for *Miranda* purposes. Alvarado had argued that as a juvenile he felt more constrained by being questioned in a police station after having been separated from his parents, and less at liberty to leave, than would a more mature adult. However, the majority opinion concluded that whether a suspect is "in custody" in the *Miranda* context is determined by whether "a reasonable person"—and not, as the Court of Appeals had concluded, "'a reasonable 17-year-old, with no prior history of arrest or police interviews'"—would "have felt he or she was not at liberty to terminate the interrogation and leave." 541 U.S., at 663. Justice O'Connor's concurrence, however, emphasized that "Alvarado was almost 18 years old at the time of his interview. It is difficult to expect police to recognize that a suspect is a juvenile when he is so close to the age of majority." She cautioned that, "There may be cases in which a suspect's age will be relevant to the 'custody' inquiry under *Miranda*...." 541 U.S., at 669. Four justices dissented.

3. In *J.D.B. v. North Carolina*, 131 S.Ct. ___, 2011 WL 2369508 (2011), the justices modified *Yarborough v. Alvarado*, ruling that the "custody" determination for purposes of *Miranda* should account for the suspect's youth in a case involving a 13-year-old boy who was questioned by police officers and school officials in a closed conference room in his middle school. Justice Sotomayor's majority opinion noted that "the pressure of custodial interrogation is so immense that it 'can induce a frighteningly high percentage of people to confess to crimes they never committed,'" and observed that this "risk is all the more troubling—and recent studies suggest, all the more acute—when the subject of custodial interrogation is a juvenile" (citations omitted). The opinion rejected the State's argument "that a child's age has no place in the custody analysis, no matter how young the child subjected to police questioning."

> In some circumstances, a child's age "would have affected how a reasonable person" in the suspect's position "would perceive his or her freedom to leave." That is, a reasonable child subjected to police questioning will sometimes feel pressured to submit when a reasonable adult would feel free to go. We think it clear that courts can account for that reality without doing any damage to the objective nature of the custody analysis. (Citation omitted.)

Justice Alito, joined by Chief Justice Roberts and Justices Scalia and Thomas, dissented.

4. In *Oregon v. Elstad*, 470 U.S. 298, 105 S.Ct. 1285, 84 L.Ed.2d 222 (1985), which is discussed in *Ross*, the police obtained a confession from the defendant in violation of his *Miranda* rights. A short time later, they secured a second confession after advising him of his rights and securing a waiver. A majority of the Court ruled that although the first confession was inadmissible, the subsequent administration of the *Miranda* warnings and the defendant's waiver of his rights rendered the second confession admissible.

> [A]bsent deliberately coercive or improper tactics in obtaining the initial statement, the mere fact that a suspect has made an unwarned admission does not warrant a presumption of compulsion. A subsequent administration of *Miranda* warnings to a suspect who has given a voluntary but unwarned statement ordinarily should suffice to remove the conditions that precluded admission of the earlier statement. In such circumstances, the finder of fact may reasonably conclude that the suspect made a rational and intelligent choice whether to waive or invoke his rights.

5. In *Missouri v. Seibert*, 542 U.S. 600, 124 S.Ct. 2601, 159 L.Ed.2d 643 (2004), a police officer deliberately withheld a murder suspect's *Miranda* rights during custodial interrogation with the hope of securing an incriminating statement. The suspect, Patrice Seibert, confessed, after which the detective advised her of her *Miranda* rights, obtained a written waiver, and then elicited a second confession. In reliance on *Elstad*, the trial court admitted the second confession and Seibert was convicted. The Missouri Supreme Court reversed and the United States Supreme Court affirmed. Justice Souter's plurality opinion cited several reasons why Seibert's second statement, unlike the second confession given in *Elstad*, should be suppressed.

> The contrast between *Elstad* and this case reveals a series of relevant facts that bear on whether *Miranda* warnings delivered midstream could be effective enough to accomplish their object: the completeness and detail of the questions and answers in the first round of interrogation, the overlapping content of the two statements, the timing and setting of the first and the second, the continuity of police personnel, and the degree to which the interrogator's questions treated the second round as continuous with the first. In *Elstad*, it was not unreasonable to see the occasion for questioning at the station house as presenting a markedly

different experience from the short conversation at home; since a reasonable person in the suspect's shoes could have seen the station house questioning as a new and distinct experience, the *Miranda* warnings could have made sense as presenting a genuine choice whether to follow up on the earlier admission.

At the opposite extreme are the facts here, which by any objective measure reveal a police strategy adapted to undermine the *Miranda* warnings. The unwarned interrogation was conducted in the station house, and the questioning was systematic, exhaustive, and managed with psychological skill. When the police were finished there was little, if anything, of incriminating potential left unsaid. The warned phase of questioning proceeded after a pause of only 15 to 20 minutes, in the same place as the unwarned segment. When the same officer who had conducted the first phase recited the *Miranda* warnings, he said nothing to counter the probable misimpression that the advice that anything Seibert said could be used against her also applied to the details of the inculpatory statement previously elicited. In particular, the police did not advise that her prior statement could not be used. Nothing was said or done to dispel the oddity of warning about legal rights to silence and counsel right after the police had led her through a systematic interrogation, and any uncertainty on her part about a right to stop talking about matters previously discussed would only have been aggravated by the way Officer Hanrahan set the scene by saying "we've been talking for a little while about what happened on Wednesday the twelfth, haven't we?" The impression that the further questioning was a mere continuation of the earlier questions and responses was fostered by references back to the confession already given. It would have been reasonable to regard the two sessions as parts of a continuum, in which it would have been unnatural to refuse to repeat at the second stage what had been said before. These circumstances must be seen as challenging the comprehensibility and efficacy of the *Miranda* warnings to the point that a reasonable person in the suspect's shoes would not have understood them to convey a message that she retained a choice about continuing to talk.

Justice Kennedy, who cast the fifth and decisive vote in agreeing that Seibert's second confession must be suppressed, concurred only in the judgment. In his view, it was critical that the police had deliberately withheld the *Miranda* rights prior to Seibert's first confession with the hope of securing a second confession, which they believed would be admissible after they read Seibert her rights and secured a waiver.

The admissibility of postwarning statements should continue to be governed by the principles of *Elstad* unless the deliberate two-step strategy was employed. If the deliberate two-step strategy has been used, postwarning statements that are related to the substance of prewarning statements must be excluded unless curative measures are taken before the postwarning statement is made. Curative measures should be designed to ensure that a reasonable person in the suspect's situation would understand the import and effect of the *Miranda* warning and of the *Miranda* waiver. For example, a substantial break in time and circumstances between the prewarning statement and the *Miranda* warning may suffice in most circumstances, as it allows the accused to distinguish the two contexts and appreciate that the interrogation has taken a new turn. Alternatively, an additional warning that explains the likely inadmissibility of the prewarning custodial statement may be sufficient. No curative steps were taken in this case, however, so the postwarning statements are inadmissible and the conviction cannot stand.

D. Recording Police Interrogation of Suspects

What, if anything, might be gained by expecting the police to audio- or videorecord their interrogation of crime suspects and then allowing judges and juries to review the recorded sessions when they deliberate about the admissibility and/or reliability of confessions? What, if anything, might be lost? Would recording interrogation sessions be feasible? Expensive and/or time consuming? Induce suspects to refrain from talking as openly as they otherwise might? Assist the police by capturing and preserving details of potentially lengthy and confusing narratives, enabling them to pursue leads or note inconsistencies they otherwise might have missed? Impede the police by discouraging them from employing potentially unseemly interrogation strategies, or by making their strategies more widely known and hence less effective? Assist finders of fact—judges and juries—by providing the best evidence of what was said and done? Risk giving a distorted or incomplete account of a suspect's statement or what motivated or preceded it? Should the law require that some or all interrogation sessions be recorded? Should local police departments be free to record or refrain from recording interrogations according to their own policy, or on a case-by-case basis at their discretion?

Stephan v. State

711 P.2d 1156 (Alaska 1985)

BURKE, Justice.

More than five years ago, in *Mallott v. State*, 608 P.2d 737 (Alaska 1980), we informed Alaska law enforcement officials that "it is incumbent upon them to tape record, where feasible, any questioning [of criminal suspects,] and particularly that which occurs in a place of detention." *Id.* at 743 n.5. This requirement (hereinafter the *Mallott* rule) was again noted in *S.B. v. State*, 614 P.2d 786 (Alaska 1980), with the observation that an electronic record of such interviews "will be a great aid" when courts are called upon to determine "the circumstances of a confession or other waiver of [a suspect's] *Miranda* rights." *Id.* at 790 n.9. In a third case, *McMahan v. State*, 617 P.2d 494 (Alaska 1980), *cert. denied*, 454 U.S. 839 (1981), the recording requirement was repeated, with the further statement that "if *Miranda* rights are read to the defendant, this too should be recorded." 617 P.2d at 499 n.11. Today, we hold that an unexcused failure to electronically record a custodial interrogation conducted in a place of detention violates a suspect's right to due process, under the Alaska Constitution, and that any statement thus obtained is generally inadmissible.

I. FACTS

The relevant facts in the two cases now before us are similar. Malcolm Scott Harris and Donald Stephan, petitioners, were arrested on unrelated criminal charges, taken to police stations and questioned by police officers. Harris was interrogated on two separate occasions; Stephan was interrogated only once. Both men made inculpatory statements. In each instance, a working audio or video recorder was in the room and was used during part, but not all, of the interrogation. The officers, in each case, offered no satisfactory excuse for their clear disregard of the *Mallott* rule.[3]

II. PROCEEDINGS BELOW

Prior to their respective trials, Harris and Stephan both moved to suppress confessions made during their interrogations. At the suppression hearings there was conflicting testimony about what occurred during the unrecorded portions of the interviews. Harris claimed that, in his first interrogation, he was not informed of his *Miranda* rights at the beginning of the session, that the questioning continued after he asserted his right to remain silent, and that the officer made threats and promises during the untaped portions. Stephan claimed that his ultimate confession was induced by promises of leniency and was obtained in the absence of an attorney, after he requested one. In both cases, the officers' testimony was to the contrary.[5] Without a full recording to resolve the conflict, the superior court was required to evaluate the credibility of the witnesses and choose which version of the unrecorded events to believe. In each case, the court chose the police officers' recollections and determined that the confession was voluntary and, thus, admissible at trial. Harris and Stephan were ultimately found guilty and filed notices of appeal.

---

3. One officer stated that it was "normal practice" to get the suspect's statement "laid out in the desired manner," and only then record the full, formal confession. Another officer explained that a suspect is more at ease and likely to talk without a tape recorder running.

5. Conflicts of this sort are typical in confession cases.

The Alaska Court of Appeals concluded, in each case, that there was a violation of the *Mallott* rule, but declined to adopt an exclusionary rule....

III. RECORDING IS A REQUIREMENT OF STATE DUE PROCESS

... The court of appeals' refusal to adopt an exclusionary rule in these circumstances is perhaps due to failure on our part to adequately explain the full significance of our prior decisions.... Such recording is a requirement of state due process when the interrogation occurs in a place of detention and recording is feasible. We reach this conclusion because we are convinced that recording, in such circumstances, is now a reasonable and necessary safeguard, essential to the adequate protection of the accused's right to counsel, his right against self incrimination and, ultimately, his right to a fair trial.

It must be emphasized that *our holding is based entirely upon the requirements of article I, section 7, of the Alaska Constitution,* as interpreted by this court. We accept the state's argument that custodial interrogations need not be recorded to satisfy the due process requirements of the United States Constitution....

When a defendant claims that his confession is involuntary, the Constitution of the United States imposes a heavy burden. Before the confession will be admitted, the prosecution must show a knowing and intelligent waiver of the defendant's federal privilege against self incrimination and his right to counsel. *Miranda v. Arizona,* 384 U.S. 436 (1966). Under the Alaska Constitution, the state's obligation is no less burdensome.

> The contents of an interrogation are obviously material in determining the voluntariness of a confession. The state usually attempts to show voluntariness through the interrogating officer's testimony that the defendant's constitutional rights were protected. The defendant, on the other hand, often testifies to the contrary. The result, then, is a swearing match between the law enforcement official and the defendant, which the courts must resolve. The difficulty in depicting what transpires at such interrogations stems from the fact that in this country they have largely taken place incommunicado.
>
> ....
>
> ... Interrogation still takes place in privacy. Privacy results in secrecy and this in turn results in a gap in our knowledge as to what in fact goes on in the interrogation rooms.
>
> *Miranda,* 384 U.S. at 445, 448. Thus, we believe a recording requirement is justified, because "a tape recording provides an objective means for evaluating what occurred during interrogation." *Harris v. State,* 678 P.2d at 414 (Singleton, J., concurring and dissenting).

Although there are undoubtedly cases where the testimony on one side or the other is intentionally false, dishonesty is not our main concern. Human memory is often faulty—people forget specific facts, or reconstruct and interpret past events differently.

> It is not because a police officer is more dishonest than the rest of us that we ... demand an objective recordation of the critical events. Rather, it is because we are entitled to assume that he is no less human—no less inclined to reconstruct and interpret past events in a light most favorable to himself—that we should not permit him to be a "judge of his own cause."

Kamisar, [*Forward: Brewer v. Williams—A Hard Look at a Discomfiting Record,* 66 Geo. L.J. 209, 242–43 (1977–78) (citation omitted).] Defendants, undoubtedly, are equally fallible.

In the absence of an accurate record, the accused may suffer an infringement upon his right to remain silent and to have counsel present during the interrogation. Also, his right to a fair trial may be violated, if an illegally obtained, and possibly false, confession is subsequently admitted. An electronic recording, thus, protects the defendant's constitutional rights, by providing an objective means for him to corroborate his testimony concerning the circumstances of the confession.

The recording of custodial interrogations is not, however, a measure intended to protect only the accused; a recording also protects the public's interest in honest and effective law enforcement, and the individual interests of those police officers wrongfully accused of improper tactics. A recording, in many cases, will aid law enforcement efforts, by confirming the content and the voluntariness of a confession, when a defendant changes his testimony or claims falsely that his constitutional rights were violated. In any case, a recording will help trial and appellate courts to ascertain the truth.

The concept of due process is not static; among other things, it must change to keep pace with new technological developments. For example, the gathering and preservation of breath samples was previously impractical. Now that this procedure is technologically feasible, many states require it, either as a matter of due process or by resort to reasoning akin to a due process analysis. The use of audio and video tapes is even more commonplace in today's society. The police already make use of recording devices in circumstances when it is to their advantage to do so. Examples would be the routine video recording of suspect behavior in drunk driving cases and, as was done in these cases, the recording of formal confessions. Furthermore, media reports indicate that many Alaska police officers have purchased their own recorders, carry them while on duty and regularly record conversations with suspects or witnesses, in order to protect themselves against false accusations. When a portable recorder has not been available, some officers have even used their patrol car radio to record conversations through the police dispatch center.

In both of the cases before us, the police were engaged in custodial interrogations of suspects in a place of detention. A working recording device was readily available, but was used to record only part of the questioning. Compliance with the recording rule is not unduly burdensome under these circumstances. Turning the recorder on a few minutes earlier entails minimal cost and effort. In return, less time, money and resources would have been consumed in resolving the disputes that arose over the events that occurred during the interrogations.

The only real reason advanced by police for their frequent failure to electronically record an entire interrogation is their claim that recordings tend to have a "chilling effect" on a suspect's willingness to talk. Given the fact that an accused has a constitutional right to remain silent, under both the state and federal constitutions, and that he must be clearly warned of that right prior to any custodial interrogation, this argument is not persuasive.[20]

In summary, the rule that we adopt today requires that custodial interrogations in a place of detention, including the giving of the accused's *Miranda* rights, must be electronically recorded. To satisfy this due process requirement, the recording must clearly indicate that it recounts the entire interview. Thus, explanations should be given at the beginning, the end and before and after any interruptions in the recording, so that courts are not left to speculate about what took place.

Since its announcement, the *Mallott* rule has always included a proviso, "when feasible." The failure to electronically record an entire custodial interrogation will, therefore, be considered a violation of the rule, and subject to exclusion, *only if the failure is unexcused.* Acceptable excuses might include an unavoidable power or equipment failure, or a situation where the suspect refused to answer any questions if the conversation is being recorded. We need not anticipate all such possible excuses here, for courts must carefully scrutinize each situation on a case-by-case basis. Any time a full recording is not made, however, the state must persuade the trial court, by a preponderance of the evidence, that recording was not feasible under the circumstances,[22] and in such cases the failure to record should be viewed with distrust.

IV. REMEDY

The court of appeals ... concluded that the determination of the appropriate "sanction" for a violation of the *Mallott* rule is best left to the sound discretion of the trial court ... We, however, reject this choice of remedy. Instead, we adopt a general rule of exclusion. While other remedies may each have their merits, we believe an exclusionary rule will best protect the suspects' constitutional rights, provide clear direction to law enforcement agencies and lower courts, and preserve the integrity of our justice system....

... We believe that a strong and certain remedy will have a considerable deterrent effect in future cases. Compliance imposes such minimal costs and burdens on law enforcement

20. Also relevant to this argument, perhaps, is the fact that, when the interrogation occurs in a place of detention and the suspect knows or has reason to know he is speaking to a police officer, there is no constitutional requirement that the suspect be informed that the interview is being recorded.

22. In each of the cases at bar, the officers failed to comply with the rule, although such compliance was clearly feasible, and no legitimate excuses were offered for their noncompliance. Thus, the defendants' confessions should not have been admitted.

agencies that they will have little to gain from noncompliance.

... Agency policy and operations must change, not simply individual behaviors. Once they are fully aware of the consequences of unexcused violations of the *Mallott* rule, we are confident that law enforcement agencies will establish effective procedures to implement the rule and provide adequate training for their personnel. Suppression of statements taken in violation of the rule will, therefore, deter continued disregard of its requirements by officers, agencies and courts.

Another purpose is also served by the rule that we now adopt. The integrity of our judicial system is subject to question whenever a court rules on the admissibility of a questionable confession, based solely upon the court's acceptance of the testimony of an interested party, whether it be the interrogating officer or the defendant. This is especially true when objective evidence of the circumstances surrounding the confession could have been preserved by the mere flip of a switch. Routine and systematic recording of custodial interrogations will provide such evidence, and avoid any suggestion that the court is biased in favor of either party.

Most importantly, an exclusionary rule furthers the protection of individual constitutional rights. Strong protection is needed to insure that a suspect's right to counsel, his privilege against self incrimination, and due process guarantees are protected. A confession is generally such conclusive evidence of guilt that a rule of exclusion is justified, when the state, without excuse, fails to preserve evidence of the interchange leading up to the formal statement. This is particularly true when, as in these cases, the defendant may have been deprived of potentially favorable evidence simply because a police officer, in his own discretion, chose to turn the recorder on twenty minutes into the interview rather than at the beginning. Exclusion is warranted under these circumstances because the arbitrary failure to preserve the entire conversation directly affects a defendant's ability to present his defense at trial or at a suppression hearing....

Thus, we conclude that exclusion is the appropriate remedy for an unexcused failure to electronically record an interrogation, when such recording is feasible. A general exclusionary rule is the only remedy that provides crystal clarity to law enforcement agencies, preserves judicial integrity, and adequately protects a suspect's constitutional rights. The necessity for this strong remedy remains, even when we consider society's interests in crime prevention and the apprehension of criminal offenders. Exclusion of reliable, yet unrecorded, statements will not occur frequently when compliance is widespread.[33]

V. EXCEPTIONS

Despite what we have said thus far, we recognize that nearly every rule must have its exceptions, and that exclusion of a defendant's statements in certain instances would be wholly unreasonable. A violation of the *Mallott* rule does not, therefore, require exclusion of the defendant's statements in all cases. Thus, the holding in this case does not bar the admission of statements obtained *before* a violation of the recording rule occurs. Where recording ceases for some impermissible reason, properly recorded statements made prior to the time recording stops may be admitted, even when the failure to record the balance of the interrogation is unexcused, since such prior statements could not be tainted by anything that occurred thereafter. Also, failure to record part of an interrogation does not bar the introduction of a defendant's recorded statements, *if the unrecorded portion of the interrogation is, by all accounts, innocuous.* In such cases, there is no reason to exclude the defendant's recorded statements, because no claim of material misconduct will be presented. For the same reason, a defendant's unrecorded statement may be admitted if no testimony is

33. *Caveat:* We recognize that many custodial interrogations must take place in the field, where recording may not be feasible. Because of this, the rule that we announce today has limited application; it applies only to *custodial interrogations conducted in a place of detention,* such as a police station or jail, where it is reasonable to assume that recording equipment is available, or can be made available with little effort. In a future case, however, we may be persuaded to extend the application of this rule, *particularly if it appears that law enforcement officials are engaging in bad faith efforts to circumvent the recording requirement set forth in this opinion.*

presented that the statement is inaccurate or was obtained improperly, apart from violation of the *Mallott* rule.

REVERSED and REMANDED for further proceedings, with orders that Harris' and Stephan's statements be suppressed.

Notes and Questions

1. With its decision in *State v. Stephan,* the Alaska Supreme Court became the first state tribunal to require the police to record "custodial interrogations conducted in a place of detention." A "place of detention" includes locations "such as a police station or jail, where it is reasonable to assume that recording equipment is available, or can be made available with little effort" (*see* footnote 33). Nearly a decade later, the Minnesota Supreme Court followed suit in *State v. Scales,* 518 N.W.2d 587, 592 (Minn. 1994): "[I]n the exercise of our supervisory power to insure the fair administration of justice, we hold that all custodial interrogation including any information about rights, any waiver of those rights, and all questioning shall be electronically recorded where feasible and must be recorded when questioning occurs at a place of detention." In *In re Jerrell C.J.*, 699 N.W.2d 110, 123 (Wis. 2005), a case we considered earlier in this chapter, the Wisconsin Supreme Court exercised its "supervisory power to require that all custodial interrogation of juveniles ... be electronically recorded where feasible, and without exception when questioning occurs at a place of detention."

2. Courts in other jurisdictions have not gone as far as requiring the police to electronically record custodial interrogations but have issued rulings encouraging or addressing aspects of that practice. For example, in *Commonwealth v. DiGiambattista*, 813 N.E.2d 516, 533–35 (Mass. 2004), the Massachusetts Supreme Judicial Court held:

> [W]hen the prosecution introduces evidence of a defendant's confession or statement that is the product of a custodial interrogation or an interrogation conducted at a place of detention (e.g., a police station), and there is not at least an audiotape recording of the complete interrogation, the defendant is entitled (on request) to a jury instruction advising that the State's highest court has expressed a preference that such interrogations be recorded whenever practicable, and cautioning the jury that, because of the absence of any recording of the interrogation in the case before them, they should weigh evidence of the defendant's alleged statement with great caution and care. Where voluntariness is a live issue ... the jury should also be advised that the absence of a recording permits (but does not compel) them to conclude that the Commonwealth has failed to prove voluntariness beyond a reasonable doubt.
>
> ...
>
> Despite our view that recording all interrogations would improve the efficiency, accuracy, and fairness of criminal proceedings, we still decline at this time to make recording of the interrogation a prerequisite to the admissibility of a defendant's statement. However, where the utilization of recording is left to the unfettered discretion of law enforcement (as it is at present), and an officer has chosen not to record a particular interrogation, we think that it is only fair to point out to the jury that the party with the burden of proof has, for whatever reason, decided not to preserve evidence of that interrogation in a more reliable form, and to tell them that they may consider that fact as part of their assessment of the less reliable form of evidence that the Commonwealth has opted to present.

In an opinion concurring in part and dissenting in part in *DiGiambattista,* 813 N.E.2d, at 450, Justice Greaney, joined by two other members of the court, noted:

> If [recording suspects' statements] is to be considered at all by the court, it should be done so only after study by a representative committee (like the study now being conducted in New Jersey, see *State v. Cook,* 179 N.J. 533, 562, 847 A.2d 530 [2004]), where all interested parties

can be heard and as many issues as possible identified and resolved in advance. Otherwise, the pronouncement of a mandatory rule without guidelines and exceptions could lead to a quagmire of litigation (with defendants seeking to gain advantage at every opportunity) over a multiplicity of issues. Experience with the criminal rules of procedure demonstrates that practices that have been studied and codified in rules and exceptions work the best. The Legislature, of course, may act at any time, and that body is uniquely suited to conduct the type of study necessary to fashion a workable procedure. I hope they will address the matter.

3. In a case in which the police videorecorded their interrogation of the defendant, the Iowa Supreme Court commented favorably on that practice and stated: "We believe electronic recording, particularly videotaping, of custodial interrogations should be encouraged, and we take this opportunity to do so." *State v. Hajtic*, 724 N.W.2d 449, 456 (Iowa 2006).

4. In *State v. Barnett*, 789 A.2d 629, 632–633 (N.H. 2001), the New Hampshire Supreme Court declined to require the police to make an electronic recording of their custodial interrogation of crime suspects, but barred the prosecution's use of an audiorecording made of a defendant's confession when the recording failed to capture the entirety of the interrogation session.

We believe ... [that] excluding all statements made during unrecorded custodial interrogations (absent certain narrow exceptions), go[es] too far. Our primary motive in establishing a recording rule is to ensure the fair and equitable presentation of evidence at trial.... Listening to a defendant be inculpated by his or her own voice has a persuasive power unrivaled by contradictory testimonial evidence.

To avoid the inequity inherent in admitting into evidence the selective recording of a post-*Miranda* interrogation, we establish the following rule: In order to admit into evidence the taped recording of an interrogation, which occurs after *Miranda* rights are given, the recording must be complete. The police need not tape the administration of a defendant's *Miranda* rights or the defendant's subsequent waiver of those rights. However, immediately following the valid waiver of a defendant's *Miranda* rights, a tape recorded interrogation will not be admitted into evidence unless the statement is recorded in its entirety.... [F]ailure to record the complete interrogation will not result in the wholesale exclusion of the interrogation. Rather, where the incomplete recording of an interrogation results in the exclusion of the tape recording itself, evidence gathered during the interrogation may still be admitted in alternative forms, subject to the usual rules of evidence. In light of our ruling, admission of the incomplete recording of the defendant's interrogation is not permissible....

5. Several jurisdictions have enacted legislation, much of which is of recent origin, which requires the electronic recording of police interrogation of suspects under designated circumstances. The statutes typically include limitations such as where the questioning occurs (*e.g.*, in a "place of detention") and the type of crime being investigated (*e.g.*, criminal homicide, designated serious felonies); authorize exceptions; and enumerate the consequences for noncompliance (*e.g.*, an adverse jury instruction, creation of a rebuttable presumption of involuntariness).[28] New Jersey has adopted an electronic recording requirement by rule of court.[29] We reproduce below Montana's statutory provisions, Mont. Code Ann. §§ 46-4-406 through 46-4-411, which became effective in October 2009.

46-4-406. Purpose

The legislature intends to require the electronic recording of custodial interrogations in felony cases based on the finding that properly recorded interrogations:

(1) provide the best evidence of the communications that occurred during an interrogation;

(2) prevent disputes about a peace officer's conduct or treatment of a suspect during the course of an interrogation;

(3) prevent a defendant from lying about the account of events originally provided to law enforcement by the defendant;

(4) spare judges and jurors the time necessary and the need to assess which account of an interrogation to believe;
(5) enhance public confidence in the criminal process; and
(6) have been encouraged by the Montana supreme court in a written opinion of that court.

46-4-407. Definitions

As used in 46-4-406 through 46-4-411, the following definitions apply:

(1) "Custodial interrogation" means an interview conducted by a peace officer in a place of detention for the purpose of investigating a felony or, in the case of a youth, an offense that would be a felony if committed by an adult if the interview is reasonably likely to elicit a response from the person being interviewed that may incriminate the person being interviewed with regard to the commission of an offense.
(2) "Electronic recording" or "electronically recorded" means an audio recording, visual recording, or audiovisual recording, if available, that is an authentic, unaltered record of a custodial interrogation.
(3) "Place of detention" means a jail, police or sheriff's station, holding cell, correctional or detention facility, office, or other structure in this state where persons are held in connection with criminal charges or juvenile delinquency proceedings.
(4) "Statement" means an oral, written, sign language, or nonverbal communication.

46-4-408. Recordings required

Except as provided in 46-4-409, all custodial interrogations must be electronically recorded. The recording must contain a peace officer advising the person being interviewed of the person's Miranda rights, a recording of the interview, and a conclusion of the interview.

46-4-409. Exceptions to custodial recording requirements

A judge shall admit statements or evidence of statements that do not conform to 46-4-408 if, at hearing, the state proves by a preponderance of the evidence that:

(1) the statements have been made voluntarily and are reliable; or
(2) one or more of the following circumstances existed at the time of the custodial interrogation:
(a) the questions put forth by law enforcement personnel and the person's responsive statements were part of the routine processing or booking of the person;
(b) before or during a custodial interrogation, the person unambiguously declared that the person would respond to the law enforcement officer's questions only if the person's statements were not electronically recorded;
(c) the failure to electronically record an interrogation in its entirety was the result of unforeseeable equipment failure and obtaining replacement equipment was not practicable;
(d) exigent circumstances prevented the making of an electronic recording of the custodial interrogation;
(e) the person's statements were surreptitiously recorded by or under the direction of law enforcement personnel;
(f) the person's statement was made during a custodial interrogation that was conducted in another state by peace officers of that state in compliance with the laws of that state; or
(g) the person's statement was made spontaneously and not in response to a question.

46-4-410. Cautionary jury instruction

If the defendant objects to the introduction of evidence under 46-4-408 and the court finds by a preponderance of the evidence that the statements are admissible, the judge shall, upon motion of the defendant, provide the jury with a cautionary instruction.

46-4-411. Handling and preservation of electronic recordings

(1) An electronic recording of a custodial interrogation must be clearly identified and catalogued by law enforcement personnel.
(2) If a criminal or youth court proceeding is brought against a person who was the subject of

an electronically recorded custodial interrogation, the electronic recording must be preserved by law enforcement personnel until all appeals and all postconviction and habeas corpus proceedings are final and concluded or until the time within which the proceedings must be brought has expired.
(3) Upon motion by the defendant, the court may order that a copy of the electronic recording be preserved for any period beyond the expiration of all appeals.
(4) If a criminal or youth court proceeding is not brought against a person who has been the subject of an electronically recorded custodial interrogation, the related electronic recording must be preserved by law enforcement personnel until all applicable state and federal statutes of limitations bar prosecution of the person.

6. Thomas Sullivan, a former U.S. Attorney, began a mission in 2003. Specifically, he and his colleagues began calling police stations around the nation in an attempt to document whether they record interrogations and the reasons for their choices to record or not to record. They have now collected information from all 50 states and the District of Columbia.[30] One of the major themes to emerge is that jurisdictions that do record interrogation sessions embrace the practice wholeheartedly and claim that they will never go back to not recording. Sullivan has received many testimonials about the positives of recording from a range of criminal justice actors (police officers to appellate judges). One police officer from Montgomery County, Maryland stated, "I am a big fan of recordings. They are quicker and more accurate than note taking. Defense attorneys challenge everything as a matter of practice, and it's always great to have a solid piece of evidence showing what occurred during the interrogations."[31]

The cited disadvantages of recording generally come from those who have never attempted it. Believed drawbacks include that suspects will "clam up," that jurors will not understand and be shocked by interrogation techniques, logistical difficulties (*e.g.*, storage space, technical problems), and the increased potential for suppressed confessions. Those perceived obstacles—which tend not to be cited by law enforcement agencies that record interrogation sessions—are rather difficult to overcome. Major departments, such as the New York City Police and the Federal Bureau of Investigation, remain skeptical about recording interrogations, although some progress has been made in recent years (*e.g.*, the NYPD is pilot testing recording in certain precincts). Although many details must be addressed before recording is implemented, such as those incorporated in the Montana statute presented above, issues such as defining when, where, who, and under what circumstances recording should occur are not insurmountable.

Many reforms to prevent false confessions have been proposed, but the principal one typically is the videotaping of interrogations from beginning to end (*i.e.*, not just recording the confession statements). In the American Psychology and Law Society-sponsored consensus paper on police-induced false confessions, the authors strongly endorsed this reform. Importantly, they also recommended having an equal camera focus on suspects and detectives.[32] In research conducted over more than 20 years, Professor G. Daniel Lassiter has consistently demonstrated that perceptions concerning confessions' voluntariness are compromised when only the suspect can be seen, as opposed to when both the suspect and detective are viewable.[33] Great Britain, New Zealand, and other nations that have made sweeping changes to their interrogation methods (for example, turning from an adversarial approach to one that is based on information-gathering) have also mandated electronic recording. The proponents of electronic recording consider the procedure as a win-win situation, one that facilitates convicting the guilty and freeing the innocent.

E. Expert Witnesses

Assume that a suspect confesses to a crime and the confession is admitted into evidence at trial during the prosecution's case. Further assume that the defendant concedes having confessed but argues that the confession was coerced and/or false. Should the defense be entitled to have an expert witness—presumably, someone with expertise in psychology and possessing other relevant knowledge—testify about the occurrence of false confessions, associated risk factors, including suspect characteristics and techniques of police interrogation, and related matters? Would such testimony have an adequate scientific foundation? Would it address matters not commonly known or understood by lay jurors? Would it inappropriately address issues of witness credibility, which traditionally are left to the trial judge or jury? Consider the following case.

Vent v. State

67 P.3d 661 (Alaska App. 2003)

COATS, Chief Judge.

A jury convicted Eugene C. Vent of second-degree murder first-degree sexual assault, second-degree assault, and two counts of first-degree robbery for the assault and robbery of Franklin Dayton and the robbery, sexual assault, and murder of J.H., a fifteen-year-old juvenile. Vent appeals his convictions, arguing that the superior court erred in denying his motion to suppress statements he made to the police, in allowing Fairbanks Detective Aaron Ring to testify to certain matters, and, in excluding Dr. Richard A. Leo from testifying at trial as an expert witness. For the reasons set forth below, we affirm Vent's convictions.

[The assaults occurred during the early morning hours of October 11, 1997. After Vent and others who allegedly participated in the assaults were arrested, Detective Ring conducted three separate interviews with Vent. Vent had been given his *Miranda* rights. The trial judge found that "Vent was 17 years and 11 months old, was a bright young man who was lucid and alert during the interviews, and did not demonstrate any mental impairment." He had prior arrests for theft and drunkenness. The judge suppressed the results of the initial interview, ruling that Vent had asked that the questioning be terminated before the interview was completed, but allowed his statements from the second and third interviews to be admitted into evidence. She rejected claims that the second and third sets of statements were either tainted by the initial, inadmissible statements, or were involuntary. "Vent confessed to Detective ... Ring that he [and his companions] hit and kicked J.H." During cross-examination, Detective Ring "admitted that he had misrepresented to Vent the evidence against him. He admitted that he had told Vent that Vent's clothes had blood splatter on them when this evidence did not exist." At trial, "Vent ... claimed that he did not assault Dayton and J.H.... He argued that Detective Ring pressured him into making a false confession by lying to him about the strength of the evidence against him." The jury returned verdicts of guilty and Vent was sentenced to a term of 48 years imprisonment, with 10 years suspended.] ...

A major portion of Vent's defense was his contention that Detective Ring pressured him into making false statements in which Vent implicated himself. Vent contends that Judge Esch erred in ruling that Dr. Richard Leo, an expert witness in the field of police interrogation practices, could not testify about the psychology of confessions and how police interrogation techniques can cause innocent people to confess to crimes they did not commit....

Based on his education and research, Dr. Leo was going to testify, *inter alia,* that:

> there is the common belief that people do not make unreliable or false statements unless they're tortured or mentally ill. And I would explain that that —that's not the case, sometimes people do make false statements, even if they're not physically tortured or mentally ill, that there—there is psy-

> chological research that explains how certain techniques can lead people to make the decision to confess whether they're guilty or innocent. And that there are certain principles of analysis that researchers use to evaluate whether or not a statement is likely reliable or likely unreliable....
>
> [The testimony would explain] how interrogation works to produce confessions, particular techniques and what their impact can be on someone's decision making.

Alaska Rule of Evidence 702(a) states that:

> [i]f scientific, technical, or other specialized knowledge will assist the trier of fact to understand the evidence or to determine a fact in issue, a witness qualified as an expert by knowledge, skill, experience, training, or education, may testify thereto in the form of an opinion or otherwise.

"To be admissible, expert testimony must (1) address an issue beyond the common knowledge of the average layman, (2) be presented by a witness having sufficient expertise, and (3) assert a reasonable opinion given the state of the pertinent art or scientific knowledge." [*United States v. Vallejo,* 237 F.3d 1008, 1019 (9th Cir.2001).] Pursuant to Rule 702, "an expert is permitted wide latitude to offer opinions, including those that are not based on firsthand knowledge or observation." [*Daubert v. Merrell Dow Pharm., Inc.,* 509 U.S. 579, 592 (1993).] "The general test regarding the admissibility of expert testimony is whether the jury can receive 'appreciable help' from such testimony." [*United States v. Amaral,* 488 F.2d 1148, 1152 (9th Cir.1973).] One of the purposes of admitting expert testimony is "to inform the court and jury about affairs not within the full understanding of the average man." [*Id.* at 1152–53.] "When the subject of inquiry is one which common knowledge would enable one to decide, it is not a proper subject for expert testimony. It is for the trial court in the exercise of a sound discretion to determine whether expert testimony is appropriate under the circumstances of the case." [*Cohen v. W. Hotels, Inc.,* 276 F.2d 26, 27 (9th Cir.1960)]....

Expert testimony should be admitted only if it is both reliable and relevant....

In the present case, after hearing Vent's offer of proof, Judge Esch determined that Dr. Leo's testimony would not appreciably aid the jury in determining whether Vent made a false confession. He indicated that he was troubled by the fact that there was no way to quantify or test Dr. Leo's conclusions that certain techniques might lead to false confessions. He also concluded that jurors would be aware that some people do make false confessions and that this proposition could be developed by questioning and argument.

Reviewing the law in other jurisdictions reveals that there is some support for and against the admissibility of false confession expert testimony. For example, in *United States v. Hall,* [93 F.3d 1337 (7th Cir.1996)], the Seventh Circuit concluded that the trial judge had excluded false confession expert testimony by improperly applying the *Daubert* standards. On remand, the district court admitted testimony similar to Dr. Leo's [974 F.Supp. 1198, 1204–05 (C.D.Ill.1997), *aff'd,* 165 F.3d 1095 (7th Cir.1999)].... Various other courts have upheld the admissibility of false confession expert testimony.[36] But in numerous other cases, appellate courts have concluded that a trial court does not abuse its discretion in refusing to admit this testimony.[37]

---

36. *See, e.g., United States v. Shay,* 57 F.3d 126, 129–30 (1st Cir.1995) (finding trial court erred in excluding expert testimony regarding defendant's mental condition that caused him to give false confession); *United States v. Raposo,* 1998 WL 879723, at 5–6 (S.D.N.Y. Dec.16, 1998) (admitting expert testimony on false confessions); *Callis v. State,* 684 N.E.2d 233, 239 (Ind.App.1997) (affirming trial court's decision to admit, on limited grounds, expert witness testimony regarding police interrogation tactics); *State v. Buechler,* 253 Neb. 727, 572 N.W.2d 65, 72–74 (1998) (holding that the trial court committed prejudicial error when it excluded expert testimony on false confessions); *State v. Baldwin,* 125 N.C.App. 530, 482 S.E.2d 1, 5 (1997) (holding that the trial court erred in excluding expert witness testimony that police interrogation tactics made defendant susceptible to giving a false confession).

37. *See, e.g., United States v. Griffin,* 50 M.J. 278, 284 (U.S.A.F.1999) (holding that testimony of defense expert on false confessions properly excluded as not sufficiently reliable); *State v. Cobb,* 43 P.3d 855, 869 (Kan.App.2002) (concluding that Dr. Leo's testimony invaded the province of the jury and that argument and cross-examination were sufficient to illicit problems with police interrogation techniques); *State v. Tellier,* 526 A.2d 941, 944 (Me.1987) (affirming trial court's ruling that false confession expert testimony

After a close examination of the science and court decisions in this area, one scholar has concluded:

> The unusual nature of the social sciences like psychology and social psychology may require a somewhat lower standard of scrutiny than the "hard" sciences like physics or chemistry, but *Daubert* remains a valid guideline for most scientific evidence, both hard and soft. For too long the behavioral sciences and the criminal justice system have neglected the phenomenon of false confessions. Professors Gudjonsson, Kassin, Wrightsman, Leo, and Ofshe, have opened a door on a new and little understood aspect of the interrogation process. This is not "voodoo science" but is not yet ready for "prime time" either.
>
> The false confession theory needs further study and refinement. Consequently, the admission of expert testimony based on this new theory is premature and therefore unreliable. Currently, the empirical base that supports the theory has too many unanswered questions, no known error rate, and just one laboratory experiment to back it up. This foundation cannot support reliable conclusions just yet.... Gudjonsson, Leo, and Ofshe present haunting tales that clearly establish the existence of false confessions. While every case of wrongful conviction from a false confession is a travesty of justice, these cases cannot be viewed in the abstract. Many of the tactics used by police that create false confessions typically result in true confessions as well. A lack of corroborating evidence may also be a sign of a weak case or a lack of evidence, but it does not necessarily mean the confession was false. To encourage further study in this area, courts should exercise their discretion as the "gatekeepers" of expert testimony and find the psychology of false confessions unreliable at this time.... [Major James R. Agar, II, *The Admissibility of False Confession Expert Testimony,* 1999 Army Law 26, 42–43 (1999); *see also* Paul G. Cassell, *The Guilty and the Innocent: An Examination of Alleged Cases of Wrongful Conviction from False Confessions,* 22 Harv. J.L. & Pub. Pol'y 523 (1999) (criticizing Dr. Leo's methodology)].

The case law and law review commentary is split over whether to admit false confession expert testimony. Our review of the authorities and the record convince us that there is merit to Judge Esch's questions concerning Dr. Leo's methodology and whether his testimony would appreciably aid the jury. We conclude that whether to admit Dr. Leo's testimony and the determination whether his testimony would appreciably aid the jury in this case is a question that fell within the broad discretion reserved to the trial court. We accordingly conclude that Judge Esch did not err in refusing to admit Dr. Leo's testimony....

MANNHEIMER, Judge, concurring.

I agree that Judge Esch acted within his proper discretion when he refused to allow Vent to present the expert testimony of Dr. Richard Leo.... Dr. Leo's proposed testimony would not appreciably aid the jury because it was based on common sense rather than scientific expertise.

Dr. Leo was extensively examined (outside the presence of the jury) concerning his proposed testimony. He stated that, if allowed to testify, he wished to dispel "the common belief that people do not make unreliable or false statements unless they're tortured or [are] mentally ill." Dr. Leo continued:

> I would explain that that's not the case. Sometimes, people do make false statements, even if they're not physically tortured or mentally ill.... There is psychological research that explains how certain [interrogation] techniques can lead people to make the decision to confess, whether they're guilty or innocent. And ... there are certain principles of analysis that researchers

---

would not be of assistance to the jury); *State v. Davis,* 32 S.W.3d 603, 608–09 (Mo.App.2000) (affirming the trial court's decision to exclude Dr. Leo's testimony on the ground that the testimony invaded the province of the jury); *State v. Free,* 351 N.J.Super. 203, 798 A.2d 83, 95–96 (2002) (reversing trial court's ruling that admitted expert false confession testimony); *Green v. State,* 55 S.W.3d, 633, 640 (Tex.App.2001) (affirming trial court's decision excluding expert's false confession testimony).

> use to evaluate whether or not a statement is likely reliable or likely unreliable.

Dr. Leo then explained that, "with regard to the question of [a confession's] reliability,

> what researchers look at is the post-admission [narrative] that the suspect gives—what the suspect says after the words, "I did it." What we call the "post-admission narrative." [We examine] whether that post-admission narrative fits the facts of the crime and demonstrates that the suspect possesses actual knowledge [of what the suspect is describing]. If the suspect is giving a truthful and reliable confession, one would expect the confession to fit the facts of the crime ... [and] to lead to new evidence where applicable, ... derivative evidence, [and] to reveal details that were only known by the police [and] the true perpetrator, ... not public knowledge, and [one would also expect the confession] to be corroborated by physical and medical evidence....

It is true that, in response to a question from Vent's attorney, Dr. Leo agreed that "there are scientifically known, provable ways to verify that a statement made to [the] police is true, accurate, and reliable." But Leo was speaking only of the principles he had enunciated before: the "fit" between the person's confession and the known facts of the crime. This became obvious when Leo offered examples of how his principles might be used to show that a confession was false. Leo offered the following examples: (1) a suspect confesses to a homicide, but later the purported victim shows up alive; (2) a suspect confesses to a crime, but later investigation shows that it would have been physically impossible for the suspect to have committed the crime—as, for instance, where the suspect was in prison or in another state at the time of the crime; and (3) a suspect confesses to a crime, but DNA analysis later shows that the suspect is definitely not the perpetrator.

At this point, Judge Esch asked Dr. Leo if there were other factors, besides the "fit" of the suspect's narrative with the facts of the case, that were relevant to assessing the truthfulness or reliability of a confession. Leo answered, "Not really." ...

Dr. Leo has earned university degrees (including a law degree) and, for several years, he has focused his studies on police interrogation techniques. But Dr. Leo's academic and research achievements are not determinative of whether Judge Esch should have allowed him to testify. The real question is whether Dr. Leo's proposed testimony was based on analysis or research that was beyond the ken of the normal juror. A witness may be an "expert" in the sense that they have specialized training or experience not shared by most people, but, under Evidence Rule 702(a), the proponent of the witness's testimony must further show that their proposed testimony is in fact grounded on this specialized training or experience....

Based on Dr. Leo's voir dire, Judge Esch could reasonably conclude that Dr. Leo's principles for determining the truthfulness or reliability of a confession amounted to nothing more than the common-sense notion that a confession must be tested against the known facts. This being so, Judge Esch did not abuse his discretion when he ruled that Leo's proposed testimony on this subject was not admissible under Evidence Rule 702(a)....

Notes and Questions

1. As the court's opinion in *Vent* notes, several other courts have ruled on the admissibility of expert testimony about false confessions, a determination that normally is entrusted to the discretion of a trial court judge pursuant to the jurisdiction's rules governing the admissibility of scientific and expert testimony. For additional decisions excluding or upholding the exclusion of expert testimony, *see United States v. Benally,* 541 F.3d 990 (10th Cir. 2008); *State v. Wright,* 247 S.W.3d 161 (Mo. App. 2008); *People v. Rosario,* 862 N.Y.S.2d 719 (Queens Co. 2008); *Edmonds v. State,* 955 So.2d 787 (Miss. 2007). For additional rulings authorizing such testimony or holding that its exclusion was erroneous, *see People v. Kogut,* 806 N.Y.S.2d 366 (Nassau Co. 2005); *Boyer v. State,* 825 So.2d 418 (Fla. App. 2002); *see also Lunbery v. Hornbeak,* 605 F.3d 754, 763–765 (9th Cir. 2010) (Hawkins, J., concurring).

2. As scientific knowledge increases about the "why" and "who" of false confessions, some have argued that the foundation for the admission of expert testimony likewise has been strengthened.[34] And, although as noted above, the majority of prospective jurors perceive that hearing expert testimony regarding police interrogations and false confessions would be useful, few empirical studies have been conducted to examine this assumption. One exception is a study[35] in which mock jurors (college students) were presented with facts based on a real case, *People v. Gonzales*.[36] Gonzales, a 20-year-old gang member, was accused of killing a police officer. He was interrogated three separate times, once after a night without food or sleep. In the real case, an expert testified, and this testimony (as well as other case facts and materials) was used in the research study. Before and after reading the expert testimony on false confessions, mock jurors made decisions about guilt. Expert testimony was found to have a significant influence: conviction rates dropped approximately 15 percentage points after expert testimony was presented. Although judges have sometimes determined that expert testimony is not needed because false confessions and the circumstances conducive to producing them are "within the ken" of average, lay jurors, there is mounting evidence that jurors (and judges) can hold misconceptions about important matters concerning interrogations and confessions. These misconceptions may be particularly pernicious (and therefore experts may be especially needed) when interrogations are not electronically captured and decision-makers are not privy to their full circumstances.

F. Conclusion

The law historically has evidenced a mistrust of self-incriminating statements, yet it also places great stock in confessions and authorizes their use in criminal trials subject to compliance with rules designed to limit governmental overreaching and guard against unreliable admissions. Due Process forbids governmental practices that are coercive and result in confessions that, under the totality of the circumstances, are determined to be involuntary. The right against compelled self-incrimination finds protection in the Fifth Amendment and the safeguards announced by the Supreme Court in *Miranda v. Arizona*. Yet those rules of admissibility are not foolproof. For various reasons, some related to police interrogation techniques and some not, individuals make false confessions. The consequences can be dramatic, resulting in the police curtailing further investigation of a crime, leading prosecutors to file charges, causing defense attorneys to forgo investigation of possible trial defenses and instead focus on negotiating guilty pleas, and ultimately conclude in wrongful convictions.

In addition to examining the constitutional rules governing police interrogation and the admissibility of confessions, we have considered measures designed to help reduce the risk of false confessions, such as ensuring that juveniles have the assistance of an interested adult prior to and during custodial police interrogation. Other interventions are designed to allow more accurate assessment of the reliability of confessions, including requirements for the electronic recording of interrogation sessions and admitting expert testimony to help educate finders of fact about the existence of false confessions and contributing factors. Social scientists have produced a wealth of valuable research bearing on these subjects, and policymakers in several jurisdictions have undertaken ambitious reforms. There promises to be continuing interest in evaluating the effectiveness of innovations that have been designed to minimize the risk of false confessions, in identifying false confessions that occur, and in correcting the wrongful convictions that they help produce.

Chapter 5

Prosecutors, Police, and Preservation of Evidence

A. Introduction

In this chapter we consider how the criminal justice system officials most closely identified with establishing offenders' guilt—prosecutors and the police—by that same token can occupy critical roles in helping guard against the erroneous conviction of the innocent. Although there are exceptions, for example, innocent people being ensnared in scandals involving fabricated evidence and the knowing use of perjury,[1] prosecutors and police officers in general have every reason to be solidly averse to wrongful convictions. No legitimate law enforcement interests are advanced by miscarriages of justice that result in innocent people being punished and the guilty remaining free.

Nevertheless, as we discussed in Chapter 2, prosecutors and the police are as susceptible as others to tunnel vision, institutional and organizational pressures, norms, and incentives, and other influences that help shape if not occasionally cloud their judgment. The inherent ambiguities associated with criminal investigations and prosecutions, pressing caseloads, and the limited time and resources at their disposal make law enforcement officials' responsibilities all the more challenging. Thus, it is not surprising that prosecutorial and policing duties sometimes are breached and errors occasionally made. Some of these violations and mistakes contribute to wrongful convictions.

We initially consider the prosecutor's duties as advocate for the government and how those duties give rise to constitutional imperatives against knowingly presenting untruthful testimony or allowing perjury to go uncorrected. We then explore the affirmative prosecutorial obligation to disclose evidence that may help defendants establish their innocence. Since evidence cannot be disclosed or used if it is not secured and retained, we next examine the police's obligations with respect to collecting and preserving evidence that may be probative of guilt or innocence. We conclude by considering policies governing the preservation of evidence and allowing defendants' access to evidence in the government's possession so it can be tested in connection with post-conviction claims of innocence.

B. The Prosecutor's Duties

1. Perjured Testimony

Miller v. Pate

386 U.S. 1, 87 S.Ct. 785, 17 L.Ed.2d 690 (1967)

Mr. Justice STEWART delivered the opinion of the Court.

On November 26, 1955, in Canton, Illinois, an eight-year-old girl died as the result of a brutal sexual attack. The petitioner was charged with her murder.

Prior to his trial in an Illinois court, his counsel filed a motion for an order permitting a scientific inspection of the physical evidence the prosecution intended to introduce. The motion was resisted by the prosecution and denied by the court. The jury trial ended in a verdict of guilty and a sentence of death. On appeal the judgment was affirmed by the Supreme Court of Illinois. On the basis of leads developed at a subsequent unsuccessful state clemency hearing, the petitioner applied to a federal district court for a writ of habeas corpus. After a hearing, the court granted the writ and ordered the petitioner's release or prompt retrial. The Court of Appeals reversed, and we granted certiorari to consider whether the trial that led to the petitioner's conviction was constitutionally valid. We have concluded that it was not.

There were no eyewitnesses to the brutal crime which the petitioner was charged with perpetrating. A vital component of the case against him was a pair of men's underwear shorts covered with large, dark, reddish-brown stains —People's Exhibit 3 in the trial record. These shorts had been found by a Canton policeman in a place known as the Van Buren Flats three days after the murder. The Van Buren Flats were about a mile from the scene of the crime. It was the prosecution's theory that the petitioner had been wearing these shorts when he committed the murder, and that he had afterwards removed and discarded them at the Van Buren Flats.

During the presentation of the prosecution's case, People's Exhibit 3 was variously described by witnesses in such terms as the 'bloody shorts' and 'a pair of jockey shorts stained with blood.' Early in the trial the victim's mother testified that her daughter 'had type 'A' positive blood.' Evidence was later introduced to show that the petitioner's blood 'was of group 'O'.'

Against this background the jury heard the testimony of a chemist for the State Bureau of Crime Identification. The prosecution established his qualifications as an expert, whose 'duties include blood identification, grouping and typing both dry and fresh stains,' and who had 'made approximately one thousand blood typing analyses while at the State Bureau.' His crucial testimony was as follows:

'I examined and tested 'People's Exhibit 3' to determine the nature of the staining material upon it. The result of the first test was that this material upon the shorts is blood. I made a second examination which disclosed that the blood is of human origin. I made a further examination which disclosed that the blood is of group 'A'.'

The petitioner, testifying in his own behalf, denied that he had ever owned or worn the shorts in evidence as People's Exhibit 3. He himself referred to the shorts as having 'dried blood on them.'

In argument to the jury the prosecutor made the most of People's Exhibit 3:

'Those shorts were found in the Van Buren Flats, with blood. What type blood? Not 'O' blood as the defendant has, but 'A'—type 'A.''

And later in his argument he said to the jury:

'And, if you will recall, it has never been contradicted the blood type of Janice May was blood type 'A' positive. Blood type 'A'. Blood type 'A' on these shorts. It wasn't 'O' type as the defendant has. It is 'A' type, what the little girl had.'

Such was the state of the evidence with respect to People's Exhibit 3 as the case went to the jury. And such was the state of the record as the judgment of conviction was reviewed by the Supreme Court of Illinois. The 'blood stained shorts' clearly played a vital part in the case for the prosecution. They were an important link in the chain of circumstantial evidence against the petitioner, and, in the context of the revolting crime with which he was charged, their gruesomely emotional impact upon the jury was incalculable.

So matters stood with respect to People's Exhibit 3, until the present habeas corpus proceeding in the Federal District Court. In this proceeding the State was ordered to produce the stained shorts, and they were admitted in evidence. It was established that their appearance was the same as when they had been introduced at the trial as People's Exhibit 3. The petitioner was permitted to have the shorts examined by a chemical microanalyst. What the microanalyst found cast an extraordinary new light on People's Exhibit 3. The reddish-brown stains on the shorts were not blood, but paint.

... He found 'no traces of human blood.' The State did not dispute this testimony, its counsel contenting himself with prevailing upon the witness to concede on cross-examination that he could not swear that there had never been any blood on the shorts.

It was further established that counsel for the prosecution had known at the time of the trial that the shorts were stained with paint. The prosecutor even admitted that the Canton police had prepared a memorandum attempting to explain 'how this exhibit contains all the paint on it.'...

The record of the petitioner's trial reflects the prosecution's consistent and repeated misrepresentation that People's Exhibit 3 was, indeed, 'a garment heavily stained with blood.' The prosecution's whole theory with respect to the exhibit depended upon that misrepresentation. For the theory was that the victim's assailant had discarded the shorts because they were stained with blood. A pair of paint-stained shorts, found in an abandoned building a mile away from the scene of the crime, was virtually valueless as evidence against the petitioner. The prosecution deliberately misrepresented the truth.

More than 30 years ago this Court held that the Fourteenth Amendment cannot tolerate a state criminal conviction obtained by the knowing use of false evidence. Mooney v. Holohan, 294 U.S. 103. There has been no deviation from that established principle. Napue v. People of State of Illinois, 360 U.S. 264; Pyle v. State of Kansas, 317 U.S. 213. There can be no retreat from that principle here.

The judgment of the Court of Appeals is reversed and the case is remanded for further proceedings consistent with this opinion. It is so ordered....

Notes and Questions

1. Lloyd Eldon Miller, Jr. was a 29-year-old taxi cab driver when he was arrested in 1955 and charged with murdering the eight-year-old child. Although initially protesting his innocence, he signed a confession to the crime two days after his arrest. He later retracted it, claiming that he signed the statement without reading it, that he feared he would be given the death penalty if he did not cooperate, and because the police confronted him with physical evidence and a witness that they maintained confirmed his guilt. His "confession" included an admission about discarding the "bloody" undershorts found near the crime scene. Many details of the signed statement later were revealed to be inconsistent with the facts of the murder. Miller testified at his trial, denied committing the crime, and offered an alibi. He was convicted and sentenced to death in 1956. Several execution dates were set and then postponed; he once came within seven and one-half hours of a scheduled electrocution. He remained incarcerated until 1967, when the Supreme Court announced its decision. In addition to the revelation about the paint-smeared underwear, a prosecution witness came forward and recanted her inculpatory trial testimony and other witnesses were located who corroborated Miller's alibi testimony. All charges against Miller were dismissed in 1971.[2]

2. The prosecutor at Miller's trial argued that the stained undershorts evidenced type "A" blood: "It wasn't 'O' type as the defendant has. It is 'A' type, what the little girl had." Justice Stewart's opinion in *Miller v. Pate* discloses that "[t]he reddish-brown stains on the shorts were not blood, but paint.... It was further established that counsel for the prosecution had known at the time of the trial that the shorts were stained with paint....

The prosecution deliberately misrepresented the truth." What could possibly explain such behavior, particularly in a murder trial where the defendant faced a sentence of death? Willard J. Lassers, one of the attorneys who represented Miller in the federal court proceedings that culminated with the Supreme Court's reversal of his conviction, theorized as follows:

> Did the prosecution suppress facts out of malice to Miller, deliberately seeking the execution of an innocent man? ... Let me attempt an answer: early in the case, the prosecution became convinced, genuinely convinced, of Miller's guilt. Evidence that we, as Miller's counsel, felt clearly favored him, or even exonerated him, was not seen in that light by the prosecution. Consequently, they did not feel compelled to reveal such evidence to the defense and the court.... In my view, the prosecution suppression of evidence was very wrong. But the prosecution did not act maliciously....[3]
>
> When a crime outrages society, it pushes the authorities to lash out, and to make a sacrifice of someone. They do so, not usually through vindictiveness, but because of the unremitting public pressures which warp their judgment.[4]

Does that explanation seem plausible? Were the prosecutor's actions malicious? Can being convinced about a defendant's guilt influence the likelihood of misconduct? In a cleverly designed laboratory experiment, Lucas, Graif and Lovaglia[5] tested whether beliefs about guilt and the importance placed on attaining a conviction would influence prosecutorial misconduct (specifically, with respect to information to be turned over to the defense). They found that stronger perceptions of guilt and stronger levels of the personal importance of winning convictions led to a higher incidence of misconduct. Thus, as Lassers surmises, the prosecutor in *Miller v. Pate* well may have felt that his actions were justifiable.

3. In *Napue v. Illinois,* 360 U.S. 264, 269, 79 S.Ct. 1173, 3 L.Ed.2d 1217 (1959), a case that we will consider in Chapter 8 in connection with informant testimony, the Court affirmed that the prohibition against the prosecution's knowing use of perjury to secure a conviction involves affirmative acts as well as omissions. "[I]t is established that a conviction obtained through use of false evidence, known to be such by representatives of the State, must fall under the Fourteenth Amendment. The same result obtains when the State, although not soliciting false evidence, allows it to go uncorrected when it appears."

4. A prosecutor's knowing reliance on perjured testimony represents a sufficient measure of governmental misconduct to trigger Due Process concerns. Even so, the Court has refrained from announcing a rule requiring automatic reversal of a conviction when prosecution witnesses commit perjury. In *Miller v. Pate,* Justice Stewart's opinion noted that "[t]here were no eyewitnesses to the brutal crime which the petitioner was charged with perpetrating," that the prosecution relied on a "chain of circumstantial evidence," and that "the prosecution's whole theory" about the stained undershorts "depended on [the] misrepresentation that the shorts contained the same blood type as the murder victim." The opinion concluded that "the Fourteenth Amendment cannot tolerate a state criminal conviction *obtained by* the knowing use of false evidence." 386 U.S., at 7 (emphasis added). In *United States v. Agurs,* 427 U.S. 97, 103, 96 S.Ct. 2392, 49 L.Ed.2d 342 (1976), the justices elaborated on that standard: "[A] conviction must be set aside if there is any reasonable likelihood that the false testimony could have affected the judgment of the jury" (footnote omitted).

5. Courts are divided about the appropriate standard for reviewing convictions when it appears that one or more prosecution witnesses may have committed perjury at trial

but there is no reason to believe that the prosecutor knew or should have known that the testimony was false when it was presented. The Nebraska Supreme Court addressed this issue in *State v. Lotter,* 771 N.W.2d 551 (Neb. 2009). Lotter was convicted of three counts of capital murder and sentenced to death. In trial testimony, Thomas Nissen claimed that he assisted Lotter in planning the murders but that Lotter actually killed the victims. Fourteen years later, Nissen signed an affidavit stating that his trial testimony was untruthful and that he, and not Lotter, was the actual killer.

> [Lotter claims] that the mere presence of perjured testimony, regardless of the State's knowledge that it was perjured, violated his rights to due process.... However, we hold that Nissen's recantation, even if proved true, does not present a constitutional claim amendable to postconviction relief. Therefore, postconviction relief on this basis was properly denied without an evidentiary hearing.
>
> Perjury per se is not a ground for collateral attack on a judgment. The guilt or innocence determination in a procedurally fair trial is "'a decisive and portentous event.'"[39] The Due Process Clause guarantees a procedurally fair trial, but does not guarantee that the verdict will be factually correct.[40] The U.S. Supreme Court, while holding that affirmative prosecutorial involvement in perjured testimony may interfere with the fairness of the trial process,[41] has never held that the prosecution's unknowing reliance at trial on perjured testimony violates any constitutional right.[42]
>
> Other courts, more directly confronted with the issue, have concluded that perjury itself, absent prosecutorial misconduct surrounding the perjury, does not constitute an independent constitutional claim.[43] For instance, the court in *Luna v. Beto*[44] rejected the defendant's claim that a conviction on perjured testimony was a constitutional violation even absent state complicity, explaining that the unknowing use of perjured testimony is simply an evidentiary mistake. In *Luna v. Beto,* the court stated:
>
>> [F]or an otherwise valid state conviction to be upset years later on federal habeas, surely something more than an evidentiary *mistake* must be shown. If *mistake* is enough, then never, simply never, will the process of repeated, prolonged, postconviction review cease. For in every trial, or at least nearly every trial, there will be, there are bound to be, some mistakes.[45]
>
> We agree. A defendant has a due process right to a trial process in which the truth-seeking function has not been corrupted. But it is axiomatic that the truth-seeking process is not defective simply because not all evidence weighed by the trier of fact was actually true. The protections of a "fair trial" granted the defendant in the criminal process are there precisely because some of the evidence against the defendant may be disputed.
>
> Lotter relies on *Ortega v. Duncan,*[46] wherein the U.S. Court of Appeals for the Second Circuit held that regardless of prosecutorial knowledge of the perjury, due process is violated when a court is left with the firm belief that but for a witness' perjured testimony, the defendant would most likely not have been convicted. In *Ortega v. Duncan,* the defendant was granted habeas relief when a key witness placing the defendant at the scene of the murder later recanted.
>
> The majority of the federal circuits, however, reject the Second Circuit's conclusion that affirmative prosecutorial involvement is not a nec-

39. *Herrera v. Collins,* 506 U.S. 390, 401 (1993).

40. *Herrera v. Collins, supra* note 39.

41. See, e.g., *Napue v. Illinois,* [360 U.S. 264 (1959)]; *United States v. Agurs,* [427 U.S. 97 (1976)]; *Alcorta v. Texas,* [355 U.S. 28 (1957)]; *Mooney v. Holohan,* [294 U.S. 103 (1935)].

42. See *Jacobs v. Scott,* 513 U.S. 1067 (1995) (Stevens, J., dissenting from denial of certiorari; Ginsburg, J., joins).

43. See, e.g., *Black v. United States,* 269 F.2d 38 (9th Cir.1959). See, also, *Burks v. Egeler,* 512 F.2d 221 (6th Cir.1975).

44. *Luna v. Beto,* 395 F.2d 35 (5th Cir. 1968).

45. *Id.* at 40 (Brown, C.J., concurring specially).

46. *Ortega v. Duncan,* [333 F.3d 102 (2d Cir.2003)].

essary element of a due process violation based on perjured testimony.[47] While some state courts allow such a claim, many do so under postconviction relief statutes that do not limit relief to constitutional claims rendering the judgment void or voidable.

In Nebraska, postconviction relief is strictly prescribed. In a different statute, the Legislature has provided defendants with the ability to file a motion for new trial based on newly discovered evidence showing that the defendant was wrongfully convicted. Unlike postconviction relief, relief under § 29-2103 is not strictly limited to constitutional claims. But a motion under § 29-2103 must be filed within 3 years of the date of the verdict. We have repeatedly held that a motion for postconviction relief cannot be used to obtain, outside of the 3-year time limitation, what is essentially a new trial based on newly discovered evidence. This can be no less true for a recently discovered recantation than for any other newly discovered evidence material to the defendant. It has been said that there is no form of proof so unreliable as recanting testimony. "'The opportunity and temptation for fraud are so obvious that courts look with suspicion upon such an asserted repudiation of the testimony of a witness for the prosecution, and this is so even though the repudiation be sworn to.'"[53]

"'Society's resources have been concentrated at [the time of trial] in order to decide, within the limits of human fallibility, the question of guilt or innocence of one of its citizens.'"[54] We will not set aside that decision more than a decade after it was made based only on the recent recantation of some portion of a key witness' testimony against Lotter. The 3-year limitation of § 29-2103 reflects the fact that with the passage of time and the erosion of memory and the dispersion of witnesses, there is no guarantee that the truth-seeking function of a new trial would be any more exact than the first trial. We do not grant postconviction relief in the absence of a constitutional violation, and the presence of perjury by a key witness does not, in and of itself, present a constitutional violation.

2. The Duty to Disclose Exculpatory Evidence

Brady v. Maryland

373 U.S. 83, 83 S.Ct. 1194, 10 L.Ed.2d 215 (1963)

Opinion of the Court by Mr. Justice DOUGLAS ...

Petitioner and a companion, Boblit, were found guilty of murder in the first degree and were sentenced to death, their convictions being affirmed by the Court of Appeals of Maryland. Their trials were separate, petitioner being tried first. At his trial Brady took the stand and admitted his participation in the crime, but he claimed that Boblit did the actual killing. And, in his summation to the jury, Brady's counsel conceded that Brady was guilty of murder in the first degree, asking only that the jury return that verdict 'without capital punishment.' Prior to the trial petitioner's counsel had requested the prosecution to allow him to examine Boblit's extrajudicial statements. Several of those statements were shown to him; but one dated July 9, 1958, in which Boblit admitted the actual homicide, was withheld by the prosecution and did not come to petitioner's notice until after he had been tried, convicted, and sentenced, and after his conviction had been affirmed.

Petitioner moved the trial court for a new trial based on the newly discovered evidence that had been suppressed by the prosecution.... [The trial court denied the motion.] On appeal the Court of Appeals held that suppression of

47. See, *Smith v. Gibson*, 197 F.3d 454 (10th Cir.1999); *Reddick v. Haws*, 120 F.3d 714 (7th Cir.1997); *Jacobs v. Singletary*, 952 F.2d 1282 (11th Cir.1992); *Smith v. Black*, 904 F.2d 950 (5th Cir.1990), *abrogated on other grounds, Stringer v. Black*, 503 U.S. 222 (1992); *Stockton v. Com. of Va.*, 852 F.2d 740 (4th Cir.1988); *Burks v. Egeler, supra* note 43; *White v. Hancock*, 355 F.2d 262 (1st Cir.1966); *United States v. Maroney*, 271 F.2d 329 (3d Cir.1959); *Pina v. Cambra*, 171 Fed.Appx. 674 (9th Cir.2006); *Billman v. Warden*, 79 A.2d 540 (Md. 1951).

53. *Fout v. Commonwealth*, 98 S.E.2d 817, 823 (Va. 1957).

54. *Herrera v. Collins*, 506 U.S. at 401.

the evidence by the prosecution denied petitioner due process of law and remanded the case for a retrial of the question of punishment, not the question of guilt. The case is here on certiorari.

The crime in question was murder committed in the perpetration of a robbery. Punishment for that crime in Maryland is life imprisonment or death, the jury being empowered to restrict the punishment to life by addition of the words 'without capital punishment.' In Maryland, by reason of the state constitution, the jury in a criminal case are 'the Judges of Law, as well as of fact.' Art. XV, § 5. The question presented is whether petitioner was denied a federal right when the Court of Appeals restricted the new trial to the question of punishment.

We agree with the Court of Appeals that suppression of this confession was a violation of the Due Process Clause of the Fourteenth Amendment....

This ruling is an extension of Mooney v. Holohan, 294 U.S. 103, 112, where the Court ruled on what nondisclosure by a prosecutor violates due process:

'It is a requirement that cannot be deemed to be satisfied by mere notice and hearing if a state has contrived a conviction through the pretense of a trial which in truth is but used as a means of depriving a defendant of liberty through a deliberate deception of court and jury by the presentation of testimony known to be perjured. Such a contrivance by a state to procure the conviction and imprisonment of a defendant is as inconsistent with the rudimentary demands of justice as is the obtaining of a like result by intimidation.'

... In Napue v. Illinois, 360 U.S. 264, 269, we extended the test formulated in Mooney v. Holohan when we said: 'The same result obtains when the State, although not soliciting false evidence, allows it to go uncorrected when it appears.'

We now hold that the suppression by the prosecution of evidence favorable to an accused upon request violates due process where the evidence is material either to guilt or to punishment, irrespective of the good faith or bad faith of the prosecution.

The principle of Mooney v. Holohan is not punishment of society for misdeeds of a prosecutor but avoidance of an unfair trial to the accused. Society wins not only when the guilty are convicted but when criminal trials are fair; our system of the administration of justice suffers when any accused is treated unfairly. An inscription on the walls of the Department of Justice states the proposition candidly for the federal domain: 'The United States wins its point whenever justice is done its citizens in the courts.' A prosecution that withholds evidence on demand of an accused which, if made available, would tend to exculpate him or reduce the penalty helps shape a trial that bears heavily on the defendant. That casts the prosecutor in the role of an architect of a proceeding that does not comport with standards of justice, even though, as in the present case, his action is not 'the result of guile,' to use the words of the Court of Appeals.

The question remains whether petitioner was denied a constitutional right when the Court of Appeals restricted his new trial to the question of punishment. In justification of that ruling the Court of Appeals stated:

... 'The appellant's sole claim of prejudice goes to the punishment imposed. If Boblit's withheld confession had been before the jury, nothing in it could have reduced the appellant Brady's offense below murder in the first degree. We, therefore, see no occasion to retry that issue.' 174 A.2d, at 171.

If this were a jurisdiction where the jury was not the judge of the law, a different question would be presented....

But, as we read the Maryland decisions, it is the court, not the jury, that passes on the 'admissibility of evidence' pertinent to 'the issue of the innocence or guilt of the accused.' In the present case a unanimous Court of Appeals has said that nothing in the suppressed confession 'could have reduced the appellant Brady's offense below murder in the first degree.' We read that statement as a ruling on the admissibility of the confession on the issue of innocence or guilt. A sporting theory of justice might assume that if the suppressed confession had been used at the first trial, the judge's ruling that it was not admissible on the issue of innocence or guilt might have been flouted by the jury just as might have been done if the court had first admitted a confession and then stricken it from the record. But we cannot raise that trial strategy to the dignity of a constitutional right and say that the deprival of this defendant of that sporting chance through the use of a bifurcated trial denies him due process or violates the Equal Protection Clause of the Fourteenth Amendment.

Affirmed....

Notes and Questions

1. Why did the Maryland Court of Appeals as well as the Supreme Court limit Brady's relief to a new sentencing hearing? Why wasn't Brady's murder conviction also reversed? What, precisely, does the portion of the *Brady* Court's holding mean that refers to the suppression of evidence that is "material" to guilt or to sentencing?

2. Brady's attorney had filed a pre-trial request to examine statements made by Boblit within the prosecution's possession. The fact that the prosecutor failed to produce the statement favorable to Brady notwithstanding this specific request appeared to be significant to the Court's holding. However, in *United States v. Agurs,* 427 U.S. 97, 96 S.Ct. 2392, 49 L.Ed.2d 342 (1976), the justices ruled that some evidence has such "obviously exculpatory character," 427 U.S., at 106, and "is so clearly supportive of a claim of innocence," 427 U.S., at 107, that the prosecution has a duty to disclose it even if the defense fails to request it. The *Agurs* Court further ruled that different standards govern when a new trial is warranted, depending on whether the defense made or failed to make a specific request for the information. Where the defense makes "a pretrial request for specific evidence," reversal of a conviction is in order when "the suppressed evidence might have affected the outcome of the trial." 427 U.S., at 104. Conversely, in cases where the defense made no request or simply made a general request for exculpatory evidence, non-disclosure of evidence is reversible error only "if the omitted evidence creates a reasonable doubt that did not otherwise exist...." 427 U.S., at 112. Nearly a decade later, in *United States v. Bagley,* 473 U.S. 667, 682, 105 S.Ct. 3375, 87 L.Ed.2d 481 (1985), Justice Blackmun's plurality opinion indicated that the different materiality tests identified in *Agurs* would be replaced by a single standard.

> We find the *Strickland* [*v. Washington,* 466 U.S. 668 (1984)] formulation of the *Agurs* test for materiality sufficiently flexible to cover the "no request," "general request," and "specific request" cases of prosecutorial failure to disclose evidence favorable to the accused: The evidence is material only if there is a reasonable probability that, had the evidence been disclosed to the defense, the result of the proceeding would have been different. A "reasonable probability" is a probability sufficient to undermine confidence in the outcome.

The "reasonable probability" standard for materiality now is the exclusive federal constitutional test used to evaluate alleged *Brady* violations. In the following case, which necessarily is quite fact-intensive, we consider the standard's application and learn more about the nature of the prosecutor's duties in the *Brady* context.

Kyles v. Whitley

514 U.S. 419, 115 S.Ct. 1555, 131 L.Ed.2d 490 (1995)

Justice SOUTER delivered the opinion of the Court.

After his first trial in 1984 ended in a hung jury, petitioner Curtis Lee Kyles was tried again, convicted of first-degree murder, and sentenced to death. On habeas review, we follow the established rule that the state's obligation under *Brady v. Maryland,* 373 U.S. 83 (1963), to disclose evidence favorable to the defense, turns on the cumulative effect of all such evidence suppressed by the government, and we hold that the prosecutor remains responsible for gauging that effect regardless of any failure by the police to bring favorable evidence to the prosecutor's attention. Because the net effect of the evidence withheld by the State in this case raises a reasonable probability that its disclosure would have produced a different result, Kyles is entitled to a new trial.

I

[After Kyles's conviction and death sentence were affirmed on appeal, the Louisiana Supreme

Court directed the trial court to conduct an evidentiary hearing to consider Kyles's newly discovered evidence, including favorable evidence that the State had failed to disclose prior to or during the trial. The trial court conducted the hearing but denied relief. The State Supreme Court declined review. The United States District Court for the Eastern District of Louisiana subsequently denied Kyles's petition for writ of habeas corpus. The Fifth Circuit Court of Appeals affirmed by a divided vote.]

.... Because "[o]ur duty to search for constitutional error with painstaking care is never more exacting than it is in a capital case," *Burger v. Kemp*, 483 U.S. 776, 785 (1987), we granted certiorari, and now reverse.

II

A

The record indicates that, at about 2:20 p.m. on Thursday, September 20, 1984, 60-year-old Dolores Dye left the Schwegmann Brothers' store (Schwegmann's) on Old Gentilly Road in New Orleans after doing some food shopping. As she put her grocery bags into the trunk of her red Ford LTD, a man accosted her and after a short struggle drew a revolver, fired into her left temple, and killed her. The gunman took Dye's keys and drove away in the LTD.

New Orleans police took statements from six eyewitnesses, who offered various descriptions of the gunman. They agreed that he was a black man, and four of them said that he had braided hair. The witnesses differed significantly, however, in their descriptions of height, age, weight, build, and hair length. Two reported seeing a man of 17 or 18, while another described the gunman as looking as old as 28. One witness described him as 5'4" or 5'5", medium build, 140–150 pounds; another described the man as slim and close to six feet. One witness said he had a mustache; none of the others spoke of any facial hair at all. One witness said the murderer had shoulder-length hair; another described the hair as "short."

Since the police believed the killer might have driven his own car to Schwegmann's and left it there when he drove off in Dye's LTD, they recorded the license numbers of the cars remaining in the parking lots around the store at 9:15 p.m. on the evening of the murder. Matching these numbers with registration records produced the names and addresses of the owners of the cars, with a notation of any owner's police record. Despite this list and the eyewitness descriptions, the police had no lead to the gunman until the Saturday evening after the shooting.

At 5:30 p.m., on September 22, a man identifying himself as James Joseph called the police and reported that on the day of the murder he had bought a red Thunderbird from a friend named Curtis, whom he later identified as petitioner, Curtis Kyles. He said that he had subsequently read about Dye's murder in the newspapers and feared that the car he purchased was the victim's. He agreed to meet with the police.

A few hours later, the informant met New Orleans Detective John Miller, who was wired with a hidden body microphone, through which the ensuing conversation was recorded. The informant now said his name was Joseph Banks and that he was called Beanie. His actual name was Joseph Wallace.

His story, as well as his name, had changed since his earlier call. In place of his original account of buying a Thunderbird from Kyles on Thursday, Beanie told Miller that he had not seen Kyles at all on Thursday, and had bought a red LTD the previous day, Friday. Beanie led Miller to the parking lot of a nearby bar, where he had left the red LTD, later identified as Dye's.

Beanie told Miller that he lived with Kyles's brother-in-law (later identified as Johnny Burns), whom Beanie repeatedly called his "partner." Beanie described Kyles as slim, about 6-feet tall, 24 or 25 years old, with a "bush" hairstyle. When asked if Kyles ever wore his hair in plaits, Beanie said that he did but that he "had a bush" when Beanie bought the car.

During the conversation, Beanie repeatedly expressed concern that he might himself be a suspect in the murder. He explained that he had been seen driving Dye's car on Friday evening in the French Quarter, admitted that he had changed its license plates, and worried that he "could have been charged" with the murder on the basis of his possession of the LTD....

Beanie seemed eager to cast suspicion on Kyles, who allegedly made his living by "robbing people," and had tried to kill Beanie at some prior time. Beanie said that Kyles regularly carried two pistols, a .38 and a .32, and that if the police could "set him up good," they could "get that same gun" used to kill Dye. Beanie rode with Miller and Miller's supervisor, Sgt. James Eaton, in an unmarked squad car to Desire Street, where he pointed out the building containing Kyles's apartment.

Beanie told the officers that after he bought the car, he and his "partner" (Burns) drove Kyles to Schwegmann's about 9 p.m. on Friday evening to pick up Kyles's car, described as an orange four-door Ford. When asked where Kyles's car had been parked, Beanie replied that it had been "[o]n the same side [of the lot] where the woman was killed at." The officers later drove Beanie to Schwegmann's, where he indicated the space where he claimed Kyles's car had been parked. Beanie went on to say that when he and Burns had brought Kyles to pick up the car, Kyles had gone to some nearby bushes to retrieve a brown purse, which Kyles subsequently hid in a wardrobe at his apartment. Beanie said that Kyles had "a lot of groceries" in Schwegmann's bags and a new baby's potty "in the car." Beanie told Eaton that Kyles's garbage would go out the next day and that if Kyles was "smart" he would "put [the purse] in [the] garbage." Beanie made it clear that he expected some reward for his help, saying at one point that he was not "doing all of this for nothing." The police repeatedly assured Beanie that he would not lose the $400 he paid for the car.

After the visit to Schwegmann's, Eaton and Miller took Beanie to a police station where Miller interviewed him again on the record, which was transcribed and signed by Beanie, using his alias "Joseph Banks." This statement, Beanie's third (the telephone call being the first, then the recorded conversation), repeats some of the essentials of the second one: that Beanie had purchased a red Ford LTD from Kyles for $400 on Friday evening; that Kyles had his hair "combed out" at the time of the sale; and that Kyles carried a .32 and a .38 with him "all the time."

Portions of the third statement, however, embellished or contradicted Beanie's preceding story and were even internally inconsistent. Beanie reported that after the sale, he and Kyles unloaded Schwegmann's grocery bags from the trunk and back seat of the LTD and placed them in Kyles's own car. Beanie said that Kyles took a brown purse from the front seat of the LTD and that they then drove in separate cars to Kyles's apartment, where they unloaded the groceries. Beanie also claimed that, a few hours later, he and his "partner" Burns went with Kyles to Schwegmann's, where they recovered Kyles's car and a "big brown pocket book" from "next to a building." Beanie did not explain how Kyles could have picked up his car and recovered the purse at Schwegmann's, after Beanie had seen Kyles with both just a few hours earlier. The police neither noted the inconsistencies nor questioned Beanie about them.

Although the police did not thereafter put Kyles under surveillance, they learned about events at his apartment from Beanie, who went there twice on Sunday. According to a fourth statement by Beanie, this one given to the chief prosecutor in November (between the first and second trials), he first went to the apartment about 2 p.m., after a telephone conversation with a police officer who asked whether Kyles had the gun that was used to kill Dye. Beanie stayed in Kyles's apartment until about 5 p.m., when he left to call Detective John Miller. Then he returned about 7 p.m. and stayed until about 9:30 p.m., when he left to meet Miller, who also asked about the gun. According to this fourth statement, Beanie "rode around" with Miller until 3 a.m. on Monday, September 24. Sometime during those same early morning hours, detectives were sent at Sgt. Eaton's behest to pick up the rubbish outside Kyles's building. As Sgt. Eaton wrote in an interoffice memorandum, he had "reason to believe the victims *[sic]* personal papers and the Schwegmann's bags will be in the trash."

At 10:40 a.m., Kyles was arrested as he left the apartment, which was then searched under a warrant. Behind the kitchen stove, the police found a .32-caliber revolver containing five live rounds and one spent cartridge. Ballistics tests later showed that this pistol was used to murder Dye. In a wardrobe in a hallway leading to the kitchen, the officers found a homemade shoulder holster that fit the murder weapon. In a bedroom dresser drawer, they discovered two boxes of ammunition, one containing several .32-caliber rounds of the same brand as those found in the pistol. Back in the kitchen, various cans of cat and dog food, some of them of the brands Dye typically purchased, were found in Schwegmann's sacks. No other groceries were identified as possibly being Dye's, and no potty was found. Later that afternoon at the police station, police opened the rubbish bags and found the victim's purse, identification, and other personal belongings wrapped in a Schwegmann's sack.

The gun, the LTD, the purse, and the cans of pet food were dusted for fingerprints. The gun had been wiped clean. Several prints were found on the purse and on the LTD, but none was identified as Kyles's. Dye's prints were not found on any of the cans of pet food. Kyles's prints were found, however, on a small piece of paper taken from the front passenger-side floorboard of the LTD. The crime laboratory recorded the paper as a Schwegmann's sales slip, but without noting what had been printed on it, which was obliterated in the chemical process of lifting the fingerprints. A second Schwegmann's receipt was found in the trunk of the LTD, but Kyles's prints were not found on it. Beanie's fingerprints were not compared to any of the fingerprints found.

The lead detective on the case, John Dillman, put together a photo lineup that included a photograph of Kyles (but not of Beanie) and showed the array to five of the six eyewitnesses who had given statements. Three of them picked the photograph of Kyles; the other two could not confidently identify Kyles as Dye's assailant.

B

Kyles was indicted for first-degree murder. Before trial, his counsel filed a lengthy motion for disclosure by the State of any exculpatory or impeachment evidence. The prosecution responded that there was "no exculpatory evidence of any nature," despite the government's knowledge of the following evidentiary items: (1) the six contemporaneous eyewitness statements taken by police following the murder; (2) records of Beanie's initial call to the police; (3) the tape recording of the Saturday conversation between Beanie and officers Eaton and Miller; (4) the typed and signed statement given by Beanie on Sunday morning; (5) the computer print-out of license numbers of cars parked at Schwegmann's on the night of the murder, which did not list the number of Kyles's car; (6) the internal police memorandum calling for the seizure of the rubbish after Beanie had suggested that the purse might be found there; and (7) evidence linking Beanie to other crimes at Schwegmann's and to the unrelated murder of one Patricia Leidenheimer, committed in January before the Dye murder.

At the first trial, in November, the heart of the State's case was eyewitness testimony from four people who were at the scene of the crime (three of whom had previously picked Kyles from the photo lineup). Kyles maintained his innocence, offered supporting witnesses, and supplied an alibi that he had been picking up his children from school at the time of the murder. The theory of the defense was that Kyles had been framed by Beanie, who had planted evidence in Kyles's apartment and his rubbish for the purposes of shifting suspicion away from himself, removing an impediment to romance with Pinky Burns, and obtaining reward money. Beanie did not testify as a witness for either the defense or the prosecution.

Because the State withheld evidence, its case was much stronger, and the defense case much weaker, than the full facts would have suggested. Even so, after four hours of deliberation, the jury became deadlocked on the issue of guilt, and a mistrial was declared.

After the mistrial, the chief trial prosecutor, Cliff Strider, interviewed Beanie. Strider's notes show that Beanie again changed important elements of his story. He said that he went with Kyles to retrieve Kyles's car from the Schwegmann's lot on Thursday, the day of the murder, at some time between 5 and 7:30 p.m., not on Friday, at 9 p.m., as he had said in his second and third statements. (Indeed, in his second statement, Beanie said that he had not seen Kyles at all on Thursday.) He also said, for the first time, that when they had picked up the car they were accompanied not only by Johnny Burns but also by Kevin Black, who had testified for the defense at the first trial. Beanie now claimed that after getting Kyles's car they went to Black's house, retrieved a number of bags of groceries, a child's potty, and a brown purse, all of which they took to Kyles's apartment. Beanie also stated that on the Sunday after the murder he had been at Kyles's apartment two separate times. Notwithstanding the many inconsistencies and variations among Beanie's statements, neither Strider's notes nor any of the other notes and transcripts were given to the defense.

In December 1984, Kyles was tried a second time. Again, the heart of the State's case was the testimony of four eyewitnesses who positively identified Kyles in front of the jury. The prosecution also offered a blown-up photograph taken at the crime scene soon after the murder, on the basis of which the prosecutors argued that a seemingly two-toned car in the background of the photograph was Kyles's. They repeatedly suggested during cross-examination of defense witnesses that Kyles had left his own car at Schwegmann's on the day of the murder and had retrieved it later, a theory for which they offered no evidence beyond the blown-up photograph. Once again, Beanie did not testify.

As in the first trial, the defense contended that the eyewitnesses were mistaken. Kyles's counsel called several individuals, including Kevin

Black, who testified to seeing Beanie, with his hair in plaits, driving a red car similar to the victim's about an hour after the killing. Another witness testified that Beanie, with his hair in braids, had tried to sell him the car on Thursday evening, shortly after the murder. Another witness testified that Beanie, with his hair in a "Jheri curl," had attempted to sell him the car on Friday. One witness, Beanie's "partner," Burns, testified that he had seen Beanie on Sunday at Kyles's apartment, stooping down near the stove where the gun was eventually found, and the defense presented testimony that Beanie was romantically interested in Pinky Burns. To explain the pet food found in Kyles's apartment, there was testimony that Kyles's family kept a dog and cat and often fed stray animals in the neighborhood.

Finally, Kyles again took the stand. Denying any involvement in the shooting, he explained his fingerprints on the cash register receipt found in Dye's car by saying that Beanie had picked him up in a red car on Friday, September 21, and had taken him to Schwegmann's, where he purchased transmission fluid and a pack of cigarettes. He suggested that the receipt may have fallen from the bag when he removed the cigarettes.

On rebuttal, the prosecutor had Beanie brought into the courtroom. All of the testifying eyewitnesses, after viewing Beanie standing next to Kyles, reaffirmed their previous identifications of Kyles as the murderer. Kyles was convicted of first-degree murder and sentenced to death. Beanie received a total of $1,600 in reward money.

... After exhausting state remedies, Kyles sought relief on federal habeas, claiming, among other things, that the evidence withheld was material to his defense and that his conviction was thus obtained in violation of *Brady*....

III

The prosecution's affirmative duty to disclose evidence favorable to a defendant can trace its origins to early 20th-century strictures against misrepresentation and is of course most prominently associated with this Court's decision in *Brady v. Maryland,* 373 U.S. 83 (1963) (relying on *Mooney v. Holohan,* 294 U.S. 103 (1935), and *Pyle v. Kansas,* 317 U.S. 213 (1942))....

In ... *United States v. Bagley,* 473 U.S. 667 (1985), the Court disavowed any difference between exculpatory and impeachment evidence for *Brady* purposes, and ... held that regardless of request, favorable evidence is material, and constitutional error results from its suppression by the government, "if there is a reasonable probability that, had the evidence been disclosed to the defense, the result of the proceeding would have been different."

Four aspects of materiality under *Bagley* bear emphasis. Although the constitutional duty is triggered by the potential impact of favorable but undisclosed evidence, a showing of materiality does not require demonstration by a preponderance that disclosure of the suppressed evidence would have resulted ultimately in the defendant's acquittal (whether based on the presence of reasonable doubt or acceptance of an explanation for the crime that does not inculpate the defendant). *Bagley's* touchstone of materiality is a "reasonable probability" of a different result, and the adjective is important. The question is not whether the defendant would more likely than not have received a different verdict with the evidence, but whether in its absence he received a fair trial, understood as a trial resulting in a verdict worthy of confidence. A "reasonable probability" of a different result is accordingly shown when the government's evidentiary suppression "undermines confidence in the outcome of the trial." *Bagley,* 473 U.S., at 678.

The second aspect of *Bagley* materiality bearing emphasis here is that it is not a sufficiency of evidence test. A defendant need not demonstrate that after discounting the inculpatory evidence in light of the undisclosed evidence, there would not have been enough left to convict. The possibility of an acquittal on a criminal charge does not imply an insufficient evidentiary basis to convict. One does not show a *Brady* violation by demonstrating that some of the inculpatory evidence should have been excluded, but by showing that the favorable evidence could reasonably be taken to put the whole case in such a different light as to undermine confidence in the verdict.[8]

Third, ... once a reviewing court applying *Bagley* has found constitutional error there is no

8. This rule is clear, and none of the Brady cases has ever suggested that sufficiency of evidence (or insufficiency) is the touchstone. And yet the dissent appears to assume that Kyles must lose because there would still have been adequate evidence to convict even if the favorable evidence had been disclosed....

need for further harmless-error review. Assuming, *arguendo,* that a harmless-error enquiry were to apply, a *Bagley* error could not be treated as harmless, since "a reasonable probability that, had the evidence been disclosed to the defense, the result of the proceeding would have been different," necessarily entails the conclusion that the suppression must have had "'substantial and injurious effect or influence in determining the jury's verdict.'" ...

The fourth and final aspect of *Bagley* materiality to be stressed here is its definition in terms of suppressed evidence considered collectively, not item by item.... [T]he Constitution is not violated every time the government fails or chooses not to disclose evidence that might prove helpful to the defense. We have never held that the Constitution demands an open file policy (however such a policy might work out in practice), and the rule in *Bagley* (and, hence, in *Brady*) requires less of the prosecution than the ABA Standards for Criminal Justice, which call generally for prosecutorial disclosures of any evidence tending to exculpate or mitigate. See ABA Standards for Criminal Justice, Prosecution Function and Defense Function 3-3.11(a) (3d ed. 1993) ("A prosecutor should not intentionally fail to make timely disclosure to the defense, at the earliest feasible opportunity, of the existence of all evidence or information which tends to negate the guilt of the accused or mitigate the offense charged or which would tend to reduce the punishment of the accused.")

While the definition of *Bagley* materiality in terms of the cumulative effect of suppression must accordingly be seen as leaving the government with a degree of discretion, it must also be understood as imposing a corresponding burden. On the one side, showing that the prosecution knew of an item of favorable evidence unknown to the defense does not amount to a *Brady* violation, without more. But the prosecution, which alone can know what is undisclosed, must be assigned the consequent responsibility to gauge the likely net effect of all such evidence and make disclosure when the point of "reasonable probability" is reached. This in turn means that the individual prosecutor has a duty to learn of any favorable evidence known to the others acting on the government's behalf in the case, including the police. But whether the prosecutor succeeds or fails in meeting this obligation (whether, that is, a failure to disclose is in good faith or bad faith), the prosecution's responsibility for failing to disclose known, favorable evidence rising to a material level of importance is inescapable.

The State of Louisiana would prefer an even more lenient rule. It pleads that some of the favorable evidence in issue here was not disclosed even to the prosecutor until after trial, and it suggested below that it should not be held accountable under *Bagley* and *Brady* for evidence known only to police investigators and not to the prosecutor. To accommodate the State in this manner would, however, amount to a serious change of course from the *Brady* line of cases. In the State's favor it may be said that no one doubts that police investigators sometimes fail to inform a prosecutor of all they know. But neither is there any serious doubt that "procedures and regulations can be established to carry [the prosecutor's] burden and to insure communication of all relevant information on each case to every lawyer who deals with it." *Giglio v. United States,* 405 U.S. 150, 154 (1972). Since, then, the prosecutor has the means to discharge the government's *Brady* responsibility if he will, any argument for excusing a prosecutor from disclosing what he does not happen to know about boils down to a plea to substitute the police for the prosecutor, and even for the courts themselves, as the final arbiters of the government's obligation to ensure fair trials....

Unless ... the adversary system of prosecution is to descend to a gladiatorial level unmitigated by any prosecutorial obligation for the sake of truth, the government simply cannot avoid responsibility for knowing when the suppression of evidence has come to portend such an effect on a trial's outcome as to destroy confidence in its result.

This means, naturally, that a prosecutor anxious about tacking too close to the wind will disclose a favorable piece of evidence. This is as it should be. Such disclosure will serve to justify trust in the prosecutor as "the representative ... of a sovereignty ... whose interest ... in a criminal prosecution is not that it shall win a case, but that justice shall be done." *Berger v. United States,* 295 U.S. 78, 88 (1935). And it will tend to preserve the criminal trial, as distinct from the prosecutor's private deliberations, as the chosen forum for ascertaining the truth about criminal accusations. The prudence of the careful prosecutor should not therefore be discouraged....

IV

In this case, disclosure of the suppressed evidence to competent counsel would have made a different result reasonably probable.

A

As the District Court put it, "the essence of the State's case" was the testimony of eyewitnesses, who identified Kyles as Dye's killer. Disclosure of their statements would have resulted in a markedly weaker case for the prosecution and a markedly stronger one for the defense. To begin with, the value of two of those witnesses would have been substantially reduced or destroyed.

The State rated Henry Williams as its best witness, who testified that he had seen the struggle and the actual shooting by Kyles. The jury would have found it helpful to probe this conclusion in the light of Williams's contemporaneous statement, in which he told the police that the assailant was "a black male, about 19 or 20 years old, about 5'4" or 5'5", 140 to 150 pounds, medium build" and that "his hair looked like it was platted." If cross-examined on this description, Williams would have had trouble explaining how he could have described Kyles, 6-feet tall and thin, as a man more than half a foot shorter with a medium build. Indeed, since Beanie was 22 years old, 5'5" tall, and 159 pounds, the defense would have had a compelling argument that Williams's description pointed to Beanie but not to Kyles.

The trial testimony of a second eyewitness, Isaac Smallwood, was equally damning to Kyles. He testified that Kyles was the assailant, and that he saw him struggle with Dye. He said he saw Kyles take a ".32, a small black gun" out of his right pocket, shoot Dye in the head, and drive off in her LTD. When the prosecutor asked him whether he actually saw Kyles shoot Dye, Smallwood answered "Yeah."

Smallwood's statement taken at the parking lot, however, was vastly different. Immediately after the crime, Smallwood claimed that he had not seen the actual murder and had not seen the assailant outside the vehicle. "I heard a lound [sic] pop," he said. "When I looked around I saw a lady laying on the ground, and there was a red car coming toward me." Smallwood said that he got a look at the culprit, a black teenage male with a mustache and shoulder-length braided hair, as the victim's red Thunderbird passed where he was standing. When a police investigator specifically asked him whether he had seen the assailant outside the car, Smallwood answered that he had not; the gunman "was already in the car and coming toward me."

A jury would reasonably have been troubled by the adjustments to Smallwood's original story by the time of the second trial. The struggle and shooting, which earlier he had not seen, he was able to describe with such detailed clarity as to identify the murder weapon as a small black .32-caliber pistol, which, of course, was the type of weapon used. His description of the victim's car had gone from a "Thunderbird" to an "LTD"; and he saw fit to say nothing about the assailant's shoulder-length hair and moustache, details noted by no other eyewitness. These developments would have fueled a withering cross-examination, destroying confidence in Smallwood's story and raising a substantial implication that the prosecutor had coached him to give it.

Since the evolution over time of a given eyewitness's description can be fatal to its reliability, cf. *Manson v. Brathwaite,* 432 U.S. 98 (1977) (reliability depends in part on the accuracy of prior description); *Neil v. Biggers,* 409 U.S. 188 (1972), the Smallwood and Williams identifications would have been severely undermined by use of their suppressed statements.... The fact that neither Williams nor Smallwood could have provided a consistent eyewitness description pointing to Kyles would have undercut the prosecution all the more because the remaining eyewitnesses called to testify (Territo and Kersh) had their best views of the gunman only as he fled the scene with his body partly concealed in Dye's car....

B

Damage to the prosecution's case would not have been confined to evidence of the eyewitnesses, for Beanie's various statements would have raised opportunities to attack not only the probative value of crucial physical evidence and the circumstances in which it was found, but the thoroughness and even the good faith of the investigation, as well. By the State's own admission, Beanie was essential to its investigation and, indeed, "made the case" against Kyles. Contrary to what one might hope for from such a source, however, Beanie's statements to the police were replete with inconsistencies and would have allowed the jury to infer that Beanie was anxious to see Kyles arrested for Dye's murder. Their disclosure would have revealed a remarkably uncritical attitude on the part of the police.

If the defense had called Beanie as an adverse witness, he could not have said anything of any significance without being trapped by his inconsistencies. A short recapitulation of some of them will make the point. In Beanie's initial meeting with the police, and in his signed statement, he said he bought Dye's LTD and helped Kyles retrieve his car from the Schwegmann's lot on Friday. In his first call to the police, he said he bought the LTD on Thursday, and in his conversation with the prosecutor between trials it was again on Thursday that he said he helped Kyles retrieve Kyles's car. Although none of the first three versions of this story mentioned Kevin Black as taking part in the retrieval of the car and transfer of groceries, after Black implicated Beanie by his testimony for the defense at the first trial, Beanie changed his story to include Black as a participant. In Beanie's several accounts, Dye's purse first shows up variously next to a building, in some bushes, in Kyles's car, and at Black's house.

Even if Kyles's lawyer had followed the more conservative course of leaving Beanie off the stand, though, the defense could have examined the police to good effect on their knowledge of Beanie's statements and so have attacked the reliability of the investigation in failing even to consider Beanie's possible guilt and in tolerating (if not countenancing) serious possibilities that incriminating evidence had been planted.

By demonstrating the detectives' knowledge of Beanie's affirmatively self-incriminating statements, the defense could have laid the foundation for a vigorous argument that the police had been guilty of negligence. In his initial meeting with police, Beanie admitted twice that he changed the license plates on the LTD. This admission enhanced the suspiciousness of his possession of the car; the defense could have argued persuasively that he was no bona fide purchaser. And when combined with his police record, evidence of prior criminal activity near Schwegmann's, and his status as a suspect in another murder, his devious behavior gave reason to believe that he had done more than buy a stolen car. There was further self-incrimination in Beanie's statement that Kyles's car was parked in the same part of the Schwegmann's lot where Dye was killed. Beanie's apparent awareness of the specific location of the murder could have been based, as the State contends, on television or newspaper reports, but perhaps it was not....

The admitted failure of the police to pursue these pointers toward Beanie's possible guilt could only have magnified the effect on the jury of explaining how the purse and the gun happened to be recovered. In Beanie's original recorded statement, he told the police that "[Kyles's] garbage goes out tomorrow," and that "if he's smart he'll put [the purse] in [the] garbage." These statements, along with the internal memorandum stating that the police had "reason to believe" Dye's personal effects and Schwegmann's bags would be in the garbage, would have supported the defense's theory that Beanie was no mere observer, but was determining the investigation's direction and success....

To the same effect would have been an enquiry based on Beanie's apparently revealing remark to police that "if you can set [Kyles] up good, you can get that same gun." While the jury might have understood that Beanie meant simply that if the police investigated Kyles, they would probably find the murder weapon, the jury could also have taken Beanie to have been making the more sinister suggestion that the police "set up" Kyles, and the defense could have argued that the police accepted the invitation. The prosecutor's notes of his interview with Beanie would have shown that police officers were asking Beanie the whereabouts of the gun all day Sunday, the very day when he was twice at Kyles's apartment and was allegedly seen by Johnny Burns lurking near the stove, where the gun was later found....

C

Next to be considered is the prosecution's list of the cars in the Schwegmann's parking lot at mid-evening after the murder. While its suppression does not rank with the failure to disclose the other evidence discussed here, it would have had some value as exculpation and impeachment, and it counts accordingly in determining whether *Bagley* 's standard of materiality is satisfied. On the police's assumption, argued to the jury, that the killer drove to the lot and left his car there during the heat of the investigation, the list without Kyles's registration would obviously have helped Kyles and would have had some value in countering an argument by the prosecution that a grainy enlargement of a photograph of the crime scene showed Kyles's car in the background....

D

In assessing the significance of the evidence withheld, one must of course bear in mind that not every item of the State's case would have been directly undercut if the *Brady* evidence had been disclosed. It is significant, however, that the physical evidence remaining unscathed would, by the State's own admission, hardly have amounted to overwhelming proof that Kyles was the murderer. Ammunition and a holster were found in Kyles's apartment, but if the jury had suspected the gun had been planted the significance of these items might have been left in doubt. The fact that pet food was found in Kyles's apartment was consistent with the testimony of several defense witnesses that Kyles owned a dog and that his children fed stray cats. The brands of pet food found were only two of the brands that Dye typically bought, and these two were common, whereas the one specialty brand that was found in Dye's apartment after her murder, was not found in Kyles's apartment. Although Kyles was wrong in describing the cat food as being on sale the day he said he bought it, he was right in describing the way it was priced at Schwegmann's market, where he commonly shopped.

Similarly undispositive is the small Schwegmann's receipt on the front passenger floorboard of the LTD, the only physical evidence that bore a fingerprint identified as Kyles's. Kyles explained that Beanie had driven him to Schwegmann's on Friday to buy cigarettes and transmission fluid, and he theorized that the slip must have fallen out of the bag when he removed the cigarettes. This explanation is consistent with the location of the slip when found and with its small size. The State cannot very well argue that the fingerprint ties Kyles to the killing without also explaining how the 2-inch-long register slip could have been the receipt for a week's worth of groceries, which Dye had gone to Schwegmann's to purchase.

The inconclusiveness of the physical evidence does not, to be sure, prove Kyles's innocence, and the jury might have found the eyewitness testimony of Territo and Kersh sufficient to convict, even though less damning to Kyles than that of Smallwood and Williams.[22] But the question is not whether the State would have had a case to go to the jury if it had disclosed the favorable evidence, but whether we can be confident that the jury's verdict would have been the same. Confidence that it would have been cannot survive a recap of the suppressed evidence and its significance for the prosecution. The jury would have been entitled to find

(a) that the investigation was limited by the police's uncritical readiness to accept the story and suggestions of an informant whose accounts were inconsistent to the point, for example, of including four different versions of the discovery of the victim's purse, and whose own behavior was enough to raise suspicions of guilt;

(b) that the lead police detective who testified was either less than wholly candid or less than fully informed;

(c) that the informant's behavior raised suspicions that he had planted both the murder weapon and the victim's purse in the places they were found;

(d) that one of the four eyewitnesses crucial to the State's case had given a description that did not match the defendant and better described the informant;

(e) that another eyewitness had been coached, since he had first stated that he had not seen the killer outside the getaway car, or the killing itself, whereas at trial he claimed to have seen the shooting, described the murder weapon exactly, and omitted portions of his initial description that would have been troublesome for the case;

(f) that there was no consistency to eyewitness descriptions of the killer's height, build, age, facial hair, or hair length.

Since all of these possible findings were precluded by the prosecution's failure to disclose the evidence that would have supported them, "fairness" cannot be stretched to the point of calling this a fair trial. Perhaps, confidence that the verdict would have been the same could survive the evidence impeaching even two eyewitnesses if the discoveries of gun and purse were above suspicion. Perhaps those suspicious circumstances would not defeat confidence in the verdict if the eyewitnesses had generally agreed on a description and were free of impeachment. But confidence that the verdict would have been unaffected cannot survive when suppressed evidence would have entitled a jury to find that the

22. On remand, of course, the State's case will be weaker still, since the prosecution is unlikely to rely on Kersh, who now swears that she committed perjury at the two trials when she identified Kyles as the murderer.

eyewitnesses were not consistent in describing the killer, that two out of the four eyewitnesses testifying were unreliable, that the most damning physical evidence was subject to suspicion, that the investigation that produced it was insufficiently probing, and that the principal police witness was insufficiently informed or candid. This is not the "massive" case envisioned by the dissent; it is a significantly weaker case than the one heard by the first jury, which could not even reach a verdict.

The judgment of the Court of Appeals is reversed, and the case is remanded for further proceedings consistent with this opinion....

Justice SCALIA, with whom the Chief Justice, Justice KENNEDY, and Justice THOMAS join, dissenting.

In a sensible system of criminal justice, wrongful conviction is avoided by establishing, at the trial level, lines of procedural legality that leave ample margins of safety (for example, the requirement that guilt be proved beyond a reasonable doubt)—not by providing recurrent and repetitive appellate review of whether the facts in the record show those lines to have been narrowly crossed. The defect of the latter system was described, with characteristic candor, by Justice Jackson:

> "Whenever decisions of one court are reviewed by another, a percentage of them are reversed. That reflects a difference in outlook normally found between personnel comprising different courts. However, reversal by a higher court is not proof that justice is thereby better done." *Brown v. Allen,* 344 U.S. 443, 540 (1953) (opinion concurring in result).

Since this Court has long shared Justice Jackson's view, today's opinion—which considers a fact-bound claim of error rejected by every court, state and federal, that previously heard it—is, so far as I can tell, wholly unprecedented....

The Court says that we granted certiorari "[b]ecause '[o]ur duty to search for constitutional error with painstaking care is never more exacting than it is in a capital case,' *Burger v. Kemp,* 483 U.S. 776, 785 (1987)." The citation is perverse, for the reader who looks up the quoted opinion will discover that the very next sentence confirms the traditional practice from which the Court today glaringly departs: "Nevertheless, when the lower courts have found that [no constitutional error occurred], ... deference to the shared conclusion of two reviewing courts prevent[s] us from substituting speculation for their considered opinions." *Burger v. Kemp,* 483 U.S. 776, 785 (1987).

The greatest puzzle of today's decision is what could have caused *this* capital case to be singled out for favored treatment. Perhaps it has been randomly selected as a symbol, to reassure America that the United States Supreme Court is reviewing capital convictions to make sure no factual error has been made. If so, it is a false symbol, for we assuredly do not do that.... The reality is that responsibility for factual accuracy, in capital cases as in other cases, rests elsewhere—with trial judges and juries, state appellate courts, and the lower federal courts; we do nothing but encourage foolish reliance to pretend otherwise....

I

Before proceeding to detailed consideration of the evidence, a few general observations about the Court's methodology are appropriate. It is fundamental to the discovery rule of *Brady v. Maryland,* 373 U.S. 83 (1963), that the materiality of a failure to disclose favorable evidence "must be evaluated in the context of the entire record." ... It is petitioner's burden to show that in light of all the evidence, including that untainted by the *Brady* violation, it is reasonably probable that a jury would have entertained a reasonable doubt regarding petitioner's guilt. The Court's opinion fails almost entirely to take this principle into account. Having spent many pages assessing the effect of the *Brady* material on two prosecution witnesses and a few items of prosecution evidence, it dismisses the remainder of the evidence against Kyles in a quick page-and-a-half.... My discussion of the record will present the half of the analysis that the Court omits, emphasizing the evidence concededly unaffected by the *Brady* violation which demonstrates the immateriality of the violation.

In any analysis of this case, the desperate implausibility of the theory that petitioner put before the jury must be kept firmly in mind. The first half of that theory—designed to neutralize the physical evidence (Mrs. Dye's purse in his garbage, the murder weapon behind his stove)—was that petitioner was the victim of a "frame-up" by the police informer and evil genius, Beanie. Now it is not unusual for a guilty person who knows that he is suspected of a crime to try to shift blame to someone else; and it is less common, but not unheard of, for a guilty person who is neither suspected nor subject to suspicion (because he has established a perfect alibi), to call attention to himself by coming forward to point the finger at an innocent person. But petitioner's theory is that the guilty Beanie, who *could* plausibly be accused of the crime (as petitioner's brief amply demonstrates), but who was *not* a suspect any more than Kyles was (the police as yet had no leads, injected both Kyles and himself into the investigation in order to get the innocent Kyles convicted. If this were not stupid enough, the wicked Beanie is supposed to have suggested that the police search his victim's premises *a full day before he got around to planting the incriminating evidence on the premises.*

The second half of petitioner's theory was that he was the victim of a quadruple coincidence, in which four eyewitnesses to the crime mistakenly identified him as the murderer—three picking him out of a photo array without hesitation, and all four affirming their identification in open court after comparing him with Beanie. The extraordinary mistake petitioner had to persuade the jury these four witnesses made was not simply to mistake the real killer, Beanie, for the very same innocent third party (hard enough to believe), but in addition to mistake him *for the very man Beanie had chosen to frame*—the last and most incredible level of coincidence....

II

The undisclosed evidence does not create a "'reasonable probability' of a different result." To begin with the eyewitness testimony: Petitioner's basic theory at trial was that the State's four eyewitnesses happened to mistake Beanie, the real killer, for petitioner, the man whom Beanie was simultaneously trying to frame. Police officers testified to the jury, and petitioner has never disputed, that three of the four eyewitnesses (Territo, Smallwood, and Williams) were shown a photo lineup of six young men four days after the shooting and, without aid or duress, identified petitioner as the murderer; and that all of them, plus the fourth eyewitness, Kersh, reaffirmed their identifications at trial after petitioner and Beanie were made to stand side by side....

The Court attempts to dispose of this direct, unqualified, and consistent eyewitness testimony in two ways. First, by relying on a theory so implausible that it was apparently not suggested by petitioner's counsel until the oral-argument-*cum*-evidentiary-hearing held before us, perhaps because it is a theory that only the most removed appellate court could love. This theory is that there is a reasonable probability that the jury would have changed its mind about the eyewitness identification because the *Brady* material would have permitted the defense to argue that the eyewitnesses only got a good look at the killer when he was sitting in Mrs. Dye's car, and thus could identify him, not by his height and build, but *only by his face.* Never mind, for the moment, that this is factually false, since the *Brady* material showed that only *one* of the four eyewitnesses, Smallwood, did not see the killer outside the car. And never mind, also, the dubious premise that the build of a man 6-feet tall (like petitioner) is indistinguishable, when seated behind the wheel, from that of a man less than 5½-feet tall (like Beanie). To assert that unhesitant and categorical identification by four witnesses who viewed the killer, close-up and with the sun high in the sky, would not eliminate reasonable doubt if it were based *only* on *facial* characteristics, and not on height and build, is quite simply absurd. Facial features are *the primary means* by which human beings recognize one another. That is why police departments distribute "mug" shots of wanted felons, rather than Ivy-League-type posture pictures; it is why bank robbers wear stockings over their faces instead of floor-length capes over their shoulders; it is why the Lone Ranger wears a mask instead of a poncho; and it is why a criminal defense lawyer who seeks to destroy an identifying witness by asking "You admit that you saw only the killer's face?" will be laughed out of the courtroom.

It would be different, of course, if there were evidence that Kyles's and Beanie's faces looked like twins, or at least bore an unusual degree of resemblance. That facial resemblance *would* explain why, if Beanie committed the crime, all four witnesses picked out Kyles at first (though not why they continued to pick him out when he and Beanie stood side-by-side in court), and would render their failure to observe the height and build of the killer relevant.... *No* court has found that Kyles and Beanie bear any facial resemblance. In fact, quite the opposite: *every* federal and state court that has reviewed the record photographs, or seen the two men, has found that they do not resemble each other in any respect....

The physical evidence confirms the immateriality of the nondisclosures. In a garbage bag outside petitioner's home the police found Mrs.

Dye's purse and other belongings. Inside his home they found, behind the kitchen stove, the .32-caliber revolver used to kill Mrs. Dye; hanging in a wardrobe, a homemade shoulder holster that was "a perfect fit" for the revolver; in a dresser drawer in the bedroom, two boxes of gun cartridges, one containing only .32-caliber rounds of the same brand found in the murder weapon, another containing .22, .32, and .38-caliber rounds; in a kitchen cabinet, eight empty Schwegmann's bags; and in a cupboard underneath that cabinet, one Schwegmann's bag containing 15 cans of pet food. Petitioner's account at trial was that Beanie planted the purse, gun, and holster, that petitioner received the ammunition from Beanie as collateral for a loan, and that petitioner had bought the pet food the day of the murder. That account strains credulity to the breaking point.

The Court is correct that the *Brady* material would have supported the claim that Beanie planted Mrs. Dye's belongings in petitioner's garbage and (to a lesser degree) that Beanie planted the gun behind petitioner's stove. But we must see the whole story that petitioner presented to the jury. Petitioner would have it that Beanie did not plant the incriminating evidence until the day *after* he incited the police to search petitioner's home. Moreover, he succeeded in surreptitiously placing the gun behind the stove, and the matching shoulder holster in the wardrobe, while *at least 10 and as many as 19 people* were present in petitioner's small apartment. Beanie, who was wearing blue jeans and either a "tank-top" shirt, or a short-sleeved shirt, would have had to be concealing about his person not only the shoulder holster and the murder weapon, but also a different gun with tape wrapped around the barrel that he showed to petitioner. Only appellate judges could swallow such a tale. Petitioner's only supporting evidence was Johnny Burns's testimony that he saw Beanie stooping behind the stove, presumably to plant the gun. Burns's credibility on the stand can perhaps best be gauged by observing that the state judge who presided over petitioner's trial stated, in a postconviction proceeding, that "[I] ha[ve] chosen to totally disregard everything that [Burns] has said." Burns, by the way, who repeatedly stated at trial that Beanie was his "best friend," Tr. 279 (Dec. 7, 1984), has since been tried and convicted for killing Beanie....

We come to the evidence of the pet food, so mundane and yet so very damning. Petitioner's confused and changing explanations for the presence of 15 cans of pet food in a Schwegmann's bag under the sink must have fatally undermined his credibility before the jury. The Court disposes of the pet food evidence as follows:

> "The fact that pet food was found in Kyles's apartment was consistent with the testimony of several defense witnesses that Kyles owned a dog and that his children fed stray cats. The brands of pet food found were only two of the brands that Dye typically bought, and these two were common, whereas the one specialty brand that was found in Dye's apartment after her murder, was not found in Kyles's apartment. Although Kyles was wrong in describing the cat food as being on sale the day he said he bought it, he was right in describing the way it was priced at Schwegmann's market, where he commonly shopped."

The full story is this. Mr. and Mrs. Dye owned two cats and a dog, for which she regularly bought varying brands of pet food, several different brands at a time. Found in Mrs. Dye's home after her murder were the brands Nine Lives, Kalkan, and Puss n' Boots. Found in petitioner's home were eight cans of Nine Lives, four cans of Kalkan, and three cans of Cozy Kitten. Since we know that Mrs. Dye had been shopping that day and that the murderer made off with her goods, petitioner's possession of these items was powerful evidence that he was the murderer. Assuredly the jury drew that obvious inference. Pressed to explain why he just happened to buy *15 cans* of pet food that very day (keep in mind that petitioner was a very poor man, who supported a common-law wife, a mistress, and four children), petitioner gave the reason that "it was on sale." The State, however, introduced testimony from the Schwegmann's advertising director that the pet food was *not* on sale that day. The dissenting judge below tried to rehabilitate petitioner's testimony by interpreting the "on sale" claim as meaning "for sale," a reference to the pricing of the pet food (*e.g.*, "3 for 89 cents"), which petitioner claimed to have read on a shelf sign in the store. But unless petitioner was parodying George Leigh Mallory, "because it was *for* sale" would have been an irrational response to the question it was given in answer to: Why did you buy *so many* cans? ... The sum of it is that petitioner, far from explaining the presence of the pet food, doubled the force of the State's evidence by perjuring himself before the jury, as the state trial judge observed.

I will not address the list of cars in the Schwegmann's parking lot and the receipt, found in the victim's car, that bore petitioner's fingerprints. These were collateral matters that provided little evidence of either guilt or innocence. The list of cars, which did not contain petitioner's automobile, would only have served to rebut the State's introduction of a photograph purporting to show petitioner's car in the parking lot; but petitioner does not contest that the list was not comprehensive, and that the photograph was taken about six hours before the list was compiled. Thus its rebuttal value would have been marginal at best. The receipt—although it showed that petitioner must at some point have been both in Schwegmann's and in the murdered woman's car—was as consistent with petitioner's story as with the State's.

* * *

The State presented to the jury a massive core of evidence (including four eyewitnesses) showing that petitioner was guilty of murder, and that he lied about his guilt. The effect that the *Brady* materials would have had in chipping away at the edges of the State's case can only be called immaterial....

I respectfully dissent.

Notes and Questions

1. The 5–4 decision in *Kyles v. Whitley* spared Curtis Kyles from execution. The division among the justices reflects differences not only in the significance they attached to the facts that were and were not known by the trial jury, but also in their views about the proper role of the Supreme Court in reviewing cases of this nature. For the dissenters, Justice Scalia opined that, "In a sensible system of criminal justice, wrongful conviction is avoided by establishing, at the trial level, lines of procedural legality that leave ample margins of safety ... [and] not by providing recurrent and repetitive appellate review of whether the facts in the record show those lines to have been narrowly crossed." 514 U.S., at 456. In a concurring opinion, 514 U.S., at 455–456, Justice Stevens, joined by Justices Ginsburg and Breyer, took exception with that perspective.

> Our duty to administer justice occasionally requires busy judges to engage in a detailed review of the particular facts of a case, even though our labors may not provide posterity with a newly minted rule of law. The current popularity of capital punishment makes this "generalizable principle" especially important. I wish such review were unnecessary, but I cannot agree that our position in the judicial hierarchy makes it inappropriate. Sometimes the performance of an unpleasant duty conveys a message more significant than even the most penetrating legal analysis.

Following the Supreme Court's reversal, Kyles was brought to trial on the murder charge on three subsequent occasions, in October 1996, September 1997, and February 1998. Each of those trials resulted in deadlocked juries, as had Kyles's first trial in November 1984. After the last mistrial in February 1998, prosecutors dropped the charges against Kyles and he was released. Curtis Kyles is one of the 138 individuals included through March 2011 on the Death Penalty Information Center's "innocence" list, comprised of death-sentenced exonerees.[6]

2. What if the police neglect to share with the prosecutor information gained during the course of their investigation, resulting in the district attorney's office being as uninformed as the defense about the existence of exculpatory evidence? What does Justice Souter's opinion in *Kyles* indicate about whether information known to the police is presumed to be known to the prosecutor in the *Brady* context?

3. In *Strickler v. Greene,* 527 U.S. 263, 119 S.Ct. 1936, 144 L.Ed.2d 286 (1999), the Court found that the prosecution had not disclosed exculpatory information that would have

helped the defense impeach the credibility of an eyewitness who testified in the petitioner's capital murder trial, but that the evidence was not sufficiently material to excuse the failure to have raised the alleged *Brady* violation in state court proceedings or to require reversal.

4. *Brady* principles are based on Due Process requirements. As noted in *Kyles*, the Court has "never held that the Constitution demands an open file [discovery] policy ... and the rule in *Bagley* (and, hence, in *Brady*) requires less of the prosecution than ... ABA Standards ..., which call generally for prosecutorial disclosures of any evidence tending to exculpate or mitigate." If the prosecution's obligation is not defined as narrowly as simply to secure convictions, but rather to ensure "that justice shall be done," *Berger v. United States*, 295 U.S. 78, 88 (1935), would it be advisable for district attorneys to maintain an open file discovery policy?

5. We consider *Brady's* application in the context of guilty pleas, and the Supreme Court's decision in *United States v. Ruiz*, 536 U.S. 622, 122 S.Ct. 2450, 153 L.Ed.2d 586 (2002), in Chapter 9.

6. Determining whether evidence is exculpatory necessarily involves subjective judgments. As argued by Burke,[7] the *Brady* doctrine invites prosecutors, even those acting in good faith, to systematically undervalue the materiality of evidence. Specifically, in evaluating the potential exculpatory value of evidence, the prosecutor must first speculate about how trial evidence generally will be developed, and then assess the fit between the evidence under consideration and other evidence tending to establish or negate guilt. Burke argues that these two decision points are influenced by cognitive biases—confirmation bias and selective information processing—to which no one is immune. The end result is that the information considered in deciding whether evidence is material and exculpatory (and therefore necessary to turn over), is biased toward the state's version of events and the conclusion that the evidence need not be supplied to the defense.

7. Prosecutorial misconduct, generally, and *Brady* violations, specifically, are difficult to track for a number of reasons. However, in 2003, the Center for Public Integrity[8] released a report finding that prosecutorial misconduct was cited in at least 2,012 cases involving dismissed charges, reversed convictions, or reduced sentences since 1970; 32 of these cases are now known to be wrongful convictions. The Center's report also noted that the most common form of misconduct was failing to turn over favorable evidence to the defense. In attempting to answer the question, "Why do [prosecutorial] violations occur?" Professor Rachel Barkow[9] noted several incentives for prosecutors not to toe the line. These factors included pressures to violate the law (*e.g.*, the desire to keep elected or appointed positions), lack of effective deterrents, and lack of oversight to ensure compliance. Because of these systemic issues and the cognitive re-interpretation of evidence that *Brady* and its progeny encourage, some prosecutors violate the law. To help overcome such issues and detect and prevent miscarriages of justice, some district attorney offices have recently established wrongful conviction units, or "Conviction Integrity Units." For example, established units of this kind now operate in Manhattan and Dallas.

C. The Duties of the Police

Arizona v. Youngblood

488 U.S. 51, 109 S.Ct. 333, 102 L.Ed.2d 281 (1988)

Chief Justice REHNQUIST delivered the opinion of the Court.

Respondent Larry Youngblood was convicted by a Pima County, Arizona, jury of child molestation, sexual assault, and kidnaping. The Arizona Court of Appeals reversed his conviction on the ground that the State had failed to preserve semen samples from the victim's body and clothing. We granted certiorari to consider the extent to which the Due Process Clause of the Fourteenth Amendment requires the State to preserve evidentiary material that might be useful to a criminal defendant.

On October 29, 1983, David L., a 10-year-old boy, attended a church service with his mother. After he left the service at about 9:30 p.m., the boy went to a carnival behind the church, where he was abducted by a middle-aged man of medium height and weight. The assailant drove the boy to a secluded area near a ravine and molested him. He then took the boy to an unidentified, sparsely furnished house where he sodomized the boy four times. Afterwards, the assailant tied the boy up while he went outside to start his car. Once the assailant started the car, albeit with some difficulty, he returned to the house and again sodomized the boy. The assailant then sent the boy to the bathroom to wash up before he returned him to the carnival. He threatened to kill the boy if he told anyone about the attack. The entire ordeal lasted about 1½ hours.

After the boy made his way home, his mother took him to Kino Hospital. At the hospital, a physician treated the boy for rectal injuries. The physician also used a "sexual assault kit" to collect evidence of the attack. The Tucson Police Department provided such kits to all hospitals in Pima County for use in sexual assault cases. Under standard procedure, the victim of a sexual assault was taken to a hospital, where a physician used the kit to collect evidence. The kit included paper to collect saliva samples, a tube for obtaining a blood sample, microscopic slides for making smears, a set of Q-Tip-like swabs, and a medical examination report. Here, the physician used the swab to collect samples from the boy's rectum and mouth. He then made a microscopic slide of the samples. The doctor also obtained samples of the boy's saliva, blood, and hair. The physician did not examine the samples at any time. The police placed the kit in a secure refrigerator at the police station. At the hospital, the police also collected the boy's underwear and T-shirt. This clothing was not refrigerated or frozen.

Nine days after the attack, on November 7, 1983, the police asked the boy to pick out his assailant from a photographic lineup. The boy identified respondent as the assailant. Respondent was not located by the police until four weeks later; he was arrested on December 9, 1983.

On November 8, 1983, Edward Heller, a police criminologist, examined the sexual assault kit. He testified that he followed standard department procedure, which was to examine the slides and determine whether sexual contact had occurred. After he determined that such contact had occurred, the criminologist did not perform any other tests, although he placed the assault kit back in the refrigerator. He testified that tests to identify blood group substances were not routinely conducted during the initial examination of an assault kit and in only about half of all cases in any event. He did not test the clothing at this time.

Respondent was indicted on charges of child molestation, sexual assault, and kidnapping. The State moved to compel respondent to provide blood and saliva samples for comparison with the material gathered through the use of the sexual assault kit, but the trial court denied the motion on the ground that the State had not obtained a sufficiently large semen sample to make a valid comparison. The prosecutor then asked the State's criminologist to perform an ABO blood group test on the rectal swab sample in an attempt to ascertain the blood type of the boy's assailant. This test failed to detect any blood group substances in the sample.

In January 1985, the police criminologist examined the boy's clothing for the first time. He found one semen stain on the boy's underwear and another on the rear of his T-shirt. The criminologist tried to obtain blood group substances from both stains using the ABO technique, but was unsuccessful. He also performed a P-30 protein molecule test on the stains, which indicated that only a small quantity of semen was present on the clothing; it was inconclusive as to the assailant's identity. The Tucson Police Department had just begun using this test, which was then used in slightly more than half of the crime laboratories in the country.

Respondent's principal defense at trial was that the boy had erred in identifying him as the perpetrator of the crime. In this connection, both a criminologist for the State and an expert witness for respondent testified as to what might have been shown by tests performed on the samples shortly after they were gathered, or by later tests performed on the samples from the boy's clothing had the clothing been properly refrigerated. The court instructed the jury that if they found the State had destroyed or lost evidence, they might "infer that the true fact is against the State's interest."

The jury found respondent guilty as charged, but the Arizona Court of Appeals reversed the judgment of conviction. It stated that "'when identity is an issue at trial and the police permit the destruction of evidence that could eliminate the defendant as the perpetrator, such loss is material to the defense and is a denial of due process.'" The Court of Appeals concluded on the basis of the expert testimony at trial that timely performance of tests with properly preserved semen samples could have produced results that might have completely exonerated respondent. The Court of Appeals reached this conclusion even though it did "not imply any bad faith on the part of the State." The Supreme Court of Arizona denied the State's petition for review, and we granted certiorari. We now reverse.

Decision of this case requires us to again consider "what might loosely be called the area of constitutionally guaranteed access to evidence." *United States v. Valenzuela-Bernal,* 458 U.S. 858, 867 (1982). In *Brady v. Maryland,* 373 U.S. 83 (1963), we held that "the suppression by the prosecution of evidence favorable to the accused upon request violates due process where the evidence is material either to guilt or to punishment, irrespective of the good faith or bad faith of the prosecution." In *United States v. Agurs,* 427 U.S. 97 (1976), we held that the prosecution had a duty to disclose some evidence of this description even though no requests were made for it, but at the same time we rejected the notion that a "prosecutor has a constitutional duty routinely to deliver his entire file to defense counsel."

There is no question but that the State complied with *Brady* and *Agurs* here. The State disclosed relevant police reports to respondent, which contained information about the existence of the swab and the clothing, and the boy's examination at the hospital. The State provided respondent's expert with the laboratory reports and notes prepared by the police criminologist, and respondent's expert had access to the swab and to the clothing.

If respondent is to prevail on federal constitutional grounds, then, it must be because of some constitutional duty over and above that imposed by cases such as *Brady* and *Agurs.* Our most recent decision in this area of the law, *California v. Trombetta,* 467 U.S. 479 (1984), arose out of a drunk-driving prosecution in which the State had introduced test results indicating the concentration of alcohol in the blood of two motorists. The defendants sought to suppress the test results on the ground that the State had failed to preserve the breath samples used in the test. We rejected this argument for several reasons: first, "the officers here were acting in 'good faith and in accord with their normal practice,'"; second, in the light of the procedures actually used the chances that preserved samples would have exculpated the defendants were slim; and, third, even if the samples might have shown inaccuracy in the tests, the defendants had "alternative means of demonstrating their innocence." In the present case, the likelihood that the preserved materials would have enabled the defendant to exonerate himself appears to be greater than it was in *Trombetta,* but here, unlike in *Trombetta,* the State did not attempt to make any use of the materials in its own case in chief.*

* In this case, the Arizona Court of Appeals ... [held] that "'when identity is an issue at trial and the police permit destruction of evidence that *could eliminate* a defendant as the perpetrator, such loss is material to the defense and is a denial of due process.'" [This] reasoning ... mark[s] a sharp departure from *Trombetta* in two respects. First, *Trombetta* speaks of evidence whose exculpatory value is "apparent." 467 U.S., at 489. The possibility that the semen samples could have exculpated respondent if preserved or tested is not enough

Our decisions in related areas have stressed the importance for constitutional purposes of good or bad faith on the part of the Government when the claim is based on loss of evidence attributable to the Government. In *United States v. Marion,* 404 U.S. 307 (1971), we said that "[n]o actual prejudice to the conduct of the defense is alleged or proved, and there is no showing that the Government intentionally delayed to gain some tactical advantage over appellees or to harass them." Similarly, in *United States v. Valenzuela-Bernal, supra,* we considered whether the Government's deportation of two witnesses who were illegal aliens violated due process. We held that the prompt deportation of the witnesses was justified "upon the Executive's good-faith determination that they possess no evidence favorable to the defendant in a criminal prosecution."

The Due Process Clause of the Fourteenth Amendment, as interpreted in *Brady,* makes the good or bad faith of the State irrelevant when the State fails to disclose to the defendant material exculpatory evidence. But we think the Due Process Clause requires a different result when we deal with the failure of the State to preserve evidentiary material of which no more can be said than that it could have been subjected to tests, the results of which might have exonerated the defendant. Part of the reason for the difference in treatment is found in the observation made by the Court in *Trombetta,* that "[w]henever potentially exculpatory evidence is permanently lost, courts face the treacherous task of divining the import of materials whose contents are unknown and, very often, disputed." Part of it stems from our unwillingness to read the "fundamental fairness" requirement of the Due Process Clause, as imposing on the police an undifferentiated and absolute duty to retain and to preserve all material that might be of conceivable evidentiary significance in a particular prosecution. We think that requiring a defendant to show bad faith on the part of the police both limits the extent of the police's obligation to preserve evidence to reasonable bounds and confines it to that class of cases where the interests of justice most clearly require it, *i.e.,* those cases in which the police themselves by their conduct indicate that the evidence could form a basis for exonerating the defendant. We therefore hold that unless a criminal defendant can show bad faith on the part of the police, failure to preserve potentially useful evidence does not constitute a denial of due process of law.

In this case, the police collected the rectal swab and clothing on the night of the crime; respondent was not taken into custody until six weeks later. The failure of the police to refrigerate the clothing and to perform tests on the semen samples can at worst be described as negligent. None of this information was concealed from respondent at trial, and the evidence—such as it was—was made available to respondent's expert who declined to perform any tests on the samples. The Arizona Court of Appeals noted in its opinion—and we agree—that there was no suggestion of bad faith on the part of the police. It follows, therefore, from what we have said, that there was no violation of the Due Process Clause.

The Arizona Court of Appeals also referred somewhat obliquely to the State's "inability to quantitatively test" certain semen samples with the newer P-30 test. If the court meant by this statement that the Due Process Clause is violated when the police fail to use a particular investigatory tool, we strongly disagree. The situation here is no different than a prosecution for drunken driving that rests on police observation alone; the defendant is free to argue to the finder of fact that a breathalyzer test might have been exculpatory, but the police do not have a constitutional duty to perform any particular tests.

The judgment of the Arizona Court of Appeals is reversed, and the case is remanded for further proceedings not inconsistent with this opinion....

Justice STEVENS, concurring in the judgment.

---

to satisfy the standard of constitutional materiality in *Trombetta.* Second, we made clear in *Trombetta* that the exculpatory value of the evidence must be apparent "*before* the evidence was destroyed." Here, respondent has not shown that the police knew the semen samples would have exculpated him when they failed to perform certain tests or to refrigerate the boy's clothing; this evidence was simply an avenue of investigation that might have led in any number of directions. The presence or absence of bad faith by the police for purposes of the Due Process Clause must necessarily turn on the police's knowledge of the exculpatory value of the evidence at the time it was lost or destroyed.

Three factors are of critical importance to my evaluation of this case. First, at the time the police failed to refrigerate the victim's clothing, and thus negligently lost potentially valuable evidence, they had at least as great an interest in preserving the evidence as did the person later accused of the crime. Indeed, at that time it was more likely that the evidence would have been useful to the police—who were still conducting an investigation—and to the prosecutor—who would later bear the burden of establishing guilt beyond a reasonable doubt—than to the defendant. In cases such as this, even without a prophylactic sanction such as dismissal of the indictment, the State has a strong incentive to preserve the evidence.

Second, although it is not possible to know whether the lost evidence would have revealed any relevant information, it is unlikely that the defendant was prejudiced by the State's omission. In examining witnesses and in her summation, defense counsel impressed upon the jury the fact that the State failed to preserve the evidence and that the State could have conducted tests that might well have exonerated the defendant. More significantly, the trial judge instructed the jury: "If you find that the State has ... allowed to be destroyed or lost any evidence whose content or quality are in issue, you may infer that the true fact is against the State's interest." As a result, the uncertainty as to what the evidence might have proved was turned to the defendant's advantage.

Third, the fact that no juror chose to draw the permissive inference that proper preservation of the evidence would have demonstrated that the defendant was not the assailant suggests that the lost evidence was "immaterial." Our cases make clear that "[t]he proper standard of materiality must reflect our overriding concern with the justice of the finding of guilt," and that a State's failure to turn over (or preserve) potentially exculpatory evidence therefore "must be evaluated in the context of the entire record." In declining defense counsel's and the court's invitations to draw the permissive inference, the jurors in effect indicated that, in their view, the other evidence at trial was so overwhelming that it was highly improbable that the lost evidence was exculpatory....

With these factors in mind, I concur in the Court's judgment. I do not, however, join the Court's opinion because it announces a proposition of law that is much broader than necessary to decide this case. It states that "unless a criminal defendant can show bad faith on the part of the police, failure to preserve potentially useful evidence does not constitute a denial of due process of law." In my opinion, there may well be cases in which the defendant is unable to prove that the State acted in bad faith but in which the loss or destruction of evidence is nonetheless so critical to the defense as to make a criminal trial fundamentally unfair. This, however, is not such a case....

Justice BLACKMUN, with whom Justice BRENNAN and Justice MARSHALL join, dissenting.

The Constitution requires that criminal defendants be provided with a fair trial, not merely a "good faith" try at a fair trial. Respondent here, by what may have been nothing more than police ineptitude, was denied the opportunity to present a full defense. That ineptitude, however, deprived respondent of his guaranteed right to due process of law....

I

The Court, with minimal reference to our past cases and with what seems to me to be less than complete analysis, announces that "unless a criminal defendant can show bad faith on the part of police, failure to preserve potentially useful evidence does not constitute a denial of due process of law." ... Regardless of intent or lack thereof, police action that results in a defendant's receiving an unfair trial constitutes a deprivation of due process....

As noted by the majority, the Court in *Brady* ruled that "the suppression by the prosecution of evidence favorable to an accused upon request violates due process where the evidence is material either to guilt or to punishment, irrespective of the good faith or bad faith of the prosecution." The *Brady* Court went on to explain that the principle underlying earlier cases is "not punishment of society for misdeeds of a prosecutor but avoidance of an unfair trial to the accused." ...

The cases in this area clearly establish that police actions taken in bad faith are not the only species of police conduct that can result in a violation of due process. As *Agurs* points out, it makes no sense to overturn a conviction because a malicious prosecutor withholds information that he mistakenly believes to be material, but which actually would have been of no help to the defense. In the same way, it makes no sense to ignore the fact that a defendant has been denied a fair trial because the State allowed evidence that was material to the defense to deteriorate beyond the point of usefulness, simply because the police were inept rather than malicious.

I also doubt that the "bad faith" standard creates the bright-line rule sought by the majority. Apart from the inherent difficulty a defendant would have in obtaining evidence to show a lack of good faith, the line between "good faith" and "bad faith" is anything but bright, and the majority's formulation may well create more questions than it answers. What constitutes bad faith for these purposes? Does a defendant have to show actual malice, or would recklessness, or the deliberate failure to establish standards for maintaining and preserving evidence, be sufficient? Does "good faith police work" require a certain minimum of diligence, or will a lazy officer, who does not walk the few extra steps to the evidence refrigerator, be considered to be acting in good faith? While the majority leaves these questions for another day, its quick embrace of a "bad faith" standard has not brightened the line; it only has moved the line so as to provide fewer protections for criminal defendants.

II

The inquiry the majority eliminates in setting up its "bad faith" rule is whether the evidence in question here was "constitutionally material," so that its destruction violates due process.... But because I do not find the question of lack of bad faith dispositive, I now consider whether this evidence was such that its destruction rendered respondent's trial fundamentally unfair....

The exculpatory value of the clothing in this case cannot be determined with any certainty, precisely because the police allowed the samples to deteriorate. But we do know several important things about the evidence. First, the semen samples on the clothing undoubtedly came from the assailant. Second, the samples could have been tested, using technology available and in use at the local police department, to show either the blood type of the assailant, or that the assailant was a nonsecreter, *i.e.*, someone who does not secrete a blood-type "marker" into other body fluids, such as semen. Third, the evidence was clearly important. A semen sample in a rape case where identity is questioned is always significant. Fourth, a reasonable police officer should have recognized that the clothing required refrigeration. Fifth, we know that an inconclusive test was done on the swab. The test suggested that the assailant was a nonsecreter, although it was equally likely that the sample on the swab was too small for accurate results to be obtained. And, sixth, we know that respondent is a secreter.

If the samples on the clothing had been tested, and the results had shown either the blood type of the assailant or that the assailant was a nonsecreter, its constitutional materiality would be clear. But the State's conduct has deprived the defendant, and the courts, of the opportunity to determine with certainty the import of this evidence: it has "interfere[d] with the accused's ability to present a defense by imposing on him a requirement which the government's own actions have rendered impossible to fulfill." Good faith or not, this is intolerable, unless the particular circumstances of the case indicate either that the evidence was not likely to prove exculpatory, or that the defendant was able to use effective alternative means to prove the point the destroyed evidence otherwise could have made....

Rather than allow a State's ineptitude to saddle a defendant with an impossible burden, a court should focus on the type of evidence, the possibility it might prove exculpatory, and the existence of other evidence going to the same point of contention in determining whether the failure to preserve the evidence in question violated due process. To put it succinctly, where no comparable evidence is likely to be available to the defendant, police must preserve physical evidence of a type that they reasonably should know has the potential, if tested, to reveal immutable characteristics of the criminal, and hence to exculpate a defendant charged with the crime....

III

Applying this standard to the facts of this case, I conclude that the Arizona Court of Appeals was correct in overturning respondent's conviction. The clothing worn by the victim contained samples of his assailant's semen. The appeals court found that these samples would probably be larger, less contaminated, and more likely to yield conclusive test results than would the samples collected by use of the assault kit. The clothing and the semen stains on the clothing therefore obviously were material.

Because semen is a body fluid which could have been tested by available methods to show an immutable characteristic of the assailant, there was a genuine possibility that the results of such testing might have exonerated respondent. The only evidence implicating respondent was the testimony of the victim.[8] There was no other eyewitness, and the only other significant physical evidence, respondent's car, was seized by police, examined, turned over to a wrecking company, and then dismantled without the victim's having viewed it. The police also failed to check the car to confirm or refute elements of the victim's testimony.[9]

Although a closer question, there was no equivalent evidence available to respondent. The swab contained a semen sample, but it was not sufficient to allow proper testing. Respondent had access to other evidence tending to show that he was not the assailant, but there was no other evidence that would have shown that it was physically impossible for respondent to have been the assailant. Nor would the preservation of the evidence here have been a burden upon the police. There obviously was refrigeration available, as the preservation of the swab indicates, and the items of clothing likely would not tax available storage space.

Considered in the context of the entire trial, the failure of the prosecution to preserve this evidence deprived respondent of a fair trial. It still remains "a fundamental value determination of our society that it is far worse to convict an innocent man than to let a guilty man go free." *In re Winship*, 397 U.S. 358, 372 (1970) (concurring opinion). The evidence in this case was far from conclusive, and the possibility that the evidence denied to respondent would have exonerated him was not remote. The result is that he was denied a fair trial by the actions of the State, and consequently was denied due process of law. Because the Court's opinion improperly limits the scope of due process, and ignores its proper focus in a futile pursuit of a bright-line rule, I dissent.

Notes and Questions

1. Larry Youngblood was wrongfully convicted. As with many other sexual assault cases prosecuted during the 1980s and earlier, DNA analysis had not been sufficiently developed for forensic application when Youngblood was tried. In 2000, the degraded material left on the clothing of the young boy who had been victimized, and who had identified Youngblood as his assailant, was subjected to DNA testing. The tests excluded Youngblood as the source. The DNA profile subsequently was entered into the national convicted offender DNA database. In 2001, it was matched to another man, Walter Cruise. Cruise was convicted of the crimes against the youngster in 2002 and was sentenced to 24 years in prison. Youngblood spent nearly a decade in prison for the crimes.[10] Of what significance is Youngblood's innocence to the Supreme Court's decision in his case? What lessons about the reliability of eyewitness identification arise from this case? About the benefits of preserving evidence used in criminal trials even after convictions and appeals are finalized? In retrospect, what should we make of Justice Stevens's assessment that "the jurors in effect indicated that, in their view, the other evidence at trial was so overwhelming that it was highly improbable that the lost evidence was exculpatory"?

---

8. This Court "has recognized the inherently suspect qualities of eyewitness identification evidence." *Watkins v. Sowders,* 449 U.S. 341, 350 (1981) (BRENNAN, J., dissenting). Such evidence is "notoriously unreliable," *ibid.;* see *United States v. Wade,* 388 U.S. 218 (1967); *Manson v. Brathwaite,* 432 U.S. 98 (1977), and has distinct impacts on juries. "All the evidence points rather strikingly to the conclusion that there is almost nothing more convincing than a live human being who takes the stand, points a finger at the defendant, and says, 'That's the one!'" E. Loftus, Eyewitness Testimony 19 (1979).

Studies show that children are more likely to make mistaken identifications than are adults, especially when they have been encouraged by adults. Other studies show another element of possible relevance in this case: "Cross-racial identifications are much less likely to be accurate than same race identifications." These authorities suggest that eyewitness testimony alone, in the absence of corroboration, is to be viewed with some suspicion.

9. The victim testified that the car had a loud muffler, that country music was playing on its radio, and that the car was started using a key. Respondent and others testified that his car was inoperative on the night of the incident, that when it was working it ran quietly, that the radio did not work, and that the car could be started only by using a screwdriver. The police did not check any of this before disposing of the car.

2. In *California v. Trombetta,* 467 U.S. 479, 104 S.Ct. 2528, 81 L.Ed.2d 413 (1984), which is discussed in *Youngblood,* the Court considered "whether the Due Process Clause requires law enforcement agencies to preserve breath samples of suspected drunken drivers in order for the results of breath-analysis tests to be admissible in criminal prosecutions." The justices answered that question in the negative and thus overturned the contrary ruling of the California Court of Appeal. Justice Marshall's opinion for a unanimous Court relied on the officers' "acting 'in good faith and in accord with their normal practice'" when they failed to preserve the breath samples. The opinion further noted the "extremely low" chance that the samples would have been exculpatory in light of the general reliability of the test results, and that "alternative means of demonstrating their innocence" were available to the respondents, including cross-examining the officers who administered the breath tests and impeaching the test results by using other strategies.

3. Note the crucial distinction between *Brady* issues (where evidence is known to be exculpatory, and the good faith or bad faith of the prosecutor in failing to disclose it is irrelevant) and *Youngblood* issues (involving evidence that is only "potentially useful"—since its destruction or unavailability precludes confirmation that it is exculpatory—and where a showing of bad faith is required to establish a constitutional violation). This distinction proved to be dispositive to the Supreme Court in *Illinois v. Fisher,* 540 U.S. 544, 124 S.Ct. 1200, 156 L.Ed.2d 1060 (2004) (*per curiam*). Gregory Fisher was arrested in Chicago in 1988 following a traffic stop in which the police seized a white, powdered substance that tests subsequently performed by police crime laboratories identified as cocaine. Fisher filed a pretrial discovery motion in which he requested access to all physical evidence the State intended to introduce at his trial. He posted bond and was released from custody but failed to appear when his case was called for trial. He remained a fugitive until November 1999, when he was arrested in Tennessee and then returned to Illinois for trial. However, "in September 1999, the police, acting in accord with established procedures, had destroyed the substance seized from him during his arrest." Fisher moved to dismiss the possession of cocaine charge based on the State's destruction of the evidence. The trial court rejected the motion and Fisher was convicted although he denied "that he ever possessed cocaine and insinuated that the police had 'framed' him." The Illinois Court of Appeals reversed the conviction. It ruled that Fisher's discovery motion had put the State on notice to preserve the powdered substance and that "the destroyed evidence provided [Fisher's] 'only hope for exoneration,' and was 'essential to and determinative of the outcome of the case.'" The court concluded that dismissal was required even though there was no showing of bad faith in the destruction of the evidence. The United States Supreme Court reversed in a *per curiam* decision.

We have held that when the State suppresses or fails to disclose material exculpatory evidence, the good or bad faith of the prosecution is irrelevant: a due process violation occurs whenever such evidence is withheld. See *Brady v. Maryland,* 373 U.S. 83 (1963); *United States v. Agurs,* 427 U.S. 97 (1976). In [*Arizona v*] .*Youngblood,* [488 U.S. 451 (1988)], by contrast, we recognized that the Due Process Clause "requires a different result when we deal with the failure of the State to preserve evidentiary material of which no more can be said than that it could have been subjected to tests, the results of which might have exonerated the defendant." We concluded that the failure to preserve this "potentially useful evidence" does not violate due process "*unless a criminal defendant can show bad faith on the part of the police.*" (emphasis added).

The substance seized from respondent was plainly the sort of "potentially useful evidence" referred to in *Youngblood,* not the material exculpatory evidence addressed in *Brady* and *Agurs.* At most, respondent could hope that, had the evidence been preserved, a *fifth* test conducted on the substance would have exonerated him. But respondent did not allege, nor did the Appellate Court find, that the Chicago police acted in bad faith when they destroyed the substance.

Quite the contrary, police testing indicated that the chemical makeup of the substance inculpated, not exculpated, respondent, and it is undisputed that police acted in "good faith and in accord with their normal practice." Under *Youngblood,* then, respondent has failed to establish a due process violation.

We have never held or suggested that the existence of a pending discovery request eliminates the necessity of showing bad faith on the part of police. Indeed, the result reached in this case demonstrates why such a *per se* rule would negate the very reason we adopted the bad-faith requirement in the first place: to "limi[t] the extent of the police's obligation to preserve evidence to reasonable grounds and confin[e] it to that class of cases where the interests of justice most clearly require it." 488 U.S., at 58.

We also disagree that *Youngblood* does not apply whenever the contested evidence provides a defendant's "only hope for exoneration" and is "'essential to and determinative of the outcome of the case.'" ... [T]he applicability of the bad-faith requirement in *Youngblood* depended not on the centrality of the contested evidence to the prosecution's case or the defendant's defense, but on the distinction between "material exculpatory" evidence and "potentially useful" evidence. As we have held, the substance destroyed here was, at best, "potentially useful" evidence, and therefore *Youngblood's* bad-faith requirement applies.

The judgment of the Appellate Court of Illinois is reversed, and the case is remanded for further proceedings not inconsistent with this opinion....

Justice STEVENS, concurring in the judgment.

While I did not join the three Justices who dissented in *Arizona v. Youngblood,* I also declined to join the majority opinion because I was convinced then, and remain convinced today, that "there may well be cases in which the defendant is unable to prove that the State acted in bad faith but in which the loss or destruction of evidence is nonetheless so critical to the defense as to make a criminal trial fundamentally unfair."* This, like *Youngblood,* is not such a case....

What must be shown to establish that the police did not preserve evidence in "bad faith"? Consider the following decision of the Georgia Supreme Court.

State v. Miller

699 S.E.2d 316 (Ga. 2010)

HINES, Justice.

We granted certiorari to the Court of Appeals in *State v. Miller,* 680 S.E.2d 627 (Ga. App. 2009), to consider the proper standard for analyzing whether the destruction of potentially exculpatory evidence rises to a violation of due process and whether that standard was met in this case. For the reasons that follow, we conclude that the appropriate standard, which has been set forth in precedent from this Court, was not applied by the Court of Appeals, and further, that such standard was not met in Miller's case.

---

* *Youngblood's* focus on the subjective motivation of the police represents a break with our usual understanding that the presence or absence of constitutional error in suppression of evidence cases depends on the character of the evidence, not the character of the person who withholds it. *United States v. Agurs,* 427 U.S. 97, 110 (1976). Since *Youngblood* was decided, a number of state courts have held as a matter of state constitutional law that the loss or destruction of evidence critical to the defense does violate due process, even in the absence of bad faith. As the Connecticut Supreme Court has explained, "[f]airness dictates that when a person's liberty is at stake, the sole fact of whether the police or another state official acted in good or bad faith in failing to preserve evidence cannot be determinative of whether the criminal defendant received due process of law." *State v. Morales,* 657 A.2d 585, 593 (Conn. 1995) (footnote omitted). See also *State v. Ferguson,* 2 S.W.3d 912, 916–917 (Tenn. 1999); *State v. Osakalumi,* 461 S.E.2d 504, 511–512 (W.Va. 1995); *State v. Delisle,* 648 A.2d 632, 642 (Vt. 1994); *Ex parte Gingo,* 605 So.2d 1237, 1241 (Ala. 1992); *Commonwealth v. Henderson,* 582 N.E.2d 496, 497 (Mass. 1991); *State v. Matafeo,* 787 P.2d 671, 673 (Haw. 1990); *Hammond v. State,* 569 A.2d 81, 87 (Del. 1989); *Thorne v. Department of Public Safety,* 774 P.2d 1326, 1330, n. 9 (Alaska 1989).

... On November 22, 2007, a Gwinnett County police officer stopped a vehicle driven by Miller because of a tag violation. Upon learning that there were outstanding warrants for Miller's arrest on charges that he had committed a simple battery on September 9, 2007, a robbery and battery on October 5, 2007, and another battery and simple battery on September 28, 2007, the officer arrested Miller, and he was incarcerated. The officer seized Miller's cell phone for use as evidence, apparently because a picture of a gun was displayed on the screen saver and the officer thought Miller had been charged with armed robbery. However, the property sheet completed by the officer stated that the cell phone could be released to Miller, and it referenced only the traffic case against Miller and not the other criminal charges. Miller's residential address, as written down by the officer on the property sheet, was incorrect.

The tag violation against Miller was resolved, and the police department sent a notice dated December 19, 2007, informing Miller that it had property in its custody that would be disposed of within 90 days if he did not retrieve it. But, the notice was sent to the incorrect address set forth on the property sheet, rather than to Miller's correct permanent address or to the facility where he remained in custody. The notice was returned to the police department with the notation "insufficient address, unable to forward."

The preliminary hearing on the outstanding charges was scheduled for December 5, 2007, by which time Miller was represented by appointed counsel. Miller told his attorney that his cell phone contained contact information for two witnesses who could provide Miller with an alibi on October 5, 2007, as well as a third witness who had information about the victim named in the indictment, which information corroborated Miller's defense.

On January 29, 2008, the police department submitted an application, pursuant to OCGA § 17-5-54, for the destruction of multiple items of personal property in the custody of the department in a number of cases. The traffic case against Miller was on the list, and one of the items of personal property was his cell phone. The application and an attached, sworn verification of the chief of police stated that the items of property to be destroyed had been "unclaimed for more than ninety (90) days after their seizure, or following the final conviction in the case of property used as evidence, and such items [were] no longer needed in a criminal investigation or for evidentiary purposes." The representations were untrue in regard to Miller's cell phone. Nonetheless, in reliance on them, the superior court signed an order on February 4, 2008, authorizing destruction of the property. Miller's cell phone was destroyed.

On February 20, 2008, Miller was indicted for one count of robbery and two counts each of battery and simple battery. At his arraignment on March 19, 2008, defense counsel informed the prosecuting attorney about the cell phone. Unaware of its destruction, defense counsel obtained the prosecutor's consent to release of the cell phone. After learning of its destruction, the defense filed a motion to dismiss the indictment based on the State's destruction of exculpatory evidence.

Following a hearing, the trial court initially determined that the State had not destroyed the cell phone with knowledge of its potentially exculpatory nature, and therefore, that the defense had not sufficiently showed the State's bad faith so as to justify dismissal of the charges, and that the appropriate remedy would be a jury instruction on spoliation of evidence. After determining that such a jury instruction was not appropriate in a criminal case, the trial court entered an order concluding that because the police officer had seized the cell phone without any real justification, the police department could have delivered the cell phone to Miller while he was being held in custody, the police department had destroyed the cell phone in violation of OCGA § 17-5-54 and through representations in the application that were inaccurate, and the police officer who seized the cell phone did not appear and testify at the hearing on Miller's motion to dismiss, acts amounting to conscious wrongdoing by the State had been shown as would justify dismissal of the two charged offenses that allegedly occurred on October 5, 2007. The trial court also found that the cell phone contained Miller's only means of contacting the three alleged exculpatory witnesses; because of the record-keeping practices of the cell phone provider, there were no call logs that could be subpoenaed. After giving the State an opportunity to present additional evidence, the trial court entered an order dismissing two of the five counts of the indictment.

The State then appealed to the Court of Appeals, which affirmed the judgment of the trial court. It concluded that the case was controlled by the decisions of the United States Supreme Court in *California v. Trombetta,* 467 U.S. 479 (1984) and *Arizona v. Youngblood,* 488 U.S. 51 (1988), which both address whether a defendant's constitutional rights to due process have been violated when the police destroy potentially exculpatory evidence. After examining these cases, the Court of Appeals concluded:

> In our opinion, *Youngblood* describes three types of evidence: (1) that which the police knew "would have exculpated" the defendant, (2) that which the police knew "could have exculpated" the defendant, and (3) that of which nothing more can be said other than that it is potentially useful evidence. *Youngblood* seems to treat the first type of evidence as "material exculpatory evidence" and to make good or bad faith irrelevant when the police destroy or fail to preserve such evidence. As to the second and third types of evidence, *Youngblood* seems to require a showing of bad faith such as the type outlined in *Trombetta,* i.e., official animus toward the defendant or a conscious effort to suppress exculpatory evidence, before the state's destruction or failure to preserve such evidence rises to the level of a due process violation. And before dismissal of criminal charges is warranted for destruction or failure to preserve any of the three types of evidence, it would seem that the *Trombetta* requirement, concerning the inability of the defendant to obtain comparable evidence by other reasonably available means, continues in effect.

It then cited Georgia cases that it said were consistent with its interpretation of *Trombetta* and *Youngblood,* and ultimately concluded that because Miller's cell phone contained information that could have led to Miller's acquisition of evidence that could have exculpated him, the cell phone was properly characterized as type two or three *Youngblood* evidence, i.e., evidence that the police knew "could have exculpated" Miller or evidence that was "potentially useful"; it further concluded that the trial court's finding that the police had engaged in conscious wrongdoing and thus acted in bad faith in destroying the cell phone was not clearly erroneous, and that the evidence supported the trial court's finding that Miller could not obtain the information stored in the cell phone by other reasonably available means.

This Court has discussed in detail what is required, under *Trombetta* and *Youngblood,* in order to find that the State's destruction of evidence potentially exculpatory to a defendant violates the defendant's rights to due process....

In [*Walker v. State,* 449 S.E.2d 845 (Ga. 1994)] ... this Court plainly addressed the interplay between *Youngblood* and *Trombetta*:

> In dealing with the failure of the state to preserve evidence which might have exonerated the defendant, a court must determine both whether the evidence was material and whether the police acted in bad faith in failing to preserve the evidence. To meet the standard of constitutional materiality, the evidence must possess an exculpatory value that was apparent before it was destroyed, and be of such a nature that the defendant would be unable to obtain comparable evidence by other reasonably available means.

Thus, the threshold inquiry in this analysis is whether the subject evidence is so material to the defense that it is of constitutional import.

> Evidence is constitutionally material when its *exculpatory value is apparent before it was lost or destroyed* and is of such a nature that a defendant would be unable to obtain other comparable evidence by other reasonably available means.

Ballard v. State, 673 S.E.2d 213 (Ga. 2009) (emphasis supplied). Therefore, the fact that evidence may be "potentially useful" in a defendant's attempt at exoneration is insufficient to sustain a claim that the defendant has suffered an abridgment of due process of law due to the destruction or loss of the evidence. The key is the "apparent exculpatory value" of the evidence prior to its destruction or loss and "apparent" in this context has been defined as "readily seen; visible; readily understood or perceived; evident; obvious." *State v. Brawner,* 678 S.E.2d 503 (Ga. App. 2009).

Applying these guidelines to the present case compels the conclusion that Miller has failed to show a violation of due process as the result of the destruction of his cell phone. There were simply no circumstances outlined by the Court of Appeals from which it could be concluded that the exculpatory value of Miller's cell phone was obvious or evident to police or any other State actor before the cell phone was destroyed. In fact, the facts point to a conclusion which is quite the contrary. The cell phone was initially seized because police believed that it was potentially inculpatory, as displaying a picture of a gun, for possible use by the State at trial for what was believed to be an armed robbery charge against Miller. What followed in regard to the cell phone and its fate is accurately characterized as an unfortunate series of mishandlings, mistakes, and negligence by police, but in no manner does the scenario presented by the Court of Appeals permit the conclusion that it was apparent to police or anyone else involved in the seizure, custody, or disposition of the cell phone that it could possibly aid Miller in the defense of any criminal charges. Consequently, the evidence was not constitutionally material.

The judgment of the Court of Appeals is reversed....

Do the police have a duty to preserve and transmit *Brady* material to the prosecutor? Can they be held civilly liable if they fail to do so? Does it matter if their obligation to preserve and deliver evidence to the prosecutor that may help establish a defendant's innocence is analyzed under *Brady* instead of *Youngblood*? Consider the following case, involving a federal civil rights action filed against the police by a Michigan man who was wrongfully convicted of abduction and sexual assault and spent nearly 12 years in prison.

Moldowan v. City of Warren

578 F.3d 351 (6th Cir. 2009), *cert. den.*, 130 S.Ct. 3504 (2010)

CLAY, Circuit Judge.

In this action, Plaintiff Jeffrey Moldowan ("Moldowan") asserts a number of claims under 42 U.S.C. § 1983.... Moldowan's claims arise out of his arrest, criminal prosecution, conviction, and retrial for the 1990 abduction and brutal sexual assault of Maureen Fournier ("Fournier"). After new evidence came to light and a key prosecution witness recanted her testimony, the Michigan Supreme Court reversed Moldowan's conviction in 2002. *People v. Moldowan,* 643 N.W.2d 570 (Mich. 2002). On retrial, in February 2003, Moldowan was acquitted of all charges and released, having served nearly twelve years in prison.

After his release, Moldowan filed the instant civil action asserting various claims against the City of Warren, the Warren Police Department, Macomb County, the Macomb County Prosecutor in his official capacity, Dr. Alan Warnick, Warren Police Detective Donald Ingles, Warren Police Officer Mark Christian, and Fournier. Moldowan subsequently amended his complaint to assert claims against Warren Police Officer Michael Schultz. Broadly speaking, Moldowan alleges that the Defendants—both acting separately and conspiring together—violated his civil rights by fabricating evidence against him, failing to disclose exculpatory evidence, and pursuing his prosecution and retrial without probable cause.

After discovery, the Defendants moved for summary judgment on all thirty-six counts asserted in Moldowan's Third Amended Complaint raising various immunity defenses. After dismissing certain counts against Detective Ingles, the City of Warren, and the Warren Police Department, and dismissing all counts against Officer Christian, the district court denied Defendants' motions for summary judgment in all other respects.... For the reasons set forth herein, we AFFIRM IN PART and REVERSE IN PART the judgment of the district court.

I.

...

A. Factual Background

On the morning of August 9, 1990, Emergency Medical Service ("EMS") found Fournier badly injured and lying in the street in the City of Detroit. EMS transported Fournier to St. John's Hospital. The medical forms completed on her admission to the hospital, as well as subsequent medical reports and testimony from her doctors, bear witness to the extreme brutality of the crime. The police determined that Fournier had been abducted from the City of Warren, brutally assaulted and raped, and left on a street in Detroit.

Because Fournier had been abducted from Warren, the matter was turned over to the Warren Police Department ("Department"), and the case was assigned to Detective Ingles. Given the extent of Fournier's injuries, officers had to wait two days before they could interview her regarding the attack. Even then, the extent of Fournier's injuries forced Detective Ingles to write questions on a board, and Fournier responded in kind. During the interview, Fournier reported that she had been abducted from Warren on the night of August 8, 1990 by four Caucasian males, all of whom she knew. Fournier stated that, while she was walking down the street, she was approached by Moldowan, who was her ex-boyfriend, thrown into a white or light-colored van, and brutally beaten and raped by three of the four assailants. Fournier identified her attackers as Michael Cristini, Jim Cristini, Tracy Tapp ("Tapp"), and Moldowan. Fournier's sister, Colleen Corcoran ("Corcoran"), confirmed Fournier's claims that Moldowan previously had assaulted and threatened Fournier.

After completing their investigation, the police arrested and charged all four individuals. The police subsequently dropped the charges against Tapp based on his alibi that he had been in Texas for several days prior to the assault, had not returned to the Michigan until the evening of August 8, and spent the rest of the night with his girlfriend. Tapp's girlfriend confirmed his alibi.

On September 17–18, 1990, the Macomb County Circuit Court held a preliminary examination to determine whether sufficient evidence existed to proceed to trial. During that hearing, Fournier testified that, prior to the assault, she had dated and lived with Moldowan for more than a year before their relationship ended when he was arrested for assaulting her. Fournier and her sister both testified that, prior to the attack, Moldowan had been abusive toward Fournier and threatened her. In describing the assault, Fournier testified that she had been walking on 11 Mile Road in Warren when a van pulled alongside her. Fournier testified that Moldowan got out of the van, grabbed her, and dragged her into the van, where she was beaten and raped. As a result of the assault, Fournier suffered significant injuries that required extensive abdominal surgery.

Corcoran also testified at the hearing, stating that she received a call from an unidentified male on August 9, 1990, the day Fournier was found in Detroit, inquiring as to Fournier's whereabouts. Corcoran claims that she immediately recognized the caller as Moldowan. Corcoran testified that, although she knew that her sister was in the hospital, she lied and told Moldowan that her sister was at home with her, and that Moldowan then exclaimed: "No, she's not.... She's at the morgue." Corcoran also testified that Moldowan had called her home the previous day looking for Fournier, and that Moldowan had stated that "he was going to get her."

At the conclusion of the examination, the court dismissed Jim Cristini as a defendant, but bound over Moldowan and Michael Cristini on all counts. A jury trial was held from April 30 to May 10, 1991, during which Fournier and Corcoran offered substantially the same testimony they provided during the preliminary examination. Fournier also testified that she had never been in the Detroit neighborhood where EMS found her, and that she had never frequented a crack house in the area.

In addition, Dr. Alan Warnick, D.D.S., a forensic odontologist and consultant for the Wayne County Medical Examiner's Office and a consultant to Macomb County, Monroe County, and the Michigan State Police, offered expert testimony that bite marks on Fournier's neck were consistent with dental impressions taken from Moldowan, and that bite marks on Fournier's right arm and right side were consistent with Michael Cristini's dentition. In describing his conclusions, Dr. Warnick testified that the "chances are ... 2.1 billion to 1 that another individual can make those same marks."

In presenting their defense, Cristini and Moldowan offered alibi witnesses who testified that the defendants were not together on the evening in question. The defense also introduced pizza delivery tickets which documented the location of the pizza deliveries Cristini had made the night of August 8, 1990, seeking to show that Cristini could not have been part of the kidnaping. The defense also presented testimony from a witness who claimed that she observed several males in the street where Fournier was found, and that the males were both Caucasian and African-American. The defense also offered expert testimony from its own forensic odontologists countering Dr. Warnick's testimony concerning the bite-mark evidence.

On rebuttal, the prosecution called Dr. Pamela Hammel, D.D.S., a colleague of Dr. Warnick, who offered testimony corroborating and supporting Dr. Warnick's conclusions.

On May 10, 1991, the jury convicted Moldowan and Cristini of kidnaping, assault with intent to commit murder, and two counts of criminal sexual conduct in the first degree. After sentencing, the court entered an order requiring that "[a]ll evidence in the custody of the Warren Police Department, the Macomb County Prosecutor's Office and the Macomb County Circuit Court[,] whether admitted into evidence or not ... [,] be preserved from this date forward until further order of the Circuit Court, Michigan Court of Appeals, or Michigan Supreme Court."

After trial, a private investigator hired by Moldowan's family located a witness, Jerry Burroughs, who reported that, on the morning of August 9, 1990, he saw four African-American males standing around a naked white female who was lying in the street, and that he saw the four men leave in a light-colored van. Burroughs further recounted that, approximately one week after the assault, he overheard two of those same men talking about the incident and bragging that they had participated in the assault. Burroughs also indicated that he had seen Fournier in that neighborhood several times that summer frequenting a crack house in the area.

In addition to this new evidence, Dr. Hammel, after being approached several years later by Moldowan's appellate counsel, also recanted her testimony. Dr. Hammel explained that she initially had trouble matching the defendants' dentitions to the bite marks on Fournier's body, but that Dr. Warnick had reassured her that Dr. Norman Sperber, a highly respected forensic odontologist, had reviewed the evidence and confirmed Dr. Warnick's conclusions. After subsequently determining that Dr. Sperber had never reviewed any evidence in the case, Dr. Hammel surmised that Dr. Warnick "had been deceptive in order to mislead [her] into testifying in support of his conclusions." In a sworn affidavit, Dr. Hammel stated that, had she known that Dr. Warnick's representation that Dr. Sperber had reviewed the evidence was untrue, she "would never have agreed to testify as a rebuttal witness in support of Dr. Warnick's conclusions."

On the basis of this new evidence and discredited testimony, Moldowan again sought review of his conviction. The Michigan Supreme Court eventually reversed Moldowan's conviction, and remanded the matter for a new trial....

On retrial, in February 2003, Moldowan was acquitted of all charges and released. All told, Moldowan spent nearly twelve years in prison.

B. Procedural History of the Instant Action

On January 28, 2005, Moldowan brought this civil action asserting numerous claims under 42 U.S.C. § 1983 and Michigan state law....

Plaintiff's current complaint (Third Amended Complaint filed February 9, 2006) alleges a total of 36 counts against several groups of defendants: City of Warren; Police Department of City of Warren (WPD); County of Macomb and its Prosecutor in his official capacity; and sued in their individual and official capacities: Alan Warnick [forensic consultant], Donald Ingles [WPD detective], Mark Christian [WPD detective], Michael Schultz [WPD sergeant in charge of the evidence room], and "other Present and Former Members of the Warren Police Department and office of the Macomb County Prosecutor as yet unidentified," and sued individually: Maureen Fournier [the crime victim]....

The complaint alleges federal violations of plaintiff's civil and constitutional rights during his criminal prosecution, as well as state claims ...

After extensive discovery, Defendants filed motions for summary judgment, asserting various qualified and absolute immunity defenses.... [T]he district court dismissed [several claims but denied Defendants' motions as to all remaining claims]....

These three interlocutory appeals followed....

III.

We review the district court's denial of summary judgment *de novo*.... Summary judgment is proper "if the pleadings, the discovery and disclosure materials on file, and any affidavits show that there is no genuine issue as to any material fact and that the movant is entitled to judgment as a matter of law." Fed.R.Civ.P. 56(c). A genuine issue of material fact exists when there are "disputes over facts that might affect the outcome of the suit under the governing law." ...

IV.

... First, we consider the qualified and absolute immunity claims raised in ... the appeal of the City of Warren, Detective Ingles, and Officer Schultz....

C. Analysis

...

1. Counts IX, X, XI, XII—*Brady* Claims (Ingles)

Moldowan asserts a number of claims against Detective Ingles under the Fourth, Fifth, Sixth, and Fourteenth Amendments based on Ingles' alleged failure to disclose exculpatory evidence. In particular, Moldowan contends that Ingles was required to disclose exculpatory statements from Burroughs, including that Burroughs recalled seeing four African-American males standing around Fournier on the morning that she was discovered in Detroit and that Burroughs later overheard two of those men discussing their involvement in the assault.

Moldowan's allegations, although asserted under various constitutional provisions, present claims under *Brady v. Maryland,* 373 U.S. 83 (1963). In *Brady,* the Court held that "the suppression by the prosecution of evidence favorable to an accused ... violates due process where the evidence is material either to guilt or to punishment, irrespective of the good faith or bad faith of the prosecution." The question we confront here is whether Detective Ingles' alleged suppression of Burroughs' statements violated the same "legal norm" underlying the due process violation recognized in *Brady.* We hold that it does.

Detective Ingles argues that Moldowan cannot demonstrate that the Due Process Clause imposes on the police a clearly established obligation to disclose exculpatory information. Superficially, that argument has some appeal. To the extent that *Brady* imposes an obligation on the state to disclose exculpatory evidence to the defense, courts consistently have determined that this duty falls squarely on the prosecutor, not the police. In *Kyles v. Whitley,* 514 U.S. 419 (1995), for instance, the Supreme Court explained that "the individual prosecutor," who "alone can know what is undisclosed, must be assigned the consequent responsibility to gauge the likely net effect of all such evidence and make disclosure when the point of 'reasonable probability' is reached." *Id.* at 437; *see also Strickler v. Greene,* 527 U.S. 263, 281 (1999) (recognizing "the special role played by the American prosecutor in the search for truth in criminal trials"). In fact, the Supreme Court has placed the responsibility to manage the state's disclosure obligations solely on the prosecutor despite acknowledging that "no one doubts that police investigators sometimes fail to inform a prosecutor of all they know." *Kyles,* 514 U.S. at 438.

This well-established rule, however, does not resolve whether the police have a concomitant or derivative duty under the constitution to turn potentially exculpatory material over to the prosecutor. In fact, Moldowan acknowledges that the duty to "disclose" exculpatory materials to defense counsel rests on the prosecutor alone, but nevertheless maintains that the police have an analogous, but just as constitutionally-significant, obligation to turn such materials over to the prosecutor's office. Underlying Moldowan's argument is the valid concern that, if the police have no constitutional obligation in this regard, then the state could sidestep its constitutionally-mandated disclosure obligations by maintaining an unstated, but nevertheless pervasive, wall of separation between the prosecutor's office and the police with regard to the existence of potentially exculpatory evidence. Ignoring the burdens that the Constitution places on the police in this context also creates a very serious risk that police officers who conceal or withhold evidence that falls within *Brady*'s ambit will never be held accountable for the independent "deprivation of any rights, privileges, or immunities secured by the Constitution," 42 U.S.C. § 1983, that their conduct causes.

As the concurrence correctly notes, however, the Supreme Court already has addressed the first of these concerns, at least to a certain extent, by imposing on the prosecutor "a duty to learn of any favorable evidence known to the others acting on the government's behalf in the case, including the police." *Kyles,* 514 U.S. at 437....

Contrary to Detective Ingles' suggestion, however, this does not imply that the police have no role to play in ensuring that the state complies with its obligations under *Brady,* or that the police cannot commit a constitutional violation analogous to the deprivation recognized in *Brady*.... Because the prosecutor's office generally lacks its own investigative machinery, prosecutors often are entirely dependent on the police to turn over the fruits of their investigation. As a result of this interdependence, the police play a different, but no less significant role in the state's "search for truth in criminal trials." *Strickler,* 527 U.S. at 281.

Because prosecutors rely so heavily on the police and other law enforcement authorities, the obligations imposed under *Brady* would be largely ineffective if those other members of the prosecution team had no responsibility to inform the prosecutor about evidence that undermined the state's preferred theory of the crime. As a practical matter then, *Brady*'s ultimate concern for ensuring that criminal defendants receive a "fundamentally fair" trial, *see United States v. Bagley,* 473 U.S. 667, 675 (1985) (explaining that the "purpose" of the *Brady* rule is "to ensure that a miscarriage of justice does not occur"), demands that "*Brady*'s protections also extend to actions of other law enforcement officers such as investigating officers," *White v. McKinley,* 519 F.3d 806, 814 (8th Cir.2008)....

In addition to this practical justification, it is evident that the constitutional principles recognized in *Brady* apply just as equally to similar conduct on the part of police, and thus support our recognizing that the police can commit a constitutional deprivation analogous to that recognized in *Brady* by withholding or suppressing exculpatory material.... As far as the Constitution is concerned, a criminal defendant is equally deprived of his or her due process rights when the police rather than the prosecutor suppresses exculpatory evidence because, in either case, the impact on the fundamental fairness of the defendant's trial is the same.

Although the prosecutor undoubtedly plays a "special role" in "the search for truth in criminal trials," *Strickler,* 527 U.S. at 281, the police also play a unique and significant role in that process, and thus also are bound by the government's constitutional obligation to "ensure that a miscarriage of justice does not occur," *Bagley,* 473 U.S. at 675....

In other words, because the police are just as much an arm of the state as the prosecutor, the police inflict the same constitutional injury when they hide, conceal, destroy, withhold, or even fail to disclose material exculpatory information.

While the concurrence is correct that the Supreme Court has held that, technically speaking, the government's "*disclosure* " obligations fall to and must be managed by the prosecutor, *Kyles,* 514 U.S. at 437 (emphasis added), that argument overlooks that the Court's decisions also make clear that the constitutional concerns underlying *Brady* reach more broadly to preclude other governmental "authorities" from making a "calculated effort to circumvent the disclosure requirements established by *Brady* [ ] and its progeny," *Trombetta,* 467 U.S. at 488. As Judge Murnaghan succinctly explained in his dissent in *Jean v. Collins,* 221 F.3d 656 (4th Cir.2000) (en banc):

> Of course, the manner in which prosecutors and police officers comply with *Brady* is different, reflecting their different functions in the criminal justice system. Police officers do not disclose evidence to criminal defendants directly. Instead, the police accumulate evidence and then ministerially deliver it to the prosecutor. The prosecutor then makes a discretionary legal judgment about whether the evidence is material and exculpatory, such that *Brady* compels its disclosure to the defendant.

Id. at 664. Although the police and prosecutor play different roles in this process, "[t]his functional differentiation ... should not obscure the fact that Brady creates a singular constitutional duty, which prosecutors and police officers are capable of breaching in factually different ways." *Id.*

In addition to these practical justifications and constitutional considerations, the police's obligation to turn over material and exculpatory evidence also follows inexorably from the Supreme Court's recognition that the police have a constitutional duty to preserve such evidence. In *Trombetta,* the Supreme Court observed that "[w]hatever duty the Constitution imposes on the States to preserve evidence, that duty must be limited to evidence that might be expected to play a significant role in the suspect's defense." 467 U.S. at 488. The Court recognized that same duty in *Arizona v. Youngblood,* 488 U.S. 51 (1988), confirming that the Constitution imposes at least a limited "obligation" on the police "to preserve evidence ... [that] could form the basis for exonerating the defendant." If the Constitution imposes a "duty" and "obligation" on the police to preserve such evidence, that duty, no matter how limited, certainly must preclude the police from concealing that exact same information from the prosecutor, the defense, and the courts. Why else would the police be required to *preserve* such evidence if they had no attendant obligation to *reveal* its existence? *Brady* and *Trombetta* would impose hollow obligations indeed if the Constitution did not also preclude police officers from concealing the same evidence that they are not permitted to destroy and that the prosecutor is required to disclose.

The concurrence argues that the police cannot share in the state's obligations under *Brady* because "the *Brady* duty is uniquely tailored to prosecutors" in that it requires the disclosure of exculpatory evidence that is constitutionally "material," and thus requires the exercise of "a judgment that prosecutors, not police officers, are trained to make." This argument misses the point. We agree that determining whether a particular piece of evidence is "material," as defined in *Bagley*, generally requires the exercise of legal judgment that the prosecuting attorney is better trained, not to mention better positioned, to make. However, that implies only that the prosecutor should be assigned the responsibility of determining what evidence ultimately should be *disclosed* to the defendant; it does not imply, as our colleague suggests, that the police cannot be expected to recognize and determine what evidence should be preserved and turned over to the prosecutor. On the contrary, the Supreme Court already has assumed as much in concluding that the police have a constitutionally-significant "duty" to "preserve evidence ... that might be expected to play a significant role in the suspect's defense." *Trombetta*, 467 U.S. at 488–89 (holding that the police were not obliged to preserve evidence because the "exculpatory value" of the evidence was not "apparent"). If the police can be expected to recognize what evidence must be preserved, certainly it is not too burdensome to demand that they simply turn that same information over to the prosecutor's office.

For most of the same reasons we have laid out here, virtually every other circuit has concluded either that the police share in the state's obligations under *Brady*, or that the Constitution imposes on the police obligations analogous to those recognized in *Brady*. ...

Having determined that Moldowan's claims against Detective Ingles implicate a clearly established constitutional right, we next must determine whether, taking the facts alleged by Moldowan as true, Moldowan can make out a violation of this right. At Moldowan's retrial, Jerry Burroughs testified that he witnessed four African-American males standing in the street around Fournier's body in the early morning hours of August 9, 1990. Burroughs also testified that he witnessed one of the men kick her, and that shortly thereafter he saw the men drive away from the scene in a light-colored van. Burroughs also testified that he later overheard two of the men he saw standing around Fournier's body talking about the incident and claiming involvement in the assault. Burroughs testified that he reported this information to a police officer, but the officer "just acted like I[was] saying nothing." Although Burroughs could not remember the name of the officer with whom he spoke, Moldowan claims that it must have been Detective Ingles. It is without question that Detective Ingles did not report any such information to the Macomb County Prosecutor, or to defense counsel for that matter.

Construing these facts in the light most favorable to Moldowan, it is evident that Burroughs' statements cast serious doubt on, if not entirely discredit, Fournier's identification of Moldowan as one of her attackers, an issue that undoubtedly was one of the most important elements of the state's case. Burroughs' statements thus should have been disclosed to the defense as they undoubtedly "would tend to exculpate" Moldowan. *See Brady*, 373 U.S. at 88.

Defendants contend that, even if we were to conclude that the legal norms underlying *Brady* can support an analogous or derivative claim against a police officer, Moldowan cannot prevail on the facts presented here because he cannot show that Detective Ingles withheld these statements in "bad faith." ...

The question we have before us is a difficult one, with, as the concurrence rightfully points out, significant policy implications on both sides. But our job is not to craft the law to fit our policy views, it is to determine what the law requires. Notwithstanding the concurrence's argument to the contrary, the cases in this area clearly establish that police actions taken in bad faith are not the only species of police conduct that can deprive criminal defendants of the due process guaranteed by the Constitution. We acknowledge that a number of courts, including the Supreme Court, have held that a showing of bad faith is required to prevail on a claim that the police deprived a defendant of due process by concealing or withholding evidence that is only "potentially useful." But, where the police are aware that the evidence in their possession is exculpatory, the Supreme Court's decisions in this area indicate that the police have an *absolute* duty to preserve and disclose that information. The critical issue in determining whether bad faith is required thus is not whether the evidence is withheld by the prosecutor or the police, but rather whether the exculpatory value of the evidence is "apparent" or not....

In other words, the critical issue in determining whether government conduct deprived a criminal defendant of a fair trial is the nature of the evidence that was withheld; it emphatically is not the mental state of the government official who suppressed the evidence.... Although both *Agurs* and *Brady* involved due process violations by the prosecutor rather than the police, the critical lesson of those decisions is that the constitutional violation arose because of the nature of the evidence, not the state of mind of the state actor.

Notwithstanding the reasoning underlying *Agurs* and *Brady*, the concurrence contends that Moldowan's due process claim should be evaluated under the "bad-faith standard" set forth in *Arizona v. Youngblood*, which the concurrence insists "requires proof that the officer engaged in 'a conscious effort to suppress exculpatory evidence.'" This heightened standard is justified, the concurrence argues, because extending *Brady*'s "absolute duty" to law enforcement officers who do not enjoy absolute immunity will "unleash" a flood of lawsuits "that will be very difficult to stop short of trial." We respectfully disagree.

However, *Youngblood* does not impose a bad faith requirement on any and all due process claims brought against police officers. On the contrary, just like *Brady* and *Agurs*, the Court's decision in *Youngblood* confirms that where "material exculpable evidence" is concerned, the mental state of the government official withholding that evidence is not relevant to determining whether a due process violation has occurred. 488 U.S. at 57–58. In discussing the scope of the police's duty to preserve evidence, the Court contrasted the state's absolute obligation to *disclose* "material exculpable evidence" with its much more limited obligation to *preserve* "potentially useful evidence," holding that a showing of bad faith was required to show a constitutional violation only in the latter context. *Id.* at 57–58. Although, as the concurrence correctly points out, the Court rejected the bad-faith requirement in the context of due process guarantees "as interpreted in *Brady*," that turn of phrase does not bear the weight that our colleague places on it. Far from suggesting that the difference in the applicable standards turns on the job title of the government official who destroyed or concealed the evidence in question, the Court's decision in *Youngblood* actually explained:

> Part of the reason for the difference in treatment is found in the observation made by the Court in *Trombetta*, that "[w]henever potentially exculpatory evidence is permanently lost, courts face the treacherous task of divining the import of materials whose contents are unknown and, very often, disputed." Part of it stems from our unwillingness to read the "fundamental fairness" requirement of the Due Process Clause, as imposing on the police an undifferentiated and absolute duty to retain and to preserve all material that might be of conceivable evidentiary significance in a particular prosecution. We think that requiring a defendant to show bad faith on the part of the police both limits the extent of the police's obligation to preserve evidence to reasonable bounds and confines it to that class of cases where the interests of justice most clearly require it, *i.e.*, those cases in which the police themselves by their conduct indicate that the evidence could form a basis for exonerating the defendant.

Id. at 57–58. In other words, Youngblood confirms that the "reason for the difference" in the applicable standards is the nature of the evidence at issue, not the title of the government official or whether the challenged conduct relates to the state's failure to disclose evidence rather that its failure to preserve it. *See Illinois v. Fisher*, 540 U.S. 544, 549 (2004) (explaining that "the applicability of the bad-faith requirement in Youngblood depended ... on the distinction between 'materially exculpatory' evidence and 'potentially useful' evidence")....

Indeed, the only way to make sense of this critical passage from *Youngblood* is to read the phrase "the police's obligation" in the last sentence as referring to the statement from the previous sentence regarding the police's "undifferentiated and absolute duty." When given a proper reading, *Youngblood* thus confirms that the police have "an undifferentiated and absolute duty to retain and preserve" certain evidence, but that "[absolute] obligation" is limited to "those cases in which the police themselves by their conduct indicate that the evidence could form a basis for exonerating the defendant."

Simply put, where the evidence withheld or destroyed by the police falls into that more serious category, the defendant is not required to make any further showing regarding the mental state of the police. As the Court explained in *Youngblood,* "[t]he presence or absence of bad faith by the police for purposes of the Due Process Clause must necessarily turn on the police's knowledge of the exculpatory value of the evidence at the time it was lost or destroyed." *Id.* at 56 n. *....

The policy risks imagined by the concurrence also stem from this fundamental misunderstanding of the "absolute" nature of the *Brady* obligation. In *Bagley,* the Court explained that "the prosecutor is not required to deliver his entire file to defense counsel, but only to disclose evidence favorable to the accused that, if suppressed, would deprive the defendant of a fair trial." 473 U.S. at 675. In other words, the Due Process Clause imposes an "absolute duty" on the prosecutor only with regard to certain evidence, *i.e.* "material exculpatory evidence."

The central lesson of all of these cases is that the critical factor in determining whether the state's obligation is "absolute" turns on the nature of the evidence at issue, not who destroyed or suppressed the evidence. The justification for imposing an absolute duty where material and exculpatory evidence is at issue is clear enough: the failure to preserve or disclose such evidence directly threatens the "fundamental fairness" of a defendant's criminal trial. Because that concern for fundamental fairness is just as strong where a defendant claims that the police destroyed or suppressed material evidence, there is no constitutionally-supportable basis for applying a different standard and requiring courts to inquire into the mental state of the police.

The only difference in the requisite inquiry is that, where the police are concerned, the "exculpatory value" of the evidence must be "apparent."[14] *Trombetta,* 467 U.S. at 489. This additional burden, however, merely reflects that materiality is a legal question that the police are not trained to make, and thereby accounts for the practical concern that the police cannot be held accountable for failing to divine the materiality of every possible scrap of evidence. It does not imply, however, that the police are entirely shielded from liability unless a defendant shows "bad faith." Where the exculpatory value of a piece of evidence is "apparent," the police have an *unwavering* constitutional duty to preserve and ultimately disclose that evidence. The failure to fulfill that obligation constitutes a due process violation, regardless of the whether a criminal defendant or § 1983 plaintiff can show that the evidence was destroyed or concealed in "bad faith." The reason no *further* showing of animus or bad faith is required is that, where the police have in their possession evidence that they know or should know "might be expected to play a significant role in the suspect's defense," *Trombetta,* 467 U.S. at 488, the destruction or concealment of that evidence can *never* be done "in good faith and in accord with their normal practice," *Killian v. United States,* 368 U.S. 231, 242 (1961). Consequently, requiring a criminal defendant or § 1983 plaintiff to show a "conscious" or "calculated" effort to suppress such evidence would be superfluous.

In any event, even if we were inclined to believe that bad faith was required, we still would not conclude that Detective Ingles is entitled to summary judgment. Because we must read the record in the light most favorable to Moldowan, we conclude that Burroughs' testimony, taken as a whole, provides sufficient evidence for Moldowan's claims to survive summary judgment because a jury could reasonably conclude that Detective Ingles acted in bad faith. Although there is no direct evidence that Detective Ingles acted intentionally in withholding these exculpatory statements, Burroughs' testimony, at least when viewed in the light most favorable to Moldowan, provides sufficient evidence for Moldowan's claim to survive summary judgment. Despite Detective Ingles' insistence to the contrary, we lack the jurisdiction to consider his claim that Burroughs never made any such statements to the police....

KETHLEDGE, Circuit Judge, concurring in the judgment in part, and dissenting in part.

Moldowan puts many labels on his claims, but his claim against Officer Ingles is essentially that he should have disclosed, presumably to the prosecutor, the fact and contents of Jerry Burroughs' alleged statement to Ingles. I agree with the majority's conclusion that, under the standard

14. In *Youngblood,* the Court suggested that this additional burden was satisfied where "the police themselves by their conduct indicate that the evidence could form a basis for exonerating the defendant." 488 U.S. at 58.

of review applicable here, Moldowan is entitled to proceed with that claim. But I respectfully disagree with how the majority gets there.

I.

A.

With a significant caveat, the majority gets there by extending the no-fault regime of *Brady v. Maryland,* 373 U.S. 83 (1963)—or at least something functionally "analogous" to it—to police officers. The caveat, as discussed below, may as a practical matter render insignificant the differences between the majority's approach and my own. I think it important, however, to explain why extending the *Brady* regime to police officers would be both unprecedented and unwise.

"The *Brady* doctrine imposes an absolute duty on the prosecutor to produce all materially favorable evidence in the State's possession." *Villasana v. Wilhoit,* 368 F.3d 976, 979 (8th Cir.2004). By its terms, therefore, *Brady* applies to prosecutors, not police officers....

The imposition of that same absolute duty on police officers, therefore, would represent an extension of *Brady* that the Supreme Court itself has not made in the 46 years since it rendered the decision. I do not think the omission is fortuitous. Not only by its terms, but also by its content, the *Brady* duty is uniquely tailored to prosecutors. It applies to exculpatory evidence that is "material"; and the Supreme Court says that "[s]uch evidence is material 'if there is a reasonable probability that, had the evidence been disclosed to the defense, *the result of the proceeding* [that is, the criminal trial] *would have been different.*'" *Strickler v. Greene,* 527 U.S. 263, 280 (1999). Whether a particular piece of evidence would have changed the result of a criminal trial, of course, is a judgment that prosecutors, not police officers, are trained to make....

The extension is also unnecessary. The *Brady* rule *already* "encompasses evidence 'known only to police investigators and not to the prosecutor.'" *Strickler,* 527 U.S. at 280–81 (quoting *Kyles v. Whitley,* 514 U.S. 419, 438 (1995)). But it is the prosecutor, not the police themselves, who bears an absolute duty to disclose it. Indeed, even as to evidence solely in police possession—which is the kind of evidence at issue here—the Supreme Court has specifically refused to impose the *Brady* duty directly upon the police, saying that to do so "would ... amount to a serious change of course from the *Brady* line of cases." *Kyles,* 514 U.S. at 438. Instead, to comply with *Brady*, "*the individual prosecutor* has a duty to learn of any favorable evidence known to the others acting on the government's behalf in the case, including the police." *Id.* at 437 (emphasis added). And any breach of that duty, no matter how diligent the prosecutor's efforts, entitles the criminal defendant to a new trial ... Moreover, as discussed below, no one disputes that police officers already have an independent duty—though not a *Brady* duty—not to conceal materially exculpatory evidence in bad faith. Thus, as a practical matter, extending *Brady* to police officers would accomplish little with respect to the fairness of criminal trials that current law does not already accomplish.

What that extension would accomplish, rather, is a significant increase in lawsuits against police officers. Prosecutors enjoy absolute immunity for actions taken in their official capacities, *see Imbler v. Pachtman,* 424 U.S. 409 (1976), whereas police officers do not. Police officers, therefore, would become the special object of attention from criminal defendants who believe that allegedly exculpatory evidence should have been, but was not, disclosed to their counsel prior to trial. And in this respect the police would present a large target. Police officers, particularly ones like Ingles who investigate violent crime in the field, obtain a great deal of information in the course of an investigation. Some of what they obtain, like shell casings, is tangible, but much of it, like things they may have seen or heard in the course of their activities, is not. As a practical matter, an officer cannot preserve, and thus pass on to the prosecutor, *everything* he sees, hears, or learns in the course of investigating a crime. He instead has to exercise judgment about what seems important and what does not. But if an officer bears an absolute duty to disclose materially exculpatory evidence, *all* of the information thus filtered by an officer's judgment, even in the purest good faith, potentially becomes the basis of a lawsuit against him. An officer's failure to recognize an exculpatory clue, for example, and thus to pass it on to the prosecutor, would be a violation of the Due Process Clause. That the officer was merely negligent, or even that no reasonable officer could have understood the clue's significance at the time, would be no defense; the *Brady* duty is absolute. So if the clue could have changed the result of the criminal defendant's first trial, the defendant would not only get a second one; he would be entitled to have the officer pay him for his troubles as well....

Once unleashed, these suits would be very difficult to stop short of trial. For in these cases the refuge of qualified immunity would be illusory. Qualified immunity requires that the officer violate "clearly established" constitutional rights to be liable, with the idea being that, by definition, such liability is usually limited to officers who knew or should have known they were violating the law. *See Saucier v. Katz,* 533 U.S. 194, 202 (2001). But it does an officer little good to be aware of the *existence* of a generic duty, if, when acting in good faith and to the best of his ability, he is not aware that he is breaching it. And because the *Brady* duty is absolute, a criminal-defendant-turned-plaintiff would need not prove that the officer knew—or even that any reasonable officer would have known—that the officer had a duty to disclose the particular information at issue. Foreknowledge of illegality would be beside the point; and thus, as a practical matter, qualified immunity would be no immunity at all.

B.

For good reason, then, no federal appellate court has extended *Brady*'s no-fault regime to police officers....

None of the cases that the majority cites actually imposes *Brady*'s absolute duty of disclosure upon police officers. Most of them instead find liability for precisely the sort of bad-faith conduct that would give rise to liability under virtually any standard....

C.

1.

The issue before us today, as the majority correctly observes, is one of law rather than policy. And I would decide it as such. The standard that I would apply—and the one the Eighth and Eleventh Circuits apply—is the one that the Supreme Court has so far *always* applied to determine officer liability in the "area of constitutionally guaranteed access to evidence": namely, bad faith. *Arizona v. Youngblood,* 488 U.S. 51 (1988). This standard requires proof that the officer engaged in "a conscious effort to suppress exculpatory evidence." *California v. Trombetta,* 467 U.S. 479, 488 (1984)....

Notwithstanding this plain language, the majority reads *Youngblood* to mean that no showing of bad faith is required to establish a violation of due process *by the police* "where 'material exculpatory evidence' is concerned[.]" But *Youngblood* does not quite say that. What *Youngblood* says is that "[t]he Due Process Clause of the Fourteenth Amendment, *as interpreted in Brady,* makes the good or bad faith of the State irrelevant when the State fails to disclose to the defendant material exculpatory evidence." 488 U.S. at 57 (emphasis added). That statement does not impose an absolute duty upon police officers—as shown above, there *was* no police conduct at issue in *Brady*—but is instead merely a restatement of the *prosecutor's* absolute duty to disclose materially exculpatory evidence to the defendant. The evidence at issue in *Youngblood* was only "potentially" exculpatory, however, so it fell outside the scope of the prosecutor's absolute duty under *Brady.* The Court therefore considered whether the *police* had violated a duty "over and above" that imposed on the prosecutor, by failing to preserve that evidence. And the Court held that, to establish such a violation, Youngblood had to prove that the police destroyed the evidence in "bad faith[.]" *Id.* at 58.

But that holding does not mean that the police violate a defendant's due-process rights when, in the *absence* of bad faith, they fail to preserve or disclose materially exculpatory evidence. To the contrary, as the *Youngblood* Court's reiteration of the *Brady* duty makes clear, the failure to provide such evidence to the defendant would merely amount to a violation of the *prosecutor's* absolute duty to disclose such evidence. Nor does the Supreme Court's holding in Trombetta impose on police officers an absolute duty to preserve or disclose materially exculpatory evidence. Instead, the Supreme Court "rejected [Trombetta's] argument for several reasons[,]" the "first" of which was that "'the officers here were *acting in good faith and in accord with their normal practice*[.]'" *Youngblood,* 488 U.S. at 56 (quoting *Trombetta,* 467 U.S. at 488) (emphasis added). That the Youngblood Court discussed the bad-faith standard in connection with potentially exculpatory evidence merely reflects the fact that, had the evidence there been materially exculpatory, there would have been no need to discuss police duties in the first place. Because in that event the prosecutor would have violated his duty under *Brady.*

2.

There remains the question whether Moldowan's claim against Ingles can proceed under *Youngblood*'s bad-faith standard. That claim is based upon Ingles' failure to convey to the prosecutor the substance of Burroughs' statement to Ingles. Two aspects of Burroughs' testimony, in my view, are critical. First, he testified that he had personally heard two men—neither of whom was Moldowan—discussing Fournier's rape while standing outside the house next to his house. That testimony, when viewed (as it must be) in the light most favorable to Moldowan, could be interpreted as meaning that the two men essentially admitted their involvement in the crime. Second, Burroughs testified that he told "my story" to Ingles. That reference, when viewed in that same light, could be understood to encompass *all* of Burroughs' story regarding the crime, including the two mens' admission on the sidewalk next door. Thus, when viewed in the light most favorable to Moldowan, and as a whole, Burroughs' testimony could be read to mean that he told Ingles that two other men had essentially admitted to committing the crime Ingles was investigating.

There is no direct evidence that Ingles withheld Burroughs' statement in bad faith. And I think courts should be wary of inferring bad faith from the mere fact of an officer's failure to disclose evidence, lest the bad-faith standard become in practice an absolute one. But I think that, under the circumstances present here, a jury could infer bad faith from Ingles' failure to disclose Burroughs' statement—whose existence, to be fair, Ingles disputes—to the prosecutor. Of course, a jury would be free *not* to make that inference, in part because they might choose to understand Burroughs' testimony in a light less favorable to Moldowan, or not to believe it at all. Given our standard of review, however, we are not so free. I therefore agree that Moldowan is entitled to proceed with his claim against Ingles.

3.

As that bottom-line agreement suggests, my disagreement with the majority may prove larger in theory than in practice. To establish an officer's conscious suppression of materially exculpatory evidence—and thus his bad faith—a plaintiff must prove, among other things, "the police's knowledge of the exculpatory value of the evidence at the time" the criminal defendant says it should have been disclosed. *Youngblood,* 488 U.S. at 56 n. *. And therein lies the common ground between my approach and that of the majority. Notwithstanding its rather extended defense of imposing an absolute duty of disclosure upon police officers, and its rejection of a bad-faith standard in this context, and its declaration that "'*Brady* creates a singular constitutional duty, which prosecutors and police officers are capable of breaching in factually different ways[,]'" the majority, to its credit, does not simply extend *Brady*'s absolute duty of disclosure to police officers. The majority instead recognizes a "practical concern that the police cannot be held accountable for failing to divine the materiality of every possible scrap of evidence." And the majority thus holds that a police officer does not breach his duty of disclosure unless the "'exculpatory value'" of the undisclosed evidence is "'apparent'" to him....

Thus, in the end, the majority extends *Brady*'s duty of absolute disclosure to police officers, but limits the scope of that duty to evidence whose materially exculpatory value was known to the particular officer sued. I think the better approach would be simply to apply the Supreme Court's bad-faith rule, rather than a modified version of an absolute rule designed for prosecutors. In practice, however, the latter rule will probably operate as the functional equivalent of the former....

Notes and Questions

1. If, pursuant to *Imbler v. Pachtman,* 424 U.S. 409 (1976), prosecutors enjoy absolute immunity from damages under 42 U.S.C. § 1983 for failing to disclose material exculpatory evidence to the defense, is the concurring opinion's prediction in *Moldowan* likely to be accurate that the police will become the target of lawsuits that essentially amount to "derivative" *Brady* violations?

2. If a witness (Jerry Burroughs) in fact told Detective Ingles that on the morning of August 9, 1990 he saw four African-American men standing over a nude, white female (presumably, Maureen Fournier), saw them drive away in a light-colored van, and later heard two of them bragging about assaulting her, would the detective's alleged failure to relay that information to the prosecutor more appropriately be characterized as the con-

cealment of evidence that was potentially useful to the defense (*Youngblood*), or as neglecting to deliver material exculpatory evidence (*Brady*)? If *Youngblood* requires that the potentially useful nature of evidence must be "apparent" for the police's failure to preserve it to be a constitutional violation, how significant is the disagreement between the majority opinion and the concurring opinion in *Moldowan* concerning whether *Brady* (which does not require a showing of "bad faith") or *Youngblood* (with its "bad faith" requirement) is the better basis for Detective Ingles's potential liability? If what is alleged in his complaint regarding Burroughs and Ingles is true, should Moldowan be entitled to recover damages against Detective Ingles under some theory of liability?

D. Post-Conviction Claims of Innocence: Preservation of and Access to Evidence

1. Is There a Post-Conviction Duty to Preserve Evidence?

Brady violations typically do not surface until after a defendant has been found guilty; indeed, a criticism leveled against the *Brady* rule is that it fails effectively to promote pre-trial discovery.[11] If evidence collected in anticipation of a trial is not preserved following a conviction, or if it is preserved but defense attorneys do not have access to it, a defendant's ability to substantiate a *Brady* claim, or even to appreciate the possible existence of one, may be lost or significantly compromised. Maintaining evidence after a conviction can be no less important in cases where the prosecution has fulfilled its *Brady* obligations. For example, many exonerations involve convictions secured before forensic DNA testing was developed or widely utilized, when the full potential value of biological evidence to bolster a defendant's claim of innocence was not appreciated. Such evidence cannot be tested following a conviction, of course, unless it was preserved. The Innocence Project has been stymied from securing evidence needed for DNA testing in roughly one-third of the potential wrongful conviction cases it has attempted to investigate because the evidence was lost or destroyed.[12]

What measures should be taken, by whom, in what kinds of cases, and for how long, to preserve and make available evidence collected in criminal cases for possible use in post-conviction proceedings that raise claims of innocence?

Lovitt v. Warden

585 S.E.2d 801 (Va. 2003)

Opinion by Justice Barbara Milano Keenan.

[Clayton Dicks was repeatedly stabbed in the chest and back while working in a pool hall in Arlington County, Virginia during the early morning hours of November 18, 1998. He died as a result of the wounds. Police responding to witnesses' 911 call found that the drawer from the pool hall's cash register was missing, as was a pair of scissors. The scissors were found, stained with blood, outside of the pool hall. Pieces of the cash register drawer were recovered two days later from Robin Lovitt's cousin, who later testified that Lovitt had brought the drawer to the cousin's home between 1:30 and 3:00 a.m. on November 18 and removed money from it. Lovitt was arrested four days later and charged with capital murder. A forensic scientist employed by the Virginia Department of

Forensic Science testified at Lovitt's trial that blood had been extracted from three areas of the jacket Lovitt was wearing at the time of his arrest, but that DNA tests were inconclusive and she could not confirm that the blood was human. The expert witness further testified that DNA extracted from the scissors found outside of the pool hall matched Clayton Dicks, the victim. After other evidence was presented at Lovitt's trial, including testimony from the witnesses who had made the 911 call and from a jailhouse informant who reported that Lovitt had confessed to the killing, Lovitt was convicted and sentenced to death. The Virginia Supreme Court affirmed the conviction and death sentence on appeal. *Lovitt v. Commonwealth,* 537 S.E.2d 866 (Va. 2000).]

In May 2001, about six months after we affirmed Lovitt's convictions, the circuit court entered an order authorizing destruction of the exhibits entered into evidence at Lovitt's trial. Pursuant to the destruction order, all exhibits received in evidence at trial, with the exception of one chart, were destroyed. On October 1, 2001, the United States Supreme Court denied Lovitt's petition for a writ of certiorari from this Court's judgment. *See Lovitt v. Virginia,* 534 U.S. 815 (2001).

[Lovitt subsequently filed a state petition for writ of habeas corpus alleging, among other claims, that the destruction of evidence prevented adequate post-conviction review in his case, violating his due process rights.]

Testimony at the habeas hearing revealed that in April 2001, Robert C. McCarthy, Chief Deputy Clerk of the Circuit Court of Arlington County, drafted an order authorizing the destruction of the exhibits received in evidence at Lovitt's trial. McCarthy, who was responsible for evidence stored in the clerk's office, testified that he thought he was authorized to destroy the trial exhibits after receiving a mandate from this Court indicating that Lovitt's convictions were affirmed. McCarthy also stated that he decided to destroy the trial exhibits to create additional space in the clerk's office evidence room.

McCarthy drafted the evidence destruction order without consulting anyone in the Commonwealth's Attorney's office, the Attorney General's office, or the Arlington County Police Department. McCarthy also did not notify any of the circuit court judges, Lovitt's trial counsel, or his habeas counsel of the impending evidence destruction.

McCarthy drafted the order before May 2, 2001, the date that Code §§ 19.2-270.4:1 and -327.1 became effective. Code § 19.2-270.4:1 provides, in relevant part:

> B. In the case of a person sentenced to death, the court that entered the judgment shall, in all cases, order any human biological evidence or representative samples to be transferred by the governmental entity having custody to the Division of Forensic Science. The Division of Forensic Science shall store, preserve, and retain such evidence until the judgment is executed....
>
> ....
>
> E. An action under this section or the performance of any attorney representing the petitioner under this section shall not form the basis for relief in any habeas corpus or appellate proceeding.

With regard to such human biological evidence, Code § 19.2-327.1 provides, in relevant part:

> A. Notwithstanding any other provision of law or rule of court, any person convicted of a felony may, by motion to the circuit court that entered the original conviction, apply for a new scientific investigation of any human biological evidence related to the case that resulted in the felony conviction....
>
> ....
>
> G. An action under this section or the performance of any attorney representing the petitioner under this section shall not form the basis for relief in any habeas corpus proceeding or any other appeal.

McCarthy took the destruction order prepared in Lovitt's case, along with between 15 and 20 other such orders, to the chambers of Judge Paul F. Sheridan. McCarthy left the orders in Judge Sheridan's chambers for entry without providing him any information concerning the relevant cases. Judge Sheridan, who did not conduct Lovitt's trial, entered the destruction orders on May 21, 2001, authorizing the destruction of all exhibits entered into evidence at Lovitt's trial. These exhibits, with the exception of the one chart, were destroyed a few days later.

Two deputy court clerks, Clifford P. Kleback and Gwendolyn Gilmore, testified that they spoke with McCarthy before he submitted the destruction orders to Judge Sheridan. Both deputy clerks told McCarthy, who was their immediate supervisor, that he should not destroy the evidence in Lovitt's case because it was a "capital case" and Lovitt had not been executed. Kleback, who was the clerk assigned to the courtroom during Lovitt's trial, stated that he told McCarthy that the case involved DNA evidence, and that he repeatedly advised McCarthy not to destroy the evidence.

Both Kleback and Gilmore testified that McCarthy told them that the evidence could be destroyed because Lovitt's appeal had ended. Kleback and Gilmore deferred to McCarthy's decision and, at that time, did not report these conversations to either the clerk of the circuit court or to anyone in the prosecutor's office.

McCarthy testified that he did not recall speaking with Kleback and Gilmore before the evidence in Lovitt's case was destroyed.... He further testified that at the time the destruction order was entered, he was not aware of any change in the law concerning the preservation of human biological evidence.

The circuit court found that there was no evidence that any official of the Commonwealth acted in bad faith or with the intent to destroy exculpatory evidence. The court stated in its findings that "McCarthy believed he had the authority to destroy the trial exhibits once he received the mandate" from this Court. The court also found that although Code § 19.2-270.4:1 became effective 20 days before entry of the destruction order, McCarthy was unaware of the statute's provisions when the evidence was destroyed....

Lovitt argues that McCarthy, an agent of the Commonwealth, procured the destruction of the trial exhibits in bad faith, and that the destruction of this evidence violated his right of due process by preventing meaningful review of his habeas corpus petition. Lovitt also observes that under Code §§ 19.2-270.4 and -270.4:1, trial evidence may not be destroyed until after all appellate remedies have been exhausted, and that DNA evidence in a death penalty case may not be destroyed until the final judgment is executed....

We first address Lovitt's due process claim. He asserts that he is entitled to habeas corpus relief because he has been deprived of an opportunity to seek new scientific testing of the DNA found on the bloody scissors and his jacket. Lovitt asserts that this testing is necessary for him to seek a writ of actual innocence under Code §§ 19.2-327.2 through -327.6. However, he ... acknowledges that the United States Supreme Court has not addressed the question whether due process rights may be asserted against the post-trial destruction of evidence.

In the absence of such authority, Lovitt relies on *Arizona v. Youngblood,* 488 U.S. 51 (1988), and *California v. Trombetta,* 467 U.S. 479 (1984), in which the Supreme Court considered due process claims involving the pre-trial destruction of evidence....

... [U]nder the *Youngblood* standard, a state's failure to preserve potentially useful evidence does not constitute a denial of due process unless a defendant can show bad faith on the part of the state. *Youngblood,* 488 U.S. at 58. The presence or absence of bad faith by the state depends on whether agents of the state had knowledge of the exculpatory value of the evidence when it was lost or destroyed. *Youngblood,* 488 U.S. at 56 n. * Thus, the possibility that evidence could have exculpated a defendant depending on future testing results is not enough to satisfy the constitutional standard of materiality.

In the present case, the circuit court concluded that "[t]here [was] no evidence that any official of the Commonwealth acted in bad faith." The court also found that "[t]here [was] no evidence to conclude that there was an intent by anyone in the Clerk's office to destroy exculpatory evidence." The court further found that while Robert McCarthy's judgment was erroneous, he "wanted to remove the box of exhibits from the evidence room to make additional space," and he "believed he had the authority to destroy the trial exhibits once he received the mandate indicating that Lovitt's appeal to the Virginia Supreme Court had been denied."

The circuit court's determination that there was an absence of bad faith was a finding of fact, not of law, because that finding rested on the knowledge of the Commonwealth's agents concerning the exculpatory value of the evidence at the time it was destroyed. Such factual findings made by the circuit court are entitled to deference and are binding in this proceeding unless they are plainly wrong or without evidence to support them.

The circuit court's findings concerning the absence of bad faith are supported by the evidence and are not plainly wrong. McCarthy's actions, and the failure of Kleback and Gilmore to report his intentions to another supervisor, do not establish that an agent of the Commonwealth had knowledge of any exculpatory value of the trial exhibits at the time they were destroyed. The mere fact that the exhibits included DNA evidence, and that Kleback may have related this information to McCarthy, does not establish that McCarthy was aware that an analysis of some of the DNA evidence had produced inconclusive results, or that such evidence may have been subject to further testing. Moreover, even if McCarthy had been aware of these considerations, such awareness would not have met the constitutional standard of materiality under *Youngblood,* because Lovitt can assert no more than the mere possibility that further testing could have exculpated him.

In addition, the circuit court found that at the time the evidence was destroyed, McCarthy was unaware that Code § 19.2-270.4:1, enacted 20 days before the destruction order was entered, mandated the storage of human biological evidence received in the case of a person sentenced to death. McCarthy's testimony adequately supports this finding.

The circuit court made an additional factual finding that no employees of either the Commonwealth's Attorney or the Attorney General knew about the destruction of evidence until after the destruction occurred.... Therefore, we hold that the record lacks any evidence that an agent of the Commonwealth acted in bad faith with regard to the destruction of the trial exhibits.

We turn now to consider Lovitt's claim that he is entitled to habeas corpus relief because the destruction of the trial exhibits violated Code §§ 19.2-270.4 and -270.4:1.Code § 19.2-270.4(A) provides, in relevant part:

> Except as provided in § 19.2-270.4:1 and unless objection with sufficient cause is made, the trial court in any criminal case may order the donation or destruction of any or all exhibits received in evidence during the course of the trial (i) at any time after the expiration of the time for filing an appeal from the final judgment of the court if no appeal is taken or (ii) if an appeal is taken, at any time after exhaustion of all appellate remedies.

In the case of a person sentenced to death, Code § 19.2-270.4:1(B) requires the Commonwealth to store, preserve, and retain any human biological evidence, or representative samples thereof, until the judgment is executed. This statute also provides that any noncompliance with the terms of the statute "shall not form the basis for relief in any habeas corpus or appellate proceeding." Code § 19.2-270.4:1(E).

In enacting Code §§ 19.2-270.4 and -270.4:1, the General Assembly provided for both the retention of trial evidence, including evidence containing DNA, and the ultimate disposal of such evidence when all appellate remedies have been exhausted and judgment has been executed. Such procedures protect the efficacy of the appellate process, as well as the need to preserve evidence for use in the event of a retrial or other proceeding allowed by law. However, in stating the procedural requirements relating to the retention of human biological evidence in Code § 19.2-270.4:1, the General Assembly also recognized that noncompliance with those procedures may occur and provided statutory language plainly excluding any such noncompliance as a basis for appellate or habeas corpus relief.

Based on this unambiguous statutory proscription, we find no merit in Lovitt's contention that the Commonwealth's failure to comply with either statute's provisions relating to human biological evidence presented at his trial entitles him to habeas corpus relief. Thus, we hold that Lovitt has failed to advance any valid basis for habeas corpus relief arising from the destruction of the trial exhibits in his case....

Notes and Questions

1. Following the state courts' disposition of his case, Lovitt's petition for a federal writ of habeas corpus was denied. *Lovitt v. True,* 330 F.Supp.2d 603 (E.D. Va. 2004), *aff'd,* 403 F.3d 171 (4th Cir.), *cert. den.,* 546 U.S. 929 (2005). In November 2009, Virginia Governor Mark Warner commuted Lovitt's death sentence to life imprisonment without parole. The governor agreed that "the courts have correctly ruled that the law requiring the maintenance of [biological] evidence does not provide relief for a defendant in Mr. Lovitt's

circumstances." However, he believed that clemency was appropriate because "an agent of the Commonwealth, in a manner contrary to the express direction of the law" caused the destruction of the evidence before Lovitt had "exhausted every post-trial remedy."[13] Under the circumstances, is clemency in the form of a reduction of Lovitt's death sentence to life imprisonment without parole an appropriate remedy?

2. Other courts have held or suggested that *Youngblood's* "bad faith" requirement applies to the post-conviction destruction of evidence. *See, e.g., Cress v. Palmer,* 484 F.3d 844, 853–854 (6th Cir. 2007); *Yarris v. County of Delaware,* 465 F.3d 129 (3d Cir. 2006); *Williams v. State,* 891 So.2d 621 (Fla. App. 2005); *People v. Barksdale,* 762 N.E.2d 669 (Ill. App. 2001). Some courts have concluded that *Youngblood* pertains only to the pre-trial destruction of evidence and does not apply to post-conviction proceedings. *See Tyler v. Purkett,* 413 F.3d 129 (8th Cir. 2005).

3. As discussed in *Lovitt,* in addition to raising constitutional challenges to the post-conviction destruction of evidence, defendants may assert a statutory basis for the preservation of evidence. The Virginia statute does not provide appellate or habeas corpus relief in the event of noncompliance. Va. Code § 19.2-270.4:1 (E). Although roughly half of the states have enacted preservation-of-evidence statutes that apply post-conviction, the rest are without legislation governing the retention of evidence after convictions have been finalized on appeal.[14]

2. Is There a Post-Conviction Right of Access to Evidence?

District Attorney's Office for the Third Judicial District v. Osborne

___ U.S. ___, 129 S.Ct. 2308, 174 L.Ed.2d 38 (2009)

Chief Justice ROBERTS delivered the opinion of the Court.

DNA testing has an unparalleled ability both to exonerate the wrongly convicted and to identify the guilty. It has the potential to significantly improve both the criminal justice system and police investigative practices. The Federal Government and the States have recognized this, and have developed special approaches to ensure that this evidentiary tool can be effectively incorporated into established criminal procedure—usually but not always through legislation.

Against this prompt and considered response, the respondent, William Osborne, proposes a different approach: the recognition of a free-standing and far-reaching constitutional right of access to this new type of evidence. The nature of what he seeks is confirmed by his decision to file this lawsuit in federal court under 42 U.S.C. § 1983, not within the state criminal justice system. This approach would take the development of rules and procedures in this area out of the hands of legislatures and state courts shaping policy in a focused manner and turn it over to federal courts applying the broad parameters of the Due Process Clause. There is no reason to constitutionalize the issue in this way. Because the decision below would do just that, we reverse.

I

A

This lawsuit arose out of a violent crime committed 16 years ago, which has resulted in a long string of litigation in the state and federal courts. On the evening of March 22, 1993, two men driving through Anchorage, Alaska, solicited sex from a female prostitute, K.G. She agreed to perform fellatio on both men for $100 and got in their car. The three spent some time looking for a place to stop and ended up in a deserted area near Earthquake Park. When K.G. demanded payment in advance, the two men pulled out a gun and forced her to perform fellatio on the driver while the passenger penetrated her vaginally, using a blue condom she had brought. The passenger then ordered K.G. out of the car and told her to lie face-down in the snow. Fearing for her life, she refused, and the two men choked her and beat her with the gun. When K.G. tried to flee, the passenger beat her with a wooden axe handle and shot her in the head while she lay on the ground. They kicked some snow on top of her and left her for dead.

K.G. did not die; the bullet had only grazed her head. Once the two men left, she found her way back to the road, and flagged down a passing car to take her home. Ultimately, she received medical care and spoke to the police. At the scene of the crime, the police recovered a spent shell casing, the axe handle, some of K.G.'s clothing stained with blood, and the blue condom.

Six days later, two military police officers at Fort Richardson pulled over Dexter Jackson for flashing his headlights at another vehicle. In his car they discovered a gun (which matched the shell casing), as well as several items K.G. had been carrying the night of the attack. The car also matched the description K.G. had given to the police. Jackson admitted that he had been the driver during the rape and assault, and told the police that William Osborne had been his passenger. Other evidence also implicated Osborne. K.G. picked out his photograph (with some uncertainty) and at trial she identified Osborne as her attacker. Other witnesses testified that shortly before the crime, Osborne had called Jackson from an arcade, and then driven off with him. An axe handle similar to the one at the scene of the crime was found in Osborne's room on the military base where he lived.

The State also performed DQ Alpha testing on sperm found in the blue condom. DQ Alpha testing is a relatively inexact form of DNA testing that can clear some wrongly accused individuals, but generally cannot narrow the perpetrator down to less than 5% of the population. The semen found on the condom had a genotype that matched a blood sample taken from Osborne, but not ones from Jackson, K. G., or a third suspect named James Hunter. Osborne is black, and approximately 16% of black individuals have such a genotype. In other words, the testing ruled out Jackson and Hunter as possible sources of the semen, and also ruled out over 80% of other black individuals. The State also examined some pubic hairs found at the scene of the crime, which were not susceptible to DQ Alpha testing, but which state witnesses attested to be similar to Osborne's.

B

Osborne and Jackson were convicted by an Alaska jury of kidnaping, assault, and sexual assault. They were acquitted of an additional count of sexual assault and of attempted murder. Finding it "'nearly miraculous'" that K.G. had survived, the trial judge sentenced Osborne to 26 years in prison, with 5 suspended. His conviction and sentence were affirmed on appeal.

Osborne then sought postconviction relief in Alaska state court. He claimed that he had asked his attorney, Sidney Billingslea, to seek more discriminating restriction-fragment-length-polymorphism (RFLP) DNA testing during trial, and argued that she was constitutionally ineffective for not doing so.[1] Billingslea testified that after investigation, she had concluded that further testing would do more harm than good. She planned to mount a defense of mistaken identity, and thought that the imprecision of the DQ Alpha test gave her "'very good numbers in a mistaken identity, cross-racial identification case, where the victim was in the dark and had bad eyesight.'" Because she believed Osborne was guilty, "'insisting on a more advanced ... DNA test would have served to prove that Osborne committed the alleged crimes.'" The Alaska Court of Appeals concluded that Billingslea's decision had been strategic and rejected Osborne's claim.

In this proceeding, Osborne also sought the DNA testing that Billingslea had failed to perform, relying on an Alaska postconviction statute, Alaska Stat. § 12.72 (2008), and the State and Federal Constitutions. In two decisions, the Alaska Court of Appeals concluded that Osborne had no right to the RFLP test. According to the court, § 12.72 "apparently" did not apply to DNA testing that had been available at trial. The court found no basis in our precedents for recognizing a federal constitutional right to DNA evidence. After a remand for further findings, the Alaska Court of Appeals concluded that Osborne could not claim a state constitutional right either, because the other evidence of his guilt was too strong and RFLP testing was not likely to be conclusive....

---

1. RFLP testing, unlike DQ Alpha testing, "has a high degree of discrimination," although it is sometimes ineffective on small samples. Billingslea testified that she had no memory of Osborne making such a request, but said she was "'willing to accept'" that he had.

The court relied heavily on the fact that Osborne had confessed to some of his crimes in a 2004 application for parole—in which it is a crime to lie. In this statement, Osborne acknowledged forcing K.G. to have sex at gunpoint, as well as beating her and covering her with snow. He repeated this confession before the parole board. Despite this acceptance of responsibility, the board did not grant him discretionary parole. In 2007, he was released on mandatory parole, but he has since been rearrested for another offense, and the State has petitioned to revoke this parole.

Meanwhile, Osborne had also been active in federal court, suing state officials under 42 U.S.C. § 1983. He claimed that the Due Process Clause and other constitutional provisions gave him a constitutional right to access the DNA evidence for what is known as short-tandem-repeat (STR) testing (at his own expense). This form of testing is more discriminating than the DQ Alpha or RFLP methods available at the time of Osborne's trial.[3] ...

... [T]he District Court concluded that "there *does* exist, *under the unique and specific facts presented,* a very limited constitutional right to the testing sought." 445 F.Supp.2d 1079, 1081 (2006). The court relied on several factors: that the testing Osborne sought had been unavailable at trial, that the testing could be accomplished at almost no cost to the State, and that the results were likely to be material. It therefore granted summary judgment in favor of Osborne.

The Court of Appeals affirmed, relying on the prosecutorial duty to disclose exculpatory evidence recognized in *Pennsylvania v. Ritchie,* 480 U.S. 39 (1987), and *Brady v. Maryland,* 373 U.S. 83 (1963). While acknowledging that our precedents "involved only the right to *pre-trial* disclosure," the court concluded that the Due Process Clause also "extends the government's duty to disclose (or the defendant's right of access) to *post-conviction* proceedings." Although Osborne's trial and appeals were over, the court noted that he had a "potentially viable" state constitutional claim of "actual innocence," and relied on the "well-established assumption" that a similar claim arose under the Federal Constitution; cf. *Herrera v. Collins,* 506 U.S. 390 (1993). The court held that these potential claims extended some of the State's *Brady* obligations to the postconviction context.

... While acknowledging that Osborne's prior confessions were "certainly relevant," the court concluded that they did not "necessarily trum[p] ... the right to obtain post-conviction access to evidence" in light of the "emerging reality of wrongful convictions based on false confessions."

We granted certiorari to decide whether Osborne's claims could be pursued using § 1983, and whether he has a right under the Due Process Clause to obtain postconviction access to the State's evidence for DNA testing. We now reverse on the latter ground.

II

Modern DNA testing can provide powerful new evidence unlike anything known before. Since its first use in criminal investigations in the mid-1980s, there have been several major advances in DNA technology, culminating in STR technology. It is now often possible to determine whether a biological tissue matches a suspect with near certainty. While of course many criminal trials proceed without any forensic and scientific testing at all, there is no technology comparable to DNA testing for matching tissues when such evidence is at issue. DNA testing has exonerated wrongly convicted people, and has confirmed the convictions of many others.

At the same time, DNA testing alone does not always resolve a case. Where there is enough other incriminating evidence and an explanation for the DNA result, science alone cannot prove a prisoner innocent. See *House v. Bell,* 547 U.S. 518 (2006). The availability of technologies not available at trial cannot mean that every criminal conviction, or even every criminal conviction involving biological evidence, is suddenly in doubt. The dilemma is how to harness DNA's power to prove innocence without unnecessarily overthrowing the established system of criminal justice.

That task belongs primarily to the legislature. "[T]he States are currently engaged in serious, thoughtful examinations," *Washington v. Glucks-*

3. STR testing is extremely discriminating, can be used on small samples, and is "rapidly becoming the standard." Osborne also sought to subject the pubic hairs to mitochondrial DNA testing, a secondary testing method often used when a sample cannot be subjected to other tests. He argues that "[a]ll of the same arguments that support access to the condom for STR testing support access to the hairs for mitochondrial testing as well," and we treat the claim accordingly.

berg, 521 U.S. 702, 719 (1997), of how to ensure the fair and effective use of this testing within the existing criminal justice framework. Forty-six States have already enacted statutes dealing specifically with access to DNA evidence. The State of Alaska itself is considering joining them. The Federal Government has also passed the Innocence Protection Act of 2004, §411, 118 Stat. 2278, codified in part at 18 U.S.C. §3600, which allows federal prisoners to move for court-ordered DNA testing under certain specified conditions. That Act also grants money to States that enact comparable statutes, and as a consequence has served as a model for some state legislation. At oral argument, Osborne agreed that the federal statute is a model for how States ought to handle the issue.

These laws recognize the value of DNA evidence but also the need for certain conditions on access to the State's evidence. A requirement of demonstrating materiality is common, *e.g.*, 18 U.S.C. §3600(a)(8), but it is not the only one. The federal statute, for example, requires a sworn statement that the applicant is innocent. §3600(a)(1). This requirement is replicated in several state statutes. States also impose a range of diligence requirements. Several require the requested testing to "have been technologically impossible at trial." Others deny testing to those who declined testing at trial for tactical reasons.

Alaska is one of a handful of States yet to enact legislation specifically addressing the issue of evidence requested for DNA testing. But that does not mean that such evidence is unavailable for those seeking to prove their innocence. Instead, Alaska courts are addressing how to apply existing laws for discovery and postconviction relief to this novel technology. The same is true with respect to other States that do not have DNA-specific statutes.

First, access to evidence is available under Alaska law for those who seek to subject it to newly available DNA testing that will prove them to be actually innocent. Under the State's general postconviction relief statute, a prisoner may challenge his conviction when "there exists evidence of material facts, not previously presented and heard by the court, that requires vacation of the conviction or sentence in the interest of justice." Alaska Stat. §12.72.010(4) (2008). Such a claim is exempt from otherwise applicable time limits if "newly discovered evidence," pursued with due diligence, "establishes by clear and convincing evidence that the applicant is innocent." §12.72.020(b)(2).

Both parties agree that under these provisions of §12.72, "a defendant is entitled to post-conviction relief if the defendant presents newly discovered evidence that establishes by clear and convincing evidence that the defendant is innocent." If such a claim is brought, state law permits general discovery. Alaska courts have explained that these procedures are available to request DNA evidence for newly available testing to establish actual innocence.

In addition to this statutory procedure, the Alaska Court of Appeals has invoked a widely accepted three-part test to govern additional rights to DNA access under the State Constitution. Drawing on the experience with DNA evidence of State Supreme Courts around the country, the Court of Appeals explained that it was "reluctant to hold that Alaska law offers no remedy to defendants who could prove their factual innocence." *Osborne I,* 110 P.3d, at 995. It was "prepared to hold, however, that a defendant who seeks post-conviction DNA testing ... must show (1) that the conviction rested primarily on eyewitness identification evidence, (2) that there was a demonstrable doubt concerning the defendant's identification as the perpetrator, and (3) that scientific testing would likely be conclusive on this issue." Thus, the Alaska courts have suggested that even those who do not get discovery under the State's criminal rules have available to them a safety valve under the State Constitution.

This is the background against which the Federal Court of Appeals ordered the State to turn over the DNA evidence in its possession, and it is our starting point in analyzing Osborne's constitutional claims.

III

The parties dispute whether Osborne has invoked the proper federal statute in bringing his claim. He sued under the federal civil rights statute, 42 U.S.C. §1983, which gives a cause of action to those who challenge a State's "deprivation of any rights ... secured by the Constitution." The State insists that Osborne's claim must be brought under 28 U.S.C. §2254, which allows a prisoner to seek "a writ of habeas corpus ... on the ground that he is in custody in violation of the Constitution." ...

While we granted certiorari on this question, our resolution of Osborne's claims does not require us to resolve this difficult issue.

Accordingly, we will assume without deciding that the Court of Appeals was correct that ... Osborne's § 1983 claim [is not barred]. Even under this assumption, it was wrong to find a due process violation.

IV

A

"No State shall ... deprive any person of life, liberty, or property, without due process of law." U.S. Const., Amdt. 14, § 1; accord Amdt. 5. This Clause imposes procedural limitations on a State's power to take away protected entitlements. Osborne argues that access to the State's evidence is a "process" needed to vindicate his right to prove himself innocent and get out of jail. Process is not an end in itself, so a necessary premise of this argument is that he has an entitlement (what our precedents call a "liberty interest") to prove his innocence even after a fair trial has proved otherwise. We must first examine this asserted liberty interest to determine what process (if any) is due....

Osborne does ... have a liberty interest in demonstrating his innocence with new evidence under state law. As explained, Alaska law provides that those who use "newly discovered evidence" to "establis[h] by clear and convincing evidence that [they are] innocent" may obtain "vacation of [their] conviction or sentence in the interest of justice." Alaska Stat. §§ 12.72.020(b)(2), 12.72.010(4). This "state-created right can, in some circumstances, beget yet other rights to procedures essential to the realization of the parent right."

The Court of Appeals went too far, however, in concluding that the Due Process Clause requires that certain familiar preconviction trial rights be extended to protect Osborne's postconviction liberty interest. After identifying Osborne's possible liberty interests, the court concluded that the State had an obligation to comply with the principles of *Brady v. Maryland,* 373 U.S. 83. In that case, we held that due process requires a prosecutor to disclose material exculpatory evidence to the defendant before trial. The Court of Appeals acknowledged that nothing in our precedents suggested that this disclosure obligation continued after the defendant was convicted and the case was closed, but it relied on prior Ninth Circuit precedent applying "*Brady* as a post-conviction right." Osborne does not claim that *Brady* controls this case, and with good reason.

A criminal defendant proved guilty after a fair trial does not have the same liberty interests as a free man. At trial, the defendant is presumed innocent and may demand that the government prove its case beyond reasonable doubt. But "[o]nce a defendant has been afforded a fair trial and convicted of the offense for which he was charged, the presumption of innocence disappears." *Herrera v. Collins,* 506 U.S. 390, 399 (1993). "Given a valid conviction, the criminal defendant has been constitutionally deprived of his liberty."

The State accordingly has more flexibility in deciding what procedures are needed in the context of postconviction relief. "[W]hen a State chooses to offer help to those seeking relief from convictions," due process does not "dictat[e] the exact form such assistance must assume." *Pennsylvania v. Finley,* 481 U.S. 551, 559 (1987). Osborne's right to due process is not parallel to a trial right, but rather must be analyzed in light of the fact that he has already been found guilty at a fair trial, and has only a limited interest in postconviction relief. *Brady* is the wrong framework.

Instead, the question is whether consideration of Osborne's claim within the framework of the State's procedures for postconviction relief "offends some principle of justice so rooted in the traditions and conscience of our people as to be ranked as fundamental," or "transgresses any recognized principle of fundamental fairness in operation." *Medina v. California,* 505 U.S. 437, 446, 448 (1992). Federal courts may upset a State's postconviction relief procedures only if they are fundamentally inadequate to vindicate the substantive rights provided.

We see nothing inadequate about the procedures Alaska has provided to vindicate its state right to postconviction relief in general, and nothing inadequate about how those procedures apply to those who seek access to DNA evidence. Alaska provides a substantive right to be released on a sufficiently compelling showing of new evidence that establishes innocence. It exempts such claims from otherwise applicable time limits. The State provides for discovery in postconviction proceedings, and has—through judicial decision—specified that this discovery procedure is available to those seeking access to DNA evidence. These procedures are not without limits. The evidence must indeed be newly available to qualify under Alaska's statute, must have been diligently pursued, and must also be sufficiently material. These procedures are similar to those provided for DNA evidence by federal law and the law of other States, and they are not inconsistent with the "traditions and conscience of our people" or with "any recognized principle of fundamental fairness."

And there is more. While the Alaska courts have not had occasion to conclusively decide the question, the Alaska Court of Appeals has suggested that the State Constitution provides an additional right of access to DNA. In expressing its "reluctan[ce] to hold that Alaska law offers no remedy" to those who belatedly seek DNA testing, and in invoking the three-part test used by other state courts, the court indicated that in an appropriate case the State Constitution may provide a failsafe even for those who cannot satisfy the statutory requirements under general postconviction procedures.

To the degree there is some uncertainty in the details of Alaska's newly developing procedures for obtaining postconviction access to DNA, we can hardly fault the State for that. Osborne has brought this § 1983 action without ever using these procedures in filing a state or federal habeas claim relying on actual innocence. In other words, he has not tried to use the process provided to him by the State or attempted to vindicate the liberty interest that is now the centerpiece of his claim. When Osborne *did* request DNA testing in state court, he sought RFLP testing that had been available at trial, not the STR testing he now seeks, and the state court relied on that fact in denying him testing under Alaska law.

His attempt to sidestep state process through a new federal lawsuit puts Osborne in a very awkward position. If he simply seeks the DNA through the State's discovery procedures, he might well get it. If he does not, it may be for a perfectly adequate reason, just as the federal statute and all state statutes impose conditions and limits on access to DNA evidence. It is difficult to criticize the State's procedures when Osborne has not invoked them.... These procedures are adequate on their face, and without trying them, Osborne can hardly complain that they do not work in practice.

As a fallback, Osborne also obliquely relies on an asserted federal constitutional right to be released upon proof of "actual innocence." Whether such a federal right exists is an open question. We have struggled with it over the years, in some cases assuming, *arguendo,* that it exists while also noting the difficult questions such a right would pose and the high standard any claimant would have to meet. *House,* 547 U.S., at 554–555; *Herrera,* 506 U.S., at 398–417. In this case too we can assume without deciding that such a claim exists, because even if so there is no due process problem. Osborne does not dispute that a federal actual innocence claim (as opposed to a DNA access claim) would be brought in habeas. If such a habeas claim is viable, federal procedural rules permit discovery "for good cause." 28 U.S.C. § 2254 Rule 6. Just as with state law, Osborne cannot show that available discovery is facially inadequate, and cannot show that it would be arbitrarily denied to him.

B

The Court of Appeals below relied only on procedural due process, but Osborne seeks to defend the judgment on the basis of substantive due process as well. He asks that we recognize a freestanding right to DNA evidence untethered from the liberty interests he hopes to vindicate with it. We reject the invitation and conclude, in the circumstances of this case, that there is no such substantive due process right.... Osborne seeks access to state evidence so that he can apply new DNA-testing technology that might prove him innocent. There is no long history of such a right, and "[t]he mere novelty of such a claim is reason enough to doubt that 'substantive due process' sustains it." *Reno v. Flores,* 507 U.S. 292, 303 (1993).

And there are further reasons to doubt. The elected governments of the States are actively confronting the challenges DNA technology poses to our criminal justice systems and our traditional notions of finality, as well as the opportunities it affords. To suddenly constitutionalize this area would short-circuit what looks to be a prompt and considered legislative response. The first DNA testing statutes were passed in 1994 and 1997. Act of Aug. 2, 1994, ch. 737, 1994 N.Y. Laws 3709 (codified at N.Y.Crim. Proc. Law Ann. § 440.30(1-a) (West)); Act of May 9, 1997, Pub. Act No. 90-141, 1997 Ill. Laws 2461 (codified at 725 Ill. Comp. Stat., ch. 725, § 5/116-3(a) (West)). In the past decade, 44 States and the Federal Government have followed suit, reflecting the increased availability of DNA testing. As noted, Alaska itself is considering such legislation. "By extending constitutional protection to an asserted right or liberty interest, we, to a great extent, place the matter outside the arena of public debate and legislative action. We must therefore exercise the utmost care whenever we are asked to break new ground in this field." *Glucksberg,* 521 U.S., at 720. If we extended substantive due process to this area, we would cast these statutes into constitutional doubt and be forced to take over the issue of DNA access ourselves. We are reluctant to enlist the Federal Judiciary in creating a new constitutional code of rules for handling DNA.

Establishing a freestanding right to access DNA evidence for testing would force us to act as policymakers, and our substantive-due-process rulemaking authority would not only have to cover the right of access but a myriad of other issues. We would soon have to decide if there is a constitutional obligation to preserve forensic evidence that might later be tested. Cf. *Arizona v. Youngblood,* 488 U.S. 51 (1988). If so, for how long? Would it be different for different types of evidence? Would the State also have some obligation to gather such evidence in the first place? How much, and when? No doubt there would be a miscellany of other minor directives.

In this case, the evidence has already been gathered and preserved, but if we extend substantive due process to this area, these questions would be before us in short order, and it is hard to imagine what tools federal courts would use to answer them. At the end of the day, there is no reason to suppose that their answers to these questions would be any better than those of state courts and legislatures, and good reason to suspect the opposite.

* * *

DNA evidence will undoubtedly lead to changes in the criminal justice system. It has done so already. The question is whether further change will primarily be made by legislative revision and judicial interpretation of the existing system, or whether the Federal Judiciary must leap ahead—revising (or even discarding) the system by creating a new constitutional right and taking over responsibility for refining it.

Federal courts should not presume that state criminal procedures will be inadequate to deal with technological change. The criminal justice system has historically accommodated new types of evidence, and is a time-tested means of carrying out society's interest in convicting the guilty while respecting individual rights. That system, like any human endeavor, cannot be perfect. DNA evidence shows that it has not been. But there is no basis for Osborne's approach of assuming that because DNA has shown that these procedures are not flawless, DNA evidence must be treated as categorically outside the process, rather than within it. That is precisely what his § 1983 suit seeks to do, and that is the contention we reject.

The judgment of the Court of Appeals is reversed, and the case is remanded for further proceedings consistent with this opinion....

Justice ALITO, with whom Justice KENNEDY joins, and with whom Justice THOMAS joins as to Part II, concurring....

The principles of federalism, comity, and finality are not the only ones at stake for the State in cases like this one. To the contrary, DNA evidence creates special opportunities, risks, and burdens that implicate important state interests. Given those interests—and especially in light of the rapidly evolving nature of DNA testing technology—this is an area that should be (and is being) explored "through the workings of normal democratic processes in the laboratories of the States."[2]

A

As the Court notes, DNA testing often produces highly reliable results. Indeed, short tandem repeat (STR) "DNA tests can, in certain circumstances, establish to a virtual certainty whether a given individual did or did not commit a particular crime." Because of that potential for "virtual certainty," Justice STEVENS argues that the State should welcome respondent's offer to perform modern DNA testing (at his own expense) on the State's DNA evidence; the test will either confirm respondent's guilt (in which case the State has lost nothing) or exonerate him (in which case the State has no valid interest in detaining him).

2. Forty-six States, plus the District of Columbia and the Federal Government, have recently enacted DNA testing statutes.... The pace of the legislative response has been so fast that two States have enacted statutes while this case was *sub judice:* The Governor of South Dakota signed a DNA access law on March 11, 2009, and the Governor of Mississippi signed a DNA access law on March 16, 2009. The only States that do not have DNA-testing statutes are Alabama, Alaska, Massachusetts, and Oklahoma; and at least three of those States have addressed the issue through judicial decisions. Because the Court relies on such evidence, Justice STEVENS accuses it of "resembl[ing]" Justice Harlan's position in *Miranda v. Arizona,* 384 U.S. 436 (1966). I can think of worse things than sharing Justice Harlan's judgment that "this Court's too rapid departure from existing constitutional standards" may "frustrat[e]" the States "long-range and lasting" legislative efforts. *Id.,* at 524.

Alas, it is far from that simple. First, DNA testing—even when performed with modern STR technology, and even when performed in perfect accordance with protocols—often fails to provide "absolute proof" of anything. As one scholar has observed:

"[F]orensic DNA testing rarely occurs [under] idyllic conditions. Crime scene DNA samples do not come from a single source obtained in immaculate conditions; they are messy assortments of multiple unknown persons, often collected in the most difficult conditions. The samples can be of poor quality due to exposure to heat, light, moisture, or other degrading elements. They can be of minimal or insufficient quantity, especially as investigators push DNA testing to its limits and seek profiles from a few cells retrieved from cigarette butts, envelopes, or soda cans. And most importantly, forensic samples often constitute a mixture of multiple persons, such that it is not clear whose profile is whose, or even how many profiles are in the sample at all. All of these factors make DNA testing in the forensic context far more subjective than simply reporting test results...." Murphy, The Art in the Science of DNA: A Layperson's Guide to the Subjectivity Inherent in Forensic DNA Typing, 58 Emory L.J. 489, 497 (2008) (footnotes omitted).

See also R. Michaelis, R. Flanders, & P. Wulff, A Litigator's Guide to DNA 341 (2008) (hereinafter Michaelis) (noting that even "STR analyses are plagued by issues of suboptimal samples, equipment malfunctions and human error, just as any other type of forensic DNA test"). Such concerns apply with particular force where, as here, the sample is minuscule, it may contain three or more persons' DNA, and it may have degraded significantly during the 24 or more hours it took police to recover it.

Second, the State has important interests in maintaining the integrity of its evidence, and the risks associated with evidence contamination increase every time someone attempts to extract new DNA from a sample. According to Professor John Butler—who is said to have written "the canonical text on forensic DNA typing," Murphy, *supra*, at 493, n. 16—"[t]he extraction process is probably where the DNA sample is more susceptible to contamination in the laboratory than at any other time in the forensic DNA analysis process," J. Butler, Forensic DNA Typing 42 (2d ed. 2005).

Indeed, modern DNA testing technology is so powerful that it actually increases the risks associated with mishandling evidence. STR tests, for example, are so sensitive that they can detect DNA transferred from person X to a towel (with which he wipes his face), from the towel to Y (who subsequently wipes his face), and from Y's face to a murder weapon later wielded by Z (who can use STR technology to blame X for the murder). Any test that is sensitive enough to pick up such trace amounts of DNA will be able to detect even the slightest, unintentional mishandling of evidence. See Michaelis 63 (cautioning against mishandling evidence because "two research groups have already demonstrated the ability to obtain STR profiles from fingerprints on paper or evidence objects"). And that is to say nothing of the intentional DNA-evidence-tampering scandals that have surfaced in recent years. It gives short shrift to such risks to suggest that anyone—including respondent, who has twice confessed to his crime, has never recanted, and passed up the opportunity for DNA testing at trial—should be given a never-before-recognized constitutional right to rummage through the State's genetic-evidence locker.

Third, even if every test was guaranteed to provide a conclusive answer, and even if no one ever contaminated a DNA sample, that still would not justify disregarding the other costs associated with the DNA-access regime proposed by respondent. As the Court notes, recognizing a prisoner's freestanding right to access the State's DNA evidence would raise numerous policy questions, not the least of which is whether and to what extent the State is constitutionally obligated to collect and preserve such evidence. But the policy problems do not end there.

Even without our creation and imposition of a mandatory-DNA-access regime, state crime labs are already responsible for maintaining and controlling hundreds of thousands of new DNA samples every year. For example, in the year 2005, the State of North Carolina processed DNA samples in approximately 1,900 cases, while the State of Virginia processed twice as many. Each case often entails many separate DNA samples. And these data—which are now four years out of date—dramatically underestimate the States' current DNA-related caseloads, which expand at an average annual rate of around 24%.

The resources required to process and analyze these hundreds of thousands of samples have created severe backlogs in state crime labs across the country. For example, the State of Wisconsin reports that it receives roughly 17,600 DNA samples per year, but its labs can process only 9,600. Similarly, the State of North Carolina reports that "[i]t is not unusual for the [State] Crime Lab to have several thousand samples waiting to be outsourced due to the federal procedures for [the State's] grant. This is not unique to North Carolina but a national issue." ...

The procedures that the state labs use to handle these hundreds of thousands of DNA samples provide fertile ground for litigation. For example, in *Commonwealth v. Duarte,* 56 Mass.App. 714, 723, 780 N.E.2d 99, 106 (2002), the defendant argued that "the use of a thermometer that may have been overdue for a standardization check rendered the DNA analysis unreliable and inadmissible" in his trial for raping a 13-year-old girl. The court rejected that argument and held "that the status of the thermometer went to the weight of the evidence, and not to its admissibility," and the court ultimately upheld Duarte's conviction after reviewing the testimony of the deputy director of the laboratory that the Commonwealth used for the DNA tests, see *ibid.* But the case nevertheless illustrates "that no detail of laboratory operation, no matter how minute, is exempt as a potential point on which a defense attorney will question the DNA evidence." Michaelis 68.

My point in recounting the burdens that postconviction DNA testing imposes on the Federal Government and the States is not to denigrate the importance of such testing. Instead, my point is that requests for postconviction DNA testing are not cost free. The Federal Government and the States have a substantial interest in the implementation of rules that regulate such testing in a way that harnesses the unique power of DNA testing while also respecting the important governmental interests noted above. The Federal Government and the States have moved expeditiously to enact rules that attempt to perform this role. And as the Court holds, it would be most unwise for this Court, wielding the blunt instrument of due process, to interfere prematurely with these efforts.

B

I see no reason for such intervention in the present case. When a criminal defendant, for tactical purposes, passes up the opportunity for DNA testing at trial, that defendant, in my judgment, has no constitutional right to demand to perform DNA testing after conviction. Recognition of such a right would allow defendants to play games with the criminal justice system. A guilty defendant could forgo DNA testing at trial for fear that the results would confirm his guilt, and in the hope that the other evidence would be insufficient to persuade the jury to find him guilty. Then, after conviction, with nothing to lose, the defendant could demand DNA testing in the hope that some happy accident—for example, degradation or contamination of the evidence—would provide the basis for seeking postconviction relief. Denying the opportunity for such an attempt to game the criminal justice system should not shock the conscience of the Court.

There is ample evidence in this case that respondent attempted to game the system. At trial, respondent's lawyer made an explicit, tactical decision to forgo restriction-fragment-length-polymorphism (RFLP) testing in favor of less-reliable DQ Alpha testing. Having forgone more accurate DNA testing once before, respondent's reasons for seeking it now are suspect. It is true that the STR testing respondent now seeks is even more advanced than the RFLP testing he declined—but his counsel did not decline RFLP testing because she thought it was not good enough; she declined because she thought it was too good....

If a state prisoner wants to challenge the State's refusal to permit postconviction DNA testing, the prisoner should proceed under the habeas statute, which duly accounts for the interests of federalism, comity, and finality. And in considering the merits of such a claim, the State's weighty interests cannot be summarily dismissed as "'arbitrary, or conscience shocking.'" *Post,* (STEVENS, J., dissenting). With these observations, I join the opinion of the Court.

Justice STEVENS, with whom Justice GINSBURG and Justice BREYER join, and with whom Justice SOUTER joins as to Part I, dissenting.

The State of Alaska possesses physical evidence that, if tested, will conclusively establish whether respondent William Osborne committed rape and attempted murder. If he did, justice has been served by his conviction and sentence. If not, Osborne has needlessly spent decades behind bars while the true culprit has not been brought to justice. The DNA test Osborne seeks is a simple one, its cost modest, and its results uniquely precise. Yet for reasons the State has been unable or unwilling to articulate, it refuses to allow Osborne to test the evidence at his own expense and to thereby ascertain the truth once and for all....

Because I am convinced that Osborne has a constitutional right of access to the evidence he wishes to test and that, on the facts of this case, he has made a sufficient showing of entitlement to that evidence, I would affirm the decision of the Court of Appeals.

I

The Fourteenth Amendment provides that "[n]o State shall ... deprive any person of life, liberty, or property, without due process of law." § 1. Our cases have frequently recognized that protected liberty interests may arise "from the Constitution itself, by reason of guarantees implicit in the word 'liberty,'... or it may arise from an expectation or interest created by state laws or policies." Osborne contends that he possesses a right to access DNA evidence arising from both these sources.

Osborne first anchors his due process right in Alaska Stat. § 12.72.010(4) (2008). Under that provision, a person who has been "convicted of, or sentenced for, a crime may institute a proceeding for post-conviction relief if the person claims ... that there exists evidence of material facts, not previously presented and heard by the court, that requires vacation of the conviction or sentence in the interest of justice." *Ibid.*[2] Osborne asserts that exculpatory DNA test results obtained using state-of-the-art Short Tandem Repeat (STR) and Mitochondrial (mtDNA) analysis would qualify as newly discovered evidence entitling him to relief under the state statute. The problem is that the newly discovered evidence he wishes to present cannot be generated unless he is first able to access the State's evidence—something he cannot do without the State's consent or a court order.

Although States are under no obligation to provide mechanisms for postconviction relief, when they choose to do so, the procedures they employ must comport with the demands of the Due Process Clause, by providing litigants with fair opportunity to assert their state-created rights. Osborne contends that by denying him an opportunity to access the physical evidence, the State has denied him meaningful access to state postconviction relief, thereby violating his right to due process.

Although the majority readily agrees that Osborne has a protected liberty interest in demonstrating his innocence with new evidence under Alaska Stat. § 12.72.010(4), it rejects the Ninth Circuit's conclusion that Osborne is constitutionally entitled to access the State's evidence. The Court concludes that the adequacy of the process afforded to Osborne must be assessed under the standard set forth in *Medina v. California,* 505 U.S. 437 (1992). Under that standard, Alaska's procedures for bringing a claim under § 12.72.010(4) will not be found to violate due process unless they "'offen[d] some principle of justice so rooted in the traditions and conscience of our people as to be ranked as fundamental,' or 'transgres[s] any recognized principle of fundamental fairness in operation.'"[3] After conducting a cursory review of the relevant statutory text, the Court concludes that Alaska's procedures are constitutional on their face.

While I agree that the statute is not facially deficient, the state courts' application of § 12.72.010(4) raises serious questions whether the State's procedures are fundamentally unfair in their operation. As an initial matter, it is not clear that Alaskan courts ordinarily permit litigants to utilize the state postconviction statute to obtain new evidence in the form of DNA tests....

Of even greater concern is the manner in which the state courts applied § 12.72.010(4) to the facts of this case. In determining that Osborne was not entitled to relief under the postconviction statute, the Alaska Court of Appeals concluded that the DNA testing Osborne wished to obtain could not qualify as "newly discovered" because it was available at the time of trial. In his arguments before the state trial court and his briefs

---

2. Ordinarily, claims under § 12.72.010(4) must be brought within one year after the conviction becomes final. § 12.72.020(a)(3)(A). However, the court may hear an otherwise untimely claim based on newly discovered evidence "if the applicant establishes due diligence in presenting the claim and sets out facts supported by evidence that is admissible and (A) was not known within ... two years after entry of the judgment of conviction if the claim relates to a conviction; ... (B) is not cumulative to the evidence presented at trial; (C) is not impeachment evidence; and (D) establishes by clear and convincing evidence that the applicant is innocent." § 12.72.020(b)(2) (2002).

3. Osborne contends that the Court should assess the validity of the State's procedures under the test set forth in *Mathews v. Eldridge,* 424 U.S. 319 (1976), rather than the more exacting test adopted by *Medina v. California,* 505 U.S. 437 (1992). In my view, we need not decide which standard governs because the state court's denial of access to the evidence Osborne seeks violates due process under either standard.

to the Alaska Court of Appeals, however, Osborne had plainly requested STR DNA testing, a form of DNA testing not yet in use at the time of his trial. The state appellate court's conclusion that the requested testing had been available at the time of trial was therefore clearly erroneous. Given these facts, the majority's assertion that Osborne "attempt[ed] to sidestep state process" by failing "to use the process provided to him by the State" is unwarranted....

Osborne made full use of available state procedures in his efforts to secure access to evidence for DNA testing so that he might avail himself of the postconviction relief afforded by the State of Alaska. He was rebuffed at every turn. The manner in which the Alaska courts applied state law in this case leaves me in grave doubt about the adequacy of the procedural protections afforded to litigants under Alaska Stat. § 12.72.010(4), and provides strong reason to doubt the majority's flippant assertion that if Osborne were "simply [to] see[k] the DNA through the State's discovery procedures, he might well get it." However, even if the Court were correct in its assumption that Osborne might be given the evidence he seeks were he to present his claim in state court a second time, there should be no need for him to do so.

II

Wholly apart from his state-created interest in obtaining postconviction relief under Alaska Stat. § 12.72.010(4), Osborne asserts a right to access the State's evidence that derives from the Due Process Clause itself. Whether framed as a "substantive liberty interest ... protected through a procedural due process right" to have evidence made available for testing, or as a substantive due process right to be free of arbitrary government action, the result is the same: On the record now before us, Osborne has established his entitlement to test the State's evidence.

The liberty protected by the Due Process Clause is not a creation of the Bill of Rights. Indeed, our Nation has long recognized that the liberty safeguarded by the Constitution has far deeper roots.... The "most elemental" of the liberties protected by the Due Process Clause is "the interest in being free from physical detention by one's own government."

... It is ... far too late in the day to question the basic proposition that convicted persons such as Osborne retain a constitutionally protected measure of interest in liberty, including the fundamental liberty of freedom from physical restraint.

Recognition of this right draws strength from the fact that 46 States and the Federal Government have passed statutes providing access to evidence for DNA testing, and 3 additional states (including Alaska) provide similar access through court-made rules alone. These legislative developments are consistent with recent trends in legal ethics recognizing that prosecutors are obliged to disclose all forms of exculpatory evidence that come into their possession following conviction. See, *e.g.*,ABA Model Rules of Professional Conduct 3.8(g)–(h) (2008); see also *Imbler v. Pachtman,* 424 U.S. 409, 427, n. 25 (1976) ("[A]fter a conviction the prosecutor also is bound by the ethics of his office to inform the appropriate authority of after-acquired or other information that casts doubt upon the correctness of the conviction"). The fact that nearly all the States have now recognized some postconviction right to DNA evidence makes it more, not less, appropriate to recognize a limited federal right to such evidence in cases where litigants are unfairly barred from obtaining relief in state court.

Insofar as it is process Osborne seeks, he is surely entitled to less than "the full panoply of rights," that would be due a criminal defendant prior to conviction. That does not mean, however, that our pretrial due process cases have no relevance in the postconviction context. In *Brady v. Maryland,* 373 U.S. 83 (1963), we held that the State violates due process when it suppresses "evidence favorable to an accused" that is "material either to guilt or to punishment, irrespective of the good faith or bad faith of the prosecution." Although *Brady* does not directly provide for a postconviction right to such evidence, the concerns with fundamental fairness that motivated our decision in that case are equally present when convicted persons such as Osborne seek access to dispositive DNA evidence following conviction.

Recent scientific advances in DNA analysis have made "it literally possible to confirm guilt or innocence beyond any question whatsoever, at least in some categories of cases." As the Court recognizes today, the powerful new evidence that modern DNA testing can provide is "unlike anything known before." ...

Observing that the DNA evidence in this case would be so probative of Osborne's guilt or innocence that it exceeds the materiality standard that governs the disclosure of evidence under *Brady*, the Ninth Circuit granted Osborne's request for access to the State's evidence. In doing so, the Court of Appeals recognized that Osborne possesses a narrow right of postconviction access to biological evidence for DNA testing "where [such] evidence was used to secure his conviction, the DNA testing is to be conducted using methods that were unavailable at the time of trial and are far more precise than the methods that were then available, such methods are capable of conclusively determining whether Osborne is the source of the genetic material, the testing can be conducted without cost or prejudice to the State, and the evidence is material to available forms of post-conviction relief." That conclusion does not merit reversal.

If the right Osborne seeks to vindicate is framed as purely substantive, the proper result is no less clear. "The touchstone of due process is protection of the individual against arbitrary action of government." When government action is so lacking in justification that it "can properly be characterized as arbitrary, or conscience shocking, in a constitutional sense," it violates the Due Process Clause. In my view, the State's refusal to provide Osborne with access to evidence for DNA testing qualifies as arbitrary.

Throughout the course of state and federal litigation, the State has failed to provide any concrete reason for denying Osborne the DNA testing he seeks, and none is apparent. Because Osborne has offered to pay for the tests, cost is not a factor. And as the State now concedes, there is no reason to doubt that such testing would provide conclusive confirmation of Osborne's guilt or revelation of his innocence.[7] In the courts below, the State refused to provide an explanation for its refusal to permit testing of the evidence, and in this Court, its explanation has been, at best, unclear. Insofar as the State has articulated any reason at all, it appears to be a generalized interest in protecting the finality of the judgment of conviction from any possible future attacks.[8]

While we have long recognized that States have an interest in securing the finality of their judgments, finality is not a stand-alone value that trumps a State's overriding interest in ensuring that justice is done in its courts and secured to its citizens. Indeed, when absolute proof of innocence is readily at hand, a State should not shrink from the possibility that error may have occurred. Rather, our system of justice is strengthened by "recogniz[ing] the need for, and imperative of, a safety valve in those rare instances where objective proof that the convicted actually did not commit the offense later becomes available through the progress of science." DNA evidence has led to an extraordinary series of exonerations, not only in cases where the trial evidence was weak, but also in cases where the convicted parties confessed their guilt

7. Justice ALITO provides a detailed discussion of dangers such as laboratory contamination and evidence tampering that may reduce the reliability not only of DNA evidence, but of any type of physical forensic evidence. While no form of testing is error proof in every case, the degree to which DNA evidence has become a foundational tool of law enforcement and prosecution is indicative of the general reliability and probative power of such testing. The fact that errors may occur in the testing process is not a ground for refusing such testing altogether—were it so, such evidence should be banned at trial no less than in postconviction proceedings. More important still is the fact that the State now concedes there is no reason to doubt that if STR and mtDNA testing yielded exculpatory results *in this case*, Osborne's innocence would be established.

8. In his concurring opinion, Justice ALITO suggests other reasons that might motivate States to resist access to such evidence, including concerns over DNA testing backlogs and manipulation by defendants. Not only were these reasons not offered by the State of Alaska as grounds for its decision in this case, but they are not in themselves compelling. While state resource constraints might justify delays in the testing of postconviction DNA evidence, they would not justify an outright ban on access to such evidence. And Justice ALITO's concern that guilty defendants will "play games with the criminal justice system" with regard to the timing of their requests for DNA evidence is not only speculative, but gravely concerning. It bears remembering that criminal defendants are under no obligation to prove their innocence at trial; rather, the State bears the burden of proving their guilt. Having no obligation to conduct pretrial DNA testing, a defendant should not be bound by a decision to forgo such testing at trial, particularly when, as in this case, the choice was made by counsel over the defendant's strong objection....

and where the trial evidence against them appeared overwhelming.[9] The examples provided by *amici* of the power of DNA testing serve to convince me that the fact of conviction is not sufficient to justify a State's refusal to perform a test that will conclusively establish innocence or guilt.

This conclusion draws strength from the powerful state interests that offset the State's purported interest in finality *per se*. When a person is convicted for a crime he did not commit, the true culprit escapes punishment. DNA testing may lead to his identification. See Brief for Current and Former Prosecutors as *Amici Curiae* 16 (noting that in more than one-third of all exonerations DNA testing identified the actual offender). Crime victims, the law enforcement profession, and society at large share a strong interest in identifying and apprehending the actual perpetrators of vicious crimes, such as the rape and attempted murder that gave rise to this case.

The arbitrariness of the State's conduct is highlighted by comparison to the private interests it denies. It seems to me obvious that if a wrongly convicted person were to produce proof of his actual innocence, no state interest would be sufficient to justify his continued punitive detention. If such proof can be readily obtained without imposing a significant burden on the State, a refusal to provide access to such evidence is wholly unjustified.

In sum, an individual's interest in his physical liberty is one of constitutional significance. That interest would be vindicated by providing post-conviction access to DNA evidence, as would the State's interest in ensuring that it punishes the true perpetrator of a crime. In this case, the State has suggested no countervailing interest that justifies its refusal to allow Osborne to test the evidence in its possession and has not provided any other nonarbitrary explanation for its conduct. Consequently, I am left to conclude that the State's failure to provide Osborne access to the evidence constitutes arbitrary action that offends basic principles of due process. On that basis, I would affirm the judgment of the Ninth Circuit.

III

The majority denies that Osborne possesses a cognizable substantive due process right "under the circumstances of this case," and offers two meager reasons for its decision. First, citing a general reluctance to "'expand the concept of substantive due process,'" the Court observes that there is no long history of postconviction access to DNA evidence. "'The mere novelty of such a claim,'" the Court asserts, "'is reason enough to doubt that "substantive due process" sustains it.'" The flaw is in the framing. Of course courts have not historically granted convicted persons access to physical evidence for STR and mtDNA testing. But, as discussed above, courts have recognized a residual substantive interest in both physical liberty and in freedom from arbitrary government action. It is Osborne's interest in those well-established liberties that justifies the Court of Appeals' decision to grant him access to the State's evidence for purposes of previously unavailable DNA testing.

The majority also asserts that this Court's recognition of a limited federal right of access to DNA evidence would be ill advised because it would "short circuit what looks to be a prompt and considered legislative response" by the States and Federal Government to the issue of access to DNA evidence. Such a decision, the majority warns, would embroil the Court in myriad policy questions best left to other branches of government. The majority's arguments in this respect bear close resemblance to the manner in which the Court once approached the now-venerable right to counsel for indigent defendants. Before our decision in *Powell v. Alabama*, 287 U.S. 45 (1932), state law alone governed the manner in which counsel was appointed for indigent defendants.... When at last this Court recognized the Sixth Amendment right to counsel for all indigent criminal defendants in *Gideon v. Wainwright*, 372 U.S. 335 (1963), our decision did not impede the ability of States to tailor their appointment processes to local needs, nor did it unnecessarily interfere with their sovereignty. It did, however, ensure that criminal defendants were provided

9. See ... Garrett, Judging Innocence, 108 Colum. L. Rev. 55, 109 (2008) (documenting that in 50% of cases in which DNA evidence exonerated a convicted person, reviewing courts had commented on the exoneree's likely guilt and in 10% of the cases had described the evidence supporting conviction as "overwhelming").

with the counsel to which they were constitutionally entitled.[10] In the same way, a decision to recognize a limited right of postconviction access to DNA testing would not prevent the States from creating procedures by which litigants request and obtain such access; it would merely ensure that States do so in a manner that is nonarbitrary.

While it is true that recent advances in DNA technology have led to a nationwide reexamination of state and federal postconviction procedures authorizing the use of DNA testing, it is highly unlikely that affirming the judgment of the Court of Appeals would significantly affect the use of DNA testing in any of the States that have already developed statutes and procedures for dealing with DNA evidence or would require the few States that have not yet done so to postpone the enactment of appropriate legislation. Indeed, a holding by this Court that the policy judgments underlying that legislation rest on a sound constitutional foundation could only be constructive.

IV

Osborne has demonstrated a constitutionally protected right to due process which the State of Alaska thus far has not vindicated and which this Court is both empowered and obliged to safeguard. On the record before us, there is no reason to deny access to the evidence and there are many reasons to provide it, not least of which is a fundamental concern in ensuring that justice has been done in this case. I would affirm the judgment of the Court of Appeals, and respectfully dissent from the Court's refusal to do so....

Notes and Questions

1. In 2010, the year after the Court's decision in *Osborne,* Alaska enacted legislation providing criminal defendants access to post-conviction DNA testing under specified circumstances. *See* Alaska Rev. Stat. §§ 12.73.010 through 12.73.090. As of July 2010, only Massachusetts and Oklahoma were without such legislation. According to the Innocence Project, "Although 48 states have post-conviction DNA-testing access statutes, many of these testing laws are limited in scope and in substance."[15]

2. Why might a prosecutor resist a defendant's post-conviction petition for access to evidence to allow DNA testing? Justice Stevens argues that the test results "will conclusively establish" guilt or innocence in cases such as Osborne's, and that the State should support testing that would substantiate either finding. Are the reasons advanced by Justice Alito in his concurring opinion persuasive?

3. The Innocence Protection Act (IPA) was enacted by Congress as a part of the Justice for All Act of 2004. The IPA, which is presented below in relevant part, specifies the circumstances under which prisoners convicted of federal crimes can secure post-conviction DNA testing (18 U.S.C. § 3600) and requires the preservation of biological evidence relating to federal criminal investigations and prosecutions in cases where defendants remain under a prison sentence (18 U.S.C. § 3600A). Other provisions within the Justice for All Act, including the Kirk Bloodsworth Post-Conviction DNA Testing Grant Program, offer financial incentives to the States to preserve biological evidence and provide post-conviction DNA testing of specified evidence (H.R. 5107, 108th Congress, §§ 412, 413).[16]

---

10. The majority's position also resembles that taken by Justice Harlan in his dissent in *Miranda v. Arizona,* 384 U.S. 436 (1966), in which he faulted the Court for its "ironic untimeliness." He noted that the Court's decision came at time when scholars, politicians, and law enforcement officials were beginning to engage in a "massive reexamination of criminal law enforcement procedures on a scale never before witnessed," and predicted that the practical effect of the Court's decision would be to "handicap seriously" those sound efforts. Yet time has vindicated the decision in *Miranda.* The Court's refusal to grant Osborne access to critical DNA evidence rests on a practical judgment remarkably similar to Justice Harlan's, and I find the majority's judgment today as profoundly incorrect as the *Miranda* minority's was yesterday.

18 U.S.C. § 3600. DNA testing

(a) **In general.**—Upon a written motion by an individual under a sentence of imprisonment or death pursuant to a conviction for a Federal offense (referred to in this section as the "applicant"), the court that entered the judgment of conviction shall order DNA testing of specific evidence if the court finds that all of the following apply:

(1) The applicant asserts, under penalty of perjury, that the applicant is actually innocent of—

(A) the Federal offense for which the applicant is under a sentence of imprisonment or death; or

(B) another Federal or State offense, if—

(i) evidence of such offense was admitted during a Federal death sentencing hearing and exoneration of such offense would entitle the applicant to a reduced sentence or new sentencing hearing; and

(ii) in the case of a State offense—

(I) the applicant demonstrates that there is no adequate remedy under State law to permit DNA testing of the specified evidence relating to the State offense; and

(II) to the extent available, the applicant has exhausted all remedies available under State law for requesting DNA testing of specified evidence relating to the State offense.

(2) The specific evidence to be tested was secured in relation to the investigation or prosecution of the Federal or State offense referenced in the applicant's assertion under paragraph (1).

(3) The specific evidence to be tested—

(A) was not previously subjected to DNA testing and the applicant did not—

(i) knowingly and voluntarily waive the right to request DNA testing of that evidence in a court proceeding after the date of enactment of the Innocence Protection Act of 2004; or

(ii) knowingly fail to request DNA testing of that evidence in a prior motion for postconviction DNA testing; or

(B) was previously subjected to DNA testing and the applicant is requesting DNA testing using a new method or technology that is substantially more probative than the prior DNA testing.

(4) The specific evidence to be tested is in the possession of the Government and has been subject to a chain of custody and retained under conditions sufficient to ensure that such evidence has not been substituted, contaminated, tampered with, replaced, or altered in any respect material to the proposed DNA testing.

(5) The proposed DNA testing is reasonable in scope, uses scientifically sound methods, and is consistent with accepted forensic practices.

(6) The applicant identifies a theory of defense that—

(A) is not inconsistent with an affirmative defense presented at trial; and

(B) would establish the actual innocence of the applicant of the Federal or State offense referenced in the applicant's assertion under paragraph (1).

(7) If the applicant was convicted following a trial, the identity of the perpetrator was at issue in the trial.

(8) The proposed DNA testing of the specific evidence may produce new material evidence that would—

(A) support the theory of defense referenced in paragraph (6); and

(B) raise a reasonable probability that the applicant did not commit the offense.

(9) The applicant certifies that the applicant will provide a DNA sample for purposes of comparison.

(**10**) The motion is made in a timely fashion, subject to the following conditions:

(**A**) There shall be a rebuttable presumption of timeliness if the motion is made within 60 months of enactment of the Justice For All Act of 2004 or within 36 months of conviction, whichever comes later. Such presumption may be rebutted upon a showing—

(**i**) that the applicant's motion for a DNA test is based solely upon

(**ii**) of clear and convincing evidence that the applicant's filing is done solely to cause delay or harass.

(**B**) There shall be a rebuttable presumption against timeliness for any motion not satisfying subparagraph (A) above. Such presumption may be rebutted upon the court's finding—

(**i**) that the applicant was or is incompetent and such incompetence substantially contributed to the delay in the applicant's motion for a DNA test;

(**ii**) the evidence to be tested is newly discovered DNA evidence;

(**iii**) that the applicant's motion is not based solely upon the applicant's own assertion of innocence and, after considering all relevant facts and circumstances surrounding the motion, a denial would result in a manifest injustice; or

(**iv**) upon good cause shown.

...

(**b**) **Notice to the Government; preservation order; appointment of counsel.**—

(**1**) **Notice.**—Upon the receipt of a motion filed under subsection (a), the court shall—

(**A**) notify the Government; and

(**B**) allow the Government a reasonable time period to respond to the motion.

(**2**) **Preservation order.**—To the extent necessary to carry out proceedings under this section, the court shall direct the Government to preserve the specific evidence relating to a motion under subsection (a).

(**3**) **Appointment of counsel.**—The court may appoint counsel for an indigent applicant under this section in the same manner as in a proceeding under section 3006A(a)(2)(B).

(**c**) **Testing procedures.**—

(**1**) **In general.**—The court shall direct that any DNA testing ordered under this section be carried out by the Federal Bureau of Investigation.

(**2**) **Exception.**—Notwithstanding paragraph (1), the court may order DNA testing by another qualified laboratory if the court makes all necessary orders to ensure the integrity of the specific evidence and the reliability of the testing process and test results.

(**3**) **Costs.**—The costs of any DNA testing ordered under this section shall be paid—

(**A**) by the applicant; or

(**B**) in the case of an applicant who is indigent, by the Government.

(**d**) **Time limitation in capital cases.**—In any case in which the applicant is sentenced to death—

(**1**) any DNA testing ordered under this section shall be completed not later than 60 days after the date on which the Government responds to the motion filed under subsection (a); and

(**2**) not later than 120 days after the date on which the DNA testing ordered under this section is completed, the court shall order any post-testing procedures under subsection (f) or (g), as appropriate.

(**e**) **Reporting of test results.**—

(**1**) **In general.**—The results of any DNA testing ordered under this section shall be simultaneously disclosed to the court, the applicant, and the Government.

(**2**) **NDIS.**—The Government shall submit any test results relating to the DNA of the applicant to the National DNA Index System (referred to in this subsection as "NDIS").

(**3**) **Retention of DNA sample....**

(f) **Post-testing procedures; inconclusive and inculpatory results.**—

(1) **Inconclusive results.**—If DNA test results obtained under this section are inconclusive, the court may order further testing, if appropriate, or may deny the applicant relief.

(2) **Inculpatory results.**—If DNA test results obtained under this section show that the applicant was the source of the DNA evidence, the court shall—

(A) deny the applicant relief; and

(B) on motion of the Government—

(i) make a determination whether the applicant's assertion of actual innocence was false, and, if the court makes such a finding, the court may hold the applicant in contempt;

(ii) assess against the applicant the cost of any DNA testing carried out under this section;

(iii) forward the finding to the Director of the Bureau of Prisons, who, upon receipt of such a finding, may deny, wholly or in part, the good conduct credit authorized under section 3632 on the basis of that finding;

(iv) if the applicant is subject to the jurisdiction of the United States Parole Commission, forward the finding to the Commission so that the Commission may deny parole on the basis of that finding; and

(v) if the DNA test results relate to a State offense, forward the finding to any appropriate State official.

(3) **Sentence.**—In any prosecution of an applicant under chapter 79 for false assertions or other conduct in proceedings under this section, the court, upon conviction of the applicant, shall sentence the applicant to a term of imprisonment of not less than 3 years, which shall run consecutively to any other term of imprisonment the applicant is serving.

(g) **Post-testing procedures; motion for new trial or resentencing.**—

(1) **In general.**—Notwithstanding any law that would bar a motion under this paragraph as untimely, if DNA test results obtained under this section exclude the applicant as the source of the DNA evidence, the applicant may file a motion for a new trial or resentencing, as appropriate....

(2) **Standard for granting motion for new trial or resentencing.**—The court shall grant the motion of the applicant for a new trial or resentencing, as appropriate, if the DNA test results, when considered with all other evidence in the case (regardless of whether such evidence was introduced at trial), establish by compelling evidence that a new trial would result in an acquittal of—

(A) in the case of a motion for a new trial, the Federal offense for which the applicant is under a sentence of imprisonment or death; and

(B) in the case of a motion for resentencing, another Federal or State offense, if evidence of such offense was admitted during a Federal death sentencing hearing and exoneration of such offense would entitle the applicant to a reduced sentence or a new sentencing proceeding.

(h) **Other laws unaffected....**

(2) **Habeas corpus.**—Nothing in this section shall provide a basis for relief in any Federal habeas corpus proceeding....

18 U.S.C. § 3600A. Preservation of biological evidence

(a) **In general.**—Notwithstanding any other provision of law, the Government shall preserve biological evidence that was secured in the investigation or prosecution of a Federal offense, if a defendant is under a sentence of imprisonment for such offense.

(b) **Defined term.**—For purposes of this section, the term "biological evidence" means—

(1) a sexual assault forensic examination kit; or

(2) semen, blood, saliva, hair, skin tissue, or other identified biological material.

(c) **Applicability.**—Subsection (a) shall not apply if—

(1) a court has denied a request or motion for DNA testing of the biological evidence by the defendant under section 3600, and no appeal is pending;

(2) the defendant knowingly and voluntarily waived the right to request DNA testing of the biological evidence in a court proceeding conducted after the date of enactment of the Innocence Protection Act of 2004;

(3) after a conviction becomes final and the defendant has exhausted all opportunities for direct review of the conviction, the defendant is notified that the biological evidence may be destroyed and the defendant does not file a motion under section 3600 within 180 days of receipt of the notice;

(4)(A) the evidence must be returned to its rightful owner, or is of such a size, bulk, or physical character as to render retention impracticable; and

(B) the Government takes reasonable measures to remove and preserve portions of the material evidence sufficient to permit future DNA testing; or

(5) the biological evidence has already been subjected to DNA testing under section 3600 and the results included the defendant as the source of such evidence.

(d) **Other preservation requirement.**—Nothing in this section shall preempt or supersede any statute, regulation, court order, or other provision of law that may require evidence, including biological evidence, to be preserved.

(e) **Regulations.**—Not later than 180 days after the date of enactment of the Innocence Protection Act of 2004, the Attorney General shall promulgate regulations to implement and enforce this section, including appropriate disciplinary sanctions to ensure that employees comply with such regulations.

(f) **Criminal penalty.**—Whoever knowingly and intentionally destroys, alters, or tampers with biological evidence that is required to be preserved under this section with the intent to prevent that evidence from being subjected to DNA testing or prevent the production or use of that evidence in an official proceeding, shall be fined under this title, imprisoned for not more than 5 years, or both.

(g) **Habeas corpus.**—Nothing in this section shall provide a basis for relief in any Federal habeas corpus proceeding.

4. As noted in part III of Chief Justice Roberts's opinion in *Osborne*, the Court did not resolve whether 42 U.S.C. § 1983, the federal civil rights statute, was an appropriate vehicle for Osborne's claim for access to the evidence in the state's possession so he could submit it to DNA testing. The government had argued that § 1983 could not be used for this purpose, but rather that the filing should have been based on 28 U.S.C. § 2254, which governs state prisoners' federal habeas corpus applications. Resolution of that question was unnecessary in *Osborne* in light of the Court's ruling on the merits, but the issue has potentially important implications involving procedural requirements that govern prisoners' filing of habeas corpus petitions and for clarifying the application of the respective statutes.[17] In *Skinner v. Switzer*, ___ U.S. ___, ___ S.Ct. ___, ___ L.Ed.2d ___, 2011 WL 767703 (2011), the Court revisited the question: "May a convicted state prisoner seeking DNA testing of crime-scene evidence assert that claim in a civil rights action under 42 U.S.C. § 1983, or is such a claim cognizable in federal court only when asserted in a petition for a writ of habeas corpus under 28 U.S.C. § 2254?" In a 6–3 decision, the justices ruled that "a postconviction claim for DNA testing is properly pursued in a § 1983 action."

Henry Skinner was sentenced to death in Texas for murdering his live-in girlfriend and her two sons. Police arrested him after they found the victims' bodies in the home that they shared. Skinner was standing in a closet, wearing blood-stained clothing. He claimed to have been so highly intoxicated and under the influence of drugs that he passed out and had no recollection of events related to the killings. He suggested that he was physically incapable of having committed the murders and identified another man, Robert Donnell, as the likely perpetrator. The State tested some items of evidence found at the murder scene, which implicated Skinner, but several other items were not tested. Following his conviction, Skinner unsuccessfully sought access to the untested evidence so it could be analyzed for DNA which, he theorized, might link Donnell to the killings. When the state courts rejected his petition for access to the evidence, he instituted federal court proceedings in reliance on § 1983. The federal district court ruled that postconviction requests for DNA evidence had to be pursued through habeas corpus rather than § 1983 and the Fifth Circuit Court of Appeals affirmed. Justice Ginsburg's majority opinion for the Supreme Court thus confronted the issue:

When may a state prisoner, complaining of unconstitutional state action, pursue a civil rights claim under § 1983, and when is habeas corpus the prisoner's sole remedy? This Court has several times considered that question. Pathmarking here is *Heck v. Humphrey*, 512 U.S. 477 (1994). Plaintiff in that litigation was a state prisoner serving time for manslaughter. He brought a § 1983 action for damages, alleging that he had been unlawfully investigated, arrested, tried, and convicted. Although the complaint in *Heck* sought monetary damages only, not release from confinement, we ruled that the plaintiff could not proceed under § 1983. Any award in his favor, we observed, would "necessarily imply" the invalidity of his conviction. See *id.*, at 487. When "a judgment in favor of the plaintiff would necessarily imply the invalidity of his conviction or sentence," the Court held, § 1983 is not an available remedy. *Ibid.* "But if ... the plaintiff's action, even if successful, will *not* demonstrate the invalidity of [his conviction or sentence], the [§ 1983] action should be allowed to proceed...." *Ibid.*

We summarized the relevant case law most recently in *Wilkinson v. Dotson*, 544 U.S. 74 (2005)....

Measured against our prior holdings, Skinner has properly invoked § 1983. Success in his suit for DNA testing would not "necessarily imply" the invalidity of his conviction. While test results might prove exculpatory, that outcome is hardly inevitable; ... results might prove inconclusive or they might further incriminate Skinner.

Respondent Switzer nevertheless argues ... that Skinner's request for DNA testing must be pursued, if at all, in an application for habeas corpus, not in a § 1983 action.... Although Skinner's *immediate* plea is simply for an order requiring DNA testing, his *ultimate* aim, Switzer urges, is to use the test results as a platform for attacking his conviction. It suffices to point out that Switzer has found no case, nor has the dissent, in which the Court has recognized habeas as the sole remedy, or even an available one, where the relief sought would "neither terminat[e] custody, accelerat[e] the future date of release from custody, nor reduc[e] the level of custody." *Dotson*, 544 U.S., at 86 (SCALIA, J., concurring).

Respondent Switzer and her *amici* forecast that a "vast expansion of federal jurisdiction ... would ensue" were we to hold that Skinner's complaint can be initiated under § 1983. See Brief for National District Attorneys Association as *Amicus Curiae* 8. In particular, they predict a proliferation of federal civil actions "seeking post-conviction discovery of evidence [and] other relief inescapably associated with the central questions of guilt or punishment." *Id.*, at 6. These fears ... are unwarranted.

In the Circuits that currently allow § 1983 claims for DNA testing, no evidence tendered by Switzer shows any litigation flood or even rainfall. The projected toll on federal courts is all the more implausible regarding DNA testing claims, for *Osborne* has rejected substantive due process as a basis for such claims.

More generally, in the Prison Litigation Reform Act of 1995 (PLRA), 110 Stat. 1321-66, Congress has placed a series of controls on prisoner suits, constraints designed to prevent sportive filings in federal court. See, *e.g.*, PLRA § 803(d) (adding 42 U.S.C. § 1997e to create new procedures and penalties for prisoner lawsuits under § 1983); PLRA § 804(a)(3) (adding 28 U.S.C. § 1915(b)(1) to require any prisoner proceeding *in forma pauperis* to pay the full filing fee out of a percentage of his prison trust account); PLRA §804(c)(3) (adding 28 U.S.C. §1915(f) to require prisoners to pay the full amount of any cost assessed against them out of their prison trust account); PLRA §804(d) (adding 28 U.S.C. §1915(g) to revoke, with limited exception, *in forma pauperis* privileges for any prisoner who has filed three or more lawsuits that fail to state a claim, or are malicious or frivolous). See also *Crawford-El v. Britton*, 523 U.S. 574, 596–597 (1998) (PLRA aims to "discourage prisoners from filing claims that are unlikely to succeed," and statistics suggest that the Act is "having its intended effect").

Nor do we see any cause for concern that today's ruling will spill over to claims relying on *Brady v. Maryland*, 373 U.S. 83 (1963); indeed, Switzer makes no such assertion. *Brady* announced a constitutional requirement addressed first and foremost to the prosecution's conduct pretrial. *Brady* proscribes withholding evidence "favorable to an accused" and "material to [his] guilt or to punishment." *Cone v. Bell*, 556 U.S. ___, ___, 129 S.Ct. 1769, 1772 (2009). To establish that a *Brady* violation undermines a conviction, a convicted defendant must make each of three showings: (1) the evidence at issue is "favorable to the accused, either because it is exculpatory, or because it is impeaching"; (2) the State suppressed the evidence, "either willfully or inadvertently"; and (3) "prejudice ... ensued." *Strickler v. Greene*, 527 U.S. 263, 281–282 (1999).

Unlike DNA testing, which may yield exculpatory, incriminating, or inconclusive results, a *Brady* claim, when successful postconviction, necessarily yields evidence undermining a conviction: *Brady* evidence is, by definition, always favorable to the defendant and material to his guilt or punishment. And parties asserting *Brady* violations postconviction generally do seek a judgment qualifying them for "immediate or speedier release" from imprisonment. See *Dotson*, 544 U.S., at 82. Accordingly, *Brady* claims have ranked within the traditional core of habeas corpus and outside the province of §1983. See *Heck*, 512 U.S., at 479, 490, 114 S.Ct. 2364 (claim that prosecutors and an investigator had "'knowingly destroyed' evidence 'which was exculpatory in nature and could have proved [petitioner's] innocence'" cannot be maintained under §1983).

E. Conclusion

Wrongful convictions represent a failure of justice. No ethical prosecutor or law enforcement officer would knowingly help cause or tolerate an innocent person's conviction. Although they most directly affect the innocent who suffer the consequent stigmatization and punishment, wrongful convictions concurrently allow the guilty to remain free and undermine societal confidence in the administration of justice. Nevertheless, the combativeness of the adversarial system, the pressures and ambiguities associated with investigating and prosecuting crimes, and limited resources for oversight and enforcement, as well as simple human error, can position prosecutors and the police at the center of wrongful conviction cases.

In this chapter, we have examined legal doctrine most closely associated with prosecutors' obligations to serve justice, a mandate entailing much more than simply to secure convictions. Prosecutors have a duty not to participate knowingly in presenting perjured testimony, and to disclose untruthful testimony if it occurs. Reversal is required "if there is any reasonable likelihood that the false testimony could have affected the judgment of the jury." *United States v. Agurs*, 427 U.S. 97, 103, 96 S.Ct. 2392, 49 L.Ed.2d 342 (1976). Under the rule of *Brady v. Maryland*, 373 U.S. 83, 83 S.Ct. 1194, 10 L.Ed.2d 215 (1963), prosecutors have an affirmative obligation to disclose "evidence favorable to an accused"—even, as later cases held, if not specifically requested—"where the evidence is material either to guilt or to punishment, irrespective of the good faith or bad faith of the prosecution." Evidence is considered "material" under this test "'if there is a reasonable probability that, had the evidence been disclosed to the defense, the result of the proceeding would have been different.'" *Kyles v. Whitley*, 514 U.S. 419, 433–434, 115 S.Ct. 1555, 131

L.Ed.2d 490 (1995), *quoting United States v. Bagley,* 473 U.S. 667, 682, 105 S.Ct. 3375, 87 L.Ed.2d 481 (1985) (plurality opinion).

The constitutional obligations of the police are different. During the course of their investigations the police come across large amounts of potentially relevant evidence, some of which they will retain and much of which they will not. In *Arizona v. Youngblood,* 488 U.S. 51, 109 S.Ct. 333, 102 L.Ed.2d 281 (1988), the justices ruled that Due Process is offended only when the police act in "bad faith" to destroy or fail to preserve evidence that is potentially useful to a defendant. The biological evidence that the police (negligently) failed to preserve could have excluded Youngblood as the perpetrator of a sexual assault against a child, even using the relatively unsophisticated blood typing tests that were available at the time of his trial. But the actual exculpatory value of the evidence remained unknown, precisely because the police failed to preserve it for testing. Years later, after Youngblood had spent a decade in prison following his conviction for the child's abduction and assault, DNA testing exonerated him and identified another man as the assailant. The *Youngblood* "bad faith" requirement remains the federal constitutional standard governing the police's obligation to preserve potentially useful evidence. This limitation is designed to narrow the scope of the police's duty to manageable proportions and it further supports an inference that the evidence in fact was exculpatory.

We lastly considered whether the government has an obligation to preserve evidence that might be used to help challenge a conviction after a trial has resulted in a guilty verdict, and whether defendants have a right of access to evidence within the government's possession for post-conviction DNA testing. The Supreme Court has not ruled on the former question, although some lower courts have evaluated claims concerning the post-conviction loss or destruction of evidence by invoking *Youngblood's* "bad faith" requirement. In *District Attorney's Office for the Third Judicial District v. Osborne,* ___ U.S. ___, 129 S.Ct. 2308, 174 L.Ed.2d 38 (2009), the Court declined to recognize a constitutional right of access to evidence for post-conviction DNA testing. In adopting that position, the majority opinion in *Osborne* relied in part on the abundance of legislative activity regulating access to evidence for DNA testing and cited the more nuanced approach that could be taken by statute than by constitutional adjudication. At present, all but two jurisdictions entitle defendants to post-conviction access to evidence for DNA testing if their cases satisfy the statutory conditions.

Chapter 6

Counsel for the Defense

A. Introduction

Among its several important safeguards, the 6th Amendment to the United States Constitution provides that: "In all criminal prosecutions, the accused shall enjoy the right ... to have the assistance of counsel for his defence." In a system of justice premised on the assumption that the clash of skilled advocates representing the opposing views of the parties is the surest path to the truth, it only makes sense to involve an attorney for the defense as a counterweight to the public prosecutor. In *Gideon v. Wainwright*, 372 U.S. 335, 83 S.Ct. 792, 9 L.Ed.2d 799 (1963), the landmark decision which held that the 6th Amendment right to counsel applies to the States and requires the appointment of trial counsel for indigents facing felony charges, the Supreme Court considered the participation of a defense attorney essential "to achieve a fair system of justice." 372 U.S., at 344.

> [I]n our adversary system of criminal justice, any person haled into court, who is too poor to hire a lawyer, cannot be assured a fair trial unless counsel is provided for him. This seems to us to be an obvious truth. Governments, both state and federal, quite properly spend vast sums of money to establish machinery to try defendants accused of crime. Lawyers to prosecute are everywhere deemed essential to protect the public's interest in an orderly society. Similarly, there are few defendants charged with crime, few indeed, who fail to hire the best lawyers they can get to prepare and present their defenses. That government hires lawyers to prosecute and defendants who have the money hire lawyers to defend are the strongest indications of the wide-spread belief that lawyers in criminal courts are necessities, not luxuries. The right of one charged with crime to counsel may not be deemed fundamental and essential to fair trials in some countries, but it is in ours. From the very beginning, our state and national constitutions and laws have laid great emphasis on procedural and substantive safeguards designed to assure fair trials before impartial tribunals in which every defendant stands equal before the law. This noble ideal cannot be realized if the poor man charged with crime has to face his accusers without a lawyer to assist him. 372 U.S., at 344.

In this chapter we will examine the more precise contours of the right to "the assistance of counsel," focusing on cases in which the unavailability or the alleged inadequacies of defense counsel may have contributed to wrongful convictions. We begin by considering the scope of indigents' federal constitutional rights to representation by court-appointed counsel in criminal trials, appeals, and post-conviction review. We then review minimal performance standards for defense counsel, focusing on the constitutional requirement for "the effective assistance of counsel." We pay special attention to cases involving scientific evidence and the measures taken by defense counsel to be prepared to challenge or present expert testimony bearing on trial issues. We conclude in a related vein by exploring whether and to what extent fundamental fairness, or the right to the effective assistance of counsel, embrace a right for indigents to secure the help of court-appointed experts in defending against criminal accusations.

B. The Right to Court-Appointed Counsel: The Criminal Trial and Beyond

The Supreme Court's first major ruling regarding a constitutional right to court-appointed counsel occurred more than three decades before *Gideon v. Wainwright*, in *Powell v. Alabama*, 287 U.S. 45, 53 S.Ct. 55, 77 L.Ed. 158 (1932). Indeed, *Powell* marked one of the Court's earliest decisions setting aside a state court judgment in a criminal case in reliance on the 14th Amendment's Due Process Clause. Under review were the convictions and death sentences returned against several black youths for raping two white women on a freight train that was travelling through northern Alabama. This was the famous Scottsboro Boys case, representing what most observers agree resulted in one of the most glaring series of wrongful convictions in this country's history.[1] Barely more than two weeks separated the alleged rapes and the youths' indictments, trials, and condemnation to death. Alabama law entitled them to court-appointed defense counsel, but which lawyers would represent them was not resolved until the opening day of the trials. The manifest unfairness of this untimely appointment caused the Court to reverse their convictions. Justice Sutherland's opinion explained that "during perhaps the most critical period of the proceedings against these defendants, that is to say, from the time of their arraignment until the beginning of their trial, when consultation, thorough-going investigation and preparation were vitally important, the defendants did not have the aid of counsel in any real sense, although they were as much entitled to such aid during that period as at the trial itself." 287 U.S., at 57.

The right to court-appointed counsel recognized in *Powell v. Alabama* was carefully limited to the facts of that case. "In the light of ... the ignorance and illiteracy of the defendants, their youth, the circumstances of public hostility, the imprisonment and the close surveillance of the defendants by the military forces, the fact that their friends and families were all in other states and communication with them necessarily difficult, and above all that they stood in deadly peril of their lives—we think the failure of the trial court to give them reasonable time and opportunity to secure counsel was a clear denial of due process." *Powell v. Alabama*, 287 U.S. 45, 71 (1932). Not until 1963, with the Court's decision in *Gideon v. Wainwright* and the Warren Court's application of the 6th Amendment right to counsel to the states, were indigents constitutionally entitled to be represented by court-appointed counsel in felony trials without limitation.[2]

Nine years later, the justices ruled in *Argersinger v. Hamlin*, 407 U.S. 25, 92 S.Ct. 2006, 32 L.Ed.2d 530 (1972) that an indigent who was required to represent himself in a Florida criminal trial on a misdemeanor charge of carrying a concealed weapon, a "petty offense" punishable by a maximum of six months in jail, was denied his 6th Amendment right to counsel upon conviction and receipt of a 90-day jail sentence. It was unclear whether the right to court-appointed counsel recognized in *Argersinger* was limited to misdemeanor cases resulting in jail time or was meant to be available more broadly. Because laypersons facing low-level criminal charges without the assistance of counsel may be ignorant of their rights, ill-equipped to defend themselves in court, feel pressure to plead guilty to avoid suffering conviction and punishment following a trial, or otherwise be at heightened risk of wrongful conviction, the resolution of this issue has special relevance to our subject matter. The Supreme Court considered whether indigent defendants have a constitutional right to court-appointed counsel in misdemeanor trials that do not result in incarceration in *Scott v. Illinois.*

Scott v. Illinois

440 U.S. 367, 99 S.Ct. 1158, 59 L.Ed.2d 383 (1979)

Mr. Justice REHNQUIST delivered the opinion of the Court.

We granted certiorari in this case to resolve a conflict among state and lower federal courts regarding the proper application of our decision in *Argersinger v. Hamlin*, 407 U.S. 25 (1972). Petitioner Scott was convicted of theft and fined $50 after a bench trial in the Circuit Court of Cook County, Ill. His conviction was affirmed by the state intermediate appellate court and then by the Supreme Court of Illinois, over Scott's contention that the Sixth and Fourteenth Amendments to the United States Constitution required that Illinois provide trial counsel to him at its expense.

Petitioner Scott was convicted of shoplifting merchandise valued at less than $150. The applicable Illinois statute set the maximum penalty for such an offense at a $500 fine or one year in jail, or both. The petitioner argues that a line of this Court's cases culminating in *Argersinger v. Hamlin, supra*, requires state provision of counsel whenever imprisonment is an authorized penalty.

The Supreme Court of Illinois rejected this contention, quoting the following language from *Argersinger*:

"We hold, therefore, that absent a knowing and intelligent waiver, no person may be imprisoned for any offense, whether classified as petty, misdemeanor, or felony, unless he was represented by counsel at his trial." 407 U.S., at 37.

"Under the rule we announce today, every judge will know when the trial of a misdemeanor starts that no imprisonment may be imposed, even though local law permits it, unless the accused is represented by counsel. He will have a measure of the seriousness and gravity of the offense and therefore know when to name a lawyer to represent the accused before the trial starts." *Id.*, at 40.

The Supreme Court of Illinois went on to state that it was "not inclined to extend *Argersinger*" to the case where a defendant is charged with a statutory offense for which imprisonment upon conviction is authorized but not actually imposed upon the defendant. We agree with the Supreme Court of Illinois that the Federal Constitution does not require a state trial court to appoint counsel for a criminal defendant such as petitioner, and we therefore affirm its judgment....

There is considerable doubt that the Sixth Amendment itself, as originally drafted by the Framers of the Bill of Rights, contemplated any guarantee other than the right of an accused in a criminal prosecution in a federal court to employ a lawyer to assist in his defense. W. Beaney, The Right to Counsel in American Courts 27–30 (1955)....

[T]he Court held in *Duncan v. Louisiana*, 391 U.S. 145 (1968), that the right to jury trial in federal court guaranteed by the Sixth Amendment was applicable to the States by virtue of the Fourteenth Amendment. The Court held, however: "It is doubtless true that there is a category of petty crimes or offenses which is not subject to the Sixth Amendment jury trial provision and should not be subject to the Fourteenth Amendment jury trial requirement here applied to the States. Crimes carrying possible penalties up to six months do not require a jury trial if they otherwise qualify as petty offenses...." *Id.*, at 159. In *Baldwin v. New York*, 399 U.S. 66, 69 (1970), the controlling opinion of Mr. Justice White concluded that "no offense can be deemed 'petty' for purposes of the right to trial by jury where imprisonment for more than six months is authorized."

In *Argersinger* the State of Florida urged that a similar dichotomy be employed in the right-to-counsel area: Any offense punishable by less than six months in jail should not require appointment of counsel for an indigent defendant. The *Argersinger* Court rejected this analogy, however, observing that "the right to trial by jury has a different genealogy and is brigaded with a system of trial to a judge alone." 407 U.S., at 29.

The number of separate opinions in *Gideon, Duncan, Baldwin,* and *Argersinger*, suggests that constitutional line drawing becomes more difficult as the reach of the Constitution is extended further, and as efforts are made to transpose lines from one area of Sixth Amendment jurisprudence to another. The process of incorporation creates special difficulties, for the state and federal contexts are often different and application of the same principle may have ramifications distinct in degree and kind. The range of human conduct regulated by state criminal laws is much broader than that of the federal criminal laws, particularly on the "petty" offense part of the spectrum. As a matter of constitutional adjudication, we are, therefore, less willing to extrapolate an already extended line when, although the general nature of the principle sought to be applied is clear, its precise limits and their ramifications become less so. We have now in our decided cases departed from the literal meaning of the Sixth Amendment. And we cannot fall back on the common law as it existed prior to the enactment of that Amendment, since it perversely gave less in the way of right to counsel to accused felons than to those accused of misdemeanors.

In *Argersinger* the Court rejected arguments that social cost or a lack of available lawyers militated against its holding, in some part because it thought these arguments were factually incorrect. But they were rejected in much larger part because of the Court's conclusion that incarceration was so severe a sanction that it should not be imposed as a result of a criminal trial unless an indigent defendant had been offered appointed counsel to assist in his defense, regardless of the cost to the States implicit in such a rule. The Court in its opinion repeatedly referred to trials "where an accused is deprived of his liberty," *id.*, at 32, and to "a case that actually leads to imprisonment even for a brief period," *id.*, at 33. The Chief Justice in his opinion concurring in the result also observed that "any deprivation of liberty is a serious matter." *Id.*, at 41.

Although the intentions of the *Argersinger* Court are not unmistakably clear from its opinion, we conclude today that *Argersinger* did indeed delimit the constitutional right to appointed counsel in state criminal proceedings. Even were the matter *res nova*, we believe that the central premise of *Argersinger*—that actual imprisonment is a penalty different in kind from fines or the mere threat of imprisonment—is eminently sound and warrants adoption of actual imprisonment as the line defining the constitutional right to appointment of counsel. *Argersinger* has proved reasonably workable, whereas any extension would create confusion and impose unpredictable, but necessarily substantial, costs on 50 quite diverse States.[5] We therefore hold that the Sixth and Fourteenth Amendments to the United States Constitution require only that no indigent criminal defendant be sentenced to a term of imprisonment unless the State has afforded him the right to assistance of appointed counsel in his defense....

Mr. Justice POWELL, concurring.

For the reasons stated in my opinion in *Argersinger v. Hamlin*, 407 U.S. 25, 44 (1972), I do not think the rule adopted by the Court in that case is required by the Constitution. Moreover, the drawing of a line based on whether there is imprisonment (even for overnight) can have the practical effect of precluding provision of counsel in other types of cases in which conviction can have more serious consequences. The *Argersinger* rule also tends to impair the proper functioning of the criminal justice system in that trial judges, in advance of hearing any evidence and before knowing anything about the case except the charge, all too often will be compelled to forgo the legislatively granted option to impose a sentence of imprisonment upon conviction. Preserving this option by providing counsel often will be impossible or impracticable—particularly in congested urban courts where scores of cases are heard in a single sitting, and in small and rural communities where lawyers may not be available.

Despite my continuing reservations about the *Argersinger* rule, it was approved by the Court in the 1972 opinion and four Justices have reaffirmed it today. It is important that this Court provide clear guidance to the hundreds of courts

---

5. Unfortunately, extensive empirical work has not been done. That which exists suggests that the requirements of *Argersinger* have not proved to be unduly burdensome. *See, e.g.*, Ingraham, The Impact of Argersinger—One Year Later, 8 Law & Soc.Rev. 615 (1974). That some jurisdictions have had difficulty implementing *Argersinger* is certainly not an argument for extending it. S. Krantz, C. Smith, D. Rossman, P. Froud & J. Hoffman, *Right to Counsel in Criminal Cases* 1–18 (1976).

across the country that confront this problem daily. Accordingly, and mindful of *stare decisis*, I join the opinion of the Court....

Mr. Justice BRENNAN, with whom Mr. Justice MARSHALL and Mr. Justice STEVENS join, dissenting....

This case presents the question whether the right to counsel extends to a person accused of an offense that, although punishable by incarceration, is actually punished only by a fine. Petitioner Aubrey Scott was charged with theft, ... an offense punishable by imprisonment up to one year or by a fine up to $500, or by both. About four months before *Argersinger* was decided, Scott had a bench trial, without counsel, and without notice of entitlement to retain counsel or, if indigent, to have counsel provided. He was found guilty as charged and sentenced to pay a $50 fine.

The Court, in an opinion that at best ignores the basic principles of prior decisions, affirms Scott's conviction without counsel because he was sentenced only to pay a fine. In my view, the plain wording of the Sixth Amendment and the Court's precedents compel the conclusion that Scott's uncounseled conviction violated the Sixth and Fourteenth Amendments and should be reversed.

I

... *Gideon v. Wainwright* held that, because representation by counsel in a criminal proceeding is "fundamental and essential to a fair trial," 372 U.S., at 342, the Sixth Amendment right to counsel was applicable to the States through the Fourteenth Amendment....

Earlier precedents had recognized that the assistance of appointed counsel was critical, not only to equalize the sides in an adversary criminal process,[2] but also to give substance to other constitutional and procedural protections afforded criminal defendants.[3] *Gideon* established the right to appointed counsel for indigent accuseds as a categorical requirement, making the Court's former case-by-case due process analysis, cf. *Betts v. Brady*, 316 U.S. 455 (1942), unnecessary in cases covered by its holding. *Gideon* involved a felony prosecution, but that fact was not crucial to the decision; its reasoning extended, in the words of the Sixth Amendment, to "*all* criminal prosecutions."

Argersinger v. Hamlin took a cautious approach toward implementing the logical consequences of *Gideon's* rationale....

... The question of the right to counsel in cases in which incarceration was authorized but would not be imposed was expressly reserved.

II

In my view petitioner could prevail in this case without extending the right to counsel beyond what was assumed to exist in *Argersinger*. Neither party in that case questioned the existence of the right to counsel in trials involving "non-petty" offenses punishable by more than six months in jail. The question the Court addressed was whether the right applied to some "petty" offenses to which the right to jury trial did not extend. The Court's reasoning in applying the right to counsel in the case before it—that the right to counsel is more fundamental to a fair proceeding than the right to jury trial and that the historical limitations on the jury trial right are irrelevant to the right to counsel—certainly cannot support a standard for the right to counsel that is more restrictive than the standard

2. "[The Sixth Amendment] embodies a realistic recognition of the obvious truth that the average defendant does not have the professional legal skill to protect himself when brought before a tribunal with power to take his life or liberty, wherein the prosecution is presented by experienced and learned counsel. That which is simple, orderly and necessary to the lawyer, to the untrained layman may appear intricate, complex and mysterious." *Johnson v. Zerbst*, 304 U.S. 458, 462–463 (1938).

3. "The right to be heard would be, in many cases, of little avail if it did not comprehend the right to be heard by counsel. Even the intelligent and educated layman has small and sometimes no skill in the science of law. If charged with crime, he is incapable, generally, of determining for himself whether the indictment is good or bad. He is unfamiliar with the rules of evidence. Left without the aid of counsel he may be put on trial without a proper charge, and convicted upon incompetent evidence, or evidence irrelevant to the issue or otherwise inadmissible. He lacks both the skill and knowledge adequately to prepare his defense, even though he have a perfect one. He requires the guiding hand of counsel at every step in the proceedings against him. Without it, though he be not guilty, he faces the danger of conviction because he does not know how to establish his innocence. If that be true of men of intelligence, how much more true is it of the ignorant and illiterate, or those of feeble intellect." *Powell v. Alabama*, 287 U.S. 45, 68–69 (1932).

for granting a right to jury trial.... *Argersinger* thus established a "two dimensional" test for the right to counsel: the right attaches to any "nonpetty" offense punishable by more than six months in jail and in addition to any offense where actual incarceration is likely regardless of the maximum authorized penalty.

The offense of "theft" with which Scott was charged is certainly not a "petty" one. It is punishable by a sentence of up to one year in jail. Unlike many traffic or other "regulatory" offenses, it carries the moral stigma associated with common-law crimes traditionally recognized as indicative of moral depravity.[10] The State indicated at oral argument that the services of a professional prosecutor were considered essential to the prosecution of this offense. Likewise, nonindigent defendants charged with this offense would be well advised to hire the "best lawyers they can get."[11] Scott's right to the assistance of appointed counsel is thus plainly mandated by the logic of the Court's prior cases, including *Argersinger* itself.

III

But rather than decide consonant with the assumption in regard to nonpetty offenses that was both implicit and explicit in *Argersinger,* the Court today retreats to the indefensible position that the *Argersinger* "actual imprisonment" standard is the *only* test for determining the boundary of the Sixth Amendment right to appointed counsel in state misdemeanor cases, thus necessarily deciding that in many cases (such as this one) a defendant will have no right to appointed counsel even when he has a constitutional right to a jury trial. This is simply an intolerable result. Not only is the "actual imprisonment" standard unprecedented as the exclusive test, but also the problems inherent in its application demonstrate the superiority of an "authorized imprisonment" standard that would require the appointment of counsel for indigents accused of any offense for which imprisonment for any time is authorized.

First, the "authorized imprisonment" standard more faithfully implements the principles of the Sixth Amendment identified in *Gideon.* The procedural rules established by state statutes are geared to the nature of the potential penalty for an offense, not to the actual penalty imposed in particular cases. The authorized penalty is also a better predictor of the stigma and other collateral consequences that attach to conviction of an offense.... Imprisonment is a sanction particularly associated with criminal offenses; trials of offenses punishable by imprisonment accordingly possess the characteristics found by *Gideon* to require the appointment of counsel. By contrast, the "actual imprisonment" standard, as the Court's opinion in this case demonstrates, denies the right to counsel in criminal prosecutions to accuseds who suffer the severe consequences of prosecution other than imprisonment.

Second, the "authorized imprisonment" test presents no problems of administration. It avoids the necessity for time-consuming consideration of the likely sentence in each individual case before trial and the attendant problems of inaccurate predictions, unequal treatment, and apparent and actual bias....

Finally, the "authorized imprisonment" test ensures that courts will not abrogate legislative judgments concerning the appropriate range of penalties to be considered for each offense. Under the "actual imprisonment" standard,

"[t]he judge will ... be forced to decide in advance of trial—and without hearing the evidence—whether he will forego entirely his judicial discretion to impose some sentence of imprisonment and abandon his responsibility to consider the full range of punishments established by the legislature. His alternatives, assuming the availability of counsel, will be to appoint counsel and retain the discretion vested in him by law, or to abandon this discretion in advance and proceed without counsel."

10. Because a theft conviction implies dishonesty, it may be a basis for impeaching petitioner's testimony in a court proceeding. Because jurors must be of "fair character" and "approved integrity," petitioner may be excluded from jury duty as a result of his theft conviction. Twelve occupations licensed under Illinois law and 23 occupations licensed under city of Chicago ordinances require the license applicant to have "good moral character" or some equivalent background qualification that could be found unsatisfied because of a theft conviction. Under federal law petitioner's theft conviction would bar him from working in any capacity in a bank insured by the Federal Deposit Insurance Corporation, or possibly in any public or private employment requiring a security clearance.

11. *Gideon v. Wainwright,* 372 U.S. 335, 344 (1963).

Argersinger v. Hamlin, supra, at 53 (Powell, J., concurring in result).

The "authorized imprisonment" standard, on the other hand, respects the allocation of functions between legislatures and courts in the administration of the criminal justice system.

The apparent reason for the Court's adoption of the "actual imprisonment" standard for all misdemeanors is concern for the economic burden that an "authorized imprisonment" standard might place on the States. But, with all respect, that concern is both irrelevant and speculative.

This Court's role in enforcing constitutional guarantees for criminal defendants cannot be made dependent on the budgetary decisions of state governments....

In any event, the extent of the alleged burden on the States is, as the Court admits, *ante,* at n. 5, speculative. Although more persons are charged with misdemeanors punishable by incarceration than are charged with felonies, a smaller percentage of persons charged with misdemeanors qualify as indigent, and misdemeanor cases as a rule require far less attorney time.[16]

Furthermore, public defender systems have proved economically feasible, and the establishment of such systems to replace appointment of private attorneys can keep costs at acceptable levels even when the number of cases requiring appointment of counsel increases dramatically.[17] The public defender system alternative also answers the argument that an authorized imprisonment standard would clog the courts with inexperienced appointed counsel.

Perhaps the strongest refutation of respondent's alarmist prophecies that an authorized imprisonment standard would wreak havoc on the States is that the standard has not produced that result in the substantial number of States that already provide counsel in all cases where imprisonment is authorized. States that include a large majority of the country's population and a great diversity of urban and rural environments. Moreover, of those States that do not yet provide counsel in all cases where *any* imprisonment is authorized, many provide counsel when periods of imprisonment longer than 30 days, 3 months, or 6 months are authorized. In fact, Scott would be entitled to appointed counsel under the current laws of at least 33 States.

It may well be that adoption by this Court of an "authorized imprisonment" standard would lead state and local governments to re-examine their criminal statutes. A state legislature or local government might determine that it no longer desired to authorize incarceration for certain minor offenses in light of the expense of meeting the requirements of the Constitution. In my view this re-examination is long overdue. In any event, the Court's "actual imprisonment" standard must inevitably lead the courts to make this re-examination, which plainly should more properly be a legislative responsibility.

IV

The Court's opinion turns the reasoning of *Argersinger* on its head. It restricts the right to counsel, perhaps the most fundamental Sixth Amendment right, more narrowly than the admittedly less fundamental right to jury trial. The abstract pretext that "constitutional line drawing becomes more difficult as the reach of the Constitution is extended further, and as efforts are made to transpose lines from one area of Sixth Amendment jurisprudence to another," cannot camouflage the anomalous result the Court reaches. Today's decision reminds one of Mr. Justice Black's description of *Betts v. Brady* : "an anachronism when handed down" that "ma[kes] an abrupt break with its own well-considered precedents." *Gideon v. Wainwright,* 372 U.S., at 345, 344.

Mr. Justice BLACKMUN, dissenting....

---

16. See Uniform Rules of Criminal Procedure, Rule 321(b), Comment, 10 U.L.A. 70 (1974) (estimates that only 10% of misdemeanor defendants, as opposed to 60%–65% of felony defendants, meet the necessary indigency standard); National Legal Aid and Defender Assn., The Other Face of Justice, Note I, pp. 82–83 (1973) (survey indicates national average is 65% indigency in felony cases and only 47% in misdemeanor cases).

The National Advisory Commission on Criminal Justice Standards and Goals adopted a maximum caseload standard of 150 felony cases or 400 misdemeanor cases per attorney per year.

17. A study conducted in the State of Wisconsin, which introduced a State Public Defender System after the Wisconsin Supreme Court in *State ex rel. Winnie v. Harris,* 75 Wis.2d 547, 249 N.W.2d 791 (1977), extended the right to counsel in the way urged by petitioner in this case, indicated that the average cost of providing counsel in a misdemeanor case was reduced from $150–$200 to $90 by using a public defender rather than appointing private counsel.

Notes and Questions

1. To date, the overwhelming majority of identified wrongful convictions have been for the serious crimes of murder and rape. Yet there is little reason to suspect that the factors recognized as contributing to these miscarriages of justice (*e.g.*, eyewitness misidentification, ineffective assistance of counsel, and others) are limited to murder and rape cases. In 2008, state courts processed approximately 16 million misdemeanor cases in comparison to approximately 3.5 million felony cases.[3] Thus, the opportunity for wrongful convictions for lower level crimes is great. For an excellent overview of the reasons for the skewed distribution of murder and rape cases among exonerations, *see* Samuel R. Gross *et al.*, "Exonerations in the United States 1989 through 2003," 95 *Journal of Criminal Law and Criminology* 523 (2005). While noting that cases with comparatively light sentences were not included in their exoneration sample, Gross and colleagues acknowledged, "Our data reflect this: nobody, it seems, seriously pursues exonerations for defendants who are falsely convicted of shoplifting, misdemeanor assault, drug possession, or routine felonies—auto thefts or run-of-the-mill burglaries—and sentenced to probation, a $2000 fine, or even six months in the county jail or eighteen months in state prison. But obviously such errors occur." *Id.*, at 535–536.

2. An uncounseled misdemeanor conviction can have serious consequences for a defendant beyond the immediate trial and the resulting stigmatization, sanctions, and criminal record. In 1983, Kenneth Nichols pled guilty to misdemeanor driving under the influence (DUI) in a state court proceeding in Georgia. He was indigent and entered his guilty plea without the benefit of counsel and without having effectively waived the right to be represented by a court-appointed lawyer. He was fined $250 following conviction but was not incarcerated. Seven years later, while represented by an attorney, Nichols pled guilty to federal felony drug charges. Under the federal Sentencing Guidelines then in effect, Nichols's prior DUI conviction increased his maximum presumptive sentence from 210 months to 235 months imprisonment, or by more than two years. The judge, taking the DUI conviction into consideration, imposed the maximum 235 month sentence. Nichols argued that the 25 month sentence enhancement resulted directly from his prior, uncounseled misdemeanor conviction and thus was in violation of his 6th Amendment right to counsel under *Gideon* and *Argersinger*. The Supreme Court disagreed. Chief Justice Rehnquist's majority opinion in *Nichols v. United States,* 511 U.S. 738, 114 S.Ct. 1921, 128 L.Ed.2d 745 (1994), concluded that "an uncounseled misdemeanor conviction, valid under *Scott* because no prison term was imposed, is also valid when used to enhance punishment at a subsequent conviction." 511 U.S., at 749. In dissent, Justice Blackmun maintained that Nichols's uncounseled DUI conviction "led directly to his imprisonment for over two years." 511 U.S., at 754. He argued that "an uncounseled misdemeanor, like an uncounseled felony, is not reliable enough to form the basis for the severe sanction of incarceration." 511 U.S., at 762. Quoting Justice Marshall's concurring opinion in *Baldasar v. Illinois,* 446 U.S. 222, 227–228, 100 S.Ct. 1585, 64 L.Ed.2d 169, he concluded: "'An uncounseled conviction does not become more reliable merely because the accused has been validly convicted of a subsequent offense. For this reason, a conviction which is invalid for purposes of imposing a sentence of imprisonment for the offense itself remains invalid for purposes of increasing a term of imprisonment for a subsequent conviction under a repeat-offender statute.'"

3. The defendant in *Alabama v. Shelton*, 535 U.S. 654, 122 S.Ct. 1764, 152 L.Ed.2d 888 (2002), an indigent who was not represented by and had not waived his right to court-appointed trial counsel, was convicted of misdemeanor assault, fined $500, and sentenced to a 30-day jail term that was suspended for two years while he was placed on unsupervised

probation. Shelton challenged the constitutional validity of the suspended jail term. Under Alabama law, indigents facing the activation of a suspended jail sentence for violating the terms of probation were entitled to the appointment of counsel at the probation revocation proceeding. Justice Ginsburg's majority opinion in the Court's 5–4 decision in *Shelton* nevertheless concluded that "a suspended sentence that may 'end up in the actual deprivation of a person's liberty' may not be imposed unless the defendant was accorded 'the guiding hand of counsel' in the prosecution for the crime charged." 535 U.S., at 658, *quoting Argersinger v. Hamlin,* 407 U.S. 25, 40, 92 S.Ct. 2006, 32 L.Ed.2d 530 (1972). Her opinion reasoned: "A suspended sentence is a prison term imposed for the offense of conviction. Once the prison term is triggered, the defendant is incarcerated not for the probation violation, but for the underlying offense. The uncounseled conviction at that point 'results in imprisonment'; it 'end[s] up in the actual deprivation of a person's liberty.' This is precisely what the Sixth Amendment, as interpreted in *Argersinger* and *Scott,* does not allow." 535 U.S., at 662 (citations omitted). In dissent, Justice Scalia protested: "We are asked to decide whether 'imposition of a suspended or conditional sentence in a misdemeanor case invoke[s] a defendant's Sixth Amendment right to counsel.' Since *imposition* of a suspended sentence does not deprive a defendant of his personal liberty, the answer to *that* question is plainly no. In the future, *if and when* the State of Alabama seeks to imprison respondent on the previously suspended sentence, we can ask whether the procedural safeguards attending the imposition of the sentence comply with the Constitution. But that question is *not* before us now." 535 U.S., at 676 (citation omitted, emphasis in original). He argued that "the Court's decision imposes a large, new burden on a majority of the States, including some of the poorest.... That burden consists not only of the cost of providing state-paid counsel in cases of such insignificance that even financially prosperous defendants sometimes forgo the expense of hired counsel; but also the cost of enabling courts and prosecutors to respond to the 'over-lawyering' of minor cases. Nor should we discount the burden placed on the minority 24 States that currently provide counsel: that they keep their current disposition forever in place, however imprudent experience proves it to be." 535 U.S., at 680–681 (citation omitted).

4. The Supreme Court has ruled that indigent criminal defendants have a constitutional right to court-appointed counsel for representation on appeal of their convictions. Although there is no constitutional right to appeal a criminal conviction, all States provide a statutory right to appeal. Because the 6th Amendment right to counsel does not apply beyond the trial, the justices based their ruling on Due Process and Equal Protection grounds. *Douglas v. California,* 372 U.S. 353, 83 S.Ct. 814, 9 L.Ed.2d 811 (1963). The Court has further ruled that there is no federal constitutional right to court-appointed counsel in criminal cases beyond the initial appeal. In *Ross v. Moffitt,* 417 U.S. 600, 94 S.Ct. 2437, 41 L.Ed.2d 31 (1974), the justices declined to extend the *Douglas* ruling to require the appointment of counsel for indigents seeking discretionary review of their convictions in a State supreme court following the initial appeal, or by petition for writ of certiorari filed in the United States Supreme Court. The Court also has rejected claims for a constitutional right to court-appointed counsel to pursue state or federal post-conviction proceedings. *See Murray v. Giarratano,* 492 U.S. 1, 109 S.Ct. 2765, 106 L.Ed.2d 1 (1989) (capital case); *Pennsylvania v. Finley,* 481 U.S. 551, 107 S.Ct. 1990, 95 L.Ed.2d 539 (1987). The justices have granted certiorari in two cases to revisit related issues. *Maples v. Thomas,* 131 S.Ct. 1718 (2011); *Martinez v. Ryan,* 131 S.Ct. ___, 2011 WL 380903 (2011). Many states nevertheless provide a statutory right to court-appointed counsel for indigent prisoners seeking post-conviction review of their convictions.[4] Prisoners do not have a constitutional right to court-appointed counsel to seek review of their convictions on federal habeas corpus, although Congress

has authorized the appointment of counsel in federal habeas corpus proceedings for state and federal prisoners under sentence of death.[5]

C. Ineffective Assistance of Counsel

The constitutional right to the assistance of counsel implicitly guarantees that the defense attorney is a capable advocate. As the Court explained in *Strickland v. Washington*, 466 U.S. 668, 685–686, 104 S.Ct. 2052, 80 L.Ed.2d 674 (1984):

> That a person who happens to be a lawyer is present at trial alongside the accused ... is not enough to satisfy the constitutional command. The Sixth Amendment recognizes the right to the assistance of counsel because it envisions counsel's playing a role that is critical to the ability of the adversarial system to produce just results. An accused is entitled to be assisted by an attorney, whether retained or appointed, who plays the role necessary to ensure that the trial is fair.
>
> For that reason, the Court has recognized that "the right to counsel is the right to the effective assistance of counsel." *McMann v. Richardson*, 397 U.S. 759, 771, n. 14, 90 S.Ct. 1441, 25 L.Ed.2d 763 (1970).

The *Strickland* Court enunciated a two-part test for assessing ineffective assistance of counsel claims, involving whether trial counsel's *performance* measured up to minimal expectations and, if not, whether the defendant thereby suffered *prejudice*. Because trial performance is so likely to be dependent on the amount and quality of a lawyer's advance preparation, it should not be surprising that ineffective assistance of counsel claims frequently include allegations that defense attorneys neglected to engage in essential pretrial investigations. The *Strickland* test and its application are at issue in the following case, involving an alleged wrongful conviction.

Towns v. Smith

395 F.3d 251 (6th Cir. 2005)

BOYCE F. MARTIN, JR., Circuit Judge.

David Smith, Warden, appeals the district court's conditional grant of Parrish Towns's petition for a writ of habeas corpus. Because Parrish Towns's two brothers also are involved in this case, we generally will refer to Parrish Towns by his first name. The district court held that Parrish's trial counsel rendered ineffective assistance in violation of the Sixth Amendment by failing to investigate a witness who had admitted to the police, among others, that he had been involved in the crimes of which Parrish was ultimately convicted and that Parrish had played no part in those crimes. For the reasons that follow, as well as those expressed in the district court's well-reasoned opinion, we AFFIRM.

I.

Parrish Towns was convicted and sentenced to life in prison for his role in the 1982 robbery and murder of Wilma Steward. The sole eyewitness to the crime was a man named Roland Higgs, who also was robbed by the perpetrators but who survived. Soon after the murder, the police arrested an individual named Michael Richard on an unrelated charge. At the time of his arrest, Richard was in possession of a handgun, which—after Richard was released from custody—was determined to be the gun used to shoot Steward. The police also learned that Richard had committed a number of robberies in the past. Collectively, this information led the police to suspect that Richard was involved in the Steward robbery and murder, and they obtained and executed a warrant for his arrest.

Although he initially denied any involvement in the crime, Richard later admitted to an officer named Sergeant Brantley that he had, in fact, driven the get-away car, but that "Willie and his brother" were the individuals who actually robbed and shot Steward. Police determined that the "Willie" to whom Richard had referred was Willie Towns, one of Parrish's brothers, whom they proceeded to arrest. Richard subsequently told two other officers, Sergeant Sterr and Lieutenant Morrison, that the "brother" who committed the murder with Willie Towns was Kevin Towns, Parrish's other brother. Based upon this revelation, about which Sterr and Morrison informed Brantley as well as the prosecutor, the police obtained an arrest warrant for Kevin Towns and a search warrant for the Towns residence.

When the police arrived at the Towns residence, they found Parrish, who, at the time, physically resembled Kevin. Both brothers were described as being 5' 10" tall and weighing 175 pounds, and there was only a one-year difference in their ages. At this point, for reasons that never have been adequately explained, the police switched their focus from Kevin to Parrish. They asked Parrish to accompany them to the police station, which he did, and proceeded to put him in a line-up. Higgs, the eyewitness, tentatively identified Parrish as one of the perpetrators, but only on the basis of Parrish's height and weight, which—as explained—were similar to Kevin's. Moreover, Higgs emphasized that he "couldn't be sure of any identification" that he made. Later, Higgs firmly identified Willie Towns as the second perpetrator in photographic and live line-ups. Willie and Parrish Towns were ultimately tried jointly for their alleged roles in the Steward murder. It remains unclear why Richard never has been prosecuted for his role in this crime, as well as why the police never executed the warrant for Kevin Towns's arrest.

The prosecutor initially intended to call Richard as a witness at trial—presumably because he had implicated Willie Towns in the Steward murder—but changed his mind at the last minute. After the court granted the prosecutor's motion to strike Richard's name as a prosecution witness, Parrish's defense counsel insisted on having the opportunity to visit Richard in the county jail, where he had been transferred in anticipation of his trial testimony, to determine what Richard's testimony would be and whether it would be beneficial to call him as a witness in Parrish's defense. Counsel explicitly stated to the trial judge that "I have to speak with him first" in order to decide whether to call Richard as a defense witness. Richard was kept in the county jail over night, at counsel's request, but counsel never made any attempt to contact him. The following day, counsel informed the court that he would not be calling Richard as a witness.

Not surprisingly, the prosecution's case against Parrish was weak. There was no direct evidence linking him to the crimes and the strongest evidence against him was Higgs's eyewitness testimony, which was equivocal at best. Parrish's primary defense was alibi, and he called several witnesses who established his whereabouts on the evening in question....

Following this alibi testimony, the prosecution called Sergeant Dunn to the stand as a rebuttal witness. Dunn testified that on the day of his arrest, Parrish denied any involvement in the Steward murder and told him that he was at an arcade on the day of the murder. Although Parrish never testified at trial, he testified at the habeas evidentiary hearing that he initially told the police he was at an arcade because that was his normal routine and he had no specific recollection of his activities on the day of the murder, which was two weeks earlier.

At the conclusion of the trial, Willie and Parrish Towns both were convicted of robbery and first degree felony murder. Approximately nineteen years after his conviction, and after the state courts declined to grant relief, Parrish filed the instant habeas petition in the district court. His petition asserted a number of claims, including a claim for ineffective assistance of trial counsel. The Warden argued in the district court—and continues to argue in this appeal—that Parrish's ineffective assistance claim should be dismissed pursuant to the doctrine of laches because critical witnesses and evidence are no longer available, thereby impairing the Warden's ability to defend against the claim. The Warden also argued—and continues to argue—that the other claims asserted in the petition are barred by procedural default. According to Parrish, however, any procedural default that may have occurred with respect to those claims should be excused because he is actually innocent of the crimes of which he was convicted.

By order of the district court, the magistrate held an evidentiary hearing on the actual innocence issue. Although the hearing focused specifically on actual innocence, much of the testimony elicited also is relevant to Parrish's ineffective assistance claim. For example, attorney Darwin Fair testified about an interview that he conducted with Michael Richard in connection with a state court motion for relief from judgment that he had filed on Parrish's behalf. According to Fair, Richard told him that he was familiar with the facts and circumstances surrounding Parrish's conviction and that he had personal knowledge that Parrish had nothing to do with the offenses for which he had been convicted. Further, Richard indicated to Fair that he was never contacted by Parrish's trial counsel, despite his willingness to testify at trial that Parrish was not involved in the Steward murder. Based upon this information, Fair prepared an affidavit for Richard to sign, although Richard never actually signed it.

Parrish's mother also testified, as she did at trial, that Parrish returned home at approximately 1:00 a.m. on the night in question, after helping his friend move. She also explained that Richard was a friend of her son Willie but not of Parrish. Finally, she testified that on the day before Parrish's trial, she received a phone call from someone identifying himself as Michael Richard, who said that he was calling from jail and informed her that Parrish was not involved in the Steward murder.

At the beginning of the second day of the habeas evidentiary hearing, Parrish's attorney indicated that he intended to call Richard as his next witness. Because Richard had expressed a reluctance to testify without a formal grant of immunity, the magistrate appointed attorney Epstein of the Federal Defender's Office to represent him. After consulting with Richard, Epstein informed the court that Richard was unwilling to testify without a grant of immunity from prosecution and that, if called without immunity, he would invoke his Fifth Amendment privilege against self-incrimination. For reasons that are unknown, the state refused to grant Richard immunity and Richard consequently refused to testify.

Parrish then took the stand and denied any involvement in the crimes of which he was convicted....

Finally, Michael Martin, an investigator hired by attorney Fair, testified that, in connection with the motion for relief from judgment, he visited Richard in prison to verify the exculpatory evidence that Richard had provided to Fair. Martin showed Richard the affidavit that Fair had prepared for his signature and Richard confirmed that its contents were true. According to Martin, Richard also made it clear that he had been involved in some way in the Steward murder, that he, Willie Towns and Kevin Towns were the only individuals involved, and that he and Willie had committed other crimes together.

Martin also testified about his second trip to visit Richard in prison, this time with habeas counsel. During that visit, Martin said, Richard was especially emphatic about Parrish's innocence....

At the conclusion of the hearing, the magistrate granted the parties additional time to consult with the Wayne County Prosecutor's Office to attempt to arrange immunity for Richard so that he could testify. The parties later informed the magistrate that no such deal could be arranged and, accordingly, Richard never testified at the evidentiary hearing. The magistrate recommended, and the district court agreed, that although Parrish had come close, he had ultimately failed to meet the high burden of proof required to excuse procedural default on actual innocence grounds. To our knowledge, the state has never justified its continued refusal to grant any sort of immunity to Richard for his role in the Steward murder. The state has known for over twenty years now that Richard possessed the gun that was used to shoot Steward and that Richard admitted to driving the get-away car. Yet, despite this evidence, the state has never prosecuted Richard and it appears that it never will. Under these circumstances, the state's refusal to grant Richard immunity is inexplicable. Not only did this refusal significantly undermine the district court's ability to determine whether Parrish was actually innocent, it compounded the danger that a murderer will remain free.

Although Parrish's actual innocence argument was rejected, which affected most of the claims asserted in the habeas petition, the district court found that Parrish's ineffective assistance claim, which was unaffected, was meritorious. The district court held that Parrish's trial counsel rendered ineffective assistance in violation of the Sixth Amendment by failing to investigate Richard as a potential defense witness. Accordingly, the court conditionally granted Parrish's petition, ordering the state to retry him within ninety days or release him from custody. Parrish was subsequently released on bond pending the Warden's appeal.

II.

...

B. ***Ineffective Assistance of Trial Counsel***

... No state court has adjudicated the merits of Parrish's ineffective assistance claim. Therefore, the deferential standard of review set forth in section 2254(d) of the Antiterrorism and Effective Death Penalty Act does not apply, as there is no state court conclusion by which our review could be circumscribed. *Wiggins v. Smith,* 539 U.S. 510 (2003). In analyzing Parrish's ineffective assistance claim, we consider "the totality of the evidence —'both that adduced at trial, and the evidence adduced in the habeas proceeding,'" *Wiggins,* 539 U.S. at 536 (quoting *Williams v. Taylor,* 529 U.S. 362, 397–98 (2000)) (emphasis omitted).

... The familiar two-prong test set forth in *Strickland v. Washington,* 466 U.S. 668 (1984), governs our analysis. The first prong requires Parrish to prove that his trial counsel's representation was deficient in that it "fell below an objective standard of reasonableness." *Strickland,* 466 U.S. at 688. We "must indulge a strong presumption that counsel's conduct falls within the wide range of reasonable professional assistance; that is, the defendant must overcome the presumption that, under the circumstances, the challenged conduct might be considered sound trial strategy." *Id.* at 689. The second prong requires Parrish to demonstrate that "there is a reasonable probability that, but for counsel's unprofessional errors, the result of [his trial] would have been different. A reasonable probability is a probability sufficient to undermine confidence in the outcome." *Id.* at 694....

Parrish argues that his trial counsel rendered ineffective assistance in two related ways: first, by failing to conduct a reasonable investigation into Michael Richard; and second, by failing to call Richard as a defense witness. In granting the petition, the district court relied upon the failure to investigate theory. It is well-established that "[c]ounsel has a duty to make reasonable investigations or to make a reasonable decision that makes particular investigations unnecessary." *Strickland,* 466 U.S. at 691. The duty to investigate derives from counsel's basic function, which is "'to make the adversarial testing process work in the particular case.'" *Kimmelman v. Morrison,* 477 U.S. 365, 384 (1986). This duty includes the obligation to investigate all witnesses who may have information concerning his or her client's guilt or innocence. "In any ineffectiveness case, a particular decision not to investigate must be directly assessed for reasonableness in all the circumstances, applying a heavy measure of deference to counsel's judgments." *Strickland,* 466 U.S. at 691. "The relevant question is not whether counsel's choices were strategic, but whether they were reasonable." *Roe v. Flores-Ortega,* 528 U.S. 470, 481 (2000). A purportedly strategic decision is not objectively reasonable "when the attorney has failed to investigate his options and make a reasonable choice between them." *Horton v. Zant,* 941 F.2d 1449, 1462 (11th Cir.1991).

Courts have not hesitated to find ineffective assistance in violation of the Sixth Amendment when counsel fails to conduct a reasonable investigation into one or more aspects of the case and when that failure prejudices his or her client. For example, in the recent case of *Wiggins v. Smith,* the Supreme Court held that the petitioner was entitled to a writ of habeas corpus because his counsel had failed to conduct a reasonable investigation into potentially mitigating evidence with respect to sentencing. According to the Court, "counsel chose to abandon their investigation at an unreasonable juncture, making a fully informed decision with respect to sentence strategy impossible." *Id.* at 527–28. Consistent with *Wiggins,* we have held, in a variety of situations, that counsel's failure to investigate constituted ineffective assistance in violation of the Sixth Amendment....

... Parrish's trial counsel's failure to conduct a reasonable investigation into Michael Richard, "a known and potentially important witness," violated Parrish's Sixth Amendment right to the effective assistance of counsel. Parrish has successfully satisfied both the deficiency and prejudice prongs of *Strickland.* With regard to the deficiency prong, the facts as recited above demonstrate that counsel made absolutely no attempt to communicate with Richard, despite requesting that Richard be kept in the county jail so that he could interview him prior to the commencement of the trial. Without even attempting to interview Richard, counsel simply decided not to call him as a witness. That decision was objectively unreasonable because it "was a decision made without undertaking a full investigation" into whether Richard could assist in Parrish's defense. By failing even to contact Richard—despite explicitly acknowledging the need to do so—counsel "abandoned his investigation at an unreasonable juncture, making a fully informed decision with respect to [whether to call Richard as a witness] impossible." *Wiggins,* 539 U.S. at 527–28.

... We do not mean to suggest that under no circumstances could counsel's failure to call Richard as a defense witness be deemed an objectively reasonable decision. We, like the district court, hold only that it was objectively unreasonable for counsel to make that decision without first investigating Richard, or at least making a reasoned professional judgment that such investigation was unnecessary....

With regard to *Strickland*'s prejudice prong, the record contains ample evidence indicating that but for counsel's ineffectiveness, there is a reasonable probability that Parrish would have been acquitted. Richard has consistently maintained to the police and to others that Parrish was not involved in the crimes for which he was convicted, and that he (Richard) had been willing to testify to that effect at Parrish's 1983 trial. Had counsel interviewed Richard, he would have discovered as much and probably would have put him on the stand—depending in part upon what other information counsel's investigation uncovered. In short, there is a reasonable probability that had the jury heard Richard's testimony, it would have acquitted Parrish....

Parrish's claim of prejudice is further supported by the notable weaknesses in the prosecution's case. The Supreme Court has explained that "a verdict or conclusion only weakly supported by the record is more likely to have been affected by errors than one with overwhelming record support." *Strickland*, 466 U.S. at 696. The only evidence linking Parrish to the crime was the eyewitness testimony of Roland Higgs. We have repeatedly expressed our "grave reservations concerning the reliability of eyewitness testimony," and Higgs's identification of Parrish in this case was particularly shaky. As discussed, that identification was admittedly tentative and was based solely on Parrish's height and weight, which were equivalent to those of his brother, Kevin, who apparently never was included in any line-up. In light of the relatively scant evidence of Parrish's guilt, his counsel's ineffectiveness must be deemed especially prejudicial.

III.

For these reasons, the district court's judgment is AFFIRMED and the state has ninety days within which to release or retry Parrish Towns.

Notes and Questions

1. Acting contrary to the advice of his court-appointed lawyer, David Washington, the defendant in *Strickland v. Washington*, 466 U.S. 668, 104 S.Ct. 2052, 80 L.Ed.2d 674 (1984), pled guilty to three counts of capital murder, waived his right under Florida law to an advisory sentencing jury, and appeared for sentencing before a judge. In preparation for the sentencing hearing, the attorney interviewed Washington and his wife and mother, but did not otherwise attempt to locate potential character witnesses. Nor did he request a psychiatric examination for his client or ask that a presentence report be prepared, concluding that there was no basis for the former and that damaging information about Washington might be uncovered and presented if a presentence report were completed. The attorney presented no mitigation evidence at the sentencing hearing, relying instead on arguments that Washington had accepted responsibility for his conduct and on his expressions of remorse. Concluding that Washington's crimes were highly aggravated and not offset by mitigating factors, the judge sentenced Washington to death. Washington thereafter challenged his death sentences, arguing that his lawyer provided him with ineffective assistance at his sentencing hearing. The Supreme Court disagreed. In announcing the two-part test for analyzing ineffective assistance of counsel claims, Justice O'Connor's majority opinion concluded that "[t]he benchmark for judging any claim of ineffectiveness must be whether counsel's conduct so undermined the proper functioning of the adversarial process that the trial cannot be relied on as having produced a just result." 466 U.S., at 686. "Judicial scrutiny of counsel's performance must be highly deferential.... [A] court must indulge a strong presumption that counsel's conduct falls within the wide range of reasonable professional assistance...." 466 U.S., at 689.

> [S]trategic choices made thorough investigation of law and facts relevant to plausible options are virtually unchallengeable; and strategic choices made after less than complete investigation are reasonable precisely to the extent that reasonable professional judgments support the limitations on investigation. In other words, counsel has a duty to make reasonable investigations or to make a reasonable decision that makes particular investigations unnecessary. In any ineffectiveness case, a particular decision not to investigate must be directly assessed for reasonableness in all the circumstances, applying a heavy measure of deference to counsel's judgments. 466 U.S., at 690–691.

2. The Court has repeatedly stressed its conclusion in *Strickland* that courts must be highly deferential in assessing the reasonableness of defense attorneys' "strategic choices made after thorough investigation of law and facts," and that those choices are "virtually unchallengeable." *See, e.g., Knowles v. Mirzayance,* ___ U.S. ___, 129 S.Ct. 1411, 1420, 173 L.Ed.2d 251 (2009); *Wiggins v. Smith,* 539 U.S. 510, 521–522, 123 S.Ct. 2527, 156 L.Ed.2d 471 (2003); *Burger v. Kemp,* 483 U.S. 776, 794–795, 107 S.Ct. 3114, 97 L.Ed.2d 638 (1987). At the same time, as we saw in *Towns v. Smith, supra,* "the investigation supporting counsel's [strategic] decision[s] ... [must] *itself [be] reasonable.*" *Wiggins v. Smith,* 539 U.S., at 523 (emphasis in original). We return to this important principle in the following case, involving an allegation of ineffective assistance of counsel based on an attorney's failure to consult with an expert to investigate issues material to his client's defense.

State v. Whittaker

158 N.H. 762, 973 A.2d 299 (2009)

DALIANIS, J.

The defendant, Kevin C. Whittaker, appeals his conviction by a jury for negligent homicide.... [H]e contends that the Superior Court (*Fauver,* J.) erred by ... denying his motion for new trial based upon ineffective assistance of counsel. We reverse and remand.

I. Background

The jury could have found the following facts. At approximately 12:50 a.m. on Sunday, November 21, 2004, a rainy and foggy night, the Durham police received a call telling them that a person was lying on Main Street. The man, later identified as Richard Hegerich, was lying parallel to the fog line, near the sidewalk curb. He was dressed in dark clothing. His face was covered with blood, and he was missing his shoes and socks. One of his shoes, a sock and his hat were in the roadway, some distance away from his body.

The police determined that Hegerich, who was twenty years old, was dead. A medical examiner later concluded that Hegerich died of multiple blunt trauma to the head caused by a motor vehicle accident. It was also determined that Hegerich had a blood alcohol content of .14. Based upon the position of his body, and the positions of his shoe, sock and hat, the police concluded that he had not been in the crosswalk when he was hit. The police found no evidence of skid marks....

At approximately 1:07 a.m., a UNH police officer stopped the defendant's car because one of its headlights was not working. The officer noticed that the car's passenger side windshield looked smashed. The defendant told the officer that a friend had been driving his car, but he could not name the friend, telling the officer instead that "it was some guy" whom he did not know very well.

While speaking to the defendant, the officer noticed that his eyes were glassy and bloodshot, he smelled of alcohol and his hands were shaking. She further observed that there were shards of glass all over the passenger seat....

The officer then administered field sobriety tests to the defendant, and, based upon his performance, arrested him for driving while intoxicated. The officer transported the defendant to the UNH police station, where he agreed to a breathalyzer test.... The breathalyzer test results showed that the defendant's blood alcohol content was .16.

After additional breathalyzer tests, the defendant was taken to the Durham police station to be interviewed....

At 8:30 a.m. the defendant volunteered that he had hit a pedestrian. He asked the booking officer, "[D]id I kill the man I hit[?]" After he was told that he had, the defendant said: "[W]hat have I done? What have I done to the victim's family? How am I going to live the rest of my life knowing I killed someone?" He then told the police that he had been drinking in Dover with his girlfriend that night and had then gone to his fraternity, where he had continued to drink. He said that the accident occurred when he was heading south on Main Street up a hill, driving under the speed limit, and that he never saw the victim until he "felt a thump." He then said, "[I]f my headlight wasn't out, I might not have killed him. Six inches, that's it. Six inches and the guy would have made it across the road and would be alive. He almost made it across the road. I saw him bounce off the corner of my car at the right ... headlight area."

The grand jury returned three indictments against the defendant: two alternative counts of negligent homicide, and one felony count of conduct after an accident. The trial court dismissed one of the negligent homicide indictments before trial.

At trial, the defendant stipulated that: (1) Hegerich died as a result of the injuries he sustained in the accident; (2) the defendant was driving the car that struck Hegerich; and (3) the defendant was impaired when he was driving. The issue for the jury on the negligent homicide charge, therefore, was whether the defendant's impairment had caused the accident. *See State v. Wong,* 125 N.H. 610, 620, 486 A.2d 262 (1984) (to sustain a conviction under RSA 630:3, II, the State must establish a causal connection between the person's driving under the influence, the subsequent collision and the resulting death).

To establish causation, the State relied, in part, upon the testimony of Joseph DiGregorio, then a deputy sheriff for Strafford County and a consultant for Collision Forensics in Somersworth, whom the court certified as an expert in traffic accident reconstruction. Based upon his review of the accident report prepared by a state trooper, reports prepared by the Durham and UNH police, the medical examiner's report, his own view of the collision site and the vehicle, and certain research and data, DiGregorio testified that: (1) the defendant was driving thirty-five miles per hour when the accident occurred, which is ten miles over the posted speed limit; (2) the defendant did not see Hegerich before hitting him; (3) Hegerich was in the roadway, not in the crosswalk, when the defendant hit him; (4) Hegerich was walking, not running, when he was hit; (5) because Hegerich was wearing blue jeans and a dark fleece jacket, it was difficult to see him on the roadway; (6) the rain and fog also made it difficult to see on the night of the accident; (7) alcohol slows down perception and reaction time; (8) although a precise point of impact could not be calculated, the area of impact was approximately twenty feet to the east of where Hegerich's hat and sock were located; (9) after hitting Hegerich, the defendant applied normal braking and came to a stop approximately 167 feet from the area of impact; and (10) Hegerich came to rest approximately 160 feet from the area of impact.

Following a five-day trial, which included an early evening view, the jury convicted the defendant of both negligent homicide and conduct after an accident. He later moved for a new trial on the negligent homicide charge on the ground that his trial counsel was ineffective because he failed to consult with an accident reconstruction expert. The trial court denied the motion, and this appeal followed.

II. Defendant's Arguments ...

B. Motion for New Trial

... The defendant's claim of ineffective assistance of counsel rests upon Part I, Article 15 of the State Constitution and the Sixth and Fourteenth Amendments to the Federal Constitution.... Because the standard for determining whether a defendant has received ineffective assistance of counsel is the same under both constitutions, necessarily, we reach the same result under the Federal Constitution as we do under the State Constitution.

The State and Federal Constitutions guarantee a criminal defendant reasonably competent assistance of counsel. To prevail upon a claim for ineffective assistance of counsel, a defendant must show, first, that counsel's representation was constitutionally deficient and, second, that counsel's deficient performance actually prejudiced the outcome of the case. To meet the first prong of this test, the defendant "must show that counsel's representation fell below an objective standard of reasonableness." *Strickland v. Washington,* 466 U.S. 668, 688 (1984). To meet the second prong, the defendant "must show that there is a reasonable probability that, but for counsel's unprofessional errors, the result of the proceeding would have been different. A reasonable probability is a probability sufficient to undermine confidence in the outcome." *Id.* at 694.

"[B]oth the performance and prejudice components of the ineffectiveness inquiry are mixed questions of law and fact." *Id.* at 698; *Dugas v. Coplan,* 428 F.3d 317, 327 (1st Cir.2005)....

1. Deficient Performance

a. Relevant Law

We first address the deficient performance prong of the *Strickland* test, which turns upon a determination of whether "counsel's assistance was reasonable considering all the circumstances." *Strickland,* 466 U.S. at 688. We must judge the reasonableness of counsel's conduct on the facts of the particular case, viewed as of the time of that conduct. *Id.* at 690.

"[T]he proper measure of attorney performance remains simply reasonableness under prevailing professional norms." *Wiggins v. Smith,* 539 U.S. 510, 521 (2003). To establish that his trial attorney's performance fell below this standard, the defendant "has to show that no competent lawyer" would have failed to consult with an accident reconstruction expert.

"Judicial scrutiny of counsel's performance must be highly deferential." *Strickland,* 466 U.S. at 689. "A fair assessment of attorney performance requires that every effort be made to eliminate the distorting effects of hindsight, to reconstruct the circumstances of counsel's challenged conduct, and to evaluate the conduct from counsel's perspective at the time." *Id.* "Because of the difficulties inherent in making the evaluation, a court must indulge a strong presumption that counsel's conduct falls within the wide range of reasonable professional assistance; that is, the defendant must overcome the presumption that, under the circumstances, the challenged action might be considered sound trial strategy." *Id.*

"We apply the *Strickland* standard to evaluate an attorney's strategic choices in light of the investigation that led to those choices." *Dugas,* 428 F.3d at 327.

> [S]trategic choices made after less than complete investigation are reasonable precisely to the extent that reasonable professional judgments support the limitations on investigation. In other words, counsel has a duty to make reasonable investigations or to make a reasonable decision that makes particular investigations unnecessary. In any ineffectiveness case, a particular decision not to investigate must be directly assessed for reasonableness in all the circumstances, applying a heavy measure of deference to counsel's judgments.

Strickland, 466 U.S. at 690–91. Thus, the issue in this case is whether the decision of the defendant's trial counsel not to consult with an accident reconstruction expert was supported by investigation that was itself reasonable. *See Dugas,* 428 F.3d at 328.

In assessing the reasonableness of trial counsel's decision not to consult with an expert, we "recognize that reasonably diligent counsel are not always required to consult an expert as part of pretrial investigation in a case involving the use of expert witnesses by the state." *Id.* A defendant's attorney is not required, in every case, to consult experts even if the State will be putting on expert witnesses. A defense attorney may have no duty to consult with an expert, for instance, when there is "no need to question the validity of the government's proposed evidence or the evidence may be so weak that it can be demolished on cross-examination." *Id.*

In *Dugas,* the First Circuit Court of Appeals ruled that defense counsel's failure to consult with an arson expert so as to investigate thoroughly a "not arson" defense was constitutionally deficient. The court reached this conclusion, in part, because creating reasonable doubt that the fire was arson was one of the only defenses available to the defendant. The only other defense was that someone else committed the arson, which, the court observed, was a difficult defense to mount. Additionally, the court noted, the arson evidence "was the cornerstone of the state's case." Further, the defendant's attorney admitted that he lacked any knowledge about arson investigation and had never before tried an arson case. Defense counsel also admitted that he was aware that there were inconsistencies in the testimony of the State's arson experts. All of these circumstances together, the court ruled, "demonstrate the inescapable need for expert consultation in this case." The court also rejected the State's claim that defense counsel's failure to consult with an expert was an informed, tactical decision entitled to deference.

Courts in other jurisdictions have ruled that the failure to consult with an expert may be ineffective assistance under similar circumstances. In *Richey v. Bradshaw,* 498 F.3d 344, 362–64 (6th Cir.2007), for instance, the court concluded that defense counsel's performance was constitutionally infirm because the scientific evidence was fundamental to the prosecution and counsel knew that there were gaps in the State's proof of arson. Under those circumstances, the court ruled that defense counsel's strategy merely to "poke holes in the State's arson case" was insufficient and that counsel had an affirmative duty to investigate the scientific bases for the State's expert's opinion.

In *Duncan v. Ornoski,* 528 F.3d 1222, 1235 (9th Cir.2008), *cert. denied,* 129 S.Ct. 1614 (2009), the issue was whether defense counsel's performance was constitutionally deficient because he failed to consult a serologist even though the police report indicated that there were antigens in the blood sample that were inconsistent with the victim's blood type. The court ruled that counsel's performance was deficient because: (1) the opinion of the State's expert was crucial to the prosecution; (2) defense counsel had no knowledge or expertise in the field; and (3) the potentially exculpatory evidence could have played a central role in the defense. *Duncan.*

In *Gersten v. Senkowski,* 426 F.3d 588, 608 (2d Cir.2005), *cert. denied,* 547 U.S. 1191 (2006), a sexual abuse case, the court ruled that defense counsel's performance was constitutionally defective because he conceded the validity of the prosecution's medical evidence without first having made any attempt to investigate whether that evidence could have been challenged. Had he consulted with an expert, the expert would have explained that there was no physical evidence of penetration. He, therefore, could have presented a strong affirmative case that the charged crime simply did not occur and that the victim's story was incredible. The court observed that, although defense counsel thought that challenging the prosecution's medical evidence would have been futile, this was not an informed decision based upon reasonable investigation and, thus, was not entitled to deference.

By contrast, the court in *Bower v. Quarterman,* 497 F.3d 459, 472 (5th Cir.2007), *cert. denied,* 128 S.Ct. 2051 (2008), ruled that failing to consult with an expert was not constitutionally defective performance when the attorney was "well aware of the issues concerning the state's ballistic evidence" and there was "little, in terms of the state's ballistic evidence," for the defendant's expert to rebut. The court held that "[u]nless a critical and important legal issue rests on the reliability of scientific evidence, ... counsel is not constitutionally required to seek a contradictory expert so long as the decision not to call an expert is informed and based on a strategic decision."

We have found only a handful of cases involving an attorney's decision whether to consult with an accident reconstruction expert. In *Lien v. Class,* 574 N.W.2d 601, 605 (S.D.1998), whether the defendant was the driver of the car that had killed the victim was a disputed issue. There was an eyewitness to the accident who said that the defendant was driving. Defense counsel found the eyewitness to be credible and did not believe that he could impeach the witness successfully. Other witnesses confirmed that the defendant had been driving the car before the accident. Additionally, the defendant had told his attorney that when he drank, which he admitted to doing before the accident, he would not let others drive his car. The court ruled that defense counsel's decision not to consult with an accident reconstruction expert was constitutionally sufficient performance because: (1) the attorney was an experienced criminal trial lawyer; (2) he was familiar with the area and with the type of jurors who would be on the panel; and (3) he knew that if he went to trial on an "expert" defense, the State had substantial evidence to overcome it.

In *Strandlien v. State,* 156 P.3d 986, 993 (Wyo.2007), on the other hand, the court ruled that there was "a clear need ... for [the defendant's] trial counsel to consult with an independent accident reconstruction expert," because "the exact nature of how the collision occurred was vital to [the] defense." In that case, the issue was whether the defendant's impairment had proximately caused the accident that killed the victim. The defendant contended at trial that the accident was unavoidable because the victim had turned into his lane. The prosecution presented the testimony of police officers who had attempted to reconstruct the accident and who testified that, but for the defendant's impairment, it would not have occurred.

Relying upon the above cases for guidance, we now turn to whether it was constitutionally deficient performance in this case not to consult with an expert in accident reconstruction, keeping in mind that in so doing, we must "indulge a strong presumption that counsel's conduct falls within the wide range of reasonable professional assistance." *Strickland,* 466 U.S. at 689.

b. Analysis

The trial court found that the defendant's trial counsel is a seasoned criminal trial attorney, and the record amply supports this finding. At the hearing on the motion for new trial, trial counsel testified that he has been a criminal trial lawyer for approximately thirty years. He also testified that he had previously tried approximately six driving while impaired cases involving pedestrian injuries or death.

The trial court also found that the defendant's trial counsel understood the issues in the case, and rather than hire an expert, chose, instead, to cross-examine the State's expert.... Trial counsel testified that he understood everything in DiGregorio's report, except the final paragraph, and that he understood his testimony. The defendant's trial counsel never explained why or what he did not understand in the final paragraph of DiGregorio's report. Trial counsel also testified that while he considered retaining an accident reconstruction expert, he decided not to do so because he believed that any testimony from such an expert would be speculative, and, therefore, inadmissible. He testified that because of the lack of physical evidence from the accident, he believed that the accident could not be reconstructed.

Thus, at least with respect to these factors, this case is distinguishable from *Dugas.* While the defense attorney in *Dugas* had never before tried an arson case, the defendant's trial counsel had previously tried cases that were similar to this one. Like defense counsel in *Lien,* 574 N.W.2d at 609, the defendant's trial counsel is an experienced criminal trial attorney. While defense counsel in *Dugas* needed expert assistance to understand and challenge the State's case, the defendant's trial counsel did not.

Dugas is distinguishable as well because in *Dugas,* "the arson evidence was the cornerstone of the state's case," while in this case, DiGregorio's testimony was not especially probative of the central question before the jury: whether the defendant's impairment had caused the accident. Although DiGregorio testified that, in his opinion, the defendant was driving his car ten miles over the posted speed limit, DiGregorio did not testify that the defendant was so doing because he was impaired. His testimony, at best, only allowed the jury to infer that the defendant exceeded the speed limit because he was impaired. Therefore, there was little in terms of the State's evidence of causation for a defense expert to rebut.

Additionally, the record demonstrates that had trial counsel consulted the expert whom the defendant presented at the hearing on his motion for a new trial, this expert would have *agreed* with DiGregorio that the defendant's car was traveling ten miles over the speed limit, and would have confirmed trial counsel's suspicion that the accident could not be reconstructed because of the lack of physical evidence.

At the motion for a new trial, the defendant presented the report and testimony of Carl Lakowicz, a partner in Northpoint Collision Consultants in Gilmanton. Lakowicz admitted that because of insufficient physical evidence, it was impossible to complete "a technical accident reconstruction." Lakowicz testified that had the defendant's trial counsel contacted him, he would have told him, "We can't help you with this case. It can't be reconstructed. We're missing evidence." He would have explained to defendant's trial counsel that the only analysis he could conduct would require him to "assume[ ] certain factors that were not in evidence."

This case is, therefore, unlike *Strandlien.* Whereas in *Strandlien,* 156 P.3d at 993, the accident *could* be reconstructed and the court found defense counsel ineffective for failing to consult with an expert in such reconstruction, here, "the exact nature of how the collision occurred" was impossible to determine.

On the other hand, trial counsel's belief that the testimony of an expert, such as Lakowicz, would have been inadmissible because it would be speculative, was not an informed one. Generally, under New Hampshire law, the assumptions upon which an expert bases an opinion "are matters which affect the weight of the evidence but do not [necessarily] ... preclude its admissibility." Provided that the trial court finds that the expert's methodology is reliable, it is up to the fact finder to determine the weight and credibility to be accorded the expert's testimony. Once the trial court has determined that the expert's methodology is reliable, "[t]he appropriate method of testing the basis of an expert's opinion is by cross-examination of the expert." Accordingly, the fact that the testimony of an expert, such as Lakowicz, is based upon certain assumptions, does not necessarily mean that it is inadmissible. Therefore, trial counsel's belief that it would have been futile to consult with an expert because any expert's opinion that is based upon assumptions is inadmissible was not an informed one.

Further, had trial counsel consulted an expert, such as Lakowicz, he could have learned that another defense was available to him—that the accident was unavoidable, regardless of the driver's impairment. Had trial counsel consulted an expert, such as Lakowicz, he could have been able to present an affirmative case that the defendant's impairment did not cause the accident.

Based upon certain calculations, Lakowicz opined that under optimum night conditions, a driver of a vehicle in good working order, going up a wet hill at thirty-five miles per hour, would need 192 feet to perceive a pedestrian and come to a safe, controlled stop. Lakowicz termed this point—the 192 feet needed to stop safely—the "point of no escape." He explained that the "point of no escape" is the point at which an accident is unavoidable, regardless of the driver's level of impairment. Based upon an experiment he conducted, Lakowicz opined that an exemplar pedestrian was not detectable at the point of no escape.

Lakowicz further opined that based upon the speed of the defendant's vehicle and the presumed speed at which Hegerich walked, the first opportunity that a driver would have had to see Hegerich, even if the incident occurred during daylight, was when they were approximately 205 feet away from one another. Lakowicz opined that at a 205-foot distance, a driver would be only two seconds away from the point of no escape (192 feet), and that the reaction time for a non-impaired person driving in daylight would be approximately two and one-half seconds. Thus, from the driver's perspective, Lakowicz opined that there was no way for the accident to have been avoided regardless of the driver's impairment.

Based upon all of these factors, even with the presumption that his performance was constitutionally sufficient, we conclude that the decision of the defendant's trial counsel not to consult with an accident reconstruction expert was constitutionally defective performance. Contrary to trial counsel's conjecture, the testimony of an expert, such as Lakowicz, *could* have been admissible, even if it was based upon assumptions. Under the unique circumstances of this case, it was not sufficient for trial counsel merely to "poke holes" in the State's case. Rather, because he knew that the State's case relied upon expert testimony that used certain assumptions, it was constitutionally deficient performance for trial counsel not to consult with an expert to learn what the expert could conclude based upon these same or similar assumptions. Had he done so, he might have been able to present an affirmative case that the defendant's impairment did not cause Hegerich's death. Under the circumstances of this case, it was constitutionally infirm performance for trial counsel to fail, at the very least, to explore this possibility with an expert in accident reconstruction.

"Defense counsel may not fail to conduct an investigation and then rely on the resulting ignorance to excuse his failure to explore a strategy that would likely have yielded exculpatory evidence." *Gersten,* 426 F.3d at 610. "[F]ailing to present exculpatory evidence is not a reasonable trial strategy." *Id.* at 611.

We do not intend to imply that defense counsel is constitutionally required to hire a consulting expert in all cases in which the prosecution calls an expert to prove an element of its case.... Our decision today "is grounded in the specifics of this case."

2. Prejudice

Because the trial court concluded that trial counsel's performance was not constitutionally infirm, it did not reach the prejudice prong of the *Strickland* test. The parties urge us to reach it in the first instance. We decline to do so. The trial court heard the testimony at the hearing on the motion for a new trial, and had an opportunity to assess the credibility of the witnesses presented in light of all of the evidence presented in support of and in opposition to the motion, and, therefore, is in a better position than we are to assess whether trial counsel's performance prejudiced the defendant.... Accordingly, we remand to the trial court for it to determine whether there is a reasonable probability that, but for trial counsel's errors, the result of the proceeding would have been different. *See Strickland,* 466 U.S. at 694....

Notes and Questions

1. If the trial court were to conclude on remand that Whittaker was "prejudiced" by his attorney's deficient performance and that his conviction consequently must be reversed,

and if Whittaker—supported by the testimony of an expert witness such as Carl Lakowicz—were to be acquitted of the negligent homicide charge on retrial, would his case qualify as a "wrongful conviction" as we defined that term in Chapter 1? Should it?

2. In 2007, Koua Fong Lee was convicted of vehicular homicide and sentenced to eight years in prison after the Toyota Camry he was driving rear-ended another vehicle at a high rate of speed as he entered a St. Paul, Minnesota freeway, killing two of the other car's occupants and seriously injuring three others. At his trial, Lee maintained that he tried desperately to stop his car but it failed to respond. His attorney suggested that Lee might have mistakenly stepped on the accelerator instead of the brake pad. In August 2010, Lee's convictions were vacated and the charges against him were dismissed. The trial judge agreed with Lee's claim that his trial attorney had provided ineffective assistance because he did not investigate and present a defense based on Toyota's widely known problems in some of its vehicles with sudden acceleration. In vacating Lee's convictions, the trial judge found that, "There were multiple errors and omissions by his attorney that necessitate this result." She concluded that testimony regarding similar problems experienced by many Toyota drivers "would 'more likely than not, or probably, or even almost certainly' have resulted in a different verdict for Lee."[6]

3. In September 2010, the Innocence Project reported that: "A review of published appeals revealed that 54 of the first 255 DNA exonerees (21%) raised claims of ineffective assistance of counsel. In the overwhelming majority of these appeals, the Courts rejected the claims (81%), however in seven cases, courts agreed with appellants and found ineffective assistance of counsel, leading to reversals of convictions for six exonerees and new representation in one case...."[7] The report argued that the *Strickland* standard "creates an extremely high burden on the defendant to establish ineffectiveness ... making it difficult for defendants to gain post conviction relief via claims of ineffective assistance of counsel."[8] *See also* Brandon L. Garrett, "Judging Innocence," 108 *Columbia Law Review* 55, 114–116 (2008).

4. There are reasons to suspect that ineffective assistance of counsel or "bad lawyering" occurs with uncommon regularity in wrongful conviction cases. Weak evidentiary cases, which in theory should typify cases involving innocent defendants, are apt to result in guilty pleas to reduced charges, making trial safeguards absent and the process much more secretive than trials. Legal scholars have argued that overburdened and often undercompensated defense attorneys are left with little choice but to enter into negotiated pleas for their clients.[9] Defense attorneys, especially public ones, often lack the time to devote to trial preparation, especially for minor crimes where a negotiated plea will result in no jail time. And, ineffective lawyers (because of inexperience or laziness) may be the most likely to encourage guilty pleas and do whatever is necessary to avoid trials.

> For an innocent defendant facing a serious felony charge, however, it is exceedingly difficult to find a lawyer willing to devote the hours necessary to prepare for and try a complicated criminal case on the lawyer's own time and money. Most of the time, therefore, the couple of hundred dollars given to defense counsel buys only a plea bargain. Even a defendant who professes innocence will usually be forced into a guilty plea by the threat of a much harsher sentence, should the defendant go to trial and be found guilty. It is very risky to go to trial facing a significant sentence knowing that defense counsel will not be prepared to conduct that trial. Regardless of guilt or innocence, most defendants are unwilling to take that risk and the vast majority plead guilty.[10]

Thus, for defendants who are innocent *and* who have the misfortune to have an overworked, undercompensated, ineffective, or disillusioned attorney, the likelihood of pleading guilty may be so high that detection of a wrongful conviction becomes extremely difficult.

D. Is There a Constitutional Right to Court-Appointed Experts for the Defense?

If indigent defendants have a right to court-appointed counsel and, as we have just seen, if counsel have an obligation under some circumstances to consult with experts to provide their clients with minimally effective assistance, does it follow that a correlative right exists to court-appointed experts for the defense? The Supreme Court confronted this question in *Ake v. Oklahoma*, 470 U.S. 68, 105 S.Ct. 1087, 84 L.Ed.2d 53 (1985), a case involving a defendant convicted of capital murder and sentenced to death who, because of his indigency, had been unable to consult with or offer the testimony of a psychiatrist or other mental health expert in connection with his insanity defense or to address his likely future dangerousness at the penalty phase of his trial. Justice Marshall's opinion for the Court concluded that the State's failure to provide Ake the assistance of a court-appointed expert under those circumstances violated his Due Process rights.

This Court has long recognized that when a State brings its judicial power to bear on an indigent defendant in a criminal proceeding, it must take steps to assure that the defendant has a fair opportunity to present his defense. This elementary principle, grounded in significant part on the Fourteenth Amendment's due process guarantee of fundamental fairness, derives from the belief that justice cannot be equal where, simply as a result of his poverty, a defendant is denied the opportunity to participate meaningfully in a judicial proceeding in which his liberty is at stake....

Meaningful access to justice has been the consistent theme of these cases. We recognized long ago that mere access to the courthouse doors does not by itself assure a proper functioning of the adversary process, and that a criminal trial is fundamentally unfair if the State proceeds against an indigent defendant without making certain that he has access to the raw materials integral to the building of an effective defense. Thus, while the Court has not held that a State must purchase for the indigent defendant all the assistance that his wealthier counterpart might buy, see *Ross v. Moffitt,* 417 U.S. 600 (1974), it has often reaffirmed that fundamental fairness entitles indigent defendants to "an adequate opportunity to present their claims fairly within the adversary system," *id.,* at 612. To implement this principle, we have focused on identifying the "basic tools of an adequate defense or appeal," *Britt v. North Carolina,* 404 U.S. 226, 227 (1971), and we have required that such tools be provided to those defendants who cannot afford to pay for them.

To say that these basic tools must be provided is, of course, merely to begin our inquiry. In this case we must decide whether, and under what conditions, the participation of a psychiatrist is important enough to preparation of a defense to require the State to provide an indigent defendant with access to competent psychiatric assistance in preparing the defense. Three factors are relevant to this determination. The first is the private interest that will be affected by the action of the State. The second is the governmental interest that will be affected if the safeguard is to be provided. The third is the probable value of the additional or substitute procedural safeguards that are sought, and the risk of an erroneous deprivation of the affected interest if those safeguards are not provided. See *Mathews v. Eldridge,* 424 U.S. 319, 335 (1976)....

... [W]ithout the assistance of a psychiatrist to conduct a professional examination on issues relevant to the defense, to help determine whether the insanity defense is viable, to present testimony, and to assist in preparing the cross-examination of a State's psychiatric witnesses, the risk of an inaccurate resolution of sanity issues is extremely high. With such assistance, the defendant is fairly able to present at least enough information to the jury, in a meaningful manner, as to permit it to make a sensible determination.

A defendant's mental condition is not necessarily at issue in every criminal proceeding, however, and it is unlikely that psychiatric assistance of the kind we have described would be of probable value in cases where it is not. The risk of error from denial of such assistance, as well as its probable value, is most predictably at its height when the defendant's mental condition is seriously in question. When the defendant is able to make an *ex parte* threshold showing to the trial court that his sanity is likely to be a significant factor in his defense, the need for the assistance of a psychiatrist is readily apparent. It is in such cases that a defense may be devastated by the absence of a psychiatric examination and testimony; with such assistance, the defendant might have a reasonable chance of success. In such a circumstance, where the potential accuracy of the jury's determination is so dramatically enhanced, and where the interests of the individual and the State in an accurate proceeding are substantial, the State's interest in its fisc must yield.

We therefore hold that when a defendant demonstrates to the trial judge that his sanity at the time of the offense is to be a significant factor at trial, the State must, at a minimum, assure the defendant access to a competent psychiatrist who will conduct an appropriate examination and assist in evaluation, preparation, and presentation of the defense. This is not to say, of course, that the indigent defendant has a constitutional right to choose a psychiatrist of his personal liking or to receive funds to hire his own. Our concern is that the indigent defendant have access to a competent psychiatrist for the purpose we have discussed, and as in the case of the provision of counsel we leave to the State the decision on how to implement this right....

Ake also was denied the means of presenting evidence to rebut the State's evidence of his future dangerousness. The foregoing discussion compels a similar conclusion in the context of a capital sentencing proceeding, when the State presents psychiatric evidence of the defendant's future dangerousness....

... On the record before us, it is clear that Ake's mental state at the time of the offense was a substantial factor in his defense, and that the trial court was on notice of that fact when the request for a court-appointed psychiatrist was made....

In addition, Ake's future dangerousness was a significant factor at the sentencing phase. The state psychiatrist who treated Ake at the state mental hospital testified at the guilt phase that, because of his mental illness, Ake posed a threat of continuing criminal violence. This testimony raised the issue of Ake's future dangerousness, which is an aggravating factor under Oklahoma's capital sentencing scheme, and on which the prosecutor relied at sentencing. We therefore conclude that Ake also was entitled to the assistance of a psychiatrist on this issue and that the denial of that assistance deprived him of due process.[13]

We next consider the scope of the right of indigent criminal defendants to court-appointed expert assistance that was recognized in *Ake v. Oklahoma.*

Moore v. State

390 Md. 343, 889 A.2d 325 (2005)

RAKER, Judge.

Petitioner, Frederick James Moore, was convicted by a jury in the Circuit Court for Howard County of first degree murder of Ashley Nicole Mason. Prior to trial, the State conducted DNA analysis on evidence found at the scene of the crime, and petitioner, who was represented by private counsel but for purposes of the motion was conceded to be indigent, requested state-funded expert assistance in the field of DNA

13. Because we conclude that the Due Process Clause guaranteed to Ake the assistance he requested and was denied, we have no occasion to consider the applicability of the Equal Protection Clause, or the Sixth Amendment, in this context.

analysis to prepare his defense. The trial court denied petitioner's motion on the grounds that the Office of the Public Defender was not required to pay for an expert when a defendant is represented by private counsel, and that the trial court had no funds to pay for an expert. The Court of Special Appeals affirmed. We granted Moore's petition for a writ of certiorari, to consider the following questions:

I. Is a criminal defendant who is unable to afford the assistance of a DNA expert, but who has retained private counsel using his limited personal funds, entitled to public funding for expert assistance under Article 27A of the Maryland Code where the most extensive testimony offered against the defendant at trial was that of the State's DNA expert?

II. Is a criminal defendant who is unable to afford the assistance of a DNA expert, but who has retained private counsel using his limited personal funds, entitled to public funding for expert assistance under the United States and Maryland Constitutions where the most extensive testimony offered against the defendant at trial was that of the State's DNA expert? ...

I. Facts

On the morning of November 3, 2000, a delivery driver discovered a pool of blood in the parking lot of a Howard County restaurant. Following a bloody trail into the woods, he discovered the lifeless body of fourteen-year-old Ashley Nicole Mason. The medical examiner later determined the cause of Mason's death to have been multiple stab wounds and strangulation.

Petitioner and Scott Jory Brill were indicted by the Grand Jury for Howard County for the murder.[1] ... [T]he State served Moore with a timely Notice of Intention to Introduce DNA Evidence. The State provided Moore with documents produced by Cellmark Diagnostics, Inc. ("Cellmark"), detailing results obtained by Cellmark in its laboratory analysis of evidence recovered from the crime scene.

Moore filed a motion captioned "Defendant's Motion To Have the Circuit Court for Howard County or the Office of the Public Defender Provide Financial Aid to the Defendant for the Purpose of Providing a DNA Expert to Testify for the Defendant" (Funding Motion). In addition to asserting Moore's inability to pay for the services of a DNA expert,[3] the Funding Motion contained the following statements:

"1. That the defendant is charged with a very serious offense of murder in the first degree.

2. That at no time did the defendant, Frederick Moore, give a statement implicating himself in the offense.

* * *

5. That ... defendant's mother, Anita Moore, was able to scrape together $1000.00, said funds which were paid to J. Thomas McClintock, Ph.D., a microbiologist and molecular biologist as well as an expert in the field of DNA testing.

6. That counsel for defendant sent to Dr. McClintock all of the materials sent to counsel by the Office of the State's Attorney for Dr. McClintock to review.

7. That after his review of the materials, Dr. McClintock provided defendant's counsel with a preliminary opinion regarding the DNA testing used in the case against Frederick Moore.

* * *

10. That the defendant believes he would be seriously prejudiced if the Court were to deny his request.

11. That the defendant believes that, BUT FOR THE FACT THAT HE IS POOR AND COMES FROM A POOR FAMILY, he would be able to hire the DNA expert which the defendant and his counsel believe would be extremely important to help explain to the jury that there are two sides to every DNA test result.

12. That the defendant believes that it is prejudicial to him if he is denied the right to have an expert witness testify on his behalf while the State is allowed to have an expert witness even though counsel for the State is not required to pay for the services of the DNA expert.

13. That counsel for defendant filed with the Honorable Court a Motion to Suppress

---

1. Brill and Moore were tried separately and each was convicted of the murder of Ashley Mason.

3. The record indicates that Moore retained counsel using funds he received in a personal injury settlement contemporaneous to his arrest for the instant offense. He asserted that he was currently "without a job or funds to pay for the services of a DNA expert" due to his incarceration pending trial.

> DNA evidence and as part of the memorandum in support of his motion, counsel for defendant listed a number of areas in which mistakes can be made by the State's expert. That unless counsel for the defendant is allowed to have an expert to support the defendant's contention, the defendant will be unjustly prejudiced."

In the Suppression Motion to which Moore refers in paragraph 13 of the Funding Motion, Moore stated, in pertinent part:

> "9. According to the FBI standards, which have not been established as proof beyond a reasonable doubt to show guilt, nine of thirteen loci are necessary to establish proof, although again NOT BEYOND A REASONABLE DOUBT, to show that the DNA recovered at a scene of a crime is associated to a particular GROUP of individuals rather than a specific individual. In fact, when providing results, so called experts of DNA testing will state, among other things, that a person CAN NOT BE EXCLUDED as the person providing the DNA. At no time can the DNA expert state conclusively that DNA evidence can be linked conclusively to any particular person or that a particular person was present at the scene of the crime.
>
> 10. That according to the results of the DNA testing, either Scott Brill or Frederick Moore could be included as the provider of the DNA found at the scene of the crime but the results do not state conclusively that Frederick Moore was present at the scene of the crime or that the DNA was conclusively the DNA of Frederick Moore."

The Circuit Court denied the Suppression Motion.

At a hearing on the Funding Motion, Moore's counsel again represented to the Circuit Court that Moore could not afford a DNA expert. With respect to Dr. McClintock, counsel stated:

> "Dr. McClintock has, in fact, worked with me on this case to a degree. We were able to come up with some funds, initially, to get the doctor to help me with some preparation. His fee is $225.00 per hour, with a minimum of four hours and a maximum of ten hours. I don't anticipate there being ten hours of work here, so I would imagine somewhere between the four and the ten at a cost of $225.00 per hour."

Regarding the usefulness or necessity of a DNA expert's services in Moore's case, Moore represented as follows:

> "[W]e got into all of the DNA testimony and evidence, rather, and it became quite obvious that Mr. Moore would be prejudiced if he were not allowed to have an expert as the State was allowed to have an expert.
>
> * * *
>
> I do feel it's a prejudice to anyone who comes before the Court on a serious matter where experts are necessary.... It's just impossible for anyone to properly defend a case unless they have thousands and thousands of dollars just to pay experts."

The District Public Defender for Carroll and Howard Counties appeared at the hearing by the consent of both parties. She informed the court that it was the Public Defender's policy not to provide funds for experts in "private counsel cases," that she had spoken to her superiors, the Public Defender and Deputy Public Defender, about Moore's case, and that these officials had been unwilling to make an exception to the policy. The State indicated, both in its written response to the Funding Motion and orally at the hearing, that it took no position as to Moore's request.

Following a brief recess, the court made the following oral ruling:

> "I just confirmed with Judge Leasure, the administrative Judge, that—with reference to the availability of Court funds and she confirms or advises me that there are no Court funds dedicated or available to provide in general for experts in cases where an individual will have private counsel and, specifically, there are not funds available—Court funds available to provide for the expert in this case.... And I would not direct the Office of the Public Defender to provide fees in this case since they are not counsel of record in the case. So, I'll specifically deny your request."

Moore did not testify at the trial. His defense, conveyed to the jury by way of argument of counsel, was that although Moore was present at the scene of the crime, Scott Brill had acted alone in killing Mason, while Moore stood by, fearing for his own life....

The State presented testimony that evidence had been collected at or near the crime scene. These items included blood recovered from the restaurant parking lot, Mason's underwear, two "do-rags" (head coverings) recovered from bushes near Mason's body, a bloody knife discovered by a garbage collector near the restaurant, clippings from Mason's fingernails, and swabs taken from Mason's ankles, vagina, and anus.

The State called Dr. Robin Cotton, forensic lab director for Cellmark. Dr. Cotton first explained the basis and methodology for conducting forensic DNA analysis using the polymerase chain reaction (PCR) method of amplification and short tandem repeats (STR) as genetic markers.[4]

Dr. Cotton next testified to the results of Cellmark's analysis of the evidence in the instant case. DNA on each of the "do-rags" was consistent with Frederick Moore's at each of the nine loci tested. Within Moore's racial category, only one individual in 79 billion could be expected to exhibit that particular DNA profile. DNA obtained from the inside of the knife was consistent with that of Ashley Mason; DNA obtained from the outside of the knife came from multiple sources. Moore was identified as a possible contributor at six of the nine loci; the outside of the knife was inconclusive as to Brill. The fingernail clippings from Ashley Mason's right and left hands both revealed a mixture of DNA, with Ashley Mason identified as the primary source. There were also indications of a male as a possible source, but no further conclusion could be made. Swabs from Mason's left ankle showed a mixture of DNA, with no primary source. Brill was included as a possible source, while Moore was excluded as a source. Swabs from Mason's right ankle also revealed a mixture of DNA, with Mason herself as the primary source. The secondary DNA was inconclusive as to Moore and as to Brill, with both men included at four of the nine loci. The vaginal swabs yielded both sperm fractions and non-sperm fractions. The sperm fractions indicated the presence of male DNA, but no further conclusions could be drawn. Sperm fractions recovered from the anal swabs revealed that Moore could be included as a possible source at five of the nine loci; no conclusion could be reached on the remaining four loci.[5] A comparison with Scott Brill's DNA was inconclusive. Sperm fractions recovered from Mason's underwear revealed a mixture of at least two sources. Although no primary source was determined, Frederick Moore was included as a possible contributor at all nine loci. Within Moore's racial category, approximately one individual in 40,000 could have contributed these sperm fractions.

In addition to the DNA evidence, the State presented testimony from [numerous other witnesses]....

Petitioner was convicted of first degree murder and was sentenced to incarceration for his natural life. He noted a timely appeal to the Court of Special Appeals, which affirmed his conviction. Before that court, he argued, *inter alia,* that the trial court erred in denying his motion requesting funding for a DNA defense expert on the grounds of indigency when he had retained and financed private counsel. He argued that the trial court (and the Public Defender) violated his federal Constitutional rights to due process, equal protection of law, and effective assistance of counsel, as well as Maryland's statutory framework providing legal aid to indigents.

The State argued that any statutory or Constitutional right to State funding for expert testimony was dependent upon indigency and that because Moore had retained private counsel, he could not be deemed indigent for any purpose. In addition, the State argued that Moore had failed to make the necessary showing in the trial court that he was indigent. The intermediate appellate court held that Moore was not indigent and was not entitled to State funding for the expert....

The Court of Special Appeals also rejected Moore's constitutional arguments and concluded that the State had complied fully with the requirements of *Ake v. Oklahoma,* 470 U.S. 68 (1985). The court reasoned that the evaluation of the samples giving rise to the DNA testimony in this case were "impartial, scientific and objective." The court concluded that "the State provided expert analysis and any constitutional duty had ended after that point."

II.

Moore argues before this Court that the federal Constitutional guarantees of effective as-

4. We reviewed this methodology at some length in *Young v. State,* 388 Md. 99, 106–112, 879 A.2d 44, 48–52 (2005).

5. Moore was not charged with any sexual offense.

sistance of counsel, due process of law, and equal protection of law include the right to a defense expert under the circumstances presented herein, without regard to whether an indigent defendant has private counsel. Relying on *Ake,* he argues that he is entitled to the "basic tools of an adequate defense" and that where, as here, DNA evidence is likely to be a significant factor, he should have been afforded expert assistance. He argues that the Court of Special Appeals was wrong in concluding that Dr. Cotton, the Cellmark expert, satisfied the State's Constitutional obligations. He asserts the Dr. Cotton did not assist with Moore's trial preparation of cross-examination and that Moore was at a distinct disadvantage and without an opportunity to prepare a defense in a case in which DNA was central to the prosecution's case. Moore also argues that the trial court and intermediate appellate court erred in holding that Moore was not entitled to expert assistance because he had private counsel. He maintains that he made the requisite showing under *Ake* that the issue of DNA would be a significant factor at trial and that he was prejudiced by the denial of these funds to secure an expert. Finally, Moore argues that he is entitled to expert funding at State expense pursuant to Md.Code (1957, 2003 Repl.Vol., 2004 Cum.Supp.), Art. 27A (governing the duties of the Public Defender). He maintains that public funding of expert costs is available to indigent defendants in Maryland without regard to a defendant's relationship with counsel or upon accepting legal representation by the Public Defender....

III.

A. *Ake v. Oklahoma*

In *Ake v. Oklahoma,* 470 U.S. 68 (1985), the Supreme Court reversed the conviction and death sentence of an indigent defendant after the trial court denied his request for a state-funded psychiatric examination. The issue in *Ake* was "whether the Constitution requires that an indigent defendant have access to the psychiatric examination and assistance necessary to prepare an effective defense based on his mental condition, when his sanity at the time of the offense is seriously in question." *Id.* at 70....

In determining whether due process demands a state-furnished psychiatrist under Ake's circumstances, the Court found several factors relevant: the private interest that will be affected by the action of the State, the governmental interest of the State that will be affected if the safeguard is to be provided, the probable value of the additional or substitute procedural safeguards that are sought, and the risk of an erroneous deprivation of the affected interest if those safeguards are not provided. Finding the defendant's interest in the accuracy of a criminal trial to be "almost uniquely compelling," the state's interest to be only economic, and the need for psychiatric assistance critical, the Court determined that due process had required provision of a psychiatrist to Ake....

The Court held as follows:

> "We therefore hold that when a defendant demonstrates to the trial judge that his sanity at the time of the offense is to be a significant factor at trial, the State must, at a minimum, assure the defendant access to a competent psychiatrist who will conduct an appropriate examination and assist in evaluation, preparation, and presentation of the defense."

Id. at 83.

B. The Scope of *Ake*

In the wake of *Ake,* several questions arise. *See generally* Paul C. Giannelli, *Ake v. Oklahoma: The Right to Expert Assistance in a Post-Daubert, Post-DNA World,* 89 Cornell L.Rev. 1305 (2004). These questions include whether *Ake* extends beyond the capital context, whether the right to expert assistance extends beyond the insanity context and to non-psychiatric experts, the nature of the assistance to which a defendant is entitled, and the threshold showing a defendant must make to trigger the right.

1. Application of *Ake* Beyond the Capital Context

... The majority of courts that have considered this question have concluded that *Ake* applies to non-capital cases....

We agree, and conclude that *Ake* extends beyond the capital context and applies to non-capital cases.

2. Application of *Ake* Beyond the Insanity/Psychiatric Context

The next question that arises is whether *Ake* is restricted to cases in which the defendant's sanity is at issue. The majority of courts have concluded that *Ake* extends beyond psychiatric experts. *See, e.g., Terry v. Rees,* 985 F.2d 283, 284 (6th Cir.1993) (pathologist); *Dunn v. Roberts,* 963 F.2d 308, 313 (10th Cir.1992) (battered-spouse syndrome expert); *Scott v. Louisiana,* 934 F.2d 631, 633 (5th Cir.1991) (ballistics expert);

Little v. Armontrout, 835 F.2d 1240, 1243 (8th Cir.1987) (hypnotism expert); *Ex parte Moody,* 684 So.2d 114, 118–19 (Ala.1996) (applicable to non-psychiatric experts generally); *Ex parte Dubose,* 662 So.2d 1189, 1194 (Ala.1995) (DNA expert); *Ex parte Sanders,* 612 So.2d 1199, 1201–02 (Ala.1993) (ballistics expert); *Prater v. State,* 307 Ark. 180, 820 S.W.2d 429, 439 (1991) (DNA expert); *Doe v. Superior Court,* 39 Cal.App.4th 538, 45 Cal.Rptr.2d 888, 892–93 (1995) (experts on battered spouse and post-traumatic stress syndromes); *Cade v. State,* 658 So.2d 550, 555 (Fla.Dist.Ct.App.1995) (DNA expert); *Bright v. State,* 265 Ga. 265, 455 S.E.2d 37, 50 (1995) (toxicologist); *Crawford v. State,* 257 Ga. 681, 362 S.E.2d 201, 206 (1987) (serologist, psychologist, survey expert); *Thornton v. State,* 255 Ga. 434, 339 S.E.2d 240, 240–41 (1986) (forensic dentist); *People v. Lawson,* 163 Ill.2d 187, 644 N.E.2d 1172, 1192 (1994) (fingerprint and shoe print experts); *James v. State,* 613 N.E.2d 15, 21 (Ind.1993) (blood spatter expert); *State v. Coker,* 412 N.W.2d 589, 593 (Iowa 1987) (expert to assist with intoxication defense); *State v. Carmouche,* 527 So.2d 307, 307 (La.1988) (fingerprint expert, serologist); *Polk v. State,* 612 So.2d 381, 393 (Miss.1992) (DNA expert); *State v. Huchting,* 927 S.W.2d 411, 419 (Mo.Ct.App.1996) (DNA expert); *People v. Tyson,* 209 A.D.2d 354, 618 N.Y.S.2d 796–97 (N.Y.App.Div.1994) (voiceprint expert); *State v. Bridges,* 325 N.C. 529, 385 S.E.2d 337, 339 (1989) (fingerprint expert); *State v. Moore,* 321 N.C. 327, 364 S.E.2d 648, 656–58 (1988) (pathologist, non-psychiatrist physician, fingerprint expert); *State v. Mason,* 82 Ohio St.3d 144, 694 N.E.2d 932, 944–45 (1998) (non-psychiatric experts generally); *Rogers v. State,* 890 P.2d 959, 966 (Okla.Crim.App.1995) (any expert necessary for adequate defense); *State v. Rogers,* 313 Or. 356, 836 P.2d 1308, 1315 (1992) (opinion polling expert); *State v. Edwards,* 868 S.W.2d 682, 697 (Tenn. Crim. App.1993) (DNA expert); *Taylor v. State,* 939 S.W.2d 148, 153 (Tex.Crim.App.1996) (DNA expert); *Rey v. State,* 897 S.W.2d 333, 338–39 (Tex.Crim.App.1995) (forensic pathologist).

The United States Supreme Court has not addressed this issue; in *Caldwell v. Mississippi,* 472 U.S. 320 (1985), the Court did not rule explicitly on whether the state had an obligation to appoint other than a psychiatric expert for an indigent defendant. The Court denied the defendant's request for the appointment of a criminal investigator on the grounds that the defendant made no showing as to the reasonableness of his request and had only generally asserted a need. *Id.* at 323 n. 1.

The United States Court of Appeals for the Eighth Circuit addressed the question and concluded that "there is no principled way to distinguish between psychiatric and non-psychiatric experts." *Little v. Armontrout,* 835 F.2d 1240, 1243 (8th Cir.1987), *cert. denied,* 487 U.S. 1210 (1988). The court focused the issue as follows:

> "The question in each case must be not what field of science or expert knowledge is involved, but rather how important the scientific issue is in the case, and how much help a defense expert could have given.

In balancing the interests of the parties, the Supreme Court reasoned that the defendant's interest is in "the accuracy of [the] criminal proceeding," and that "the host of safeguards fashioned ... over the years to diminish the risk of erroneous conviction stands as a testament to that concern." *Ake* at 78. Wrongful convictions are not limited to cases involving psychiatric issues. Where the defendant's mental state excuses an otherwise criminal act, a psychiatrist often will be the relevant expert. But where the defendant's guilt turns on the interpretation of physical evidence within the competence of some other profession or learned field, an expert in that area may be no less indispensable. Accordingly, we join the vast majority of those jurisdictions having considered this issue and hold that the right announced in *Ake* is not limited to providing psychiatric experts. The principles enunciated in *Ake* apply in cases of non-psychiatric expert assistance when an indigent defendant makes the requisite showing that the requested assistance is needed for him or her to have "a fair opportunity to present his defense." *Ake,* 470 U.S. at 76.

C. Establishment of the Right to Expert Assistance

1. The Necessary Showing

We turn now to another issue left substantially unresolved in *Ake*—the level and specificity of the threshold showing a defendant must make to establish entitlement to expert assistance.... Reading *Ake* and *Caldwell* together require that the State provide indigent defendants with the "basic tools of an adequate defense," *Ake,* 470 U.S. at 77, and, when the required showing is made, require the appointment of non-psychiatric experts. Due process and equal protection require the State to provide non-psychiatric experts to indigent defendants when the defendant makes a particularized showing of the need for assistance of such experts.

It is clear that *Ake* does not mandate handing over the State's checkbook to indigent defendants and their attorneys. The Supreme Court reiterated that it has never "held that a State must purchase for the indigent defendant all the assistance that his wealthier counterpart might buy, *see Ross v. Moffitt,* 417 U.S. 600 (1974)" but had rather "focused on identifying the 'basic tools of an adequate defense or appeal.' " *Ake* at 77 (quoting *Britt v. North Carolina,* 404 U.S. 226, 227 (1971)). Significantly, the Court's holding in *Ake* was predicated on the defendant having "demonstrat[ed] to the trial judge that his sanity at the time of the offense is to be a significant factor at trial." *Ake* at 83. Thus, in *Caldwell,* the Court terminated its inquiry when it found that "petitioner offered little more than undeveloped assertions that the requested assistance would be beneficial." *Caldwell,* 472 U.S. at 323 n. 1.

The test that seems to have been adopted by the majority of courts considering the issue is the one enunciated by the United States Court of Appeals for the Eleventh Circuit in *Moore v. Kemp,* 809 F.2d 702 (11th Cir.1987). The court concluded that *Ake* and *Caldwell* require that a defendant must show the trial court that there exists a reasonable probability both that an expert would be of assistance to the defense and that denial of expert assistance would result in a fundamentally unfair trial. The court explained as follows:

> "[A] defendant must show the trial court that there exists a reasonable probability both that an expert would be of assistance to the defense and that denial of expert assistance would result in a fundamentally unfair trial. Thus, if a defendant wants an expert to assist his attorney in confronting the prosecution's proof—by preparing counsel to cross-examine the prosecution's experts or by providing rebuttal testimony—he must inform the court of the nature of the prosecution's case and how the requested expert would be useful. At the very least, he must inform the trial court about the nature of the crime and the evidence linking him to the crime. By the same token, if the defendant desires the appointment of an expert so that he can present an affirmative defense, such as insanity, he must demonstrate a substantial basis for the defense, as the defendant did in *Ake.* In each instance, the defendant's showing must also include a specific description of the expert or experts desired; without this basic information, the court would be unable to grant the defendant's motion, because the court would not know what type of expert was needed. In addition, the defendant should inform the court why the particular expert is necessary. We recognize that defense counsel may be unfamiliar with the specific scientific theories implicated in a case and therefore cannot be expected to provide the court with a detailed analysis of the assistance an appointed expert might provide. We do believe, however, that defense counsel is obligated to inform himself about the specific scientific area in question and to provide the court with as much information as possible concerning the usefulness of the requested expert to the defense's case."

Id. at 712.

We agree with this formulation, and join those courts that have adopted it.

The manner in which the defendant may make this required showing will depend necessarily upon the purpose for which the defendant seeks the expert assistance. For example, if the defendant seeks an expert in order to confront the prosecution's proof, the defendant must inform the court how the expert would be useful in light of the prosecution's case. This is not to say that a defendant must predict to a certainty every detail of the prosecution's theory, or display a highly sophisticated understanding of the contribution the requested expert would make to the defense. Defense counsel does have, however, an obligation to become informed of the specific scientific area in question in order to explain the necessity of any requested expert to the court.

The analysis of whether a defendant has fulfilled this obligation will be a dynamic one, dependent on the amount of discovery received, the extent to which a likely prosecution theory is obvious, the complexity of the scientific or technical issues, and other case-specific factors....

2. Availability of *Ex Parte* Proceedings

The Supreme Court, in *Ake,* referred to an *ex*

parte hearing, stating that "[w]hen the defendant is able to make an *ex parte* threshold showing to the trial court that his sanity is likely to be a significant factor in his defense, the need for the assistance of a psychiatrist is readily apparent." *Ake,* 470 U.S. at 82–83. Defendants may be required to reveal to the court the defense theory in order to demonstrate entitlement to expert assistance. A defendant may request that these disclosures be made *ex parte.*

Courts have split as to the necessity of *ex parte* hearings. Several states have statutes requiring an *ex parte* hearing when an indigent defendant requests appointment of an expert.

The courts in Alabama, Arkansas, Florida, Georgia, Hawaii, Indiana, Michigan, Oklahoma, Tennessee, Texas, and Washington have held that an *ex parte* hearing is required.

The courts in Arizona, South Dakota, and Virginia have held that whether to hold an *ex parte* hearing is within the trial court's discretion. Louisiana requires an indigent defendant to show that he or she would be prejudiced if the hearing was not held *ex parte.* The North Carolina Supreme Court has held that an *ex parte* hearing is required when the request is for a psychiatrist, but not required when the request is for a non-psychiatric expert.

We believe the better view is that an *ex parte* hearing, when timely requested, is required. Indigent defendants seeking state funded experts should not be required to disclose to the State the theory of the defense when non-indigent defendants are not required to do so....

IV. Article 27A and State Funding of Experts

Before considering whether the State had a constitutional duty to fund Moore's request, we must address Moore's contention that it had a statutory duty to do so through the O.P.D. Moore contends that Art. 27A, which governs the powers and responsibilities of the Office of the Public Defender, mandated that the Public Defender fund his request even though he was not a client of the O.P.D....

We ... hold that the O.P.D. is not required to pay for expert assistance or other ancillary services if the defendant is not represented by the O.P.D. (or a panel attorney assigned by the O.P.D.) ... In order for the defendant to qualify for the benefits provided under the Act and thereby require the O.P.D. to pay for services, the defendant must be without independent means to obtain counsel.

V. Satisfaction of Moore's *Ake* Rights in the Instant Case

A. Provision of Expert Services Through the O.P.D.

The bottom line question in this case is whether the State has satisfied its constitutional obligations by establishing the O.P.D., making expert services available to clients of that Office, and requiring that, in order for an indigent to receive State-funded expert services, the defendant *must* seek representation by O.P.D. We conclude that the State has not deprived petitioner of any of his constitutional rights by requiring that he apply to the O.P.D. for representation before he is entitled as an indigent to State funded expert witness services. The Supreme Court contemplated in *Ake* that States could place restrictions on indigent defendants' access to state-funded expert services. The Court stated as follows:

> "This is not to say, of course, that the indigent defendant has a constitutional right to choose a psychiatrist of his personal liking or to receive funds to hire his own. Our concern is that the indigent defendant have access to a competent psychiatrist for the purpose we have discussed, and as in the case of the provision of counsel we leave to the State the decision on how to implement this right."

Ake, 470 U.S. at 83. Thus, while a State might provide funds enabling indigent defendants with retained counsel to hire experts of their own choosing, *Ake* does not require this approach.

Moore is correct that, if he is indigent, he has a right under *Ake* to state-paid supporting services necessary to an adequate defense.[8] As we have indicated, *supra,* Maryland has established a State-wide public defender system which provides legal representation, investigative services, and expert assistance to persons deemed indigent under Art. 27A § 2....

State v. Miller, 337 Md. 71, 651 A.2d 845 (1994), is instructive on the question of whether the State may condition the receipt of constitutionally mandated services on representation by

8. We do not reach the question of whether Moore made the required showing, as discussed *supra,* that the services he requested were in fact necessary to an adequate defense.

the O.P.D. The indigent petitioner in that case, Bernard Miller, had been convicted at trial of kidnapping, robbery, murder, and other related offenses. On appeal, as at trial, he was represented by private counsel on a *pro bono* basis. Miller had refused the representation of the O.P.D., and further refused to permit his attorney to seek appointment as an assigned public defender and thereby submit to the supervision of the O.P.D. Had Miller's counsel taken this step, the O.P.D. would have borne the costs of obtaining a stenographic transcript of the trial proceedings.

Miller filed in the Circuit Court a motion requesting that the court furnish a transcript without charge. The Circuit Court denied the motion....

On appeal, Miller argued that the requirement that he be represented by, or denied representation by, the O.P.D. before receiving a free transcript violated his rights to equal protection and assistance of counsel. We affirmed the Circuit Court....

> "Miller *is* entitled to a free transcript, but he cannot receive it on his own terms; he must go through the Office of the Public Defender. The State is free to place reasonable restrictions on the exercise of Miller's rights, and Rule 1-325(b) is neither arbitrary nor unreasonable in its language or application. There can be no equal protection violation when an individual is denied a right simply because of his own failure to comply with reasonable state procedures and regulations."

Miller, 337 Md. at 85–86, 651 A.2d at 852.

Turning to Miller's Sixth Amendment claim, we noted that the Supreme Court has held that although an indigent criminal defendant enjoys the right to assistance of counsel, this entitlement does not translate into an absolute right to counsel of the defendant's choosing. *[S]ee Wheat v. United States,* 486 U.S. 153, 159 (1988) ("the essential aim of the Amendment is to guarantee an effective advocate for each criminal defendant rather than to ensure that a defendant will inexorably be represented by the lawyer whom he prefers"). We concluded as follows:

> "Failure to provide a free transcript to the indigent appellant cannot interfere with the right to choice of counsel where no such absolute right exists. In the absence of such a right to choice of counsel, there is no constitutional violation when the State requires that an indigent defendant avail himself of the services of the Office of the Public Defender in order to obtain a free transcript.

The State has set up a system by which all indigent appellants are provided effective assistance of counsel, whether represented by the Public Defender's Office or by a private attorney under the supervision of that office. Miller cannot pick and choose which of the State-provided services he wishes to receive; he must accept the available resources as provided under Art. 27A and the Maryland Rules....

Our holding in *Miller* governs the outcome of the case *sub judice*.... Indigent defendants may utilize the O.P.D.'s complete "package" of services, or forgo them entirely. While such defendants may face difficult choices, the Constitution does not bar the State of Maryland from requiring them to choose between counsel of their choice and ancillary services provided by the O.P.D.

Assuming *arguendo* that the assistance of a DNA expert was necessary to an adequate defense in the instant case, the State did not deny Moore that assistance. Rather, expert assistance was available to him so long as he complied with the procedural requirement that he apply for legal representation through the O.P.D. Imposing this requirement on Moore did not violate his constitutional rights.

B. Insufficiency of Discovery and Cross-Examination Alone

Although we affirm the judgment of the Court of Special Appeals, we disagree with one significant aspect of its opinion. The intermediate appellate court agreed with the State's contention that Moore's constitutional rights were satisfied by the State's disclosure of the Cellmark documents and reports during discovery. The court stated as follows:

> "[T]here is nothing to indicate that Cellmark's evaluation of the samples was not impartial, scientific, and objective. Additionally, appellant's counsel was provided with all the DNA documents and reports generated by Cellmark prior to trial in order to prepare a defense. Thus, the State provided expert analysis and any constitutional duty had ended after that point."

Moore v. State, 154 Md.App. 578, 598, 841 A.2d 31, 42 (2004)....

In light of *Ake,* ... it appears to us that ... the report of a State-employed expert who does not "assist in evaluation, preparation, and presentation of the defense" [is not] constitutionally sufficient.

We find numerous passages from *Ake* supportive of the proposition that due process requires the provision of a defense expert. We find the following language particularly revealing:

> "We therefore hold that when a defendant demonstrates to the trial judge that his sanity at the time of the offense is to be a significant factor at trial, the State must, at a minimum, assure the defendant access to a competent psychiatrist who will conduct an appropriate examination *and assist in evaluation, preparation, and presentation of the defense.*" ...

The weight of authority among courts that have considered the issue suggests that the services of a defense expert are required.

In his comprehensive and thoroughly researched law review article, Professor Paul Giannelli addresses this issue as follows:

> "Appellate courts often cite the fact that the cross-examination of the prosecution expert was effective as a reason why a defense expert was not needed.
>
> * * *
>
> First, the same reasoning applies when prosecutors seek a psychiatric evaluation of an accused who has raised an insanity defense ... and yet virtually every jurisdiction has procedures recognizing the prosecution's right to have the accused examined by a state psychiatrist—a prosecution expert. The rationale for this procedure is obvious: the adversary system would be undermined if the prosecution was deprived of its own expert.
>
> Second, effective cross-examination of a prosecution expert frequently requires the advice of a defense expert....
>
> Third, there is a significant difference between attacking the opinion of an opponent's expert through cross-examination and attacking that opinion through the testimony of your own expert....
>
> Finally, if this factor is relevant at all, it would only be so on appellate review under a harmless error analysis. After all, a trial court cannot wait to review the defense counsel's cross-examination before appointing a defense expert."
>
> Paul C. Giannelli, *Ake v. Oklahoma: The Right to Expert Assistance in a Post-Daubert, Post-DNA World,* 89 Cornell L.Rev. 1305, 1376–78 (2004).

When a defendant has made the threshold showing described *supra,* the State must, at a minimum, assure the defendant access to a defense expert who will assist in evaluation, preparation, and presentation of the defense. We reject the holding of the Court of Special Appeals—relied upon by the State before this Court—that Moore's *Ake* rights were satisfied by discovery and the opportunity to cross-examine Dr. Cotton. The State satisfied the Due Process Clause, as interpreted in *Ake,* by making expert assistance available to Moore through the O.P.D., conditioned on representation by that agency....

JUDGMENT OF THE COURT OF SPECIAL APPEALS AFFIRMED....

Dissenting Opinion by BELL, C.J....

Although concluding that there is a right to State-funded expert services, the majority accepts the Court of Special Appeals' holding that Moore's *Ake* rights—his entitlement to State-funded expert services—were satisfied. This is so, the majority says, because the Office of the Public Defender ("OPD") will provide these services, so long as he is represented by an OPD attorney. This conclusion is dictated, it submits, by *State v. Miller,* 337 Md. 71, 651 A.2d 845 (1994) and the Public Defender statute, Art. 27A. I disagree with this conclusion....

C.

When explaining its application of the *Miller* holding to the case *sub judice,* the majority states that defendants properly may be put to the choice of counsel and the ancillary services required to be supplied at State expense to ensure an effective defense, because the constitution does not bar the State of Maryland from doing so. I do not agree.

The Sixth Amendment of the United States Constitution guarantees that, "[i]n all criminal prosecutions, the accused shall enjoy the right ... to have the Assistance of Counsel for his defence," *Wheat v. United States,* 486 U.S. 153, 158 (1988), the purpose of which is to ensure fairness in the criminal justice. Pursuant to that Amendment, the right to counsel is secured by the appointment of counsel, as necessary.

Inherent in the constitutional right to counsel is the right to be represented by counsel of choice. That right of choice is not limited to persons with means.... [T]o be sure, an indigent defendant's right of choice is significantly restricted....

The Supreme Court has recognized that the Sixth Amendment right to counsel of choice, in certain situations, is qualified, that "the essential aim of the Amendment is to guarantee an effective advocate for each criminal defendant rather than to ensure that a defendant will inexorably be represented by the lawyer whom he prefers." *Wheat,* 486 U.S. at 159. *See also Morris v. Slappy,* 461 U.S. 1 (1983). Thus,

> "The Sixth Amendment right to choose one's own counsel is circumscribed in several important respects. Regardless of his persuasive powers, an advocate who is not a member of the bar may not represent clients (other than himself) in court. Similarly, a defendant may not insist on representation by an attorney he cannot afford or who for other reasons declines to represent the defendant. Nor may a defendant insist on the counsel of an attorney who has a previous or ongoing relationship with an opposing party, even when the opposing party is the Government."

Wheat, 486 U.S. at 159. Moreover, notwithstanding that the right to counsel ordinarily encompasses a right to retain counsel of one's choice, the latter right does not trump, and will not be permitted to frustrate, the orderly administration of criminal justice....

Certainly, the petitioner's insistence on counsel of choice, which, by the way, does not burden the State's resources, does not implicate any of the recognized qualifications on the right to choice. Clearly, it does not come close to frustrating the orderly administration of the criminal justice system.

D.

The majority holds, as we have seen, "that the O.P.D. is not required to pay for expert assistance or other ancillary services if the defendant is not represented by the O.P.D. (or a panel attorney assigned by the O.P.D.)" ...

As I interpret this holding, to qualify for State-funded services, a defendant must be represented by the OPD or one of its panel attorneys, but to qualify for OPD representation, he or she "must be without independent means to obtain counsel." Thus, a defendant, though now indigent, who retained counsel when able to do so, would not qualify because, already having counsel, he or she would not be without independent means to obtain counsel. Similarly, a defendant who was always indigent, but had family who retained counsel for him or her or who was able to obtain *pro bono* counsel, would not qualify because he or she was not represented by the OPD or a panel attorney. The majority rejoins that the defendant is not without recourse, he or she could accept OPD representation, with which comes the ancillary services, and that only requires either that the defendant forego the counsel of choice, whether retained when able, supplied by a third party or provided *pro bono,* who is willing and able to continue the representation and with whose services the defendant is satisfied, or that counsel become a panel attorney subject to the supervision of the OPD.

This scheme infringes on the indigent defendant's Sixth Amendment rights to counsel of choice, for the reasons discussed. In addition, it uses the wrong test of eligibility for ancillary services; rather than indigency and necessity, the factors identified and addressed in *Ake,* the majority predicates entitlement to ancillary services on the status of the attorney representing the indigent defendant. At least as important, the majority's interpretation of Article 27A produces anomalous and absurd results....

The ... Iowa Supreme Court ..., in *English v. Missildine,* 311 N.W.2d at 294, ... observed:

> "It would be strange if the Constitution required the government to furnish both counsel and investigative services in cases where the indigent needs and requests public payment for only investigative services. The State's theory would impose an unreasonable and unnecessary additional burden on the public treasury." ...

For the preceding reasons, I dissent.

Notes and Questions

1. For a viewpoint agreeing with the dissenting opinion in *Moore v. State, see* Aimee Kumer, "Reconsidering *Ake v. Oklahoma*: What Ancillary Defense Services Must States Provide to Indigent Defendants Represented by Private or Pro Bono Counsel?" 18 *Temple Political and Civil Rights Law Review* 783 (2009). For commentary discussing the scope of indigent criminal defendants' right to court-appointed expert assistance under *Ake, see* Emily J. Groendyke, "*Ake v. Oklahoma*: Proposals for Making the Right a Reality," 10 *New York University Journal of Legislation and Public Policy* 367 (2006–2007); Paul C. Giannelli, "*Ake v. Oklahoma*: The Right to Expert Assistance in a Post-*Daubert*, Post-DNA World," 89 *Cornell Law Review* 1305 (2004); Carlton Bailey, "*Ake v. Oklahoma* and an Indigent Defendant's 'Right' to an Expert Witness: A Promise Denied or Imagined?" 10 *William and Mary Bill of Rights Journal* 401 (2002).

2. In *Dugas v. Coplan*, 428 F.3d 317 (1st Cir. 2005), the First Circuit Court of Appeals ruled that a retained lawyer's performance was constitutionally deficient under *Strickland* because the attorney failed to consult with an expert or otherwise equip himself adequately to understand the likely origins of the fire at issue in a state arson prosecution. In dissent (428 F.3d, at 348), Judge Howard protested that:

> there is reason for concern that, notwithstanding the majority's minimalist assurances, defense attorneys will read today's opinion as embracing, at the least, a presumption that they must spend precious time and money on constitutionally required double checks of most prosecution science experts—double checks that never before were required and reasonably may be eschewed in many circumstances. So too is there reason to fear that trial judges will read this opinion as constraining their discretion in deciding, in the case of indigent defendants, whether and when to expend limited public funds on court-appointed defense experts for purposes of double-checking the prosecution. And thus would the already slow and costly criminal trial process unnecessarily become slower and more costly.

The majority opinion, 428 F.3d, at 332, n. 21, countered with the rejoinder:

> The dissent worries about the implications of this decision, predicting that defense attorneys and trial judges will read it to require attorneys to hire experts in every case where the prosecution uses an expert, and to require judges in court-appointed cases to grant funds to hire such experts whenever such funds are requested. As our references to the ample precedents indicate, this is far from the first case where the failure of defense counsel to use experts in preparation for trial was the basis for a finding of ineffective assistance of counsel. Despite the insistence of the dissent to the contrary, this decision, like those precedents, is grounded in the specifics of this case. It is true that attorneys in future cases will try to make use of this precedent to argue that there has been ineffective assistance of counsel, and that they are entitled to funds for expert witnesses in cases involving indigent defendants. That phenomenon is a normal part of the legal process. It is not a reason to avoid applying well-established legal principles to the facts of this case.

3. In *Moore*, the majority states: "The State has set up a system by which all indigent appellants are provided effective assistance of counsel." Some have questioned, however, whether indigents instead confront systemic disadvantages regarding assistance for their defense. Appellate courts rejected ineffective assistance of counsel claims in most of the DNA-exoneration cases in which those claims were raised, including a case in which a court-appointed lawyer obtained money from the defendant's family for independent

DNA testing, did not complete the testing, and then kept the money.[11] In juvenile court, where substandard representation is not uncommon, the potential for inadequate representation and wrongful adjudication (or conviction) may be even higher than in criminal court. *See* Barbara Fedders, "Losing Hold of the Guiding Hand: Ineffective Assistance of Counsel in Juvenile Delinquency Representation," 14 *Lewis & Clark Law Review* 771 (2010); Steven A. Drizin & Greg Luloff, "Are Juvenile Courts a Breeding Ground for Wrongful Convictions?" 34 *Northern Kentucky Law Review* 257 (2007). Both Fedders and Drizin and Luloff describe attorneys in juvenile delinquency cases as routinely not investigating cases, interviewing witnesses, visiting crime scenes, filing pre-trial motions, or preparing for dispositional hearings, and generally being ill-equipped to serve as zealous and effective advocates for their clients. The system-wide problems concerning public and retained defense counsel inherent in both the adult and juvenile legal systems may inadvertently contribute to the factually innocent being wrongfully convicted.

E. Conclusion

Defense attorneys are guardians of the legal rights and interests of persons accused and convicted of committing crimes. In an adversarial system wedded to the premise that justice is best served by the clash of equally matched opposing advocates, it is easy to understand how and why defense attorneys' failure to discharge their important duties can contribute to miscarriages of justice. Deficient representation all too often is associated with fundamental, systemic problems, including the crushing workloads and resource constraints under which public defenders and other lawyers who represent the indigent frequently must operate.[12] Nevertheless, as illustrated by some of the cases we have considered in this chapter, individual errors and shortcomings, including by retained attorneys, also can result in inadequate representation.

Some criminal defendants lack legal representation altogether. Under the rule of *Scott v. Illinois*, 440 U.S. 367, 99 S.Ct. 1158, 59 L.Ed.2d 383 (1979), individuals facing misdemeanor trials that do not result in incarceration on conviction have no constitutional right to court-appointed counsel and may be required to defend themselves without legal assistance. In addition, uncounseled misdemeanor convictions can be used to enhance a defendant's sentence upon conviction for a subsequent crime or support a prosecution under three-strikes or other recidivist legislation. *Nichols v. United States,* 511 U.S. 738, 114 S.Ct. 1921, 128 L.Ed.2d 745 (1994). Nor is there a federal constitutional right to court-appointed counsel beyond the initial appeal of a criminal conviction, although legislation in many jurisdictions authorizes the appointment of counsel during later stages of judicial review.

In *Strickland v. Washington*, 466 U.S. 668, 104 S.Ct. 2052, 80 L.Ed.2d 674 (1984), the Supreme Court announced a two-part test for assessing claims of constitutionally ineffective assistance of trial counsel. To prevail, the defendant must establish that the attorney's *performance* was deficient ("in light of all the circumstances, the identified acts or omissions [of counsel] were outside the wide range of professionally competent assistance," 466 U.S., at 690), with resulting *prejudice* ("there is a reasonable probability that, but for counsel's unprofessional errors, the result of the proceeding would have been different," 466 U.S., at 694). Ineffective assistance of counsel claims can be based on the attorney's failure to make adequate investigation of potential defenses as well as on substandard trial conduct, although courts are especially deferential to the strategic or tactical decisions that lawyers inevitably make during the course of their representation.

Some criminal trials involve issues that require scientific or other expertise that attorneys lack or that must be explained to juries or judges by expert witnesses. Due Process entitles indigent defendants to the assistance of court-appointed experts when necessary for "a fair opportunity to present [a] defense." *Ake v. Oklahoma,* 470 U.S. 68, 76, 105 S.Ct. 1087, 84 L.Ed.2d 53 (1985). Several lower court decisions have extended the right recognized in *Ake* beyond the context of that case, a capital murder trial in which the indigent defendant's sanity and future dangerousness were central issues and he lacked the resources to obtain independent expert psychiatric assistance. The Supreme Court nevertheless has required "more than undeveloped assertions that the requested assistance would be beneficial" to establish a Due Process violation when court-appointed experts are not made available to indigent criminal defendants. *Caldwell v. Mississippi,* 472 U.S. 320, 323, n. 1, 105 S.Ct. 2633, 86 L.Ed.2d 231 (1985).

Chapter 7

Scientific and Forensic Evidence

A. Introduction

On March 11, 2004, terrorists' bombs claimed 191 lives and injured thousands more when they exploded on trains operating in Spain's capital city, Madrid. Because American citizens were among the casualties, the FBI became involved in the investigation. Spanish police found fingerprints on a bag containing detonation materials linked to the bombings and electronically transmitted images of them to the FBI's crime laboratory in Quantico, Virginia. There, investigators concluded that the latent fingerprint images secured from the bag were a "100 percent match" with the fingerprints of Brandon Mayfield, a 37-year-old Portland, Oregon lawyer and convert to Islam whose clients included a man recently convicted on federal terrorism charges. Mayfield was arrested as a "material witness" to the bombings on May 6, 2004. He was incarcerated for two weeks, while law enforcement authorities obtained a warrant to search his law office, including his business files. In the meantime, Spanish police had independently examined the fingerprint evidence and disagreed with the FBI's analysis; they concluded that Mayfield's fingerprints did not match those found on the incriminating bag. On May 24, 2004, the United States government acknowledged that the FBI's fingerprint identification was erroneous and dismissed the charges against Mayfield. More than two years later, the government apologized to Mayfield and his family and paid him $2 million in damages for his wrongful arrest.[1]

In some respects, Mayfield was lucky. Although he was jailed, suffered a loss of privacy through the searches of his office and files, and incurred the reputational damage associated with being a suspected terrorist, the flawed fingerprint analysis did not result in his wrongful conviction. Others have experienced far greater hardships because of faulty forensic evidence. For example, Stephen Buckley, whose case we presented in Chapter 2 (*Buckley v. Fitzimmons*, 509 U.S. 259, 113 S.Ct. 2606, 125 L.Ed.2d 209 (1993)) on the issue of prosecutorial immunity from damages under 42 U.S.C. § 1983, was arrested and brought to trial for capital murder in Illinois. The charges against him eventually were dismissed after his trial resulted in a hung jury, but not until he spent nearly three years in jail. "The principal evidence against him [at his trial] was provided by [Dr. Louise] Robbins," an anthropologist "who was allegedly well known for her willingness to fabricate unreliable expert testimony." *Id.*, 509 U.S., at 263–264.

> Robbins had noticed that people wear down the bottoms of their shoes in various ways because they walk differently. Some people wear down the outside of the heel first, for example, while others rub away the inside. She also knew that the bone structures of people's feet vary. Robbins decided this meant each individual has a unique "wear pattern" that could be used to match a person to any of his or her shoeprints, even if they changed shoes.... [S]he claimed she could determine the sex, race, and socioeconomic status of a person just by looking at a shoeprint.[2]

Robbins' testimony was crucial. "[T]hree separate studies by experts from the DuPage County Crime Lab, the Illinois Department of Law Enforcement, and the Kansas Bureau of Identification, all ... were unable to make a reliable connection between" a bootprint left on the front door of the home from which the murder victim—a 10-year-old child—had been abducted, and Buckley's boot. *Buckley v. Fitzimmons*, 509 U.S., at 262. Robbins, conversely, had no hesitation in opining that the print left on the door matched Buckley's boot. The problem, however, was that Robbins' testimony was wrong. Neither her theory nor the methodology she used in making her analyses had any basis in science. Two of Buckley's co-defendants, Rolando Cruz and Alejandro Hernandez, were convicted and sentenced to death for the murder that the three men had been accused of jointly committing. They subsequently were exonerated. Brian Dugan, who was linked to the murder by DNA evidence and confessed to having committed it alone, later pleaded guilty to the crime.[3]

Controversy swirls around whether Texas may have executed two men in error following murder convictions supported by questionable forensic evidence. Cameron Todd Willingham was executed in 2004 for the arson murder of his three children in Corsicana, a small city northeast of Waco. Willingham was at home with his children when the fire broke out. He maintained that the fire's origin must have been accidental and insisted that he was innocent of any wrongdoing. His 1992 conviction depended heavily on the testimony of fire investigators that the blaze that engulfed the home had been set intentionally. Scientists and arson investigation experts have since cast doubt on the validity and scientific bases of those conclusions.[4]

Claude Jones was convicted for a robbery-murder committed in a liquor store near Houston in 1989. His conviction was supported by a forensic expert's testimony that a hair found at the crime scene "matched" Jones's hair. The expert's conclusion also was used to corroborate the trial testimony of an alleged accomplice that Jones had committed the murder. Jones maintained his innocence. The purported accomplice subsequently admitted that he had lied. Jones was executed in 2000. A posthumous mitochondrial DNA analysis of the hair in question, completed in 2010, excluded Jones as its source and instead pointed to the hair belonging to the murder victim.[5]

According to the Innocence Project, "Of the first 225 wrongful convictions overturned by DNA testing, more than 50% (116 cases) involved unvalidated or improper forensic science."[6] Problems have surfaced in cases involving multiple forensic techniques including bite mark analysis, hair sample comparisons, blood testing, voice identification, soil analysis, DNA testing, fingerprint identification, shoe print analysis, and others.[7] There is no question that forensic evidence can be highly probative and help establish both guilt and innocence. Yet its misuse or misinterpretation, including testimony overstating its conclusiveness, also can help produce wrongful convictions.

In 2009, a distinguished panel of experts commissioned by the National Academy of Sciences (NAS) issued a comprehensive report focusing on the forensic sciences and the use of forensic evidence in court, *Strengthening Forensic Science in the United States: A Path Forward*.[8] The report addressed numerous issues, including:

(a) the fundamentals of the scientific method as applied to forensic practice—hypothesis generation and testing, falsifiability and replication, and peer review of scientific publications;

(b) the assessment of forensic methods and technologies—the collection and analysis of forensic data; accuracy and error rates of forensic analyses; sources of potential bias and human error in interpretation by forensic experts; and proficiency testing of forensic experts;

(c) infrastructure and needs for basic research and technology assessment in forensic science;

(d) current training and education in forensic science;

(e) the structure and operation of forensic science laboratories;

(f) the structure and operation of the coroner and medical examiner systems;

(g) budget, future needs, and priorities of the forensic science community and the coroner and medical examiner systems;

(h) the accreditation, certification, and licensing of forensic science operations, medical death investigation systems, and scientists;

(i) Scientific Working Groups (SWGs) and their practices;

(j) forensic science practices—

pattern/experience evidence

- fingerprints (including the interoperability of AFIS)
- firearms examination
- toolmarks
- bite marks
- impressions (tires, footwear)
- bloodstain pattern analysis
- handwriting
- hair

analytical evidence

- DNA
- coatings (e.g., paint)
- chemicals (including drugs)
- materials (including fibers)
- fluids
- serology
- fire and explosive analysis

digital evidence;

(k) the effectiveness of coroner systems as compared with medical examiner systems;

(l) the use of forensic evidence in criminal and civil litigation—

- the collection and flow of evidence from crime scenes to courtrooms
- the manner in which forensic practitioners testify in court
- cases involving the misinterpretation of forensic evidence
- the adversarial system in criminal and civil litigation
- lawyers' use and misuse of forensic evidence

- judges' handling of forensic evidence;

(m) forensic practice and projects at various federal agencies ...;

(n) forensic practice in state and local agencies;

(o) nontraditional forensic service providers; and

(p) the forensic science community in the United Kingdom.[9]

The NAS report noted the considerable breadth of disciplines nested within the forensic sciences, and the vast differences in their substance and methods as well as among their practitioners.

> The term "forensic science" encompasses a broad range of forensic disciplines, each with its own set of technologies and practices.... [T]here is wide variability across forensic science disciplines with regard to techniques, methodologies, reliability, types and numbers of potential errors, research, general acceptability, and published material. Some of the forensic science disciplines are laboratory based (e.g., nuclear and mitochondrial DNA analysis, toxicology and drug analysis); others are based on expert interpretation of observed patterns (e.g., fingerprints, writing samples, toolmarks, bite marks, and specimens such as hair). The "forensic science community," in turn, consists of a host of practitioners, including scientists (some with advanced degrees) in the fields of chemistry, biochemistry, biology, and medicine; laboratory technicians; crime scene investigators; and law enforcement officers. There are very important differences, however, between forensic laboratory work and crime scene investigations. There are also sharp distinctions between forensic practitioners who have been trained in chemistry, biochemistry, biology, and medicine (and who bring these disciplines to bear in their work) and technicians who lend support to forensic science enterprises.[10]

Those differences, in turn, have important implications for the potential validity of forensic evidence and its use in court. The report continued:

> Two very important questions should underlie the law's admission of and reliance upon forensic evidence in criminal trials: (1) the extent to which a particular forensic discipline is founded on a reliable scientific methodology that gives it the capacity to accurately analyze evidence and report findings and (2) the extent to which practitioners in a particular forensic discipline rely on human interpretation that could be tainted by error, the threat of bias, or the absence of sound operational procedures and robust performance standards. These questions are significant. Thus, it matters a great deal whether an expert is qualified to testify about forensic evidence and whether the evidence is sufficiently reliable to merit a fact finder's reliance on the truth that it purports to support. Unfortunately, these important questions do not always produce satisfactory answers in judicial decisions pertaining to the admissibility of forensic science evidence proffered in criminal trials.[11]

The committee's several detailed recommendations to ensure more uniform rigor and reliability among the proliferation of disciplines and methods comprising the forensic sciences centered on the creation of a new, independent federal agency—a National Institute of Forensic Science. That agency would have multiple functions, including:

(a) establishing and enforcing best practices for forensic science professionals and laboratories;

(b) establishing standards for the mandatory accreditation of forensic science laboratories and the mandatory certification of forensic scientists and medical examiners/forensic pathologists—and identifying the entity/entities that will develop and implement accreditation and certification;

(c) promoting scholarly, competitive peer-reviewed research and technical development in the forensic science disciplines and forensic medicine;

(d) developing a strategy to improve forensic science research and educational programs, including forensic pathology;

(e) establishing a strategy, based on accurate data on the forensic science community, for the efficient allocation of available funds to give strong support to forensic methodologies and practices in addition to DNA analysis;

(f) funding state and local forensic science agencies, independent research projects, and educational programs as recommended in this report, with conditions that aim to advance the credibility and reliability of the forensic science disciplines;

(g) overseeing education standards and the accreditation of forensic science programs in colleges and universities;

(h) developing programs to improve understanding of the forensic science disciplines and their limitations within legal systems; and

(i) assessing the development and introduction of new technologies in forensic investigations, including a comparison of new technologies with former ones.[12]

With few signs that the emergence of a National Institute of Forensic Science is imminent—and many have expressed doubt about whether adequate political support and resources exist to make establishment of such an agency likely—the numerous issues surrounding the integrity of forensic evidence almost certainly will continue to be addressed less systematically and with mixed success. In this chapter we consider several legal and scientific issues concerning the admissibility and use of forensic evidence; issues that bear directly on the potential for justice to be served or else to miscarry in criminal cases.

B. Scientific Evidence: Standards Governing Admissibility—*Frye* and *Daubert*

Jurors typically will not be well versed in the technical underpinnings of science. Most laypersons are unlikely to have a detailed understanding of physics, chemistry, medicine, neurobiology, or related disciplines, or to have intimate knowledge of the procedures, methods, and analytical techniques of the natural and social sciences. Such limitations not only may hamper jurors' ability to understand the foundations of scientific evidence, but also may dispose them to credit expert testimony without critical evaluation, resulting in undue deference to a presumed "aura of scientific infallibility." Scientific testimony also can be time-consuming, not to mention expensive, when the services of retained or court-appointed experts are required. Expert testimony additionally can threaten to dominate a trial and hence divert fact-finders from considering other important evidence and issues.

The law consequently has been wary of allowing expert and scientific testimony into evidence unless it first satisfies threshold criteria for admissibility. Those criteria typically include that: (a) the subject of the testimony is "beyond the ken" of the average lay juror (or, alternatively, that the proffered testimony will "assist" the finder of fact); (b) the witness has appropriate qualifications to testify as an expert; (c) the involved science is sufficiently reliable to provide a foundation for the testimony; and (d) the probative value of the testimony is not significantly outweighed by its potential for unfair prejudice.[13] Although the courts regularly confront such issues, they may resolve them differently in light of the particular standards that govern the admissibility of scientific evidence within their respective jurisdictions. The state and federal courts do not follow a single, uniform approach in ruling on the admissibility of expert testimony. One of the important jurisdictional differences involves how the courts determine whether the science on which the offered testimony is based is sufficiently reliable to allow the jury to consider it. The two most widely used approaches—applying "the *Frye* test" or "the *Daubert* factors"—are named after the judicial decisions announcing them.

In *Frye v. United States,* 293 F. 1013 (D.C. Cir. 1923), the District of Columbia Court of Appeals affirmed a trial court's refusal to admit the results of a "systolic blood pressure deception test" into evidence at the request of a murder defendant who had argued that the test results supported his claim of innocence. The court concluded that "the systolic blood pressure deception test has not yet gained such standing and scientific recognition among physiological and psychological authorities as would justify the courts in admitting expert testimony" relating to it. The court's brief opinion, which cited neither legal nor scientific authority, famously announced the "general acceptance" test to govern the admissibility of expert scientific testimony, a standard that rapidly gained favor in jurisdictions throughout the country and remained essentially unchallenged for half a century.

> Just when a scientific principle or discovery crosses the line between the experimental and demonstrable stages is difficult to define. Somewhere in this twilight zone the evidential force of the principle must be recognized, and while courts will go a long way in admitting expert testimony deduced from a well-recognized scientific principle or discovery, the thing from which the deduction is made must be sufficiently established to have gained general acceptance in the particular field in which it belongs. 293 F., at 1014.

In contrast, *Daubert v. Merrell Dow Pharmaceuticals,* 509 U.S. 579, 113 S.Ct. 2786, 125 L.Ed.2d 469 (1993) eschewed reliance on a single standard and instead instructed trial courts to consider several factors in assessing whether expert scientific testimony is sufficiently reliable to be admitted into evidence. Although a United States Supreme Court decision, *Daubert* involved an interpretation of a Federal Rule of Evidence. It is not a constitutional ruling and consequently is binding only in the federal courts. Nevertheless, many states, through legislation or judicial decision, have embraced the *Daubert* criteria and rely on them to determine the admissibility of expert, scientific testimony in their courts. *Daubert* was a civil case in which the plaintiffs sought to have expert testimony admitted at trial in support of their claim that their child's birth defects could be linked to the antinausea medication manufactured by the defendant drug company. The trial court, relying on the *Frye* "general acceptance" test, excluded the offered testimony, and the court of appeals affirmed. The Supreme Court reversed, concluding that "the *Frye* test was superseded by the adoption of the Federal Rules of Evidence." 509 U.S., at 587.

The specific rule at issue, Federal Rule of Evidence 702, was adopted in 1975 and, when *Daubert* was decided, provided:

> If scientific, technical, or other specialized knowledge will assist the trier of fact to understand the evidence or to determine a fact in issue, a witness qualified as

> an expert by knowledge, skill, experience, training, or education, may testify thereto in the form of an opinion or otherwise.[14]

Under *Daubert,* "[m]any factors" bear on a trial court's obligation to make "a preliminary assessment of whether the reasoning or methodology underlying the testimony is scientifically valid and of whether that reasoning or methodology properly can be applied to the facts in issue." 509 U.S., at 592–593. "'[G]eneral acceptance' can yet have a bearing on the inquiry," 509 U.S., at 594, although that consideration alone is not determinative. Other relevant factors include whether the scientific theory or technique in question "can be (and has been) tested"; "whether the theory or technique has been subjected to peer review and publication"; and the "known or potential rate of error, and the existence and maintenance of standards controlling the technique's operation." 509 U.S., at 593–594.

> The inquiry envisioned by Rule 702 is, we emphasize, a flexible one. Its overarching subject is the scientific validity—and thus the evidentiary relevance and reliability—of the principles that underlie a proposed submission. The focus, of course, must be solely on principles and methodology, not on the conclusions that they generate. 509 U.S., at 594–595.

The *Frye* and *Daubert* tests governing the admissibility of scientific evidence, including their asserted strengths and weaknesses, are discussed at greater length in the following case. Perhaps fittingly, in light of the "systolic blood pressure deception test" at issue in *Frye, State v. Porter* involves a criminal defendant's request to have the results of a modern polygraph examination admitted into trial evidence in support of his claimed innocence. The case also provides us with the opportunity to consider whether the scientific principles and techniques on which polygraph examinations are premised are sufficiently reliable to justify the admissibility of the test results in criminal trials.

State v. Porter

698 A.2d 739 (Conn. 1997)

BORDEN, Justice.

The issues in this certified appeal are: (1) whether Connecticut should adopt as the standard for the admissibility of scientific evidence the standard set forth by the United States Supreme Court in *Daubert v. Merrell Dow Pharmaceuticals, Inc.,* 509 U.S. 579 (1993); and (2) whether Connecticut should abandon its traditional per se rule that polygraph evidence is inadmissible at trial. The defendant, Christian E. Porter, appeals from the judgment of the Appellate Court affirming his conviction for arson in the first degree ... [He] claims that: (1) the Appellate Court incorrectly concluded that the trial court properly denied his request for an evidentiary hearing regarding the admissibility of polygraph evidence; and (2) in light of the United States Supreme Court's decision in *Daubert*..., this court should reconsider its test for determining the admissibility of scientific evidence, which is currently based on *Frye v. United States,* 293 F. 1013 (D.C.Cir.1923), and should conclude that polygraph evidence is admissible under the *Daubert* test....

The defendant's home in Norwich was destroyed by a fire on July 20, 1992. The defendant was subsequently charged with two counts of arson in the first degree ...

Before trial, the defendant retained Leighton Hammond, a polygrapher, to conduct a polygraph examination to determine whether the defendant was telling the truth when he claimed that he had no guilty knowledge of, and had not participated in, the burning of his home. The defendant did not give the state advance notification of the examination. The pertinent test questions asked of the defendant were: (1) "Did you set fire to your home?"; (2) "Did you tell even one lie, in your statement to the Norwich Police?"; and (3) "Do you know for sure, if any person deliberately set fire to your home?" In the opinion of Hammond, the defendant was telling the truth when he answered "no" to each of these questions.

The defendant then moved that the trial court admit the results of the polygraph examination. After a hearing, the trial court denied the defendant's motion, stating that it was not the place of a trial court to reconsider Connecticut's traditional per se ban on the admissibility of polygraph evidence.

Following a jury trial, at which the defendant did not testify, he was convicted of arson in the first degree.... The Appellate Court affirmed the trial court's judgment ...

I

The *Daubert* Standard

The defendant argues that Connecticut should adopt the federal test for the admissibility of scientific evidence, as set forth by the United States Supreme Court in *Daubert v. Merrell Dow Pharmaceuticals, Inc.,* 509 U.S. 579. We agree that, when read and applied correctly, *Daubert* provides the proper approach to the threshold admissibility of scientific evidence.

A

... The standard enunciated in *Frye v. United States* was predominant in both state and federal courts for the seventy years from its formulation until the decision in *Daubert* in 1993. *Frye* itself was a lie detector case; indeed, it was the first appellate case in the United States to address the admissibility of lie detector examination results. In *Frye,* the defendant appealed from his murder conviction on the grounds that the trial court had improperly disallowed expert testimony that he had passed a "systolic blood pressure deception test," the precursor of the modern polygraph examination.[5]

In considering the defendant's claim in *Frye,* the Court of Appeals for the District of Columbia first determined that "general acceptance" in the scientific community was a precondition to the admissibility of any scientific evidence. *Frye v. United States,* supra, 293 F. at 1014. "Just when a scientific principle or discovery crosses the line between the experimental and demonstrable stages is difficult to define. Somewhere in this twilight zone the evidential force of the principle must be recognized, and while courts will go a long way in admitting expert testimony deduced from a well-recognized scientific principle or discovery, the thing from which the deduction is made must be sufficiently established to have gained general acceptance in the particular field in which it belongs." The court affirmed the trial court's exclusion of the systolic blood pressure evidence because the blood pressure device had "not yet gained such standing and scientific recognition among physiological and psychological authorities as would justify the courts in admitting expert testimony deduced from the discovery, development, and experiments thus far made." Subsequently, *Frye* and its "general acceptance" standard were expressly adopted by a number of state and federal courts.

In 1993, however, the federal standard for the admissibility of scientific evidence changed as a result of the decision of the United States Supreme Court in *Daubert v. Merrell Dow Pharmaceuticals, Inc.* In *Daubert,* the court held that rule 702[6] of the Federal Rules of Evidence, which was enacted in 1975, had superseded the *Frye* test. The court concluded that "[n]othing in the text of [rule 702] establishes 'general acceptance' as an absolute prerequisite to admissibility.... That austere standard, absent from, and incompatible with, the Federal Rules of Evidence, should not be applied in federal trials."

Instead, a federal trial court has a responsibility to determine, pursuant to rule 702, whether the proffered evidence will "assist the trier of fact." This entails a two part inquiry: "whether the reasoning or methodology underlying the [scientific theory or technique in question] is scientifically valid and ... whether that reasoning or methodology properly can be applied to the facts in issue." In other words,

---

5. The systolic blood pressure deception test was simply a sphygmomanometer—a device that records blood pressure. The theory behind this device was that if a person lied, the resulting stress and fear of detection would cause that person's blood pressure to rise. The systolic blood pressure deception test was developed by William Marston, and was actually administered by Marston in *Frye.* Marston was also the creator of the "Wonder Woman" comic book character, who is well known for her truth-inducing magic lasso.

6. Rule 702 of the Federal Rules of Evidence provides: "Testimony by Experts"

> "If scientific, technical, or other specialized knowledge will assist the trier of fact to understand the evidence or to determine a fact in issue, a witness qualified as an expert by knowledge, skill, experience, training, or education, may testify thereto in the form of an opinion or otherwise."

before it may be admitted, the trial judge must find that the proffered scientific evidence is both reliable and relevant.

More specifically, the first requirement for scientific evidence to be admissible under rule 702 is that the subject of the testimony must be scientifically valid, meaning that it is scientific knowledge rooted "in the methods and procedures of science"; and is "more than subjective belief or unsupported speculation."[7] This requirement "establishes a standard of evidentiary reliability" as, "[i]n a case involving scientific evidence, *evidentiary reliability* will be based upon *scientific validity*." (Emphasis in original.)

The court listed four nonexclusive factors for federal judges to consider in determining whether a particular theory or technique is based on scientific knowledge: (1) whether it can be, and has been, tested; (2) whether the theory or technique has been subjected to peer review and publication; (3) the known or potential rate of error, including the existence and maintenance of standards controlling the technique's operation; and (4) whether the technique is, in fact, generally accepted in the relevant scientific community. The court emphasized, however, that the inquiry is "a flexible one. Its overarching subject is the scientific validity—and thus the evidentiary relevance and reliability—of the principles that underlie a proposed submission." Indeed, the court explicitly noted that other factors "may well have merit ... [t]o the extent that they focus on the reliability of evidence as ensured by the scientific validity of its underlying principles...." *Id.*, at 594–95 n. 12.

The second condition that scientific evidence must satisfy in order to be admissible under rule 702 is that it must "fit" the case in which it is presented. In other words, proposed scientific testimony must be demonstrably relevant to the facts of the particular case in which it is offered, and not simply be valid in the abstract....

Finally, the court emphasized that even if a scientific theory or technique satisfied both of the previous criteria and thus would be admissible under a rule 702 analysis, it can still be excluded for failure to satisfy some other federal rule of evidence. Most important, it can still be excluded for failure to satisfy rule 403, which allows for the exclusion of relevant evidence "'if its probative value is substantially outweighed by the danger of unfair prejudice, confusion of the issues, or misleading the jury....'"[8]

Because *Daubert* was premised on an interpretation of a federal rule of evidence, its rejection of *Frye* is not binding authority on state courts. Nonetheless, subsequent to the *Daubert* decision, several states that had theretofore followed *Frye* reconsidered the issue and adopted the *Daubert* standard.

B

We now address the question of the proper standard for the threshold admissibility of scientific evidence in this state. We begin by noting that, at present, Connecticut nominally follows the *Frye* rule....

It is clear that we have been moving toward a validity standard for a number of years.... [W]e conclude that the *Daubert* approach should govern the admissibility of scientific evidence in Connecticut.

1

We first discuss why a special standard for the admissibility of scientific evidence is required at all. Implicit in both *Frye* and *Daubert* is the notion that a trial judge should, by one method or another, serve as a "gatekeeper" and make a preliminary assessment of the validity of scientific testimony before allowing the fact finder even to consider it. A number of commentators, however, have suggested that the validity of proffered scientific evidence should go solely to its *weight*, not to its admissibility, and thus the fact finder should have a chance to consider all scientific evidence that is submitted....

We disagree ... and conclude that the validity of the methodologies underlying proffered scientific evidence should be considered in determining the admissibility of such evidence, as

7. The court emphasized that "[t]he focus, of course, must be solely on principles and methodology, not on the conclusions that they generate." 509 U.S. at 595.

8. Rule 403 of the Federal Rules of Evidence provides: "Exclusion of Relevant Evidence on Grounds of Prejudice, Confusion, or Waste of Time"

> "Although relevant, evidence may be excluded if its probative value is substantially outweighed by the danger of unfair prejudice, confusion of the issues, or misleading the jury, or by considerations of undue delay, waste of time, or needless presentation of cumulative evidence."

well as in determining its weight. Accordingly, we also conclude that it is proper for a trial judge to serve a gatekeeper function.

a

In this regard, we first note the concern expressed by many authorities that juries will be overwhelmed by complex scientific evidence and will give such evidence more weight than it deserves. We acknowledge, however, that other commentators have specifically asserted that juries will *not* be overly impressed by such evidence. At present, empirical data regarding the impact of scientific testimony on juries is almost entirely lacking. As a consequence, whether jurors will unduly credit scientific evidence is quite uncertain. Indeed, direct empirical evidence regarding the impact of scientific evidence on judges is also lacking.

Although the effect of scientific evidence with regard to both judges and juries is uncertain, we note that, purely as a procedural matter, a judge is in a much better position than a juror to assess accurately the fundamental validity of such evidence. This is due to the different roles each serves at trial and the concomitant powers each has....

For example, juries mainly have to rely on in-court testimony for their understanding of scientific evidence; that is, they are largely dependent upon the presentations of the parties and their experts. There is evidence, however, that expert presentations may often be misleading and, at the same time, that cross-examination of experts may often be difficult and ineffective in bringing out flaws in the expert's reasoning.

Judges, on the other hand, have the benefit of reviewing briefs and other documents.... Furthermore, a judge presiding over a criminal case [has the authority] to appoint an independent expert when necessary. Such an appointment could certainly be made to assist the judge in evaluating proposed scientific testimony.

Moreover, "[a]n important element in adjudication ... is the development of judicial expertise through repeated exposure to and familiarity with similar scientific issues." Judges, on the one hand, are likely to gain familiarity with various common procedures, and with scientific techniques in general, by virtue of presiding over multiple cases involving such issues.... On the other hand, "[t]aking the time required to educate jurors and to present them with similarly detailed information could easily overwhelm the other issues in a case."

Given this background, we conclude that a gatekeeping role for trial judges in relation to scientific evidence is appropriate....

b

In addition, we believe it is proper for trial judges to serve as gatekeepers for scientific evidence because a relevance standard of admissibility inherently involves an assessment of the validity of the proffered evidence. More specifically, if scientific evidence has no grounding in scientific fact, but instead is based on conjecture and speculation, it cannot in any meaningful way be relevant to resolving a disputed issue....

2

Having concluded that Connecticut judges should exercise a gatekeeper function with regard to scientific evidence, we now briefly explain our conclusion that the *Frye* "general acceptance" standard is not adequate for this role. We note that even before the decision in *Daubert*, the *Frye* rule was widely criticized.... These critics observe that scientific pioneers and dissenters are occasionally right.... Excluding scientific views simply because they are not "generally accepted," without *any* further consideration of their validity, thus contravenes "the liberal nature ... of modern evidentiary law."

We are persuaded by these criticisms of the *Frye* test. We conclude that an admissibility test for scientific evidence premised *solely* on its "general acceptance" is conceptually flawed and therefore must be rejected....

3

... Our reasons for adopting *Daubert* are based upon our understanding of that case. By its own terms, the opinion of the United States Supreme Court in *Daubert* sets forth a conceptual *approach* to the admissibility of scientific evidence, and not a functional *test* therefore.... [T]he essential holding of the Supreme Court is the general principle that, as a threshold matter, and subject still to the rules of evidence generally, scientific evidence should be admitted in court only upon some showing of its scientific validity. Although the court provides "general observations" as to some factors that might be relevant to this determination, it explicitly states that "[m]any factors will bear on the inquiry, *and we do not presume to set out a definitive checklist or test*." (Emphasis added.) ...

Critics of *Daubert* emphasize this indefiniteness....

We view *Daubert* 's indefiniteness not as a flaw, but as a necessity. The term "scientific evidence" covers a large variety of subjects. The Federal Judicial Center, for example, included in its Reference Manual on Scientific Evidence essays on the broad topics of epidemiology, toxicology, survey research, DNA evidence, multiple regression, and estimation of economic losses in damages awards. In addition to those subjects, courts have also treated as scientific evidence testimony on subjects ranging from the causation of a plaintiff's cataracts; to an analysis of bloodstain patterns at a crime scene; to, of course, polygraph evidence; and beyond.

... No purely mechanical test based on a finite number of set considerations can, in and of itself, truly guide judges with regard to the admissibility of all of the varied and eclectic types of scientific evidence....

We conclude that a test embodying a general, overarching approach to the threshold admissibility of scientific evidence is required. Although such a standard is more vague on its surface, it will in fact discourage untrammeled discretion by giving trial courts a workable principle to follow. Moreover, we believe that *Daubert*'s focus on scientific validity properly directs trial judges to the core issue that they should address as gatekeepers of scientific evidence. For, as explained previously, scientific evidence is likely neither relevant nor helpful to the fact finder if it does not meet some minimum standard of validity.

C

We now examine, pursuant to our conception of the *Daubert* approach, the mechanics and scope of a *Daubert* assessment....

1

We begin by noting the distinction under the *Daubert* approach between the methodologies underlying an expert's scientific testimony and the expert opinion itself. As the court in *Daubert* noted, the focus of a validity assessment "must be solely on principles and methodology, not on the conclusions that they generate." So long as the methodology underlying a scientific opinion has the requisite validity, the testimony derived from that methodology meets the *Daubert* threshold for admissibility, even if the judge disagrees with the ultimate opinion arising from that methodology, *and even if there are other methodologies that might lead to contrary conclusions*....

Of course, even where a particular technique has been shown to satisfy *Daubert*, the proponent must also establish that the specific scientific testimony at issue is, in fact, *derived from* and based upon that methodology. The Supreme Court in *Daubert* referred to this concept as the "fit" requirement. "[A]lthough some conclusions can be reasonably inferred from the methodology employed, others cannot." ...

2

We now set forth some of the factors that various courts have considered in conducting a methodological analysis. We emphasize, however, that these factors are *not* exclusive. Some will not be relevant in particular cases; and some cases will call for considerations not discussed herein....

Even under *Daubert*, courts should continue to consider whether a scientific principle has gained "general acceptance" in making admissibility determinations. Although "general acceptance" is no longer an absolute prerequisite to the admission of scientific evidence, it should, in fact, be an important factor in a trial judge's assessment.... [I]f a trial court determines that a scientific methodology *has* gained general acceptance, then the *Daubert* inquiry will generally end and the conclusions derived from that methodology will generally be admissible. If a principle has *not* gained general acceptance, however, we emphasize that "a proponent of [the] scientific opinion ... may [still] demonstrate the reliability or validity of the underlying scientific theory or process by some other means, that is, without establishing general acceptance."

Several other factors may properly play a role in a court's assessment of the validity of a scientific methodology. The remaining factors listed in *Daubert*—whether that methodology has been tested and subjected to peer review, and the known or potential rate of error—are of course important. Moreover, the prestige and background of the expert witness supporting the evidence can play a role in determining whether a novel technique employed by that individual is likely to have any scientific merit. The extent to which the scientific technique in question relies on subjective interpretations and judgments by the testifying expert, rather than on objectively verifiable criteria, can also be a factor. In the same vein, courts have looked at whether a testifying expert can present and explain the data and methodology underlying his or her scientific testimony in such a manner that the fact finder can reasonably and realistically draw its own conclusions therefrom. Several courts have also considered whether the scientific technique underlying the proffered expert testimony was developed and implemented solely to develop evidence for in-court use, or whether the technique has been developed or used for extrajudicial purposes.

We appreciate that many of these factors lack precision, but this indefiniteness is unavoidable. The actual operation of each factor, as is the determination of which factors should be considered at all, depends greatly on the specific context of each case in which each particular *Daubert* analysis is conducted. So long as trial judges remain focused on the underlying purpose behind the *Daubert* analysis—to establish whether a scientific methodology has sufficient validity to be helpful to the fact finder—we are confident that the previously mentioned uncertainties are not so overwhelming as to render *Daubert* functionally inoperative.

3

We now turn to the threshold burden that a proponent of scientific testimony bears to establish that the testimony is admissible....

In addressing the showing that a proponent of scientific evidence must make, we are largely guided by the fundamental tenets of the law of evidence regarding admissibility. "Evidence is admissible when it tends to establish a fact in issue or to corroborate other direct evidence in the case." "Evidence is not rendered inadmissible because it is not conclusive. All that is required is that evidence *tend* to support a relevant fact even to a slight degree, so long as it is not prejudicial or merely cumulative." ...

These concepts are as applicable to scientific testimony as to other types of evidence. Thus, questions about the methodological validity of proffered scientific testimony will generally go to the *weight* of such evidence, not to its admissibility. Courts should exclude scientific evidence, however, when such concerns render the technique, and the resulting evidence, incapable of assisting the fact finder in a sufficiently meaningful way....

A trial judge should ... deem scientific evidence inadmissible only when the methodology underlying such evidence is sufficiently invalid to render the evidence incapable of helping the fact finder determine a fact in dispute. We adopt the *Daubert* approach, however, specifically because we conclude that a sufficient showing of validity *is* necessary for scientific evidence to be helpful. The interplay between these principles—a general policy in favor of admission of helpful evidence, and a specific policy of requiring a showing of a certain level of validity before scientific testimony can properly be presented to a fact finder—cannot be resolved by an absolute statement or rule. Instead, a case-by-case analysis will be necessary.

D

It is important to remember that *Daubert* only provides a *threshold* inquiry into the admissibility of scientific evidence. Even evidence that has met the *Daubert* inquiry into its methodological validity, and thus has been shown to have some probative value, may be excluded for failure to satisfy other evidentiary rules. In particular, scientific evidence, like all evidence, is properly excluded if its prejudicial impact outweighs its probative value, even if it is otherwise admissible.

E

Finally, we address the concern that, by requiring trial courts to conduct a *Daubert* validity assessment, we are improperly requiring them to become amateur scientists....

We conclude that this concern is unfounded. Under *Daubert,* trial judges are not required to make a determination of the ultimate scientific validity of any scientific propositions. Instead, they need only make a much more limited inquiry: whether sufficient indicia of legitimacy exist to support the conclusion that evidence derived from the principle may be profitably considered by a fact finder at trial....

Moreover, to the extent that our adoption of *Daubert* does "[signal] that the time has come for courts and lawyers to learn the basic principles of science" we see this as an unavoidable necessity. As science and technology have advanced and become increasingly prevalent in our society, the number of cases, both civil and criminal, in which scientific testimony plays a role has also grown.... Only by being knowledgeable, in at least a basic way, about the issues surrounding the scientific evidence before them, can judges discharge their duties properly. Accordingly, *Daubert,* at its most fundamental level, merely directs "trial judges consciously [to] do what is in reality a basic task of a trial judge—ensure the reliability and relevance of evidence without causing confusion, prejudice or mistake."

II

Admissibility of Polygraph Evidence

We now turn to the defendant's claim that Connecticut should abandon its traditional per se rule against the admission of polygraph evidence at trial....

Without deciding, we will assume, for the purposes of this opinion, that polygraph evidence satisfies the admissibility threshold established by *Daubert.* After reviewing the case law and the current, extensive literature on the polygraph test, however, we are convinced that the prejudicial impact of polygraph evidence greatly exceeds its probative value. Accordingly, we see no reason to abandon our well established rule of exclusion, and we conclude that polygraph evidence should remain per se inadmissible in all trial court proceedings in which the rules of evidence apply, and for all trial purposes, in Connecticut courts....

B

... [W]e turn now to an assessment of the threshold validity, probative value, and prejudicial impact of polygraph evidence. In order to do so, it is necessary to understand some of the mechanics and theory behind the modern polygraph test.

1

Modern polygraph theory rests on two assumptions: (1) there is a regular relationship between deception and certain emotional states; and (2) there is a regular relationship between those emotional states and certain physiological changes in the body that can be measured and recorded. These physiological changes include fluctuations in heart rate and blood pressure, rate of breathing, and flow of electrical current through the body, and they are measured by a cardiosphygmograph, a pneumograph and a galvanometer, respectively. These instruments, bundled together, form the basis of most modern polygraphs.

There is no question that a high quality polygraph is capable of accurately measuring the relevant physical characteristics. Even polygraph advocates, however, acknowledge that "[n]o known physiological response or pattern of responses is unique to deception." Indeed, "there is no reason to believe that lying produces distinctive physiological changes that characterize it and only it.... [T]here is no set of responses—physiological or otherwise—that humans omit only when lying or that they produce only when telling the truth.... No doubt when we tell a lie many of us experience an inner turmoil, but we experience similar turmoil when we are falsely accused of a crime, when we are anxious about having to defend ourselves against accusations, when we are questioned about sensitive topics—and, for that matter, when we are elated or otherwise emotionally stirred." Thus, while a polygraph machine can accurately gauge a subject's *physiological* profile, it cannot, on its own, determine the nature of the underlying *psychological* profile. "The instrument cannot itself detect deception."

The polygraph examiner, therefore, is responsible for transforming the output of a polygraph machine from physiological data into an assessment of truth or deception. This mission actually involves two separate tasks. First, the examiner must design and implement a polygraph test in such a way that the physiological data produced is properly linked to a subject's deceptiveness, and not just to his nervousness or other unrelated emotional responses. Second, even if the data produced *is* linked to a subject's deception, the examiner must interpret the data, that is, grade the test, correctly.

The "control question test" is the polygraph method most commonly used in criminal cases to link physiological responses to deception. The control question test is based on the theory that fear of detection causes psychological stress. Under that test, therefore, the "polygraph instrument is measuring the fear of detection *rather than deception per se.*"

In the control question test procedure, the polygrapher first conducts a pretest interview with the subject wherein the accuracy and reliability of the polygraph are emphasized. This is done to aggravate the deceptive subject's fear of detection while calming the innocent subject, which is crucial given that the test's efficacy is based entirely on the subject's emotional state. All exam questions are then reviewed with the subject, in order to minimize the impact of surprise on the test results and to ensure that the subject understands the questions. The actual control question test consists of a sequence of ten to twelve questions, repeated several times. There are three categories of questions: neutral; relevant; and control. All questions are formulated by the polygrapher conducting the examination based on a review of the facts of the case.

A neutral question is entirely nonconfrontational and is designed to allow the polygrapher to get a baseline reading on the subject's physiological responses. A neutral question addresses a subject's name, age, address, or similar topic.

A relevant question is accusatory and directed specifically at the subject under investigation. "For example, in an assault investigation, a relevant question might be: 'On May 1, 1986, did you strike Mr. Jones (the alleged victim) with any part of your body?'"

A control question concerns "an act of wrongdoing of the same general nature as the main incident under investigation," and is designed to be "one to which the subject, in all probability, will lie or to which his answer will be of dubious validity in his own mind." Control questions "cover many years in the prior life of the subject and are deliberately vague. Almost anyone would have difficulty answering them truthfully with a simple 'No.'" In an assault case, a control question might be: "Did you ever want to see anyone harmed?" Although few people honestly could deny these control questions categorically, they are "presented to the subject in a manner designed to lead him to believe that admissions would negatively influence the examiner's opinion and that strong reactions to those questions during the test would produce a deceptive result."[42]

The theory behind the control question test is that "the truthful person will respond more to the control questions than to the relevant questions because they represent a greater threat to that person. For the same reason the deceptive person will respond more to the relevant questions than to the control questions." Thus, in order for the test to work properly, both truthful and deceptive examinees must have particular mind sets during the exam. "The innocent examinee [must fear] that the polygraph examiner will pick up his deception [on the control question] and incorrectly conclude that he is also being deceptive about the relevant question." As a result, the innocent subject's physiological responses to the control question, stemming from this fear, will be greater than those to the relevant question, which the subject can answer honestly. A guilty subject, however, will be more worried about having his crime and deception exposed by the relevant question than he is about any control question issues. Accordingly, his physiological responses—prompted by his fear of detection—will be greater with regard to the relevant question than to the control question.

Under the control question test, the absolute measure of the subject's physiological responses to each question is unimportant. For example, the mere fact that a subject has a strong response to a relevant question can simply be indicative of nervousness and does not, by itself, indicate deception. Instead, the polygrapher looks to the *relative* strength of the responses to the control and relevant questions in order to determine truth or deception.[43] The art of the polygrapher lies in composing control and relevant questions that elicit the appropriate relative responses from truthful and deceitful parties.

A control question exam ordinarily pairs relevant and control questions with some neutral questions interspersed. For example, a typical progression would be:

"1. (Neutral) Do you understand that I will ask only the questions we have discussed?

"2. (Pseudo-Relevant) Regarding whether you took that ring, do you intend to answer all of the questions truthfully?

"3. (Neutral) Do you live in the United States?

"4. (Control) During the first twenty-four years of your life, did you ever take something that did not belong to you?

"5. (Relevant) Did you take a ring from the Behavioral Sciences Building on July 1, 1985?

"6. (Neutral) Is your name Joanne?

"7. (Control) Between the ages of ten and twenty-four, did you ever do anything dishonest or illegal?

---

42. In other words, the control question test process requires that the examiner, during the pretest interview, manipulate the subject into both (1) lying on the control questions, out of fear that the examiner will otherwise react negatively to the subject's prior antisocial conduct, and (2) fearing that this same deception will taint the entire exam.

43. This process is what separates the control question test from the relevant-irrelevant polygraph test. In the latter test, there are no control questions, only relevant and irrelevant questions. A subject whose responses to the relevant questions are greater than those to the irrelevant questions is considered deceptive. Although still practiced by some polygraphers today the relevant-irrelevant test is almost universally rejected in the literature. ("A variety of factors might cause individuals to react more strongly to questions about crimes of which they are accused than to innocuous questions.... There is no clear and systematic way to interpret the outcome of a relevant-irrelevant test, and the result is subject to a great deal of error.").

"8. (Relevant) Did you take that diamond ring from a desk in the Behavioral Sciences Building on July 1?

"9. (Neutral) Were you born in the month of February?

"10. (Control) Before 1984 did you ever lie to get out of trouble or to cause a problem for someone else?

"11. (Relevant) Were you in any way involved in the theft of that diamond ring from the Behavioral Sciences Building last July?"

The entire sequence is normally gone through three times, after which the examiner scores the result to attempt to reach a determination of truthfulness or deception.

The most common technique for scoring polygraph charts is pure numerical grading. In the most prevalent numerical system, the polygrapher assigns a numerical value along the range of -3 to +3 to each pair of relevant and control questions. A score of +3 indicates a much stronger reaction to the control question than to the relevant question and, therefore, truthfulness; a score of -3 indicates a much stronger reaction to the relevant question and, therefore, deception; and a score of 0 indicates that there was no significant difference in response. The examiner considers only the polygraph chart in assigning these scores; no consideration is given to any subjective impressions regarding the subject's truthfulness that the examiner develops over the course of the exam. The scores for all question pairs in all three sequences are then totaled. If the sum is +6 or greater, the subject is classified as truthful; if the sum is -6 or lower, the subject is classified as deceptive; scores of -5 to +5 are deemed inconclusive. Computers are sometimes used to give more precise numerical scores to polygraph charts.[44]

If an analysis of the first three charts produces inconclusive results, the examiner will often repeat the question sequence twice more. After that, however, further repetitions are generally considered meritless, as the subject will have become habituated to the test questions and, therefore, will no longer have sufficiently strong emotional responses for polygraph purposes.[45]

44. We note that there is disagreement in the literature even as to what method of scoring is proper. Most authorities agree that numerical scoring is the only valid approach. Nonetheless, many examiners still use "global scoring." Under this approach, the examiner looks at the subject's relative reactions to the control and relevant questions, but also considers various "clinical impressions," such as the subject's demeanor, in arriving at a conclusion of truthfulness or deception. A few authors, albeit generally polygraph detractors, suggest that the global method is, in fact, more accurate.

45. The other main type of polygraph examination used in criminal matters is the guilty knowledge test. The guilty knowledge test "does not attempt to determine whether the [subject] is lying but, rather, whether he or she possesses guilty knowledge, that is, whether the [subject] recognizes the correct answers, from among several equally plausible but incorrect alternatives, to certain questions relating to a crime. For example, escaping through an alley a bank robber drops and leaves behind his hat. A likely suspect is later apprehended and, while attached to the polygraph, he is interrogated as follows:

> "1. 'The robber in this case dropped something while escaping. If you are that robber, you will know what he dropped. Was it: a weapon? a face mask? a sack of money? his hat? his car keys?'...
>
> "Unlike the control question test, the accuracy of the guilty knowledge test does not depend upon the nature or degree of the subject's emotional concern. The physiological variables employed are not intended to measure emotional response but, rather, to signal the cognitive processes involved in the recognition of the correct alternative."
>
> "The guilty knowledge test assumes that the guilty subject will have a greater physical response to the 'significant alternative' than would a subject without any guilty knowledge." Advocates claim that the primary advantage of the guilty knowledge test is that recognition can be more directly measured by physiological data than can truth or deception.
>
> For the guilty knowledge test to work, however, there must be "concealed knowledge" that only the guilty party would know and recognize. This requirement greatly limits the number of cases in which the test can be utilized. In any event, although the guilty knowledge test does have its advocates the guilty knowledge test's validity is as hotly debated as that of the control question test. Because the validity of the guilty knowledge test is so uncertain, and because all of the prejudicial effects of allowing control question test evidence apply to guilty knowledge test evidence as well we conclude that guilty knowledge test evidence must also be excluded from use in our courts.

2

We now examine the validity of the results produced by the polygraph test.[46] The word "validity" has two meanings in the polygraph context: for the purposes of this discussion, they will be labeled "accuracy" and "predictive value." Courts generally do not specify to which concept they are referring when they address polygraph issues. Maintaining this distinction is essential, however, if one is to evaluate fairly the validity of the polygraph test.

a

The "accuracy" of the polygraph test itself has two components: *sensitivity* and *specificity*. The polygraph's sensitivity is its ability to tell that a guilty person is, in fact, lying. If the polygraph test had a 90 percent sensitivity, then it would correctly label a deceptive subject as being deceptive 90 percent of the time. Thus, the test would incorrectly label a deceptive subject as being truthful 10 percent of the time; this mislabeling is called a "false negative" error. The polygraph's specificity is its ability to tell that an innocent person is, in fact, being truthful. If the polygraph test had an 80 percent specificity, then it would label a truthful subject as being truthful 80 percent of the time. The test would thus incorrectly label a truthful subject as being deceptive 20 percent of the time; this mislabeling is called a "false positive" error. It is generally agreed in the literature, by both advocates and critics, that polygraphs have greater sensitivity than specificity; that is, that false positives outnumber false negatives.

There is wide disagreement, however, as to what the sensitivity and specificity values actually are for a well run polygraph exam. Dozens of studies of polygraph accuracy have been conducted. They fall into two basic types, namely, laboratory simulations of crimes[47] and field studies based on data from polygraph examinations in actual criminal cases.[48] The variance in expert opinion regarding polygraph accuracy arises from disagreements as to which methods and which studies within each method are methodologically valid.

Polygraph supporters base their accuracy estimates on both laboratory simulation and field studies. These advocates acknowledge that field studies are theoretically preferable for establishing the polygraph test's field accuracy, but they conclude that serious methodological difficulties inherent in such studies, such as establishing the actual guilt or innocence of the study subjects, make most of these studies unreliable. They think, however, that laboratory studies, when designed to approximate field conditions and when carefully conducted, *can* provide useful and valid data. David Raskin, perhaps the foremost polygraph advocate in the United States, recently reviewed the literature on polygraph studies and concluded that eight laboratory studies and four field studies of the control question test polygraph technique were methodologically valid. D. Raskin, "The Scientific Status of Research on Polygraph Techniques," in West Companion to Scientific Evidence 2 (Faigman et al. eds. 1996). The laboratory studies that Raskin cites, taken together, indicate that the polygraph test has an 89 percent sensitivity rate and a 91 percent specificity rate; the field studies give an 87 percent sensitivity and a 59 percent specificity.[50] Other studies indicate higher levels of accuracy....

---

46. Although courts generally use the word "reliability" when discussing the polygraph test, the concept to which the courts are referring is actually the test's "validity." In the polygraph context, reliability and validity have specialized meanings. Reliability refers only to reproducibility of results, or consistency, while validity relates to the test's actual ability to do what it claims to do, namely, detect deception. Reliability is important, but the polygraph debate really centers around the test's validity.

47. "The most accepted type of laboratory study simulates a real crime in which subjects are randomly assigned to guilty and innocent treatment conditions.... Guilty subjects enact a realistic crime, and innocent subjects are merely told about the nature of the crime and do not enact it. All subjects are motivated to produce a truthful outcome, usually by a substantial cash bonus for passing the test."

48. "The best available method for field research uses cases in which suspects were administered polygraph tests after which their guilt or innocence was established when the guilty person confessed. Other polygraph examiners are then asked to make diagnoses based solely on the polygraph charts from those tests without knowledge of the guilt or innocence of the subjects or the opinions of the original examiners. The decisions from these blind analyses are then compared to the confession criterion to estimate the accuracy of the polygraph tests."

50. Pursuant to standard practice in calculating specificity and sensitivity, we exclude all of the inconclusive outcomes in the raw data from our calculations, because inconclusive results are not conclusions.

Critics, however, view the existing body of polygraph studies quite differently. First, although polygraph detractors agree with the advocates that most field studies are invalid due to methodological concerns, they disagree as to which tests *are* valid. David Lykken, a prominent polygraph critic, has concluded from the field tests he deems valid that the polygraph has a sensitivity of 84 percent and a specificity of only 53 percent. D. Lykken, "The Validity of Tests: Caveat Emptor," 27 Jurimetrics J. 263, 264 (1987).... After its own thorough review of the polygraph field studies, the United States Office of Technology Assessment concluded that "the cumulative research evidence suggest that ... the polygraph test detects deception better than chance, but with significant error rates."

Moreover, polygraph critics argue that laboratory simulation studies are almost completely invalid. They point out that, although the accuracy of the control question test turns entirely on the subject having the "right" emotional responses, the emotional stimuli in the laboratory are completely different from those in the field.... Raskin has admitted that these concerns with laboratory simulations are significant.

Even if one accepts Raskin's field study estimates of accuracy over those of the polygraph critics, polygraph evidence is of questionable validity. Raskin's 87 percent sensitivity indicates a 13 percent false negative rate. In other words, 13 percent of those who are in fact deceptive will be labeled as truthful. Moreover, Raskin's 59 percent specificity indicates a 41 percent false positive rate. In other words, 41 percent of subjects who are, in fact, truthful will be labeled as deceptive.

b

In the previous section, we demonstrated that the basic *accuracy* of the polygraph test is still open to considerable debate. The actual *probative value* of polygraph evidence as a signifier of guilt or innocence, moreover, is even more questionable. This is because sensitivity, for example, only tells how likely a polygraph is to label accurately a person as deceptive *given that* the person really is lying. At trial, however, we would not yet know that a subject is deceptive—indeed, making that determination may be the entire point of the trial. Knowing how accurately the polygraph test labels deceptive people as deceptive is not, therefore, directly helpful. We are instead interested in a related, but distinct, question: how likely is it that a person really is lying given that the polygraph labels the subject as deceptive? This is called the "predictive value positive." Similarly, at trial we are not directly interested in the polygraph test's specificity, but rather in its "predictive value negative": how likely is it that a subject really is truthful given that the polygraph labels the subject as not deceptive?

Predictive value positive and predictive value negative depend on the sensitivity and specificity of the polygraph test, but also turn on the "base rate"[53] of deceptiveness among the people tested by the polygraph. Unfortunately, no reliable

53. The term "base rate" refers to the prevalence of a condition among the relevant tested population. In the context of the polygraph test, the base rate is the percentage of people who submit to a polygraph exam who are, in fact, deceptive on the exam. If, out of every 100 people who take a polygraph test, we could empirically demonstrate that fifty are, in fact, giving deceptive responses, then the base rate of deception would be 50 percent.

The base rate is important because it can greatly accentuate the impact of the false positive and false negative rates arising from any given specificity and sensitivity values. If one assumes base rates progressively higher than 50 percent, then, by definition, the number of deceptive examinees increases and the number of honest examinees decreases. A logical consequence is that, even holding specificity and sensitivity rates constant, as the base rate increases the number of false negatives (the labeling of deceptive subjects as truthful) also rises and the number of false positives (the labeling of truthful subjects as deceptive) falls, because only deceptive subjects produce false negatives and only truthful subjects produce false positives. Likewise, if one were to assume base rates progressively lower than 50 percent, then, even holding sensitivity and specificity constant, as the base rate falls the number of false positives will necessarily rise and the number of false negatives will fall.

For example, a very low base rate would dramatically emphasize the problem of false positives, even if sensitivity and specificity were both relatively high. Suppose that the polygraph has a sensitivity of 90 percent (and thus a false negative rate of 10 percent) and a specificity of 80 percent (and thus a false positive rate of 20 percent), and that the base rate of deception is 10 percent. If 100 subjects are tested, then the 10 percent base rate signifies that ten subjects are deceptive and ninety are truthful. Given the specificity of 80 percent, seventy-two of the ninety truthful subjects will be labeled accurately as truthful (80 percent of ninety is seventy-two); the remaining eighteen truthful subjects will be mislabeled as deceptive due to the 20 percent

measure of this base rate currently exists if, indeed, one is possible at all. Raskin has claimed, on the basis of an analysis of a United States Secret Service study and on the basis of his own empirical experience, that only about 40 to 60 percent of criminal defendants who are willing to submit to polygraph tests are actually guilty. If a base rate of about 50 percent were correct, then, using Raskin's own field derived figures of 87 percent sensitivity and 59 percent specificity, the predictive value positive of the polygraph test would only be 68 percent and the predictive value negative would be 82 percent. That is, even if we were to agree with all of Raskin's figures, we should only be 68 percent confident that a subject really is lying if the subject fails a polygraph exam, and only 82 percent confident that the subject is being truthful if the subject passes. Therefore, although the probative value of the polygraph test may be greater than that of a coin toss, it is not significantly greater, especially for failed tests.

Furthermore, the 50 percent base rate that Raskin posits is far from universally accepted.... Lykken posits, albeit with as equally sparse evidence as Raskin, that the base rate of guilt among people volunteering for a polygraph exam is 80 percent. Using this base rate, the polygraph test's predictive value positive is 89 percent and its predictive value negative is 53 percent. Lykken's base rate, therefore, makes a failed test more probative than it is under Raskin's base rate, but makes a passed test much less probative.

The *specific* predictive value positive and predictive value negative figures generated by a particular set of assumptions, however, is not the significant point for the legal determination of whether to admit polygraph evidence. The point is that, given the complete absence of reliable data on base rates, we have no way of assessing the probative value of the polygraph test. Under one set of assumptions, a failed test has some significance, while a passed test does not; under another, the situation is reversed. The figures are further muddied when one recalls that the sensitivity and specificity of the polygraph are also hotly debated.

C

Countermeasures are also a concern with regard to polygraph validity. A countermeasure is any technique used by a deceptive subject to induce a false negative result and thereby pass the test. For a countermeasure to work on the control question test, all it must do is "change the direction of the differential reactivity between the relevant and control questions...."

It may be true that "subjects *without special training* in countermeasures are unable to beat the polygraph test, even if they have been provided with extensive information and suggestions on how they might succeed. Yet as one polygraph supporter ... concedes, "studies have indicated that [expert-conducted] training in specific point countermeasures designed to increase [physiological responses to control questions] is effective in producing a substantial number of false negative outcomes...." Specifically, "[s]ubjects in these studies were informed about the nature of the control question test and were trained to recognize control and relevant questions. Countermeasure subjects were then instructed to employ a countermeasure (e.g., bite their tongue, press their toes to the floor, or count backward by seven) during the control question zones of a control question test. In one study, none of the guilty subjects who received this brief training was correctly detected.... Across all of the studies more than 50% of the decisions on countermeasures subjects were incorrect." ...

3

With the foregoing information in mind, we will assume, without deciding, that polygraph evidence satisfies *Daubert.* Although the subjective nature and highly questionable predictive value of the polygraph test weigh heavily against admission, we assume that polygraph evidence may have enough demonstrated validity to pass the *Daubert* threshold for admissibility.

We conclude, however, that admission of the polygraph test would be highly detrimental to the operation of Connecticut courts, both procedurally and substantively. Moreover, as illustrated in ... this opinion, the probative value

---

false positive rate. Similarly, given the sensitivity of 90 percent, nine of the ten deceptive subjects will be labeled accurately as deceptive (90 percent of ten is nine); the remaining deceptive subject will be mislabeled as truthful due to the 10 percent false negative rate....

"A hundred people are tested: 81 percent are correctly classified; 90 percent of the guilty fail; 80 percent of the innocent pass. And yet of these who fail, only one in three is guilty." S. Blinkhorn, "Lie Detection As a Psychometric Procedure," in The Polygraph Test (A. Gale ed., 1988) pp. 29, 34.

of polygraph evidence is very low, even if it satisfies *Daubert*. Accordingly, we also conclude that any limited evidentiary value that polygraph evidence does have is substantially outweighed by its prejudicial effects. We therefore reaffirm our per se rule against the use of polygraph evidence in Connecticut courts.

a

The most significant, and fundamental, problem with allowing polygraph evidence in court is that it would invade the fact-finding province of the jury. The jury has traditionally been the sole arbiter of witness credibility.... ...

A determination of whether a witness is telling the truth is well within the province of all jurors' understanding and abilities.... Most scientific testimony is facially different from polygraph evidence, however, in that it involves matters that jurors *cannot* assess on their own. A juror cannot, for example, determine whether a blood stain contains DNA consistent with that of a particular individual without expert assistance and testimony.

Very few studies have been done on the influence that polygraph evidence has over juries, and the cumulative results of those studies are inconclusive. In view of the importance of maintaining the role of the jury, this uncertainty alone justifies the continued exclusion of polygraph evidence. Moreover, polygraph evidence so directly abrogates the jury's function that its admission is offensive to our tradition of trial by jury....

A polygrapher can ascertain a witness' deception or truth only indirectly, through physical manifestations thereof. It is unfair, however, to label a person as truthful or a liar based solely on such indirect, secondary indicia as a polygraph provides. Although a juror also considers secondary indicia, like demeanor, in assessing a witness' credibility, the juror has access to the rest of the evidence in the case as well, giving the juror several points of reference on which to base an assessment. In this way, a witness is not wrongly condemned, or elevated, solely because his or her body does not act in the "right" way.

Moreover, we afford criminal defendants the right to trial by a panel of several jurors partly out of the recognition that, although one person may be misled when a witness gives the "incorrect" physical signals, the cumulative impressions of the group are likely to lead to the truth. It violates the premise of this entire system to allow a single person—the polygrapher—to label a witness as honest or as dishonest based solely on the same type of indirect evidence that we generally maintain takes an entire jury to evaluate.

In this regard, we do not dispute that polygraphers may often reach a correct *conclusion* regarding a subject's guilt or innocence.[63] We conclude, however, that this fact, in and of itself, is irrelevant. As illustrated in ... this opinion, the ability of the polygraph *technique* to tell whether a subject is lying or telling the truth is still highly questionable. Thus, one cannot say with any degree of certainty that a polygrapher's ultimate conclusion about a subject's veracity is in fact based upon the polygraph machine—that is, based upon science. It is just as likely, if not more likely, that a polygrapher's conclusion will be based either on chance or on his or her general impressions of the subject's credibility. An assessment of witness credibility based simply on chance or on intuition is not, however, admissible at trial. Indeed, forming impressions and intuitions regarding witnesses is the quintessential jury function; moreover, to the extent possible, luck should be excluded from the assessment process altogether.

---

63. It is interesting to note that critics of the *Frye* rule and critics of polygraph exclusion in general have on occasion asserted Frye's factual innocence as part of their arguments. "The premise appears to be that if, in truth, Frye was innocent of the crime charged, then the rule in the case is the culprit, for it permitted an innocent man to be convicted when science was ready and able to exonerate him. In the absence of the *Frye* court's parochial, constraining attitude toward the efficacy of scientific evidence, or so the proponents of this position seem to say, an innocent man would not have been unjustly convicted of murder and punished for it." J. Starrs, "'A Still-Life Watercolor': *Frye v. United States*," 27 J. Forensic Sci. 684, 687 (1982). Thus, authors have at various times asserted that someone else confessed to the murder for which Frye was convicted.

Subsequent scholarship has demonstrated, however, that both the third party confession and the pardon arising therefrom are nothing more than "folklore," and that, in fact, Frye served eighteen years in jail before being paroled. See generally J. Starrs, supra, 27 J. Forensic Sci. 690, 692. Moreover, even if Frye had, in fact, been innocent, we conclude, for the reasons discussed in the text of this opinion, that the court in *Frye* was nonetheless correct to exclude the sphygmomanometer evidence.

... Because one cannot say with a high degree of certainty that a polygrapher's conclusion is based firmly in objective, scientific truth, and because one therefore cannot say that polygraph evidence provides a better informed assessment of a witness' credibility than the personal observations of each juror, allowing polygraph testimony would be a direct invasion of the province of the jury.

b

Furthermore, admission of polygraph test results at trial would likely produce regular, and immensely time consuming, "battles of the experts." Admittedly, such a battle is common whenever scientific evidence is offered in court, and many types of scientific evidence are nonetheless routinely admitted at trials. In those instances, however, the probative value of the evidence is such that the delay attendant to the admission of the evidence is warranted. Because polygraph evidence is of such dubious probative value, however, the prejudicial impact of the likely delays weighs more heavily against admission....

c

Finally, there is a risk that, if polygraph evidence were admissible, juries would come to expect it with regard to *all* witnesses, a possibility that implicates both of the aforementioned concerns. Indeed, one wonders whether juries would draw adverse inferences against the witness whenever such evidence was not presented ...

Our decision to maintain our per se rule of exclusion with regard to polygraph evidence is consistent with the conclusion of the majority of courts that have considered this issue. State appellate courts, for whom *Daubert* is not mandatory authority, largely agree with our assessment that the prejudicial impact of polygraph evidence outweighs its probative value. As a result, approximately one half of the states have an absolute rule barring admission of polygraph evidence in criminal cases. Several of these courts have specifically held that the *Daubert* standard does not require admission of polygraph evidence, in light of the polygraph's questionable reliability and prejudicial impact.

The majority of the remaining states that have considered the issue admit polygraph evidence at trial only when its admission is stipulated to in advance by all parties.[68] Even the jurisdictions that allow polygraph evidence by stipulation, however, generally do not assert that the evidence is probative, or that it gains validity by means of the stipulation. Instead, the allowance is simply based on the parties' right to waive evidentiary objections. We are unpersuaded by this rationale. In our view, the limited reliability of polygraph evidence, taken together with its significant potential for prejudicial effect, compel the conclusion that such evidence should remain inadmissible even pursuant to a stipulation.

Of the states that do allow polygraph evidence without a stipulation, most allow it only in proceedings other than at trial. Only a very few states actually allow polygraph evidence that has not been stipulated to at the trial itself. These states have concluded that, at least under certain circumstances, polygraph evidence is sufficiently more probative than prejudicial to warrant admission. For the reasons discussed in ... this opinion, however, we disagree, and instead conclude in agreement with the majority of states that such a balance in favor of admissibility is not, in fact, ever reached.

In this regard, it is particularly instructive to note that several courts, after experimenting with polygraph admissibility for several years, rejected its admissibility and reinstated the traditional rule of inadmissibility. In each case, the court realized that its earlier assessment, namely, that the probative value of polygraph evidence outweighed its prejudicial impact, was mistaken....

Federal appellate courts generally grant trial judges more leeway to admit polygraph evidence than do their state counterparts, especially in the wake of *Daubert*. Indeed, the majority of federal courts of appeals do not have a per se rule that polygraph evidence is inadmissible at trial. Nonetheless, most maintain that, although admission is within the discretion of the trial court, such evidence should, as a general policy, be excluded under rule 403 of the Federal Rules of Evidence....

III

The defendant's final claim is that the right to compulsory process, as guaranteed under the sixth amendment to the United States constitution and as applied to the states through the fourteenth amendment to the United States

68. "Stipulation" in this context refers to a practice whereby both parties agree, *before* a subject takes a polygraph exam, that the results thereof will be admissible, but that the adversely affected party retains the right to cross-examine the polygraph witness and otherwise to attempt to impeach the polygraph evidence.

constitution, and also as accorded by article first, § 8, of the Connecticut constitution, guarantees him the right to present a defense, and that the exclusion of favorable polygraph results violates that right.... We disagree.

Although an accused does, of course, have a federal constitutional right to present a defense, "the right to present relevant testimony is not without limitation." *Rock v. Arkansas,* 483 U.S. 44, 55 (1987).[78] "Rules for the admission and exclusion of evidence should be found offensive to notions of fundamental fairness embodied in the United States Constitution only when, (1) without a rational basis, they disadvantage the defendant more severely than they do the State, or (2) [they] arbitrarily exclude reliable defensive evidence without achieving a superior social benefit." *Perkins v. State,* 902 S.W.2d 88, 94 (Tex.App.1995).... [T]here is a very strong basis for excluding polygraph evidence, and such exclusion is not arbitrary given the polygraph test's demonstrated lack of probative value.

... We acknowledge that several different polygraph testing techniques currently exist, and that lie detection technology continues to evolve. If, at some future date, *substantial* evidence indicates that some polygraph or other lie detection technique has reached a sufficiently high level of validity that the probative value of such evidence potentially outweighs its prejudicial impact, we may be forced to revisit this issue. Until then, however, we see no purpose in requiring the trial courts of this state to undertake evidentiary hearings every time a defendant proffers polygraph evidence.

The judgment of the Appellate Court is affirmed.

BERDON, J., concurring and dissenting.

The court today retains a per se rule that bars from evidence the results of a polygraph test under any circumstances. This per se rule infringes on the defendant's constitutional right to present a defense. The significance—and indeed the absurdity—of this rule barring polygraph evidence under any circumstances is demonstrated by hypothesizing the following factual scenario. A defendant is accused of a capital felony subject to the death penalty and the only issue is one of identification—that is, whether he was incorrectly identified by a witness as the perpetrator of the crime. The defendant submits to a properly administered polygraph examination that indicates that he is telling the truth when he says that he did not kill the victim. He also submits to a polygraph examination administered by the state that confirms the truthfulness of his statement that he was not the perpetrator. Notwithstanding the results of these two polygraph tests, the state continues with its prosecution of the defendant because of the strong identification testimony of its sole eyewitness. The thought of executing a person found guilty under these circumstances would shock anyone's conscience, whether the polygraph is 91 percent or merely 59 percent accurate.... This per se rule of the court collides with the "'fundamental value determination of our society,' given voice in Justice Harlan's concurrence in *Winship,* that 'it is far worse to convict an innocent man than to let a guilty man go free.'" *Francis v. Franklin,* 471 U.S. 307, 313 (1985), quoting *In re Winship,* 397 U.S. 358, 372 (1970) (Harlan, J., concurring)....

Indeed, if the defendant in the present case was an African-American, ... and the case involved crossracial identification, not to allow the jury to consider the properly administered polygraph test results when considering the reliability of the identification of the accused is simply unacceptable, whether the accused's life is at stake or whether he faces the loss of his liberty. Furthermore, it is well known that the frailties of eyewitness identification are not limited to cross-racial identification....

In concluding that the traditional reasons for the per se rule are unpersuasive, one commentator has stated: "The most frequently mentioned [criticism] is that the technique is 'unreliable' due to inherent failings, a shortage of qualified operators, and the prospect that 'coaching' and practicing

78. Some authorities have argued that *Rock* provides a "strong constitutional impetus" for polygraph admission. We disagree. In *Rock,* the Supreme Court struck down Arkansas' per se ban on hypnotically refreshed testimony, concluding that such testimony could be reliable under certain conditions, and thus that a per se rule barring admission was unconstitutional. *Rock* arose, however, in the context of a manslaughter case in which the defendant wished to testify on her own behalf. In reaching its conclusion, the court emphasized that Arkansas' rule had impermissibly infringed on the right "of a defendant to testify"; the "rule had a significant adverse effect on [the defendant's] ability to testify"; and that no other state had a per se rule barring the hypnotically refreshed "testimony of a *defendant.*" (Emphasis in original.) By excluding polygraph evidence, we in no way restrict any defendant's right or ability to testify.

would become commonplace if the evidence were generally admissible. Yet, by themselves, such doubts are not sufficient to warrant a rigid exclusionary rule. A great deal of lay testimony routinely admitted is at least as unreliable and inaccurate, and other forms of scientific evidence involve risks of instrumental or judgmental error." Indeed, with respect to psychiatric testimony used to predict a defendant's future potential for dangerous behavior, the United States Supreme Court has stated, despite the unanimous expert opinion that such conclusions were accurate only one out of three times; *Barefoot v. Estelle,* 463 U.S. 880, 920–22 (1983) (Blackmun, J., dissenting); that "[a]ll of these professional doubts about the usefulness of psychiatric predictions can be called to the attention of the jury. Petitioner's entire argument, as well as that of Justice Blackmun's dissent, is founded on the premise that a jury will not be able to separate the wheat from the chaff. We do not share in this low evaluation of the adversary process." *Id.*, at 899–901 n. 7.

Second, the claims that it will be time-consuming for our courts can be disposed of in short shrift. The need to conserve precious court time pales in significance when a person's liberty or life is at stake. Surely, we cannot be that callous to a person who may be innocent. Any problems with polygraph evidence can be overcome through rules developed by this court regarding its admissibility, the availability of a polygraph examination conducted by the state, cross-examination and jury instructions.

The greatest tragedy in our judicial system, with all its fallibility and misidentifications, would be to take away the life or liberty of one innocent person for the sake of preventing guilty persons from escaping punishment. See 4 W. Blackstone, Commentaries on the Laws of England (1769) c. 27, p. 352 ("it is better that ten guilty persons escape, than that one innocent suffer").

Finally, the majority curiously rejects polygraph evidence on the ground that it invades the fact-finding province of the jury. There are three answers to that argument. First, any reliable device that can aid the jury in its truth seeking mission should be available under rules and standards set forth by this court.... Second, as we approach the twenty-first century, "science, for better or for worse, has become more a part of our daily lives. Scientific evidence, in turn, has become more a part of the ordinary trial so that jurors may be more likely to use polygraph evidence with discretion." Third, we allow the prosecution to introduce expert testimony, which is far less reliable than the polygraph, to bolster the credibility of the state's case in other situations. See, e.g., *State v. Ali,* 233 Conn. 403, 660 A.2d 337 (1995) (expert allowed to testify as to typical behavior patterns of victims of sexual assault); *State v. Borrelli,* 227 Conn. at 173–74, 629 A.2d 1105 (expert allowed to testify as to typical behavior patterns of victims of battered women's syndrome); *State v. Spigarolo,* 210 Conn. 359, 556 A.2d 112, cert. denied, 493 U.S. 933 (1989) (expert allowed to testify that it is not unusual for child sexual abuse victim to give inconsistent or incomplete statements)....

V

Finally, by not allowing the defendant an opportunity to have a hearing before the trial court in order to demonstrate the reliability of the polygraph evidence, he is deprived of his right to present a defense under the sixth amendment to the federal constitution and article first, § 8, of the state constitution....

VI

In conclusion, I would remand this case to the trial court in order to furnish the defendant with an opportunity to prove the validity of his polygraph examination and to demonstrate that it was correctly administered in this case. Both the state and the defendant should have the opportunity to be heard on the issue of accuracy and the conditions for the admissibility of the polygraph evidence. Only then do I believe that a court would be in the position to rule on its admissibility....

Notes and Questions

1. A majority of the states have now adopted *Daubert* or apply closely related factors to determine the admissibility of scientific testimony, although a substantial minority remain faithful to the *Frye* "general acceptance" test.[15] The federal courts, of course, are required to observe *Daubert* and its interpretation of F.R.Ev. 702.

2. Critics of the *Frye* test cite reasons in addition to those mentioned in *State v. Porter* to adopt different standards to govern the admissibility of scientific evidence. The asserted drawbacks include: (a) reducing the judicial gatekeeping rule to a simple "nose-counting" of scientists in determining whether the general acceptance test has been met, a consequence of which is abdicating what is appropriately a legal judgment to the scientific community; (b) the imprecision and ambiguity surrounding the concept of "general acceptance"; (c) identifying the "particular field" that should be consulted in connection with the general acceptance inquiry—for example, in a case such as *Porter*, should the opinions of certified polygraphers be sought, or psychologists, or physiologists, or representatives of another field?; (d) the lack of necessary correspondence between general acceptance and scientific validity—for example, not only can a technique that historically has been widely credited become suspect when examined anew with greater rigor, but the time lag between the development of a new technique, such as DNA analysis, and its general acceptance might produce undue delay in judicial recognition of valid science, to the prejudice of parties involved in a legal dispute; and (e) whether scientific principles or techniques that cannot fairly be characterized as new or novel elude scrutiny altogether under the *Frye* test.[16]

3. As indicated in *State v. Porter*, the principal criticisms of *Daubert* involve the arguable lack of guidance courts are given in applying the identified factors to draw conclusions about the crucial question of whether evidence has crossed the threshold of scientific reliability, and whether judges have sufficient expertise to understand and resolve complicated issues of science.[17] For example, in *Daubert*, Chief Justice Rehnquist expressed the following reservation:

> The Court speaks of its confidence that federal judges can make a "preliminary assessment of whether the reasoning or methodology underlying the testimony is scientifically valid and of whether that reasoning or methodology properly can be applied to the facts in issue." The Court then states that a "key question" to be answered in deciding whether something is "scientific knowledge" "will be whether it can be (and has been) tested." Following this sentence are three quotations from treatises, which not only speak of empirical testing, but one of which states that the "'criterion of the scientific status of a theory is its falsifiability, or refutability, or testability.'"
>
> I defer to no one in my confidence in federal judges; but I am at a loss to know what is meant when it is said that the scientific status of a theory depends on its "falsifiability," and I suspect some of them will be, too. *Daubert v. Merrell Dow Pharmaceuticals*, 509 U.S. 579, 600 (1993) (concurring in part and dissenting in part) (citations omitted).

Research provides some support for Chief Justice Rehnquist's reservations about the ability of judges to serve as accurate gatekeepers of the ever-changing advances in science and technology. In a now seminal study, Gatowski and her colleagues surveyed 400 state court judges about their understanding of the *Daubert* components.[18] The authors found that only 4–5% of the judges had a clear and accurate understanding of falsifiability and error rate, although higher proportions (71–82%) understood the peer review process and the concept of general acceptance. Another potential problem area highlighted by the research was that individual judges gave differential weight to the components. For example, 17% indicated they gave equal weight to the four *Daubert* criteria, 21% were unsure about how to combine the four, and the remaining 62% were divided regarding which of the four criteria they gave the most weight to in their decision-making.

4. As discussed in *State v. Porter,* most jurisdictions observe a *per se* rule of exclusion regarding polygraph examination results in trials, although several states admit them into evidence upon the parties' prior agreement or stipulation.[19] In New Mexico, polygraph examination results generally are admissible, subject to the trial court's discretion, if a qualified polygrapher administered the exam.[20] The United States Supreme Court found no constitutional infirmity in a United States Military Rule of Evidence that makes polygraph evidence *per se* inadmissible in court-martial proceedings. *United States v. Scheffer,* 523 U.S. 303, 118 S.Ct. 1261, 140 L.Ed.2d 413 (1998).

5. Is there a persuasive response to the observation made in Justice Berdon's dissenting opinion in *State v. Porter* that if eyewitness identification testimony is admissible in criminal trials notwithstanding serious questions surrounding its reliability, then polygraph evidence should similarly be admissible? Is there merit in Justice Berdon's further argument that a *per se* rule of exclusion heightens the risk of convicting innocent people? If Porter had been allowed to present evidence that he had passed the polygraph test administered to him in connection with the charged arson, should the jury be trusted to evaluate that evidence along with other evidence presented at the trial?

C. The Admissibility of Forensic Evidence: Different Disciplines and Their Techniques

We cannot consider the entire array of forensic science disciplines, several of which are identified in the National Academy of Sciences report discussed earlier in this chapter. We instead examine select types of forensic evidence, including kinds that have played a role in known cases of wrongful conviction.

1. Fingerprints

United States v. Baines

573 F.3d 979 (10th Cir. 2009)

HOLLOWAY, Circuit Judge.

After a jury trial in federal district court, defendant-appellant Robert Abdul Baines was convicted on five counts: conspiracy to possess marijuana with intent to distribute; possession of marijuana with intent to distribute; possessing a firearm in furtherance of a drug trafficking crime; possession of a firearm after former conviction of a felony; and possession of ammunition after former conviction of a felony....

Concluding that the district court did not abuse its discretion in allowing the government to present expert evidence that a thumb print found on some of the contraband recovered by the authorities was a match to Baines' print, we affirm the judgment of the district court.

I

Because the sole issue Baines raises in this appeal is the admissibility at trial of fingerprint analysis as expert testimony, a brief overview of the facts underlying the convictions, as established in the trial testimony, will suffice to provide context for our discussion.

Baines recruited two young women to travel with him and two male friends from Pennsylvania to Arizona, offering the women $1,000 each for the trip. Both young women testified at trial that they realized that the purpose of the trip was to transport drugs, although Baines did not tell them any details....

Baines had told the two young women to plan a route for their trip back to Pennsylvania. One of them decided that they should go through

Texas rather than return the way that they had come. That decision proved fateful because this route took them through Las Cruces, New Mexico, and near there they unexpectedly entered a border checkpoint.

When the trunk of the Ford was opened at the border checkpoint, the agent immediately noticed the scent of fresh marijuana.... One of the agents had asked one of the women about the van that was behind them at the checkpoint and learned that the two vehicles were traveling together.... Accordingly, the van and its three occupants were also directed to the secondary inspection center. Officers found packages of marijuana ... and a black duffle bag ... also contained two pistols and ammunition. The two women were arrested.

When it appeared that the men were going to be released, one of the young women decided to tell the officers about defendant's role in arranging the trip and his apparent role in acquiring and loading the marijuana. Both women also told the agents that during the trip defendant had said that he was "in the business."

With the testimony of the two young women and other evidence, such as records of calls made from cell phones, the jury was persuaded to convict Mr. Baines of the drug counts. But neither of the women had seen Mr. Baines with the black duffle bag in which the guns and ammunition were found ... So the government relied on fingerprint evidence to connect Baines with the guns and ammunition.

Two fingerprints were discovered on one of the magazines found with the two pistols in the black duffle bag. Defendant filed a motion before trial to bar the government from presenting evidence that a fingerprint specialist had determined that one of the recovered "latent" prints matched the "known" fingerprint of defendant Baines. Defendant's motion invoked Rules 104(a) and 702 of the Federal Rules of Evidence and *Daubert v. Merrell Dow Pharm., Inc.*, 509 U.S. 579 (1993). Defendant requested a pretrial hearing on the admissibility of the government's expert testimony, and the district court granted the request.

II

A

Two witnesses testified at the pretrial hearing on defendant's motion to exclude the fingerprint evidence, Mr. Fullerton, the state-employed fingerprint examiner who later testified at trial, and FBI Agent Meagher, who is a fingerprint specialist with the bureau. Agent Meagher's testimony was wide-ranging, explaining basic concepts underlying fingerprint identification, the procedure followed by fingerprint examiners, and branching out from there to respond to inquiries aimed at some of the factors suggested in *Daubert* as relevant to the consideration of expert testimony.

Agent Meagher defined "fingerprint" as the "ridged skin which appears on the palmar side of the hand for each of the fingers." He used a photograph to demonstrate that the ridges are visible on the hand. He explained that the ridge pattern can then be "transferred to an object when it is touched, or intentionally recorded on a known fingerprint card."

To explore the issues involved in fingerprint identification, it is first necessary to understand the difference between what the witnesses called latent prints and known prints. A known print is the kind that is made intentionally, as when a person is arrested. Law enforcement agencies and others taking fingerprints will attempt to get full prints of each finger. Agent Meagher explained that this seemingly simple task is actually not so simple; practice and training are needed to develop the skill of recording prints to obtain a clear and complete image. In previous years prints were normally taken by applying ink to the fingers and then applying the fingers to a paper card with a rolling motion. In recent years, some agencies have adopted a digital photo scanning technique in place of the old method. Even with trained personnel recording the prints, the quality of known prints varies substantially.

Latent fingerprints are partial prints like those found at crime scenes and often are invisible to the naked eye. One study determined that a latent print is only, on average, about 22% of a known print. The gist of defendant's challenge is that the government in this case did not establish that the method for matching the latent print at issue with defendant's known print was reliable.

The field of fingerprint identification ultimately rests on two premises: that each individual's fingerprints are unique and that the unique pattern of a person's prints does not change over time. These basic principles are essentially unchallenged in this appeal. Nor does defendant contest that the latent print found on the magazine in this case was accurately reproduced for analysis. Defendant's challenge is to the reliability of the process of comparing the latent print to known prints.

Agent Meagher described the approach used in fingerprint comparison. The first step a fingerprint examiner takes is a close observation of the characteristics of the latent print under study. A latent print may have three levels of detail. The first level is the "ridge flow" or pattern of the ridges. There are three basic patterns, known as arch, loop, and whirl. An "individualization"[2] cannot be based on this level alone although a decision to exclude a candidate may be made on Level 1 detail alone.

The second level of detail is "the ridge path of the individual ridges." The examiner chooses ridges on the print, follows them, and makes observations. For example, the examiner may note points where a ridge ends or divides into two ridges. Agent Meagher testified that an examiner can "individualize" or establish an identity at this point. The third level of detail is observed by "zooming in" more closely to gather additional information about an individual ridge, including features like sweat pores and differences in size and shape of the ridge.

The process used for determining whether a latent print matches a known print has been given the acronym ACE-V, with the letters standing for the steps in a four-stage process: (1) analysis, (2) comparison, (3) evaluation, and (4) verification. In the initial analysis step, the examiner looks at the latent print and the known print separately. The purpose of this step is to discern characteristics at all three levels of detail and to evaluate the quality and quantity of information on each print. The examiner may find a disparity in characteristics that compels the conclusion that the prints cannot be a match, or may find that one or the other—usually the latent—is of too poor a quality or simply reveals too little information for further examination to be fruitful. If, however, the examiner determines that there is nothing to exclude the possibility of a match and that the quantity and quality of the information is sufficient, then he moves to the next step.

The second step in the process is comparison, a side-by-side examination of the latent print and the known print. The examiner looks for reasons to exclude the known print and for similarities between the two. As Mr. Fuller later explained in his trial testimony, the examiner at this stage is determining if there could be a match between the known print and the latent print. If it appears possible that they might match, the examiner goes to the third step, evaluation, where the examiner actually tries to reach a conclusion as to whether there is a match or not.

Verification, the fourth stage, involves having a second examiner look at the prints being compared. In this appeal, defendant stresses that the verification process is not truly independent. Not only is the second examiner usually with the same law enforcement agency, but in this case at least the second examiner did not conduct a "blind" comparison, but rather was given all the work notes and other work product of the first examiner.

Agent Meagher was asked about the error rate for friction ridge identification. His answer (as to many questions during the hearing, all without objection) was a rambling narrative covering almost six pages of transcript. He began by positing that there are two types of errors, practitioner error and methodological error. He then pronounced by his *ipse dixit* that the subject of the hearing was methodological error, not practitioner error, and that the error rate for the method was "either no error, or it's a zero error." He went on to acknowledge that practitioners do make mistakes, but then asserted that the "practitioner error rate goes to the individual, not to the whole of the practitioners applying the methodology." It would be "inappropriate," he testified, to "take the accumulation of those who have made errors and assign it to those who have not made errors," thus at least implying that most practitioners have achieved a level of perfection that is rather rare, to say the least, in other complex human endeavors. Agent Meagher did go on to cite one published report in which 92 participants performed a total of 5,861 individualizations, out of which there were two errors, both of which were noticed and corrected by verifiers.

On cross-examination Agent Meagher testified that the FBI has no statistics from which error rates of its analysts could be calculated. He said that each analyst would know his or her error rate from the proficiency examination taken at the end of training and annually thereafter. With respect to errors in actual cases, Mr.

---

2. Agent Meagher explained that in the "fingerprint discipline" the term "individualization" is used (instead of "identification") and that the term means that the examiner has identified the "donor" of the latent print to the exclusion of all other possible donors.

Meagher first explained that there were three possible types of errors to consider: false or mistaken identifications in which the analyst incorrectly identifies a person as the source of a latent print; missed identifications, where the analyst fails to make an identification when she should have; and clerical errors. Of these, the first is the proper focus for the court, "the only error of consequence," the agent testified. As to these "false positives," Meagher testified that the FBI had "made, on average, about one erroneous identification every 11 years." The total number of identifications made has been about one million per year, he continued, so that the known actual error rate was about one per eleven million identifications. He further testified that he knew of no erroneous identifications in proficiency testing of the FBI's examiners in the last ten years that he has been in a managerial position to have access to that information. There were one or two missed identifications during the ten-year period.

The second witness at the *Daubert* hearing was Mr. Fullerton of the New Mexico forensic lab, who conducted the actual process in this case. His testimony covered some of the same ground as Agent Meagher's in describing the ACE-V procedure in general, for example. Fullerton also testified that he was able to conclude that the latent print at issue matched the known left thumb print of defendant Baines.

Mr. Fullerton testified that he could not even determine the basic pattern of the latent print at level 1 because the left side of the print was not available. The latent print was an impression of such a small portion of the print that Fullerton could not say whether it was a part of a left slant loop or a whorl. Moreover, Fullerton testified, in this case the known prints were also of poor quality. However, on re-direct examination at trial he further explained that, although the prints of several fingers on Baines' card were very poor images, the left thumb print was of good quality and could be matched to the latent print.

Notwithstanding these challenges, Fullerton testified, he was able to conclude that the latent print was from Mr. Baines's left thumb, based on eleven points of comparison. Verification was accomplished by giving the data—and Fullerton's marks on the copies of the prints and other work notes—to another examiner in the same lab. Fullerton admitted that this was not an "independent identification" and that his sharing of his work product with the second examiner had suggested findings.

The defense presented no witnesses at the hearing.

B

The district court's ruling.

The district judge ... held that the evidence was shown to be relevant and reliable, meeting the requirements of Fed.R.Evid. 702. In closing, the judge addressed the core of defendant's argument, that fingerprint analysis rests substantially on the subjective interpretations of the examiner. The judge said that this argument went to the weight of the evidence, not its admissibility, and she quoted *Daubert*'s observation that "[v]igorous cross-examination, presentation of contrary evidence and careful instruction on the burden of proof are the traditional and appropriate means of attacking shaky but admissible evidence." *Daubert,* 509 U.S. at 596.

At trial, Mr. Fullerton testified to his opinion that the latent print from the magazine matched the known left thumb print of defendant Baines.

III

As noted, the only issue in this appeal is whether the trial court should have excluded the fingerprint evidence. As with other evidentiary rulings, we review the district court's decisions to admit expert testimony only for abuse of discretion. *See Kumho Tire Co. v. Carmichael,* 526 U.S. 137 (1999). The issue in this case is whether the district court properly fulfilled its duty, as established in *Daubert v. Merrell Dow Pharmaceuticals, Inc.,* 509 U.S. 579 (1993), to ensure that expert testimony "rests on a reliable foundation and is relevant to the task at hand."

General principles.

Expert testimony is admissible only if it is potentially helpful to the jury and "(1) the testimony is based upon sufficient facts or data, (2) the testimony is the product of reliable principles and methods, and (3) the witness has applied the principles and methods reliably to the facts of the case." Fed.R.Evid. 702. The burden of proof is on the proponent of the evidence, here the government.

The Court has suggested some factors, which are not necessarily exhaustive, that will be helpful to the trial courts in determining whether proposed expert testimony is based on reliable methods and principles: (1) whether the particular theory can be and has been tested; (2) whether the theory has been subjected to peer review and publication; (3) the known or potential rate of error; (4) the existence and maintenance of standards controlling the technique's operation; and (5) whether the technique has achieved general acceptance in the relevant scientific or expert community. *Daubert v. Merrell Dow Pharm.*, 509 U.S. 579 (1993). These factors do not constitute a "definitive checklist or test." The gatekeeping inquiry must be "tied to the facts of a particular case." The factors "may or may not be pertinent in assessing reliability, depending on the nature of the issue, the expert's particular expertise, and the subject of his testimony." *Kumho Tire*, 526 U.S. at 150.

Daubert was limited to scientific evidence. In *Kumho Tire Co.*, the Court held that the district courts' "gatekeeping" obligation as described in *Daubert* applies to all expert testimony and that in performing this function in particular cases, the district courts may consider the specific *Daubert* factors to the extent relevant. The Court specifically noted that "no clear line" divides "scientific" and "technical or other specialized" knowledge, all of which are treated together under Fed.R.Evid. 702.

Defendant's argument.

... First, defendant asserts that fingerprint identification lacks objective standards and so must rely largely on the subjective impressions of the individual examiner. Agent Meagher admitted that the FBI does not use any objective standard for the number of similarities between a latent print and a known print necessary to make a match, and also that the subjective views of the individual examiner play a significant role in the process.

Meagher identified only two standards, both of which involve subjective determinations, defendant contends. First, Meagher testified that the examiner must not find any discrepancy between the two prints. But Meagher explained that "no discrepancy" really means no discrepancy without a "viable or plausible or valid explanation," and whether an explanation meets that amorphous standard is a subjective judgment by the examiner.

Second, Meagher testified that there must be "agreement of sufficient friction ridge details in sequence," but again it is up to the examiner to determine what is "sufficient." Defendant cites one scholar who opines that the fingerprint community has been unable to answer the "crucial question" of "where the boundary lies between insufficient and sufficient correspondences." Simon A. Cole, *More Than Zero: Accounting For Error in Latent Fingerprint Identification*, 95 J.Crim. L. & Criminology 985, 993–94 (Spring 2005) [hereinafter Cole, *More Than Zero*]. Indeed, one appellate court that held the evidence admissible found that this factor weighed against admissibility. *See United States v. Mitchell*, 365 F.3d 215, 241 (3d Cir.2004).

Turning to the other *Daubert* factors, defendant contends that the government failed to show that the process for latent fingerprint identification has been tested. As one judge said, "there have not been any studies to establish how likely it is that partial prints taken from a crime scene will be a match for only one set of fingerprints in the world." *United States v. Crisp*, 324 F.3d 261, 273 (4th Cir.2003) (Michael, J., dissenting).

Defendant then turns to attacking the one survey and one study that the government, through Agent Meagher, proffered as evidence of reliability. In the survey, the FBI polled law enforcement agencies in all 50 states, the District of Columbia, Canada and the United Kingdom and learned that none of these agencies had ever found two different people with the same fingerprints and that none of the agencies had ever found that a latent fingerprint had been identified with two different people.[6] But, defendant says, this is not the same as saying that latent prints had never been misidentified.

The government also relied on a statistical study commissioned by the FBI and conducted by Lockheed Martin. Studying 50,000 prints and comparing each by computer against every other one, this study confirmed to an extremely high degree of probability that no two persons' fingerprints are identical. Again, defendant responds that is not at issue here.

In the second part of this study, an attempt was made to simulate latent prints by extracting about 20% of the data from each print and then comparing these partial prints to every other print in the database.[8] The study concluded, with a very high degree of certainty, that there is

---

6. The FBI conducted this survey in preparation for the exhaustive *Daubert* hearing described in *United States v. Mitchell*, 365 F.3d 215, 223–225 (3d Cir.2004).

8. The researchers had determined that the average latent print has just over 20% of the image of a known print.

almost no chance of ever finding two persons to have the same print, even when based on such partial prints. But defendant points out that a leading case found these "pseudo-latent" prints are "poor approximations of real latent prints." *Mitchell,* 365 F.3d at 237. Because the study did not adequately model real-world conditions, it does not provide significant support for the government's position, *Mitchell* held.

Nor has fingerprint identification been subject to peer review, defendant continues. The government claimed that the verification step in the ACE-V process is peer review, but defendant insists this is not accurate. The Court in *Daubert* referred to a process that serves to assess the scientific validity of the methodology, which is not accomplished merely by having two persons apply the same technique, defendant argues. Consistency of results does not prove that the results are valid.

Moreover, the verification at issue here is not truly independent. In fact, it fails to show independence in two ways. Often, as here, the reviewer is associated with the first examiner and both are employed by the same agency. Second, unlike true peer review in the scientific process, the reviewer in this system is not independent in that he receives all of the examiner's work product, rather than perform the analysis himself. Indeed, Mr. Fullerton admitted in his testimony that this was not an "independent identification" and that giving his work product to the verifier was suggestive. In a truly independent verification process, the reviewer should not even know the conclusion of the first examiner, much less all the steps taken on the path to that conclusion, defendant asserts.

Next, defendant contends that the government failed to show a meaningful rate of error for latent fingerprint identification. Mr. Meagher testified that the rate of error for latent fingerprint identifications is zero, yet he admitted that innocent people have been convicted based on misidentification of their fingerprints. Defendant cites one study that describes 22 cases of latent fingerprint misidentification. Cole, *More Than Zero,* 95 J.Crim. L. & Criminology at 985–87, 1001–16. Those include the much-publicized recent case where the FBI identified a Portland lawyer as a suspect in the terrorist bomb attack on the Madrid train station that killed 191 people, in spite of the fact that the Spanish authorities insisted, correctly, that the fingerprints did not match.[9]

Defendant criticizes Agent Meagher's attempt to distinguish between methodological error and practitioner error. Defendant argues that this is a false and meaningless distinction. One scholar, expressing the same view, said that because the method "depends so heavily on subjective human judgment ... the method literally is the people who employ it." Jonathan J. Koehler, *Fingerprint Error Rates and Proficiency Tests: What They Are And Why They Matter,* 59 Hastings L.J. 1077, 1090 (May 2008). In any event, defendant goes on, the purported distinction is irrelevant under *Daubert.*

The government produced no evidence, defendant says, about error rates in real-world cases. Mr. Meagher admitted that the FBI's only actual error rates are based on proficiency tests the examiner candidates take under controlled conditions. The FBI does not compile error rates for examinations in real cases. As Judge Michael observed in his *Crisp* dissent, "where tests have attempted to imitate actual conditions, the error rates have been alarmingly high." 324 F.3d at 275.[10]

In sum, defendant contends that the error rate is not zero, and the government failed to establish an actual error rate. Moreover, Baines argues that the effort by fingerprint examiners to create an aura of infallibility has the potential to seriously mislead jurors.

Finally, Baines argues that the government failed to show that fingerprint identification has been generally accepted in any unbiased scientific or technical community. It is not enough, according to him, that courts have accepted the technique.

The government's argument.

The *Daubert* inquiry is a flexible one, the government notes, and the factors that case set out "do not all necessarily apply" in every case. *Kumho Tire,* 526 U.S. at 150–51. Every published decision to address this issue has found the ev-

9. The incident is described in Cole, *More Than Zero,* 95 J.Crim. L. & Criminology at 985–87, where the author notes that the mistaken identification was made by a total of four examiners, each of whom had considerable experience in the field.

10. Defendant does not directly challenge Meagher's claim that the FBI analysts have cumulatively made only one mistaken identification every eleven years or one per each eleven million cases.

idence admissible. Fingerprint evidence has been admissible in this country for almost 100 years. The government urges this court to adopt the reasoning of *United States v. Mitchell,* 365 F.3d 215 (3d Cir.2004), which it says was based on substantially the same expert testimony, chiefly from Agent Meagher, that was presented in this case.

First, the *Mitchell* court found that the theories underlying fingerprint identification—that fingerprints are unique and permanent, and that identification matches can be made from fingerprints containing sufficient detail—are testable and have actually been tested by experience. On the second *Daubert* factor, the *Mitchell* court found that the ACE-V protocol constituted peer review and weighed in favor of admission.

The *Mitchell* court then considered the factor of established error rate for the procedure. Although a precise error rate has not been established, the court found that various estimates of the error rate all suggested that it was very low. The court cited evidence which the government characterizes as indistinguishable from the evidence in this record: the absence of significant numbers of false identifications in practice, the absence of "false positives" in an FBI survey of state agencies, and the Lockheed study discussed *supra.* Agent Meagher testified that the FBI's own monitoring has revealed approximately one false identification every eleven years. About one million comparisons per year were made, he said, so that the error rate was approximately one for every 11 million comparisons.

On the fourth *Daubert* factor, the government points to testimony from Agent Meagher that the ACE-V procedure is a widely accepted standard governing operation of the methodology. Meagher also testified that additional standards for conclusions are set by the Scientific Working Group on Friction Ridge Analysis, Study and Technology (SWGFRAST), a professional group. Meagher testified that the standards for positive identifications of the latter group included agreement of sufficient friction ridge details in sequence, as determined by a competent examiner, and applied to "common area and both impressions" (a phrase that was not explained), and absent any discrepancies.

Finally, the *Mitchell* court found that general acceptance in the fingerprint community weighed in favor of admissibility. The court rejected the argument Baines makes here—that the community is not an impartial, scientific community....

Analysis.

Our task is not to determine the admissibility or inadmissibility of fingerprint analysis for all cases but merely to decide whether, on this record, the district judge in this case made a permissible choice in exercising her discretion to admit the expert testimony. Although this record raises multiple questions regarding whether fingerprint analysis can be considered truly scientific in an intellectual, abstract sense, nothing in the controlling legal authority we are bound to apply demands such an extremely high degree of intellectual purity. Instead, courts applying Fed.R.Evid. 702, *Daubert,* and *Kumho Tire,* are charged only with determining that the expert witness "employs in the courtroom the same level of intellectual rigor that characterizes the practice of an expert in the relevant field." *Kumho Tire,* 526 U.S. at 152....

The first *Daubert* question is whether the technique can be and has been tested. We have seriously considered defendant's argument that the testing of fingerprint analysis that has been reported mostly falls short of the rigors demanded by the ideals of science. On the other hand, the core proposition—that reliable identifications may be made from comparison of latent prints with known prints—is testable. And unquestionably the technique has been subject to testing, albeit less rigorous than a scientific ideal, in the world of criminal investigation, court proceedings, and other practical applications, such as identification of victims of disasters.

Thus, while we must agree with defendant that this record does not show that the technique has been subject to testing that would meet all of the standards of science, it would be unrealistic in the extreme for us to ignore the countervailing evidence. Fingerprint identification has been used extensively by law enforcement agencies all over the world for almost a century. Fingerprint analysts such as Mr. Fullerton, who have been certified by the FBI, have undergone demanding training culminating in proficiency examinations, followed by further proficiency examinations at regular intervals during their careers. Although these proficiency examinations have been criticized on several grounds, most notably that they do not accurately represent conditions encountered in the field, we see no basis in this record for totally disregarding these proficiency tests.

In conclusion, on this record we believe that the first *Daubert* factor weighs somewhat in favor of admissibility, although not powerfully.

The second *Daubert* factor is whether the theory or process has been subject to peer review and publication. We find little in the record to guide us in consideration of this factor. Defendant argues persuasively that the verification stage of the ACE-V process is not the independent peer review of true science. Agent Meagher's testimony included some references to professional publications, but these were too vague and sketchy to enable us to assess the nature of the professional dialogue offered. In short, the government did not show in this case that this factor favors admissibility.

The third *Daubert* factor is the known or potential error rate of the procedure. As recited *supra,* testing has been done in training programs and other environments that are not shown to be accurate facsimiles of the tasks undertaken by fingerprint analysts in actual cases. Nevertheless, the accumulated data is impressive. Very few mistakes are reported in testing that trainees must complete before progressing to actual casework. Mr. Fullerton, who made the actual identification in this case, testified that he has always attained a perfect score in his proficiency tests.

More significantly, Agent Meagher testified to an error rate of one per every 11 million cases, and the defense did not—either in the evidentiary hearing or in the briefs on appeal—challenge that testimony. There may have been erroneous identifications that never came to light. Defense attorneys rarely have the resources to hire independent experts for trial, and in the interests of finality our system has created obstacles to post-conviction review. But even allowing for the likelihood that the actual error rate for FBI examiners may be higher than reflected in Mr. Meagher's testimony, the known error rate remains impressively low. We are not aware of any attempt to quantify the maximum error rate that could meet *Daubert* standards, but surely a rate considerably higher than one per 11 million could still pass the test. We conclude that the evidence of the error rate on this record strongly supported the judge's decision to admit the expert testimony.

The fourth *Daubert* factor is the existence and maintenance of standards controlling the technique's operation. On this point, we are persuaded by the analysis of the Third Circuit in *United States v. Mitchell,* 365 F.3d at 241. The ACE-V system is a procedural standard but not a substantive one. Critical steps in the process depend on the subjective judgment of the analyst. We hasten to add that subjectivity does not, in itself, preclude a finding of reliability. But in searching this record for evidence of standards that guide and limit the analyst in exercise of these subjective judgments, we find very little. Because in the end determination of this factor is not critical to our decision, we will assume *arguendo* that this factor does not support admissibility.

The fifth *Daubert* factor is whether the technique has attained general acceptance in the relevant scientific or expert community. Conceding the general acceptance of fingerprint analysis by law enforcement officials nationwide and internationally, defendant contends that fingerprint analysis has not been accepted in "any unbiased scientific or technical community" and cites to the *Daubert* formulation of the standard, which was limited to the "relevant scientific community." 509 U.S. at 594. This distinction is significant in this case because the field of fingerprint analysis is dominated by agents of law enforcement, with apparently little presence of disinterested experts such as academics.

But in *Kumho Tire,* the Court—dealing with proffered expert testimony that was characterized as technical rather than scientific—referred with apparent approval to a lower court's inquiry into general acceptance in the "relevant expert community," and then the Court discussed its own search in the record for evidence of acceptance of the controverted test by "other experts in the industry." Consequently, while we acknowledge that acceptance by a community of unbiased experts would carry greater weight, we believe that acceptance by other experts in the field should also be considered. And when we consider that factor with respect to fingerprint analysis, what we observe is overwhelming acceptance....

In reaching a conclusion after this process of focusing on each of the *Daubert* factors in turn, we must return to two overriding principles. The first is that our review here is deferential, limited to the question of whether the district judge abused her considerable discretion. The second is that the Rule 702 analysis is a flexible one, as both *Daubert* and *Kumho Tire* teach. The *Daubert* factors are "meant to be helpful, not definitive," and not all of the factors will be pertinent in every case. *Kumho Tire,* 526 U.S. at 150–51. On the whole, it seems to us that the record supports the district judge's finding that fingerprint analysis is sufficiently reliable to be admissible. Thus, we find no abuse of discretion....

In closing, we echo the thoughts of Judge Pollak, who said regarding the desirability of research to provide the scrutiny and independent verification of the scientific method to aid in assessing the reliability of fingerprint evidence, that such efforts would be "all to the good. But to postpone present in-court utilization of this 'bedrock forensic identifier' pending such research would be to make the best the enemy of the good." *United States v. Llera Plaza,* 188 F.Supp.2d 549, 572 (E.D.Pa.2002).

Conclusion

Having found no abuse of discretion in admission of the disputed evidence, the only issue raised in this appeal, we AFFIRM the judgment of the district court.

Notes and Questions

1. In addition to the authorities cited in *United States v. Baines,* other courts, applying *Daubert, Frye,* or closely related tests, have recently permitted fingerprint identification testimony over objections that the analytical techniques and standards lack rigor and that insufficient systematic research has evaluated error and validity rates. *See, e.g., Commonwealth v. Gambora,* 933 N.E.2d 50 (Mass. 2010) (declining to reconsider prior ruling on admissibility in *Commonwealth v. Patterson,* 840 N.E.2d 12 (Mass. 2005), although noting concerns raised in 2009 NAS report); *Markham v. State,* 984 A.2d 262, 272–277 (Md. App. 2009); *United States v. Pena,* 586 F.3d 105, 109–111 (1st Cir. 2009), *cert. den.,* 130 S.Ct. 1919 (2010); *United States v. Rose,* 672 F.Supp.2d 723 (D. Md. 2009).

2. Several commentators also have analyzed fingerprint identification testimony in light of the legal standards governing admissibility of scientific evidence.[21]

3. Although the court did not accept Agent Meagher's error rate of one in 11 million as truth, it did conclude that a "rate considerably higher than one per 11 million could still pass the test." In a creatively designed experiment, five experienced fingerprint examiners were asked to evaluate a set of fingerprints they had evaluated several years earlier (the examiners were unaware that they had already examined the fingerprints and also were unaware of their original conclusion).[22] The examiners were led to believe that the prints would not match. Only one of the five examiners was unaffected by the manipulation (*i.e.,* the non-match information) in that this person did not alter his or her previous conclusion. Three of the five changed from reporting a match to reporting a non-match and one changed to "cannot decide." These findings highlight the subjective nature of fingerprint analysis, and therefore the large potential for error.

4. In a study of the first 232 cases of wrongful convictions that resulted in DNA-based exonerations, Professor Brandon Garrett and Innocence Project Co-Director Peter Neufeld identified 159 cases—involving 156 trial convictions and three individuals who pled guilty—in which forensic evidence was presented. They located trial transcripts in 137 of the cases and collected details regarding the forensic evidence testimony. Their study found that two of the wrongful conviction cases "involved troubling testimony or analysis" pertaining to fingerprint identification. Brandon L. Garrett & Peter J. Neufeld, "Invalid Forensic Science Testimony and Wrongful Convictions," 95 *Virginia Law Review* 1, 72–73 (2009). Neither wrongful conviction was based on a simple misidentification, but rather appeared to involve deliberate misconduct by a fingerprint examiner. In one of those cases, Stephan Cowans was convicted for shooting a police officer in Massachusetts, based in part on erroneous testimony that a latent thumb print found on a glass mug linked to the officer's assailant matched his known print. "After Cowans was exonerated by post-conviction DNA testing, the District Attorney asked the Massachusetts State Police to re-

examine the thumb print. The State Police declared that Cowans was clearly excluded." *Id.*, at 73. A subsequent investigation supported the conclusion that the expert who had testified at trial about the thumb print "match" realized prior to testifying "that Cowans was excluded, but ... nevertheless concealed that fact in his trial testimony." *Id.*, at 73–74. The other case involved Gene Bibbins' conviction in Louisiana for rape. At Bibbins' trial, a fingerprint examiner for the Baton Rouge police "testified that the comparison between [Bibbins'] fingerprints and latent prints found on the window fan in the victim's room was non-probative, when in fact the Louisiana State Crime Lab had excluded Bibbins and documented its contrary finding in a report not disclosed to the defense." *Id.*, at 73; *see id.*, at 78.

2. Comparative Bullet Lead Analysis

Clemons v. State

896 A.2d 1059 (Md. 2006)

BATTAGLIA, J.

This case presents us with the task of determining whether certain conclusory aspects of comparative bullet lead analysis ("CBLA") are admissible under the standard enunciated in *Frye v. United States*, 293 F. 1013 (D.C.Cir. 1923), and adopted by this Court in *Reed v. State*, 283 Md. 374, 391 A.2d 364 (1978), which makes evidence emanating from a novel scientific process inadmissible absent a finding that the process is generally accepted by the relevant scientific community....

Background

On January 8, 2002, Kenya Bryant and his thirteen-year-old son Brandon were packing their vehicle outside Mr. Bryant's home in Suitland, Maryland in preparation for Brandon's return home to North Carolina after visiting his father during his winter break from school. Brandon went inside the house to retrieve more things, heard ten gunshots, and remained inside the home until the police arrived and informed him that his father had been killed.

Approximately eighteen hours after Mr. Bryant was shot, Lachrisha Williams notified Prince George's County Police that she had witnessed the shooting. During her interview with police, Ms. Williams provided a description of the driver, although she did not know his name at the time.

Two days after the shooting, on January 10, 2002, District of Columbia Metropolitan Police Department officers seized a Lorcin nine-millimeter handgun and bullets from an automobile in conjunction with an investigation of a traffic accident in the District of Columbia. Gemar Clemons, the petitioner, was a passenger in that vehicle and, among other offenses, was charged under the District of Columbia Code with the alleged possession of an unregistered handgun (the Lorcin) as well as possession of ammunition. Clemons was subsequently acquitted by a jury of all charges associated with the traffic stop, including the charges involving the possession of the handgun and ammunition.

Thereafter, police were able to determine that the Lorcin handgun seized in the District of Columbia was consistent with that used to shoot Mr. Bryant, but could not conclusively identify it as the weapon. After Clemons was arrested in the District, Ms. Williams also was asked to view a photographic array, and she selected Clemons's picture as that of the man who shot Mr. Bryant. Clemons was arrested on July 2, 2002, and on August 6, 2002 was charged with ... the Bryant murder....

... Clemons ... filed [a] motion *in limine* in which he asked the court to exclude the testimony of the State's expert witness, Charles A. Peters, a forensic chemist from the Federal Bureau of Investigation ("FBI"), who was represented to be an expert on CBLA, a three-step process that involves the comparison of the elemental composition of bullets in an effort to determine whether different bullets originated from the same vat of lead. In his motion, Clemons specifically challenged the admissibility of CBLA. At the pretrial hearing, Clemons agreed to the court's decision to defer addressing the motion to exclude Peters's testimony until trial.[6]

At trial, the State called Peters to testify as an expert witness. Immediately prior to Peters's testimony, both parties recognized that the scientific process providing the foundation for Peters's testimony was subject to examination.... The judge permitted the challenge to the admissibility of Peters's testimony and required that it occur in the presence of the jury. During Peters's voir dire examination, he described the methods that he employs in CBLA ...

Overruling defense counsel's objection to the witness's qualifications and the general acceptance of the scientific process that was the subject of his testimony, the court noted:

> Comparative bullet lead analysis. All right. I'll tell you what I'm going to do. I'll admit him as an expert. I heard a lot of voir dire on these interesting questions, challenges. So I'm going to admit him as an expert in this field because he's been in this field for a long time. He's done tens of thousands of these analyses. He's been around since the '70s. This test called ICP, Inductively Coupled Plasma, OES[[8]] version is what this witness intends to testify about. And the fact that there are some challenges, it doesn't mean that it's such a novel and scientific kind of test that the court finds as a matter of law that it shouldn't be submitted to the jury. And I'm going to accept the witness's qualifications in this field and of course limit his testimony to this particular test in this particular field.

Immediately following this statement, Peters testified as follows with respect to the comparison of Exhibit 50, unfired cartridges containing bullets recovered on January 10, 2002, in the District of Columbia and Exhibits 26 and 27, bullet fragments numbered K101 and K102, respectively, recovered from Mr. Bryant's body:

[THE STATE]: And as a result of that examination, were you able to reach any conclusion?

[PETERS]: Yes, I was.

Q. Can you go through each one of your conclusions?

A. In this particular case there were exhibit —

Q. State's exhibit number 50. Showing you what's been admitted into evidence, which will be the ammunition recovered from the District of Columbia.

A. There were five of these cartridges. A cartridge is an unfired round. It has a bullet, the gunpowder, the primer, and it hasn't been fired. We took ammunition from them and compared them to bullets that were physically the same. One of the bullets that was physically the same was exhibit number 26.

Q. Is that K101 as well?

A. Yes.

Q. Okay.

A. We compared this to these five cartridges and one of the five cartridges from here was analytically the same. And basically the way I can explain it to you, if I gave you these two samples and said put them in your hand behind your back and give them back. I can tell you which one was which and analyze them. Elementally I couldn't tell them apart. That elements such as antimony, arsenic, silver, and copper was analytically the same in both of those samples. And that tells me that this likely came from the same pot of lead at the manufacturer, but in this case is Winchester....

THE COURT: Is it likely or is it the same? I thought that likely was you compared it

6. Judges have discretion to defer a pre-trial ruling on a motion *in limine* and ordinarily do so where the issue can be better developed or achieve a better context based on what occurs at trial. Where evidence is subject to challenge under *Frye-Reed*, however, the issue should, whenever possible, be dealt with prior to trial. The evidence bearing on whether the challenged evidence is actually the product of a novel scientific technique and, if so, whether that technique is generally accepted in the relevant scientific community will usually be collateral to the substantive issues at trial and may, itself, be inadmissible with respect to those substantive issues. That alone justifies resolving the issue prior to trial. Dealing with the issue pre-trial also avoids delays and diversions at trial that may inconvenience both witnesses and the jury....

8. Inductively Coupled Plasma-Optical Emission Spectoscopy was the technique used for CBLA up to the time of its discontinuation by the FBI Laboratory. National Research Council, FORENSIC ANALYSIS: WEIGHING BULLET LEAD EVIDENCE 15–16 (2004).

to bullets that are physically the same. Physically likely the same or physically the same? What is your testimony?

[PETERS]: Where the bullet and the cartridges are analytically indistinguishable so they're the same in the composition. What does that mean? It means they're likely or consistent as my report says. Well, it came from the same smelt of lead....

[THE STATE]: Now with State's exhibit—State's exhibit number 27, K102, did you have occasion to analyze that?

A. Yes.

Q. And what were your results with that?

A. Here again this is another bullet and I analyzed it and compared it to these five cartridges. And one of these cartridges was analytically indistinguishable to each other. Different composition that the first group I talked about. So they would each come basically from a different smelt of lead made at Winchester.

Q. So they're consistent with having been originated or made from the same manufactured source?

A. Yes....

To counter Peters's testimony, Clemons presented the testimony of William Tobin, a consulting forensic metallurgist who had been a special agent at the FBI for twenty-seven years and who had been assigned to the FBI Laboratory in Quantico, Virginia as a forensic metallurgist prior to his retirement in 1998. Tobin testified that when he retired he initiated a study of CBLA because he noticed a "contradiction between metallurgic [principles] and the [principles] required to accept the practice of comparing bullet leads." After collaborating with other chemists in the lead industry, Tobin had concluded that the practice was "seriously flawed"....

... And it's our general conclusion that the practice of comparing bullet lead has limited, if any, forensic value....

At the close of the trial, the jury convicted Clemons of second degree murder and use of a handgun in the commission of a felony.... [T]he court imposed an aggregate sentence of forty-two years imprisonment....

... We hold that CBLA is not admissible under the *Frye-Reed* standard because it is not generally accepted within the scientific community as valid and reliable....

To better understand the scientific procedures at issue in the case *sub judice* and the application of the *Frye-Reed* standard, a brief discussion of the bullet manufacturing process and the development of CBLA is required. The lead used to manufacture bullets is derived from secondary lead smelters which salvage lead from recycled automobile batteries. Charles A. Peters, *The Basis for Compositional Bullet Lead Comparisons,* 4 Forensic Sci. Communications (2002). After separating the batteries into their main components, plastic, acid, and lead, the smelters mix the lead derived from batteries with lead from other sources and melt the mixture in kettles with capacities up to one hundred tons. The scrap lead is then processed into ingots[10] (also called "pigs" in relevant publications). *Id.*

The lead is provided to bullet manufacturers in one of several forms: ingots, which vary from sixty-five to eighty pounds; billets, which range from one hundred to three hundred pounds; and sows, which are approximately two thousand pounds. If the lead is provided in one of the latter two forms, it is remelted in seven- to ten-ton pots and combined with lead remnants from the bullet manufacturing process, which may include rejected bullets, excess lead from the bullet molding process, or other scrap lead in the facility. "The molten lead is then poured into a billet mold and allowed to cool and solidify." The quantities of lead are made into wire by squeezing them through a narrow opening, which is then cut into slugs. Slugs are shaped into bullets through a process called "swaging," which involves a die that applies compressive force by hammering radially on the slug, then tumbled for smoothness and loaded along with gunpowder into cartridge cases. *Id.* The cartridges are loaded into boxes and stamped with a packing code. The number of bullets manufactured from a single melt varies widely. "For example, a melt pot of 200,000 lbs will yield 35,000,000 .22-caliber bullets, which a pig or ingot will yield 10,000 to 20,000 bullets. The yield for larger caliber bullets will be smaller." Michael O. Finkelstein & Bruce Levin, *Compositional Analysis of Bullet Lead as Forensic Evidence,* 13 J.L. & Pol'y 119, 121 (2005).

With this manufacturing process in mind, we turn to the origin and processes of CBLA. During

10. Ingot is defined as "a mass of metal cast into a convenient shape for storage or transportation to be later remitted for casting or finished." Webster's Third New Int'l Dictionary, 1162 (2002).

the 1960's, researchers at Gulf General Atomic explored the possibility of analyzing the elements found in bullet lead as a forensic tool in criminal investigations through neutron activation analysis ("NAA") under a contract with the United States Atomic Energy Commission. William A. Tobin, *Comparative Bullet Lead Analysis: A Case Study in Flawed Forensics,* 28 Champion 12, 15 (July, 2004); Edward J. Imwinkelried & William A. Tobin, *Comparative Bullet Lead Analysis (CBLA) Evidence: Valid Inference or Ipse Dixit?,* 28 Okla. City U.L. Rev. 43, 48 (2003). Gulf General Atomic used a nuclear reactor to irradiate the lead alloy and then analyzed the radiation emitted from the lead to identify the chemicals present and measure their concentration. The Gulf General Atomic researchers stated:

> It has been found that the number of (chemical) elements observable (in lead analysis by NAA), and thus the number of points of comparison, is generally limited to three elements, due to the dominance of antimony radioisotopes in the activated bullet lead specimens. This factor, coupled with a high degree of composition uniformity of bullet lead from at least one major manufacturer, imposes some limitations on the method.... (T)wo bullets with the same patter of only three identification points are not usually definitively identified as having a common source. (M)atching concentrations of all three elements does not indicate that two bullets came from the same lot.

In the late 1980s and early 1990s, analysts shifted from NAA to a different methodology, inductively coupled plasma-optical emission spectroscopy ("ICP-OES"). The National Research Council described the process for ICP-OES as:

> For analysis, samples generally are dissolved to form an aqueous solution of known weight and dilution. The solution is aspired into the nebulizer, which transforms it into an aerosol. The aerosol then proceeds into the plasma, it is transformed into atoms and ions in the discharge, and the atoms (elements) are excited and emit light at characteristic wavelengths. The intensity of the light at the wavelengths associated with each element is proportional to that element's concentration.
>
> The ICP-OES torch consists of three concentric tubes—known as the outer, middle, and inner tubes—usually made of fused silica. The torch is positioned in a coil of a radio-frequency generator. The support gas that flows through the middle annulus, argon, is seeded with free electrons collide with the argon gas and form Ar+ ions. Continued interaction of the electrons and ions with the radiofrequency field increases the energy of the particles and forms and sustains a plasma, a gas in which some fraction of the atoms are present in an ionized state. At the same time, the sample is swept through the inner loop by the carrier gas, also argon, and is introduced into the plasma, allowing the sample to become ionized and subsequently emit light.
>
> * * *
>
> Each element emits several specific wavelengths of light in the ultraviolet-visible spectrum that can be used for analysis. The selection of the optical wavelength for a sample depends on a number of factors, such as the other elements present in the sample matrix. The light emitted by the atoms of an element must be converted to an electric signal that can be measured quantitatively. That is achieved by resolving the light with a diffraction grating then using a solid-state diode array or other photoelectric detector to measure wavelength-specific intensity for each element emission line. The concentration of the elements in the sample is determined by comparing the intensity of the emission signals from the sample with that from a solution of a known concentration of the element (standard).

National Research Council, FORENSIC ANALYSIS: WEIGHING BULLET LEAD EVIDENCE 14 (2004) ("NRC Report"). The main purported advantage of ICP-OES over NAA was that ICP-OES permitted the laboratory to analyze six or seven elements present in the lead alloy: antimony, arsenic, bismuth, cadmium, copper, silver, and tin.

After obtaining the elemental composition numbers, the samples are categorized "according to similarity of compositional presence." *Tobin, supra,* at 13. "Compositions similar to a crime scene bullet(s) are put in one group and considered 'analytically indistinguishable'; compositions considered dissimilar are placed in different groups and considered 'analytically distinguishable.'" From that data, the expert witness will draw a conclusion as to the probative significance of "finding 'analytically indistinguishable' (similar) compositions in both crime scene and 'known' bullet samples." The entire process is premised upon three assumptions: the fragment being analyzed is representative of "the composition of the source from which it originated"; the source from which the sample is derived is compositionally homogeneous; and "no two molten sources are ever produced with the same composition." *Id.* at 13–14.

Recently the assumptions regarding that uniformity or homogeneity of the molten source and the uniqueness of each molten source that provide the foundation for CBLA have come under attack by the relevant scientific community of analytical chemists and metallurgists.

In 1991, at the International Symposium on the Forensic Aspects of Trace Evidence, hosted by the FBI, various experts in the field "cautioned that 'the variability (of the elemental mix) within a production run ... has not been addressed in a comprehensive study.'" In 2002, another study was published which detailed the metallurgical phenomena that occur in the lead refining and casting processes and result in inhomogeneity within a single smelt as well as analytically indistinguishable lots produced with relative frequency by lead smelters. E. Randich, Wayne Duerfeldt, Wade McLendon & William Tobin, *A Metallurgical Review of the Interpretation of Bullet Lead Compositional Analysis,* 127 Forensic Sci. Int'l 174, 182 (2002) ("The Randich Study"). That study derived its conclusions from an analysis of secondary lead refiners' production data, which is currently the only source of molten source composition data in existence. This analysis revealed that the elemental composition of samples taken from the beginning, middle, and end of 100-ton molten source pours at a single refiner "could vary in antimony by almost 12 percent, copper by 142 percent, tin by 1,871 percent, or arsenic by 31 percent, from the beginning to the end of the pour." *See* William A. Tobin & Wayne Duerfeldt, *How Probative is Comparative Bullet Lead Analysis?,* 17 Crim. Just. 26, 28 (Fall, 2002). Moreover, the Randich Study noted that

> [v]ariability in composition within each individual pig [ingot] is also caused by a phenomenon known as segregation that occurs during the solidification of the pig. As the cast pig cools, it solidifies first at the (cooler) exterior surface. The center of the pig is the last region to solidify. Impurity elements that are more soluble in the liquid phase and hence become more concentrated at the center of the pig. Because of the nature of the various binary elemental phase diagrams ... and depending on the amounts of each element present in the alloy, this phenomenon is expected to be more pronounced for elements like antimony, to have only a minor effect for elements like [bismuth], and to have little effect on elements that are present at less that 10 [parts per million] level such as tin and arsenic.... The effects for the other elements of interest would strongly depend on the amounts present and on cooling rates. Segregation thus increases the lack of homogeneity in each individual pig. This is a basic metallurgical phenomenon and tendency known to exist in all casting processes. Note, also, that differences in cooling rate alone can result in significantly different compositions from the surface of the pig to the center, and between samples taken from two different pigs of identical, overall (average) composition.

Randich, et al., supra, at 179. Thus, as these studies indicate, the assumption that an ingot or vat of lead is homogenous as required for CBLA to be valid is not generally accepted by the scientific community.

The assumption that each molten lead source is unique is also being questioned by analytical chemists and metallurgists. A recent article in the Oklahoma City Law Review noted that the use of lead reclaimed from automobile batteries undermines the confidence in the assumption of uniqueness. The authors observed that "secondary refiners obtain their bullet lead from scrap automobile batteries. Battery manufacturers observe 'relatively tight specifications because of electrical conductivity, corrosion, (and) processing.'" Moreover, Professor Imwinkelried and Mr. Tobin concluded that because most lead produced by secondary refiners is used in the manufacture of new automobile batteries and the manufacturers follow "stringent compositional specifications" with respect to the lead intended for both battery and bullet manufacturing, "the probability increases that in a given year manufacturers will produce coincidental repeats whose compositions are analytically indistinguishable." Essentially, the higher quality of lead produced by manufacturers of automobile batteries increases the probability that coincidental identical compositions will occur.

This suspected probability was borne out in the research published in the Randich Study. Randich and his colleagues determined that "multiple indistinguishable shipments of lead alloys from secondary lead refiners to the ammunition manufacturers are made each year and over a period of many years." Similarly, FBI researchers discovered two sets of bullets manufactured seven months and fifteen months apart respectively that were analytically indistinguishable.

Furthermore, at least one study conducted by Dr. Robert D. Koons, a research chemist with the FBI Laboratory in Quantico, Virginia, and Dr. Diana M. Grant, a forensic examiner with the FBI Laboratory in Washington, D.C., observed an error rate, which includes false positives and negatives, of twenty-five to thirty-three percent. *See* Robert D. Koons & Diana M. Grant, *Compositional Variation in Bullet Lead Manufacture,* 47 J. Forensic Sci. 950 (2002). There has been no study of the error rate for the process when used in the field. Moreover, there is no incentive to finance such a study because currently the FBI, which was the only laboratory engaging in CBLA analysis in the United States, has ceased conducting CBLA for forensic purposes.

The only consensus that can be derived from all of this is that more studies must be conducted regarding the validity and reliability of CBLA. Although scientific unanimity is not required to satisfy the *Frye-Reed* test's requirement of general acceptance, it is clear that a genuine controversy exists within the relevant scientific community about the reliability and validity of CBLA. Based on the criticism of the processes and assumptions underlying CBLA, we determine that the trial court erred in admitting expert testimony based on CBLA because of the lack of general acceptance of the process in the scientific community.

The State argues that any error, under the circumstances of the case at bar, would be harmless error in light of the testimony of an eyewitness to the murder. In *Reed,* however, we observed that "[l]ay jurors tend to give considerable weight to 'scientific' evidence when presented by 'experts' with impressive credentials." The same holds true in the case at bar. Although the case *sub judice* was not entirely dependent upon the expert testimony at issue, we are unable "to declare a belief, beyond a reasonable doubt, that the error in no way influenced the verdict."

Conclusion

We conclude that CBLA does not satisfy the requirement under the *Frye-Reed* test for the admissibility of scientific expert testimony because several fundamental assumptions underlying the process are not generally accepted by the scientific community. Therefore, we reverse the judgment of the Court of Special Appeals and remand the case to the Circuit Court for Prince George's County for a new trial....

Notes and Questions

1. As noted in *Clemons,* in 2004 the National Research Council (NRC) of the National Academies of Science issued a report, *Forensic Analysis Weighing Bullet Lead Evidence,* which was stimulated by a request from the FBI regarding the appropriate use of comparative bullet lead analysis. The report, completed by a Committee on Scientific Assessment of Bullet Lead Elemental Composition Comparison, specifically noted that, "Variations among and within lead bullet manufacturers make any modeling of the general manufacturing process unreliable and potentially misleading in [compositional analysis of bullet lead] comparisons."[23] The report included the following findings and recommendations:

Finding: Although it has been demonstrated that there are a large number of different compositionally indistinguishable volumes of lead (CIVL), there is evidence that bullets from different CIVLs can sometimes coincidentally be analytically indistinguishable.

Recommendation: The possible existence of coincidentally indistinguishable CIVLs should be acknowledged in the laboratory report and by the expert witness on direct examination.

Finding: Compositional analysis of bullet lead data alone does not permit any definitive statement concerning the date of bullet manufacture.

Finding: Detailed patterns of distribution of ammunition are unknown, and as a result, an expert should not testify as to the probability that a crime scene bullet came from the defendant. Geographic distribution data on bullets and ammunition are needed before such testimony can be given.

Finding: The available data do not support any statement that a crime bullet came from, or is likely to have come from, a particular box of ammunition, and references to "boxes" of ammunition in any form are seriously misleading.... Testimony that the crime bullet came from the defendant's box or from a box manufactured at the same time, is also objectionable because it may be understood as implying a substantial probability that the bullet came from the defendant's box.[24]

In November 2007, the *Washington Post* and the CBS news program, *60 Minutes*, publicized the results of their joint investigation regarding what ensued in the aftermath of the NRC report. They reported that, in response to the report's findings, the FBI had stopped using comparative bullet lead analysis (CBLA) in 2005. The FBI laboratory director then issued a memorandum stating that prosecutors should be discouraged from presenting CBLA in future criminal prosecutions, explaining that, "We cannot afford to be misleading to a jury." "Despite those private concerns, the [FBI] told defense lawyers in a general letter dated Sept. 1, 2005, that although it was ending the technique, it 'still firmly supports the scientific foundation of bullet lead analysis.' And in at least two cases, the bureau has tried to help state prosecutors defend past convictions by using court filings that experts say are still misleading. The government has fought releasing the list of the estimated 2,500 cases over three decades in which it performed the analysis."[25]

2. In early 2010, it was reported that:

Three people convicted of murder have been released from prison because their cases were tainted by a now discredited theory that bullets found at a crime scene could be linked to bullets found in possession of suspects.

Nearly five years after the FBI abandoned its so-called comparative bullet lead analysis, the FBI has yet to complete its review of nearly 2,500 cases where law enforcement used such evidence to investigate a case.

So far, the agency has found 187 cases where so-called comparative bullet lead analysis evidence was not only used in the investigation, but came into play at trial where FBI experts provided testimony. It has notified prosecutors in those cases where testimony from its experts "exceeds the limits of science and cannot be supported by the FBI," one agency letter says.[26]

3. In the wake of the NRC report and its expressed doubts about the reliability of CBLA, some courts have upset criminal convictions based on expert testimony using that technique

to link bullets found at a crime scene to ammunition found in a defendant's possession. *See Smith v. State,* 23 So.3d 1277 (Fla. App. 2010); *State v. Behn,* 868 A.2d 329 (N.J. Super. 2005); *Ragland v. Commonwealth,* 191 S.W.3d 569 (Ky. 2006) (raising doubts about reliability of CBLA but reversing murder conviction based on expert's false testimony). Other courts have been unwilling to treat the revealed deficiencies in CBLA as newly discovered evidence for purposes of post-conviction review, or for other reasons have declined to overturn convictions that were based in part on CBLA testimony. *See Scott v. State,* 788 N.W.2d 497 (Minn. 2010); *Gassler v. State,* 787 N.W.2d 575 (Minn. 2010); *Higgs v. United States,* 711 F.Supp.2d 479 (D. Md. 2010); *Commonwealth v. Lykus,* 885 N.E.2d 769 (Mass. 2008); *Commonwealth v. Fisher,* 870 A.2d 864 (Pa. 2005); *Commonwealth v. Kretchmar,* 971 A.2d 1249 (Pa. Super. 2009).

3. Bite Marks

Brooks v. State

748 So.2d 736 (Miss. 1999)

PITTMAN, Presiding Justice, for the Court:

[Levon Brooks was charged with the capital murder of three-year-old Courtney Smith, who was abducted from the bed she shared with her two sisters on September 15, 1990. The victim's five-year-old sister identified Brooks, an ex-boyfriend of the children's mother, as the man who had abducted Courtney. The child's body was found two days later. An autopsy concluded that the cause of death was drowning. It further revealed vaginal injuries as well as apparent bite marks on the victim's wrist. Dr. Michael West, a forensic odontologist, "gave extensive testimony regarding the tests he had conducted in reaching the conclusion that the bite marks had been made by Brooks." Based primarily on this evidence, Brooks was convicted of capital murder and was sentenced to life in prison. Among other issues raised on appeal, Brooks argued that Dr. West's testimony had erroneously been received into evidence.]

... At trial, the State offered Dr. West as an expert in the subject of forensic odontology. Brooks, after briefly questioning Dr. West, made no objection to Dr. West being designated an expert. Because there was no contemporaneous objection made at trial, this issue is procedurally barred. However, because of the controversial nature of bite-mark evidence, this Court will address the issue on the merits.

This Court has never affirmatively stated that bite-mark evidence is admissible in Mississippi. It has intimated that such expert testimony regarding bite-mark evidence will be allowed:

> Because the opinions concerning the methods of comparison employed in a particular case may differ, it is certainly open to defense counsel to attack the qualifications of the expert, the methods and data used to compare the bite marks to persons other than the defendant, and the factual and logical bases of the expert's opinions. Also, **where such expert testimony is allowed by the trial court,** it should be open to the defendant to present evidence challenging the reliability of bite-mark comparisons. *State v. Ortiz,* 502 A.2d 400, 403 (Conn. 1985). Only then will the jury be able to give the proper weight, if any, to this evidence.

Howard v. State, 701 So.2d 274, 288 (Miss. 1997) (emphasis added). We now take the opportunity to state affirmatively that bite-mark identification evidence is admissible in Mississippi.

Dr. West outlined the procedures he used in determining that Brooks made the bite marks found on Courtney's wrist. He testified that he excised the portion of skin containing the bite marks. He then took the dental casts of twelve people, including Sonja Smith, Courtney's mother, and Brooks. Dr. West then photographed the skin portion and compared the molds he had made to the photographs, effectively eliminating everyone except Brooks as suspects.

... If expert testimony regarding bite-mark evidence is allowed by the trial court, the defense should be given the opportunity to present evidence that challenges the reliability of bite-mark comparisons, as was done in [this] case....

Brooks accepted Dr. West as an expert in forensic odontology. Brooks further cross-examined Dr. West on the field of odontology. In an attempt to challenge the reliability of bite-mark comparisons, Brooks brought out that there are no established guidelines in evaluating bite-mark evidence. He also brought out that the American Dental Association recognizes the field of forensic odontology but does not view it as a specialty.

Brooks called Dr. Harry Mincer as his expert in forensic odontology. Dr. Mincer testified that he used the same procedures as Dr. West in examining the bite-mark evidence. Dr. Mincer also testified that while he could not say with medical certainty that Brooks made the bite marks found on Courtney, he **did find consistencies** between the mold of Brooks' teeth and the bite marks on Courtney. Dr. Mincer further testified on cross-examination that he could **not** exclude Brooks as the biter and that, in his opinion, he could exclude the teeth from the other persons tested as the ones that had inflicted the bite marks in question.

Dr. Mincer noted that Dr. West had taught him how to interpret bite marks and that he used basically the same procedures as Dr. West in evaluating the bite marks. These admissions by Dr. Mincer, including his testimony that he could not specifically exclude Brooks as having made the bite marks, made it difficult to challenge the reliability of the bite-mark evidence.

... The trial court did not abuse its discretion in admitting Dr. West's testimony. This issue is without merit....

SMITH, Justice, concurring.

I concur with the majority view that bite-mark evidence is now admissible in this state. I have long espoused that view, but have previously been unable to convince a majority of this Court that we should adopt this view.... I write further here in support of the majority view, to simply point out the extent of the universal acceptance by our courts nationwide of the admissibility of bite-mark evidence.

Bite-mark evidence has been repeatedly accepted as scientific evidence and held to be admissible. *Handley v. State,* 515 So.2d 121, 130 (Ala. Crim. App. 1987) (forensic odonatologist [sic] testimony admissible as evidence is in the nature of physical comparisons as opposed to scientific tests or experiments); *State v. Richards,* 804 P.2d 109, 111 (Ariz. App. 1990) (a *Frye* hearing is not required where bite-mark evidence is presented by a qualified expert); *Verdict v. State,* 868 S.W.2d 443, 447 (Ark. 1993) (bite-mark evidence is not novel scientific evidence and was relevant and reliable); *People v. Marsh,* 441 N.W.2d 33, 36 (Mich. App. 1989) (general reliability of bite-mark evidence as a means of positive identification is sufficiently established that a court is authorized to take judicial notice of reliability without conducting hearing on same); *State v. Armstrong,* 369 S.E.2d 870, 877 (W. Va. 1988) (reliability of bite-mark evidence is sufficiently established that a court is authorized to take judicial notice of same); *State v. Stinson,* 397 N.W.2d 136, 140 (Wis. App.1986) (bite-mark identification evidence presented by an expert witness can be a valuable aid to a jury in understanding and interpreting evidence)....

The majority view is correct and long overdue.... I am confident that our learned trial judges will properly determine, on a case-by-case basis, whether an expert may testify to certain matters if the proper procedures are followed by the parties seeking the admission of such expert's testimony. I am equally persuaded that our juries are quite capable to determine what weight and credibility to give to the expert witness and his testimony....

McRAE, Justice, dissenting.

The majority takes the opportunity to conclude once and for all that forensic ondontology evidence is universally admissible, essentially the same as fingerprints and DNA testing, and is permissible in Mississippi regardless of the quality of that evidence and regardless of the fact that the proponent of that evidence claims that two indentations are teeth marks unique to one person in the world. This is done despite the fact that the discipline is without any universal criteria or methodology. I dissent because, not only do I have qualms about proclaiming that bite-mark evidence is admissible to specifically identify a person and exclude everyone else, I also have reservations about Michael West's unmatched ability to conclude that no one other than the defendant could have produced the marks on the deceased especially where, as here, other experts are unwilling to testify that the marks could **only** be bite marks and not something else.

I recognize that a majority of courts taking up this issue have ruled that bite-mark evidence is admissible. Nonetheless, as pointed out in Faigman, Kaye, Saks & Sanders, MODERN SCIENTIFIC EVIDENCE: THE LAW AND SCIENCE OF EXPERT TESTIMONY, § 24-1.0, at 156 (West 1997), courts that have admitted bite-mark evidence have done so despite the fact that forensic odontologists "were more doubtful about whether the state of their knowledge permitted them to successfully accomplish the challenging task of identifying a perpetrator 'to the exclusion of all others.'" The admission by the courts of this testimony "apparently convinced the forensic odontology community that, despite their doubts, they really were able to perform bite mark identifications." *Id.* at 157–58. Notwithstanding the fact that the experts themselves were sorely divided over whether a defendant could be uniquely identified on the basis of his teeth marks, courts routinely held that such disagreements went to the weight of the evidence rather than its admissibility.

Thus, courts routinely admit bite-mark evidence even though there are many areas in forensic bite-mark identification about which there is still disagreement among its practitioners.[2] One of these areas, and a not insignificant one, is what constitutes a bite mark. In the instant case, Brooks's expert testified that he could not be certain that the marks, consisting of only "two linear marks," were human bite marks. They "could have been made by any number of things," Dr. Mincer opined. Dr. West, of course, testified that with the aid of ultraviolet light he was able to identify marks that could have been made by nothing other than Brooks's teeth.

This is not the first time that Dr. West has been able to boldly go where no expert has gone before. In *Harrison v. State,* 635 So.2d 894, 897 (Miss.1994), West testified that the victim's body was covered in teeth marks inflicted by the defendant. On appeal, Dr. Mincer gave an affidavit to the effect that the marks appeared to be ant bites. In *Davis v. State,* 611 So.2d 906, 910 (Miss.1992), West concluded that "the wound was a bite mark consistent with having been inflicted approximately three weeks previously." But Dr. Richard Souviron, a forensic odontologist from Miami, Florida, "testified that the wound on Davis' arm was not a bite mark, but even if it were, it was inconsistent with Mrs. Davis' teeth."

West's propensity for testifying with a confidence seen in no other expert has been documented by Paul Gianelli in *The Abuse of Scientific Evidence in Criminal Cases: The Need for Independent Crime Laboratories,* 4 VA. J. SOC. POL'Y & LAW 439 (1997). *See also* Marcia Coyle, "Expert" Science Under Fire in Capital Cases, Nat'l L.J., July 11, 1994, at A23....

West estimates that he has testified about fifty-five times over the past decade. A third to one half of these cases were capital prosecutions, and he has only "lost" one case. In 1992, West matched a bite mark found on a rape victim with the teeth of Jonny Bourn, a positive identification, but DNA analysis of skin taken from fingernail scrapings of the victim conclusively excluded Bourn....

It is also worth mentioning that West seems to have difficulty in keeping up with evidence. In the instant case, he lost the not only the mold to Brooks's lower teeth but also the mold of another suspect's teeth. In *Banks v. State,* 725 So.2d 711, 715–16 (Miss.1997), this Court was forced to reverse where West testified that the defendant's teeth correlated to marks in a sandwich left at the crime scene but failed to preserve the sandwich so that the defense could make its own comparisons.

Furthermore, West's opinion that "it could be no one else but Levon Brooks that bit this girl's arm" was rendered despite the fact that the wound was comprised of a mere two

2. Faigman et al. list the following areas as those lacking a consensus in the community of forensic odontologists: 1. The timing of the bite mark injury; 2. Enhancement procedures and techniques (note that in this case, West testified that he used ultraviolet light to enhance the wound enabling him to find "several unique marks" that corresponded to the flaws on the back side of Brooks's teeth; this technique is what allowed West to be positive that only Brooks could have made the two indentations); 3. The type of material for test bites or the accuracy of test bites under various mockup conditions; 4. The pressure necessary to produce the various levels of tissue injury under normal and unusual circumstances has not been reliably measured; 5. Manipulation of various types of distortion to produce correction; 6. The problem faced by forensic dentists today is not necessarily one of matching the bite mark to a set of teeth. It is demonstrating whether another set of teeth could have produced the same or similar mark; 7. There is not universal agreement on which injuries are bite mark related; 8. Research on the minimum number of points of concordance or the minimum number of teeth marks needed in a bite mark for certainty is not as well established as the uniqueness of the dentition. Faigman, et al. § 24-2.3 at 178–80.

indentations. As a general rule, the more teeth registered on the wound, the better the comparison. De La Cruz, *Forensic Dentistry and the Law: Is Bite Mark Evidence Here to Stay?*, 24 AM.CRIM. L. REV. 983, 1005 n. 7 (1987) (citing Rawson, Vale, Sperber, Herschaft & Yfantis, *Reliability of Scoring System of the American Board of Forensic Odontology for Human Bite Marks*, 31 J. FORENSIC SCI. 1235, 1238–39 (1986)). Even West admitted that the typical bite mark consists of indentations made by six teeth.

This Court's apparent willingness to allow West to testify to anything and everything so long as the defense is permitted to cross-examine him may be expedient for prosecutors but it is harmful to the criminal justice system. I believe it is time we did a careful analysis of bite mark testimony—especially that coming from Dr. West—now rather than later or we risk having West become the Ralph Erdmann[5] of Mississippi with the attendant consequence of having to re-examine every case in which West has ever testified.

... [B]ecause I believe the introduction of West's testimony was reversible error, I dissent.

Notes and Questions

1. In an opinion cited in *Brooks v. State,* above, the Mississippi Supreme Court invalidated Eddie Lee Howard, Jr.'s capital murder conviction and death sentence, concluding that Howard's waiver of the right to counsel was not voluntary, that the trial court erred in allowing Howard to represent himself without conducting a competency hearing, and that the trial court's refusal to allow Howard's standby counsel to deliver closing argument violated his right to counsel. *Howard v. State,* 701 So.2d 274 (Miss. 1997). Howard, then represented by counsel, was retried in 2000. As in his original trial, Dr. Michael West "testified that Howard's dentition matched the bite marks on [the murder victim's] neck, breast, and arm." *Howard v. State,* 853 So.2d 781, 796 (Miss. 2003). Howard again was convicted and sentenced to death. Finding no error in the admission of Dr. West's testimony or in other respects, the Mississippi Supreme Court affirmed the conviction and death sentence. Justice McRae dissented and, as in his dissenting opinion in *Brooks,* argued that Dr. West's bite mark testimony should not have been admitted into evidence. *Howard v. State,* 853 So.2d 781, 799–807 (Miss. 2003).

McRAE, Presiding Justice, Dissenting.

The "expert odontology testimony" of Dr. West should not have been submitted to the jury as it is "junk science" and not generally accepted by the scientific community as required by then Rule 702 of the Mississippi Rules of Evidence and *Frye v. United States,* 293 F. 1013 (D.C.Cir.1923). Likewise, neither Dr. West nor his "junk science" meet the standards and requirements for admission under *Daubert v. Merrell Dow Pharmaceuticals, Inc.,* 509 U.S. 579 (1993), and revised Rule 702 of the Mississippi Rules of Evidence....

Bite mark identification is not a reliable discipline and lacks generally recognized criteria or methodology....

It is clear that this Court's ruling concerning bite mark evidence goes too far and gives little guidance or checks with regard to such testing and subsequent testimony. Even with DNA evidence, we require an independent control check of any materials or regents used in the performance of the test; the running of known control samples in parallel with the unknown samples to check for errors in test performance; and the calculation of the statistical probability which

5. Ralph Erdmann was a Texas pathologist who faked autopsies. Erdmann's misconduct was discovered only when he listed the weight of a deceased's spleen in an autopsy report. The deceased's relatives were puzzled since they knew that the deceased's spleen had been removed years before. Paul Gianelli, *The Abuse of Scientific Evidence in Criminal Cases: The Need for Independent Crime Laboratories,* 4 VA.J.SOC.POL'Y & LAW at 449–50 (1997). In another case, Erdmann reported that a man found dead in a dumpster had died of pneumonia and hypothermia. A second autopsy showed that the deceased had died from a bullet wound to the head. Erdmann Faces New Legal Woes, 81 A.B.A. J. 32 (1995).

signifies the statistical probability that a person picked randomly from the population would have a DNA profile identical to the DNA profile generated from the forensic sample. Under the methodology employed by Dr. West, there is no statistical probability, no control group, and no check on the materials and regents used in performance. Essentially, there are no independent checks on Dr. West's scientific findings and opinions. He is given free rein to account for himself without any independent confirmation of his methodology or techniques. Furthermore, in his expert opinion testimony the jury is told that the victim's bite mark is "identical" to the teeth of the defendant and is given no statistical probability regarding the margin of error for the techniques employed or the probability that another individual may have left similar bite marks. How can this be? How can Dr. West testify outright that these marks were left by this individual; yet an expert testifying to DNA evidence (the most special and unique makeup of our bodies) is not allowed to testify that the blood is the defendants or the victims, but rather has to give a statistical probability regarding the likelihood that the blood is the defendant's or victims? This makes no sense.

Even under this Court's recent adoption of revised Rule 702 and *Daubert,* 509 U.S. 579, Dr. West's methodology and opinion will not meet the requirements for expert opinion. Revised Rule 702 provides that:

> If scientific, technical, or other specialized knowledge will assist the trier of fact to understand the evidence or to determine a fact in issue, a witness qualified as an expert by knowledge, training, or education, may testify thereto in the form of an opinion or otherwise; if (1) the testimony is based upon sufficient facts or data; (2) the testimony is the product of reliable principles and methods; and (3) the witness has applied the principles and methods reliably to the facts of the case.

... With the application of the principles established in *Daubert,* it is clear that Dr. West's expert opinion does not meet the standards governing admissibility under revised Rule 702. First, "scientific knowledge" implies some sort of objective rather than subjective standard of measurement and means of assessment. Dr. West, through his own testimony acknowledged that bite mark identification is not governed by an objective standard but rather is a "subjective art and science" with no computable margin of error.

Second, scientific testimony must be based on "good grounds,"—i.e. "what is known." *See Daubert,* 509 U.S. at 590. As stated earlier, the forensic odontology community is still in discussions as to whether the methodology and procedures used by Dr. West are sincerely grounded in good science and reliable, therefore Dr. West's methodology is not grounded in "what is known."

Third, Dr. West's methodology cannot meet the criteria requirements as provided in *Daubert.* Dr. West's methodology and procedure have to a small degree been tested. During his testimony, Dr. West repeatedly emphasized the studies done by Dr. Reider Sognnaes at UCLA which studied and compared the dental impressions of 100 twins to determine whether the dental imprints of these twins were distinguishable and identifiable by detailed and unique characteristics. He offered no other studies where the margin of error has been calculated for forensic bite mark identification. Dr. West only continually emphasized that each dental impression is unique to an individual without any other evidence of studies which support his methodology and techniques. Furthermore, it was never revealed whether the UCLA study Dr. West emphasized used the same methodology and techniques employed by himself. Likewise, Dr. West has conducted no independent blind control group studies to verify his techniques or methodology. Additionally, the techniques and methodologies employed by Dr. West are "not capable" of being calculated with a margin of error as "it's a subjective art and science." Dr. West, in his own words, acknowledges that his procedures and methodology are subjective and no margin of error has been calculated to determine how often he is right or wrong. This fact alone tells a lot about Dr. West's so called science. Also, despite this Court's finding that bite mark evidence is "generally accepted," Dr. West's methodologies, procedures, and techniques are not generally accepted in the forensic odontology community. Dr. West himself acknowledges that many of the forensic odontologists that testify regarding bite mark evidence do not agree with his methods. Despite Dr. West's failure to meet the two requirements of *Daubert* discussed above, his theories, methods, and procedure have been subjected to peer review by way of publication. However, publication does not mean that his peers have actually concurred in his methodology and accepted it as a general procedure for bite mark identification. Under the three factors enunciated in *Daubert,* the methodology and procedures used by Dr. West in forming his so called expert opinions are not admissible under revised Rule 702.

Additionally, Rule 403 of the Mississippi Rules of Evidence also supports the exclusion of Dr. West's opinion testimony. Rule 403 provides that "[a]lthough relevant, evidence may be excluded if its probative value is substantially outweighed by the danger of unfair prejudice, confusion of the issues, or misleading the jury, or by considerations of undue delay, waste of time, or needless presentation of cumulative evidence." M.R.E. 403. Under Rule 403, the probative value of Dr. West's testimony does not outweigh the unfair prejudice and possible misleading of the jury. Dr. West all but tells the jury "Howard did it." Despite his efforts to limit his testimony to "consistency," Dr. West during testimony characterized Howard's dental impressions as "identical" to those found on the victim....

2. On December 29, 1991, the nude body of a young woman was found in the restroom of the Phoenix nightclub where she had worked as a bartender. "The killer had left very little behind.... There was one crucial piece of evidence. [The victim] had been bitten on the neck and left breast with sufficient force to leave teeth marks." *State v. Krone,* 897 P.2d 621, 621–622 (Ariz. 1995). Ray Krone emerged as a suspect when the police learned that he had offered to help the victim close the bar on the night of the murder. He supplied the police with a Styrofoam impression of his teeth as well as teeth casts. He was arrested after "[a] comparison of the casts to [the victim's] wounds suggested that Krone had made the marks." *Id.,* at 622. Krone maintained his innocence at his 1992 trial for capital murder. However, two prosecution experts offered their opinions that the bite marks on the victim's body had been made by Krone. One of the experts testified, "That's as nice a match ... as we really ever see in a bite mark case." The other opined, "I say that there is a match. Okay? I'm saying there's a definite match."[27] "The bite marks ... were critical to the State's case. Without them, there likely would have been no jury submissible case against Krone." *State v. Krone,* 897 P.2d, at 624. The jury found Krone guilty of capital murder and he was sentenced to death. The Arizona Supreme Court overturned his conviction in 1995, finding reversible error in the prosecution's failure to provide timely disclosure to defense counsel of a videotape made by one of the expert witnesses and displayed to the jury that illustrated how the expert had concluded that the bite marks found on the body were made by Krone. Krone was retried in 1996. As in his original trial, the primary evidence against him was the expert testimony regarding the bite marks. He again was convicted but this time was sentenced to life in prison. In 2002, "after Krone had served more than ten years in prison, ... DNA testing would prove his innocence. DNA testing conducted on the saliva and blood found on the victim excluded Krone as the source and instead matched a man ... [who] was incarcerated on an unrelated sex crime...."[28] Krone was released from prison in April 2002 and the charges against him were dismissed.[29]

3. Including Ray Krone's case, at least six DNA-based exonerations have involved convictions supported by expert testimony concerning bite mark comparisons. In two of the cases, the experts testified only that they had observed a "consistency" between the defendants' teeth and the bite marks at issue; in the remaining cases, "the odontologists provided invalid testimony," including two cases in addition to Krone's in which they "testified they were certain that the defendant left the bite marks."[30]

4. In *Ege v. Yukins,* 485 F.3d 364 (6th Cir. 2007), the Sixth Circuit Court of Appeals affirmed a federal district court's decision granting habeas corpus relief to a defendant convicted of first-degree murder in Michigan. The defendant's attorney had failed to object to a prosecution witness's expert testimony regarding bite mark comparisons. The

expert, Dr. Alan Warnick, "was asked by the prosecution, 'Let's say you have the Detroit Metropolitan Area, three, three and a half million people. Would anybody else within that kind of number match like [the defendant] did?' He responded, 'No, in my expert opinion, nobody else would match up.'" *Id.*, 485 F.3d, at 368. The district court ruled that the defense attorney's failure to object to that testimony constituted ineffective assistance of counsel. "'There can be no question that the bite mark evidence together with Dr. Warnick's 3.5-million-to-one odds making was powerful evidence.... Dr. Warnick's evidence was unreliable and grossly misleading. The evidence was so extremely unfair that its admission violates fundamental concepts of justice.'" *Id.*, 485 F.3d, at 370.

5. As noted by the Mississippi Supreme Court in *Brooks v. State,* courts in other jurisdictions have regularly upheld the admissibility of expert testimony concerning bite mark comparisons. *See also Milone v. Camp,* 22 F.3d 693 (7th Cir. 1994); *People v. Marx,* 54 Cal. App.3d 100 (1975); Marjorie A. Shields, "Admissibility and Sufficiency of Bite Mark Evidence as Basis for Identification of Accused," 1 A.L.R.6th 657 (2005). The reliability of bite mark analysis, however, is disputed, and some commentators have expressed skepticism about whether expert testimony should be admissible.[31]

6. The 2009 report issued by the National Academy of Sciences, *Strengthening Forensic Science in the United States: A Path Forward,* included the following observations about forensic odontology.

> More research is needed to confirm the fundamental basis for the science of bite mark comparison. Although forensic odontologists understand the anatomy of teeth and the mechanics of biting and can retrieve sufficient information from bite marks on skin to assist in criminal investigations and provide testimony at criminal trials, the scientific basis is insufficient to conclude that bite mark comparisons can result in a conclusive match....
>
> Despite the inherent weaknesses involved in bite mark comparison, it is reasonable to assume that the process can sometimes reliably exclude suspects. Although the methods of collection of bite mark evidence are relatively noncontroversial, there is considerable dispute about the value and reliability of the collected data for interpretation. Some of the key areas of dispute include the accuracy of human skin as a reliable registration material for bite marks, the uniqueness of human dentition, the techniques used for analysis, and the role of examiner bias. The [American Board of Forensic Odontology] has developed guidelines for the analysis of bite marks in an effort to standardize analysis, but there is still no general agreement among practicing forensic odontologists about national or international standards for comparison.
>
> Although the majority of forensic odontologists are satisfied that bite marks can demonstrate sufficient detail for positive identification, no scientific studies support this assessment, and no large population studies have been conducted. In numerous instances, experts diverge widely in their evaluations of the same bite mark evidence, which has led to questioning of the value and scientific objectivity of such evidence.
>
> ... The committee received no evidence of an existing scientific basis for identifying an individual to the exclusion of all others. That same finding was reported in a 2001 review, which "revealed a lack of valid evidence to support many of the assumptions made by forensic dentists during bite mark comparisons." Some research is warranted in order to identify the circumstances within which the methods of forensic odontology can provide probative value.[32]

4. Microscopic Hair Analysis

In December 1982, the body of Debra Sue Carter was found in her Ada, Oklahoma apartment. The 21-year-old had been sexually assaulted and beaten. A blood-soaked washcloth was lodged in her throat. The cause of death was suffocation. The apartment showed signs of a violent struggle. Someone—apparently the killer or killers—had used nail polish and catsup to write messages on the apartment walls, kitchen table, and on her back. Police found a bloody palm print and secured several hairs from the apartment. They had few other leads. More than four years elapsed before Ronald Williamson and Dennis Fritz were arrested for the crime, in May 1987.

Williamson, a star athlete during high school who had a brief professional baseball career, had a significant history of substance abuse and mental illness. Fritz, whose wife had been murdered years earlier by a neighbor, had been a school teacher. The two men were friends. The arrests followed information police received from jailhouse informants who had reported overhearing Williamson make incriminating statements while he was incarcerated for unrelated offenses. In addition, although he had mentioned nothing about Williamson when first interviewed, a year later Ada resident Glen Gore volunteered to the police that he remembered Ms. Carter telling him on the night she was last seen alive that Williamson had asked her to dance and had made her feel uncomfortable. Following his arrest, while being interrogated by the police, Williamson made a statement in which he described having a dream about killing Ms. Carter.

Fritz and Williamson were tried separately on capital murder charges in April 1988. Each was found guilty. Fritz was sentenced to life imprisonment, and Williamson to death. Their respective convictions were affirmed by the Oklahoma Court of Criminal Appeals.[33] In 1995, a federal district court vacated Williamson's conviction, ruling that a hearing to determine his competency to stand trial should have been conducted and that he had been provided ineffective assistance of counsel. We reproduce a portion of the district court's opinion below, which addresses the expert testimony regarding hair analysis that was admitted at his trial. Similar testimony had been offered at Fritz's trial. Williamson remained incarcerated following the district court's ruling pending appeal of that decision and a possible retrial. Then, as reported by the Innocence Project:

> DNA testing revealed that neither Fritz nor Williamson deposited the spermatozoa found in the victim. Further testing proved that none of the many hairs that were labeled "matches" belonged to them. The profile obtained from the semen evidence matched Glenn [sic] Gore, one of the state's witnesses at trial....
>
> Dennis Fritz and Ron Williamson were exonerated and released in April 1999. Williamson had, at one point, come within five days of execution. The two had been wrongfully incarcerated, respectively, for eleven years.
>
> Five years after his release, Williamson was diagnosed with cirrhosis of the liver. On December 4, 2004, he died in an Oklahoma nursing home, surrounded by his family.[34]

Ronald Williamson's case is the subject of John Grisham's book, *The Innocent Man: Murder and Injustice in a Small Town* (New York: Doubleday 2006). Dennis Fritz recounts his own case history in *Journey Toward Justice* (Santa Anna, CA: Seven Locks Press 2006). Following the exoneration of Williamson and Fritz, Glen Gore was convicted of Ms. Carter's murder and he was sentenced to death. His conviction was reversed when, ironically, the Oklahoma Court of Criminal Appeals ruled that he had unfairly been denied the opportunity to offer evidence to attempt to establish that a third party—Williamson, Fritz, or Ricky Simmons (a mentally ill individual who had volunteered to the police that he had killed Ms. Carter)—had committed the crime.[35] Gore again was convicted on retrial, and was sentenced to life imprisonment without parole when the jury was unable to reach a unanimous penalty decision.[36]

Williamson v. Reynolds

904 F.Supp. 1529 (E.D. Okla. 1995)

SEAY, Chief Judge....

Petitioner alleges ... that the unreliability and inherent subjectivity of microscopic hair comparison should prohibit its admissibility....

The prosecution's only physical evidence, apart from the semen evidence, were hairs allegedly found to be "microscopically consistent" with Petitioner and his co-defendant Dennis Fritz. Dennis Smith, retired detective captain of the Ada Police Department, testified that he and OSBI [Oklahoma State Bureau of Investigation] Agent Gary Rogers collected several hundred hairs at the crime scene. Individual hairs were placed in paper bindles which are pieces of paper that have been folded over several times. The victim's stuffed animals which had hairs attached to them were placed in bags. Head hair, pubic hair and saliva samples were taken from the victim's family and friends shortly after the murder. Samples were also collected from Glen Gore, who likely was the last person seen with the victim, and Mike Carpenter, whose fingerprint was found in her car. Smith and Rogers transported these samples to the Oklahoma State Crime Bureau.

In March 1983 the police department asked Petitioner and Dennis Fritz to submit hair and saliva samples, and they complied. These samples were also taken to the OSBI for analysis. Rogers testified that about three days later, Petitioner complied with a request for additional pubic hair samples, because not enough had been obtained earlier. About a year and one half after the murder, Smith could not remember whether Gore's samples had been submitted, so additional samples were taken and sent to the crime bureau.

Mary Long, OSBI criminalist, testified that she collected pubic combings from the victim and hairs from articles found in the victim's apartment. She also collected known pubic hair and known scalp hair from the victim.[10] Long sent this evidence to Susan Land, another OSBI criminalist. In all, Long submitted 45 hair sample containers to Land.

Susan Land testified that although she had hair samples from many individuals, the only samples she mounted on microscope slides were those from the victim, Petitioner and Fritz. She stated that she may have commenced a microscopic examination of some of the hair samples, but stopped because she did not feel she could be objective in her analysis due to the "stress and strain" from working on numerous homicide cases. Consequently, she turned the mounted and unmounted hair samples over to Melvin Hett on September 19, 1983.

Hett, the third OSBI criminalist to examine the evidence, testified that he had been engaged in the science of hair identification approximately 13 years and that about 90% of his time was devoted to hair and fiber comparisons and analysis. He brought charts prepared at his request to demonstrate the major racial characteristics of hair: Caucasian, Negroid and Mongoloid. He stated that in Oklahoma, however, there are many mixtures of the three racial types. He explained that a cross section of a human hair shows the three areas of human hairs: the cuticle or outer layer of scales, the cortex which gives hair its color, and the medulla which is usually just an air sack running down the center of the hair. Hett further testified that there are approximately 25 characteristics used in hair comparisons. He used his exhibits to demonstrate other characteristics and variations used in hair analysis and discussed factors such as bleaching, dying, sun bleaching and brushing which can change the characteristics of an individual hair. He explained that the root of an individual hair can have dif-

10. Hairs collected directly from an individual are called his "known" hairs. Unidentified hairs collected at the scene are called "questioned" hairs.

ferent characteristics from its far tip, and the hairs on an individual's head do not all look exactly the same. Therefore, when a known hair sample is to be used for comparison, the OSBI usually requests at least 30 hairs to account for variations of an individual's hair.

Hett testified he uses a stereo microscope which magnifies approximately 30 times for low power hair comparisons and a comparison microscope which allows the viewer to look at and compare 2 different hair samples simultaneously at a magnification of 50 to 400 times. He stated he spent several hundred hours in his examination of the hair samples in this investigation.

Hett said he received hair samples from Susan Land on September 19, 1983, some of which were mounted on slides and some of which were in bindles. He also received additional samples directly from the Ada Police Department. Mary Long also sent him scalp and pubic hair samples from Ricky Simmons in October 1987.

When asked by the prosecutor whether he found any pubic hairs from the washcloth from the victim's mouth that "matched" Fritz's pubic hairs, Hett testified he found 1 that was "consistent microscopically" with Fritz's pubic hairs and "could have the same source." Defense counsel objected to Hett's answer or the form of the question, and the objection was sustained. Hett then testified that he found 2 pubic hairs "consistent" with Fritz's pubic hairs on the panties found at the scene and 1 pubic hair on the floor under the victim's body that was also "consistent" with Fritz's. He found 7 pubic hairs removed from bedding and mounted on slides by Susan Land which were "consistent" with Fritz's pubic hair. In all, there were 11 hairs that he found "consistent" with Fritz's pubic hair. He also found 1 scalp hair from the bedding and 1 scalp hair from the floor that were "consistent microscopically" with Fritz's scalp hair and could have the same source.

With regard to Petitioner's hair, Hett testified he found 2 pubic hairs from the bedding that were "consistent microscopically and *could have* the same source as Ron Williamson's known pubic hair." He also found 2 scalp hairs on the washcloth which were "consistent microscopically and *could have* the same source" as Petitioner's known scalp hair (emphasis added).

The prosecutor questioned Hett about what "could have the same source" meant. Hett explained, "When a hair *matches,* if you will, it is consistent microscopically to a known source" (emphasis added). After an objection by defense counsel, Hett went on to say he meant that

> [T]he hairs either did originate from that [known] source, or there could be or might be another individual in the world somewhere that might have the same microscopic characteristics. In other words, hairs are not an absolute identification, but they either came from this individual or there is—could be another individual somewhere in the world that would have the same characteristics to their hair.

Hett testified he received scalp and pubic hairs from a number of individuals, including Glen Gore. These persons were eliminated as possible sources of the questioned hairs after Hett's "direct comparisons" indicated the known samples were not "microscopically consistent" with the questioned hairs.

Under cross-examination, Hett stated he completed three reports for this investigation, but only the first two were submitted by the prosecution as a trial exhibit. The first two reports were dated December 1985 and January 9, 1986. The third report, covering evidence received by OSBI from 1985 through 1987, was dated April 7, 1988, the day after Fritz's trial began. Defense counsel was unaware of the third report until this cross-examination and did not receive a copy until then.

Under cross-examination, Hett testified that he could not determine with certainty that a particular hair came from a certain person, but he could only state whether a questioned hair "might" have come from a certain individual. He admitted that hair comparisons are not absolute identifications like fingerprints....

Petitioner argues that the State's hair evidence presented by its expert was inadmissible due to its unreliability and inherently subjective nature. The State asserts that the reliability of hair evidence is a jury question, rather than an admissibility issue.

Of the hundreds of hairs submitted to OSBI for analysis, 2 scalp hairs and 2 pubic hairs were found to be "consistent microscopically" with Petitioner's known scalp and pubic hairs. However, the State's expert did not explain which of the "approximately" 25 characteristics were consistent, any standards for determining whether the samples were consistent, how many persons could be expected to share this same combination of characteristics, or how he arrived at his conclusions.[11] Hett did acknowledge that "consistent microscopically" is not the same as a positive identification.

Forensic examination of human hair was conducted as early as 1861. Hair comparison in a criminal prosecution was first considered over one hundred years ago by the Wisconsin Supreme Court. *Knoll v. State,* 12 N.W. 369 (Wis. 1882). The hair expert in *Knoll* visually compared hair samples and concluded that they came from a common source. On appeal the court held that "such evidence is of a most dangerous character," and reversed the conviction. *Knoll,* 12 N.W. at 371–72.

At the time of the *Knoll* decision, hair analysis was a new area of forensics. Since then, it has become a familiar and common component of criminal prosecutions with contemporary hair analysis relying heavily upon conventional microscopes. Modern hair experts generally state their results in testimony that samples are "similar" and "could have" come from the "same source." Critics of hair evidence have criticized the admission of hair evidence on the grounds that it is too subjective and it has a high error rate.[13]

In 1993, the United States Supreme Court held that "the trial judge must ensure that any and all scientific testimony or evidence admitted is not only relevant, but reliable." *Daubert v. Merrell Dow Pharmaceuticals,* 509 U.S. 579, 113 S.Ct. 2786, 2795 (1993). *See also Taylor v. State,* 889 P.2d 319, 328–29 (Okla. Crim. App. 1995) (expressly adopting the *Daubert* holding). Reliability refers to trustworthiness of the evidence. "In a case involving scientific evidence, evidentiary reliability will be based upon scientific validity." *Daubert,* 113 S.Ct. at 2795 n. 9. This standard applies both to "'novel' scientific techniques" and "well-established propositions." *Daubert,* 113 S.Ct. at 2796 n. 11.

Acknowledging that it would not be reasonable to require scientific testimony to be "'known' to a certainty," the Supreme Court held that

> [I]n order to qualify as "scientific knowledge," an inference or assertion must be derived by the scientific method. Proposed testimony must be supported by appropriate validation—i.e., "good grounds," based on what is known. In short, the requirement that an expert's testimony pertain to "scientific knowledge" establishes a standard of evidentiary reliability. *Daubert,* 509 U.S. at ___, 113 S.Ct. at 2795.

In deciding whether proffered expert testimony is admissible, the trial judge must initially determine "whether the reasoning or methodology underlying the testimony is scientifically valid" and "whether that reasoning or methodology properly can be applied to the facts in issue." *Daubert,* 113 S.Ct. at 2796....

[I]n analyzing Petitioner's case under the guidelines of *Daubert,* this court has found an apparent scarcity of scientific studies regarding the reliability of hair comparison testing. The few available studies reviewed by this court tend to point to the method's unreliability. Although probability standards for fingerprint and serology evidence have been established and recognized by the courts, no such standards exist for human hair identification. Since the evaluation of hair evidence remains subjective, the weight the examiner gives to the presence or absence of a particular characteristic depends upon the examiner's subjective opinion. Consequently, any conclusion regarding whether a particular hair sample came from a certain individual depends upon the value judgment and expertise of the examiner.[15]

In response to studies indicating a high percentage of error in forensic analysis, The Law Enforcement Assistance Administration sponsored its own Laboratory Proficiency Testing Program. Between 235 and 240 crime

---

11. There is an apparent lack of consensus among hair examiners about the number of characteristics, and it has been suggested that there is a need for more accurate definitions of hair features in microscopic hair examination. *See* Aitken & Robertson, *The Value of Microscopic Features in the Examination of Human Head Hairs: Statistical Analysis of Questionnaire Returns,* 31 J. Forensic Sci. 546 (1986); Robertson & Aitken, *The Value of Microscopic Features in the Examination of Human Head Hairs: Analysis of Comments in Questionnaire Returns,* 31 J. Forensic Sci. 563 (1986).

13. Imwinkelried, *Forensic Hair Analysis: The Case Against the Underemployment of Scientific Evidence,* 39 Wash. & Lee L.Rev. 41, 41–44 (1982).

15. Miller, *Procedural Bias in Forensic Science Examinations of Human Hair,* 11 Law & Human Behavior 157, 157–58 (1987).

laboratories throughout the United States participated in the program which compared police laboratories' reports with analytical laboratories' findings on different types of evidence, including hair. Overall, the police laboratories' performance was weakest in the area of hair analysis. The error rates on hair analysis were as high as 67% on individual samples, and the majority of the police laboratories were incorrect on 4 out of 5 hair samples analyzed. Such an accuracy level was below chance.[16]

Two studies by B.D. Gaudette of the Royal Canadian Mounted Police attempted to establish the probability of error when a questioned hair sample is found to be microscopically similar to known hair samples. Gaudette placed the probability that a single head hair which is microscopically similar to samples from a known source actually came from another source at about 1 in 4,500.[17] The estimated probability for this type of error in pubic hair analysis was 1 in 800.[18] Courts have disagreed on whether these probability estimates are admissible, and other researchers have severely criticized the studies, concluding that they are invalid.[19] Assertions have even been made that the Canadian probability estimates are virtually meaningless and grossly in error due to experimental bias resulting in an inaccurately low probability estimate.[20] Gaudette has conceded that hair comparison is "still somewhat subjective," and that "hair is not generally a basis for positive personal identification."[21] He contends his critics misunderstood his research, but he did revise his probability figures to 1 in 57 for scalp hair and 1 in 17 for pubic hair for the relevant population of individuals.[22]

In one revealing study students enrolled in advanced college crime laboratory courses were trained to examine hair samples. All the students received training that met the level required for qualification to testify as human hair experts. This study found a 30.4% error rate in conventional hair comparisons when a questioned hair from a fictitious crime scene was compared with known hair samples from a fictitious suspect. The examiners' error rate fell to 3.8%, however, when the method of comparison was changed to the "lineup" method. In this second method, examiners were presented with hair from a fictitious crime scene and samples from 5 fictitious suspects which were similar to the questioned hair in comparison characteristics.[23]

The researcher in this study concluded that the conventional method is subject to unintentional bias among hair examiners. As with eyewitness identification, it appears that the accuracy rate for hair identification increases when multiple suspects are presented. Also, as with eyewitness identifications, erroneous conclusions can increase when the examiner is told which hair sample is from the suspect in the crime. A preconceived conclusion that questioned hairs and known hairs are from the same individual may affect the examiner's evaluation.[24] This court notes that hair expert Melvin Hett testified in the preliminary hearing that this conventional method of comparison was precisely the procedure used in Petitioner's case.

Other forms of expert examination and testimony have been criticized because jurors may be awed by an "aura of special reliability and trustworthiness" which may cause undue prejudice, confuse the issues or mislead the jury. In the case of hair expert testimony the jurors do not have the opportunity for direct evaluation. Instead, they hear an abbreviated summary of the characteristics of hair and testimony of the expert's overall conclusions.

The clear implication from the expert's testimony in Petitioner's trial was that 4 of the hairs found at the victim's apartment belonged to Petitioner. As witness to the incorrect conclusion

16. Imwinkelried, 39 Wash. & Lee L.Rev. at 44.

17. Gaudette & Keeping, *An Attempt at Determining Probabilities in Human Scalp Hair Comparison,* 19 J. Forensic Sci. 514 (1974).

18. Gaudette, *Probabilities and Human Pubic Hair Comparisons,* 21 J. Forensic Sci. 514 (1976).

19. Moellenberg, [*Splitting Hairs in Criminal Trials: Admissibility of Hair Comparison Probability Estimates,*] 1984 Ariz.St.L.J. [521,] 521–22.

20. Barnett and Ogle, *Probabilities and Human Hair Comparisons,* 27 J. Forensic Sci. 272, 273–74 (1982).

21. Gaudette, *Some Further Thoughts on Probabilities and Human Hair Comparisons,* 23 J. Forensic Sci. 758, 759–61 (1978).

22. Gaudette, *A Supplementary Discussion of Probabilities and Human Hair Comparisons,* 27 J. Forensic Sci. 279, 283 (1982).

23. Miller, 11 Law & Human Behavior at 160–61.

24. *Id.* at 161–62.

that could result from this testimony, the prosecutor said in his closing argument, "[T]here's a match." Even the Court of Criminal Appeals misinterpreted and overstated the hair evidence by writing, "Hair evidence *placed [Petitioner] at the decedent's apartment.*" *Williamson* [*v. State*], 812 P.2d [384,] 397 [(Okla. Crim. App. 1991)] (emphasis added).

This court finds that the prosecutor's mischaracterization of the hair evidence misled the jury, the trial court and the appellate court to believe "microscopically consistent" equates with reliability and to conclude there was a "match" between questioned hairs and Petitioner's hairs. Actually, the most to be drawn from Hett's testimony was that the questioned hair samples could have come from Petitioner. This also means, of course, that the hair samples might not have been his. While it may be possible to exclude an individual as the source of a hair sample, it is not possible to prove questioned hairs are from a particular person.

This court has been unsuccessful in its attempts to locate *any* indication that expert hair comparison testimony meets *any* of the requirements of *Daubert.* Not even the "general acceptance" standard is met, since any general acceptance seems to be among hair experts who are generally technicians testifying for the prosecution, not scientists who can objectively evaluate such evidence.[25]

This court has previously addressed the issue of hair expert testimony in the context of a criminal proceeding where the death penalty was sought. Such testimony by a special agent with the Federal Bureau of Investigation in Washington, D.C. was held inadmissible. *United States v. Hutching,* No. CR-92-32-S (E.D.Okla.) (Tr. of Testimony of D.W. Deedrick, Feb. 25, 1993, 34–69). Based in part on the hair expert's own testimony that there is no research to indicate with any certainty the probabilities that two hair samples are from the same individual, this court held that hair expert testimony was too speculative to be admissible. Admission of such testimony would have been "extremely unfair" and could "prejudice the defendants without any real probative value." (Tr. of Deedrick at 67, *Hutching*). This court is not persuaded to change those conclusions.

This court, therefore, finds that the introduction into evidence of expert hair testimony at Petitioner's trial was irrelevant, imprecise and speculative, and its probative value was outweighed by its prejudicial effect. The state of the art of hair analysis has not reached a level of certainty to permit such testimony. Although the hair expert may have followed procedures accepted in the community of hair experts, the human hair comparison results in this case were, nonetheless, scientifically unreliable. This court recognizes the long history of admissibility of such evidence, but as the *Daubert* Court stated, "[H]ypotheses ... that are incorrect will eventually be shown to be so." *Daubert,* 113 S.Ct. at 2798. Based on the reasons above, this court holds that hair comparison evidence based on forensic procedures employed in Petitioner's case is inadmissible....

EPILOGUE

While considering my decision in this case I told a friend, a layman, I believed the facts and law dictated that I must grant a new trial to a defendant who had been convicted and sentenced to death.

My friend asked, "Is he a murderer?"

I replied simply, "We won't know until he receives a fair trial."

God help us, if ever in this great country we turn our heads while people who have not had fair trials are executed. That almost happened in this case.

ACCORDINGLY, the Writ of Habeas Corpus shall issue, unless within one hundred twenty (120) days of the entry of this Order the State grants Petitioner a new trial or, in the alternative, orders his permanent release from custody....

Notes and Questions

1. On appeal, the 10th Circuit Court of Appeals affirmed the district court's order granting Williamson a new trial, relying exclusively on the 6th Amendment ground of ineffective assistance of trial counsel. *Williamson v. Ward,* 110 F.3d 1508 (10th Cir. 1997).

---

25. *See* Moenssens, *Novel Scientific Evidence in Criminal Cases: Some Words of Caution,* 84 J.Crim.L. & Criminology 1, 5 (1993).

However, in the course of its ruling, the Court of Appeals agreed with the State's argument "that the district court applied the wrong standard in ruling that the hair analysis evidence was inadmissible." 110 F.3d, at 1522.

When the admission of evidence in a state trial is challenged on federal habeas, the question is whether the error, if any, was so grossly prejudicial that it fatally infected the trial and denied the fundamental fairness that is the essence of due process. This assessment requires examining both the reliability of the evidence and the significance it had at trial. The district court here, however, did not perform its analysis under a due process/fundamental fairness standard. Instead, it incorrectly assessed the issue in evidentiary terms under *Daubert v. Merrell Dow Pharmaceuticals, Inc.*, 509 U.S. 57 (1993). Because the court employed the wrong standard, we reverse its ruling that the hair analysis was inadmissible. That evidentiary determination is properly left to the state court in the event of a retrial.

2. Microscopic comparison of hairs has largely been supplanted by mitochondrial DNA (mtDNA) analysis, which has been available since the mid-1990s, or by nuclear DNA analysis when hair roots are available for testing.[37] Courts overwhelmingly have upheld the admissibility of expert testimony concerning microscopic hair analysis, even in the post-DNA era.[38]

3. Of the 137 DNA-based exonerations reviewed by Garrett and Neufeld that involved forensic testimony and for which trial transcripts were available, 65 "involved microscopic hair comparison analysis. Of those, 25—or 38%—had invalid hair comparison testimony. Most (18) of those cases involved invalid individualizing claims."[39] Another commentator has observed:

> The subjectivity inherent in microscopic [hair] comparisons leaves the technique open to inconsistencies among examiners and problems such as expectation bias.
>
> The few studies on the reliability of microscopic hair analysis have shown it to have extremely high error rates, perhaps in large part because of this subjectivity. A proficiency testing program in the 1970s reported 54% and 67% error rates, which are (remarkably) worse than chance. A recent 2002 study showed that in nine instances out of eighty in which hair was found consistent via microscopy, further mtDNA analysis excluded the suspect.
>
> Microscopic hair analysis has one other serious drawback.... [W]ell-accepted statistics do not exist on the distribution of various types of hair in the population. As a result, experts confine themselves to vague terms such as "consistent" or "similar." ... [F]actfinders receive no guidance as to what weight to give a finding of "consistent." Unlike with observable traits such as hair color, factfinders have no innate sense of the rarity or commonality of the trait in the population.[40]

4. The National Academy of Sciences report, *Strengthening Forensic Science in the United States: A Path Forward*, summarized its assessment of microscopic hair analysis as follows:

> No scientifically accepted statistics exist about the frequency with which particular characteristics of hair are distributed in the population. There appear to be no uniform standards on the number of features on which hairs must agree before an examiner may declare a "match." ... The categorization of hair features depends heavily on examiner proficiency and practical experience.

> An FBI study found that, of 80 hair comparisons that were "associated" through microscopic examinations, 9 of them (12.5%) were found in fact to come from different sources when reexamined through mtDNA analysis. This illustrates not only the imprecision of microscopic hair analyses, but also the problem with using imprecise reporting terminology such as "associated with," which is not clearly defined and which can be misunderstood to imply individualization.
>
> ... In cases where there seems to be a morphological match (based on microscopic examination), it must be confirmed using mtDNA analysis; microscopic studies alone are of limited probative value. The committee found no scientific support for the use of hair comparisons for individualization in the absence of nuclear DNA....[41]

5. Deoxyribonucleic Acid: DNA

The forensic use of DNA analysis and resulting exonerations have been central to galvanizing public interest in wrongful convictions and helping stimulate criminal justice reforms. "The advent of DNA testing and the window it opens onto the errors of the legal system have altered the nature and study of miscarriages of justice in America. Most fundamentally, DNA testing has established factual innocence—as opposed to procedural innocence—with certainty...."[42] By the end of 2010, at least 266 wrongfully convicted individuals in the United States had been exonerated following post-conviction DNA testing.[43] DNA evidence of course also is a powerful tool in helping to establish guilt. DNA analyses were first used to investigate and prosecute crimes in England in the mid-1980s[44] and were used in criminal prosecutions in this country shortly thereafter.[45] They now routinely are admitted into evidence in criminal cases.[46]

The National Academies of Science report, *Strengthening Forensic Science in the United States: A Path Forward*, concluded that "DNA typing is now universally recognized as the standard against which many other forensic individualization techniques are judged."[47]

> DNA analysis is scientifically sound for several reasons: (1) there are biological explanations for individual-specific findings; (2) the 13 STR [Short Tandem Repeat] loci used to compare DNA samples were selected so that the chance of two different people matching on all of them would be extremely small; (3) the probabilities of false positives have been explored and quantified in some settings (even if only approximately); (4) the laboratory procedures are well specified and subject to validation and proficiency testing; and (5) there are clear and repeatable standards for analysis, interpretation, and reporting. DNA analysis also has been subjected to more scrutiny than any other forensic science discipline, with rigorous experimentation and validation performed prior to its use in forensic investigations. As a result of these characteristics, the probative power of DNA is high. Of course, DNA evidence is not available in every criminal investigation, and it is still subject to errors in handling that can invalidate the analysis.... [48]

We next consider case law that describes the basic science of DNA analysis as well as how the results of DNA testing should be interpreted and communicated—issues that are vital with respect to both prosecutions and exonerations. Although DNA has been recognized as the gold standard, the analysis of it contains elements of subjectivity and is dependent on the interpreter's training and experience. Of the 116 cases involving unvalidated or improper forensic evidence examined by Garrett and Neufeld, four percent of the exonerees were wrongly convicted because of incorrect DNA analysis.

In Chapter 5, we presented *District Attorney's Office for the Third Judicial District v. Osborne*, ___ U.S. ___, 129 S.Ct. 2308, 174 L.Ed.2d 38 (2009), in which the Supreme Court concluded that criminal defendants do not have a constitutional right of access to DNA evidence within the government's possession to test the evidence for potential use in post-conviction proceedings. In light of the material that follows, you may wish to reconsider *Osborne*, as well the observations made by Justice Alito in his concurring opinion about the probative value of forensic DNA analyses.

a. DNA Analysis: Is There a "Match"?

Young v. State

879 A.2d 44 (Md. 2005)

RAKER, Judge.

The primary issue we address in this appeal is whether the trial court erred in admitting evidence that there was a DNA "match" in the absence of accompanying statistical evidence. We conclude that the court did not err and hold that when a DNA method analyzes genetic markers at sufficient locations to arrive at an infinitesimal random match probability, expert opinion testimony of a match and of the source of the DNA evidence is admissible.

I.

... At trial, the State presented the following evidence: On September 27, 2001, a thirteen-year-old boy participated in an internet chat room called "Gay Twenties." Young, who was thirty-seven at the time, participated in the chat room as well. Young contacted the boy via instant messenger and telephone and arranged a rendezvous at the boy's apartment. The next day, Young visited the boy's home, and the two engaged in oral and anal sex. On October 2, Young visited the boy's home unannounced and again engaged him in anal sex. During the second encounter, the boy's mother returned home from work. After Young left, the boy eventually disclosed to his mother what had occurred. Later that night, the mother and child contacted the police. The boy was taken to the hospital where he was examined.

Identification was the primary issue at trial. The State offered three types of identification evidence. First, the State presented testimonial evidence, primarily that of the boy. Young challenged the testimonial evidence, emphasizing the boy and his mother's failure to identify Young in a police photo array and claiming that the boy was not credible. Second, the State tendered evidence that Young participated in the chat room. Young did not dispute that evidence. Third, the State presented DNA evidence.

The DNA evidence consisted of an analysis of two DNA samples. The first was obtained from the boy by a forensic nurse who examined him at the hospital and took a swab of his rectal area. The second was procured by an officer of the Prince George's County Police Department who, with Young's consent, took two swabs of Young's mouth.

In this appeal, Young challenges the testimony of Rupert Page, a forensic DNA analyst for the Prince George's County Police Department, who examined the samples on behalf of the State. The court received Page as an expert in profiling and forensic serology. Page testified that other than identical twins, no two people have the same DNA profile. He then described his testing of the anal swabs from the boy and the oral swabs from Young. Page explained that he used a process called differential extraction to separate the sperm cells from the boy's skin cells on the anal swab. He testified that he made a microscope slide of the sperm cells, obtained a DNA profile from the slide, and compared the profile to Young's profile obtained from the oral swabs.

In response to the State's questions, Page repeatedly testified that the two DNA profiles "matched." Page did not provide any basis for this conclusion, other than to state that his conclusion was based on his comparison of the two samples. He did not identify which DNA sequences he reviewed, and only on cross-examination did he note that he employed the polymerase chain reaction ("PCR") method. Page did not testify to the probability that a random person's profile would have matched the profile taken from the boy. Defense counsel objected repeatedly, arguing that, based on *Armstead v. State,* 342 Md. 38, 673 A.2d 221 (1996), the witness was required to provide probability statistics to accompany and support his conclusion....

The court permitted the witness to testify that the DNA profiles "matched," but did not allow him to testify that Young was the source of the DNA obtained from the anal swab. Instead, the court admitted into evidence Page's DNA report, over defense counsel's objection. In this report, Page noted that he employed the PCR method and the AmpFISTR Profiler Plus PCR Amplification Kit and AmpFISTR Cofiler PCR Amplification Kit to examine DNA markers along a combined thirteen loci and a gender identification locus.[3] Page concluded, "The sperm fraction of the Anal Swab (R1) contains DNA from a male. To a reasonable degree of scientific certainty (in the absence of an identical twin), Anthony Young (K1) is the source of the DNA obtained from the sperm fraction of the Anal Swab (R1)."[4] Page's report contained no statistical data to support his conclusion.

... The jury found Young guilty of one count of second degree sexual offense. The court sentenced Young to a term of twenty years incarceration.

Young noted a timely appeal to the Court of Special Appeals. In an unreported opinion, that court affirmed....

We granted Young's petition for a Writ of Certiorari. Young raises the following issue:

"Whether it was error to admit 'expert testimony' that there was a DNA 'match' in the absence of any foundation for such an assertion." ...

We conclude that scientific advances in DNA profiling enable an examiner employing particular methods and analyzing genetic markers at a sufficient number of loci to testify, to a reasonable degree of scientific certainty, to the source of the DNA evidence. We hold that in such circumstances, as in the instant case, the expert is not required to accompany his "match" testimony with contextual statistics. Accordingly, the Circuit Court did not err in admitting the expert's testimony of a match.

III.

We have described the science of DNA evidence as follows:

> "Deoxyribonucleic acid ('DNA') is the organic material that provides the genetic instructions for all individual hereditary characteristics. The importance of DNA for forensic purposes is that DNA does not vary within an individual and, with the exception of identical twins, no two individuals have the same DNA configuration.
>
> "The molecular structure of DNA is commonly referred to as a 'double helix,' which resembles a spiraling ladder, and which is composed of twisted double strands of repeated sequences of 'nucleotides.' The sides of the ladder are composed of the 'nucleotides,' which are organic bases that pair with one another to form the 'rungs' of the double helix. It is the repeating sequence of base pairs along the DNA double helix that comprise 'genes,' which determine the unique physiological traits of human beings. The specific position that a gene occupies is called its 'locus.' An individual's entire complement of DNA is known as the 'genome.'
>
> "The vast majority of the base pair sequences of human DNA are identical for all people. There are, however, a few DNA segments or genes, called 'polymorphic loci,' which are highly variable among individuals. The alternative forms of these individual polymorphic gene fragments are called 'alleles.' It is these polymorphisms that have great significance for forensic DNA analysis because they provide the basis for DNA identification.

3. AmpFISTR Profiler Plus PCR Amplification Kit and AmpFISTR Cofiler PCR Amplification Kit are commercial products marketed by Applied Biosystems.

4. Young later testified that he did not have an identical twin.

Gross v. State, 371 Md. 334, 339 n. 1, 809 A.2d 627, 630 n. 1 (2002).[5]

The polymerase chain reaction ("PCR") method of DNA analysis is an amplification procedure that reproduces repeatedly a short segment of DNA, making it possible to analyze minute or degraded samples. *See* ... Committee on DNA Forensic Science, National Research Council, *The Evaluation of Forensic DNA Evidence* 70 (1996) [hereinafter "NRC II"].

PCR analysis begins with a three-step process to amplify the DNA sample: (1) denaturization (the DNA is heated to separate the two strands); (2) annealing (primers containing nucleotide sequences that are complementary to the DNA region being amplified are added to the DNA sample, which bond to the gene when cooled); (3) extension (the gene is "copied" repeatedly in order to produce a larger sample of DNA for analysis). The PCR method can be carried out in a laboratory, with results obtained in a significantly shorter time than with the previously common restriction fragment length polymorphism ("RFLP") analysis. Additionally, the PCR method usually permits an exact identification of each allele, sidestepping RFLP's measurement uncertainties. These advantages, along with the method's utility for analyzing minute DNA samples, have resulted in a vast expansion in the use of the PCR method.

Once PCR amplification has been completed, analysis of the DNA profile and match determination can be conducted through the utilization of several different genetic markers. The markers employed by the laboratory in the instant case are short tandem repeats ("STR"). STRs are DNA sequences consisting of two to six base pairs. STRs particularly are useful in analyzing small DNA samples, because loci containing STRs are present with great frequency throughout the chromosomes. The loci have a large number of alleles and usually are susceptible to unique identification. *Id.* The FBI has designated thirteen core STR loci and a sex-typing marker (amelogenin) for identification in its national database of convicted felons, the Combined DNA Index System ("CODIS").[7]

DNA profiling typically is used to compare a suspect's DNA with a sample of DNA taken from a crime scene. "DNA profiling" is a catch-all term for a wide range of methods employed to study genetic variations, including RFLP and PCR/STR typing. All types of DNA analysis involve three basic steps: (1) processing or typing of the DNA samples (to produce x-ray films that indicate the lengths of the polymorphic fragments); (2) match determination (comparison of the films to determine whether any sets of fragments match); and (3) statistical analysis (to determine the statistical significance of any match between the two DNA samples). This three-step process produces two distinct, but interrelated, types of information: (1) molecular biological information (whether a match exists between an unknown DNA sample and a sample taken from a suspect); and (2) population genetics information (if a match exists, the statistical probability that the unknown sample came from a third party with the same DNA pattern as the suspect).

DNA evidence cannot be attributed conclusively to one person unless examiners analyze the entire DNA molecules of the DNA evidence and the DNA sample from that person respectively. Two unrelated individuals can have identical DNA fragments that are examined in a particular type of DNA analysis—*i.e.,* identical DNA patterns at the targeted loci. The underlying theory of the forensic use of DNA testing is that as the number and variability of the polymor-

5. At the time of our decision in *Armstead v. State,* 342 Md. 38, 673 A.2d 221 (1996), restriction fragment length polymorphism ("RFLP") analysis was the most common method used in forensic DNA analysis. RFLP involves the use of the DNA loci that contain "variable number tandem repeat" ("VNTR") sequences, which are stretches of DNA in which a short nucleotide core sequence of base pairs is repeated in tandem along the chromosome. As a result of VNTR sequencing, the length of a given allele, which is measured by the number of repeated base pairs, varies from person to person. VNTR loci particularly are useful in forensic DNA analysis because they have a very large number of different alleles. RFLP analysis yields distinct DNA profiles because the exact number of repeats, and therefore the length of the VNTR region, varies from one allele to another, and different VNTR alleles can be identified by their length. DNA fragments containing VNTRs are detected by specially constructed molecular "probes," which are short segments of single-stranded DNA with radioactive components that bind to specific DNA sequences.

7. Due to the small number of alleles on many of the loci used in PCR-based tests, more loci are required for the same statistical power provided by a few loci using RFLP/VNTRs. Twelve STR loci have a comparable discriminatory power to four or five VNTR loci.

phisms analyzed increases, the odds of two people coincidentally sharing the same DNA profile becomes vanishingly small.

Therefore, when a DNA "match" has been declared, a conclusive identification of a crime suspect as the source of the unknown DNA sample is not being made. Rather, the suspect simply has been "included" as a possible source of the DNA material, because the suspect's DNA sample has matched the crime scene DNA sample at a certain number of critical alleles. The issue still remains of just how many other people in the population could share the same DNA profile with the suspect.

Once a DNA match determination has been made, forensic scientists perform statistical analysis of population frequencies to estimate the statistical significance of the match, by calculating the likelihood that a random person (*i.e.,* not the person whose DNA actually was left at the crime scene) would match the crime scene sample, commonly referred to as the "random match probability." In order to make a statistical evaluation of a declared match, it is necessary to know how frequently a genotype occurs in the relevant reference population. Genotype frequency calculations are performed to determine the relative frequency of a random match within a sample population database.

The statistical significance of a match is determined by a two-step process: first, an initial determination is made regarding the random match probability of each polymorphic locus (the "individual allele frequency"); second, the individual allele frequencies are combined to determine the overall probability of possessing the entire matched DNA segment (the "aggregate DNA profile frequency"). These probability estimates are achieved using theoretical population genetics models in order to determine the frequency with which a given genetic pattern will occur in a defined population.

Probability calculations generally are made using the "product rule." The product rule, also known as the "multiplication method," states that the likelihood of a match occurring for an entire DNA segment can be determined by calculating the match probability for each polymorphic allele and then multiplying those probabilities together. To give a basic example, if a matching DNA sample contains two independent alleles, and there is a 10% chance of a random match of the first allele and a 20% chance of a random match of the second, the product rule would suggest that there was a two percent chance that a random person in the population shared the same DNA profile (.10 × .20 = .02).

IV.

The State argues that recent scientific advances in DNA analysis have resulted in infinitesimal random match probabilities, thus eliminating the necessity for the State to accompany match evidence with statistical evidence. The State is correct, to a large degree. The State is incorrect, however, in claiming that *all* techniques for analyzing DNA evidence produce infinitesimal random match probabilities.

Nine years have passed since *Armstead* was decided. As DNA analysis technology advances, examiners can utilize more precise techniques and view more loci. The fact remains that a match cannot identify the source of the relevant DNA sample conclusively unless the entire DNA molecule is viewed. Under certain circumstances, however, new technologies result in infinitesimal random match probabilities that would be deemed conclusive by all but mathematicians and philosophers. The instant case thus confronts us with the question of whether and to what extent these scientific advances have altered the holding of *Armstead* that contextual statistics *must* accompany match testimony.

Central to this question is whether, in such cases, a trial court may permit testimony of "source attribution." A witness testifying to "source attribution" or "uniqueness"[9] would state that in the absence of identical twins, it can be concluded to a reasonable scientific certainty that the evidence sample and the defendant sample came from the same person (*i.e.*, from the same source). Source attribution would fulfill

9. The terms "source attribution" and "uniqueness" appear to be used interchangeably. To the extent that the terms have been distinguished, authors have preferred "source attribution," in order to emphasize that the relevant reference population depends on the context of the case. Thus, the expert should calculate the probability that another person within the relevant population of potential sources of the DNA sample would share the DNA profile. The relevant population typically will not be the entire world population. For that reason, the expert attributes the source of the sample, rather than claiming that the defendant's DNA profile is "unique."

the need to give meaning to the term "match." Source attribution would inform the jury that the matching patterns are as unique as the Mona Lisa, and not as common as a picture with two eyes or even a four-leaf clover.

The first report of the National Research Council unambiguously presented accompanying statistical testimony as necessary and emphasized the inappropriateness of testifying to the uniqueness of the genotype. The National Research Council recognized the potential for unique identification, but noted that the typing systems employed at that time did not examine enough loci. The report stated as follows:

> "Can DNA typing uniquely identify the source of a sample? Because any two human genomes differ at about 3 million sites, no two persons (barring identical twins) have the same DNA sequence. Unique identification with DNA typing is therefore possible provided that enough sites of variation are examined.
>
> "However, the DNA typing systems used today examine only a few sites of variation and have only limited resolution for measuring the variability at each site."

Committee on DNA Forensic Science, National Research Council, *DNA Technology in Forensic Science* 74 (1992) [hereinafter "NRC I"]. The report then concluded that "[t]o say that two patterns match, without providing any scientifically valid estimate (or, at least, an upper bound) of the frequency with which such matches might occur by chance, is meaningless." *Id.* As a consequence of its comments about uniqueness, the report stated that the current DNA methods did not permit experts to testify to uniqueness. The report stated as follows: "Regardless of the calculated frequency, an expert should—given ... the relatively small number of loci used and the available population data—avoid assertions in court that a particular genotype is unique in the population." NRC I at 92.

With the rapid scientific advances in DNA typing, the National Research Council presented an updated view of uniqueness in its 1996 report. Defining "uniqueness," the Committee stated that an evidentiary profile "might be said to be unique if it is so rare that it becomes unreasonable to suppose that a second person in the population might have the same profile." [Committee on DNA Forensic Science, National Research Council, *The Evaluation of Forensic DNA Evidence* 70 (1996) [hereinafter "NRC II"]], at 136. Addressing the comment of the 1992 report that, given the small number of loci used, an expert should not testify to uniqueness, the 1996 report stated as follows:

> "Because more population data and loci already are available, and still more will be available soon, we are approaching the time when many scientists will wish to offer opinions about the source of incriminating DNA....
>
> "We can say only that after one reaches some threshold, the point at which DNA testing is extensive enough to warrant an opinion as to the identity of the source becomes a matter of judgment. Does a profile frequency of the reciprocal of twice the Earth's population suffice? Ten times? One hundred times? There is no 'bright-line' standard in law or science that can pick out exactly how small the probability of the existence of a given profile in more than one member of a population must be before assertions of uniqueness are justified.... There might already be cases in which it is defensible for an expert to assert that, assuming that there has been no sample mishandling or laboratory error, the profile's probable uniqueness means that the two DNA samples come from the same person.
>
> "Opinion testimony about uniqueness would simplify the presentation of evidence by dispensing with specific estimates of population frequencies or probabilities. If the basis of an opinion were attacked on statistical grounds, however, or if frequency or probability estimates were admitted, this advantage would be lost. Nevertheless, because the difference between a vanishingly small probability and an opinion of uniqueness is so slight, courts that decide on a criterion for uniqueness and determine that the criterion has been met may choose to allow the latter along with, or instead of, the former, when the scientific findings support such testimony." *Id.* at 194–95

The National Research Council's conclusions make clear that once profile frequency reaches a certain level of infinitesimalness, there is no scientific basis for requiring statistical testimony to accompany match testimony. The 1996 report accepted the concern about scientific justifiability articulated in the 1992 report and adopted as a rationale in *Armstead;* the 1996 report stated that "it would not be scientifically justifiable to speak of a match as proof of identity in the absence of underlying data that permit some reasonable estimate of how rare the matching characteristics actually are." NRC II at 192. It concluded, however, that once a profile may be considered unique, it is scientifically justifiable to testify to a match without accompanying statistics. *Id.* (stating that "[o]nce science has established that a methodology has some individualizing power, the legal system must determine whether and how best to import that technology into the trial process"). Additionally, the National Research Council concluded that at the point in which the profile is considered unique, source attribution would be an appropriate means to explain a match to the jury. *Id.* at 195. As the excerpt from the NRC II report indicates, there appears to be wide agreement that defining "uniqueness" is not a statistical task; rather courts or legislatures can determine under what circumstances and with less than what statistical probability a profile can be considered "unique."

... [F]ollowing the NRC II report, the FBI adopted a policy that its expert witnesses may testify to a match without citing statistics, when the probability of a match is less than one in 260 billion.

We conclude that there exist methods of DNA analysis employing certain markers that, when tested along a minimum number of loci, yield DNA profiles with an astonishingly small random match probability. When the random match probability is sufficiently minuscule, the DNA profile may be deemed unique. In such circumstances, testimony of a match is admissible without accompanying contextual statistics. In place of the statistics, the expert may inform the jury of the meaning of the match by identifying the person whose profile matched the profile of the DNA evidence as the source of that evidence; *i.e.* the expert may testify that in the absence of identical twins, it can be concluded to a reasonable scientific certainty that the evidence sample and the defendant sample came from the same person.[12]

A defendant is not without recourse when the State's expert identifies the defendant as the source of the DNA evidence. The defendant has the opportunity, and the right, to challenge the expert's conclusion in cross-examination. Md. Code § 10-915 of the Courts and Judicial Proceedings Article provides additional means for the defendant to challenge the expert's testimony that the defendant was the source of the DNA evidence. Under § 10-915(c), the party seeking to introduce the DNA evidence must, upon written request at least thirty days prior to the pro-

---

12. Under certain circumstances, the expert's caveat should take into account the higher random match probability for close relatives, not only identical twins. *See* L.M. Goos et al., *The Influence of Probabilistic Statements on the Evaluation of the Significance of a DNA Match,* 35 Can. Soc'y Forensic Sci. 77, 81 (2002). The FBI's DNA Advisory Board recommends the following approach for considering the impact of close relatives on source attribution:

> "[T]he possibility of a close relative (typically a brother) of the accused being in the pool of potential contributors of crime scene evidence should be considered in case-specific context. It is not appropriate to proffer that a close relative is a potential contributor of the evidence when there are no facts in evidence to suggest this instance is relevant. However, if a relative had access to a crime scene and there is reason to believe he/she could have been a contributor of the evidence, then the best action to take is to obtain a reference sample from the relative.... Typing ... will resolve the question of whether or not the relative carries the same DNA profile as the accused.
>
> "When a legitimate suspected relative cannot be typed, a probability statement can be provided. Given the accused DNA profile, the conditional probability that the relative has the same DNA profile can be calculated."

DNA Advisory Board, [*Statistical and Population Genetics Issues Affecting the Evaluation of the Frequency of Occurrence of DNA Profiles Calculated From Pertinent Population Database(s),* 2 Forensic Sci. Comm. No. 3 (July 2000), *at* http://www.fbi.gov/hq/lab/fsc/backissu/july2000/dnastat.htm].

When sufficient loci are analyzed, an expert can identify the defendant as the source of the DNA evidence, even taking into account related individuals.

ceeding, provide the other party with a "statement setting forth the genotype data and the profile frequencies for the databases utilized." § 10-915(c)(2)(v). The defendant may cross-examine the expert on the statistics and the expert's conclusions based on those statistics. Additionally, the defendant can challenge the weight of the DNA evidence, by, for example, questioning the expert about laboratory errors and contamination....

The method and marker employed in the instant case, PCR/STR along the thirteen loci recommended by the FBI and the sex-typing marker, produce "exceedingly small" random match probabilities. The thirteen STR loci selected by the FBI yield an average match probability of one in 180 trillion. When thirteen STR loci are analyzed, the random match probability for related individuals, even including siblings, is sufficiently low as to be characterized as unique.[13]

In the instant case, the State's witness testified, without citing any statistics, that the DNA sample taken from the victim's rectum matched the DNA sample provided by Young to the police. The State sought repeatedly to elicit testimony from Rupert Page that Young was the source of the DNA sample taken from the victim. While the Circuit Court sustained Young's objections to this questioning, the Circuit Court admitted Page's report. Page's report stated that he conducted a PCR/STR test to examine the anal swab from the victim and the oral swab from Young. The report contained a list of the thirteen STR loci and gender marker typed. Finally, in the report, Page concluded to a "reasonable degree of scientific certainty (in the absence of an identical twin)" that Young was the source of the DNA obtained from the boy. In other words, Page's testimony and his report (1) informed the Circuit Court that he had employed a DNA analysis technique that results in infinitesimal probabilities; (2) announced to the jury his conclusion that the DNA samples "matched"; and (2) explained to the jury that by "match" he meant that Young was the source of the DNA evidence. We hold that the Circuit Court did not err in admitting the testimony and the report, and, accordingly, we affirm the decision of the Court of Special Appeals....

Notes and Questions

1. Several accessible explanations of the science underlying DNA analysis are available. Sources include: Max M. Houck & Jay A. Siegel, *Fundamentals of Forensic Science* 255–281 (New York: Elsevier, 2d ed. 2010); Paul C. Giannelli & Edward J. Imwinkelried, 2 *Scientific Evidence* 1-133 (Newark, NJ: LexisNexis, 4th ed. 2007); Victor W. Weedn, "DNA Analysis," in Cyril H. Wecht & John T. Rago (eds.), *Forensic Science and Law: Investigative Applications in Criminal, Civil, and Family Justice* 419–429 (Boca Raton, FL: Taylor & Francis 2006); Lawrence Koblinsky, Thomas F. Liotti & Jamel Oeser-Sweat, *DNA: Forensic and Legal Applications* (Hoboken, NJ: John Wiley & Sons 2005); National Research Council, Committee on DNA Forensic Science, *The Evaluation of Forensic DNA Evidence* (Washington, DC: National Academy Press 1996). *See also* David H. Kaye, *The Double Helix and the Law of Evidence* (Cambridge, MA: Harvard University Press 2010).

2. In *Young v. State*, the Maryland Court of Appeals approved the admissibility of expert testimony opining that there was "a DNA 'match'" between the defendant and a crime scene sample notwithstanding the absence of statistical evidence providing context for

13. *See* [Bruce Budowle et al., *Source Attribution of a Forensic DNA Profile*, 2 Forensic Sci. Comm. No. 3 (July 2000), *at* http://www.fbi.gov/hq/lab/fsc/backissu/july2000/source.htm] (citing probabilities for thirteen STR loci as one in 40,000 among full siblings and one in a billion for other relatives and concluding that "source attribution should be possible routinely for scenarios where relatives of the suspect cannot be typed with typing results of the suspect from 11–13 of the CODIS STR loci"). We hold that a PCR/STR test along thirteen loci produces a sufficiently minuscule random match probability to make expert testimony of uniqueness admissible.

that conclusion. In contrast, when DNA analysis does not identify a defendant as the likely source of biological evidence—but instead results in the conclusion that the defendant "cannot be excluded" as the source, or that the defendant's DNA is "consistent with" that found at a crime scene—courts have been reluctant to allow expert testimony that is not accompanied by explanatory statistics. Thus, in *Commonwealth v. Mattei*, 920 N.E.2d 845 (Mass. 2010), the prosecution's forensics expert testified that DNA found on the sweatshirt of the victim of a sexual assault "showed a 'match' with DNA samples from the defendant and the victim." *Id.*, 920 N.E.2d, at 852. That testimony was supported by accompanying statistical probabilities.

> The expert testified that the probability of a randomly selected person having a DNA profile that, like the victim's, matched the profile of the DNA in the sample from the sweatshirt sleeve was one in 1.373 quadrillion for the Caucasian population, one in 135.9 quadrillion for the African-American population, and one in 662.3 quadrillion for the Hispanic population. The probability of a randomly selected person having a DNA profile that, like the defendant's, matched the profile of the DNA in the sample from the sweatshirt front was one in 631.7 quadrillion for the Caucasian population, one in 5.152 quintillion for the African-American population, and one in 13.51 quintillion for the Hispanic population. 920 N.E.2d, at 852, n. 17.

Biological evidence found elsewhere, on the defendant's sweatshirt and on a doorknob within the victim's apartment, contained DNA from at least two sources. The expert testified that she could not distinguish between the profiles in those mixtures. With respect to the evidence found on the defendant's sweatshirt, "the expert testified that the *victim* was 'included' or 'could not be excluded' as a potential source of" the DNA.

> As to the swabbing of blood found on the ... doorknob ..., the expert testified that this also showed the presence of DNA from more than one source, and a DNA test showed the mixture was 'consistent with' DNA from the victim and from the defendant. According to the expert, the victim and the defendant were both "included" as "potential contributor[s]" to the mixture, i.e., neither the victim nor the defendant "were excluded as a potential contributor to the DNA mixture on the interior of the doorknob." ... The expert did not testify as to the probability that an individual randomly selected from the population would also 'not be excluded' by these tests, nor did she provide any other indication as to the meaning of a "not excluded" result. 920 N.E.2d, at 853–854.

The Massachusetts Supreme Judicial Court found reversible error in the admission of that testimony.

We have ... held that in a criminal trial we will "not permit the admission of test results showing a DNA match (a positive result) without telling the jury anything about the likelihood of that match occurring." *Commonwealth v. Curnin*, 409 Mass. 218, 222 n. 7, 565 N.E.2d 440 (1991). We have explained our approach by stating that "[e]vidence of a match based on correctly used testing systems is of little or no value without reliable evidence indicating the significance of the match, that is, 'evidence of the probability of a random match of [the victim's or] the defendant's DNA in the general population.'" *Commonwealth v. Rosier*, 425 Mass. 807, 813, 685 N.E.2d 739 (1997).

The same reasoning applies to evidence that a DNA test, although resulting in less than a complete "match," could not exclude a particular individual as a potential contributor. Without reliable accompanying evidence as to the likelihood that the test could not exclude other individuals in a given population, the jury have no way to evaluate the meaning of the result. As the dissent in *Commonwealth v. Mattei,* 72 Mass. App. 510, 522, 892 N.E.2d 826 (2008) (Rubin, J., dissenting), noted, there is no way to determine whether the results of nonexclusion in this case mean "that half the people in the world could have left the DNA that was found in the mixture[s]" on the interior doorknob or on the defendant's sweatpants. We simply do not know.

Further, admitting evidence of a failure to exclude without accompanying evidence that properly interprets that result creates a greater risk of misleading the jury and unfairly prejudicing the defendant than admission of a "match" without accompanying statistics. As to "matches," it is "generally well known that DNA testing often allows scientists to identify a particular individual from among millions." *Peters v. State,* 18 P.3d 1224, 1227 (Alaska Ct.App.2001). Jurors are routinely presented with exceedingly infinitesimal random match probabilities. See, e.g., *Commonwealth v. Gaynor,* 443 Mass. 245, 249, 820 N.E.2d 233 (2005) ("one in 64 quadrillion African-Americans"); *Commonwealth v. Girouard,* 436 Mass. 657, 669 n. 4, 766 N.E.2d 873 (2002) ("one in fifty-seven trillion" Caucasians); *Commonwealth v. Thad T.,* 59 Mass. App. 497, 505, 796 N.E.2d 869 (2003) ("one in 320 trillion" African-Americans). Indeed in this case, as to the "matches" identified on the sweatshirt, the Commonwealth's expert testified to random match probabilities as small as one in 13.51 quintillion. If the jury are not provided with similar statistical evidence where the DNA test result is a "nonexclusion," there is a real risk that jurors will be misled into thinking that these DNA test results are similarly significant and that the nonexclusion evidence is similarly conclusive as to the "matched" contributor's identity, when in fact the actual meaning of such results can vary substantially.[28]

The *Mattei* opinion notes that courts in different jurisdictions have arrived at varying conclusions on the issue presented, and that under some circumstances have allowed "nonexclusion" results to be admitted without accompanying statistics. 920 N.E.2d, at 855–856 & nn. 25 & 26. For a decision agreeing with the result reached in *Mattei, see Deloney v. State,* 938 N.E.2d 724 (Ind. App. 2010) (but finding the expert testimony to be harmless error).

3. In the NAS report, *Strengthening Forensic Science,* the Committee on Identifying the Needs of the Forensic Science Community, reported that "FBI quality guidelines require that reports from forensic DNA analysis must contain, at a minimum, a description of the evidence examined, a listing of the loci analyzed, a description of the methodology, results and/or conclusions, and an interpretative statement (either quantitative or qualitative) concerning the inference to be drawn from the analysis."[49]

28. The Commonwealth argues that requiring the presentation of statistical analysis as an accompaniment to testimony that DNA test results could not exclude an individual as a potential source "could prove highly damaging to defendants as a class," given advancements in technology allowing results short of a complete "match" nevertheless to be strongly discriminating among potential contributors. There is nothing in the record to support the claim, and our own precedents reveal that not all DNA tests result in extremely low random match probabilities. See, e.g., *Commonwealth v. O'Laughlin,* 446 Mass. 188, 197, 843 N.E.2d 617 (2006) ("one in two of any randomly selected individuals"); *Commonwealth v. Gaynor, supra* at 250, 820 N.E.2d 233 ("one in 490 African-Americans"); *Commonwealth v. McNickles,* 434 Mass. 839, 851, 753 N.E.2d 131 (2001) ("one out of eighty-three Hispanics").

b. The Prosecutor's Fallacy

McDaniel v. Brown

___ U.S. ___, 130 S.Ct. 665, 175 L.Ed.2d 582 (2010)

PER CURIAM.

In *Jackson v. Virginia,* 443 U.S. 307 (1979), we held that a state prisoner is entitled to habeas corpus relief if a federal judge finds that "upon the record evidence adduced at the trial no rational trier of fact could have found proof of guilt beyond a reasonable doubt." *Id.,* at 324. A Nevada jury convicted respondent of rape; the evidence presented included DNA evidence matching respondent's DNA profile. Nevertheless, relying upon a report prepared by a DNA expert over 11 years after the trial, the Federal District Court applied the *Jackson* standard and granted the writ. A divided Court of Appeals affirmed. *Brown v. Farwell,* 525 F.3d 787 (C.A.9 2008). We granted certiorari to consider whether those courts misapplied *Jackson.* Because the trial record includes both the DNA evidence and other convincing evidence of guilt, we conclude that they clearly did.

I

Around 1 a.m. on January 29, 1994, 9-year-old Jane Doe was brutally raped in the bedroom of her trailer. Respondent Troy Brown was convicted of the crime. During and since his trial, respondent has steadfastly maintained his innocence.[1] He was, however, admittedly intoxicated when the crime occurred, and after he awoke on the following morning he told a friend "'he wished that he could remember what did go on or what went on.'"

Troy and his brother Travis resided near Jane Doe in the same trailer park. Their brother Trent and his wife Raquel lived in the park as well, in a trailer across the street from Jane Doe's. Both Troy and Trent were acquainted with Jane Doe's family; Troy had visited Jane Doe's trailer several times. Jane did not know Travis. The evening of the attack, Jane's mother, Pam, took Jane to Raquel and Trent's trailer to babysit while the three adults went out for about an hour. Raquel and Trent returned at about 7:30 p.m. and took Jane home at about 9:30 p.m. Pam stayed out and ended up drinking and playing pool with Troy at a nearby bar called the Peacock Lounge. Troy knew that Jane and her 4-year-old sister were home alone because he answered the phone at the bar when Jane called for her mother earlier that evening.

Troy consumed at least 10 shots of vodka followed by beer chasers, and was so drunk that he vomited on himself while he was walking home after leaving the Peacock at about 12:15 a.m. Jane called her mother to report the rape at approximately 1 a.m. Although it would have taken a sober man less than 15 minutes to walk home, Troy did not arrive at his trailer until about 1:30 a.m. He was wearing dark jeans, a cowboy hat, a black satin jacket, and boots. Two witnesses saw a man dressed in dark jeans, a cowboy hat, and a black satin jacket stumbling in the road between the two trailers shortly after 1 a.m.

The bedroom where the rape occurred was dark, and Jane was unable to conclusively identify her assailant. When asked whom he reminded her of, she mentioned both Troy and his brother Trent. Several days after the rape, she identified a man she saw on television (Troy) as her assailant but then stated that the man who had sent flowers attacked her. It was Trent and Raquel who had sent her flowers, not Troy. She was unable to identify Troy as her assailant out of a photo lineup, and she could not identify her assailant at trial. The night of the rape, however, she said her attacker was wearing dark jeans, a black jacket with a zipper, boots, and a watch. She also vividly remembered that the man "stunk real, real bad" of "cologne, or some beer or puke or something."

Some evidence besides Jane's inconsistent identification did not inculpate Troy. Jane testified that she thought she had bitten her assailant, but Troy did not have any bite marks on his hands when examined by a police officer approximately four hours after the attack. Jane stated that her assailant's jacket had a zipper (Troy's did not) and that he wore a watch (Troy claimed he did not). Additionally, there was conflicting testimony as to when Troy left the Peacock and when Pam received Jane's call re-

1. He denied involvement when a police officer claimed (wrongly) that the police had found his fingerprints in Jane's bedroom, and he even denied involvement when the sentencing judge told him that acceptance of responsibility would garner him leniency.

porting the rape. The witnesses who saw a man stumbling between the two trailers reported a bright green logo on the back of the jacket, but Troy's jacket had a yellow and orange logo. Finally, because Jane thought she had left a night light on when she went to bed, the police suspected the assailant had turned off the light. The only usable fingerprint taken from the light did not match Troy's and the police did not find Troy's fingerprints in the trailer.

Other physical evidence, however, pointed to Troy. The police recovered semen from Jane's underwear and from the rape kit. The State's expert, Renee Romero, tested the former and determined that the DNA matched Troy's and that the probability another person from the general population would share the same DNA (the "random match probability") was only 1 in 3,000,000. Troy's counsel did not call his own DNA expert at trial, although he consulted with an expert in advance who found no problems with Romero's test procedures. At some time before sentencing, Troy's family had additional DNA testing done. That testing showed semen taken from the rape kit matched Troy's DNA, with a random match probability of 1 in 10,000.

The jury found Troy guilty of sexual assault and sentenced him to life with the possibility of parole after 10 years. On direct appeal, the Nevada Supreme Court considered Troy's claim that his conviction was not supported by sufficient evidence, analyzing "whether the jury, acting reasonably, could have been convinced of [Troy's] guilt beyond a reasonable doubt." *Brown v. Nevada*, 934 P.2d 235, 241 (Nev. 1997) *(per curiam)*. The court rejected the claim....

In 2001, respondent sought state postconviction relief, claiming, *inter alia*, that his trial counsel was constitutionally ineffective for failing to object to the admission of the DNA evidence.... The state postconviction court denied relief, and the Nevada Supreme Court affirmed.

Respondent thereafter filed this federal habeas petition, claiming there was insufficient evidence to convict him on the sexual assault charges and that the Nevada Supreme Court's rejection of his claim was both contrary to, and an unreasonable application of, *Jackson*. He did not bring a typical *Jackson* claim, however. Rather than argue that the totality of the evidence admitted against him at trial was constitutionally insufficient, he argued that some of the evidence should be excluded from the *Jackson* analysis. In particular, he argued that Romero's testimony related to the DNA evidence was inaccurate and unreliable in two primary respects: Romero mischaracterized the random match probability and misstated the probability of a DNA match among his brothers. Absent that testimony, he contended, there was insufficient evidence to convict him.

In support of his claim regarding the accuracy of Romero's testimony, respondent submitted a report prepared by Laurence Mueller, a professor in ecology and evolutionary biology (Mueller Report). The District Court supplemented the record with the Mueller Report, even though it was not presented to any state court....

Relying upon the Mueller Report, the District Court set aside the "unreliable DNA testimony" and held that without the DNA evidence "a reasonable doubt would exist in the mind of any rational trier of fact." The court granted respondent habeas relief on his *Jackson* claim.[3]

The Ninth Circuit affirmed. 525 F.3d 787. The court held the Nevada Supreme Court had unreasonably applied *Jackson*. The Court of Appeals first reasoned "the admission of Romero's unreliable and misleading testimony violated Troy's due process rights," so the District Court was correct to exclude it. It then "weighed the sufficiency of the remaining evidence," including the District Court's "catalogu[e] [of] the numerous inconsistencies that would raise a reasonable doubt as to Troy's guilt in the mind of any rational juror." In light of the "stark" conflicts in the evidence and the State's concession that there was insufficient evidence absent the DNA evidence, the court held it was objectively unreasonable for the Nevada Supreme Court to reject respondent's insufficiency-of-the-evidence claim.

We granted certiorari to consider two questions: the proper standard of review for a *Jackson* claim on federal habeas, and whether such a claim may rely upon evidence outside the trial record that goes to the reliability of trial evidence.

---

3. The District Court also granted habeas relief on respondent's claim that he was denied effective assistance of counsel with respect to his attorney's handling of the DNA evidence and failure to adequately investigate the victim's stepfather as an alternative suspect. The Court of Appeals did not consider those claims on appeal and they are not now before us.

II

Respondent's claim has now crystallized into a claim about the import of two specific inaccuracies in the testimony related to the DNA evidence, as indicated by the Mueller Report. The Mueller Report does not challenge Romero's qualifications as an expert or the validity of any of the tests that she performed. Mueller instead contends that Romero committed the so-called "prosecutor's fallacy" and that she underestimated the probability of a DNA match between respondent and one of his brothers.

The prosecutor's fallacy is the assumption that the random match probability is the same as the probability that the defendant was not the source of the DNA sample. See Nat. Research Council, Comm. on DNA Forensic Science, The Evaluation of Forensic DNA Evidence 133 (1996) ("Let P equal the probability of a match, given the evidence genotype. The fallacy is to say that P is also the probability that the DNA at the crime scene came from someone other than the defendant"). In other words, if a juror is told the probability a member of the general population would share the same DNA is 1 in 10,000 (random match probability), and he takes that to mean there is only a 1 in 10,000 chance that someone other than the defendant is the source of the DNA found at the crime scene (source probability), then he has succumbed to the prosecutor's fallacy. It is further error to equate source probability with probability of guilt, unless there is no explanation other than guilt for a person to be the source of crime-scene DNA. This faulty reasoning may result in an erroneous statement that, based on a random match probability of 1 in 10,000, there is a .01% chance the defendant is innocent or a 99.99% chance the defendant is guilty.

The Mueller Report does not dispute Romero's opinion that only 1 in 3,000,000 people would have the same DNA profile as the rapist. Mueller correctly points out, however, that some of Romero's testimony—as well as the prosecutor's argument—suggested that the evidence also established that there was only a .000033% chance that respondent was innocent. The State concedes as much. For example, the prosecutor argued at closing the jury could be "99.999967 percent sure" in this case. And when the prosecutor asked Romero, in a classic example of erroneously equating source probability with random match probability, whether "it [would] be fair to say ... that the chances that the DNA found in the panties—the semen in the panties—and the blood sample, the likelihood that it is not Troy Brown would be .000033," Romero ultimately agreed that it was "not inaccurate" to state it that way.

Looking at Romero's testimony as a whole, though, she also indicated that she was merely accepting the mathematical equivalence between 1 in 3,000,000 and the percentage figure. At the end of the colloquy about percentages, she answered affirmatively the court's question whether the percentage was "the same math just expressed differently." She pointed out that the probability a brother would match was greater than the random match probability, which also indicated to the jury that the random match probability is not the same as the likelihood that someone other than Troy was the source of the DNA.

The Mueller Report identifies a second error in Romero's testimony: her estimate of the probability that one or more of Troy's brothers' DNA would match. Romero testified there was a 1 in 6,500 (or .02%) probability that one brother would share the same DNA with another. When asked whether "that change[s] at all with two brothers," she answered no. According to Mueller, Romero's analysis was misleading in two respects. First, she used an assumption regarding the parents under which siblings have the lowest chance of matching that is biologically possible, but even under this stingy assumption she reported the chance of two brothers matching (1 in 6,500) as much lower than it is (1 in 1,024 under her assumption). Second, using the assumptions Mueller finds more appropriate, the probability of a single sibling matching respondent is 1 in 263, the probability that among two brothers one or more would match is 1 in 132, and among four brothers it is 1 in 66.

In sum, the two inaccuracies upon which this case turns are testimony equating random match probability with source probability, and an underestimate of the likelihood that one of Troy's brothers would also match the DNA left at the scene.

III

Although we granted certiorari to review respondent's *Jackson* claim, the parties now agree that the Court of Appeals' resolution of his claim under *Jackson* was in error. Indeed, respondent argues the Court of Appeals did not decide his case under *Jackson* at all, but instead resolved the question whether admission of Romero's inaccurate testimony rendered his trial fundamentally unfair and then applied *Jackson* to determine whether that error was harmless....

Respondent no longer argues it was proper for the District Court to admit the Mueller Report for the purpose of evaluating his *Jackson* claim, and concedes the "purpose of a *Jackson* analysis is to determine whether the jury acted in a rational manner in returning a guilty verdict based on the evidence before it, not whether improper evidence violated due process".....

Respondent therefore correctly concedes that a reviewing court must consider all of the evidence admitted at trial when considering a *Jackson* claim....

Even if the Court of Appeals could have considered it, the Mueller Report provided no warrant for entirely excluding the DNA evidence or Romero's testimony from that court's consideration. The Report did not contest that the DNA evidence matched Troy. That DNA evidence remains powerful inculpatory evidence even though the State concedes Romero overstated its probative value by failing to dispel the prosecutor's fallacy. And Mueller's claim that Romero used faulty assumptions and underestimated the probability of a DNA match between brothers indicates that two experts do not agree with one another, not that Romero's estimates were unreliable.

Mueller's opinion that "the chance that among four brothers one or more would match is 1 in 66," is substantially different from Romero's estimate of a 1 in 6,500 chance that one brother would match. But even if Romero's estimate is wrong, our confidence in the jury verdict is not undermined. First, the estimate that is more pertinent to this case is 1 in 132—the probability of a match among two brothers—because two of Troy's four brothers lived in Utah. Second, although Jane Doe mentioned Trent as her assailant, and Travis lived in a nearby trailer, the evidence indicates that both (unlike Troy) were sober and went to bed early on the night of the crime. Even under Mueller's odds, a rational jury could consider the DNA evidence to be powerful evidence of guilt.

Furthermore, the Court of Appeals' discussion of the non-DNA evidence departed from the deferential review that *Jackson* and § 2254(d)(1) demand.....

For example, the court highlights conflicting testimony regarding when Troy left the Peacock. It is true that if a juror were to accept the testimony of one bartender that Troy left the bar at 1:30 a.m., then Troy would have left the bar after the attack occurred. Yet the jury could have credited a different bartender's testimony that Troy left the Peacock at around 12:15 a.m. Resolving the conflict in favor of the prosecution, the jury must have found that Troy left the bar in time to be the assailant. It is undisputed that Troy washed his clothes immediately upon returning home. The court notes this is "plausibly consistent with him being the assailant" but also that he provided an alternative reason for washing his clothes. Viewed in the light most favorable to the prosecution, the evidence supports an inference that Troy washed the clothes immediately to clean blood from them.

To be sure, the court's *Jackson* analysis relied substantially upon a concession made by the State in state postconviction proceedings that "absent the DNA findings, there was insufficient evidence to convict [Troy] of the crime." But that concession posited a situation in which there was no DNA evidence at all, not a situation in which some pieces of testimony regarding the DNA evidence were called into question. In sum, the Court of Appeals' analysis failed to preserve "the factfinder's role as weigher of the evidence" by reviewing "*all of the evidence* ... in the light most favorable to the prosecution," *Jackson, supra*, at 319, and it further erred in finding that the Nevada Supreme Court's resolution of the *Jackson* claim was objectively unreasonable.

IV

Resolution of the *Jackson* claim does not end our consideration of this case because respondent asks us to affirm on an alternative ground. He contends the two errors "in describing the statistical meaning" of the DNA evidence rendered his trial fundamentally unfair and denied him due process of law....

As respondent acknowledges, in order to prevail on this claim, he would have to show that the state court's adjudication of the claim was "contrary to, or involved an unreasonable application of, clearly established Federal law." 28 U.S.C. § 2254(d)(1). The clearly established law he points us to is *Manson v. Brathwaite*, 432 U.S. 98, 114 (1977), in which we held that when the police have used a suggestive eyewitness identification procedure, "reliability is the linchpin in determining" whether an eyewitness identification may be admissible, with reliability determined according to factors set out in *Neil v. Biggers*, 409 U.S. 188 (1972). Respondent argues that the admission of the inaccurate DNA testimony violated *Brathwaite* because the testimony was "identification testimony," 432 U.S., at 114, was "unnecessarily suggestive," *id.*, at 113, and was unreliable.

Respondent has forfeited this claim, which he makes for the very first time in his brief on the merits in this Court. Respondent did not present his new "DNA due process" claim in his federal habeas petition, but instead consistently argued that Romero's testimony should be excluded from the *Jackson* analysis simply because it was "unreliable" and that the due process violation occurred because the remaining evidence was insufficient to convict.... Recognizing that his *Jackson* claim cannot prevail, respondent tries to rewrite his federal habeas petition. His attempt comes too late, however, and he cannot now start over.

* * *

We have stated before that "DNA testing can provide powerful new evidence unlike anything known before." *District Attorney's Office for Third Judicial Dist. v. Osborne,* 557 U.S. ___, ___, 129 S.Ct. 2308, 2316 (2009). Given the persuasiveness of such evidence in the eyes of the jury, it is important that it be presented in a fair and reliable manner. The State acknowledges that Romero committed the prosecutor's fallacy, and the Mueller Report suggests that Romero's testimony may have been inaccurate regarding the likelihood of a match with one of respondent's brothers. Regardless, ample DNA and non-DNA evidence in the record adduced at trial supported the jury's guilty verdict under *Jackson,* and we reject respondent's last minute attempt to recast his claim under *Brathwaite.* The Court of Appeals did not consider, however, the ineffective-assistance claims on which the District Court also granted respondent habeas relief. Accordingly, the judgment of the Court of Appeals is reversed, and the case is remanded for further proceedings consistent with this opinion....

Notes and Questions

1. In the ruling overturned by the Supreme Court, *Brown v. Farwell,* 525 F.3d 787, 795–796 (9th Cir. 2008), the court of appeals explained "the prosecutor's fallacy," as reflected in the testimony and argument presented in Troy Brown's trial, as follows:

... Romero testified that there was a 99.99967 percent chance that Troy's DNA was the same as the DNA discovered in Jane's underwear—or, in other words, that the science demonstrated a near 100 percent chance of Troy's guilt. This assertion was incorrect, as it falls directly into what has become known as the "prosecutor's fallacy." The prosecutor's fallacy occurs when the prosecutor elicits testimony that confuses source probability with random match probability. Put another way, a prosecutor errs when he "presents statistical evidence to suggest that the [DNA] evidence indicates the likelihood of the defendant's guilt rather than the odds of the evidence having been found in a randomly selected sample." *United States v. Shonubi,* 895 F.Supp. 460, 516 (E.D.N.Y.1995) (internal quotation marks and citation omitted), *vacated on other grounds,* 103 F.3d 1085 (2d Cir.1997); *see also United States v. Chischilly,* 30 F.3d 1144, 1157 (9th Cir.1994) ("To illustrate, suppose the ... evidence establishes that there is a one in 10,000 chance of a random match. The jury might equate this likelihood with source probability by believing that there is a one in 10,000 chance that the evidentiary sample did not come from the defendant. This equation of random match probability with source probability is known as the prosecutor's fallacy."); Richard Lempert, *Some Caveats Concerning DNA as Criminal Identification Evidence,* 13 CARDOZO L. REV. 303, 305–06 (1991). Such a fallacy is dangerous, as the probability of finding a random match can be much higher than the probability of matching one individual, given the weight of the non-DNA evidence. *See* William C. Thompson and Edward L. Schumann, *Interpretation of Statistical Evidence in Criminal Trials,* 11 L. AND HUM. BEHAV. 167, 170–71 (1987) (noting that the prosecutor's fallacy "could lead to serious error, particularly where the other evidence in the case is weak and therefore the prior probability of guilt is low").

Here, Romero initially testified that Troy's DNA matched the DNA found in Jane's underwear, and that 1 in 3,000,000 people randomly selected from the population would also match the DNA found in Jane's underwear (random match probability). After the prosecutor pressed her to put this another way, Romero testified that there was a 99.99967 percent chance that the DNA found in Jane's underwear was from Troy's blood (source probability). This testimony was misleading, as it improperly conflated random match probability with source probability. In fact, the former testimony (1 in 3,000,000) is the probability of a match between an innocent person selected randomly from the population; this is not the same as the probability that Troy's DNA was the same as the DNA found in Jane's underwear, which would prove his guilt. Statistically, the probability of guilt given a DNA match is based on a complicated formula known as Bayes's Theorem, *see id.* at 170–71 n. 2, and the 1 in 3,000,000 probability described by Romero is but one of the factors in this formula. Significantly, another factor is the strength of the non-DNA evidence. Here, Romero improperly conflated random match and source probability, an error that is especially profound given the weakness of the remaining evidence against Troy. In sum, Romero's testimony that Troy was 99.99967 percent likely to be guilty was based on her scientifically flawed DNA analysis, which means that Troy was most probably convicted based on the jury's consideration of false, but highly persuasive, evidence.

2. The seminal scholarly article describing the prosecutor's fallacy and related misstatements or misinterpretations of statistical information based on forensic test results is William C. Thompson & Edward L. Schumann, "Interpretation of Statistical Evidence in Criminal Trials: The Prosecutor's Fallacy and the Defense Attorney's Fallacy," 11 *Law & Human Behavior* 167 (1987). Another helpful source is Dawn McQuiston-Surrett & Michael J. Saks, "Communicating Opinion Evidence in the Forensic Identification Sciences: Accuracy and Impact," 59 *Hastings Law Journal* 1159 (2008). Those authors offer another example of the prosecutor's fallacy, as well as its counterpart, "the defense attorney's fallacy."

> These [fallacies] can occur when an expert opines that a match exists between crime scene evidence and evidence known to originate with the defendant, and data are offered so that the fact finders have some basis for evaluating the likelihood that the two samples shared a common source, namely, the defendant. As an example, a long blond hair is found at a crime scene and a suspect with long blond hair is arrested. The significance of the long blond hair depends, to an important degree, on how common or how rare that trait is in the population; such evidence would be more probative in China than it would be in Sweden.
>
> In the Prosecutor's Fallacy, fact finders mistakenly think that the frequency of the trait in the population tells them something about the probability of guilt or innocence of the particular defendant. For example, if fact finders learn that a trait shared by the perpetrator and the defendant occur in 2% of the population, many of them infer that the chance that the defendant is not the source is only 2%. In the Defense Attorney's Fallacy, fact finders might realize that a population rate of 2% would mean that in a city of, say, 1,000,000 people, 20,000 would have the trait, and mistakenly regard the evidence as having virtually no probative value on the question of identity. The first error overvalues the evidence and the second undervalues it. *Id.,* at 1178–79 (footnotes omitted).

Other useful references include Robert Aronson & Jacqueline McMurtrie, "The Use and Misuse of High-Tech Evidence by Prosecutors: Ethical and Evidentiary Issues," 76 *Fordham Law Review* 1453, 1477–1480 (2007); Dale A. Nance & Scott B. Morris, "Juror Understanding of DNA Evidence: An Empirical Assessment of Presentation Formats for Trace Evidence With a Relatively Small Random-Match Probability," 34 *Journal of Legal Studies* 395 (2005); Jonathan J. Koehler, "The Psychology of Numbers in the Courtroom: How to Make DNA-Match Statistics Seem Impressive or Insufficient," 74 *Southern California Law Review* 1275 (2001); Margaret A. Berger, "Laboratory Error Seen Through the Lens of Science and

Policy," 30 *University of California at Davis Law Review* 1081, 1106–1108 (1997). For a compelling example of the misuse of the likelihood ratio, see William C. Thompson, "Painting the Target Around the Matching Profile: The Texas Sharpshooter Fallacy in Forensic DNA Interpretation," 8 *Law, Probability and Risk* 257 (2009).

3. When the prosecutor and/or defense attorney misrepresent likelihood ratios, matching statistics, and the like, it stands to reason that triers of fact also will misunderstand. In an article entitled, "When Are People Persuaded by DNA Match Statistics?," Jonathan J. Koehler demonstrated that the manner in which the DNA evidence was framed influenced ratings of guilt.[50] Koehler created four conditions in which the DNA match statistic was exactly the same but framed and presented differently: 1) single-target probability (*i.e.*, the probability that the suspect would match is 0.1%); 2) single-target frequency (*i.e.*, the frequency with which the suspect would match is 1 in 1,000; 3) multi-target probability (*i.e.*, 0.1% of the people would also match); and 4) multi-target frequency (*i.e.*, 1 in 1,000 people would also match). When the DNA match statistics were presented in the multi-target frequency condition, only 3% voted guilty; in contrast, in the other three conditions, guilty rates were approximately 25% despite the fact that all match statistics were the same. The study suggests that the conviction or acquittal of a defendant can be heavily dependent on whether DNA match statistics are presented accurately by the expert, and in turn, interpreted correctly by the prosecuting or defense attorneys.

D. Laboratory Scandals and Forensic Fraud

When forensic evidence contributes to wrongful convictions the typical problems involve simple error in the collection or analysis of the evidence, mistaken or overstated conclusions about the link between the evidence and the defendant, or jurors' misunderstanding or confusion about the probative value of the evidence. Sometimes, however, the explanations are more sinister. Laboratory scandals, including inexcusable lapses in procedure and oversight, as well as affirmative misconduct and fraud, also have resulted in miscarriages of justice.

In February 2010, Gregory Taylor, who had been found guilty of murder in North Carolina in 1993 and incarcerated since then, "became the first convicted felon in U.S. history to be exonerated by a state-mandated innocence commission."[51] A three-judge panel ruled that he had been wrongfully convicted following an investigation conducted by the North Carolina Innocence Inquiry Commission. Taylor's exoneration helped shed light on a practice followed in hundreds of cases by the North Carolina State Bureau of Investigation's (SBI) crime laboratory of withholding laboratory reports that were potentially favorable to defendants. At Taylor's trial, evidence was presented that human blood was found on the vehicle Taylor was driving on the night of the murder. A follow-up test, which concluded that no blood was on the vehicle, was not divulged. An audit commissioned by North Carolina's Attorney General "showed that the crime lab's failures to conduct tests or inform court officials of blood test results that might help the defendant may have involved as many as 229 cases."[52] A legislative committee subsequently recommended numerous changes in the State's crime laboratory operating procedures, including:

- changing state law to make clear all data calculations and writings related to lab tests on evidence should be made available to a defendant during the discovery process, and to make it grounds for obstruction of justice if certain data is deliberately withheld.

- allowing other accreditation agencies to certify labs that perform forensic work for the state....
- requiring individual lab scientists get certified in scientific fields by June 1, 2012.
- appointing an ombudsman who would listen to complaints about the SBI from the public, attorneys and law enforcement and make recommendations to the agency and the lab....
- making clear in state law that lab workers serve the public and the criminal justice system, and not solely law enforcement.
- changing the SBI lab's name to the North Carolina State Crime Laboratory.
- creating a forensic science advisory board comprised of the SBI lab director and 12 scientists and other forensic scientists to review SBI lab procedures and recommend new testing procedures or remove outdated ones....
- directing the attorney general to form an advisory board on practicing forensic law to access the needs of the field statewide.
- the Legislature giving more than $40 million to the SBI to provide 40 hours of training annually to nearly 400 forensic scientists and field agents; meet a higher level of outside accreditation; replace aging lab equipment; upgrade electronic case record systems; and pay for the ombudsman.[53]

North Carolina is not the only jurisdiction that has experienced crime laboratory problems ranging from gross negligence to fraud. "A state audit of the [Houston] crime laboratory, completed in December 2002, has found that DNA technicians there misinterpreted data, were poorly trained and kept shoddy records."[54] Problems also surfaced with blood, hair, and other types of analyses conducted by the Houston crime lab, likely encompassing thousands of cases and contributing to an unknown number of wrongful convictions, including that of George Rodriguez, who served 17 years in prison for the rape of a 14-year-old girl. Rodriguez subsequently was exonerated based on post-conviction DNA testing.[55] In Oklahoma City, the integrity of numerous convictions was called into question because of the work of former crime lab analyst Joyce Gilchrist.[56] "Systemic problems, indeed scandals, have occurred at DNA laboratories in at least seventeen states."[57] The following case describes the misconduct of former West Virginia State Police Crime Laboratory analyst Fred Zain, and its impact on that state's criminal justice system.

In the Matter of an Investigation of the West Virginia State Police Crime Laboratory, Serology Division

438 S.E.2d 501 (W. Va. 1993)

MILLER, Justice:

This case is an extraordinary proceeding arising from a petition filed with this Court on June 2, 1993, by William C. Forbes, Prosecuting Attorney for Kanawha County, requesting the appointment of a circuit judge to conduct an investigation into whether habeas corpus relief should be granted to prisoners whose convictions were obtained through the willful false testimony of Fred S. Zain, a former serologist with the Division of Public Safety. On June 3, 1993, in response to the petition, we entered an order appointing the Honorable James O. Holliday, a retired circuit judge, to supervise an investigation of the Serology Division at the West Virginia State Police Crime Laboratory. On November 4, 1993, after an extensive, five-month investigation, Judge Holliday filed his report with this Court, a copy of which is attached as an Appendix to this opinion.

The report chronicles the history of allegations of misconduct on the part of Trooper Zain, beginning with the wrongful conviction of Glen Dale Woodall, who was eventually released after DNA testing conclusively established his innocence. The report further discusses allegations of misconduct and incompetence by Trooper Zain's subordinates during his tenure with the Division of Public Safety. Finally, the report summarizes the findings of James McNamara, Laboratory Director of the Florida Department of Law Enforcement, and Ronald Linhart, Supervisor of Serology in the Crime Laboratory for the Los Angeles County Sheriff's Department, who were selected by Barry Fisher, Chairman of the Laboratory Accreditation Board of the American Society of Crime Laboratory Directors (ASCLD), to conduct an analysis of the policies, procedures, practices, and records of the Serology Division during Trooper Zain's tenure.

The ASCLD report and the deposition testimony of fellow officers in the Serology Division during Trooper Zain's tenure support the multiple findings of fact by Judge Holliday regarding Trooper Zain's long history of falsifying evidence in criminal prosecutions. Specifically, the report states:

> "The acts of misconduct on the part of Zain included (1) overstating the strength of results; (2) overstating the frequency of genetic matches on individual pieces of evidence; (3) misreporting the frequency of genetic matches on multiple pieces of evidence; (4) reporting that multiple items had been tested, when only a single item had been tested; (5) reporting inconclusive results as conclusive; (6) repeatedly altering laboratory records; (7) grouping results to create the erroneous impression that genetic markers had been obtained from all samples tested; (8) failing to report conflicting results; (9) failing to conduct or to report conducting additional testing to resolve conflicting results; (10) implying a match with a suspect when testing supported only a match with the victim; and (11) reporting scientifically impossible or improbable results." (Footnote omitted).

The report by Judge Holliday further notes that the ASCLD team concluded that these irregularities were "'the result of systematic practice rather than an occasional inadvertent error'" and discusses specific cases that were prosecuted in which Serology Division records indicate that scientifically inaccurate, invalid, or false testimony or reports were given by Trooper Zain.

In addition to investigating what occurred during Trooper Zain's tenure in the Serology Division, Judge Holliday also explored how these irregularities could have happened. The report notes that many of Trooper Zain's former supervisors and subordinates regarded him as "pro-prosecution." The report further states: "It appears that Zain was quite skillful in using his experience and position of authority to deflect criticism of his work by subordinates." Although admittedly beyond the scope of the investigation, the report by Judge Holliday notes that there was evidence that Trooper Zain's supervisors may have ignored or concealed complaints of his misconduct. Finally, the report discusses ASCLD criticisms of certain operating procedures during Trooper Zain's tenure, which the report concludes "undoubtedly contributed to an environment within which Zain's misconduct escaped detection." According to the report, these procedural deficiencies included:

> "(1) no written documentation of testing methodology; (2) no written quality assurance program; (3) no written internal or external auditing procedures; (4) no routine proficiency testing of laboratory technicians; (5) no technical review of work product; (6) no written documentation of instrument maintenance and calibration; (7) no written testing procedures manual; (8) failure to follow generally-accepted scientific testing standards with respect to certain tests; (9) inadequate record-keeping; and (10) failure to conduct collateral testing."

Judge Holliday's report correctly concludes that Trooper Zain's pattern and practice of misconduct completely undermined the validity and reliability of any forensic work he performed or reported, and thus constitutes newly discovered evidence. It further recognizes the appropriate standard of review in cases of newly discovered evidence as set forth by this Court most recently in ... *State v. O'Donnell,* 189 W.Va. 628, 433 S.E.2d 566 (1993):

> "A new trial will not be granted on the ground of newly-discovered evidence unless the case comes within the following rules: (1) The evidence must appear to have been discovered since the trial, and, from the affidavit of the

> new witness, what such evidence will be, or its absence satisfactorily explained. (2) It must appear from facts stated in his affidavit that [defendant] was diligent in ascertaining and securing his evidence, and that the new evidence is such that due diligence would not have secured it before the verdict. (3) Such evidence must be new and material, and not merely cumulative; and cumulative evidence is additional evidence of the same kind to the same point. (4) The evidence must be such as ought to produce an opposite result at a second trial on the merits. (5) And the new trial will generally be refused when the sole object of the new evidence is to discredit or impeach a witness on the opposite side."

Newly discovered evidence is not the only ground on which habeas relief can be afforded. It has long been recognized by the United States Supreme Court that it is a violation of due process for the State to convict a defendant based on false evidence....

In *Giglio v. United States,* 405 U.S. 150 (1972), a unanimous Court again concluded that the Government was responsible for false testimony on the part of one of its witnesses even though the prosecutor was unaware of its falsity....

Thus, in this case, it matters not whether a prosecutor using Trooper Zain as his expert ever knew that Trooper Zain was falsifying the State's evidence. The State must bear the responsibility for the false evidence. The law forbids the State from obtaining a conviction based on false evidence.

It is also recognized that, although it is a violation of due process for the State to convict a defendant based on false evidence, such conviction will not be set aside unless it is shown that the false evidence had a material effect on the jury verdict....

We agree with Judge Holliday's recommendation that in any habeas corpus hearing involving Zain evidence, the only issue is whether the evidence presented at trial, independent of the forensic evidence presented by Trooper Zain, would have been sufficient to support the verdict. As we have earlier stated, once the use of false evidence is established, as here, such use constitutes a violation of due process. The only inquiry that remains is to analyze the other evidence in the case ... to determine if there is sufficient evidence to uphold the conviction.

In those cases in which Zain evidence was presented and a guilty plea was entered, the habeas court's task will require a different analysis. The issue then becomes whether the defendant should be allowed to withdraw the guilty plea. We recognized in ... *State v. Pettigrew,* 284 S.E.2d 370 (W. Va. 1981), that after a defendant enters a guilty plea and is sentenced, an attempt to withdraw the guilty plea only can be done on a showing of manifest necessity....

Ordinarily, at a guilty plea hearing there is no formal testimony given by the State to establish the defendant's guilt, although the defendant is generally called upon to provide a factual basis for the acceptance of the plea. The focus of such a hearing is to determine whether the plea is voluntary, whether the defendant understands the rights he is waiving by virtue of the plea and the nature of the charge against him, and whether the court is satisfied that a factual basis exists for accepting the plea....

Obviously, there are many factors that may be considered in determining, in the guilty plea context, whether a manifest injustice has occurred. In those instances where a defendant made his guilty plea without any knowledge of the Zain material, it cannot be said to have influenced the plea. It would seem that only in those instances where a defendant can show that the Zain material was communicated to him prior to the guilty plea would the habeas court have to consider the matter further. Even where such further action is warranted, the test still will be whether all the circumstances surrounding the plea and the evidence of the defendant's involvement in the crime warrant a conclusion that manifest injustice occur if the guilty plea is not set aside.

As Judge Holliday's report recognizes, in these cases it has not been possible to identify the final outcome from the forensic reports. Nor do these reports cover every case in which Trooper Zain may have been involved. Finally, it was not the function of Judge Holliday's inquiry to determine the current status of such defendants.

In order to resolve these matters, we will direct the Clerk of this Court to prepare and cause to be distributed to the Division of Corrections an appropriate post-conviction habeas corpus form. This form will be designed to identify those individuals who desire to seek habeas relief on a Zain issue. As a condition for obtaining such relief, the form will require the relator to consent to a DNA test.... This Court will then determine an appropriate independent laboratory to conduct the DNA test at the State's expense....

The matters brought before this Court by Judge Holliday are shocking and represent egregious violations of the right of a defendant to a fair trial. They stain our judicial system and mock the ideal of justice under law. We direct Prosecutor Forbes to pursue any violation of criminal law committed by Trooper Zain and urge that he consult with the United States District Attorney for the Southern District of West Virginia. We direct our Clerk to send all relevant papers to both of them. This conduct should not go unpunished.

This corruption of our legal system would not have occurred had there been adequate controls and procedures in the Serology Division. Judge Holliday's report is replete with the deficiencies and derelictions that existed and as were uncovered by the American Society of Crime Laboratory Directors whose team reviewed the forensic data.[6] To ensure that this event does not recur, we direct the Superintendent of the Division of Public Safety to file with the Clerk of this Court a report outlining the steps that are to be taken to obtain certification of the State Police forensic laboratory by the American Society of Crime Laboratory Directors. We direct that this report be filed within sixty days from the date of the entry of this opinion.

Finally, we wish to commend Judge Holliday for the thoroughness of his report and the quality of the investigation he conducted.... We adopt Judge Holliday's report and order its immediate implementation....

Notes and Questions

1. Fred Zain worked at the West Virginia Crime Lab from 1979 until 1989, heading the serology department the last three years of his employment. He then moved to Bexar County, Texas, where he worked in a similar capacity from 1989 to 1993, until he was fired. He testified for the prosecution in at least a dozen states over the course of his career. Subsequent review of his testimony revealed numerous cases in which "Zain claimed tests had been performed when they had not been done. He stated that samples of biological evidence were 'conclusive' proof of someone's guilt when he hadn't tested the evidence...."[58] Through 1996, at least seven convictions in West Virginia were overturned based on Zain's having testified, including that of Glen Woodall, who was convicted of rape in 1987 and sentenced to life imprisonment without parole. Woodall was exonerated in 1992 based on post-conviction DNA testing.[59] "Zain died of cancer in 2002 ... while awaiting retrial on charges of obtaining money from the State of West Virginia under false pretenses. He was also charged with perjury in Texas, but the case was dismissed because of statute of limitations issues."[60]

---

6. Judge Holliday in note 7 of his report outlines the work of this organization:

"The American Society of Crime Laboratory Directors, a national association, has established a voluntary Crime Laboratory Accreditation Program in which any crime laboratory may participate in order to demonstrate that its management, operations, personnel, procedures, instruments, physical plant, security, and safety procedures meet certain standards. These standards, which are incorporated into an Accreditation Manual, represent the consensus of the members of ASCLD. For example, the two major requirements for ASCLD/LAB accreditation include (1) periodic, internal case report and case note review and (2) proficiency testing in which blind and/or open samples of which the 'true' results are unknown to the examiner prior to the analysis. State police laboratories which have received ASCLD/LAB accreditation include the Illinois State Police, the Arizona Department of Public Safety, the Washington State Patrol, the Missouri State Highway Patrol, the Michigan State Police, the Oregon State Police, the Texas Department of Public Safety, the North Carolina State Bureau of Investigation, the Virginia Bureau of Forensic Sciences, the Florida Department of Law Enforcement, the Wisconsin State Crime Laboratory, and the Indiana State Police."

2. The National Academy of Sciences report, *Strengthening Forensic Science in the United States: A Path Forward*, focused extensively on crime laboratories, their operating procedures, and their personnel. The report noted:

> The majority of forensic science laboratories are administered by law enforcement agencies, such as police departments, where the laboratory administrator reports to the head of the agency. This system leads to significant concerns related to the independence of the laboratory and its budget. Ideally, public forensic science laboratories should be independent of or autonomous within law enforcement agencies.[61]

After observing that accreditation of crime laboratories was required in only three states (New York, Oklahoma, and Texas), and that certification of practitioners was not uniformly required, the report recommended that "[l]aboratory accreditation and individual certification of forensic science professionals should be mandatory...."[62] It called for a code of ethics to govern forensic science disciplines, with an appropriate mechanism for enforcement.[63] In addition:

> Forensic laboratories should establish routine quality assurance and quality control procedures to ensure the accuracy of forensic analyses and the work of forensic practitioners. Quality control procedures should be designed to identify mistakes, fraud, and bias; confirm the continued validity and reliability of standard operating procedures and protocols; ensure that best practices are being followed; and correct procedures and protocols that are found to need improvement.[64]

The report ambitiously proposed the creation of a new federal agency, a National Institute of Forensic Science, that would be invested with a host of functions and responsibilities, including several bearing on the accreditation of crime laboratories, the certification of forensic practitioners, the establishment and enforcement of best practices, and helping support education and research in forensics.[65]

E. Conclusion

At the beginning of this chapter we presented the lengthy roster of forensic science practices reviewed in the 2009 National Academy of Sciences report, *Strengthening Forensic Science in the United States: A Path Forward.* The categories included "pattern/experience evidence" (*e.g.*, fingerprints, firearms, toolmarks, bite marks, tire and footwear impressions, bloodstain pattern analysis, handwriting, hair), "analytical evidence" (*e.g.*, DNA, paint and other coatings, drugs and other chemicals, fibers and other materials, fluids, serology, fire and explosive analysis), and "digital evidence."[66] We could not hope to cover the numerous disciplines and techniques subsumed by science and forensics in this chapter, nor examine all of the ways that related evidence might contribute to wrongful convictions. We have attempted to identify several of the important relevant legal and scientific issues.

Many predicted that the Supreme Court's decision in *Daubert v. Merrell Dow Pharmaceuticals,* 509 U.S. 579, 113 S.Ct. 2786, 125 L.Ed.2d 469 (1993) would result in more liberal admission of scientific evidence than under the *Frye* "general acceptance" test. Somewhat surprisingly, *Daubert* invited reconsideration of the reliability and hence the admissibility of numerous types of venerable forensic evidence, including fingerprint identification, hair analysis, and many other traditionally unquestioned techniques. Much as *Daubert* helped usher in a new era of law, in science, few developments have been more significant in altering public perceptions about wrongful convictions, and have had more practical importance, than the forensic application of DNA analysis. DNA-based exonerations have forcefully demonstrated that factually innocent people have been erroneously convicted and punished. The scientific reliability of DNA testing is widely regarded as "the gold standard" against which other disciplines are measured.

Of course, no scientific technique, including DNA testing, is infallible. Nor does the presence (or absence) of an individual's DNA or other trace evidence at a crime scene definitively establish guilt (or innocence). Still, scientific evidence can be especially powerful in criminal trials, much as the expert witnesses who present it can further enhance its credibility in the eyes of lay jurors. Therein lies the potential value, as well as the attendant dangers, of scientific and forensic evidence in the investigation and prosecution of crimes.

Chapter 8

Informants

A. Introduction

There is nothing inherently disagreeable or suspicious about being considered an "informant". Defined simply as "a person who informs or gives information,"[1] every witness interviewed by the police or who testifies in court is subsumed within this term. However, our focus in this chapter is not on disinterested witnesses who supply information, but rather on those whose motives may be questionable: informants "who receive benefits from the government for their testimony."[2] Commonly known as "snitches" ("jailhouse snitches" if incarcerated), or less pejoratively as "incentivized" witnesses, individuals who provide information in expectation of or pursuant to an agreement for consideration from the authorities may perceive (correctly) that their testimony will be valued, and rewarded, only if it helps produce an arrest or secure a conviction.

Reliance on information provided by incentivized witnesses, and perhaps especially by jailhouse informants, presents criminal justice officials with a dilemma. As one federal judge has observed, "[c]riminals are likely to say and do almost anything to get what they want, especially when what they want is to get out of trouble with the law."[3] On the other hand, as distinguished federal jurist Learned Hand has noted: "Courts have countenanced the use of informers from time immemorial; in cases of conspiracy, or in other cases when the crime consists of preparing for another crime, it is usually necessary to rely upon them or upon accomplices because the criminals will almost certainly proceed covertly."[4] Whether these countervailing tendencies can be reconciled, and if so, how, are of obvious importance for both promoting justice and guarding against miscarriages of justice.

"Snitches contributed to wrongful convictions" in 51 of the 266 (19.2%) DNA-based exonerations reported by the Innocence Project through early 2011.[5] In their analysis of 340 wrongful conviction cases that resulted in exoneration between 1989 and 2003—owing to DNA analysis or otherwise—Professor Gross and colleagues found that "[i]n at least seventeen exoneration cases [5.0%] the real criminal lied under oath to get the defendant convicted; in at least ninety-seven cases [28.5%] a civilian witness who did not claim to be directly involved in the crime committed perjury—usually a jailhouse snitch or another witness who stood to gain from the false testimony."[6] Another study concluded that 51 of the first 111 (45.9%) individuals since the early 1970s who were found guilty of capital murder and sentenced to death, but subsequently exonerated, were convicted "based in whole or part on the testimony of witnesses with incentives to lie—in the vernacular, snitches.... That makes snitches the leading cause of wrongful convictions in U.S. capital cases...."[7]

It may seem odd that systems of justice countenance witnesses whose testimony is conditioned on the government providing a *quid pro quo* in the form of a charge or sentence reduction or other consideration. Does bartering for justice risk subverting it? Would we (understandably) not look askance at defense witnesses whose testimony was similarly conditioned on compensation or reward? We begin by presenting case decisions that evoke such fundamental questions. We next consider the prosecution's obligation to disclose promises made to witnesses in exchange for testimony, and whether prosecutors can be liable for failing to monitor the snitches on whom they rely when their false or duplicitous testimony contributes to wrongful convictions. We conclude by examining various procedures designed to diminish the risk that unreliable informant testimony will corrupt the truth-seeking process—measures that include pre-trial screening and discovery, corroboration requirements, and special jury instructions.

B. Snitches for Hire: Are Incentives to Testify Bribery? Are Incentives Fundamentally Unfair?

A federal criminal statute, 18 U.S.C. § 201, prohibits the "[b]ribery of public officials and witnesses." In particular, 18 U.S.C. § 201(c)(2) provides:

> Whoever ... directly or indirectly, gives, offers, or promises anything of value to any person, for or because of the testimony under oath or affirmation given or to be given by such person as a witness upon a trial, hearing, or other proceeding, before any court ... authorized by the laws of the United States to hear evidence or take testimony ... shall be fined under this title or imprisoned for not more than two years, or both.

Sonya Singleton was charged in a federal indictment with multiple counts of money laundering and conspiracy to distribute cocaine. Allegations centered on her use of Western Union facilities in Wichita, Kansas to wire money to California in exchange for cocaine, which was intended for sale in the Wichita area. One of the government's witnesses at Singleton's trial was an alleged co-conspirator, Napoleon Douglas. As provided in a written plea agreement approved by the government, Douglas's testimony was procured following three promises:

> First, the government promised not to prosecute Mr. Douglas for any other violations of the Drug Abuse Prevention and Control Act stemming from his activities currently under investigation, except perjury or related offenses. Second, it promised "to advise the sentencing court, prior to sentencing, of the nature and extent of the cooperation provided" by Mr. Douglas. Third, the government promised "to advise the Mississippi parole board of the nature and extent of the cooperation provided" by Mr. Douglas. Mr. Douglas agreed, "in consideration of the items listed ... [to] testify[] truthfully in federal and/or state court"....[8]

Singleton filed a pretrial motion to suppress Douglas's testimony, contending that the government's promises made in exchange for his testimony were unlawful under 18 U.S.C. § 201(c)(2). The trial judge denied the motion, Douglas testified at Singleton's trial, and she was convicted. On appeal, a three-judge panel of the 10th Circuit Court of Appeals sent shockwaves through the legal community by agreeing with Singleton's argument and reversing her conviction. *United States v. Singleton*, 144 F.3d 1343 (10th Cir.1998). The repercussions were short-lived. Acting on its own motion, the 10th Circuit Court of Appeals reconsidered the case *en banc* and in short order overturned the panel decision, thus restoring approval of the long-observed practice of prosecutors' offering consideration to informants in exchange for their trial testimony. We present portions of the majority, concurring, and dissenting opinions of the court's *en banc* decision below.

United States v. Singleton

165 F.3d 1297 (10th Cir. 1999) (en banc)

PORFILIO, Circuit Judge.

... Ms. Singleton takes the position that when Mr. Douglas testified after receiving the government's promise of lenient treatment in exchange for his truthful testimony, he became a "paid 'occurrence' witness," and testimony from those of such ilk is contrary to the fundamental precepts of American justice because the payment of something of value would give the witness a strong motivation to lie. She reasons [18 U.S.C.] section 201(c)(2) was enacted to deter that result, and we need only apply plain meaning to the word "whoever" contained in the statute to conclude it must apply broadly and encompass the government and its representatives.

In contrast, the United States argues to allow section 201(c)(2) to sweep so broadly would not only be a radical departure from the ingrained legal culture of our criminal justice system but would also result in criminalizing historic practice and established law. The government maintains Congress did not intend to hinder the sovereign's authority to prosecute violations against the United States in this fashion....

As correctly argued by Ms. Singleton, "whoever" is a broad term which by its ordinary definition would exclude no one. Indeed, if one were to take the word at face value, defendant's argument becomes colorable, at least. However, the defendant's approach, while facially logical, ignores a crucial point that must be considered in any attempt to apply the statute to the issues of this case. She argues the breadth of the word " 'whoever' includes within its scope the assistant United States attorney who offered Douglas something of value in exchange for his testimony." To begin the parsing of the statute with this assumption, however, ignores a fundamental fact: the capacity in which the government's lawyer appears in the courts.

The prosecutor, functioning within the scope of his or her office, is not simply a lawyer advocating the government's perspective of the case. Indeed, the prosecutor's function is far more significant. Only officers of the Department of Justice or the United States Attorney can represent the United States in the prosecution of a criminal case. Indeed, a federal court cannot even assert jurisdiction over a criminal case unless it is filed and prosecuted by the United States Attorney or a properly appointed assistant. Therefore, the government's sovereign authority to prosecute and conduct a prosecution is vested solely in the United States Attorney and his or her properly appointed assistants.... We thus infer in criminal cases that an Assistant United States Attorney, acting within the scope of authority conferred upon that office, is the alter ego of the United States exercising its sovereign power of prosecution. Hence, in the attempt to apply section 201(c)(2), the United States and the Assistant United States Attorney cannot be separated....

Put into proper context, then, the defendant's argument is: in a criminal prosecution, the word "whoever" in the statute includes within its scope the United States acting in its sovereign capacity. Extending that premise to its logical conclusion, the defendant implies Congress must have intended to subject the United States to the provisions of section 201(c)(2), and, consequently, like any other violator, to criminal prosecution. Reduced to this logical conclusion, the basic argument of the defendant is patently absurd.

There is even a more fundamental reason for arriving at the same conclusion, however. Although Congress may, by legislative act, add to or redefine the meaning of any word, it did not do so in the passage of section 201(c)(2). Therefore, we must presume it intended to employ the common meaning of the word. The word "whoever" connotes a being. ***See* Webster's Third New International Dictionary** 2611 (1993) (defining "whoever" as "whatever ***person***: any ***person***" (emphasis added)). The United States is an inanimate entity, not a being. The word "whatever" is used commonly to refer to an inanimate object. Therefore, construing "whoever" to include the government is semantically anomalous. Looking beyond definitions, though, there are rules of statutory construction that will lead to the same conclusion.

Statutes of general purport do not apply to the United States unless Congress makes the application clear and indisputable....

The next question, then, is whether applying the statute to the government would deprive the sovereign of a recognized or established prerogative, title, or interest. The answer to that question is, inescapably yes.

From the common law, we have drawn a longstanding practice sanctioning the testimony of accomplices against their confederates in exchange for leniency. Indeed,

> [n]o practice is more ingrained in our criminal justice system than the practice of the government calling a witness who is an accessory to the crime for which the defendant is charged and having that witness testify under a plea bargain that promises him a reduced sentence.

United States v. Cervantes-Pacheco, 826 F.2d 310, 315 (5th Cir.1987); *United States v. Juncal,* 1998 WL 525800, at *1 (S.D.N.Y. Aug. 20, 1998) ("The concept of affording cooperating accomplices with leniency dates back to the common law in England and has been recognized and approved by the United States Congress, the United States Courts and the United States Sentencing Commission.").

This ingrained practice of granting lenience in exchange for testimony has created a vested sovereign prerogative in the government. It follows that if the practice can be traced to the common law, it has acquired stature akin to the special privilege of kings. However, in an American criminal prosecution, the granting of lenience is an authority that can only be exercised by the United States through its prosecutor; therefore, any reading of section 201(c)(2) that would restrict the exercise of this power is surely a diminution of sovereignty not countenanced in our jurisprudence.

Moreover, in light of the longstanding practice of leniency for testimony, we must presume if Congress had intended that section 201(c)(2) overturn this ingrained aspect of American legal culture, it would have done so in clear, unmistakable, and unarguable language....

... We simply believe the general principles we have set forth so completely undercut defendant's reading that further exposition would be redundant.

Our conclusion in no way permits an agent of the government to step beyond the limits of his or her office to make an offer to a witness other than one traditionally exercised by the sovereign. A prosecutor who offers something other than a concession normally granted by the government in exchange for testimony is no longer the alter ego of the sovereign and is divested of the protective mantle of the government. Thus, fears our decision would permit improper use or abuse of prosecutorial authority simply have no foundation.[2] It is noteworthy, then, that defendant's premise relies upon the shibboleth "the government is not above the law." While we agree with that notion, we simply believe this particular statute does not exist for the government. Accordingly, we **AFFIRM** the district court's denial of the motion to suppress on 18 U.S.C. § 201(c)(2) grounds....

LUCERO, J., with whom Judge HENRY joins, concurring.

I concur in the judgment that the United States and its agent, an Assistant United States Attorney, did not violate 18 U.S.C. § 201(c)(2) by offering in a plea agreement to exchange leniency for the testimony of Singleton's co-conspirator. But I write separately to state my disagreement with the majority's holding that the word "whoever" in 18 U.S.C. § 201(c)(2), as it is used to define the class of persons who can violate the statute, cannot include the government or its agents. The majority's interpretation would permit the conclusion that consistent with the provisions of § 201, a United States Attorney may pay a prosecution witness for false testimony.

I cannot join the dissent, however, because § 201(c)(2) operates in conjunction with other statutes to allow the government, upon proper disclosure and/or with court approval, to trade certain items of value for testimony. These statutes include 18 U.S.C. § 3553(e) and 28 U.S.C. § 994(n), passed as part of the Sentencing Reform Act of 1984, which allow

---

2. The concurrence expresses a concern our disposition would "permit the conclusion that consistent with the provisions of § 201, a United States Attorney may pay a prosecution witness for false testimony." We believe the concern is misplaced. It is inconceivable that any court would hold that a prosecutor who pays for the *false* testimony of a witness is carrying out an official function of the government. Our disposition protects only those prosecutorial acts of the government which have been recognized in common law or authorized by statute. A prosecutor who goes beyond those limitations is clearly not performing a governmental function. Moreover, a prosecutor who procures false testimony is surely subject to penalty under 18 U.S.C. § 1622.

The dissent's observation that both statutes employ the word "whoever" misses our point. "Whoever" includes the prosecutor in § 1622 because subornation of perjury is not an official governmental function.

courts, acting pursuant to the Sentencing Guidelines and upon motion of the government, to reduce sentences for individuals who provide "substantial assistance in the investigation or prosecution of another"; the federal immunity statutes, 18 U.S.C. §§ 6001–6005, passed as part of the Organized Crime Control Act of 1970, which require courts, upon the request of the government, to confer immunity upon witnesses for their testimony in aid of the prosecution; and the Witness Relocation and Protection Act, 18 U.S.C. §§ 3521–3528, passed as part of the Comprehensive Crime Control Act of 1974, which allows the government to bestow various benefits for the protection of cooperating witnesses. Because these specific statutes are in conflict with the general prohibitions of § 201(c)(2), the specific statutes control, and permit the prosecution's actions in this case....

KELLY, Circuit Judge, with whom SEYMOUR, Chief Judge, and EBEL, Circuit Judge, join, dissenting.

The court holds that 18 U.S.C. § 201(c)(2) does not apply to the government because government prosecutors are inseparable from the sovereign, and that its application would deprive the sovereign of its power to grant leniency in exchange for testimony and would conflict with various statutory provisions. Because courts must apply unambiguous statutes as they are written and § 201(c) does not admit of an exception for the government or its prosecutors, I respectfully dissent.

As an initial observation, since the panel issued its opinion in this case, prosecutors from coast to coast have attempted to portray it as the death knell for the criminal justice system as we know it. These are the same grave forecasts made by prosecutors after the Supreme Court's decision in *Miranda v. Arizona,* 384 U.S. 436 (1966), and the advent of the exclusionary rule. But experience has proven that the government, just like the private citizens it regulates and prosecutes, can live within the rules. No one would suggest that the criminal justice system has ceased to function because the Court or Congress has effectuated constitutional or statutory guarantees designed to promote a more reliable outcome in criminal proceedings.

In holding that § 201(c)(2) simply does not apply to the government, the court does not hold that leniency in exchange for testimony does not constitute "anything of value." To be sure, the investigation and prosecution of criminal wrongdoing is an important societal function. Yet, largely missing from the debate since the panel opinion was issued is any concern for the other deeply held values that § 201(c) was intended to protect and which, I believe, the panel opinion honored by applying § 201(c) as Congress wrote it. Those concerns center on maintaining the integrity, fairness, and credibility of our system of criminal justice. Criminal judgments are accepted by society at large, and even by individual defendants, only because our system of justice is painstakingly fair. An additional core value honored by the panel opinion is the preservation of the separation of powers carefully articulated in the Constitution between the legislative and judicial branches, and the proper role of the judiciary as the law-interpreting, rather than lawmaking, branch of the federal government.

Contrary to the concerns expressed by some commentators and courts, a straight-forward interpretation of § 201(c), which encompasses a prohibition against the government buying witness testimony with leniency, actually aids the search for truth. In theory, the leniency is only in exchange for "truthful" testimony. But as the Supreme Court has recognized: "Common sense would suggest that [an accused accomplice] often has a greater interest in lying in favor of the prosecution rather than against it, especially if he is still awaiting his own trial or sentencing. To think that criminals will lie to save their fellows but not to obtain favors from the prosecution for themselves is indeed to clothe the criminal class with more nobility than one might expect to find in the public at large." *Washington v. Texas,* 388 U.S. 14, 22–23 (1967). To be sure, there are devices that partially ameliorate the problem. The government is required to disclose exculpatory information, including impeachment information, to a defendant. Testifying accomplices may be cross-examined. Their credibility may be impeached, and the jury is instructed that it may regard such testimony with caution. However, all of these devices have limitations. In the real world of trial and uncertain proof, and in view of § 201(c), a witness's demeanor and actual testimony are simply too important to hinge upon promises of leniency. Although the court notes that a prosecutor who procures false testimony could be prosecuted for subornation of perjury, 18 U.S.C. § 1622,[2] such a remedy offers little practical advantage to a defendant facing trial. By barring an exchange of leniency for testimony, Congress in § 201(c) has sought to eliminate, *at the source*, the most obvious incentive for false testimony.

On the other side of the ledger is my concern for the institutional role of Article III courts. Much of this case has been about policy. I accept the government's position that accomplices can provide important information and interpreting § 201(c) to include prosecutors might require some changes to elicit testimony of some witnesses. While it would be up to the Department of Justice to devise ways of compliance, the government is not precluded from offering leniency in exchange for information and assistance short of actual testimony at trial. Likewise, the government could prosecute accomplices first, then compel their testimony by subpoena against co-conspirators. Finally, the government could request that the district court order an accomplice to testify under a grant of immunity. Surely the Department has the ability and resources to come up with effective and lawful means for procuring necessary accomplice testimony. However, I also accept the defense attorneys' position that government leniency in exchange for testimony can create a powerful incentive to lie and derail the truth-seeking purpose of the criminal justice system. The very nature and complexity of this policy debate reinforces my initial belief that this is an argument better left to Congress. This court must perform its constitutional duties and no more. Ours is not to explore the farthest meanings that the term "whoever" can bear so as to effectuate the policy we think best. Our duty is to interpret the plain meaning of the statute. I continue to believe that meaning is clear: § 201(c), as written, applies to prosecutors and criminal defendants alike. If the balance struck by § 201 is to be reweighed, that reweighing should be done by the policymaking branch of government—the Congress, and not the courts. In that regard, it bears repeating that the panel's original opinion was purely a matter of *statutory* construction, not constitutional analysis, and it remains completely open for Congress to reweigh the conflicting values sought to be addressed in § 201.

I. "Whoever" Means Whoever

The government argues that construing the word "whoever" to include the government is semantically anomalous because "whoever" connotes a being. As a textual and contextual matter, this is wrong. Textually, "whoever" clearly connotes more than a being and in fact denotes inanimate entities. The Dictionary Act, 1 U.S.C. § 1, definition of "whoever" includes, but is not limited to, corporations, companies, associations, firms, partnerships, societies, and joint stock companies—all inanimate entities. Contextually, the government concedes that "whoever" in § 201(b) applies to the government and it acknowledges that § 201(c) applies to the government if the government pays an informant money to testify. It makes absolutely no sense to give "whoever" one meaning in § 201(b) (and in § 201(c) when the inducement offered by the government is money) and to give the very same word a completely different meaning in § 201(c) when the inducement offered is leniency or some other promise to improve the informant's position....

The court suggests that the prosecutor and the sovereign are inseparable, and therefore the word "whoever" cannot apply because the United States cannot be prosecuted for providing leniency in exchange for testimony.... To suggest that government attorneys performing prosecutorial functions are beyond scrutiny because of who they represent is anomalous because it merges attorney and client. No one would suggest that an accused and his attorney are one in the same for purposes of compliance with constitutional, statutory and ethical norms. As discussed below, constraints on government prosecutors are not unusual, notwithstanding that the sovereign is the client. Merely because the government cannot be prosecuted if its agents violate a rule does not mean that the rule may be disregarded; to the contrary, the rule may be enforced by means other than prosecution, here by exclusion of evidence. The remedy of exclusion serves as a deterrent, protects a court's integrity and allows a federal court the only means it has to enforce federal law....

Beyond the government's sui generis definition of "whoever," the government's argument rests upon the predicate that the

2. Like § 201(c)(2), the subornation of perjury statute applies to "[w]hoever," and makes no exception for federal prosecutors.

government has the sovereign authority to prosecute criminal conduct, and applying § 201(c) to the government would impermissibly curtail that prerogative. However, applying § 201(c) to the government does not affect the core prerogative to prosecute or to withhold prosecution. The government erroneously conflates two distinct concepts: the vested sovereign prerogative of the government *to prosecute* and the obvious non-prerogative of *how to prosecute.* Prohibiting the government from granting witnesses leniency in exchange for testimony leaves the right to prosecute unfettered; the government can still prosecute anybody it wants and charge any way it wants. The anti-gratuity statute only limits *how* the government may prosecute its case and the government clearly has no vested sovereign prerogative to prove a case in any way it wishes. How the government proves its case is frequently restricted. Federal prosecutors must follow the Constitution, state codes of conduct, the rules of the individual courts, and the rules of evidence....

Thus, the anti-gratuity statute leaves unfettered the sovereign's established prerogative to charge; it merely places a restriction on one method of gathering admissible evidence, here testimony, *for* or *against* an accused. A federal prosecutor is not above the law and is not free to prove a case by any process he or she wants. Once the government falls into the crucible of the trial, the government, like the defendant, must follow the generally applicable rules governing the process. The government's argument that discontinuing the pervasive practice of buying testimony for leniency would jeopardize law enforcement is just another way of saying that the end justifies the means; not only is such a premise unsound policy, it also serves to demean the profession and all who strive to continue our system of justice as the fairest in the world.

II. Section 201(c)(2) in Relation to Other Statutes

Contrary to the government's contentions, the defendant's reading of § 201(c)(2) can be reconciled with 18 U.S.C. § 3553(e)[5] and U.S.S.G. § 5K1.1(a)(2).[8] It has been argued that this collection of enactments demonstrates Congress' sanction of the practice of offering various forms of leniency to a defendant in exchange for the defendant's agreement to testify in the government's prosecution of other individuals.

... As noted in the panel opinion, nowhere in 18 U.S.C. § 3553(e) [or other statutes] is "substantial assistance" defined to include testimony. The conspicuous absence of the word "testimony" from any of these sources would indicate that "substantial assistance" simply does not include testimony—a conclusion that avoids any conflict between these provisions and § 201(c)(2). In contrast, U.S.S.G. § 5K1.1(a)(2) does permit a court to consider "the truthfulness, completeness, and reliability of any information or testimony provided by the defendant" in deciding whether to depart from the guideline range in sentencing a defendant who has "provided substantial assistance" to the government. Even so, the fact that "substantial assistance" encompasses a defendant's testimony still does not place § 5K1.1 in conflict with § 201(c)(2). Given the duty to reconcile seemingly conflicting statutes whenever possible, it appears that § 5K1.1 creates a narrow exception to § 201(c)(2) by permitting a *court* to reward a defendant's truthful testimony *after* it has been given. This narrow exception does not affect § 201(c)(2)'s prohibition against the prosecutor offering or promising leniency in advance to a defendant in exchange for his agreement to testify.

---

5. 18 U.S.C. § 3553(e) provides:

Upon motion of the Government, the court shall have the authority to impose a sentence below a level established by statute as minimum sentence so as to reflect a defendant's substantial assistance in the investigation or prosecution of another person who has committed an offense. Such sentence shall be imposed in accordance with the guidelines and policy statements issued by the Sentencing Commission pursuant to section 994 of title 28, United States Code.

8. U.S.S.G. § 5K1.1(a)(2) provides:

Upon motion of the government stating that the defendant has provided substantial assistance in the investigation or prosecution of another person who has committed an offense, the court may depart from the guidelines.

(a) The appropriate reduction shall be determined by the court for reasons stated that may include, but are not limited to, consideration of the following:

(2) the truthfulness, completeness, and reliability of any information or testimony provided by the defendant.

Likewise, the defendant's reading of §201(c)(2) can be harmonized with 18 U.S.C. §§6001–6005, the statutes dealing with federal immunity. Under these statutes, where an individual has refused to testify on the basis of his Fifth Amendment privilege against self-incrimination, and where, in the judgment of the federal prosecuting attorney, the testimony may be necessary to the public interest, the prosecutor may, with approval of the Attorney General, request the district court to order that individual to testify under a grant of immunity. These statutes allow the government to compel an unwilling witness to cooperate by precluding use of the Fifth Amendment privilege. This function is entirely distinct from promising or offering leniency ex ante in exchange for a defendant's testimony, so the prohibition expressed in §201(c)(2) does not conflict with the grant of immunity authorized by the §§6001–6005. Sections 6000–6005 provide a mechanism to *take away* from a defendant a right he otherwise would have—the right not to incriminate himself. Constitutionally, the only way that right can be taken from a defendant is by offering immunity in exchange. Thus, the *quid pro quo* there is an exchange of immunity for a person's Fifth Amendment privilege. Once that exchange is made, the government can *compel* the witness to testify even against his wishes. That is very different, both conceptually and in terms of the risks presented, from purchasing voluntary testimony with leniency....

III. Tradition

The government relies on the common law practice of sanctioning the testimony of accomplices against their confederates in exchange for leniency. Apparently, this practice has not always been an unquestioned part of the common law. The seventeenth century English common law scholar and judge, Sir Matthew Hale, reasoned:

> If a reward be promised to a person for giving his evidence before he gives it, this, if proved disables his testimony. And so for my own part I have always thought, that if a person have a promise of a pardon if he give evidence against one of his own confederates, this disables his testimony, if it be proved upon him.[9]

II Sir Matthew Hale, *The History of Pleas of the Crown* 280 (Sollom Emlyn ed. 1736) (footnote omitted). A narrow focus on this practice, however, ignores two other equally compelling traditions: the common law prohibition against paying fact witnesses, and the fundamental policy of ensuring a level playing field between the government and defendant in a criminal case.

Under the common law in most jurisdictions, "it is improper to pay an occurrence witness any fee for testifying." *Model Rules of Professional Conduct* Rule 3.4 cmt. [3]. "Fair competition in the adversary system is secured by prohibitions against destruction or concealment of evidence, improperly influencing witnesses, obstructive tactics in discovery procedure, and the like." *Model Rules* Rule 3.4 cmt. [1]. The prohibition against improperly influencing witnesses is also expressed in the law of contracts, which invalidates agreements to pay fact witnesses on grounds of public policy and for lack of consideration, as well as in ethical rules which bar an attorney from offering a witness compensation or other illegal inducements to testify—even for truthful testimony, *see, e.g., Model Rules of Professional Conduct* Rule 3.4(b) (1996); *Model Code of Professional Responsibility* DR 7-109(C) (1981).[10]

Congress has expressed its desire that government attorneys comply with state and local federal court rules governing the practice of law. These ethical norms not only protect the individual, but also our system of justice within a democracy....

Constitutional law manifests another vital legal tradition which the government's position undercuts—the policy of ensuring a level play-

9. Sir Matthew Hale acknowledged that "the contrary opinion hath prevailed." II *History of Pleas of the Crown* 280 n.(c).

10. The Model Code provides that "[a] lawyer shall not pay, offer to pay, or acquiesce in the payment of compensation to a [fact] witness contingent upon the content of his testimony or the outcome of the case." *Model Code of Professional Responsibility* DR 7-109(C) (1981). It also suggests that "[w]itnesses should always testify truthfully and should be free of any financial inducements that might tempt them to do otherwise" and that "in no event should a lawyer pay or agree to pay a contingent fee to any witness." *Id.* at EC 7-28. This rule is well served by an interpretation of §201(c)(2) that prohibits payment of compensation in the form of leniency.

ing field between the government and defendant in a criminal case. The Supreme Court long ago recognized that impartiality in criminal cases requires that "[b]etween [the accused] and the state the scales are to be evenly held." *Hayes v. Missouri,* 120 U.S. 68, 70 (1887). Such a policy dates back to the Bill of Rights, which was "designed to level the playing field between the defendant and the state," Susan Bandes, *Empathy, Narrative, and Victim Impact Statements,* 63 U. Chi. L.Rev. 361, 402 (1996), and indeed the policy has animated landmark constitutional decisions.... Simply put, ours is an adversarial legal system, and implicit in this system, which pits the government against the defendant in a court of law, is the notion of fair play.

Remaining faithful to the important common law prohibition against paying fact witnesses and the fundamental policy of ensuring a level playing field between the government and defendant requires applying § 201(c)(2) to the government as its plain language suggests.

For the above reasons, I respectfully dissent....

Notes and Questions

1. The three-judge panel's ruling in *Singleton I,* finding that the government's offer of leniency to a prosecution witness to secure testimony was a form of bribery proscribed by 18 U.S.C. § 201(c)(2) "sparked widespread controversy. Prosecutors [were] ... shocked by the ruling.... Attorneys for defendants across the country applauded the ruling.... Within days, two separate Senate bills were proposed to amend the statute so as to exempt prosecutors from its application."[9] For scholarly commentary on *Singleton I,* its denouement with the 10th Circuit Court of Appeals' *en banc* decision in *Singleton II,* and related issues, *see* George C. Harris, "Testimony for Sale: The Law and Ethics of Snitches and Experts," 28 *Pepperdine Law Review* 1 (2000); Ian Weinstein, "Regulating the Market for Snitches," 47 *Buffalo Law Review* 563 (1999).

2. Judge Paul J. Kelly, Jr., who was appointed to the 10th Circuit Court of Appeals by President George H. W. Bush, wrote the panel decision in *Singleton I* and dissented from the *en banc* ruling in *Singleton II.* His opinion in *Singleton I* addressed "the government's vague argument that some overriding policy should prevent application of [18 U.S.C. § 201 (c) (2)] to the government's conduct...." *United States v. Singleton,* 144 F.3d 1343, 1352–1354 (10th Cir. 1998), *vacated,* 165 F.3d 1297 (10th Cir. 1999) (en banc).

"Criminal prohibitions do not generally apply to reasonable enforcement actions by officers of the law." *Brogan [v. United States,* 522 U.S. 398, 118 S.Ct. 805, 811 (1998)]. If the justification applies, conduct which violates the terms of a criminal statute is nevertheless not forbidden. The justification can be generally described as follows: a peace officer, prison guard, or private citizen authorized to act as a peace officer may, to the extent necessary to make an arrest, prevent an escape, or prevent the commission of a crime, violate a criminal statute if the conduct which constitutes the violation is reasonable in relation to the gravity of the evil threatened and the importance of the interest to be furthered. The government's conduct does not fall within this justification for at least two reasons: it was not undertaken by a peace officer or one acting in that capacity, and it was not required by an exigent need to make an arrest or prevent an escape or other crime.

The Supreme Court's more general statement of the rule that "[c]riminal prohibitions do not generally apply to reasonable enforcement actions by officers of the law," embraces field enforcement activity. *Brogan,* 118 S.Ct. at 811. The Court has held, for example, that the government's limited undercover participation in an unlawful drug operation is "a recognized and permissible means of investigation." *United States v. Russell,* 411 U.S. 423, 432 (1973). *Brogan* itself states that 18 U.S.C. § 1001 "does not make it a crime for an undercover narcotics agent to make a false statement to a drug peddler." *Brogan,* 118 S.Ct. at 811 (internal quotes and alterations omitted); *see United States v. Monaco,* 700 F.2d 577, 580–81 (10th Cir.1983) ("To obtain evidence of certain crimes undercover agents frequently must participate in illegal activities.").

The conduct of police, investigators, and law enforcement agents is regularly evaluated against the standard of what is legitimate and reasonably necessary to enforce the law. But we have found no case in which prosecutors, in their role as lawyers representing the government after the initiation of criminal proceedings, have been granted a justification to violate generally applicable laws.

The law enforcement justification exists to allow field officers a practically necessary means to detect and prevent crime, and to apprehend suspects. It is justified by the difficulties inherent in detecting certain types of crime. *See Russell,* 411 U.S. at 432, 93 S.Ct. 1637 (narcotics); *United States v. Kelly,* 707 F.2d 1460, 1468 (D.C.Cir.) (public corruption), *cert. denied,* 464 U.S. 908 (1983); *Monaco,* 700 F.2d at 580–81 (prostitution). The government's violation of § 201(c)(2), however, is entirely unrelated to detecting crime. Once the exigencies of field enforcement are satisfied, we can find no policy by which prosecutors may be excused from statutes regulating testimony presented to the federal courts. Although there are difficulties inherent in proving certain types of crimes, violating § 201(c)(2) is not necessary to overcome those difficulties: compulsory process is lawful and available, and avoids the taint on truthfulness which attends unlawful witness gratuities. The law enforcement justification has never altered the playing field on which crimes are proved in court. We decline to expand the meaning of "enforcement action" beyond its historical scope of detection, apprehension, and prevention of crime.

Because the government's statutory violation occurred not in a field investigation but in the context of testimony which was to be presented to the court, we further hold its action was not "reasonable." The chasm between the government's present conduct and reasonable law enforcement actions can be illustrated by analogy to the FBI's Abscam operation, under which operatives and undercover agents offered bribes to public officials and arrested those who accepted the bribes. *See Kelly,* 707 F.2d at 1461–63. Although Abscam created controversy and dissent in the courts, it was held a legitimate means of detecting public corruption. The government's present inducement for testimony goes much further. Reasonable law enforcement actions stop with detecting crime and observing enough to prove it. The government's statutory violation unreasonably exceeds this purpose, and is the more egregious because the intended product of the violation is testimony presented in court. We conclude the government's violation of § 201(c)(2) was neither "reasonable" nor an "enforcement action." *Brogan,* 118 S.Ct. at 811. Consequently it falls outside the scope of legitimate investigatory practices and is not justified by law enforcement authority.

3. Judge Kelly further argued in his dissenting opinion in *Singleton II* that "[r]emaining faithful to the important common law prohibition against paying fact witnesses and the fundamental policy of ensuring a level playing field between the government and defendant requires applying § 201(c)(2) to the government...." 165 F.3d, at 1314. If Ms. Singleton had offered "anything of value to any person, for or because of the testimony ... to be given by such person as a witness upon a trial," 18 U.S.C. § 210(c)(2), would she have been guilty of violating the statute? If she would have, but a federal prosecutor is not guilty of such an offense, is there "a level playing field between the government and defendant"? *Should* the defense similarly be allowed to offer consideration to a witness if necessary to secure the witness's (truthful) testimony? *See* H. Richard Uviller, "No Sauce for the Gander: Valuable Consideration for Helpful Testimony from Tainted Witnesses in Criminal Cases," 23 *Cardozo Law Review* 771 (2002).

Even if not a form of "bribery" under federal law, might the inducements offered to a witness in exchange for testimony threaten to undermine the fairness of trials in which that testimony plays a central role? Consider the following case.

Sheriff, Humboldt County v. Acuna

819 P.2d 197 (Nev. 1991)

STEFFEN, Justice:

Respondent Raul Acuna allegedly sold cocaine to an individual who was motivated by his own criminal involvement with the law to cooperate with the police. The alleged transaction was monitored electronically and Acuna was arrested and charged with selling a controlled substance. After a preliminary hearing, Acuna filed a pretrial petition for a writ of habeas corpus based upon an asserted violation of this court's holding in *Franklin v. State,* 94 Nev. 220, 577 P.2d 860 (1978). The district court agreed that *Franklin* was dispositive and issued the writ. Having reevaluated the *Franklin* rule and concluded that it should not be further perpetuated, we reverse without determining whether the district court erred in finding a violation of the *Franklin* standard.

FACTS

Phillip Crawford, a "cooperating individual" who was working with W. Kent Brown, an investigator for the Tri-County Narcotics Task Force, told Brown that he had arranged to buy a small quantity of cocaine from Acuna. The alleged transaction occurred at a parking lot in the Winnemucca area and was monitored by police through means of an electronic listening device carried on Crawford's person. On April 11, 1990, Acuna was arrested and charged with selling a controlled substance. The following month, after a preliminary hearing, Acuna filed a pretrial petition for a writ of habeas corpus based upon a violation of the *Franklin* rule arising out of the State's arrangement with Crawford.

At the hearing on the petition, Acuna contended that because Crawford had not as yet been formally charged and was allowed to enter a guilty plea, Crawford was under compulsion to testify against Acuna in a particular manner. The State opposed the petition on the ground that the *Franklin* rule applied only to an accomplice and that Crawford did not fit in that category. The district court rejected the State's position, ruling that *Franklin* was not limited to accomplice testimony. Thereafter the petition was granted and the State appealed.

DISCUSSION

Our ruling in *Franklin* was a takeoff from the case of *People v. Medina,* 41 Cal.App.3d 438, 116 Cal.Rptr. 133 (1974). The *Medina* court held, and we so quoted in *Franklin,* "that a defendant is denied a fair trial if the prosecution's case depends substantially upon accomplice testimony and the accomplice is placed, either by the prosecution or the court, under a strong compulsion to testify in a particular fashion." However, the *Franklin* court substantially expanded the *Medina* ruling by condemning the use of testimony secured from a witness through means of an executory plea bargain. Specifically, we stated that the application of the *Medina* rationale

> may not be limited solely to situations where immunity is expressly conditioned on specific testimony. As a matter of logic, if the circumstances of the plea bargain would reasonably cause the alleged accomplice to believe he must testify in a particular fashion, then a less explicit arrangement also violates the defendant's due process rights.

We thereafter concluded that

> [b]y bargaining for specific testimony to implicate a defendant, and withholding the benefits of the bargain until after the witness has performed, the prosecution becomes committed to a theory quite possibly inconsistent with the truth and the search for truth. We deem this contrary to public policy, to due process, and to any sense of justice.

[*Franklin*], 577 P.2d at 863. The concern thus expressed by the *Franklin* majority was the lack of reliability inherent in an arrangement where "the prosecutor must simultaneously purchase and coerce testimony in order to obtain a conviction...."

The *Franklin* court is not to be criticized for its zeal in seeking to promote and protect the truth-seeking objective of a criminal trial. Indeed, criminal justice may never be consistently attained at the expense of truth. We nevertheless conclude that our rather isolated *Franklin* rule is of limited benefit to the search for truth, and that it in fact may tend to frustrate truth and create incentives for dissembling at trial. The *Franklin* constraints, noted above, do nothing to restrain the incentives of a defendant and the State to consummate bargains deemed advantageous to both. The State understandably desires testimony from persons vulnerable to prosecution that will be of assistance in bringing other malefactors to justice. Such persons are also motivated to bargain in order to ease the consequences that may ensue as a result of their own criminal conduct. The stage is thus set, at least potentially, for the cooperating individual to provide the State with information helpful to the prosecution of one or more other defendants in exchange for some form of leniency concerning his own criminal involvement.

We realize that persons vulnerable to criminal prosecution have incentives to dissemble as an inducement for more favorable treatment by the State. It is thus clear that at least during the negotiating stages of a plea bargain or other arrangements for leniency, the potential witness will provide information that he or she deems to be of value to the State in the prosecution of one or more other criminally involved persons. We must assume that the prosecutor will evaluate the veracity of the information and bargain for its use in the form of trial testimony only if there is a basis for concluding that the information is reliable. In no event would we expect our prosecutors to enter into agreements for perjured testimony.

Moreover, we view as unrealistic the proposition that withholding the benefit of the bargain until after the promisee testifies tends to commit the prosecution to a theory that may be inconsistent with truth or the search for truth. It is difficult to envision a responsible prosecutor proceeding to trial without having carefully developed a trial plan or strategy designed to prove the truth of a theory upon which the prosecution is based.... It seems clear, therefore, that one of the few instances when a prosecutor could improperly adhere to a predetermined factual theory during trial would be where the prosecution is based upon perjured testimony knowingly bargained for as a means of securing a conviction. In the latter case, the problem arises from the prosecutor's dishonesty and lack of ethics as opposed to the withholding of benefits until after the witness testifies.

If the State is required to provide the benefit of the bargain prior to the time the promisee testifies at trial, the State's expectations may be frustrated by an uncooperative or "forgetful" witness. Although it is true, as observed by the court in *Franklin,* that withholding the benefit of the bargain until after the promisee testifies may create pressure to testify in a particular manner, it would be neither realistic nor fair to expect the State to enter into a bargain without assurances that the promisee's trial testimony would be consistent with the information he or she provided to prosecutors as a basis for leniency. We are simply unwilling to assume, and therefore base a rule of law upon, the proposition that our prosecutors will sit down with persons vulnerable to prosecution and commit them to testifying perjuriously. If the person seeking the bargain purports to have true information, and the State concludes that such information is reliable and would be of assistance in prosecuting other persons, the State, in return for a commitment of leniency, would have every right to expect that the promisee's trial testimony would be essentially consistent with the original information upon which the State's promise was induced. If the promisee reneges on the commitment to provide truthful and consistent trial testimony, the State will be free to withdraw from the bargain.

We now conclude that bargaining for specific trial testimony, i.e., testimony that is essentially consistent with the information represented to be factually true during negotiations with the State, and withholding the benefits of the bargain until after the witness has testified, is not inconsistent with the search for truth or due process. However, we emphasize that our ruling does not countenance a bargain for testimony conforming to a predetermined script or for leniency or other consideration contingent upon the State obtaining a conviction. We hold only that when our prosecutors bargain in good faith for testimony represented to be factually accurate, it is not a violation of due process or public policy to withhold the benefit of the bargain until after the witness testifies.

Although we have concluded that executory plea agreements are acceptable under Nevada law, we are not unmindful of the danger posed by perjured testimony concocted by persons seeking lenient treatment in connection with their own criminal problems. We have already noted that the State may properly enter into plea arrangements when the putative witness persuasively professes to have truthful information of value and a willingness to accurately relate such information at trial. The less than remote possibility remains, however, that the recipient of the State's promise has fabricated his or her information and will repeat it at trial as a perjurer. Courts across the land have, in part, sought to deal with the incentive to commit perjury by requiring at trial the baring of all aspects of the bargain pursuant to which the testimony is given. As a result, it is generally determined that the terms of the State's bargain concern only the weight, and not the admissibility of the testimony.

In accordance with the foregoing, we now embrace the rule generally prevailing in both state and federal courts, and hold that any consideration promised by the State in exchange for a witness's testimony affects only the weight accorded the testimony, and not its admissibility. Second, we also hold that the State may not bargain for testimony so particularized that it amounts to following a script, or require that the testimony produce a specific result. Finally, the terms of the *quid pro quo* must be fully disclosed to the jury, the defendant or his counsel must be allowed to fully cross-examine the witness concerning the terms of the bargain, and the jury must be given a cautionary instruction.[4]

In reevaluating *Franklin,* we have concluded that it is both fair and prudent to align Nevada with the general rule of law prevailing in other jurisdictions....

Recently, the California Supreme Court focused on the issue addressed in *People v. Medina, supra,* and concluded that plea bargains consummated in exchange for testimony are unacceptable only where "the testimony must be confined to a predetermined formulation" or must produce "a given result, that is to say, a conviction." *People v. Garrison,* 47 Cal.3d 746, 765 P.2d 419, 428 (1989). The *Garrison* holding is reflective of what appears to be a national consensus disavowing plea bargains in exchange for testimony only where the bargain compels the witness to provide particularized testimony. As noted above, we remain concerned over the prospects of vulnerable persons fabricating testimony as an inducement for leniency by the State, but are convinced that the safeguards provided in the instant ruling will be more effective in ferreting out false testimony than the restrictive rule in *Franklin.* Finally, we reemphasize that it is not improper for the State to require the promisee to testify in a general manner that is consistent with the information provided to the State as an inducement for the bargain, subject, of course, to any change mandated by truth if the promisee subsequently admits to falsifying the information upon which the bargain is based. In the latter event, the State is under no obligation to provide the witness with the benefit of a bargain resulting from disinformation. The testimony condemned by the courts generally, and now this court in particular, is that which must be played according to a predetermined script and irrespective of its truthfulness. The witness must understand that he is not free to commit perjury, and that the plea bargain may not be based upon false testimony.

In the hearing before the district court, testimony established that Crawford was not placed under a compulsion to testify according to preformulated, particularized, and dubious facts. Of course, Crawford was aware of the fact that the State was privy to the transaction concerning which he would testify, and that any deviation from the known, true facts would result in a loss of the concessions he expected to receive from the State. He was nevertheless under no compulsion to testify in accordance with a manufactured script or in any way contrary to the truth. Crawford's agreement with the State compelled him only to be truthful in his testimony.

In view of our ruling, the district court's order granting Acuna's petition for a writ of habeas corpus is reversed and the case is remanded for further proceedings....

ROSE, Justice, with whom SPRINGER, Justice, agrees, concurring:

I am concurring in the result reached by the majority because I do not think the conduct of the law enforcement officers violated the *Franklin* rule. The granting of the writ of habeas corpus should be reversed on that basis rather than overruling the *Franklin* decision.

In *Franklin,* this court balanced the reliability of accomplice testimony with the strong desire of law enforcement to use such testimony, even when the accomplice was given express or implied direction to testify in a specific way. We concluded that an executory plea bargain agreement in which the state bargains for specific testimony is improper, and the accomplice should not be permitted to testify. According to *Franklin,* whether the agreement was a bargain for specific testimony would depend on the express agreement between law enforcement and the ac-

4. We are confident that the rule adopted by this opinion will adequately safeguard a defendant's right to a fair trial. Therefore, to the extent that *Franklin* is inconsistent with our ruling in the instant case, *Franklin* is overruled.

complice, and the circumstances of the entire transaction. *Franklin* was a reasonable decision to help ensure that truthful testimony would be presented at trial.

The State attempts to distinguish this case from *Franklin* by arguing that the *Franklin* rule should be limited to accomplice testimony and not to other informants. However, informant testimony presents the same reliability concerns as accomplice testimony....

In this case, law enforcement bargained for Crawford's cooperation, not his testimony. The agreement was that Crawford would attempt to purchase drugs from Acuna, and law enforcement would then recommend that Crawford receive probation for his involvement in a prior drug sale. Crawford then made a controlled purchase of marijuana from Acuna. Since this transaction with Acuna was monitored, there is a minimum chance of Crawford's fabrication for or against law enforcement. Crawford then testified at trial about this purchase from Acuna.

While it is true that the agreement with Crawford was executory to the extent that he had not been charged with or sentenced for any felony, I do not believe this transaction violated *Franklin.* First, it was a bargain for cooperation, not testimony. When the bargain was struck, there was no testimony to bargain for, since the transaction had not even occurred. Second, there is no suggestion that Crawford was obligated to testify in any particular manner. And, since the transaction Crawford testified about was closely monitored, there is minimum chance of fabrication....

The majority elects to overrule *Franklin,* rather than decide the case on this basis or limit the *Franklin* ruling to accomplice testimony, even though nothing has transpired to diminish the concern for the reliability of this type of testimony since *Franklin* was decided in 1978. In fact, many situations have come to light that justify our suspicions. For example, in the celebrated case of Leslie Vernon White, the Los Angeles district attorney's office found itself in a difficult situation. White admitted that he frequently lied on the witness stand when testifying as a jailhouse informant, which resulted in the convictions of many possibly innocent people.[1] Such revelations are all too frequent and confirm our concern about accomplice and informant testimony.

... [W]e should avoid overturning a long standing decision by judicial fiat, without compelling reason.

Notes and Questions

1. In *Hoffa v. United States,* 385 U.S. 293, 87 S.Ct. 408, 17 L.Ed.2d 374 (1966), the Supreme Court considered a multi-pronged challenge to the government's reliance on the testimony of an undercover informant in a federal criminal trial. The case involved the prosecution of Teamsters president Jimmy Hoffa for endeavoring to bribe members of the jury impaneled to determine whether Hoffa had violated the Taft-Hartley Act in a

1. Over the past decade, Leslie White has testified against at least a dozen California inmates whom he claimed confessed their guilt to him. However, he later disclosed that at least some of the information he passed on to lawmen was nothing but lies. He demonstrated how easy it is for a "snitch" to concoct a false confession simply by using a telephone in the prison chaplain's office. Identifying himself as a bail bondsman, White called the sheriff's document-control center and got an accused murderer's case number and date of arrest. Then, he called the district attorney's records bureau, identifying himself as a deputy district attorney to obtain names of witnesses and the prosecutors handling the case. In order to obtain details of the murder, White called the coroner's office and told them he was a police officer.

After he falsely testified about a confession or damaging admission made in jail by the defendant which would be consistent with the facts he had learned, White would receive special privileges, including early release from his frequent prison terms. As a result of White's revelations of fabricated testimony, Los Angeles is having to review more than 130 cases from the past ten years for possible taint. *A Snitch's Story,* Time Magazine, December 12, 1988.

Furthermore, there is some indication that informants are more frequently used when a case is weak, and therefore, the risk of convicting innocent people is increased. *Use of Jailhouse Informers Reviewed in Los Angeles,* New York Times, January 3, 1989. Of the 225 people convicted of murder and other felonies as a result of Mr. White and other jailhouse informers' testimony over the last 10 years in Los Angeles, 30 are on death row. *California Shaken over an Informer,* New York Times, February 16, 1989.

case referred to as "the Test Fleet trial." While the Test Fleet trial was underway in Nashville, Tennessee, Edward Partin, a Teamsters official from Louisiana, visited with Hoffa on several occasions. The Test Fleet trial ultimately ended in a hung jury. Hoffa subsequently was brought to trial and convicted for endeavoring to bribe members of the Test Fleet trial jury. Partin provided crucial testimony at the bribery trial regarding conversations he had had with Hoffa. Although it was disputed whether Partin was acting as an undercover government informant when he engaged in those conversations or instead decided to assist the prosecution sometime thereafter, the Court proceeded "upon the premise that Partin was a government informer from the time he first arrived in Nashville ... and that the Government compensated him for his services as such." 385 U.S., at 299. After rejecting Hoffa's arguments that the government's use of an undercover informant in such a capacity violated his rights under the Fourth, Fifth, and Sixth Amendments, Justice Stewart's majority opinion addressed Hoffa's Due Process argument.

... The 'totality' of the Government's conduct during the Test Fleet trial operated, it is said, to "offend those canons of decency and fairness which express the notions of justice of English-speaking peoples even toward those charged with the most heinous offenses" (Rochin v. California, 342 U.S. 165, 169 [1952]).

The argument boils down to a general attack upon the use of a government informer as 'a shabby thing in any case,' and to the claim that in the circumstances of this particular case the risk that Partin's testimony might be perjurious was very high. Insofar as the general attack upon the use of informers is based upon historic 'notions' of 'English-speaking peoples,' it is without historical foundation....

This is not to say that a secret government informer is to the slightest degree more free from all relevant constitutional restrictions than is any other government agent. See Massiah v. United States, 377 U.S. 201 [(1964)]. It is to say that the use of secret informers is not per se unconstitutional.

The petitioner is quite correct in the contention that Partin, perhaps even more than most informers, may have had motives to lie. But it does not follow that his testimony was untrue, nor does it follow that his testimony was constitutionally inadmissible. The established safeguards of the Anglo-American legal system leave the veracity of a witness to be tested by cross-examination, and the credibility of his testimony to be determined by a properly instructed jury. At the trial of this case, Partin was subjected to rigorous cross-examination, and the extent and nature of his dealings with federal and state authorities were insistently explored. The trial judge instructed the jury, both specifically[13] and generally,[14] with regard to assessing Partin's credibility. The Constitution does not require us to upset the jury's verdict....

Chief Justice Warren dissented. His opinion elaborated on the circumstances surrounding Partin's interactions with Hoffa and his incentives to provide favorable testimony for the government.

---

13. The judge instructed the jury that it was petitioner's contention that he 'did not invite Edward Partin to come to Nashville, Tennessee, during the trial of (the Test Fleet case) but that the said Edward Partin came of his own accord under the pretense of attempting to convince Mr. Hoffa that the Teamsters local union in Baton Rouge, Louisiana should not be placed in trusteeship by reason of Partin's being under indictment and other misconduct on Partin's part, but for the real purpose of fabricating evidence against Hoffa in order to serve his own purposes and interests.'

14. The jury was instructed: 'You should carefully scrutinize the testimony given and the circumstances under which each witness has testified, and every matter in evidence which tends to indicate whether the witness is worthy of belief. Consider each witness' intelligence, his motives, state of mind, his demeanor and manner while on the witness stand. Consider also any relation each witness may bear to either side of the case * * *. All evidence of a witness whose self-interest is shown from either benefits received, detriments suffered, threats or promises made, or any attitude of the witness which might tend to prompt testimony either favorable or unfavorable to the accused should be considered with caution and weighed with care.'

... At this late date in the annals of law enforcement, it seems to me that we cannot say either that every use of informers and undercover agents is proper or, on the other hand, that no uses are. There are some situations where the law could not adequately be enforced without the employment of some guile or misrepresentation of identity. A law enforcement officer performing his official duties cannot be required always to be in uniform or to wear his badge of authority on the lapel of his civilian clothing. Nor need he be required in all situations to proclaim himself an arm of the law. It blinks the realities of sophisticated, modern-day criminal activity and legitimate law enforcement practices to argue the contrary. However, one of the important duties of this Court is to give careful scrutiny to practices of government agents when they are challenged in cases before us, in order to insure that the protections of the Constitution are respected and to maintain the integrity of federal law enforcement....

Here, Edward Partin, a jailbird languishing in a Louisiana jail under indictments for such state and federal crimes as embezzlement, kidnapping, and manslaughter (and soon to be charged with perjury and assault), contacted federal authorities and told them he was willing to become, and would be useful as, an informer against Hoffa who was then about to be tried in the Test Fleet case. A motive for his doing this is immediately apparent—namely, his strong desire to work his way out of jail and out of his various legal entanglements with the State and Federal Governments. And it is interesting to note that, if this was his motive, he has been uniquely successful in satisfying it. In the four years since he first volunteered to be an informer against Hoffa he has not been prosecuted on any of the serious federal charges for which he was at that time jailed, and the state charges have apparently vanished into thin air.

Shortly after Partin made contact with the federal authorities and told them of his position in the Baton Rouge Local of the Teamsters Union and of his acquaintance with Hoffa, his bail was suddenly reduced from $50,000 to $5,000 and he was released from jail. He immediately telephoned Hoffa, who was then in New Jersey, and, by collaborating with a state law enforcement official, surreptitiously made a tape recording of the conversation. A copy of the recording was furnished to federal authorities. Again on a pretext of wanting to talk with Hoffa regarding Partin's legal difficulties, Partin telephoned Hoffa a few weeks later and succeeded in making a date to meet in Nashville where Hoffa and his attorneys were then preparing for the Test Fleet trial. Unknown to Hoffa, this call was also recorded and again federal authorities were informed as to the details.

Upon his arrival in Nashville, Partin manifested his 'friendship' and made himself useful to Hoffa, thereby worming his way into Hoffa's hotel suite and becoming part and parcel of Hoffa's entourage. As the 'faithful' servant and factotum of the defense camp which he became, he was in a position to overhear conversations not directed to him, many of which were between attorneys and either their or prospective defense witnesses. Pursuant to the general instructions he received from federal authorities to report 'any attempts at witness intimidation or tampering with the jury,' anything illegal,' or even 'anything of interest,' Partin became the equivalent of a bugging device which moved with Hoffa wherever he went. Everything Partin saw or heard was reported to federal authorities and much of it was ultimately the subject matter of his testimony in this case. For his services he was well paid by the Government, both through devious and secret support payments to his wife and, it may be inferred, by executed promises not to pursue the indictments under which he was charged at the time he became an informer.

This type of informer and the uses to which he was put in this case evidence a serious potential for undermining the integrity of the truth-finding process in the federal courts. Given the incentives and background of Partin, no conviction should be allowed to stand when based heavily on his testimony. And that is exactly the quicksand upon which these convictions rest, because without Partin, who was the principal government witness, there would probably have been no convictions here.... [T]he affront to the quality and fairness of federal law enforcement which this case presents is sufficient to require an exercise of our supervisory powers. As we said in ordering a new trial in Mesarosh v. United States, 352 U.S. 1, 14 (1956), a federal case involving the testimony of an unsavory informer who, the Government admitted, had committed perjury in other cases:

'This is a federal criminal case, and this Court has supervisory jurisdiction over the proceedings of the federal courts. If it has any duty to perform in this regard, it is to see that the waters of justice are not polluted. Pollution having taken place here, the condition should be remedied at the earliest opportunity.

'The government of a strong and free nation does not need convictions based upon such testimony. It cannot afford to abide with them.'

I do not say that the Government may never use as a witness a person of dubious or even bad character. In performing its duty to prosecute crime the Government must take the witnesses as it finds them. They may be persons of good, bad, or doubtful credibility, but their testimony may be the only way to establish the facts, leaving it to the jury to determine their credibility. In this case, however, we have a totally different situation. Here the Government reaches into the jailhouse to employ a man who was himself facing indictments far more serious (and later including one for perjury) than the one confronting the man against whom he offered to inform. It employed him not for the purpose of testifying to something that had already happened, but rather for the purpose of infiltration to see if crimes would in the future be committed. The Government in its zeal even assisted him in gaining a position from which he could be a witness to the confidential relationship of attorney and client engaged in the preparation of a criminal defense. And, for the dubious evidence thus obtained, the Government paid an enormous price. Certainly if a criminal defendant insinuated his informer into the prosecution's camp in this manner he would be guilty of obstructing justice. I cannot agree that what happened in this case is in keeping with the standards of justice in our federal system and I must, therefore, dissent.

2. Social scientists have begun to address the question of why and when informants "snitch." In a cleverly designed laboratory study, the influence of offering an incentive to provide a "secondary confession" (*i.e.*, a witness stating that the suspect committed the mock crime) was examined. Swanner, Beike and Cole[10] found that the provided incentive—in this case, not getting in trouble—increased the number of false secondary confessions but did not increase true ones. More specifically, when the suspect denied committing the mock crime, the number of incentivized snitches who informed on the suspect went up. When the suspect confessed, incentives did not influence rates of informants snitching. This finding has special relevance to the risk of wrongful convictions.

3. Professor Alexandra Natapoff has written that "[c]riminal informants are a potent and sometimes necessary crime-fighting tool.... Offering lenience to low-level offenders is sometimes the only way to get information about high-level criminals." Alexandra Natapoff, *Snitching: Criminal Informants and the Erosion of American Justice* 2 (New York: New York University Press 2009). But she also has warned:

> At the same time, using criminal informants exacerbates some of the worst features of the U.S. justice system. The practice is clandestine and unregulated, inviting inaccuracy, crime, and sometimes corruption. It inflicts special harms on vulnerable individuals such as racial minorities, substance abusers, and poor defendants who lack robust legal representation. Because of its secretive and discretionary nature, it evades the traditional checks and balances of judicial and public scrutiny, even as it determines the outcomes of millions of investigations and cases. And finally, like the criminal system itself, it is rapidly expanding. *Id.*, at 3.

C. Informant Testimony and Prosecutors' Duties: Disclosure and Oversight

1. The Duty to Disclose

Giglio v. United States

405 U.S. 150, 92 S.Ct. 763, 31 L.Ed.2d 104 (1972)

Mr. Chief Justice BURGER delivered the opinion of the Court.

Petitioner was convicted of passing forged money orders and sentenced to five years' imprisonment. While appeal was pending in the Court of Appeals, defense counsel discovered new evidence indicating that the Government had failed to disclose an alleged promise made to its key witness that he would not be prosecuted if he testified for the Government. We granted certiorari to determine whether the evidence not disclosed was such as to require a new trial under the due process criteria of Napue v. Illinois, 360 U.S. 264 (1959), and Brady v. Maryland, 373 U.S. 83 (1963).

The controversy in this case centers around the testimony of Robert Taliento, petitioner's alleged coconspirator in the offense and the only witness linking petitioner with the crime. The Government's evidence at trial showed that in June 1966 officials at the Manufacturers Hanover Trust Co. discovered that Taliento, as teller at the bank, had cashed several forged money orders. Upon questioning by FBI agents, he confessed supplying petitioner with one of the bank's customer signature cards used by Giglio to forge $2,300 in money orders; Taliento then processed these money orders through the regular channels of the bank. Taliento related this story to the grand jury and petitioner was indicted; thereafter, he was named as a coconspirator with petitioner but was not indicted.

Trial commenced two years after indictment. Taliento testified, identifying petitioner as the instigator of the scheme. Defense counsel vigorously cross-examined, seeking to discredit his testimony by revealing possible agreements or arrangements for prosecutorial leniency:

'(Counsel.) Did anybody tell you at any time that if you implicated somebody else in this case that you yourself would not be prosecuted?

'(Taliento.) Nobody told me I wouldn't be prosecuted.

'Q. They told you you might not be prosecuted?

'A. I believe I still could be prosecuted.

...

'Q. Were you ever arrested in this case or charged with anything in connection with these money orders that you testified to?

'A. Not at that particular time.

'Q. To this date, have you been charged with any crime?

'A. Not that I know of, unless they are still going to prosecute.'

In summation, the Government attorney stated, '(Taliento) received no promises that he would not be indicted.'

The issue now before the Court arose on petitioner's motion for new trial based on newly discovered evidence. An affidavit filed by the Government as part of its opposition to a new trial confirms petitioner's claim that a promise was made to Taliento by one assistant, DiPaola, that if he testified before the grand jury and at trial he would not be prosecuted.[2] DiPaola presented the Government's case to the grand jury but did not try the case in the District Court, and Golden, the assistant who took over the case for trial, filed an affidavit stating that DiPaola

---

2. DiPaola's affidavit reads, in part, as follows:

'It was agreed that if ROBERT EDWARD TALIENTO would testify before the Grand Jury as a witness for the Government, ... he would not be ... indicted.... It was further agreed and understood that he, ROBERT EDWARD TALIENTO, would sign a Waiver of Immunity from prosecution before the Grand Jury, and that if he eventually testified as a witness for the Government at the trial of the defendant, JOHN GIGLIO, he would not be prosecuted.'

assured him before the trial that no promises of immunity had been made to Taliento.[3] The United States Attorney, Hoey, filed an affidavit stating that he had personally consulted with Taliento and his attorney shortly before trial to emphasize that Taliento would definitely be prosecuted if he did not testify and that if he did testify he would be obliged to rely on the 'good judgment and conscience of the Government' as to whether he would be prosecuted.

The District Court did not undertake to resolve the apparent conflict between the two Assistant United States Attorneys, DiPaola and Golden, but proceeded on the theory that even if a promise had been made by DiPaola it was not authorized and its disclosure to the jury would not have affected its verdict. We need not concern ourselves with the differing versions of the events as described by the two assistants in their affidavits. The heart of the matter is that one Assistant United States Attorney—the first one who dealt with Taliento—now states that he promised Taliento that he would not be prosecuted if he cooperated with the Government.

As long ago as Mooney v. Holohan, 294 U.S. 103, 112 (1935), this Court made clear that deliberate deception of a court and jurors by the presentation of known false evidence is incompatible with 'rudimentary demands of justice.' This was reaffirmed in Pyle v. Kansas, 317 U.S. 213 (1942). In Napue v. Illinois, 360 U.S. 264 (1959), we said, '(t)he same result obtains when the State, although not soliciting false evidence, allows it to go uncorrected when it appears.' Id., at 269. Thereafter Brady v. Maryland, 373 U.S., at 87, held that suppression of material evidence justifies a new trial 'irrespective of the good faith or bad faith of the prosecution.' When the 'reliability of a given witness may well be determinative of guilt or innocence,' nondisclosure of evidence affecting credibility falls within this general rule. We do not, however, automatically require a new trial whenever 'a combing of the prosecutors' files after the trial has disclosed evidence possibly useful to the defense but not likely to have changed the verdict....' United States v. Keogh, 391 F.2d 138, 148 (CA2 1968). A finding of materiality of the evidence is required under Brady. A new trial is required if 'the false testimony could ... in any reasonable likelihood have affected the judgment of the jury ...' Napue, supra, at 271.

In the circumstances shown by this record, neither DiPaola's authority nor his failure to inform his superiors or his associates is controlling. Moreover, whether the nondisclosure was a result of negligence or design, it is the responsibility of the prosecutor. The prosecutor's office is an entity and as such it is the spokesman for the Government. A promise made by one attorney must be attributed, for these purposes, to the Government. To the extent this places a burden on the large prosecution offices, procedures and regulations can be established to carry that burden and to insure communication of all relevant information on each case to every lawyer who deals with it.

Here the Government's case depended almost entirely on Taliento's testimony; without it there could have been no indictment and no evidence to carry the case to the jury. Taliento's credibility as a witness was therefore an important issue in the case, and evidence of any understanding or agreement as to a future prosecution would be relevant to his credibility and the jury was entitled to know of it.

For these reasons, the due process requirements enunciated in Napue and the other cases cited earlier require a new trial, and the judgment of conviction is therefore reversed and the case is remanded for further proceedings consistent with this opinion....

Notes and Questions

1. Assume that the explicit agreement between the witness Taliento and Assistant United States Attorney DiPaola, as reflected in the affidavit quoted in footnote 2 of Chief Justice Burger's opinion in *Giglio*, had not been made and that Taliento nevertheless had testified with the hope and expectation that his testimony would be rewarded by the government.

---

3. Golden's affidavit reads, in part, as follows:
'Mr. DiPaola ... advised that Mr. Taliento had not been granted immunity but that he had not indicted him because Robert Taliento was very young at the time of the alleged occurrence and obviously had been overreached by the defendant Giglio.'

Under those facts, would either Taliento's testimony or the argument of the Assistant U.S. Attorney who represented the government at trial, that the witness "received no promises that he would not be indicted," have been problematic? Consider the following:

> One of the most difficult areas to regulate involves the unstated expectations and *sub rosa* understandings [between prosecuting attorneys and testifying witnesses].... One commentator has observed:
>
> To enhance the credibility of his testimony, an informant often testified that there have been no promises of benefits made to them in return for their testimony [sic]. Even though nothing may be explicitly stated, both the prosecutor and the informant knew that there will be some compensation for the testimony. "The practice (of promising rewards) was done by a wink and a nod and it was never necessary to have any kind of formal understanding."
>
> As one court wrote: "We are not unaware of the reality that the Government has ways of indicating to witness's [sic] counsel the likely benefits from cooperation without making bald promises...."

Paul C. Giannelli, "*Brady* and Jailhouse Snitches," 57 *Case Western Reserve Law Review* 593, 607 (2007) (citations omitted).

2. In 1980, Delma Banks, Jr. was convicted of capital murder in Texas and sentenced to death. Robert Farr, a key prosecution witness, testified at both the guilt and penalty phases of Banks's trial. While undergoing cross-examination during the guilt trial, Farr was asked "whether he had 'ever taken any money from some police officers,' or 'give[n] any police officers a statement.' Farr answered no to both questions; he asserted emphatically that police officers had not promised him anything and that he had 'talked to no one about this [case]' until a few days before trial. These answers were untrue, but the State did not correct them. Farr was the paid informant who told Deputy Sheriff Huff that Banks would travel to Dallas in search of a gun." *Banks v. Dretke,* 540 U.S. 668, 678, 124 S.Ct. 1256, 157 L.Ed.2d 1166 (2004).

> Farr's trial testimony, critical at the penalty phase, was cast in large doubt by the declaration Banks ultimately obtained from Farr and introduced in the federal habeas proceeding. In the guilt phase of Banks's trial, Farr had acknowledged his narcotics use. In the penalty phase, Banks's counsel asked Farr if, "drawn up tight over" previous drug-related activity, he would "testify to anything anybody want[ed] to hear"; Farr denied this. Farr's declaration supporting Banks's federal habeas petition, however, vividly contradicts that denial: "I assumed that if I did not help [Huff] ... he would have me arrested for drug charges." Had jurors known of Farr's continuing interest in obtaining Deputy Sheriff Huff's favor in addition to his receipt of funds to "set [Banks] up," they might well have distrusted Farr's testimony, and, insofar as it was uncorroborated, disregarded it. *Id.*, 540 U.S., at 701.

During closing arguments at the guilt-phase trial, "the prosecution called the jury's attention to Farr's admission, at trial, that he used narcotics. Just as Farr had been truthful about his drug use, the prosecution suggested, he was also 'open and honest with [the jury] in every way in his penalty-phase testimony.' Farr's testimony, the prosecution emphasized, was 'of the utmost significance' because it showed '[Banks] is a danger to friends and strangers alike.'" *Id.*, 540 U.S., at 681–682.

Focusing on these aspects of Farr's testimony, the Supreme Court ruled that the court of appeals erred in dismissing the habeas corpus relief granted Banks by the federal district court. Justice Ginsburg's opinion for the Court elaborated on the importance of fact-finders being provided with information necessary to assess informants' reliability.

The jury, moreover, did not benefit from customary, truth-promoting precautions that generally accompany the testimony of informants. This Court has long recognized the "serious questions of credibility" informers pose. *On Lee v. United States,* 343 U.S. 747, 757 (1952). See also Trott, Words of Warning for Prosecutors Using Criminals as Witnesses, 47 Hastings L.J. 1381, 1385 (1996) ("Jurors suspect [informants'] motives from the moment they hear about them in a case, and they frequently disregard their testimony altogether as highly untrustworthy and unreliable...."). We have therefore allowed defendants "broad latitude to probe [informants'] credibility by cross-examination" and have counseled submission of the credibility issue to the jury "with careful instructions." *On Lee,* 343 U.S., at 757, 72 S.Ct. 967; accord *Hoffa v. United States,* 385 U.S. 293, 311–312 (1966). See also 1A K. O'-Malley, J. Grenig, & W. Lee, Federal Jury Practice and Instructions, Criminal § 15.02 (5th ed.2000) (jury instructions from the First, Fifth, Sixth, Seventh, Eighth, Ninth, and Eleventh Circuits on special caution appropriate in assessing informant testimony).

The State argues that "Farr was heavily impeached [at trial]," rendering his informant status "merely cumulative." The record suggests otherwise. Neither witness called to impeach Farr gave evidence directly relevant to Farr's part in Banks's trial. The impeaching witnesses, Kelley and Owen, moreover, were themselves impeached, as the prosecution stressed on summation. Further, the prosecution turned to its advantage remaining impeachment evidence concerning Farr's drug use. On summation, the prosecution suggested that Farr's admission "that he used dope, that he shot," demonstrated that Farr had been "open and honest with [the jury] in every way."

At least as to the penalty phase, in sum, one can hardly be confident that Banks received a fair trial, given the jury's ignorance of Farr's true role in the investigation and trial of the case. See *Kyles* [*v. Whitley,* 514 U.S. 419, 434 (1995)] ("The question is not whether the defendant would more likely than not have received a different verdict with the evidence, but whether in its absence he received a fair trial, understood as a trial resulting in a verdict worthy of confidence."). On the record before us, one could not plausibly deny the existence of the requisite "reasonable probability of a different result" had the suppressed information been disclosed to the defense. *Ibid.* (citing [*United States v.*] *Bagley,* 473 U.S. [667], 678 [(1985)]. Accordingly, as to the suppression of Farr's informant status and its bearing on "the reliability of the jury's verdict regarding punishment," ... [the] elements of a *Brady* claim are satisfied.

2. A Duty to Monitor?

In Chapter 2, we considered several Supreme Court decisions addressing the scope of prosecutors' immunity from liability in cases arising under 42 U.S.C. § 1983, the federal civil rights statute. We now revisit that issue in connection with a § 1983 lawsuit seeking damages from a prosecutor and his assistant based on their alleged failure "adequately to train and to supervise the prosecutors who worked for them as well as their failure to establish an information system about informants."

Van de Kamp v. Goldstein

__ U.S.__, 129 S.Ct. 855, 172 L.Ed.2d 706 (2009)

Justice BREYER delivered the opinion of the Court.

We here consider the scope of a prosecutor's absolute immunity from claims asserted under 42 U.S.C. § 1983. See *Imbler v. Pachtman,* 424 U.S. 409 (1976). We ask whether that immunity extends to claims that the prosecution failed to disclose impeachment material, see *Giglio v. United States,* 405 U.S. 150 (1972), due to: (1) a failure properly to train prosecutors, (2) a failure properly to supervise prosecutors, or (3) a failure to establish an information system containing potential impeachment material about informants. We conclude that a prosecutor's absolute immunity extends to all these claims.

I

In 1998, respondent Thomas Goldstein (then a prisoner) filed a habeas corpus action in the Federal District Court for the Central District of California. He claimed that in 1980 he was convicted of murder; that his conviction depended in critical part upon the testimony of Edward Floyd Fink, a jailhouse informant; that Fink's testimony was unreliable, indeed false; that Fink had previously received reduced sentences for providing prosecutors with favorable testimony in other cases; that at least some prosecutors in the Los Angeles County District Attorney's Office knew about the favorable treatment; that the office had not provided Goldstein's attorney with that information; and that, among other things, the prosecution's failure to provide Goldstein's attorney with this potential impeachment information had led to his erroneous conviction.

After an evidentiary hearing the District Court agreed with Goldstein that Fink had not been truthful and that if the prosecution had told Goldstein's lawyer that Fink had received prior rewards in return for favorable testimony it might have made a difference. The court ordered the State either to grant Goldstein a new trial or to release him. The Court of Appeals affirmed the District Court's determination. And the State decided that, rather than retry Goldstein (who had already served 24 years of his sentence), it would release him.

Upon his release Goldstein filed this § 1983 action against petitioners, the former Los Angeles County district attorney and chief deputy district attorney. Goldstein's complaint (which for present purposes we take as accurate) asserts in relevant part that the prosecution's failure to communicate to his attorney the facts about Fink's earlier testimony-related rewards violated the prosecution's constitutional duty to "insure communication of all relevant information on each case [including agreements made with informants] to every lawyer who deals with it." *Giglio, supra,* at 154. Moreover, it alleges that this failure resulted from the failure of petitioners (the office's chief supervisory attorneys) adequately to train and to supervise the prosecutors who worked for them as well as their failure to establish an information system about informants. And it asks for damages based upon these training, supervision, and information-system related failings.

Petitioners, claiming absolute immunity from such a § 1983 action, asked the District Court to dismiss the complaint. The District Court denied the motion to dismiss on the ground that the conduct asserted amounted to "administrative," not "prosecutorial," conduct; hence it fell outside the scope of the prosecutor's absolute immunity to § 1983 claims. The Ninth Circuit ... affirmed the District Court's "no immunity" determination. We now ... reverse....

II

A half-century ago Chief Judge Learned Hand explained that a prosecutor's absolute immunity reflects "a balance" of "evils." *Gregoire v. Biddle,* 177 F.2d 579, 581 (C.A.2 1949). "[I]t has been thought in the end better," he said, "to leave unredressed the wrongs done by dishonest officers than to subject those who try to do their duty to the constant dread of retaliation." In *Imbler,* this Court considered prosecutorial actions that are "intimately associated with the judicial phase of the criminal process." And, referring to Chief Judge Hand's views, it held that prosecutors are absolutely immune from liability in § 1983 lawsuits brought under such circumstances.

The § 1983 action at issue was that of a prisoner freed on a writ of habeas corpus who subsequently sought damages from his former prosecutor.... In particular, the prisoner claimed that the trial prosecutor had permitted a fingerprint expert to give false testimony, that the prosecutor was responsible for the expert's having suppressed important evidence, and that the prosecutor had introduced a misleading artist's sketch into evidence.

In concluding that the prosecutor was absolutely immune, the Court pointed out that legislators have long "enjoyed absolute immunity for their official actions," that the common law granted immunity to "judges and ... jurors acting within the scope of their duties," and that the law had also granted prosecutors absolute immunity from common-law tort actions, say, those underlying a "decision to initiate a prosecution." The Court then held that the "same considerations of public policy that underlie" a prosecutor's common-law immunity "countenance absolute immunity under § 1983." Those considerations, the Court said, arise out of the general common-law "concern that harassment by unfounded litigation" could both "cause a deflection of the prosecutor's energies from his public duties" and also lead the prosecutor to "shade his decisions instead of exercising the independence of judgment required by his public trust."

Where § 1983 actions are at issue, the Court said, both sets of concerns are present and serious. The "public trust of the prosecutor's office would suffer" were the prosecutor to have in mind his "own potential" damages "liability" when making prosecutorial decisions—as he might well were he subject to § 1983 liability. This is no small concern, given the frequency with which criminal defendants bring such suits, ... and the "substantial danger of liability even to the honest prosecutor" that such suits pose when they survive pretrial dismissal ... A "prosecutor," the Court noted, "inevitably makes many decisions that could engender colorable claims of constitutional deprivation. Defending these decisions, often years after they were made, could impose unique and intolerable burdens upon a prosecutor responsible annually for hundreds of indictments and trials." The Court thus rejected the idea of applying the less-than-absolute "qualified immunity" that the law accords to other "executive or administrative officials," noting that the "honest prosecutor would face greater difficulty" than would those officials "in meeting the standards of qualified immunity." Accordingly, the immunity that the law grants prosecutors is "absolute."

The Court made clear that absolute immunity may not apply when a prosecutor is not acting as "an officer of the court," but is instead engaged in other tasks, say, investigative or administrative tasks. To decide whether absolute immunity attaches to a particular kind of prosecutorial activity, one must take account of the "functional" considerations discussed above. See *Burns v. Reed,* 500 U.S. 478 (1991) (collecting cases applying "functional approach" to immunity); *Kalina v. Fletcher,* 522 U.S. 118 (1997). In *Imbler,* the Court concluded that the "reasons for absolute immunity appl[ied] with full force" to the conduct at issue because it was "intimately associated with the judicial phase of the criminal process." The fact that one constitutional duty at issue was a positive duty (the duty to supply "information relevant to the defense") rather than a negative duty (the duty not to "use ... perjured testimony") made no difference. After all, a plaintiff can often transform a positive into a negative duty simply by reframing the pleadings; in either case, a constitutional violation is at issue.

Finally, the Court specifically reserved the question whether or when "similar reasons require immunity for those aspects of the prosecutor's responsibility that cast him in the role of an administrator ... rather than that of advocate." It said that "[d]rawing a proper line between these functions may present difficult questions, but this case does not require us to anticipate them."

In the years since *Imbler,* we have held that absolute immunity applies when a prosecutor prepares to initiate a judicial proceeding, *Burns, supra,* or appears in court to present evidence in support of a search warrant application, *Kalina, supra.* We have held that absolute immunity does not apply when a prosecutor gives advice to police during a criminal investigation, see *Burns, supra,* when the prosecutor makes statements to the press, *Buckley v. Fitzsimmons,* 509 U.S. 259 (1993), or when a prosecutor acts as a complaining witness in support of a warrant application, *Kalina* (SCALIA, J., concurring). This case, unlike these earlier cases, requires us to consider how immunity applies where a prosecutor is engaged in certain administrative activities.

III

Goldstein claims that the district attorney and his chief assistant violated their constitutional obligation to provide his attorney with impeachment-related information, see *Giglio,* 405 U.S. 150, because, as the Court of Appeals wrote, they failed "to adequately train and supervise deputy district attorneys on that subject," and because, as Goldstein's complaint adds, they "failed to create any system for the Deputy District Attorneys handling criminal cases to access information pertaining to the benefits provided to jailhouse informants and other impeachment information." We agree with Goldstein that, in making these claims, he attacks the office's administrative procedures. We are also willing to assume with Goldstein, but purely for argument's sake, that *Giglio* imposes certain obligations as to training, supervision, or information-system management.

Even so, we conclude that prosecutors involved in such supervision or training or information-system management enjoy absolute immunity from the kind of legal claims at issue here. Those claims focus upon a certain kind of administrative obligation—a kind that itself is directly connected with the conduct of a trial. Here, unlike with other claims related to administrative decisions, an individual prosecutor's error in the plaintiff's specific criminal trial constitutes an essential element of the plaintiff's claim. The administrative obligations at issue here are thus unlike administrative duties concerning, for example, workplace hiring, payroll administration, the maintenance of physical facilities, and the like. Moreover, the types of activities on which Goldstein's claims focus necessarily require legal knowledge and the exercise of related discretion, *e.g.*, in determining what information should be included in the training or the supervision or the information-system management. And in that sense also Goldstein's claims are unlike claims of, say, unlawful discrimination in hiring employees. Given these features of the case before us, we believe absolute immunity must follow.

A

We reach this conclusion by initially considering a hypothetical case that involves supervisory or other office prosecutors but does not involve administration. Suppose that Goldstein had brought such a case, seeking damages not only from the trial prosecutor but also from a supervisory prosecutor or from the trial prosecutor's colleagues—all on the ground that they should have found and turned over the impeachment material about Fink. *Imbler* makes clear that all these prosecutors would enjoy absolute immunity from such a suit. The prosecutors' behavior, taken individually or separately, would involve "[p]reparation ... for ... trial," and would be "intimately associated with the judicial phase of the criminal process" because it concerned the evidence presented at trial. And all of the considerations that this Court found to militate in favor of absolute immunity in *Imbler* would militate in favor of immunity in such a case.

The only difference we can find between *Imbler* and our hypothetical case lies in the fact that, in our hypothetical case, a prosecutorial supervisor or colleague might himself be liable for damages *instead of* the trial prosecutor. But we cannot find that difference (in the pattern of liability among prosecutors within a single office) to be critical. Decisions about indictment or trial prosecution will often involve more than one prosecutor within an office. We do not see how such differences in the pattern of liability among a group of prosecutors in a single office could alleviate *Imbler*'s basic fear, namely, that the threat of damages liability would affect the way in which prosecutors carried out their basic court-related tasks. Moreover, this Court has pointed out that "it is the interest in protecting the proper functioning of the office, rather than the interest in protecting its occupant, that is of primary importance." *Kalina*, 522 U.S., at 125. Thus, we must assume that the prosecutors in our hypothetical suit would enjoy absolute immunity.

B

Once we determine that supervisory prosecutors are immune in a suit directly attacking their actions related to an individual trial, we must find they are similarly immune in the case before us. We agree with the Court of Appeals that the office's *general* methods of supervision and training are at issue here, but we do not agree that that difference is critical for present purposes. That difference does not preclude an intimate connection between prosecutorial activity and the trial process. The management tasks at issue, insofar as they are relevant, concern how and when to make impeachment information available at a trial. They are thereby directly connected with the prosecutor's basic trial advocacy duties. And, in terms of *Imbler*'s functional concerns, a suit charging that a supervisor made a mistake directly related to a particular trial, on the one hand, and a suit charging that a supervisor trained and supervised inadequately, on the other, would seem very much alike.

That is true, in part, for the practical reason that it will often prove difficult to draw a line between *general* office supervision or office training (say, related to *Giglio*) and *specific* supervision or training related to a particular case. To permit claims based upon the former is almost inevitably to permit the bringing of claims that include the latter. It is also true because one cannot easily distinguish, for immunity purposes, between claims based upon training or supervisory failures related to *Giglio* and similar claims related to other constitutional matters (obligations under *Brady v. Maryland*, 373 U.S. 83 (1963), for example). And that being so, every consideration that *Imbler* mentions militates in favor of immunity.

As we have said, the type of "faulty training" claim at issue here rests in necessary part upon a consequent error by an individual prosecutor in the midst of trial, namely, the plaintiff's trial. If, as *Imbler* says, the threat of damages liability for such an error could lead a trial prosecutor to take account of that risk when making trial-related decisions, so, too, could the threat of more widespread liability throughout the office (ultimately traceable to that trial error) lead both that prosecutor and other office prosecutors as well to take account of such a risk. Indeed, members of a large prosecutorial office, when making prosecutorial decisions, could have in mind the "consequences in terms of" damages liability whether they are making general decisions about supervising or training or whether they are making individual trial-related decisions.

Moreover, because better training or supervision might prevent most, if not all, prosecutorial errors at trial, permission to bring such a suit here would grant permission to criminal defendants to bring claims in other similar instances, in effect claiming damages for (trial-related) training or supervisory failings. Further, given the complexity of the constitutional issues, inadequate training and supervision suits could, as in *Imbler,* "pose substantial danger of liability even to the honest prosecutor." Finally, as *Imbler* pointed out, defending prosecutorial decisions, often years after they were made, could impose "unique and intolerable burdens upon a prosecutor responsible annually for hundreds of indictments and trials."

At the same time, to permit this suit to go forward would create practical anomalies. A trial prosecutor would remain immune, even for *intentionally* failing to turn over, say *Giglio* material; but her supervisor might be liable for *negligent* training or supervision. Small prosecution offices where supervisors can personally participate in all of the cases would likewise remain immune from prosecution; but large offices, making use of more general office-wide supervision and training, would not. Most important, the ease with which a plaintiff could restyle a complaint charging a trial failure so that it becomes a complaint charging a failure of training or supervision would eviscerate *Imbler.*

We conclude that the very reasons that led this Court in *Imbler* to find absolute immunity require a similar finding in this case. We recognize, as Chief Judge Hand pointed out, that sometimes such immunity deprives a plaintiff of compensation that he undoubtedly merits; but the impediments to the fair, efficient functioning of a prosecutorial office that liability could create lead us to find that *Imbler* must apply here.

C

We treat separately Goldstein's claim that the Los Angeles County District Attorney's Office should have established a system that would have permitted prosecutors "handling criminal cases to access information pertaining to the benefits provided to jailhouse informants and other impeachment information." We do so because Goldstein argues that the creation of an information management system is a more purely administrative task, less closely related to the "judicial phase of the criminal process," than are supervisory or training tasks. He adds that technically qualified individuals other than prosecutors could create such a system and that they could do so prior to the initiation of criminal proceedings.

In our view, however, these differences do not require a different outcome. The critical element of any information system is the information it contains. Deciding what to include and what not to include in an information system is little different from making similar decisions in respect to training. Again, determining the criteria for inclusion or exclusion requires knowledge of the law.

Moreover, the absence of an information system is relevant here if, and only if, a proper system would have included information about the informant Fink. Thus, were this claim allowed, a court would have to review the office's legal judgments, not simply about *whether* to have an information system but also about *what kind* of system is appropriate, and whether an appropriate system would have included *Giglio*-related information *about one particular kind of trial informant.* Such decisions—whether made prior to or during a particular trial—are "intimately associated with the judicial phase of the criminal process." And, for the reasons set out above, all *Imbler*'s functional considerations (and the anomalies we mentioned earlier) apply here as well.

We recognize that sometimes it would be easy for a court to determine that an office's decision about an information system was inadequate. Suppose, for example, the office had no system at all. But the same could be said of a prosecutor's trial error. Immunity does not exist to help prosecutors in the easy case; it exists because the easy cases bring difficult cases in their wake. And, as *Imbler* pointed out, the likely presence of too many difficult cases threatens, not prosecutors, but the public, for the reason that it threatens to undermine the necessary independence and integrity of the prosecutorial decision-making process. Such is true of the kinds of claims before us, to all of which *Imbler*'s functional considerations apply. Consequently, where a § 1983 plaintiff claims that a prosecutor's management of a trial-related information system is responsible for a constitutional error at his or her particular trial, the prosecutor responsible for the system enjoys absolute immunity just as would the prosecutor who handled the particular trial itself.

* * *

For these reasons we conclude that petitioners are entitled to absolute immunity in respect to Goldstein's claims that their supervision, training, or information-system management was constitutionally inadequate. Accordingly, the judgment of the Court of Appeals is reversed, and the case is remanded for further proceedings consistent with this opinion....

Notes and Questions

1. The Supreme Court's rulings on the scope of prosecutorial immunity from damages under 42 U.S.C. § 1983 have centered on the essential function the prosecutor was performing in connection with the alleged constitutional violation. Thus, in *Imbler v. Pachtman,* 424 U.S. 409, 430 (1976), the justices exempted prosecutors from § 1983 liability for activities defined as "intimately associated with the judicial phase of the criminal process," even (if the allegations in that case were true) suppressing favorable evidence and knowingly using false testimony. The justices, however, had made "clear that absolute immunity may not apply when a prosecutor is not acting as 'an officer of the court,' but is instead engaged in other tasks, say investigative or administrative tasks." *Van de Kamp v. Goldstein,* 129 S.Ct. 855, 861 (2009). Goldstein had argued that the Los Angeles County prosecutors' alleged lapses involved essentially administrative tasks, that were rooted squarely in the *Giglio* Court's observation that prosecutors could ease their "burden" in making required disclosures about informants by establishing "procedures and regulations ... to insure communication of all relevant information on each case to every lawyer who deals with it." *Giglio v. United States,* 405 U.S. 150, 154 (1972). In *Van de Kamp v. Goldstein,* the justices acknowledged that the prosecutorial function at issue was administrative, yet nevertheless concluded that absolute immunity was in order because the administrative obligation was of "a kind that itself is directly connected with the conduct of a trial."

> Here, unlike with other claims related to administrative decisions, an individual prosecutor's error in the plaintiff's specific criminal trial constitutes an essential element of the plaintiff's claim. The administrative obligations at issue here are thus unlike administrative duties concerning, for example, workplace hiring, payroll administration, the maintenance of physical facilities, and the like. Moreover, the types of activities on which Goldstein's claims focus necessarily require legal knowledge and the exercise of related discretion, *e.g.,* in determining what information should be included in the training or the supervision or the information-system management.... [W]e believe absolute immunity must follow. 129 S.Ct., at 862.

Are these distinctions between the different kinds of administrative functions persuasive? Is the following assessment accurate? "[A]fter *Van de Kamp,* prosecutors have immunity for anything they do in the course of presenting evidence or argument in court. Their supervisors have immunity for implementing office-wide managerial or administrative policies that cause such violations to occur. The only possible *individual* liability that prosecutors may still have for their involvement in criminal matters is for the investigative function." Joel B. Rudin, "Suing for Prosecutorial Misconduct," 34 *Champion* 24, 26 (March 2010).

2. The litigation at issue in *Van de Kamp v. Goldstein* had roots in a lengthy investigation conducted by the Los Angeles County Grand Jury, which issued a public report in 1990 chronicling "the misuse of jailhouse informants by the Los Angeles County District

Attorney's Office. One of the shortcomings the grand jury identified was the failure of the district attorney to maintain any centralized index of potential impeachment information about informants.... [E]ventually the L.A. District Attorney's Office adopted stringent policies and procedures governing its use." Albert Locher, "The Case of Thomas Goldstein: A Murder, a Fink, and Prosecutorial Liability," 43 *Prosecutor* 12, 12–13 (June 2009). Those policies and procedures, of course, came too late to benefit Goldstein, who spent 24 years in prison after being wrongfully convicted of murder. Does the Supreme Court's resolution of the "'... balance' of 'evils'... [in which] 'it has been thought in the end better ... to leave unredressed the wrongs done by dishonest officers than to subject those who try to do their duty to the constant dread of retaliation'" *Van de Kamp,* 129 S.Ct., at 859, *quoting Gregoire v. Biddle,* 177 F.2d 579, 581 (2d Cir. 1949), strike you as appropriate? Would it help to know more about the circumstances surrounding Goldstein's wrongful conviction? More facts are provided in *Goldstein v. Superior Court,* 195 P.3d 588 (Cal. 2008), where the California Supreme Court rejected Goldstein's petition for the release of the evidentiary materials considered by the Los Angeles County Grand Jury during its investigation into the misuse of jailhouse informants.

In 1979 Goldstein was an engineering student and Marine Corps veteran with no criminal history. He became a murder suspect after an eyewitness to an unrelated shooting saw the gunman enter Goldstein's apartment building. No witness or forensic evidence connected Goldstein with the murder victim, but Long Beach police detectives showed Goldstein's photograph, among others, to Loran Campbell, an eyewitness to the homicide. Campbell did not recognize anyone in the photo lineup, and Goldstein did not match Campbell's description of the suspect. However, a detective asked if Goldstein could have been the person Campbell saw running from the scene. Campbell said it was possible, though he was not certain.

Goldstein was arrested and placed in a jail cell with Edward Floyd Fink, a heroin addict and convicted felon. At Goldstein's trial, Fink testified that Goldstein said he was in jail because he shot a man in a dispute over money. Fink claimed he received no benefit as a result of his testimony. Goldstein was convicted of murder in 1980. In 1988, the Los Angeles County Grand Jury began an investigation into the use of jailhouse informants. In 1990, it issued a public report concluding that misuse of jailhouse informants had been pervasive over the preceding 10 years. The grand jury found that the Los Angeles County District Attorney's office had demonstrated a "deliberate and informed declination to take the action necessary to curtail the misuse of jailhouse informant testimony." Among other deficiencies, it had failed to create a centralized index of potential impeachment information about informants, including any benefit they received for their testimony and their history of cooperation with law enforcement....

After the grand jury released its report, Goldstein sought a writ of habeas corpus in federal court. At an evidentiary hearing in August 2002, Loran Campbell recanted his identification of Goldstein. Campbell admitted he had been overanxious to help the police. He had identified Goldstein based on what the police told him and his desire to be a good citizen, not on his observations on the night of the murder. Goldstein also presented evidence that Fink had received benefits for cooperating with law enforcement. The magistrate found Campbell credible, and stated: "It is readily apparent to this Court that Fink fits the profile of the dishonest jailhouse informant that the Grand Jury Report found to be highly active in Los Angeles County at the time of [Goldstein's] conviction." Goldstein's petition was granted. He was released from custody in April of 2003, after serving 24 years in prison.

D. Procedural Reforms

1. Pre-Trial Screening

In Chapter 7 we considered various "gatekeeping" measures designed to insulate juries from expert testimony that failed to meet threshold criteria for reliability. Analogous proposals have been made with respect to the testimony of incentivized informants. Some proposals focus on prosecutors as the gatekeepers and others rely on the courts, although those approaches are not mutually exclusive.

In October 1984, a nine-year-old girl disappeared from her home in the small Canadian town of Queensville, Ontario, approximately 35 miles north of Toronto. Her body was found more than two months later. She had been stabbed to death and sexually assaulted. Guy Paul Morin, age 25, lived with his parents in the house next door to the victim and her family. He was employed, had no criminal record, and had an alibi corresponding to the time that the child apparently was abducted. He nevertheless was arrested and charged with murder, based largely on forensic analysis of hair, fibers, and blood associated with the crime. He was acquitted at an initial trial but a new trial was authorized following the prosecution's appeal (Canada does not have a prohibition against double jeopardy). He was convicted on retrial, where the testimony of two jailhouse informants who swore that Morin had confessed to committing the murder during his pretrial incarceration was central to the prosecution's case. Morin was exonerated in 1995, after spending a decade in prison, based on DNA evidence that excluded him as the source of the semen found on the murdered child's underwear.[11]

An official inquiry was conducted into the circumstances resulting in Morin's wrongful conviction. The Hon. Fred Kaufman, a former judge of the Quebec Court of Appeal, presided over the inquiry. The eventual Kaufman Commission Report contained extensive findings and made 119 recommendations. Several recommendations focused on the use of jailhouse informants, including a mechanism and the criteria to be used for prosecutorial screening of informants prior to relying on their testimony.

Report of the Kaufman Commission on Proceedings Involving Guy Paul Morin[12]

Recommendation 40: Approval of supervising Crown counsel for informer use

The current Crown policy provides that, if the Crown's case is based exclusively, or principally, on evidence of an in-custody informer, the prosecutor must bring the case to the attention of their supervising Director of Crown Operations as soon as practicable and the Director's approval must be obtained before taking the case to trial. The policy should, instead, reflect that, if the prosecutor determines that the prosecution case *may rely, in part*, on in-custody informer evidence, the prosecutor must bring the case to the attention of their supervising Director of Crown Operations as soon as practicable and the Director's approval must be obtained before taking the case to trial. The Ministry of the Attorney General should also consider the feasibility of establishing an In-Custody Informer Committee (composed of senior prosecutors from across the province) to approve the use of in-custody informers and to advise prosecutors on issues relating to such informers, such as means to assess their reliability or unreliability, and the appropriateness of contemplated benefits for such informers.

Recommendation 41: Matters to be considered in assessing informer reliability

The current Crown policy lists matters which Crown counsel may take into account in assessing the reliability of an in-custody informer. Those matters do not adequately address the assessment of reliability and place undue reliance upon matters which do little to enhance the reliability of an informer's claim. The Crown policy should be amended to reflect that the prosecutor, the supervisor or any Committee constituted should consider the following elements:

1. The extent to which the statement is confirmed in the sense earlier defined;

2. The specificity of the alleged statement. For example, a claim that the accused said "I killed A.B." is easy to make but extremely difficult for any accused to disprove;

3. The extent to which the statement contains details or leads to the discovery of evidence known only to the perpetrator;

4. The extent to which the statement contains details which could reasonably be accessed by the in-custody informer, other than through inculpatory statements by the accused. This consideration need involve an assessment of the information reasonably accessible to the in-custody informer, through media reports, availability of the accused's Crown brief in jail, etc. Crown counsel should be mindful that, historically, some informers have shown great ingenuity in securing information thought to be unaccessible to them. Furthermore, some informers have converted details communicated by the accused in the context of an exculpatory statement into details which purport to prove the making of an inculpatory statement;

5. The informer's general character, which may be evidenced by his or her criminal record or other disreputable or dishonest conduct known to the authorities;

6. Any request the informer has made for benefits or special treatment (whether or not agreed to) and any promises which may have been made (or discussed with the informer) by a person in authority in connection with the provision of the statement or an agreement to testify;

7. Whether the informer has, in the past, given reliable information to the authorities;

8. Whether the informer has previously claimed to have received statements while in custody. This may be relevant not only to the informer's reliability or unreliability but, more generally, to the issue whether the public interest would be served by utilizing a recidivist informer who previously traded information for benefits;

9. Whether the informer has previously testified in any court proceeding, whether as a witness for the prosecution or the defence or on his or her behalf, and any findings in relation to the accuracy and reliability of that evidence, if known;

10. Whether the informer made some written or other record of the words allegedly spoken by the accused and, if so, whether the record was made contemporaneous to the alleged statement of the accused.

11. The circumstances under which the informer's report of the alleged statement was taken (*e.g.* report made immediately after the statement was made, report made to more than one officer, etc.);

12. The manner in which the report of the statement was taken by the police (*e.g.* through use of non-leading questions, thorough report of words spoken by the

accused, thorough investigation of circumstances which might suggest opportunity or lack of opportunity to fabricate a statement). Police should be encouraged to address all of the matters relating to the Crown's assessment of reliability with the informer at the earliest opportunity. Police should also be encouraged to take an informer's report of an alleged in-custody statement under oath, recorded on audio or videotape, in accordance with the guidelines set down in *R. v. K.G.B.* However, in considering items 10 to 12, Crown counsel should be mindful that an accurate, appropriate and timely interview by police of the informer may not adequately address the dangers associated with this kind of evidence;

13. Any other known evidence that may attest to or diminish the credibility of the informer, including the presence or absence of any relationship between the accused and the informer;

14. Any relevant information contained in any available registry of informers.[13]

Citing the above recommendations of the Kaufman Commission Report approvingly, the American Bar Association Criminal Justice Section's Ad Hoc Innocence Committee has endorsed the proposition that "[t]he first (and perhaps the most important) check on unreliable testimony by informants is the prosecutor."[14]

Other reform measures require judicial screening and approval of proposed informant testimony, under limited circumstances. Illinois legislation prohibits jailhouse informant testimony in capital cases[15] unless, at a pre-trial hearing, the prosecution establishes the informant's reliability by a preponderance of the evidence.

725 Illinois Compiled Stat. Ann. § 5/115-21 (2003)

(a) For the purposes of this Section, "informant" means someone who is purporting to testify about admissions made to him or her by the accused while incarcerated in a penal institution contemporaneously.

(b) This Section applies to any capital case in which the prosecution attempts to introduce evidence of incriminating statements made by the accused to or overheard by an informant.

(c) In any case under this Section, the prosecution shall timely disclose in discovery:

(1) the complete criminal history of the informant;

(2) any deal, promise, inducement, or benefit that the offering party has made or will make in the future to the informant;

(3) the statements made by the accused;

(4) the time and place of the statements, the time and place of their disclosure to law enforcement officials, and the names of all persons who were present when the statements were made;

(5) whether at any time the informant recanted that testimony or statement and, if so, the time and place of the recantation, the nature of the recantation, and the names of the persons who were present at the recantation;

(6) other cases in which the informant testified, provided that the existence of such testimony can be ascertained through reasonable inquiry and whether the informant received any promise, inducement, or benefit in exchange for or subsequent to that testimony or statement; and

(7) any other information relevant to the informant's credibility.

(d) In any case under this Section, the prosecution must timely disclose its intent to introduce the testimony of an informant. The court shall conduct a hearing to determine whether the testimony of the informant is reliable, unless the defendant waives such a hearing. If the prosecution fails to show by a preponderance of the evidence that the informant's testimony is reliable, the court shall not allow the testimony to be heard at trial. At this hearing, the court shall consider the factors enumerated in subsection (c) as well as any other factors relating to reliability.

(e) A hearing required under subsection (d) does not apply to statements covered under subsection (b) that are lawfully recorded.

Consider the following decision by the Nevada Supreme Court regarding the prosecution's use of jailhouse informant testimony in capital penalty hearings.

D'Agostino v. State

823 P.2d 283 (Nev. 1991)

PER CURIAM:

This case involves the robbery and murder of a woman in Las Vegas. Appellant, Frank D'Agostino, was convicted of the murder and sentenced to death by a jury. Appellant raises numerous issues on appeal, challenging both his conviction and sentence of death.

... [W]e affirm appellant's convictions. We do, however, find error with respect to appellant's penalty hearing. Thus, we reverse appellant's sentence of death and remand the case to the district court for a new penalty hearing.

The penalty hearing was contaminated by the testimony of one Michael Gaines, a prisoner who shared a cell with D'Agostino. The prosecution called Gaines as a witness to testify, over objection, that D'Agostino had admitted to Gaines several killings unrelated to the present case. According to Gaines' testimony, D'Agostino, while Gaines and D'Agostino were in jail, admitted killing some unidentified man at some unspecified time and place in New York. Gaines also testified that D'Agostino told him, while they were jailmates, that D'Agostino cut a woman's throat and threw her body off of a cruise ship.

There is, of course, no way that D'Agostino could have defended himself against these kinds of unverifiable accusations. Gaines might just as well have told the jury that D'Agostino had admitted to him a number of serial, chain-saw massacres. Absent any details as to time, place and victim, an accused who must face this kind of incriminating testimony is seriously and unfairly prejudiced when the jury comes together to deliberate as to whether he should live or die.

By reason of Gaines' testimony, D'Agostino went before the penalty jury as a two-time murderer. A legally unsophisticated jury has little knowledge as to the types of pressures and inducements that jail inmates are under to "cooperate" with the state and to say anything that is "helpful" to the state's case. It is up to the trial judge to see that there are sufficient assurances of reliability prior to admitting the kind of amorphous testimony presented to keep this kind of unreliable evidence out of the hands of the jury, especially when the supposedly admitted crimes of the accused cannot be reasonably described in terms of where, when, against whom (other than "some old man in New York") and the circumstances under which the crimes were committed. More and more frequently, it seems, we are confronted with cases in which a jailbird comes forward to testify that the accused admitted to him that he not only committed the crime that he is accused of but also several other assorted crimes. We think it is time that this practice is examined more carefully.

We are not suggesting any impropriety or collusion on the part of prosecutors; but, it appears to us that a jail-house incrimination is now available in a fairly large number of homicide cases. Some limitations ought to be placed on this practice. Protections against this kind of unreliable evidence are afforded by our case law relating to proof of other crimes, but it should be remembered that in death cases the proof of other crimes is intended not to show the guilt of the accused but, rather, to display the character of the convict and to show culpability and just deserts on the party of the homicidal convict. Past criminal activity is one of the most critical factors in the process of assessing punishment, for whatever purpose punishment might be inflicted. Past misconduct relates to the criminal's blameworthiness for the charged homicide and relates, as well, to whether the jury deems it necessary for public safety to impose an irrevocable, permanent quarantine upon the murderer. The point is that past homicidal conduct of the subject of a death penalty hearing goes to the very heart of the jury's decision-making process. Improperly admitted evidence of past criminal conduct is even more damaging in a penalty hearing than it is in a guilt-determining proceeding because the past conduct goes to the substance of whether the murder should or should not be punished by death.

While past murders are relevant, even vital, to the penalty hearing when properly called to the jury's attention, unreliably demonstrated past killings are harmful in the extreme and simply cannot be overlooked by a reviewing court.

Based on the foregoing considerations, we now hold that testimony in a penalty hearing relating to supposed admissions by the convict as to past homicidal criminal conduct may not be heard by the jury unless the trial judge first determines that the details of the admissions supply a sufficient indicia of reliability or there is some credible evidence other than the admission itself to justify the conclusion that the convict committed the crimes which are the subject of the admission. Absent either criteria in the instant penalty hearing, we reverse the judgment of execution and remand to the trial court for a new penalty hearing.

Notes and Questions

1. Should the jailhouse informant reliability hearing mandated in the Illinois statute be limited to capital murder cases? Should the reliability determination required in *D'Agostino v. State* be even more limited, applying only to the penalty phase of a capital trial, and only to "supposed admissions by the convict as to past homicidal criminal conduct"?

2. Is the recommendation made by the Kaufman Commission regarding prosecutorial screening of the reliability of in-custody informants likely to be effective or enforceable? Should a hearing and judicial determination of reliability also be required?

2. Pre-Trial Discovery

As exemplified in 725 Ill. Comp. Stat. § 5/115-21 (c), presented above, the requirement for a pre-trial hearing and determination of the reliability of a jailhouse informant also provides discovery by putting the defense on notice of the proposed testimony and accompanying circumstances. Yet reliability hearings are rarely required, and pre-trial discovery regarding informants and their intended testimony can be especially critical in their absence. In *Dodd v. State,* the Oklahoma Court of Criminal Appeals initially held that trial judges must conduct pre-trial hearings to consider the reliability of jailhouse informant testimony and determine its admissibility, but then rescinded that ruling in favor of a more limited holding requiring only pre-trial disclosure.

Dodd v. State

993 P.2d 778 (Okla. Crim. App. 2000)

JOHNSON, Judge

[Rocky Eugene Dodd was convicted of two counts of capital murder and sentenced to death. To secure the convictions, the prosecution relied in part on the testimony of Kenneth Bryant, who was incarcerated in the Oklahoma County Jail while Dodd also was incarcerated there awaiting trial.]

... Bryant testified that while watching the O.J. Simpson trial on television in the jail common area, Dodd appeared interested in the DNA portion of the trial and asked Bryant if he thought police could obtain DNA evidence if blood got on a nugget ring or the velcro portion of a watch band. Bryant testified he asked Dodd if he committed the murders to which Dodd replied, "Yes ... but proving it will be a different thing." Dodd allegedly told Bryant that he had gone to the victims' apartment to retrieve the checks he had given Shane [McInturff, one of the victims] and to take whatever drugs were there and that things "went wrong." Dodd explained that he did not want his wife to find out about the checks. He was worried she would find out he was using drugs. Bryant further testified that Dodd stated he figured his co-worker, who had loaned him the hunting knife, would know that he had the murder weapon.

On appeal, Dodd raises eighteen propositions of error. However, finding error requiring reversal, we need only address Proposition IV(E) which deals specifically with informant Bryant's testimony. After Dodd's preliminary hearing, Bryant recanted his testimony that Dodd had admitted killing the victims. The recantation occurred during an interview with investigators for another capital murder case. Bryant later reasserted the truthfulness of his original testimony. Bryant testified at trial about his recantation and the circumstances surrounding the recantation. Bryant explained that he told the investigator "what she wanted to hear" in hope that she would arrange for him to get an ["own recognizance"] bond so he could get out of jail and return to his dying wife.

Proposition IV(E) deals specifically with two letters written by Bryant regarding his recantations. Defendant's Exhibit 20 is a letter dated August 29, 1995, written to Stephanie Brown, an investigator involved with the Carter murder case. In this letter Bryant expresses his belief that regardless of his recantations, he will still receive favorable treatment from the District Attorney's Office in exchange for his testimony in the Dodd and Carter capital murder cases. Defendant's Exhibit 21 is a letter also dated August 29, 1995, written to an assistant in the District Attorney's Office regarding the Carter murder case. Bryant discusses in this letter his long history of testifying in first degree murder trials in Oklahoma County. He states he is no longer "afraid ... and no longer [has] to lie ... for anyone in this world—especially the OK County D.A.'s Office." He further states, "The testimony from me in this case about a confession that you both asked & wanted from me—you'll not get-because as you very well know—there wasn't one."

During the trial, the State objected to the admission of these letters and the court sustained the objection finding the letters had not been properly provided in discovery. Dodd contends ... that the trial court improperly prevented defense counsel from impeaching informant Bryant with the prior inconsistent statements contained in these letters. We agree.

... The excluded evidence was admissible for impeachment purposes.... Bryant's credibility was a pivotal issue in this case. The evidence in this case was wholly circumstantial and Bryant was a key witness for the State. To deny Dodd the opportunity to fully attack Bryant's credibility was error....

... Courts should be exceedingly leery of jailhouse informants, especially if there is a hint that the informant received some sort of a benefit for his or her testimony. This problem is even greater here when we look at the error that is discussed above as to the withdrawal of the statements by the informant and what the informant has to say about promises made to the informant. The Court should look to how many times the informant has testified before for the District Attorney's office. Here we very clearly have two letters that may or may not be true but should have been in evidence. Consequently, under the unique circumstances of this case, we find Dodd's murder conviction must be reversed.

The Constitution of the United States prohibits a jailhouse informant from testifying to a defendant's statements when the informant works for the government and "deliberately elicits" or coerces statements related to a crime for which an accused has been indicted. While the state action affected by such a government/informant relationship triggers careful constitutional scrutiny, it permits equally insidious reliability problems to escape attention. Consider the more common example of the informant who does not work for the government when procuring incriminating statements. In these cases, there is no state action and therefore no constitutional concern. But, this distinction matters little in terms of informant reliability or trustworthiness. Irrespective of whether initially contacted by the state, most informants relay incriminating statements to the state in expectation of benefit in exchange.

Today we adopt a procedure to ensure complete disclosure so that counsel will be prepared to cross-examine an informant-witness. The following procedures shall apply to all jailhouse informant testimony not specifically excluded by the United States Constitution.

At least ten days before trial, the state is required to disclose in discovery: (1) the complete criminal history of the informant; (2) any deal, promise, inducement, or benefit that the offering party has made or may make *in the future* to the informant (emphasis added); (3) the specific statements made by the defendant and the time, place, and manner of their disclosure; (4) all other cases in which the informant testified or offered statements against an individual but was not called, whether the statements were admitted in the case, and whether the informant received any deal, promise, inducement, or benefit in exchange for or subsequent to that testimony or statement; (5) whether at any time the informant recanted that testimony or statement, and if so, a transcript or copy of such recantation; and (6) any other information relevant to the informant's credibility.

In all cases, where a court admits jailhouse informant testimony, [the following instruction] shall be given:

> The testimony of an informer who provides evidence against a defendant must be examined and weighed by you with greater care than the testimony of an ordinary witness. Whether the informer's testimony has been affected by interest or prejudice against the defendant is for you to determine. In making that determination, you should consider: (1) whether the witness has received anything (including pay, immunity from prosecution, leniency in prosecution, personal advantage, or vindication) in exchange for testimony; (2) any other case in which the informant testified or offered statements against an individual but was not called, and whether the statements were admitted in the case, and whether the informant received any deal, promise, inducement, or benefit in exchange for that testimony or statement; (3) whether the informant has ever changed his or her testimony; (4) the criminal history of the informant; and (5) any other evidence relevant to the informer's credibility.

Upon review, we are unable to find this error harmless beyond a reasonable doubt. Defendant's Exhibit 21 directly called into question the truthfulness of Bryant's testimony. It further demonstrates the pressure under which Bryant may have been to lie for the State. The information contained in Defendant's Exhibit 21 was not cumulative to any other impeachment evidence presented. While defense counsel was able to impeach Bryant with his numerous convictions, his prior history as an informant, and by calling into question Bryant's possible motives for testifying, the State's case was far from overwhelming. Consequently, under the unique circumstances of this case, we find Dodd's murder convictions must be **REVERSED**....

STRUBHAR, P.J.: specially concurring.

... This case illustrates the problems associated with the use of jailhouse informants who often play a pivotal role in an accused's conviction. While I recognize the need to use jailhouse informants' testimony, we must take certain precautions to ensure a citizen is not convicted on the testimony of an unreliable professional jailhouse informant, or snitch, who routinely trades dubious information for favors. The use of such untrustworthy witnesses carries considerable costs, especially in death-penalty cases, by undermining the foundation of cases where the stakes are the highest. The misuse of such informants also adds financial costs to taxpayers when convictions based on their testimony are reversed to be retried. Therefore, to ensure the utmost reliability in the admission of jailhouse informant testimony, I would also mandate the reliability hearing prescribed in the original opinion in this matter. *Dodd v. State*, 1999 OK CR 29, *rehearing granted vacating and withdrawing opinion*, 70 OBJ 2952 (Oct. 6, 1999). As with the use of *Dauber* [*v. Merrell Dow Pharmaceuticals, Inc.*, 509 U.S. 579, 597 (1993)] hearings to ensure the relevance and reliability of novel scientific expert testimony, this reliability hearing will allow the trial court to perform its gatekeeping function and filter out prejudicial jailhouse informant testimony that is more probably false than true. I am authorized to state that Judge Johnson joins in this writing.

LUMPKIN, Vice-Presiding Judge: concurs in part/dissents in part.

... I dissent to the Court's disregard of the provisions and procedures of the Oklahoma Criminal Discovery Code by *sua sponte* implementing the automatic disclosure requirement regarding a particular class of witnesses. That procedure is not necessary, is outside the scope of the issues raised in this appeal, is not shown by the evidence in this case to be a needed procedure, and is already well encompassed within the current Discovery Code provisions....

CRAIG, M.C., Assigned Judge: specially concurring.

I concur in the Court's opinion and write only to comment on my reasons for joining the majority of the Court, as now constituted, in receding from the reliability hearing prescribed in the original opinion in this matter. *Dodd v. State,* 1999 OK CR 29, rehearing granted vacating and withdrawing opinion, 70 OBJ 2952 (Oct. 6, 1999).

The original opinion established a procedure for and mandated that before a jailhouse informant could be called to testify, the court would make a determination, under prescribed criteria, as to the reliability of the proffered witness and whether such witness should be allowed to testify.

Arguments are made that such procedure will allow the trial court to perform gatekeeping functions, as in [the case] of *Daubert v. Merrell Dow Pharmaceuticals, Inc.,* 509 U.S. 579 (1993), in ensuring reluctance [sic] and reliability of novel scientific expert testimony; or *Idaho v. Wright,* 497 U.S. 805 (1990), in determining the trustworthiness of testimony of a minor child; or *Jackson v. Denno,* 378 U.S. 368 (1964), in allowing the trial court to make a threshold determination of the admissibility of a confession. Compelling reasons prompted each of the provisions for these threshold determinations, which do not extend to the use of a jailhouse informant as a witness, and adequate protection is afforded by the discovery procedure and the use of cautionary jury instructions as mandated in the majority opinion.

Many witnesses, in addition to jailhouse informants, may have a motive to lie. That is not a sufficient reason to remove the trier of fact from making a determination of the credibility of such witness.

Notes and Questions

1. The opinions of the different judges in *Dodd* run the gamut, from endorsing a pretrial reliability hearing and gatekeeping ruling by the trial judge, to the specific discovery required under the court's ruling, to treating the testimony of jailhouse informants no differently from the testimony of other witnesses. Which approach represents the preferred policy?

2. In addition to its discovery mandate, the majority opinion in *Dodd* requires trial judges to deliver specific cautionary instructions to jurors regarding the credibility of informants and their testimony. Some other jurisdictions require similar cautionary jury instructions, as we consider in the following section.

3. Could other measures be taken to better equip participants in the criminal justice process—be they prosecutors, trial judges, defense attorneys, or jurors—to assess the credibility of jailhouse informants? As discussed above, the Kaufman Commission was convened following the wrongful conviction of Guy Paul Morin in Ontario. In addition to recommending procedures and criteria for prosecutors to screen the proposed testimony of in-custody informants before introducing such testimony at trial, the Commission urged that "all contacts between police officers and in-custody informers must, absent exceptional circumstances, be videotaped or, where that is not feasible, audiotaped. This policy should also provide that officers receive statements from such informers under oath, where reasonably practicable."[16] The Commission further recommended that "[t]he Ministry of the Attorney General should amend its Crown Policy Manual to encourage all contacts between prosecutors and in-custody informers to be videotaped or, where that is not feasible, audiotaped."[17] A commission conducting an inquiry following another

Canadian wrongful murder conviction—that of Thomas Sophonow—made similar suggestions, although it expressed fundamental misgivings about allowing the testimony of in-custody informants except in "rare" cases. The Sophonow Commission made the following recommendations concerning reliance on "jailhouse informants":

1. As a general rule, jailhouse informants should be prohibited from testifying.

   They might be permitted to testify in a rare case, such as kidnapping, where they have, for example, learned of the whereabouts of the victim. In such a situation, the police procedure adopted should be along the following lines.

   Upon learning of the alleged confession made to a jailhouse informant, the police should interview him. The interview should be videotaped or audiotaped from beginning to end. At the outset, the jailhouse informant should be advised of the consequences of untruthful statements and false testimony. The statement would then be taken with as much detail as can be ascertained.

   Before it can even be considered, the statement must be reviewed to determine whether this information could have been garnered from media reports of the crime, or from evidence given at the preliminary hearing or from the trial if it is underway or has taken place.

   If the police are satisfied that the information could not have been obtained in this way, consideration should then be given to these factors:

   Has the purported statement by the accused to the informant:

   a. revealed material that could only be known by one who committed the crime;

   b. disclosed evidence that is, in itself, detailed, significant and revealing as to the crime and the manner in which it was committed; and

   c. been confirmed by police investigation as correct and accurate.

   Even then, in those rare circumstances, such as a kidnapping case, the testimony of the jailhouse informant should only be admitted, provided that the other conditions suggested by Justice Kaufman in his Inquiry have been met. In particular, the Trial Judge will have to determine on a voir dire whether the evidence of the jailhouse informant is sufficiently credible to be admitted, based on the criteria suggested by Justice Kaufman.

2. Further, because of the unfortunate cumulative effect of alleged confessions, only one jailhouse informant should be used.

3. In those rare cases where the testimony of a jailhouse informant is to be put forward, the jury should still be instructed in the clearest of terms as to the dangers of accepting this evidence. It may be advisable as well to point specifically to both the Morin case and the Sophonow case as demonstrating how convincing, yet how false, the evidence was of jailhouse informants.

4. There must be a very strong direction to the jury as to the unreliability of this type of evidence. In that direction, there should be a reference to the ease with which jailhouse informants can, on occasion, obtain access to information which would appear that only the accused could know. Because of the weight jurors attach to the confessions and statements allegedly made to these unreliable witnesses, the failure to give the warning should result in a mistrial.[18]

3. Corroboration Requirements and Cautionary Instructions

Premised on the "determination that the testimony of individuals who may themselves be criminally liable is inherently suspect,"[19] several states prohibit defendants from being convicted based solely on the uncorroborated testimony of an alleged accomplice to the charged offense.[20] The American Bar Association's Criminal Justice Section has advocated extending the accomplice corroboration requirement, proposing that "no prosecution should occur based solely upon uncorroborated jailhouse informant testimony."[21] This recommendation arguably is largely symbolic—evidence can be quite tangential to establishing guilt yet nevertheless "corroborate" a witness's testimony, and few prosecutions are based "solely" upon informant testimony, or any other form of evidence.[22] It stops somewhat short of the Kaufman Commission's analogous proposal:

> ... [I]t will never be in the public interest to initiate or continue a prosecution based only upon the unconfirmed evidence of an in-custody informer....
>
> The current Crown policy notes that confirmation, in the context of an in-custody informer, is not the same as corroboration. Confirmation is defined as evidence or information available to the Crown which contradicts a suggestion that the inculpatory aspects of the proposed evidence of the informer was fabricated.... Confirmation should be defined as *credible* evidence or information, available to the Crown, *independent of the in-custody informer,* which *significantly supports* the position that the inculpatory aspects of the proposed evidence were not fabricated. One in-custody informer does not provide confirmation for another.[23]

When the testimony of jailhouse or other incentivized informants is admitted into evidence, several jurisdictions authorize or require that cautionary instructions be administered to jurors, directing that they scrutinize that testimony with special care. We have seen one form of such instructions in the Oklahoma Court of Appeals' decision in *Dodd v. State.* California law provides:

> In any criminal trial or proceeding in which an in-custody informant testifies as a witness, upon the request of a party, the court shall instruct the jury as follows:
>
> "The testimony of an in-custody informant should be viewed with caution and close scrutiny. In evaluating such testimony, you should consider the extent to which it may have been influenced by the receipt of, or expectation of, any benefits from the party calling that witness. This does not mean that you may arbitrarily disregard such testimony, but you should give it the weight to which you find it to be entitled in the light of all the evidence in the case."[24]

Do such instructions go far enough? Consider the following case, decided by the Connecticut Supreme Court.

State v. Arroyo

973 A.2d 1254 (Conn. 2009)

ROGERS, C.J.

The defendant, Reynaldo Arroyo, was convicted, after a jury trial, of felony murder, conspiracy to commit robbery in the first degree, and larceny in the fifth degree.... The defendant appealed from the judgment to the Appellate Court, which affirmed the judgment of conviction. Thereafter, this court granted the defendant's petition for certification to appeal limited to the following issues: (1) "Did the Appellate Court properly determine that the special credibility instruction mandated in *State v. Patterson,* 276 Conn. 452, 886 A.2d 777 (2005), was not applicable?".... With respect to the first claim, we conclude that, although *Patterson* does not require a special credibility instruction if a jailhouse informant has not received a promise of a benefit in exchange for his testimony, the *Patterson* rule should now be expanded to apply to all jailhouse informant testimony. We also conclude, however, that the absence of such an instruction in the present case was harmless....

As set forth in the Appellate Court's opinion, the jury reasonably could have found the following facts. "On the afternoon of March 28, 2001, the defendant asked his neighbor [Charles Smith] if he could borrow money, stating that he would pay the money back after he went on 'a mission.' Later that evening, the defendant and Richmond Perry drove to Mike's Package Store in Middlefield. At the counter, an argument ensued between the defendant and the owner of the store, Edmund Caruso, over the amount of change the defendant received from his purchase. The argument escalated, and the defendant pulled out a handgun and jumped over the counter. The defendant pushed Caruso, who then sprayed Mace at both the defendant and Perry. During the altercation, Caruso was shot several times and subsequently died as a result of his injuries. Following the shooting, the defendant and Perry fled from the scene with the cash register. The defendant was arrested several weeks later."

Thereafter, the ... jury found him guilty of felony murder, larceny in the fifth degree and conspiracy to commit robbery in the first degree....

On appeal to the Appellate Court, the defendant claimed ... that the trial court improperly had: (1) denied his request for a special credibility instruction concerning the testimony of two jailhouse informants pursuant to *State v. Patterson*.... The Appellate Court rejected the defendant's first claim because it concluded that a *Patterson* charge is required only when the state has promised some benefit to the jailhouse informant in exchange for testifying, and there was no evidence of such a promise in this case....

This certified appeal followed....

We disagree with the defendant that *Patterson* applies even when a jailhouse informant has not received a promise of a benefit in exchange for his testimony, but agree with him that the *Patterson* rule should be expanded and that the trial court must give a special credibility instruction even when the informant has not received an express promise of a benefit. We agree with the state, however, that the absence of a *Patterson* charge in the present case was harmless....

I

We first address the defendant's claim that the Appellate Court improperly determined that the trial court properly had refused to give a special credibility instruction concerning the testimony of the jailhouse informants pursuant to *Patterson.* The opinion of the Appellate Court sets forth the following additional facts and procedural history that are relevant to our resolution of this claim. "At trial, the state presented the testimony of Thomas Moran and Ronald Avery. While awaiting their trials, Moran and Avery shared a courthouse lockup cell with the defendant. Both Moran and Avery testified that while in the lockup, on different occasions, the defendant confessed to them that he and Perry had robbed the package store and had shot Caruso.

"Prior to his conversations with the defendant in the lockup, Moran had known the defendant and had lived with him for a short period of time earlier that year. Moran testified that although he had an extensive criminal record, he did not 'believe in violence' and was testifying because 'it was the right thing to do.' The jury heard evidence that Moran had attempted to use the information three different times in an effort to negotiate an agreement with the state, even though from the beginning, he was told, 'you'll get nothing.' Moran's attempts to obtain benefits in exchange for his cooperation were futile.

"Avery met the defendant for the first time while in the lockup at the Norwich courthouse. Avery testified that he did not believe the defendant initially, but decided to come forth with the information after seeing the incident reported on the news. Avery testified that he thought there would be a monetary reward for the information, and, furthermore, he had hoped to use the information to 'get some play' on his case.

"Prior to the conclusion of the trial, the defendant requested that the judge instruct the jury that it should weigh, examine and view Moran's and Avery's testimony with great caution, care and scrutiny to determine whether the testimony had been affected by bias or prejudice against the defendant, and to consider whether Moran and Avery testified to serve their own self-interest because they believed or hoped that they would benefit by falsely implicating the defendant.

"The court denied the defendant's request but instructed the jury to consider the motives of any witness and the credibility of his or her testimony, taking into account all the evidence as well as any inconsistencies in the witness' testimony and whether the witness had an interest in the outcome of the trial or any bias or prejudice toward any party or any matter in the case." ...

In *State v. Patterson,* this court stated that "an informant who has been promised a benefit by the state in return for his or her testimony has a powerful incentive, fueled by self-interest, to implicate falsely the accused. Consequently, the testimony of such an informant, like that of an accomplice, is inevitably suspect." We concluded, therefore, that the defendant in that case was entitled to a jury instruction that the testimony of the informant, who had received a promise of a sentence reduction, should "be reviewed with particular scrutiny and weighed ... with greater care than the testimony of an ordinary witness."

The defendant in the present case contends that, under *Patterson,* a special credibility instruction is required even when a jailhouse informant has not received a promise of a benefit. He contends that the mere expectation of a benefit is sufficient. Alternatively, the defendant contends that Moran expressly was promised that he would receive a benefit in exchange for his testimony.[5] Finally, the defendant contends that, if *Patterson* does not apply, this court should expand its application to all jailhouse informant testimony. Although we do not agree with the defendant that *Patterson* applies even when a jailhouse informant has not received a promise of a benefit, we conclude that *Patterson's* requirement for a special credibility instruction now should be extended to apply to the testimony of all jailhouse informants.[6]

In recent years, there have been a number of high profile cases involving wrongful convictions based on the false testimony of jailhouse informants. See, e.g., R. Bloom, "Jailhouse Informants," 18 Crim. Just. 20 (Spring 2003).[7] Several of these cases resulted in formal investigations that shed much needed light on the extensive use of jailhouse informants in criminal prosecutions, an issue that previously had been "largely a closeted aspect of the criminal justice system." One such investigation, by a grand jury in Los Angeles county, California, revealed an "appalling number of instances of perjury or other falsifications to law enforcement...."[8] C. Sherrin, "Jailhouse Informants, Part I: Problems with their Use," 40 Crim. L.Q. 106, 113 (1997). The grand jury also "found that a particularly clever informant realizes that a successful performance on the witness stand is enhanced if it appears he or she is not benefiting from the testimony.... These informants wait until after they've testified to request favors—a request that is generally answered.... And, because the reward is not offered before the testimony, the jury has no way to measure the informant's motivation to fabricate testimony, as the prosecutor ... is under no obligation to disclose nonexisting exculpatory evidence." R. Bloom, supra, 18 Crim. Just. at 24. Thus, the expectation of a "[r]eward for testifying is a systemic reality" even where the informant

5. In support of this claim, the defendant points to the testimony of Moran's counsel that she was told that "'the court *may* take judicial notice of his cooperation in an ongoing investigation at his sentencing.'"

6. Accordingly, we need not reach the defendant's claim that Moran received a promise of a benefit in exchange for his testimony.

7. Bloom discusses the case of Leslie Vernon White, who fabricated the confessions of a *large* number of fellow prisoners while incarcerated in California in the 1980s, the false convictions of Guy Paul Morin and Thomas Sophonow in Canada, based on the testimony of a jailhouse informant, and the reversal of a *large* number of capital felony convictions in Illinois, forty-six of which had involved the testimony of jailhouse informants. R. Bloom, 18 Crim. Just. at 20–21; see also E. Dodds, note, "I'll Make You a Deal: How Repeat Informants Are Corrupting the Criminal Justice System and What To Do About It," 50 Wm. & Mary L.Rev. 1063, 1073–79 (2008).

8. See also A. Natapoff, "Beyond Unreliable: How Snitches Contribute to Wrongful Convictions," 37 Golden Gate U.L.Rev. 107, 109 (2006) (estimating that approximately 21 percent of wrongful capital convictions are influenced by jailhouse informant testimony and 20 percent of all California wrongful convictions result from false jailhouse informant testimony).

has not received an explicit promise of a reward.[9] In addition, several commentators have pointed out that jailhouse informants frequently have motives to testify falsely that may have nothing to do with the expectation of receiving benefits from the government.[10]

In light of this growing recognition of the inherent unreliability of jailhouse informant testimony, we are persuaded that the trial court should give a special credibility instruction to the jury whenever such testimony is given, regardless of whether the informant has received an express promise of a benefit.[11] As we indicated in *Patterson,* the trial court should instruct the jury that the informant's testimony must "be reviewed with particular scrutiny and weighed ...

9. See also R. Warden, Northwestern University School of Law, Center on Wrongful Convictions, "The Snitch System: How Snitch Testimony Sent Randy Steidl and Other Innocent Americans to Death Row" (2004), available at www.law.northwestern.edu/wrongfulconvictions/issues/causesandremedies/snitches/SnitchSystemBooklet.pdf, p. 15 (last visited July 6, 2009) ("[T]he snitch system sometimes operates on implicit promises. Even absent a formal understanding, the reward inevitably comes—because failing to deliver in one case would chill prospective future snitches."); S. Skurka, "A Canadian Perspective on the Role of Cooperators and Informants," 23 Cardozo L.Rev. 759, 766 (2002) ("[J]ailhouse informant is a term that conveniently captures a number of factors that are highly relevant to the need for caution. These include the facts that the jailhouse informant is already in the power of the state, is looking to better his or her situation in a jailhouse environment where bargaining power is otherwise hard to come by, and will often have a history of criminality." [Internal quotation marks omitted.]); V. Wefald, "Watch Out! How Prosecutors and Informants Use Winking and Nodding to Try to Get Around *Brady* and *Giglio,*" 58 Guild Practitioner 234, 239–40 (2001) ("once the informant has finished testifying that he has not been promised anything ... the prosecutor *must* go about getting the informant what he wants or 'risk' the informant 'recanting' his testimony" [emphasis in original]); C. Zimmerman, "Toward a New Vision of Informants: A History of Abuses and Suggestions for Reform," 22 Hastings Const. L. Q. 81, 144 (Fall 1994) ("[t]he [police] handler has no desire and sees little benefit in formalizing the informant relationship").

10. See S. Skurka, "A Canadian Perspective on the Role of Cooperators and Informants," 23 Cardozo L.Rev. 759, 762–63 (2002) ("jailhouse informants are almost invariably motivated by self-interest and ... historically such evidence has been shown to be untruthful and to produce miscarriages of justice"); J. Call, "Legal Notes," 22 Just. Syst. J. 73, 74 (2001) ("[b]ecause jailhouse informants are already incarcerated, they are likely to feel that they have nothing to lose and much to gain by providing information to the government"); C. Sherrin, "Jailhouse Informants in the Canadian Criminal Justice System, Part II: Options for Reform," 40 Crim. L.Q. 157, 172–73 (1997) ("what may seem trivial to those on the outside, may still act as an invitation to perjury to those on the inside"); C. Zimmerman, "Toward a New Vision of Informants: A History of Abuses and Suggestions for Reform," 22 Hastings Const. L.Q. 81, 139 (1994) (informant's motivations for testifying "can include ... some emotional impetuses ... [such as] the thrill of playing detective, fear, and survival").

11. One other state court also has reached this conclusion. See *Dodd v. State,* 993 P.2d 778, 784 (Okla.Crim.App.2000); see also *State v. Grimes,* 295 Mont. 22, 31, 982 P.2d 1037 (1999) ("when a government informant motivated by personal gain rather than some independent law enforcement purpose provides testimony, a cautionary instruction is the more prudent course of action"), citing *People v. Dela Rosa,* 644 F.2d 1257, 1259 (9th Cir.1980) ("courts have long recognized that the definition of an informer includes persons who provide evidence against a defendant for some personal advantage or vindication, as well as for pay or immunity"); cf. *People v. Payton,* 3 Cal.4th 1050, 1059 and n. 2, 839 P.2d 1035 (1992) (trial court was not required to give cautionary instruction on jail-house informant sua sponte, but state statute enacted after trial requires trial court to give cautionary instruction upon request); but see *United States v. Brooks,* 928 F.2d 1403, 1409 (4th Cir.) ("informer cautionary instruction is only appropriate when the individual supplying the information generally is either paid for his services or, having been a participant in the unlawful transaction, is granted immunity in exchange for his testimony"), cert. denied, 502 U.S. 845 (1991); *State v. Saenz,* 271 Kan. 339, 348, 22 P.3d 151 (2001) (cautionary instruction is required only when informant acted as agent of state); *West v. Commonwealth,* 161 S.W.3d 331, 336 (Ky.App.2005) (cautionary instruction on jailhouse informant testimony not required); *Moore v. State,* 787 So.2d 1282, 1287 (Miss.2001) (although trial court is not required to give cautionary instruction if jailhouse informant did not receive benefit in exchange for testifying, court recognizes that jailhouse informant testimony "is becoming an increasing problem in this state, as well as throughout the American criminal justice system" and court "does not view inmate testimony favorably"); *Lovitt v. Warden,* 266 Va. 216, 252, 585 S.E.2d 801 (2003) (Virginia "does not require a fact finder to give different consideration to the testimony of a government informant than to the testimony of other witnesses"), cert. denied, 541 U.S. 1006 (2004).

with greater care than the testimony of an ordinary witness." In addition, the trial court may ask the jury to consider: the extent to which the informant's testimony is confirmed by other evidence; the specificity of the testimony; the extent to which the testimony contains details known only by the perpetrator; the extent to which the details of the testimony could be obtained from a source other than the defendant; the informant's criminal record; any benefits received in exchange for the testimony; whether the informant previously has provided reliable or unreliable information; and the circumstances under which the informant initially provided the information to the police or the prosecutor, including whether the informant was responding to leading questions.

Having concluded that the defendant in the present case was entitled to this cautionary instruction, we must next determine whether the trial court's denial of the defendant's request for such an instruction was harmful...." Several factors guide our determination of whether the trial court's failure to give the requested instruction was harmful. These considerations include: (1) the extent to which [the jailhouse informant's] apparent motive for falsifying his testimony was brought to the attention of the jury, by cross-examination or otherwise; (2) the nature of the court's instructions on witness credibility; (3) whether [the informant's] testimony was corroborated by substantial independent evidence; and (4) the relative importance of [the informant's] testimony to the state's case." *State v. Patterson,* at 472, 886 A.2d 777....

With respect to the first factor, the state claims that defense counsel cross-examined both Moran and Avery extensively as to their motive for testifying and addressed their incentive to lie in closing argument. Indeed, the defendant concedes that the jury "was aware that [the] informants ... both hoped for and anticipated a benefit from the [s]tate when they made their statements to the police upon which their testimony was based. The desired benefits were expressed both during direct and cross-examination."

With respect to the second factor, the trial court instructed the jurors that, in determining whether a witness was credible, it should consider whether the witness had "an interest in the outcome of this case or any bias or prejudice concerning any party or any matter involved in the case." As in *State v. Patterson,* these instructions "were not extensive, and they contained no reference to [the informants] specifically." Unlike *Patterson,* however, the trial court instructed the jury that Moran and Avery had been convicted of prior felonies and that the jury "may consider that everything else being equal, you would not believe the testimony of a person who has committed a serious crime as readily as you would a person of good character. However, you are not required to disbelieve a witness because he has been previously convicted of a felony." Thus, the jury was specifically instructed that it should subject Moran's and Avery's testimony to greater scrutiny than the testimony of an ordinary witness.

With respect to the third and fourth factors, the state claims that the evidence strongly supported the defendant's conviction even without the informants' testimony....

We conclude that all four factors support a conclusion that the trial court's denial of the defendant's request for a jailhouse informant instruction regarding the testimony of Moran and Avery could not have substantially affected the verdict. The jury was made aware of the fact that the informants hoped for a benefit from the state, the court specifically instructed the jury that their testimony should be considered with caution because they were convicted felons and there was strong evidence to support the conviction even without the informants' testimony. Even if Smith's testimony was not a model of consistency and clarity,[14] the defendant has not identified any motive for him to have lied about the defendant's involvement in the murder. Although Perry had a motive to testify falsely about the defendant's involvement, his testimony was not incredible as a matter of law.[15] Moreover, the jury reasonably could have believed Perry's testimony that the defendant had participated in the robbery even if it was unsure about his testimony that the defendant had shot Caruso. Finally, the presence of the cash register and the

14. The defendant points out that Smith was an admitted drug dealer and claims that Smith's testimony was inconsistent with his statement to the police, with crime scene evidence and with the testimony of other witnesses.

15. The defendant claims that Perry's testimony was incredible because he previously had given four inconsistent statements to the police and he admitted at trial that he had lied in all of them.

jacket contaminated by Mace at the defendant's house, and Perry's willingness to share the proceeds from the robbery and from the sale of the murder weapon with him, all constituted strong evidence that the defendant had participated in the robbery. Accordingly, we conclude that the trial court's denial of the defendant's request for a special credibility charge was harmless and affirm the judgment of the Appellate Court on this alternate ground....

Notes and Questions

1. Do you agree with the Court's conclusion? Would an instruction to the jury about jailhouse informants likely have made a difference in the *Arroyo* verdict? In research investigating the influence of informant testimony that was incentivized (either through leniency or monetary reward), it was found that reliance on incentive information had no effect on verdicts. That is, whether mock jurors were told explicitly that informants' testimony against the defendant was incentivized did not appreciably affect their decisions about the defendant's guilt. This result was obtained even when mock jurors recognized that the informant's motives were based on self-interest rather than concerns for justice, and even when mock jurors clearly were made aware of the incentive. In discussing their findings, the authors conclude that the safeguard of judicial instructions "will be effective only if jurors can perceive the enormous incentive to fabricate evidence in exchange for leniency and differentiate between honest and dishonest witnesses."[25]

2. Although several states now require cautionary judicial instructions regarding the reliability of informant testimony, Professor Paul Giannelli notes the wide variation in these special instructions:

> In some jurisdictions, a cautionary instruction is not required where there is corroboration of accomplice testimony. For example, in Virginia, in the absence of corroboration, it is the duty of the court to give a cautionary instruction. In Mississippi, cautionary instructions are discretionary, but that discretion can be abused where the state's evidence rests solely on accomplice testimony and there is some question as to the reasonableness and consistency of that testimony. In Utah, giving a cautionary instruction generally falls within the discretion of the court, but it must be given if the judge finds the testimony "self-contradictory, uncertain or improbable." Federal cases set forth various versions of such instructions, some using the language "particular caution" and others employing phrases such as "great caution" or "great caution and care."[26]

Another pertinent issue is the timing of the jury instructions. Some research indicates that instructions are most effective when delivered at the time of the witness's testimony, and not just at the conclusion of the trial, when they are separated from the testimony and included among numerous other instructions.[27]

E. Conclusion

If the practice of offering incentives to witnesses to collect information for the investigation of crimes and secure their testimony in criminal prosecutions is sometimes necessary, it also is sometimes problematic. Police and prosecutors may have few choices but to rely on witnesses who consort with criminals and perhaps even partake in criminal activity. Those witnesses may not cooperate without reciprocation. At the same time, unreliable informants—including jailhouse snitches as well as other individuals who provide information or testify with the expectation that their assistance will be rewarded—have helped produce many known wrongful convictions and have doubtlessly contributed to untold numbers of additional miscarriages of justice. Their management by and within the criminal justice process thus poses stark challenges.

We have considered arguments in this chapter that the government's providing consideration to witnesses in exchange for testimony itself is a violation of the criminal law—representing a form of bribery—and so threatens the integrity of the criminal justice process that it runs afoul of fundamental fairness. Courts have not been receptive to such claims, focusing attention on procedural reforms rather than a policy of exclusion. Of course, for procedural safeguards to be effective, the promises made by the government to secure a witness's testimony must, at a minimum, be disclosed. In *Giglio v. United States*, the Supreme Court recognized that Due Process requires the prosecution to make such disclosures as part of its duties under *Brady v. Maryland.* Among the procedures recommended to minimize the risks associated with reliance on incentivized informants are judicial and/or prosecutorial pre-trial screening, comprehensive and timely discovery, corroboration requirements, and forceful cautionary instructions to jurors. Although some reforms regarding the use of incentivized witnesses have been adopted in some jurisdictions, for the most part reliance has been placed on vigorous cross-examination, argumentation, and the commonsense judgment of juries, or the traditional truth-seeking mechanisms of the adversarial process.

Part III

Adjudication; Capital Cases; Post-adjudication Detection and Redress

Chapter 9

Adjudication: Trials and Guilty Pleas

A. Introduction

To this point, we have examined several factors that are prominently associated with wrongful convictions: mistaken eyewitness identifications, false confessions, the malfeasance and misfeasance of prosecutors and defense counsel, faulty forensics, and unreliable informants. Although ultimately contributing to erroneous guilty verdicts, these problem areas are largely rooted outside of the adjudication process. We now alter our focus to consider attributes of the judicial guilt-determination process—both trials and guilty pleas—that can help spawn miscarriages of justice. The adjudication process can misfire in diverse ways to help result in innocent people being convicted. We examine several important potential sources of error in trial verdicts and convictions based on guilty pleas in the following sections.

B. Trial-Related Issues

1. Prejudicial Publicity

United States v. Carona

571 F.Supp.2d 1157 (C.D. Cal. 2008)

ANDREW J. GUILFORD, District Judge.

The essence of American culture lies in our founding documents. A principal feature of those documents is that when the government, with its immense power, accuses a person of a crime, that person is presumed innocent until proven guilty in a trial before an unbiased jury. These principles are not mere platitudes taught to school children, but are central to our nation's commitment to the protection of individual liberty. Including such concepts in the opening of this Order may seem unnecessarily obvious and sentimental. But sadly, it is not. For in this case some have disgraced our collective American heritage by actively seeking to deny the Defendants their right to a fair trial by an unbiased jury. This has been done by some seeking the money that comes with fame, and sponsored by others seeking profit. The conduct includes encouraging citizens to lie under oath in one of our country's courts. These selfish acts dishonor not only our country, but those who have made great sacrifices to preserve the freedoms and rights that define who we are as a people.

But the Court finds that the advocates of such lawlessness are not nearly as important as they pretend, and their listeners are not the gullible audience they suppose. The Court will not overreact to bait offered by largely satirical commentators. Cynicism will not prevail, and the Court is confident that the population of Orange

County will produce twelve jurors who will embrace their obligation as citizens of this country to provide the Defendants with a trial before an unbiased jury. The Court intends to take all necessary precautions to ensure that the promise of a fair trial is delivered in this case. The Motion to Transfer Venue ("Motion") is therefore DENIED.

BACKGROUND

Defendants Michael Carona, Deborah Carona, and Debra Hoffman ("Defendants") face trial on a series of charges relating to their alleged conspiracy to use Michael Carona's office as Orange County Sheriff to enrich themselves and other co-conspirators, thereby depriving the residents of Orange County of the honest services of an elected official. In this Motion, Defendants contend that the extent and nature of pretrial publicity related to the case requires the Court to presume that Defendants' right to an impartial jury has been prejudiced, leaving the Court "no choice but to transfer venue."

In general, pretrial publicity in this case has been similar to other criminal cases involving a high-profile member of society. Defendants have submitted a compilation of what they describe as "a sampling of the prejudicial newspaper articles and other media that have pervaded the Central District both before and after the indictment was unsealed on October 30, 2007." These articles include many viewpoint-neutral factual accounts of the case, along with negative portrayals of Defendant Michael Carona in articles with the following headlines: "A Sheriff's Rising Star is Dimmed by Scandal," *Los Angeles Times;* "Dumb and Dumber: The stupidity of ex-sheriff Mike Carona, forever preserved on FBI Surveillance tape," *OC Weekly;* and "Inside Orange County Jails: Grand Jury transcripts underscore just how low Michael Carona dragged the O.C. Sheriff's Department," *Los Angeles Times.*

While some degree of negative publicity is inevitable, and most of the media attention in this case has been unremarkable, Defendants contend that the unprecedented actions taken by a few individuals in the media have made pretrial publicity in this case exceptionally prejudicial. A talk radio program has encouraged potential jurors to conceal their biases toward Defendants during the jury selection process in an effort to increase the likelihood that they will be chosen for the jury in this case, and to unthinkingly find Defendants guilty if selected to the jury. Specifically, they have advocated that potential jurors lie under oath to the Court and the attorneys about their knowledge and preconceptions regarding the case, and about whether they listen to the offending radio program.

LEGAL STANDARD

Due process requires that a criminal defendant "receive a trial by an impartial jury free from outside influences." *Sheppard v. Maxwell,* 384 U.S. 333, 362 (1966); *see also Rideau v. Louisiana,* 373 U.S. 723, 724–26 (1963) (finding that failure to transfer venue violated defendant's due process rights where proceedings occurred "in a community so pervasively exposed" to prejudicial publicity that the trial was "but a hollow formality"). A court must grant a motion to change venue "if prejudicial pretrial publicity makes it impossible to seat an impartial jury," *Ainsworth v. Calderon,* 138 F.3d 787, 795 (9th Cir.1998), and the burden is on the defendant seeking a change of venue to establish that he cannot obtain a fair trial without a change.

In *Daniels v. Woodford,* 428 F.3d 1181, 1211 (9th Cir.2005), *cert. denied,* 127 S.Ct. 2876 (2007), the Ninth Circuit held that to support a change of venue the defendant "must demonstrate either actual or presumed prejudice." Actual prejudice exists where the jurors have "demonstrated actual partiality or hostility that could not be laid aside." Because this motion for change of venue is brought before a jury has been selected, and even before the voir dire process, Defendants cannot establish actual prejudice and must make a showing of presumed prejudice. "Prejudice is presumed only in extreme instances 'when the record demonstrates that the community where the trial [is to be] held [is] saturated with prejudice and inflammatory media about the crime.'" A court is to consider three factors when determining presumed prejudice: (1) whether there was a "barrage of inflammatory publicity immediately prior to trial, amounting to a huge ... wave of public passion"; (2) whether the news accounts were primarily factual because such accounts tend to be less inflammatory than editorial or cartoons; and (3) whether the media accounts contained inflammatory or prejudicial material not admissible at trial. *Daniels,* 428 F.3d at 1211. A district judge has broad discretion in ruling on a motion for change of venue.

ANALYSIS

... Having considered the particular facts of this case under the factors from *Daniels,* the

Court declines to find a presumption of prejudice.

Under the first *Daniels* factor, courts consider whether there has been a "barrage of inflammatory publicity" that amounts to "wave of public passion." While there has clearly been heightened public interest in this case, such interest is expected when a prominent elected official is charged with criminal wrongdoing. It is natural, and indeed healthy, for citizens to express concern when the integrity of our public servants falls under suspicion. The attention of the public and the media to this case is not unusual in this regard. The Court is also influenced by the fact that the crimes alleged in this case, such as bribery, corruption, and witness tampering, are of a character less likely to incite a "wave of public passion." In contrast to the facts of this case, the typical case requiring a transfer of venue involves a crime, such as rape or murder, that is likely to evoke a visceral response from the public. *See, e.g., ... Sheppard v. Maxwell,* 384 U.S. 333, 335–37 (requiring change of venue in case where defendant physician was accused of bludgeoning his pregnant wife to death, and "news media inflamed and prejudiced the public"). The potential for public outrage and indignation spawned by allegations of government corruption should not be downplayed. But the public response to acts of physical violence is of an inherently different character, involving passion that heightens the risk of bias and prejudice trumping rational thought.

Another factor in the *Daniels* analysis is whether news accounts of the case are "primarily factual, because such accounts tend to be less inflammatory than editorials or cartoons." As with any high-profile case, the media coverage here does include editorials and other opinionated statements expressing bias and hostility against the Defendants. But the majority of media accounts are factual in nature, following the progress of the case as it moves toward trial. Further, the Court finds that the volume of editorialization and expressions of opinion in the media has generally declined since charges were brought against Defendants in October 2007.

Finally, *Daniels* is concerned with whether media accounts of the case contain "inflammatory or prejudicial material not admissible at trial." Defendants contend that media accounts of Michael Carona include a "wide range" of prejudicial materials not admissible at trial. But many of the materials Defendants cite in this regard were published well before charges were brought against Defendants in this case, dating back to as early as 2005. As the elected sheriff of one of the nation's most populous counties, Michael Carona was certain to be the focus of media attention, both positive and negative. That he was at times portrayed in a negative light regarding events and allegations unrelated to the criminal charges in this trial does not establish a presumption of prejudice. And the nonexistence of a presumption of prejudice is especially strong regarding media attention before June 2006, when public perception of Michael Carona was sufficiently positive that he was elected to a third consecutive term as Orange County Sheriff. The Court's ruling here might be different if the secretly recorded conversations between Michael Carona and cooperating witness Don Haidl had been suppressed, and would not be available at trial. But because the Court has ruled that these conversations may be presented to the jury, media coverage of this admissible evidence is not inherently unduly prejudicial.

In sum, the Court does not find that the community is "so saturated with inflammatory and prejudicial media" that prejudice against Defendants must be presumed. In reaching this conclusion the Court notes that Orange County is home to a diverse population of over three million people, providing a substantial jury pool for Defendants' trial. The Ninth Circuit has recognized that the size of the relevant community is an important factor in determining whether the community is "so saturated" with negative media that a presumption of prejudice should apply, as large metropolitan areas are able to absorb the effects of prejudicial publicity in ways that smaller and more insular communities could not....

A stone thrown into a small pond disturbs the entire body of water, while the same stone thrown into a large lake will have little effect beyond the immediate place of impact. In contrast to small rural communities that may find themselves engulfed by the ripple effects of prejudicial publicity, the "size and heterogeneity" of Orange County neutralize these effects.

In finding that Defendants have not established a presumption of prejudice based on pretrial publicity in this case, the Court assumes that careful pretrial screening, including voir dire, will effectively identify the biases of potential jurors. Defendants contend that this assumption is faulty because the efficacy of pretrial screening to identify biases in potential jurors has been undermined by a radio show encouraging its listeners to act as "stealth" jurors. While recognizing the peculiar challenges of this case, the Court is confident that through diligent and comprehensive pretrial screening a fair and impartial jury can be selected. The power of the voir dire process to illicit [sic] honest answers should not be underestimated, especially when the threat of federal perjury charges looms. Voir dire is "the prime safeguard," and the "method we have relied on from the beginning" to identify juror bias. *Fields v. Brown,* 503 F.3d 755, 772 (9th Cir.2007); *Patton v. Yount,* 467 U.S. 1025, 1038 (1984). The Court agrees with the sentiments from *Application of Cohn,* 332 F.2d 976, 977 (2d Cir.1964), that "[i]t would indeed be a cynical approach to believe that jurors, who give their assurance that they can fairly and impartially decide the fact issues before them, would deliberately conceal deep prejudices." By accepting the possibility that potential jurors would perjure themselves to satisfy the whim of a radio personality, the Court would cast doubt on the integrity of the very foundations of the jury trial system. This it will not do.

CONCLUSION

Because the citizens of Orange County can and should provide the unbiased jury guaranteed to Defendants, the Motion to Transfer Venue is DENIED....

Notes and Questions

1. *Sheppard v. Maxwell,* 384 U.S. 333, 86 S.Ct. 1507, 16 L.Ed.2d 600 (1966), which is cited in *Carona,* involved the prosecution of Dr. Sam Sheppard for the murder of his pregnant wife, Marilyn, who was found bludgeoned to death in 1954 in their upscale home outside of Cleveland. Sheppard reported that he had fallen asleep on a living room couch while watching television after his wife had gone to bed, that he awakened on hearing his wife cry out, that he saw a "form" standing in the bedroom, and that he was knocked unconscious after chasing and struggling with the intruder. The authorities did not believe Sheppard's story and, amidst a sea of sensational media publicity, including a televised coroner's inquiry conducted in a school gymnasium, Sheppard was charged with the murder. He was brought to trial two weeks before the November election in which the chief prosecutor was running for judge against the jurist presiding at Sheppard's trial.

The courtroom in which the trial was held measured 26 by 48 feet. A long temporary table was set up inside the bar, in back of the single counsel table. It ran the width of the courtroom, parallel to the bar railing, with one end less than three feet from the jury box. Approximately 20 representatives of newspapers and wire services were assigned seats at this table by the court. Behind the bar railing there were four rows of benches. These seats were likewise assigned by the court for the entire trial. The first row was occupied by representatives of television and radio stations, and the second and third rows by reporters from out-of-town newspapers and magazines. One side of the last row, which accommodated 14 people, was assigned to Sheppard's family and the other to Marilyn's. The public was permitted to fill vacancies in this row on special passes only. Representatives of the news media also used all the rooms on the courtroom floor, including the room where cases were ordinarily called and assigned for trial. Private telephone lines and telegraphic equipment were installed in these rooms so that reports from the trial could be speeded to the papers. Station WSRS was permitted to set up broadcasting facilities on the third floor of the courthouse next door to the jury room, where the jury rested during recesses in the trial and deliberated. Newscasts were made from this room throughout the trial, and while the jury reached its verdict.

On the sidewalk and steps in front of the courthouse, television and newsreel cameras were occasionally used to take motion pictures of the participants in the trial, including the jury and the judge.... In the corridors outside the courtroom there was a host of photographers and television personnel with flash cameras, portable lights and motion picture cameras. This group photographed the prospective jurors during selection of the jury. After the trial opened, the witnesses, counsel, and jurors were photographed and televised whenever they entered or left the courtroom. Sheppard was brought to the courtroom about 10 minutes before each session began; he was surrounded by reporters and extensively photographed for the newspapers and television....

All of these arrangements with the news media and their massive coverage of the trial continued during the entire nine weeks of the trial. The courtroom remained crowded to capacity with representatives of news media. Their movement in and out of the courtroom often caused so much confusion that, despite the loudspeaker system installed in the courtroom, it was difficult for the witnesses and counsel to be heard. Furthermore, the reporters clustered within the bar of the small courtroom made confidential talk among Sheppard and his counsel almost impossible during the proceedings. They frequently had to leave the courtroom to obtain privacy. And many times when counsel wished to raise a point with the judge out of the hearing of the jury it was necessary to move to the judge's chambers.... The reporters vied with each other to find out what counsel and the judge had discussed, and often these matters later appeared in newspapers accessible to the jury.

The daily record of the proceedings was made available to the newspapers and the testimony of each witness was printed verbatim in the local editions, along with objections of counsel, and rulings by the judge. Pictures of Sheppard, the judge, counsel, pertinent witnesses, and the jury often accompanied the daily newspaper and television accounts....

The jurors themselves were constantly exposed to the news media. Every juror, except one, testified at voir dire to reading about the case in the Cleveland papers or to having heard broadcasts about it. Seven of the 12 jurors who rendered the verdict had one or more Cleveland papers delivered in their home; the remaining jurors were not interrogated on the point. Nor were there questions as to radios or television sets in the jurors' homes, but we must assume that most of them owned such conveniences. As the selection of the jury progressed, individual pictures of prospective members appeared daily. During the trial, pictures of the jury appeared over 40 times in the Cleveland papers alone. The court permitted photographers to take pictures of the jury in the box, and individual pictures of the members in the jury room.... The day before the verdict was rendered—while the jurors were at lunch and sequestered by two bailiffs—the jury was separated into two groups to pose for photographs which appeared in the newspapers.

The jury found Sheppard guilty of his wife's murder and he was sentenced to life imprisonment. His appeal was denied by the Ohio Supreme Court. A federal district court granted Sheppard's habeas corpus petition, although the Sixth Circuit Court of Appeals reversed. The Supreme Court reviewed his case in 1966 and ruled that the massive, prejudicial publicity prior to and throughout the case proceedings had deprived Sheppard of a fair trial.

The principle that justice cannot survive behind walls of silence has long been reflected in the 'Anglo-American distrust for secret trials.' In re Oliver, 333 U.S. 257, 268 (1948). A responsible press has always been regarded as the handmaiden of effective judicial administration, especially in the criminal field.... The press does not simply publish information about trials but guards against the miscarriage of justice by subjecting the police, prosecutors, and judicial processes to extensive public scrutiny and criticism. This Court has, therefore, been unwilling to place any direct limitations on the freedom traditionally exercised by the news media for '(w)hat transpires in the court room is public property.' Craig v. Harney, 331 U.S. 367, 374 (1947). The 'unqualified prohibitions laid down by the framers were intended to give to liberty of the press * * * the broadest scope that could be countenanced in an orderly society.' Bridges v. California, 314 U.S. 252, 265 (1941). And where there was 'no threat or menace to the integrity of the trial,' Craig v. Harney, 331 U.S. at 377, we have consistently required that the press have a free hand, even though we sometimes deplored its sensationalism.

But the Court has also pointed out that '(l)egal trials are not like elections, to be won through the use of the meeting-hall, the radio, and the newspaper.' Bridges v. California, supra, 314 U.S. at 271. And the Court has insisted that no one be punished for a crime without 'a charge fairly made and fairly tried in a public tribunal free of prejudice, passion, excitement, and tyrannical power.' Chambers v. Florida, 309 U.S. 227, 236–237 (1940). '[F]reedom of discussion should be given the widest range compatible with the essential requirement of the fair and orderly administration of justice.' Pennekamp v. Florida, 328 U.S. 331, 347 (1946). But it must not be allowed to divert the trial from the 'very purpose of a court system * * * to adjudicate controversies, both criminal and civil, in the calmness and solemnity of the courtroom according to legal procedures.' Cox v. Louisiana, 379 U.S. 559, 583 (1965) (Black, J., dissenting). Among these 'legal procedures' is the requirement that the jury's verdict be based on evidence received in open court, not from outside sources....

... [W]e note that unfair and prejudicial news comment on pending trials has become increasingly prevalent. Due process requires that the accused receive a trial by an impartial jury free from outside influences. Given the pervasiveness of modern communications and the difficulty of effacing prejudicial publicity from the minds of the jurors, the trial courts must take strong measures to ensure that the balance is never weighed against the accused. And appellate tribunals have the duty to make an independent evaluation of the circumstances. Of course, there is nothing that proscribes the press from reporting events that transpire in the courtroom. But where there is a reasonable likelihood that prejudicial news prior to trial will prevent a fair trial, the judge should continue the case until the threat abates, or transfer it to another county not so permeated with publicity. In addition, sequestration of the jury was something the judge should have raised sua sponte with counsel. If publicity during the proceedings threatens the fairness of the trial, a new trial should be ordered. But we must remember that reversals are but palliatives; the cure lies in those remedial measures that will prevent the prejudice at its inception. The courts must take such steps by rule and regulation that will protect their processes from prejudicial outside interferences. Neither prosecutors, counsel for defense, the accused, witnesses, court staff nor enforcement officers coming under the jurisdiction of the court should be permitted to frustrate its function. Collaboration between counsel and the press as to information affecting the fairness of a criminal trial is not only subject to regulation, but is highly censurable and worthy of disciplinary measures.

Since the state trial judge did not fulfill his duty to protect Sheppard from the inherently prejudicial publicity which saturated the community and to control disruptive influences in the courtroom, we must reverse the denial of the habeas petition. The case is remanded to the District Court with instructions to issue the writ and order that Sheppard be released from custody unless the State puts him to its charges again within a reasonable time....

Dr. Sheppard was acquitted following the retrial. He had spent 10 years in prison. He died in 1970, at age 46. The television series, and later the movie, "The Fugitive," were loosely based on Sheppard's case. Dr. Sheppard's son, Sam Reese Sheppard, filed a lawsuit in 1999 seeking damages for his father's wrongful conviction and imprisonment. A jury rejected the claim. For more on this case, *see* Cynthia L. Cooper & Sam Reese Sheppard, *Mockery of Justice: The True Story of the Sheppard Murder Case* (Boston: Northeastern University Press 1995); Jonathan L. Entin, "Being the Government Means (Almost) Never Having to Say You're Sorry: The Sam Sheppard Case and the Meaning of Wrongful Imprisonment," 38 *Akron Law Review* 139 (2005).

2. With Marilyn Sheppard's murder and Sam Sheppard's original trial occurring in 1954, and the case coming before the Supreme Court in 1966, *Sheppard v. Maxwell* unfolded well before the development of the Internet, in an era when newspapers, television, and radio were the primary means for disseminating news. The ready availability of information on the Internet and its widespread accessibility have added to the challenge of securing jurors whose verdicts will not be influenced by preconceived opinions or extrajudicial facts.[1] In *Skilling v. United States,* ___ U.S. ___, 130 S.Ct. 2896, 177 L.Ed.2d 619 (2010), the former CEO of the Houston-based Enron Corporation, Jeffrey Skilling, had been convicted of violating the "honest services" law, 18 U.S.C. § 1346, for engaging in fraudulent

conduct in connection with his corporate responsibilities. The Court vacated his conviction because his "alleged misconduct entailed no bribe or kickback, [and hence] it does not fall within § 1346's proscription." 130 S.Ct., at 2907. In another portion of their ruling, however, the justices rejected (by vote of 6–3) Skilling's claim that the district court had erred in denying his change of venue motion because "hostility toward him in Houston, coupled with extensive pretrial publicity, had poisoned potential jurors." 130 S.Ct., at 2908. Although the extensive discussion devoted to the issue of prejudicial pretrial publicity and juror impartiality in Justice Ginsburg's majority opinion and in Justice Sotomayor's dissent gave scant attention to the Internet as a source of news and opinions, the potential of Internet news, blogs, and other postings to affect the fairness of trials cannot be ignored in contemporary cases.[2]

3. In a meta-analytic review of empirical studies on pretrial publicity on juror verdicts, the authors summarize their methods and findings as follows:

> The effect of pretrial publicity (PTP) on juror verdicts was examined through a meta-analysis of 44 empirical tests representing 5,755 subjects. In support of the hypothesis, subjects exposed to negative PTP were significantly more likely to judge the defendant guilty compared to subjects exposed to less or no negative PTP. Greater effect sizes were produced in studies which included a pretrial verdict assessment, use of the potential juror pool as subjects, multiple points of negative information included in the PTP, real PTP, crimes of murder, sexual abuse, or drugs, and greater length of time between PTP exposure and judgment. The effect was attenuated with student subjects, use of general rather than specific PTP information, certain types of PTP content, a post-trial predeliberation verdict, and specific types of crimes.

Nancy M. Steblay, Jasmina Besirevic, Solomon M. Fulero & Belia Jiminez-Lorente, "The Effects of Pretrial Publicity on Juror Verdicts: A Meta-Analytic Review," 23 *Law and Human Behavior* 219 (1999).

4. Commentators have argued that the intensive publicity surrounding capital murder cases helps contribute to the comparatively high rate of known wrongful convictions in those cases, in part because police and prosecutors are under commensurately greater pressure to make arrests and secure convictions, and in part because the publicity compromises jurors' ability to be impartial. *See* Samuel L. Gross, "The Risks of Death: Why Erroneous Convictions are Common in Capital Cases," 44 *Buffalo Law Review* 469, 475 (1996). *See generally* Jeffrey L. Kirchmeier, Stephen R. Greenwald, Harold Reynolds & Jonathan Sussman, "Vigilante Justice: Prosecutor Misconduct in Capital Cases," 55 *Wayne Law Review* 1327, 1342–49 (2009).

2. Courtroom Spectators

The right to a public trial, guaranteed in the Sixth Amendment, helps protects the accused by guarding against governmental abuses that may flourish in secretive, closed-door proceedings. Yet the Supreme Court also has ruled that the First Amendment provides the public with an independent right of access to criminal trials, even over the accused's objection,[3] so that citizens can partake of the important business of the courts and their administration of justice.

> [T]he right of access to criminal trials plays a particularly significant role in the functioning of the judicial process and the government as a whole. Public scrutiny of a criminal trial enhances the quality and safeguards the integrity of

> the factfinding process, with benefits to both the defendant and to society as a whole. Moreover, public access to the criminal trial fosters an appearance of fairness, thereby heightening public respect for the judicial process. And in the broadest terms, public access to criminal trials permits the public to participate in and serve as a check upon the judicial process—an essential component in our structure of self-government. *Globe Newspaper Co. v. Superior Court*, 457 U.S. 596, 606, 102 S.Ct. 2613, 73 L.Ed.2d 248 (1982) (footnotes omitted).

As with other constitutional rights, the right of the public to observe criminal trials is "not absolute." *Id.*, 457 U.S., at 606. Trial judges have broad discretion to maintain order and appropriate decorum within their courtrooms, and hence to exclude and/or sanction observers who are unruly or disruptive. The following case involves an issue presenting a potential clash between the fairness of a criminal trial—and the consequent risk of a wrongful conviction—and citizens' expressive rights and their right to attend and observe court proceedings.

State v. Lord

165 P.3d 1251 (Wash. 2007)

J.M. JOHNSON, J.

The right to a fair trial by an impartial jury is a foundation of our criminal justice system. Today we must decide whether the courtroom presence of lapel buttons, showing a picture of the victim, deprived the defendant of this fundamental right. We conclude, as did the courts below, there was no inherent prejudice and affirm the conviction.

Our constitution also guarantees that a trial will be public, allowing the attendance of spectators who have an interest in the trial. Courts must presume that the jurors we entrust with determining guilt both understand, and have the fortitude to withstand, the potential influence from spectators who show sympathy or affiliation. An underlying presumption is that jurors are intelligent and responsible individuals. A similar assumption about voters, from which jurors are chosen, underlies our democracy. As further protection, jury panels are instructed and solemnly charged by the court with the duty to avoid bias or prejudice.[2] A simple picture button, a sign of support or sympathy that does not expressly advocate guilt or innocence, does not alone impermissibly bias a jury.

In determining whether a jury has been unduly influenced, there is an important distinction between the potential impact of a "state-sponsored" message and a message from private citizens.[3] The special influence of the imprimatur of the State is often troubling, while private acts are more likely understood as private expressions.

We hold that spectator signs of affiliation—here through buttons showing a victim's picture

---

2. *See* 11 *Washington Practice: Washington Pattern Jury Instructions: Criminal* 1.01, at 4, 5, 7 (2d ed. Supp. 2005):

> The only evidence you are to consider consists of testimony of witnesses and exhibits admitted into evidence....
>
> You must not consider or discuss any evidence that I do not admit or that I tell you to disregard....
>
> You must keep your mind free of outside influences so that your decision will be based entirely on the evidence presented during trial and on my instructions to you about the law....
>
> As jurors, you are officers of this court. *As such you must not let your emotions overcome your rational thought process. You must reach your decision based on the facts proved to you and on the law given to you, not on sympathy, prejudice, or personal preference.* (Emphasis added.)

3. "[A]lthough the Court articulated the test for inherent prejudice that applies to state conduct in *Williams* and *Flynn*, we have never applied that test to spectators' conduct. Indeed, part of the legal test of *Williams* and *Flynn*—asking whether the practices furthered an essential *state* interest—suggests that those cases apply *only to state-sponsored practices.*" *Carey v. Musladin*, 549 U.S. 70, ___ ___(2006) (emphasis added).

—do not automatically present "'an unacceptable risk ... of impermissible factors coming into play.'" *Holbrook v. Flynn,* 475 U.S. 560, 570 (1986) (quoting *Estelle v. Williams,* 425 U.S. 501, 505 (1976) (inherent prejudice requires an unacceptable risk of impermissible factors)). Here, Lord was not denied a fair trial or the constitutionally guaranteed presumption of innocence....[4]

FACTS AND PROCEDURAL HISTORY

Brian Keith Lord seeks review of the Court of Appeals decision affirming an aggravated first degree murder conviction. Lord asserts his right to a fair trial was violated because several trial spectators were allowed to wear buttons depicting a picture of the victim for three days of his month long trial....

Lord was convicted for the first degree murder of Tracy Parker and sentenced to death on August 18, 1987. On appeal, this court affirmed the conviction and sentence. On habeas review, the Ninth Circuit Court of Appeals reversed Lord's conviction on the grounds his trial counsel failed to present three witnesses who would have testified they thought they saw the victim alive after Lord was supposed to have killed her. *Lord v. Wood,* 184 F.3d 1083 (9th Cir.1999).

The case was remanded to the Kitsap County Superior Court, and this second trial included the testimony from the disputed three witnesses, as well as some additional deoxyribonucleic acid (DNA) analysis of blood and other evidence. The jury found Lord guilty, and the court sentenced Lord to life imprisonment without the possibility of parole. The Washington Court of Appeals affirmed. Lord then appealed to this court.

The State's basic theory of the crime remained the same. On September 16, 1986, Ms. Parker went to the residence of Wayne and Sharon Frye for her usual horse ride. Lord abducted Ms. Parker and took her to his brother's nearby residence where Lord had a workshop. He raped and killed Ms. Parker in the workshop and then drove to Clear Creek Road to deposit the body. He then returned to his brother's home.

In addition to evidence from the first trial, the State introduced newly available DNA analysis at the second trial. Since the initial investigation in 1986, forensic technology had progressed significantly and several different laboratories were able to test the blood and hair samples from the crime.[7]

In the new trial, the State experts applied more advanced DNA technology to the original evidence further implicating Lord. Mitotyping Technologies tested a hair from the bath towel found at Island Lake for mitochondrial DNA. The results matched Lord, excluding 99.94 percent of the population. LabCorp also tested a hair from the orange U-Haul blanket found near Ms. Parker's clothes, and the DNA matched Lord, excluding 99.94 percent of the population. Finally, LabCorp tested a blood splatter found in Lord's workshop where the victim was allegedly killed. The test produced a complete DNA genetic profile consistent with Ms. Parker's blood and excluded Lord as the source.

During the first three days of the trial, many of the spectators wore buttons with a picture of the victim. The effect on the jury of these buttons is central to our first issue today. The buttons were approximately two and one-half inches in diameter and bore an in-life photograph of victim Tracy Parker. They were picture buttons only and had no message or writing of any kind. Defense counsel objected and moved the judge to remove the buttons from the courtroom. The trial court denied the motion, allowing the buttons to remain for the first three days of trial. Lord did not move for mistrial nor later request a curative jury instruction.

On the third day, the trial court noted on the record that the jury could see the buttons worn by spectators in the courtroom and expressed concern that the buttons might invoke undue sympathy from the jury. On the morning of the

4. Our holding that such displays are not a *per se* indication of inherent prejudice does not undermine a trial court judge's authority to control the courtroom (subject to an abuse of discretion review). Determination of inherent or actual prejudice is the practical provenance of the trial court judge, who is in the best position to monitor the atmosphere of the courtroom. Shirts, buttons, and other behavior may create an overtly hostile atmosphere that could prejudice the jury or intimidate witnesses. Therefore, the trial court judge's examination of the circumstances surrounding the display must be given considerable weight.

7. During the initial investigation, a search group found the victim's jacket, red sweatshirt, jeans, underpants, and shoes near Island Lake. Nearby they discovered a bath towel like the towel used as a curtain in the Frye's garage, the last location where Ms. Parker was seen alive. Another search party found an orange U-Haul blanket near Ms. Parker's clothes. It appeared to have blood stains and was singed. Ms. Parker's body was ultimately found a short distance from the Island Lake site.

fourth day, the court excluded the buttons from the courtroom for the remainder of the 31 day trial....

ANALYSIS ...

A. *Buttons Worn by Trial Spectators*

It is beyond dispute that "[t]he constitutional safeguards relating to the integrity of the criminal process ... embrace the fundamental conception of a fair trial, and ... exclude influence or domination by either a hostile or friendly mob." *Cox v. Louisiana,* 379 U.S. 559, 562 (1965). However, a silent showing of sympathy or affiliation in a courtroom, without more, is not inherently prejudicial. The trial court did not abuse its discretion when it allowed the presence of spectator buttons for a portion of the trial. *See Flynn,* 475 U.S. at 570 (inherent prejudice requires an unacceptable risk of impermissible factors). We affirm the Court of Appeals decision in this case and thereby reaffirm our recent and controlling Washington precedent, *In re Pers. Restraint of Woods,* 154 Wash.2d 400, 416, 114 P.3d 607 (2005). Additionally, United States Supreme Court precedent is consistent with our conclusion and confirms that this issue is appropriate for state court resolution.[9]

1. *United States Supreme Court and Federal Circuit Court Cases*

The United States Supreme Court has analyzed two cases with different facts that are relevant to our constitutional analysis. In *Williams,* 425 U.S. at 530, the State forced a defendant to wear an orange prison jumpsuit in front of the jury. The court held this action was "inherently prejudicial" and denied defendant due process. A contrasting opinion, *Holbrook v. Flynn,* held that the courtroom presence of four uniformed and armed state troopers, who sat directly behind the defendants for the duration of the trial, did not deny defendants due process. 475 U.S. at 571. These two cases can be used as bookends to demonstrate the range of impermissible and permissible courtroom behavior. Note that both cases involved direct action by the state, unlike the private spectator buttons at issue in the instant case.

When courtroom conduct is challenged as inherently prejudicial to the defendant, we must determine whether "'an unacceptable risk is presented of impermissible factors coming into play'" to affect the jury. *Flynn,* 475 U.S. at 570. A reviewing court must consider the courtroom scene presented to the jury and determine whether it was "*so inherently prejudicial* as to pose an *unacceptable threat* to defendant's right to a fair trial." *Flynn,* 475 U.S. at 572 (emphasis added). As the language indicates, some small risk of inherent prejudice is not automatically fatal as long as inherent prejudice does not pose an unacceptable threat to the outcome.

In *Flynn,* the United States Supreme Court held that the presence of the uniformed and armed state troopers did not deny due process because of the "wider range of inferences that a juror might reasonably draw from the officers' presence." *Id.* at 569. Here, picture buttons worn by the spectators more closely resembles the circumstances in *Flynn* than those in *Williams.* The natural reaction of grieving for a family member or friend is one of the "wider range" of inferences that can be derived reasonably from a picture button in the spectator gallery. Many immediate analogues come to mind; the common tradition of wearing black clothing or armband to mourn resonates as the most obvious. The jury would understand this as a sign of loss, but not automatically find it inherently prejudicial or as urging conviction of defendant.

Another important distinction in this case is the difference between the prejudicial effect of State or *litigant* behavior versus restrictions necessary on private *spectator* behavior. Our courtrooms are constitutionally required to be open to the public, thereby eschewing a tightly controlled, sterile trial environment in favor of open public access. *See* WASH. CONST. art. I, § 22; U.S. CONST. amend. VI.

United States Supreme Court cases have considered various state actions, such as requiring a defendant to appear in court wearing shackles or prison clothes or positioning armed and uniformed state troopers in the courtroom.[12] The

9. *See Carey v. Musladin,* 549 U.S. 70 (2006), which dealt with a similar case, and reverses a Ninth Circuit Court of Appeals decision that held such buttons were prejudicial.

12. *See Illinois v. Allen,* 397 U.S. 337, 344 (1970) ("Not only is it possible that the sight of shackles and gags might have a significant effect on the jury's feelings about the defendant, but the use of this technique is itself something of an affront to the very dignity and decorum of judicial proceedings that the judge is seeking to uphold."); *Flynn,* 475 U.S. 560; *Estelle v. Williams,* 425 U.S. 501 (1976).

Court has never held or even suggested it is a constitutional violation to allow picture buttons to be worn in the courtroom by private citizens. The Court has instead expressly allowed state appellate courts to determine and follow their own constitutional precedent regarding spectator buttons. *See Carey v. Musladin,* 549 U.S. 70 (2006). We do so today.

Lord claims that the mere presence of picture buttons in the courtroom denied him a fair trial. He does not argue, nor does the record support, that he suffered actual prejudice. Instead, he asserts that the buttons were an "inherently prejudicial factor." Lord based his argument on Ninth Circuit Court of Appeals cases that are neither controlling nor persuasive....

Lord first cites *Norris v. Risley,* 918 F.2d 828, 830 (9th Cir.1990), *overruled in part by Musladin,* 549 U.S. 70, where spectators wore buttons with the phrase "Women against *Rape*" for the entire trial, sold refreshments outside the courtroom, and had contact with jurors in the elevator and restrooms. The actions of those spectators were held to be inherently prejudicial because the wording on the buttons implied the defendant was guilty.

The circuit court opinion in *Norris* is otherwise distinguishable. Here, we do not have buttons with an overt message underlined with a bold red stroke. Instead, the photographs here had no words and portray an ambiguous message that would be reasonably understood as a show of sympathy and support for the victim's family. In-life photographs of the victim are not considered inherently prejudicial in Washington, and photos of victims are often admissible.... The *Lord* buttons were removed by the trial judge after the third day of a 31 day trial. This is also in contrast with *Norris* where supporters wore the "Women Against *Rape*" buttons throughout the trial, inside and around the courtroom, including the elevator the jury used.

Lord also argued that *Musladin v. LaMarque,* 427 F.3d 647, 651 (9th Cir.2005) *vacated sub nom. Carey v. Musladin,* 549 U.S. 70, supported his claim. In *Musladin,* the Ninth Circuit Court of Appeals on a habeas corpus review had reversed a decision by California courts that allowed courtroom spectators to wear buttons bearing a photograph of the deceased. Three members of the victim's family wore buttons similar to those worn in the instant case, throughout multiple days of the trial, and in plain view of the jury.

The United States Supreme Court vacated the Ninth Circuit Court decision in *Musladin.* The Court held that the California State Court of Appeals decision allowing spectator buttons was an appropriate interpretation of established law as determined by the United States Supreme Court and that a federal circuit court may not overturn such a state court decision. This ruling confirms that this court appropriately follows our own carefully considered jurisprudence....

2. *Washington Law*

Washington law is clear on this matter. We have recently ruled that silent displays of affiliation by trial spectators, which do not explicitly advocate guilt or innocence, are permissible. *Woods,* 154 Wash.2d at 416, 114 P.3d 607. In *Woods,* the defendant complained of black and orange remembrance ribbons worn by spectators during a murder trial. *Woods* objected to the presence of the ribbons. The trial judge allowed them, with the caveat that the judge could provide a jury instruction, if necessary, to mitigate any prejudicial effects. In that case, we applied the Supreme Court's decision in *Flynn* as the controlling law and upheld the conviction. We reaffirm this holding.

In *Woods,* we also found the ribbons were distinguishable from the printed buttons in *Norris* because the "ribbons did not contain any inscription. They were simply ribbons that the wearers indicated they wore in memory of the victims."

The picture button in this case, like the ribbons in *Woods,* did not bear *any message* regarding guilt or innocence. The facts before us are directly analogous to *Woods.* The holding in *Woods* was also informed by our exhaustive review of numerous states' treatment of trial spectators who silently signal their affiliation. Though not binding, this court did summarize many foreign cases that were consistent with our analysis:

> Many courts have used the *Holbrook* [*Flynn*] standard and have found that no inherent prejudice exists so as to taint the defendant's right to fair trial from the wearing of buttons or other displays. *See, e.g., Buckner v. State,* 714 So.2d 384, 389 (Fla.1998) (spectators holding up victim's picture was not inherently prejudicial); *Pachl v. Zenon,* 929 P.2d 1088, 1093 (Or. App. 1996) (spectators wearing buttons with inscription "Crime Victims United" was

> not prejudicial and counsel was not ineffective for failing to challenge the issue); *State v. Braxton,* 477 S.E.2d 172, 177 (N.C. 1996) (spectators wearing badges with victim's picture on them was not prejudicial). In most cases involving violent crime, there is at least one grieving family present at the trial and the presence of such persons should not come as any surprise to the jury members. *See, e.g., State v. Richey,* 298 S.E.2d 879, 889 (W.Va. 1982) ("We must assume that a jury has the fortitude to withstand this type of public scrutiny, and cannot presume irreparable harm to the defendant's right to a fair jury trial by the presence of spectators who may have some type of associational identity with the victim of the crime.").

Woods, 154 Wash.2d at 418, 114 P.3d 607.

Thus, this court has previously decided where picture buttons and ribbons fall along the spectrum of permissible courtroom behavior. Using *Woods* as our guide, we reaffirm that there is no per se "inherent prejudice [to] the defendant's right to fair trial from the wearing of buttons or other displays."

Moreover, this court has also held in other decisions that jury viewing of in-life photographs of the victim is not inherently prejudicial, especially in a case where the jury will see crime scene photographs of the victim. In the instant case, both crime scene and in-life photographs were admitted into evidence and seen by the jury. Because the buttons in controversy carried an in-life photograph of the victim, they were not inherently prejudicial. Therefore, there was no unconstitutional infringement of defendant's right to a fair trial.[14]

Finally, Lord did not make a motion for mistrial or for a curative jury instruction. Such inaction has been held to constitute waiver, unless manifest constitutional error is found.... A defendant generally cannot decline to ask for a mistrial or jury instruction, gamble on the outcome, and when convicted, reassert the waived objection....

CONCLUSION

We cannot guarantee a perfect trial, but we shall always endeavor to assure a fair and constitutional proceeding. On review, complaints regarding courtroom conduct under the supervision of trial courts require reversal only when a court is presented with an *unacceptable* risk. The requisite unacceptable risk of inherent prejudice to reverse requires more than the mere presence of photo buttons worn by grieving family members and spectators....

CHAMBERS, J. (concurring in part/dissenting in part).

... [W]hile I concur with the majority's resolution of the jury taint issue, I write separately to set forth my reasons.

A trial is not a sporting event where fans wave signs, logos, and photographs declaring their allegiance for one team or another. I would hold that when a court effectively permits spectators to participate in a trial, prejudice will be presumed. Because I find the thought of courtroom spectators wearing buttons communicating their views on a central issue before the court abhorrent to a fair and impartial trial, I cannot join the majority.

Courts have a constitutional obligation to ensure a fair and impartial trial. Spectators help ensure that courts are fulfilling their constitutional role by being the eyes and ears of the public, watching justice be done. The decision makers in our trials must be impartial. Constitutionally, spectators, especially those who support one side or another, may not participate in the trial. *Cf. Patterson v. Colorado,* 205 U.S. 454, 462 (1907) ("The theory of our system is that the conclusions to be reached in a case will be induced only by evidence and argument in open court, and not by any outside influence, whether of private talk or public print."). When spectators become participants, fairness and impartiality are jeopardized and the constitutional promise of due process under law is undermined.

"Justice in all cases shall be administered openly...." CONST. art I, § 10. This prevents secret trials, ensures that judges perform their constitutional role, and fosters public confidence in the administration of justice. Justice must be administered openly. Though in the courtroom, the right of the accused to a fair and impartial trial is paramount and the expressive right of spectators is subordinate. The constitutional role of the spectator is to

14. Our constitutional "Victims of crimes—Rights" amendment requires the court or jury to consider the victim during some proceedings. WASH. CONST. art. I, § 35.

be an observer and nothing more. Any effort on the part of the spectators to communicate with the jury should be scrupulously prevented by the judge.

Brian Lord was on trial for murder. For the first three days of his trial, many spectators, over Lord's objection, wore large buttons bearing photographs of the murder victim, Tracy Parker. The buttons carried no message other than the message implicit in the presence of the photograph. On the third day, the able trial judge must have begun having second thoughts about allowing the buttons. She knew by then that jurors could see the buttons and was rightly concerned that the buttons might evoke undue sympathy from the jury, compromising Lord's right to an impartial process. On the fourth day, the judge excluded the buttons from the courtroom.

We have found the wearing of black and orange remembrance ribbons by trial spectators permissible because the ribbons did not advocate a finding of guilt or innocence. *In re Pers. Restraint of Woods,* 154 Wash.2d 400, 416, 114 P.3d 607 (2005). But in *Norris,* spectators wore buttons with the phrase "Woman Against Rape," and the court rightly held the communications were inherently prejudicial.[1] *Norris v. Risley,* 918 F.2d 828, 830 (9th Cir.1990). The majority concludes that wearing buttons bearing Tracy Parker's picture is more like wearing black and orange ribbons than buttons saying, "Woman Against Rape." Certainly, wearing buttons condemning rape during a rape trial is more pointed but wearing the victim's image in a trial for the rape and murder of that victim is fairly pointed itself. Allowing either is to allow courtroom spectators to present a planned, organized effort to communicate with—and sway—the jury. In my view, signs, logos, and buttons with photographs have no place in a courtroom during a trial. *Accord Carey v. Musladin,* 549 U.S. 70 (2006) (Stevens, J., concurring). As the Supreme Court said more than half a century ago, "[d]ue process requires that the accused receive a trial by an impartial jury free from outside influences." *Sheppard v. Maxwell,* 384 U.S. 333, 362 (1966). In my view, judges should not permit spectators to communicate to the jury in any overt, organized, and concerted fashion.[2]

However, law is often an exercise is balancing. While I would begin from the assumption that such buttons cause undue prejudice, I would allow the presumption to be rebutted. In this case, I am satisfied that the prejudice was constrained by the trial court's decision to order the buttons removed 4 days into a 31-day trial. Further, counsel made no motion for mistrial or request for a curative instruction. Since this appears to be a reasonable strategic decision, I cannot say the omissions rise to ineffective assistance of counsel. Thus, I concur with the majority insofar as it holds that Lord is not entitled to relief on this ground.

1. I recognize that after our oral argument, the United States Supreme Court denied habeas relief to a petitioner whose case bears a striking similarity to this one, notwithstanding *Woods* and *Norris. See Carey v. Musladin,* 549 U.S. 70 (2006). In *Carey,* the United States Supreme Court denied habeas relief because the wearing of buttons with the victim's image did not violate "'clearly established Federal law, as determined by the Supreme Court of the United States,'" as required by the Antiterrorism and Effective Death Penalty Act of 1996 before a state court's ruling could be overruled. *Carey,* 127 S.Ct. at 652–53 (quoting 28 U.S.C. § 2254(d)(1)). Whether or not clearly established federal constitutional minimums have been violated, of course, does not answer whether our own state constitutional standards have been met. For those reasons, I also respectfully disagree with the majority's characterization of the holding in *Carey.*

2. Signs, logos, buttons, and the like are forms of expression and communication. I agree that some spectator "communication" is inherent in the constitutional guaranty of a public trial and thus part of the constitutional landscape. For example, the quiet presence of a person sharing traits with the defendant or the victim sitting behind the prosecutor or the defense attorney may play an acceptable, if subtle, role in a trial.

Notes and Questions

1. As discussed in *State v. Lord,* the murder conviction at issue in *Carey v. Musladin,* 549 U.S. 70, 127 S.Ct. 649, 166 L.Ed.2d 482 (2006), was affirmed within the California state court system and later was challenged in the federal courts on Musladin's petition for a writ of habeas corpus. Consequently, the state court ruling was not to be disturbed unless it "was contrary to, or involved an unreasonable application of, clearly established federal law." 28 U.S.C. § 2254 (d) (1). At issue in both *Lord* and *Musladin* was the courtroom conduct of private citizens, rather than state actors. Previous Supreme Court decisions, *Estelle v. Williams,* 425 U.S. 501, 96 S.Ct. 1691, 48 L.Ed.2d 126 (1976) and *Holbrook v. Flynn,* 475 U.S. 560, 106 S.Ct. 1340, 89 L.Ed.2d 525 (1986), had "dealt with government-sponsored practices: In *Williams,* the State compelled the defendant to stand trial in prison clothes, and in *Flynn,* the State seated [four uniformed state] troopers immediately behind the defendant." *Carey v. Musladin,* 549 U.S., at 75. The justices had never before ruled on "a claim that ... private-actor conduct was so inherently prejudicial that it deprived a defendant of a fair trial." *Id.,* 549 U.S., at 76. Given "the lack of guidance from" the Supreme Court, the justices simply concluded in *Musladin* "that the state court [had not] 'unreasonabl[y] appli[ed] clearly established Federal law.'" *Id.,* 549 U.S., at 77. At Musladin's murder trial, "several members of [the shooting victim's] family sat in the front row of the spectator's gallery. On at least some of the trial's 14 days, some members of [the] family wore buttons with a photo of [the victim] on them." *Id.,* 549 U.S., at 72. The trial court denied defense counsel's motion to order the family members to remove the buttons during the trial, concluding that there was "'no possible prejudice to the defendant.'" *Id.,* 549 U.S., at 72–73. Relying on *Holbrook v. Flynn,* the California Court of Appeal affirmed, concluding that the buttons were not inherently prejudicial because the buttons "had not 'branded defendant "with an unmistakable mark of guilt" in the eyes of the jurors' because 'the simple photograph ... was unlikely to have been taken as a sign of anything other than the normal grief occasioned by the loss of [a] family member.'" *Id.,* 549 U.S., at 73. Had the procedural posture of this case been different, not requiring the federal courts to be so deferential to the state court ruling, is it possible that the outcome would have been different? Should it have been different?

2. Consider the following facts in *Shootes v. State,* 20 So.3d 434 (Fla. App. 2009):

> On February 15, 2007, officers of the Jacksonville Sheriff's Office Narcotics Unit ("JSO") prepared to execute a search warrant upon a residence. The officers preferred that the home be unoccupied for the search, but they had learned from the resident of the home that Appellant was inside. Accordingly, the officers arranged for the home's resident to call Appellant and ask him to leave the home, and when he did so, the officers would temporarily hold or detain Appellant away from the premises. Unaware of the impending search or the officers' plans, Appellant walked away from the home and proceeded down the street. Two unmarked police cars with heavily tinted windows advanced upon Appellant and hemmed him in, one car pulling abruptly in front of, and the other behind, Appellant. As the cars came to a halt around Appellant, an officer jumped out of one car with what Appellant described as a "big old gun." Other officers exited as well, wearing "tactical gear." The officers testified that they shouted "Police!" as they exited the vehicles, but Appellant denied ever hearing any announcement from the officers.
>
> In reaction to the situation, which Appellant testified he assumed was an attack by robbers, he drew a handgun and fired at the officers. The officers returned fire and Appellant was shot, subdued and arrested. Appellant testified that he did not realize until after the shooting stopped that the men were not criminals attacking him but were in fact police officers, in essence advancing a theory of self-defense. There was conflicting evidence about the officers' clothing and whether their clothing and appearance should have alerted Appellant to their identities as police

officers. The visual presentation of the officers was thus a feature of the trial and was pivotal to Appellant's theory of defense.

The first three days of the jury trial proceedings were held in one courtroom, but upon arriving at the courthouse for the final day of trial, defense counsel discovered that the proceedings had been moved to a larger courtroom. No explanation for this change of location is contained in the record of the trial proceedings.

Courtroom observers stated—via affidavits—that during those final stages of the trial, one side of the gallery began filling with officers of the JSO. According to these affiants, the officers sat together in the front rows of the gallery, closest to the jury. One affiant stated that there were between 35 and 50 officers in the gallery, and the other three affiants stated that between 50 and 70 officers attended. The affiants consistently swore that the officers were identifiable as JSO personnel because some wore the formal blue JSO uniforms and some wore undercover uniform shirts with bright yellow letters reading "Narcotics Officer, Police, Jacksonville Sheriff's Office" and insignia of the JSO.

In his motion for new trial, Appellant asserted, among other things, that his Sixth Amendment right to a fair trial was denied by the presence of the large number of JSO officers in the courtroom on the last day of trial.

The trial judge denied Shootes's motion for a new trial and Shootes appealed. The Florida Court of Appeals reversed, concluding that "Appellant's fundamental right to a fair and impartial trial, including a verdict based solely upon the evidence developed at the trial, was prejudiced and that the trial court abused its discretion in denying the motion for a new trial." 20 So.3d, at 440.

The presence of courtroom observers wearing uniforms, insignia, buttons, or other indicia of support for the accused, the prosecution, or the victim of the crime does not automatically constitute denial of the accused's right to a fair trial. *Holbrook v. Flynn,* 475 U.S. 560 (1986) (four uniformed officers seated immediately behind defendant); *Carey v. Musladin,* 549 U.S. 70 (2006) (fair trial not denied by wearing of buttons with photo of victim by some members of victim's family). However, there are situations where the atmosphere in the courtroom might infringe on the defendant's right to a fair trial. When this issue is raised, a case-by-case approach is required to allow courts to consider the "totality of the circumstances." *Sheppard v. Maxwell,* 384 U.S. 333, 352 (1966); *Holbrook v. Flynn,* 475 U.S., [at 569].

Considering the circumstances, a defendant claiming he was denied a fair trial must show "either actual or inherent prejudice." *Woods v. Dugger,* 923 F.2d [1454, 1457 (11th Cir. 1991)]. Actual prejudice requires some indication or articulation by a juror or jurors that they were conscious of some prejudicial effect. Inherent prejudice, on the other hand, requires a showing by the defendant that there was an unacceptable risk of impermissible factors coming into play.

... The appearance of the considerable number of JSO officers in various modes of official Sheriff's Office attire presented an unacceptable risk of impermissible factors coming into play.

The number of spectators identifiable as law enforcement personnel was substantial in this case, comparable to the number of officers in *Woods v. Dugger,* 923 F.2d 1454 (11th Cir.1991)—where "about half of the spectators" in the overflowing gallery wore prison guard uniforms—and distinguishes this case from those cases involving the appearance of a relatively few officers visible in the gallery. *Compare Holbrook v. Flynn,* 475 U.S. 560 (1986) (supplemental security of four officers in trial of six defendants not inherently prejudicial); *Davis v. State,* 223 S.W.3d 466 (Tex.App.2006) (no inherent prejudice when up to eight uniformed officers sat in gallery over course of trial, vastly outnumbered by civilian spectators; no indication that officers "gravitated towards" jury or that prosecution "had a role in the presence of the officers during trial").

The record also shows that in Appellant's trial, the officers sat together as a group in the seats closest to the jury, and they were not present as added security or to provide testimony. *Compare Pratt v. State,* 492 S.E.2d 310 (Ga. App. 1997) (no inherent prejudice denying fair trial where twenty-five uniformed correctional officers in gallery to observe closing arguments were in back of room, away from jury, and several had been witnesses sequestered during testimony phase of trial); *Hill v. Ozmint,* 339 F.3d 187 (4th Cir.2003) (no inherent prejudice when nothing in record indicated courtroom was filled with "an array of police officers"; officers present were "dispersed throughout the courtroom"; at least seventeen of the officers had been witnesses). Where a substantial number of uniformed or otherwise identifiably garbed officers are not present for the purpose of preserving order in the courtroom or to provide testimony in the proceedings, a jury is susceptible to the impression that the officers are there "to communicate a message to the jury." *Woods v. Dugger,* 923 F.2d at 1459. In *Woods v. Dugger,* the court concluded that in that case, "[t]he jury could not help but receive the message" that the officers wanted a conviction. *Id.* at 1460. *See also, Norris v. Risley,* 878 F.2d 1178 (9th Cir.1989) (unacceptable risk of improper factors where, during rape trial, twenty to twenty-five spectators wore buttons stating "Women Against Rape"). The only messages a jury should be sent are those from the judge, from evidence presented and admitted, and from proper argument of counsel.

Finally, unlike cases where clothing or accessories worn by spectators might merely have shown support for the victim or another party in general, in this case the officers' apparel was actually a feature of the trial, directly related to Appellant's theory of self-defense. Appellant testified that at the time he fired on the officers, he did not recognize them as such, that he believed he was acting in self-defense, and that only after the confrontation was over did he realize they were not robbers or worse. Witnesses for the State testified that the officers wore tee shirts, vests, or other official apparel with visible identifying markings or letters, but whether the markings were visible to Appellant was in dispute. Under these circumstances, the courtroom scene presented to the jurors of dozens of officers literally clothed with the authority of the JSO could not only have sent the jury a message of official interest and desire for a conviction, but the display of various formal and informal JSO uniforms could easily have been seen by the jury as a live demonstration of the appearance of the officers involved in the altercation with Appellant. Together with the conspicuous crowd of officers present, in close proximity to the jury, the display of undercover police clothing created an unacceptable risk that the jury's determinations of the credibility of witnesses and findings of fact would be tainted by impermissible factors not introduced as evidence or subject to cross-examination.

The totality of the circumstances in the courtroom on the final day of the jury trial resulted in an unacceptable risk of impermissible factors influencing the jury's decision and thus constituted inherent prejudice to Appellant's right to a fair trial resulting in fundamental error....

Following the Florida Court of Appeals' decision and the reversal of Shootes' conviction, the President of the Jacksonville Fraternal Order of Police was quoted as saying: "I believe that our jurors are much smarter than that, and I don't think they would be intimidated because we're sitting there supporting one of our own.... How can somebody stop us from doing that? We have the same rights as other American citizens."[4] For another case involving a defendant's claim that the presence of "a large number of uniformed troopers and police officers attended [his] trial—implicitly informing the jury that the law enforcement community wanted to see [him] convicted" on the charge of murdering a police officer, *see Phillips v. State,* 70 P.3d 1128 (Alaska App. 2003) (rejecting the claim and affirming the conviction).

3. Several commentators have addressed issues concerning courtroom spectators, symbolic displays, and the resulting threats to fair trials.[5]

3. Children as Witnesses

Several attributes of youth, including the blurred line that some children maintain between fact and fantasy, children's heightened suggestibility, particularly with respect to adults in positions of authority, and the inability of some children to appreciate fully their obligation to be truthful and the consequences of being untruthful, led to the common law rule that disqualified children younger than 14 from serving as witnesses in legal proceedings. In due course, that rigid rule gave way to one requiring judges to make competency rulings on a case-by-case basis after probing a prospective child witness's understanding of his or her obligation to tell the truth.[6] Most jurisdictions now adhere to that more flexible approach, although in some states the jury is invited to assess a child's credibility as a witness without a prior judicial competency determination.[7]

When a child is not only a witness, but also the alleged victim of a crime, decisions about the competency of the child to testify are particularly weighty. Especially in sex abuse prosecutions, the child who is the alleged victim might also be the only witness. The stakes are thus heightened for all concerned. As the Wisconsin Supreme Court noted in a case involving a father's alleged sexual assault of his four-year-old daughter, who was five when called as a prosecution witness in a preliminary hearing:[8]

> The case before us involves the most taboo form of pedophilia, incest.
>
> The problem of children testifying in cases such as this is one that will continue to tax the ingenuity of legislatures, the bar, and the courts. The rules and their application are bound to undergo change and modification as our knowledge of the ramification of child sexual exploitation increases. One cannot help but notice the increasing awareness of the lifetime emotional and psychological scars that victims of incest report in later life. Great damage also results to one innocent of such conduct being erroneously convicted or even charged with such a crime.

The Missouri Supreme Court voiced similar concerns in a case involving the appeal of a man's conviction for the sexual assault of his eight-year-old stepdaughter.[9]

> Scholars and legislators alike have for many years debated the propriety, or at least the permissible scope, of a child's testimony. The goal has always been to attain a proper balance between the competing interests of the child and those of the accused. The harsh confrontation between those interests arises predominantly in cases where, as here, the child is the only eyewitness to the crime. More often than not in these cases the only direct evidence connecting the accused with the crime is the testimony of the child. Other circumstantial evidence merely shows that the crime occurred. Consequently, offenders, who have chosen a young child as their victim, often avoid conviction when the child's testimony is unavailable. On the other hand, there is the accused's interest in obtaining a fair trial. Proponents of the accused's interest argue that the testimony of a truly incompetent young child increases the danger of sentencing an innocent man.

The dilemma is clear. Few crimes are as serious or reprehensible as the sexual assault of a child; such offenders deserve prosecution and punishment. At the same time, little could be worse than to be wrongfully accused and convicted of a crime of this nature based on a child's erroneous perceptions or testimony. Professor Gross and his colleagues did not include "mass child molestation prosecutions [where] the identity of the perpetrators is not an issue" in their study of exonerations in the United States between 1989 and 2003.[10] In describing a few such incidents, they observed that the central question in such cases was: "Did the crimes really happen at all?"

> In many of these child-molestation cases, the accusations were bizarre if not impossible on their face. Some children at the Little Rascals Day Care Center in Edenton, North Carolina, for example, said that they had seen babies killed at the day-care center, children taken out on boats and thrown overboard to feed sharks, and children taken to outer space in a hot air balloon. In Kern County, California, children described mass orgies with as many as fourteen adults who forced groups of children to inhale eighteen-inch lines of cocaine or heroin, gave them injections with syringes that left large bruises, and hung the children from hooks as the adults repeatedly sodomized them.... In other cases, the accusations

> were merely implausible, and appear to ... have been generated by over-eager prosecutors and therapists who demanded that the young children they examined tell them that they had been molested, and would not take No for an answer.[11]

One of the most famous "mass child molestation prosecutions"—which ultimately failed to result in convictions—involved claims made by more than 350 children that they had been molested during the 1980s at the McMartin Preschool in Los Angeles.

> Following indictment and an eighteen month preliminary hearing, [the judge] ordered ... seven [preschool staff members] to stand trial on 135 of the more than 300 charged counts of sexual abuse. Prosecutors ultimately dropped charges against five of the defendants, leaving only Raymond Buckey and his mother, Peggy McMartin Buckey, to be tried. Thirty-three months, 124 witnesses, 974 exhibits, and almost 64,000 pages of transcript later, the Buckeys were acquitted on fifty-two counts of abuse. The jury deadlocked on the remaining thirteen, all of which were against Raymond Buckey. Two new prosecutors retried Buckey on eight counts involving only three children. Another jury deadlocked on these charges, and the judge declared a mistrial.
>
> On July 28, 1990, the McMartin case ended without a single conviction, despite the fact that seven of the jurors believed the children had been molested "in some sense, by someone." An assistant district attorney acknowledged that it was "quite possible that there were some people in this case who were wrongfully accused."[12]

Consider the following case, which discusses practices that can threaten securing reliable testimony from the alleged victims of child sexual abuse.

State v. Michaels

642 A.2d 1372 (N.J. 1994)

HANDLER, J.

In this case a nursery school teacher was convicted of bizarre acts of sexual abuse against many of the children who had been entrusted to her care. She was sentenced to a long prison term with a substantial period of parole ineligibility. The Appellate Division reversed the conviction and remanded the case for retrial. 264 *N.J.Super.* 579, 625 A.2d 489 (1993).

... In setting aside the conviction, the Appellate Division ordered that if the State decided to retry the case, a pretrial hearing would be necessary to determine whether the statements and testimony of the child-sex-abuse victims must be excluded because improper questioning by State investigators had irremediably compromised the reliability of that testimonial evidence....

I

In September 1984, Margaret Kelly Michaels was hired by Wee Care Day Nursery ("Wee Care") as a teacher's aide for preschoolers. Located in St. George's Episcopal Church, in Maplewood, Wee Care served approximately fifty families, with an enrollment of about sixty children, ages three to five.

Michaels, a college senior from Pittsburgh, Pennsylvania, came to New Jersey to pursue an acting career. She responded to an advertisement and was hired by Wee Care, initially as a teacher's aide for preschoolers, then, at the beginning of October, as a teacher. Michaels had no prior experience as a teacher at any level.

Wee Care had staff consisting of eight teachers, numerous aides, and two administrators. The nursery classes for the three-year-old children were housed in the basement, and the kindergarten class was located on the third floor. During nap time, Michaels, under the supervision of the head teacher and the director, was responsible for about twelve children in one of the basement classrooms. The classroom assigned to Michaels was separated from an adjacent occupied classroom by a vinyl curtain.

During the seven month period that Michaels worked at Wee Care, she apparently performed satisfactorily. Wee Care never received a complaint about her from staff, children, or parents. According to the State, however, between October 8, 1984, and the date of Michaels's resignation on April 26, 1985, parents and teachers began observing behavioral changes in the children.

On April 26, 1985, the mother of M.P., a four-year-old in Michaels's nap class, noticed while awakening him for school, that he was covered with spots. She took the child to his pediatrician and had him examined. During the examination, a pediatric nurse took M.P.'s temperature rectally. In the presence of the nurse and his mother, M.P. stated, "this is what my teacher does to me at nap time at school." M.P. indicated to the nurse that his teacher, Kelly (the name by which Michaels was known to the children), was the one who took his temperature. M.P. added that Kelly undressed him and took his temperature daily. On further questioning by his mother, M.P. said that Kelly did the same thing to S.R.

The pediatrician, Dr. Delfino, then examined M.P. He informed Mrs. P. that the spots were caused by a rash. Mrs. P. did not tell Dr. Delfino about M.P.'s remarks; consequently, he did not examine M.P.'s rectum. In response to further questioning from his mother after they had returned home, M.P., while rubbing his genitals, stated that "[Kelly] uses the white jean stuff." Although M.P. was unable to tell his mother what the "white jean stuff" was, investigators later found vaseline in Wee Care's bathroom and white cream in the first-aid kit. During the same conversation, M.P. indicated that Kelly had "hurt" two of his classmates, S.R. and E.N.

M.P.'s mother contacted the New Jersey Division of Youth and Family Services ("DYFS") and Ms. Spector, Director of Wee Care, to inform them of her son's disclosures. On May 1, 1985, the Essex County Prosecutor's office received information from DYFS about the alleged sexual abuse at Wee Care. The Prosecutor's office assumed investigation of the complaint.

The Prosecutor's office interviewed several Wee Care children and their parents, concluding their initial investigation on May 8, 1985. During that period of investigation, Michaels submitted to approximately nine hours of questioning. Additionally, Michaels consented to taking a lie detector test, which she passed. Extensive additional interviews and examinations of the Wee Care children by the prosecutor's office and DYFS then followed.

Michaels was charged on June 6, 1985, in a three count indictment involving the alleged sexual abuse of three Wee Care boys. After further investigation, a second indictment was returned July 30, 1985, containing 174 counts of various charges involving twenty Wee Care boys and girls. An additional indictment of fifty-five counts was filed November 21, 1985, involving fifteen Wee Care children. Prior to trial the prosecution dismissed seventy-two counts, proceeding to trial on the remaining 163 counts.

After several pretrial hearings, the trial commenced on June 22, 1987. The bulk of the State's evidence consisted of the testimony of the children. That testimony referred extensively to the pretrial statements that had been elicited from the children during the course of the State's investigations. The State introduced limited physical evidence to support the contention that the Wee Care children had been molested.

By the time the trial concluded nine months later, another thirty-two counts had been dismissed, leaving 131 counts. On April 15, 1988, after twelve days of deliberation, the jury returned guilty verdicts on 115 counts, including aggravated sexual assault (thirty-eight counts), sexual assault (thirty-one counts), endangering the welfare of children (forty-four counts), and terroristic threats (two counts). The trial court sentenced Michaels to an aggregate term of forty-seven years imprisonment with fourteen years of parole ineligibility.

II

The focus of this case is on the manner in which the State conducted its investigatory interviews of the children. In particular, the Court is asked to consider whether the interview techniques employed by the state could have undermined the reliability of the children's statements and subsequent testimony, to the point that a hearing should be held to determine whether either form of evidence should be admitted at retrial.

The question of whether the interviews of the child victims of alleged sexual-abuse were unduly suggestive and coercive requires a highly nuanced inquiry into the totality of circumstances surrounding those interviews. Like confessions and identification, the inculpatory capacity of statements indicating the occurrence of sexual abuse and the anticipated testimony about those occurrences requires that special care be taken to ensure their reliability.

The Appellate Division carefully examined the record concerning the investigatory interviews.

It concluded that the interrogations that had been conducted were highly improper. The court determined from the record that the children's accusations were founded "upon unreliable perceptions, or memory caused by improper investigative procedures," and that testimony reflecting those accusations could lead to an unfair trial. Accordingly, it held that in the event of a re-trial, a pretrial hearing would be required to assess the reliability of the statements and testimony to be presented by those children to determine their admissibility. The State appeals that determination.

Woven into our consideration of this case is the question of a child's susceptibility to influence through coercive or suggestive questioning. As the Appellate Division noted, a constantly broadening body of scholarly authority exists on the question of children's susceptibility to improper interrogation. The expanse of that literature encompasses a variety of views and conclusions. Among the varying perspectives, however, the Appellate Division found a consistent and recurrent concern over the capacity of the interviewer and the interview process to distort a child's recollection through unduly slanted interrogation techniques. The Appellate Division concluded that certain interview practices are sufficiently coercive or suggestive to alter irremediably the perceptions of the child victims.

A.

Like many other scientific and psychological propositions that this Court has addressed in different contexts, the notion that a child is peculiarly susceptible to undue influence, while comporting with our intuition and common experience is in fact a hotly debated topic among scholars and practitioners....

... This Court has been especially vigilant in its insistence that children, as a class, are not to be viewed as inherently suspect witnesses. We have specifically held that age *per se* cannot render a witness incompetent. We declined to require or allow, absent a strong showing of abnormality, psychological testing of child-victims of sexual abuse as a predicate to a determination of the credibility of the child-victim as a witness. We have also recognized that under certain circumstances children's accounts of sexual abuse can be highly reliable. Nevertheless, our common experience tells us that children generate special concerns because of their vulnerability, immaturity, and impressionability, and our laws have recognized and attempted to accommodate those concerns, particularly in the area of child sexual abuse.

The broad question of whether children as a class are more or less susceptible to suggestion than adults is one that we need not definitively answer in order to resolve the central issue in this case. Our inquiry is much more focused. The issue we must determine is whether the interview techniques used by the State in this case were so coercive or suggestive that they had a capacity to distort substantially the children's recollections of actual events and thus compromise the reliability of the children's statements and testimony based on their recollections.

We begin our analyses by noting ... that the "investigative interview" is a crucial, perhaps determinative, moment in a child-sex-abuse case. A decision to prosecute a case of child sexual abuse often hinges on the information elicited in the initial investigatory interviews with alleged victims, carried out by social workers or police investigators.

... If a child's recollection of events has been molded by an interrogation, that influence undermines the reliability of the child's responses as an accurate recollection of actual events.

A variety of factors bear on the kinds of interrogation that can affect the reliability of a child's statements concerning sexual abuse. We note that a fairly wide consensus exists among experts, scholars, and practitioners concerning improper interrogation techniques. They argue that among the factors that can undermine the neutrality of an interview and create undue suggestiveness are a lack of investigatory independence, the pursuit by the interviewer of a preconceived notion of what has happened to the child, the use of leading questions, and a lack of control for outside influences on the child's statements, such as previous conversations with parents or peers.

The use of incessantly repeated questions also adds a manipulative element to an interview. When a child is asked a question and gives an answer, and the question is immediately asked again, the child's normal reaction is to assume that the first answer was wrong or displeasing to the adult questioner. The insidious effects of repeated questioning are even more pronounced when the questions themselves over time suggest information to the children.

The explicit vilification or criticism of the person charged with wrongdoing is another factor that can induce a child to believe abuse has occurred. Similarly, an interviewer's bias with respect to a suspected person's guilt or innocence can have a marked effect on the accuracy of a child's statements. The transmission of suggestion can also be subtly communicated to children through more obvious factors such as the interviewer's tone of voice, mild threats, praise, cajoling, bribes and rewards, as well as resort to peer pressure.

The Appellate Division recognized the considerable authority supporting the deleterious impact improper interrogation can have on a child's memory. Other courts have recognized that once tainted the distortion of the child's memory is irremediable.

The critical influence that can be exerted by interview techniques is also supported by the literature that generally addresses the reliability of children's memories. Those studies stress the importance of *proper* interview techniques as a predicate for eliciting accurate and consistent recollection.

The conclusion that improper interrogations generate a significant risk of corrupting the memories of young children is confirmed by government and law enforcement agencies, which have adopted standards for conducting interviews designed to overcome the dangers stemming from the improper interrogation of young children. The National Center for the Prosecution of Child Abuse, in cooperation with the National District Attorney's Association and the American Prosecutor's Research Institute has adopted protocols to serve as standards for the proper interrogation of suspected child-abuse victims. Those interview guidelines require that an interviewer remain "open, neutral and objective." American Prosecutors Research Institute, National Center for Prosecution of Child Abuse, *Investigation and Prosecution of Child Abuse* at 7 (1987); an interviewer should avoid asking leading questions; an interviewer should never threaten a child or try to force a reluctant child to talk; and an interviewer should refrain from telling a child what others, especially other children, have reported. The New Jersey Governor's Task Force on Child Abuse and Neglect has also promulgated guidelines. It states that the interviewer should attempt to elicit a child's feelings about the alleged offender, but that the interviewer should not speak negatively about that person. Further, multiple interviews with various interviewers should be avoided.

Finally, we can acknowledge judicial recognition of the very same concerns expressed in the academic literature and addressed by the guidelines established by governmental authorities with respect to the improper interrogation of alleged child sex abuse victims. The United States Supreme Court in *Idaho v. Wright*, 497 *U.S.* 805, 812–13 (1990), noted with approval the conclusion of the Idaho Supreme Court that the failure to video tape interviews with alleged child victims, the use of blatantly leading questions, and the presence of an interviewer with a preconceived idea of what the child should be disclosing, in addition to children's susceptibility to suggestive questioning, all indicate the potential for the elicitation of unreliable information.

We therefore determine that a sufficient consensus exists within the academic, professional, and law enforcement communities, confirmed in varying degrees by courts, to warrant the conclusion that the use of coercive or highly suggestive interrogation techniques can create a significant risk that the interrogation itself will distort the child's recollection of events, thereby undermining the reliability of the statements and subsequent testimony concerning such events.

B.

... The interrogations undertaken in the course of this case utilized most, if not all, of the practices that are disfavored or condemned by experts, law enforcement authorities and government agencies.

The initial investigation giving rise to defendant's prosecution was sparked by a child volunteering that his teacher, "Kelly," had taken his temperature rectally, and that she had done so to other children. However, the overwhelming majority of the interviews and interrogations did not arise from the spontaneous recollections that are generally considered to be most reliable. Few, if any, of the children volunteered information that directly implicated defendant. Further, none of the child victims related incidents of actual sexual abuse to their interviewers using "free recall." Additionally, few of the children provided any tell-tale details of the alleged abuse although they were repeatedly prompted to do so by the investigators. We note further that the investigators were not trained in interviewing young children. The earliest interviews with children were not recorded and in some instances the original notes were destroyed.[1] Many of the interviewers demonstrated ineptness in dealing with the challenges presented by preschoolers, and displayed their frustration with the children.

Almost all of the interrogations conducted in the course of the investigation revealed an obvious lack of impartiality on the part of the interviewer. One investigator, who conducted the majority of the interviews with the children, stated that his interview techniques had been based on the premise that the "interview process is in essence the beginning of the healing process." He considered it his "professional and ethical responsibility to alleviate whatever anxiety has arisen as a result of what happened to them." A lack of objectivity also was indicated by the interviewer's failure to pursue any alternative hypothesis that might contradict an assumption of defendant's guilt, and a failure to challenge or probe seemingly outlandish statements made by the children.

The record is replete with instances in which children were asked blatantly leading questions that furnished information the children themselves had not mentioned. All but five of the thirty-four children interviewed were asked questions that indicated or strongly suggested that perverse sexual acts had in fact occurred.... In addition, many of the children, some over the course of nearly two years leading up to trial, were subjected to repeated, almost incessant, interrogation. Some children were re-interviewed at the urgings of their parents.

The record of the investigative interviews discloses the use of mild threats, cajoling, and bribing. Positive reinforcement was given when children made inculpatory statements, whereas negative reinforcement was expressed when children denied being abused or made exculpatory statements.

Throughout the record, the element of "vilification" appears. Fifteen of the thirty-four children were told, at one time or another, that Kelly was in jail because she had done bad things to children; the children were encouraged to keep "Kelly" in jail. For example, they were told that the investigators "needed their help" and that they could be "little detectives." Children were also introduced to the police officer who had arrested defendant and were shown the handcuffs used during her arrest; mock police badges were given to children who cooperated.

In addition, no effort was made to avoid outside information that could influence and affect the recollection of the children.... [T]he children were in contact with each other and, more likely than not, exchanged information about the alleged abuses. Seventeen of the thirty-four children were actually told that other children had told investigators that Kelly had done bad things to children. In sum, the record contains numerous instances of egregious violations of proper interview protocols.

We thus agree with the Appellate Division that the interviews of the children were highly improper and employed coercive and unduly suggestive methods. As a result, a substantial likelihood exists that the children's recollection of past events was both stimulated and materially influenced by that course of questioning. Accordingly, we conclude that a hearing must be held to determine whether those clearly improper interrogations so infected the ability of the children to recall the alleged abusive events that their pretrial statements and in-court testimony based on that recollection are unreliable and should not be admitted into evidence.

IV ...

A.

... The determination of the reliability of pretrial statements must take into account all relevant circumstances....

... Among the factors that bear on that determination are: (1) the person to whom the child made the statement; (2) whether the statement was made under conditions likely to elicit truthfulness; (3) whether the child's recitation exhibits unusual or above-age-level familiarity with sex or sexual functions; (4) post-event and post-recitation distress; (5) any physical evidence of abuse; and (6) any congruity between a defendant's confession or statement.... [Other] factors that should be considered in assessing the reliability of a complaint regarding sexual offenses ... are: (1) the age of the victim, (2) circumstances of the questioning; (3) the victim's

---

1. As a matter of sound interviewing methodology, nearly all experts agree that initial interviews should be videotaped....

In this case, ... [t]he Court is aware of 39 transcripts of interviews with thirty-four children, or about one-half of those interviewed by DYFS. The rest were apparently unrecorded.

relationship with the interrogator; and (4) the type of questions asked.

In this case we are equally concerned about the reliability of anticipated in-court testimony that may be derived from the out-of-court statements and antecedent interrogations. The considerations that are germane to the assessment of the reliability of in-court testimony parallel those that inform the determination of the reliability of out-of-court statements.

The law governing the admissibility of eyewitness identification testimony provides a helpful perspective in addressing the concerns at issue here. The United States Supreme Court has insisted that a pretrial hearing be held to determine the reliability and admissibility of proffered in-court testimony based on unduly suggestive identification procedures. *Manson* [*v. Brathwaite,* 432 *U.S.* 98, 114 (1977)]....

We are confronted in this case with pretrial events relating not to the identification of an offender but, perhaps more crucially, to the occurrence of the offense itself. Those events—investigatory interviews—are fraught with the elements of untoward suggestiveness and the danger of unreliable evidentiary results.... [T]o ensure defendant's right to a fair trial a pretrial taint hearing is essential to demonstrate the reliability of the resultant evidence.

B.

[At the] pretrial hearing ... [t]he basic issue to be addressed ... is whether the pretrial events, the investigatory interviews and interrogations, were so suggestive that they give rise to a substantial likelihood of irreparably mistaken or false recollection of material facts bearing on defendant's guilt.

Consonant with the presumption that child victims are to be presumed no more or less reliable than any other class of witnesses, the initial burden to trigger a pretrial taint hearing is on the defendant. The defendant must make a showing of "some evidence" that the victim's statements were the product of suggestive or coercive interview techniques.

That threshold standard has been met with respect to the investigatory interviews and interrogations that occurred in this case. Without limiting the grounds that could serve to trigger a taint hearing, we note that the kind of practices used here—the absence of spontaneous recall, interviewer bias, repeated leading questions, multiple interviews, incessant questioning, vilification of defendant, ongoing contact with peers and references to their statements, and the use of threats, bribes and cajoling, as well as the failure to videotape or otherwise document the initial interview sessions—constitute more than sufficient evidence to support a finding that the interrogations created a substantial risk that the statements and anticipated testimony are unreliable, and therefore justify a taint hearing.

Once defendant establishes that sufficient evidence of unreliability exists, the burden shall shift to the State to prove the reliability of the proffered statements and testimony by clear and convincing evidence. Hence, the ultimate determination to be made is whether, despite the presence of some suggestive or coercive interview techniques, when considering the totality of the circumstances surrounding the interviews, the statements or testimony retain a degree of reliability sufficient to outweigh the effects of the improper interview techniques.... To make that showing, the State is entitled to call experts to offer testimony with regard to the suggestive capacity of the suspect investigative procedures. The defendant, in countering the State's evidence, may also offer experts on the issue of the suggestiveness of the interrogations. However, the relevance of expert opinion focusing essentially on the propriety of the interrogation should not extend to or encompass the ultimate issue of the credibility of an individual child as a witness. The State is also entitled to demonstrate the reliability of the child's statements or testimony by proffering independent indicia of reliability....

In choosing the burden of proof to be imposed on the State, we are satisfied that the clear-and-convincing-evidence standard serves to safeguard the fairness of a defendant's trial without making legitimate prosecution of child sexual abuse impossible....

Finally, if it is determined by the trial court that a child's statements or testimony, or some portion thereof, do retain sufficient reliability for admission at trial, then it is for the jury to determine the probative worth and to assign the weight to be given to such statements or testimony as part of their assessment of credibility. Experts may thus be called to aid the jury by explaining the coercive or suggestive propensities of the interviewing techniques employed, but not of course, to offer opinions as to the issue of a child-witness's credibility, which remains strictly a matter for the jury....

C.

In conclusion, we find that the interrogations that occurred in this case were improper and there is a substantial likelihood that the evidence derived from them is unreliable. We therefore hold that in the event the State seeks to re-prosecute this defendant, a pretrial hearing must be held in which the State must prove by clear and convincing evidence that the statements and testimony elicited by the improper interview techniques nonetheless retains a sufficient degree of reliability to warrant admission at trial. Given the egregious prosecutorial abuses evidenced in this record, the challenge that the State faces is formidable. If the statements and proffered testimony of any of the children survive the pretrial hearing, the jury will have to determine the credibility and probative worth of such testimony in light of all the surrounding circumstances....

APPENDIX

This Appendix presents a detailed summary of several interviews....

Notes and Questions

1. Michaels spent five years in prison before her convictions were overturned. The prosecution elected not to retry her.[13]

2. In *Harrison v. State,* 33 So.2d 727 (Fla. App. 2010), the Florida Court of Appeals ruled (2–1) that the trial court abused its discretion when it excluded the testimony of the defendant's proffered expert witness regarding factors affecting the reliability of children's memory in a case involving an 11-year-old child who testified that she had been sexually assaulted by the defendant several years earlier, when she was only three or four years old.

3. As mentioned in the *Michaels* decision, there is general consensus among scientists that children, like adults, can be suggestible and that there are proper and improper methods of interview. In general, the research demonstrates that asking open-ended questions as opposed to leading or suggestive questions is more likely to yield accurate information, albeit sometimes less complete (particularly from younger children). For example, the National Institute of Child Health and Human Development (NICHD) Investigative Interview Protocol, which places a premium on open-ended questions, has been shown in several studies to improve the quality of the information obtained. The authors of the interview protocol state, "The NICHD Protocol operationalizes the principles about which there has been clear expert professional consensus and has been shown to improve the behavior of investigative interviewers by helping them to elicit information that is more likely to be accurate because it is recalled by the child freely rather than in response to information and probes provided by the interviewer. In addition, interviewers are better able to judge whether victims are telling the truth when the interviews are conducted using the Protocol, perhaps because the children are thereby encouraged to provide more information in the narrative form which is more amenable to credibility assessment."[14]

Research has also clearly demonstrated the ways in which children should not be interviewed. In one study, researchers took techniques used in the *Michaels* case interviews and examined their influence on children's likelihood of false allegations in a laboratory situation. Specifically, Garven and her colleagues examined the influence of *Reinforcement* (both positive and negative consequences) and *Co-witness information* on 5- to 7-year-old children.[15] A verbatim example of negative consequences used in the *Michaels* case is as follows:

I = Interviewer. C = Child.

I: Heck, everybody was playing naked games in their school. Then they were just little kids, and they played, too, and some of the naked games were fun. The kids had a good time. And they were kind of silly. Do you remember that Bear [a puppet], some of those fun silly games?

C: [Shakes Bear puppet's head, "no".]

I: Oh, Bear, maybe you don't have a very good memory ...

C: [Laughs]

I: ... and your memory must not be as good as Patsy's friend's memories ...

(Interview Number 111, pp. 19–20)

An example of the co-witness information technique from *Michaels* is:

I: ... Mr. Floppy Family person [a puppet]. Have you ever seen anything so floppy as that? That's ridiculous, isn't it?

C: I'm going to choke him.

I: You're going to choke him? You know, some of the kids said they got choked.

Both of these techniques can convey to children that their original answers were wrong or insufficient and that similar others are responding differently (and more appropriately). In the laboratory study, Garven and colleagues found that whereas reinforcement had dramatic and repeated effects on false allegations, the co-witness information did not. Children exposed to reinforcement were about 3 to 10 times more likely to make false allegations than those children not exposed.

For more information about children's legal capacities, and investigative interviewing, see the following resources: Ceci, S. J., Bruck, M., Kulkfsky, S. C., Klemfuss, J. Z., & Sweeney, C., "Unwarranted Assumptions About Children's Testimonial Accuracy," 3 *Annual Review of Clinical Psychology* 311 (2008); Goodman, G. S., & Quas, J. A., "It's When and How, Not Just How Many: Repeated Interviews and Children's Memory," *Current Directions in Psychology* (2008); Lyon, T.D., "Applying Suggestibility Research to the Real World: The Case of Repeated Questions," 65 *Law & Contemporary Problems* 97 (2002); Poole, D. A., & Lamb, M. E., *Investigative Interviews of Children: A Guide for Helping Professionals* (Washington, DC: American Psychological Association 1998).

4. Impeachment: Cross-Examination About Prior Convictions

A common law rule, grounded on the notion that the testimony of interested parties is inherently suspect, flatly prohibited individuals accused of a crime from testifying on their own behalf. Defendants instead were allowed to make unsworn statements that were not subject to cross-examination. That rule eventually yielded to one acknowledging that criminal defendants have a right to testify in their own defense, although they of course cannot be compelled to do so.[16] If a defendant elects to testify, the prosecution has a corresponding right of cross-examination. A traditional function of cross-examination is testing witnesses' veracity, including by asking about prior criminal convictions, a tack justified on the premise that past criminality reflects unfavorably on a witness's testimonial credibility.

Defendants with a record of prior criminal convictions who are brought to trial on new charges thus confront a vexing choice. If they do not testify, although the law does not permit the judge or prosecutor to comment on that decision,[17] the jury may nevertheless infer that their silence suggests they cannot truthfully deny guilt and must have something to hide. If they do testify, their prior criminal record—which otherwise is not (except under unusual circumstances) made known to the jury—is exposed pursuant to the rules of evidence observed in most jurisdictions.[18] Although jurors are instructed to consider the prior record only insofar as it may reflect on testimonial veracity, they may instead draw the (impermissible) inference that the past convictions help evidence guilt on the present charge.[19]

Individuals with a criminal history are often disadvantaged within the criminal justice system for other reasons, as well. While investigating unsolved crimes, the police may focus attention on known past offenders. Such a propensity is artfully captured in the famous admonition of Captain Renault, the French prefect of police, in the film classic *Casablanca*, who instructed his officers to "round up the usual suspects" following the shooting of a Nazi officer—a humane gesture in that context designed to deflect suspicion from Humphrey Bogart's character, Rick Blaine.[20] One scholar has argued that, "In reality, most innocent defendants are recidivists, because institutional biases select for the arrest and charge of these repeat players."[21] Once the police make an arrest, "tunnel vision" and confirmation bias may combine to fuel a self-fulfilling prophecy that the guilty party has been identified.

Such influences may enhance the risk of wrongful conviction for individuals with a record of committing past crimes. Professor John Blume examined 119 cases of wrongful conviction revealed through post-conviction DNA testing in which he was able to ascertain whether the defendant testified. Seventy-three of those defendants (61%) testified, a higher percentage than reflected in a control sample involving presumptively guilty defendants (49%). The remaining defendants who subsequently were exonerated did not testify. John H. Blume, "The Dilemma of the Criminal Defendant with a Prior Record—Lessons from the Wrongfully Convicted," 5 *Journal of Empirical Legal Studies* 477, 489–490 (2008). Blume then attempted to determine how many among the 119 DNA-exonerated defendants had criminal records and whether the presence or absence of prior convictions might have influenced their decisions about testifying.

> ... Of the 56 innocent defendants who did testify for which information is available, only 24 (43 percent) had prior criminal records that the prosecution could have put before the jury for the purpose of testing the defendant's credibility. Of the innocent wrongfully convicted defendants who failed to testify for which information was available, 32 of 35 (91 percent) had prior convictions that potentially could have been used for impeachment purposes had they exercised their constitutional right to tell their story.
>
> ... In almost all instances in which a defendant with a prior record did not testify, counsel for the wrongfully convicted defendant indicated that avoiding impeachment was the principal reason the defendant did not take the stand....
>
> Subject to [the stated] limitations, the currently available data, therefore, suggest that many demonstrably innocent defendants did not testify at trial because, had they done so, they would have been impeached with their prior convictions. *Id.*, at 490–492 (footnotes omitted).

What limitations, if any, should be placed on cross-examination of defendants about prior criminal convictions for impeachment purposes?

State v. Hardy

946 P.2d 1175 (Wash. 1997)

SANDERS, Justice.

Patrick Hardy appeals a second degree robbery conviction, asserting a prior drug conviction was improperly admitted into evidence contrary to ER 609(a)(1). The Court of Appeals affirmed, but we reverse. As held in *State v. Jones,* 101 Wash.2d 113, 122, 677 P.2d 131(1984) prior drug convictions "have little to do with a defendant's credibility as a witness...."

FACTS

At trial complaining witness Shamsa Wilkins testified that as she stood on a downtown Seattle street corner at 4:30 in the morning, Hardy approached her, spoke with her for a few minutes, and then robbed her of her jewelry....

Seattle police officer Stewart testified he was summoned to the scene and arrived within a minute of the call. Officer Stewart testified the alleged victim and her female companion Margaret Smith were "very, very, distraught and upset ... break[ing] down into tears" and "excited" as they told him what allegedly happened.... While alleged victim Wilkins testified at trial, her friend Margaret Smith did not.

Police also testified Hardy was found a few minutes after the alleged robbery at a nearby intersection passed out in his black Camaro. Wilkins' jewelry was found in Hardy's pockets.

Hardy took the stand and testified to a different version of events. He claimed Wilkins was in a push and shove match with her female friend and he had simply helped out by picking up loose jewelry from the ground. He did not deny he left the scene with the jewelry in his pocket, but such would not constitute robbery.

Before trial the State moved to introduce Hardy's prior felony drug conviction for impeachment purposes should he choose to testify. Defense counsel objected claiming the prior drug conviction was not only irrelevant to Hardy's credibility but very prejudicial as well. The court stated on the record "[t]he impeachment value of the prior crime is almost nil" and as a drug crime it would be particularly prejudicial given the anti-drug "fever." The court, nevertheless, admitted the prior conviction as an unnamed felony, reasoning "the jury should be entitled to know that there is some prior conviction." Responding to the court's ruling, Hardy's counsel elicited the unnamed prior conviction on direct.[2] The jury convicted Hardy. Hardy appealed to the Court of Appeals, but for naught.

The appellate court affirmed, reasoning all prior drug convictions are relevant to the defendant's credibility because drug convictions necessarily show secrecy and deceit....

ER 609

Evidence of prior felony convictions is generally inadmissible against a defendant because it is not relevant to the question of guilt yet very prejudicial, as it may lead the jury to believe the defendant has a propensity to commit crimes. ER 609 represents a narrow exception to this rule against admitting evidence of prior convictions.

> For the purpose of attacking the credibility of a witness in a criminal or civil case, evidence that the witness has been convicted of a crime shall be admitted if elicited from the witness or established by public record during examination of the witness but only if the crime (1) was punishable by death or imprisonment in excess of 1 year under the law under which the witness was convicted, *and the court determines that the probative value of admitting this evidence outweighs the prejudice to the party against whom the evidence is offered,* or (2) involved dishonesty or false statement, regardless of the punishment.
>
> ER 609(a) (emphasis added).

Drug convictions are not crimes of "dishonesty or false statement" like perjury or criminal fraud and thus ER 609(a)(2) does not apply. Rather the inquiry focuses on ER 609(a)(1), which allows admittance of prior felony convictions only if "the probative value of admitting this evidence outweighs the prejudice to the party against whom the evidence

2. The fact that defense counsel brought out the damaging impeachment evidence on direct does not foreclose defendant's subsequent challenge in light of the trial court's ruling that it was admissible.

is offered...." ER 609(a)(1). *State v. Jones,* 101 Wash.2d 113, 677 P.2d 131 (1984) is dispositive.[4]

Probative value

ER 609(a)(1) requires the prior conviction have "probative value." When assessing probative value it is critical to understand "the sole purpose of impeachment evidence [under ER 609(a)(1)] is to enlighten the jury with respect to the defendant's credibility as a witness." *Jones,* 101 Wash.2d at 118, 677 P.2d 131.[5] Credibility in this context refers to truthfulness. Prior convictions are therefore only "probative" under ER 609(a)(1) to the extent they are probative of the witness's truthfulness.

State v. Begin, 59 Wash.App. 755, 759–60, 801 P.2d 269 (1990) declared all prior felonies "'are evidence of non-law-abiding character'" and thus "probative" under ER 609(a)(1). However, the proper inquiry under ER 609(a)(1) is not whether the prior conviction shows a "non-law-abiding character"[6] but whether it shows the witness is not truthful. To the extent *Begin* suggests all criminal convictions go to truthfulness or that every criminal act is evidence of an untruthful personality it is disapproved.[7] "Simply because a defendant has committed a crime in the past does not mean the defendant will lie when testifying." *Jones,* 101 Wash.2d at 119, 677 P.2d 131. To the contrary, we have held "few prior offenses that do not involve crimes of dishonesty or false statement are likely to be probative of a witness' veracity." *Id.* at 120, 677 P.2d 131. We again affirm that position and caution prior convictions not involving dishonesty or false statements are not probative of the witness's veracity until the party seeking admission thereof shows the opposite by demonstrating the prior conviction disproves the veracity of the witness.

Jones held "the trial court must state, for the record, the factors which favor admission or exclusion of prior conviction evidence." The court must consider such factors to assess whether probative value outweighs prejudice. It is imperative the court state, on the record, how the proffered evidence is probative of veracity to allow appellate review.

Some of the *Jones* and *Alexis* factors may also be useful to assess probative value.[8] For example, factor one focuses attention on the nature of the prior crime while factors two (remoteness) and four (age and circumstances) may indicate an otherwise probative conviction is less probative because it is chronologically remote.

... We find nothing inherent in ordinary drug convictions to suggest the person convicted is untruthful and conclude prior drug convictions, in general, are not probative of a witness's veracity under ER 609(a)(1). Numerous sister jurisdictions are in accord.

Prejudicial effect

[9] If the prior conviction is probative of veracity under ER 609(a)(1) the court must still assess prejudicial effect. "[P]rior conviction evidence is inherently prejudicial" when the defendant is the witness because it tends to shift the jury focus "from the merits of the charge to the defendant's general propensity for criminality."

---

4. *Jones* was overruled in part by *State v. Ray,* 116 Wash.2d 531, 806 P.2d 1220 (1991). *Ray* addressed crimes of dishonesty under ER 609(a)(2) and overruled *Jones* only on the remedy issue.

5. *See also State v. Alexis,* 95 Wash.2d 15, 19, 621 P.2d 1269 (1980) ("[T]he only purpose of impeaching evidence is to aid the jury in evaluating a witness' credibility, including a defendant when he elects to take the witness stand. Its purpose is not to persuade the jury in a substantive manner.").

6. See ER 404(a) ("Evidence of a person's character ... is not admissible for the purpose of proving action in conformity therewith on a particular occasion...."); Alan D. Hornstein, *Between Rock and a Hard Place: The Right to Testify and Impeachment by Prior Conviction,* 42 Vill. L.Rev. 1, 2 (1997) ("It is a long-standing principle of the law of evidence that a defendant's character for law breaking may not be used as evidence that the defendant committed the particular offense for which he or she is being tried.").

7. Jeremy Bentham provided an early example with his "man so proud of his truthfulness that he challenges a person who called him a liar to a duel. He wins the duel but is subsequently convicted of murder. Several years later, after release from prison, he is indicted on another crime." In the second trial is his prior conviction evidence of untruthfulness? *State v. McAboy,* 236 S.E.2d 431, 435 n. 6 (W.Va. 1977) (citing 2 Wigmore, *Evidence* § 519, at 610 (3d ed.1940) and citing Jeremy Bentham, *Rationale of Judicial Evidence* (Bowring's ed. 1827)), *overruled by State v. Kopa,* 311 S.E.2d 412 (W.Va. 1983).

8. The *Jones/Alexis* factors include: (1) the type and nature of the prior crime; (2) the remoteness of the prior conviction; (3) the similarity of the prior crime to the current charge; (4) the age and circumstances of the defendant when previously convicted; (5) whether the defendant testified at the previous trial; and (6) the length of defendant's criminal record.

Jones, 101 Wash.2d at 120, 677 P.2d 131.[11] Several studies confirm the prejudice.[12] One commentator observed "[i]f the jury learns that a defendant previously has been convicted of a crime, the probability of conviction increases dramatically." Alan D. Hornstein, *Between Rock and a Hard Place: The Right to Testify and Impeachment by Prior Conviction,* 42 Vill. L.Rev. 1 (1997). The threat of admitting inherently prejudicial prior convictions places the accused in a catch-22 where he must either forego testifying in his defense or testify and risk portrayal as a criminal. Forcing the accused to such a Hobson's choice is not favored.

Additionally, the trial court must assess whether even greater prejudice may result from the particular nature of the prior conviction. Several of the *Jones* and *Alexis* factors help identify particularly prejudicial scenarios. For example, factor three points out the more similar the prior crime to the one presently charged, the greater the prejudice. Likewise, factor six highlights the fact that the longer the record the greater the prejudicial prospect the jury will use such as evidence to infer guilt.

Admissible only if probative value outweighs prejudice

Prior convictions are inadmissible under ER 609(a)(1) until the party seeking admission affirmatively demonstrates (1) the prior conviction bears on the witness's veracity and (2) the probative value outweighs the prejudice. *Jones,* 101 Wash.2d at 120, 677 P.2d 131.

With the burden on the party seeking admission the trial court must conduct an on-the-record analysis of probative value versus prejudicial effect. Such requires an articulation of exactly how the prior conviction is probative of the witness's truthfulness.

Unnamed felonies

The trial court attempted to lessen the prejudice by admitting the prior conviction under ER 609(a)(1) as an unnamed felony. But unnaming a felony "is not a substitute for the balancing process required" under ER 609(a)(1). If the balance merits admission, it is anomalous to unname the felony as it is generally the nature of the prior felony which renders it probative of veracity. Courts should not admit unnamed felonies under ER 609(a)(1) unless they can articulate how unnaming the felony still renders it probative of veracity.

Remedy

... Reversal is required if, within reasonable probabilities, the error affected the trial's outcome. Here Hardy's credibility was important because it was virtually his word against the alleged victim's as to whether he forcefully took the jewelry. The victim was the only other eyewitness to testify. The State did not produce the female companion who was the other alleged eyewitness. There was not overwhelming evidence that Hardy forcefully took the jewelry as alleged. But the prior crime was the only impeachment of Hardy's veracity and was thus critical. We conclude there was at least a reasonable probability that this improper impeachment affected the jury's determination. Accordingly, reversal is the remedy....

TALMADGE, Justice (dissenting).

... The Court's settled method for deciding the admissibility of prior convictions under ER 609(a)(1) is not a rule of per se admissibility or inadmissibility of prior felony drug convictions, but rather a case-by-case weighing on the record of probative value versus prejudice....

It is very difficult for me to discern a reasonable probability that a passing reference to a prior unnamed felony conviction designed to impeach Hardy's testimony in this case would constitute prejudicial error....

---

11. *See also* Jack B. Weinstein, Margaret A. Berger & Joseph M. McLaughlin, 3 *Weinstein's Evidence* § 609[02], at 609–29 (1996) ("In a criminal case, the accused with a record risks that the jury may wish to punish him because he is bad regardless of his present guilt.").

12. Edith Greene & Mary Dodge, *The Influence of Prior Record Evidence on Juror Decision Making,* 19 Law & Human Behavior 67, 76 (1995) (in controlled mock trial study "jurors who learned that the defendant had been previously convicted were significantly more likely to convict him of a subsequent offense than were jurors without this information."); Harry Kalven, Jr. & Hans Zeisel, *The American Jury* 161 (1966) (acquittal of defendant is far less likely when jury knows about prior criminal convictions than when no record of prior crimes revealed).

Notes and Questions

1. Washington Rule of Evidence 609, which is quoted in *State v. Hardy*, is modeled after Federal Rule of Evidence 609. In relevant part, the federal rule provides:

> **Rule 609. Impeachment by Evidence of Conviction of Crime**
>
> **(a) General rule.**—For the purpose of attacking the character for truthfulness of a witness,
>
> (1) evidence that a witness other than an accused has been convicted of a crime shall be admitted, subject to Rule 403, if the crime was punishable by death or imprisonment in excess of one year under the law under which the witness was convicted, and evidence that an accused has been convicted of such a crime shall be admitted if the court determines that the probative value of admitting this evidence outweighs its prejudicial effect to the accused; and
>
> (2) evidence that any witness has been convicted of a crime shall be admitted regardless of the punishment, if it readily can be determined that establishing the elements of the crime required proof or admission of an act of dishonesty or false statement by the witness.
>
> **(b) Time limit.** Evidence of a conviction under this rule is not admissible if a period of more than ten years has elapsed since the date of the conviction or of the release of the witness from the confinement imposed for that conviction, whichever is the later date, unless the court determines, in the interests of justice, that the probative value of the conviction supported by specific facts and circumstances substantially outweighs its prejudicial effect. However, evidence of a conviction more than 10 years old as calculated herein, is not admissible unless the proponent gives to the adverse party sufficient advance written notice of intent to use such evidence to provide the adverse party with a fair opportunity to contest the use of such evidence....

Federal Rule of Evidence 403, to which reference is made in FREv 609, provides:

> **Rule 403. Exclusion of Relevant Evidence on Grounds of Prejudice, Confusion, or Waste of Time**
>
> Although relevant, evidence may be excluded if its probative value is substantially outweighed by the danger of unfair prejudice, confusion of the issues, or misleading the jury, or by considerations of undue delay, waste of time, or needless presentation of cumulative evidence.

For cases interpreting and applying these Federal Rules of Evidence, which govern the admissibility of evidence of prior crimes for impeachment purposes, *see United States v. Linares,* 367 F.3d 941 (D.C. Cir. 2004); *United States v. Brown,* 606 F.Supp.2d 306 (E.D.N.Y. 2009).

2. In *Green v. State,* 527 S.E.2d 98 (S.C. 2000), the South Carolina Supreme Court concluded that the defendant's attorney had provided ineffective assistance of counsel by failing to object that the prejudicial effect of allowing cross-examination of the defendant about his prior convictions outweighed its probative value. It thus reversed the defendant's conviction for distributing crack cocaine. The defendant had testified at his trial, denying that he had sold cocaine, and subsequently was cross-examined about two prior convictions for possession of crack cocaine. The court noted that the evidence offered at trial made the defendant's "credibility ... critical, as the jury had to choose between his version of events and that of" the testifying police officers. It further noted that the prejudicial effect

of the prior convictions was heightened because of the similarity between those offenses and the charged offense, and enumerated the factors trial courts should consider in determining whether to allow impeachment based on prior convictions:

1. The impeachment value of the prior crime.
2. The point in time of the conviction and the witness's subsequent history.
3. The similarity between the past crime and the charged crime.
4. The importance of the defendant's testimony.
5. The centrality of the credibility issue

527 S.E.2d, at 101.

3. For an extensive discussion of the history, benefits, costs, and application of evidentiary rules concerning impeachment of testifying defendants by cross-examination about prior convictions, *see People v. Allen,* 420 N.W.2d 499 (Mich. 1988). Another helpful state court ruling is *State v. Hamilton,* 937 A.2d 965 (N.J. 2008).

4. A review of jury studies conducted between 1955 and 1999 reports that seven studies have examined the influence of defendants' prior convictions on trial verdicts. All but one of the studies found that juries exposed to defendants' criminal histories were more inclined to vote guilty than juries not similarly exposed; one study noted a 40% increase in conviction rates. This research included laboratory studies, mock trials, as well as studies of actual juries. The one study that did not find a relationship between prior criminal history and guilt utilized a prior charge unrelated to the current charge. *See* Dennis J. Devine, Laura D. Clayton, Benjamin B. Dunford, Rasmy Seying & Jennifer Pryce, "Jury Decision Making: 45 Years of Empirical Research on Deliberating Groups," 7 *Psychology, Public Policy, and Law* 622 (2001).

In addition, jurors tend not to use impeachment evidence about prior crime to make decisions about credibility but rather to make inferences about criminal dispositions. Professors Edith Greene and Kirk Heilbrun discuss three possible reasons why criminal history increases conviction rates.[22] First, some jurors see past criminal behaviors as indicative of criminality, that is, of persons being prone to engage in criminal behavior. Second, some jurors may use the prior records as evidence bearing on the current charge, which in turn, increases perceptions of guilt. And finally, relevant to wrongful convictions, some jurors may view an erroneous conviction for defendants who have prior convictions as a less serious miscarriage of justice than for defendants who do not have past convictions.

5. Evidence of Third-Party Guilt

"Innocence is typically claimed in two ways at trial: through an alibi defense or through evidence of third-party guilt."[23] Yet, for various reasons, including maintaining the focus of a trial on the accused party and his or her conduct, limiting the scope of evidence, avoiding juror confusion, and guarding against fabricated testimony, rules of evidence typically place limitations on evidence that is offered to prove that a specific third party committed the crime with which the defendant has been charged.[24] Are these justifications sufficient to prevent evidence of third-party guilt from being introduced as a part of the accused's defense?

Holmes v. South Carolina

547 U.S. 319, 126 S.Ct. 1727, 164 L.Ed.2d 503 (2006)

Justice ALITO delivered the opinion of the Court.

This case presents the question whether a criminal defendant's federal constitutional rights are violated by an evidence rule under which the defendant may not introduce proof of third-party guilt if the prosecution has introduced forensic evidence that, if believed, strongly supports a guilty verdict.

I

On the morning of December 31, 1989, 86-year-old Mary Stewart was beaten, raped, and robbed in her home. She later died of complications stemming from her injuries. Petitioner was convicted by a South Carolina jury of murder, first-degree criminal sexual conduct, first-degree burglary, and robbery, and he was sentenced to death. The South Carolina Supreme Court affirmed his convictions and sentence, and this Court denied certiorari. Upon state post-conviction review, however, petitioner was granted a new trial.

At the second trial, the prosecution relied heavily on the following forensic evidence:

"(1) [Petitioner's] palm print was found just above the door knob on the interior side of the front door of the victim's house; (2) fibers consistent with a black sweatshirt owned by [petitioner] were found on the victim's bed sheets; (3) matching blue fibers were found on the victim's pink nightgown and on [petitioner's] blue jeans; (4) microscopically consistent fibers were found on the pink nightgown and on [petitioner's] underwear; (5) [petitioner's] underwear contained a mixture of DNA from two individuals, and 99.99% of the population other than [petitioner] and the victim were excluded as contributors to that mixture; and (6) [petitioner's] tank top was found to contain a mixture of [petitioner's] blood and the victim's blood."

In addition, the prosecution introduced evidence that petitioner had been seen near Stewart's home within an hour of the time when, according to the prosecution's evidence, the attack took place.

As a major part of his defense, petitioner attempted to undermine the State's forensic evidence by suggesting that it had been contaminated and that certain law enforcement officers had engaged in a plot to frame him. Petitioner's expert witnesses criticized the procedures used by the police in handling the fiber and DNA evidence and in collecting the fingerprint evidence. Another defense expert provided testimony that petitioner cited as supporting his claim that the palm print had been planted by the police.

Petitioner also sought to introduce proof that another man, Jimmy McCaw White, had attacked Stewart. At a pretrial hearing, petitioner proffered several witnesses who placed White in the victim's neighborhood on the morning of the assault, as well as four other witnesses who testified that White had either acknowledged that petitioner was " 'innocent' " or had actually admitted to committing the crimes. One witness recounted that when he asked White about the "word ... on the street" that White was responsible for Stewart's murder, White "put his head down and he raised his head back up and he said, well, you know I like older women." According to this witness, White added that "he did what they say he did" and that he had "no regrets about it at all." Another witness, who had been incarcerated with White, testified that White had admitted to assaulting Stewart, that a police officer had asked the witness to testify falsely against petitioner, and that employees of the prosecutor's office, while soliciting the witness' cooperation, had spoken of manufacturing evidence against petitioner. White testified at the pretrial hearing and denied making the incriminating statements. He also provided an alibi for the time of the crime, but another witness refuted his alibi.

The trial court excluded petitioner's third-party guilt evidence citing *State v. Gregory,* 198 S.C. 98, 16 S.E.2d 532 (1941), which held that such evidence is admissible if it "'raise[s] a reasonable inference or presumption as to [the defendant's] own innocence'" but is not admissible if it merely "'cast[s] a bare suspicion upon another'" or "'raise[s] a conjectural inference as to the commission of the crime by another.'" On appeal, the South Carolina Supreme Court found no error in the exclusion of petitioner's third-party guilt evidence. Citing both *Gregory* and its later decision in *State v. Gay,* 343 S.C. 543, 541 S.E.2d 541 (2001), the State Supreme Court held that "where there is strong evidence of an appellant's guilt, especially where there is strong forensic evidence, the proffered evidence about a third party's alleged guilt does not raise a reasonable inference as to the appellant's own innocence." Applying this standard, the court held that petitioner could not "overcome the forensic evidence against him to raise a reasonable inference of his own innocence." We granted certiorari.

II

"[S]tate and federal rulemakers have broad latitude under the Constitution to establish rules excluding evidence from criminal trials." *United States v. Scheffer,* 523 U.S. 303, 308 (1998); see also *Crane v. Kentucky,* 476 U.S. 683 (1986); *Marshall v. Lonberger,* 459 U.S. 422 (1983); *Chambers v. Mississippi,* 410 U.S. 284 (1973); *Spencer v. Texas,* 385 U.S. 554 (1967). This latitude, however, has limits. "Whether rooted directly in the Due Process Clause of the Fourteenth Amendment or in the Compulsory Process or Confrontation Clauses of the Sixth Amendment, the Constitution guarantees criminal defendants 'a meaningful opportunity to present a complete defense.'" *Crane, supra,* at 690 (quoting *California v. Trombetta,* 467 U.S. 479, 485 (1984); citations omitted). This right is abridged by evidence rules that "infring[e] upon a weighty interest of the accused" and are "'arbitrary' or 'disproportionate to the purposes they are designed to serve.'" *Scheffer, supra,* at 308 (quoting *Rock v. Arkansas,* 483 U.S. 44, 58, 56 (1987)).

This Court's cases contain several illustrations of "arbitrary" rules, *i.e.,* rules that excluded important defense evidence but that did not serve any legitimate interests. In *Washington v. Texas,* 388 U.S. 14 (1967), state statutes barred a person who had been charged as a participant in a crime from testifying in defense of another alleged participant unless the witness had been acquitted. As a result, when the defendant in *Washington* was tried for murder, he was precluded from calling as a witness a person who had been charged and previously convicted of committing the same murder. Holding that the defendant's right to put on a defense had been violated, we noted that the rule embodied in the statutes could not "even be defended on the ground that it rationally sets apart a group of persons who are particularly likely to commit perjury" since the rule allowed an alleged participant to testify if he or she had been acquitted or was called by the prosecution. *Id.,* at 22–23.

A similar constitutional violation occurred in *Chambers v. Mississippi, supra.* A murder defendant called as a witness a man named McDonald, who had previously confessed to the murder. When McDonald repudiated the confession on the stand, the defendant was denied permission to examine McDonald as an adverse witness based on the State's "'voucher' rule," which barred parties from impeaching their own witnesses. In addition, because the state hearsay rule did not include an exception for statements against penal interest, the defendant was not permitted to introduce evidence that McDonald had made self-incriminating statements to three other persons. Noting that the State had not even attempted to "defend" or "explain [the] underlying rationale" of the "voucher rule," this Court held that "the exclusion of [the evidence of McDonald's out-of-court statements], coupled with the State's refusal to permit [the defendant] to cross-examine McDonald, denied him a trial in accord with traditional and fundamental standards of due process," *id.,* at 302.

Another arbitrary rule was held unconstitutional in *Crane v. Kentucky, supra.* There, the defendant was prevented from attempting to show at trial that his confession was unreliable because of the circumstances under which it was obtained, and neither the State Supreme Court nor the prosecution "advanced any rational justification for the wholesale exclusion of this body of potentially exculpatory evidence." *Id.,* at 691.

In *Rock v. Arkansas, supra,* this Court held that a rule prohibiting hypnotically refreshed testimony was unconstitutional because "[w]holesale inadmissibility of a defendant's testimony is an arbitrary restriction on the right to testify in the absence of clear evidence by the State repudiating the validity of all post-hypnosis recollections." *Id.,* at 61. By contrast, in *Scheffer, supra,* we held that a rule excluding all polygraph evidence did not abridge the right to present a defense because the rule "serve [d] several legitimate interests in the criminal trial process," was "neither arbitrary nor disproportionate in promoting these ends," and did not "implicate a sufficiently weighty interest of the defendant." *Id.,* at 309.

While the Constitution thus prohibits the exclusion of defense evidence under rules that serve no legitimate purpose or that are disproportionate to the ends that they are asserted to promote, well-established rules of evidence permit trial judges to exclude evidence if its probative value is outweighed by certain other factors such as unfair prejudice, confusion of the issues, or potential to mislead the jury. See, *e.g.,* Fed. Rule Evid. 403.... Plainly referring to rules of this type, we have stated that the Constitution permits judges "to exclude evidence that is 'repetitive..., only marginally relevant' or poses an undue risk of 'harassment, prejudice, [or] confusion of the issues.'" *Crane,* 476 U.S., at 689–690....

A specific application of this principle is found in rules regulating the admission of evidence proffered by criminal defendants to show that someone else committed the crime with which they are charged. See, *e.g.,* 41 C.J.S., Homicide § 216, pp. 56–58 (1991) ("Evidence tending to show the commission by another person of the crime charged may be introduced by accused when it is inconsistent with, and raises a reasonable doubt of, his own guilt; but frequently matters offered in evidence for this purpose are so remote and lack such connection with the crime that they are excluded"); 40A Am.Jur.2d, Homicide § 286, pp. 136–138 (1999) ("[T]he accused may introduce any legal evidence tending to prove that another person may have committed the crime with which the defendant is charged.... [Such evidence] may be excluded where it does not sufficiently connect the other person to the crime, as, for example, where the evidence is speculative or remote, or does not tend to prove or disprove a material fact in issue at the defendant's trial" (footnotes omitted)). Such rules are widely accepted, and neither petitioner nor his *amici* challenge them here.

In *Gregory,* the South Carolina Supreme Court adopted and applied a rule apparently intended to be of this type, given the court's references to the "applicable rule" from Corpus Juris and American Jurisprudence:

"'[E]vidence offered by accused as to the commission of the crime by another person must be limited to such facts as are inconsistent with his own guilt, and to such facts as raise a reasonable inference or presumption as to his own innocence; evidence which can have (no) other effect than to cast a bare suspicion upon another, or to raise a conjectural inference as to the commission of the crime by another, is not admissible.... [B]efore such testimony can be received, there must be such proof of connection with it, such a train of facts or circumstances, as tends clearly to point out such other person as the guilty party.'" 16 S.E.2d, at 534–535 (quoting 16 C.J., Criminal Law § 1085, p. 560 (1918), and 20 Am.Jur., Evidence § 265, p. 254 (1939)).

In *Gay* and this case, however, the South Carolina Supreme Court radically changed and extended the rule. In *Gay,* after recognizing the standard applied in *Gregory,* the court stated that "[i]n view of the strong evidence of appellant's guilt—especially the forensic evidence—... the proffered evidence ... did not raise 'a reasonable inference' as to appellant's own innocence." Similarly, in the present case, as noted, the State Supreme Court applied the rule that "where there is strong evidence of [a defendant's] guilt, especially where there is strong forensic evidence, the proffered evidence about a third party's alleged guilt" may (or perhaps must) be excluded.

Under this rule, the trial judge does not focus on the probative value or the potential adverse effects of admitting the defense evidence of third-party guilt. Instead, the critical inquiry concerns the strength of the prosecution's case: If the prosecution's case is strong enough, the evidence of third-party guilt is excluded even if that evidence, if viewed independently, would have great probative value and even if it would not pose an undue risk of harassment, prejudice, or confusion of the issues.

Furthermore, as applied in this case, the South Carolina Supreme Court's rule seems to call for little, if any, examination of the credibility of the prosecution's witnesses or the reliability of its evidence. Here, for example, the defense strenuously claimed that the prosecution's forensic evidence was so unreliable (due to mishandling and a deliberate plot to frame petitioner) that the evidence should not have even been admitted. The South Carolina Supreme Court responded that these challenges did not entirely "eviscerate" the forensic evidence and that the defense challenges went to the weight and not to the admissibility of that evidence. Yet, in evaluating the prosecution's forensic evidence and deeming it to be "strong"—and thereby justifying exclusion of petitioner's third-party guilt evidence—the South Carolina Supreme Court made no mention of the defense challenges to the prosecution's evidence.

Interpreted in this way, the rule applied by the State Supreme Court does not rationally serve the end that the *Gregory* rule and its analogues in other jurisdictions were designed to promote, *i.e.,* to focus the trial on the central issues by excluding evidence that has only a very weak logical connection to the central issues. The rule applied in this case appears to be based on the following logic: Where (1) it is clear that only one person was involved in the commission of a particular crime and (2) there is strong evidence that the defendant was the perpetrator, it follows that evidence of third-party guilt must be weak. But this logic depends on an accurate evaluation of the prosecution's proof, and the true strength of the prosecution's proof cannot be assessed without considering challenges to the reliability of the prosecution's evidence. Just because the prosecution's evidence, *if credited*, would provide strong support for a guilty verdict, it does not follow that evidence of third-party guilt has only a weak logical connection to the central issues in the case. And where the credibility of the prosecution's witnesses or the reliability of its evidence is not conceded, the strength of the prosecution's case cannot be assessed without making the sort of factual findings that have traditionally been reserved for the trier of fact and that the South Carolina courts did not purport to make in this case.

The rule applied in this case is no more logical than its converse would be, *i.e.*, a rule barring the prosecution from introducing evidence of a defendant's guilt if the defendant is able to proffer, at a pretrial hearing, evidence that, if believed, strongly supports a verdict of not guilty. In the present case, for example, petitioner proffered evidence that, if believed, squarely proved that White, not petitioner, was the perpetrator. It would make no sense, however, to hold that this proffer precluded the prosecution from introducing its evidence, including the forensic evidence that, if credited, provided strong proof of petitioner's guilt.

The point is that, by evaluating the strength of only one party's evidence, no logical conclusion can be reached regarding the strength of contrary evidence offered by the other side to rebut or cast doubt. Because the rule applied by the State Supreme Court in this case did not heed this point, the rule is "arbitrary" in the sense that it does not rationally serve the end that the *Gregory* rule and other similar third-party guilt rules were designed to further. Nor has the State identified any other legitimate end that the rule serves. It follows that the rule applied in this case by the State Supreme Court violates a criminal defendant's right to have "'a meaningful opportunity to present a complete defense.'" *Crane,* 476 U.S., at 690 (quoting *Trombetta,* 467 U.S., at 485).

III

For these reasons, we vacate the judgment of the South Carolina Supreme Court and remand the case for further proceedings not inconsistent with this opinion.

Notes and Questions

1. Does the Court's ruling in *Holmes*—centering, as it seems to, on the "arbitrary" application of a rule restricting evidence of third-party guilt that "does not focus on the probative value or the potential adverse effects of admitting the defense evidence of third-party guilt ... [but instead on] the strength of the prosecution's case"—go far enough in protecting defendants' fair trial rights?

2. For the perspective that, even after *Holmes*, "the states' treatment of this wrong-person defense [is likely to remain] confusing, inconsistent, and insufficiently protective of a defendant's constitutional right to present a complete defense," *see* Lissa Griffin, "Avoiding Wrongful Convictions: Re-Examining the 'Wrong Person' Defense," 39 *Seton Hall Law Review* 129, 130 (2009). Professor Griffin argues:

> The ability of a criminal defendant to present a credible wrong-person defense is more pressing today with the mounting evidence of wrongful convictions through DNA proof. Paradoxically, as it becomes increasingly apparent that innocent people are convicted, the courts continue to refuse to admit proof that someone else really is guilty. Moreover, although a prosecution witness is almost always permitted to point the finger at the defendant with only the barest of reliability protections and no corroboration at all, defense witnesses are routinely prohibited from pointing the finger at someone else. An evolved notion of parity—which lies at the core of due process—requires a fairer judicial inquiry into the admissibility of wrong-person-defense evidence. *Id.*, at 132–133 (footnotes omitted).

6. Should Jurors Be Allowed to Submit Questions for Witnesses?

In most trials, the jurors who will be called upon to resolve contested facts and determine the sufficiency of the evidence sit as passive listeners while the advocates examine and cross-examine witnesses. If the lawyers overlook a line of questioning that the jurors would find helpful, or even essential to their task, the quality of their decision may suffer. On the other hand, if jurors are allowed to pose questions, there may be a risk that their neutrality and roles as impartial fact-finders somehow will be compromised, or that the lawyers for one side will gain an advantage by altering their trial strategy in response to what they perceive has prompted the questions. If jurors have an opportunity to submit questions—for prior review and screening by the judge and the advocates—to be posed to the witnesses at a trial, what is the likely effect, if any, on the trial's dynamics, the jurors' deliberations, and (of particular relevance to the risk of wrongful conviction) the eventual verdict's reliability?

People v. Medina

114 P.3d 845 (Colo. 2005)

Justice BENDER delivered the Opinion of the Court....

I. Facts and Proceedings Below

These two cases raise questions about the validity of allowing jurors to ask witnesses questions during a criminal trial. In September of 2000, Chief Justice Mary J. Mullarkey authorized a pilot project to study the effects of permitting jurors to submit written questions to witnesses during certain criminal trials.[1] The Colorado Jury Reform Pilot Project Subcommittee provided a list of policies and procedures that the district court was to follow when jurors asked questions. Pursuant to these policies, jurors were allowed to submit written questions to the court before a particular witness was excused from the witness stand. Trial courts were not required to ask all questions submitted by jurors. Rather, courts were instructed that the purpose behind the project was to clarify testimony and to help jurors understand the evidence. Thus, before asking a question, the court first reviewed the questions and heard all objections from counsel, on the record, outside the jury's hearing. Keeping in mind the rights of all parties to due process and the right to a fair trial, the trial court then was directed to apply the applicable rules of law and evidence, and if the question was proper in light of these considerations, the court asked the witness the question. Once the question was answered, the attorneys were given an opportunity to ask follow-up questions of the witness. At the conclusion of the trial, the jurors, judge, and attorneys completed survey forms about their experience with jurors asking questions in that particular case. These two cases in this consolidated opinion were randomly selected at the trial level to be part of the pilot project.

In this opinion, we first set forth the facts that led to the petitioners' cases before us. We then give an overview of juror questioning in this country and establish the standard of review for determining if a defendant is prejudiced by a juror's question. We then apply that standard to the cases of the respective petitioner.

---

1. This pilot project culminated in the adoption of Rule 24(g) to the Colorado Rules of Criminal Procedure, effective July 1, 2004. This rule states that jurors will be allowed to submit written questions of a witness to the court pursuant to the rules adopted by the trial court. The rule further states that the trial court has the discretion to prohibit or limit questioning of a witness. Crim. P. 24(g) states:

> Jurors shall be allowed to submit written questions to the court for the court to ask of witnesses during trial, in compliance with procedures established by the trial court. The trial court shall have the discretion to prohibit or limit questioning in a particular trial for reasons related to the severity of the charges, the presence of significant suppressed evidence or for other good cause.

A. Yvonne Medina

Yvonne Medina was convicted by a jury of second degree assault, crime of violence, criminal mischief, first degree criminal trespass, and menacing. The court sentenced her to five and one-half years in the Department of Corrections. The evidence presented at trial showed that the victim, her ex-boyfriend, was home in his apartment when Medina knocked at his door. The victim refused to let her in because his new girlfriend was in the apartment. Medina then broke a window next to the door, reached in, and unlocked the front door. Once inside, she picked up a piece of glass, approached her ex-boyfriend, and stabbed him several times while the other woman hid in a closet. The victim then left his apartment to seek help and when he returned, he found his apartment vandalized.

At the beginning of the trial, the court advised counsel and the jury that jurors would be allowed to submit questions to witnesses through the court pursuant to the pilot project guidelines authorized by the Chief Justice. Defense counsel objected to the procedure. Only one question was asked by the jury throughout the trial.

Medina's theory of defense was that the victim and the other woman concocted the story about what had occurred and that Medina was not at the ex-boyfriend's apartment the night of the incident. In support of this theory, Medina called the district attorney's investigator to testify about pre-trial interviews he had with the witnesses. She stated that the victim and the woman made a number of inconsistent statements during these interviews with the investigator. After being examined by the attorneys for the defense and prosecution, a juror submitted a written question to the court asking how frequently witnesses change their stories or make inconsistent statements. The question asked:

> Roughly what percentage of reports that you have taken in your career reflect some inconsistencies from witnesses, i.e., how common is it for witnesses to add or subtract information from their original statements?

Pursuant to the procedures set forth by the pilot project guidelines, a bench conference was held where defense counsel objected to the juror's question. First the defense reasserted its general objection to jurors asking questions and second the defense argued that the question was not relevant. The prosecution did not comment on the objection. The court overruled defense counsel's objection and asked the question. The investigator responded that people do change their stories and that individuals involved in domestic violence cases are more likely to change their story than in other situations. She said:

> It probably depends on the type of case. Domestic violence, it probably happens more so than your vehicular homicide or your vehicular assault case or a DUI or something. I hadn't really thought about that....
>
> I'm trying to think percentage-wise about how many percentages of people would change their story. It's a high percentage. I don't think it's up to 50 percent, but I hadn't thought about how many people change. But it's probably more than 10 percent. Somewhere maybe even more than 20 percent, but you know, that's probably the best I can do. Sorry.

Medina appealed her conviction and in an unpublished opinion the court of appeals affirmed....

B. Philip Moses

Philip Moses was at his place of work, a car dealership in Aurora, Colorado, when two police officers arrived to arrest him for a municipal violation. Moses was seated in his car and when the officers approached, he put his car in reverse and backed out of his parking space. One of the officers approached the car and Moses accelerated forward, hit the officer with the vehicle, and knocked him to the ground. Moses drove off and was stopped by a police roadblock where he got out of his car and fled on foot. Law enforcement then found Moses hiding in some bushes a short time later and arrested him.

Moses was charged with first degree assault on a peace officer, felony menacing, and mandatory sentencing for a crime of violence. Early in the trial, the court overruled defense counsel's general objection to the practice of allowing jurors to ask questions and allowed the jury to ask questions through the court of the various witnesses according to the terms of the pilot project. The record in this case contains seventeen written questions from the jury with some containing multiple sub-questions. Four of the written questions were denied by the trial court. Not all of the bench conferences were held on the record.

After the second witness was called, jurors submitted several written questions to the court. Counsel approached the bench to discuss the admissibility of the jurors' questions. Before discussing the questions, Moses's attorney stated to the court that the defendant was able to hear the attorneys and the court at the first bench conference where the parties discussed the admissibility of four questions from the jury. The court acknowledged to the parties that the volume to the headset was set too loud and suggested that the attorneys try and keep their voices down. There is no other indication in the record that the jury had in fact heard the previous bench conference or heard any subsequent bench conference.

The jury acquitted Moses of first degree assault on a peace officer but convicted him of felony menacing, resisting arrest, and reckless driving. The court sentenced him to three years in the Department of Corrections and he appealed. The court of appeals affirmed these convictions....

II. Analysis....

A. Juror Questions-Past and Present

To set the stage for our decision, we give a brief history of how the manner in which the jury conducts its charge has evolved over time. The current criminal justice system has progressed from one where bad luck and poor social status were factors that were more likely to result in a conviction than actual proof of a criminal act. In Sir William Blackstone's *Commentaries on the Laws of England,* the noted jurist gives an account of the many ways in which a criminal trial proceeded prior to our understanding of the adversarial criminal trial. 4 William Blackstone, *Commentaries on the Laws of England,* *342–351 (Cooley ed. 1899). These early tests of guilt incorporated society's preoccupation with the supernatural and included trial by ordeal, test of the morsel, and trial by battel.[6] The presumption underlying these tests was that God would intervene and, through a miraculous sign, indicate which party was in the right. Such methods of determining guilt by way of divine intervention fell out of use as the age of reason made clear the "folly and impiety of pronouncing a man guilty, unless he was cleared by a miracle." Blackstone, *Commentaries,* at *343.

The early Anglo-American jury system originated sometime in the twelfth century. The trial by jury in the English system of justice grew out of a general apprehension of state power denigrating the rights of the common man. "Our law has therefore wisely placed this strong and two-fold barrier, of a presentment and a trial by jury, between the liberties of the people and the prerogative of the crown." Blackstone *Commentaries,* at *349.

These juries were composed of qualified individuals, chosen by the king, and who reported to the court on facts or issues in dispute. Jurors did not hear witnesses, but rather conducted investigations of those who had knowledge of the facts.[7] Then, in the fifteenth century, juries began hearing the testimony of witnesses in court, a practice that became commonplace in the sixteenth century. Thus as part of the search for truth, jurors, judges, and counsel in the English courts were allowed to ask questions and call witnesses. *See* John Langbein, *The Origins of Adversary Criminal Trial* 319 (A.W. Brian Simpson, Oxford University Press, 2003).

Concern over state power in the administration of justice carried over to the framers of the United States Constitution who consistently agreed on the right of an individual to be tried by a jury. *See* Albert W. Alshuler & Andrew G. Deiss, *A Brief History of the Criminal Jury in the United States,* 61 U. Chi. L.Rev. 867, 870–71 (1994). The jury provided protection against failures inherent in our system, and served to "guard against the exercise of arbitrary power —to make available the commonsense judgment of the community as a hedge against the overzealous or mistaken prosecutor and in preference to the professional or perhaps over-conditioned or biased response of a judge." *Taylor v. Louisiana,*

6. In the trial by ordeal the defendant was subjected to a physical challenge, such as a burning, and he was deemed innocent if he escaped unhurt. Blackstone, *Commentaries* at *342–44. In the test of the morsel, the defendant was given a piece of consecrated cheese or bread and the defendant was pronounced innocent if he was able to digest the food. *Id.* at *345. The trial by battel required the defendant to fight his accuser and if the defendant lost, then he was considered guilty and hung immediately. *Id.* at *346–48. *See also* Landsman, *A Brief Survey of the Development of the Adversary System,* 44 Ohio St. L.J. 713, 717–720 (1983) (discussing various methods of determining guilt prior to jury system).

7. *See,* Jeffrey S. Berkowitz, Note, *Breaking the Silence: Should Jurors be Allowed to Question Witnesses During Trial,* 44 Vand. L.Rev. 117, 123 (1991) (discussing transition away from investigatory role of jury due to problems with achieving convictions under attaint process where jurors could be put on trial for rendering an incorrect verdict after the collection of evidence).

419 U.S. 522, 530–31 (1975). The jury's presence thus provides a formidable restraint on government power in our criminal courts. Therefore, it is only logical that jurors who are the arbiters of truth and hedge against government power also have the tools available to think critically and to seek clarification of the issues presented to them.

Allowing jurors to ask witnesses questions is "neither radical nor a recent innovation." *State v. Doleszny,* 844 A.2d 773, 778 (Vt. 2004). It is a practice with "deeply entrenched" roots in the common law. *United States v. Bush,* 47 F.3d 511, 515 (2nd Cir.1995)....

The purpose of the jury "in criminal cases [is] to prevent government oppression" and "to assure a fair and equitable resolution of factual issues." *Colgrove v. Battin,* 413 U.S. 149, 157 (1973). While the manner in which the jury conducts its charge of finding facts in a criminal case has changed over time—from being inquisitors directly involved in the gathering of evidence and testifying to that evidence, to a more passive role where it considers the evidence presented by the government and the defendant—jurors have consistently been empowered to ask questions of witnesses so as to satisfy their weighty responsibility and purpose.

This historical trend continues to the modern day where the vast majority of courts from other jurisdictions allow jurors to ask questions in criminal cases with only a handful of states disallowing the practice. While the United States Supreme Court has not specifically decided the constitutionality of juror questioning, none of the federal circuits prohibit the practice. In addition, the majority of state courts also allow jurors to ask witnesses questions[9] and several states specifically provide for juror questions in court rules or state statute.[10]

The reasons for adopting the practice vary, however, a general theme appears from these jurisdictions. These courts do not believe that allowing jurors to ask questions prejudices a criminal defendant nor does it deprive a defendant of his right to an impartial jury. Instead, these jurisdictions believe that if proper procedures are put in place by the trial court to screen objectionable questions, a number of benefits from jury questioning may be realized without prejudice to the defendant.

"Juror inspired questions may serve to advance the search for truth by alleviating uncertainties in the jurors' minds, clearing up confusion or alerting the attorneys to points that bear further elaboration." *Richardson,* 233 F.3d at 1290 (quoting *United States v. Sutton,* 970 F.2d 1001, 1005 n. 3 (1st Cir.1992)). Commentators also agree that juror questioning facilitates the search for truth and justice, clarifies the facts in complex cases, provides the jury with an essential tool to fulfill its role as the finder of fact, and increases juror attentiveness during trial and satisfaction with the judicial process.[11]

---

9. *See, e.g., State v. LeMaster,* 669 P.2d 592, 596–98 (Ariz. Ct. App. 1983); *Nelson v. State,* 513 S.W.2d 496, 498 (Ark. 1974); *People v. McAlister,* 167 Cal.App.3d 633, (1985); *Gurliacci v. Mayer,* 590 A.2d 914, 930 (Conn. 1991); *Scheel v. State,* 350 So.2d 1120, 1121 (Fla. App. 1977); *Trotter v. State,* 733 N.E.2d 527, 531 (Ind.App.2000); *Rudolph v. Iowa Methodist Med. Ctr.,* 293 N.W.2d 550, 556 (Iowa 1980); *State v. Culkin,* 35 P.3d 233, 253 (Ha. 2001); *Transit Auth. of River City v. Montgomery,* 836 S.W.2d 413, 416 (Ky. 1992); *Commonwealth v. Urena,* 632 N.E.2d 1200, 1206 (Mass. 1994); *People v. Heard,* 200 N.W.2d 73, 76 (Mich. 1972); *Callahan v. Cardinal Glennon Hosp.,* 863 S.W.2d 852, 867 (Mo.1993); *State v. Graves,* 907 P.2d 963, 966–67 (Mont. 1995); *State v. Jumpp,* 619 A.2d 602, 610–12 (N.J. Super. 1993); *People v. Bacic,* 608 N.Y.S.2d 452 (Appel. Div. 1994); *State v. Howard,* 360 S.E.2d 790, 795 (N.C. 1987); *State v. Fisher,* 789 N.E.2d 222, 230 (Ohio 2003); *Cohee v. State,* 942 P.2d 211, 214–15 (Okla. Crim. App. 1997); *State v. Anderson,* 158 P.2d 127, 128 (Utah 1945); *State v. Doleszny,* 844 A.2d 773 (Vt. 2004); *State v. Munoz,* 837 P.2d 636, 639 (Wash. App. 1993).

10. *See e.g.,* Ariz.R.Crim.P. 18.6(e) (2004) ("Jurors shall be instructed that they are permitted to submit to the court written questions directed to witnesses ..."); Indiana Evidence Rule 614(d) (2004) ("A juror may be permitted to propound questions to a witness by submitting them in writing to the judge ..."); Nevada Short Trial Rule 24 (2005) ("[T]he court will allow members of the jury to ask written questions of any witness called to testify in this case."); Utah R.Crim.P. 17(i) (2004) ("A judge may invite jurors to submit written questions to a witness ...").

11. *See* Nicole L. Mott, *The Current Debate on Juror Questions: "To Ask Or Not To Ask, That Is The Question",* 78 Chi.-Kent L.Rev. 1099 (2003); Kristen Debarba, Note, *Maintaining The Adversarial System: The Practice Of Allowing Jurors To Question Witnesses During Trial,* 55 Vand. L.Rev. 1521 (2002); Emma Cano, *Speaking Out: Is Texas Inhibiting The Search For Truth By Prohibiting Juror Questioning Of Witnesses In Criminal Cases?,* 32 Tex. Tech L.Rev. 1013 (2001); Steven D. Penrod & Larry Heuer, *Tweaking Commonsense: Assessing Aids To Jury Decision Making,* 3 Psychol. Pub. Pol'y & L. 259 (1997).

Despite this national trend toward allowing jurors to ask questions through the court, a handful of state courts have decided to prohibit the practice of allowing jurors to ask questions altogether.[12] These courts have held that juror questioning has the potential of disrupting the neutral role that jurors play in the adversarial system of justice.

B. Reasons to Prohibit Juror Questioning

The defendants in these cases claim that allowing jurors to ask questions undermines the traditional role of the jury. First, they argue that the practice encourages the jury to decide facts and form opinions about the case before all of the evidence is presented. Second, it allows the prosecution to restructure its case according to the questions asked. Juror questioning also can put counsel in the awkward position of choosing between objecting to a juror's question, and risk antagonizing a juror, or choosing not to object because he wants to keep the juror "on his side" despite the effect that a failure to object would have on appeal.

These arguments were adopted in large part by the Minnesota Supreme Court in *State v. Costello.* That court reasoned that juror questioning encourages jurors to create a tentative opinion of the case before all the evidence is presented. This creates the risk that jurors will "draw conclusions or settle on a given legal theory before the parties have completed their presentations, and before the court has instructed the jury on the law of the case." *Costello,* 646 N.W.2d at 211. Second, the court concluded that the practice can upset the burden of production and persuasion in a criminal case.

These concerns, while theoretically plausible, were not verified in the scholarly work which has examined juror questioning. Professors Steven Penrod and Larry Heuer conducted two separate empirical studies where they solicited data from judges, lawyers, and jurors about the impact that juror questioning had on the trial. Steven D. Penrod & Larry Heuer, *Tweaking Commonsense Assessing Aids to Jury Decision Making,* 3 Psychol. Pub. Pol'y & L. 259 (1997); Larry Heuer & Steven Penrod, *Increasing Juror Participation in Trials Through Note Taking and Question Asking,* 79 Judicature 256 (1996); *see also* Nicole L. Mott, *The Current Debate on Juror Questions: "To Ask Or Not To Ask, That Is The Question",* 78 Chi.-Kent L.Rev. 1099 (2003) (discussing, and confirming, results of Heuer and Penrod studies).

One of the Heuer and Penrod studies examined the effects of juror questioning in 29 courtrooms in Wisconsin and the other study solicited input from 103 courtrooms in 33 different states around the United States. These studies, based on empirical evidence, concluded that the purported harmful consequences of juror questioning are wholly unsupported by the data and that the "effects of [juror questioning are] really rather innocuous." *Tweaking Commonsense,* 3 Psychol. Pub. Pol'y & L. at 280.

In addition to these two studies, this court also commissioned a study which followed 239 randomly selected trials in Colorado which participated in the Juror Reform Pilot Project. This study gathered empirical evidence from the selected trials and culminated in a report which found that juror questioning had little negative effect on the impact of trial proceedings and may improve courtroom dynamics. Mary Dodge, *Should Jurors Ask Questions in Criminal Cases? A Report Submitted to the Colorado Supreme Court's Jury System Committee* (Fall 2002), *available at* http://www.courts. state.co.u s/supct/committees/jury reformdocs/dodge report.pdf (hereinafter *Dodge Report*).

With respect to the assertion that juror questioning encouraged jurors to decide facts and form opinions about the case, the data collected by Heuer and Penrod demonstrated that juror questioning did not impact the verdicts given and that jurors' questions were only modestly helpful come deliberation time. These findings, they concluded, contradicted the general assertion that jurors become advocates rather than remain neutral and that juror questions did not have a prejudicial effect on the trial. *Tweaking Commonsense,* 3 Psychol. Pub. Pol'y & L. at 278–79. This same result was realized in the *Dodge Report* which also concluded that juror

12. *See Matchett v. State,* 364 S.E.2d 565 (Ga. 1988) (recognizing that state does not allow juror questioning but reviewing juror's improper question for harmless error); *State v. Zima,* 468 N.W.2d 377, 380 (Neb. 1991) (prohibiting practice); *Wharton v. State,* 734 So.2d 985 (Miss. 1998) (holding that although the practice of allowing juror questions is prohibited, court will review instances where questions are asked for harmless error); *State v. Costello,* 646 N.W.2d 204 (Minn.2002) (exercising supervisory power to prohibit juror questions); *Morrison v. State,* 845 S.W.2d 882 (Tex.Cr.App. 1992).

questioning does not influence jury verdicts and that factors other than juror questions ultimately influenced the outcome.

Heuer and Penrod also found that juror questions were not very helpful in getting jurors to the truth and that judges and attorneys both agreed that juror questions did not provide useful information of the jury's thinking. Nor did questions alert counsel to issues requiring further development. In Colorado, while the *Dodge Report* noted that juror questions provided attorneys with information about what evidence may have confused the jurors, the findings also indicated that juror questions Thus, according to the data accumulated from these empirical studies, jury questions did not cause either party to restructure its case according to the questions asked.

These studies also discredit the defendants' arguments that a juror may become antagonistic to one side should counsel object to his question. The majority of the jurors in the Heuer and Penrod studies who asked questions stated that they were not embarrassed or angry when counsel objected and that they typically understood the basis for the objection. Nor does the data suggest that attorneys shied away from objecting to questions. The findings showed that the attorneys and judges did not believe that juror questioning caused the jury to become prejudiced against a particular side. Again, the *Dodge Report* corroborates these findings. Judges and Attorneys did not report unfavorable reactions from jurors when a question was declined. Furthermore, the majority of jurors reported that they did not have an adverse reaction when their questions were not asked.

These studies all agreed that juror questioning encourages jurors to become more engaged in the trial and attentive to witnesses. It also promotes juror understanding of the facts and issues of the case. In addition, the data shows that the act of asking a question does not necessarily transform an otherwise passive juror into an advocate.[13] As with any empirical analysis, these studies cannot provide a conclusive answer to the issue we confront. However, what we can learn from these studies is that the empirical data does not support the argument that juror questions are per se unconstitutional. We should therefore not wholly dismiss the value of juror questioning. Thus, we agree with the Supreme Court of Vermont which dismissed the assertion that a juror may become biased if allowed to ask a question because this argument "trades a speculative increase in neutrality for a likely reduction in juror comprehension of the evidence." *Doleszny,* 844 A.2d at 785.

The rationales which the Minnesota and Texas Courts have used as reasons to disallow jury questions are not supported by the empirical studies. More importantly, those courts which prohibit the practice have based their decisions primarily upon policy reasons and not upon constitutional grounds. These jurisdictions do not provide empirical support for their policy conclusions, but rather base their decisions to prohibit jury questions on possibilities and speculation regarding factual scenarios not present in the cases before them.

With this understanding of the history and broad support recognizing that juror questioning of witnesses does not violate a defendant's right to a fair trial and may provide actual benefits to the trial process, we now address whether the Colorado Constitution prohibits juror questioning in all criminal cases.

C. Colorado

Medina and Moses both argue that Colorado should break from the majority of states and presume a prejudice inherent in juror questioning. They suggest that a defendant's constitutional rights are violated when a juror is allowed to ask a question irrespective of the question asked and the effect of that question on a juror, the jury, or the trial as a whole.

The Colorado Constitution states that the criminally accused "shall have the right to ... [a] trial by an impartial jury." Colo. Const. art. II § 16; *see also* Colo. Const. art. II § 23 ("The right to a trial by jury shall remain inviolate in criminal cases"); Colo. Const. art. II § 25 ("No person shall be deprived of life, liberty or property, without due process of law."). We have held that this right to a jury trial entitles a defendant to a jury drawn from a fair cross section of the members of his or her community. And, counsel may not

13. Asking a question is one of the "tools of inquiry and aids to decision making that are used every day by members of a literate society." *Tweaking Commonsense,* 3 Psychol. Pub. Pol'y & L. at 262. *See also* Steven L. Friedland, *The Competency and Responsibility of Jurors in Deciding Cases,* 85 Nw. U.L.Rev. 190, at 209–212 (1990) (analogizing the learning process of a student who is allowed to ask questions and take notes to that of the juror and finding that an active learner is more effective than a passive one).

discriminate based on race, gender, national origin, religion, age, economic status, or occupation when selecting jurors from the jury pool.

But, we have also held that where a juror can put aside his personal opinion or preconceived notion as to guilt or innocence and render a verdict based upon the evidence presented and the law at hand, the defendant's right to a fair trial is not violated....

It is the trial court's duty to determine the competency and credibility of each juror. The trial court's decision to deny a challenge for cause in the jury selection process or decision to excuse a juror will not be disturbed absent an abuse of discretion. The fact that the jury may have been exposed to pretrial publicity or is familiar with the general nature of the case does not by itself cause a jury to be constitutionally defective.

Our precedent recognizes that juries are formed out of the various members of the community, with each juror bringing his or her own life experiences and understanding of human behavior. In a criminal case, jurors are instructed that they should bring these life experiences and observations when considering the evidence presented at trial....

In addition to a trial by jury, due process entitles a defendant to a fair trial but not a perfect trial. Due process also requires that the prosecution prove every element of a charged offense beyond a reasonable doubt. This does not mean that the government's burden is lessened simply because a juror asks a question which solicits additional relevant evidence in a criminal case. To hold otherwise would undermine the rule that an appellate court is required to consider the evidence as a whole—not simply the evidence presented by the prosecution—before determining if there was sufficient evidence to support a finding of guilt beyond a reasonable doubt by a rational finder of fact.

Thus, while a defendant does have a right to an unbiased jury, he is not entitled to have his case presented to a jury that sits as a passive receptacle of information. Nor does it mean that once a juror forms a bias about a piece of evidence introduced at trial or about the credibility of a witness, that the defendant's rights have been violated.

Juror questioning undoubtedly changes courtroom dynamics but not to the extent that it renders a criminal trial constitutionally infirm. Minor delays for bench conferences to discuss whether a piece of evidence is admissible or a party's decision to reorganize its theory of the case based upon new evidence adduced at trial are not foreign concepts to a criminal trial. Our system also provides a mechanism to weed out potentially biased jurors during voir dire—a practice which is closely controlled by the trial judge and subject to appellate review. Jurors are instructed that they are not to discuss the case or come to conclusions until the end of all evidence. We choose not to adopt the defendants' position and speculate about a juror's state of mind or that juries wholeheartedly disregard the trial judge's instructions and their serious and weighty responsibility in a criminal trial simply because a question is or is not asked. Therefore, we hold that the fact that a juror asks a question during a criminal trial, in and of itself, does not violate a defendant's constitutional rights to a fair trial and an impartial jury.

We are confident that, with adequate safeguards in place, a defendant's constitutional rights will be protected should a juror propound an inadmissible question or should a juror's bias manifest itself through the questioning of a witness. Under the terms of the pilot project, the court was not required to ask all questions submitted by jurors. Rather, the trial judge, with the advice of counsel, screened the jurors' written questions before asking the witness the question. Then, keeping in mind the rights of all parties, the court was instructed to apply the applicable law and rules of evidence before determining whether a question was proper before asking the witness. With these safeguards in place, the defendant still has the ability for appellate review should a trial court allow an otherwise impermissible question from the jury; a course of action which is not different from instances where trial counsel asks an impermissible question. Trial courts will also continue to have the power to dismiss and replace jurors who are unable to continue with their duties as jurors. Thus, where errors do arise, our trial and appellate courts will continue to have the responsibility to review the impact of the error to assure that a defendant's constitutional rights are protected.

D. Standard of Review

Having determined that the practice of allowing jurors to ask questions of witnesses through the court is not per se unconstitutional, we now turn to the question of the appropriate standard for appellate courts to review the impact of an improper question from a juror....

... [W]e reject the defendants' assertion that we should apply structural error when an improper question from the jury is asked of a witness....

... [L]ike other erroneous evidentiary rulings made by the trial court, we hold that where the court errs by asking an improper question from the jury, the impact of that question shall be reviewed for harmless error. Under this standard of review, reversal is required unless the appellate court determines that the trial court's evidentiary ruling was harmless—that is, viewing the evidence as a whole, the error did not substantially influence the verdict or impair the fairness of the trial....

III. Application

A. Yvonne Medina

... The evidence admitted in this case concerned the likelihood that a witness would change his or her story and make inconsistent statements. The juror's question asked "how common is it for witnesses to add or subtract information from their original statements?" This question sought the police investigator's opinion with respect to the frequency that a witness would change his or her story. Generally, a witness is precluded from providing an opinion on issues that are based on scientific, technical, or other specialized knowledge unless that witness is qualified as an expert. The answer to the question in this case is not based upon the witness's first-hand impressions, such as the time of day or weather conditions when the event occurred, but based on specialized training or education of how witnesses behave when giving statements to police investigators.

Turning to the record, the witness who responded to this juror's question was not qualified by the defense as an expert. Furthermore, the question was irrelevant to the facts of the case. Whether ten percent or even fifty percent of people have inconsistencies in their recollection of events has no bearing on whether the witnesses in this case made inconsistent statements or whether the statements from these witnesses can be believed. Therefore, we hold that the trial court erred in allowing the question because it called for irrelevant expert testimony.

Even though the trial court erred and should not have allowed the question, we do not see how the answer to the question substantially influenced the verdict or impaired the fairness of Medina's trial. The evidence is not probative of the witnesses' credibility because it could be interpreted two different ways. One interpretation is that it is common for witnesses to have inconsistent statements and that despite the inconsistencies in these witnesses' statements they are still truthful. The second understanding is that the witnesses cannot be relied upon and that they were lying. It is thus not reasonably possible that the solicited testimony substantially influenced the verdict in this case.

Hence, we hold that although the trial court erred in allowing the juror's question, the answer to the question in this case was harmless.

B. Phillip Moses

Apart from the general objection to jury questioning addressed above, Moses does not challenge any of the trial court's rulings with respect to particular juror questions which were asked by the trial court. Rather, he argues that the jury may have overheard the first bench conference where defense counsel objected to one of the juror's questions causing prejudice to the defendant. At the second bench conference defense counsel notified the court that Moses heard the first bench conference from his seat in the courtroom. There is no indication that the jury had in fact heard this first bench conference or any other bench conference during the trial....

Moses concedes that the jury did not hear any other bench conference after the judge advised counsel to keep their voices down and he turned down the volume to his headphones at this second conference. At the first bench conference, which may have been overheard by the jury, the court and counsel discussed the admissibility of the juror's questions. Four questions were submitted of which defense counsel objected to one based on relevance and lack of foundation and the prosecutor agreed. The court sustained the objection. The following conversation appears in the record.

> THE COURT: For our record, we have four questions proposed to [the witness]. And by agreement, questions 1, 3, and 4 are being given without objection. Though, I want to give [defense counsel] an opportunity to make a general objection, and then—specifically, he's objecting to question number 2. So let's start with the general objection.
>
> [DEFENSE COUNSEL]: My objection is generally to this procedure. I understand the Supreme Court authorized this procedure, but I'm objecting to

the jury being allowed to ask questions whatsoever. My client's constitutional-affective [sic] assistance of—and the Colorado Constitution?

THE COURT: Thank you, sir.

Then the question, number 2, for [the witness] is: The dents were made as a result of the knife stick—I would change that to night stick—would have—they been smaller or larger? You object, sir?

[DEFENSE COUNSEL]: Object, calls for speculation on the part of the officer. Also lacking foundation that he's a qualified expert in this area. I think it calls for speculation-foundation.

THE COURT: Do you wish to make any record?

[PROSECUTION]: Briefly. Your Honor, the evidence has been that the officer tapped on the hood which he obviously observed. I think he can testify to that—but it calls for something that he, at the time, he may or may not know the answer.

THE COURT: Thank you. After reflection, I agree it calls for speculation. Therefore deny the question.

During this conference neither party criticizes the juror asking the question or makes statements about the question other than it calls for speculation. No statements about testimony not already admitted into evidence were made. Furthermore, the defense and prosecution both agreed that the question called for speculation on behalf of the officer. Thus, we decline to find an error simply because the jury may have overheard a bench conference where no prejudicial statements were made.

IV. Conclusion

For the reasons stated, the decisions of the court of appeals are affirmed....

Notes and Questions

1. If you were on a jury would you want to have a chance to submit questions that might be posed to witnesses? If you were a prosecutor or a defense attorney, would you want jurors to have that option? If you were on trial? On balance, do the potential benefits of a process such as the one observed in Colorado in *Medina* appear to outweigh the possible drawbacks?

2. If the issue of allowing jurors to submit questions that they would like to have posed to witnesses is somewhat controversial, should there be any reservations about allowing trial jurors to take notes while they listen to testimony? Many jurisdictions now permit juror note-taking, which is designed to enhance recollection of evidence, particularly in lengthy trials.[25]

3. We have not addressed important issues concerning the composition of trial juries, including how the jury venire is determined, the exercise of peremptory challenges, and other matters that could relate to fact-finding reliability and potential biases, and hence influence the likelihood of wrongful convictions. We consider one such issue, the "death qualification" of jurors in capital trials, in the following chapter.

4. Psycholegal scholars have conducted hundreds, if not thousands, of studies on jury decision-making. Indeed, some have lamented what they perceive to be a near-exclusive research focus on trials, which are rare in comparison to guilty pleas.[26] It is beyond our scope to review this body of research here. In the comprehensive review of 45 years of empirical research on jury decision-making mentioned above, completed by Devine and colleagues, the authors describe the extant research relevant to procedural characteristics (*e.g.*, legal definitions, jury size and involvement, and verdict/sentence options), participant characteristics (*e.g.*, juror demographics and attitudes, victim and defendant characteristics), case characteristics (*e.g.*, inadmissible material, expert testimony, evidence), and deliberation characteristics (*e.g.*, deliberation structure and polling). The authors developed four emergent themes based on the review of this extensive research.

Theme 1: Jurors often do not make decisions in the manner intended by the courts, regardless of how they are instructed.

Theme 2: Dispositional characteristics may predict jury outcomes better than juror verdict preferences.

Theme 3: Kalven and Zeisel's "liberation" hypothesis is alive and well. (The liberation hypothesis states that when evidence is ambiguous (does not clearly favor the prosecution or the defense), jurors are "liberated" from the evidence and are more susceptible to extraneous, extralegal influences.) *See* Harry Kalven, Jr. & Hans Zeisel, *The American Jury* (Boston: Little, Brown & Co. 1966).

Theme 4: Deliberation processes do influence jury outcomes in some situations.

C. Guilty Pleas

1. Would Innocent People Plead Guilty to a Crime They Did Not Commit?

The number of criminal cases disposed of by guilty pleas easily dwarfs that of cases that go to trial: in both the federal and state courts, in the neighborhood of 95% of felony convictions result from guilty pleas.[27] If nothing else, the sheer volume of guilty pleas makes them important to study as a potential vehicle for contributing to wrongful convictions. The Innocence Project reports that 22 of the first 265 individuals exonerated (8.3%) through post-conviction DNA testing pled guilty,[28] whereas 20 exonerees (5.9%) in the larger but overlapping database of wrongful convictions compiled by Professor Gross and his colleagues pled guilty, including 15 innocent murder defendants and four innocent rape defendants.[29] Not included in these totals are exonerees whose wrongful convictions were part of widespread scandals involving official misconduct, including 31 individuals who pled guilty to drug charges in Tulia, Texas, and a "majority of the 100 or more exonerated defendants [who pled guilty] in the Rampart scandal in Los Angeles."[30]

Reasons in addition to the simple prevalence of guilty pleas exist to investigate them as a source of wrongful convictions. As we shall see, various structural incentives embedded in the criminal justice process itself may induce innocent people to plead guilty. For example, innocent defendants might plead guilty to avoid risking onerous sentences, including death, that are threatened to follow a trial conviction; lawyers too busy to conduct a full case investigation, who may presume their client is guilty, might pursue a guilty plea as the preferred litigation option and advise their clients accordingly; deadlines for accepting seemingly favorable plea offers may expire prior to the completion of discovery and the disclosure of *Brady* material that would reveal a potentially successful trial defense. Many additional considerations could be influential. The case below helps illuminate some of the formidable systemic pressures that could cause defendants to plead guilty to crimes they did not commit.

United States v. Speed Joyeros
S.A., 204 F.Supp.2d 412 (E.D.N.Y. 2002)

Weinstein, Senior District Court J.

I. Introduction

The questions posed are whether acceptance of a plea of guilty and a departure downward in sentencing were appropriate in this substantial money laundering case. Serious factual and legal issues are presented by evidence of the defendant's long pretrial incarceration under onerous conditions, the government's control over funding for her counsel and the threat of much greater punishment without a plea.

This case illustrates the danger of due process violations by intensive pressure on defendants to plead guilty because of lengthy pretrial incarcerations and the offer of advantageous deals for lesser terms of imprisonment. The stick and carrot—largely controlled by prosecutors—produces a danger of excessive coercion of a defendant and undue pressures on defense counsel to avoid trial. It requires particularly close supervision by the court to ensure voluntariness of the plea. In evaluating the need for sentencing departures the unusual tensions some defendants face while in custody awaiting trial also must be considered.

The virtual elimination of federal criminal trials, substituting administrative decisions not to prosecute or pleas of guilty, has substantially changed our federal criminal law system. Increased prosecutorial discretion and power have raised the percent of guilty pleas from 86% of all federal convictions in 1971 to 95% in 2001. Discretion not to prosecute for the crime committed is widely exercised. Enhancement of control of sentencing by the prosecutor as a result of sentencing guidelines and minimum sentences has increased the government's power to coerce defendants. There has been a change from the paradigmatic concept of investigation and accusation by the government of almost all persons believed to have committed crimes, trial by jury with a strong role for defense counsel, and discretion in sentencing by the court, to a system sharply reducing the role of defense counsel, the jury and the judge, and whatever protections they can afford a defendant.

Defendant Hebroni and codefendants were charged with using jewelry businesses in Panama to launder some $10,000,000 of drug money. The prosecution was controlled by the Narcotics and Dangerous Drugs section of the United States Department of Justice, from Washington, D.C., rather than by the district's United States Attorney.

After lengthy pre-trial proceedings, drawn out over a period of more than a year and a half largely because of failure of the government to produce the huge amount of documents seized by the government of Panama; successive grants of bail by the trial court which were overturned on appeal; and strong government opposition to payment of defense counsel from defendant's known assets, all of which had been seized; defendant and the government entered into a plea agreement. It required defendant to be incarcerated for a term of somewhere between 33 and 41 months under the guidelines, and to give up all her assets. Without such an agreement, upon conviction she would have faced a prison sentence of 151 to 188 months and possibly more, based on a level of 34 or higher. See U.S. Sentencing Guidelines Manual §§2S1.1(b)(1) & 2S1.1(b)(2)(I) (2001) (hereinafter "Guidelines Manual").

The court entertained doubts about 1) defendant's capacity and desire to sign the plea agreement and 2) a possible conflict of interest of defense counsel in recommending a plea. Accordingly, the defendant was ordered to undergo a psychiatric evaluation to determine her fitness. Additional defense counsel was appointed to ensure that defendant's rights were fully protected and that she was being appropriately advised.

Ultimately defendant's plea was accepted by the court. While defendant agreed not to seek a downward departure, the agreement did not limit the court's independent authority to consider such a departure. On the basis of the presentence report, briefs by both sides and sentencing hearings, the court departed downward 2 levels and sentenced the defendant to a total of 27 months in prison and forfeiture of all her personal and business assets, a fine, and a term of supervised release of three years, during which time defendant may not engage in the jewelry or rare metals business, nor conduct any business in Panama.

II. Facts

A. Background

Defendant Hebroni is a citizen of Israel domiciled in Panama. She is forty-nine years old and recently widowed. Her immediate family is her 6-year-old son, now a resident of Israel, who was conceived after many years of medical intervention. Defendant appears to be an intelligent woman, though physically frail.

The court was presented with no admissible evidence. From the contentions of government counsel and concessions by defendant, the facts can be briefly summarized as follows:

Co-defendant Speed Joyeros, S.A., is a jewelry business fully owned by defendant Hebroni. Speed Joyeros, S.A., engaged in the sale of gold and silver jewelry and precious metals to many retail and wholesale customers throughout Central and South America and in Europe and the Middle East....

Hebroni received cash, checks and electronic money transfers in a money laundering scheme. A primary modus was to sell jewelry to drug lords, knowing that it was being paid for with drug money, thus allowing them to convert dirty money into sparkling clean jewelry. Financial institutions in the United States and other countries were employed in these conversions....

B. Procedural History

On September 22, 2000, Hebroni was arrested and detained on money laundering charges. She had voluntarily come to this country from Panama to defend against forfeiture proceedings commenced here against millions of dollars of her assets, mainly in Panama....

On October 10, 2000, defendant pled not guilty. After various pretrial motions, defendant sought bail. On July 2, 2001, bail was denied by the judge previously assigned to the case.

The case lagged, with large numbers of the basic business records from Panama unavailable in this country. All the documents used by defendants in their Panamanian businesses had been seized by the government of Panama. Despite repeated attempts by the defendant to retrieve and examine these many thousands of papers in preparation for trial, they had still not been fully examined by the defense up to the time of plea.

After new bail hearings, on December 12, 2001, defendant was ordered released if she could satisfy specified conditions.... The court was particularly concerned that without bailed release there was a serious possibility that defendant would not be able to properly defend herself. Her defense as well as the prosecution was to be based on the documents seized from her place of business by Panamanian authorities. They had not yet been provided to her. In addition, her incarceration limited her ability to work with her attorneys, accountants, and the necessary calculators and computers required to analyze the extensive business records in this complex case. Trial was set for March 11, 2002, giving defendant just under three months to prepare.

The government appealed from the order of December 12, 2001 granting release on conditions. Release was stayed by the court of appeals. By its decision of January 8, 2002, it vacated the district court's order....

Important events bearing on defendant's ability to defend had occurred. First, over strong government objection, the court ordered the release of sufficient of the defendants' funds to pay her attorneys for work done to that time.

Second, the government began to make available to defendant numerous boxes of papers. Since she was unable to study these documents except while she was detained, the court made available a room in the courthouse. She was brought to and from prison each day to view her business writings under the guard of the marshals. This procedure was burdensome since defendant was given limited space and she did not have the necessary equipment and assistance. Trial would have required introduction and analysis of thousands of documents, tracing transactions running through institutions in many countries.

Third, defendant suffered physically. She submitted evidence indicating that she was being held in the open in cold weather for lengthy periods each day with inadequate clothing awaiting transportation between jail and court, and was not being provided with appropriate food. The court observed her physical and emotional deterioration....

Conditions of incarceration of the defendant and the nature of the case raised doubts that due process could be served without some form of release. The defendant had to be able to prepare for her impending trial. In the court's view the bail terms were sufficient to assure her presence at trial. The district court again granted bail on February 12, 2002 with detailed findings as required by the court of appeals. The conditions were stringent. Defendant was to be detained under house arrest; monitored by Pretrial Services with an electronic bracelet at her own cost; subject to telephone monitoring; subject to a curfew; guarded at all times if the government wished; required to place her passport in government custody; and required to post bail of $10,000,000 guaranteed by substantial real property.

At the time bail was granted this second time, the court noted that defendant was only a month away from trial, so that further detention would seriously hinder her ability to present a defense. Delays in release on bail worked in the government's favor since it shortened the time when defendant and her counsel could analyze the evidence in an appropriate environment.

The government appealed from the district court's February 12, 2002 order granting release on bail. The court of appeals stayed the order. Ultimately the court of appeals, on March 13, 2002, reversed the district court's order....

As the defense's difficulty in adequately preparing for trial under these conditions became more evident, and the date of trial grew closer, the parties notified the court that they wished to enter into a plea agreement. Defendant agreed to plead guilty to count one of the indictment. Count one contains allegations of millions of dollars in money laundering, but the parties agreed that the guilty plea would be limited to $474,000 of specific money laundering events. Defendant agreed "not to contest that the Government would have proven beyond a reasonable doubt at trial in this case that the funds identified in Count One of the indictment were derived from drug trafficking."

The agreement incorporated contemplated terms of a sentence for the defendant. As already noted, the prospective guideline was at level 20, carrying a range of imprisonment of 33 to 41 months; it included a downward adjustment for acceptance of responsibility. Defendant agreed not to seek a downward departure or to appeal her sentence if it was not greater than 41 months. She also agreed to forfeit all of her own ownership of assets in the defendant companies (estimated at some $6,000,000) which had been seized by Panamanian authorities, as well as the remaining more than $600,0000 [sic] of assets in a United States bank. The indicted corporations also pleaded guilty as part of the deal.

A hearing was held on March 1, 2002 to review the plea.... [T]he court ordered that the defendant be examined by a physician to assist in determining if her plea was voluntary. The resulting report of Dr. Sanford L. Drob was illuminating.

Dr. Drob noted that Ms. Hebroni had suffered physically during her incarceration, especially in recent months when she was shuttled back and forth from jail to court daily to review papers. He also pointed out that Ms. Hebroni was exceedingly anxious to be reunited with her infant son. She told Dr. Drob that the reason she had agreed to a plea was to be reunited with her son sooner. She was, according to the Doctor, under the erroneous impression that she would be sentenced to time served. She stated, according to his report, that she believed that "you can't win" at trial. Dr. Drob concluded that defendant would have been far less likely to accept a plea agreement if she had been allowed to leave jail on bail while awaiting trial.

Dr. Drob noted that "several factors" were involved in defendant's decision to plead. The primary reason was concern for her son. She had suffered unusual stress as a result of separation from him—her only child and the result of years of fertility treatments. Since she was widowed, her son depended on her as his only parent; she had already had to explain an absence of 18 months. She also felt physically worn down and ill-equipped to undergo a lengthy trial.

Since the report indicated that defendant had an erroneous understanding of the plea agreement—which did not, as she reportedly thought, require immediate release—the court ordered defense counsel to make clear to their client the effect of the agreement. The court appointed supplemental counsel to ensure that defendant's rights were adequately protected. It was concerned that the lack of defendant's assets to pay legal and other costs of a trial might have produced an inclination of defense counsel to reduce their own obligations and potential financial risk were there a full trial, by recommending a plea.

On March 20, 2002, the court held a second hearing on the plea agreement.... Defense counsel stated that defendant was aware of the effect of the plea agreement and was capable of making the agreement. Based on this affirmation; the medical report; an oral report of supplemental defense counsel that defendant understood the plea and that her counsel's advice was based solely on her welfare; and close questioning of the defendant by the court, the defendant's plea was accepted....

III. Law

A. Conflicts of Interest

Attorneys are subject to strict rules designed to prevent them from having conflicts of interest with their clients. The American Bar Association

Model Code of Professional Responsibility demands that a lawyer "shall not accept [or continue in] employment if the exercise of his professional judgment on behalf of his client will be or reasonably may be affected by his own financial, business, property, or personal interests." ABA Model Code DR 5-101. This principle is one of the pillars of our judicial system—that an attorney should not have any reservation in giving unalloyed support to the client he is representing....

Forfeiture cases may be particularly amenable to conflicts of interest. In these cases, all of a defendant's assets may be seized, preventing the attorney from recovering any fee if the defendant loses. The attorney has a financial incentive to ensure that fees are paid, and thus an incentive to advise a defendant in a manner likely to protect fees—a position which may diverge from the best interests of the defendant....

B. Plea Bargains

1. Plea Bargaining and Coercion

The Federal Rules of Criminal Procedure allow a defendant to "plead guilty, not guilty, or nolo contendere." F.R.Cr.P. 11(a)(1). Any plea of guilty must be shown to the court to be "voluntary":

> The court shall not accept a plea of guilty or nolo contendere without first, by addressing the defendant personally in open court, determining that the plea is voluntary and not the result of force or threats or of promises apart from a plea agreement. The court shall also inquire as to whether the defendant's willingness to plead guilty or nolo contendere results from prior discussions between the attorney for the government and the defendant or the defendant's attorney.

F.R.Cr.P. 11(d). While the rule warns of coercion as a "result of force or threats or of promises apart from a plea agreement," the court's obligation to determine "voluntariness" is not limited by these examples. The word "voluntary" is itself laden with ambiguity; it is an antonym of "coerced" which may be due to various forms of non-force or non-threats. The second sentence starting with the words, "the court shall also" inquire about prior "discussions," suggests that inappropriate coercion may exist even where there is no "force or threats or ... promises apart from a plea agreement."

There is no single clear definition of "voluntary" for all legal purposes. Even in the criminal-law-plea context, it is unclear whether "voluntary" means freedom from any coercion or whether it means freedom only from "wrongful" or "undue" coercion. A pristine rule of "no coercion" would preclude many plea agreements. Requiring plea negotiations to be free from "any coercion" would contradict the basic notions of bargaining. Contract law theory suggests that no bargaining process is completely devoid of coercion in some form. The problem is one of discerning what level of coercion is so inappropriate as to render a plea agreement invalid.

The seventh edition of Black's Law Dictionary's definition of "voluntary" as something done "unconstrained by interference ... not compelled by outside influence," is not helpful in determining whether a guilty plea was "voluntary" since a defendant is always "influenced" by many factors including family demands and other social pressures as well as by the hope of minimizing punishment. To conclude that a plea agreement is made "unconstrained by interference" or "not compelled by outside influence" would be to ignore the reality that such an agreement is a bargain made between an often relatively powerless defendant and a prosecutor who can exercise a great deal of influence over the accused's future happiness....

One court of appeals has realistically declared that a plea is involuntary only if it is obtained through "wrongful coercion." *United States v. Hernandez,* 203 F.3d 614, 619 (9th Cir.2000). This implies that some coercion is implicit in the plea bargaining process and only "wrongful coercion"—however defined—invalidates a plea....

An illegally coerced plea may be analogized to an illegally obtained confession....

In addressing confessions as well as pleas, "voluntary" can not be defined by freedom from "coercion," rather than by acknowledging appropriate levels of coercion. Determining whether a confession or plea is the product of illegitimate coercion requires consideration of the state of mind of the defendant as well as the techniques used for extracting agreement. More "coercion" may be allowable in the form of bargained for benefits in pleas than would be allowed in confessions because the plea is developed with counsel's advice and with time to reflect and formalize the decision.

A closer equivalence to "plea bargains" than confessions is suggested by contract law. *Cf. Brady* [*v. United States,* 397 U.S. 742, 752 (1970)] (plea bargains involve "mutuality of advantage"). The law recognizes that some degree of coercion exists in contract formation, but that the level of duress or threat may not be such that a party is "unfairly" (however defined) induced to enter into an agreement....

"Coercion" and "voluntary" are, in short, vague terms of limited value in deciding whether to accept a plea. The critical question is whether the defendant was in a position to rationally weigh the advantages and disadvantages of the plea and whether a reasonable person in that position might make the same decision. This is a rather imprecise standard. In addition, certain tactics are considered incompatible with the etiquette of criminal justice, including overt threats and physical abuse. In accepting the plea the court must try to be as fully cognizant as practicable of the circumstances leading to the plea and of the nature and the background of the particular defendant, including age, education, social class, family pressures, and other relevant factors that might have affected the decision. The defense attorney's position is critical for he or she provides defendant with the crutch of cool rationality.

"Coercion" within limits is an available tool for prosecutors. It is appropriate so long as it does not shock the judicial conscience and does not depart substantially from commonly held beliefs of what is appropriate pressure for the government to apply to supposed miscreants. "Voluntary" under these circumstances means a capacity of the defendant and his counsel under the circumstances to rationally and fairly weigh the benefits of the plea against risks of not pleading. If "coerced" is too strong a word, one that leaves members of the justice system uncomfortable, many pleas are, to put the matter more politely, "induced" by strong promises of great value (e.g., a lesser term of incarceration, or life rather than death)—offers that, to paraphrase a famous movie line, most defendants cannot refuse.

2. Competency to Plead

Voluntariness is comprised of at least two separate elements. First, the plea may not be "coerced" in the sense already described.... Coercion is a fact-intensive inquiry which will depend on the particular case.

Second, a defendant must be competent to plead....

In making these two inquiries, courts are instructed to err on the side of caution and use "the 'utmost solicitude of which courts are capable in canvassing the matter with the accused to make sure [the defendant] has a full understanding of what the plea connotes and of its consequence.'" *Boykin v. Alabama,* 395 U.S. 238, 243–44 (1969).

There is a lively debate among scholars over whether plea bargaining is systemically unreasonably coercive in nature. *Compare, e.g.,* John H. Langbein, Torture and Plea Bargaining, 46 U. Chi. L.Rev. 3, 12–19 (1978) (plea bargaining is similar to medieval European torture), *and* Stephen J. Schulhofer, Plea Bargaining as Disaster, 101 Yale L.J.1979, 1980 (1992) (plea bargaining should be abolished), *with* Frank H. Easterbrook, Plea Bargaining as Compromise, 101 Yale L.J.1969, 1978 (1992) (plea bargaining is an efficient compromise and maintains defendant autonomy).

Langbein's view, while perhaps overly dramatic, is relevant to the present inquiry. He notes that:

> Like the Europeans of distant centuries who did employ [torture], we make it terribly costly for an accused to claim his right to the constitutional safeguard of trial. We threaten him with a materially increased sanction if he avails himself of his right and is thereafter convicted. This sentencing differential is what makes plea bargaining coercive. There is, of course, a difference between having your limbs crushed if you refuse to confess, or suffering some extra years of imprisonment if you refuse to confess, but the difference is of degree, not kind. *Plea bargaining, like torture, is coercive.*

Langbein at 12–13 (emphasis added). Langbein further notes the irony in requiring that plea bargains be labeled "voluntary" and "not coerced" before they can be approved by a court. "The plea agreement is the source of the coercion," he notes, "and already embodies the involuntariness." His critique is rejected by the American system of criminal justice as it has evolved; it is now firmly bottomed on coercively induced pleas.

3. Changes in the Criminal Justice System

When the Sentencing Guidelines were introduced, some judges expressed doubts about their constitutionality and fairness....

One concern of some judges was that if it made no difference to the sentence under the guidelines whether a defendant was tried, or pleaded guilty, then the new process would lead to a substantial increase in the number of criminal trials. Defendants would, it was suggested, have no incentive to plead, since the sentence would be the same under the guidelines.

In fact, just the opposite result occurred. The number of criminal jury trials has radically decreased since the guidelines were implemented. There are now relatively few criminal trials. In the meantime, the number of guilty pleas has increased dramatically.

One explanation for this largely unforeseen result is based on a series of related factors: The government often works out deals to avoid prosecution or drop more serious charges; 5K.1 letters (which are issued, in accordance with U.S.S.G. § 5K.1 for defendants who cooperate with the government, and which grant a judge broad discretion to depart downward) are issued to many cooperating defendants; the government often does not contest findings of fact essential to lower sentences, such as "cooperation" or "minor role," which can favor defendants; the government does not appeal many downward departures; and the government readily agrees to "safety valve" provisions (guidelines and statutes allowing for sentence reductions for certain defendants who cooperate with government, and for making inapplicable harsh statutory minimums). All of these benefits are available to the pleading defendant rather than to one taking the case to trial. Between safety valve and other reductions, defendants can often reduce their guidelines calculation by 6 or more levels, in effect cutting many sentences in half or more. The message to defendants is clear: "Don't insist on your right to trial." Since the sentencing judges' ability to impose a sentence other than the one the government insists on under the guidelines is sharply reduced, the government's power to induce pleas has been magnified....

The power of the prosecutor is particularly enhanced in connection with informers. If the government is satisfied that a putative defendant has made early admissions, particularly if accompanied by a promise to testify against other persons in the criminal enterprise, the government can provide a 5K.1 letter that permits probation for even the most heinous crimes accompanied by a waiver of any minimum sentence. The pressure on the informer to shade the truth to assist the government in obtaining convictions of others is enormous. While the government does all it can to ensure against false accusations, the use of informers does place greater pressure on informed against defendants to plead guilty. The court must guard particularly against pleas coerced in such situations. (In the instant case there was a strong hint of former employees of defendant informing on her.)

Statistics available from the United States Sentencing Commission illustrate this trend to avoid the guidelines in order to induce pleas. The number of sentences within guideline range has dropped from 82% in 1989 to 64% in 2000.... The majority of departures are granted for substantial assistance to authorities.... Since substantial assistance departures require a letter from the government, the government has control over whether or not to grant a defendant the single most effective tool for receiving a sentence below the guideline range....

There may, of course, be other explanations for the reduction in the relative number of trials besides utilization of the guidelines by the prosecutors to induce pleas—perhaps prosecutions are now those commenced only in the clearest cases of guilt, or perhaps now the mix of cases, emphasizing drug violations or illegal entry into the United States, has increased the ease of successful prosecution.

At the same time that it essentially controls the sentence, the government can often block bail. In some cases this opposition is justified... Still, the combination of pretrial incarceration, plus higher periods of potential incarceration after conviction, when compared with a relatively easy plea and a known relatively short period of incarceration, create intense pressure on a defendant to plead. In most cases, this pressure does not result in a serious concern that the innocent are being found guilty.

The 1994 Sentencing Commission study on plea negotiations conceded the existence of problems. Its study stated that "prosecutors exercise a considerable degree of sentencing discretion through charging and bargaining decisions. This discretion, if unchecked, has the potential to re-create the very disparities that the Sentencing Reform Act was intended to alleviate." Plea Negotiations Study at 6. The report further noted that "circumvention" of the guidelines occurs, through bargaining by prosecutors in charging defendants. It stated bluntly, "our research uncovered *unequivocal evidence that bargaining and charging practices undercut the sentencing guidelines.* There is simply no way to deny the existence of this problem in every jurisdiction we studied." Inappropriate use of minor role reductions and § 5K1 letters was found to lead to circumvention of the guidelines....

... [B]etween 1971 and 2001, the number of criminal defendants convicted in federal district courts rose from 78% of total defendants charged in 1971, and 75% of those charged in the next three years, to 90% of defendants charged in 2001....

This ratio of convicted defendants to charged defendants has been driven up in part by large increases in the relative number of guilty pleas....

Overall, the percent of convictions resulting from guilty pleas has increased from 86% in 1971 (27,544 pleas in a total of 32,103 convictions) to 95% in 2001 (64,402 pleas in a total of 67,731 convictions)....

These numbers should not surprise anyone familiar with the current criminal law system....

Numbers of pleas and trials for state courts, while not readily available, are likely to be similar to those for Federal courts....

When examining the criminal justice system in its report on the Speedy Trial Act the House Judiciary Committee noted the danger signal flashed by our increased reliance on pleas. It declared:

> Whether the negotiated plea is a desirable element within the system or one of the basic causes of delay and court-clogging is another question. The National Advisory Commission in its *Courts* report found that plea bargaining constitutes a triple danger to the system:
>
> > (1) *Danger to the Defendant's Rights* — A survey of more that 3,400 criminal justice practitioners in four states — California, Michigan, New Jersey, and Texas — revealed that 61 percent of those polled agreed that it was probable or somewhat probable that most defense attorneys engage in plea bargaining primarily to expedite the movement of cases. Furthermore, 8 percent agreed that it was probable or somewhat probable that most defense attorneys in plea bargaining negotiations pressure clients into entering a plea that the client feels is unsatisfactory.
> >
> > (2) *Danger to Court Administration* — Very simply, the Commission found that plea bargaining resulted in the need to pull cases out of the process — sometimes on the morning of trial — making efficient scheduling of cases difficult or impossible. Thus, plea bargaining makes it difficult to use judicial and prosecutorial time effectively.
> >
> > (3) *Danger to Society's Need for Protection* — The conclusion of the commission in this regard is that, because defendants are often dealt with less severely than might normally be the case, plea bargaining results in leniency that reduces the deterrent effect of the law and may have a less direct effect on corrections programs.

Speedy Trial Act History at 7412 (emphasis supplied). Because of these factors, the Commission recommended the prohibition of plea bargaining. Rejecting this radical recommendation, the House Committee suggested only that the report deserved "weight."

The Sentencing Commission found that the result of "charge bargaining" by prosecutors was that "the amount of [sentence reduction] is taken out of the hands of the judge, where the Guidelines intended to place it, and left more under control of the prosecutor, where neither the Congress nor the Commission intended the discretion to be." Plea Negotiations Study at 30–31.

Most pleas of guilty are fully justified. There is often clear evidence of guilt. Often the defendant agrees on his or her guilt at the time of arrest. The catharsis of prompt acknowledgment of wrongdoing and its potential first step on the road to rehabilitation should not be underestimated as a value of the truly "voluntary" plea.

Occasionally, as in the case at hand, the coercive nature of the system is such as to give serious cause for concern that we are utilizing excessive coercion to avoid trials. Yet, there is no injustice on any appreciable scale through conviction of the innocent that can be demonstrated. Neither prosecution nor defense, nor the trial nor appellate courts, seem blameworthy. Nevertheless, the end result of the "new criminal justice system" in almost eliminating trials is disquieting. Such massive shifts may in practice require development of new judicial techniques, ethical rules or attitudes.

C. Bail

1. Law Governing Bail

Bail in Federal courts is governed by section 3142 of Title 18 of the United States Code. Section 3142 establishes a general policy of release of prisoners pending trial. Prisoners may be released on their own recognizance (subsection (b)) or on conditions (subsection (c)). Only if, after conducting hearings, the judge decides that release presents a danger to the security of the public or that "no condition or combination of conditions will reasonably assure that appearance of the person as required," may the defendant be detained without bail. 18 U.S.C. §3142(e). This provision codifies the longstanding norm in our justice system that bail is the rule, and that few cases are to be exceptions. The Constitution itself prohibits the use of excessive bail. U.S. Const. Am. VIII....

2. History of Bail Reform

Despite these protections, many poor defendants were often unable to make bail. A disparity based upon social status led to widespread dissatisfaction. Public interest organizations urged increased release before trial.

There were several reasons why bail reform was urged. A primary concern was that expressed by the Supreme Court earlier in *Stack* [*v. Boyle*, 342 U.S. 1, 4 (1951)], that defendants who are held in pretrial custody are less able to defend themselves. This correlation was shown in several studies prior to passage of the Bail Reform Act in 1964. *See, e.g.*, Anne Rankin, The Effect of Pretrial Detention, 39 N.Y.U. L.Rev. 641 (1964). Ms. Rankin, a Research Associate from the Vera Institute, relied upon data from New York. She pointed out that "previous studies of bail have indicated that an accused who has been detained in jail between his arraignment and the final adjudication of his case is more likely to receive a conviction or a jail sentence than an accused who has been free on bail." She used standard statistical techniques to attempt to neutralize the effect of other variables. An initial reading of the statistics showed that for the period in question, sixty-four percent of non-bailed defendants were sentenced to prison time, while only seventeen percent of bailed defendants were sentenced to prison. This difference of forty-seven percent was largely attributable, the study concluded, to the different decisions made on bail. Factors one might think would cause a difference, such as the race of the defendant and the type of offense charged, were not statistically significant. Rankin identified five factors which did have a statistical correlation with disposition: defendant's previous record, the bail amount, type of counsel, family integration, and employment stability. After controlling for each of these variables, the study found that for sizable numbers of defendants, the decision between bail and pretrial detention still accounted for a difference unfavorable to those unreleased of thirty-five to thirty-seven percent in final disposition. Based on these findings, the study concluded that "a causal relationship exists between [pretrial] detention and unfavorable disposition."

Similar finding were developed in other studies.... These studies supported the 1964 Bail Reform Act....

The national bail laws were amended in 1984. The bail reform provisions of the crime control statute passed in 1984 were part of a massive crime control statute which included, among other things, the statutory authorization for the Sentencing Guidelines.... [T]he Bail Reform Act of 1984 was designed to allow judges discretion to deny bail in the case of dangerous defendants.... The legislative history contains no mention of Congressional repudiation of its earlier aims in the 1964 Act, which included the need to enable defendants to prepare adequately for trial.

The 1984 Act dealt with a very different kind of defendant than Ms. Hebroni—the currently dangerous defendant. No one has suggested that Ms. Hebroni is or was dangerous after her indictment and seizure of her business and assets. Thus the concerns expressed about excessive bail in the history of the prior legislation cannot be ignored in a case such as hers.

In sum, the bail provisions as now written authorize the detention of defendants without bail only for a severely restricted class of defendants for whom no amount of bail would suffice to assure their appearance, and for a small group of defendants who present a danger of criminal activity while they await disposition of criminal charges against them. The presumption in favor of bail—the "traditional right to freedom" of which the *Stack* court spoke—has remained in force. The need for a general policy of release has remained the same: With narrow exceptions, defendants should be released in order to be able to adequately prepare their defense.

3. Constitutional Requirements

... The Constitution, in its guarantee that excessive bail should not be required, established the default rule that defendants should not be detained prior to trial unless necessary. This is because the right to freedom before conviction is basic. Similarly, the right to release on bail is inextricably related to the presumption of innocence of an accused....

Even fundamental rights such as the right to freedom may be limited if there is a compelling state interest....

Assuring the presence of a defendant at trial is a compelling interest, but infringements of basic rights, in the name of compelling interests, must be narrowly tailored. For example, defendants should be denied their freedom only where the trial court has a basis for its finding that detention is clearly necessary to ensure presence at trial.

Government also has an interest in acquitting innocent defendants and a corollary interest in assuring that all defendants have time and conditions that will allow for the defense necessary in our adversarial system. If either side has too great a systemic advantage, then the fairness of the system itself is at risk....

Finally, the analysis of bail must take into account the seismic modifications of the criminal law which have occurred in the last few decades.... The major shift is that there are now significantly fewer trials and more pleas. This alteration could mean different things in the bail context. One possible change is that defendants might need the freedom bail provides in order to effectively prepare a defense—not for trial, but rather as a starting bargaining position in plea bargaining. Where a court denies bail it places defendant in a weaker bargaining position in constructing the plea bargain which will largely determine the sentence.

4. Use of Pretrial Services

In considering whether bail is appropriate judges in this district take into account the close supervision of bailed defendants by Pretrial Services....

... [T]he prosecutor's power to successfully oppose bail—at the trial and appellate level—for those who will not cooperate or plead, suggests the enormous influence of the government on bail as well as on pleas and sentences.

D. Speedy Trial

1. Constitutional Aspects

The right to a speedy trial is guaranteed by the Constitution. *See* U.S. Const., Am. 6 ("In all criminal prosecutions, the accused shall enjoy the right to a speedy and public trial.")....

2. Statutes and Rules

The Speedy Trial Act was passed in 1974 in order to ensure that defendants' right to a speedy trial was enforced. The Act ... states at the outset that courts are to "assure a speedy trial." 18 U.S.C. § 3161(a). In general, no defendant may be held before trial more than 90 days. Certain endemic and other delays are not factored into this calculation.

The legislative history of the Act shows that it was designed to satisfy a variety of purposes. It was "to assist in reducing crime and the danger of recidivism by requiring speedy trials and by strengthening the supervision over persons released pending trial." Speedy Trial Act History at 7402. Such a law was necessary, the House Committee felt, "in order to give real meaning to the Sixth Amendment right [to a speedy trial]." ...

The House Committee was concerned that jail time would disrupt family life, retard rehabilitation, and punish the innocent; significantly, the Committee also relied upon the fact that pretrial detention, "hinders the defendant's ability to gather evidence, contact witnesses, and otherwise prepare his case." ...

E. Sentencing

This case raises issues in several distinct areas of the law of sentencing, including departure, fines, and terms of supervised release....

IV. Application of Law to Facts

A. Defendant's Ability to Plead

The defendant's ability to "voluntarily" enter into a plea agreement was affected by her bail situation as her trial grew increasingly closer. The adverse effect on defendant has been apparent.

An example of stresses on her was produced by separation from her only child. Defendant's young son traveled from Israel to New York; he was to live with defendant and other family members prior to her trial if she complied with the bail decision of the trial court under supervised conditions, similar to strict house arrest. Her affection for her son, and the difficulty that the separation caused because of her detention was apparent.

Living with her son was part of the highly restrictive bail package this court approved on February 12, 2002. It was designed to satisfy the demands of the appellate court that bail be related to appearance at trial; the package satisfied this court that defendant would be likely to appear at trial. The court was also aware of other important considerations. Contact with her son would have been therapeutic for a woman now incarcerated a year and a half pending trial, whose trial was only a month away. Defendant's deterioration placed in jeopardy her ability to prepare effectively for trial, including her mental ability to make important decisions. Instead of any family contact, the defendant was then subjected to an emotionally wrenching thwarted near-reunion.

It was under a combination of trying circumstances that defendant decided to plead. She agreed to plead guilty to charges which would lead to a sentence of 33 to 47 months in prison. She also agreed that she would not request a downward departure—a routine clause in such agreements.

Rule 11(f) makes clear that a plea may be accepted where there is a "factual basis" for it. The court is not required to believe that the defendant is actually guilty, or even likely to be found guilty. The documents so far produced in court do not convincingly establish guilt. Nevertheless, the admission of guilt when combined with the proffers of the government of what cooperating witnesses will say and the huge number of boxes of documents, which may or may not contain authenticable incriminating records, provide a factual basis for the plea which satisfies Rule 11(f). The court is not prepared to conclude on the basis of what it has examined that defendant is likely to be guilty. It decides merely that Rule 11(f)'s standard of a "factual basis" has been met so that the plea may be accepted.

B. Conflicts of Interest

At the time defendant's counsel were originally retained, their representation was not marred by a conflict of interest. Even though incarceration may have hampered her counsel's ability to effectively advise defendant regarding a plea agreement, it did not create a conflict.

More serious was the government's declared intent to take title to all of defendant's funds, and to withhold her assets from use as attorneys fees. Were defendant to proceed to trial and lose her case, all of her assets would have been lost. In that event, her counsel risked not being paid.

Her attorney was thus forced to choose between two equally unpalatable alternatives. He could advise his client to proceed to a complex and long trial, aware that preparation had been severely hindered by defendant's detention, risking a huge financial loss of his own from representation over many months with no substantial hope for a fee. Or he could advise her to plead guilty and cut his potential losses. This apparent conflict was forced upon defense counsel by government's declared position that it now owned essentially all of defendant's assets through forfeiture.

The court attempted to mitigate the conflict problem by appointing additional counsel, pursuant to the Criminal Justice Act. 18 U.S.C. § 3006A. Appointed counsel is not subject to the same potential conflict since compensation comes from the government, not from the defendant's seized assets.

C. Sentencing

... [T]hree factors, the destruction of livelihood, the rigor of pretrial detention and the denial of bail creating unusual difficulties in this case, are independent reasons for departure. Based on these reasons individually and collectively, the court departs downward two levels. This leaves an offense level after departures of 18, which translates to a sentence between 27 and 33 months....

V. Conclusion

The defendant is sentenced to 27 months in prison and a fine of $250,000. She should receive credit for time served and for good behavior if appropriate.

Following incarceration, she will serve a term of three years of supervised release. Supervised release may be served abroad. As a special condition of supervised release, she may not conduct business in Panama, nor engage in the jewelry or precious metals businesses anywhere or violate any law of the United States or of the country where she resides. Any illegal entry into the United States will be a violation of the terms of supervised release. Further details are spelled out in the judgment of conviction.

SO ORDERED....

Notes and Questions

1. The federal Sentencing Guidelines discussed in Judge Weinstein's opinion in *Speed Joyeros* were subsequently declared unconstitutional by the Supreme Court insofar as they allowed trial judges to make an upward departure from the presumptive sentencing range based on fact findings that were not made by the trial jury. *United States v. Booker,* 543 U.S. 220, 125 S.Ct. 738, 160 L.Ed.2d 621 (2005). Following *Booker,* the Sentencing Guidelines are only advisory although they remain influential and can provide a frame of reference for sentences that are challenged on appeal as being unreasonable. Sentencing reductions, in the form of downward departures from the Sentencing Guidelines, do not directly threaten the protections associated with the right to trial by jury that was at issue in *Booker.* Significant incentives thus remain for defendants to plead guilty, thereby accepting responsibility for their conduct, to curry favorable sentencing consideration and avoid the so-called "trial tax" represented by more onerous sentences that typically are imposed on defendants who are convicted after they opt for a trial. *See* Ricardo J. Bascuas, "The American Inquisition: Sentencing After the Federal Guidelines," 45 *Wake Forest Law Review* 1, 41–48 (2010); Nancy J. King, David A. Soule, Sara Steen & Robert R. Weidner, "When Process Affects Punishment: Differences in Sentences After Guilty Plea, Bench Trial, and Jury Trial in Five Guidelines States," 105 *Columbia Law Review* 959 (2005).

2. In one Canadian study of prosecutorial bail decision-making, researchers found that detained defendants were more likely to be offered pleas than defendants who had been released. The authors viewed pretrial detention as a way to encourage or "coerce" pleas.[31] Although not seemingly common, at least one state, Minnesota, requires defendants pleading guilty to attend to the following statement: "I do/do not make the claim that the fact I have been held in jail since my arrest and could not post bail caused me to decide to plead guilty in order to get the thing over with rather than waiting my turn at trial."[32]

3. Although there is a shortage of empirical studies on guilty pleas generally, and on false guilty pleas, specifically, studies have been conducted comparing guilty and innocent subjects' willingness to consider entering a plea of guilty. In one set of studies, Gregory, Mowen, and Linder asked male college students to imagine that they were guilty or innocent of armed robbery, listen to a tape of the defense attorney's arguments, and then reject or accept a plea offer.[33] Number of charges and sanction severity were also manipulated. They found that when the number of charges was high versus low (four versus one charge) and when the sanctions were high versus low (10–15 versus 1–2 years in prison), both guilty and innocent participants were more likely to plead guilty: 100% for guilty subjects and 33% for innocent subjects. In a separate experiment, Gregory *et al.* manipulated the guilt or innocence of subjects in regard to cheating on a test. After all the participants (16 male college students) were accused of cheating, they were told they would have to go before the department ethics committee, and if the committee determined the subject had cheated, his final grade in the class would be dropped. However, the subjects were told that if they admitted guilt, the experimenter would be willing to drop the matter and forgo the referral to the committee. Of the eight innocent subjects, none accepted the deal. In comparison, six of the eight guilty subjects admitted to cheating. For a more recent study with similar findings, *see* Melissa Russano, Christian A. Meissner, Fadia M. Narchet & Saul M. Kassin, "Investigating True and False Confessions within a Novel Experimental Paradigm," 16 *Psychological Science* 481 (2005). Unlike Gregory *et al.*, Russano and colleagues found that the offered deal alone was sufficient to induce some (14%) of the innocent subjects to admit guilt.

Additionally, Tor and colleagues examined the impact of substantive and comparative fairness-related concerns on young adults' (college and law students) willingness to plead guilty when guilty and innocent.[34] Across four studies, Tor *et al.* found that participants asked to imagine that they were innocent of a mock crime demonstrated increased risk seeking (in that they were willing to take their chances at trial and not accept pleas) compared to those asked to imagine they were guilty. However, when the probability of conviction was high—95%—innocent and guilty participants displayed risk neutrality (and had comparable plea acceptance rates). Tor *et al.* reasoned that innocents prefer risk because they perceive the choice between plea and trial (two negative outcomes) to be substantively unfair. Tor *et al.* also tested the notion of comparative fairness by manipulating whether the sentence associated with a plea was shorter than, similar to, or longer than sentences typically offered by the prosecutor. They found that, despite the value of the sentence being fixed, those who were offered the comparatively "worse" and "similar" deals were significantly less likely to plead guilty than those offered the "better" deal, a pattern that emerged for both guilty and innocent participants. Thus, in general, research has supported the anecdotal contention that innocent persons will plead guilty under certain conditions.

2. Knowing, Intelligent, and Voluntary Pleas

Defendants who plead guilty relinquish several fundamental constitutional rights, including the right to remain silent while the government is put to its burden of proving guilt beyond a reasonable doubt, the right to trial by jury, and to confront and cross-examine adverse witnesses. To safeguard those rights, it is important that defendants who enter guilty pleas do so in a "knowing, intelligent, and voluntary" fashion. We explore the meaning of those terms, as construed by the courts, in the rules and cases that follow.

In *Boykin v. Alabama*, 395 U.S. 238, 89 S.Ct. 1709, 23 L.Ed.2d 274 (1969), the defendant, an indigent "27-year-old Negro" who was represented by court-appointed counsel, pled guilty to five counts of common law robbery, a crime then punishable by death in Alabama. "So far as the record shows, the judge asked no questions of [the defendant] concerning his plea" before accepting it. A jury thereupon sentenced Boykin to death and the Alabama Supreme Court affirmed the conviction and death sentence on appeal. The United States Supreme Court reversed in an opinion written by Justice Douglas.

It was error, plain on the face of the record, for the trial judge to accept petitioner's guilty plea without an affirmative showing that it was intelligent and voluntary....

A plea of guilty is more than a confession which admits that the accused did various acts; it is itself a conviction; nothing remains but to give judgment and determine punishment. Admissibility of a confession must be based on a "reliable determination on the voluntariness issue which satisfies the constitutional rights of the defendant." Jackson v. Denno, 378 U.S. 368, 387 [(1964)]. The requirement that the prosecution spread on the record the prerequisites of a valid waiver is no constitutional innovation. In Carnley v. Cochran, 369 U.S. 506, 516 [(1962)] we dealt with a problem of waiver of the right to counsel, a Sixth Amendment right. We held: "Presuming waiver from a silent record is impermissible. The record must show, or there must be an allegation and evidence which show, that an accused was offered counsel but intelligently and understandingly rejected the offer. Anything less is not waiver."

We think that the same standard must be applied to determining whether a guilty plea is voluntarily made. For, as we have said, a plea of guilty is more than an admission of conduct; it is a conviction. Ignorance, incomprehension, coercion, terror, inducements, subtle or blatant threats might be a perfect cover-up of unconstitutionality. The question of an effective waiver of a federal constitutional right in a proceeding is of course governed by federal standards.

Several federal constitutional rights are involved in a waiver that takes place when a plea of guilty is entered in a state criminal trial. First, is the privilege against compulsory self-incrimination guaranteed by the Fifth Amendment and applicable to the States by reason of the Fourteenth. Second, is the right to trial by jury. Third, is the right to confront one's accusers. We cannot presume a waiver of these three important federal rights from a silent record.

What is at stake for an accused facing death or imprisonment demands the utmost solicitude of which courts are capable in canvassing the matter with the accused to make sure he has a full understanding of what the plea connotes and of its consequence. When the judge discharges that function, he leaves a record adequate for any review that may be later sought and forestalls the spin-off of collateral proceedings that seek to probe murky memories.

The three dissenting justices in the Alabama Supreme Court stated the law accurately when they concluded that there was reversible error "because the record does not disclose that the defendant voluntarily and understandingly entered his pleas of guilty." ...

Federal Rule of Criminal Procedure 11 governs the entry of guilty pleas in federal court and includes provisions designed to ensure that a defendant's guilty plea (or plea of nolo contendere, or "no contest") is knowing, intelligent, and voluntary. Most states follow similar procedures. The federal rule provides:

Rule 11. Pleas

(a) **Entering a Plea.**

(1) **In General.** A defendant may plead not guilty, guilty, or (with the court's consent) nolo contendere.

(2) **Conditional Plea.** With the consent of the court and the government, a defendant may enter a conditional plea of guilty or nolo contendere, reserving in writing the right to have an appellate court review an adverse determination of a specified pretrial motion. A defendant who prevails on appeal may then withdraw the plea.

(3) **Nolo Contendere Plea.** Before accepting a plea of nolo contendere, the court must consider the parties' views and the public interest in the effective administration of justice.

(4) **Failure to Enter a Plea.** If a defendant refuses to enter a plea or if a defendant organization fails to appear, the court must enter a plea of not guilty.

(b) **Considering and Accepting a Guilty or Nolo Contendere Plea.**

(1) **Advising and Questioning the Defendant.** Before the court accepts a plea of guilty or nolo contendere, the defendant may be placed under oath, and the court must address the defendant personally in open court. During this address, the court must inform the defendant of, and determine that the defendant understands, the following:

(A) the government's right, in a prosecution for perjury or false statement, to use against the defendant any statement that the defendant gives under oath;

(B) the right to plead not guilty, or having already so pleaded, to persist in that plea;

(C) the right to a jury trial;

(D) the right to be represented by counsel—and if necessary have the court appoint counsel—at trial and at every other stage of the proceeding;

(E) the right at trial to confront and cross-examine adverse witnesses, to be protected from compelled self-incrimination, to testify and present evidence, and to compel the attendance of witnesses;

(F) the defendant's waiver of these trial rights if the court accepts a plea of guilty or nolo contendere;

(G) the nature of each charge to which the defendant is pleading;

(H) any maximum possible penalty, including imprisonment, fine, and term of supervised release;

(I) any mandatory minimum penalty;

(J) any applicable forfeiture;

(K) the court's authority to order restitution;

(L) the court's obligation to impose a special assessment;

(M) in determining a sentence, the court's obligation to calculate the applicable sentencing-guideline range and to consider that range, possible departures under the Sentencing Guidelines, and other sentencing factors under 18 U.S.C. § 3553(a); and

(N) the terms of any plea-agreement provision waiving the right to appeal or to collaterally attack the sentence.

(2) **Ensuring That a Plea Is Voluntary.** Before accepting a plea of guilty or nolo contendere, the court must address the defendant personally in open court and determine that the plea is voluntary and did not result from force, threats, or promises (other than promises in a plea agreement).

(3) **Determining the Factual Basis for a Plea.** Before entering judgment on a guilty plea, the court must determine that there is a factual basis for the plea.

(c) **Plea Agreement Procedure.**

(1) **In General.** An attorney for the government and the defendant's attorney, or the defendant when proceeding pro se, may discuss and reach a plea agreement. The court must not participate in these discussions. If the defendant pleads guilty or nolo contendere to either a charged offense or a lesser or related offense, the plea agreement may specify that an attorney for the government will:

(A) not bring, or will move to dismiss, other charges;

(B) recommend, or agree not to oppose the defendant's request, that a particular sentence or sentencing range is appropriate or that a particular provision of the Sentencing Guidelines, or policy statement, or sentencing factor does or does not apply (such a recommendation or request does not bind the court); or

(C) agree that a specific sentence or sentencing range is the appropriate disposition of the case, or that a particular provision of the Sentencing Guidelines, or policy statement, or sentencing factor does or does not apply (such a recommendation or request binds the court once the court accepts the plea agreement).

(2) **Disclosing a Plea Agreement.** The parties must disclose the plea agreement in open court when the plea is offered, unless the court for good cause allows the parties to disclose the plea agreement in camera.

(3) **Judicial Consideration of a Plea Agreement.**

(**A**) To the extent the plea agreement is of the type specified in Rule 11(c)(1)(A) or (C), the court may accept the agreement, reject it, or defer a decision until the court has reviewed the presentence report.

(**B**) To the extent the plea agreement is of the type specified in Rule 11(c)(1)(B), the court must advise the defendant that the defendant has no right to withdraw the plea if the court does not follow the recommendation or request.

(4) **Accepting a Plea Agreement.** If the court accepts the plea agreement, it must inform the defendant that to the extent the plea agreement is of the type specified in Rule 11(c)(1)(A) or (C), the agreed disposition will be included in the judgment.

(5) **Rejecting a Plea Agreement.** If the court rejects a plea agreement containing provisions of the type specified in Rule 11(c)(1)(A) or (C), the court must do the following on the record and in open court (or, for good cause, in camera):

(**A**) inform the parties that the court rejects the plea agreement;

(**B**) advise the defendant personally that the court is not required to follow the plea agreement and give the defendant an opportunity to withdraw the plea; and

(**C**) advise the defendant personally that if the plea is not withdrawn, the court may dispose of the case less favorably toward the defendant than the plea agreement contemplated.

(**d**) **Withdrawing a Guilty or Nolo Contendere Plea.** A defendant may withdraw a plea of guilty or nolo contendere:

(1) before the court accepts the plea, for any reason or no reason; or

(2) after the court accepts the plea, but before it imposes sentence if:

(**A**) the court rejects a plea agreement under Rule 11(c)(5); or

(**B**) the defendant can show a fair and just reason for requesting the withdrawal.

(**e**) **Finality of a Guilty or Nolo Contendere Plea.** After the court imposes sentence, the defendant may not withdraw a plea of guilty or nolo contendere, and the plea may be set aside only on direct appeal or collateral attack.

(**f**) **Admissibility or Inadmissibility of a Plea, Plea Discussions, and Related Statements.** The admissibility or inadmissibility of a plea, a plea discussion, and any related statement is governed by Federal Rule of Evidence 410.

(**g**) **Recording the Proceedings.** The proceedings during which the defendant enters a plea must be recorded by a court reporter or by a suitable recording device. If there is a guilty plea or a nolo contendere plea, the record must include the inquiries and advice to the defendant required under Rule 11(b) and (c).

(**h**) **Harmless Error.** A variance from the requirements of this rule is harmless error if it does not affect substantial rights.

Note that F.R.Crim.Pro. 11(b)(2) requires the trial judge to determine that the defendant's plea of guilty or nolo contendere "is voluntary and did not result from force, threats, or promises (other than promises in a plea agreement)." Recall also that Judge Weinstein discussed the concept and various possible meanings of "voluntariness" at some length in his opinion in *Speed Joyeros*. The Supreme Court has considered the voluntariness requirement in the context of guilty pleas in several important cases.

Brady v. United States

397 U.S. 742, 90 S.Ct. 1463, 25 L.Ed.2d 747 (1970)

Mr. Justice WHITE delivered the opinion of the Court.

In 1959, petitioner was charged with kidnaping in violation of 18 U.S.C. s 1201(a). Since the indictment charged that the victim of the kidnaping was not liberated unharmed, petitioner faced a maximum penalty of death if the verdict of the jury should so recommend. Petitioner, represented by competent counsel throughout, first elected to plead not guilty. Apparently because the trial judge was unwilling to try the case without a jury, petitioner made no serious attempt to reduce the possibility of a death penalty by waiving a jury trial. Upon learning that his codefendant, who had confessed to the authorities, would plead guilty and be available to testify against him, petitioner changed his plea to guilty. His plea was accepted after the trial judge twice questioned him as to the voluntariness of his plea.[2] Petitioner was sentenced to 50 years' imprisonment, later reduced to 30.

In 1967, petitioner sought relief under 28 U.S.C. § 2255, claiming that his plea of guilty was not voluntarily given because § 1201(a) operated to coerce his plea, because his counsel exerted impermissible pressure upon him, and because his plea was induced by representations with respect to reduction of sentence and clemency. It was also alleged that the trial judge had not fully complied with Rule 11 of the Federal Rules of Criminal Procedure.[3]

After a hearing, the District Court for the District of New Mexico denied relief. According to the District Court's findings, petitioner's counsel did not put impermissible pressure on petitioner to plead guilty and no representations were made with respect to a reduced sentence or clemency. The court held that § 1201(a) was constitutional and found that petitioner decided to plead guilty when he learned that his codefendant was going to plead guilty: petitioner pleaded guilty 'by reason of other matters and not by reason of the statute' or because of any acts of the trial judge. The court concluded that 'the plea was voluntarily and knowingly made.'

The Court of Appeals for the Tenth Circuit affirmed.... We granted certiorari to consider the claim that the Court of Appeals was in error in not reaching a contrary result on the authority

---

2. Eight days after petitioner pleaded guilty, he was brought before the court for sentencing. At that time, the court questioned petitioner for a second time about the voluntariness of his plea:

> 'THE COURT: * * * Having read the presentence report and the statement you made to the probation officer, I want to be certain that you know what you are doing and you did know when you entered a plea of guilty the other day. Do you want to let that plea of guilty stand, or do you want to withdraw it and plead not guilty?
> 'DEFENDANT BRADY: I want to let that plea stand, sir.
> 'THE COURT: You understand that in doing that you are admitting and confessing the truth of the charge contained in the indictment and that you enter a plea of guilty voluntarily, without persuasion, coercion of any kind? Is that right?
> 'DEFENDANT BRADY: Yes, your Honor.
> 'THE COURT: And you do do that?
> 'DEFENDANT BRADY: Yes, I do.
> 'THE COURT: You plead guilty to the charge?
> 'DEFENDANT BRADY: Yes, I do.'

3. ... Rule 11 was amended in 1966 and now reads as follows:

> 'A defendant may plead not guilty, guilty or, with the consent of the court, nolo contendere. The court may refuse to accept a plea of guilty, and shall not accept such plea or a plea of nolo contendere without first addressing the defendant personally and determining that the plea is made voluntarily with understanding of the nature of the charge and the consequences of the plea.... The court shall not enter a judgment upon a plea of guilty unless it is satisfied that there is a factual basis for the plea.'

In McCarthy v. United States, 394 U.S. 459 (1969), we held that a failure to comply with Rule 11 required that a defendant who had pleaded guilty be allowed to plead anew. In Halliday v. United States, 394 U.S. 831 (1969), we held that the McCarthy rule should apply only in cases where the guilty plea was accepted after April 2, 1969, the date of the McCarthy decision.

of this Court's decision in United States v. Jackson, 390 U.S. 570 (1968). We affirm.

I

In United States v. Jackson, the defendants were indicted under § 1201(a). The District Court dismissed the § 1201(a) count of the indictment, holding the statute unconstitutional because it permitted imposition of the death sentence only upon a jury's recommendation and thereby made the risk of death the price of a jury trial. This Court held the statute valid, except for the death penalty provision; with respect to the latter, the Court agreed with the trial court 'that the death penalty provision * * * imposes an impermissible burden upon the exercise of a constitutional right * * *.' The problem was to determine 'whether the Constitution permits the establishment of such a death penalty, applicable only to those defendants who assert the right to contest their guilt before a jury.' The inevitable effect of the provision was said to be to discourage assertion of the Fifth Amendment right not to plead guilty and to deter exercise of the Sixth Amendment right to demand a jury trial. Because the legitimate goal of limiting the death penalty to cases in which a jury recommends it could be achieved without penalizing those defendants who plead not guilty and elect a jury trial, the death penalty provision 'needlessly penalize(d) the assertion of a constitutional right,' and was therefore unconstitutional.

Since the 'inevitable effect' of the death penalty provision of § 1201(a) was said by the Court to be the needless encouragement of pleas of guilty and waivers of jury trial, Brady contends that Jackson requires the invalidation of every plea of guilty entered under that section, at least when the fear of death is shown to have been a factor in the plea. Petitioner, however, has read far too much into the Jackson opinion.

The Court made it clear in Jackson that it was not holding § 1201(a) inherently coercive of guilty pleas: 'the fact that the Federal Kidnaping Act tends to discourage defendants from insisting upon their innocence and demanding trial by jury hardly implies that every defendant who enters a guilty plea to a charge under the Act does so involuntarily.'...

Moreover, the Court in Jackson rejected a suggestion that the death penalty provision of § 1201(a) be saved by prohibiting in capital kidnaping cases all guilty pleas and jury waivers, 'however clear (the defendants') guilt and however strong their desire to acknowledge it in order to spare themselves and their families the spectacle and expense of protracted courtroom proceedings.' '(T)hat jury waivers and guilty pleas may occasionally be rejected' was no ground for automatically rejecting all guilty pleas under the statute, for such a rule 'would rob the criminal process of much of its flexibility.'

Plainly, it seems to us, Jackson ruled neither that all pleas of guilty encouraged by the fear of a possible death sentence are involuntary pleas nor that such encouraged pleas are invalid whether involuntary or not. Jackson prohibits the imposition of the death penalty under § 1201(a), but that decision neither fashioned a new standard for judging the validity of guilty pleas nor mandated a new application of the test theretofore fashioned by courts and since reiterated that guilty pleas are valid if both 'voluntary' and 'intelligent.' See Boykin v. Alabama, 395 U.S. 238, 242 (1969).[4]

That a guilty plea is a grave and solemn act to be accepted only with care and discernment has long been recognized. Central to the plea and the foundation for entering judgment against the defendant is the defendant's admission in open court that he committed the acts charged in the indictment. He thus stands as a witness against himself and he is shielded by the Fifth Amendment from being compelled to do so—hence the minimum requirement that his plea be the voluntary expression of his own choice. But the plea is more than an admission of past conduct; it is the defendant's consent that judgment of conviction may be entered without a trial—a waiver of his right to trial before a jury or a judge. Waivers of constitutional rights not only must be voluntary but must be knowing, intelligent acts done with sufficient awareness of the relevant circumstances and likely consequences. On neither score was Brady's plea of guilty invalid.

II

The trial judge in 1959 found the plea voluntary before accepting it; the District Court in 1968, after an evidentiary hearing, found that the plea was voluntarily made; the Court of Ap-

4. The requirement that a plea of guilty must be intelligent and voluntary to be valid has long been recognized. The new element added in Boykin was the requirement that the record must affirmatively disclose that a defendant who pleaded guilty entered his plea understandingly and voluntarily....

peals specifically approved the finding of voluntariness. We see no reason on this record to disturb the judgment of those courts. Petitioner, advised by competent counsel, tendered his plea after his codefendant, who had already given a confession, determined to plead guilty and became available to testify against petitioner. It was this development that the District Court found to have triggered Brady's guilty plea.

The voluntariness of Brady's plea can be determined only by considering all of the relevant circumstances surrounding it. One of these circumstances was the possibility of a heavier sentence following a guilty verdict after a trial. It may be that Brady, faced with a strong case against him and recognizing that his chances for acquittal were slight, preferred to plead guilty and thus limit the penalty to life imprisonment rather than to elect a jury trial which could result in a death penalty. But even if we assume that Brady would not have pleaded guilty except for the death penalty provision of § 1201(a), this assumption merely identifies the penalty provision as a 'but for' cause of his plea. That the statute caused the plea in this sense does not necessarily prove that the plea was coerced and invalid as an involuntary act.

The State to some degree encourages pleas of guilty at every important step in the criminal process. For some people, their breach of a State's law is alone sufficient reason for surrendering themselves and accepting punishment. For others, apprehension and charge, both threatening acts by the Government, jar them into admitting their guilt. In still other cases, the post-indictment accumulation of evidence may convince the defendant and his counsel that a trial is not worth the agony and expense to the defendant and his family. All these pleas of guilty are valid in spite of the State's responsibility for some of the factors motivating the pleas; the pleas are no more improperly compelled than is the decision by a defendant at the close of the State's evidence at trial that he must take the stand or face certain conviction.

Of course, the agents of the State may not produce a plea by actual or threatened physical harm or by mental coercion overbearing the will of the defendant. But nothing of the sort is claimed in this case; nor is there evidence that Brady was so gripped by fear of the death penalty or hope of leniency that he did not or could not, with the help of counsel, rationally weigh the advantages of going to trial against the advantages of pleading guilty. Brady's claim is of a different sort: that it violates the Fifth Amendment to influence or encourage a guilty plea by opportunity or promise of leniency and that a guilty plea is coerced and invalid if influenced by the fear of a possibly higher penalty for the crime charged if a conviction is obtained after the State is put to its proof.

Insofar as the voluntariness of his plea is concerned, there is little to differentiate Brady from (1) the defendant, in a jurisdiction where the judge and jury have the same range of sentencing power, who pleads guilty because his lawyer advises him that the judge will very probably be more lenient than the jury; (2) the defendant, in a jurisdiction where the judge alone has sentencing power, who is advised by counsel that the judge is normally more lenient with defendants who plead guilty than with those who go to trial; (3) the defendant who is permitted by prosecutor and judge to plead guilty to a lesser offense included in the offense charged; and (4) the defendant who pleads guilty to certain counts with the understanding that other charges will be dropped. In each of these situations,[8] as in Brady's case, the defendant might never plead guilty absent the possibility or certainty that the plea will result in a lesser penalty than the sentence that could be imposed after a trial and a verdict of guilty. We decline to hold, however, that a guilty plea is compelled and invalid under the Fifth Amendment whenever motivated by the defendant's desire to accept the certainty or probability of a lesser penalty rather than face a wider range of possibilities extending from acquittal to conviction and a higher penalty authorized by law for the crime charged.

The issue we deal with is inherent in the criminal law and its administration because guilty pleas are not constitutionally forbidden, because

8. We here make no reference to the situation where the prosecutor or judge, or both, deliberately employ their charging and sentencing powers to induce a particular defendant to tender a plea of guilty. In Brady's case there is no claim that the prosecutor threatened prosecution on a charge not justified by the evidence or that the trial judge threatened Brady with a harsher sentence if convicted after trial in order to induce him to plead guilty.

the criminal law characteristically extends to judge or jury a range of choice in setting the sentence in individual cases, and because both the State and the defendant often find it advantageous to preclude the possibility of the maximum penalty authorized by law. For a defendant who sees slight possibility of acquittal, the advantages of pleading guilty and limiting the probable penalty are obvious—his exposure is reduced, the correctional processes can begin immediately, and the practical burdens of a trial are eliminated. For the State there are also advantages—the more promptly imposed punishment after an admission of guilt may more effectively attain the objectives of punishment; and with the avoidance of trial, scarce judicial and prosecutorial resources are conserved for those cases in which there is a substantial issue of the defendant's guilt or in which there is substantial doubt that the State can sustain its burden of proof. It is this mutuality of advantage that perhaps explains the fact that at present well over three-fourths of the criminal convictions in this country rest on pleas of guilty,[10] a great many of them no doubt motivated at least in part by the hope or assurance of a lesser penalty than might be imposed if there were a guilty verdict after a trial to judge or jury.

Of course, that the prevalence of guilty pleas is explainable does not necessarily validate those pleas or the system which produces them. But we cannot hold that it is unconstitutional for the State to extend a benefit to a defendant who in turn extends a substantial benefit to the State and who demonstrates by his plea that he is ready and willing to admit his crime and to enter the correctional system in a frame of mind that affords hope for success in rehabilitation over a shorter period of time than might otherwise be necessary.

A contrary holding would require the States and Federal Government to forbid guilty pleas altogether, to provide a single invariable penalty for each crime defined by the statutes, or to place the sentencing function in a separate authority having no knowledge of the manner in which the conviction in each case was obtained. In any event, it would be necessary to forbid prosecutors and judges to accept guilty pleas to selected counts, to lesser included offenses, or to reduced charges. The Fifth Amendment does not reach so far....

Bram [v. United States, 168 U.S. 532 (1897)] is not inconsistent with our holding....

... Brady first pleaded not guilty; prior to changing his plea to guilty he was subjected to no threats or promises in face-to-face encounters with the authorities. He had competent counsel and full opportunity to assess the advantages and disadvantages of a trial as compared with those attending a plea of guilty; there was no hazard of an impulsive and improvident response to a seeming but unreal advantage. His plea of guilty was entered in open court and before a judge obviously sensitive to the requirements of the law with respect to guilty pleas. Brady's plea ... was voluntary.

The standard as to the voluntariness of guilty pleas must be essentially that defined by Judge Tuttle of the Court of Appeals for the Fifth Circuit:

"(A) plea of guilty entered by one fully aware of the direct consequences, including the actual value of any commitments made to him by the court, prosecutor, or his own counsel, must stand unless induced by threats (or promises to discontinue improper harassment), misrepresentation (including unfulfilled or unfulfillable promises), or perhaps by promises that are by their nature improper as having no proper relationship to the prosecutor's business (e.g. bribes)." [*Shelton v. United States,* 242 F.2d 101, 115 (5th Cir. 1957) (dissenting opinion), *judgment set aside,* 246 F.2d 571 (5th Cir. 1957), *reversed,* 356 U.S. 26 (1958)].

Under this standard, a plea of guilty is not invalid merely because entered to avoid the possibility of a death penalty.

III

The record before us also supports the conclusion that Brady's plea was intelligently made. He was advised by competent counsel, he was made aware of the nature of the charge against him, and there was nothing to indicate that he was incompetent or otherwise not in control of his mental faculties; once his confederate had pleaded guilty and became available to testify, he chose to plead guilty, perhaps to ensure that he would face no more than life imprisonment or a term of years. Brady was aware of precisely

10. It has been estimated that about 90%, and perhaps 95%, of all criminal convictions are by pleas of guilty; between 70% and 85% of all felony convictions are estimated to be by guilty plea. D. Newman, Conviction, The Determination of Guilt or Innocence Without Trial 3 and n. 1 (1966).

what he was doing when he admitted that he had kidnaped the victim and had not released her unharmed.

It is true that Brady's counsel advised him that § 1201(a) empowered the jury to impose the death penalty and that nine years later in United States v. Jackson, the Court held that the jury had no such power as long as the judge could impose only a lesser penalty if trial was to the court or there was a plea of guilty. But these facts do not require us to set aside Brady's conviction.

Often the decision to plead guilty is heavily influenced by the defendant's appraisal of the prosecution's case against him and by the apparent likelihood of securing leniency should a guilty plea be offered and accepted. Considerations like these frequently present imponderable questions for which there are no certain answers; judgments may be made that in the light of later events seem improvident, although they were perfectly sensible at the time. The rule that a plea must be intelligently made to be valid does not require that a plea be vulnerable to later attack if the defendant did not correctly assess every relevant factor entering into his decision. A defendant is not entitled to withdraw his plea merely because he discovers long after the plea has been accepted that his calculus misapprehended the quality of the State's case or the likely penalties attached to alternative courses of action. More particularly, absent misrepresentation or other impermissible conduct by state agents, a voluntary plea of guilty intelligently made in the light of the then applicable law does not become vulnerable because later judicial decisions indicate that the plea rested on a faulty premise. A plea of guilty triggered by the expectations of a competently counseled defendant that the State will have a strong case against him is not subject to later attack because the defendant's lawyer correctly advised him with respect to the then existing law as to possible penalties but later pronouncements of the courts, as in this case, hold that the maximum penalty for the crime in question was less than was reasonably assumed at the time the plea was entered.

The fact that Brady did not anticipate United States v. Jackson, supra, does not impugn the truth or reliability of his plea. We find no requirement in the Constitution that a defendant must be permitted to disown his solemn admissions in open court that he committed the act with which he is charged simply because it later develops that the State would have had a weaker case than the defendant had thought or that the maximum penalty then assumed applicable has been held inapplicable in subsequent judicial decisions.

This is not to say that guilty plea convictions hold no hazards for the innocent or that the methods of taking guilty pleas presently employed in this country are necessarily valid in all respects. This mode of conviction is no more foolproof than full trials to the court or to the jury. Accordingly, we take great precautions against unsound results, and we should continue to do so, whether conviction is by plea or by trial. We would have serious doubts about this case if the encouragement of guilty pleas by offers of leniency substantially increased the likelihood that defendants, advised by competent counsel, would falsely condemn themselves. But our view is to the contrary and is based on our expectations that courts will satisfy themselves that pleas of guilty are voluntarily and intelligently made by competent defendants with adequate advice of counsel and that there is nothing to question the accuracy and reliability of the defendants' admissions that they committed the crimes with which they are charged. In the case before us, nothing in the record impeaches Brady's plea or suggests that his admissions in open court were anything but the truth.

Although Brady's plea of guilty may well have been motivated in part by a desire to avoid a possible death penalty, we are convinced that his plea was voluntarily and intelligently made and we have no reason to doubt that his solemn admission of guilt was truthful.

Affirmed....

On the same day the Supreme Court decided *Brady v. United States*, it affirmed the voluntariness of a guilty plea entered under similar circumstances (in that it was motivated, in part, to avoid the risk of a capital sentence), in *Parker v. North Carolina*, 397 U.S. 790, 90 S.Ct. 1458, 25 L.Ed.2d 785 (1970). We present relevant portions of Justice Brennan's opinion in these cases below.

Mr. Justice BRENNAN, with whom Mr. Justice DOUGLAS and Mr. Justice MARSHALL join, dissenting in [Parker v. North Carolina] and concurring in the result in [Brady v. United States]....

I

The Court properly notes the grave consequences for a defendant that attach to his plea of guilty; for the plea constitutes a simultaneous surrender of numerous constitutional rights, including the privilege against compulsory self-incrimination and the right to a trial by jury, with all of its attendant safeguards. Indeed, we have pointed out that a guilty plea is more serious than a confession because it is tantamount to a conviction. Accordingly, we have insisted that a guilty plea, like any surrender of fundamental constitutional rights, reflect the unfettered choice of the defendant. In deciding whether any illicit pressures have been brought to bear on a defendant to induce a guilty plea, courts have traditionally inquired whether it was made 'voluntarily' and 'intelligently' with full understanding and appreciation of the consequences.

The concept of 'voluntariness' contains an ambiguous element, accentuated by the Court's opinions in these cases, because the concept has been employed to analyze a variety of pressures to surrender constitutional rights, which are not all equally coercive or obvious in their coercive effect. In some cases where an 'involuntary' surrender has been found, the physical or psychological tactics employed exerted so great an influence upon the accused that it could accurately be said that his will was literally overborne or completely dominated by his interrogators, who rendered him incapable of rationally weighing the legal alternatives open to him.

There is some intimation in the Court's opinions in the instant cases that, at least with respect to guilty pleas, 'involuntariness' covers only the narrow class of cases in which the defendant's will has been literally overborne. At other points, however, the Court apparently recognizes that the term 'involuntary' has traditionally been applied to situations in which an individual, while perfectly capable of rational choice, has been confronted with factors that the government may not constitutionally inject into the decision-making process. For example, in Garrity v. New Jersey, 385 U.S. 493 (1967), we held a surrender of the self-incrimination privilege to be involuntary when an individual was presented by the government with the possibility of discharge from his employment if he invoked the privilege. So, also, it has long been held that certain promises of leniency or threats of harsh treatment by the trial judge or the prosecutor unfairly burden or intrude upon the defendant's decision-making process. Even though the defendant is not necessarily rendered incapable of rational choice, his guilty plea nonetheless may be invalid.

Thus the legal concept of 'involuntariness' has not been narrowly confined but refers to a surrender of constitutional rights influenced by considerations that the government cannot properly introduce. The critical question that divides the Court is what constitutes an impermissible factor, or, more narrowly in the context of these cases, whether the threat of the imposition of an unconstitutional death penalty is such a factor.

Even after the various meanings of 'involuntary' have been identified, application of voluntariness criteria in particular circumstances remains an elusory process because it entails judicial evaluation of the effect of particular external stimuli upon the state of mind of the accused....

... Of course, the presence of counsel is a factor to be taken into account in any overall evaluation of the voluntariness of a confession or a guilty plea. However, it hardly follows that the support provided by counsel is sufficient by itself to insulate the accused from the effect of any threat or promise by the government.

It has frequently been held, for example, that a guilty plea induced by threats or promises by the trial judge is invalid because of the risk that the trial judge's impartiality will be compromised and because of the inherently unequal bargaining power of the judge and the accused. The assistance of counsel in this situation, of course, may improve a defendant's bargaining ability, but it does not alter the underlying inequality of power.... Here, the government has promised the accused, through the legislature, that he will receive a substantially reduced sentence if he pleads guilty. In fact, the legislature has simultaneously threatened the accused with the ultimate penalty—death—if he insists upon a jury trial and has promised a penalty no greater than life imprisonment if he pleads guilty.

It was precisely this statutorily imposed dilemma that we identified in Jackson as having the 'inevitable effect' of discouraging assertion of the right not to plead guilty and to demand a jury trial. As recognized in Jackson, it is inconceivable that this sort of capital penalty scheme will not have a major impact upon the decisions of many defendants to plead guilty. In any particular case, therefore, the influence of this unconstitutional factor must necessarily be given weight in determining the voluntariness of a plea.

To be sure, we said in Jackson that 'the fact that the Federal Kidnapping Act tends to discourage defendants from insisting upon their innocence and demanding trial by jury hardly implied that every defendant who enters a guilty plea to a charge under the Act does so involuntarily.' ... But that statement merely emphasized the obvious fact that it is perfectly possible that a defendant pleaded guilty for reasons entirely unrelated to the penalty scheme, for example, because his guilt was clear or because he desired to spare himself and his family 'the spectacle and expense of protracted courtroom proceedings.' The converse, however, is equally clear: not every defendant who pleaded guilty under the Act did so voluntarily, that is, uninfluenced by the highly coercive character of the penalty scheme. This much is merely the teaching of Jackson.

... Today the Court appears to distinguish sharply between a guilty plea that has been 'encouraged' by the penalty scheme and one that has been entered 'involuntarily.' However, if the influence of the penalty scheme can never render a plea involuntary, it is difficult to understand why in Jackson we took the extraordinary step of invalidating part of that scheme....

Of course, whether in a given case the penalty scheme has actually exercised its pernicious influence so as to make a guilty plea involuntary can be decided only by consideration of the factors that actually motivated the defendant to enter his plea. If a particular defendant can demonstrate that the death penalty scheme exercised a significant influence upon his decision to plead guilty, then, under Jackson, he is entitled to reversal of the conviction based upon his illicitly produced plea.

The Court attempts to submerge the issue of voluntariness of a plea under an unconstitutional capital punishment scheme in a general discussion of the pressures upon defendants to plead guilty which are said to arise from, inter alia, the venerable institution of plea bargaining. The argument appears to reduce to this: because the accused cannot be insulated from all inducements to plead guilty, it follows that he should be shielded from none.

The principal flaw in the Court's discourse on plea bargaining, however, is that it is, at best, only marginally relevant to the precise issues before us. There are critical distinctions between plea bargaining as commonly practiced and the situation presently under consideration—distinctions which, in constitutional terms, make a difference. Thus, whatever the merit, if any, of the constitutional objections to plea bargaining generally, those issues are not presently before us.

We are dealing here with the legislative imposition of a markedly more severe penalty if a defendant asserts his right to a jury trial and a concomitant legislative promise of leniency if he pleads guilty. This is very different from the give-and-take negotiation common in plea bargaining between the prosecution and defense, which arguably possess relatively equal bargaining power. No such flexibility is built into the capital penalty scheme where the government's harsh terms with respect to punishment are stated in unalterable form.

Furthermore, the legislatively ordained penalty scheme may affect any defendant, even one with respect to whom plea bargaining is wholly inappropriate because his guilt is uncertain. Thus the penalty scheme presents a clear danger that the innocent, or those not clearly guilty, or those who insist upon their innocence, will be induced nevertheless to plead guilty. This hazard necessitates particularly sensitive scrutiny of the voluntariness of guilty pleas entered under this type of death penalty scheme.

The penalty schemes involved here are also distinguishable from most plea bargaining because they involve the imposition of death—the most severe and awesome penalty known to our law. This Court has recognized that capital cases are treated differently in some respects from noncapital cases....

III

... An independent examination of the record in the instant case convinces me that the conclusions of the lower courts are not clearly erroneous. Although Brady was aware that he faced a possible death sentence, there is no evidence that this factor alone played a significant role in his decision to enter a guilty plea. Rather, there is considerable evidence, which the District Court credited, that Brady's plea was triggered by the confession and plea decision of his codefendant and not by any substantial fear of the death penalty. Moreover, Brady's position is dependent in large measure upon his own assertions, years after the fact, that his plea was motivated by fear of the death penalty and thus rests largely upon his own credibility. For example, there is no indication, contemporaneous with the entry of the guilty plea, that Brady thought he was innocent and was pleading guilty merely to avoid possible execution. Furthermore, Brady's plea was accepted by a trial judge who manifested some sensitivity to the seriousness of a guilty plea and questioned Brady at length concerning his guilt and the voluntariness of the plea before it was finally accepted.

In view of the foregoing. I concur in the result reached by the Court in the Brady case.

Notes and Questions

1. Is it possible to reconcile *United States v. Jackson,* 390 U.S. 570, 88 S.Ct. 1209, 20 L.Ed.2d 138 (1968) and *Brady v. United States*? If the federal kidnapping statute, 18 U.S.C. § 1201(a), was ruled unconstitutional in *Jackson* because only defendants who pled not guilty risked a sentence of death—a scheme characterized by the *Jackson* Court as having "the inevitable effect ... to discourage assertion of the Fifth Amendment right not to plead guilty and to deter exercise of the Sixth Amendment right to demand a jury trial" (390 U.S., at 581)—how could a guilty plea entered by a defendant such as Brady be considered "voluntary"? And if Brady did plead guilty, at least in part, to avoid risking a death sentence and did not know that the statutory scheme in that respect was unconstitutional, how could his guilty plea be considered "intelligent"?

2. *Is* entering a plea of guilty a "voluntary" choice when the defendant knows that the failure to do so—that is, if he or she pleads not guilty and is convicted following a trial—presents a real risk of execution? In October 1988, a 20-year-old woman who worked as the assistant manager of a Pizza Hut in Austin, Texas was raped and murdered in the establishment, and the restaurant was robbed of cash proceeds. A few weeks later, homicide detectives interrogated 22-year-old Christopher Ochoa after he and his friend, Richard Danzinger, asked a security guard at the Pizza Hut several questions about the killing and the guard considered them suspicious.

> According to Ochoa, ... the police interrogated him for more than twelve hours. After asserting that they had convincing evidence of his guilt, the interrogating officers "threatened him with a capital-murder prosecution if he did not cooperate, showing him photos of death row and even pointing out the spot on his left arm where the needle would be inserted." Ochoa said that the detectives also promised him he would not die if he admitted what he had done....
>
> ... So, in response to the interrogators' threats and other tactics, he agreed to a deal. He would avoid the death penalty by pleading guilty to second degree murder and providing "truthful" testimony against Danzinger.[35]

Ochoa did plead guilty to the murder and was sentenced to life imprisonment. He testified against Danzinger, who had denied guilt, at the latter's trial. Danzinger was convicted of rape and was sentenced to 99 years in prison. While serving his sentence, Danzinger was severely beaten by other prisoners, resulting in permanent brain damage. In a series of letters written between 1996 and 1998, a man imprisoned for other crimes, Achim Josef Marino, confessed to having committed the crimes to which Ochoa had confessed and for which Ochoa and Danzinger had been convicted. Marino sent one of those letters to then-Governor George W. Bush, stating:

> Governor Bush, sir, I do not know these men [Ochoa and Danzinger] nor why they would plead guilty to a crime they never committed.... I can only assume

> that they must have been facing a capital murder trial with a poor chance of acquittal, but I tell you this, sir, I did this awful crime and I was alone.[36]

Although Marino's letters prompted no response, DNA testing subsequently excluded Ochoa and Danzinger as the source of the semen found in the victim of the rape-murder. Ochoa's guilty plea was vacated and Danzinger's conviction was overturned in 2001, and they were released from prison. Each had been incarcerated for more than 12 years. Ochoa later graduated from the University of Wisconsin Law School, the site of the Innocence Project that had worked to help free him. Marino subsequently stood trial for and was found guilty, as he had admitted in his letters, of committing the rape-murder for which Ochoa and Danziger had been convicted.[37]

3. Footnote 8 in Justice White's majority opinion in *Brady v. United States* includes the caveat:

> We here make no reference to the situation where the prosecutor or judge, or both, deliberately employ their charging and sentencing powers to induce a particular defendant to tender a plea of guilty. In Brady's case there is no claim that the prosecutor threatened prosecution on a charge not justified by the evidence or that the trial judge threatened Brady with a harsher sentence if convicted after trial in order to induce him to plead guilty.

Does a "threat" to impose a harsher sentence on a defendant who stands trial instead of pleading guilty have to be delivered explicitly to come within the above reservation? Would it suffice to demonstrate that, in practice, more onerous sentences routinely are imposed on defendants who are convicted following trial convictions than after pleading guilty? And what if a prosecutor "deliberately employ[ed]" his or her "charging ... powers to induce a particular defendant to tender a plea of guilty"? Would such a tactic be unconstitutional? Consider the following case.

Bordenkircher v. Hayes

434 U.S. 357, 98 S.Ct. 663, 54 L.Ed.2d 604 (1978)

Mr. Justice STEWART delivered the opinion of the Court.

The question in this case is whether the Due Process Clause of the Fourteenth Amendment is violated when a state prosecutor carries out a threat made during plea negotiations to reindict the accused on more serious charges if he does not plead guilty to the offense with which he was originally charged.

I

The respondent, Paul Lewis Hayes, was indicted by a Fayette County, Ky., grand jury on a charge of uttering a forged instrument in the amount of $88.30, an offense then punishable by a term of 2 to 10 years in prison. After arraignment, Hayes, his retained counsel, and the Commonwealth's Attorney met in the presence of the Clerk of the Court to discuss a possible plea agreement. During these conferences the prosecutor offered to recommend a sentence of five years in prison if Hayes would plead guilty to the indictment. He also said that if Hayes did not plead guilty and "save[d] the court the inconvenience and necessity of a trial," he would return to the grand jury to seek an indictment under the Kentucky Habitual Criminal Act, which would subject Hayes to a mandatory sentence of life imprisonment by reason of his two prior felony convictions.[2] Hayes chose not to plead guilty, and the prosecutor did obtain an indictment charging him under the Habitual Criminal Act. It is not disputed that the recidivist charge

---

2. At the time of Hayes' trial the statute provided that "[a]ny person convicted a ... third time of felony ... shall be confined in the penitentiary during his life." That statute has been replaced by Ky.Rev.Stat. § 532.080 (Supp. 1977) under which Hayes would have been sentenced to, at most, an indeterminate term of 10 to 20 years....

was fully justified by the evidence, that the prosecutor was in possession of this evidence at the time of the original indictment, and that Hayes' refusal to plead guilty to the original charge was what led to his indictment under the habitual criminal statute.

A jury found Hayes guilty on the principal charge of uttering a forged instrument and, in a separate proceeding, further found that he had twice before been convicted of felonies. As required by the habitual offender statute, he was sentenced to a life term in the penitentiary. The Kentucky Court of Appeals rejected Hayes' constitutional objections to the enhanced sentence, holding in an unpublished opinion that imprisonment for life with the possibility of parole was constitutionally permissible in light of the previous felonies of which Hayes had been convicted,[3] and that the prosecutor's decision to indict him as a habitual offender was a legitimate use of available leverage in the plea-bargaining process.

On Hayes' petition for a federal writ of habeas corpus, the United States District Court for the Eastern District of Kentucky agreed that there had been no constitutional violation in the sentence or the indictment procedure, and denied the writ. The Court of Appeals for the Sixth Circuit reversed the District Court's judgment.... We granted certiorari....

II

It may be helpful to clarify at the outset the nature of the issue in this case. While the prosecutor did not actually obtain the recidivist indictment until after the plea conferences had ended, his intention to do so was clearly expressed at the outset of the plea negotiations. Hayes was thus fully informed of the true terms of the offer when he made his decision to plead not guilty. This is not a situation, therefore, where the prosecutor without notice brought an additional and more serious charge after plea negotiations relating only to the original indictment had ended with the defendant's insistence on pleading not guilty. As a practical matter, in short, this case would be no different if the grand jury had indicted Hayes as a recidivist from the outset, and the prosecutor had offered to drop that charge as part of the plea bargain.

The Court of Appeals nonetheless drew a distinction between "concessions relating to prosecution under an existing indictment," and threats to bring more severe charges not contained in the original indictment—a line it thought necessary in order to establish a prophylactic rule to guard against the evil of prosecutorial vindictiveness. Quite apart from this chronological distinction, however, the Court of Appeals found that the prosecutor had acted vindictively in the present case since he had conceded that the indictment was influenced by his desire to induce a guilty plea. The ultimate conclusion of the Court of Appeals thus seems to have been that a prosecutor acts vindictively and in violation of due process of law whenever his charging decision is influenced by what he hopes to gain in the course of plea bargaining negotiations.

III

We have recently had occasion to observe: "[W]hatever might be the situation in an ideal world, the fact is that the guilty plea and the often concomitant plea bargain are important components of this country's criminal justice system. Properly administered, they can benefit all concerned." *Blackledge v. Allison*, 431 U.S. 63, 71. The open acknowledgment of this previously clandestine practice has led this Court to recognize the importance of counsel during plea negotiations, *Brady v. United States*, 397 U.S. 742, the need for a public record indicating that a plea was knowingly and voluntarily made, *Boykin v. Alabama*, 395 U.S. 238, and the requirement that a prosecutor's plea-bargaining promise must be kept, *Santobello v. New York*, 404 U.S. 257. The decision of the Court of Appeals in the present case, however, did not deal with considerations such as these, but held that the substance of the plea offer itself violated the limitations imposed by the Due Process Clause of the Fourteenth Amendment. For the reasons that follow, we have concluded that the Court of Appeals was mistaken in so ruling.

IV

This Court held in *North Carolina v. Pearce*, 395 U.S. 711, that the Due Process Clause of the Fourteenth Amendment "requires that vindictiveness against a defendant for having

3. According to his own testimony, Hayes had pleaded guilty in 1961, when he was 17 years old, to a charge of detaining a female, a lesser included offense of rape, and as a result had served five years in the state reformatory. In 1970 he had been convicted of robbery and sentenced to five years' imprisonment, but had been released on probation immediately.

successfully attacked his first conviction must play no part in the sentence he receives after a new trial." The same principle was later applied to prohibit a prosecutor from reindicting a convicted misdemeanant on a felony charge after the defendant had invoked an appellate remedy, since in this situation there was also a "realistic likelihood of 'vindictiveness.'" *Blackledge v. Perry*, 417 U.S., at 27.

In those cases the Court was dealing with the State's unilateral imposition of a penalty upon a defendant who had chosen to exercise a legal right to attack his original conviction—a situation "very different from the give-and-take negotiation common in plea bargaining between the prosecution and defense, which arguably possess relatively equal bargaining power." *Parker v. North Carolina*, 397 U.S. 790, 809 (opinion of Brennan, J.). The Court has emphasized that the due process violation in cases such as *Pearce* and *Perry* lay not in the possibility that a defendant might be deterred from the exercise of a legal right, but rather in the danger that the State might be retaliating against the accused for lawfully attacking his conviction.

To punish a person because he has done what the law plainly allows him to do is a due process violation of the most basic sort, see *North Carolina v. Pearce,* 395 U.S., at 738, and for an agent of the State to pursue a course of action whose objective is to penalize a person's reliance on his legal rights is "patently unconstitutional." *Chaffin v. Stynchcombe,* 412 U.S., at 32–33, n. 20. See *United States v. Jackson*, 390 U.S. 570. But in the "give-and-take" of plea bargaining, there is no such element of punishment or retaliation so long as the accused is free to accept or reject the prosecution's offer.

Plea bargaining flows from "the mutuality of advantage" to defendants and prosecutors, each with his own reasons for wanting to avoid trial. *Brady v. United States,* 397 U.S., at 752. Defendants advised by competent counsel and protected by other procedural safeguards are presumptively capable of intelligent choice in response to prosecutorial persuasion, and unlikely to be driven to false self-condemnation. Indeed, acceptance of the basic legitimacy of plea bargaining necessarily implies rejection of any notion that a guilty plea is involuntary in a constitutional sense simply because it is the end result of the bargaining process. By hypothesis, the plea may have been induced by promises of a recommendation of a lenient sentence or a reduction of charges, and thus by fear of the possibility of a greater penalty upon conviction after a trial.

While confronting a defendant with the risk of more severe punishment clearly may have a "discouraging effect on the defendant's assertion of his trial rights, the imposition of these difficult choices [is] an inevitable"—and permissible—"attribute of any legitimate system which tolerates and encourages the negotiation of pleas." *Chaffin v. Stynchcombe, supra*, 412 U.S., at 31. It follows that, by tolerating and encouraging the negotiation of pleas, this Court has necessarily accepted as constitutionally legitimate the simple reality that the prosecutor's interest at the bargaining table is to persuade the defendant to forgo his right to plead not guilty.

It is not disputed here that Hayes was properly chargeable under the recidivist statute, since he had in fact been convicted of two previous felonies. In our system, so long as the prosecutor has probable cause to believe that the accused committed an offense defined by statute, the decision whether or not to prosecute, and what charge to file or bring before a grand jury, generally rests entirely in his discretion.[8] Within the limits set by the legislature's constitutionally valid definition of chargeable offenses, "the conscious exercise of some selectivity in enforcement is not in itself a federal constitutional violation" so long as "the selection was [not] deliberately based upon an unjustifiable standard such as race, religion, or other arbitrary classification." *Oyler v. Boles*, 368 U.S. 448, 456. To hold that the prosecutor's desire to induce a guilty plea is an "unjustifiable standard," which, like race or religion, may play no part in his charging decision, would contradict the very premises that underlie the concept of plea bargaining itself. Moreover, a rigid constitutional rule that would prohibit a prosecutor from acting forthrightly in his dealings with the defense could only invite un-

8. This case does not involve the constitutional implications of a prosecutor's offer during plea bargaining of adverse or lenient treatment for some person *other* than the accused, see ALI Model Code of Pre-Arraignment Procedure, Commentary to § 350.3, pp. 614–615 (1975), which might pose a greater danger of inducing a false guilty plea by skewing the assessment of the risks a defendant must consider. Cf. *Brady v. United States*, 397 U.S. 742, 758.

healthy subterfuge that would drive the practice of plea bargaining back into the shadows from which it has so recently emerged.

There is no doubt that the breadth of discretion that our country's legal system vests in prosecuting attorneys carries with it the potential for both individual and institutional abuse. And broad though that discretion may be, there are undoubtedly constitutional limits upon its exercise. We hold only that the course of conduct engaged in by the prosecutor in this case, which no more than openly presented the defendant with the unpleasant alternatives of forgoing trial or facing charges on which he was plainly subject to prosecution, did not violate the Due Process Clause of the Fourteenth Amendment....

Mr. Justice BLACKMUN, with whom Mr. Justice BRENNAN and Mr. Justice MARSHALL join, dissenting....

In [*North Carolina v. Pearce*, 395 U.S. 711, 725 (1969)] ... it was held that "vindictiveness against a defendant for having successfully attacked his first conviction must play no part in the sentence he receives after a new trial." Accordingly, if on the new trial, the sentence the defendant receives from the court is greater than that imposed after the first trial, it must be explained by reasons "based upon objective information concerning identifiable conduct on the part of the defendant occurring after the time of the original sentencing proceeding," other than his having pursued the appeal or collateral remedy. On the other hand, if the sentence is imposed by the jury and not by the court, if the jury is not aware of the original sentence, and if the second sentence is not otherwise shown to be a product of vindictiveness, *Pearce* has no application. *Chaffin v. Stynchcombe*, 412 U.S. 17 (1973).

Then later, in [*Blackledge v. Perry*, 417 U.S. 21, 27 (1974)], the Court applied the same principle to prosecutorial conduct where there was a "realistic likelihood of 'vindictiveness.' " It held that the requirement of Fourteenth Amendment due process prevented a prosecutor's reindictment of a convicted misdemeanant on a felony charge after the defendant had exercised his right to appeal the misdemeanor conviction and thus to obtain a trial *de novo*. It noted the prosecution's "considerable stake" in discouraging the appeal.

The Court now says, however, that this concern with vindictiveness is of no import in the present case, despite the difference between five years in prison and a life sentence, because we are here concerned with plea bargaining where there is give-and-take negotiation, and where, it is said, "there is no such element of punishment or retaliation so long as the accused is free to accept or reject the prosecution's offer." Yet in this case vindictiveness is present to the same extent as it was thought to be in *Pearce* and in *Perry*; the prosecutor here admitted that the sole reason for the new indictment was to discourage the respondent from exercising his right to a trial. Even had such an admission not been made, when plea negotiations, conducted in the face of the less serious charge under the first indictment, fail, charging by a second indictment a more serious crime for the same conduct creates "a strong inference" of vindictiveness.... I therefore do not understand why, as in *Pearce*, due process does not require that the prosecution justify its action on some basis other than discouraging respondent from the exercise of his right to a trial....

It might be argued that it really makes little difference how this case, now that it is here, is decided. The Court's holding gives plea bargaining full sway despite vindictiveness. A contrary result, however, merely would prompt the aggressive prosecutor to bring the greater charge initially in every case, and only thereafter to bargain. The consequences to the accused would still be adverse, for then he would bargain against a greater charge, face the likelihood of increased bail, and run the risk that the court would be less inclined to accept a bargained plea. Nonetheless, it is far preferable to hold the prosecution to the charge it was originally content to bring and to justify in the eyes of its public.

Mr. Justice POWELL, dissenting....

Respondent was charged with the uttering of a single forged check in the amount of $88.30. Under Kentucky law, this offense was punishable by a prison term of from 2 to 10 years, apparently without regard to the amount of the forgery. During the course of plea bargaining, the prosecutor offered respondent a sentence of five years in consideration of a guilty plea. I observe, at this point, that five years in prison for the offense charged hardly could be characterized as a generous offer. Apparently respondent viewed the offer in this light and declined to accept it; he protested that he was innocent and insisted on going to trial. Respondent adhered to this position even when the prosecutor advised that he would seek a new indictment under the State's

Habitual Criminal Act which would subject respondent, if convicted, to a mandatory life sentence because of two prior felony convictions.

The prosecutor's initial assessment of respondent's case led him to forgo an indictment under the habitual criminal statute. The circumstances of respondent's prior convictions are relevant to this assessment and to my view of the case. Respondent was 17 years old when he committed his first offense. He was charged with rape but pleaded guilty to the lesser included offense of "detaining a female." One of the other participants in the incident was sentenced to life imprisonment. Respondent was sent not to prison but to a reformatory where he served five years. Respondent's second offense was robbery. This time he was found guilty by a jury and was sentenced to five years in prison, but he was placed on probation and served no time. Although respondent's prior convictions brought him within the terms of the Habitual Criminal Act, the offenses themselves did not result in imprisonment; yet the addition of a conviction on a charge involving $88.30 subjected respondent to a mandatory sentence of imprisonment for life. Persons convicted of rape and murder often are not punished so severely.

No explanation appears in the record for the prosecutor's decision to escalate the charge against respondent other than respondent's refusal to plead guilty. The prosecutor has conceded that his purpose was to discourage respondent's assertion of constitutional rights, and the majority accepts this characterization of events.

It seems to me that the question to be asked under the circumstances is whether the prosecutor reasonably might have charged respondent under the Habitual Criminal Act in the first place. The deference that courts properly accord the exercise of a prosecutor's discretion perhaps would foreclose judicial criticism if the prosecutor originally had sought an indictment under that Act, as unreasonable as it would have seemed.[2] But here the prosecutor evidently made a reasonable, responsible judgment not to subject an individual to a mandatory life sentence when his only new offense had societal implications as limited as those accompanying the uttering of a single $88 forged check and when the circumstances of his prior convictions confirmed the inappropriateness of applying the habitual criminal statute. I think it may be inferred that the prosecutor himself deemed it unreasonable and not in the public interest to put this defendant in jeopardy of a sentence of life imprisonment....

... Here, any inquiry into the prosecutor's purpose is made unnecessary by his candid acknowledgment that he threatened to procure and in fact procured the habitual criminal indictment because of respondent's insistence on exercising his constitutional rights. We have stated in unequivocal terms ... that ... if the only objective of a state practice is to discourage the assertion of constitutional rights it is 'patently unconstitutional.'" *Chaffin v. Stynchcombe*, 412 U.S. 17, 32 n. 20 (1973)....

The plea-bargaining process, as recognized by this Court, is essential to the functioning of the criminal-justice system. It normally affords genuine benefits to defendants as well as to society. And if the system is to work effectively, prosecutors must be accorded the widest discretion, within constitutional limits, in conducting bargaining. This is especially true when a defendant is represented by counsel and presumably is fully advised of his rights. Only in the most exceptional case should a court conclude that the scales of the bargaining are so unevenly balanced as to arouse suspicion. In this case, the prosecutor's actions denied respondent due process because their admitted purpose was to discourage and then to penalize with unique severity his exercise of constitutional rights. Implementation of a strategy calculated solely to deter the exercise of constitutional rights is not a constitutionally permissible exercise of discretion. I would affirm the opinion of the Court of Appeals on the facts of this case.

2. The majority suggests that this case cannot be distinguished from the case where the prosecutor initially obtains an indictment under an enhancement statute and later agrees to drop the enhancement charge in exchange for a guilty plea. I would agree that these two situations would be alike *only if* it were assumed that the hypothetical prosecutor's decision to charge under the enhancement statute was occasioned not by consideration of the public interest but by a strategy to discourage the defendant from exercising his constitutional rights. In theory, I would condemn both practices. In practice, the hypothetical situation is largely unreviewable. The majority's view confuses the propriety of a particular exercise of prosecutorial discretion with its unreviewability. In the instant case, however, we have no problem of proof.

Notes and Questions

1. Is *Bordenkircher v. Hayes* more aptly characterized as a case of "prosecutorial vindictiveness" or one reflecting the "mutually advantageous" nature of negotiated guilty pleas and "the simple reality that the prosecutor's interest at the bargaining table is to persuade the defendant to forgo his right to plead not guilty"?

2. Is the majority opinion correct that, "As a practical matter, ... this case would be no different if the grand jury had indicted Hayes as a recidivist from the outset, and the prosecutor had offered to drop that charge as part of the plea bargain"? Is it accurate to describe the plea-bargaining process as one in which "'the prosecution and defense ... arguably possess relatively equal bargaining power'"?

3. Was the prosecutor's offer to recommend a prison sentence of five years in exchange for Hayes's guilty plea to the charge of uttering a forged check in the amount of $88.30 a fair one? In this regard, how "serious" is Hayes's record of prior convictions? To what extent should a defendant's prior criminal record figure in the plea-bargaining and sentencing process?

3. Alford Pleas

North Carolina v. Alford

400 U.S. 25, 91 S.Ct. 160, 27 L.Ed.2d 162 (1970)

Mr. Justice WHITE delivered the opinion of the Court.

On December 2, 1963, Alford was indicted for first-degree murder, a capital offense under North Carolina law.[1] The court appointed an attorney to represent him, and this attorney questioned all but one of the various witnesses who appellee said would substantiate his claim of innocence. The witnesses, however, did not support Alford's story but gave statements that strongly indicated his guilt. Faced with strong evidence of guilt and no substantial evidentiary support for the claim of innocence, Alford's attorney recommended that he plead guilty, but left the ultimate decision to Alford himself. The prosecutor agreed to accept a plea of guilty to a charge of second-degree murder, and on December 10, 1963, Alford pleaded guilty to the reduced charge.

Before the plea was finally accepted by the trial court, the court heard the sworn testimony of a police officer who summarized the State's case. Two other witnesses besides Alford were also heard. Although there was no eyewitness to the crime, the testimony indicated that shortly before the killing Alford took his gun from his house, stated his intention to kill the victim, and returned home with the declaration that he had carried out the killing. After the summary presentation of the State's case, Alford took the stand and testified that he had not committed the murder but that he was pleading guilty because he faced the threat of the death

1. Under North Carolina law, first-degree murder is punished with death unless the jury recommends that the punishment shall be life imprisonment....

At the time Alford pleaded guilty, North Carolina law provided that if a guilty plea to a charge of first-degree murder was accepted by the prosecution and the court, the penalty would be life imprisonment rather than death. The provision permitting guilty pleas in capital cases was repealed in 1969. See Parker v. North Carolina, 397 U.S. 790 (1970). Though under present North Carolina law it is not possible for a defendant to plead guilty to a capital charge, it seemingly remains possible for a person charged with a capital offense to plead guilty to a lesser charge.

penalty if he did not do so.[2] In response to the questions of his counsel, he acknowledged that his counsel had informed him of the difference between second- and first-degree murder and of his rights in case he chose to go to trial. The trial court then asked appellee if, in light of his denial of guilt, he still desired to plead guilty to second-degree murder and appellee answered, 'Yes, sir. I plead guilty on—from the circumstances that he (Alford's attorney) told me.' After eliciting information about Alford's prior criminal record, which was a long one,[4] the trial court sentenced him to 30 years' imprisonment, the maximum penalty for second-degree murder.

Alford sought post-conviction relief in the state court. Among the claims raised was the claim that his plea of guilty was invalid because it was the product of fear and coercion.... In 1967, Alford again petitioned for a writ of habeas corpus in the District Court for the Middle District of North Carolina. That court, without an evidentiary hearing, ... denied relief on the grounds that the guilty plea was voluntary and waived all defenses and nonjurisdictional defects in any prior stage of the proceedings and that the findings of the state court in 1965 clearly required rejection of Alford's claim that that he was denied effective assistance of counsel prior to pleading guilty. On appeal, a divided panel of the Court of Appeals for the Fourth Circuit reversed on the ground that Alford's guilty plea was made involuntarily. In reaching its conclusion, the Court of Appeals relied heavily on United States v. Jackson, 390 U.S. 570 (1968), which the court read to require invalidation of the North Carolina statutory framework for the imposition of the death penalty because North Carolina statutes encouraged defendants to waive constitutional rights by the promise of no more than life imprisonment if a guilty plea was offered and accepted. Conceding that Jackson did not require the automatic invalidation of pleas of guilty entered under the North Carolina statutes, the Court of Appeals ruled that Alford's guilty plea was involuntary because its principal motivation was fear of the death penalty. By this standard, even if both the judge and the jury had possessed the power to impose the death penalty for first-degree murder or if guilty pleas to capital charges had not been permitted, Alford's plea of guilty to second-degree murder should still have been rejected because impermissibly induced by his desire to eliminate the possibility of a death sentence.... We vacate the judgment of the Court of Appeals and remand the case for further proceedings.

We held in Brady v. United States, 397 U.S. 742 (1970), that a plea of guilty which would not have been entered except for the defendant's desire to avoid a possible death penalty and to limit the maximum penalty to life imprisonment or a term of years was not for that reason compelled within the meaning of the Fifth Amendment. Jackson established no new test for determining the validity of guilty pleas. The standard was and remains whether the plea represents a voluntary and intelligent choice among the alternative courses of action open to the defendant. That he would not have pleaded except for the opportunity to limit the possible penalty does not necessarily demonstrate that the plea of guilty

---

2. After giving his version of the events of the night of the murder, Alford stated:

> 'I pleaded guilty on second degree murder because they said there is too much evidence, but I ain't shot no man, but I take the fault for the other man. We never had an argument in our life and I just pleaded guilty because they said if I didn't they would gas me for it, and that is all.'

In response to questions from his attorney, Alford affirmed that he had consulted several times with his attorney and with members of his family and had been informed of his rights if he chose to plead not guilty. Alford then reaffirmed his decision to plead guilty to second-degree murder:

> 'Q. (by Alford's attorney). And you authorized me to tender a plea of guilty to second degree murder before the court?
>
> 'A. Yes, sir.
>
> 'Q. And in doing that, that you have again affirmed your decision on that point?
>
> 'A. Well, I'm still pleading that you all got me to plead guilty. I plead the other way, circumstantial evidence; that the jury will prosecute me on—on the second. You told me to plead guilty, right. I don't—I'm not guilty but I plead guilty.'

4. Before Alford was sentenced, the trial judge asked Alford about prior convictions. Alford answered that, among other things, he had served six years of a ten-year sentence for murder, had been convicted nine times for armed robbery, and had been convicted for transporting stolen goods, forgery, and carrying a concealed weapon.

was not the product of a free and rational choice, especially where the defendant was represented by competent counsel whose advice was that the plea would be to the defendant's advantage. The standard fashioned and applied by the Court of Appeals was therefore erroneous and we would, without more, vacate and remand the case for further proceedings with respect to any other claims of Alford which are properly before that court, if it were not for other circumstances appearing in the record which might seem to warrant an affirmance of the Court of Appeals.

As previously recounted after Alford's plea of guilty was offered and the State's case was placed before the judge, Alford denied that he had committed the murder but reaffirmed his desire to plead guilty to avoid a possible death sentence and to limit the penalty to the 30-year maximum provided for second-degree murder. Ordinarily, a judgment of conviction resting on a plea of guilty is justified by the defendant's admission that he committed the crime charged against him and his consent that judgment be entered without a trial of any kind. The plea usually subsumes both elements, and justifiably so, even though there is no separate, express admission by the defendant that he committed the particular acts claimed to constitute the crime charged in the indictment. Here Alford entered his plea but accompanied it with the statement that he had not shot the victim.

If Alford's statements were to be credited as sincere assertions of his innocence, there obviously existed a factual and legal dispute between him and the State. Without more, it might be argued that the conviction entered on his guilty plea was invalid, since his assertion of innocence negatived any admission of guilt, which, as we observed last Term in Brady, is normally '[c]entral to the plea and the foundation for entering judgment against the defendant * * *.' 397 U.S., at 748.

In addition to Alford's statement, however, the court had heard an account of the events on the night of the murder, including information from Alford's acquaintances that he had departed from his home with his gun stating his intention to kill and that he had later declared that he had carried out his intention. Nor had Alford wavered in his desire to have trial court determine his guilt without a jury trial. Although denying the charge against him, he nevertheless preferred the dispute between him and the State to be settled by the judge in the context of a guilty plea proceeding rather than by a formal trial. Thereupon, with the State's telling evidence and Alford's denial before it, the trial court proceeded to convict and sentence Alford for second-degree murder.

State and lower federal courts are divided upon whether a guilty plea can be accepted when it is accompanied by protestations of innocence and hence contains only a waiver of trial but no admission of guilt....

This Court has not confronted this precise issue, but prior decisions do yield relevant principles....

The issue in Hudson v. United States, 272 U.S. 451 (1926), was whether a federal court has power to impose a prison sentence after accepting a plea of nolo contendere, a plea by which a defendant does not expressly admit his guilt, but nonetheless waives his right to a trial and authorizes the court for purposes of the case to treat him as if he were guilty.[8] The Court held that a trial court does have such power.... Implicit in the nolo contendere cases is a recognition that the Constitution does not bar imposition of a prison sentence upon an accused who is unwilling expressly to admit his guilt but who, faced with grim alternatives, is willing to waive his trial and accept the sentence.

These cases would be directly in point if Alford had simply insisted on his plea but refused to admit the crime. The fact that his plea was denominated a plea of guilty rather than a plea of nolo contendere is of no constitutional significance with respect to the issue now before us, for the Constitution is concerned with the practical consequences, not the formal categorizations, of state law. Thus, while most pleas of guilty consist of both a waiver of trial and an express admission of guilt, the latter element is not a constitutional requisite to the imposition of

8. ... Throughout its history, ... the plea of nolo contendere has been viewed not as an express admission of guilt but as a consent by the defendant that he may be punished as if he were guilty and a prayer for leniency. Fed.Rule Crim.Proc. 11 preserves this distinction in its requirement that a court cannot accept a guilty plea 'unless it is satisfied that there is a factual basis for the plea'; there is no similar requirement for pleas of nolo contendere, since it was thought desirable to permit defendants to plead nolo without making any inquiry into their actual guilt.

criminal penalty. An individual accused of crime may voluntarily, knowingly, and understandingly consent to the imposition of a prison sentence even if he is unwilling or unable to admit his participation in the acts constituting the crime.

Nor can we perceive any material difference between a plea that refuses to admit commission of the criminal act and a plea containing a protestation of innocence when, as in the instant case, a defendant intelligently concludes that his interests require entry of a guilty plea and the record before the judge contains strong evidence of actual guilt. Here the State had a strong case of first-degree murder against Alford. Whether he realized or disbelieved his guilt, he insisted on his plea because in his view he had absolutely nothing to gain by a trial and much to gain by pleading. Because of the overwhelming evidence against him, a trial was precisely what neither Alford nor his attorney desired. Confronted with the choice between a trial for first-degree murder, on the one hand, and a plea of guilty to second-degree murder, on the other, Alford quite reasonably chose the latter and thereby limited the maximum penalty to a 30-year term. When his plea is viewed in light of the evidence against him, which substantially negated his claim of innocence and which further provided a means by which the judge could test whether the plea was being intelligently entered, see McCarthy v. United States, [394 U.S. 459], 466–467 (1969),[10] its validity cannot be seriously questioned. In view of the strong factual basis for the plea demonstrated by the State and Alford's clearly expressed desire to enter it despite his professed belief in his innocence, we hold that the trial judge did not commit constitutional error in accepting it.[11]

Relying on United States v. Jackson, Alford now argues in effect that the State should not have allowed him this choice but should have insisted on proving him guilty of murder in the first degree. The States in their wisdom may take this course by statute or otherwise and may prohibit the practice of accepting pleas to lesser included offenses under any circumstances. But this is not the mandate of the Fourteenth Amendment and the Bill of Rights. The prohibitions against involuntary or unintelligent pleas should not be relaxed, but neither should an exercise in arid logic render those constitutional guarantees counterproductive and put in jeopardy the very human values they were meant to preserve.

The Court of Appeals for the Fourth Circuit was in error to find Alford's plea of guilty invalid because it was made to avoid the possibility of the death penalty. That court's judgment directing the issuance of the writ of habeas corpus is vacated and the case is remanded to the Court of Appeals for further proceedings consistent with this opinion....

Mr. Justice BLACK ... concurs in the judgment and in substantially all of the opinion in this case.

Mr. Justice BRENNAN, with whom Mr. Justice DOUGLAS and Mr. Justice MARSHALL join, dissenting.

Last Term, this Court held, over my dissent, that a plea of guilty may validly be induced by an unconstitutional threat to subject the defendant to the risk to death, so long as the plea is entered in open court and the defendant is represented by competent counsel who is aware of the threat, albeit not of its unconstitutionality. Brady v. United States, 397 U.S. 742 (1970); Parker v. North Carolina, 397 U.S. 790 (1970). Today the Court makes clear that its previous holding was intended to apply even when the record demonstrates that the actual effect of the unconstitutional threat was to induce a guilty plea from a defendant who was unwilling to admit his guilt.

---

10. Because of the importance of protecting the innocent and of insuring that guilty pleas are a product of free and intelligent choice, various state and federal court decisions properly caution that pleas coupled with claims of innocence should not be accepted unless there is a factual basis for the plea, and until the judge taking the plea has inquired into and sought to resolve the conflict between the waiver of trial and the claim of innocence.

In the federal courts, Fed. Rule Crim. Proc. 11 expressly provides that a court 'shall not enter a judgment upon a plea of guilty unless it is satisfied that there is a factual basis for the plea.'

11. Our holding does not mean that a trial judge must accept every constitutionally valid guilty plea merely because a defendant wishes so to plead. A criminal defendant does not have an absolute right under the Constitution to have his guilty plea accepted by the court, although the States may by statute or otherwise confer such a right. Likewise, the States may bar their courts from accepting guilty pleas from any defendants who assert their innocence, cf. Fed. Rule Crim. Proc. 11, which gives a trial judge discretion to 'refuse to accept a plea of guilty * * *.' We need not now delineate the scope of that discretion.

I adhere to the view that, in any given case, the influence of such an unconstitutional threat 'must necessarily be given weight in determining the voluntariness of a plea.' And, without reaching the question whether due process permits the entry of judgment upon a plea of guilty accompanied by a contemporaneous denial of acts constituting the crime, I believe that at the very least such a denial of guilt is also a relevant factor in determining whether the plea was voluntarily and intelligently made. With these factors in mind, it is sufficient in my view to state that the facts set out in the majority opinion demonstrate that Alford was 'so gripped by fear of the death penalty' that his decision to plead guilty was not voluntary but was 'the product of duress as much so as choice reflecting physical constraint.' Accordingly, I would affirm the judgment of the Court of Appeals.

Notes and Questions

1. Most jurisdictions—47 states, Washington D.C., and the federal jurisdiction—allow courts to accept *Alford* pleas.[38] A majority of the states (approximately 38), Washington D.C., and the federal jurisdiction also permit nolo contendere pleas.[39] The courts nevertheless retain discretion not to accept *Alford* and nolo contendere pleas (as well as guilty pleas in which defendants admit responsibility). *See* footnote 11 of the majority opinion in *Alford.* In 2004, an estimated 76,000 inmates in state prison claimed to have been convicted via an *Alford* plea, which accounted for about 7% of all pleas (including not guilty pleas).[40]

2. Justice White's majority opinion in *Alford* maintains that, "An individual accused of crime may voluntarily, knowingly, and understandingly consent to the imposition of a prison sentence even if he is unwilling or unable to admit his participation in the acts constituting the crime." Why would an individual do so? Even if good reasons exist in some cases to enter such a plea, when Alford told the judge, "I ain't shot no man, but I take the fault for the other man.... I just pleaded guilty because they said if I didn't they would gas me for it," is it fair to conclude that his plea was "voluntary"? How important is it in *Alford* that the State demonstrated "a strong factual basis" for Alford's guilt?

3. Judges have considerable discretion in deciding whether to accept *Alford* pleas. Courts are expected find a sufficient factual basis of guilt before allowing the plea. Although *Alford* pleas are guilty pleas, with traditional guilty pleas the admission of guilt accompanying the plea itself or the defendant's in-court allocution contributes to the factual basis for the conviction. With *Alford* pleas, the judge must determine through other means that there is sufficient evidence of guilt to support the plea. However, as Shipley[41] argues, "sufficient" is not defined, guidelines were never forthcoming, and as a result, the pleas are accepted—or not accepted—for a variety of reasons, with differential standards applied. Further, the judge often relies on a summary of the evidence provided only by the state without a similar summary provided by the defense. In the *Alford* case, the Supreme Court noted that "strong" and "overwhelming" evidence against the defendant met the sufficient factual basis criterion. However, it is unknown whether in practice judges who have since accepted *Alford* pleas actively gauge the strength of the evidence against these defendants or, if they do, what threshold of strength is sufficient.

4. *Alford* and no contest pleas often are discussed together. The *Alford* Court noted that it perceived no material difference between the two in its decision. However, important differences between the pleas exist. For example, defendants who enter *Alford* pleas assert their innocence whereas defendants who enter no contest pleas typically do not (rather, they just do not acknowledge guilt). The future legal implications of the pleas also differ. Whereas no contest pleas do not represent an admission of guilt in future proceedings (*e.g.* in civil litigation), *Alford* pleas do.[42]

If new evidence of a defendant's innocence surfaces following conviction, should defendants who pled guilty be foreclosed from challenging their guilt pursuant to post-conviction procedures that are available to defendants who were convicted following trial? Should it matter whether the guilty plea was an *Alford* plea, involving a refusal to admit responsibility at the time the plea was accepted?

Norris v. State

896 N.E.2d 1149 (Ind. 2008)

DICKSON, Justice.

Four years after his guilty plea, conviction, and sentence for child molesting, the defendant sought post-conviction relief on grounds of newly discovered evidence. The post-conviction court granted the State's motion for summary disposition, and the defendant appealed. The Court of Appeals reversed and remanded for an evidentiary hearing before the post-conviction court. We granted transfer and now hold that a guilty plea may not be challenged in post-conviction proceedings by a claim of newly discovered evidence regarding the events that constituted the crime.

In June 2004, the State filed a delinquency petition charging that the defendant, prior to his eighteenth birthday, had performed an act that, if committed by an adult, would constitute Child Molesting, a class C felony. The juvenile court waived jurisdiction and child molesting charges were filed against the defendant in adult court. On December 9, 2004, the defendant pleaded guilty in accordance with a plea agreement calling for a maximum executed sentence of two years, which was imposed by the trial court. The defendant did not attempt a direct appeal but in December 2006 filed a Petition for Post-Conviction Relief on the grounds of newly discovered evidence to show "that the events with which the Petitioner was charged did not happen, and that the testimony and evidence was manufactured and that the Petitioner is innocent of all charges filed against him." The defendant's post-conviction petition did not allege ineffective assistance of counsel. He is not seeking to withdraw his plea and proceed to trial but rather to set aside and vacate his conviction. The State moved for summary disposition, to which the defendant responded with various items, including an affidavit from Colleen Norris, mother of the victim and sister of the defendant, recanting allegations she had made to police in 2004 accusing the defendant of sexually molesting her daughter. In its order granting the State's motion for summary disposition, the trial court found "that there is no genuine issue of material fact, that the Petitioner did indeed do what he admitted, and the State is entitled to judgment as a matter of law."

... In opposition to the State's motion for summary disposition, the defendant submitted an affidavit from his sister declaring that she had lied to police and that the defendant had not committed any act of molestation, and a psychological evaluation that the defendant contends shows that, "because of his limited mental capacity and personality, [he] could be convinced to say anything she wanted him to believe." The defendant argues that these submissions entitled him to an evidentiary hearing on his petition for post-conviction relief....

A conviction entered pursuant to a guilty plea stands on grounds substantially different from one entered based on a determination of guilt following the presentation of evidence. The former does not rest upon any factual evidence other than a defendant's testimony establishing the factual basis for his plea. Of course, the sentence imposed following such conviction is based on sentencing facts, but the essence of the present appeal is a challenge to the conviction, not the sentence. The defendant's petition for post-conviction relief is seeking to vacate his sentence by presenting "evidence of material fact which had not previously been presented to or heard by the court which would have proven he did not commit the crime." His conviction was based, however, only on his plea of guilty, not upon the testimony of his sister whose recantation he now presents to support his claim. He thus wishes to now contest the factual accuracy of his own guilty plea. This challenge implicates the nature and purpose of a guilty plea.

In 1970, the United States Supreme Court found that the federal Constitution did not bar a court from accepting a guilty plea when the defendant maintains innocence. *North Carolina v. Alford,* 400 U.S. 25 (1970). But *Alford* explicitly recognizes that the individual states may refuse to accept guilty pleas that accompany protestations of innocence. Indiana law has long refused to accept such "Alford" pleas. Over fifty years ago, this Court held that "a plea of guilty tendered by one who in the same breath protests his innocence, or declares he does not actually know whether or not he is guilty, is no plea at all." *Harshman v. State,* 232 Ind. 618, 621, 115 N.E.2d 501, 502 (1953).... Indiana jurisprudence has insisted that a factual basis must exist for a guilty plea, and that a judge may not accept a guilty plea while a defendant claims actual innocence. This rule was designed to both increase the reliability of guilty pleas and prevent the diminishment of respect for the court system as jailing people who committed no crime.

A defendant's plea of guilty is thus not merely a procedural event that forecloses the necessity of trial and triggers the imposition of sentence. It also, and more importantly, conclusively establishes the fact of guilt, a prerequisite in Indiana for the imposition of criminal punishment. The defendant here is seeking to undermine the sanctity of his own guilty plea by seeking to challenge facts that were presented to police and led to his arrest and the filing of criminal charges against him. He is not contesting any testimonial evidence at trial that resulted in a determination of guilt notwithstanding a not-guilty plea.

Our post-conviction procedures do not expressly address this distinction....

In establishing the extraordinary remedy of post-conviction relief, we intended the phrase "material facts, not previously presented and heard," in Section 1(a)(4), to refer to evidentiary facts presented to the trial court and which had a sufficient causative effect on a resulting determination of guilt. More significantly, post-conviction relief generally may not be based upon any "ground ... knowingly, voluntarily, and intelligently waived in the proceeding that resulted in the conviction." P-C.R. 1(8). A plea of guilty thus forecloses a post-conviction challenge to the facts adjudicated by the trial court's acceptance of the guilty plea and resulting conviction. The facts established by a plea of guilty may not be later challenged in post-conviction proceedings.[2]

Though this defendant now claims that new evidence would require that his conviction be vacated, we cannot harmonize this new position taken by the defendant with the fact that he originally admitted to committing the crime by his guilty plea. It is inconsistent to allow defendants who pleaded guilty to use post-conviction proceedings to later revisit the integrity of their plea in light of alleged new evidence seeking to show that they were in fact not guilty. Both his confession and his new claims cannot be true. A defendant knows at the time of his plea whether he is guilty or not to the charged crime. With a trial court's acceptance of a defendant's guilty plea, the defendant waives the right to present evidence regarding guilt or innocence. This constitutes a waiver under P-C.R. 1(1)(8)....

To reinforce his claim of newly discovered evidence that the defendant's sister (whose report to law enforcement which led to his arrest and the filing of charges) has now recanted, the defendant claims that such evidence would show that, because of his limited verbal and non-verbal skills, low intellectual functioning, and mild mental retardation, the defendant's sister "could convince [him] to say what she wanted him to say." A defendant may have recourse to post-conviction proceedings to seek a withdrawal of his guilty plea whenever the plea was not knowingly and voluntarily made. I.C. § 35-35-1-4(c)(3). But here the defendant is not asserting a claim challenging the knowing and voluntary nature of his plea nor seeking to withdraw his plea. The defendant has already served his sentence of imprisonment and does not wish to set aside his guilty plea and proceed to trial, but rather seeks only to set aside and vacate his conviction.... The issue of whether the defendant's plea was knowing and voluntary is therefore not presented.

We affirm the trial court's granting of the State's motion for summary disposition and the resulting denial of the defendant's petition for post-conviction relief.

BOEHM, Justice, concurring in result.

I agree with the majority that Norris has not shown that the post-conviction court erred in dismissing his petition. I do not agree with the

2. This appeal does not involve any request for post-conviction DNA testing that pursuant to statute, if favorable to the defendant, may result in "a new trial or any other relief as may be appropriate under Indiana law or court rule." Ind.Code § 35-38-7-19(3).

majority that a guilty plea precludes a court from granting post-conviction relief on a claim of actual innocence. Any system of justice must allow for correction of injustice based on clear and convincing evidence of innocence, even if the defendant can be said to have contributed to his own plight by pleading guilty.

The easiest example of such circumstances is irrefutable physical evidence of innocence where the defendant pleaded to a lesser charge in the face of highly persuasive but not conclusive evidence of guilt of a crime carrying a far higher penalty. An example posited at oral argument in this case assumed a defendant charged with rape. The victim is intelligent and articulate, and identifies the defendant as the perpetrator without equivocation or hesitancy. She also testifies that she had intercourse with no one other than the perpetrator within the month preceding the crime, and that the sample taken from her by examiners is from the perpetrator. The defendant has no alibi, and faced with a Class A felony conviction, pleads guilty to a Class C battery felony. DNA technology now establishes to a virtual certainty that the sample did not come from the defendant. The State in oral argument seemed to concede these circumstances would establish a claim for relief despite a guilty plea. If a more persuasive example is needed, add to these facts a confession by a third party whose DNA turns out to match the sample from the victim's rape kit. I recognize that DNA presents special issues and may permit relief where other forms of evidence do not. I cite this example simply as a case that demonstrates that not all guilty pleas should be immunized from subsequent attack, regardless of whether the convincing evidence is derived from DNA testing.

The only basis for denying relief to a defendant presenting convincing evidence of innocence is the convenience of the system in avoiding having to sort out which of such claims is indeed of sufficient merit to permit the courts to entertain them. There is no doubt that all sorts of cases will arise where evidence not adduced at trial is claimed to demonstrate innocence. But in my view, where there is a very high degree of confidence that justice did indeed misfire, no civilized system of justice would deny all relief. The United States Supreme Court has assumed that, at least in some circumstances, the federal Constitution may require relief for a defendant making a persuasive claim of actual innocence. *Herrera v. Collins,* 506 U.S. 390 (1993) ("We may assume, for the sake of argument in deciding this case, that in a capital case a truly persuasive demonstration of 'actual innocence' made after trial would render the execution of a defendant unconstitutional, and warrant habeas relief if there were no state avenue open to process such a claim."). We need not look to the federal or state constitutions for such a requirement. Our Post-Conviction Rule 1(a)(4) acknowledges the need for relief on a showing of "evidence of material facts, not previously presented and heard, that requires vacation of the conviction or sentence in the interest of justice." The interest of justice surely requires overturning a conviction of an innocent person.

I recognize that this state has long held that an *Alford* plea—"I plead guilty but I didn't do it"—is not to be accepted. That rule is not based on the notion that such pleas do not occur. Nor does it, as the majority claims, "conclusively establish the fact of guilt." The law treats it as having that effect, but it is a fiction to claim that it has that effect in every case. The rule against accepting *Alford* pleas is not based on the idea that a person pleading guilty is always guilty. Rather, it is designed to cause the courts to identify such a false plea when it occurs and reject it in the interest of achieving a truly just result. The wisdom of that rule is not the point here. Assuming that rejection of *Alford* pleas serves to further the correct resolution of criminal cases in the first place, it cannot be said with confidence that no innocent person has ever pleaded guilty in this state. If that occurs because of prosecutorial misconduct, the law provides some paths to redress. But not every plea by an innocent person is the product of wrongdoing. Such a plea may occur because the person mistakenly believes himself to be guilty. It can also occur because the probability of a far worse result is too great if a plea bargain is rejected. The hypothetical situation discussed above is an example of the latter. In either case, while one may fault the defendant for pleading guilty when he is not, by far the greater fault lies in an imperfect system of justice that often relies on eyewitness testimony and other forms of proof that can, with the best of intentions, produce wrong results. Post-conviction relief under Post-Conviction Rule 1 is the only path under our rules to redress such an injustice. I would not close that door.

Having said that, I do not believe Norris has presented evidence that meets the standards required by Post-Conviction Rule 1(a)(4), which permits relief on a showing of new evidence that "requires vacation of the conviction or sentence in the interest of justice." The interest of justice is served by finality as well as accuracy. We therefore should upset a guilty plea only where we have a very high degree of confidence that it was in fact incorrect. *Cf. Herrera*, 506 U.S. at 417 ("[T]he threshold showing for such an assumed right [to habeas relief if state relief were foreclosed] would necessarily be extraordinarily high.").

The evidence presented here is the affidavit of the defendant's sister, who now says she vindictively wrongly accused Norris of misconduct with her daughter. She also says that Norris is susceptible of being influenced and pleaded guilty due to her domination. Norris also presents the affidavit of his father, who states that the molestation could not have occurred because of the home's layout, and that Norris is mentally retarded and easily influenced. Additionally, Norris presents a psychological evaluation concluding that he functions between "the extremely low and borderline range of intellectual functioning." This is not the sort of evidence that is sufficient to overcome a guilty plea. It is itself inherently somewhat suspect, coming as it does after the fact and from relatives of the defendant, but not from the victim.[3] I therefore conclude that the showing presented here is insufficient to overcome the strong presumption that a guilty plea is in fact a truthful admission of guilt.

RUCKER, J., concurs.

Notes and Questions

1. Considerable variation exists among jurisdictions concerning whether convictions based on guilty pleas later can be challenged on grounds of newly discovered evidence (even including the results of DNA analysis—an issue expressly reserved in footnote 2 in *Norris*) and actual innocence, illustrating the tension between considerations of finality, the relevance attached to the defendant's admission of guilt (in non-*Alford* pleas), and the desirability of correcting miscarriages of justice.[43] Did the court in *Norris* strike the right balance? Is the more flexible rule urged by Justice Boehm in his concurring opinion a better approach? Do you agree with Justice Boehm's application of that rule, and his conclusion that the showing made by Norris "is insufficient to overcome the strong presumption that a guilty plea is in fact a truthful admission of guilt"?

2. Do Norris's relative youth and his diminished mental capabilities diminish the measure of confidence that should attach to the reliability of his guilty plea?

Although there are few, if any, direct empirical studies on the relationship between vulnerabilities like youth and mental impairment, and the likelihood of falsely pleading guilty, there is a wealth of information on these groups' proclivity for false confessions and on their understanding and appreciation of the legal system. In many ways, false guilty pleas are false confessions, as acknowledged in the *Speed Joyeros* case ("An illegally coerced plea may be analogized to an illegally obtained confession...."). The same rationales explaining the risk of false confessions also likely explain the risk of false guilty pleas: traits such as impulsivity, immaturity, obedience to authority, and possible impairments in decision-making capabilities can influence individuals' decisions to accept guilty plea offers even though they are innocent.[44] Findings from the adjudicative competence literature are also highly relevant in this context. Juveniles and persons with mental illness and with mental retardation are significantly more likely to have deficits in competence than their adult and non-disordered counterparts.[45] Simply put,

3. At oral argument, Norris pointed out that the appendix contains a letter from the victim to the trial court several months before the post-conviction petition was filed stating that she lied to police under threats from her mother. This letter was not written under oath, and Norris submitted no statement from the victim in support of his petition for post-conviction relief.

individuals who do not understand and appreciate the guilty plea process may be more likely to enter false guilty pleas.

D. Conclusion

Aspects of the adjudication process—both contested trials and guilty pleas—can affect the reliability of verdicts reached in criminal cases and consequently can contribute to miscarriages of justice. The issues that we have considered in this chapter frequently require a careful balancing of interests. For example, just as extensive pretrial publicity can be prejudicial to the accused and undermine the fairness of a trial, a vibrant, free press serves many invaluable functions, including helping to ensure accountability for actors in the criminal justice system and informing the public about issues of great importance to government and the community. Similar interest balancing arises with respect to guilty pleas, such as the tension between achieving finality of judgments and respecting the integrity of the guilty plea process, and a willingness to acknowledge that innocent people sometimes falsely admit guilt and hence are unjustly punished, suggesting that guilty pleas should not in all cases foreclose the consideration of persuasive new evidence inconsistent with guilt.

Some threats to the reliability of the adjudication process tend to be case-specific, while others are more structural or systemic in nature. For example, relatively few trials may evoke reactions that lead friends or family members of crime victims to demonstrate sympathy or support by wearing buttons to court or engaging in related symbolic displays. On the other hand, the looming "trial tax" in the form of more onerous punishment for defendants convicted after contesting guilt than for those who plead guilty, and pre-trial occurrences such as an inability to gain release from jail on bail or being assigned a lawyer more interested in an efficient resolution of a criminal charge than a just one, are recurrent process issues that might induce innocent defendants to plead guilty. While factors that precede the formal adjudication of guilt, such as eyewitness misidentification, false confessions, and others that we have considered, are traditional focal points for explaining wrongful convictions, important attributes of the adjudication process itself also merit attention as potential sources of miscarriages of justice.

Chapter 10

Capital Cases

A. Introduction

In *Furman v. Georgia,* 408 U.S. 238, 92 S.Ct. 2726, 33 L.Ed.2d 346 (1972), the United States Supreme Court ruled that the "the imposition and carrying out of the death penalty in [*Furman* and its companion] cases constitute cruel and unusual punishment in violation of the Eighth and Fourteenth Amendments." *Id.,* 408 U.S., at 239–240 (per curiam). The five justices who arrived at that conclusion did so for different reasons (each wrote individually, without joining the others' opinions). *Furman* now is commonly interpreted as invalidating death-penalty laws that fail to constrain sentencing discretion adequately, thus risking arbitrary capital punishment decisions. As a result of this momentous ruling, the death-penalty statutes in effect throughout the country were declared unconstitutional and more than 600 prisoners awaiting execution had their death sentences commuted to life imprisonment.[1]

Legislatures in a majority of the states quickly re-enacted death-penalty statutes that were designed to comply with *Furman's* uncertain mandate. In 1976, the Supreme Court approved newly enacted laws that narrowed the range of death-eligible crimes and incorporated standards to guide capital sentencing discretion.[2] At the same time, the Court declared unconstitutional legislation that made capital punishment mandatory on conviction for designated crimes.[3] In arriving at those decisions, using language that would be echoed repeatedly in later rulings, the justices announced that, for purposes of constitutional analysis, "death is different" from other forms of criminal punishment.

> [T]he penalty of death is qualitatively different from a sentence of imprisonment, however long. Death, in its finality, differs more from life imprisonment than a 100-year prison term differs from one of only a year or two. Because of that qualitative difference, there is a corresponding difference in the need for reliability in the determination that death is the appropriate punishment in a specific case. *Woodson v. North Carolina*, 428 U.S. 280, 305, 96 S.Ct. 2978, 49 L.Ed.2d 944 (1976) (plurality opinion).

Because the death penalty is uniquely severe as well as irrevocable, many people would agree that wrongful convictions in capital cases are "qualitatively different" from other miscarriages of justice, and that "a corresponding difference in the need for reliability" attaches to capital murder trials. We know, however, that erroneous capital murder convictions not only have occurred in the post-*Furman* era, but have been revealed with uncommon regularity. In 2008, Professors Samuel Gross and Barbara O'Brien explained:

> Since 1973, 128 U.S. criminal defendants who were sentenced to death have been exonerated. This is a startlingly high number, considering that death sentences amount to less than one-tenth of 1 percent of prison sentences in the United States. Most likely, this extraordinary number of capital exonerations is caused

> in part by a higher underlying error rate among capital convictions and in part by a higher rate of detection of those errors after conviction. It is well known that more resources are devoted to capital defense than to other cases, before and after conviction, but it is hard to believe that better review alone explains the capital exoneration rate. If that were the whole story, it would mean, for example, that if we had reviewed prison sentences with the same level of care that we devoted to death sentences, there would have been approximately 87,000 non-death-row exonerations from 1989 through 2003 rather than the 266 that were reported in a comprehensive study in 2005.[4]

We have discussed reports that shed light on the incidence and causes of wrongful capital convictions in earlier chapters and we already have encountered many such cases. With the possible exception of the emergence of DNA exonerations, the awful prospect of executing an innocent person has been unrivaled in helping to focus attention on wrongful convictions in the United States.[5] In the following sections, we examine a number of issues relating to miscarriages of justice in capital cases.

B. The Constitution and the Risk of Erroneous Executions

1. *Quinones I, II,* and *III*

United States v. Quinones

196 F.Supp.2d 416 (S.D.N.Y. 2002) [*Quinones I*]

RAKOFF, District Judge.

The Federal Death Penalty Act, 18 U.S.C. §§ 3591–3598, serves deterrent and retributive functions, or so Congress could reasonably have concluded when it passed the Act in 1994. But despite the important goals, and undoubted popularity, of this federal act and similar state statutes, legislatures and courts have always been queasy about the possibility that an innocent person, mistakenly convicted and sentenced to death under such a statute, might be executed before he could vindicate his innocence—an event difficult to square with basic constitutional guarantees, let alone simple justice. As Justice O'Connor, concurring along with Justice Kennedy in *Herrera v. Collins,* 506 U.S. 390 (1993), stated: "I cannot disagree with the fundamental legal principle that executing the innocent is inconsistent with the Constitution. Regardless of the verbal formula employed—'contrary to contemporary standards of decency,' 'shocking to the conscience,' or offensive to a 'principle of justice so rooted in the traditions and conscience of our people as to be ranked as fundamental'—the execution of a legally and factually innocent person would be a constitutionally intolerable event." *Id.* at 870.

To the majority in *Herrera,* however, as to most judges and legislators at the time (1993), the possibility that an innocent person might be executed pursuant to a death penalty statute seemed remote. Thus, Chief Justice Rehnquist, writing for the Court in *Herrera,* discounted as potentially unreliable a study that had concluded that 23 innocent persons were executed in the United States between 1900 and 1987. *See Herrera,* 113 S.Ct. at 868, n. 15. While recognizing that no system of justice is infallible, the majority in *Herrera* implicitly assumed that the high standard of proof and numerous procedural protections required in criminal cases, coupled with judicial review, post-conviction remedies, and, when all else failed, the possibility of executive clemency, rendered it highly unlikely that an executed person would subsequently be discovered to be innocent.

That assumption no longer seems tenable. In just the few years since *Herrera,* evidence has emerged that clearly indicates that, despite all the aforementioned safeguards, innocent people—mostly of color—are convicted of capital crimes they never committed, their convictions affirmed, and their collateral remedies denied, with a frequency far greater than previously supposed.

Most striking are the results obtained through the use of post-conviction testing with deoxyribonucleic acid ("DNA"). Although DNA testing is of remarkably high reliability, its value as a forensic tool in criminal investigations was not demonstrated until 1985 and its use in re-evaluating prior convictions was only beginning at the time *Herrera* was decided in 1993. Yet in just the few years since then, DNA testing has established the factual innocence of no fewer than 12 inmates on death row, some of whom came within days of being executed and all of whom have now been released.[4] This alone strongly suggests that more than a few people have been executed in recent decades whose innocence, otherwise unapparent to either the executive or judicial branches, would have been conclusively established by DNA testing if it had been available in their cases.

The problem, however, goes well beyond the issue of the availability of DNA testing. Indeed, the success of DNA testing in uncovering the innocence of death row defendants has itself helped spark reinvestigation of numerous other capital cases as to which DNA testing is unavailable or irrelevant but as to which other techniques can be applied. Partly as a result, in just the past decade, at least 20 additional defendants who had been duly convicted of capital crimes and were facing execution have been exonerated and released.[5] Again, the inference is unmistakable that numerous innocent people have been executed whose innocence might otherwise have been similarly established, whether by newly-developed scientific techniques, newly-discovered evidence, or simply renewed attention to their cases.

Moreover, even the frequency of these recent exonerations resulting from DNA testing and from fresh attention to neglected cases hardly captures either the magnitude of the problem or how little it was recognized until recently. It was not until the year 2000, for example, that Professor James S. Liebman and his colleagues at Columbia Law School released the results of the first comprehensive study ever undertaken of modern American capital appeals (4,578 appeals between 1973 and 1995). That study, though based only on those errors judicially identified on appeal, concluded that "the overall rate of prejudicial error in the American capital punishment system" is a remarkable 68%. James S. Liebman, et al., *A Broken System: Error Rates in Capital Cases* (2000) at ii. No system so "persistently and systematically fraught with error," *id.*, can warrant the kind of reliance that would justify removing the possibility of future exoneration by imposing death.

Just as there is typically no statute of limitations for first-degree murder—for the obvious reason that it would be intolerable to let a cold-blooded murderer escape justice through the mere passage of time—so too one may ask whether it is tolerable to put a time limit on when someone wrongly convicted of murder must prove his innocence or face extinction. In constitutional terms, the issue is whether—now that we know the fallibility of our system in capital cases—capital punishment is unconstitutional because it creates an undue risk that a meaningful number of innocent persons, by being put to death before the emergence of the techniques or evidence that will establish their innocence, are thereby effectively deprived of the opportunity to prove their innocence—and thus

4. Defendants' statistics and summaries of such releases, derived from data kept and continuously updated by the Death Penalty Information Center at its website, http://www.deathpenaltyinfo.org/innoccases, have not been disputed by the Government on this motion. *Cf.* S.486, at § 101(a)(5)(more than 80 defendants, including 10 who had been sentenced to death, exonerated by DNA testing between 1994 and 2001). *See generally* National Institute of Justice, Office of Justice Programs, U.S. Department of Justice, *Convicted by Juries, Exonerated by Science: Case Studies in the Use of DNA Evidence to Establish Innocence After Trial* (1996).

5. Defendants claim that the figures are even higher, but a review of the underlying data on the website of the Death Penalty Information Center, *supra*, shows that the defendants' figures include cases in which the basis of the exoneration is not clearly discernible. On any fair analysis of the website data, however, at least 20 of the 51 death-sentenced defendants who have been released from prison since 1991 were released on grounds indicating factual innocence derived from evidence other than DNA testing.

deprived of the process that is reasonably due them in these circumstances under the Fifth Amendment.[6]

In the instant case, the Government has announced its unalterable intention to seek the death penalty with respect to defendants Alan Quinones and Diego Rodriguez, the only two of the eight defendants originally named in this narcotics/murder case who have not pled guilty to the underlying charges....

... The Government asserts ... that the thrust of defendants' argument is contrary to the positions taken by the Supreme Court in *Herrera,* where the Court affirmed the denial of petitioner's second petition for habeas relief in which he alleged that his pending execution in the face of new evidence of his alleged innocence would violate the Eighth and Fourteenth Amendments.

This Court is not persuaded that *Herrera* provides the guidance necessary to resolve the instant issue....

Ironically, it was only a year or so after *Herrera* was decided that the new availability of DNA testing began to supply the kind of "truly persuasive demonstration" of actual innocence to which Chief Justice Rehnquist had hypothetical alluded. Thus, not only did *Herrera* not reach the issue here presented, but also it was premised on a series of factual assumptions about the unlikelihood that proof of actual innocence would emerge long after conviction that no longer seem sustainable. More generally, as already discussed, it implicitly premised a degree of unlikelihood of wrongful capital convictions that no longer seems tenable.[9]

The issue—not addressed by *Herrera* or, so far as appears, anywhere else—boils down to this. We now know, in a way almost unthinkable even a decade ago, that our system of criminal justice, for all its protections, is sufficiently fallible that innocent people are convicted of capital crimes with some frequency. Fortunately, as DNA testing illustrates, scientific developments and other innovative measures (including some not yet even known) may enable us not only to prevent future mistakes but also to rectify past ones by releasing wrongfully-convicted persons—but only if such persons are still alive to be released. If, instead, we sanction execution, with full recognition that the probable result will be the state-sponsored death of a meaningful number of innocent people, have we not thereby deprived these people of the process that is their due? Unless we accept—as seemingly a majority of the Supreme Court in *Herrera* was unwilling to accept—that considerations of deterrence and retribution can constitutionally justify the knowing execution of innocent persons, the answer must be that the federal death penalty statute is unconstitutional.

Consequently, if the Court were compelled to decide the issue today, it would, for the foregoing reasons, grant the defendants' motion to dismiss all death penalty aspects of this case on the ground that the federal death penalty statute

6. "No person shall ... be deprived of life, liberty, or property without due process of law...." While this language—drafted when capital punishment for such offenses as burglary, arson, counterfeiting and theft, was common, *see* Stuart Banner, *The Death Penalty: An American History* (2002) at 5—clearly implies that some capital punishment is compatible with due process, due process is, virtually by definition, an evolving concept that takes account of current conditions and new discoveries, as well as heightened moral awareness. In *Herrera,* the concurring and dissenting justices (a majority of the Court), in describing the execution of the innocent as a constitutionally intolerable event, used terms like "shock the conscience," suggesting that they view it as a denial of substantive due process.

9. As the Government notes, Chief Justice Rehnquist's opinion for the Court, while acknowledging the fallibility of any fact-finding system, takes solace not only in the putative unlikelihood of frequent mistakes but also in the availability of executive clemency when all legal remedies are exhausted. In the Chief Justice's view, "Clemency ... is the historic remedy for preventing miscarriages of justice where judicial process has been exhausted." But subsequent studies show that there has been a precipitous decline in the number of clemencies granted in recent years. As summarized by Professor Banner: "The most noticeable [change in recent years] was the sudden decline of clemency. For centuries governors commuted death sentences in significant numbers. That pattern continued for the first two-thirds of the twentieth century ... [but] dropped close to zero under the new sentencing schemes [enacted after 1972]." Banner, *supra,* at 291. This is hardly surprising in an age when "law and order" is a political issue, for the executive branch, far more than the judiciary, is inherently sensitive to political pressure. In any event, clemency has no real relevance to the issue now before this Court, for it would be unusual for an executive to stay an execution simply because proof of innocence might *thereafter* develop; yet it is this very real possibility, as demonstrated by the emergence of DNA testing, that creates the constitutional problem here addressed.

is unconstitutional. But prudence dictates that in a matter of such importance, the Court should give the Government—which only now has the benefit of the Court's views on this issue—one last opportunity to be heard before a final determination is reached....

United States v. Quinones

205 F.Supp.2d 256 (S.D.N.Y. 2002) [*Quinones II*]

RAKOFF, District Judge.

In its Opinion dated April 25, 2002, the Court, upon review of the parties' written submissions and oral arguments, declared its tentative decision to grant defendants' motion to dismiss the death penalty aspects of this case on the ground that the Federal Death Penalty Act, 18 U.S.C. §§ 3591–3598, is unconstitutional. *United States v. Quinones,* 196 F.Supp.2d 416, 420 (S.D.N.Y. 2002).... [A]fter careful consideration, the Court adheres to its prior view and declares the Federal Death Penalty Act unconstitutional....

... [T]he Government argues that because, in the Government's view, the Framers of the Constitution, the Congress that enacted the Federal Death Penalty Act, and the Supreme Court that addressed that Act in *Herrera v. Collins,* 506 U.S. 390 (1993), all accepted the constitutionality of administering capital punishment despite the inherent fallibility of the judicial system, even the likelihood that innocent people may mistakenly be executed does not mean that they did not receive the process that was their due or that the statute is inherently flawed....

With respect to the "Framers of the Constitution," the Government argues that, because the Fifth Amendment mandates that no person shall "be deprived of *life,* liberty, or property without due process of law" (emphasis supplied), therefore "the drafters of the Constitution themselves assumed the existence of capital punishment, doubtless against a backdrop in which they did not expect flawless administration of the penalty." But to "assume the existence" of the death penalty is not the same as endorsing it, and to "not expect flawless administration" is not the same as countenancing the execution of numerous innocent people.

There is, indeed, no indication that the Framers of the Constitution ever considered the issue of the death penalty as a substantive matter; they were simply concerned with extending due process to the full range of existing proceedings.... [A]t the time the Constitution was drafted in 1787 the death penalty was a common punishment in the various states for a wide variety of personal and property offenses, ranging from murder and rape to fraud and theft. *See* Stuart Banner, *The Death Penalty: An American History* 5–23, 88–111 (2002). There was no reason to believe that federal actions would be any different. Consequently, in guaranteeing due process of law to all deprivations of life, liberty and property, the drafters of the Constitution were simply applying due process to the full panoply of anticipated actions, rather than endorsing or even commenting on any particular kind of deprivation.

Furthermore, nothing suggests that the Framers regarded due process as a static concept, fixed for all time by the conditions prevailing in 1787. Just as it is settled law that the Eighth Amendment's prohibition of "cruel and unusual punishment" must be interpreted in light of "evolving standards of decency," *Trop v. Dulles,* 356 U.S. 86, 100–101 (1958), so too it is settled law that the Fifth Amendment's broad guarantee of "due process" must be interpreted in light of evolving standards of fairness and ordered liberty. To freeze "due process" in the precise form it took in 1787 would be to freeze it to death.

With respect to the Congress that enacted the Federal Death Penalty Act in 1994, the Government argues that it was "a Congress that well understood—and fully debated—whether the FDPA should be given effect despite the risk that innocent individuals might be sentenced to death" and that "Congress determined that enactment was warranted, based at least in part upon a balancing of defendant's rights against the rights of innocent victims."....

The simple fact is that none of the committee reports that comprise the primary legislative history of the Federal Death Penalty Act contains even a single passage supporting the Government's claim. Indeed, the total absence of the

Government's hypothesized "debate" from the formal history of the Act tends, if anything, to confirm the Court's view that members of Congress had no occasion in 1994 to weigh, in Benthamite fashion, a supposed balance of innocent lives saved and innocent lives lost as a result of the imposition of the death penalty.[4] Had they done so, moreover, the debate would have been entirely speculative, for whatever the merits of the studies supporting the deterrent effect of the death penalty, it was not until after the enactment of the Federal Death Penalty Act in 1994 that the most clear and compelling evidence of innocent people being sentenced to death chiefly emerged, *i.e.*, the DNA testing that established conclusively that numerous persons who had been convicted of capital crimes (by "proof beyond a reasonable doubt") were, beyond any doubt, innocent.

Moreover, even if one were to suppose, contrary to fact, that the Congress that enacted the Federal Death Penalty Act undertook a "death calculus" and somehow weighed (through sheer speculation) the number of innocent lives that would be saved by the presumed added deterrent impact of the death penalty against the number of innocent lives that would be lost by innocent people being mistakenly executed, this would not be dispositive of the issue before this Court.... If protection of innocent people from state-sponsored execution is a protected liberty, and if such protected liberty includes the right of an innocent person not to be deprived, by execution, of the opportunity to demonstrate his innocence, then Congress may not override such liberty absent a far more clear and compelling need than any presented here.

Which brings us to the Supreme Court's 1993 decision in *Herrera v. Collins*.... [T]he Government proclaims that *Herrera* is "fatal to defendants' motion" and not only "does not lend support to this Court's preliminary ruling; it forecloses it." These new contentions are, however, entirely unsupportable.

While much of *Herrera* is *dictum*, its actual holding is not difficult to discern. Ten years after his conviction of capital murder, and quite some years after having exhausted his state and federal, direct and collateral appeals, Herrera, who was facing imminent execution in Texas, sought to reopen his case on the basis of belatedly-produced largely-hearsay affidavits. After the Texas courts denied his application as untimely, he sought federal habeas corpus relief, contending that, notwithstanding the belated and successive nature of his petition, his claim of actual innocence entitled him, under the Eighth and Fourteenth Amendments, to re-open his case. While the Supreme Court, in rejecting this claim, spent considerable time in describing putative shortcomings in petitioner's approach, the Court's actual holding was as follows:

> We may assume, for the sake of argument in deciding this case, that in a capital case a truly persuasive demonstration of "actual innocence" made after trial would render the execution of a defendant unconstitutional, and warrant federal habeas relief if there were no state avenue open to process such a claim. But because of the very disruptive effect that entertaining claims of actual innocence would have on the need for finality in capital cases, and the enormous burden that having to retry cases based on often stale evidence would place on the States, the threshold showing for such an assumed right would necessarily be extraordinarily high. The showing made by petitioner in this case falls far short of any such threshold. 506 U.S. at 417.

Any doubt that this is the Court's holding (and that, indeed, such language was necessary to obtain the assent of two of the five justices, O'Connor and Kennedy, who joined in the majority) is laid to rest by the concurring opinion of Justice O'Connor, joined in by Justice Kennedy, which expressly states that "the execution of a legally and factually innocent person would be a constitutionally intolerable event" but that petitioner has failed to make the kind of persuasive

4. Such cold-blooded utilitarianism would have been uncharacteristic of Congress, which, experience suggests, is much more likely to favor the Kantian, "Golden Rule" approach characteristic of the world's great religions. Under that latter approach, the relevant question would presumably be: "Are you prepared to apply to yourself a legal process that would execute you for a crime you never committed before you were able to finally prove your innocence?"

showing necessary to consider such a claim at this belated stage. 506 U.S. at 420. Justice O'Connor continues:

> Ultimately, two things about this case are clear. First is what the Court does *not* hold. Nowhere does the Court state that the Constitution permits the execution of an actually innocent person. Instead, the Court assumes for the sake of argument that a truly persuasive demonstration of actual innocence would render any such execution unconstitutional and that federal habeas relief would be warranted if no state avenue were open to process the claim. Second is what petitioner has not demonstrated. Petitioner has failed to make a persuasive showing of actual innocence. 506 U.S. at 427.

So too, Justice White, declining to join in the five-justice majority opinion, stated in his opinion concurring in the judgment that "In voting to affirm, I assume that a persuasive showing of 'actual innocence' made after trial, even though made after the expiration of the time provided by law for the presentation of newly discovered evidence, would render unconstitutional the execution of petitioner in this case." 506 U.S. at 429.

As for the dissent by Justice Blackmun, joined by Justices Stevens and Souter, it too confirms that "the long and general discussion that precedes the Court's disposition of this case ... is dictum because the Court assumes ... 'that in a capital case a truly persuasive demonstration of "actual innocence" made after trial would render the execution of a defendant unconstitutional.'" 506 U.S. at 430....

In sum, the Court remains unpersuaded that anything in *Herrera,* the legislative history of the Federal Death Penalty Act, or the Due Process clause itself precludes the decision here reached. If anything, the combined view of five justices in *Herrera* that execution of the innocent is constitutionally impermissible supports the instant decision.

Finally, ... the Government argues that the evidence on which the Court premises its legal conclusions is either unreliable, irrelevant, or both....

Regarding the DNA testing that has exonerated at least 12 death row inmates since 1993, the Government argues that, since such testing is now available prior to trial in many cases, its effect, going forward, will actually be to reduce the risk of mistaken convictions. This completely misses the point. What DNA testing has proved, beyond cavil, is the remarkable degree of fallibility in the basic fact-finding processes on which we rely in criminal cases. In each of the 12 cases of DNA-exoneration of death row inmates referenced in *Quinones,* the defendant had been found guilty by a unanimous jury that concluded there was proof of his guilt beyond a reasonable doubt; and in each of the 12 cases the conviction had been affirmed on appeal, and collateral challenges rejected, by numerous courts that had carefully scrutinized the evidence and the manner of conviction. Yet, for all this alleged "due process," the result, in each and every one of these cases, was the conviction of an innocent person who, because of the death penalty, would shortly have been executed (some came within days of being so) were it not for the fortuitous development of a new scientific technique that happened to be applicable to their particular cases.

DNA testing may help prevent some such near-tragedies in the future; but it can only be used in that minority of cases involving recoverable, and relevant, DNA samples. Other scientific techniques may also emerge in the future that will likewise expose past mistakes and help prevent future ones, and in still other cases, such as those referenced below, exoneration may be the result of less scientific and more case-specific developments, such as witness recantations or discovery of new evidence. But there is no way to know whether such exoneration will come prior to (or during) trial or, conversely, long after conviction.[9] What is certain is that, for the foreseeable future, traditional trial methods and appellate review will not prevent the conviction of numerous innocent people.

Where proof of innocence is developed long after both the trial and the direct appeal are con-

9. In one Government study of 28 cases of post-conviction exoneration of various crimes based on DNA testing, the average defendant had spent 7 years in prison before his innocence was uncovered. National Institute of Justice, Office of Justice Programs, U.S. Department of Justice, *Convicted by Juries, Exonerated by Science: Case Studies in the Use of DNA Evidence to Establish Innocence After Trial* (1996)("National Institute of Justice DNA Study") at iii.

cluded, it is entirely appropriate that the defendant make a truly persuasive showing of innocence, as *Herrera* requires, before his case can be reopened. But given what DNA testing has exposed about the unreliability of the primary techniques developed by our system for the ascertainment of guilt, it is quite something else to arbitrarily eliminate, through execution, any possibility of exoneration after a certain point in time. The result can only be the fully foreseeable execution of numerous innocent persons.

While the DNA evidence alone is sufficient to establish this basic point, the Court, in its Opinion of April 25, also relied on the even larger number of death row inmates who have been exonerated over the past decade by investigations that, while inspired by the DNA testing, used more conventional methods. Although, as the Government notes in its Memorandum and as the Court itself noted in its prior Opinion, the website of the Death Penalty Information Center ("DPIC") that lists these cases may be over-inclusive,[10] the Court, upon review of the underlying case summaries, conservatively concluded that at least 20 such defendants released from death row over the past decade for reasons unrelated to DNA testing were factually innocent. *Quinones* at 418.[11] These included people like Joseph Burrows, who was released after 5 years on death row only after the state's chief witness against him confessed to the murder; Anthony Porter, who spent no less than 16 years on death row until prosecutors decided they had made a mistake (upon which determination they then brought murder charges against a different suspect, who confessed); and Gary Drinkard, whose 1995 conviction and death sentence were overturned in 2001 only after an entire team of lawyers and investigators uncovered conclusive proof that he was at home at the time of the murder for which he was charged. Because, moreover, DNA testing was not applicable to these cases and they therefore required a more onerous investigation before innocence could be proved to the high degree necessary to satisfy the relevant court or prosecutor, these additional 20 innocent convicts served an average of 10 years in prison before their innocence was established.

The Government does not deny that an increasing number of death row defendants have been released from prison in recent years for reasons other than DNA testing. Nor does the Government, despite its quibbles with the DPIC website, directly contest the Court's conservative conclusion that at least 20 of these non-DNA exonerations likely involved the capital convictions of innocent persons. Instead, the Government argues that both the DNA and non-DNA exonerations are irrelevant to consideration of the Federal Death Penalty Act because the exonerated defendants were all state convicts, rather than federal. This, moreover, is no accident, argues the Government, but is rather the result of the allegedly greater protections that federal procedure generally, and the Federal Death Penalty Act in particular, afford defendants.

Upon analysis, however, the Government's distinction proves ephemeral, for several reasons. To begin with, while it true that none of the 31

10. This is not to say, however, that there is any basis for the Government's contention that the data and case summaries set forth in the DPIC website (as opposed to DPIC's interpretations of those data and summaries) are unreliable. Upon review of the substantial record provided by the parties, the Court is satisfied that the DPIC employs, as it attests, reasonably strict and objective standards in listing and describing the data and summaries that appear on its website.

11. Exhibit A to the Def. Mem. lists the names and details of the 12 death row defendants exonerated since 1993 by DNA testing, plus 20 other, non-DNA death row exonerations since *Herrera* that defendants have correctly intuited satisfy the Court's conservative criterion of prisoners who were "released on grounds indicating factual innocence." The 32 names (with numbers corresponding to their DPIC website listings) are: 53. Kirk Bloodsworth; 54. Federico M. Macias; 55. Walter McMillian; 59. Andrew Golden; 60. Joseph Burrows; 63. Rolando Cruz; 64. Alejandro Hernandez; 66. Verneal Jimerson; 67. Dennis Williams; 68. Roberto Miranda; 69. Gary Gauger; 70. Troy Lee Jones; 72. Ricardo Aldape Guerra; 73. Benjamin Harris; 76. Robert Lee Miller, Jr.; 78. Shareef Cousin; 79. Anthony Porter; 80. Steven Smith; 81. Ronald Keith Williamson; 82. Ronald Jones; 83. Clarence Richard Dexter; 86. Steve Manning; 88. Joseph Nahume Green; 89. Earl Washington; 91. Frank Lee Smith; 92. Michale Graham; 93. Albert Burrell; 94. Peter Limone; 97. Jeremy Sheets; 98. Charles Irvin Fain; 99. Juan Robert Melendez; and 100. Ray Krone. Moreover, even under the Court's cautious approach, substantial arguments could be made for adding at least 8 other names to the list, namely: 56. Gregory R. Wilhoit; 65. Sabrina Butler; 74. Robert Hayes; 77. Curtis Kyles; 85. Alred Rivera; 90. William Nieves; 95. Gary Drinkard; and 101. Thomas H. Kimbell, Jr.

persons so far sentenced to death under the Federal Death Penalty Act has been subsequently exonerated (though five of the sentences have already been reversed, the sample is too small, and the convictions too recent, to draw any conclusions therefrom). The 32 exonerated death row inmates identified by the Court in its prior Opinion, are part of a relevant pool of anywhere from around 800 to around 3,700 death row inmates, depending on how you look at it.[12] As previously noted, moreover, the time-lag between conviction and exoneration for the 32 exonerated inmates averaged somewhere in the range of 7 to 10 years after conviction. Consequently, if federal practices were equally as vulnerable to wrongful capital convictions as state practices, still, on any reasonable statistical analysis, one would not expect any exonerations to have yet emerged with respect to a sample as small as 31 federal capital convicts, none of whom was sentenced before 1995.[13]

More fundamentally, there is no logical reason to suppose that practices and procedures under the Federal Death Penalty Act will be materially more successful in preventing mistaken convictions than the deficient state procedures that have already been shown to be wanting. By virtue of the Fourteenth Amendment, all the primary protections are the same in both systems: proof beyond a reasonable doubt, trial by jury, right to effective assistance of counsel, right of confrontation, etc.

If anything, certain federal practices present a greater risk of wrongful capital convictions than parallel state practices. For example, federal practice, in contrast to that of many states that allow the death penalty, permits conviction on the uncorroborated testimony of an accomplice. Similarly, federal practice treats circumstantial evidence identically to direct evidence and permits conviction based solely on such evidence, whereas many states that allow the death penalty permit a conviction based solely on circumstantial evidence only if such evidence excludes to a moral certainty every other reasonable inference except guilt.

Even more fundamentally, it appears reasonably well established that the single most common cause of mistaken convictions is inaccurate eye-witness testimony. As recently summarized by Senior Circuit Judge Jon O. Newman of the Second Circuit:

> Experience has shown that in some cases juries have been persuaded beyond a reasonable doubt to convict and vote the death penalty even though the defendant is innocent. The most common reason is that one or more eyewitnesses said they saw the defendant commit the crime, but it later turned out that they were mistaken, as eyewitnesses sometimes are.

Newman, "Make Judges Certify Guilt In Capital Cases," Newsday, July 5, 2000, p. A25.[15] *See also, e.g., National Institute of Justice DNA Study, supra,* at 15. The federal rules of evidence are no less receptive to such eye-witness testimony than state rules, and federal courts, at both the trial and appellate levels, apply, even more than state courts, highly deferential standards to jury findings premised on such testimony.

Accordingly, there is no good reason to believe the federal system will be any more successful at avoiding mistaken impositions of the death

12. According to the DPIC website, the total of state and federal convicts on death row increased by 811 between 1994 and the end of 2001. According to yesterday's New York Times, the total number of persons (state and federal) sentenced to death since the death penalty was revived in 1976 is 3,701. *See N.Y. Times,* June 30, 2002, chart at section 4, p. 16.

13. It may also be noted that, as the Government concedes, at least one of the 31 federal death row inmates, David Ronald Chandler, had a colorable claim of actual innocence, but his sentence was commuted by President Clinton. However, although the commutation was seemingly prompted by serious doubts about Chandler's guilt, it should also be noted that Chandler was not granted a full pardon. More generally, as noted in the Court's prior Opinion, the use of executive clemency to rectify wrongful death penalty convictions, always a haphazard remedy at best, has significantly diminished in recent years, notwithstanding the greater number of cases of proven innocence. Clemency, moreover, cannot address the problem of the mistakenly convicted defendant who is executed before he can prove his innocence.

15. Judge Newman's "op-ed" piece, prompted by the controversial execution of Gary Graham in Texas, suggests that legislatures might be able to reduce the risk of wrongful capital convictions to arguably acceptable levels by requiring the trial judge to certify, as a precondition to imposing the death penalty, that guilt has been proved, not only beyond reasonable doubt, but to a certainty. Whether such a legislative solution could solve the due process problems here presented is well beyond the scope of this Opinion.

penalty than the error-prone state systems already exposed.

In its Opinion of April 25, the Court also supported its overall conclusions by reference to the unusually high rate of legal error (68%) detected in appeals (both state and federal) from death penalty convictions, as shown by the comprehensive study of those appeals released in 2000 by Professor James Liebman and his colleagues. While legal error is not a direct measure of factual error, Liebman's study was concerned with errors that the appellate courts had determined were not harmless and that therefore could be outcome-determinative. *See* James S. Liebman, et al., *A Broken System: Error Rates In Capital Cases, 1973–1995* (2000) at 32. That such errors could infect nearly 7 out of every 10 capital cases strongly suggests that, at a minimum, the trial process appears to operate with less reliability in the context of capital cases than elsewhere. Moreover, Liebman and his colleagues conclude, in a recently-released follow-up analysis of their data, that the 68% error rate if anything understates the extent of the problem so far as factually mistaken capital convictions are concerned. *See* James S. Liebman, et al., *A Broken System, Part II: Why There Is So Much Error In Capital Cases, And What Can Be Done About It* (2002), at 25.

In response, the Government launches an extended, and remarkably personal attack on Liebman and his study, annexing critical press releases from elected officials such as the Attorney General of Montana and the Governor of Florida, and even arguing that the study is suspect because Liebman (though only one of the six authors of the study) is, allegedly, an avowed opponent of the death penalty. As convincingly shown, however, in the Brief Amicus Curiae of 42 Social Scientists filed in response, the Liebman study, commissioned at the behest of the Chairman of the U.S. Senate Judiciary Committee, is by far the most careful and comprehensive study in this area, and one based, moreover, exclusively on public records and court decisions.

When it comes to something as fundamental as protecting the innocent, press releases and ad hominem attacks are no substitute for reasoned discourse, and the fatuity of the Government's attacks on Liebman's study only serves to highlight the poverty of the Government's position. At the same time, no judge has a monopoly on reason, and the Court fully expects its analysis to be critically scrutinized. Still, to this Court, the unacceptably high rate at which innocent persons are convicted of capital crimes, when coupled with the frequently prolonged delays before such errors are detected (and then often only fortuitously or by application of newly-developed techniques), compels the conclusion that execution under the Federal Death Penalty Act, by cutting off the opportunity for exoneration, denies due process and, indeed, is tantamount to foreseeable, state-sponsored murder of innocent human beings.

Accordingly, the Court grants defendant's motion to strike all death penalty aspects from this case, on the ground that the Federal Death Penalty Act is unconstitutional....

United States v. Quinones

313 F.3d 49 (2d Cir. 2002), *reh. den.*,
317 F.3d 86 (2d. Cir. 2003) [*Quinones III*]

JOSÉ A. CABRANES, Circuit Judge:

We consider here a challenge to the constitutionality of the Federal Death Penalty Act of 1994 ("FDPA") (codified at 18 U.S.C. §§3591–3598).

Defendants Alan Quinones and Diego Rodriguez were indicted for, *inter alia*, murder in aid of racketeering, in violation of 18 U.S.C. §§1959(a)(1) and 2. Shortly thereafter, the Government filed notices of its intention to seek the death penalty against them. In response, Quinones and Rodriguez filed a motion to strike the death penalty notices on the ground that the FDPA is unconstitutional.... [T]he United States District Court for the Southern District of New York (Jed S. Rakoff, *Judge*) ... held that ... the FDPA violates substantive and procedural due process rights guaranteed by the Fifth Amendment. The Government timely filed this appeal.

... We hold that, to the extent the defendants' arguments rely upon the Eighth Amendment, their argument is foreclosed by the Supreme

Court's decision in *Gregg v. Georgia,* 428 U.S. 153 (1976). With respect to the defendants' Fifth Amendment due process claim, we observe that the language of the Due Process Clause itself recognizes the possibility of capital punishment. Moreover, the defendants' argument that execution deprives individuals of the opportunity for exoneration is not new at all—it repeatedly has been made to the Supreme Court and rejected by the Supreme Court. Most notably, the Supreme Court expressly held in *Herrera v. Collins,* 506 U.S. 390 (1993), that, while the Due Process Clause protects against government infringement upon rights that are "so rooted in the traditions and conscience of our people as to be ranked as fundamental," there is no fundamental right to a continued opportunity for exoneration throughout the course of one's natural life. Because neither the Court of Appeals nor the District Court is authorized to disregard or overturn the Supreme Court's holding in *Herrera,* we reverse the order of the District Court....

II.

...

C. *Constitutionality of the Federal Death Penalty Act*

... In holding that the FDPA violates the Constitution, the District Court relied upon the Due Process Clause of the Fifth Amendment. But three separate provisions in the Fifth Amendment—including the Due Process Clause itself—expressly contemplate the existence of capital punishment:

> No person shall be held to answer for a *capital,* or otherwise infamous crime, unless on a presentment or indictment of a Grand Jury ... nor shall any person be subject for the same offence to be twice put in jeopardy of *life* or limb ... nor be deprived of *life,* liberty, or property without due process of law....
> U.S. Const. amend. V (emphasis added).

Accordingly, "it is apparent from the text of the Constitution itself that the existence of capital punishment was accepted by the Framers." *Gregg v. Georgia,* 428 U.S. 153, 177 (1976) (joint opinion of Stewart, Powell, and Stevens, JJ.).

While admitting that the Framers "assume[d] the existence" of the death penalty, the District Court declared that "it is settled law that the Fifth Amendment's broad guarantee of 'due process' must be interpreted in light of evolving standards of fairness and ordered liberty." Applying this standard, it found that the death penalty no longer comports with due process of law because of recent evidence demonstrating the frequency with which innocent people are convicted and sentenced to death.

The District Court erred in looking to "evolving standards" in conducting its due process analysis: It is the Eighth Amendment—not the Due Process Clause of the Fifth Amendment—that requires consideration of "evolving standards" in determining whether a particular punishment conforms to principles of decency "that mark the progress of a maturing society." And the Supreme Court expressly held in *Gregg* that, to the extent our standards of decency have evolved since the enactment of the Constitution, they still permit punishment by death for certain heinous crimes such as murder.

While the Supreme Court has held that "the concept of due process of law is not final and fixed," *Rochin v. California,* 342 U.S. 165, 170 (1952), it has also made it clear that a criminal law violates the constitutional command of the Due Process Clause only if it offends some principle of justice "so rooted in the traditions and conscience of our people as to be ranked as fundamental." *Id.* at 169. While the District Court failed to mention this standard expressly, it held that an innocent person sentenced to death has a liberty interest in the opportunity to seek exoneration during the course of his or her natural life and implied that this liberty interest amounts to a fundamental right.

Despite suggestions by the District Court and the defendants that they are embracing a novel challenge to the constitutionality of capital punishment, the idea that a convicted person has a right to the continued opportunity for exoneration during the course of his natural life is not new: Because this proposition has been presented to the Supreme Court on a number of occasions and repeatedly rejected by the Court, we hold that the continued opportunity to exonerate oneself throughout the natural course of one's life is not a right "so rooted in the traditions and conscience of our people as to be ranked as fundamental."

"Our primary guide in determining whether the principle in question is fundamental is, of course, historical practice," *Montana v. Egelhoff,* 518 U.S. 37, 43–44 (1996). The majority of states as well as the federal government have provided for capital punishment for over two hundred years. The defendants try to belittle the significance of this fact by arguing that courts have never before considered "the constitutional implications of the execution of innocent defendants in light of new evidence that this is a problem of crisis proportions." But the argument that innocent people may be executed—in small or large numbers—is not new; it has been central to the centuries-old debate over both the wisdom and the constitutionality of capital punishment, and binding precedents of the Supreme Court prevent us from finding capital punishment unconstitutional based solely on a statistical or theoretical possibility that a defendant might be innocent.

Even before the founding of our country, European nations from which we derived our laws recognized that capital punishment inherently entails a risk that innocent people will be executed. *See generally* Hugo Adam Bedau & Michael L. Radelet, *Miscarriages of Justice in Potentially Capital Cases,* 40 Stan. L.Rev. 21, 22 (1987). In the mid-1770s, the British scholar Jeremy Bentham argued that capital punishment differs from all other punishments because "[f]or death, there is no remedy." Jeremy Bentham, *The Rationale of Punishment* 186 (Robert Heward ed., 1830) (circa 1775). Bentham recognized that there could be no "system of penal procedure which could insure the Judge from being misled by false evidence or the fallibility of his own judgment," *id.* at 187, and he argued that execution prevents "the oppressed [from meeting] with some fortunate event by which his innocence may be proved," *id.* at 189.

In the United States, opponents of capital punishment "began to argue that innocent people were often executed by mistake" as early as the mid-Nineteenth Century. Stuart Banner, *The Death Penalty: An American History* 121 (2002). These abolitionists maintained that "[the] government ought to abandon capital punishment in general because so many innocent people were going to their deaths on the gallows." Since that time, there has been a prodigious scholarly debate over whether the likelihood that innocent people will be executed justifies abolition of the death penalty. *See, e.g.,* Edwin M. Borchard, *Convicting the Innocent: Errors of Criminal Justice* Intro., *passim* (1932) (chronicling sixty-five prosecutions and convictions of "completely innocent people," *id.* at xiii, and noting that, although exactly "[h]ow many wrongfully convicted persons have actually been executed ... is impossible to say ... these cases offer a convincing argument for the abolition of the death penalty," *id.* at xix); E. Roy Calvert, *Capital Punishment in the Twentieth Century* 123–134 (5th red. Patterson Smith 1973) (1936) (arguing that "no human tribunal is ever competent to impose an irrevocable penalty," *id.* at 123, and noting that "it is surprising how many cases are actually known of the execution of the innocent" given that, "[b]y the infliction of the capital penalty the person primarily concerned is prevented from urging his claim," *id.* at 125–26); George R. Scott, *The History of Capital Punishment* 248–63 (1950) (chronicling cases in which innocent persons have been executed and insisting that "we have no means of knowing whether or not other persons have been wrongly convicted and executed [because].... [t]he accused is dead and, therefore, unable to supply information and evidence which may be necessary [for his or her exoneration,]" *id.* at 251–52); Jerome & Barbara Frank, *Not Guilty* 248–49 (1957) (noting "the intolerably monstrous nature of any death sentence ... [because] [i]t cannot be undone" and insisting that "[n]o one knows how many innocent men, erroneously convicted of murder, have been put to death by American governments [because].... once a convicted man is dead, all interest in vindicating him usually evaporates"); Charles L. Black, Jr., *Capital Punishment: The Inevitability of Caprice and Mistake passim* (1974) (arguing that the death penalty, no matter how it is administered, inherently encounters the possibility of mistake in its application); Hugo Adam Bedau & Michael L. Radelet, *Miscarriages of Justice in Potentially Capital Cases,* 40 Stan. L.Rev. 21 (1987) (citing their own study for the proposition that, from 1900 through 1985, at least 139 innocent persons were sentenced to death and at least 23 innocent persons were executed).[12]

Further, prior to the FDPA's enactment, Congress had been presented with extensive evidence in support of the argument that innocent individuals might be executed. *See, e.g.,* 140 Cong. Rec. S10394-02 (Aug. 2, 1994) (Statement of Sen. Simon) (discussing generally "False Convictions and the Death Penalty" and placing on the record

---

12. The study by Bedau and Radelet has sparked a significant amount of scholarly controversy over the extent to which innocent persons are executed. *See, e.g.,* Stephen J. Markman & Paul G. Cassell, *Protecting the Innocent: A Response to the Bedau-Radelet Study,* 41 Stan. L.Rev. 121 (1988).

a 1994 *USA Today* article that noted "at least 85 instances in the past 20 years in which prosecutors—knowingly or unknowingly—relied on fabricated, mishandled, or tampered evidence to convict the innocent or free the guilty" and suggesting that "such miscarriages of justice are more common than we might like to believe"); 140 Cong. Rec. H2322-02, *H2330 (April 14, 1994) (Statement of Rep. Nadler) ("The death penalty, once imposed, can never be recalled.... We have no way of judging how many innocent persons have been executed, but we can be certain that there were some."); *id.* at *H2327 (Statement of Rep. Mfume) ("a large body of evidence shows that innocent people are often convicted of crimes, including capital crimes, and that some of them have been executed. There have been, on the average, more than four cases per year in which an entirely innocent person was convicted of murder, and many of those persons were sentenced to death."); *id.* at *H2326 (April 14, 1994) (Statement of Rep. Kopetski) ("Stanford Law Review documented hundreds of cases in which innocent individuals were sentenced to death, 23 of whom were wrongly executed. Let me repeat that, because it's a staggering number: 23 people lay dead who were later exonerated of wrongdoing."); 139 Cong. Rec. S15745-01, *S15766 (Nov. 16, 1993) (Statement of Sen. Levin) (noting "case after case after case in which people have been sentenced to death only later to be found innocent and released" and placing on the record an October 21, 1993 study by the Subcommittee on Civil and Constitutional Rights of the House Judiciary Committee that "describes 48 cases in the past 20 years where a convicted person has been released from death row either because their innocence was proven or because there was a reasonable doubt that was raised as to their guilt"). While not determinative, it is noteworthy that Congress enacted the FDPA against the backdrop of repeated assertions by some members that innocent people have been executed. This informed, deliberative legislative action itself casts doubt on the assertion that the right to a continued opportunity for exoneration throughout the course of one's natural life is "rooted in the ... conscience of our people."

Most importantly, the Supreme Court has upheld state and federal statutes providing for capital punishment for over two hundred years, and it has done so despite a clear recognition of the possibility that, because our judicial system—indeed, any judicial system—is fallible, innocent people might be executed and, therefore, lose any opportunity for exoneration....

The Supreme Court first expressly acknowledged the argument pressed here—namely, that capital punishment might deprive innocent persons of the ability to exonerate themselves—in *Furman v. Georgia,* 408 U.S. 238 (1972). In *Furman,* all nine Justices, each writing separately, found that application of a *particular* state death penalty statute was so arbitrary that it violated the Eighth Amendment. Despite this, only two members of the Court—Justice Thurgood Marshall and Justice William J. Brennan—were willing to hold the death penalty unconstitutional *per se.* And, although the argument before us today was squarely before the Court in *Furman,* only Justice Marshall indicated any possibility that this argument, standing alone, might be sufficient to render the death penalty unconstitutional.

The opinions of Justice Marshall and Justice Brennan make clear that the *Furman* Court was presented with, considered, and declined to adopt the argument that capital punishment unconstitutionally deprives innocent persons who have been sentenced to death of the opportunity to exonerate themselves. In his opinion, Justice Marshall expressly recognized that "there is evidence that innocent people have been executed before their innocence can be proved." 408 U.S. at 364 (Marshall, J., concurring):

> Just as Americans know little about who is executed and why, they are unaware of the potential dangers of executing an innocent man. Our 'beyond a reasonable doubt' burden of proof in criminal cases is intended to protect the innocent, but we know it is not foolproof. Various studies have shown that people whose innocence is later convincingly established are convicted and sentenced to death....
>
> No matter how careful courts are, the possibility of perjured testimony, mistaken honest testimony, and human error remain all too real. We have no way of judging how many innocent persons have been executed but we can be certain that there were some. *Id.* at 366–68 (footnotes omitted).

Justice Brennan took the argument one step further, expressly acknowledging that execution deprives innocent persons of the opportunity for exoneration:

> [d]eath is truly an awesome punishment. The calculated killing of a human being by the State involves, by its very nature, a denial of the executed person's humanity. The contrast with the plight of a person punished by imprisonment is evident. *An individual in prison does not lose 'the right to have rights.'* A prisoner retains, for example, the constitutional rights to the free exercise of religion, to be free of cruel and unusual punishments, *and to treatment as a 'person' for purposes of due process of law* and the equal protection of the laws. A prisoner remains a member of the human family. Moreover, *he retains the right of access to the courts. His punishment is not irrevocable.* Apart from *the common charge, grounded upon the recognition of human fallibility, that the punishment of death must inevitably be inflicted upon innocent men,* we know that death has been the lot of men whose convictions were unconstitutionally secured in view of later, retroactively applied, holdings of this Court. The punishment itself may have been unconstitutionally inflicted, yet *the finality of death precludes relief. An executed person has indeed 'lost the right to have rights.'* 408 U.S. at 290 (internal citation omitted) (emphasis added).

These excerpts demonstrate beyond any possible doubt that the basic thesis of the District Court's opinion—that capital punishment is unconstitutional because it denies individuals the opportunity for exoneration—is not a new one. The *Furman* Court understood that innocent persons may be executed before obtaining evidence necessary to exonerate themselves. Nevertheless, seven justices declined to find that "the death penalty is unconstitutional *per se.*" In doing so, they effectively denied the existence of a fundamental right to the opportunity for exoneration over the course of one's natural life.

More importantly, just four years after *Furman,* the Court expressly held in *Gregg v. Georgia* that capital punishment does not constitute a *per se* violation of the Eighth Amendment. The Court reached this conclusion despite the petitioner's argument that the death penalty "entail[s] both mistake and caprice," and that "some people will be killed wrongly," Br. for Petitioner in *Gregg* at 10a, and despite its own acknowledgment that "[t]here is no question that death as a punishment is unique in its severity and irrevocability." 428 U.S. at 187 (joint opinion of Stewart, Powell, and Stevens, JJ.). Moreover, in his dissent in *Gregg,* Justice Brennan reiterated his view that the death penalty is excessive because "[a]n executed person has indeed 'lost the right to have rights.'" 428 U.S. at 230. The *Gregg* Court was therefore keenly aware of the argument asserted here, that execution terminates any asserted right to the opportunity for exoneration during one's natural life. Despite this awareness, the Court rejected the proposition that capital punishment is unconstitutional *per se.*

More recently, in *Herrera v. Collins,* 506 U.S. 390 (1993), the Supreme Court affirmed the denial of a petition for a writ of habeas corpus in which the petitioner claimed that his execution would violate both the Due Process Clause and the Eighth Amendment because new evidence could prove his "actual innocence." The Court noted that "[c]laims of actual innocence based on newly discovered evidence have never been held to state a ground for federal habeas relief *absent an independent constitutional violation occurring in the underlying state criminal proceeding.*" *Id.* at 400 (emphasis added). The Court then declined to hold that "execution of a person who is innocent of the crime for which he was convicted" amounts to an independent violation of either the Eighth Amendment *or* the Due Process Clause. *Id.* at 398. The Court noted that "[t]his proposition has an element of appeal, as would the similar proposition that the Constitution prohibits the imprisonment of one who is innocent of the crime for which he was convicted...." *Id.* But the Court recognized that it had previously "observed that '[d]ue process does not require that every conceivable step be taken, at whatever cost, to eliminate the possibility of convicting an innocent person.'" *Id.* at 398–99.

The *Herrera* Court recognized that "a petitioner otherwise subject to defenses of abusive or successive use of the writ may have his federal constitutional claim considered on the merits if he makes a proper showing of actual innocence." *Id.* at 404. It emphasized, however, that "our habeas jurisprudence [thus far] makes clear that *a claim of 'actual innocence' is not itself a constitutional claim....*'" *Id.* (emphasis added).

Despite this precedent, the *Herrera* Court "*assume[d], for the sake of argument* in deciding [that] case, that in a capital case a truly persuasive demonstration of 'actual innocence' made after trial would render the execution of a defendant unconstitutional...." *id.* at 417 (emphasis added). But, while the Court assumed, *only for the sake of its analysis,* that capital punishment of a person who is able to demonstrate his innocence *prior to execution* violates the Constitution, it made no such holding. It follows, therefore, that *Herrera* did not suggest, much less hold, that the mere speculative possibility that one might be able to demonstrate his innocence at some point in the future renders capital punishment unconstitutional.

... *Herrera* therefore establishes, at a minimum, that it is lawful under the Due Process Clause to end the judicial review process at some point, despite the purely theoretical possibility that the defendant might have been able to demonstrate his innocence in the future.

Further, despite its recognition of the "unalterable fact that our judicial system, like the human beings who administer it, is fallible," *id.* at 415, the Court held in *Herrera* that a state's refusal to grant a new trial to a capital defendant based upon newly-discovered evidence that could prove his innocence does not "transgress[ ] a principle of fundamental fairness rooted in the traditions and conscience of our people," *id.* at 411. The Supreme Court thereby made clear that, once an individual has exhausted his available legal remedies, the Due Process Clause no longer entitles him to an opportunity to demonstrate his innocence. Accordingly, the Supreme Court established in *Herrera* that there is no fundamental right to the opportunity for exoneration even before one's execution date, much less during the entire course of one's natural lifetime.

The District Court found the Supreme Court's decision in *Herrera* to be inapposite because it was "not informed by the ground-breaking DNA testing and other exonerative evidence developed in the years since." *Quinones II,* 205 F.Supp.2d at 263. Yet, *Herrera* prevents us from finding capital punishment unconstitutional based solely on a statistical or theoretical possibility that a defendant might be innocent.... Accordingly, in light of *Herrera,* the District Court erred in recognizing a "[fundamental] right of an innocent person not to be deprived, by execution, of the opportunity to demonstrate his innocence," and we likewise would err if we were to ignore or reject the jurisprudence of the Supreme Court on this subject.

In sum, if the well-settled law on this issue is to change, that is a change that only the Supreme Court or Congress is authorized to make....

Notes and Questions

1. In light of the sweeping implications of Judge Rakoff's ruling in *Quinones II* that the federal death penalty statute violates Due Process because it exposes innocent people to the risk of execution—"and, indeed, is tantamount to foreseeable, state-sponsored murder of innocent human beings"—most observers were not surprised by the Second Circuit Court of Appeals' rapid reversal in *Quinones III.* In July 2004, a federal jury sitting in Manhattan convicted Alan Quinones and his codefendant Diego Rodriguez of the capital murder of a New York City Police Department confidential informant in connection with racketeering and drug-related activities. Following a six-day penalty hearing, the jury sentenced each man to life imprisonment without the possibility of parole. Judge Rakoff presided at the trial.[6] As of January 1, 2010, fifty-nine persons awaited execution on the federal death row in Terre Haute, Indiana, having been sentenced to death under United States law. Three people, including Timothy McVeigh, have been executed under federal authority in the post-*Furman* era.[7]

2. If the Second Circuit Court of Appeals was correct in *Quinones III* when it said, "if the well-settled law on this issue is to change, that is a change that only the Supreme Court or Congress is authorized to make," 313 F.3d, at 69, in light of the issues raised in the various *Quinones* opinions, *should* either the Supreme Court or Congress step in to invalidate or rescind the federal death penalty statute? Should additional procedural

safeguards at least be required to help guard against the conviction and execution of innocent persons?

3. After considering but rejecting a bill to abolish the state's death penalty, the Maryland Legislature enacted the following provisions, which became effective October 1, 2009.

> **Maryland Code, Criminal Law § 2-202**
>
> (a) A defendant found guilty of murder in the first degree may be sentenced to death only if: ...
>
> (3) the State presents the court or jury with:
>
> (i) biological evidence or DNA evidence that links the defendant to the act of murder;
>
> (ii) a video taped, voluntary interrogation and confession of the defendant to the murder; or
>
> (iii) a video recording that conclusively links the defendant to the murder....

Are these measures likely to be effective in guarding against erroneous executions? Do they go too far in attempting to protect the innocent, by effectively gutting the capital punishment statute, restricting the pool of death-eligible offenders so radically and for reasons that have so little to do with the death penalty's principal justifications—retribution, deterrence, and incapacitation—that they are a step in the wrong direction? Do they ensure a "foolproof" death penalty law that entirely eliminates the risk of executing an innocent person?

4. In 2004, a special commission appointed by former Massachusetts Governor Mitt Romney issued a set of recommendations that, according to the report, "if adopted in their entirety, can allow creation of a fair capital punishment statute ... that is as narrowly tailored, and as infallible, as humanly possible."[8] The commission's ten recommendations represent a markedly different approach than the Maryland Legislature adopted in proposing a viable death penalty statute while simultaneously minimizing the risk of executing innocent parties. The Massachusetts Legislature declined to act on the recommendations and Massachusetts remains one of 16 states that currently do not authorize capital punishment. For additional commentary on the Massachusetts commission and its recommendations, *see* Joseph L. Hoffmann, "Protecting the Innocent: The Massachusetts Governor's Council Report," 95 *Journal of Criminal Law & Criminology* 561 (2005); Franklin E. Zimring, "Symbol and Substance in the Massachusetts Commission Report," 80 *Indiana Law Journal* 115 (2005).

2. Perspectives from the United States Supreme Court

The *Quinones* opinions offer a lengthy discussion of the Supreme Court's decision in *Herrera v. Collins,* 506 U.S. 390, 113 S.Ct. 853, 122 L.Ed.3d 203 (1993), a case that we considered in Chapter 2. In 2002, when the *Quinones* litigation was unfolding, *Herrera* represented the justices' most extensive discussion of the risk of wrongful convictions within the capital punishment context. But in 2006, in a death penalty case that had nothing to do with a claim of innocence, several of the justices reached out to revisit that subject. The narrow issue and the Court's holding in *Kansas v. Marsh,* 548 U.S. 163, 126 S.Ct. 2516, 165 L.Ed.2d 429 (2006) are concisely stated at the outset of Justice Thomas's majority opinion, below. Issues bearing on the death penalty and actual innocence are considered more extensively in Justice Scalia's concurring opinion and in Justice Souter's dissent.

Kansas v. Marsh

548 U.S. 163, 126 S.Ct. 2516, 165 L.Ed.2d 429 (2006)

Justice THOMAS delivered the opinion of the Court.

Kansas law provides that if a unanimous jury finds that aggravating circumstances are not outweighed by mitigating circumstances, the death penalty shall be imposed. We must decide whether this statute, which requires the imposition of the death penalty when the sentencing jury determines that aggravating evidence and mitigating evidence are in equipoise, violates the Constitution. We hold that it does not....

V

Justice SOUTER (hereinafter dissent) argues that the advent of DNA testing has resulted in the "exoneratio[n]" of "innocent" persons "in numbers never imagined before the development of DNA tests." Based upon this "new empirical argument about how 'death is different,'" the dissent concludes that Kansas' sentencing system permits the imposition of the death penalty in the absence of reasoned moral judgment.

But the availability of DNA testing, and the questions it might raise about the accuracy of guilt-phase determinations in capital cases, is simply irrelevant to the question before the Court today, namely, the constitutionality of Kansas' capital *sentencing* system. Accordingly, the accuracy of the dissent's factual claim that DNA testing has established the "innocence" of numerous convicted persons under death sentences —and the incendiary debate it invokes—is beyond the scope of this opinion.[7]

The dissent's general criticisms against the death penalty are ultimately a call for resolving all legal disputes in capital cases by adopting the outcome that makes the death penalty more difficult to impose. While such a bright-line rule may be easily applied, it has no basis in law. Indeed, the logical consequence of the dissent's argument is that the death penalty can only be just in a system that does not permit error. Because the criminal justice system does not operate perfectly, abolition of the death penalty is the only answer to the moral dilemma the dissent poses. This Court, however, does not sit as a moral authority. Our precedents do not prohibit the States from authorizing the death penalty, even in our imperfect system. And those precedents do not empower this Court to chip away at the States' prerogatives to do so on the grounds the dissent invokes today....

Justice SCALIA, concurring....

III

Finally, I must say a few words (indeed, more than a few) in response to Part III of Justice SOUTER's dissent. This contains the disclaimer that the dissenters are not *(yet)* ready to "generaliz[e] about the soundness of capital sentencing across the country," but that is in fact precisely what they do. The dissent essentially argues that capital punishment is such an undesirable institution—it results in the condemnation of such a large number of innocents—that any legal rule which eliminates its pronouncement, including the one favored by the dissenters in the present case, should be embraced.

As a general rule, I do not think it appropriate for judges to heap either praise or censure upon a legislative measure that comes before them, lest it be thought that their validation, invalidation, or interpretation of it is driven by their desire to expand or constrict what they personally approve or disapprove as a matter of policy. In the present case, for example, people might leap to the conclusion that the dissenters' views on whether Kansas's equipoise rule is constitutional are determined by their personal disapproval of an institution that has been democratically adopted by 38 States and the United States. But of course that requires no leap;

7. But see The Penalty of Death, in Debating the Death Penalty: Should America Have Capital Punishment? The Experts on Both Sides Make Their Best Case 117, 127–132, 134 (H. Bedau & P. Cassell eds. 2004). See also Markman & Cassell, Protecting the Innocent: A Response to the Bedau-Radelet Study, 41 Stan. L. Rev. 121, 126–145 (1988) (examining accuracy in use of the term "innocent" in death penalty studies and literature); Marquis, The Myth of Innocence, 95 J.Crim. L. & C. 501, 508 (2005) ("Words like 'innocence' convey enormous moral authority and are intended to drive the public debate by appealing to a deep and universal revulsion at the idea that someone who is genuinely blameless could wrongly suffer for a crime in which he had no involvement"); *People v. Smith*, 708 N.E.2d 365, 371 (Ill. 1999) ("While a not guilty finding is sometimes equated with a finding of innocence, that conclusion is erroneous.... Rather, [a reversal of conviction] indicates simply that the prosecution has failed to meet its burden of proof").

just a willingness to take the dissenters at their word. For as I have described, the dissenters' very argument is that imposition of the death penalty should be minimized by invalidation of the equipoise rule because it is a bad, "risk[y]," and "hazard[ous]" idea. A broader conclusion that people should derive, however (and I would not consider this much of a leap either), is that the dissenters' encumbering of the death penalty in *other* cases, with unwarranted restrictions neither contained in the text of the Constitution nor reflected in two centuries of practice under it, will be the product of their policy views—views not shared by the vast majority of the American people. The dissenters' proclamation of their policy agenda in the present case is especially striking because it is nailed to the door of the wrong church—that is, set forth in a case litigating a rule that has nothing to do with the evaluation of guilt or innocence.... But as the Court observes, guilt or innocence is logically disconnected to the challenge in *this* case to *sentencing* standards. The *only* time the equipoise provision is relevant is when the State has proved a defendant guilty of a capital crime.

There exists in some parts of the world sanctimonious criticism of America's death penalty, as somehow unworthy of a civilized society. (I say sanctimonious, because most of the countries to which these finger-waggers belong had the death penalty themselves until recently—and indeed, many of them would still have it if the democratic will prevailed.[3]) It is a certainty that the opinion of a near-majority of the United States Supreme Court to the effect that our system condemns many innocent defendants to death will be trumpeted abroad as vindication of these criticisms. For that reason, I take the trouble to point out that the dissenting opinion has nothing substantial to support it.

It should be noted at the outset that the dissent does not discuss a single case—not one—in which it is clear that a person was executed for a crime he did not commit. If such an event had occurred in recent years, we would not have to hunt for it; the innocent's name would be shouted from the rooftops by the abolition lobby. The dissent makes much of the new-found capacity of DNA testing to establish innocence. But in every case of an executed defendant of which I am aware, that technology has *confirmed* guilt.

This happened, for instance, only a few months ago in the case of Roger Coleman. Coleman was convicted of the gruesome rape and murder of his sister-in-law, but he persuaded many that he was actually innocent and became the posterchild for the abolitionist lobby. Around the time of his eventual execution, "his picture was on the cover of Time magazine ('This Man Might Be Innocent. This Man Is Due to Die'). He was interviewed from death row on 'Larry King Live,' the 'Today' show, 'Primetime Live,' 'Good Morning America' and 'The Phil Donahue Show.'" Even one Justice of this Court, in an opinion filed shortly before the execution, cautioned that "Coleman has now produced substantial evidence that he may be innocent of the crime for which he was sentenced to die." *Coleman v. Thompson,* 504 U.S. 188, 189 (1992) (Blackmun, J., dissenting). Coleman ultimately failed a lie-detector test offered by the Governor of Virginia as a condition of a possible stay; he was executed on May 20, 1992.

In the years since then, Coleman's case became a rallying point for abolitionists, who hoped it would offer what they consider the "Holy Grail: proof from a test tube that an innocent person had been executed." But earlier this year, a DNA test ordered by a later Governor of Virginia proved that Coleman was guilty, even though his defense team had "proved" his innocence and had even identified "'the real killer'" (with whom they eventually settled a defamation suit). And Coleman's case is not unique. See Truth and Consequences: The Penalty of Death, in Debating the Death Penalty: Should America Have Capital Punish-

3. It is commonly recognized that "[m]any European countries ... abolished the death penalty in spite of public opinion rather than because of it." Bibas, Transparency and Participation in Criminal Procedure, 81 N.Y.U.L.Rev. 911, 931–932 (2006). Abolishing the death penalty has been made a condition of joining the Council of Europe, which is in turn a condition of obtaining the economic benefits of joining the European Union. The European Union advocates against the death penalty even *in America*; there is a separate death-penalty page on the Web site of the Delegation of the European Commission to the U.S.A. See http://www.eurunion.org/legislat/deathpenalty/deathpenhome.htm (all Internet materials as visited June 17, 2006). The views of the European Union have been relied upon by Justices of this Court (including all four dissenters today) in narrowing the power of the American people to impose capital punishment. See, *e.g., Atkins v. Virginia*, 536 U.S. 304, 317, n. 21 (2002) (citing, for the views of "the world community," the Brief for the European Union as *Amicus Curiae*).

ment? The Experts on Both Sides Make Their Best Case 117, 128–129 (H. Bedau & P. Cassell eds. 2004) (discussing the cases of supposed innocents Rick McGinn and Derek Barnabei, whose guilt was also confirmed by DNA tests).

Instead of identifying and discussing any particular case or cases of mistaken execution, the dissent simply cites a handful of studies that bemoan the alleged prevalence of wrongful death sentences. One study (by Lanier and Acker) is quoted by the dissent as claiming that "'more than 110' death row prisoners have been released since 1973 upon findings that they were innocent of the crimes charged, and 'hundreds of additional wrongful convictions in potentially capital cases have been documented over the past century.'" (opinion of SOUTER, J.). For the first point, Lanier and Acker cite the work of the Death Penalty Information Center (more about that below) and an article in a law review jointly authored by Radelet, Lofquist, and Bedau (two professors of sociology and a professor of philosophy). For the second point, they cite only a 1987 article by Bedau and Radelet. See Miscarriages of Justice in Potentially Capital Cases, 40 Stan. L. Rev. 21. In the very same paragraph which the dissent quotes, Lanier and Acker also refer to that 1987 article as "hav[ing] identified 23 individuals who, in their judgment, were convicted and executed in this country during the 20th century notwithstanding their innocence." Lanier & Acker, Capital Punishment, the Moratorium Movement, and Empirical Questions, 10 Psychology, Public Policy & Law 577, 593 (2004). This 1987 article has been highly influential in the abolitionist world. Hundreds of academic articles, including those relied on by today's dissent, have cited it. It also makes its appearance in judicial decisions—cited recently in a six-judge dissent in *House v. Bell,* 386 F.3d 668, 708 (C.A.6 2004) (en banc) (Merritt, J., dissenting), for the proposition that "the system is allowing some innocent defendants to be executed." The article therefore warrants some further observations.

The 1987 article's obsolescence began at the moment of publication. The most recent executions it considered were in 1984, 1964, and 1951; the rest predate the Allied victory in World War II. (Two of the supposed innocents are Sacco and Vanzetti.) Bedau & Radelet, *supra,* at 73. Even if the innocence claims made in this study were true, all except (perhaps) the 1984 example would cast no light upon the functioning of our current system of capital adjudication. The legal community's general attitude toward criminal defendants, the legal protections States afford, the constitutional guarantees this Court enforces, and the scope of federal habeas review are all vastly different from what they were in 1961. So are the scientific means of establishing guilt, and hence innocence—which are now so striking in their operation and effect that they are the subject of more than one popular TV series. (One of these new means, of course, is DNA testing—which the dissent seems to think is primarily a way to identify defendants erroneously convicted, rather than a highly effective way to avoid conviction of the innocent.)

But their current relevance aside, this study's conclusions are unverified. And if the support for its most significant conclusion—the execution of 23 innocents in the 20th century—is any indication of its accuracy, neither it, nor any study so careless as to rely upon it, is worthy of credence. The only execution of an innocent man it alleges to have occurred after the restoration of the death penalty in 1976—the Florida execution of James Adams in 1984—is the easiest case to verify. As evidence of Adams' innocence, it describes a hair that could not have been his as being "clutched in the victim's hand," Bedau & Radelet, *supra,* at 91. The hair was *not* in the victim's hand; "[i]t was a remnant of a sweeping of the ambulance and so could have come from another source." Markman & Cassell, Protecting the Innocent: A Response to the Bedau-Radelet Study, 41 Stan. L.Rev. 121, 131 (1988). The study also claims that a witness who "heard a voice inside the victim's home at the time of the crime" testified that the "voice was a woman's," Bedau & Radelet, *supra,* at 91. The witness's actual testimony was that the voice, which said "'"In the name of God, don't do it"'" (and was hence unlikely to have been the voice of anyone but the male victim), "'sounded "kind of like a woman's voice, kind of like strangling or something. . . ."'" Markman & Cassell, 41 Stan. L. Rev., at 130. Bedau and Radelet failed to mention that upon arrest on the afternoon of the murder Adams was found with some $200 in his pocket—one bill of which "was stained with type O blood. When Adams was asked about the blood on the money, he said that it came from a cut on his finger. His blood was type AB, however, while the victim's was type O." *Id.,* at 132. Among the other unmentioned, incriminating details: that the victim's *eyeglasses* were found in Adams' car, along with jewelry belonging to the victim, and clothing of Adams' stained with type O blood. *Ibid.* This is just a sample of the evidence arrayed against this "innocent." See *id.*, at 128–133, 148–150.

Critics have questioned the study's findings with regard to all its other cases of execution of alleged innocents for which "appellate opinions ... set forth the facts proved at trial in detail sufficient to permit a neutral observer to assess the validity of the authors' conclusions." *Id.*, at 134. (For the rest, there was not "a reasonably complete account of the facts ... readily available," *id.*, at 145.) As to those cases, the only readily verifiable ones, the authors of the 1987 study later acknowledged, "We agree with our critics that we have not 'proved' these executed defendants to be innocent; we never claimed that we had." Bedau & Radelet, The Myth of Infallibility: A Reply to Markman and Cassell, 41 Stan. L.Rev. 161, 164 (1988). One would have hoped that this disclaimer of the study's most striking conclusion, if not the study's dubious methodology, would have prevented it from being cited as authority in the pages of the United States Reports. But alas, it is too late for that. Although today's dissent relies on the study only indirectly, the two dissenters who were on the Court in January 1993 have already embraced it. "One impressive study," they noted (referring to the 1987 study), "has concluded that 23 innocent people have been executed in the United States in this century, including one as recently as 1984." *Herrera v. Collins*, 506 U.S. 390, 430, n. 1 (1993) (Blackmun, J., joined by STEVENS and SOUTER, JJ., dissenting).[4]

Remarkably avoiding any claim of erroneous executions, the dissent focuses on the large numbers of *non*-executed "exonerees" paraded by various professors. It speaks as though exoneration came about through the operation of some outside force to correct the mistakes of our legal system, rather than *as a consequence of the functioning of our legal system.* Reversal of an erroneous conviction on appeal or on habeas, or the pardoning of an innocent condemnee through executive clemency, demonstrates not the failure of the system but its success. Those devices are part and parcel of the multiple assurances that are applied before a death sentence is carried out.

Of course even in identifying exonerees, the dissent is willing to accept anybody's say-so. It engages in no critical review, but merely parrots articles or reports that support its attack on the American criminal justice system. The dissent places significant weight, for instance, on the Illinois Report (compiled by the appointees of an Illinois Governor who had declared a moratorium upon the death penalty and who eventually commuted all death sentences in the State, see Warden, Illinois Death Penalty Reform: How It Happened, What It Promises, 95 J.Crim. L. & C. 381, 406–407, 410 (2005)), which it claims shows that "false verdicts" are "remarkable in number." (opinion of SOUTER, J.). The dissent claims that this report identifies 13 inmates released from death row after they were determined to be innocent. To take one of these cases, discussed by the dissent as an example of a judgment "as close to innocence as any judgments courts normally render," *post*, at n. 2: In *People v. Smith*, 185 Ill.2d 532, 708 N.E.2d 365 (1999), the defendant was twice convicted of murder. After his first trial, the Supreme Court of Illinois "reversed [his] conviction based upon certain evidentiary errors" and remanded his case for a new trial. *Id.*, 708 N.E.2d, at 366. The second jury convicted Smith again. The Supreme Court of Illinois again reversed the conviction because it found that the evidence was insufficient to establish guilt beyond a reasonable doubt. *Id.*, 708 N.E.2d, at 370–371. The court explained:

> "While a not guilty finding is sometimes equated with a finding of innocence, that conclusion is erroneous. Courts do not find people guilty or innocent.... A not guilty verdict expresses no view as to a defendant's innocence. Rather, [a reversal of conviction] indicates simply that the prosecution has failed to meet its burden of proof." *Id.*, 708 N.E.2d, at 371.

This case alone suffices to refute the dissent's claim that the Illinois Report distinguishes between "exoneration of a convict because of actual innocence, and reversal of a judgment because of legal error affecting conviction or sentence but not inconsistent with guilt in fact," *post*, at n. 2. The broader point, however, is that it is ut-

4. See also *Callins v. Collins*, 510 U.S. 1141, 1158, n. 8 (1994) (Blackmun, J., dissenting from denial of certiorari) ("Innocent persons *have* been executed, see Bedau & Radelet, Miscarriages of Justice in Potentially Capital Cases, 40 Stan. L.Rev. 21, 36, 173–179 (1987), perhaps recently, see *Herrera v. Collins*, 506 U.S. 390 (1993), and will continue to be executed under our death penalty scheme").

terly impossible to regard "exoneration"—however casually defined—as a failure of the capital justice system, rather than as a vindication of its effectiveness in releasing not only defendants who are innocent, but those whose guilt has not been established beyond a reasonable doubt.

Another of the dissent's leading authorities on exoneration of the innocent is Gross, Jacoby, Matheson, Montgomery, & Patil, Exonerations in the United States 1989 Through 2003, 95 J. Crim. L. & C. 523 (2005) (hereinafter Gross). The dissent quotes that study's self-congratulatory "criteria" of exoneration seemingly so rigorous that no one could doubt the study's reliability. See *post,* at n. 3 (opinion of SOUTER, J.). But in fact that article, like the others cited, is notable not for its rigorous investigation and analysis, but for the fervor of its belief that the American justice system is condemning the innocent "in numbers," as the dissent puts it, "never imagined before the development of DNA tests." *Post,* (opinion of SOUTER, J.). Among the article's list of 74 "exonerees," Gross 529, is Jay Smith of Pennsylvania. Smith—a school principal—earned three death sentences for slaying one of his teachers and her two young children. See *Smith v. Holtz,* 210 F.3d 186, 188 (C.A.3 2000). His retrial for triple murder was barred on double-jeopardy grounds because of prosecutorial misconduct during the first trial. But Smith could not leave well enough alone. He had the gall to sue, under 42 U.S.C. § 1983, for false imprisonment. The Court of Appeals for the Third Circuit affirmed the jury verdict for the defendants, observing along the way that "our confidence in Smith's convictions is not diminished in the least. We remain firmly convinced of the integrity of those guilty verdicts." 210 F.3d, at 198.

Another "exonerated" murderer in the Gross study is Jeremy Sheets, convicted in Nebraska. His accomplice in the rape and murder of a girl had been secretly tape recorded; he "admitted that he drove the car used in the murder..., and implicated Sheets in the murder." *Sheets v. Butera,* 389 F.3d 772, 775 (C.A.8 2004). The accomplice was arrested and eventually described the murder in greater detail, after which a plea agreement was arranged, conditioned on the accomplice's full cooperation. The resulting taped confession, which implicated Sheets, was "[t]he crucial portion of the State's case," *State v. Sheets,* 618 N.W.2d 117, 122 (Neb. 2000). But the accomplice committed suicide in jail, depriving Sheets of the opportunity to cross-examine him. This, the Nebraska Supreme Court held, rendered the evidence inadmissible under the Sixth Amendment. After the central evidence was excluded, the State did not retry Sheets. Sheets brought a § 1983 claim; the U.S. Court of Appeals for the Eighth Circuit affirmed the District Court's grant of summary judgment against him. *Id.,* at 780. Sheets also sought the $1,000 he had been required to pay to the Nebraska Victim's Compensation Fund; the State Attorney General—far from concluding that Sheets had been "exonerated" and was entitled to the money—refused to return it. The court action left open the possibility that Sheets could be retried, and the Attorney General did "not believe the reversal on the ground of improper admission of evidence... is a favorable disposition of charges."

In its inflation of the word "exoneration," the Gross article hardly stands alone; mischaracterization of reversible error as actual innocence is endemic in abolitionist rhetoric, and other prominent catalogues of "innocence" in the death-penalty context suffer from the same defect. Perhaps the best known of them is the List of Those Freed From Death Row, maintained by the Death Penalty Information Center. See http://www.deathpenaltyinfo.org/article.php?scid=6&did=110. This includes the cases from the Gross article described above, but also enters some dubious candidates of its own. Delbert Tibbs is one of them. We considered his case in *Tibbs v. Florida,* 457 U.S. 31 (1982), concluding that the Double Jeopardy Clause does not bar a retrial when a conviction is "revers[ed] based on the weight, rather than the sufficiency, of the evidence," *id.,* at 32. The case involved a man and a woman hitchhiking together in Florida. A driver who picked them up sodomized and raped the woman, and killed her boyfriend. She eventually escaped and positively identified Tibbs. The Florida Supreme Court reversed the conviction on a 4-to-3 vote. *Tibbs v. State,* 337 So.2d 788 (Fla.1976). The Florida courts then grappled with whether Tibbs could be retried without violating the Double Jeopardy Clause. The Florida Supreme Court determined not only that there was no double-jeopardy problem, but that the *very basis on which it had reversed the conviction was no longer valid law,* and that its action in "reweigh[ing] the evidence" in Tibbs' case had been "clearly improper." After we affirmed the Florida Supreme Court, however, the State felt compelled to drop the charges. The state attorney explained this to the Florida Commission on Capital Cases: "'By the time of the retrial, [the] witness/victim ... had progressed from a marijuana smoker to a crack user and I could not put her up on the stand, so I declined to prosecute. Tibbs, in my opinion, was never an innocent man wrongfully accused. He was a lucky human being. He was guilty, he was lucky and now he is free. His 1974 conviction was not a miscarriage of justice.'" Florida Commission on Capital Cases, Case Histories: A Review of 24 Individuals Released From Death Row 136–137 (rev. Sept. 10, 2002), http://www.floridacapitalcases.state.fl.us/Publications/innocentsproject.pdf. Other state officials involved made similar points.

Of course, even with its distorted concept of what constitutes "exoneration," the claims of the Gross article are fairly modest: Between 1989 and 2003, the authors identify 340 "exonerations" *nationwide*—not just for capital cases, mind you, nor even just for murder convictions, but for various felonies. Joshua Marquis, a district attorney in Oregon, recently responded to this article as follows:

> "[L]et's give the professor the benefit of the doubt: let's assume that he understated the number of innocents by roughly a factor of 10, that instead of 340 there were 4,000 people in prison who weren't involved in the crime in any way. During that same 15 years, there were more than 15 million felony convictions across the country. That would make the error rate .027 percent—or, to put it another way, a success rate of 99.973 percent." The Innocent and the Shammed, N.Y. Times, Jan. 26, 2006, p. A23.

The dissent's suggestion that capital defendants are *especially* liable to suffer from the lack of 100% perfection in our criminal justice system is implausible. Capital cases are given especially close scrutiny at every level, which is why in most cases many years elapse before the sentence is executed. And of course capital cases receive special attention in the application of executive clemency. Indeed, one of the arguments made by abolitionists is that the process of finally completing all the appeals and reexaminations of capital sentences is so lengthy, and thus so expensive for the State, that the game is not worth the candle. The proof of the pudding, of course, is that as far as anyone can determine (and many are looking), *none* of the cases included in the .027% error rate for American verdicts involved a capital defendant erroneously executed.

Since 1976 there have been approximately a half million murders in the United States. In that time, 7,000 murderers have been sentenced to death; about 950 of them have been executed; and about 3,700 inmates are currently on death row. See Marquis, The Myth of Innocence, 95 J. Crim. L. & C. 501, 518 (2005). As a consequence of the sensitivity of the criminal justice system to the due-process rights of defendants sentenced to death, almost two-thirds of all death sentences are overturned. "Virtually none" of these reversals, however, are attributable to a defendant's "'actual innocence.'" Most are based on legal errors that have little or nothing to do with guilt. See *id.*, at 519–520. The studies cited by the dissent demonstrate nothing more.

Like other human institutions, courts and juries are not perfect. One cannot have a system of criminal punishment without accepting the possibility that someone will be punished mistakenly. That is a truism, not a revelation. But with regard to the punishment of death in the current American system, that possibility has been reduced to an insignificant minimum. This explains why those ideologically driven to ferret out and proclaim a mistaken modern execution have not a single verifiable case to point to, whereas it is easy as pie to identify plainly guilty murderers who have been set free. The American people have determined that the good to be derived from capital punishment—in deterrence, and perhaps most of all in the meting out of condign justice for horrible crimes—outweighs the risk of error. It is no proper part of the business of this Court, or of its Justices, to second-guess that judgment, much less to impugn it before the world, and less still to frustrate it by imposing judicially invented obstacles to its execution....

Justice SOUTER, with whom Justice STEVENS, Justice GINSBURG, and Justice BREYER join, dissenting....

III

[The Court's relevant] precedent, demanding reasoned moral judgment, developed in response to facts that could not be ignored, the kaleidoscope of life and death verdicts that made no sense in fact or morality in the random sentencing before *Furman* [*v. Georgia,* 408 U.S. 238] was decided in 1972. Today, a new body of fact must be accounted for in deciding what, in practical terms, the Eighth Amendment guarantees should tolerate, for the period starting in 1989 has seen repeated exonerations of convicts under death sentences, in numbers never imagined before the development of DNA tests. We cannot face up to these facts and still hold that the guarantee of morally justifiable sentencing is hollow enough to allow maximizing death sentences, by requiring them when juries fail to find the worst degree of culpability: when, by a State's own standards and a State's own characterization, the case for death is "doubtful."

A few numbers from a growing literature will give a sense of the reality that must be addressed. When the Governor of Illinois imposed a moratorium on executions in 2000, 13 prisoners under death sentences had been released since 1977 after a number of them were shown to be innocent, as described in a report which used their examples to illustrate a theme common to all 13, of "relatively little solid evidence connecting the charged defendants to the crimes." State of Illinois, G. Ryan, Governor, Report of the Governor's Commission on Capital Punishment: Recommendations Only 7 (Apr. 2002) (hereinafter Report); see also *id.*, at 5–6, 7–9. During the same period, 12 condemned convicts had been executed. Subsequently the Governor determined that four more death row inmates were innocent. See *id.*, at 5–6; Warden, Illinois Death Penalty Reform, 95 J. Crim. L. & C. 381, 382, and n. 6 (2005).[2] Illinois had thus wrongly convicted and condemned even more capital defendants than it had executed, but it may well not have been otherwise unique; one recent study reports that between 1989 and 2003, 74 American prisoners condemned to death were exonerated, Gross, Jacoby, Matheson, Montgomery, & Patil, Exonerations in the United States 1989 Through 2003, 95 J. Crim. L. & C. 523, 531 (2006) (hereinafter Gross), many of them cleared by DNA evidence, *ibid.*[3] Another report states that "more

---

2. The Illinois Report emphasizes the difference between exoneration of a convict because of actual innocence, and reversal of a judgment because of legal error affecting conviction or sentence but not inconsistent with guilt in fact. See Report 9 (noting that, apart from the 13 released men, a "broader review" discloses that more than half of the State's death penalty cases "were reversed at some point in the process"). More importantly, it takes only a cursory reading of the Report to recognize that it describes men released who were demonstrably innocent or convicted on grossly unreliable evidence. Of one, the Report notes "two other persons were subsequently convicted in Wisconsin of" the murders. *Id.*, at 8. Of two others, the Report states that they were released after "DNA tests revealed that none of them were the source of the semen found in the victim. That same year, two other men confessed to the crime, pleaded guilty and were sentenced to life in prison, and a third was tried and convicted for the crime." *Ibid.* Of yet another, the Report says that "another man subsequently confessed to the crime for which [the released man] was convicted. He entered a plea of guilty and is currently serving a prison term for that crime." *Id.*, at 9.

> A number were subject to judgments as close to innocence as any judgments courts normally render. In the case of one of the released men, the Supreme Court of Illinois found the evidence insufficient to support his conviction. See *People v. Smith*, 708 N.E.2d 365 (Ill. 1999). Several others obtained acquittals, and still more simply had the charges against them dropped, after receiving orders for new trials.
>
> At least 2 of the 13 were released at the initiative of the executive. We can reasonably assume that a State under no obligation to do so would not release into the public a person against whom it had a valid conviction and sentence unless it were certain beyond all doubt that the person in custody was not the perpetrator of the crime. The reason that the State would forgo even a judicial forum in which defendants would demonstrate grounds for vacating their convictions is a matter of common sense: evidence going to innocence was conclusive.

3. The authors state the criteria for their study: "As we use the term, 'exoneration' is an official act declaring a defendant not guilty of a crime for which he or she had previously been convicted. The exonerations we have studied occurred in four ways: (1) In forty-two cases governors (or other appropriate executive officers) issued pardons based on evidence of the defendants' innocence. (2) In 263 cases criminal charges were dismissed by courts after new evidence of innocence emerged, such as DNA. (3) In thirty-one cases the defendants were acquitted at a retrial on the basis of evidence that they had no role in the crimes for which they were originally convicted. (4) In four cases, states posthumously acknowledged the innocence of defendants who had already died in prison...." Gross 524 (footnote omitted). The authors exclude from their list of exonerations "any case in which a dismissal or an acquittal appears to have been based on a decision that while the defendant was not guilty of the charges in the original conviction, he did play a role in the crime and may be guilty of some lesser crime that is based on the same conduct. For our purposes, a defendant who is acquitted of murder on retrial, but convicted of involuntary manslaughter, has not been exonerated. We have also excluded any case in which a dismissal was entered in the absence of strong evidence of factual innocence, or in which—despite such evidence—there was unexplained physical evidence of the defendant's guilt." *Id.*, at 524, n. 4.

than 110" death row prisoners have been released since 1973 upon findings that they were innocent of the crimes charged, and "[h]undreds of additional wrongful convictions in potentially capital cases have been documented over the past century." Lanier & Acker, Capital Punishment, the Moratorium Movement, and Empirical Questions, 10 Psychology, Public Policy & Law 577, 593 (2004). Most of these wrongful convictions and sentences resulted from eyewitness misidentification, false confession, and (most frequently) perjury, Gross 544, 551–552, and the total shows that among all prosecutions homicide cases suffer an unusually high incidence of false conviction, *id.*, at 532, 552, probably owing to the combined difficulty of investigating without help from the victim, intense pressure to get convictions in homicide cases, and the corresponding incentive for the guilty to frame the innocent, *id.*, at 532.

We are thus in a period of new empirical argument about how "death is different," *Gregg*, 428 U.S., at 188 (joint opinion of Stewart, Powell, and STEVENS, JJ.): not only would these false verdicts defy correction after the fatal moment, the Illinois experience shows them to be remarkable in number, and they are probably disproportionately high in capital cases. While it is far too soon for any generalization about the soundness of capital sentencing across the country, the cautionary lesson of recent experience addresses the tie-breaking potential of the Kansas statute: the same risks of falsity that infect proof of guilt raise questions about sentences, when the circumstances of the crime are aggravating factors and bear on predictions of future dangerousness.

In the face of evidence of the hazards of capital prosecution, maintaining a sentencing system mandating death when the sentencer finds the evidence pro and con to be in equipoise is obtuse by any moral or social measure. And unless application of the Eighth Amendment no longer calls for reasoned moral judgment in substance as well as form, the Kansas law is unconstitutional.

Notes and Questions

1. In Chapter 7, while addressing issues involving scientific and forensic evidence, we discussed the recent controversy over whether Cameron Todd Willingham, executed in Texas in 2004, and Claude Jones, executed in Texas in 2000, may have been innocent. Justice Scalia's opinion in *Kansas v. Marsh* emphasizes the absence of proof that an innocent person has been executed in the post-*Furman* era of capital punishment. Do you think Justice Scalia's opinion about the constitutionality of the death penalty would be different if such proof were to emerge? If we accept his premise—that "[l]ike other human institutions, courts and juries are not perfect. One cannot have a system of criminal punishment without accepting the possibility that someone will be punished mistakenly"—which conclusion seems more defensible: that the death penalty should be retained, or that it should be replaced with a punishment such as life imprisonment without parole, where erroneous judgments are not no so final and irrevocable?

2. Justice Scalia's opinion refers to the *New York Times* op-ed piece by Oregon prosecutor Joshua Marquis in which Marquis, attempting to determine a wrongful conviction rate in felony cases states, "That would make the error rate .027 percent—or, to put it another way, a success rate of 99.973 percent." In responding to Scalia and Marquis, Professor D. Michael Risinger attempted to calculate an empirical estimate of the number of people wrongly sentenced to death over an eight-year period. Using only capital rape-murder cases in which there was likely to be DNA available for testing as the denominator (479 cases between 1982 and 1989) and the number of identified exonerees divided in half during this time period as the numerator (10.5), Risinger estimates a 3.3% wrongful conviction rate for capital rape-murders; a rate which he refers to as, "A conservative minimum factual innocence rate, derived from a real, not insignificant, set of serious criminal convictions, and capital convictions to boot."[9] Professor Samuel Gross, whose study formed the basis of Marquis' calculations, took exception with logic employed to arrive at the estimated .027 error rate:

> [E]stimates ... based on some version of dividing the number of known false convictions—exonerations—by the total of all convictions [ignores] the fact that almost all of these exonerations occurred in a few narrow categories of crimes (primarily murder and rape) and that even within those categories many false convictions remain unknown, perhaps the great majority. By this logic we could estimate the number of baseball players who have used steroids by dividing the number of major league baseball players who have been caught by the total of all baseball players at all levels: major league, minor leagues, semipro, college, and Little League—and maybe throwing in football and basketball players as well.[10]

3. Justice Souter's opinion in *Kansas v. Marsh* refers to the spate of death row exonerations, including several supported by DNA analysis, as "a new body of fact [that] must be accounted for in deciding what ... the Eighth Amendment guarantees should tolerate...." If DNA and other forms of evidence have helped expose wrongful convictions in some post-*Furman* capital cases, what does this fact suggest about convictions and executions in cases where there was no DNA to test, including those in the pre-*Furman* era: that they should be considered reliable, or simply that the means may have been lacking to help identify wrongful convictions? If we can safely assume that the Framers of the 8th Amendment were aware that miscarriages of justice could occur, including in capital cases, have the "evolving standards of decency" made the risk of executing innocent persons of greater constitutional significance in contemporary society? Or, as Justice Scalia suggests, should decisions about the perpetuation of capital punishment be left to the states and their legislative bodies, assigning weight as they deem appropriate to the risk of executing the innocent and the death penalty's perceived retributive, deterrent, or incapacitation benefits?

Justice John Paul Stevens began his tenure on the Supreme Court in 1975. The following year, in *Gregg v. Georgia*, 428 U.S. 153, 93 S.Ct. 2909, 49 L.Ed.2d 859 (1976) and its companion cases, he joined six other members of the Court in upholding "guided discretion" death-penalty legislation that was enacted in several states after *Furman* invalidated their earlier capital sentencing laws. More than three decades later, just two years before his retirement, Justice Stevens repudiated his earlier views. He did so in *Baze v. Rees*, 553 U.S. 35, 128 S.Ct. 1520, 170 L.Ed.2d 420 (2008), a case—much like *Kansas v. Marsh*—that presented an issue that seems unlikely to have provoked such a wide-ranging opinion; the question before the Court involved the constitutionality of Kentucky's use of lethal injection as a method of execution. And, much as he did in response to Justice Souter's discussion of innocence in *Kansas v. Marsh*, Justice Scalia issued a spirited rejoinder to Justice Stevens' opinion.

Baze v. Rees

553 U.S. 35, 128 S.Ct. 1520, 170 L.Ed.2d 420 (2008)

... Justice STEVENS, concurring in the judgment.

When we granted certiorari in this case, I assumed that our decision would bring the debate about lethal injection as a method of execution to a close. It now seems clear that it will not. The question whether a similar three-drug protocol may be used in other States remains open, and may well be answered differently in a future case on the basis of a more complete record. Instead of ending the controversy, I am now convinced that this case will generate debate not only about the constitutionality of the three-drug protocol, and specifically about the justification for the use of the paralytic agent, pancuronium bromide, but also about the justification for the death penalty itself....

II

The thoughtful opinions written by THE CHIEF JUSTICE and by Justice GINSBURG have persuaded me that current decisions by state legislatures, by the Congress of the United States, and by this Court to retain the death penalty as a part of our law are the product of habit and inattention rather than an acceptable deliberative process that weighs the costs and risks of administering that penalty against its identifiable benefits, and rest in part on a faulty assumption about the retributive force of the death penalty.

In *Gregg v. Georgia,* 428 U.S. 153 (1976), we explained that unless a criminal sanction serves a legitimate penological function, it constitutes "gratuitous infliction of suffering" in violation of the Eighth Amendment. We then identified three societal purposes for death as a sanction: incapacitation, deterrence, and retribution. In the past three decades, however, each of these rationales has been called into question.

While incapacitation may have been a legitimate rationale in 1976, the recent rise in statutes providing for life imprisonment without the possibility of parole demonstrates that incapacitation is neither a necessary nor a sufficient justification for the death penalty.[10] Moreover, a recent poll indicates that support for the death penalty drops significantly when life without the possibility of parole is presented as an alternative option.[11] And the available sociological evidence suggests that juries are less likely to impose the death penalty when life without parole is available as a sentence.[12]

The legitimacy of deterrence as an acceptable justification for the death penalty is also questionable, at best. Despite 30 years of empirical research in the area, there remains no reliable statistical evidence that capital punishment in fact deters potential offenders.[13] In the absence of such evidence, deterrence cannot serve as a sufficient penological justification for this uniquely severe and irrevocable punishment.

We are left, then, with retribution as the primary rationale for imposing the death penalty. And indeed, it is the retribution rationale that animates much of the remaining enthusiasm for the death penalty.[14] As Lord Justice Denning argued in 1950, "'some crimes are so outrageous that society insists on adequate punishment, because the wrong-doer deserves it, irrespective of whether it is a deterrent or not.'" Our Eighth Amendment jurisprudence has narrowed the class of offenders eligible for the death penalty to include only those who have committed outrageous crimes defined by specific aggravating factors. It is the cruel treatment of victims that

10. Forty-eight States now have some form of life imprisonment without parole, with the majority of statutes enacted within the last two decades. See Note, A Matter of Life and Death: The Effect of Life-Without-Parole Statutes on Capital Punishment, 119 Harv. L.Rev. 1838, 1839, 1841–1844 (2006).

11. See R. Dieter, Sentencing For Life: Americans Embrace Alternatives to the Death Penalty (Apr.1993), http://www.deathpenaltyinfo.org/article.php?scid=45&did=481.

12. In one study, potential capital jurors in Virginia stated that knowing about the existence of statutes providing for life without the possibility of parole would significantly influence their sentencing decision. In another study, a significant majority of potential capital jurors in Georgia said they would be more likely to select a life sentence over a death sentence if they knew that the defendant would be ineligible for parole for at least 25 years. See Note, 119 Harv. L.Rev., at 1845....

13. Admittedly, there has been a recent surge in scholarship asserting the deterrent effect of the death penalty, see, *e.g.,* Mocan & Gittings, Getting Off Death Row: Commuted Sentences and the Deterrent Effect of Capital Punishment, 46 J. Law & Econ. 453 (2003); Adler & Summers, Capital Punishment Works, Wall Street Journal, Nov. 2, 2007, p. A13, but there has been an equal, if not greater, amount of scholarship criticizing the methodologies of those studies and questioning the results, see, *e.g.,* Fagan, Death and Deterrence Redux: Science, Law and Causal Reasoning on Capital Punishment, 4 Ohio St. J.Crim. L. 255 (2006); Donohue & Wolfers, Uses and Abuses of Empirical Evidence in the Death Penalty Debate, 58 Stan. L.Rev. 791 (2005).

14. Retribution is the most common basis of support for the death penalty. A recent study found that 37% of death penalty supporters cited "an eye for an eye/they took a life/fits the crime" as their reason for supporting capital punishment. Another 13% cited "They deserve it." The next most common reasons—"sav[ing] taxpayers money/cost associated with prison" and deterrence—were each cited by 11% of supporters. See Dept. of Justice, Bureau of Justice Statistics, Sourcebook of Criminal Justice Statistics 147 (2003) (Table 2.55), online at http://www.albany.edu/sourcebook/pdf/t255.pdf.

provides the most persuasive arguments for prosecutors seeking the death penalty. A natural response to such heinous crimes is a thirst for vengeance.[15]

At the same time, however, ... our society has moved away from public and painful retribution towards ever more humane forms of punishment. State-sanctioned killing is therefore becoming more and more anachronistic. In an attempt to bring executions in line with our evolving standards of decency, we have adopted increasingly less painful methods of execution, and then declared previous methods barbaric and archaic. But by requiring that an execution be relatively painless, we necessarily protect the inmate from enduring any punishment that is comparable to the suffering inflicted on his victim.[16] This trend, while appropriate and required by the Eighth Amendment's prohibition on cruel and unusual punishment, actually undermines the very premise on which public approval of the retribution rationale is based. See, *e.g.*, Kaufman-Osborn, Regulating Death: Capital Punishment and the Late Liberal State, 111 Yale L.J. 681, 704 (2001) (explaining that there is "a tension between our desire to realize the claims of retribution by killing those who kill, and ... a method [of execution] that, because it seems to do no harm other than killing, cannot satisfy the intuitive sense of equivalence that informs this conception of justice"); A. Sarat, When the State Kills: Capital Punishment and the American Condition 60–84 (2001).

Full recognition of the diminishing force of the principal rationales for retaining the death penalty should lead this Court and legislatures to reexamine the question recently posed by Professor Salinas, a former Texas prosecutor and judge: "Is it time to Kill the Death Penalty?" See Salinas, 34 Am. J.Crim. L. 39 (2006). The time for a dispassionate, impartial comparison of the enormous costs that death penalty litigation imposes on society with the benefits that it produces has surely arrived.[17]

15. For example, family members of victims of the Oklahoma City bombing called for the Government to "'put [Timothy McVeigh] inside a bomb and blow it up.'" Walsh, One Arraigned, Two Undergo Questioning, Washington Post, Apr. 22, 1995, pp. A1, A13. Commentators at the time noted that an overwhelming percentage of Americans felt that executing McVeigh was not enough. Linder, A Political Verdict: McVeigh: When Death Is Not Enough, L.A. Times, June 8, 1997, p. M1.

16. For example, one survivor of the Oklahoma City bombing expressed a belief that "'death by [lethal] injection [was] "too good" for McVeigh.'" A. Sarat, When the State kills: Capital Punishment and the American Condition 64 (2001). Similarly, one mother, when told that her child's killer would die by lethal injection, asked: "Do they feel anything? Do they hurt? Is there any pain? Very humane compared to what they've done to our children. The torture they've put our kids through. I think sometimes it's too easy. They ought to feel something. If it's fire burning all the way through their body or whatever. There ought to be some little sense of pain to it." *Id.*, at 60 (emphasis deleted).

17. For a discussion of the financial costs as well as some of the less tangible costs of the death penalty, see Kozinski & Gallagher, Death: The Ultimate Run-On Sentence, 46 Case W. Res. L.Rev. 1 (1995) (discussing, *inter alia*, the burden on the courts and the lack of finality for victim's families). Although a lack of finality in death cases may seem counterintuitive, Kozinski and Gallagher explain:

> "Death cases raise many more issues, and far more complex issues, than other criminal cases, and they are attacked with more gusto and reviewed with more vigor in the courts. This means there is a strong possibility that the conviction or sentence will be reconsidered—seriously reconsidered—five, ten, twenty years after the trial.... One has to wonder and worry about the effect this has on the families of the victims, who have to live with the possibility—and often the reality—of retrials, evidentiary hearings, and last-minute stays of execution for decades after the crime." *Id.*, at 17–18 (footnotes omitted).

Thus, they conclude that "we are left in limbo, with machinery that is immensely expensive, that chokes our legal institutions so they are impeded from doing all the other things a society expects from its courts, [and] that visits repeated trauma on victims' families...." *Id.*, at 27–28; see also Block, A Slow Death, N.Y. Times, Mar. 15, 2007, p. A27 (discussing the "enormous costs and burdens to the judicial system" resulting from the death penalty).

Some argue that these costs are the consequence of judicial insistence on unnecessarily elaborate and lengthy appellate procedures. To the contrary, they result "in large part from the States' failure to apply constitutionally sufficient procedures at the time of initial [conviction or] sentencing." *Knight v. Florida,* 528 U.S. 990, 998 (1999) (BREYER, J., dissenting from denial of certiorari). They may also result from a general reluctance by States to put large numbers of defendants to

III

"[A] penalty may be cruel and unusual because it is excessive and serves no valid legislative purpose." *Furman v. Georgia,* 408 U.S. 238, 331 (1972) (Marshall, J., concurring). Our cases holding that certain sanctions are "excessive," and therefore prohibited by the Eighth Amendment, have relied heavily on "objective criteria," such as legislative enactments.... [We also have] acknowledged that "objective evidence, though of great importance, did not 'wholly determine' the controversy, 'for the Constitution contemplates that in the end our own judgment will be brought to bear on the question of the acceptability of the death penalty under the Eighth Amendment.' " *Atkins* [*v. Virginia,* 536 U.S. 304], 312 [(2002)]....

Our decisions in 1976 upholding the constitutionality of the death penalty relied heavily on our belief that adequate procedures were in place that would avoid the danger of discriminatory application identified by Justice Douglas' opinion in *Furman,* of arbitrary application identified by Justice Stewart, and of excessiveness identified by Justices Brennan and Marshall. In subsequent years a number of our decisions relied on the premise that "death is different" from every other form of punishment to justify rules minimizing the risk of error in capital cases. Ironically, however, more recent cases have endorsed procedures that provide less protections to capital defendants than to ordinary offenders.

Of special concern to me are rules that deprive the defendant of a trial by jurors representing a fair cross section of the community. Litigation involving both challenges for cause and peremptory challenges has persuaded me that the process of obtaining a "death qualified jury" is really a procedure that has the purpose and effect of obtaining a jury that is biased in favor of conviction. The prosecutorial concern that death verdicts would rarely be returned by 12 randomly selected jurors should be viewed as objective evidence supporting the conclusion that the penalty is excessive.[18]

Another serious concern is that the risk of error in capital cases may be greater than in other cases because the facts are often so disturbing that the interest in making sure the crime does not go unpunished may overcome residual doubt concerning the identity of the offender. Our former emphasis on the importance of ensuring that decisions in death cases be adequately supported by reason rather than emotion, has been undercut by more recent decisions placing a thumb on the prosecutor's side of the scales. Thus, in *Kansas v. Marsh,* 548 U.S. 163 (2006), the Court upheld a state statute that requires imposition of the death penalty when the jury finds that the aggravating and mitigating factors are in equipoise. And in *Payne v. Tennessee,* 501 U.S. 808 (1991), the Court overruled earlier cases and held that "victim impact" evidence relating to the personal characteristics of the victim and the emotional impact of the crime on the victim's family is admissible despite the fact that it sheds no light on the question of guilt or innocence or on the moral culpability of the defendant, and thus serves no purpose other than to encourage jurors to make life or death decisions on the basis of emotion rather than reason.

A third significant concern is the risk of discriminatory application of the death penalty. While that risk has been dramatically reduced, the Court has allowed it to continue to play an unacceptable role in capital cases. Thus, in *McCleskey v. Kemp,* 481 U.S. 279 (1987), the Court upheld a death sentence despite the "strong probability that [the defendant's] sentencing jury ... was influenced by the fact that [he was] black and his victim was white." *Id.,* at 366 (STEVENS, J., dissenting).

Finally, given the real risk of error in this class of cases, the irrevocable nature of the consequences is of decisive importance to me. Whether or not any innocent defendants have

death, even after a sentence of death is imposed. Cf. Tempest, Death Row Often Means a Long Life; California condemns many murderers, but few are ever executed, L.A. Times, Mar. 6, 2006, p. B1 (noting that California death row inmates account for about 20% of the Nation's total death row population, but that the State accounts for only 1% of the Nation's executions). In any event, they are most certainly not the fault of judges who do nothing more than ensure compliance with constitutional guarantees prior to imposing the irrevocable punishment of death.

18. See *Uttecht v. Brown,* 551 U.S. 1, 35 (2007) (STEVENS, J., dissenting) (explaining that "[m]illions of Americans oppose the death penalty," and that "[a] cross section of virtually every community in the country includes citizens who firmly believe the death penalty is unjust but who nevertheless are qualified to serve as jurors in capital cases").

actually been executed, abundant evidence accumulated in recent years has resulted in the exoneration of an unacceptable number of defendants found guilty of capital offenses. See Garrett, Judging Innocence, 108 Colum. L.Rev. 55 (2008); Risinger, Innocents Convicted: An Empirically Justified Factual Wrongful Conviction Rate, 97 J.Crim. L. & C. 761 (2007). The risk of executing innocent defendants can be entirely eliminated by treating any penalty more severe than life imprisonment without the possibility of parole as constitutionally excessive.

In sum, just as Justice White ultimately based his conclusion in *Furman* on his extensive exposure to countless cases for which death is the authorized penalty, I have relied on my own experience in reaching the conclusion that the imposition of the death penalty represents "the pointless and needless extinction of life with only marginal contributions to any discernible social or public purposes. A penalty with such negligible returns to the State [is] patently excessive and cruel and unusual punishment violative of the Eighth Amendment." *Furman,* 408 U.S., at 312 (White, J., concurring).[19]

IV

The conclusion that I have reached with regard to the constitutionality of the death penalty itself makes my decision in this case particularly difficult. It does not, however, justify a refusal to respect precedents that remain a part of our law. This Court has held that the death penalty is constitutional, and has established a framework for evaluating the constitutionality of particular methods of execution. Under those precedents, ... I am persuaded that the evidence adduced by petitioners fails to prove that Kentucky's lethal injection protocol violates the Eighth Amendment. Accordingly, I join the Court's judgment.

Justice SCALIA, with whom Justice THOMAS joins, concurring in the judgment.

... I write separately to provide what I think is needed response to Justice STEVENS' separate opinion.

I

Justice STEVENS concludes as follows: "[T]he imposition of the death penalty represents the pointless and needless extinction of life with only marginal contributions to any discernible social or public purposes. A penalty with such negligible returns to the State [is] patently excessive and cruel and unusual punishment violative of the Eighth Amendment."

This conclusion is insupportable as an interpretation of the Constitution, which generally leaves it to democratically elected legislatures rather than courts to decide what makes significant contribution to social or public purposes. Besides that more general proposition, the very text of the document recognizes that the death penalty is a permissible legislative choice. The Fifth Amendment expressly requires a presentment or indictment of a grand jury to hold a person to answer for "a capital, or otherwise infamous crime," and prohibits deprivation of "life" without due process of law. U.S. Const., Amdt. 5. The same Congress that proposed the Eighth Amendment also enacted the Act of April 30, 1790, which made several offenses punishable by death. Writing in 1976, Professor Hugo Bedau — no friend of the death penalty himself — observed that "[u]ntil fifteen years ago, save for a few mavericks, no one gave any credence to the possibility of ending the death penalty by judicial interpretation of constitutional law." The Courts, the Constitution, and Capital Punishment 118 (1977). There is simply no legal authority for the proposition that the imposition of death as a criminal penalty is unconstitutional other than the opinions in *Furman v. Georgia,* 408 U.S. 238 (1972), which established a nationwide moratorium on capital punishment that Justice STEVENS had a hand in ending four years later in *Gregg.*

II

What prompts Justice STEVENS to repudiate his prior view and to adopt the astounding position that a criminal sanction expressly mentioned in the Constitution violates the Constitu-

19. Not a single Justice in *Furman* concluded that the mention of deprivation of "life" in the Fifth and Fourteenth Amendments insulated the death penalty from constitutional challenge. The five Justices who concurred in the judgment necessarily rejected this argument, and even the four dissenters, who explicitly acknowledged that the death penalty was not considered impermissibly cruel at the time of the framing, proceeded to evaluate whether anything had changed in the intervening 181 years that nevertheless rendered capital punishment unconstitutional. And indeed, the guarantees of procedural fairness contained in the Fifth and Fourteenth Amendments do not resolve the substantive questions relating to the separate limitations imposed by the Eighth Amendment.

tion? His analysis begins with what he believes to be the "uncontroversial legal premise" that the "'extinction of life with only marginal contributions to any discernible social or public purposes ... would be patently excessive' and violative of the Eighth Amendment." Even if that were uncontroversial in the abstract (and it is certainly not what occurs to me as the meaning of "cruel and unusual punishments"), it is assuredly controversial (indeed, flat-out wrong) as applied to a mode of punishment that is explicitly sanctioned by the Constitution. As to that, *the people* have determined whether there is adequate contribution to social or public purposes, and it is no business of unelected judges to set that judgment aside. But even if we grant Justice STEVENS his "uncontroversial premise," his application of that premise to the current practice of capital punishment does not meet the "heavy burden [that] rests on those who would attack the judgment of the representatives of the people." *Gregg, supra,* at 175 (joint opinion of Stewart, Powell, and STEVENS, JJ.). That is to say, Justice STEVENS' policy analysis of the constitutionality of capital punishment fails on its own terms.

According to Justice STEVENS, the death penalty promotes none of the purposes of criminal punishment because it neither prevents more crimes than alternative measures nor serves a retributive purpose. He argues that "the recent rise in statutes providing for life imprisonment without the possibility of parole" means that States have a ready alternative to the death penalty. Moreover, "[d]espite 30 years of empirical research in the area, there remains no reliable statistical evidence that capital punishment in fact deters potential offenders." Taking the points together, Justice STEVENS concludes that the availability of alternatives, and what he describes as the unavailability of "reliable statistical evidence," renders capital punishment unconstitutional. In his view, the benefits of capital punishment—as compared to other forms of punishment such as life imprisonment—are outweighed by the costs.

These conclusions are not supported by the available data. Justice STEVENS' analysis barely acknowledges the "significant body of recent evidence that capital punishment may well have a deterrent effect, possibly a quite powerful one." Sunstein & Vermeule, Is Capital Punishment Morally Required? Acts, Omissions, and Life-Life Tradeoffs, 58 Stan. L.Rev. 703, 706 (2006); see also *id.*, at 706, n. 9 (listing the approximately half a dozen studies supporting this conclusion). According to a "leading national study," "each execution prevents some eighteen murders, on average." *Id.*, at 706. "If the current evidence is even roughly correct ... then a refusal to impose capital punishment will effectively condemn numerous innocent people to death." *Ibid.*

Of course, it may well be that the empirical studies establishing that the death penalty has a powerful deterrent effect are incorrect, and some scholars have disputed its deterrent value. But that is not the point. It is simply not our place to choose one set of responsible empirical studies over another in interpreting the Constitution. Nor is it our place to demand that state legislatures support their criminal sanctions with foolproof empirical studies, rather than commonsense predictions about human behavior. "The value of capital punishment as a deterrent of crime is a complex factual issue the resolution of which properly rests with the legislatures, which can evaluate the results of statistical studies in terms of their own local conditions and with a flexibility of approach that is not available to the courts." *Gregg, supra,* at 186 (joint opinion of Stewart, Powell, and STEVENS, JJ.). Were Justice STEVENS' current view the constitutional test, even his own preferred criminal sanction—life imprisonment without the possibility of parole—may fail constitutional scrutiny, because it is entirely unclear that enough empirical evidence supports that sanction as compared to alternatives such as life with the possibility of parole.

But even if Justice STEVENS' assertion about the deterrent value of the death penalty were correct, the death penalty would yet be constitutional (as he concedes) if it served the appropriate purpose of retribution. I would think it difficult indeed to prove that a criminal sanction fails to serve a retributive purpose—a judgment that strikes me as inherently subjective and insusceptible of judicial review. Justice STEVENS, however, concludes that, because the Eighth Amendment "protect[s] the inmate from enduring any punishment that is comparable to the suffering inflicted on his victim," capital punishment serves no retributive purpose at all. The infliction of any pain, according to Justice STEVENS, violates the Eighth Amendment's prohibition against cruel and unusual punishments, but so too does the imposition of capital punishment *without pain* because a criminal penalty lacks a retributive purpose unless it inflicts pain commensurate with the pain that the criminal has caused. In other words, if a punishment is not retributive enough, it is not retributive at all. To state this proposition is to refute it, as Justice STEVENS once understood. "[T]he decision that capital punishment may be the appropriate sanction in extreme cases is an expression of the community's belief that certain crimes are themselves so grievous an affront to humanity that the only adequate response may be the penalty of death." *Gregg,* 428 U.S., at 184 (joint opinion of Stewart, Powell, and STEVENS, JJ.).

Justice STEVENS' final refuge in his cost-benefit analysis is a familiar one: There is a risk that an innocent person might be convicted and sentenced to death—though not a risk that Justice STEVENS can quantify, because he lacks a single example of a person executed for a crime he did not commit in the current American system. His analysis of this risk is thus a series of sweeping condemnations that, if taken seriously, would prevent any punishment under any criminal justice system. According to him, "[t]he prosecutorial concern that death verdicts would rarely be returned by 12 randomly selected jurors should be viewed as objective evidence supporting the conclusion that the penalty is excessive." But prosecutors undoubtedly have a similar concern that *any* unanimous conviction would rarely be returned by 12 randomly selected jurors. That is why they, like defense counsel, are permitted to use the challenges for cause and peremptory challenges that Justice STEVENS finds so troubling, in order to arrive at a jury that both sides believe will be more likely to do justice in a particular case. Justice STEVENS' concern that prosecutors will be inclined to challenge jurors who will not find a person guilty supports not his conclusion, but the separate (and equally erroneous) conclusion that peremptory challenges and challenges for cause are unconstitutional. According to Justice STEVENS, "the risk of error in capital cases may be greater than in other cases because the facts are often so disturbing that the interest in making sure the crime does not go unpunished may overcome residual doubt concerning the identity of the offender." That rationale, however, supports not Justice STEVENS' conclusion that the death penalty is unconstitutional, but the more sweeping proposition that any conviction in a case in which facts are disturbing is suspect—including, of course, convictions resulting in life without parole in those States that do not have capital punishment. The same is true of Justice STEVENS' claim that there is a risk of "discriminatory application of the death penalty." The same could be said of any criminal penalty, including life without parole; there is no proof that in this regard the death penalty is distinctive.

But of all Justice STEVENS' criticisms of the death penalty, the hardest to take is his bemoaning of "the enormous costs that death penalty litigation imposes on society," including the "burden on the courts and the lack of finality for victim's families." Those costs, those burdens, and that lack of finality are in large measure the creation of Justice STEVENS and other Justices opposed to the death penalty, who have "encumber[ed] [it] ... with unwarranted restrictions neither contained in the text of the Constitution nor reflected in two centuries of practice under it"—the product of their policy views "not shared by the vast majority of the American people." *Kansas v. Marsh,* 548 U.S. 163, 186 (2006) (SCALIA, J., concurring).

III

But actually none of this really matters. As Justice STEVENS explains, " 'objective evidence, though of great importance, [does] not wholly determine the controversy, for the Constitution contemplates that in the end *our own judgment will be brought to bear on the question of the acceptability of the death penalty under the Eighth Amendment.*' " *Ante,* (quoting *Atkins v. Virginia,* 536 U.S. 304, 312 (2002); emphasis added). "I have relied *on my own experience* in reaching the conclusion that the imposition of the death penalty" is unconstitutional. (emphasis added).

Purer expression cannot be found of the principle of rule by judicial fiat. In the face of Justice STEVENS' experience, the experience of all others is, it appears, of little consequence. The experience of the state legislatures and the Congress—who retain the death penalty as a form of punishment—is dismissed as "the product of habit and inattention rather than an acceptable deliberative process." The experience of social scientists whose studies indicate that the death penalty deters crime is relegated to a footnote. The experience of fellow citizens who support the death penalty is described, with only the most thinly veiled condemnation, as stemming from a "thirst for vengeance." It is Justice STEVENS' experience that reigns over all.

* * *

I take no position on the desirability of the death penalty, except to say that its value is eminently debatable and the subject of deeply, indeed passionately, held views—which means, to me, that it is preeminently not a matter to be resolved here. And especially not when it is explicitly permitted by the Constitution....

Notes and Questions

1. As a policy issue, does it make sense for a decision about the death penalty's retention or abolition to hinge on balancing its presumed benefits against its presumed costs, including the risk of executing innocent parties? Is a similar balancing approach appropriate for constitutional analysis?

2. Justice Stevens states in his opinion: "given the real risk of error in [capital] cases, the irrevocable nature of the consequences is of decisive importance to me.... The risk of executing innocent defendants can be entirely eliminated by treating any penalty more severe than life imprisonment without the possibility of parole as constitutionally excessive." 553 U.S., at 85–86. If the death penalty were eliminated as a sentencing option—as it has been in several states, Washington D.C., and in almost all Western industrialized countries except for the United States—might one ironic consequence be that the quest to discover and exonerate wrongfully convicted individuals, and enact corresponding systemic reforms, will lose some vigor? Consider the report of the Governor's Commission on Capital Punishment in Illinois, comprising a comprehensive set of procedural reforms that were recommended after 13 death-sentenced individuals in that state were exonerated (ultimately leading to former Governor George Ryan's decision to commute the death sentences of all individuals then on Illinois' death row).[11]

> ... [T]he recommendations in this Report focus primarily on issues that relate to the capital punishment process....
>
> During some of its discussions, Commission members were struck by the fact that particular cases received a much higher level of scrutiny because capital punishment was involved. Had those same defendants been sentenced to life imprisonment, or a term of years, their cases might not have been reviewed as carefully and by so many different parties. As a result, some of the injustices with which the public has recently become acquainted might not have been corrected....
>
> ... [T]he punishment [a defendant who is sentenced to life in prison without the possibility of parole] receives is severe, and the possibility that innocent persons may suffer as a result exists, albeit to a different degree than in a case involving the death penalty. In light of this, recommendations made in this Report with respect to gathering of evidence, avoiding tunnel vision, protection against false confessions, eyewitness evidence, DNA evidence and the caution about problems associated with certain types of cases, such as those involving in-custody informants, apply with equal force to cases where non-death sentences are imposed.[12]

3. Jurors who have concluded "beyond a reasonable doubt" that a defendant is guilty of capital murder, and accordingly have voted to convict, nevertheless sometimes harbor a "lingering doubt" or "residual doubt" about the correctness of their verdict. Research evidence suggests that lingering doubt about guilt can powerfully influence punishment decisions, helping sway jurors to impose a sentence of life imprisonment instead of death.[13] Supreme Court rulings have been less than definitive about whether defendants have a constitutional right to present evidence or arguments that focus on residual doubt at the punishment phase of capital trials, although several justices have suggested that lingering doubt about guilt is not properly considered a factor mitigating punishment and hence that no such right exists.[14]

C. Death-Qualified Juries

A juror's obligation is to apply the facts proven at a trial to the law governing the case and render a verdict accordingly. A prospective juror who is unwilling or unable to follow the law is not allowed to serve; he or she is disqualified "for cause." Deeply held personal views about the death penalty may be strong enough to interfere with a capital trial juror's obligation to adhere to the law as instructed by the judge. A prospective juror whose personal opposition to capital punishment "would 'prevent or substantially impair the performance of his duties as a juror in accordance with his instructions and his oath'"[15] is not "death qualified" and consequently can be excused for cause in trials in which the prosecution is seeking the death penalty. Conversely, a prospective juror who believes that the death penalty should automatically be imposed in all cases of murder, and is unwilling to consider mitigation evidence or the possibility of a sentence other than death, is not "life qualified" and also can be excused for cause in capital murder trials.[16] Studies typically, although not invariably, find that the number of potential jurors who are not "death qualified" substantially exceeds the number who are not "life qualified."[17]

Excluding a significant segment of the population from jury service in capital trials because those individuals' personal opinions about the death penalty trump their willingness to follow the law not only has implications for capital sentencing decisions, but also for juries' guilt-phase decisions. The explanations for why a juror's attitudes about capital punishment might influence his or her judgment about a defendant's guilt are discussed at length in the following opinion. In *Lockhart v. McCree,* 479 U.S. 162, 106 S.Ct. 1758, 90 L.Ed.2d 137 (1986), the Supreme Court rejected a capital murder defendant's claim that the death-qualification process violated his Sixth and Fourteenth Amendment rights to a trial by a representative and impartial jury. McCree had argued that the death-qualification of his jury resulted in a "conviction prone" panel and that the removal of individuals with strong anti-death penalty views should have been postponed until the penalty phase of the trial (which would become necessary, of course, only if the guilt-phase jury convicted him of capital murder). In *State v. Griffin,* below, the Connecticut Supreme Court considered a similar claim that was raised under the state constitution.

State v. Griffin

741 A.2d 913 (Conn. 1999)

CALLAHAN, C.J.

The defendant appeals from the judgment of conviction, after a jury trial, of one count of capital felony in violation of General Statutes § 53a-54b (8) and of two counts of murder in violation of General Statutes § 53a-54a. In her appeal, the defendant claims that ... the trial court improperly permitted the state to "death qualify"[2] potential jurors prior to the guilt phase of her trial, thereby denying her right, under the Connecticut constitution, to trial by an impartial jury ...

The jury reasonably could have found the following facts....

The defendant shot and attacked both of the victims as they entered the kitchen. During the scuffle, the telephone answering machine located on the kitchen counter was activated and recorded some of the audible portion of the events that were taking place in the kitchen. The

2. The term "death qualified" jury has been used to refer to a jury from which prospective jurors have been excluded for cause on the basis of their opposition to the death penalty. See *Lockhart v. McCree,* 476 U.S. 162, 167 (1986).

defendant shot Steller once and King three times. When the gun had been emptied, the defendant, realizing that the victims were still alive, asked Fruean for assistance. Fruean took a butcher's knife from a knife block located on the kitchen counter and handed it to the defendant, who proceeded to stab Steller and King several times. The defendant also used a serrated paring knife and a carving knife to stab the victims. Realizing that the victims, even then, still were alive, the defendant smashed a ceramic lamp on Steller's head and broke a glass mason jar over King's head....

The defendant was charged with two counts of murder and one count of capital felony. She entered a plea of not guilty and elected to be tried by a jury. On November 3, 1995, she filed a motion in limine seeking an order prohibiting counsel from asking potential venirepersons: (1) "[a]ny questions concerning attitudes and beliefs for or against the imposition of the death penalty"; and (2) "[a]ny questions by which it is directly or indirectly suggested that the defendant, if convicted of [c]apital felony, in violation of [§]53a-54b (8) might suffer the penalty of death." The motion also sought to prohibit the excusal for cause, *prior to the guilt phase of the trial,* of prospective jurors who were unalterably opposed to capital punishment. That motion was denied.

Jury selection for the defendant's trial consumed some forty court days, during which more than 150 venirepersons were voir dired. The trial court, over the defendant's objections, excused for cause twelve venirepersons on the ground that their opposition to the death penalty would prevent or substantially impair the performance of their duties as jurors during the sentencing phase of the trial. The trial court also excused for cause three venirepersons who stated that if the defendant was found guilty, the death penalty should be imposed automatically. In light of the capital felony charges, the court granted each party thirty peremptory challenges. Of those, the state used thirty and the defendant used twenty-seven.

The jury returned a verdict of guilty on all counts. Thereafter, the trial court conducted a separate sentencing hearing ... before the same jury. The jury returned a special verdict finding that the state had proved aggravating factors beyond a reasonable doubt regarding both the murder of Steller and the murder of King, and that the defendant had proved mitigating factors by a preponderance of the evidence. The trial court merged the two murder counts with the capital felony count and rendered a judgment of conviction accordingly, and imposed a sentence of life imprisonment without the possibility of release pursuant to §53a-46a (g). This appeal followed.

I

The defendant claims that article first, §§8 and 19,[7] of the Connecticut constitution prohibits the identification and excusal for cause, prior to the *guilt phase* of a bifurcated capital felony trial, of venirepersons whose beliefs concerning the death penalty would prevent or substantially impair the performance of their duties as jurors during the *sentencing phase* of the trial. Specifically, the defendant maintains that questioning venirepersons, prior to the guilt phase

7. Article first, §8, of the constitution of Connecticut, as amended by articles seventeen and twenty-nine of the amendments, provides in relevant part: "a. In all criminal prosecutions, the accused shall have a right to be heard by himself and by counsel; to be informed of the nature and cause of the accusation; to be confronted by the witnesses against him; to have compulsory process to obtain witnesses in his behalf; to be released on bail upon sufficient security, except in capital offenses, where the proof is evident or the presumption great; and in all prosecutions by information, to a speedy, public trial by an impartial jury. No person shall be compelled to give evidence against himself, nor be deprived of life, liberty or property without due process of law, nor shall excessive bail be required nor excessive fines imposed. No person shall be held to answer for any crime, punishable by death or life imprisonment, unless upon probable cause shown at a hearing in accordance with procedures prescribed by law, except in the armed forces, or in the militia when in actual service in time of war or public danger...."

Article first, §19, of the constitution of Connecticut, as amended by article four of the amendments, provides: "The right of trial by jury shall remain inviolate, the number of such jurors, which shall not be less than six, to be established by law; but no person shall, for a capital offense, be tried by a jury of less than twelve jurors without his consent. In all civil and criminal actions tried by a jury, the parties shall have the right to challenge jurors peremptorily, the number of such challenges to be established by law. The right to question each juror individually by counsel shall be inviolate."

of the trial, about their beliefs regarding the death penalty, and excusing for cause those venirepersons whose opposition to the death penalty would interfere with the performance of their duties as jurors at the sentencing phase of the trial, results in a guilt phase jury that is not impartial because it is: (1) more "conviction prone" than a jury that is not death qualified; and (2) not composed of a representative cross section of the community. The defendant argues that such venirepersons properly may be identified and excused for cause only at the sentencing phase of a bifurcated capital felony trial. We disagree.

In *State v. Geisler,* 222 Conn. 672, 684–86, 610 A.2d 1225 (1992), we adopted an analytic framework for determining whether our state constitution affords Connecticut citizens greater individual liberties than does its federal counterpart. Specifically, we enumerated six factors to be considered: (1) persuasive relevant federal precedents; (2) the text of relevant constitutional provisions; (3) historical insights into the intent of our constitutional forebears; (4) related Connecticut precedents; (5) persuasive precedents of other state courts; and (6) contemporary understandings of applicable economic and sociological norms. None of those factors supports the defendant's state constitutional claim.

A

Relevant Federal Precedent

The United States Supreme Court first addressed the issue of "death qualification" of jurors in capital cases in *Witherspoon v. Illinois,* 391 U.S. 510 (1968). In *Witherspoon,* a state statute permitted the excusal for cause of "any [venireperson] who shall, on being examined, state that he has conscientious scruples against capital punishment, or that he is opposed to the same." Thus, the statute at issue in *Witherspoon* not only permitted the excusal of venirepersons whose beliefs concerning the death penalty would prevent or substantially impair their ability to perform their duties as jurors, it also allowed the excusal for cause of venirepersons who were opposed to the death penalty even if their scruples against the death penalty would not interfere with the performance of their duties as jurors.[8]

The petitioner in *Witherspoon* argued that excusal for cause, *prior to the guilt phase of the trial,* of all venirepersons with scruples against the death penalty results in a jury "necessarily ... biased in favor of conviction," thereby violating a defendant's right under the sixth amendment to the United States constitution to have his innocence or guilt determined by an impartial jury. The court, however, concluded that the petitioner had not presented sufficient evidence to support a conclusion that the excusal, prior to the guilt phase, of venirepersons with scruples against the death penalty necessarily results in a more "conviction prone" jury. Consequently, the court rejected the petitioner's claim that the "death qualification" process utilized at his trial deprived defendants of their federal constitutional right to have their innocence or guilt determined by an impartial jury.

The court also considered, however, the effect that the "death qualification" process utilized at the petitioner's trial had at the sentencing phase. *Witherspoon* was decided before the court's decisions in *Furman v. Georgia,* 408 U.S. 238 (1972), and *Gregg v. Georgia,* 428 U.S. 153 (1976), and the then current Illinois death penalty statute provided jurors "broad discretion to decide whether or not [to impose the death penalty] in a given case." *Witherspoon v. Illinois,* 391 U.S. at 519. Noting that under the Illinois statutory scheme, "a juror's general views about capital punishment [played] an inevitable role in any such decision"; *id.*; the court concluded that the excusal for cause of all venirepersons with scruples against the death penalty resulted in a jury that at sentencing was "uncommonly willing to condemn a man to die." On that basis, the court held that "a sentence of death cannot be carried out if the jury that imposed or recommended it was chosen by excluding veniremen for cause simply because they voiced general objections to the death penalty or expressed conscientious or religious scruples against its infliction." The court stated, however, that this conclusion did not "render invalid the *conviction,* as opposed to the *sentence,* in [*Witherspoon*] or any other case."

The court also suggested in a footnote in *Witherspoon* that the federal constitution did not prohibit the excusal for cause of venirepersons "who [make] unmistakably clear (1) that they would *automatically* vote against the imposition

8. At the trial of the petitioner in *Witherspoon,* the state used the statute to excuse for cause forty-seven venirepersons, nearly one half of the entire venire panel, each of whom had expressed concerns about the death penalty. *Witherspoon v. Illinois,* supra, 391 U.S. at 513–14.

of capital punishment without regard to any evidence that might be developed at the trial of the case before them, or (2) [whose] attitude toward the death penalty would prevent them from making an impartial decision as to the defendant's *guilt.*" (Emphasis in original.) *Id.*, at 522–23 n. 21. Thus, the court's decision in *Witherspoon* indicated that in capital criminal trials, two categories of venirepersons properly could be excused for cause on the basis of their opposition to the death penalty: (1) individuals whose beliefs would prevent them from performing their duties as jurors during the guilt phase of the trial; and (2) individuals whose beliefs automatically would prevent them from performing their duties as jurors during the sentencing phase of the trial.

In *Wainwright v. Witt,* 469 U.S. 412 (1985), which was decided after *Furman* and *Gregg,* the United States Supreme Court again considered the effect that a prospective juror's beliefs concerning the death penalty have on that individual's eligibility to serve as a juror in a capital case. In *Witt,* the court noted that its statement in *Witherspoon* that a venireperson could be excused for cause if his beliefs "automatically" would prevent him from imposing a sentence of death was best understood in the context of the death penalty statute at issue in that case. The court clarified the standard for determining whether a venireperson properly may be challenged for cause on the basis of his beliefs regarding the death penalty. Specifically, the court concluded that the federal constitution permits the excusal for cause of venirepersons whose opposition to capital punishment would prevent or substantially impair the performance of their duties as jurors in accordance with the court's instructions and the juror's oath. Thus, as interpreted in *Witherspoon* and *Witt,* the federal constitution permits the excusal for cause of venirepersons whose opposition to the death penalty would prevent or substantially impair the performance of their duties as jurors during either: (1) the guilt phase of the trial; *or* (2) the sentencing phase of the trial....

In 1986, the United States Supreme Court again addressed the issue of "death qualification" of venirepersons in *Lockhart v. McCree,* 476 U.S. 162 (1986). At the trial of the petitioner in *Lockhart,* the court had excused certain venirepersons for cause in accordance with the *Witt* test. On appeal, the petitioner did not claim that any of the jurors who had served at his trial had been "partial" in the sense that they had been unable to render a verdict based solely on the evidence and the trial court's instructions. Instead, relying on social science evidence, the petitioner contended that the excusal for cause, prior to the guilt phase, of venirepersons whose opposition to the death penalty would prevent them from performing their duties as jurors only at the sentencing phase of a capital criminal trial, results in a more "conviction prone" guilt phase jury, thereby depriving the defendant of his rights under the sixth amendment to have his guilt or innocence decided by: (1) a jury composed of a representative cross section of the community; and (2) an impartial jury. The United States Supreme Court disagreed, concluding that: (1) although the sixth amendment requires that juries be fairly selected from a venire pool comprising a representative cross section of the community, it does not require that the actual jury so selected be composed of a representative cross section of the community; (2) the petitioner had not presented social science evidence establishing the hypothesis that "death qualification" of venirepersons prior to the guilt phase of a bifurcated trial results in juries that are more "conviction prone"; (3) the sixth amendment right to trial by an "impartial" jury requires only a trial by "jurors who will conscientiously apply the law and find the facts"; and (4) consequently, even if the social science evidence had been capable of supporting a finding that the excusal for cause, prior to the guilt phase of the trial, of venirepersons whose beliefs preclude them from serving as jurors only during the sentencing phase of the trial results in juries that are more "conviction prone," such a finding would not have been a ground for concluding that death qualified juries are not "impartial" within the meaning of the sixth amendment. Thus, the court concluded that the federal constitution did not prohibit the excusal for cause, prior to the guilt phase, of venirepersons whose opposition to the death penalty would preclude them from serving as jurors at the sentencing phase of a capital trial.

In 1992, the United States Supreme Court examined once again the issue of "death qualification" of venirepersons in bifurcated capital felony trials. *Morgan v. Illinois,* 504 U.S. 719 (1992). At the trial of the petitioner in *Morgan,* the court had permitted the state, prior to the guilt phase of the trial, to ask potential jurors whether their opposition to the death penalty would prevent them from performing their duties as jurors. The trial court, however, had refused the petitioner's request to ask potential jurors whether, if the petitioner was convicted, they automatically would vote to impose the death penalty regardless of the facts. The United States Supreme Court concluded that the federal constitution guarantees defendants in capital cases the right to question and excuse for cause any venireperson who, upon conviction, would *automatically* vote to apply the death penalty regardless of the facts....

It is useful at this juncture to identify what the defendant's state constitutional claim does not involve. The defendant does not argue that she was deprived of a trial by an impartial jury because the individuals who served as jurors at her trial were not "impartial" in the sense that they were incapable of finding facts solely on the basis of the evidence presented and applying the law in accordance with the court's instructions. Nor does she contend that the venire panels from which the jury that served at her trial was selected did not consist of a representative cross section of the community. Instead, the defendant asks us to conclude that, as a matter of law, the identification[9] and excusal for cause, prior to the guilt phase of a bifurcated capital felony trial, of venirepersons whose views about the death penalty would substantially impair their ability to serve as jurors at the sentencing phase results in a jury that is not "impartial" because: (1) it is more "conviction prone"; and (2) it is not composed of a fair cross section of the community. In effect, the defendant maintains that the state constitution requires that "proprosecution" and "prodefense" attitudes be balanced across the jury that is selected to decide a defendant's innocence or guilt. Thus, the defendant contends that our state constitution incorporates a meaning of "impartial jury" that the United States Supreme Court refused to adopt under the federal constitution in *Lockhart.* Federal precedent, therefore, does not support the defendant's state constitutional claim; indeed, it is directly contrary to that claim....

F

Economic and Sociological Factors

We consider now the last *Geisler* factor, economic and sociological norms. The defendant's state constitutional claim is based on the proposition that, as a matter of fact, identifying and excusing for cause, prior to the guilt phase, venirepersons whose beliefs would substantially impair their ability to serve as jurors at the sentencing phase, but not the guilt phase of the trial, results in a jury that is more "conviction prone." We reject that hypothesis.

The defendant presented no evidence at trial to support her contention that identification and excusal for cause, prior to the guilt phase, of venirepersons whose beliefs concerning the death penalty preclude them from serving as jurors during the sentencing phase of a capital felony trial results in a more "conviction prone" jury. Moreover, the defendant explicitly declined the trial court's invitation to provide such evidence. Instead, the defendant now relies entirely upon findings made by two federal district courts on the basis of certain social science evidence that "death qualified juries" are "conviction prone." See *Keeten v. Garrison,* 578 F.Supp. 1164 (W.D.N.C.), rev'd, 742 F.2d 129 (4th Cir.1984), cert. denied, 476 U.S. 1145 (1986); *Grigsby v. Mabry,* 569 F.Supp. 1273 (E.D.Ark.1983), aff'd, 758 F.2d 226 (8th Cir.1985), rev'd sub nom. *Lockhart v. McCree,* 476 U.S. 162. In effect, the defendant asks us to take judicial notice of those findings....

The social science evidence on which the defendant now relies consists of fourteen studies. Five of the studies[11] did not even identify the

9. Paradoxically, the defendant acknowledges that the state constitution permits the excusal for cause, prior to the guilt phase of the trial, of venirepersons whose views about the death penalty would prevent or substantially impair the performance of their duties as jurors during the guilt phase of the trial. It is difficult to square this acknowledgment with the defendant's claims.

11. H. Zeisel, "Some Data on Juror Attitudes Toward Capital Punishment," University of Chicago Law School: Center for Studies in Criminal Justice (1988) (data collected in 1954 and 1955); W. Wilson, "Belief in Capital Punishment and Jury Performance," University of Texas (1964) (unpublished) (data collected from 187 college students in 1964); F. Goldberg, "Toward Expansion of *Witherspoon:* Capital Scruples, Jury Bias, and Use of Psychological Data to Raise Presumptions in the Law," 5 Harv. C.R.-C.L. L.Rev. 53 (1970) (data collected from college students in 1966 and 1967); G. Jurow, "New Data on the Effect of a 'Death Qualified' Jury on the Guilt Determination Process," 84 Harv. L.Rev. 567 (1971) (data collected prior to 1970 from 211 New York employees of Sperry Rand Corporation); L. Harris & Associates, Inc., "Study No.2016" (1971), reported in W. White, "The Constitutional Invalidity of Convictions, Imposed by Death-Qualified Juries," 58 Cornell L.Rev. 1176 (1973) (data collected in 1971 from 2068 adults throughout United States).

participants whose beliefs concerning the death penalty would supposedly preclude them from serving as jurors at the sentencing phase, but not at the guilt phase, of a capital trial. Thus, those five studies are incapable of establishing the defendant's hypothesis that identification and excusal of venirepersons at issue in the present case—individuals whose beliefs concerning the death penalty preclude them from serving as jurors at the sentencing phase, but not at the guilt phase, of the trial—results in a more "conviction prone" jury.

Furthermore, eight of the nine remaining studies[12] only attempted to establish a correlation between views on the death penalty and attitudes regarding certain other aspects of the criminal justice process, the *untested assumption* being that persons with "proprosecution" attitudes vote to convict criminal defendants more often than persons with "prodefense" attitudes. None of the eight studies involved an actual, or even a simulated, jury experience in which study participants: (1) were instructed as to the presumption of innocence and the obligation to decide the case solely on the evidence and in accordance with the court's instructions regarding the law; or (2) participated, under oath, in deliberations regarding a "defendant's" innocence or guilt. We are not persuaded that the correlation these studies purport to have established between death penalty attitudes and certain other criminal justice attitudes is capable of either: (1) predicting jury voting behavior; or (2) establishing the defendant's hypothesis regarding the effect that identification and excusal for cause of certain venirepersons—individuals whose views on the death penalty would preclude them for serving as jurors at the sentencing phase, but not at the guilt phase, of the trial—has upon jury voting behavior.

The final study on which the defendant relies is documented in C. Cowan, W. Thompson & P. Ellsworth, "The Effects of Death Qualification on Jurors' Predisposition to Convict and on the Quality of Deliberation," 8 Law & Hum. Behav. 53, 62–63 (1984) (Ellsworth Conviction Proneness Study). This study is not based on current Connecticut data. Instead, it is based on data that was collected twenty years ago in California from only 240 individuals. "Voir dire" took place during *telephone interviews in which subjects were asked only two multiple choice questions:* (1) "'Is your attitude toward the death penalty such that as a juror you would never be willing to impose it in any case, no matter what the evidence was, or would you consider voting to impose it in at least some cases? a) I would be unwilling to vote to impose it in any case. b) I would consider voting to impose it in some cases'"; and (2) "'Which of the following expresses what you would do if you were a juror for the first part of the trial? a) I would follow the [court's] instructions and decide the question of guilt or innocence in a fair and impartial manner based on the evidence and the law. or b) I would not be fair and impartial in deciding the question of guilt or innocence, knowing that if the person was convicted he or she might get the death penalty.'" No *further* attempt was made to verify that the respondents were willing and able to put aside preconceived notions and decide a case solely on the basis of the evidence presented and in accordance with a court's instructions regarding the law. In addition, no attempt was made to ascertain whether respondents would be unable to serve as jurors because their views

12. E. Bronson, "On the Conviction Proneness and Representativeness of the Death-Qualified Jury: An Empirical Study of Colorado Veniremen," 42 U. Colo. L.Rev. 1 (1970) (data collected in 1968 and 1969 in Colorado); E. Bronson, "Does the Exclusion of Scrupled Jurors in Capital Cases Make the Jury More Likely to Convict? Some Evidence from California," 3 Woodrow Wilson J.L. 11 (1980) (data collected in 1969 and 1970 in California); R. Fitzgerald & P. Ellsworth, "Due Process vs. Crime Control: Death Qualification and Jury Attitudes," 8 Law & Hum. Behav. 31 (1984) (data collected in 1979); P. Ellsworth, R. Bukaty, C. Cowan & W. Thompson, "The Death-Qualified Jury and the Defense of Insanity," 8 Law & Hum. Behav. 81 (1984) (data collected in California; thirty-five participants); W. Thompson, C. Cowan, P. Ellsworth & J. Harrington, "Death Penalty Attitudes and Conviction Proneness: The Translation of Attitudes into Verdicts," 8 Law & Hum. Behav. 95 (1984) (data collected in California; thirty-six participants); C. Haney, "On the Selection of Capital Juries: The Biasing Effects of the Death-Qualification Process," 8 Law & Hum. Behav. 121 (1984) (data collected in California; sixty-seven participants); L. Harris & Associates, Inc., "Study No. 814002" (1981) (unpublished); R. Seltzer, G. Lopes, M. Dayan & R. Canan, "The Effect of Death Qualification on the Propensity of Jurors to Convict: The Maryland Example," 29 How. L.J. 571 (1986) (data collected in 1983).

in favor of the death penalty would cause them automatically to impose a sentence of death. See *Morgan v. Illinois,* 504 U.S. at 735–36. Even assuming, without deciding, that the Ellsworth Conviction Proneness Study is methodologically sound, we do not believe that the "death qualification" process utilized in the study, which entailed *only two multiple choice questions posed over the telephone,* reasonably can be said to be representative of either the process by which venirepersons in Connecticut are questioned during voir dire about their death penalty attitudes or of the process by which venirepersons who have preconceived notions and biases that would preclude them from serving as jurors are culled from a Connecticut venire panel. For example, jury selection in the present case consumed forty full days during which the questioning of individual venirepersons lasted as long as two hours. We also are not persuaded that a single study based on data collected approximately twenty years ago from 240 California residents provides a proper basis for taking judicial notice that, despite the state constitutional guarantee of individual voir dire and peremptory challenges, the excusal for cause, prior to the guilt phase of a capital felony trial, of venirepersons whose views about the death penalty would prevent or substantially impair the performance of their duties as jurors during the sentencing phase, but not at the guilt phase, of the trial, results in a more "conviction-prone" jury in Connecticut in 1999. The individuals questioned for the Ellsworth Conviction Proneness Study did not serve under oath as jurors in an actual capital trial and, once they had given two multiple choice answers regarding their beliefs concerning the death penalty, were not subjected to further voir dire scrutiny to ensure that they were capable of deciding the case solely on the basis of the evidence and in accordance with the law.

Connecticut experience, moreover, does not support the defendant's hypothesis that the death qualification procedure utilized at her trial results in a more "conviction prone" jury. For example, in a capital felony case now pending before this court, *State v. Johnson,* Docket No. SC 14801, the trial court excused for cause twenty-seven venirepersons who stated during voir dire that the death penalty should be imposed automatically in that case. Only seventeen venirepersons were excused on the basis of their opposition to the death penalty. Put another way, in *State v. Johnson,* the death qualification process resulted in the excusal for cause of twenty-seven supposedly "proconviction" venirepersons and only seventeen supposedly "proacquittal" venirepersons. Thus, even if we were to assume, without deciding, that, as the defendant maintains, death penalty beliefs are predictive of jury voting behavior, we still could not conclude that "death qualification" results in a Connecticut jury that is more, rather than less, "conviction prone."

... The state has a valid and important interest in having the same jury serve at the guilt and penalty phases of a capital felony trial. See *State v. Webb,* 238 Conn. at 467, 680 A.2d 147 ("In most capital cases, the evidence presented to demonstrate the defendant's guilt also will be relevant to the determination of the existence of aggravating factors.... Thus, if different juries were required to consider the guilt and penalty issues, much of the same evidence would be likely to be presented to each of the juries." [Citation omitted.]). We conclude that article first, § 8, of the constitution of Connecticut incorporates the standard of "impartial jury" provided by the federal constitution, namely, a jury that is: (1) composed of individuals able to decide the case solely on the evidence and in accordance with the court's instructions regarding the law; and (2) properly selected from a venire panel that is composed of a representative cross section of the community. Identification and excusal for cause, prior to the guilt phase of a capital felony trial, of venirepersons whose views concerning the death penalty preclude them from serving as jurors at the sentencing phase, but not at the guilt phase, of the trial does not violate the state constitutional guarantee of trial by an impartial jury.

Finally, we note that, as a practical matter, the standard of "impartial jury" advocated by the defendant would require not only that jurors be able to set aside preconceived notions and decide a case solely on the evidence and in accordance with the court's instructions, but also that "proprosecution" and "prodefense" attitudes—the very attitudes that the jurors have been determined to be capable of setting aside and that the jurors are sworn to set aside—be balanced across the jury. Even if we were to assume, without deciding, that it somehow would be possible to ascertain and balance jurors' criminal justice attitudes across a jury, the defendant's proposed standard of "impartial jury" still would not be workable because it effectively would require the elimination of the use of peremptory challenges—challenges that are guaranteed by article first, § 19, of the constitution of Connecticut....

BERDON, J., dissenting.

The majority today holds, for the first time under our state constitution, that the state may death qualify the jury that decides the *guilt* of the defendant in a capital case by allowing the court to excuse for cause those persons who, because of their opposition to the death penalty, are incapable of voting for it. The death qualified jury is "tilted in favor of the prosecution by the exclusion of a group of prospective jurors [who are] uncommonly aware of an accused's constitutional rights but quite capable of determining his culpability without favor or bias." *Lockhart v. McCree*, 476 U.S. 162, 185 (1986) (Marshall, J., dissenting). Although the *Lockhart* court held that such a jury passes federal constitutional muster, I believe that the death qualification of the jury violates article first of the Connecticut constitution, which, pursuant to § 8 and § 19, guarantees the right to an impartial jury drawn from a representative cross section of the people and due process of law.

I

The majority would have us believe that in those cases in which the state seeks the death penalty, the accused cannot have the benefit of a jury selected from a cross section of the population that determines his guilt. Any other criminal defendant, that does not face this ultimate penalty, has the benefit of a group of persons summoned to serve potentially as jurors that includes those who are opposed to the death penalty on moral or other grounds and would not vote for it. Similarly, if the state decides not to seek the death penalty, the defendant is able to have a representative venire. The trial court in this case needlessly excluded those prospective jurors (venirepersons) from the guilt phase of the trial thereby violating the defendant's state constitutional rights.[5]

The significance of that exclusion as explained by Justice Marshall (joined by Justices Brennan and Stevens), is that there is "overwhelming evidence that death-qualified juries are substantially more likely to convict or to convict on more serious charges than juries on which unalterable opponents of capital punishment are permitted to serve." *Id.*, at 184 (Marshall, J., dissenting). I agree with Justice Marshall who cogently wrote in dissent: "With a glib nonchalance ill suited to the gravity of the issue presented and the power of [the] respondent's claims, [this] Court upholds a practice that allows the State a special advantage in those prosecutions where the charges are the most serious and the possible punishments, the most severe. The State's mere announcement that it intends to seek the death penalty if the defendant is found guilty of a capital offense will, under today's decision, give the prosecution license to empanel a jury especially likely to return that very verdict. Because I believe that such a blatant disregard for the rights of a capital defendant offends logic, fairness, and the Constitution, I dissent."

The consequences of the majority upholding this automatic exclusion can be significant—in Connecticut, those persons who are opposed to the death penalty and who potentially could not put that belief aside amount to approximately 39 percent of our state population[6] as measured by the legislators who voted against the death penalty. Based on this assumption, Connecticut voters are less supportive of the death penalty than the national population.[8]

II

Before I proceed with my state constitutional analysis, let me put this case in its proper perspective. The defendant, Janet Griffin, like the defendant in *Lockhart*, does not claim that those who are opposed to the death penalty and cannot put that belief aside should *not* be excluded from

---

5. As a result of the trial court's voir dire of the venirepersons regarding their opposition to the death penalty in this case, twelve out of 157, or nearly 8 percent, were excused from serving because they opposed the death penalty and could not put that belief aside if selected.

6. In 1973, there was a vote on House Bill No. 8297, the bill underlying General Statutes § 53a-54b, which provides for the penalty of death. In the House of Representatives, 37 percent of the legislators and in the Senate, 47 percent of the senators voted against the death penalty. Overall, based on the total number of senators and representatives, 39 percent were not in favor of the death penalty.

8. According to a Gallup Poll conducted in 1999, 22 percent of the population answered that they were "against" when asked: "Are you in favor of the death penalty for a person convicted of murder?" The sample was 543 adults. The statistic's margin of error was plus or minus five percentage points. See M. Gillespie, Public Opinion Supports Death Penalty, Gallup News Service, February 24, 1999, p. 2.

the *penalty* phase of the trial if the defendant is found guilty of capital felony pursuant to General Statutes § 53a-54b. Rather, the defendant maintains that her constitutional rights are violated if the jury that deliberates her guilt at trial is death qualified. All that the defendant asks, as in *Lockhart,* is that her guilt or innocence be determined by a jury like those that sit in noncapital cases—one whose composition is not prosecution oriented and conviction prone.

Our state statutory scheme can accommodate both the defendant's constitutional right to have her guilt or innocence decided by a jury that is drawn from a representative cross section of the population and the state's right to exclude in the penalty phase of a capital case those who could not put aside their opposition in deciding whether to impose the death penalty. If the defendant is found guilty of a capital felony by a jury that includes jurors who would not vote for the penalty of death based upon moral or other grounds, General Statutes § 53a-46a (b) clearly authorizes the trial court to impanel a second jury that could be death qualified to determine the penalty.[9] Similarly, the United States Supreme Court, in *Witherspoon v. Illinois,* 391 U.S. 510, 520 n. 18 (1968), recognized the appropriateness of a bifurcated trial when a death qualified jury could not be impartial.[10]....

III

Despite the majority's failure to ensure that the defendant's trial was fair by ordering a bifurcation of her trial under our supervisory powers, the state constitution requires that a death qualified jury cannot decide the defendant's guilt or innocence in a capital case....

D

Sociological Considerations

A distinctive group of death qualified jurors emerges from the examination of sociological studies. This evidence suggests that death qualified jurors are systematically excluded from the jury selection process in violation of the fair cross sectional requirement.

Under the first part of the *Duren* [*v. Missouri,* 439 U.S. 357 (1979)] test, death qualified jurors form a distinctive group in the community. The results of a national survey indicate that 22 percent of the population are against the death penalty for a person convicted of murder.[18] After the *Witherspoon* decision, researchers who sought to put a face on those who opposed the death penalty found that more African-Americans and women are excluded because of their opposition to the death penalty despite their ability to serve impartially during the guilt phase.

Beyond sheer numbers, researchers consistently find that the attitudes of death qualified jurors are distinguishable from those of other jurors. Attitudinal surveys that have sampled venirepersons, individuals who were eligible for jury service and members of the general population, consistently found that those who support the death penalty are more likely to hold prosecution perspectives.[19] They are "more likely to believe that a defendant's failure to testify is

---

9. General Statutes § 53a-46a (b)(2)(C) provides that such hearing to determine the penalty shall be conducted before another jury "if the jury which determined the defendant's guilt has been discharged by the court for good cause...."

10. "Even so, a defendant convicted by such a jury in some future case might still attempt to establish that the jury was less than neutral with respect to guilt. If he were to succeed in that effort, the question would then arise whether the State's interest in submitting the penalty issue to a jury capable of imposing capital punishment may be vindicated at the expense of the defendant's interest in a completely fair determination of guilt or innocence-given the possibility of accommodating both interests by means of a bifurcated trial, using one jury to decide guilt and another to fix punishment. That problem is not presented here, however, and we intimate no view as to its proper resolution." *Witherspoon v. Illinois,* 391 U.S. at 520 n. 18.

18. See M. Gillespie, Public Opinion Supports Death Penalty, Gallup News Service, February 24, 1999, p. 2.

19. In *Grigsby v. Mabry,* 758 F.2d at 232–33, the court described the results of a number of "Attitudinal and Demographic Surveys" as follows:

> "1. Bronson, 'On the Conviction Proneness and Representativeness of the Death-Qualified Jury: An Empirical Study of Colorado Veniremen,' 42 U. Colo. L.Rev. 1 (1970). (Bronson-Colorado).
> "The subjects of this study were 718 Colorado venirepersons. Interviews were done by trained students from the University of Colorado in 1968 and 1969. Each subject was asked whether they strongly favored, favored, opposed, or strongly opposed the death penalty. This was followed by five questions regarding attitudes on criminal justice issues. On each of the five questions the

indicative of his guilt, more hostile to the insanity defense, more mistrustful of defense attorneys, and less concerned about the danger of erroneous convictions. [*Grigsby v. Mabry,* 569 F. Sup. 1273, 1283, 1293, 1304 (E.D.Ark.1983)]." *Lockhart v. McCree,* 476 U.S. at 188 (Marshall, J., dissenting). In addition, "[t]his proprosecution bias is reflected in the greater readiness of death-qualified jurors to convict or to convict on more serious charges. [*Grigsby v. Mabry,* 569 F. Supp. at 1294–1302]; *Grigsby v. Mabry,* [758 F.2d at 233–36].[20] ... [Even] the very process of death qualification—which focuses attention on the death penalty before the trial has even begun—has been found to predispose the jurors that survive the process to believe that the defendant is guilty. [*Grigsby v. Mabry,* 569 F. Supp. at 1302–1305; *Grigsby v. Mabry,* 758 F.2d at 234]." *Lockhart v. McCree,* at 188 (Marshall, J., dissenting).

The majority's critique of the sociological evidence raises the question of whether any study would be satisfactory short of an admission by the jurors who sat on the case and who favored

---

survey found the stronger the subjects' support for the death penalty, the stronger their support for positions most favorable to the prosecution.

"2. Bronson, 'Does the Exclusion of Scrupled Jurors in Capital Cases Make the Jury More Likely to Convict? Some Evidence from California,' 3 Woodrow Wilson L.J. 11 (1980). (Bronson-California)....

"Trained students interviewed 755 Butte County, California, venirepersons regarding their position on the death penalty. Seven attitudinal questions, much like those used in Bronson-Colorado, followed. Once again a direct and significant correlation between death penalty beliefs and criminal justice attitudes was found.

"The second survey involved interviews of 707 venirepersons from Los Angeles, Sacramento and Stockton, California. The results were consistent with the prior studies: the more strongly the subjects favored the death penalty, the more likely they were to endorse pro-prosecution positions.

"3. Louis Harris & Associates, Inc., Study No.2016 (1971).

"Harris randomly polled 2,068 adults throughout the United States in 1971. The respondents were asked about their attitudes on the death penalty and other criminal justice issues. The results parallel those of the Bronson surveys. In addition, Harris found more blacks than whites, and more women than men, would be excluded from jury service by death qualification.

"4. Fitzgerald & Ellsworth, 'Due Process vs. Crime Control: Death Qualification and Jury Attitudes,' 8 Law & Hum. Behav. 31 (1984). (Fitzgerald-1979).

"The survey upon which this article is based was a sample of 811 jury eligible persons in Alameda County, California, in 1979. An independent professional polling organization, Field Research Corporation of San Francisco, drew the sample and interviewed the subjects. Respondents who could not be fair and impartial, i.e., nullifiers, were excluded. Of the remaining 717 subjects, over seventeen percent were found to be [*Witherspoon*-excludables]. Questions regarding attitudes on criminal justice issues showed that death qualified respondents were more favorable to the prosecution than the [*Witherspoon*-excludables].

"5. Precision Research, Inc., Survey No. 1286 (1981). (Precision Survey).

"This survey was conducted by an Arkansas polling organization in 1981. A sample of 407 adults in the state of Arkansas were asked the same questions used in Fitzgerald-1979. The survey found that approximately eleven percent of those who could be fair and impartial in determining guilt-innocence were [*Witherspoon*-excludables]."

20. The court in *Grigsby v. Mabry,* 758 F.2d at 233–34, noted the findings of several "Conviction-Proneness Surveys" as follows:

"1. H. Zeisel, Some Data on Juror Attitudes Toward Capital Punishment (University of Chicago Monograph 1968). (Zeisel).

"In 1954 and 1955 Zeisel questioned jurors who had served on felony juries in Brooklyn, New York, and Chicago, Illinois. The subjects were asked about the first ballot votes of their jury and whether they had scruples against the death penalty. The study controlled for the weight of evidence in each case and found jurors with conscientious scruples against the death penalty voted to acquit more often than jurors without such scruples.

"2. W. Wilson, Belief in Capital Punishment and Jury Performance (1964) (unpublished). (Wilson).

"This study presented 187 college students with written descriptions of five capital cases in 1964. Each student was asked whether he or she had scruples against the death penalty. They were then asked to assume that they were jurors in the five cases. The students without death penalty scruples voted for conviction more often than those with scruples.

the death penalty that they have a bias for conviction. The majority maintains that their "own thorough examination ... persuades [them] that the social science evidence presented in [*Grigsby* and *Keeten*, that is relied upon by the defendant] is not capable of establishing the defendant's hypothesis ... that in Connecticut in 1999, the removal for cause, prior to the guilt phase of a capital felony trial, of venirepersons whose beliefs concerning the death penalty would prevent or substantially impair the performance of their duties as jurors during the sentencing phase of a capital felony trial results in a more 'conviction prone' jury." My simple answer to the majority's conclusion is that, putting the studies aside, anyone with any common sense and who has the experience of life, would be compelled to come to the conclusion that venirepersons who favor the death penalty are more conviction prone than those who oppose it.

Furthermore, their criticism unfairly minimizes the value of those sociological studies examining the relationship between attitudes and human behavior. The majority argues that in five of the studies, researchers did not identify participants who would be death qualified. While this is true, the subjects of these studies were either jurors or members of the general population who are potentially members of the jury pool. The majority also criticizes the remaining studies that correlate subjects' attitudes toward the death penalty with attitudes toward the criminal justice system but do not assess whether they would be more likely to vote for conviction. This criticism ignores the finding that the beliefs of those subjects are internally consistent; if subjects support the death penalty, they are more likely to hold proprosecution beliefs. A reasonable inference from these studies is that jurors with these beliefs are more likely to convict.

The majority fails to recognize the "essential unanimity of the results obtained by researchers using diverse subjects and varied methodologies." *Lockhart v. McCree*, 476 U.S. at 189 (Marshall, J., dissenting). They would have us put common sense aside and a defendant's life on hold while we wait for the definitive sociological study of whether jurors who hold positive attitudes toward the death penalty are more likely to favor the prosecution and thus, vote to convict. "The evidence thus confirms, and is itself corroborated by, the more intuitive judgments of scholars and

"3. Goldberg, 'Toward Expansion of *Witherspoon:* Capital Scruples, Jury Bias, and Use of Psychological Data to Raise Presumptions in the Law,' 5 Harv. C.R.-C.L.L.Rev. 53 (1970).

"A set of sixteen written descriptions were given to 100 white and 100 black college students in Georgia. Those without scruples voted to convict in seventy-five percent of cases, compared to sixty-nine percent for those with scruples.

"4. Jurow, 'New Data on the Effect of a "Death Qualified" Jury on the Guilt Determination Process,' 84 Harv. L.Rev. 567 (1971). (Jurow).

"Audio recordings of two simulated murder trials were played for 211 employees of Sperry Rand Corporation in New York. The subjects filled out questionnaires which measured their attitudes toward the death penalty and various criminal justice issues. The subjects were then asked to listen to each 'trial' and vote on guilt-innocence. Those persons who more strongly favored the death penalty were found to be more likely to convict.

"5. Cowan, Thompson & Ellsworth, 'The Effects of Death Qualification on Jurors' Predisposition to Convict and on the Quality of Deliberation,' 8 Law & Hum. Behav. 53 (1984). (Cowan-Deliberation).

"This 1979 study began by identifying the [*Witherspoon*-excludables] in its sample of jury eligible residents of San Mateo and Santa Clara Counties, California. Those [*Witherspoon*-excludables] who could not be fair and impartial in determining guilt-innocence (nullifiers) were excluded from the sample. The remaining 288 subjects were shown a realistic two and one-half hour videotape of a murder trial. The subjects filled out questionnaires regarding their criminal justice attitudes and were assigned to panels of twelve in order to simulate jury deliberations. Some panels were death qualified, while others included [*Witherspoon*-excludables]. Ballot forms were filled out by each subject before and after the panel deliberations as a means of examining the quality and importance of the deliberations.

"The study found that death penalty attitudes were closely linked to conviction proneness—subjects favoring the death penalty were more likely to convict. In addition, the study concluded that jury panels containing a mix of [*Witherspoon*-excludables] and death-qualified subjects tended to view all witnesses more critically and remember the facts of the case more accurately than death-qualified jury panels."

of so many of the participants in capital trials—judges, defense attorneys, and prosecutors." *Lockhart v. McCree,* at 188 (Marshall, J., dissenting).

Turning to the second prong of the *Duren* test,[21] it is not fair and reasonable to allow our trial courts to exclude death qualified jurors from the jury pool given the significant number of persons who oppose the death penalty. In addition, by allowing prosecutors to eliminate these jurors there has been an expansion of the number of potential jurors who are excluded through peremptory challenges and those that are eliminated for cause.[22] See *Lockhart v. McCree,* 476 U.S. at 190–92 (Marshall, J., dissenting).

Finally, the state of course does not deny that the third prong of the *Duren* test has been satisfied—that is, these venirepersons that are death qualified are systematically excluded for cause.[23]

Under the *Duren* test, once the defendant has established a prima facie case, the burden then shifts to the state to prove that the selection system resulting in a nonrepresentative array furthers a significant state interest. The majority claims that "[t]he state has a valid and important

21. The Eighth Circuit, in *Grigsby v. Mabry,* 758 F.2d at 231–32, considered that "[t]he second element of the *Duren* test relates to venires. However, given our earlier discussion and finding that there is no practical difference between exclusion from the venire and systematic exclusion for cause from the petit jury, we analyze the resultant petit juries. In this case we find the representation of [*Witherspoon*-excludables] on the juries is not 'fair and reasonable in relation to the number of such persons in the community....' *Duren* [*v. Missouri,* 439 U.S. at 364]. The district court found [*Witherspoon*-excludables] constitute between eleven and seventeen percent of the population. However, [*Witherspoon*-excludables] are totally excluded from guilt-innocence juries in Arkansas."

22. "The true impact of death qualification on the fairness of a trial is likely even more devastating than the studies show. *Witherspoon* placed limits on the State's ability to strike scrupled jurors for cause, unless they state 'unambiguously that [they] would automatically vote against the imposition of capital punishment no matter what the trial might reveal,' [*Witherspoon v. Illinois,* 391 U.S. at 516 n. 9]. It said nothing, however, about the prosecution's use of peremptory challenges to eliminate jurors who do not meet that standard and would otherwise survive death qualification. See Gillers, 'Deciding Who Dies,' 129 U. Pa. L.Rev. 1, 85 n. 391 (1980). There is no question that peremptories have indeed been used to this end, thereby expanding the class of scrupled jurors excluded as a result of the death-qualifying voir dire challenged here. See, e.g., *People v. Velasquez,* 26 Cal.3d 425 [438 n. 9, 606 P.2d 341, 162 Cal.Rptr. 306] (1980) (prosecutor informed court during voir dire that if a venireperson expressing scruples about the death penalty 'were not a challenge for cause, I would kick her off on a peremptory challenge'). The only study of this practice has concluded: 'For the five-year period studied a prima facie case has been demonstrated that prosecutors in Florida's Fourth Judicial Circuit systematically used their peremptory challenges to eliminate from capital juries venirepersons expressing opposition to the death penalty.' Winick, 'Prosecutorial Peremptory Challenge Practices in Capital Cases: An Empirical Study and a Constitutional Analysis,' 81 Mich. L.Rev. 1, 39 (1982).

> "Judicial applications of the *Witherspoon* standard have also expanded the class of jurors excludable for cause. While the studies produced by respondent generally classified a subject as a *Witherspoon*-excludable only upon his unambiguous refusal to vote death under any circumstance, the courts have never been so fastidious. Trial and appellate courts have frequently excluded jurors even in the absence of unambiguous expressions of their absolute opposition to capital punishment. Schnapper, 'Taking *Witherspoon* Seriously: The Search for Death-Qualified Jurors,' 62 Texas L.Rev. 977, 993–1032 (1984). And this less demanding approach will surely become more common in the wake of this Court's decision in *Wainwright v. Witt,* 469 U.S. 412 (1985). Under *Witt,* a juror who does not make his attitude toward capital punishment 'unmistakably clear,' *Witherspoon* [*v. Illinois,* supra, 391 U.S. at 522 n. 21], may nonetheless be excluded for cause if the trial court is left with the impression that his attitude will '"prevent or substantially impair the performance of his duties as a juror in accordance with his instructions and his oath."' [*Wainwright* v.] *Witt,* [at 433] (quoting *Adams v. Texas,* 448 U.S. 38, 45 [1980]). It thus 'seems likely that *Witt* will lead to more conviction-prone panels' since '"scrupled" jurors—those who generally oppose the death penalty but do not express an unequivocal refusal to impose it—usually share the pro-defendant perspective of excludable jurors.' See Finch & Ferraro, 'The Empirical Challenge to Death Qualified Juries: On Further Examination,' 65 Neb. L.Rev. 21, 63 (1986)." *Lockhart v. McCree,* 476 U.S. at 190–92 (Marshall, J., dissenting).

23. The Eighth Circuit, in *Grigsby v. Mabry,* 758 F.2d at 232, considered that "*Duren* requires the petitioners to establish that the [*Witherspoon*-excludables] are systematically excluded. Here, the district court found the systematic exclusion results from the voir dire at trial. *Grigsby* [*v. Mabry,* 569 F. Supp. at 1286]. There is little argument offered by the state that in capital cases the exclusion is not systematic."

interest in having the same jury serve at the guilt and penalty phases of a capital felony trial.... In most capital cases, the evidence presented to demonstrate the defendant's guilt also will be relevant to the determination of the existence of aggravating factors.... Thus, if different juries were required to consider the guilt and penalty issues, much of the same evidence would be likely to be presented to each of the juries." The majority indicates that the state's interest in judicial efficiency, that is, not presenting the same evidence to two different juries, is more important than the defendant's right to an impartial jury. Clearly, the state has not satisfied their burden of proving a significant interest.... [W]hen we must choose between justice and judicial efficiency, we come down strongly on the side of justice....

IV

Although I do not believe that the death penalty can be constitutionally imposed under our state constitution, common decency should dictate that, at the very least, when this extreme and barbaric punishment is sought by the state, we level the playing field so the defendant can at least receive a fair trial in the determination of his guilt or innocence. Today, the majority compounds the brutality of the penalty of death by ensuring that a jury is death qualified and therefore, more likely to convict the defendant at the guilt phase of the trial. In order to gain this tactical advantage, the state will from this day forward be encouraged to seek death in those marginal cases in which such a penalty should not have been sought.

This probably will be the last case before my retirement in which I will have the opportunity to express my views with respect to the dreadful punishment of death and related matters. Civilized nations have barred this horrible punishment. Some of our sister states have also banned death as a punishment, including all of the New England states except one—Connecticut. I have pointed out ... that the penalty of death fails to comport with contemporary standards of decency and that it constitutes cruel and unusual punishment in violation of our state constitution. I leave this court heartbroken because, as a result of one vote,[24] Connecticut is not among those enlightened states and nations to put an end to the death penalty. But those who would have it must live with this stain of blood. The determination of the constitutionality of the death penalty is not in the control of the legislature but, rather, in this court and the majority has failed to recognize its unconstitutionality.

I dissent.

NORCOTT, J., with whom KATZ, J., joins, dissenting.

I respectfully dissent from the conclusion of the majority that the practice of "death qualification," that is, the exclusion from capital juries of an entire group of potential jurors who express beliefs in opposition to the death penalty during voir dire questioning, does not violate the state constitution. While it is clear that this question has been resolved against the defendant's claim under the federal constitution I hold to the belief that the majority opinion's analysis of the practice does not stand up under our state constitution....

At the outset, I must say that I simply cannot overcome my intuitive agreement with the claim that death qualified juries are disposed to convict at the guilt phase. In my opinion, the empirical support for this claim, first set forth in *McCree* and supplemented by the defendant in this appeal, merits far more consideration than that given by the majority....

As one commentary observed, "[f]rom a social scientist's viewpoint the empirical question [whether death qualified juries are biased against the defendant on the issue of guilt] has been conclusively answered." R. Seltzer, G. Lopes, M. Dayan & R. Canan, "The Effect of Death Qualification on the Propensity of Jurors to Convict: The Maryland Example," 29 How. L.J. 571, 581 (1986). It seems to me that the cost of ignoring the direction in which the empirical data leads us is too great. While I do not believe that a minute dissection of these studies is warranted in this dissent, I do contend that the empirical evidence raises serious questions about the practice of the death qualification of juries. A succinct summarization of these studies reflects the following: (1) jurors who withstand death qualification tend to be less solicitous of a defendant's due process rights and significantly

24. See *State v. Cobb,* 251 Conn. 285, 743 A.2d 1 (four to three decision); *State v. Webb,* 238 Conn. 389, 680 A.2d 147 (four to three decision).

more eager to convict; see *State v. Young*, 853 P.2d 327, 389 (Utah 1993) (Durham, J., dissenting); (2) death qualification disproportionately excludes blacks and women, groups who statistically have been shown to be more opposed to the death penalty than whites and men; see W. White, "The Constitutional Invalidity of Convictions Imposed by Death-Qualified Juries," 58 Cornell L. Rev. 1176, 1187 (1973); (3) jury deliberations do not "neutralize the voting propensities of individual death-qualified or excludable jurors"; *Grigsby v. Mabry*, 569 F. Supp. 1273, 1302 (E.D.Ark.1983), aff'd, 758 F.2d 226 (8th Cir.1985), rev'd sub nom. *Lockhart v. McCree*, 476 U.S. 162; (4) jury panels that included *Witherspoon* excludables were able to remember facts more accurately than their death qualified counterparts; *id.*, at 1302; (5) death qualified jurors, as opposed to "*Witherspoon* excludables," were more prone to believe prosecution than defense witnesses; see *Hovey v. Superior Court*, 28 Cal.3d 1, 59–60, 616 P.2d 1301, 168 Cal.Rptr. 128 (1980); and (6) death qualified jurors maintained a higher standard of the concept of reasonable doubt than did jurors who were not death qualified; *id.*, at 59, 616 P.2d 1301; see also W. White, 58 Cornell L. Rev. 1188.

I am of the further opinion that the concerns of the state in opposition to alternatives to death qualification do not overcome my belief that the practice violates our state constitutional guarantees of a fair trial.

While I am cognizant of the state's interest in the protection of "neutrality" on the penalty issue, and while I further acknowledge that the concerns about cost, time and judicial resources are valid ones, I do not believe that, given the stakes involved, these concerns are compelling enough to change my position. Indeed, the idea that separate juries decide the issues of guilt and punishment ... seems most prudent. If the concern for assuring fairness in capital cases is to be taken seriously, surely implementing such an additional measure makes sense. Given the extraordinary delay that exists from the date of conviction to the date of actual execution of sentence in death penalty cases around the country, the concern about the excessive time factor involved in impaneling two juries is minimal....

Notes and Questions

1. The death- and life-qualification of capital jurors, as well as questioning prospective jurors to better inform the parties' exercise of peremptory challenges, frequently results in prolonged jury selection in trials where the death penalty is sought. In *Griffin*, for example, "[j]ury selection for the defendant's trial consumed some forty court days, during which more than 150 venirepersons were voir dired." Note that examination of jurors about their willingness to impose a death (or life) sentence is one factor helping explain why death-qualified juries might be "conviction prone." Questions that focus intensively and repeatedly on attitudes about punishment risk instilling a "presumption of guilt" by creating an expectation that the jurors' principal task will be to choose between a sentence of death and life imprisonment and that the defendant's culpability is a foregone conclusion.[18] On the other hand, since most parties agree that "nullifiers"—*i.e.*, individuals whose views about the death penalty are so strong that their ability to make a fair decision at the guilt phase of a trial would be affected—are properly excluded from capital jury service, some questioning of prospective jurors about their death-penalty attitudes prior to the guilt-phase trial may be inevitable.[19]

2. In light of the research evidence offered, as well as the "common sense" perspective that individuals with strong views against the death penalty are less likely than others to hold "pro-prosecution" attitudes that would make them inclined to convict the accused, and convict on the highest charge, who has the stronger argument about whether death qualification should be deferred until the trial's penalty phase (if there is a capital murder conviction)? How substantial are the state's interests in having the same jury consider the defendant's guilt as well as his or her punishment? Would impaneling enough alternate jurors at the guilt phase to allow for the replacement of jurors, prior to penalty-phase de-

liberations, who are not death- or life-qualified be a feasible way to avoid duplicating the presentation of evidence and incurring the time and financial costs associated with having two distinct juries?

3. Both the majority and the dissent in *Griffin* rely on social science studies that were cited in *Lockhart v. McCree* and thus had been conducted more than a decade earlier. Indeed, the majority opinion takes specific issue with the "Ellsworth Conviction Prone Study" noting that the data were 20 years old (and involved California residents, and not Connecticut residents). However, between 1984 (the publication year of the Ellsworth study) and 1999 (the year of the *Griffin* decision), additional scientific studies on death qualified jurors had been published. *See, e.g.*, Craig Haney, Aida Hurtado & Luis Vega, "'Modern' Death Qualification: New Data on Its Biasing Effects," 18 *Law & Human Behavior* 619 (1994); Robert J. Robinson, "What Does 'Unwilling to Impose the Death Penalty' Mean Anyway? Another Look at Excludable Jurors," 17 *Law & Human Behavior* 471 (1993).[20] Although the Court claimed only to be responding to the defendant's request that it take judicial notice of the relevant facts, the Court also was considering the *Geisler* factors, the last of which is "*contemporary* understandings of applicable economic and sociological norms" (emphasis added). More recent research (*i.e.*, post-1999) on death qualified jurors and their attitudes also has been completed, including several studies by Dr. Brooke Butler.[21]

4. Does the "death is different" refrain have ironic application in the present context? Note that the death-qualification of jurors occurs exclusively in murder prosecutions where a capital sentence is sought, and in no other criminal trials. Consider Justice Marshall's observations in his dissenting opinion in *Lockhart v. McCree*, 476 U.S. 162, 206 (1986).

> On occasion, this Court has declared what I believe should be obvious—that when a State seeks to convict a defendant of the most serious and severely punished offenses in its criminal code, any procedure that "diminish[es] the reliability of the guilt determination" must be struck down. *Beck v. Alabama*, 447 U.S. [625, 638 (1980)]. But in spite of such declarations, I cannot help thinking that respondent here would have stood a far better chance of prevailing on his constitutional claims had he not been challenging a procedure peculiar to the administration of the death penalty. For in no other context would a majority of this Court refuse to find any constitutional violation in a state practice that systematically operates to render juries more likely to convict, and to convict on the more serious charges.

D. Conclusion

Recent years have seen a dramatic decline in capital prosecutions and the number of new death sentences imposed. Whereas 326 death sentences were returned nationally in 1995, that number dropped to 235 in 2000, and plunged to approximately 114 in 2010,[22] or barely one-third of the total registered 15 years earlier. One factor helping to account for this precipitous fall in new yearly death sentences almost certainly is the concern shared by jurors, prosecutors, and the American public that innocent people are at risk of execution.[23] There is no doubt that the enormity and finality of the capital sanction magnifies concerns associated with wrongful convictions.

Capital punishment remains in effect in a sizeable majority of jurisdictions within the United States, including 34 states, under federal authority, and in the U.S. Military. In 2010, the nation's death row population stood at 3,261. Forty-six executions were carried out that year, bringing the total number since 1977, *i.e.,* during the modern, or post-*Furman* era of capital punishment, to 1,234.[24] The Supreme Court has repeatedly affirmed that the death penalty is not inherently unconstitutional, although the justices also have recognized that death is qualitatively different from other punishments, thus imposing a corresponding requirement for heightened reliability in capital sentencing proceedings. For the most part, nevertheless, the Court has not demanded commensurately higher reliability with respect to the determination of guilt in capital murder trials.[25] One scholar has even argued that, in light of the publicity associated with capital crimes, the intense pressures they generate in the community for the apprehension and punishment of the offender, and other factors, "the nature of capital cases multiplies the likelihood of error"[26] instead of reducing the chances of wrongful convictions.

Of course, not everyone agrees that death penalty cases are more prone than others to result in miscarriages of justice.[27] And, as we have seen, controversy swirls around whether a wrongful capital conviction has resulted in an innocent person being executed, at least in modern times. The result has been an uneasy tension between balancing the presumed benefits of the death penalty—its contributions to the retributive, deterrence, and incapacitation functions of punishment—and its perceived costs, including the risk of wrongful conviction and execution.

Chapter 11

Beyond Adjudication: Clemency, Innocence Commissions, and Compensation

A. Introduction

The courts, through trials and pretrial proceedings, are primary in determining whether individuals who have been charged with crimes are in fact guilty of committing them. Through appeals and post-conviction review, the courts also are primary in deciding whether individuals found guilty of crimes were convicted erroneously. While attention to procedural error is the norm, appeals and collateral challenges also can test the sufficiency of the evidence supporting a conviction. Subject to compliance with statutory prerequisites, post-conviction proceedings allow defendants to introduce newly discovered evidence of innocence. Judicial remedies for erroneous convictions normally include reversal and ordering a new trial, or outright dismissal of charges. We now turn our attention beyond these staples of the judicial process to explore alternative avenues for detecting, re-examining, and correcting wrongful convictions, and to consider additional remedies that may be available to innocent people who have been convicted and punished in error. We will examine executive clemency, innocence commissions, and compensating the wrongfully convicted.

B. Executive Clemency

In Chapter 2, we considered *Herrera v. Collins,* 506 U.S. 390, 113 S.Ct. 853, 122 L.Ed.2d 203 (1993), the important Supreme Court case in which Leonel Herrera, who had been convicted of murder and sentenced to death in a Texas state court, sought federal habeas corpus relief based on his claim that he was innocent. Herrera argued that to allow his execution to go forward would violate his Due Process rights and his Eighth Amendment right to be free from cruel and unusual punishments. Chief Justice Rehnquist's opinion for the Court assumed, "for the sake of argument" (506 U.S., at 417), that the federal Constitution would be offended by the execution of an innocent person. However, a majority of the justices agreed that the evidence offered in support of Herrera's petition "falls far short" of the "extraordinarily high" threshold to be satisfied before a federal court would be authorized to examine a claim of actual innocence on habeas corpus (506 U.S., at 417). Such a demanding showing would be required "because of the very disruptive effect that entertaining claims of actual innocence would have on the need for finality in capital cases, and the enormous burden that having to retry cases based on often stale evidence would place on the States" (506 U.S., at 417).

While strongly discouraging judicial review of "free-standing" claims of actual innocence, Chief Justice Rehnquist's opinion observed that Herrera was not "left without a forum to raise his actual innocence claim" (506 U.S., at 411).

> For under Texas law, petitioner may file a request for executive clemency. Clemency is deeply rooted in our Anglo-American tradition of law, and is the historic remedy for preventing miscarriages of justice where judicial process has been exhausted....
>
> Executive clemency has provided the "fail safe" in our criminal justice system.... [H]istory is replete with examples of wrongfully convicted persons who have been pardoned in the wake of after-discovered evidence establishing their innocence. 506 U.S., at 411–415 (cites and footnotes omitted).

While judicial review of convictions necessarily adheres to rules of law, executive clemency is discretionary and subject to no such constraints. Indeed, clemency decisions often explicitly embrace extralegal considerations.[1] "[T]he heart of executive clemency... is to grant clemency as a matter of grace, thus allowing the executive to consider a wide range of factors not comprehended by earlier judicial proceedings and sentencing determinations." *Ohio Adult Parole Authority v. Woodard,* 523 U.S. 272, 280–281, 118 S.Ct. 1244, 140 L.Ed.2d 387 (1998) (plurality opinion). As noted by the Court in *Herrera,* doubts about the reliability of a conviction represent one time-honored reason for grants of executive clemency.

Clemency can take various forms, including a *reprieve* (a delay for a specified period of time in carrying out a punishment, normally to allow for its review); a *commutation* (a reduction of punishment, such as from death to life imprisonment); and a *pardon* (which forgives or nullifies a judgment of guilt or criminal responsibility).[2] Logically, an innocent person who suffered a criminal conviction would be an appropriate candidate for a pardon. Yet, as we repeatedly have noted, the line demarcating "doubts about guilt" and "actual innocence" can be elusive. And precisely because clemency decisions are not rule-bound, and are subject to political and many other influences, a pardon might not issue even in the face of compelling evidence that an individual was wrongly convicted. A grant of clemency in such cases thus might take the alternative form of a commuted sentence, or be withheld altogether. Such decisions are not reviewable by the courts.[3]

Clemency authority exists under federal law and in all states, although it resides in various officials or administrative bodies. The United States Constitution vests that authority in the President, providing in Art. II, § 2[1] that the President "shall have Power to grant Reprieves and Pardons for Offenses against the United States, except in Cases of Impeachment." Most states grant their governors exclusive clemency authority, although in several the governor must first consider (but is not bound by) the recommendation made by a board of pardons or analogous administrative body, which typically is appointed by the governor. In a few states, the governor can grant clemency if and only if a board of pardons first makes a favorable recommendation, and in some states—including a few that have experienced scandals—clemency powers inhere in a pardon board alone rather than the governor.[4]

In an earlier era, distinguished by limited procedural safeguards, the unavailability of appeals, and mandatory sentencing, executive clemency was an integral part of the criminal justice process. For example, in England toward the turn of the 19th century, the Crown regularly spared condemned offenders from the gallows, commuting as many as seven out of every eight death sentences imposed.[5] Capital case clemency decisions varied markedly throughout the United States in the era preceding *Furman v. Georgia*, 408 U.S. 238, 92 S.Ct. 2726, 33 L.Ed.2d 346 (1972). Commutations were relatively common in some states; for example, North Carolina governors reduced 229 out of the 585 (39.1%) death sentences imposed in the state between 1903 and 1963 to life imprisonment, as did Texas governors in 100 of the 461 (21.7%) death sentences they reviewed between 1923 and 1972.[6] More recently, however—with the notable exception of former Illinois Governor George Ryan's blanket commutation of 167 capital offenders' sentences in that state in 2003, and other widespread death row commutations in New Mexico, Ohio, New Jersey, and again in Illinois in 2011 when its death penalty law was repealed—many observers have noted a precipitous decline in capital case clemency.[7] The Death Penalty Information Center reports that "[s]ince 1976, [267] death row inmates have been granted clemency for humanitarian reasons"—reasons which "include doubts about the defendant's guilt or conclusions of the governor regarding the death penalty process."[8] However, excluding Governor Ryan's and four other governors' "broad grants of clemency,"[9] the number of such commutations drops to 64, compared to (through early March 2011) 1242 executions.[10]

Death-sentenced prisoners comprise a tiny fraction of individuals convicted of crimes. And, as we have noted, a pardon rather than a commuted sentence is the type of clemency that logically would be available to persons wrongfully convicted of crimes. Statistics describing the commutation of capital sentences thus are not as informative for our purposes as would be data about grants of executive clemency in criminal cases generally, especially clemency decisions grounded on possible innocence. Unfortunately, such information is not readily available. One scholar, relying on available statistical compilations, noted:

> At both the state and federal level, grants of executive clemency have plummeted in recent decades. For much of the nation's history, clemency was used routinely at the federal level. But the percentage of federal grants of clemency applications has declined sharply, with the biggest drop occurring from President Nixon's presidency until today. State level pardons have also fallen in recent decades. "Pardons are granted on more than a token basis in only 13 states and are a realistically available remedy in only about half of those." This same time period has been characterized by the dominance of tough-on-crime politics, and one cannot deny the relationship between this trend and the decline of executive clemency. No governor or President wants to be viewed as soft on crime or to be blamed if a pardoned individual goes on to commit another crime.[11]

Concerns about "tough-on-crime politics" or that a pardoned individual might commit "another" crime, of course, are not logically warranted when clemency is used to remedy an innocent person's wrongful conviction. Nevertheless, in politics as in other callings, perceptions matter. Executive officials often grapple with the risk of adverse public reaction and political backlash when making their clemency decisions.[12] Between the Truman (1945–1953) and Carter (1977–1981) administrations, the annual number of federal pardons typically exceeded 100 (the high point was 1950, when President Truman granted 400). However, only once since 1980 did subsequent presidents grant more than 100 pardons, when President Clinton issued 258 on leaving office in 2001, and they usually conferred far fewer.[13] Governors in many states have been similarly chary in their clemency decisions. For example, in populous New York, where nearly 200,000 felony and misdemeanor convictions were recorded in one recent year alone, governors issued a total of just 11 pardons between 1974 and 2008.[14]

The following cases, the first from North Carolina and the second from Tennessee, present issues concerning the exercise of clemency that arise within the context of capital convictions and sentences. They help illuminate the history and purposes of executive clemency as they discuss the scope of discretion retained by clemency authorities in the respective states.

Bacon v. Lee

549 S.E.2d 840 (N.C. 2001)

MARTIN, Justice.

Plaintiffs [(three death-sentenced prisoners)] instituted the instant civil action to challenge the constitutionality of the Governor's exercise of his clemency power under Article III, Section 5(6) of the Constitution of North Carolina....

Plaintiffs allege in their first claim for relief that they have "the right to petition for [executive] clemency at any time after conviction, pursuant to Art. III, § 5(6) of the North Carolina Constitution," and that they have a due process right under Article I, Sections 1, 19, 21, 27, and 35 of the North Carolina Constitution and the Eighth and Fourteenth Amendments to the United States Constitution for their clemency petition to "be considered and decided by a neutral and impartial decision maker, untainted by his prior participation in [any] Plaintiff's prosecution." Plaintiffs allege that because Governor Easley "was the Attorney General of North Carolina throughout part, or all, of each and every Plaintiff's appellate and post-conviction review proceedings in state and/or federal court, and was also the local prosecutor in the initial trial proceedings of Plaintiff McLaughlin, he has an inherent conflict of interest that precludes him from fairly considering any Plaintiff's clemency request, and [therefore] does not qualify as a neutral and impartial decision maker."

Plaintiffs' second claim for relief is "grounded in each of the Plaintiffs' [sic] cognizable liberty interest in his continued life and existence, and his right, under the North Carolina Constitution and the U.S. Constitution, to equal protection of law against deprivation of such cognizable interest." ...

Plaintiffs, in their third claim for relief, allege a "cruel and unusual punishment [claim] under the Eighth and Fourteenth Amendments to the U.S. Constitution, and under Art. I, §§ 19 & 27 of the North Carolina Constitution."

In their prayer for relief, plaintiffs seek injunctive relief and entry of "a declaratory judgment that the exercise of the power of clemency by Defendant Easley with respect to any of the Plaintiffs would constitute a violation of such Plaintiff's rights to due process, equal protection of the law and freedom from cruel and unusual punishment under the state and federal constitutions, and in violation of 42 U.S.C. § 1983." ...

I.

Before addressing the allegations raised in the instant complaint, we briefly consider the background of the doctrine of executive clemency and the justiciability of clemency procedures. First, the genesis of executive clemency in the United States is found in the English common law. *See, e.g., Herrera v. Collins,* 506 U.S. 390, 411–12 (1993); *Schick v. Reed,* 419 U.S. 256, 262 (1974); *Ex parte Grossman,* 267 U.S. 87, 110 (1925); *United States v. Wilson,* 32 U.S. (7 Pet.) 150, 160 (1833). In *Wilson,* Chief Justice Marshall stated:

> As this power had been exercised from time immemorial by the executive of that nation whose language is our language, and to whose judicial institutions ours bear a close resemblance; we adopt their principles respecting the operation and effect of a pardon, and look into their books for the rules prescribing the manner in which it is to be used by the person who would avail himself of it.

32 U.S. (7 Pet.) at 160.

In England the power to grant pardons belonged almost exclusively to the Monarch. *See Schick,* 419 U.S. at 260–62 ("by 1787 the English prerogative to pardon was unfettered except for a few specifically enumerated limitations" such as impeachments). Traditionally, the exercise of clemency authority has been considered "a matter of grace," *see, e.g., Ohio Adult Parole Auth. v. Woodard,* 523 U.S. 272, 280–81 (1998), or "an act of grace," *see, e.g., Wilson,* 32 U.S. (7 Pet.) at 160. Clemency was designed to give the executive the authority to exempt "the individual on whom it is bestowed from the punishment the law inflicts for a crime he has committed." *Id.* In *Ex parte Grossman,* the United States Supreme Court observed that clemency "may afford relief from [the] undue harshness or evident mistake in the operation or enforcement of the criminal law." 267 U.S. at 120.

The United States Supreme Court recently reaffirmed the traditional conception of clemency as an Executive Branch function separate from adjudicatory proceedings within the Judicial Branch. *See Herrera,* 506 U.S. at 411–13. The Court noted that one of the great advantages of clemency in England was "'that there is a magistrate, who has it in his power to extend mercy, wherever he thinks it is deserved: holding a court of equity in his own breast, to soften the rigour of the general law, in such criminal cases as merit an exemption from punishment.'" *Id.* at 412 (quoting 4 William Blackstone, *Commentaries on the Laws of England* *397). Consequently, "pardon and commutation decisions have not traditionally been the business of courts; as such, they are rarely, if ever, appropriate subjects for judicial review." *Connecticut Bd. of Pardons v. Dumschat,* 452 U.S. 458, 464 (1981).

We observe that all fifty states have incorporated clemency provisions in their respective constitutions. The people of North Carolina have vested their Governor with virtually absolute clemency authority since the adoption of their first Constitution in 1776.... Under the Constitution of 1971, the third and present State Constitution, the power to grant pardons, reprieves, and commutations continues to be the exclusive prerogative of the executive. The Constitution provides in part:

> The Governor may grant reprieves, commutations, and pardons, after conviction, for all offenses (except in cases of impeachment), upon such conditions as he may think proper, subject to regulations prescribed by law relative to the manner of applying for pardons. N.C. Const. art. III, § 5(6).[4]

Plaintiffs contend that the United States Supreme Court effectively overruled its prior jurisprudence regarding executive clemency procedures in *Ohio Adult Parole Auth. v. Woodard,* 523 U.S. 272 (1998). According to plaintiffs, "*Woodard* completely changed the landscape, and swept away the precedential value of any cases decided before it that turned on the notion that clemency proceedings were immune from due process safeguards."

In *Woodard,* the defendant was sentenced to death in the state courts of Ohio for an aggravated murder committed in the course of a carjacking. When he failed to obtain a stay of execution more than forty-five days prior to his scheduled execution date, the Ohio Adult Parole Authority (the Authority) informed the defendant, with three days' notice, that on 9 September 1994 he could have a clemency interview, followed by a hearing on 16 September. In response, the defendant did not request an interview but instead objected to the proposed date for the interview and requested that his counsel be permitted to attend, and participate in, the clemency interview and hearing. The Authority failed to respond to the defendant's requests. On 14 September 1994 the defendant filed suit in the United States District Court for the Southern District of Ohio alleging that Ohio's clemency process violated, among other things, his Fourteenth Amendment due process rights.

The district court granted the State of Ohio's motion for judgment on the pleadings. On appeal, the United States Court of Appeals for the Sixth Circuit affirmed in part and reversed in part. The court determined that there was no federally created life or liberty interest in clemency (relying on *Dumschat,* 452 U.S. at 464–65). Because the Governor's decision to grant clemency remained within his sole discretion, regardless of the Authority's recommendation, the court also determined that the defendant did not have any state-created life or liberty interest in clemency. The court then considered a "second strand" of due process analysis "center[ed] on the role of clemency in the entire punitive scheme." Relying on *Evitts v. Lucey,* 469 U.S. 387 (1985), the Sixth Circuit observed that "[t]he Constitution does not require a state ... to provide a system of appeals, but if the state chooses to do so, the appeal, too, must comply

4. N.C.G.S. § 147-21 prescribes the form and content of a pardon application. It provides:

> Every application for pardon must be made to the Governor in writing, signed by the party convicted, or by some person in his behalf. And every such application shall contain the grounds and reasons upon which the executive pardon is asked, and shall be in every case accompanied by a certified copy of the indictment, and the verdict and judgment of the court thereon.

with the basic requirements of due process." According to the court, this reasoning applied to other post-conviction avenues of relief made available by the government, including clemency. The court determined that "due process at the clemency stage will necessarily be minimal ... because of the great distance from the truly fundamental process." As a result, the Sixth Circuit remanded the case to the district court to address defendant's due process claim under this "second strand of due process analysis."

The United States Supreme Court reversed the Sixth Circuit's decision. The Court's principal opinion, a plurality opinion of four justices authored by Chief Justice Rehnquist, reaffirmed the *Dumschat* holding—that clemency decisions "'have not traditionally been the business of courts; as such, they are rarely, if ever, appropriate subjects for judicial review.'" *Woodard,* 523 U.S. at 276 (quoting *Dumschat,* 452 U.S. at 464). According to the principal opinion, "[c]lemency proceedings are not part of the trial—or even of the adjudicatory process. They do not determine the guilt or innocence of the defendant.... They are conducted by the executive branch, independent of direct appeal and collateral relief proceedings." *Id.* at 284. If the procedural constraints that Woodard requested were implemented, "the executive's clemency authority would cease to be a matter of grace committed to the executive authority." *Id.* at 285. Accordingly, the Court determined that Ohio's clemency procedures did not violate the Fourteenth Amendment Due Process Clause.

Justice O'Connor, concurring by separate opinion, determined that a prisoner under a death sentence retains a life interest after proper conviction to which due process safeguards attach. She concluded that "some *minimal* procedural safeguards apply to clemency proceedings." "Judicial intervention might, for example, be warranted in the face of a scheme whereby a state official flipped a coin to determine whether to grant clemency, or in a case where the State arbitrarily denied a prisoner any access to its clemency process." *Id.* Justice O'Connor ultimately concluded, however, that none of the defendant's allegations "amount[ed] to a due process violation" as a matter of law. *See id.* at 290 (no remand to district court necessary in order to make factual determinations on Woodard's due process claim).

Justice Stevens, concurring in part and dissenting in part, stated that a prisoner retained a "life interest protected by the Due Process Clause." *Id.* at 292 (Stevens, J., concurring in part and dissenting in part). He concluded that because clemency proceedings involved the "final stage of the decisional process that precedes an official deprivation of life," they must satisfy the basic requirements of due process. *Id.* at 295. Accordingly, Justice Stevens stated in dissent that the case should be remanded to the district court to determine "whether Ohio's procedures meet the minimum requirements of due process."

Justice O'Connor's concurring opinion represents the holding of the Court because it was decided on the narrowest grounds and provided the fifth vote. Three justices joined in the principal opinion authored by Chief Justice Rehnquist, and three justices concurred in Justice O'Connor's concurring opinion. Thus, eight justices essentially concluded that Woodard's due process allegations failed as a matter of law.

II.

The primary question presented by the instant case is whether Governor Easley's consideration of clemency requests from plaintiffs or putative class members violates the Fourteenth Amendment Due Process Clause in light of the *Woodard* decision. More particularly, we must determine whether the minimal due process applicable to state clemency procedures includes the right of an inmate seeking clemency to have his or her request reviewed by an executive possessing the level of impartiality normally required of a judge presiding over an adjudicatory proceeding.

As a preliminary matter, we note that, pursuant to Article III, Section 5(6) of the State Constitution, the Governor may grant clemency at any time "after conviction." N.C. Const. art. III, § 5(6). Nevertheless, we take judicial notice of the fact that the executive in North Carolina does not ordinarily consider clemency requests in capital cases until the applicant has exhausted all avenues of relief within the federal and state judiciary....

Apart from Bacon, the instant record does not reflect that Cagle, McLaughlin, or any putative class member has exhausted his or her federal and state post-conviction remedies. In the absence of this threshold showing, the claims asserted by these named plaintiffs and putative class members are not ripe for review.... Accordingly, we remand the claims asserted by Cagle and McLaughlin to the trial court for entry of an order of dismissal without prejudice.

We review Bacon's claims pursuant to our supervisory authority under Article IV of the Constitution of North Carolina and N.C. R.App. P. 2....

We initially note that, since *Woodard*, the federal courts have generally followed a cautious approach to the question of the amount of process due inmates seeking clemency. For instance, in *Roll v. Carnahan*, 225 F.3d 1016 (8th Cir.2000), prisoners in Missouri contended their Governor could not be fair and impartial when considering clemency petitions because he was engaged in a campaign for the United States Senate where one of the issues was clemency in capital cases. While recognizing that *Woodard* ensured minimal due process rights within clemency proceedings, the court concluded the "complaint that the governor will not be objective fail[ed]" because clemency decisions were left to the sole discretion of the Governor under the Missouri Constitution.

Similarly, in *Duvall v. Keating*, 162 F.3d 1058 (10th Cir.), *cert. denied*, 525 U.S. 1061 (1998), a prisoner argued he was denied due process in his pursuit of clemency because the Governor of Oklahoma had previously stated he would not grant clemency to murderers. The Oklahoma Constitution provided for a clemency petition to be reviewed by the Pardon and Parole Board (the Board) following an impartial investigation. Although the Governor's decision was discretionary, he could commute a sentence only upon the favorable recommendation of the Board. In that case, the Board deadlocked and thus did not send a recommendation to the Governor. The court, relying on *Woodard*, held:

> Because clemency proceedings involve acts of mercy that are not constitutionally required, the minimal application of the Due Process Clause only ensures a death row prisoner that he or she will receive the clemency procedures explicitly set forth by state law, and that the procedure followed in rendering the clemency decision will not be wholly arbitrary, capricious or based upon whim, for example, flipping a coin.

Id. at 1061. The court declined to review "the substantive merits of the clemency decision." Because the prisoner had not shown he was deprived of any procedure allowed him by the State Constitution or otherwise shown that the procedures used were arbitrary, the court concluded that the prisoner had not been denied due process.

In another case, a prisoner alleged he had been denied due process in pursuit of clemency for various reasons, including that the State Attorney General had formerly served as his prosecutor and later as counsel to the Parole Board and counsel to the Governor. *Workman v. Summers*, 136 F.Supp.2d 896, 897 (M.D.Tenn.2001). The court held that "[t]he decision of the Governor to grant or deny clemency is not reviewable" and limited its analysis to a review of state clemency procedures. Because the prisoner had not shown that he had been denied access to the clemency process or had been subjected to an arbitrary determination or arbitrary procedure, the court held that he had received "the minimal due process required for a clemency proceeding."

The United States Court of Appeals for the Fourth Circuit considered, and rejected, a similar claim in *Buchanan v. Gilmore*, 139 F.3d 982 (4th Cir. 1998), albeit before the issuance of *Woodard*....

We find the rationale of these decisions persuasive and conclude that Bacon has not alleged any cognizable violation of his due process rights in connection with the clemency procedures available to him under North Carolina law. We do not believe *Woodard* intended to repudiate entirely the cardinal principle that clemency decisions are normally not a matter to be litigated in courts of law. Instead, we conclude, after review of *Woodard*, that state clemency procedures generally comport with due process when a prisoner is afforded notice and the opportunity to participate in clemency procedures, and the clemency decision, though substantively a discretionary one, is not reached by means of a procedure such as a coin toss. *See Woodard*, 523 U.S. at 289–90 (O'Connor, J., concurring). Our consideration of the amount of process due Bacon incidental to his clemency request is guided in part by Justice O'Connor's observation in *Woodard:* "It is clear that 'once society has validly convicted an individual of a crime and therefore established its right to punish, the demands of due process are reduced accordingly.'" 523 U.S. at 288 (quoting *Ford v. Wainwright*, 477 U.S. 399, 429 (1986) (O'Connor, J., concurring in result in part and dissenting in part)).

In our view, Bacon's due process rights are not violated by Governor Easley's consideration of his clemency request. It is undisputed that

Bacon received notice of clemency procedures and that he has fully availed himself of these procedures. Moreover, Bacon has not alleged that Governor Easley has, or will, render a decision in a manner that violates *Woodard.* Bacon contends, however, that Governor Easley "has an inherent conflict of interest that precludes him from fairly considering" Bacon's clemency request because of his prior service as Attorney General of North Carolina.

We disagree with Bacon's assertion that the people's elected executive could be divested of one of his or her express constitutional powers, in this case the exclusive authority over clemency decisions under Article III, Section 5(6) of the Constitution of North Carolina, because he or she previously served as Attorney General. All executives assume office after a unique composite of life experiences which undoubtedly influence their discharge of clemency power. Despite the potential for the executive's previous roles—whether as attorney, chemist, farmer, or otherwise—to influence his or her clemency determinations, the people of North Carolina have nonetheless opted to vest their Governor with virtually plenary clemency authority.

Significantly, Governor Easley is not the first North Carolina executive to have served previously as Attorney General. In 1917 former Attorney General Thomas Bickett assumed the office of Governor of North Carolina. As Governor, Bickett considered, and granted, a number of clemency, pardon, and reprieve petitions from prisoners whose appeals he had handled while serving as Attorney General.... Both then, and now, acceptance of Bacon's argument would undeniably repudiate the people's constitutional election concerning the role of their elected executive within the clemency process. After careful review, we are unpersuaded that *Woodard* intended to disrupt the orderly role of the executive in discharging clemency power by making his or her background or previous life experiences a justiciable controversy under the Due Process Clause of the Fourteenth Amendment. Our holding remains unaltered regardless of whether Bacon's due process allegations are premised on an "inherent conflict of interest" theory, as alleged in the complaint, or on an "actual bias" theory, as asserted in brief before this Court.

Our conclusion is supported by the nature of executive clemency and its constitutional placement within our tripartite system of government. The nature of executive clemency is fundamentally different than adjudicatory proceedings within the Judicial Branch of government. A primary goal of adjudicatory proceedings is the uniform application of law. In furtherance of this objective, courts generally consider themselves bound by prior precedent, *i.e.,* the doctrine of *stare decisis.* Furthermore, courts generally consider only evidence of record in their disposition of adjudicatory proceedings....

In contrast, because the nature of clemency is inherently one of executive "grace" or "mercy," the decision to grant or deny a clemency request does not bind the executive, or his or her successor, in future clemency reviews....

Also, unlike judicial proceedings, the clemency decision-maker is generally not limited in discharging his or her extrajudicial function by rules of evidence, rules of procedure, or other indicia of judicial proceedings.... Finally, the clemency decision is necessarily influenced by the unique background and life experiences, and presumably the social and political philosophy, of the executive decision-maker.

As one commentator stated in highlighting differences between judicial proceedings and the exercise of clemency authority:

> *Mercy cannot be quantified or institutionalized.* It is properly left to the conscience of the executive entitled to consider pleas and should not be bound by court decisions meant to do justice....
>
> *Mercy is not the same as justice nor is it the opposite. Executive clemency allows for discretion in a way that courtroom procedure cannot.* It broadens the relevance of the philosophical and moral implications of an individual crime in a way that a judicial determination of guilt or innocence should not. As one clemency applicant eloquently describes it: When a chief executive considers clemency, he or she acts as the "distilled conscience" of the citizenry.

Brown, *The Quality of Mercy,* 40 UCLA L.Rev. at 328–30 (footnotes omitted) (emphasis added).

In sum, clemency determinations by the Executive Branch are fundamentally different than adjudicatory proceedings within the Judicial Branch. Bacon's unilateral attempt, therefore, to superimpose recusal principles developed by, and applicable to, judges is wholly foreign to the executive's consideration of clemency requests.

Moreover, we do not read *Woodard* to diminish substantially the undeniable textual commitment of clemency to the Executive Branch of government. By analogy to presidential clemency powers, see U.S. Const. art. II, §2(1) (President has the "power to grant reprieves and pardons for offenses against the United States, except in cases of impeachment"), we do not believe that Bacon's proposed expansion of the range of justiciable matters relating to executive clemency would be consistent with the federal separation of powers doctrine....

In view of the foregoing, we conclude that Bacon's demand for the equivalent of a judicial arbiter to consider his clemency request does not fall within the minimal due process rights applied by *Woodard* to state clemency procedures. Bacon's due process claim therefore fails as a matter of law.

Alternatively, even if Bacon adequately alleges a *Woodard* violation, the Governor cannot delegate the exercise of the clemency authority under Article III, Section 5(6) of the State Constitution. As such, the Rule of Necessity applies, enabling Governor Easley to consider Bacon's clemency request....

III.

Bacon alleges, in his second claim for relief, that Governor Easley's consideration of his clemency request violates his right to equal protection of the law under the United States Constitution. Specifically, Bacon alleges that equal protection is denied where "one group of convicted capital defendants will have their clemency petitions decided by a neutral and impartial decision-maker, and another group, similarly situated, by a decision-maker who does not qualify as neutral and impartial because of his previous involvement in their cases as Attorney General, or local prosecutor."

We observe, as an initial matter, that *Woodard* did not recognize an equal protection claim within the context of executive clemency. In any event, Bacon's equal protection claim fails because we cannot conclude that Bacon has been, or will be, treated differently for purposes of pursuing clemency than other similarly situated death row inmates....

Bacon also alleges, in his third claim for relief, a violation of his right to be free from cruel and unusual punishment under the Eighth and Fourteenth Amendments to the United States Constitution. Bacon's claim rests upon the premise that "a capital punishment system without clemency would constitute cruel and unusual punishment." Accordingly, he argues, "the Constitution must give some structural limitation to what constitutes a clemency proceeding."

Bacon's basic premise—that clemency is constitutionally required in a capital punishment system—is erroneous as a matter of law. In *Herrera* the United States Supreme Court observed that "although the Constitution vests in the President a pardon power, it does not require the States to enact a clemency mechanism." 506 U.S. at 414; *see also Young v. Hayes,* 218 F.3d 850, 853 (8th Cir.2000) ("The Constitution of the United States does not require that a state have a clemency procedure...."); *Duvall v. Keating,* 162 F.3d at 1062 (finding no basis for the plaintiffs' allegation of an Eighth Amendment violation within the clemency context). Consequently, Bacon's Eighth Amendment claim fails as a matter of law....

Notes and Questions

1. The court reached only Bacon's claims for relief, ruling that since Cage and McLaughlin had not yet exhausted potential avenues of relief in the federal or state courts, their cases were not ripe for adjudication. It appears that Governor Easley, prior to his election to that office, served as "the local prosecutor in the initial trial proceedings" that culminated in McLaughlin's murder conviction and death sentence. If McLaughlin were to exhaust all judicial opportunities for relief and thus was left to petition Governor Easley for clemency—the same man who had worked as a prosecutor to secure his conviction and death sentence—would he have a stronger constitutional claim than Bacon? How would you expect the court to rule under those circumstances?

2. If Bacon's clemency petition had been based primarily on a claim of innocence, to what extent would the court's discussion of the role of mercy in clemency decisions be germane? What bearing would the *Herrera* decision have on Bacon's petition?

3. What opportunity, if any, must be provided to a prisoner who petitions for executive clemency to establish facts—such as those bearing on his or her innocence—that may be critical to a clemency decision? In *Ohio Adult Parole Authority v. Woodard,* 523 U.S. 272, 118 S.Ct. 1244, 140 L.Ed.2d 387 (1998), which is discussed at some length in *Bacon v. Lee,* the Supreme Court rejected a death-sentenced prisoner's claim that Ohio's clemency procedures violated his Due Process rights. Chief Justice Rehnquist's plurality opinion observed that: "Clemency proceedings are not part of the trial—or even of the adjudicatory process.... [T]he executive's clemency authority would cease to be a matter of grace committed to the executive authority if it were constrained by the sort of procedural requirements that respondent urges." 523 U.S., at 284–285. Justice O'Connor, joined by three other justices, concurred only in the judgment. She expressed the opinion that "some *minimal* procedural safeguards apply to clemency proceedings. Judicial intervention might, for example, be warranted in the face of a scheme whereby a state official flipped a coin to determine whether to grant clemency, or in a case where the State arbitrarily denied a prisoner any access to its clemency process." 523 U.S., at 289. Justice Stevens, concurring in part and dissenting in part, argued most forcefully for procedural safeguards in the clemency proceedings made available to death-sentenced prisoners, but even he concluded that "only the most basic elements of fair procedure are required." 523 U.S., at 292.

Two years before *Woodard* was decided, the Texas Court of Appeals denied Gary Graham's claim that the Texas Board of Pardons and Paroles was constitutionally "required to hold a hearing to consider his claim for executive clemency." *Graham v. Texas Board of Pardons and Paroles,* 913 S.W.2d 745, 747 (Tex. App. 1996). Graham had been convicted of capital murder and sentenced to death for a robbery-murder committed in Houston. He was 17 years old at the time of the crime (the Supreme Court would later rule—but not in time to benefit Graham—that the Constitution forbids the execution of offenders who committed their crimes before turning 18 years of age[15]). He had admitted committing a series of violent robberies close in time to the murder, but he consistently maintained his innocence of the murder. Virtually the only trial evidence linking him to the killing was the testimony of a single eyewitness whose reliability was brought into serious question.[16] Ruling that Graham had sufficient opportunity to litigate his claim of actual innocence in a judicial forum, the court rejected his contention. "[W]e do not mean to imply that Graham is not entitled to meaningful review of his clemency petition by the Board, but only that the Texas Constitution does not require the Board to grant Graham a due course of law hearing where such a hearing is already provided by way of state habeas corpus procedure." 913 S.W.2d, at 751–752 (footnote omitted).

Graham's case drew special attention because George W. Bush, then Governor of Texas, was running for President in 2000, when Graham was executed.[17] Graham fought the execution team that transported him to the execution chamber, protesting that "I'm an innocent black man that is being murdered."[18] Under Texas law, the Governor cannot commute a death sentence without the prior recommendation of the Board of Pardons and Parole; the Board had denied Graham's clemency application. Because Graham already had been issued one 30-day reprieve, state law precluded additional reprieves. Governor Bush thus had no formal authority to halt or delay Graham's execution,[19] but the publicity attending Graham's claims of innocence and other aspects of his case brought important elements of Texas's clemency procedures during Governor Bush's administration under scrutiny.

During Bush's six years as governor 150 men and two women were executed in Texas—a record unmatched by any other governor in modern American history. Each time a person was sentenced to death, Bush received from his legal counsel [Alberto Gonzales] a document summarizing the facts of the case, usually on the morning of the day scheduled for the execution, and was then briefed on those facts by his counsel; based on this information Bush allowed the execution to proceed in all cases but one. The first fifty-seven of these summaries were prepared by Gonzales....

A close examination of the Gonzales memoranda suggest that Governor Bush frequently approved executions based on only the most cursory briefings on the issues in dispute. In fact, in these documents Gonzales repeatedly failed to apprise the governor of crucial issues in the cases at hand: ineffective counsel, conflict of interest, mitigating evidence, even actual evidence of innocence.[20]

In light of the importance of clemency as a possible "fail safe" in guarding against miscarriages, should more regular fact-finding procedures be required in the decision-making process?[21] In this vein, of what relevance are the Supreme Court's recent decisions addressing whether state prisoners have a post-conviction right of access to DNA evidence in *District Attorney's Office for the Third Judicial District v. Osborne,* 557 U.S. ___, 129 S. Ct. 2308, 174 L.Ed.2d 38 (2009), and *Skinner v. Switzer,* ___ U.S. ___, 2011 WL 767703 (2011), which we considered in Chapter 5? One of the amicus curiae briefs filed in *Osborne* was submitted on behalf of "Eleven Individuals Who Have Received Clemency Through DNA Testing."[22] While rejecting Osborne's claim that he had a constitutional right of access to DNA evidence for a post-conviction challenge to his convictions for kidnapping, assault, and sexual assault, Chief Justice Roberts' majority opinion noted:

In identifying his potential liberty interest, Osborne first attempts to rely on the Governor's constitutional authority to "grant pardons, commutations, and reprieves." Alaska Const., Art. III, § 21. We have held that noncapital defendants do not have a liberty interest in traditional state executive clemency, to which no particular claimant is *entitled* as a matter of state law. *Connecticut Bd. of Pardons v. Dumschat,* 452 U.S. 458, 464 (1981). Osborne therefore cannot challenge the constitutionality of any procedures available to vindicate an interest in state clemency. 129 S.Ct., at 2319 (emphasis in original).

Workman v. State

22 S.W.3d 807 (Tenn. 2000)

ORDER

This cause came on to be heard upon the motion of the State of Tennessee requesting that an execution date be set in the above-styled case.

The respondent, Philip Workman, filed a "Response to Motion to Set Execution Date and Motion for Certificate of Commutation," alleging that he was convicted upon perjured testimony and that he is not guilty of capital murder. The State filed a reply and response, arguing that the respondent is not entitled to further delay in the imposition of his sentence of death and that his case is not an appropriate one for this Court to consider issuance of a certificate of commutation.

Under the Tennessee Constitution, the power to commute a death sentence is vested in the Governor. Tenn. Const. Art. III, § 6. In addition, the Tennessee General Assembly has passed enabling legislation providing the Governor with several options for granting clemency. Tennessee Code Annotated Section 40-27-101 confers upon the Governor the general "power to grant reprieves, commutations and pardons in all criminal cases after conviction, except impeachment." Section 40-27-104 grants the Governor the discretion to remit a portion of a prisoner's sentence upon the recommendation of the board of probation and parole. Two statutes speak directly to the issue of commutation of death sentences. Pursuant to Tenn. Code Ann. § 40-27-105, upon application for a pardon by a person sentenced to death, the Governor may commute the sentence to life imprisonment if he or she "is of [the] opinion that the facts and circumstances adduced are not sufficient to warrant a total pardon." This Court has no role in clemency proceedings except for that provided by Tenn. Code Ann. § 40-27-106. Under that provision, the governor may commute the punishment from death to life imprisonment upon the certificate of this Court, "that in its opinion, there are extenuating circumstances attending the case, and that the punishment ought to be commuted."

The respondent alleges several reasons why this Court should issue a certificate of commutation. First, he asserts that Harold Davis, who testified at trial that he saw the respondent shoot the victim, has since recanted his testimony. Second, citing the opinion of two experts, he contends that the fatal shot was not fired from his gun. Finally, he challenges this Court's and the Sixth Circuit Court of Appeal's prior characterizations of his testimony at trial as a "confession." *See State v. Workman*, 667 S.W.2d 44 (Tenn. 1984); *Workman v. Bell*, 160 F.3d 276 (6th Cir. 1998). The State counters that the respondent's assertions are inherently suspect and that the Court should consider only record facts.

While members of this Court disagree regarding the role of the Court in recommending commutation, we all agree on two basic precepts: first, on the issue of recommending commutation, the Court should consider only facts contained in the record, or facts which are uncontroverted. Second, we all agree there is no legal basis why an execution date should not be set because the respondent has exhausted all judicial remedies and the conviction and sentence are final as a matter of law....

... [C]ertificates of commutation are issued pursuant to Tenn. Code Ann. § 40-27-106 only when the "extenuating circumstances attending the case" are based upon the facts in the record, or a combination of record facts and new evidence that is uncontroverted. Section 40-27-106 does not authorize relief when a death-sentenced prisoner, in what amounts to an original action, relies upon extra-judicial facts and challenges the accuracy of the jury's verdict and the credibility of the evidence upon which his or her conviction was based. In contrast, we note that the Governor may review a request for commutation without being bound by such limitations.[1]

After careful review of the record of the proceedings in this case, the majority concludes that the record supports both the conviction and sentence. The respondent has presented no extenuating circumstances that warrant issuance of a certificate of commutation. Accordingly, the Motion for Certificate of Commutation is DENIED....

... There exists no procedure, no method, and no means by which the conviction or the sentence can be further tested or scrutinized under the procedural guidelines within which this Court must function. His case is therefore ripe for the setting of an execution date. Accordingly, the State's motion to set an execution date is GRANTED. It is hereby ORDERED, ADJUDGED and DECREED by this Court that the Warden of the Riverbend Maximum Security Institution, or his designee, shall execute the sentence of death as provided by law on the 6th day of April, 2000, unless otherwise ordered by this Court or other appropriate authority....

/s/ Riley Anderson
Chief Justice

DROWOTA, Justice, concurring.

I fully concur with the Court's order setting an execution date and denying the respondent's request for a certificate of commutation pursuant to Tenn. Code Ann. § 40-27-106 (1997). However, I write separately to explain the jurisprudential landscape that existed at the time Section 40-27-106 was enacted, to discuss the important role of *executive* clemency and commutation in the Anglo-American tradition of law, and to emphasize that the respondent should take the opportunity to file an application for executive clemency. A final decision on the application should be rendered only after careful review and full consideration by the Governor of the facts

1. Despite the limitations on this Court's consideration of new facts, we note that when evidence supporting the respondent's current allegations was presented in appropriate proceedings, it was considered and rejected by both state and federal courts.

and circumstances of this case and the circumstances of other similar first degree murder cases in Tennessee, regardless of the sentence imposed. *See* Tenn. Code Ann. § 40-27-105 (1997).

The respondent's request for a certificate of commutation is grounded upon Tenn. Code Ann. § 40-27-106 (1997), which provides that "[t]he governor may, likewise, commute the punishment from death to imprisonment for life, upon the certificate of the supreme court, entered on the minutes of the court, that in its opinion, there were extenuating circumstances attending the case, and that the punishment ought to be commuted." Although the statute has been applied in a handful of prior cases by this Court, none of those cases, nor any other Tennessee authority, contains a comprehensive discussion of the statute. Furthermore, there appears to be no similar statute in any other state although some states have constitutional provisions which are analogous.

The statutory provision was originally enacted in 1858. At the time of its enactment, there were few judicial avenues of review and relief available to persons convicted of first degree murder....

Even though the statute upon which the respondent now relies was, at the time of its enactment, one of only a few avenues of relief available to prisoners sentenced to death, the statute has always been applied sparingly by this Court. The respondent has not cited, nor has independent research revealed, any case in which the statute has been applied since the Post-Conviction Procedure Act was adopted in 1967. Moreover, Section 40-27-106 has never been previously applied to afford relief to a death-sentenced prisoner who files what amounts to an original action in this Court and relies upon extra-judicial "new evidence" to challenge the accuracy of the jury's verdict and the credibility of the evidence upon which his or her conviction was based. Research reveals that certificates of commutation pursuant to Tenn. Code Ann. § 40-27-106 have been issued only when the "extenuating circumstances attending the case" are based upon facts contained in the record of the judicial proceedings, or upon a combination of record facts and new evidence that is uncontroverted.

Assuming for the sake of argument, however, that the respondent's extra-judicial "new evidence" could be considered, such evidence is disfavored because it was "obtained without the benefit of cross-examination and an opportunity to make credibility determinations." *Herrera v. Collins,* 506 U.S. 390 (1993). Moreover, the evidence was obtained over eighteen years after commission of the crime. *Cf. McCleskey v. Zant,* 499 U.S. 467, 491 (1991) ("[T]he 'erosion of memory and dispersion of witnesses that occur with the passage of time' prejudice the government and diminish the chances of a reliable criminal adjudication.") In addition, the evidence is itself internally inconsistent thereby further undermining its reliability. Finally, the "new evidence" must be considered in light of the proof of the respondent's guilt at trial, proof that included the eyewitness testimony of Officers Stoddard and Parker. The recantation of witness Harold Davis notwithstanding, the evidence of the respondent's guilt is overwhelming. Officer Stoddard was in close proximity to the victim, Officer Oliver, and the respondent, Workman, at the time the victim was shot. Not only did Officer Stoddard hear the shots fired and see the victim lying on the ground, but he was also fired upon and wounded by the respondent. Although not in close proximity when the victim was shot, Officer Parker came around the corner after hearing shots fired and saw Officer Oliver fall to the ground. There is no evidence that either of these witnesses fired a weapon during the struggle between the victim and the respondent. Furthermore, the evidence includes testimony by the respondent, who admits to pulling the trigger and firing all the bullets from his gun. This testimony combined with all other evidence leaves no doubt that the respondent killed Officer Oliver. Accordingly, the respondent's claim that his testimony has been improperly characterized as a "confession" is without merit. As to the new expert testimony concerning the consistency of the appearance of the fatal wound with bullets fired from the respondent's gun, this evidence merely conflicts with the testimony of the medical examiner at trial that the wound was consistent with a bullet fired from a high caliber weapon. The respondent has presented no uncontroverted evidence that someone else fired the fatal shot. Even considering the "new evidence", the respondent has presented no extenuating circumstances that warrant issuance of a certificate of commutation from this Court.

Consequently, in light of the many avenues of judicial review which now exist and are available to prisoners sentenced to death and in light of the fact that the respondent relies solely upon extra-judicial "new evidence" that is aimed at impeaching the verdict of the original jury, I fully concur in the Court's denial of the respondent's request for a certificate of commutation pursuant to Tenn. Code Ann. § 40-27-106.

Having so stated, I emphasize that executive clemency operates outside the letter of the law. The executive clemency process is a vehicle for mercy. The executive is not required to confine his or her clemency determination to those facts contained in the record of the judicial proceeding. Executive clemency has been appropriately described by the United States Supreme Court both as the "'fail safe' in our criminal justice system" and "the traditional remedy for claims of innocence based on new evidence, discovered too late in the day to file a new trial motion...." *Herrera*, 506 U.S. at 415–17.

The clemency power in England was vested in the Crown and can be traced back to the 700's. Blackstone characterized executive clemency as "one of the great advantages of monarchy in general, above any other form of government." 4 W. Blackstone, *Commentaries* *397. Because there was no right of appeal until 1907, clemency provided the principal avenue of relief for individuals convicted of criminal offenses, most of which were capital crimes.

Both the Constitution of the United States and the Constitution of Tennessee adopt the British model and give to the executive the power to grant reprieves and pardons. United States Const. Art. 2, sec. 2, cl. 1; Tenn. Const. Art. III, sec. 6. In an early case, Chief Justice Marshall provided the following explanation of the relationship between the executive clemency power and the judicial process.

> A pardon is an act of grace, proceeding from the power entrusted with the execution of the laws, which exempts the individual, on whom it is bestowed, from the punishment the law inflicts for a crime he has committed. It is the private, though official act of the executive magistrate, delivered to the individual for whose benefit it is intended, and not communicated officially to the court. *It is a constituent part of the judicial system, that the judge sees only with judicial eyes, and knows nothing respecting any particular case, of which he is not informed judicially. A private deed, not communicated to him, whatever may be its character, whether a pardon or release, is totally unknown and cannot be acted on. The looseness which would be introduced into judicial proceedings, would prove fatal to the great principles of justice, if the judge might notice and act upon facts not brought regularly into the cause. Such a proceeding, in ordinary cases, would subvert the best established principles, and overturn those rules which have been settled by the wisdom of ages.*

United States v. Wilson, 32 U.S. (7 Pet.) 150, 160–61 (1833) (emphasis added).

Although Justice Marshall made this statement more than 150 years ago, the pronouncement remains sound....

Although I fully realize that executive clemency decisions are outside the domain of the courts, in this separate concurring order, I feel it is appropriate to state my concerns. In almost twenty years of service as a justice on the Tennessee Supreme Court, I have participated in reviewing the sentences in 117 death penalty cases and have been the author of the majority opinion of this Court in thirty-one of those cases and the author of the minority opinion in five of those cases. In addition, I have reviewed innumerable reports of trial judges in first degree murder cases in which a sentence of life imprisonment or life imprisonment without the possibility of parole was imposed. I have no hesitation in observing that the circumstances of this case are by no means as egregious as most of the death penalty cases I have reviewed. Furthermore, the circumstances of this case are less egregious than many of the life sentence cases I have reviewed. Clearly, these observations provide no legal ground for relief. The issue of statutory comparative proportionality was addressed and rejected in the respondent's direct appeal to this Court. However, with respect to any executive clemency application that may be filed by the respondent, it is my belief that a final decision should be rendered only after full scrutiny and careful consideration has been given to both the circumstances of the respondent's particular case and the circumstances of other similar first degree murder cases in Tennessee, regardless of the sentence imposed. The date set for execution of the sentence of death, April 6, 2000, affords the Governor sufficient time to carefully consider any executive clemency application that may be filed by the respondent.

BARKER, Justice, concurring.

I concur with the Court's order setting an execution date in this case and denying the respondent's request for a certificate of commutation pursuant to Tennessee Code Annotated section 40-27-106 (1997). Because my reasons for denying the respondent's request for a certificate of commutation are somewhat different from those of my colleagues, I write separately to explain my views.

Each member of this Court has carefully read the transcript of the original trial in this case. We have also reviewed the opinions and orders which have resulted from the respondent's nearly twenty years of litigation in both the state and federal systems. Each member of this Court agrees that the respondent has availed himself of all possible procedures and venues in an effort to seek judicial relief from his sentence of death. There are no more judicial avenues, either state or federal, available to the respondent. Recognizing that, the respondent is now requesting this Court to recommend by certification in accordance with Tennessee Code Annotated section 40-27-106 that the Governor commute his sentence to something less than death. In support of his request, counsel for the respondent have filed in this Court "evidence" which the respondent claims raises doubt about his guilt in this case. All of the members of this Court agree that we are not a fact-finding body and are in no position to consider those documents.... If any "extenuating circumstances" exist warranting this Court's issuing of a certificate of commutation, they must be based upon facts which have been established in the record. Not only do I see no such facts in the record, but the record fully supports the jury's sentence of death.

Moreover, in my view the statute authorizing this Court to certify to the Governor that a sentence of death ought to be commuted, *see* Tenn. Code Ann. § 40-27-106, has largely become obsolete. The statute was originally enacted in 1858 and has remained unchanged in our Code since 1932. Since that time, the trial and appellate procedures used in capital cases have been vastly expanded and improved. The trial in a capital case is now bifurcated with the jury first required to determine guilt or innocence, and if a defendant is found guilty, then a separate sentencing hearing is conducted. Before a jury may sentence an accused to death, it must find the presence of at least one statutorily defined aggravating circumstance, and the aggravating circumstance or circumstances must outweigh any mitigating circumstances. When the statute in question was originally enacted, there was no bifurcated trial and the jury was given little or no guidance in determining whether the defendant would be sentenced to life or death.

Likewise, the appellate process today affords a defendant multiple opportunities for thorough appellate review....

All of the procedural safeguards now in place are designed to, and in my opinion do, allow the judiciary to prevent a defendant from being executed unjustly....

Tennessee Code Annotated section 40-27-106 allowing for a certificate of commutation was enacted at a time when this Court did not have the ability to review or modify a sentence of death based upon arbitrariness, proportionality, or evidentiary support. As such, the only avenue available to the courts to correct a manifest injustice was through a recommendation of executive clemency. Since 1977, however, this Court has possessed the statutory authority to evaluate the appropriateness of a death sentence on direct review and even to modify such a sentence on its own if the statutory and procedural requirements are met. Virtually every "extenuating circumstance" warranting modification can reasonably fit within the four factors that this Court is required to consider in all death penalty reviews, and consequently, the statute providing for a certificate of commutation has been rendered obsolete in most all cases....

Finally, I am also of the opinion that there exists a serious question concerning the constitutionality of Tennessee Code Annotated section 40-27-106. The statute may represent an unconstitutional infringement upon the doctrine of separation of powers. I believe that application of section 40-27-106 is constitutionally suspect because a recommendation from this Court respecting the executive's commutation power, although granted by statute, may be wholly without the constitutional power of the judiciary in this State.

The Constitution grants the power to "grant reprieves and pardons" solely to the governor, *see* Tenn. Const. art. III, § 6, and this power is to be exercised by the governor alone "without reference to the Board of Paroles or anyone else." *Rowell v. Dutton*, 688 S.W.2d 474, 476–77 (Tenn. Crim. App. 1985). The very purpose of granting to the executive the exclusive exercise of the clemency power is so that some authority other than the courts is empowered to ameliorate or avoid particular criminal judgments. In this respect, the governor's clemency power is an important check entrusted to the executive to afford relief from undue harshness or evident mistake occurring during the normal administration of the criminal law by the courts. *Cf. Ex Parte Grossman,* 267 U.S. 87, 120–21 (1925).

Because the governor's clemency power serves as a check on the exercise of judicial power by this Court, I believe that it is inappropriate for this Court to obtrude in the executive's exercise of the clemency power by recommendation or otherwise.... I recognize that a certificate issued by this Court recommending clemency can have no force of law and in no way compels any executive action; nevertheless, to the extent that any statute authorizes this Court to attempt to influence a governor's clemency decision, that statute may overstep the constitutional authority given the judicial branch of our government.

The Governor is fully capable of reviewing the record in the respondent's case independently of this Court. Therefore, should the respondent choose, he may seek a commutation of his sentence pursuant to the procedure contained in Tennessee Code Annotated section 40-27-105. The procedure outlined in that section does not involve this Court, but rather it is a procedure established for the Governor's independent decision....

BIRCH, Justice, concurring in part and dissenting in part.

On March 20, 1982, a jury convicted Philip R. Workman of first degree murder and thereafter imposed a sentence of death. Since then, the conviction and sentence have together been reviewed to the fullest extent allowable under state and federal procedural guidelines....

Given the state of the record, there exists, in my view, no procedure, no method, no means by which the conviction or the sentence or the process through which they were produced can be further tested or scrutinized under the procedural guidelines within which this Court must function. Therefore, the conviction and sentence are, in my opinion, final as a matter of law.

In most civilized societies, the power to commute a death sentence is within the prerogative of the executive....

To complement the Governor's constitutional power to commute a sentence of death, our General Assembly has, in its wisdom, seen fit to provide, by statute, the means by which the Supreme Court may certify to the Governor that, in the opinion of the Court, there were extenuating circumstances attending the case and the punishment ought to be commuted....

Because the Court is not of one mind on the commutation issue, I am firmly convinced that it is my duty to separately address Workman's request for a recommendation of commutation and to do so on the record.

Now, therefore, in accordance with that duty described above, pursuant to and independent of the enabling statute cited herein, and after a careful consideration of the pertinent parts of the entire record, I do hereby certify to His Excellency, the Honorable Don Sundquist, Governor of the State of Tennessee, that there were extenuating circumstances attending this case and that the punishment of death ought to be commuted.

Notes and Questions

1. As explained in *Workman,* the Tennessee statute authorizing the Governor to commute a capital sentence to life imprisonment upon the Tennessee Supreme Court's certifying "that in its opinion, there are extenuating circumstances attending the case, and that the punishment ought to be commuted," Tenn. Code Ann. § 40-27-106, operates independently of the Governor's general authority "to grant reprieves, commutations and pardons in all criminal cases after conviction, except impeachment," Tenn. Code Ann. § 40-27-101, as well as the Governor's authority to commute a death sentence to life imprisonment if, in his or her opinion "the facts and circumstances adduced are not sufficient to warrant a total pardon." Tenn. Code Ann. § 40-27-105. These multiple legislative executive clemency provisions are unusual and, at least in the opinion of Judge Barker, the section allowing the Tennessee Supreme Court to issue a certificate of extenuating circumstances and a recommendation for commutation, which was enacted in 1858, "has largely become

obsolete." An additional statutory mechanism pertaining to executive clemency, not mentioned in *Workman*, is available in Tennessee.

> Tenn. Code Ann. § 40-27-109. Exoneration
>
> (a) After consideration of the facts, circumstances and any newly discovered evidence in a particular case, the governor may grant exoneration to any person whom the governor finds did not commit the crime for which the person was convicted. No person may apply for nor may the governor grant exoneration until the person has exhausted all possible state judicial remedies.
>
> (b) Exoneration granted pursuant to subsection (a) shall as a matter of law be unconditional, shall without application having to be made therefore expunge all records of the person's arrest, indictment and conviction, and shall automatically restore all rights of citizenship to the person.
>
> (c)(1) The governor has the authority to review and reconsider any pardon the governor has previously granted for the purpose of determining whether the recipient of the pardon qualifies for and merits the granting of exoneration in lieu of a pardon. If the governor so determines, the governor shall have the authority to convert any pardon previously granted into exoneration as defined by this section.
>
> (2) Nothing in this section shall be construed as preventing the governor from granting exoneration to a person who applied for a pardon if the person qualifies under subsection (a) and if the governor determines the person merits exoneration.

2. Tennessee has not been immune from improprieties relating to grants of executive clemency, some of which were dramatized in the 1985 movie, "Marie," starring Sissy Spacek as Marie Ragghianti, the Chairwoman of the Tennessee Board of Pardon and Paroles during Governor Ray Blanton's administration who helped expose official wrongdoing.[23]

> "These are not very happy days for Tennessee," said Lamar Alexander as he was sworn in as governor in a secret ceremony arranged three days early in 1979 to block outgoing Governor Ray Blanton from granting executive clemency to more convicted criminals in the waning hours of his term. With just days left before the planned inauguration of his successor, Blanton—already under investigation by a federal grand jury for selling pardons—had freed fifty-two prison inmates, including twenty-three murderers, in a late-night signing session. (Blanton was later convicted on federal mail fraud charges for demanding kickbacks to issue liquor licenses while he was in office, although some counts were overturned on appeal; two of his aides were also convicted for accepting bribes in exchange for paroling prisoners.)[24]

3. Does allowing for judicial input to governors regarding clemency decisions, as under Tenn. Code Ann. § 40-20-106, more closely resemble an additional safeguard against unjust or erroneous executions or, as Justice Barker suggests, does it present separation of power issues that raise "a serious question concerning the [statute's] constitutionality"? Particularly when capital punishment followed automatically on conviction, depriving the sentencing authority of discretion to impose or recommend a sentence of life imprisonment, it was not uncommon for appellate courts, trial judges, and even prosecutors, to express their opinions to executive authorities that the convicted offender would be a suitable candidate for a sentence commutation.[25]

4. Philip Workman was executed in 2007. Based largely on factual allegations that were outside of the official case record, to which reference is made in the Tennessee Supreme Court's opinion, five of the original trial jurors had signed affidavits stating that they would not have sentenced Workman to death had they known about the assertions. The extra-record allegations cast doubts on whether Workman fired the shots that killed Officer Oliver.[26]

C. Innocence Commissions

The tragic consequences of wrongful convictions, experienced most directly by the individuals falsely accused and punished, extend well beyond their immediate cases. They ripple widely, embracing the injustice of the actual culprit escaping apprehension and punishment, the risk that the true offender will commit additional crimes while still at large, and threatening to undermine public confidence in the justice system. As harmful and regrettable as miscarriages of justice are, they also present an opportunity, if not an obligation, for officials and citizens alike to gain further understanding about the factors that contribute to wrongful convictions and how to prevent their recurrence. Yet in many jurisdictions, such critical reviews are lacking. As Barry Scheck and Peter Neufeld, the co-founders of the Innocence Project, observed nearly a decade ago:

> In the United States there are strict and immediate investigative measures taken when an airplane falls from the sky, a plane's fuel tank explodes on a runway, or a train derails. Serious inquiries are swiftly made by the National Transportation Safety Board (NTSB), an agency with subpoena power, great expertise, and real independence to answer the important and obvious questions: What went wrong? Was it system error or an individual's mistake? Was there any official misconduct? And, most important of all, what can be done to correct the problem and prevent it from happening again? ...
>
> The American criminal justice system, in sharp contrast, has no institutional mechanism to evaluate its equivalent of a catastrophic plane crash, the conviction of an innocent person.[27]

Criminal justice institutions that would occupy the National Transportation Safety Board-like role of investigating the causes of wrongful convictions and ensuring that appropriate corrective and preventive measures are taken, are commonly referred to as "Innocence Commissions." Two different models, which are not necessarily mutually exclusive,[28] have been envisioned. One approach focuses on error correction in individual cases; such commissions have the authority to investigate or serve as fact-finding bodies for individual claims of wrongful conviction and/or to recommend that the contested conviction be upset or reaffirmed. The other model is more future- and policy-oriented, proposing and advocating systemic reforms designed to improve the administration of justice generally and minimize the risk of wrongful convictions.[29]

The lone "error correction" Innocence Commission presently operating within the United States is the North Carolina Innocence Inquiry Commission (NCIIC), which was created legislatively in 2006 (*see* N.C.G.S. §§ 15A-1461 through 15A-1470). In Chapter 7 we discussed the exoneration of Gregory Taylor following a review conducted by the NCIIC, the first such outcome in connection with the Commission's functioning. The North Carolina statute provides for the appointment of an eight-member Commission, including a superior court judge, a prosecutor, a criminal defense attorney, a victim advocate, a sheriff, one member of the public who is neither an attorney nor employed by the Judicial Department, and two people chosen at the discretion of the Chief Justice of the North Carolina Supreme Court.[30] The Commission's duties include:

(1) To establish the criteria and screening process to be used to determine which cases shall be accepted for review.

(2) To conduct inquiries into claims of factual innocence, with priority to be given to those cases in which the convicted person is currently incarcerated solely for the crime for which he or she claims factual innocence.

(3) To coordinate the investigation of cases accepted for review.

(4) To maintain records for all case investigations.

(5) To prepare written reports outlining Commission investigations and recommendations to the trial court at the completion of each inquiry.[31]

The Commission has the discretion to dismiss claims of factual innocence or to order a formal inquiry.[32] Formal inquiries are conducted pursuant to procedures that include the appointment of counsel for the convicted person, notification of the victim in the case, subpoena powers, discovery, and examination of witnesses under oath.[33] The statute further provides:

> After hearing the evidence, the full Commission shall vote to establish further case disposition as provided by this subsection. All eight voting members of the Commission shall participate in that vote.
>
> Except in cases where the convicted person entered and was convicted on a plea of guilty, if five or more of the eight voting members of the Commission conclude there is sufficient evidence of factual innocence to merit judicial review, the case shall be referred to the senior resident superior court judge in the district of original jurisdiction by filing with the clerk of court the opinion of the Commission with supporting findings of fact, as well as the record in support of such opinion, with service on the district attorney in noncapital cases and service on both the district attorney and Attorney General in capital cases. In cases where the convicted person entered and was convicted on a plea of guilty, if all of the eight voting members of the Commission conclude there is sufficient evidence of factual innocence to merit judicial review, the case shall be referred to the senior resident superior court judge in the district of original jurisdiction.
>
> If less than five of the eight voting members of the Commission, or in cases where the convicted person entered and was convicted on a guilty plea less than all of the eight voting members of the Commission, conclude there is sufficient evidence of factual innocence to merit judicial review, the Commission shall conclude there is insufficient evidence of factual innocence to merit judicial review. The Commission shall document that opinion, along with supporting findings of fact, and file those documents and supporting materials with the clerk of superior court in the district of original jurisdiction, with a copy to the district attorney and the senior resident superior court judge.... [34]

The Commission does not have the authority to vacate a conviction. "If the Commission concludes there is sufficient evidence of factual innocence to merit judicial review," it requests the Chief Justice of the North Carolina Supreme Court "to appoint a three-judge panel ... to hear evidence relevant to the Commission's recommendation."[35] Then, pursuant to N.C.G.S. § 15A-1469:

> (d) The three-judge panel shall conduct an evidentiary hearing. At the hearing, the court, and the defense and prosecution through the court, may compel the testimony of any witness, including the convicted person. All evidence relevant to the case, even if considered by a jury or judge in a prior proceeding, may be presented during the hearing. The convicted person may not assert any privilege or prevent a witness from testifying. The convicted person has a right to be present at the evidentiary hearing and to be represented by counsel. A waiver of the right to be present shall be in writing....
>
> (h) The three-judge panel shall rule as to whether the convicted person has proved by clear and convincing evidence that the convicted person is innocent of the charges. Such a determination shall require a unanimous vote. If the vote is unanimous, the panel shall enter dismissal of all or any of the charges. If the vote is not unanimous, the panel shall deny relief.

"Unless otherwise authorized..., the decisions of the Commission and of the three-judge panel are final and are not subject to further review by appeal, certification, writ, motion, or otherwise."[36]

The North Carolina Innocence Inquiry Commission was modeled loosely on an analogous body created in England in 1995, the Criminal Cases Review Commission (CCRC).[37] The charge of the CCRC is "to review the applications of convicted defendants who claim they have been wrongfully convicted and to refer cases to the court of appeal for review where there is a 'real possibility that the conviction, verdict, finding or sentence would not be upheld were the reference to be made.'"[38] The "real possibility" test is not defined legislatively, although it has been interpreted judicially as "'more than an outside chance or a bare possibility but which may be less than a probability or a likelihood or a racing certainty' that the conviction, verdict, finding or sentence would be found 'unsafe.'"[39] Judicial review of criminal convictions in England is much more limited than in the United States; for example, there is no right to an appeal, although if an appeal is granted, the defendant faces less daunting prospects for relief.[40] Unlike the North Carolina Innocence Inquiry Commission, the CCRC is not restricted to considering only claims based on actual innocence.[41]

In part because relatively few avenues for challenging convictions are available, concerns arose that the CCRC, and ultimately the Court of Appeal, would be inundated with cases. Experience suggests otherwise. The Court of Appeal, in particular, has been spared reviewing an extravagant number of applications. Moreover, most of the cases referred by the CCRC for judicial review were considered meritorious. The CCRC began accepting cases in 1997.

> As of September 30, 2010, the CCRC has taken in a total of 13,004 applications. Of those, it has referred 445 cases to the Court of Appeal, which in turn has heard 411 of those cases. Of those 411 cases, the Court of Appeal has quashed 290, upheld 118, and has reserved judgment on three awaiting further hearing. In sum, the Court of Appeal has quashed convictions in close to three-quarters of the cases it has received from the CCRC.[42]

The NCIIC similarly has referred few cases for judicial consideration. Between 2007, when it began operating, and December 2010, the Commission received 850 claims; 724 of those claims were "closed," 23 were being investigated, and only three had proceeded through a Commission hearing. Gregory Taylor's case remained the only one forwarded for judicial review and resulting in exoneration.[43]

As the isolated existence in this country of North Carolina's Innocence Inquiry Commission suggests, questions and objections have been raised about Innocence Commissions that function to review actual innocence claims and recommend judicial relief in appropriate cases. One concern involves whether scarce fiscal, administrative, and judicial resources should be invested to staff, maintain, and support their operation.[44] The NCIIC, a state agency with a staff of five, was allotted $372,879 for its 2009 operating budget. It received an additional federal grant from the National Institute of Justice in the amount of $566,980 for DNA testing in cases of claimed innocence.[45]

Another concern is the familiar one about achieving the proper balance between the finality of criminal convictions and elementary fairness. In a case arising early in the operation of the CCRC, *Regina v. CCRC ex parte Pearson,* [1999] 3 All ER 498, 1999 WL 477999, Lord Chief Justice Bingham of the Queen's Bench observed:

> The "real possibility" test prescribed in section 13(1)(a) of the 1995 Act as the threshold which the Commission must judge to be crossed before a conviction may be referred to the Court of Appeal is imprecise but plainly denotes a contingency which, in the Commission's judgment, is more than an outside chance or a bare possibility but which may be less than a probability or a likelihood or a racing certainty. The Commission must judge that there is at least a reasonable prospect of a conviction, if referred, not being upheld. The threshold test is carefully chosen: if the Commission were almost automatically to refer all but the most obviously threadbare cases, its function would be mechanical rather than judgmental and the Court of Appeal would be burdened with a mass of hopeless appeals; if, on the other hand, the Commission were not to refer any case unless it judged the applicant's prospect of success on appeal to be assured, the cases of some deserving applicants would not be referred to the Court and the beneficial object which the Commission was established to achieve would be to that extent defeated. The Commission is entrusted with the power and the duty to judge which cases cross the threshold and which do not.

Related, principled objections have been raised about Innocence Commissions generally, particularly those having an "error correction" function such as the CCRC and the NCIIC.

> There are at least three reasons for concern with respect to creation of innocence commissions: 1) their presence may serve to diffuse public disaffection, thereby stifling movements for change; 2) for those considering creation of an innocence commission to conduct post-mortem investigations of cases that may lead to exonerations, they create an additional institutional decision-making body to filter cases through, thereby delaying and/or potentially quashing remedies in wrongful conviction cases; and 3) they may be established in such a way that the composition of the Commission is geared toward maintaining the status quo institutional arrangement.[46]

Innocence Commissions that examine the causes of wrongful convictions and recommend systemic reforms, rather than investigating individual claims of innocence, are more prevalent within the United States but still have been created in a minority of jurisdictions. Official bodies charged with such functions have operated in at least ten states: California, Connecticut, Florida, Illinois, Louisiana, New York, North Carolina, Pennsylvania, Texas, and Wisconsin; most were created as short-term rather than permanent institutions.[47] Over the past two decades, provincial governments in Canada have appointed at least seven inquiry commissions to investigate individual cases of wrongful conviction and make corresponding recommendations for reforms.[48] In Chapter 8 we considered portions of the report of the Kaufman Commission, which was established in the wake of Guy Paul Morin's wrongful conviction for murder in Ontario. Some Innocence Commissions that adhere to the "systemic reform" model, such as the Innocence Commission for Virginia, were organized and operate independently of state governments.[49]

The Innocence Project has endorsed the creation of official "criminal justice reform commissions" by state governments, recommending that they "include experts from all parts of the criminal justice system—including crime victims and concerned members of the public," and that they function "to study wrongful convictions and advocate for changes in the system."[50] "The key features of Criminal Justice Reform Commissions are subpoena power, access to first-rate investigative resources, and political independence. These commissions must be trusted to speak out about cases where the system fails.... [T]hey must consist of distinguished players from all aspects of the criminal justice system, so that their findings will be trusted, respected, and acted upon."[51] Reports issued by such commissions have called for numerous systemic reforms in jurisdictions' investigative and judicial processes. They have met with mixed success regarding implementation of the recommended reforms.[52]

D. Compensating the Wrongfully Convicted

Jeffrey Deskovic was 16 years old and a sophomore in high school in Peekskill, New York in November 1989 when the body of a 15-year-old classmate was found in a wooded area; the girl had been beaten, raped, and strangled. Deskovic was charged with the murder more than two months later. He confessed to the crime following several hours of police interrogation; he was alone and told that he had failed a polygraph exam. He eventually was reduced to rocking on the floor while curled into a fetal position. DNA analysis subsequently excluded him as the source of the semen found in the victim but the prosecution proceeded to trial, speculating that the victim may have had consensual sexual relations with another boy.

"No physical evidence or eyewitness testimony was found to connect Deskovic to [the] rape and murder. The scientific evidence exonerated him."[53] Protesting his innocence, he nevertheless was convicted of the rape and murder in January 1991. He was sentenced to 15 years to life imprisonment. Years later, the DNA sample found in the murder victim was matched to a man serving a life sentence for an unrelated murder. The man subsequently confessed to the crimes for which Deskovic had been wrongfully convicted and incarcerated. Deskovic was released from prison in November 2006 and the indictment against him was dismissed. "Deskovic was 33 years old. He had been incarcerated half his life for a crime he did not commit."[54]

> As a boy, Jeffrey Mark Deskovic could swim the length of a pool underwater without coming up for air. On sultry days at the Elmira state prison, where he spent most of his 16 years behind bars for a rape and murder he did not commit, Mr. Deskovic would close his eyes under a row of outdoor showers and imagine himself swimming....
>
> Having walked out of Westchester County Courthouse vindicated yet petrified of the unpredictable tomorrow ahead, Mr. Deskovic found that his first year on the outside was more turbulent than triumphant. Still trying to recover what was stolen from him, he is, at 34, a free man who has yet to feel truly free.[55]

Wrongful convictions exact an enormous toll. Exoneration cannot restore the years lost to incarceration nor fully erase the many other harms suffered. Exonerees commonly endure continuing stigmatization resulting from their wrongful conviction and imprisonment, have trouble securing employment and housing, find familial relationships disrupted or irreparably broken, encounter difficulties adjusting to technological and other societal changes that have passed them by while they were incarcerated, and experience significant and continuing physical and mental health problems, sometimes including symptoms reminiscent of post-traumatic stress disorders.[56] It is difficult not to empathize with individuals such as Jeffrey Deskovic who have been accused, convicted, and punished for crimes they did not commit.

More difficult, perhaps, is determining how the wrongfully convicted should be compensated. Monetary compensation for wrongful conviction and incarceration varies widely across jurisdictions. Differences exist not only in the amount awarded, but also in the circumstances under which compensation can be secured, and whether it is made available by statute or instead only through successful litigation or special legislative authorization. The availability of post-release services and other assistance for exonerees also varies markedly. In many jurisdictions, individuals who are released from prison following exoneration have access to fewer forms of assistance in securing jobs or housing, and qualify for fewer services and programs, than offenders who are released on parole.[57] Those who do qualify for assistance sometimes must wait years before it is provided.[58]

Only 27 states have enacted legislation authorizing compensation for innocent persons who have been wrongfully convicted and incarcerated; in the remaining states, exonerees must pursue often lengthy and uncertain litigation, or obtain relief through special legislative bills if they hope to secure monetary damages in compensation for the harms they have endured.[59] Where legislation exists, damage awards are available in varying amounts and typically are subject to numerous preconditions. Under federal law, "The amount of damages awarded shall not exceed $100,000 for each 12-month period of incarceration for any plaintiff who was unjustly sentenced to death and $50,000 for each 12-month period of incarceration for any other plaintiff." 28 U.S.C. § 2513 (e) (2004). Amounts provided in compensation for wrongful conviction and incarceration under state legislation differ markedly. "Many states place limits on the amount of damages that can be recovered per year in prison, ranging from $5,000 per year in Wisconsin to $80,000 per year in Texas."[60]

> The statutes grant a sum per day, a sum per year, a maximum of $20,000, a maximum of $1,000,000, or provide only vague guidance, or no guidance at all, on the question of damages. Montana, uniquely, provides only educational aid at the state's expense.[61]

Various prerequisites and disqualifications confront exonerees who seek compensation for their wrongful conviction and incarceration. Exonerees must demonstrate more than simply that their convictions were vacated; typically, they are required to establish their actual innocence by clear and convincing evidence or by a preponderance of the evidence.[62] "Illinois, Maryland, and North Carolina demand a full pardon from the governor, while Maine mandates both a pardon and judicial finding of innocence. Missouri's compensation statute ... awards compensation only to individuals exonerated through the use of DNA evidence."[63] Many states preclude damages if the claimant "caused or contributed to" his or her conviction, a provision frequently interpreted to bar recovery for exonerees who pled guilty or falsely confessed.[64] Florida law prohibits recovery for wrongfully convicted individuals who have a prior felony conviction.[65] Several jurisdictions require that claims be made within two or three years following exoneration or they are barred by a statute of limitations.[66] The Innocence Project reports that, as of 2010:

> [M]ore than 240 people have been proven innocent and exonerated through post-conviction DNA testing. They spent on average 13 years, and as many as

> 31 years in prison. Forty percent of them have not received any compensation, and many received only a paltry amount that fell far short of repaying their losses or helping them get re-established in the free world.[67]

Below, we consider cases that include discussion and interpretation of the statutes defining eligibility and authorizing compensation for wrongfully convicted persons in Iowa and Massachusetts.

State v. McCoy

742 N.W.2d 593 (Iowa 2007)

CADY, Justice.

In this appeal, we must determine whether the district court erred in determining that an individual was not a "wrongfully imprisoned person" entitled to bring a claim for damages under the Iowa Tort Claims Act....

I. Background Facts and Proceedings.

Darryl McCoy was charged by a trial information with the first-degree murder and willful injury of Jonathan Johnson. Johnson was found dead in the backseat of his car on January 27, 2002, in Davenport. He was covered with a blanket and had a plastic bag over his head. Johnson had been shot multiple times, stabbed, cut, and struck with blunt force to the head.

On September 13, 2002, McCoy was convicted of the charges following a jury trial. The evidence at trial revealed McCoy was at an apartment in Davenport with his brother and an individual named Chance Barnes. Johnson and an individual named Jerome Wilson came to the apartment and knocked on the door. A dispute quickly erupted between McCoy's brother and Johnson, and Wilson was instructed to leave the premises. Wilson complied and went outside the apartment building. He then heard loud noises emanating from the apartment. Barnes subsequently exited the apartment, and Wilson asked him about the whereabouts of Johnson. Barnes told Wilson not to worry about Johnson and not to enter the apartment. McCoy made numerous incriminating statements to police following his arrest, and these statements were introduced into evidence at the trial. Essentially, McCoy told police he observed his brother and Barnes engage in a fight with Johnson in the apartment before they shot and stabbed him. McCoy also confessed to helping dispose of the dead body and cleaning the apartment after the murder.

McCoy was sentenced by the district court to a term of life imprisonment on October 10, 2002. He was placed in one of the state correctional institutions to serve his sentence. McCoy appealed the conviction and sentence.

On February 4, 2005, we reversed the judgment of conviction and sentence against McCoy and remanded the case for a new trial. *See State v. McCoy*, 692 N.W.2d 6 (Iowa 2005). We concluded McCoy received ineffective assistance of counsel at his trial because his trial counsel failed to seek suppression of the incriminating statements made to police. We determined the statements were involuntary and the admission of the statements at trial was prejudicial.

Following the remand for a new trial, the county attorney filed a motion to dismiss the charges against McCoy in the interest of justice. The county attorney believed the State could not obtain a conviction on retrial without the incriminating statements found to be inadmissible on appeal. The district court granted the motion and dismissed the charges against McCoy on March 23, 2005. McCoy was released from imprisonment after being confined for over three years.

On October 3, 2005, McCoy filed an application with the district court requesting a determination that he was a "wrongfully imprisoned person" and entitled to seek compensation from the state. The Attorney General of Iowa filed a resistance to the application, and the application was scheduled for a hearing. McCoy submitted the trial transcript of the underlying criminal trial as evidence to support his application, excluding the evidence of his incriminating statements.

The district court agreed with McCoy that the incriminating statements could not be considered as evidence at the hearing in determining McCoy's right to seek compensation as a wrongfully imprisoned person. Nevertheless, the district court found McCoy failed to establish he was entitled to bring an action as a "wrongfully imprisoned person." The district court determined McCoy was not a "wrongfully imprisoned person" because it was possible for the State to refile a murder charge against him in the future. The district court also found McCoy failed to establish he did not commit the murder or the willful injury.

McCoy appealed and raises two claims. First, he claims the evidence supported a finding that he was a "wrongfully imprisoned person." Second, he claims the evidence established he did not commit murder or any lesser included offense....

III. Wrongful Imprisonment.

The Iowa wrongful imprisonment statute creates a cause of action for wrongful imprisonment that permits a person to commence an action for damages under the State Tort Claims Act. *See generally* Iowa Code ch. 663A (2005). We have previously considered the framework of our statute and observed that Iowa was one of a growing number of states to enact wrongful imprisonment compensation legislation. *Dohlman,* 725 N.W.2d [428, 430–31 (Iowa 2006)] (discussing statutory framework); *Cox v. State,* 686 N.W.2d 209, 212 (Iowa 2004). The statutes are a response to the mounting evidence of innocent persons who have been wrongfully convicted and imprisoned in this country. *See generally* Adele Bernhard, *Justice Still Fails: A Review of Recent Efforts to Compensate Individuals Who Have Been Unjustly Convicted and Later Exonerated,* 52 Drake L. Rev. 703, 711–13 (2004). Iowa's statute was enacted in 1997.

Like other persons permitted to bring a tort action against the state, a wrongfully imprisoned person is given the right to sue the state in district court for damages after first presenting the claim to the State Appeals Board. *See* Iowa Code §§ 669.3–.5. However, a wrongfully imprisoned person must first clear a hurdle not set for other state tort claimants. A wrongfully imprisoned person may not proceed with a lawsuit under the State Tort Claims Act until the district court has conducted a predicate review and assessment of the claim and found the person is entitled to commence a civil action based on two preliminary findings. This additional procedure permits the district court to serve as a gatekeeper of such claims to insure only meritorious claims for damages will be filed with the State Appeals Board.

The first essential finding required to be made by the district court in its gatekeeping function is the claimant must be a "wrongfully imprisoned person." Iowa Code § 663A.1(3). The statute provides five criteria that must be satisfied to be a "wrongfully imprisoned person." *Id.* § 663A.1(1). Generally, those criteria consider the seriousness of the charge, form of conviction, term of incarceration, disposition of the conviction, and reason for the imprisonment. The second essential finding is the claimant did not commit the offense or the offense was not committed by any person. *Id.* § 663A.1(2). Both findings must be made. Otherwise, the person has no right to pursue a claim under the State Tort Claims Act. *Id.* § 663A.1(3).

The two separate findings reveal that the right to sue the state under the State Tort Claims Act as a "wrongfully imprisoned person" not only requires the person qualify as a "wrongfully imprisoned person," but also requires the person be a "wrongfully imprisoned person" who did not commit the offense or whose offense of conviction was not committed by any person. This distinction reveals the crux of the right to seek recovery as a wrongfully imprisoned person is the second finding that requires the person to be an "innocent man" or woman.

The second finding under the statute must be based on "clear and convincing evidence."Ó Iowa Code § 663A.1(2). The statute, however, does not provide for any standard of proof to make the first finding of a "wrongfully imprisoned person." This approach signals the second finding is a product of a fact-intensive process, while the first finding is primarily met through an examination of court records and documents by the district court that confirm each criterion. In fact, the statute does not require the district court to make the second finding until presented with "an order vacating, dismissing, or reversing the conviction and sentence in a case for which no further proceedings can be or will be held against an individual on any facts and circumstances alleged in the proceedings which resulted in the conviction." *Id.* § 663A.1(2).

In this case, the district court determined McCoy was not a "wrongfully imprisoned person" and then proceeded to also determine that he failed to establish that the offenses of conviction were not committed by him.... [W]e proceed to review the decision by the district court that McCoy failed to establish the offenses of conviction were not committed by him.[5]

The lynchpin of a wrongful imprisonment proceeding before the district court is innocence. Under the statute, innocence may be established in one of two ways. The person seeking authorization to file a tort claim against the state must establish by clear and convincing evidence either the person did not commit the offense (for which the person was convicted, sentenced, and imprisoned), including a lesser offense, or that the offense was not committed by any person. Iowa Code § 663A.1(2). Generally, this means there must be proof the person did not commit the acts charged or that the acts committed did not constitute a crime.

The burden imposed on a wrongfully imprisoned person is difficult to meet because it requires the person to prove a negative. Essentially, it means the person must show he or she was actually innocent of the crime, or no crime occurred.... [I]t is not enough for the person seeking the right to sue for compensation as a wrongfully imprisoned person to merely establish that a reviewing court determined the conviction was not supported by substantial evidence. Such a finding only signifies a reasonable fact finder could not be convinced of guilt beyond a reasonable doubt. When the crime of conviction was committed by someone, the person seeking the right to sue as a wrongfully imprisoned person must affirmatively establish by clear and convincing evidence that he or she did not commit the crime or any lesser included crime.

McCoy claims the transcript of the evidence at his criminal trial, stripped of the inadmissible evidence of his involuntary statements, establishes he did not commit the murder or willful injury, or any lesser included offense. In other words, McCoy claims the absence of proof of his criminal guilt in the trial transcript constitutes evidence of his innocence.

... The district court ... refused to consider McCoy's incriminating statements at the wrongfully imprisoned person hearing. Nevertheless, the district court found the redacted transcript failed to establish by clear and convincing evidence that McCoy did not commit the crimes. Accordingly, we need not decide the evidentiary dispute if the redacted record supports the trial court finding.[6]

Normally, a transcript of the evidence at a criminal trial, by itself, will not provide the evidence necessary to establish innocence under section 663A.1(2). As determined in *Dohlman,* a wrongfully imprisoned person must establish more than the absence of guilt in law to establish innocence under section 668A.1(2). The person must be factually innocent, not merely procedurally free from reprosecution or not guilty. *See* Hugo Adam Bedau, Michael A. Radelet & Constance E. Putnam, *Convicting the Innocent in Capital Cases: Criteria, Evidence, and Inference,* 52 Drake L.Rev. 587, 598 (2004) (recognizing an acquittal or reversal of a conviction may constitute an adjudication of "procedural innocence," but "[w]hether such a defendant was also factually innocent is a further question never settled just by the fact that some appellate court correctly found procedural or due process objections to the defendant's conviction or sentence"). Thus, we turn to the record presented at the hearing to determine if it supported the district court finding that McCoy failed to show he did not commit the murder or willful injury.

In this case, the district court found McCoy failed to establish his innocence due to the evidence in the trial transcript that he was present at the scene of the murder at the time it may have taken place. This finding is based on the trial testimony of a witness who accompanied the murder victim to an apartment occupied by McCoy and others. This was the last time the witness saw the victim alive. The evidence suggests a fight involving the victim occurred in the apartment during the time McCoy was present and after the witness was instructed to leave the apartment. The witness was also later instructed not to return to the apartment.

Our review of this evidence supports the con-

---

5. McCoy did not claim that the offenses of murder and willful injury were "not committed by any person." Iowa Code § 663A.1(2)(*b*). McCoy's brother and Chance Barnes were successfully prosecuted for the murder of Jonathan Johnson.

6. Some state compensation statutes have been interpreted to preclude recovery by persons who voluntarily confess to the crime, based on statutory language that disqualifies persons from compensation who have contributed to their own conviction in some way. *See* Bernhard, *Justice Still Fails,* at 717–18. The Iowa wrongful imprisonment statute does not contain such language, but does disqualify a person who has pled guilty from being a "wrongfully imprisoned person" under section 663A.1(1)(*b*).

clusion of the district court. This evidence presents too many unanswered questions about McCoy's role in the murder, which the wrongfully-imprisoned-person hearing failed to answer. To prove a negative by clear and convincing evidence, it is not enough for a wrongfully imprisoned person to merely create questions and doubts about his or her involvement in the crime of conviction. Instead, the person must affirmatively answer those doubts and questions to the point that the district court will be convinced the person did not commit the crime or any lesser included crime.[7] McCoy has failed to do this. There was ample evidence to support the finding of the district court.

IV. Conclusion.

Substantial evidence supports the finding by the district court that McCoy failed to establish his right to sue the State as a wrongfully imprisoned person. We affirm the district court.

Notes and Questions

1. In *State v. Dohlman,* 725 N.W.2d 428 (Iowa 2006), which is cited in *McCoy,* the Iowa Supreme Court affirmed a district court's dismissal of a claim for compensation filed by a defendant whose conviction for homicide by vehicle had been reversed on appeal following the appellate court's conclusion that the prosecution had presented insufficient evidence to establish guilt beyond a reasonable doubt. Dohlman had served 17 months in prison during the pendency of his appeal. The court emphasized the distinction between "an appellate court finding that there is not substantial evidence to support a criminal conviction" and the statutory requirement that the claimant prove that he or she is a "wrongfully imprisoned person" by clear and convincing evidence. The opinion explained the requirements for qualifying as a wrongfully convicted person under Iowa's statutory framework. 725 N.W.2d, at 430–431.

The first step in qualifying as a wrongfully imprisoned person requires an individual to meet the following criteria:

1. As used in this section, a "*wrongfully imprisoned person*" means an individual who meets all of the following criteria:

a. The individual was charged, by indictment or information, with the commission of a public offense classified as an aggravated misdemeanor or felony.

b. The individual did not plead guilty to the public offense charged, or to any lesser included offense, but was convicted by the court or by a jury of an offense classified as an aggravated misdemeanor or felony.

c. The individual was sentenced to incarceration for a term of imprisonment not to exceed two years if the offense was an aggravated misdemeanor or to an indeterminate term of years under chapter 902 if the offense was a felony, as a result of the conviction.

d. The individual's conviction was vacated or dismissed, or was reversed, and no further proceedings can be or will be held against the individual on any facts and circumstances alleged in the proceedings which had resulted in the conviction.

e. The individual was imprisoned solely on the basis of the conviction that was vacated, dismissed, or reversed and on which no further proceedings can be or will be had.

Iowa Code § 663A.1(1).

If these criteria are met, the court then proceeds to the second inquiry: whether that person meets the requirements of section 663A.1(2). Section 663A.1(2) provides:

2. Upon receipt of an order vacating, dismissing, or reversing the conviction and sentence in a case for

7. The district court must have no serious or substantial doubt about the person's criminal involvement in the crime of conviction to find the person did not commit the crime. *See In re C.B.,* 611 N.W.2d 489, 492 (Iowa 2000)....

which no further proceedings can be or will be held against an individual on any facts and circumstances alleged in the proceedings which resulted in the conviction, the district court shall make a determination whether there is clear and convincing evidence to establish either of the following findings:

a. That the offense for which the individual was convicted, sentenced, and imprisoned, including any lesser included offenses, was not committed by the individual.

b. That the offense for which the individual was convicted, sentenced, and imprisoned was not committed by any person, including the individual.

Id. § 663A.1(2). If the criteria of both section 663A.1(1) and section 663A.1(2) are met, the individual qualifies as a wrongfully imprisoned person. *Id.* § 663A.1(3)(*a*).

2. How difficult is it, in the words of the court in *McCoy,* "[t]o prove a negative by clear and convincing evidence"? To qualify for compensation, should it be sufficient for a person to demonstrate the legal insufficiency of the evidence to support a conviction, as in *McCoy* and *Dohlman*?

Guzman v. Commonwealth

937 N.E.2d 441 (Mass. 2010)

CORDY, J.

In this case, we interpret one of the eligibility provisions of the recently enacted Massachusetts Erroneous Convictions Law, which provides legal redress to certain individuals who can show that they have been wrongfully convicted of a felony and incarcerated. See G.L. c. 258D (c. 258D). The plaintiff, Humberto Guzman, whose convictions of trafficking, distribution, and conspiracy to distribute cocaine were vacated after he served nearly four years in prison, brought this lawsuit claiming that he was entitled to recover under c. 258D.

The Commonwealth filed a motion to dismiss the claim.... At the hearing on the motion, the parties agreed ... that the motion should be treated as one for summary judgment. The judge allowed the Commonwealth's motion, concluding that Guzman would be unable to prove that he is within the class of persons eligible for relief. Guzman appealed. The Appeals Court reversed and reinstated Guzman's claim, *Guzman v. Commonwealth,* 907 N.E.2d 1140 (Mass App. 2009) (*Guzman*).... We agree with the Appeals Court's well-reasoned opinion, and for similar reasons, we reverse....

1. *The Erroneous Convictions Law.* In 2004, in the wake of a growing number of exonerations both in Massachusetts and across the nation, the Legislature enacted c. 258D, which created a remedy, in the form of a new cause of action (and a corresponding waiver of sovereign immunity) that could be brought against the Commonwealth by persons who had been wrongfully convicted and imprisoned.[2,3] The statute provides a variety

---

2. Representative Patricia Jehlen first filed a bill in 1999 providing for compensation to those individuals wrongfully convicted and later released. In her testimony before the Committee on Public Safety, she explained that, in part, the motivation for the filing of the bill stemmed from the "disparate treatment" of two men, Bobby Joe Leaster and Lawyer Johnson, who were both convicted of murder in 1971 and released after spending more than ten years in prison. The Legislature awarded Leaster compensation by special act in 1992 but never acted on a similar petition for Johnson. See Fisher, Convictions of Innocent Persons in Massachusetts: An Overview, 12 B.U. Pub. Int. L.J. 1, 9–10, 34–38 (2002) (discussing Leaster and Johnson cases).

3. As evidenced by the two cases discussed in note 2, *supra,* traditional civil and tort remedies have been noted to be lacking in providing sufficient redress. See Wisneski, "That's Just Not Right": Monetary Compensation for the Wrongfully Convicted in Massachusetts, 88 Mass. L.Rev. 138, 139–140, 145–148 (2004).

of remedies for a person so harmed, including the recovery of up to $500,000 in damages from the Commonwealth.[4] G.L. c. 258D, § 5.

Relevant here are certain subsections of G.L. c. 258D, § 1. General Laws c. 258D, § 1(A), authorizes certain claims to be brought against the Commonwealth, thereby waiving the Commonwealth's sovereign immunity as to such claims. General Laws c. 258D, § 1(B), is the eligibility provision, which limits "[t]he class of persons eligible to obtain relief" to:

> "(i) those that have been granted a full pardon pursuant to section 152 of chapter 127, if the governor expressly states in writing his belief in the individual's innocence, or
>
> "(ii) those who have been granted judicial relief by a state court of competent jurisdiction, *on grounds which tend to establish the innocence* of the individual as set forth in clause (vi) of subsection (C), and if (*a*) the judicial relief vacates or reverses the judgment of a felony conviction, and the felony indictment or complaint used to charge the individual with such felony has been dismissed, or if a new trial was ordered, the individual was not retried and the felony indictment or complaint was dismissed or a nolle prosequi was entered, or if a new trial was ordered the individual was found not guilty at the new trial; and (*b*) at the time of the filing of an action under this chapter no criminal proceeding is pending or can be brought against the individual by a district attorney or the attorney general for any act associated with such felony conviction" (emphasis added).

General Laws c. 258D, § 1(C), sets out the elements of the claimant's case and the applicable burden of proof. For present purposes, the salient language is found in the introduction to § 1(C) and subsections (i) and (vi):

> "In order for an individual to prevail and recover damages against the [C]ommonwealth in a cause of action brought under this chapter, the individual must establish, by clear and convincing evidence, that:—(i) he is a member of the class of persons defined in subsection (B); [and] ... (vi) he did not commit the crimes or crime charged in the indictment or complaint or any other felony arising out of or reasonably connected to the facts supporting the indictment or complaint, or any lesser included felony. ..."

Guzman contends that he is eligible to bring this action because his conviction was vacated or reversed "on grounds which tend to establish [his] innocence" and his case was subsequently dismissed. As is more fully explained below, Guzman filed a motion for a new trial in the underlying criminal case, which was allowed by the trial judge on October 13, 1994. In allowing the motion, the judge concluded that Guzman had been denied the effective assistance of counsel at trial because a conflicting interest of his trial counsel prejudiced Guzman's defense of misidentification. Subsequent to the allowance of the motion for a new trial, a different judge dismissed the felony indictments against Guzman with prejudice.[5]

---

4. The other remedies enumerated in G.L. c. 258D include furnishment of "services" by the Commonwealth to address "deficiencies in the [claimant's] physical and emotional condition that are shown to be directly related to the [claimant's] erroneous felony conviction and resulting incarceration" (G.L. c. 258D, § 5[A]); a fifty per cent reduction in tuition and fees at State and community colleges in the Commonwealth, including the University of Massachusetts at Amherst and its satellite campuses (*id.*); and the expungement or sealing of the criminal records pertaining to the erroneous felony conviction (G.L. c. 258D, § 7).

5. The investigating police detectives in Guzman's case, Kenneth Acerra and Walter Robinson, faced Federal indictments on multiple charges in March, 1997, relating to their falsification of affidavits filed in support of search warrants and the theft of evidence, including cash and drugs, seized after execution of the warrants. The indictments against Acerra and Robinson specifically referenced the case against Guzman and alleged that the officers stole a large amount of cash during this investigation. Acerra and Robinson pleaded guilty to these charges in 1998. The indictments against Guzman were dismissed with prejudice on March 25, 1997, because the testimony of the detectives was considered to be "essential" to the case against Guzman, and their unavailability due to the then pending Federal indictments against them precluded any retrial.

2. *Guzman's eligibility.* a. *Statutory language.* In determining whether Guzman was eligible to bring his claim, we must interpret and then apply the statutory language requiring that the judicial relief granted (in this case a new trial) was "on grounds which tend to establish the [plaintiff's] innocence." G.L. c. 258D, § 1(B)(ii). In the process of enacting c. 258D, the wording of this provision was the subject of a specific exchange between the legislative and executive branches. The version of the bill initially passed by the Legislature and sent to the Governor for signature provided for eligibility where judicial relief had been granted "on grounds consistent with ... innocence." The Governor returned the bill with a number of proposed amendments "to clarify and improve certain ambiguous portions of the bill so that it will accomplish its intended goals." Among the proposed changes sought by the Governor was the replacement of the phrase "consistent with" with the phrase "which tend to establish" in § 1(B)(ii).

The Governor's amendment, eventually adopted into law, was plainly intended to limit the scope of the bill's original language. As the Appeals Court recognized, "[p]ropositions are 'consistent with' each other if they are compatible and can coexist harmoniously," see *Guzman,* 907 N.E.2d 1140, quoting Merriam-Webster's Collegiate Dictionary 266, 253 (11th ed. 2005), and under the language of the bill as originally passed, it is possible to envision many potential claimants whose convictions are reversed because of procedural or evidentiary errors or structural deficiencies at their trials that could well be "consistent" with innocence without *any* tendency to establish it. The adoption of the gubernatorial amendment had the effect of limiting the class of claimants to those who received judicial relief on grounds that directly implicate innocence. We agree with the Appeals Court that even with the "more stringent" language, the statute does not express an intent to limit *eligibility,* a threshold question, to individuals whose convictions were vacated or reversed strictly on the basis "of compelling or overwhelming exculpatory evidence," that is, on the grounds that they were actually innocent.

The Commonwealth argues that the eligibility requirements of § 1(B), including the one relative to judicial relief, were intended by the Legislature as gatekeeping provisions, the importance of which is apparent from the structure of the statute, which recognizes the difficulties inherent in litigating cases in which the purported evidence may be difficult to marshal, given the passage of time and the sensitivity required for victims of crime. Drawing on comparisons to similar statutes from other States, particularly New York, the Commonwealth contends that the statute was designed to foreclose from proceeding those cases lacking affirmative evidence of innocence. Viewing the eligibility provision as a screening mechanism, it argues, would serve the dual purposes of providing compensation to truly deserving individuals and limiting the class of potential claimants. Relying on what it views as the plain words of the statute, the statutory structure and scheme, the legislative intent, principles of statutory construction, and the historical context in which the law was enacted,[10] the Commonwealth essentially contends that in order to proceed with a claim the plaintiff must show that the judicial relief he was granted rested on affirmative evidence of innocence.... He must demonstrate that the grounds for relief had some "meaningful tendency" to establish innocence, not just a tendency to assist the defendant's chances for acquittal.

While we agree that the eligibility requirements of c. 258D were intended to limit the class of persons entitled to pursue relief, and in this sense perform a screening function, and that the relief granted must be on grounds tending to do more than merely assist the defendant's chances of acquittal, we do not discern a legislative intent that the determination of eligibility be tantamount to a testing of the merits of a claimant's case. If the Legislature intended

10. The Commonwealth observes that c. 258D was enacted as part of a national trend to provide compensation for erroneous convictions in recognition of the government's moral responsibility to provide redress. According to the Commonwealth, nearly all the statutes of other States express a purpose to compensate only those who are actually innocent, a purpose undoubtedly relied on by the Legislature in enacting c. 258D.

it to be so, it could have structured the statute to specifically reflect this intent.[11]

Our inquiry begins with the language adopted by the Legislature. Where the language of the statute is clear, we interpret it according to its ordinary meaning. Where a statute fails to specifically define its terms, "we give them their usual and accepted meanings, as long as these meanings are consistent with the statutory purpose." *Commonwealth v. Zone Book, Inc.,* 361 N.E.2d 1239 (Mass. 1977)....

To apply these principles to the phrase, "grounds which tend to establish" the actual innocence of the plaintiff, it is necessary to separate the phrase into its component parts. The term "grounds" refers to "the foundation or basis on which knowledge, belief, or conviction rests." Webster's Third New Int'l Dictionary 1002 (1993).... We conclude that the Legislature used the term "grounds" to mean "basis." The phrase "tend to establish" combines the verb "tend" with the verb "establish." "Tend" means "to exhibit a direction or approach toward an object or effect." Merriam-Webster's Collegiate Dictionary 1287 (11th ed. 2005)...."Establish" means "to prove." Merriam-Webster's Collegiate Dictionary, at 427. Taking these definitions collectively, ... the phrase is properly understood to mean judicial relief on "grounds resting upon facts and circumstances probative of the proposition that the claimant did not commit the crime."

b. *Application.* In determining whether Guzman is among the class of persons eligible to seek relief under c. 258D, we review the summary judgment record, including the relevant portions of the trial and motion transcripts, the trial judge's written memorandum of decision on Guzman's motion for new trial, and the Appeals Court's affirmance of the same....

i. *Guzman's criminal case....* Essentially, the Commonwealth's case against Guzman was based on a theory of constructive possession of cocaine. Guzman's defense was that he had been mistaken for his cousin, Esteban Maffeo. In support of this defense, he produced a number of witnesses (but not Maffeo) to testify that Maffeo was a separate person and that Guzman was not a drug dealer, but a businessman who owned a beauty salon and towing business. The prosecution sought to show that Guzman and Maffeo were the same person.

The primary witnesses against Guzman were two Boston police detectives, Kenneth Acerra and Walter Robinson,[14] who had seized cocaine and cash as the result of searches they had conducted of two apartments, a safe deposit box, and an automobile registered to Maffeo but allegedly driven by Guzman on occasion. Importantly, the detectives also testified that they had observed Guzman selling cocaine in separate instances to two other individuals, Arthur Logue and James Spencer, neither of whom testified at the trial. Those individuals had been arrested at different times before Guzman and had been the subjects of separate prosecutions. Spencer, as it developed, had been represented in his criminal case by Guzman's trial attorney.

Guzman was convicted on January 29, 1992. He subsequently filed a motion for a new trial claiming that his counsel was ineffective due to a conflict of interest that prejudiced his defense.

After an evidentiary hearing, the trial judge granted Guzman a new trial on grounds that are not in dispute. She found that the central issue in the case was identification (or misidentification), and that Guzman's attorney's personal concerns regarding a potential conflict arising from his representation of Spencer had led him to take steps contrary to the interests of Guzman at trial. More specifically, she found that Guzman's trial attorney declined to call Spencer and Logue as witnesses at Guzman's trial, even knowing that they likely would have contradicted the testimony of Detectives Acerra and Robinson that Guzman was the person who sold them (Spencer and Logue) drugs, solely because he

11. The New York statute, for example, explicitly includes a screening mechanism that addresses the full merits of a claimant's case. It requires that a claim "shall state facts in sufficient detail to permit the court to find that claimant is likely to succeed at trial in proving that (a) he did not commit any of the acts charged in the accusatory instrument..., and (b) he did not by his own conduct cause or bring about his conviction. The claim shall be verified by the claimant. If the court finds after reading the claim that claimant is not likely to succeed at trial, it shall dismiss the claim, either on its own motion or on the motion of the state." N.Y. Ct. Cl. Act § 8-b(4) (McKinney 1989). Had the Legislature wanted to structure c. 258D to do the same, it could have done so, especially given the other similarities between that statute and c. 258D.

14. See note 5, *supra.*

desired to avoid the appearance of a conflict of interest. The judge concluded that this conduct constituted ineffective assistance of counsel which prejudiced Guzman's right to a fair trial by causing the exclusion of testimony crucial to his defense of mistaken identity.

ii. *Guzman's civil claim under c. 258D.* As noted, Guzman subsequently brought this claim against the Commonwealth, alleging that he was in the class of persons entitled to recover under c. 258D. Summary judgment was granted to the Commonwealth only on the ground that Guzman would be unable to establish that he met the eligibility requirement of having received judicial relief on grounds that tended to establish his innocence. G.L. c. 258D, § 1(B)(ii). The motion judge first found that, "while Guzman claims he is innocent of all charges, he has submitted neither new evidence nor affidavits showing genuine material facts in dispute," and then concluded, "as a matter of law," that Guzman was not eligible under the statute "because the charges against him were not dismissed on grounds which tend to show innocence." The judge reasoned that Guzman's motion for new trial was allowed because "he may have been prejudiced" by his attorney's conflict of interest,[18] and that the eligibility requirements were not met because there had been evidence at trial corroborating the salient points of the detectives' testimony regarding Guzman's guilt. The judge ultimately determined Guzman's failure to "adduce evidence sufficient to create a question of fact as to whether ... the charges against him were dismissed on grounds" tending to establish his innocence excluded him from seeking compensation under c. 258D.

The Appeals Court reversed, explaining that in determining eligibility, the statute did not require that the "grounds for relief be examined in relation to the strength of the evidence of guilt adduced at the claimant's criminal trial," *Guzman*, 907 N.E.2d 1140, and that the language of the statute did not "import[ ] into the eligibility provision a preliminary assessment" of the ultimate merits of the claim.[19] *Id.* We agree.

Where the grounds for relief are not in dispute, the question whether they "tend to establish" that the plaintiff did not commit the crime is primarily a question of law. Here, there is no dispute that the judge granted a new trial because Guzman's defense of misidentification was prejudiced by defense counsel's conflicting interests that resulted in his failure to call witnesses who likely would have testified that Guzman was not the person identified by the detectives as the person they claimed to observe selling them drugs. In these circumstances, it cannot be said that these grounds did not rest on facts and circumstances probative of the proposition that Guzman did not commit the crimes charged as required by G.L. c. 258D, § 1(B)(ii). Although presented in the context of a claim of ineffective assistance of counsel, the relief granted to Guzman rested on the assumption, articulated by the trial judge, that the erroneously omitted evidence was probative of the conclusion that the culprit was someone else.[20]

Where Guzman's eligibility to bring the lawsuit was the only ground on which the Commonwealth's motion for summary judgment was brought, it was error to grant it.... The case is remanded to the Superior Court for further proceedings consistent with this decision....

---

18. In her written decision, the motion judge alluded to the indictments against Detectives Acerra and Robinson and noted these indictments "certainly" would have affected the detectives' credibility and "potentially the validity" of the search warrants obtained in their investigation of Guzman. In ultimately concluding that Guzman was not eligible to seek relief, the motion judge cited G.L. c. 258D, § 1(F), which allows the admission of evidence obtained in violation of a defendant's constitutional rights, and explained that such a requirement "manifest[ed] a legislative intent to exclude from compensation" those individuals whose convictions are overturned because of illegally obtained evidence. Although the motion for a new trial was not based on the invalidity of search warrants, or the consequent inadmissibility of evidence, we agree that c. 258D explicitly provides for the admission of such evidence at the trial of the c. 258D claim.

19. The Appeals Court recognized that, to be sure, "all the evidence relied on by the parties on the issue of actual innocence, including any inculpatory evidence from the criminal trial that the Commonwealth may choose to introduce, eventually must be weighed and evaluated to determine whether the claimant has met his burden of proof [that he is actually innocent] and is entitled to recover." *Guzman*, 907 N.E.2d 1140.

20. Not all cases in which a new trial is granted on ineffective assistance grounds necessarily will result in eligibility to bring suit under G.L. c. 258D. Essential to our analysis here is that counsel's ineffective assistance took the form of depriving Guzman of the introduction of evidence tending to establish his actual innocence.

Notes and Questions

1. Note the difference in the provisions of the Massachusetts Erroneous Convictions Law that govern "eligibility" to file a claim for relief, and "to prevail and recover damages." The "eligibility" provision, at issue in *Guzman*, requires the claimant to rely "on grounds which tend to establish ... innocence." To "prevail and recover damages" the claimant must "establish, by clear and convincing evidence, that ... he did not commit the crime or crimes charged...." Why would compensation legislation include sequential requirements, instead of relying exclusively on the latter provision?

2. Would the trial court's ruling dismissing Guzman's claim likely have been upheld had Massachusetts' statute more closely resembled New York's legislation, which is set forth in relevant part in footnote 11 of the Supreme Judicial Court's opinion? Which approach—that reflected in the Massachusetts law or in New York's—seems preferable?

3. As discussed in *Guzman*, Massachusetts enacted its Erroneous Convictions Law in 2004. Prior to this legislation, wrongfully convicted individuals were required to seek redress through other means, described by one commentator as follows:

> [T]he only remedy available to [wrongfully convicted individuals] is to appeal to the legislature for redress through a special law. However, such awards are rare. In 1904, Cornelius Usher was pardoned and received $1,000 compensation through a special bill in the legislature. In 1957, Santos Rodriguez was released from prison, and the Massachusetts legislature subsequently awarded him a $12,500 indemnity. In 1992, Bobby Joe Leaster was awarded a $500,000 annuity through a special bill, in order "to discharge the moral obligation of the Commonwealth." Usher, Rodriguez and Leaster are the only former inmates ever to receive compensation awards from the Massachusetts legislature. Further, the approval process for these awards took a very long time; for example, Leaster's case was pending for nine years before relief was granted. Apart from the long delays inherent in obtaining relief under a special law, the ad hoc character of the system makes it impossible for claims to be reviewed by reference to any sort of uniform standard.[68]

4. Katharina Brow was found stabbed to death in her home in Ayer, Massachusetts in 1980. Items of jewelry, her purse, and cash were missing. Two years later, Kenneth Waters was arrested for the crimes. He was convicted and sentenced to life imprisonment. The Massachusetts Supreme Judicial Court affirmed his conviction in 1987.[69] Convinced of his innocence, Waters' sister, Betty Anne Waters, put herself through college and law school, became a licensed attorney, and eventually uncovered blood-stained exhibits from the trial that were subjected to DNA testing in 2000. The tests excluded Kenneth Waters as the source of the biological evidence found at the crime scene. Prosecutors did not oppose Waters' motion for a new trial, which was granted in 2001. "Although prosecutors would not concede Waters' innocence, they declined to retry him for the reason that there was 'insufficient evidence to proceed.' After eighteen years in prison, Waters was free."[70] Waters received no compensation. "Tragically, ... Mr. Waters died from an accidental fall six months [after his release]."[71] The movie "Conviction," starring Hilary Swank as Betty Anne Waters, portrayed events surrounding Kenneth Waters' exoneration. The movie was released in 2010.

Douglas Warney was convicted of second-degree murder and burglary in Rochester, New York in 1996. The murder victim had been stabbed 19 times and a bloody knife and bloody clothing were found at the crime scene. Warney was sentenced to 25 years to life imprisonment. Affirming his conviction, the Appellate Division of the New York Supreme Court rejected Warney's claim that the guilty verdict was against the weight of the evidence.

> Defendant confessed to the crime and gave accurate descriptions of many details of the crime scene. Defendant testified at trial that the police threatened him and forced him to confess to the crime. Two police detectives, however, testified that they did not threaten defendant, and that defendant was cooperative with them. In fact, defendant does not dispute that it was he who contacted the police in the first instance and provided them with information about the murder. *People v. Warney,* 750 N.Y.S.2d 731, 733 (A.D. 2002), *leave to appeal denied,* 790 N.E.2d 289 (N.Y. 2003).

Post-conviction DNA testing of scrapings from the victim's fingernails and bloody items found at the crime scene excluded Warney as the source of the biological evidence. The analysis produced a match to Eldred Johnson, Jr., who was serving a life term prison sentence. Johnson confessed to the murder for which Warney had been convicted when he was confronted with the DNA results. Warney was released from prison and his conviction was vacated in 2006.[72]

The Innocence Project describes Warney and circumstances related to his confession to police detectives, as follows:

> Douglas Warney, a man with a history of mental health issues, an eighth-grade education, and advanced AIDS, called the police stating that he had information about a homicide. He knew the victim: he had cleaned the victim's house and shoveled snow from his driveway just two years before the murder. Warney was interrogated for 12 hours by police, he confessed and provided details that only the killer could know—that the victim was wearing a nightgown, that he had been cooking chicken, and that the killer cut himself with a knife and wiped it with a tissue in the bathroom. He also mentioned a second man, who was later found to have been confined to a clinic at the time of the murder. Warney's confession contained other inconsistencies, such as the location of the murder and the disposal of clothing after the crime.[73]

Warney filed a claim for damages in the New York Court of Claims for his wrongful conviction and imprisonment. Among other provisions, New York's authorizing legislation specifies: "The claim shall state facts in sufficient detail to permit the court to find that claimant is likely to succeed at trial in proving that (a) he did not commit any of the acts charged in the accusatory instrument ... and (b) he did not by his own conduct cause or bring about his conviction." N.Y. Ct. Claims Act § 8-b (4) (2007). In reliance on this section, and citing Warney's confession to the murder, the Court of Claims dismissed Warney's claim for damages. The Appellate Division affirmed.

People v. Warney

894 N.Y.S.2d 274 (A.D. 2010)

MEMORANDUM:

The Court of Claims properly granted defendant's motion to dismiss this claim seeking damages for unjust conviction and imprisonment pursuant to Court of Claims Act § 8-b. The claim was brought after claimant's conviction of two counts of murder in the second degree was vacated based on newly found evidence, i.e., the DNA analysis of the blood evidence from the crime scene that implicated another person.

Claimant had confessed to the crimes, which in large part led to his conviction. The new evidence was discovered after claimant had been incarcerated for a period of time, whereupon the person implicated by the new evidence confessed and pleaded guilty to the crimes. "To survive [defendant's] dismissal motion, ... claimant [was required by Court of Claims Act § 8-b(3) to] state facts in sufficient detail to permit the court to find that [he] was likely to succeed at trial in proving[, inter alia,] that [he] by [his] own conduct [did not] cause or bring about [the] conviction" (*Reed v. State of New York,* 78 N.Y.2d 1, 7, 574 N.E.2d 433). "[F]or example, an innocent criminal defendant may cause or bring about his or her own conviction by making an uncoerced false confession of guilt that is presented to the jury at trial" (*O'Donnell v. State of New York,* 26 A.D.3d 59, 62–63, 808 N.Y.S.2d 266; *see generally Ausderau v. State of New York,* 130 Misc.2d 848, 851–852, 498 N.Y.S.2d 253, *affd.* 127 A.D.2d 980, 512 N.Y.S.2d 790, *lv. denied* 69 N.Y.2d 613, 511 N.E.2d 87). We therefore conclude that claimant has failed to state facts in sufficient detail to permit the court to find that he is likely to succeed at trial in proving that he did not by his own conduct cause or bring about his conviction (*see* § 8-b[4]). Indeed, he merely surmises that his confession must have been coerced because it was later shown to be false when someone else confessed to the crime and, apart from claimant's actual confession, there was evidence that claimant approached the police in the first instance with information about the crimes and made incriminating statements to police officers....

Notes and Questions

1. Should Warney's claim be dismissed because "his own conduct"—*i.e.*, the incriminating statements he made to the police that were admitted into evidence at his trial—"cause[d] or [brought] about his conviction"?

2. On appeal, the New York Court of Appeals reversed the Appellate Division's judgment, concluding that Warney was entitled to present evidence in the Court of Claims in support of his allegation that his false confession had been coerced. *Warney v. State,* ___ N.E.2d ___, 2011 WL 1157701 (N.Y. 2011).

CIPARICK, J.

... Warney ... seeks damages under Court of Claims Act § 8-b for the years he spent wrongly incarcerated. His claim alleges that he "did not cause or contribute to his own wrongful arrest, conviction, or incarceration," but rather his conviction "was the direct result of the intentional and malicious actions of members of the [Rochester Police Department] [RPD] who fabricated and coerced a false confession from ... a man whom they knew had a history of serious mental health problems." The State moved to dismiss the claim for failing to state facts in sufficient detail to demonstrate that Warney is likely to succeed at trial in proving that he did not bring about his own conviction.

Court of Claims granted the State's motion and dismissed the claim. It was "not convinced" that only the perpetrator and police could have known many of the details contained in the confession, and noted that Warney "does not indicate how he was coerced by police to give a false confession." Moreover, the court held that Warney, "by his own actions, which included calling the police to tell them he had information about the murder, trying to frame an innocent man for the crime, and ... volunteering that he had 'a body'... did cause or bring about his own conviction."...

The Appellate Division affirmed, reasoning that a criminal defendant who gave an uncoerced false confession that was presented to the jury at trial could not subsequently bring an action under section 8-b, and that Warney failed to adequately allege that his confession was coerced. The Appellate Division also found that Warney brought about his own conviction by making other incriminating statements, and by approaching the police falsely claiming to have information about the murder. We ... now reverse.

Court of Claims Act (CCA) § 8-b, the Unjust Conviction and Imprisonment Act, provides a mechanism for "innocent persons who can demonstrate by clear and convincing evidence that they were unjustly convicted and imprisoned ... to recover damages against the state" (CCA § 8-b [1]). It offers claimants who meet its strict pleading and evidentiary burdens "an available avenue of redress over and above the existing tort remedies" (CCA § 8-b [1]).

To present a claim under the statute, a claimant must "establish by documentary evidence" that (a) the claimant was convicted of a crime, sentenced to a term of imprisonment, and served at least part of the sentence; (b) the claimant was pardoned on the ground of innocence or, alternatively, the conviction was reversed or vacated and the accusatory instrument was dismissed; and (c) the claim is not time-barred (CCA § 8-b [3]). Here, the State does not dispute that Warney met this initial burden.

The statute further requires that the claim "state facts in sufficient detail to permit the court to find that claimant is likely to succeed" in meeting his or her burden at trial of proving by clear and convincing evidence that, as relevant here, (a) "he did not commit any of the acts charged in the accusatory instrument" and (b) that "he did not by his own conduct cause or bring about his conviction" (CCA § 8-b [4]). "If the court finds after reading the claim that claimant is not likely to succeed at trial, it shall dismiss the claim" (CCA § 8-b [4]).

The parties here debate whether, in addition to being sufficiently detailed, the allegations in the pleading must have evidentiary support. We now clarify that no such support is necessary, except where expressly indicated by the statute. Although a claimant must submit documentary evidence supporting certain facts pursuant to CCA § 8-b (3), the pleading standard articulated in CCA § 8-b (4) lacks any analogous requirement. Because the State, in waiving its sovereign immunity from suit, has consented to have its liability "determined in accordance with the same rules of law as applied to actions in the supreme court," except where superseded by the Court of Claims Act or Uniform Rules of the Court of Claims (CCA § 8), we presume that the familiar standard governing motions to dismiss in Supreme Court is appropriate here. Therefore, Court of Claims, like other trial courts, should "accept the facts as alleged in the [claim] as true" (*Leon v. Martinez,* 84 N.Y.2d 83, 87 [1994]).

Of course, section 8-b still imposes a higher pleading standard than the CPLR [Civil Practice Law and Rules]. Court of Claims must consider whether the allegations are sufficiently detailed to demonstrate a likelihood of success at trial (*see* CCA § 8-b [4]). "[T]he allegations in the claim must be of such character that, if believed, they would clearly and convincingly establish the elements of the claim, so as to set forth a cause of action" (*Solomon v. State of New York,* 146 A.D.2d 439, 442, 541 N.Y.S.2d 384 [1st Dept 1989]). In evaluating the likelihood of success at trial, Court of Claims should avoid making credibility and factual determinations. In short, a claimant who meets the evidentiary burdens described in CCA § 8-b (3) and makes detailed allegations with respect to the elements described in section 8-b (4) is entitled to an opportunity to prove the allegations at trial (CCA § 8-b [5]). With these principles in mind, we turn to the claim at issue here.

Court of Claims' dismissal was based in large part on factual determinations that were inappropriate at this stage of the litigation. First, although Warney alleges in detail that his confession was coerced, the court concluded that "the evidence presented" did not "indicate" that it was. The court was "not convinced" that, as Warney alleges, "only the police and the true perpetrator could have known many of the factual details" in the confession. These findings were premature; the proper inquiry was whether Warney's allegations, if true, demonstrate a likelihood of success at trial, not whether they were supported by convincing evidence. As the State concedes, a coerced false confession does not bar recovery under section 8-b because it is not the claimant's "own conduct" within the meaning of the statute.[3] Assuming the truth of Warney's allegations, as we must, the police used "coercive tactics" and threats to induce his confession. The allegations describe how no member of the public other than the perpetrator could have known all the details contained in the confession—whether negligently or through intentional manipulation, police misconduct led to the inclusion of these details in Warney's state-

3. Warney argues that the word "conduct" in the statute should be read as "misconduct," as this reading is in line with clear Legislative intent (*see* 1984 Report of N.Y. Law Rev Commn, 1984 McKinney's Session Laws of N.Y. at 2932 [claimant should "have to establish that he did not cause or bring about his prosecution by reason of his own misconduct"]). Because he alleges that no conduct of his brought about his conviction, however, we find it unnecessary to consider whether such conduct must rise to the level of misconduct.

ment. Thus, Warney has adequately pleaded that he was coerced into adopting the false confession.[4]

Second, Court of Claims determined that Warney's statement to an RPD officer, "I've got a body," which was introduced against him at trial, was conduct contributing to his conviction. Warney has never admitted to making that statement, however, and his claim alleges that, as he maintained at trial, he actually said "I'm being charged with a body." Accepting Warney's allegations as true, we presume that he never made this inculpatory statement. Determining what Warney said is purely a credibility determination, pitting his account against the officer's. The officer's testimony is no more or less convincing, at this pleading stage, than Warney's account of the conversation.

The State further argues that Warney's initial interactions with the RPD ought to bar him from recovery. We disagree. A claimant's statutory obligation to prove that "he did not ... cause or bring about his own conviction" (CCA § 8-b [4]) could conceivably be read as barring recovery when *any* action by the claimant caused or brought about the underlying conviction, no matter how indirectly. This reading, however, would bar recovery by every innocent claimant who inadvertently and unforeseeably played some small role in the chain of events leading to his or her conviction. Instead, as we have previously suggested, a claimant's conduct bars recovery under the statute only if it was the "proximate cause of conviction" (*Ivey* [*v. State of New York*], 80 N.Y.2d [474], at 482, 591 N.Y.S.2d 969, 606 N.E.2d 1360 [(1992)]). Warney's early conversations with the RPD, as the events are described in his claim, did not cause or bring about his conviction within the meaning of the statute. While Warney acknowledges that he initiated contact with the RPD, triggering the questioning that ultimately led to his false confession and conviction, he alleges that he was "severely mentally impaired," and that the RPD knew of his mental illness. Moreover, it was the RPD's alleged mishandling of the ensuing investigation that ultimately resulted in Warney's conviction.

In sum, the courts below inappropriately made credibility and factual findings, dismissing Warney's claim without giving him the opportunity to prove his detailed allegations that he did not cause or bring about his conviction. Because these allegations, taken as true, demonstrate a likelihood of success at trial, Warney is entitled to proceed with his claim, secure discovery, and obtain a disposition on the merits....

E. Conclusion

The judicial process, through appeals and post-conviction review, offers the principal mechanisms for correcting error in its earlier determinations of guilt. However, the executive branch, through clemency powers recognized in all states and federally, also can correct error. Clemency historically has been regarded as an important "fail safe" for innocent people convicted of crimes. Skeptics have questioned whether executive clemency in reality functions as a meaningful safeguard for the innocent, citing infrequent use of the pardoning power, haphazard fact-finding procedures, and a reluctance by chief executives to be perceived as being "soft on crime" by granting clemency.

Innocence commissions also function extrajudicially. Although lacking the authority to vacate a criminal conviction, innocence commissions that conform to the "error correction" model exemplified by the North Carolina Innocence Inquiry Commission and Britain's Criminal Cases Review Commission are empowered to review claims of innocence, investigate and make determinations of fact, and recommend judicial relief.

4. The State contends that since Supreme Court ruled at a suppression hearing prior to the criminal trial that the confession was voluntarily given, it cannot be found in this action to have been coerced. We reject that contention and conclude that although the statement was admissible at the criminal trial, the judge there lacked many of the facts now stated in Warney's claim. Most importantly, the question of coercion must now be viewed in light of Warney's innocence.

Innocence commissions appointed in several states have a different function, to examine known cases of wrongful conviction and make system-wide recommendations designed to help jurisdictions avoid and correct miscarriages of justice. The Innocence Project has advocated that all jurisdictions create official "criminal justice reform commissions," and provide those bodies with appropriate authority and political independence.

Wrongful convictions and punishment cause deep and often irreparable harm to the individuals suffering them. Surprisingly, perhaps, statutes authorizing compensation for wrongfully imprisoned individuals have been enacted in only slightly more than half of the states; aggrieved individuals elsewhere must sue for damages, often encountering difficult jurisdictional and procedural hurdles, or else rely on special legislation authorizing them to recover damages, another process fraught with uncertainties. The wrongfully convicted typically must affirmatively establish their actual innocence, demonstrate that their own conduct did not cause or contribute to their conviction, and meet other prerequisites to recoup damages. Damage awards are capped legislatively at widely disparate levels throughout the country. Large numbers of wrongfully convicted individuals receive no assistance in recovering or reintegrating into society following release from prison, nor monetary damages. Such individuals arguably are forced to experience multiple miscarriages of justice, involving not only their wrongful conviction and punishment, but also the societal indifference exhibited following their exoneration.

Endnotes

Chapter 1

1. For further information about the case involving Jesse and Stephen Boorn, *see* Rob Warden, *America's First Wrongful Murder Conviction Case*, available at Northwestern University Center on Wrongful Convictions, http://www.law.northwestern.edu/wrongfulconvictions/exonerations/vtBoornSummary.html (last visited June 3, 2010); Edwin M. Borchard, *Convicting the Innocent: Sixty-Five Actual Errors of Criminal Justice* 14–21 (Garden City, NY: Garden City Publishing Co. 1932); Gerald M. McFarland, *The Counterfeit Man: The True Story of the Boorn-Colvin Murder* (Amherst, MA: University of Massachusetts Press 1990). McFarland speculates that the man whose return to Vermont spared the Boorn brothers may not, in fact, have been Russell Colvin, the alleged murder victim.

2. *See* Susan Levine, "Ex-Death Row Inmate Hears Hoped-for Words: We Found Killer," *Washington Post* A1, Sept. 6, 2003, available at http://truthinjustice.org/bloodsworth.htm (last visited June 4, 2010); "Kirk Bloodsworth," available at The Justice Project, http://www.thejusticeproject.org/kirk/kirk-bloodsworth-story/ (last visited June 4, 2010); Tim Junkin, *Bloodsworth: The True Story of the First Death Row Inmate Exonerated by DNA* (Chapel Hill, NC: Algonquin Books of Chapel Hill 1998); *Bloodsworth v. State*, 543 A.2d 392 (Md. App.), *cert. den.*, 548 A.2d 128 (Md. 1988); *Bloodsworth v. State*, 512 A.2d 1056 (Md. 1986).

3. *See* "Woman Not Guilty in Retrial in the Deaths of Her 5 Children," *New York Times*, July 27, 2006, available at http://www.nytimes.com/2006/07/27/us/27yates.html (last visited June 4, 2010); *Ex parte Yates*, 193 S.W.3d 149 (Tex. App. 2006); Suzanne O'Malley, *"Are You There Alone?" The Unspeakable Crime of Andrea Yates* (New York: Simon & Schuster 2004); Timothy Roche, "Andrea Yates: More to the Story," *Time*, March 18, 2002, available at http://www.time.com/time/nation/article/0,8599,218445,00.html (last visited June 4, 2010); Jim Yardley, "Mother Who Drowned 5 Children in Tub Avoids a Death Sentence," *New York Times*, March 16, 2002, available at http://www.nytimes.com/2002/03/16/us/mother-who-drowned-5-children-in-tub-avoids-a-death-sentence.html (last visited June 4, 2010); Jim Yardley, "Texas Jury Convicts Mother Who Drowned Her Children," *New York Times*, March 13, 2002, available at http://www.nytimes.com/2002/03/13/us/texas-jury-convicts-mother-who-drowned-her-children.html (last visited June 4, 2010); Tex. Penal Code Ann. § 8.01 (1993).

4. *People v. Caruso*, 164 N.E. 106 (N.Y. 1928).

5. *See Brewer v. Williams*, 430 U.S. 387 (1977); *State v. Williams*, 182 N.W.2d 396 (Iowa 1971). Following the Supreme Court's ruling, Williams was retried and once again was convicted of murder. Testimony concerning the child's body and its condition was allowed into evidence by the trial judge on the theory that the body inevitably would have been discovered by the police through the efforts of ongoing search parties, and that the violation of Williams's Sixth Amendment right consequently did not require suppression of this evidence. Williams's case once again was reviewed by the U.S. Supreme Court, and a majority of the justices agreed that the trial court had correctly admitted evidence concerning the body in reliance on the inevitable discovery doctrine, resulting in the affirmance of Williams's murder conviction. *See Nix v. Williams*, 467 U.S. 431 (1984). *See generally* Thomas N. McInnis, *The Christian Burial Case: An Introduction to Criminal and Judicial Procedure* (Westport, CT: Praeger 2001).

6. For a more current "no crime" case involving a purported criminal homicide, *see* "'Murdered' Chinese Man Reappears After Ten Years," ABC News/Reuters (May 9, 2010), available at http://abcnews.go.com/International/wireStory?id=10595834 (last visited June 19, 2010) ("A Chinese man who was supposedly hacked to death in a fight has reappeared in his hometown after 10 years, ... raising questions about police torture to extract a confession from the alleged killer. Zhao Zuohai, the supposed killer, was acquitted of the crime and released by a Henan court on Saturday.... He had

served 10 years of a 29-year sentence after confessing to killing Zhao Zhenshang in a hatchet fight in central China's Henan province.... A headless body was found in a village well about a year after the fight, at which point Zhao was arrested and confessed to the killing. The victim, Zhao Zhenshang, reappeared in the village on May 2 to seek welfare support. He had fled after the fight because he feared he had killed the now-imprisoned Zhao. Convictions in the Chinese court system are strongly dependent on confessions, motivating police to use force to get a confession and close the case.... The imprisoned Zhao's brother told the local Dahe Newspaper that police had forced him to drink chili water and set off fireworks over his head to force the confession. The imprisoned Zhao narrowly escaped being executed for the crime. His sentence was commuted from a death penalty with two years' reprieve. While in prison, his wife left him for another man and three of his four children were given to other families for adoption....").

7. *See* Samuel R. Gross, "Convicting the Innocent," 4 *Annual Review of Law and Social Science* 173, 182–184 (2008).

8. *See* Tony G. Poveda, "Estimating Wrongful Convictions," 18 *Justice Quarterly* 689, 691–92 (2001); Stanley Z. Fisher, "Convictions of Innocent Persons in Massachusetts: An Overview," 12 *Boston University Public Interest Law Journal* 1, 5 & n. 13 (2002).

9. *See* Charles L. Black, Jr., *Capital Punishment: The Inevitability of Caprice and Mistake* 46–50 (New York: Norton 1974).

10. Poveda, *supra*, at 703.

11. *Id.* at 703–04.

12. Robert J. Ramsey & James Frank, "Wrongful Conviction: Perceptions of Criminal Justice Professionals Regarding the Frequency of Wrongful Conviction and the Extent of System Errors," 53 *Crime & Delinquency* 436 (2007).

13. C. Ronald Huff, Arye Rattner & Edward Sagarin, "Guilty Until Proven Innocent: Wrongful Conviction and Public Policy," 32 *Crime & Delinquency* 518 (1986); C. Ronald Huff, Arye Rattner & Edward Sagarin, *Convicted But Innocent: Wrongful Conviction and Public Policy* 53–62 (Thousand Oaks, CA: Sage Publications 1996).

14. *Id.* at 62.

15. Keith A. Findley & Michael S. Scott, "The Multiple Dimensions of Tunnel Vision in Criminal Cases," 2006 *Wisconsin Law Review* 291, 291.

16. State v. Hennis, 372 S.E.2d 523, 528 (N.C. 1988) (*quoting* N.C.G.S. § 15A-1443 (a) (1983)).

17. Death Penalty Information Center, *Innocence and the Crisis in the American Death Penalty*, available at http://www.deathpenaltyinfo.org/innocence-and-crisis-american-death-penalty#Sec05a (bolding in original) (last visited June 12, 2010).

18. John Schwartz, "In 3rd Trial, Conviction in Murders from 1985," *New York Times*, April 8, 2010, available at http://www.nytimes.com/2010/04/09/us/09soldier.html (last visited June 12, 2010); Paul Woolverton, "Hennis Sentenced to Death for 1985 Eastburn Murders," *Fayetteville Observer*, April 16, 2010, available at http://fayobserver.com/Articles/2010/04/15/991361 (last visited June 12, 2010).

19. Schwartz, *supra*.

20. *See* Lorraine Hope, Edith Greene, Melanie Gavisk, Amina Memon & Kate Houston, "A Third Verdict Option: Exploring the Impact of the Not Proven Verdict on Mock Juror Decision Making," 32 *Law & Human Behavior* 241 (2008); Joseph M. Barbato, "Scotland's Bastard Verdict: Intermediacy and the Unique Three-Verdict System," 15 *Indiana International & Comparative Law Review* 543 (2005); Samuel Bray, "Not Proven: Introducing a Third Verdict," 72 *University of Chicago Law Review* 1299 (2005).

21. Death Penalty Information Center, *Former Death Row Inmate Acquitted in One Court, Now Convicted in Another,* available at http://www.deathpenaltyinfo.org/former-death-row-inmate-acquitted-one-court-now-convicted-another (last visited June 12, 2010).

22. Hugo Adam Bedau & Michael L. Radelet, "Miscarriages of Justice in Potentially Capital Cases," 40 *Stanford Law Review* 21, 25 (1987) (footnote omitted).

23. *Id.*

24. *Id.* at 47.

25. Stephen J. Markman & Paul G. Cassell, "Protecting the Innocent: A Response to the Bedau-Radelet Study," 41 *Stanford Law Review* 121, 126 (1988). For the original authors' rejoinder, *see* Hugo Adam Bedau & Michael L. Radelet, "The Myth of Infallibility: A Reply to Markman and Cassell," 41 *Stanford Law Review* 161 (1988).

26. *See* Fisher, *supra*, at 6–12.

27. *See, e.g.*, Huff, Rattner & Sagarin, *supra*; Ayre Rattner, "Convicted But Innocent: Wrongful Conviction and the Criminal Justice System," 12 *Law & Human Behavior* 283 (1988).

28. Samuel R. Gross, Kristen Jacoby, Daniel J Matheson, Nicholas Montgomery & Sujata Patil, "Exonerations in the United States 1989 Through 2003," 95 *Journal of Criminal Law & Criminology* 523, 524 (2005) (footnote omitted).

29. Innocence Project, *About the Innocence Project*, available at http://www.innocenceproject.org/about/ (last visited June 16, 2010).

30. Innocence Project, *Fact Sheet: Facts on Post-Conviction DNA Exoneration*, available at http://www.innocenceproject.org/Content/Facts_on_PostConviction_DNA_Exonerations.php (last visited March 9, 2011).

31. Innocence Project, *Gary Dotson*, available at http://www.innocenceproject.org/Content/89.php (last visited June 16, 2010). *See also* Rob Warden, "The Revolutionary Role of Journalism in Identifying and Rectifying Wrongful Convictions," 70 *University of Missouri at Kansas City Law Review* 803, 829–843 (2002).

32. *See* Daniel S. Medwed, "Innocentrism," 2008 *University of Illinois Law Review* 1549, 1560 (2008); Hillary S. Ritter, "It's the Prosecution's Story, But They're Not Sticking To It: Applying Harmless Error and Judicial Estoppel to Exculpatory Post-Conviction DNA Testing Cases," 74 *Fordham Law Review* 825 (2005); Gross *et al., supra,* at 525–526.

33. Innocence Project, *Eyewitness Misidentification,* available at http://www.innocenceproject.org/understand/Eyewitness-Misidentification.php (last visited June 16, 2010).

34. Innocence Project, *Unvalidated or Improper Forensic Science*, available at http://www.innocenceproject.org/understand/Unreliable-Limited-Science.php (last visited June 16, 2010).

35. Innocence Project, *False Confessions*, available at http://www.innocenceproject.org/understand/False-Confessions.php (last visited June 16, 2010).

36. Innocence Project, *Informants/Snitches*, available at http://www.innocenceproject.org/understand/Snitches-Informants.php (last visited June 16, 2010).

37. Innocence Project, *Government Misconduct*, available at http://www.innocenceproject.org/understand/Government-Misconduct.php (last visited June 16, 2010).

38. Innocence Project, *Bad Lawyering*, available at http://www.innocenceproject.org/understand/Bad-Lawyering.php (last visited June 16, 2010).

39. Tonja Jacobi & Gwendolyn Carroll, "Acknowledging Guilt: Forcing Self-Identification in Post-conviction DNA Testing," 102 *Northwestern University Law Review* 263, 281 & n. 49 (2008).

40. Gross *et al., supra,* at 525.

41. *Id.* at 527

42. *Id,* at 533.

43. *Id.* at 528–529.

44. Gross, *supra,* at 179 (citation omitted).

45. Gross *et al., supra,* at 530–531.

46. *Id., supra* at 544, Table 3.

47. Samuel R. Gross & Barbara O'Brien, "Frequency and Predictors of False Conviction: Why We Know So Little, and New Data on Capital Cases," 5 *Journal of Empirical Legal Studies* 927, 932–933 (2008) (emphasis in original).

48. 408 U.S. 238 (1972).

49. Northwestern University School of Law Center on Wrongful Convictions, *The Snitch System* 3 (2004), available at http://www.law.northwestern.edu/wrongfulconvictions/issues/causesandremedies/snitches/SnitchSystemBooklet.pdf (last visited June 17, 2010).

50. Bedau & Radelet, *supra,* at 36.

51. *Id.* at 57, Table 6.

52. *See* Samuel R. Gross, "The Risks of Death: Why Erroneous Convictions are Common in Capital Cases," 44 *Buffalo Law Review* 469 (1996). *See also* James S. Liebman, "Rates of Reversible Error and the Risk of Wrongful Execution," 86 *Judicature* 78 (Sept.–Oct. 2002).

53. *See* James R. Acker, "Actual Innocence: Is Death Different?", 27 *Behavioral Sciences and the* Law 297 (2009) (questioning whether the Supreme Court's expressed concerns for heightened reliability in capital cases have effectively been applied to the guilt-determination phase of capital trials or whether they instead have been confined to the penalty phase of capital proceedings); Richard A. Rosen, "Innocence and Death," 82 *North Carolina Law Review* 61 (2003) (discussing but rejecting the argument that procedural protections in capital cases help protect innocent defendants against wrongful conviction).

54. Gross & O'Brien, *supra,* at 942 ("Most likely, this extraordinary number of capital exonerations is caused in part by a higher underlying error rate among capital convictions and in part by a higher rate of detection of those errors after conviction."). *Cf.,* Kansas v. Marsh, 548 U.S. 163, 193 (2006)

(Scalia, J., concurring) ("Reversal of an erroneous conviction on appeal or on habeas, or the pardoning of an innocent condemnee through executive clemency, demonstrates not the failure of the system but its success. Those devices are part and parcel of the multiple assurances that are applied before a death sentence is carried out."). *But see* Lawrence C. Marshall, "Do Exonerations Prove that 'The System Works?'" 86 *Judicature* 83 (Sept.–Oct. 2002).

55. Gross & O'Brien, *supra.*

56. D. Michael Risinger, "Innocents Convicted: An Empirically Justified Factual Wrongful Conviction Rate," 97 *Journal of Criminal Law & Criminology* 761 (2007) (in reliance on DNA exonerations between 1982 and 1989 of death-sentenced individuals convicted of rape-murder, estimating that the wrongful conviction rate for capital rape-murder is 3.3% and perhaps as high as 5%).

57. The Justice Project, *Convicting the Innocent: Texas Justice Derailed—Stories of Injustice and the Reforms That Can Prevent Them* 2–4 (2006), available at http://www.thejusticeproject.org/wp-content/uploads/convicting-the-innocent.pdf (last visited June 21, 2010).

58. Edwin M. Borchard, *Convicting the Innocent: Sixty-Five Actual Errors of Criminal Justice* (Garden City, NY: Garden City Publishing Company 1932).

59. United States v. Garsson, 291 F. 646, 649 (S.D.N.Y. 1923). *See also* James R. Acker & Catherine L. Bonventre, "Protecting the Innocent in New York: Moving Beyond Changing Only Their Names," 73 *Albany Law Review* 1245, 1253 & n. 35 (2010).

60. Erle Stanley Gardner, *The Court of Last Resort* (New York: William Sloane Associates 1952).

61. Jerome Frank & Barbara Frank, *Not Guilty* 38 (Garden City, NY: Doubleday & Co. 1957).

62. Richard A. Leo, "Rethinking the Study of Miscarriages of Justice: Developing a Criminology of Wrongful Conviction," 21 *Journal of Contemporary Criminal Justice* 201 (2005).

63. *See* Jon B. Gould & Richard A. Leo, "One Hundred Years Later: Wrongful Convictions After a Century of Research," 100 *Journal of Criminal Law & Criminology* 825 (2010); Marvin Zalman, "Criminal Justice Reform and Wrongful Conviction: A Research Agenda," 17 *Criminal Justice Policy Review* 468 (2006); Leo, *supra* note 62.

64. *See, e.g.,* Kent Roach, "The Role of Innocence Commissions: Error Discovery, Systemic Reform, or Both?", 85 *Chicago-Kent Law Review* 89 (2010); Stephanie Roberts & Lynne Weathered, "Assisting the Factually Innocent: The Contradictions and Compatibility of Innocence Projects and the Criminal Cases Review Commission," 29 *Oxford Journal of Legal Studies* 43 (2009); Jerome M. Maiatico, "All Eyes On Us: A Comparative Critique of the North Carolina Innocence Inquiry Commission," 56 *Duke Law Journal* 1345 (2007); American Bar Association Criminal Justice Section, *Achieving Justice: Freeing the Innocent, Convicting the Guilty: Report of the ABA Criminal Justice Section's Ad Hoc Innocence Committee to Ensure the Integrity of the Criminal Justice Process* (Washington, DC: American Bar Association 2006); Keith A. Findley, "The Pedagogy of Innocence: Reflections on the Role of Innocence Projects in Clinical Legal Education," 13 *Clinical Law Review* 231 (2006).

Chapter 2

1. *Atwater v. City of Lago Vista,* 532 U.S. 318, 121 S.Ct. 1536, 149 L.Ed.2d 549 (2001).

2. *United States v. Watson,* 423 U.S. 411, 96 S.Ct. 820, 46 L.Ed.2d 598 (1976).

3. See generally, Nickerson, R. S. (1998). Confirmation bias: A ubiquitous phenomenon in many guises. *Review of General Psychology, 2,* 175–220. O'Brien, B. (2009). Prime suspect: An examination of factors that aggravate and counteract confirmation bias in criminal investigations. *Psychology, Public Policy, and Law, 15,* 315–334.

4. Keith A. Findley & Michael S. Scott, "The Multiple Dimensions of Tunnel Vision in Criminal Cases," 2006 *Wisconsin Law Review* 291, 292 (2006) (internal citations omitted).

5. *Id.,* at 329–330.

6. Robert H. Jackson, speech at the Second Annual Conference of United States Attorneys, Washington D.C. (April 1, 1940), *reprinted in* Robert H. Jackson, "The Federal Prosecutor," 24 *Journal of the American Judicature Society* 18 (1940).

7. For additional information about these cases, *see* Thomas Frisbie & Randy Garrett, *Victims of Justice Revisited* (Evanston, IL: Northwestern University Press 2005); The Justice Project, *Rolando Cruz and Alejandro Hernandez,* available at http://www.thejusticeproject.org/profiles/rolando-cruz-and-alejandro-hernandez/ (last visited June 23, 2010); Death Penalty Information Center, *Innocence Cases: 1994–2003 (57. Rolando Cruz; 58. Alejandro Hernandez),* available at http://www.deathpenaltyinfo.org/innocence-cases-1994-2003 (last visited June 23, 2010); Art Barnum & Ted Gregory, "Jeanine Nicarico Murder: Tears of Joy as Brian

Dugan Gets Death Penalty," *Chicago Tribune* (Nov. 12, 2009), available at http://articles.chicagotribune.com/2009-11-12/news/0911111045_1_patricia-nicarico-brian-dugan-penalty (last visited June); Christy Gutowski, "Dugan Gets Death Sentence for Nicarico Murder," *Chicago Daily Herald* (Nov. 11, 2009), available at http://www.dailyherald.com/story/?id=335585 (last visited June 23, 2010).

8. McGhee entered a so-called *Alford* plea, pleading guilty while maintaining that he actually was innocent. We will discuss *North Carolina v. Alford*, 400 U.S. 25, 91 S.Ct. 160, 27 L.Ed.2d 162 (1970) and *Alford* pleas in Chapter 9.

9. *Brief for Petitioners, Pottawattamie County v. McGhee*, at p. i (U.S. Supreme Court, No. 08-1065, 2009).

10. "Deal in Case of Prosecutor Immunity," *New York Times* (Jan. 5, 2010), available at http://www.nytimes.com/2010/01/05/us/05scotus.html (last visited June 24, 2010).

11. *Pottawattamie County v. McGhee*, 130 S.Ct. 1047 (2010).

12. *See United States v. Salerno*, 481 U.S. 739, 107 S.Ct. 2095, 95 L.Ed.2d 697 (1987) (authorizing preventive detention of qualifying individuals charged with federal crimes, subject to accompanying procedural safeguards); *Schall v. Martin*, 467 U.S. 253, 104 S.Ct. 2403, 81 L.Ed.2d 207 (1984) (authorizing pretrial detention of suspected juvenile offenders pursuant to state law).

13. Weld, H. P., & Roff, M. (1938). A study in the formation of opinion based upon legal evidence. *The American Journal of Psychology, LI*, 609–628.

14. For a general review, see Steblay, N., Besirevic, J., Fulero, S. M., & Jiminez-Lorente, B. (1999). The effects of pretrial publicity on juror verdicts: A meta-analytic review. *Law and Human Behavior, 23*, 219–235.

15. Dane, F. C. (1989). In search of reasonable doubt: A systematic examination of selected quantification approaches. *Law and Human Behavior, 9*, 141–158. See also, Simon, R. J. (1970). "Beyond a reasonable doubt" An experimental attempt at quantification. *Journal of Applied Behavioral Science, 6*, 203–209 and Thomas, E. A. C., & Hogue, A. (1976). Apparent weight of evidence, decision criteria, and confidence ratings in juror decision making. *Psychological Review, 83*, 442–465.

16. Champagne, A., & Nagel, S. (1982). The psychology of judging. In N. L. Kerr & R. M. Bray (Eds.), *The psychology of the courtroom*. New York: Academic Press.

17. Kagehiro, D. K., & Stanton, W. C. (1985). Legal vs. quantified definitions of standards of proof. *Law and Human Behavior, 9*, 159–178.

18. C. Ronald Huff, "Wrongful Conviction in the United States," in C. Ronald Huff & Martin Killias, eds., *Wrongful Conviction: International Perspectives on Miscarriages of Justice* 59, 65 (Philadelphia: Temple University Press 2008).

19. *See, e.g.*, George C. Thomas III, Gordon G. Young, Keith Sharfman & Kate B. Briscoe, "Is It Ever Too Late for Innocence? Finality, Efficiency, and Claims of Innocence," 64 *University of Pittsburgh Law Review* 263 (2003). *See also Herrera v. Collins*, 506 U.S. 390, 408–411 (1993).

20. *See People v. Phillips*, 30 A.D.3d 621, 817 N.Y.S.2d 373 (2006).

21. Order of the Suffolk County Supreme Court, Indict. Nos. 1535–88, 1290–88 (July 22, 2008), available at http://www.courts.state.ny.us/courts/10jd/suffolk/decisions/TankleffJuly22.pdf (last visited June 28, 2010). *See also* Bruce Lambert, "No Retrial in '88 Double Killing on Long Island," *New York Times* (July 1, 2008), available at http://www.nytimes.com/2008/07/01/nyregion/01tankleff.html?_r=1&ref=arlene_tankleff (last visited June 28, 2010).

22. First Judiciary Act, ch. 20, § 14, 1 Stat. 73, 81–82 (1789).

23. The Judiciary Act of February 5, 1867, ch. 28 § 1, 14 Stat. 385–386.

24. *See, e.g.*, "Habeas Relief for State Prisoners," 38 *Georgetown Law Journal Annual Review of Criminal Procedure* 892 (2009); Anne R. Traum, "Last Best Chance for the Great Writ: Equitable Tolling and Federal Habeas Corpus," 68 *Maryland Law Review* 545 (2009); Lee Kovarsky, "AEDPA's Wrecks: Comity, Finality, and Federalism," 82 *Tulane Law Review* 443 (2007).

25. *House v. Bell*, 547 U.S. 518, 538, 126 S.Ct. 2064, 165 L.Ed.2d 1 (2006). *See also Schlup v. Delo*, 513 U.S. 298, 327, 115 S.Ct. 851, 130 L.Ed.2d 808 (1995).

26. *In re Davis*, 565 F.3d 810, 814 (11th Cir. 2009) (per curiam).

27. *Davis v. State*, 660 S.E.2d 354 (Ga. 2008).

28. *In re Davis*, 565 F.3d 810, 813 (11th Cir. 2009) (per curiam).

29. *Id.*, 565 F.3d, at 827 (Barkett, J., dissenting).

30. Bill Rankin, "Witnesses Back Off Testimony Against Troy Davis," *The Atlanta Journal-Constitution* (June 23, 2010), available at http://www.ajc.com/news/atlanta/witnesses-back-off-testimony-555778.html (last visited June 29, 2010).

Chapter 3

1. Innocence Project, *Eyewitness Misidentification*, available at http://www.innocenceproject.org/understand/Eyewitness-Misidentification.php (last visited June 30, 2010).

2. *Id.*

3. Stern, L. W. (1910). Abstracts of lectures in the psychology of testimony and on the study of individuality. *American Journal of Psychology, 21*, 270–282. Stern, L. W. (1939). The psychology of testimony. *Journal of Abnormal and Social Psychology, 34*, 3–20.

4. Loftus, E. F. (1975). Leading questions and the eyewitness report. *Cognitive Psychology, 7*, 560–572.

5. Wells, G. (1978). Applied eyewitness testimony research: System variables and estimator variables. *Journal of Personality and Social Psychology, 36*, 1546–1577.

6. Wells, G., Small, M., Penrod, S., Malpass, R. S., Fulero, S. M., & Brimacombe, C. A. E. (1998). Eyewitness identification procedures: Recommendations for lineups and photospreads. *Law and Human Behavior, 22*, 603–647.

7. Available at http://www.ncjrs.gov/pdffiles1/nij/178240.pdf.

8. Although Wells *et al.* (1998) acknowledge that sequential lineups would be their fifth recommendation.

9. Mecklenburg, S. (2006). Report to the legislature of the state of Illinois: The Illinois pilot program on sequential double-blind identification procedures. Available at http://www.psychology.iastate.edu/faculty/gwells/Illinois_Report.pdf.

10. See special issue of *Law and Human Behavior, Volume 32, Issue* 1. e.g, Schacter, D. L., Dawes, R., Jacoby, L. L., Kahneman, D., Lempert, R., Roediger, H. L., & Rosenthal., R. (2007). Policy forum: Studying eyewitness investigations in the field. *Law and Human Behavior*. Available at http://www.jjay.cuny.edu/extra/policyforum.pdf.

11. Steblay, N. K. (2010). What we know now: The Evanston Illinois field lineups. *Law and Human Behavior*. Published online 23 February 2010.

12. E.g., O'Toole, T. P. (2006). What's the matter with Illinois? How an opportunity was squandered to conduct an important study on eyewitness identification procedures. *Champion Magazine, August*, p. 18. Available at http://www.nacdl.org/public.nsf/01c1e7698280d20385256d0b00789923/03c451bfa6487584852571e300634d51?OpenDocument.

13. *See also* New Jersey Dept. of Public Safety, Attorney General Guidelines for Preparing and Conducting Photo and Live Lineup Identification Procedures, available at http://www.state.nj.us/lps/dcj/agguide/photoid.pdf (last visited July 3, 2010).

14. Report of the Special Master, *State v. Henderson*, available at http://www.judiciary.state.nj.us/pressrel/HENDERSON%20FINAL%20BRIEF%20.PDF%20%2800621142%29.PDF (last visited July 3, 2010).

Chapter 4

1. Gerald W. McFarland, *The "Counterfeit" Man: The True Story of the Boorn-Colvin Murder Case* 166 (New York: Pantheon Books 1990), *quoting* the *Rutland Herald*. The wrongful convictions of Jesse and Stephen Boorn for murdering Russell Colvin are discussed in Chapter 1.

2. Tom Wells & Richard A. Leo, *The Wrong Guys: Murder, False Confessions, and the Norfolk Four* 251 (New York: The New Press 2008). *See also* James R. Acker & Catherine L. Bonventre, "Protecting the Innocent in New York: Moving Beyond Changing Only Their Names," 73 *Albany Law Review* 101, 160–163 (2010).

3. Innocence Project, *The Causes of Wrongful Conviction*, available at http://www.innocenceproject.org/understand/ (last visited July 6, 2010). *See also,* Innocence Project, *False Confessions*, available at http://www.innocenceproject.org/understand/False-Confessions.php (last visited July 6, 2010). Another authority reports that, through early 2010, "postconviction DNA testing has exonerated 252 convicts, forty-two of whom falsely confessed to rapes and murders." Brandon L. Garrett, "The Substance of False Confessions," 62 *Stanford Law Review* 1051, 1052 (2010) (footnote omitted).

4. Saul M. Kassin, "False Confessions: Causes, Consequences, and Implications for Reform," 17 *Current Directions in Psychological Science* 249, 249 (2008). *See also* Saul M. Kassin & Lawrence S. Wrightsman, "Confession Evidence," in Saul M. Kassin & Lawrence S. Wrightsman, eds., *The Psychology of Evidence and Trial Procedure* 67, 76–80 (Beverly Hills, CA: Sage Publications 1985).

5. *See* Richard A. Leo, Steven A. Drizin, Peter J. Neufeld, Bradley R. Hall & Amy Vatner, "Bringing Reliability Back In: False Confessions and Legal Safeguards in the Twenty-First Century," 2006 *Wisconsin*

Law Review 479 (2006); Steven A. Drizin & Richard A. Leo, "The Problem of False Confessions in the Post-DNA World," 82 *North Carolina Law Review* 891 (2004).

6. *See* Saul M. Kassin, Steven A. Drizin, Thomas Grisso, Gisli H. Gudjonsson, Richard A. Leo & Allison D. Redlich, "Police-Induced Confessions: Risk Factors and Recommendations," 34 *Law & Human Behavior* 3 (2010); Richard A. Leo & Brittany Liu, "What Do Potential Jurors Know About Police Interrogation Techniques and False Confessions?" 27 *Behavioral Sciences and the Law* 381 (2009); Saul M. Kassin, Christian A. Meissner & Rebecca J. Norwick, "'I'd Know a False Confession if I Saw One': A Comparative Study of College Students and Police Investigators," 29 *Law & Human Behavior* 211 (2005).

7. *See* Brandon L. Garrett, "Judging Innocence," 108 *Columbia Law Review* 55, 61 (2008).

8. William T. Pizzi, "*Colorado v. Connelly*: What Really Happened?" 7 *Ohio State Journal of Criminal Law* 377, 389 (2009).

9. For more about these cases and others, see Rob Warden & Steven A. Drizin, *True Stories of False Confessions* (Evanston, IL: Northwestern University Press 2009). *See also* innocenceproject.org; www.martytankleff.org; Edds, Margaret. 2003. *An Expendable Man: The Near-Execution of Earl Washington, Jr.* New York: New York University Press; Grisham, John. 2006. *The Innocent Man: Murder and Injustice in a Small Town.* New York: Doubleday; Firstman, Richard & Jay Salpeter. 2008. *A Criminal Injustice: A True Crime, a False Confession, and the Fight to Free Marty Tankleff.* New York: Ballantine Books; Sullivan, Timothy. 1992. *Unequal Verdicts: The Central Park Jogger Trials.* New York: Simon & Schuster.

10. Drizin & Leo, *supra* note 5.

11. Allison D. Redlich and Gail S. Goodman (2003). Taking responsibility for an act not committed: The influence of age and suggestibility. *Law and Human Behavior, 27*, 141–156.

12. *See* Richard Firstman & Jay Salpeter, *A Criminal Injustice: A True Crime, a False Confession, and the Fight to Free Marty Tankleff* 562–581 (New York: Ballantine Books 2008).

13. Allison D. Redlich and Christian Meissner (2009). Techniques and controversies in the interrogation of suspects: The artful practice versus the scientific study. In J.L. Skeem, K. Douglas, and S. Lilienfeld (Eds). *Psychological science in the courtroom: Controversies and concerns* (pp. 124–148). New York: The Guilford Press.

14. See generally, Bond, C. F., & DePaulo, B. M. (2006). Accuracy of deception judgments. *Personality and Social Psychology Bulletin, 10*, 214–234.; DePaulo, B. M., Lindsay, J. J., Malone, B. E., Muhlenbruck, L., Charlton, K., & Cooper, H. (2003). Cues to deception. *Psychological Bulletin, 129*, 74–118.; Vrij, A. (2000). *Detecting lies and deceit: The psychology of lying and its implications for professional practice.* Chichester: Wiley; Vrij, A., Granhag, P. A., & Porter, S. (2010). Pitfalls and opportunities in nonverbal and verbal lie detection. *Psychological Science in the Public Interest, 11*, 89–121.

15. Saul M. Kassin and Gisli H. Gudjonsson (2004). The psychology of confessions: A review of the literature and issues. *Psychological Science in the Public Interest, 5*, 33–67.

16. Drizin & Leo, *supra* note 5.

17. Kassin, S. M., Meissner, C. A., & Norwick, R. J. (2005). "I'd know a false confession if I saw one": A comparative study of college students and police investigators. *Law and Human Behavior, 29*, 211–227.

18. Garrett, *supra* note 3.

19. *Id.*, at 1086 (footnotes and internal citations omitted).

20. Mark Costanzo, Netta Shaked-Schroer, and Katherine Vinson (2010). Juror beliefs about police interrogations, false confessions, and expert testimony. *Journal of Empirical Legal Studies, 7*, 231–247.

21. E.g., Chojnacki, D. E., Cicchini, M. D., and White, L. T. (2008). An empirical basis for the admission of expert testimony on false confessions. *Arizona State Law Journal, 40*, 1–45.

22. *See, e.g., Yarborough v. Alvarado*, 541 U.S. 652, 124 S.Ct. 2140, 158 L.Ed.2d 958 (2004); *Berkemer v. McCarty*, 468 U.S. 420, 104 S.Ct. 3138, 82 L.Ed.2d 317 (1984).

23. *See, e.g., Arizona v. Mauro*, 481 U.S. 520, 107 S.Ct. 1931, 95 L.Ed.2d 458 (1987); *Rhode Island v. Innis*, 446 U.S. 291, 100 S.Ct. 1682, 64 L.Ed.2d 297 (1980).

24. *See, e.g., Florida v. Powell*, ___ U.S. ___, 130 S.Ct. 1195, ___ L.Ed.2d ___ (2010); *Duckworth v. Eagan*, 492 U.S. 195, 109 S.Ct. 2875, 106 L.Ed.2d 166 (1989).

25. *See, e.g., Berghuis v. Thompkins*, ___ U.S. ___, 130 S.Ct. 2250, 176 L.Ed.2d 1098 (2010); *Maryland v. Shatzer*, ___ U.S. ___, 130 S.Ct. 1213, 175 L.Ed.2d 1045 (2010); *Davis v. United States*, 512 U.S. 452, 114 S.Ct. 2350, 129 L.Ed.2d 362 (1994); *Fare v. Michael C.*, 442 U.S. 707, 99 S.Ct. 2560, 61 L.Ed.2d 197 (1979).

26. *Washington v. Commonwealth*, 323 S.E.2d 577, 585–586 (Va. 1984).

27. *See* Garrett, *supra* note 3, at 1075–1077; Rob Warden & Steven A. Drizin, eds., *True Stories of False Confessions* 235–248 (Evanston, IL: Northwestern University Press 2009); Jon B. Gould, *The Innocence Commission: Preventing Wrongful Convictions and Restoring the Criminal Justice System* 79–83, 155–156 (New York: New York University Press 2008); Virginia Law School, *Wrongfully Convicted Death Row Inmate Wins Civil Suit with Help from Virginia Law Students*, available at http://www.law.virginia.edu/html/news/

2006_spr/washington.htm (last visited July 10, 2010); Margaret Edds, *An Expendable Man: The Near-Execution of Earl Washington, Jr.* (New York: New York University Press 2003); Paul T. Hourihan, "Earl Washington's Confession: Mental Retardation and the Law of Confessions," 81 *Virginia Law Review* 1471 (1995).

28. *See, e.g.*, D.C. Code § 5-116.01 (2005); 725 ILCS 5/103-2.1 (2005); Me. Rev. Stat. Ann. § 2803-B (1)(K) (2005); Md. Code Crim. Pro. § 2-402 (2009); Mo Rev. Stat. §§ 590.701.1-590.701.7 (2009); Mont. Code Ann. §§ 46-4-406 through 46-4-411 (2009); Neb. Rev. Stat. §§ 29-4501 through 29-4508 (2008); N.M. Stat. Ann. § 29-1-16 (2006); N.C.G.S. § 15A-211 (2008); Ohio Rev. Code Ann. § 2933.81 (2010); Or. Rev. Stat. § 133.400 (2010); Tex. Code Crim. Pro. Art. 38.22 (3) (a) (2005); Wis. Stat. Ann. § 968.073 (2005).

29. N.J. Rule of Court 3:17 (2010).

30. For a list of states and individual jurisdictions that record interrogations, see Appendix B in Thomas P. Sullivan and Andrew W. Vail (2009). The consequence of law enforcement officials' failure to record custodial interviews as required by law. *The Journal of Criminal Law and Criminology, 99*, 215–234.

31. Thomas Sullivan (2010). The wisdom of custodial recording. In G. D. Lassiter and C. A. Meissner (Eds.) *Police interrogations and false confessions* (pp. 174–127). Washington, DC: APA Press.

32. Kassin *et al.*, *supra* note 6.

33. For an overview, see Lassiter, G. D. (in press). Psychological science and sound public policy: Video recording custodial interrogations. *American Psychologist.*

34. Costanzo, Mark, and Richard A. Leo. 2007. Research and expert testimony on Interrogations and confessions. In *Expert Psychological Testimony for the Courts*. Edited by Mark Costanzo, Daniel Krauss, and Kathy Pezdek, 69–98. Mahwah, NJ: Erlbaum.

35. Blandon-Gitlin, Iris, Katheryn Sperry, and Richard Leo. 2010. Jurors believe interrogation tactics are not likely to elicit false confessions: Will expert witness testimony inform them otherwise? *Psychology, Crime, and Law, 16*, 1477–2744. See also, Moffa, M.S. and Platania, J. (2007). Effects of expert testimony on interrogation tactics on perceptions of confessions. *Psychological Reports, 100*, 563–570.

36. *People of the State of California v. Catarino Gonzalez.* Los Angeles County Superior Court. Los Angeles, CA.

Chapter 5

1. *See* Samuel R. Gross, Kristen Jacoby, Daniel J. Matheson, Nicholas Montgomery & Sujata Patil, "Exonerations in the United States 1989 Through 2003," 95 *Journal of Criminal Law & Criminology* 523, 533–535 (2005) (discussing scandals involving the Los Angeles Police Department Ramparts Division (Community Resources Against Street Hoodlums, or "CRASH" unit) and police in Tulia, Texas, that resulted in numerous wrongful convictions for firearms and drug offenses); Peter A. Joy, "The Relationship Between Prosecutorial Misconduct and Wrongful Convictions: Shaping Remedies for a Broken System," 2006 *Wisconsin Law Review* 399, 399 (2006), *quoting* Ken Armstrong & Maurice Possley, "Trial & Error; How Prosecutors Sacrifice Justice to Win; The Verdict: Dishonor," *Chicago Tribune* § 1, p. 1 (Jan. 10, 1999):

> With impunity, prosecutors across the country have violated their oaths and the law, committing the worst kinds of deception in the most serious of cases.
>
> They have prosecuted black men, hiding evidence the real killers were white. They have prosecuted a wife, hiding evidence her husband committed suicide. They have prosecuted parents, hiding evidence their daughter was killed by wild dogs.
>
> They do it to win.
>
> They do it because they won't get punished.
>
> They have done it to defendants who came within hours of being executed, only to be exonerated.

2. Miller's case is discussed in detail in Willard J. Lassers, *Scapegoat Justice: Lloyd Miller and the Failure of the American Legal System* (Bloomington, IN: Indiana University Press 1973), and it is summarized in Michael J. Radelet, Hugo Adam Bedau & Constance E. Putnam, *In Spite of Innocence: The Ordeal of 400 Americans Wrongly Convicted of Crimes Punishable by Death* 141–152 (Boston: Northeastern University Press 1992). In addition to the Supreme Court's 1967 ruling in *Miller v. Pate*, court decisions relating to Miller's case include *People v. Miller,* 148 N.E.2d 455 (Ill. 1958) (affirming his conviction and death sentence); *United States ex rel. Miller v. Pate,* 226 F.Supp. 541 (N.D. Il. 1963) (vacating Miller's conviction on federal habeas corpus); and *United States ex rel. Miller v. Pate,* 342 F.2d 646 (7th Cir. 1965) (reversing the district court's order granting relief).

3. Lassers, *supra,* at 3–4.

4. *Id.*, at 228 (footnote omitted).

5. Jeffrey W. Lucas, Corina Graif, and Michael J. Lovaglia (2008). Prosecutorial misconduct in serious cases: Theory and design of a laboratory experiment. In C. Horne & M. J. Lovaglia (Eds.), *Experiments in criminology and law* (pp. 119–135). Lanham, MD: Rowman & Littlefield Publishers, Inc.

6. Death Penalty Information Center, *Innocence: Curtis Kyles*, available at http://www.deathpenaltyinfo.org/innocence-cases-1994-2003 (last visited March 10, 2011).

7. Alafair Burke (2007). *Brady*'s brainteaser: The accidental prosecutor and cognitive bias. *Case Western Law Review*, 57, 575.

8. The Center for Public Integrity (2003). Harmful error: Investigating America's local prosecutors. http://projects.publicintegrity.org/pm/. See also The Justice Project's *Improving prosecutorial accountability: A policy review.* http://www.thejusticeproject.org/national/solution/ensuring-proper-safeguards-against-prosecutorial-misconduct.

9. Rachel E. Barkow (2010). Organizational guidelines for the prosecutor's office. *Cardozo Law Review, 31*, 2089–2118.

10. *See* Innocence Project, *Larry Youngblood,* available at http://www.innocenceproject.org/Content/303.php (last visited July 20, 2010); Religion & Ethics, *DNA and Fair Trials,* available at http://www.pbs.org/wnet/religionandethics/week941/feature.html (last visited July 20, 2010); Tim O'Brien, "Reasonable Doubt and DNA," *Washington Post* (Sept. 7, 2000), available at http://www.deathpenaltyinfo.org/node/646 (last visited July 20, 2010).

11. *See, e.g.,* Bennett L. Gershman, "Litigating *Brady v.* Maryland: Games Prosecutors Play," 57 *Case Western Reserve Law Review* 531 (2007); Eugene Cerruti, "Through the Looking-Glass at the *Brady* Doctrine: Some New Reflections on White Queens, Hobgoblins, and Due Process," 94 *Kentucky Law Journal* 211 (2005–2006); Scott E. Sundby, "Fallen Superheroes and Constitutional Mirages: The Tale of *Brady v. Maryland,*" 33 *McGeorge Law Review* 643 (2002).

12. "The Innocence Project recently concluded a preliminary review of its closed cases from the last 10 years. Initial findings show that 32% of all closed cases were closed due to reports that evidence had been lost or destroyed.... When the Innocence Project closes a case, efforts to prove a prisoner's innocence through DNA testing end—because no evidence can be located for DNA testing, despite repeated searches that usually last several years." Innocence Project, *DNA Exoneration Cases Where Evidence Was Believed Lost or Destroyed,* available at http://www.innocenceproject.org/Content/396.php (last visited July 21, 2010).

13. Clemency statement of Governor Mark R. Warner, *quoted in* Cynthia E. Jones, "The Right Remedy for the Wrongly Convicted: Judicial Sanctions for Destruction of DNA Evidence," 77 *Fordham Law Review* 2893, 2896 (2009).

14. *See* Innocence Project, *Preservation of Evidence,* available at http://www.innocenceproject.org/Content/Preservation_Of_Evidence.php# (last visited July 21, 2010); Norman C. Bay, "Old Blood, Bad Blood, and *Youngblood*: Due Process, Lost Evidence, and the Limits of Bad Faith," 86 *Washington University Law Review* 241, 284–285 (2008).

15. Innocence Project, *Access to Post-Conviction DNA Testing,* available at http://www.innocenceproject.org/Content/304.php# (last visited July 21, 2010).

16. *See generally* Michael E. Kleinert, Note, "Improving the Quality of Justice: The Innocence Protection Act of 2004 Ensures Post-Conviction DNA Testing, Better Legal Representation, and Increased Compensation for the Wrongfully Imprisoned," 44 *Brandeis Law Journal* 491 (2006).

17. *See Heck v. Humphrey,* 512 U.S. 477, 114 S.Ct. 2364, 129 L.Ed.2d 383 (1994).

Chapter 6

1. *See, e.g.,* James R. Acker, *Scottsboro and Its Legacy: The Cases that Challenged American Legal and Social Justice* (Westport, CT: Praeger Publishers 2008); Dan T. Carter, *Scottsboro: A Tragedy of the American South* (Baton Rouge, LA: Louisiana State University Press, rev. ed. 1979); James Goodman, *Stories of Scottsboro* (New York: Vintage Books 1994).

2. *Gideon* overruled *Betts v. Brady,* 316 U.S. 455, 62 S.Ct. 1252, 86 L.Ed. 1595 (1942), which had conditioned the right to court-appointed counsel on the presence of "special circumstances" that would cause a layperson being required to represent him- or herself at a criminal trial to be fundamentally unfair under Due Process principles.

3. See National Center for State Courts, Court Statistics Project http://www.ncsconline.org/D_Research/csp/2008_files/Criminal.pdf.

4. *See generally* Emily Garcia Uhrig, "A Case for a Constitutional Right to Counsel in Habeas Corpus," 60 *Hastings Law Journal* 541 (2009); Sarah L. Thomas, "A Legislative Challenge: A Proposed Model Statute

to Provide for the Appointment of Counsel in State Habeas Corpus Proceedings for Indigent Prisoners," 54 *Emory Law Journal* 1139 (2005).

5. 18 U.S.C. § 3599 (a) (2) (2006); *see generally McFarland v. Scott,* 512 U.S. 849, 114 S.Ct. 2568, 129 L.Ed.2d 666 (1994) (reviewing case brought under 21 U.S.C. § 841q (4) (b) (1988) (since repealed)).

6. Martiga Lohn, "Koua Fong Lee, 'Toyota Defense' Driver Who Killed Three in Crash, Will Go Free," *Huffington Post,* Aug. 6, 2010, available at http://www.huffingtonpost.com/2010/08/06/koua-fong-lee-toyota-defe_0_n_673040.html, last visited November 27, 2010; Peter Whoriskey, "Recalls Cast New Light on Toyota Crash Case," *Washington Post,* Aug. 5, 2010, available at http://www.washingtonpost.com/wp-dyn/content/article/2010/08/05/AR2010080503502.html, last visited November 27, 2010.

7. Emily M. West, *Court Findings of Ineffective Assistance of Counsel Claims in Post-Conviction Appeals Among the First 255 DNA Exoneration Cases* 3 (Innocence Project 2010), available at http://www.innocenceproject.org/docs/Innocence_Project_IAC_Report.pdf, last visited November 27, 2010.

8. *Id.* at 1.

9. Stephanos Bibas, "Plea Bargaining Outside the Shadow of Trial," 117 *Harvard Law Review* 2463 (2004); Rodney Uphoff, "Convicting the Innocent: Aberration or Systemic Problem?" 2006 *Wisconsin Law Review* 739 (2006).

10. Uphoff, *supra* note 9, at 752 (citations omitted).

11. See note 7.

12. *See, e.g.,* American Bar Association Criminal Justice Section, *Achieving Justice: Freeing the Innocent, Convicting the Guilty* 87–89 (Chicago: American Bar Association 2006).

Chapter 7

1. Eric Lichtblau, "U.S. Will Pay $2 Million to Lawyer Wrongly Jailed," *New York Times* (Nov. 30, 2006); Steven T. Wax & Christopher J. Schatz, "A Multitude of Errors: The Brandon Mayfield Case," *Champion Magazine* 6 (Sept./Oct. 2004); Sarah Kershaw, "Spain and U.S. at Odds on Mistaken Terror Arrest," *New York Times* (June 5, 2004).

2. Thomas Frisbie & Randy Garrett, *Victims of Justice Revisited* 68 (Evanston, IL: Northwestern University Press 2005).

3. *See* authorities cited in Chapter 2, n. 4. With particular respect to Dr. Robbins' discredited testimony, *see* Thomas Frisbie & Randy Garrett, *Victims of Justice Revisited* 67–70, 200–208 (Evanston, IL: Northwestern University Press 2005); Paul C. Giannelli, "The Abuse of Scientific Evidence in Criminal Cases: The Need for Independent Crime Laboratories," 4 *Virginia Journal of Social Policy & Law* 439, 457–462 (1997).

4. *See* David Grann, "Trial by Fire: Did Texas Execute an Innocent Man?" *The New Yorker* (Sept. 7, 2009), available at http://www.newyorker.com/reporting/2009/09/07/090907fa_fact_grann (last visited December 31, 2010). *See also* Craig L. Beyler, *Analysis of the Fire Investigation Methods and Procedures Used in the Criminal Arson Cases Against Ernest Ray Willis and Cameron Todd Willingham* (submitted to the Texas Forensic Science Commission, Aug. 17, 2009), available at http://alt.coxnewsweb.com/sharedblogs/austin/investigative/upload/2009/08/execution_based_on _bad_investi/D_Beyler%20FINAL%20REPORT%20082509.pdf (last visited December 31, 2010). A broadcast of a PBS Frontline program featuring Willingham's case, *Death by Fire,* is available for viewing at http://www.pbs.org/wgbh/pages/frontline/death-by-fire/ (last visited December 31, 2010).

5. *See* Allan Turner, Cindy Horswell & Mike Tolson, "Hair Casts Doubt on Executed Man's Guilt," *Houston Chronicle* (Nov. 12, 2010), available at http://www.chron.com/disp/story.mpl/metropolitan/7290273.html (last visited December 31, 2010); Barry C. Scheck, "Capital Punishment and Human Fallibility," *Wall Street Journal* (Nov. 27, 2010), available at http://online.wsj.com/article/SB10001424052748704638304575636720145607414.html (last visited December 31, 2010).

6. Innocence Project, *Wrongful Convictions Involving Unvalidated or Improper Forensic Science that Were Later Overturned through DNA Testing,* available at http://www.innocenceproject.org/docs/DNA_Exonerations_Forensic_Science.pdf (last visited December 31, 2010).

7. *Id. See also* Brandon J. Garrett & Peter J. Neufeld, "Invalid Forensic Science Testimony and Wrongful Convictions," 95 *Virginia Law Review* 1 (2009).

8. Committee on Identifying the Needs of the Forensic Sciences Community, National Research Council, *Strengthening Forensic Science in the United States: A Path Forward* (Washington, DC: United States Dept. of Justice 2009), available at http://www.ncjrs.gov/pdffiles1/nij/grants/228091.pdf (last visited December 31, 2010).

9. *Id.,* at 3–4.

10. *Id.*, at 6–7.

11. *Id.*, at 9.

12. *Id.*, at 19–20.

13. *See generally,* Paul C. Giannelli & Edward J. Imwinkelried, *Scientific Evidence* 1–90, 289–307 (Newark, NJ: LexisNexis 2007); Edward W. Cleary (Ed.), *McCormick on Evidence* 30–45 (St. Paul, MN: West Publishing Co., 3d ed. 1984).

14. Congress amended Federal Rule of Evidence 702 in 2000. The Rule now provides: "If scientific, technical, or other specialized knowledge will assist the trier of fact to understand the evidence or to determine a fact in issue, a witness qualified as an expert by knowledge, skill, experience, training, or education, may testify thereto in the form of an opinion or otherwise, if (1) the testimony is based upon sufficient facts or data, (2) the testimony is the product of reliable principles and methods, and (3) the witness has applied the principles and methods reliably to the facts of the case."

15. Alice B. Lustre, "Post-*Daubert* Standards for Admissibility of Scientific and Other Expert Testimony in State Courts," 90 A.L.R.5th 453 (2001 and cumulative supplement).

16. *See, e.g.*, Simon A. Cole, "Out of the *Daubert* Fire and Into the *Fryeing* Pan? Self-Validation, Meta-Expertise and the Admissibility of Latent Print Evidence in *Frye* Jurisdictions," 8 *Minnesota Journal of Law, Science & Technology* 453 (2008); Paul C. Giannelli, "The Admissibility of Novel Scientific Evidence: *Frye v. United States*, a Half-Century Later," 80 *Columbia Law Review* 1197 (1980); Robert J. Goodwin, "Fifty Years of *Frye* in Alabama: The Continuing Debate Over Adopting the Test Established in *Daubert v. Merrell Dow Pharmaceuticals, Inc.*," 35 *Cumberland Law Review* 231 (2004–2005).

17. *See, e.g.*, Michael F. Baumeister & Dorothea M. Capone, "Admissibility Standards as Politics—The Imperial Gate Closers Arrive!!!," 33 *Seton Hall Law Review* 1025 (2003); David Crump, "The Trouble With *Daubert-Kumho*: Reconsidering the Supreme Court's Philosophy of Science," 68 *Missouri Law Review* 1 (2003); A. Leah Vickers, "*Daubert*, Critique and Interpretation: What Empirical Studies Tell Us About the Application of *Daubert*," 40 *University of San Francisco Law Review* 109 (2005).

18. Sophie I. Gatowski, Shirley A. Dobbin, James T. Richardson, Gerald P. Ginsburg, Mara L. Merlino & Veronica Dahir, "Asking the Gatekeepers: A National Survey of Judges on Judging Expert Evidence in a Post-*Daubert* World," 25 *Law and Human Behavior* 433 (2001).

19. *See State v. A.O.*, 965 A.2d 152 (N.J. 2009) (collecting cases); George L. Blum, "Admissibility in State Criminal Case of Results of Polygraph (Lie Detector) Test—Post-*Daubert* Cases," 10 A.L.R.6th 463 (2006 and cumulative supplement); Vincent V. Vigluicci, "Calculating Credibility: *State v. Sharma* and the Future of Polygraph Admissibility in Ohio and Beyond," 42 *Akron Law Review* 319 (2009).

20. *Lee v. Martinez*, 96 P.3d 291 (N.M. 2004).

21. *See, e.g.*, Simon A. Cole, "Out of the *Daubert* Fire and Into the *Fryeing* Pan? Self-Validation, Meta-Expertise and the Admissibility of Latent Print Evidence in *Frye* Jurisdictions," 8 *Minnesota Journal of Law, Science & Technology* 453 (2008); Jennifer L. Mnookin, "The Courts, the NAS, and the Future of Forensic Science," 75 *Brooklyn Law Review* 1209 (2010); Dorothy E. Schmidt, "A Dark and Stormy Night: The Mystery of the Missing Science in Fingerprint Identification," 75 *Defense Counsel Journal* 47 (2008); Katherine Schwinghammer, "Fingerprint Identification: How 'The Gold Standard of Evidence' Could Be Worth Its Weight," 32 *American Journal of Criminal Law* 265 (2005).

22. Itiel E. Dror, David Charlton & Ailsa E. Peron, "Contextual Information Renders Experts Vulnerable to Making Erroneous Identifications," 156 *Forensic Science International* 74 (2006).

23. Committee on Scientific Assessment of Bullet Lead Elemental Composition Comparison, National Research Council of the National Academies of Science, *Forensic Analysis Weighing Bullet Lead Evidence* 5 (Washington, DC: The National Academies Press 2004).

24. *Id.*, at 112–113.

25. John Solomon, "FBI's Forensic Test Full of Holes," *Washington Post* (Nov. 18, 2007), available at http://www.washingtonpost.com/wp-dyn/content/article/2007/11/17/AR2007111701681.html (last visited January 6, 2011). *See also* CBS News, 60 Minutes, "Evidence of Injustice" (Nov. 18, 2007; updated Sept. 14, 2008), available at http://www.cbsnews.com/stories/2007/11/16/60minutes/main3512453.shtml (last visited January 6, 2011).

26. Associated Press, "Discredited Bullet Evidence: 5 Years In, FBI Still Hasn't Finished Review of 2,500 Cases" (Jan. 18, 2010), available at http://blog.cleveland.com/nationworld_impact/print.html?entry=/2010/01/discredited_bullet_evidence_5.html (last visited January 6, 2011). *See also* Innocence Project, "Oregon Man Freed After 10 Years" (Dec. 22, 2009), available at http://www.innocenceproject.org/Content/Oregon_Man_Freed_After_10_Years.php (last visited January 6, 2011).

27. Brandon J. Garrett & Peter J. Neufeld, "Invalid Forensic Science Testimony and Wrongful Convictions," 95 *Virginia Law Review* 1, 70 (2009) (footnotes omitted).

28. Innocence Project, "Ray Krone," available at http://www.innocenceproject.org/Content/Ray_Krone.php (last visited January 22, 2011).

29. *Id.*

30. Garrett & Neufeld, *supra*, 95 *Virginia Law Review*, at 69.

31. *See, e.g.*, Erica Beecher-Monas, "Reality Bites: The Illusion of Science in Bite-Mark Evidence," 30 *Cardozo Law Review* 1369 (2009); Adam Deitch, "An Inconvenient Tooth: Forensic Odontology Is an Inadmissible Junk Science When It Is Used to 'Match' Teeth to Bitemarks in Skin," 2009 *Wisconsin Law Review* 1205 (2009).

32. Committee on Identifying the Needs of the Forensic Sciences Community, National Research Council, *Strengthening Forensic Science in the United States: A Path Forward* 175–176 (Washington, DC: United States Dept. of Justice 2009) (footnotes omitted), available at http://www.ncjrs.gov/pdffiles1/nij/grants/228091.pdf (last visited January 22, 2011).

33. *Fritz v. State*, 811 P.2d 1353 (Okla. Crim. App. 1991); *Williamson v. State*, 812 P.2d 384 (Okla. Crim. App. 1991).

34. Innocence Project, "Ron Williamson," available at http://www.innocenceproject.org/Content/Ron_Williamson.php (last visited January 24, 2011). *See also* Innocence Project, *Dennis Fritz*, available at http://www.innocenceproject.org/Content/Dennis_Fritz.php (last visited January 24, 2011).

35. *Gore v. State*, 119 P.3d 1268 (Okla. Crim. App. 2005).

36. Kristi Eaton, "Life Without Parole Meted Out to Gore," *NewsOK* (June 23, 2006), available at http://newsok.com/life-without-parole-meted-out-to-gore/article/1877021 (last visited January 24, 2011).

37. Margaret A. Berger, "Expert Testimony in Criminal Proceedings: Questions *Daubert* Does Not Answer," 33 *Seton Hall Law Review* 1125, 1134 (2003).

38. *See, e.g., State v. West*, 877 A.2d 787, 806–809 (Conn. 2005); *United States v. Santiago*, 156 F.Supp.2d 145 (D. Puerto Rico 2001); Gregory G. Sarno, "Admissibility and Weight, in Criminal Cases, of Expert or Scientific Evidence Respecting Characteristics and Identification of Human Hair," 23 *A.L.R.4th* 1199 (1983 & 2010 Supp.);

39. Brandon J. Garrett & Peter J. Neufeld, "Invalid Forensic Science Testimony and Wrongful Convictions," 95 *Virginia Law Review* 1, 47 (2009).

40. Edward K. Cheng, "Mitochondrial DNA: Emerging Legal Issues," 13 *Journal of Law and Policy* 99, 108–110 (2005) (footnotes omitted). *See also* Paul C. Giannelli, "Forensic Science: Under the Microscope," 34 *Ohio Northern University Law Review* 315, 331 (2008) ("The number of [DNA-based] exoneration cases which involved the use of microscopic hair analysis (43 out of 200) is remarkable.")

41. Committee on Identifying the Needs of the Forensic Sciences Community, National Research Council, *Strengthening Forensic Science in the United States: A Path Forward* 160–161 (Washington, DC: United States Dept. of Justice 2009) (footnotes omitted), available at http://www.ncjrs.gov/pdffiles1/nij/grants/228091.pdf (last visited January 25, 2011).

42. Richard A. Leo, "Rethinking the Study of Miscarriages of Justice: Developing a Criminology of Wrongful Conviction," 21 *Journal of Contemporary Criminal Justice* 201, 205 (2005).

43. Innocence Project, "Fact Sheet," available at http://www.innocenceproject.org/Content/Facts_on_Post-Conviction_DNA_Exonerations.php# (last visited January 26, 2011).

44. *See* Denise A. Filocoma, "Unravelling the DNA Controversy: *People v. Wesley*, A Step in the Right Direction," 3 *Journal of Law and Policy* 537, 542 & n. 18 (1995); Sally E. Renskers, "Trial by Certainty: Implications of Genetic DNA Fingerprints," 39 *Emory Law Journal* 309, 314 (1990).

45. *See Andrews v. State*, 533 So.2d 841 (Fla. App. 1988), *review denied*, 542 So.2d 1332 (Fla. 1989); *People v. Wesley*, 533 N.Y.S.2d 643 (Misc. 1988), *aff'd*, 633 N.E.2d 451 (N.Y. 1994).

46. *See* Donald E. Shelton, "Twenty-First Century Forensic Science Challenges for Trial Judges in Criminal Cases: Where the 'Polybutadiene' Meets the 'Bitumen'," 18 *Widener Law Journal* 309, 320–321 (2009); Thomas M. Fleming, "Admissibility of DNA Identification Evidence," 84 *A.L.R.4th* 313 (1991 & 2010 Supp.).

47. Committee on Identifying the Needs of the Forensic Sciences Community, National Research Council, *Strengthening Forensic Science in the United States: A Path Forward* 130 (Washington, DC: United States Dept. of Justice 2009), available at http://www.ncjrs.gov/pdffiles1/nij/grants/228091.pdf (last visited January 26, 2011).

48. *Id.*, at 133.

49. *Id.*

50. Jonathan J. Koehler, "When Are People Persuaded by DNA Match Statistics?" 25 *Law and Human Behavior* 493 (2001).

51. David Zucchino, "North Carolina Man Exonerated After 17 Years," *Los Angeles Times* (Feb. 17, 2010), available at http://articles.latimes.com/print/2010/feb/17/nation/la-na-innocence18-2010feb18 (last visited January 28, 2011).

52. "N.C. SBI Lab Must Report Whole Truth," *Charlotte Observer* (Dec. 29, 2010), available at http://www.charlotteobserver.com/2010/12/29/v-print/1939768/nc-sbi-lab-must-report-whole-truth.html (last visited January 28, 2011).

53. "A Look at NC Crime Lab Committee's Recommendations," *Charlotte Observer* (Jan. 18, 2011), available at http://www.charlotteobserver.com/2011/01/18/v-print/1990383/a-look-at-nc-crime-lab-committees.html (last visited January 28, 2011).

54. Adam Liptak & Ralph Blumenthal, "New Doubt Cast on Testing in Houston Police Crime Lab," *New York Times* (Aug. 5, 2004), available at http://www.nytimes.com/2004/08/05/us/new-doubt-cast-on-testing-in-houston-police-crime-lab.html?pagewanted=print&src=pm (last visited January 28, 2011).

55. *Id.;* Innocence Project, "George Rodriguez," available at http://www.innocenceproject.org/Content/George_Rodriguez.php (last visited January 28, 2011). *See also* Erin Murphy, "The New Forensics: Criminal Justice, False Certainty, and the Second Generation of Scientific Evidence," 95 *California Law Review* 721, 767 & n.202 (2007).

56. *See* Paul C. Giannelli, "Wrongful Convictions and Forensic Science: The Need to Regulate Crime Labs," 86 *North Carolina Law Review* 163, 174–182 (2007); Mark Furhman, *Death and Justice: An Expose of Oklahoma's Death Row Machine* (New York: William Morrow 2003). *See also McCarty v. State,* 114 P.3d 1089 (Okla. Crim. App. 2005).

57. Brandon L. Garrett, "Judging Innocence," 108 *Columbia Law Review* 55, 64 (2008) (footnote omitted). *See also* James R. Acker & Catherine L. Bonventre, "Protecting the Innocent in New York: Moving Beyond Changing Only Their Names," 73 *Albany Law Review* 1245, 1301–02 (2010); Paul C. Giannelli, "Forensic Science: Under the Microscope," 34 *Ohio Northern University Law Review* 315, 334–335 (2008).

58. Barry Scheck, Peter Neufeld & Jim Dwyer, *Actual Innocence: Five Days to Execution, and Other Dispatches from the Wrongly Convicted* 113 (New York: Doubleday 2000). *See also* Innocence Project, "Forensic Science Misconduct," available at http://www.innocenceproject.org/understand/Forensic-Science-Misconduct.php (last visited January 28, 2011).

59. *See* Paul C. Giannelli, "The Abuse of Scientific Evidence in Criminal Cases: The Need for Independent Crime Laboratories," 4 *Virginia Journal of Social Policy and the Law* 439, 442–449 (1997).

60. Innocence Project, "A Trail of Misconduct and the Need for Reform," available at http://www.innocenceproject.org/Content/A_Trail_of_Misconduct_and_the_Need_for_Reform.php (last visited January 28, 2011).

61. Committee on Identifying the Needs of the Forensic Sciences Community, National Research Council, *Strengthening Forensic Science in the United States: A Path Forward* 182–183 (Washington, DC: United States Dept. of Justice 2009), available at http://www.ncjrs.gov/pdffiles1/nij/grants/228091.pdf (last visited January 28, 2011).

62. *Id.*, at 215.

63. *Id.*, at 216.

64. *Id.*, at 215.

65. *Id.*, at 19–20.

66. Committee on Identifying the Needs of the Forensic Sciences Community, National Research Council, *Strengthening Forensic Science in the United States: A Path Forward* 3 (Washington, DC: United States Dept. of Justice 2009), available at http://www.ncjrs.gov/pdffiles1/nij/grants/228091.pdf (last visited January 28, 2011).

Chapter 8

1. *Webster's College Dictionary* 691 (New York: Random House 1991).

2. American Bar Association, Criminal Justice Section, *Achieving Justice: Freeing the Innocent, Convicting the Guilty—Report of the ABA Criminal Justice Section's Ad Hoc Innocence Committee to Ensure the Integrity of the Criminal Process* 67 (Washington, DC: American Bar Association 2006). *See also* James R. Acker & Catherine L. Bonventre, "Protecting the Innocent in New York: Moving Beyond Changing Only Their Names," 73 *Albany Law Review* 1245, 1316 (2010).

3. Stephen S. Trott, "Words of Warning for Prosecutors Using Criminals as Witnesses," 47 *Hastings Law Journal* 1381, 1383 (1996). The author, the Hon. Steven S. Trott, was a Circuit Judge on the United States Court of Appeals for the Ninth Circuit.

4. *United States v. Dennis,* 183 F.2d 201, 224 (2d Cir. 1950), *aff'd,* 341 U.S. 494 (1951).

5. Innocence Project, *Facts on Post-Conviction DNA Exonerations*, available at http://www.innocenceproject.org/Content/Facts_on_PostConviction_DNA_Exonerations.php (last visited February 3, 2011).

6. Samuel R. Gross, Kristen Jacoby, Daniel J. Matheson, Nicholas Montgomery & Sujata Patil, "Exonerations in the United States 1989 Through 2003," 95 *Journal of Criminal Law & Criminology* 523, 543–544 (2005).

7. Center on Wrongful Convictions, *The Snitch System* 3 (Chicago: Northwestern University School of Law 2004–2005), available at http://www.law.northwestern.edu/wrongfulconvictions/issues/causesandremedies/snitches/SnitchSystemBooklet.pdf (last visited February 3, 2011).

8. *United States v. Singleton,* 144 F.3d 1343, 1344 (10th Cir. 1998), *vacated,* 165 F.3d 1297 (10th Cir. 1999) (en banc).

9. Camille Knight, "The Federal Bribery Statute and the Ethics of Purchasing Testimony," 33 *John Marshall Law Review* 209, 211–212 (1999) (footnotes omitted). *See also* Melissa W. Rawlinson, "*United States v. Singleton* and the Witness Gratuity Statute: What is the Best Approach for the Criminal Justice System?" 14 *Brigham Young University Journal of Public Law* 227, 228 (2000).

10. Jessica K. Swanner, Denise R, Beike, and Alexander T. Cole (2010). Snitching, lies, and computer crashes: An experimental investigation of secondary confessions. *Law and Human Behavior, 34,* 53–65. See also, Jessica K. Swanner and Denise R. Beike (2010). Incentives increase the rate of false but not true secondary confessions from informants with an allegiance to a suspect. *Law and Human Behavior, 34,* 418–428.

11. *Report of the Kaufman Commission on Proceedings Involving Guy Paul Morin, Executive Summary* 1–4 (1996), available at http://www.attorneygeneral.jus.gov.on.ca/english/about/pubs/morin/morin_esumm.pdf (last visited February 5, 2011). *See generally* Steven Skura, "A Canadian Perspective on the Role of Cooperators and Informants," 23 *Cardozo Law Review* 759 (2002); Keith A. Findley, "Learning From Our Mistakes: A Criminal Justice Commission to Study Wrongful Convictions," 38 *California Western Law Review* 333 (2002); Dianne L. Martin, "Distorting the Prosecution Process: Informers, Mandatory Minimum Sentences, and Wrongful Convictions," 39 *Osgoode Hall Law Journal* 513, 525 (2001).

12. Available at http://www.attorneygeneral.jus.gov.on.ca/english/about/pubs/morin/ (last visited February 5, 2011).

13. *Report of the Kaufman Commission on Proceedings Involving Guy Paul Morin, Recommendations* 13–15 (1996), available at http://www.attorneygeneral.jus.gov.on.ca/english/about/pubs/morin/morin_recom.pdf (last visited February 5, 2011).

14. American Bar Association, Criminal Justice Section, *Achieving Justice: Freeing the Innocent, Convicting the Guilty—Report of the ABA Criminal Justice Section's Ad Hoc Innocence Committee to Ensure the Integrity of the Criminal Process* 67 (Washington, DC: American Bar Association 2006).

15. In March 2011, Governor Pat Quinn signed legislation abolishing capital punishment in Illinois.

16. *Report of the Kaufman Commission on Proceedings Involving Guy Paul Morin, Recommendations* 21 (1996), available at http://www.attorneygeneral.jus.gov.on.ca/english/about/pubs/morin/morin_recom.pdf (last visited February 7, 2011).

17. *Id.,* at 23. *See also* Sam Roberts, "Should Prosecutors Be Required to Record Their Pretrial Interviews with Accomplices and Snitches?" 74 *Fordham Law Review* 257 (2005).

18. Manitoba Justice,*The Inquiry Regarding Thomas Sophonow, Recommendations, Jailhouse Informants,* available at http://www.gov.mb.ca/justice/publications/sophonow/recommendations/english.html#jailhouse (last visited February 7, 2011).

19. *People v. Cona,* 399 N.E.2d 1167, 1170 (N.Y. 1979). *See* Acker & Bonventre, *supra,* 73 *Albany Law Review,* at 1317 & n. 327.

20. *See* R. Michael Cassidy, "'Soft Words of Hope:' *Giglio,* Accomplice Witnesses, and the Problem of Implied Inducements," 98 *Northwestern University Law Review* 1129, 1164 & n. 200 (2004).

21. American Bar Association, Criminal Justice Section, *Achieving Justice: Freeing the Innocent, Convicting the Guilty—Report of the ABA Criminal Justice Section's Ad Hoc Innocence Committee to Ensure the Integrity of the Criminal Process* 63 (Washington, DC: American Bar Association 2006).

22. Cassidy, *supra,* 98 *Northwestern University Law Review,* at 1164–65; Erik Lillquist, "Improving Accuracy in Criminal Cases," 41 *University of Richmond Law Review* 897, 918–921 (2007).

23. *Report of the Kaufman Commission on Proceedings Involving Guy Paul Morin, Recommendations* 12 (1996) (emphasis in original), available at http://www.attorneygeneral.jus.gov.on.ca/english/about/pubs/morin/morin_recom.pdf (last visited February 7, 2011).

24. Cal. Penal Code § 1127a(b) (2004).

25. Jeffrey S. Neuschatz, Deah S. Lawson, Jessica K. Swanner, Christian A. Meissner, and Joseph S. Neuschatz, "The Effects of Accomplice Witnesses and Jailhouse Informants on Jury Decision Making," 32 *Law and Human Behavior* 137, 148 (2008).

26. Paul C. Giannelli, "*Brady* and Jailhouse Snitches," 57 *Case Western Reserve Law Review* 593, 611 (2007) (internal citations and footnotes omitted).

27. *Id.,* at 611 n. 93.

Chapter 9

1. Adam Liptak, "Finding Untainted Jurors in the Age of the Internet," *New York Times* (Feb. 28, 2010), available at http://www.nytimes.com/2010/03/01/us/01venue.html (last visited February 11, 2011).

2. *See* Matthew Mastromauro, "Pre-Trial Prejudice 2.0: How YouTube Generated News Coverage Is Set to Complicate the Concepts of Pre-Trial Prejudice Doctrine and Endanger Sixth Amendment Fair Trial Rights," 10 *Journal of High Technology Law* 289 (2010); Gary A. Hengstler, "*Sheppard v. Maxwell* Revisited—Do the Traditional Rules Work for Nontraditional Media?" 71 *Law & Contemporary Problems* 171 (Fall 2008); Gavin Phillipson, "Trial by Media: The Betrayal of the First Amendment's Purpose," 71 *Law & Contemporary Problems* 15 (Fall 2008).

3. *Richmond Newspapers, Inc. v. Virginia,* 448 U.S. 555, 100 S.Ct. 2814, 65 L.Ed.2d 973 (1980).

4. "Appeals Court: Officers' Presence Tainted Jacksonville Man's Trial," *Blackwatch News* (Oct. 22, 2009), available at http://westchesterblackwatch.wordpress.com/2009/10/22/appeals-court-officers%E2%80%99-presence-tainted-jacksonville-man%E2%80%99s-trial/ (last visited February 11, 2011).

5. *See, e.g.,* Jody Lynee Madeira, "When It's Hard to Relate: Can Legal Systems Mitigate the Trauma of Victim-Offender Relationships?" 46 *Houston Law Review* 401, 411–412 (2009); Sierra Elizabeth, "The Newest Spectator Sport: Why Extending Victims' Rights to the Spectators' Gallery Erodes the Presumption of Innocence," 58 *Duke Law Journal* 275 (2008); Meghan E. Lind, "Hearts on Their Sleeves: Symbolic Displays of Emotion by Spectators in Criminal Trials," 98 *Journal of Criminal Law & Criminology* 1147 (2008); Scott Kitner, "The Need and Means to Restrict Spectators from Wearing Buttons at Criminal Trials," 27 *Review of Litigation* 733 (2008); Janet Morrow & Robert Morrow, "A Narrow Grave: Texas Punishment Law in Capital Murder Cases," 43 *South Texas Law Review* 979, 1098–1100 (2002).

6. Jane Dever Prince, "Competency and Credibility: Double Trouble for Child Victims of Sexual Offenses," 9 *Suffolk Journal of Trial and Appellate Advocacy* 113, 114–115 (2004).

7. Several states have enacted statutes providing that children are competent to testify in the criminal cases in which they are the alleged victims of sexual abuse. *See* Michelle L. Morris, "Li'l People, Little Justice: The Effect of the Witness Competency Standard in California in Sexual Abuse Cases," 22 *Journal of Juvenile Law* 113 (2001–2002).

8. *State v. Hanson,* 439 N.W.2d 133, 134 (Wis. 1989).

9. *State v. Williams,* 729 S.W.2d 197, 199 (Mo. 1987).

10. Samuel R. Gross, Kristen Jacoby, Daniel J. Matheson, Nicholas Montgomery & Sujata Patil, "Exonerations in the United States 1989 Through 2003," 95 *Journal of Criminal Law and Criminology* 523, 539 (2005).

11. *Id.,* at 539 (footnotes omitted).

12. Meredith Felise Sopher, "'The Best of All Possible Worlds': Balancing Victims' and Defendants' Rights in the Child Sexual Abuse Case," 63 *Fordham Law Review* 633, 657 (1994) (footnotes omitted). *See also* Jacqueline McMurtrie, "The Role of the Social Sciences in Preventing Wrongful Convictions," 42 *American Criminal Law Review* 1271, 1283 n. 60 (2005) (discussing the McMartin Preschool case, and noting that although the prosecution produced no convictions, Raymond Buckey spent five years in jail over the course of the lengthy proceedings, and Peggy McMartin Buckey spent two years in jail. "The trial proceedings lasted three years and cost taxpayers between $13 million and $15 million."); Edgar W. Butler, Hiroshi Fukurai, Jo-Ellan Dimitrius & Richard Krooth, *Anatomy of the McMartin Child Molestation Case* (New York: University Press of America 2001).

13. Sopher, *supra,* 63 *Fordham Law Review,* at 654–655; McMurtrie, *supra,* 42 *American Criminal Law Review,* at 1283 n. 61.

14. See http://www.ncbi.nlm.nih.gov/pmc/articles/PMC2180422/#APP1; Michael E. Lamb, Yael Orbach, Irit Hershkowitz, Phillip W. Esplin, and Dvora Horowitz, "Structured Forensic Interview Protocols Improve the Quality and Informativeness of Investigative Interviews with Children: A Review of Research Using the NICHD Investigative Interview Protocol," 31 *Child Abuse and Neglect* 1201 (2007).

15. Garven, S., Wood, J. M., & Malpass, R. S., "Allegations of Wrongdoing: The Effects of Reinforcement on Children's Mundane and Fantastic Claims," 85 *Journal of Applied Psychology* 38 (2000).

16. *See Rock v. Arkansas,* 483 U.S. 44, 107 S.Ct. 2704, 97 L.Ed.2d 37 (1987); *Ferguson v. Georgia,* 365 U.S. 570, 81 S.Ct. 756, 5 L.Ed.2d 783 (1961); Edward Roslak, "Game Over: A Proposal to Reform Federal Rule of Evidence 609," 39 *Seton Hall Law Review* 695, 698–701 (2009).

17. *Griffin v. California,* 380 U.S. 609, 85 S.Ct. 1229, 14 L.Ed.2d 106 (1965).

18. John H. Blume, "The Dilemma of the Criminal Defendant with a Prior Record—Lessons from the Wrongfully Convicted," 5 *Journal of Empirical Legal Studies* 477, 483, 499–505 (2008).

19. *See* Edith Green & Mary Dodge, "The Influence of Prior Record Evidence on Juror Decision Making," 19 *Law & Human Behavior* 67 (1995); Roselle L. Wissler & Michael J. Saks, "On the Inefficacy of Limiting Instructions: When Jurors Use Prior Conviction Evidence to Decide on Guilt," 9 *Law & Human Behavior* 37 (1985).

20. *See* "The Usual Suspects," available at http://www.phrases.org.uk/meanings/the-usual-suspects.html (last visited February 14, 2011); "Memorable Quotes for Casablanca," available at http://www.imdb.com/title/tt0034583/quotes (last visited February 14, 2011).

21. Josh Bowers, "Punishing the Innocent," 156 *University of Pennsylvania Law Review* 1117–18 (2008).

22. Edie Greene and Kirk Heilbrun, *Wrightsman's Psychology and the Legal System* (Belmont, CA: Wadworth, 7th ed. 2011).

23. Brandon L. Garrett, "Claiming Innocence," 92 *Minnesota Law Review* 1629, 1655 (2008).

24. *See* John H. Blume, Sheri L. Johnson & Emily Paavola, "Every Juror Wants a Story: Narrative Relevance, Third Party Guilt and the Right to Present a Defense," 44 *American Criminal Law Review* 1069 (2007).

25. *See, e.g.*, Valerie P. Hans, "Empowering the Active Jury: A Genuine Tort Reform," 13 *Roger Williams University Law Review* 39 (2008); Ron Bailey, "Note-Taking by Jurors: Should It Be a Universal Practice?" 46 *Federal Lawyer* 3 (Feb. 1999); Steven D. Penrod & Larry Heuer, "Tweaking Commonsense: Assessing Aids to Jury Decision Making," 3 *Psychology, Public Policy, and Law* 259 (1997); Leonard Pertnoy, "The Jurors' Need to Know vs. The Constitutional Right to a Fair Trial," 97 *Dickinson Law Review* 627 (1993); Leonard B. Sand & Steven Alan Reiss, "A Report on Seven Experiments Conducted by District Court Judges in the Second Circuit," 60 *New York University Law Review* 423 (1985).

26. Ogloff, J, "Two Steps Forward and One Step Backward: The Law and Psychology Movement in the 20th Century," 24 *Law and Human Behavior* 457 (2000); Small, M. A., "Legal Psychology and Therapeutic Jurisprudence," 37 *Saint Louis University Law Journal* 675 (1993).

27. *See Padilla v. Kentucky*, ___ U.S. ___, 130 S.Ct. 1473, 1485 & n. 13, 176 L.Ed.2d 284 (2010) ("[Guilty pleas] account for nearly 95% of all criminal convictions." (*citing* Dept. of Justice, Bureau of Justice Statistics, Sourcebook of Criminal Justice Statistics 2003, p. 418 (31st ed. 2005) (Table 5.17) (only approximately 5%, or 8,612 out of 68,533, of federal criminal prosecutions go to trial); *id.*, at 450 (Table 5.46) (only approximately 5% of all state felony criminal prosecutions go to trial)).

28. Innocence Project, "Facts on Post-Conviction DNA Exonerations," available at http://www.innocenceproject.org/Content/Facts_on_PostConviction_DNA_Exonerations.php (last visited February 16, 2011); Innocence Project, "When the Innocent Plead Guilty," available at http://www.innocenceproject.org/Content/When_the_Innocent_Plead_Guilty.php (last visited February 16, 2011).

29. Samuel R. Gross, Kristen Jacoby, Daniel J. Matheson, Nicholas Montgomery & Sujata Patil, "Exonerations in the United States 1989 Through 2003," 95 *Journal of Criminal Law and Criminology* 523, 536 (2005).

30. *Id.*

31. Kellough, G., & Wortley, S., "Remand for Plea: Bail Decisions and Plea Bargaining as Commensurate Decisions," 42 *British Journal of Criminology* 186 (2002).

32. http://www.mncourts.gov/forms/public/forms/Criminal/Plea_Petition/CRM101.pdf

33. Gregory, W. L., Mowen, J. C., & Linder, D. E., "Social Psychology and Plea Bargaining: Applications, Methodology, and Theory," 36 *Journal of Personality and Social Psychology* 1521 (1978).

34. Avishalom Tor, Oren Gazal-Ayal, & Stephen M. Garcia, "Fairness and Willingness to Accept Plea Bargain Offers," 7 *Journal of Empirical Legal Studies* 97 (2010).

35. Welsh S. White, "Confessions in Capital Cases," 2003 *University of Illinois Law Review* 979, 1009–10 (2003) (footnotes omitted).

36. Daina Borteck, "Pleas for DNA Testing: Why Lawmakers Should Amend State Post-Conviction DNA Testing Statutes to Apply to Prisoners Who Pled Guilty," 25 *Cardozo Law Review* 1429, 1443 (2004) (*quoting* Henry Weinstein, "DNA Testing Clears Texas Murderer and 'Accomplice'," *Los Angeles Times* A10 (Oct. 14, 2000)).

37. *See* White, *supra*, 2003 *University of Illinois Law Review*, at 1010–11; Borteck, *supra*, 25 *Cardozo Law Review*, at 1443–44; Innocence Project, "Christopher Ochoa," available at http://www.innocenceproject.org/Content/Christopher_Ochoa.php (last visited February 18, 2011); The Justice Project, "Christopher Ochoa and Richard Danziger," available at http://www.thejusticeproject.org/texas/christopher-ochoa-and-richard-danziger/ (last visited February 19, 2011); Mark Donald, "Lethal Rejection," *Dallas Observer* (Dec. 12, 2002), available at http://www.dallasobserver.com/2002-12-12/news/lethal-rejection/5/ (last visited February 19, 2011).

38. Stephanos Bibas, "Harmonizing Substantive-Criminal-Law Values and Criminal Procedure: The Case of *Alford* and Nolo Contendere Pleas," 88 *Cornell Law Review* 1361, 1372–1373 & n. 52 (2003) (citing judicial decisions authorizing *Alford* pleas from all states except Indiana, New Jersey, and North Dakota);

Andrew D. Leipold, "How the Pretrial Process Contributes to Wrongful Convictions," 42 *American Criminal Law Review* 1123, 1156 & n. 176 (2005).

39. Bibas, *supra,* 88 *Cornell Law Review,* at 1371 n. 44; Leipold, *supra,* 42 *American Criminal Law Review,* at 1154 n. 165.

40. Redlich, A. D., & Ozdogru, A., "*Alford* Pleas in the Age of Innocence," 27 *Behavioral Sciences and the Law* 467 (2009).

41. Shipley, C. J., "The *Alford* Plea: A Necessary but Unpredictable Tool for the Criminal Defendant," 72 *Iowa Law Review* 1063 (1987).

42. *Id.*

43. *See* JH Dingfelder Stone, "Facing the Uncomfortable Truth: The Illogic of Post-Conviction DNA Testing for Individuals Who Pleaded Guilty," 45 *University of San Francisco Law Review* 47, 50–52 (2010); Brandon L. Garrett, "Claiming Innocence," 92 *Minnesota Law Review* 1629, 1680–81 (2008); Eunyung Theresa Oh, "Innocence After 'Guilt': Postconviction DNA Relief for Innocents Who Pled Guilty," 55 *Syracuse Law Review* 161 (2004); Daina Borteck, "Pleas for DNA Testing: Why Lawmakers Should Amend State Post-Conviction DNA Testing Statutes to Apply to Prisoners Who Pled Guilty," 25 *Cardozo Law Review* 1429 (2004).

44. Generally, see Appelbaum, K. L. & Appelbaum, P. S. (1994). Criminal justice-related competencies in defendants with mental retardation. *Journal of Psychiatry and Law, 22,* 483–503.; Kassin, S. M., Drizin, S., Grisso, T., Gudjonsson, G., Leo, R. A., & Redlich, A. D. (2010). APLS-Approved White Paper, Police-induced confessions: Risk factors and recommendations. *Law and Human Behavior, 34,* 3–38.; Owen-Kostelnik, J., Reppucci, N. D., & Meyer, J. R. (2006). Testimony and interrogation of minors: Assumptions about maturity and morality. *American Psychologist, 61,* 286–304.; Perske, R. (2004). Understanding persons with intellectual disabilities in the criminal justice system: Indicators of progress? *Mental Retardation, 42,* 484–487. Redlich, A. D. (2004). Mental illness, police interrogations, and the potential for false confession. *Psychiatric Services, 55,* 19–21.

45. For example, see, Grisso, T., Steinberg, L., Woolard, J., Cauffman, E., Scott, E., Graham, S., Lexcen, F., Reppucci, N.D., & Schwartz, R. (2003). Juveniles' competence to stand trial: A comparison of adolescents' and adults' capacities as trial defendants. *Law and Human Behavior, 27,* 333–363.; Hoge, S. K., Poythress, N. G., Bonnie, R. J., Monahan, J., Eisenberg, M., & Feucht-Haviar, T. (1997). The MacArthur adjudicative competence study: Diagnosis, psychopathology, and competence-related abilities. *Behavioral Sciences and the Law, 15,* 329–345.

Chapter 10

1. *See generally,* David M. Oshinsky, *Capital Punishment on Trial:* Furman v. Georgia *and the Death Penalty in Modern America* (Lawrence, Kansas: University Press of Kansas 2010); Michael Meltsner, *Cruel and Unusual: The Supreme Court and Capital Punishment* (New York: Random House 1973).

2. *Gregg v. Georgia,* 428 U.S. 153, 96 S.Ct. 2909, 49 L.Ed.2d 859 (1976); *Proffitt v. Florida,* 428 U.S. 242, 96 S.Ct. 2960, 49 L.Ed.2d 913 (1976); *Jurek v. Texas,* 428 U.S. 262, 96 S.Ct. 2950, 49 L.Ed.2d 929 (1976).

3. *Woodson v. North Carolina,* 428 U.S. 280, 96 S.Ct. 2978, 49 L.Ed.2d 944 (1976); *Roberts v. Louisiana,* 428 U.S. 325, 96 S.Ct. 3001, 49 L.Ed.2d 974 (1976).

4. Samuel R. Gross & Barbara O'Brien, "Frequency and Predictors of False Conviction: Why We Know So Little, and New Data on Capital Cases," 5 *Journal of Empirical Legal Studies* 927, 942–943 (2008) (footnotes omitted).

5. *See, e.g.,* Frank R. Baumgartner, Suzanna L. DeBoef & Amber E. Boydstun, *The Decline of the Death Penalty and the Discovery of Innocence* (New York: Cambridge University Press 2008); Michael L. Radelet, "The Role of Innocence in Contemporary Death Penalty Debates," 41 *Texas Tech Law Review* 199 (2008).

6. United States Attorney, Southern District of New York, "Defendants to Face Life in Prison for Murder of Confidential Informant," available at http://www.justice.gov/usao/nys/pressreleases/August04/quinonessentencepr.pdf (last visited February 21, 2011).

7. Death Penalty Information Center, *The Death Penalty in 2010: Year End Report* 3 (Dec. 2010), available at http://www.deathpenaltyinfo.org/documents/2010YearEnd-Final.pdf (last visited February 21, 2011); Death Penalty Information Center, *Number of Executions by State and Region Since 1976,* available at http://www.deathpenaltyinfo.org/number-executions-state-and-region-1976 (last visited February 21, 2011).

8. Governor's Council on Capital Punishment, *Final Report of the Massachusetts Governor's Council on Capital Punishment* 3 (2004), available at http://www.lawlib.state.ma.us/docs/5-3-04Governorsreportcapitalpunishment.pdf (last visited February 21, 2011).

9. D. Michael Risinger, "Innocents Convicted: An Empirically Justified Factual Wrongful Conviction Rate," 97 *Journal of Criminal Law & Criminology* 761, 778 (2007). Risinger cut the number for the numerator in half "to give some cushion against the criticism that it is not beyond every doubt that every person exonerated by DNA was factually innocent." *Id.*, at 774.

10. Samuel R. Gross, "Convicting the Innocent," 4 *Annual Review of Law and Social Science* 173, 176 (2008).

11. *See, e.g.*, Leigh B. Bienen, "Capital Punishment in Illinois in the Aftermath of the Ryan Commutations: Reforms, Economic Realities, and a New Saliency for Issues of Cost," 100 *Journal of Criminal Law & Criminology* 1301 (2010); Rob Warden, "Illinois Death Penalty Reform: How It Happened, What It Promises," 95 *Journal of Criminal Law & Criminology* 381 (2005); Austin Sarat, "Putting a Square Peg in a Round Hole: Victims, Retribution, and George Ryan's Clemency," 84 *North Carolina Law Review* 1345 (2004). Legislation repealing capital punishment in Illinois became effective in 2011.

12. Governor's Commission on Capital Punishment, *Report of the Governor's Commission on Capital Punishment* 188 (Springfield, IL: State of Illinois 2002), available at http://www.idoc.state.il.us/ccp/ccp/reports/commission_report/index.html (last visited February 23, 2011).

13. *See, e.g.*, Margery Malkin Koosed, "Averting Mistaken Executions by Adopting the Model Penal Code's Exclusion of Death in the Presence of Lingering Doubt," 21 *Northern Illinois University Law Review* 41, 54–69 (2001); William J. Bowers, Marla Sandys & Benjamin D. Steiner, "Foreclosed Impartiality in Capital Sentencing: Jurors' Predispositions, Guilt-Trial Experience, and Premature Decision Making," 83 *Cornell Law Review* 1476, 1535–36 (1998).

14. *See Oregon v. Guzek*, 546 U.S. 517, 528–530, 126 S.Ct. 1226, 163 L.Ed.2d 1112 (2006) (Scalia, J., concurring in the judgment); *Franklin v. Lynaugh*, 487 U.S. 164, 174, 108 S.Ct. 2320, 101 L.Ed.2d 155 (1988) (plurality opinion); *Lockhart v. McCree*, 476 U.S. 162, 205, 106 S.Ct. 1758, 90 L.Ed.2d 137 (1986) (Marshall, J., dissenting).

15. *Wainwright v. Witt*, 469 U.S. 412, 424, 105 S.Ct. 844, 83 L.Ed.2d 841 (1985), *quoting Adams v. Texas*, 448 U.S. 38, 45, 100 S.Ct. 2521, 65 L.Ed.2d 581 (1980).

16. *Morgan v. Illinois*, 504 U.S. 719, 112 S.Ct. 2222, 119 L.Ed.2d 492 (1992).

17. *See* Marla Sandys & Scott McClelland, "Stacking the Deck for Guilt and Death: The Failure of Death Qualification to Ensure Impartiality," in James R. Acker, Robert M. Bohm & Charles S. Lanier, eds., *America's Experiment With Capital Punishment: Reflections on the Past, Present, and Future of the Ultimate Penal Sanction* 395 (Durham, NC: Carolina Academic Press, 2d ed. 2003); John H. Blume, Sheri Lynn Johnson & A. Brian Threlkeld, "Probing 'Life Qualification' Through Expanded Voir Dire," 29 *Hofstra Law Review* 1209, 1220–31 (2001).

18. *See id.*, 29 *Hofstra Law Review*, at 1231–47; Craig Haney, "On the Selection of Capital Juries: The Biasing Effects of the Death-Qualification Process," 8 *Law & Human Behavior* 121 (1984); Craig Haney, "Examining Death Qualification: Further Analysis of the Process Effect," 8 *Law & Human Behavior* 133 (1984).

19. *Lockhart v. McCree*, 476 U.S. 162, 170 n. 7 (1986) ("McCree concedes that the State may challenge for cause prospective jurors whose opposition to the death penalty is so strong that it would prevent them from impartially determining a capital defendant's guilt or innocence. *Ipso facto*, the State must be given the opportunity to identify such prospective jurors by questioning them at *voir dire* about their views of the death penalty."); *id.*, 476 U.S., at 293 (Marshall, J., dissenting) (arguing that the majority opinion "overlooks the ease with which nullifiers could be identified before trial without any extended focus on how jurors would conduct themselves at a capital sentencing proceeding. Potential jurors could be asked, for example, 'if there be any reason why any of them could not fairly and impartially try the issue of defendant's guilt in accordance with the evidence presented at the trial and the court's instructions on the law.'" (citation and footnote omitted).

20. It should be noted, however, that both of these studies were of California residents, and suffered from some of the same weaknesses cited by the *Lockhart* Court.

21. Brooke Butler, "Death Qualification and Prejudice: The Effect of Implicit Racism, Sexism, and Homophobia on Capital Defendants' Right to Due Process," 25 *Behavioral Sciences and the Law* 857 (2007); Brooke Butler & Gary Moran, "The Role of Death Qualification and Need for Cognition in Venirepersons' Evaluations of Expert Scientific Testimony in Capital Trials," 25 *Behavioral Sciences and the Law* 561 (2007); Brooke Butler & Gary Moran, "The Impact of Death Qualification, Belief in a Just World, Legal Authoritarianism, and Locus of Control on Venirepersons' Evaluations of Aggravating and Mitigating Circumstances in Capital Trials," 25 *Behavioral Sciences and the Law* 57 (2007); Brooke Butler, "The Role of Death Qualification in Capital Trials Involving Juvenile Defendants," 37 *Journal of Applied Social Psychology* 549 (2007); Brooke Butler, "The Role of Death Qualification in Jurors' Susceptibility to Pretrial Publicity," 37 *Journal of Applied Social Psychology* 115 (2007).

22. Death Penalty Information Center, *The Death Penalty in 2010: Year End Report* 1 (2010), available at http://www.deathpenaltyinfo.org/documents/2010YearEnd-Final.pdf (last visited February 24, 2011).

23. *See* William J. Bowers & Scott E. Sundby, "Why the Downturn in Death Sentences?" in Charles S. Lanier, William J. Bowers & James R. Acker, *The Future of America's Death Penalty: An Agenda for the Next Generation of Capital Punishment Research* 47 (Durham, NC: Carolina Academic Press 2009); Michael L. Radelet, "The Role of the Innocence Argument in Contemporary Death Penalty Debates," 41 *Texas Tech Law Review* 199 (2008); Scott E. Sundby, "The Death Penalty's Future: Charting the Crosscurrents of Declining Death Sentences and the McVeigh Factor," 84 *Texas Law Review* 1929 (2006).

24. Death Penalty Information Center, *The Death Penalty in 2010: Year End Report* 1 (2010), available at http://www.deathpenaltyinfo.org/documents/2010YearEnd-Final.pdf (last visited February 24, 2011).

25. *See* James R. Acker, "Actual Innocence: Is Death Different?" 27 *Behavioral Sciences and the Law* 297 (2009).

26. Samuel R. Gross, "The Risks of Death: Why Erroneous Convictions Are Common in Capital Cases," 44 *Buffalo Law Review* 469, 472 (1996).

27. *See, e.g.*, Joshua Marquis, "The Myth of Innocence," 95 *Journal of Criminal Law & Criminology* 501 (2005); Stephen J. Markman & Paul G. Cassell, "Protecting the Innocent: A Response to the Bedau-Radelet Study," 41 *Stanford Law Review* 121 (1988).

Chapter 11

1. James R. Acker, Talia Harmon & Craig Rivera, "Merciful Justice: Lessons from 50 Years of New York Death Penalty Commutations," 35 *Criminal Justice Review* 183, 184–188 (2010).

2. Kathleen Dean Moore, *Pardons: Justice, Mercy, and the Public Interest* 4–5 (New York: Oxford University Press 1989).

3. *See, e.g., Connecticut Board of Pardons v. Dumschat,* 452 U.S. 458, 464, 101 S.Ct. 2460, 69 L.Ed.2d 158 (1981); *Ex parte Grossman,* 267 U.S. 87, 120–121, 45 S.Ct. 332, 69 L.Ed. 527 (1925).

4. *See* Gavriel B. Wolfe, "I Beg Your Pardon: A Call for Renewal of Executive Clemency and Accountability in Massachusetts," 27 *Boston College Third World Law Journal* 417, 428 (2007); Daniel Kobil, "Chance and the Constitution in Capital Clemency Cases," 28 *Capital University Law Review* 567, 570–571 (2000); Allen L. Williamson, "Clemency in Texas—A Question of Mercy?" 6 *Texas Wesleyan Law Review* 131, 136–137 (1999) ("Of the fifty states, twenty-eight place the clemency power in the governor alone, although many have an advisory board that will issue non-binding opinions. In sixteen states, the governor shares power with some sort of administrative board. In the five remaining states, a panel, usually appointed by the governor, has the principle [sic] authority to make clemency decisions.") (Footnotes omitted.)

5. *See* James R. Acker & Charles S. Lanier, "May God—or the Governor—Have Mercy: Executive Clemency and Executions in Modern Death-Penalty Systems," 36 *Criminal Law Bulletin* 200, 211–212 (2000); Leon Radzinowicz, 1 *A History of English Criminal Law and Its Administration from 1750,* 107–164 (London: Stevens & Sons Limited 1948).

6. James R. Acker, Talia Harmon & Craig Rivera, "Merciful Justice: Lessons from 50 Years of New York Death Penalty Commutations," 35 *Criminal Justice Review* 183, 187 (2010).

7. *See* Austin Sarat, "Memorializing Miscarriages of Justice: Clemency Petitions in the Killing State," 42 *Law & Society Review* 183, 187 (2008); William A. Pridemore, "An Empirical Examination of Commutations and Executions in Post-*Furman* Capital Cases," 17 *Justice Quarterly* 159, 181 (2000); Victoria J. Palacios, "Faith in Fantasy: The Supreme Court's Reliance on Commutation to Ensure Justice in Death Penalty Cases," 49 *Vanderbilt Law Review* 311 (1996). *See generally* John Kraemer, "An Empirical Examination of the Factors Associated with the Commutation of State Death Row Prisoners' Sentences Between 1986 and 2005," 45 *American Criminal Law Review* 1389 (2008); Michael Heise, "Mercy by the Numbers: An Empirical Analysis of Mercy and Its Structure," 89 *Virginia Law Review* 239 (2003).

8. Death Penalty Information Center, "Clemency," available at http://www.deathpenaltyinfo.org/clemency (last visited March 11, 2011). On March 9, 2011 Illinois Governor Pat Quinn signed legislation abolishing the death penalty in that state, and commuted the death sentences of 15 individuals on Illinois' death row to life imprisonment without parole. We have updated the Death Penalty Information Center's total of "humanitarian" commutations to include this recent action. *See generally* Michael L. Radelet & Barbara A. Zsembik, "Executive Clemency in Post-*Furman* Capital Cases," 27 *University of Richmond Law Review* 289, 293–303 (1993).

9. Death Penalty Information Center, *supra* note 8.

10. *Id.*; Death Penalty Information Center, "Executions by Year," available at http://www.deathpenalty info.org/executions-year (last visited March 2, 2011).

11. Rachel E. Barkow, "The Ascent of the Administrative State and the Demise of Mercy," 121 *Harvard Law Review* 1332, 1348–49 (2008) (citation and footnotes omitted).

12. *See* Joanna M. Huang, "Correcting Mandatory Injustice: Judicial Recommendation of Executive Clemency," 60 *Duke Law Journal* 131, 149–152 (2010); Cathleen Burnett, "The Failed Failsafe: The Politics of Executive Clemency," 8 *Texas Journal on Civil Liberties and Civil Rights* 191 (2003); Susan L. Pilcher, "Ignorance, Discretion and the Fairness of Notice: Confronting 'Apparent Innocence' in the Criminal Law," 33 *American Criminal Law Review* 1, 45 (1995).

13. *Sourcebook of Criminal Justice Statistics Online,* Tables 5.72.1969 and 5.72.2010, available at http://www.albany.edu/sourcebook/pdf/t5721969.pdf, and http://www.albany.edu/sourcebook/pdf/t5722010.pdf (last visited March 3, 2011).

14. James R. Acker & Catherine L. Bonventre, "Protecting the Innocent in New York: Moving Beyond Changing Only Their Names," 73 *Albany Law Review* 1245, 1352–53 (2010).

15. *Roper v. Simmons,* 543 U.S. 551, 125 S.Ct. 1183, 161 L.Ed.2d 1 (2005).

16. *See* Mandy Welch & Richard Burr, "The Politics of Finality and the Execution of the Innocent: The Case of Gary Graham," in David R. Dow & Mark Dow (eds.), *Machinery of Death: The Reality of America's Death Penalty Regime* 127 (New York: Routledge 2002).

17. Jeffrey L. Kirchmeier, "Another Place Beyond Here: The Death Penalty Moratorium Movement in the United States," 73 *University of Colorado Law Review* 1, 50 (2002).

18. *Quoted in* Melynda J. Price, "Litigating Salvation: Race, Religion and Innocence in the Karla Faye Tucker and Gary Graham Cases," 15 *Southern California Review of Law & Social Justice* 267, 270 (2006).

19. *See* Death Penalty Information Center, "Capital Punishment in Context: The Case of Gary Graham," available at http://capitalpunishmentincontext.org/cases/graham (last visited March 3, 2011).

20. Alan Berlow, "The Texas Clemency Memos," *The Atlantic Online* (July/August 2003), available at http://www.theatlantic.com/magazine/archive/2003/07/the-texas-clemency-memos/2755/ (last visited March 3, 2011).

21. *See, e.g.,* Daniel T. Kobil, "The Evolving Role of Clemency in Capital Cases," in James R. Acker, Robert M. Bohm & Charles S. Lanier (eds.), *America's Experiment With Capital Punishment: Reflections on the Past, Present, and Future of the Ultimate Penal Sanction* 673, 686–689 (Durham, NC: Carolina Academic Press, 2d. ed. 2003); Daniel T. Kobil, "Due Process in Death Penalty Commutations: Life, Liberty, and the Pursuit of Clemency," 27 *University of Richmond Law Review* 201 (1993).

22. *Brief of Eleven Individuals Who Have Received Clemency Through DNA Testing as Amici Curiae in Support of Respondent,* filed in *District Attorney's Office for the Third Judicial District v. Osborne* (U.S. Supreme Court, No. 08-6 (Feb. 2, 2009).

23. *See* Peter Maas, *Marie, A True Story* (New York: Random House 1983).

24. Gregory C. Sisk, "Suspending the Pardon Power During the Twilight of a Presidential Term," 67 *Missouri Law Review* 13, 13 (2002) (citation and footnotes omitted). *See also* Daniel T. Kobil, "The Quality of Mercy Strained: Wresting the Pardoning Power from the King," 69 *Texas Law Review* 569, 607 (1991).

25. James R. Acker, Talia Harmon & Craig Rivera, "Merciful Justice: Lessons from 50 Years of New York Death Penalty Commutations," 35 *Criminal Justice Review* 183, 189–191 (2010); Elkan Abramowitz & David Paget, "Executive Clemency in Capital Cases," 39 *New York University Law Review* 136 (1964).

26. *See* Dwight Aarons, "Adjudicating Claims of Innocence for the Capitally Condemned in Tennessee: Embracing a Truth Forum," 76 *Tennessee Law Review* 511, 526 (2009); Death Penalty Information Center, "Judge Stays Workman Execution, Doubts About Case Remain," available at http://www.deathpenaltyinfo.org/node/492 (last visited March 3, 2011); *Workman v. Bell,* 484 F.3d 837 (6th Cir. 2007); *State v. Workman,* 111 S.W.3d 10 (Tenn. App. 2002).

27. Barry C. Scheck & Peter J. Neufeld, "Toward the Formation of 'Innocence Commissions' in America," 86 *Judicature* 98, 98 (No. 2) (2002). *See also* James M. Doyle, "Learning from Error in American Criminal Justice," 100 *Journal of Criminal Law & Criminology* 109 (2010).

28. Stephanie Roberts & Lynne Weathered, "Assisting the Factually Innocent: The Contradictions and Compatibility of Innocence Projects and the Criminal Case Review Commission," 29 *Oxford Journal of Legal Studies* 43 (2009).

29. *See* Kent Roach, "The Role of Innocence Commissions: Error Discovery, Systemic Reform or Both?" 85 *Chicago-Kent Law Review* 80 (2010).

30. N.C.G.S. § 15A-1463 (a) (2006).

31. N.C.G.S. § 15A-1466 (2006).

32. N.C.G.S. § 15A-1467 (a) (2006).

33. N.C.G.S. § 15A-1467 (b)–(f) (2006).

34. N.C.G.S. § 15A-1468 (c) (2006).

35. N.C.G.S. § 15A-1469 (a) (2006).

36. N.C.G.S. § 15A-1470 (a) (2006).

37. Jerome M. Maiatico, "All Eyes on Us: A Comparative Critique of the North Carolina Innocence Inquiry Commission," 56 *Duke Law Journal* 1345 (2007); Christine C. Mumma, "The North Carolina Actual Innocence Commission: Uncommon Perspectives Joined by a Common Cause," 52 *Drake Law Review* 647 (2004).

38. Lissa Griffin, "The Correction of Wrongful Convictions: A Comparative Perspective," 16 *American University International Law Review* 1241, 1276 (2001) (citation omitted).

39. Maiatico, *supra* note 37, at 1365 (2007) (citation omitted).

40. Griffin, *supra* note 38, at 1267–69.

41. Roach, *supra* note 29, at 101.

42. David Wolitz, "Innocence Commissions and the Future of Post-Conviction Review," 52 *Arizona Law Review* 1027, 1045 (2010) (footnotes omitted). *See also* Maiatico, *supra* note 37, at 1367–68; Acker & Bonventre, *supra* note 14, at 1337.

43. The North Carolina Innocence Inquiry Commission, *NC Innocence Inquiry Commission Case Statistics*, available at http://www.innocencecommission-nc.gov/stats.html (last visited March 5, 2011). *See also* Roach, *supra* note 29, at 103.

44. Wolitz, *supra* note 42, at 1060–63

45. The North Carolina Innocence Inquiry Commission, *Report to the 2009–2010 Short Session of the General Assembly of North Carolina*, App. G, p. XVI, available at http://www.innocencecommission-nc.gov/gar.html (last visited March 5, 2011). *See also* Roach, *supra* note 29, at 103.

46. Robert Carl Schehr, "The Criminal Cases Review Commission as a State Strategic Selection Mechanism," 42 *American Criminal Law Review* 1289, 1300 (2005). *See also* Robert Carl Schehr & Lynne Weathered, "Should the United States Establish a Criminal Cases Review Commission?" 88 *Judicature* 122 (2004).

47. Innocence Project, *Criminal Justice Reform Commissions: Case Studies,* available at http://www.innocenceproject.org/Content/Criminal_Justice_Reform_Commissions_Case_Studie s.php (last visited March 5, 2011); Robert J. Norris, Catherine L. Bonventre, Allison D. Redlich & James R. Acker, "'Than That One Innocent Suffer': Evaluating State Safeguards Against Wrongful Convictions," 74 *Albany Law Review* ___ (2011) (forthcoming). *See also* Roach, *supra* note 29, at 108–110.

48. Roach, *supra* note 29, at 104–108.

49. *See* Jon B. Gould, *The Innocence Commission: Preventing Wrongful Convictions and Restoring the Criminal Justice System* (New York: New York University Press 2008); Roach, *supra* note 29, at 110–112.

50. Innocence Project, *Criminal Justice Reform Commissions,* available at http://www.innocenceproject.org/Content/Criminal_Justice_Reform_Commissions.php# (last visited March 5, 2011).

51. Innocence Project, *Fact Sheet: Criminal Justice Reform Commissions,* available at http://www.innocenceproject.org/Content/Criminal_Justice_Reform_Commissions.php (last visited March 5, 2011).

52. Innocence Project, *Criminal Justice Reform Commissions: Case Studies, supra* note 47; Roach, *supra* note 29, at 108–112; Leigh B. Bienen, "Capital Punishment in Illinois in the Aftermath of the Ryan Commutations: Reforms, Economic Realities, and a New Saliency for Issues of Cost," 100 *Journal of Criminal Law & Criminology* 1301 (2010).

53. Report on the Conviction of Jeffrey Deskovic, Prepared at the Request of Janet DiFiore, Westchester County District Attorney 2 (June 2007), available at http://www.westchesterda.net/Jeffrey%20Deskovic%20Comm%20Rpt.pdf (last visited March 7, 2011).

54. *Id.*, at 4.

55. Fernanda Santos, "Vindicated by DNA, but a Lost Man on the Outside," *New York Times* (Nov. 25, 2007), available at http://www.nytimes.com/2007/11/25/us/25jeffrey.html (last visited March 7, 2011).

56. *See* Saundra D. Westervelt & Kimberly J. Cook, "Framing Innocents: The Wrongly Convicted as Victims of State Harm," 53 *Crime, Law & Social Change* 259, 264–271 (2010); Mary C. Delaney, Keith A. Findley & Sheila Sullivan, "Exonerees' Hardships After Freedom," 83 *Wisconsin Lawyer* 18 (Feb. 2010); Heather Weigand, "Rebuilding a Life: The Wrongfully Convicted and Exonerated," 18 *Public Interest Law Journal* 427 (2009); Kathryn Campbell & Myriam Denov, "The Burden of Innocence: Coping with a Wrongful Imprisonment," 2004 *Canadian Journal of Criminology and Criminal Justice* 139 (2004). *See also* Saundra D. Westervelt & Kimberly Cook, "Coping with Innocence after Death Row," 7 *Contexts* 32 (2008); Janet Roberts & Elizabeth Stanton, "Free and Uneasy: A Long Road Back After Exoneration, and Justice Is Slow to Make Amends," *New York Times* (Nov. 25, 2007), available at http://www.nytimes.com/2007/11/25/us/25dna.html (last visited March 7, 2011).

57. Weigand, *supra* note 56, at 429; Jeffrey Chinn & Ashley Ratliff, "'I Was Put Out the Door With Nothing' — Addressing the Needs of the Exonerated Under a Refugee Model," 45 *California Western Law Review* 405, 406–407 (2009).

58. Innocence Project, *Making Up for Lost Time: What the Wrongfully Convicted Endure and How to Provide Fair Compensation* 17–18 (2010), available at http://www.innocenceproject.org/Content/Executive_Summary_Making_up_for_Lost_Time_What_the_Wrongfully_Convicted_Endure_and_How_to_Provide_Fair_Compensation.php (last visited March 7, 2011).

59. *Id.*, at 12–15; Jessica L. Lonergan, "Protecting the Innocent: A Model for Comprehensive, Individualized Compensation of the Exonerated," 11 *Legislation and Public Policy* 405 (2008).

60. Daniel S. Kahn, "Presumed Guilty Until Proven Innocent: The Burden of Proof in Wrongful Conviction Claims Under State Compensation Statutes," 44 *University of Michigan Journal of Law Reform* 123, 142 (2010) (footnotes omitted).

61. *Id.*, at 411–412 (footnotes omitted). *See also* Innocence Project, *supra* note 57, at 27–31; Fernanda Santos & Janet Roberts, "Putting a Price on a Wrongful Conviction," *New York Times* (Dec. 2, 2007), available at http://www.nytimes.com/2007/12/02/weekinreview/02santos.html (last visited March 7, 2011).

62. Kahn, *supra* note 60, at 145.

63. Lonergan, *supra* note 59, at 412 (footnotes omitted).

64. Innocence Project, *supra* note 58, at 18–19; Kahn, *supra* note 60, at 140–142.

65. Innocence Project, *supra* note 58, at 19.

66. Kahn, *supra* note 60, at 144–145.

67. Innocence Project, *supra* note 58, at 3. *See also* Roberts & Stanton, *supra* note 56.

68. Ashley H. Wisneski, "'That's Just Not Right': Monetary Compensation for the Wrongly Convicted in Massachusetts," 88 *Massachusetts Law Review* 138, 139 (2004) (footnotes omitted).

69. *Commonwealth v. Waters,* 506 N.E.2d 859 (Mass. 1987).

70. Stanley Z. Fisher, "Convictions of Innocent Persons in Massachusetts: An Overview," 12 *Boston University Public Interest Law Journal* 1, 46–47 (2002) (citation and footnotes omitted).

71. *Id.*, at 47 (footnote omitted).

72. Innocence Project, "Know the Cases: Douglas Warney," available at http://www.innocenceproject.org/Content/Douglas_Warney.php (last visited March 8, 2011).

73. *Id.*

About the Authors

James R. Acker is a Distinguished Teaching Professor at the University at Albany School of Criminal Justice. He earned his JD at Duke Law School and his PhD at the University at Albany. His academic interests include the integration of law and social science, capital punishment, criminal law, criminal procedure, and the legal rights of children. He has authored, co-authored, and co-edited several scholarly articles and books addressing those subjects, including three previous volumes published by Carolina Academic Press: *America's Experiment With Capital Punishment: Perspectives on the Past, Present, and Future of the Ultimate Penal Sanction* (2d ed. 2003) (with Robert M. Bohm and Charles S. Lanier); *Wounds That Do Not Bind: Victim-Based Perspectives on the Death Penalty* (2006) (with David R. Karp); and *The Future of America's Death Penalty: An Agenda for the Next Generation of Capital Punishment Research* (2009) (with Charles S. Lanier and William J. Bowers).

Allison D. Redlich is an Associate Professor at the University at Albany School of Criminal Justice. She received her PhD in Developmental Psychology at the University of California, Davis and completed a postdoctoral fellowship at Stanford University. Her current program of research addresses miscarriages of justice with an emphasis on actual innocence and due process right violations. The majority of her work concerns the vulnerable populations of juveniles and persons with mental illness. With an eye towards advancing knowledge on these topics, she publishes extensively, presents to national audiences of criminal justice practitioners, and provides expert courtroom testimony.

Index

E

K

L

M

N